International Directory of

COMPANY HISTORIES

INTERNATIONAL DIRECTORY OF COMPANY HISTORIES

VOLUME I
ADVERTISING-DRUGS

VOLUME II
ELECTRICAL & ELECTRONICS-FOOD SERVICES & RETAILERS

VOLUME III
HEALTH & PERSONAL CARE-MATERIALS

VOLUME IV
MINING & METALS-RETAIL

VOLUME V
RUBBER & TIRE-WASTE

International Directory of COMPANY HISTORIES

VOLUME II

Editor
Lisa Mirabile

Assistant Editors
Diane Pascal
Noelle Watson

Writers and Researchers
Angel Abcede, Joseph Bator, Elaine Belsito, Kate Berney, Robin Carre, Ellen Cothran, Peter Cunningham, Thomas Derdak, Vera Emmons, Michael Fitzgerald, Sean Francis, Joyce Goldenstern, Mary Hynes-Berry, Tony Jeffris, Jerome Kaminski, Joy Kammerling, Roberta Lamanna, Suzanne Leibundguth, Jeanne Lewis, Marie MacNee, Kim Magon, Jonathan Martin, Mary Sue Mohnke, Betty T. Moore, Anne Morddel, Frances Norton, George Robb, Ginger Rodriguez, Lea Ann Rogala, Wallace Ross, Elizabeth Rourke, Sandra Schusteff, John Simley, René Steinke, Douglas Sun, Mary Sworsky, Thomas Tucker, Ray Walsh, Nina Wendt, Paul Zaccarine

ST. JAMES PRESS
CHICAGO AND LONDON
St J

For further information, write:

ST. JAMES PRESS
233 East Ontario Street
Chicago, IL 60611
U.S.A.

or

3 Percy Street
London W1P 9FA
England

British Library Cataloguing in Publication Data

International directory of company histories. Vol. 2
1. Large companies, to 1990
I. Mirabile, Lisa
338.7′4′09

ISBN 1-55862-012-5

First published in the U.S.A. and U.K. 1990
Typeset by Florencetype Ltd., Kewstoke, Avon, England
Printed by BookCrafters, Chelsea, Michigan, U.S.A.

INDUSTRIES COVERED IN THE DIRECTORY

VOLUME I

Advertising
Aerospace
Airlines
Automotive
Beverages
Chemicals
Conglomerates
Construction
Containers
Drugs

VOLUME II

Electrical & Electronics
Entertainment & Leisure
Financial Services
—Bank
—Non-Bank
Food Products
Food Services & Retailers

VOLUME III

Health & Personal Care
Health Care Services
Hotels
Information Technology
Insurance
Manufacturing
Materials

VOLUME IV

Mining & Metals
Paper & Forestry
Petroleum
Publishing & Printing
Real Estate
Retail

VOLUME V

Rubber & Tire
Steel
Telecommunications
Textiles & Apparel
Tobacco
Transport Services
Utilities
Waste

CONTENTS

EDITOR'S NOTE

The *International Directory of Company Histories* provides accurate and detailed information on the development of the world's largest and most influential companies. When completed, the *Directory*'s five volumes will cover some 1,200 companies.

The companies chosen for inclusion in the *Directory* meet one or both of the following criteria: they have achieved a minimum of two billion U.S. dollars in annual sales (financial services companies are measured by assets: banks have a minimum of $30 billion in assets, and non-banks $10 billion); or they are leading influences in their respective industries or geographical locations.

Each entry begins with a company's legal name, the mailing address of its headquarters, its telephone number, and whether the company is publicly or privately owned. Wholly owned subsidiaries of other companies are included if they meet the requirements mentioned above and have been independent within the past five years. A very limited number of state-owned companies that are major competitors in their industries and operate much like public or private companies are also included.

The company's earliest incorporation date and the number of its employees and its sales (or assets) for fiscal year 1988 are also included. Sales figures are given in local currencies and also translated into U.S. dollars at the exchange rate on December 30, 1988. Finally, a list of the cities where a company's stock is traded is given.

Throughout the *Directory* spelling is according to American style and the word "billion" is used in its American sense of a thousand million.

The histories were compiled from publicly accessible sources such as magazines, general and academic periodicals, books, and annual reports, as well as from material supplied by the companies themselves. St. James Press would like to thank the staffs of the Chicago Public Library, the University of Chicago Library, the Northwestern University Library (Evanston, Illinois), the Illinois Institute of Technology Library (Chicago), and the Financial Times Editorial Library (London) for their courteous assistance and invaluable guidance.

St. James Press does not endorse any of the companies or products mentioned in this book. Likewise, the companies that appear in the *Directory* were selected without reference to their wishes and have in no way endorsed their entries. The companies were all given the opportunity to read their entries for factual inaccuracies, and we are indebted to many of them for their corrections. We also thank them for allowing the use of their logos for identification purposes.

This *Directory* is intended for reference and research, for those students, job candidates, business people, librarians, historians, investors, and others who want to learn more about the historical development of the world's most important companies.

Lisa Mirabile

ABBREVIATIONS FOR FORMS OF COMPANY INCORPORATION

A.B.	Akiebolaget (Sweden)
A.G.	Aktiengesellschaft (West Germany, Switzerland)
A.S.	Atieselskab (Denmark)
A/S	Aksjeselskap (Denmark, Norway)
A.Ş.	Anonim Şirket (Turkey)
B.V.	Besloten Vennootschap met beperkte, Aansprakelijkheid (The Netherlands)
Co.	Company (United Kingdom, United States)
Corp.	Corporation (United States)
G.I.E.	Groupement d'Intérêt Economique (France)
GmbH.	Gesellschaft mit beschränkter Haftung (Germany)
H.B.	Handelsbolaget (Sweden)
Inc.	Incorporated (United States)
K.K.	Kabushiki Kaisha (Japan)
Ltd.	Limited (Canada, Japan, United Kingdom, United States)
N.V.	Naamloze Vennootschap (The Netherlands)
PLC	Public Limited Company (United Kingdom)
PTY.	Proprietary (Australia, Hong Kong, South Africa)
S.A.	Société Anonyme (Belgium, France, Switzerland)
SpA	Società per Azioni (Italy)

ABBREVIATIONS FOR CURRENCY

A$	Australian dollar
BFr	Belgian franc
Cz	Brazilian cruzado
C$	Canadian dollar
DKr	Danish krone
FIM	Finnish markka
FFr	French franc
DM	German mark
HK$	Hong Kong dollar
L	Italian lira
¥	Japanese yen
W	Korean won
Dfl	Netherlands florin
R	South African rand
Pts	Spanish peseta
SKr	Swedish krone
SFr	Swiss franc
TL	Turkish lira
£	United Kingdom pound
$	United States dollar
B	Venzuelan bolivar

International Directory of
COMPANY HISTORIES

ELECTRICAL & ELECTRONICS

ABB ASEA Brown Boveri Ltd.
Alps Electric Co., Ltd.
AMP, Inc
Bicoastal Corporation
Compagnie Générale d'Électricite
Cooper Industries, Inc.
Emerson Electric Co.
Fuji Electric Co., Ltd.
General Electric Company, PLC
General Electric Company
GM Hughes Electronics Corporation
Harris Corporation
Honeywell Inc.
Intel Corporation
Koor Industries Ltd.
Kyocera Corporation
Lucky-Goldstar
Matsushita Electric Industrial Co., Ltd.
Mitsubishi Electric Corporation
Motorola, Inc.
National Semiconductor Corporation
NEC Corporation
Nokia Corporation
Oki Electric Industry Company, Limited
Omron Tateisi Electronics Company
N. V. Philips Gloeilampemfabrieken
The Plessey Company, PLC
Racal Electronics PLC
Raytheon Company
RCA Corporation
Sanyo Electric Company, Ltd.
Schneider S.A.
Sharp Corporation
Siemens A.G.
Sony Corporation
Sumitomo Electric Industries, Ltd.
Tandy Corporation
TDK Corporation
Texas Instruments Incorporated
Thomson S.A.
Victor Company of Japan, Ltd.
Westinghouse Electric Corporation
Zenith Electronics Corporation

ENTERTAINMENT & LEISURE

Capital Cities/ABC Inc.
CBS Inc.
Columbia Pictures Entertainment, Inc.
Granada Group PLC
Ladbroke Group PLC
MCA Inc.
MGM/UA Communications Company
National Broadcasting Company Inc.
Paramount Pictures Corporation
Rank Organisation PLC
Tele-Communications, Inc.
Touristik Union International GmbH. and Company K.G.
Turner Broadcasting System, Inc.
Twentieth Century Fox Film Corporation
Walt Disney Company
Warner Communications Inc.

FINANCIAL SERVICES: BANKS

H.F. Ahmanson & Company
Algemene Bank Nederland N.V.
Amsterdam-Rotterdam Bank N.V.
Australia and New Zealand Banking Group Ltd.
Banca Commerciale Italiana SpA
Banco Bilbao Vizcaya, S.A.
Banco Central
Banco do Brasil S.A.
Bank Brussels Lambert
Bank Hapoalim B.M.
Bank of Boston Corporation
Bank of Montreal
Bank of New England Corporation
The Bank of New York Company, Inc.
The Bank of Nova Scotia
Bank of Tokyo, Ltd.
BankAmerica Corporation
Bankers Trust New York Corporation
Banque Nationale de Paris S.A.
Barclays PLC
Bayerische Hypotheken- und Wechsel-Bank AG
Bayerische Vereinsbank A.G.
Canadian Imperial Bank of Commerce
The Chase Manhattan Corporation
Chemical Banking Corporation
Citicorp
Commerzbank A.G.
Compagnie Financiere de Paribas
Continental Bank Corporation
Crédit Agricole
Credit Suisse
Credito Italiano
The Dai-Ichi Kangyo Bank Ltd.
The Daiwa Bank, Ltd.
Deutsche Bank A.G.
Dresdner Bank A.G.
First Chicago Corporation

First Interstate Bancorp
The Fuji Bank, Ltd.
Generale Bank
The Hongkong and Shanghai Banking Corporation Limited
The Industrial Bank of Japan, Ltd.
Kansallis-Osake-Pankki
Kredietbank N.V.
Lloyds Bank PLC
Long-Term Credit Bank of Japan, Ltd.
Manufacturers Hanover Corporation
Mellon Bank Corporation
Midland Bank PLC
The Mitsubishi Bank, Ltd.
The Mitsubishi Trust & Banking Corporation
The Mitsui Bank, Ltd.
The Mitsui Trust & Banking Company, Ltd.
J.P. Morgan & Co. Incorporated
National Westminster Bank PLC
NCNB Corporation
Nippon Credit Bank
Norinchukin Bank
PNC Financial Corporation
The Royal Bank of Canada
The Sanwa Bank, Ltd.
Security Pacific Corporation
Skandinaviska Enskilda Banken
Société Générale
Standard Chartered PLC
The Sumitomo Bank, Ltd.
The Sumitomo Trust & Banking Company, Ltd.
Svenska Handelsbanken
Swiss Bank Corporation
The Taiyo Kobe Bank, Ltd.
The Tokai Bank, Ltd.
The Toronto-Dominion Bank
Union Bank of Switzerland
Wells Fargo & Company
Westdeutsche Landesbank Girozentrale
Westpac Banking Corporation
The Yasuda Trust and Banking Company, Ltd.

FINANCIAL SERVICES: NON-BANKS

American Express Company
Bear Stearns Companies, Inc.
CS First Boston Inc.
Daiwa Securities Company, Limited
Drexel Burnham Lambert Incorporated
Federal National Mortgage Association
Fidelity Investments
Goldman, Sachs & Co.
Household International, Inc.
Kleinwort Benson Group PLC
Merrill Lynch & Co. Inc.
Morgan Grenfell Group PLC
Morgan Stanley Group Inc.
The Nikko Securities Company Limited
Nippon Shinpan Company, Ltd.
Nomura Securities Company, Limited
Orix Corporation
PaineWebber Group Inc.
Salomon Inc.
Shearson Lehman Hutton Holdings Inc.
Student Loan Marketing Association
Trilon Financial Corporation
Yamaichi Securities Company, Limited

FOOD PRODUCTS

Ajinomoto Co., Inc.
Associated British Foods PLC
Beatrice Company
Borden, Inc.
BSN Groupe S.A.
Cadbury Schweppes PLC
Campbell Soup Company
Canada Packers Inc.
Carnation Company
Castle & Cook, Inc.
Conagra, Inc.
CPC International Inc.
Dalgety, PLC
General Mills, Inc.
George A. Hormel and Company
H.J. Heinz Company
Hershey Foods Corporation
Hillsdown Holdings, PLC
IBP, inc.
Itoham Foods Inc.
Jacobs Suchard AG
Kellogg Company
Koninklijke Wessanen N.V.
Kraft General Foods Inc.
Land O'Lakes, Inc.
Meiji Milk Products Company, Limited
Meiji Seika Kaisha, Ltd.
Nabisco Brands, Inc.
Nestlé S.A.
Nippon Meat Packers, Inc.
Nippon Suisan Kaisha, Limited
Nisshin Flour Milling Company, Ltd.
Pillsbury Company
Quaker Oats Company

Ralston Purina Company
Ranks Hovis McDougall PLC
Reckitt & Colman PLC
Rowntree Mackintosh
Sara Lee Corporation
Snow Brand Milk Products Company, Limited
SODIMA
Taiyo Fishery Company, Limited
Tate & Lyle PLC
Tyson Foods, Incorporated
Unigate PLC
Unilever
United Biscuits (Holdings) PLC
United Brands Company

FOOD SERVICES & RETAILERS

Albertson's, Inc.
American Stores Company
ARA Services
Argyll Group PLC
Asda Group PLC
Burger King Corporation
Cargill, Inc.
The Circle K Corporation
Edeka Zentrale A.G.
Fleming Companies, Inc.
Food Lion, Inc.
The Gateway Corporation Ltd.
George Weston Limited
Giant Food Inc.
The Great Atlantic & Pacific Tea Company, Inc.
ICA AB
Koninklijke Ahold N. V.
The Kroger Company
McDonald's Corporation
The Oshawa Group Limited
Provigo Inc.
Safeway Stores Incorporated
J Sainsbury PLC
The Southland Corporation
Steinberg Incorporated
The Stop & Shop Companies, Inc.
Super Valu Stores, Inc.
Supermarkets General Holdings Corporation
Sysco Corporation
Tesco PLC
TW Services, Inc.
Wetterau Incorporated
Winn-Dixie Stores, Inc.

ELECTRICAL & ELECTRONICS

ABB ASEA BROWN BOVERI LTD.
ALPS ELECTRIC CO., LTD.
AMP, INC
BICOASTAL CORPORATION
COMPAGNIE GÉNÉRALE D'ÉLECTRICITE
COOPER INDUSTRIES, INC.
EMERSON ELECTRIC CO.
FUJI ELECTRIC CO., LTD.
GENERAL ELECTRIC COMPANY, PLC
GENERAL ELECTRIC COMPANY
GM HUGHES ELECTRONICS CORPORATION
HARRIS CORPORATION
HONEYWELL INC.
INTEL CORPORATION
KOOR INDUSTRIES LTD.
KYOCERA CORPORATION
LUCKY-GOLDSTAR
MATSUSHITA ELECTRIC INDUSTRIAL CO., LTD.
MITSUBISHI ELECTRIC CORPORATION
MOTOROLA, INC.
NATIONAL SEMICONDUCTOR CORPORATION
NEC CORPORATION
NOKIA CORPORATION
OKI ELECTRIC INDUSTRY COMPANY, LIMITED
OMRON TATEISI ELECTRONICS COMPANY
N. V. PHILIPS GLOEILAMPEMFABRIEKEN
THE PLESSEY COMPANY, PLC
RACAL ELECTRONICS PLC
RAYTHEON COMPANY
RCA CORPORATION
SANYO ELECTRIC COMPANY, LTD.
SCHNEIDER S.A.
SHARP CORPORATION
SIEMENS A.G.
SONY CORPORATION
SUMITOMO ELECTRIC INDUSTRIES, LTD.
TANDY CORPORATION
TDK CORPORATION
TEXAS INSTRUMENTS INCORPORATED
THOMSON S.A.
VICTOR COMPANY OF JAPAN, LTD.
WESTINGHOUSE ELECTRIC CORPORATION
ZENITH ELECTRONICS CORPORATION

ABB ASEA BROWN BOVERI LTD.

Post Office Box 8131
CH-8050 Zurich
Switzerland
Switzerland
(01) 317–71–11

Wholly owned subsidiary of ASEA A.B. and BBC Brown, Boveri Ltd.
Incorporated: 1988
Employees: 180,000
Sales: SKr110 billion (US$17.98 billion)

Formerly fierce competitors in the heavy-electrical and power-generation fields, Sweden's ASEA A.B. and Switzerland's BBC Brown, Boveri Ltd. announced in August, 1987 that the two companies would combine their assets to form a new company, called ABB Asea Brown Boveri Ltd. (ABB). The merger took effect on January 1, 1988. ABB is headquartered in Switzerland and owned equally by the two parent companies, which maintain separate stock listings in their own countries and act as holding companies for ABB. The merger, which created Europe's largest heavy-electrical combine, was designed to take advantage of ASEA's management strengths and Brown Boveri's technological and marketing expertise. Although both Sweden and Switzerland are outside the European Economic Community, the integration of the two companies has been watched closely by analysts as a prototype of the international corporation that will become increasingly common as the EEC advances towards the unification of the European market.

ASEA

Elektriska Aktiebolaget in Stockholm was established in 1883 by Ludwig Fredholm to manufacture dynamos based on the designs of a young engineer named Jonas Wenstrom. Wenstrom's innovative designs quickly led to financial success, and Fredholm soon wanted to expand the scope of his firm's operations. He arranged a merger with Wenstroms & Granstroms Elektriska Kraftbolag, a company founded by Jonas Wenstrom's brother Goran.

Allmanna Svenska Elektriska Aktiebolaget (ASEA) was created on November 18, 1890 to provide electrical equipment for Swedish industry. Goran Wenstrom shared presidential responsibilities with Fredholm, who also served as chairman of the board. After Fredholm's death in 1891, Wenstrom become sole president and Oscar F. Wijkman was appointed chairman.

The dawning of the electrical age provided ASEA with large new markets as the industrial and residential use of electricity became commonplace in Sweden. The company quickly established itself as a pioneer in the industrial field: ASEA's installation of electricity at a rolling mill in the town of Hofors is believed to be the first of its kind in the world, and in 1893, ASEA built Sweden's first three-phase electrical transmission, between Hellsjon and Crangesberg.

ASEA's early success was short-lived. In 1896 one of Sweden's leading inventors and industrialists, Gustaf de Laval, acquired a 50% interest in the company and both Wenstrom and Wijkman were ousted in a management reorganization. But Laval's mismanagement of ASEA soon led the company into severe financial difficulties. With the help of the Stockholms Enskilda Bank, management opposed to Laval eventually extricated the company from his control. Disorganized and deeply in debt, the firm lost a significant share of the electrical equipment market in Sweden.

Stockholms Enskilda Bank played a major role in ASEA's financial recovery. In fact, it was only after the bank agreed to guarantee his salary that J. Sigfrid Edstrom, the former manager of the Gothenburg Tramways Company, agreed to become president of ASEA in 1903. Under Edstrom's direction, the company began to show a substantial profit by 1907. In addition, he expanded the firm's markets in Europe: subsidiaries were established in Great Britain, Spain, Denmark, Finland, and Russia between 1910 and 1914.

Although Sweden remained neutral during World War I, the company was adversely affected by the conflict. ASEA prospered during the early years of the war since the scarcity of coal stimulated the development of electricity, including the company's first major railway electrification project. Eventually, however, the firm lost many of its European markets due to the success of German submarine warfare. In Russia, all of ASEA's operations were interrupted by the revolution beginning in 1917.

The postwar years brought a deep recession to Sweden that lasted from 1920 to 1923. Yet Edstrom's cautious spending policies enabled the company to survive. By the late 1920s, ASEA was once again on the road to profitability and growth. In 1926 the company provided the electric locomotives and converter equipment for the first electric trains on the Stockholm–Gothenburg line, and in 1932 ASEA built the world's largest naturally-cooled three-phase transformer.

During the 1930s, company management decided to concentrate on expanding and improving its domestic operations. After several years of negotiations, ASEA and LM Ericsson Telephone Company signed a pact in 1933 stipulating that the two companies would not compete with each other in certain sectors of the electrical market. As part of the agreement, ASEA purchased Elektromekano from Ericsson, giving ASEA undisputed control over a large portion of the electrical-equipment market in Sweden.

In addition to its production of electric locomotives and rail equipment for Sweden's national railway electrification program, the firm expanded into new markets. ASEA purchased A.B. Svenska Flaktfabriken, a firm specializing in air-freight handling technology, and a large electric-motor manufacturer in Poland to augment its domestic production. In 1934, Edstrom was named chairman of the board and Arthur Linden, executive vice-president and a close Edstrom associate for many years, was named president. These two men directed the company's successful growth and expansion strategy until World War II.

The Swedish government once again voted to remain neutral during the war, but once again, war severely affected the country's economy. The Nazi occupation effectively curtailed ASEA's operations throughout Europe, and even to a significant extent in Sweden. A new president, Thorsten Ericson, was appointed in 1943, but this management change had little impact on the company's fortunes for the remainder of the war.

During the immediate postwar years, domestic power demands skyrocketed and forced utility companies to expand rapidly. ASEA was unable to meet this demand for electrical equipment due to shortages of material. To make matters worse, a five-month strike by metal workers played havoc with the company's delivery schedule, leaving ASEA unable to meet the demand from the Soviet Union for electric equipment based on a 1946 trade agreement between Sweden and the U.S.S.R.

In 1947 ASEA broke into the American market by signing a licensing agreement with the Ohio Brass Company for the local production of surge arrestors. During this time, ASEA also received substantial orders for the first stage of the massive Aswan Dam project in Egypt.

In 1949 Ake T. Vrethem, formerly with the Swedish State Power Board, was named president of ASEA and Ericson became chairman of the board. Under their direction, the company continued its pioneering efforts in several areas: ASEA supplied electrical equipment and technical expertise to the world's first 400 kilovolt AC transmission, between Harspranget and Hallsberg in 1952; the company also claims to have produced the world's first synthetic diamonds using high-pressure technology in 1953, two years before General Electric announced a similar achievement in the United States; and ASEA supplied the first permanent high-voltage, direct current (HVDC) transmission, linking the Swedish mainland with the island of Gotland in 1954.

The company continued to play a critical role in Sweden's rail transit system. ASEA's locomotives accounted for virtually all the traffic on the country's rail network. In the mid-1950s, the firm introduced its "Ra" light-class electric locomotive, which was an immediate success and gave a boost to ASEA's efforts to market competitive locomotive models internationally.

In 1961 Curt Nicolin was appointed president. Nicolin restructured the parent company, introduced a new divisional organization, and relocated some of ASEA's manufacturing facilities. The company formed an electronics division, signaling the start of ASEA's transition from a traditional heavy electrical equipment manufacturer to an electronics company in which high-technology played an increasingly important role.

In the mid-1960s, ASEA's American market expanded considerably and became more important to the company's overall sales strategy. After serving customers such as the Tennessee Valley Authority, the company firmly established itself in the United States when it was chosen to supply HVDC equipment for the Pacific Internie Project on the West Coast.

ASEA also received an order to build Sweden's first full-scale nuclear power station during this period. The company then merged its nuclear division with the state-owned Atom-Energi to form ASEA-ATOM in 1968. ASEA acquired the remaining 50% state interest in Atom-Energi in 1982.

In 1963, ASEA achieved a major technological breakthrough with the introduction of an improved thyristor able to handle substantially more electrical current than existing devices. As a result, the company began manufacturing thyristor locomotives for Swedish and European rail systems. In the mid-1970s, ASEA worked with its American licensee, the electro-motive division of General Motors, to secure an order for 47 thyristor locomotives for use on Amtrak lines in the Boston–New York–Washington, D.C. corridor.

Nuclear power became a increasingly controversial issue in Sweden during the late 1970s. ASEA continued to manufacture nuclear reactors and received its first foreign order, from Finland. But in a 1980 national referendum Sweden voted to phase out nuclear power programs over a period of 25 years. The company is still allowed to complete orders for foreign reactors, but ASEA-ATOM's future looks bleak.

Curt Nicolin was also appointed chairman of the board in 1976. However, during the 1970s, Nicolin's management style was overwhelmed by the fast pace of changing technology. A large number of utility and electrical equipment manufacturing companies, including ASEA, experienced falling profits and lackluster growth.

ASEA began to revive in 1980, when 39-year-old Percy Barnevik was named managing director and, eventually, CEO. Barnevik immediately began a reorganization of the company's management strategy: from now on the company would emphasize high profit margin projects (ASEA had previously bid on projects with low profit margins for the sake of maintaining a minimum sales level and a certain number of employees). Barnevik's strategy began to pay off quickly.

Under Barnevik's direction, ASEA initiated a major expansion into high-tech areas, investing heavily in robotics and other state-of-the-art electronics. The development costs of robotics at first held profits down in that sector, but Barnevik viewed robotics as a long-term, high-growth area.

Barnevik also considered ASEA's industrial controls business, with products such as large automation controls, a high-growth sector. ASEA already had a major share of the rapidly expanding market for industrial energy controls, such as those that recycle waste heat. In addition, the company has positioned itself to take advantage of a growing demand for pollution controls, spurred in part by the acid-rain controversy in Europe and North America.

In 1985, the company was accused of an illegal diversion of proprietary U.S. technology to the Soviet Union. A former ASEA vice-president was charged by Swedish authorities with tax evasion and violation of foreign exchange regulations in connection with the sale of six sophisticated computers with possible military applications. Barnevik insisted that the diversions occurred without management's approval. If U.S. officials investigating the case decide otherwise, ASEA's reliance on American electrical components and sensitive technology could be dealt a severe blow.

BBC BROWN BOVERI

BBC Brown Boveri was established in 1891. The company's development is interesting because it is one of only a few multinational corporations to operate subsidiaries that are larger than the parent company. Because of the limitations of the Swiss domestic market, Brown Boveri established subsidiaries throughout Europe relatively early in its history, and at times has had difficulty maintaining managerial control over some of its larger operating units. The merger with ASEA, a company which has been praised for its strong management, is expected to help Brown Boveri reorganize and reassert control over its vast international network.

Brown Boveri's early activities included manufacturing electrical components such as electrical motors for locomotives and power-generating equipment for Europe's railway systems. In 1919, the company entered into a licensing agreement with the British manufacturing firm Vickers that gave the British firm the right to manufacture and sell Brown Boveri products throughout the British Empire and in some parts of Europe. The agreement gave Brown Boveri a significant amount of money and the promise of substantial annual revenue, and also helped the company expand into markets where it did not yet have subsidiaries at a time when protectionist policies inhibited international expansion.

In the early 1920s, Brown Boveri, already a geographically diversified company with successful operating subsidiaries in Italy, Germany, Norway, Austria, and the Balkans, suffered losses due to the devaluation of the French franc and the German mark. At the same time, in the Swiss domestic market, production costs increased while sales remained static, causing the company further losses. In 1924 Brown Boveri devalued its capital by 30% to cover the losses it had incurred. In 1927 the agreement with Vickers ran out and was not renewed.

During the same time, Brown Boveri's various subsidiaries grew rapidly. Industrialization throughout Europe created strong demand for the company's heavy electrical equipment. Italy's burgeoning railroad industry provided a particularly strong boost to Brown Boveri's Italian subsidiary, and the company's German facility, catering to the large German market, actually did considerably more business than the Swiss parent. For the next few decades Brown Boveri grew as fast as technological developments in electrical engineering, accustoming itself to the cyclical nature of capital investment. Each of the company's subsidiaries tended to develop individually, as if it were a domestic company in the country in which it operated, and broad geographic coverage helped insulate the parent from severe crises when a certain region experienced economic difficulties.

This sort of segmented development had its drawbacks, however. After World War II, the cold war presented a variety of business opportunities for defense-related electrical contractors. But Brown Boveri's subsidiaries were seen as foreign companies in many of the countries in which they operated, sometimes making it difficult for the company to win lucrative contracts involving sensitive technology and other government contracts. The company, nevertheless, excelled at power generation, including nuclear power generators, and prospered in this field. Electrification efforts in the Third World also provided Brown Boveri with substantial profits.

In 1970 Brown Boveri began an extensive reorganization. Its subsidiaries were divided into five groups: German, French, Swiss, "medium-sized" (seven manufacturing bases in Europe and Latin America), and Brown Boveri International (the remaining facilities). Each of these groups was further broken down into five product divisions: power generation, electronics, power distribution, traction equipment, and industrial equipment.

Throughout the 1970s, Brown Boveri struggled to expand into the U.S. market. The company negotiated a joint venture with Rockwell, the American manufacturer of high-tech military and aerospace applications, but the deal fell through when the two companies could not agree on financial terms. While Brown Boveri counted a handful of major U.S. customers as its clients, among them large utilities like the Tennessee Valley Authority and American Electric, Brown Boveri's American market share was dismal considering the company's international standing (North American sales accounted for only 3.5% of total sales in 1974 and 1975), and the company continued to search for a means of effectively entering U.S. markets.

In 1974 Brown Boveri acquired the British controls and instrument manufacturer George Kent. The deal at first raised concern in Britain over foreign ownership of such highly sensitive technology, but Brown Boveri prevailed with the encouragement of George Kent's rank-and-file employees, who feared the alternative of being bought by Britain's General Electric Company (GEC). The newly acquired company was renamed Brown Boveri Kent and made an excellent addition to the parent company's already-diverse product line.

In the mid-1970s growing demand in the Middle East for large power-generating facilities distracted the company from its North American thrust. Oil-rich African nations like Nigeria also increased demand for Brown Boveri's heavy electrical engineering expertise when they attempted to diversify their manufacturing capabilities.

In the early 1980s Brown Boveri's sales flattened out and the company began to register declines in earnings. In 1983, Brown Boveri's German subsidiary in Mannheim,

West Germany, which accounted for nearly half of the entire parent company's sales, rebounded, but although orders were up, the company was in need of rationalization. In 1985 the subsidiary's performance improved as a result of cost-cutting. Price decreases in the international market and unfavorable shifts in currency exchanges rates offset the increased orders. In 1986 the parent company acquired a significant block of shares in the Mannheim subsidiary, brings its total stake to 75%. Despite promising results in the Italian and Brazilian units, profits for the parent company were disappointing in 1986.

In the later 1980s Brown Boveri took steps to reduce duplication of research and development among its various groups. While each subsidiary continued to do some product-development research for its individual market, theoretical research was unified under the parent company, making more efficient use of research funding. In 1987 the company introduced a supercharging system for diesel engines called Comprex. This system was capable of increasing an engine's horsepower by 35% and delivering up to 50% more torque at lower speeds. The Japanese automaker Mazda planned to use the new supercharger in its new diesel passenger models.

In August, 1987 ASEA and Brown Boveri announced their intent to merge their assets for shares in a new company, Asea-Brown Boveri, to be owned equally by each parent company. When the merger took effect, on January 1, 1988, Asea's Curt Nicolin and Brown Boveri's Fritz Leutwiler became joint chairmen. Asea's CEO, Percy Barnevik, became the new operating company's CEO, while his Brown Boveri counterpart became deputy CEO.

The joint venture between these two former competitors allowed them to combine expensive research-and-development efforts in superconductors, high-voltage chips, and control systems used in power plants. In addition, ASEA's strength in Scandinavia and northern Europe balanced Brown Boveri's strong presence in Austria, Italy, Switzerland, and West Germany.

The integration of the giant was the new management's first task. CEO Barnevik had been applauded for his excellent job of rationalization at ASEA. When he took the helm of that company in 1980 it was struggling; by 1986 it was earning 5.5% of total sales, compared to Brown Boveri's 1.5%. The companies hoped Barnevik would have similar success with Brown Boveri's operations.

In 1989 Asea Brown Boveri formed a joint venture with the American electrical firm Westinghouse. ABB owned 45% of the new subsidiary, which manufactures electricity distribution systems for international markets. This gave the company the foothold in North America that both halves of ABB had struggled to achieve for the past two decades. Then, several months later, ABB exercized its option to buy Westinghouse out of the venture, leaving ABB the sole owner of the company.

Asea Brown Boveri has continued to expand aggressively throughout the world, buying companies in Europe and North America in preparation for the unification of the European Economic Community in 1992 and the increased global competition that will bring.

As Asea Brown Boveri moves into the 1990s, the eyes of industrial analysts are upon it. As the largest cross-border merger in history, the company will serve as a model for the type of international combinations which are likely to increase in frequency after the relaxation of European trade borders in 1992. Demand for heavy electrical equipment is expected to increase over the long term as systems installed in the early part of the century wear out. Asea Brown Boveri's size gives it the kind of muscle it will need to survive in the meantime, but its aggressive management will no doubt be looking to develop new products, such as robotics, and tap new markets, like North America.

Principal Subsidiaries: Asea Brown Boveri S.A. (Belgium); Asea Brown Boveri AG (West Germany); Asea Brown Boveri S.p.A. (Italy); SAE/SADELMI S.A. Elettrificazione S.p.A. (Italy); Asea Brown Boveri B.V. (Netherlands); Asea Brown Boveri S.A. (Spain); Asea Brown Boveri Ltd. (U.K.); ABB Kent (Holdings) PLC (U.K.); Asea Brown Boveri AG (Austria); ABB Strömberg Drives Oy (Finland); Elektrisk Bureau A/S (Norway); Asea Brown Boveri (Sweden); Asea Brown Boveri AG (Switzerland); Asea Brown Boveri Inc. (Canada); Asea Brown Boveri, Inc. (U.S.A.); ABB Asea Brown Boveri Pty. Ltd. (Australia); Asea Brown Boveri Ltd. (Hong Kong); Asea Brown Boveri S.A. (Argentina); Asea Brown Boveri Ltda. (Brazil).

ALPS

ALPS ELECTRIC CO., LTD.

1–7, Yukigaya–Otsuka–Cho
Ota-ku
Tokyo 145
Japan
(03) 726–1211

Public Company
Incorporated: 1948 as Kataoka Electric Company
Employees: 6,694
Sales: ¥376.65 billion (US$3.01 billion)
Stock Index: Tokyo Osaka Nagoya

Alps is one of the largest electronics companies in the world; it is, among other things, the world's largest manufacturer of floppy disk drives. Alps produces tens of thousands of different parts and components for manufacturers as diverse as Honda, General Motors, Goldstar, Matsushita, and Hitachi.

As one of the few secondary manufacturers to remain independent of client companies and other industrial groups, Alps is an oddity in Japanese industry. In order to maintain this independence, the company has had to avoid a "vertical" diversification. Instead of moving from parts manufacturing to finished products, which would have put Alps squarely in competition with its clients, the company expanded "horizontally," developing a wider and more sophisticated array of components and preserving harmony with its customers.

Alps's customers are some of the largest companies in the world; these companies could certainly establish their own parts manufacturing subsidiaries. The fact that they haven't tried to replace Alps testifies to the company's many strengths. It need only be concerned with a very narrow function, and it can benefit from greater economies of scale by selling the same product to several different customers.

The man behind Alps Electric is Katsutaro Kataoka, a self-styled industrial revolutionary in the mold of Sony's Akio Morita. A displaced war veteran and mechanical engineer, Kataoka worked briefly for Toshiba. He was uncomfortable working for a large firm, so he left Toshiba, borrowed $1,400 from his family, and set up a small manufacturing shop in Ohta, a drab industrial suburb of Tokyo. The company opened for business in November, 1948 as the Kataoka Electric Company.

Kataoka's original product line consisted of an unimpressive variety of simple-technology components such as light switches and variable capacitors. He peddled these items to a number of larger manufacturers, offering a reliable product at low unit costs. The company's business grew steadily during the 1950s, but while its volume increased, its technology changed very little.

But as the products manufactured by Kataoka's customers became more complex, these customers began to pressure Kataoka to develop a wider variety of more durable, high-quality parts. Kataoka began investing more heavily in research and development and expanded its operations with new factories. A subsidiary, Tohoku Alps, was established in August of 1964, and the following December Kataoka Electric changed its name to the more English-sounding Alps.

Alps Electric began a period of unprecedented growth during the mid-1960s as the Japanese consumer electronics industry took off. Alps components were incorporated into thousands of products, and it established significant market shares in new sectors, such as radio tuners. A technical agreement with General Instrument in 1963 led to Alps's acquisition of UHF television tuner technology; today Alps is the world's leader in TV tuner manufacturing. Eager to capitalize on its profitability and take advantage of promising markets, Alps entered into an agreement to produce car radios with Motorola in 1967. The venture was moderately successful, and it gave Alps a chance to learn about many new technologies developed by Motorola. Alps also established joint ventures with local manufacturers in developing countries, including India (1964), Taiwan (1970), and South Korea (1970).

By 1970 the company was the largest independent component manufacturer in Japan, but it was unable to win the respect usually accorded a company of its size. Because it was limited to producing components, and therefore a captive of its customers' business, analysts and industrialists considered Alps a secondary company, regardless of its sales volume.

In fact, it was Alps and secondary manufacturers like it that made Japan's export-led boom in electronics possible on such a scale. Their billions of simple pieces, produced at very low cost, were essential to final manufacturers. Alps was constantly motivated to maintain its high quality and low prices by the unspoken threat that its customers could find other suppliers.

During the 1970s, Alps established subsidiaries and joint venture companies in the United States, Brazil, and West Germany. It operated a joint venture to produce semiconductors with Motorola from 1973 to 1975, and in 1978 took over Motorola's share of the car stereo venture, changing its name to Alpine Electronics. Alpine subsequently introduced a line of successful upmarket radios under its own name for Honda, BMW, Volvo, Chrysler, and GM.

When exchange rates have depressed the sale of Japanese electronic goods in foreign markets, final manufacturers have often protected their profit margins by demanding lower prices from suppliers such as Alps. While these suppliers were in many cases powerless to argue, Alps began to seize the initiative on several fronts. It began to develop special components, such as automobile electronics devices and to contribute to research on new end-products. No longer just a supplier but now an active participant in the design process, Alps is not in a position to have its prices dictated by its customers anymore.

The company's graduation to a higher position in Japanese industry had an immediate effect on its business. Alps developed computer keyboards for IBM and Apple, and later took over Apple's keyboard and "mouse" plant in Garden Grove, California. Alps began to produce floppy disk drives in 1980 and steadily built market share; its customers include IBM, Apple, and Commodore. By 1985 it was the world's largest producer of floppy disk drives.

That year the company decided to try to exploit certain sectors of the market as a primary manufacturer. The computer market slumped during 1987, however, and the company was compelled to take losses in most of its computer-related product lines.

Alps intends to reduce its reliance on secondary manufacturing gradually, but for now, its major products are still secondary: switches (23% of sales), floppy disk drives and printers (21%), car audio sets (19%), and VCR parts, including magnetic heads and cylinders (14%).

As a supplier, Alps has many strengths. The company's main plants are located in a rural area of northern Honshu. It has little trouble finding more plant space near existing facilities, and has access to cheaper labor. It makes great use of subcontractors, particularly in labor-intensive and marginally profitable processes. Assembly lines are being automated, as are the warehouses. Alps is likely to retain these advantages for many years; they will bolster the company's sales while it undertakes the difficult task of establishing itself as a primary manufacturer under the energetic leadership of its president, Masataka Katoaka.

Principal Subsidiaries: Tohoku Alps Co., Ltd.; Alpine Electronics Inc.; Alpine Electronics Manufacturing of America, Inc. (U.S.A.); Alps Electric (U.S.A.) Inc. (U.S.A.); Alpine Electronics of America, Inc. (U.S.A.)

AMP

AMP, INC

Harrisburg, Pennsylvania 17105–3608
U.S.A.
(717) 564–0100

Public Company
Incorporated: 1956
Employees: 24,100
Sales: $2.67 billion
Stock Index: New York

AMP is the leading manufacturer of an essential and often overlooked line of electrical components: connections. AMP has developed highly versatile and durable "smart" connections that perform many functions more economically than other alternatives.

The founder of AMP was Uncas A. Whitaker, a former employee of Westinghouse Electric and the Hoover Company who held degrees in mechanical and electrical engineering and law. In 1941, after two years as a senior engineer for American Machine & Foundry in New York, Whitaker decided to start his own company. Aircraft Marine Products, as the company was called, specialized in solderless, uninsulated electrical connections for aircraft and boat manufacturers: a short metal tube with a ring on the end and a crimping tool. The device allowed electricians to make quick, removable wire connections without a heating element or flux. It was simple, unique, and very popular.

From a small office in New Jersey, Aircraft Marine established supply contracts with some of the largest industrial manufacturers in the world. Less than three months after the company was created, the United States entered World War II. Companies such as Boeing, Consolidated Vultee, Ford, and Electric Boat redirected their production toward the war effort, developing new products and accelerating output. More than ever before, warplanes, battleships and field equipment incorporated electrical devices, and increasingly these were assembled with solderless connections.

With its business thriving from war production, Aircraft Marine soon moved to a larger facility in Glen Rock, Pennsylvania. It then moved its headquarters to Harrisburg in 1943, after winning over the city's chamber of commerce, which didn't want new business in the city, complaining about inadequate housing. A fire at the Glen Rock plant and the trauma of relocation overshadowed the introduction of the pre-insulated terminal, an improved version of AMP's existing product that left all but the terminal ring exposed—an improvement which reduced the incidence of shorted circuits.

The end of the war brought a termination of contracts across a broad spectrum of American industry. Many of Aircraft Marine's customers went bankrupt, were acquired, or were forced into mergers—in general they were compelled to reduce the scale of their operations drastically. Aircraft Marine, however, required little product conversion in order to adapt to the postwar economy since its connections were versatile components rather than more specialized finished products.

Still, the transition was stressful for Aircraft Marine. It was able to survive the sudden drop in orders through drastic austerity measures and additional underwriting from Midland Investment Company, its primary benefactor. Whitaker became bitter about the company's experience with military contracts and procurement controls.

Aircraft Marine re-entered the commercial market with another new product, the strip-formed terminal. During 1952, the company created a marketing unit called AMP Special Industries, and established sales of existing products and the introduction of connectors for pin and sockets, coaxial cables, and printed circuits resulted in unprecedented growth. Expanding through sales-led growth rather than by acquisition, in the 1950s Aircraft Marine added subsidiaries in Australia, Britain, the Netherlands, Italy, Japan, Mexico, and West Germany.

Aircraft Marine changed its name to AMP upon incorporation as a public company in 1956. The company thereafter raised additional capital through share offerings. AMP improved and expanded its plant space and began a more ambitious research and development effort. Having demonstrated brisk and stable growth, AMP was listed on the New York Stock Exchange in October 1959.

Whitaker relinquished the company presidency to George A. Ingalls in 1961. Although he remained chairman, Whitaker wished to emphasize a more democratic form of leadership. He assigned many of his own managerial responsibilities to other managers and slowly removed himself from the company's daily operations.

AMP made a conscious decision during the 1960s against diversification into a wider range of products. Instead, management elected to concentrate on the "passive components" market it had come to dominate. AMP had experienced 15% annual growth in the ten years since the mid-1950s and anticipated an increasingly difficult "active component" market in the ensuing decades. Indeed, while Japanese electronics manufacturers were developing new capabilities in active components—particularly transistors—they neglected to take advantage of trade regulations which would have allowed them to establish an enduring position in passive components. As a result, AMP became the largest passive component manufacturer in Japan, a position it holds to this day.

AMP continued to make frequent management changes; presidents and chief executives served only for about five years before changing jobs. Whitaker, however, served as chairman until his death in 1975. His death neither interrupted the company's business nor caused a management battle for power. Under the leadership of Joseph D. Brenner, AMP maintained its stable course, but devoted increasing sums of money toward research into new "semi-passive" systems.

Among the products to materialize from this intensified effort were more advanced coaxial connections for the growing cable TV market, fiber-optic terminals for improved telecommunications systems, and more durable membrane switches. To some extent, however, AMP did not take full advantage of military sales. Like Whitaker, Brenner refused to seek Pentagon sales because the government negotiated special prices on the basis of margin. This necessitated inspection of AMP's books—something Whitaker viewed as interference in the company's business. Instead, AMP was, in effect, a secondary supplier; it sold to companies that did hold Pentagon contracts. Insulated from the vagaries of defense procurement, AMP was better able to maintain stable growth, which continued at an annual rate of about 16%.

Walter Raab, a CPA with nearly 30 years of service to AMP, was named chairman and CEO upon Brenner's retirement in 1982. A cautious planner, in the mold of his predecessors, Raab presided over AMP during a delicate period. Major customers, such as IBM, Ford, and Digital, sought to cut supply costs by reducing stocks and numbers of suppliers. AMP, and its principal competitors Molex and Thomas & Betts, were expected to benefit most. Already the largest suppliers to the industry, they were most likely to survive. In fact, they stood to gain market share as smaller suppliers were eliminated.

AMP invested heavily in the development of integrated sub-assemblies and new automated application methods. The system was originally conceived for use in automotive manufacture. The installation of automotive wiring harnesses, or electrical systems, was complex and labor-intensive. Sub-assemblies, however, were simple and cut down on man-hours. AMP had to wait more than ten years, however, before auto manufacturers were willing to incorporate the system.

Suddenly, in 1985 components customers initiated a drastic reorganization. They switched to automated sub-assemblies in a very short period of time. AMP, the least affected, suffered an 18% drop in sales, but recovered quickly as new products were brought on line.

Recognizing the potential sales which came with the Reagan Administration's military expansion, AMP created a special group, open to Pentagon scrutinization, whose specific purpose is to engage in government sales. But less than 5% of its sales come from the military. In late 1987, both AMP and Molex purchased shares in Matrix, a defense-oriented connection manufacturer. Neither competitor has yet moved to absorb Matrix, but their interest in the company demonstrates the importance each attaches to future military sales.

AMP's new president, James Marley, was trained in manufacturing rather than finance. He believes AMP's future lies in the development of "smarter" connections—ones that perform as switches or regulators. In addition, he told *Financial World*, "If we focus on being good vendors to our customers, we won't ever have to worry about competition."

Principal Subsidiaries: AMP Products Corp.; AMP Keyboard Technologies, Inc.; Carroll Touch Inc.; Mark Eyelet Inc.; Matrix Science Corp.; AMP Packaging Sys., Inc.; AMP of Canada Ltd.; AMP de Mexico, S.A.; AMP S.A. Argentina; AMP do Brasil Ltda.; AMP de France S.A.; AMP-Holland B.V.; AMP of Great Britain Ltd.; AMP Italia S.p.A.; AMP Deutschland G.m.b.H.; AMP Espanola, S.A.; AMP Osterrich Handelsges M.b.H.; AMP Schweiz A.G.; AMP (Japan) Ltd.; Australian AMP Pty. Ltd.; AMP Finland OY; AMP Norge A/S; AMP Portugal, LDA; AMP Svenska A.B.; AMP Belgium; AMP Danmark; AMP Singapore Pte. Ltd.; AMP Products Pacific Ltd., Hong Kong; AMP Korea; New Zealand AMP Ltd.; AMP Ireland Limited; AMP Taiwan.

Further Reading: Cohn, W. H. *The End is Just Beginning*, Carnegie-Mellon Press, 1980; Barton, Michael. *Life by the Moving Road: A History of the Harrisburg Area*, Woodland Hills, California, Windsor Publications, 1983.

BICOASTAL CORPORATION

15438 North Florida Avenue
Tampa, Florida 33613
U.S.A.
(813) 264–7100

Public Company
Incorporated: 1863 as the Singer Manufacturing Company
Employees: 3,800
Sales: $301.9 million
Stock Index: New York

Bicoastal Corporation is better known as the Singer Company, which was its name until the fall of 1989. Singer, of course, is the company that brought the world the sewing machine. While Mahatma Gandhi was imprisoned by India's British colonial government in the early 1930s, he learned to sew on a Singer Sewing Machine—it is said that he called the machine "one of the few useful things ever invented." There are Singer sewing machines in almost every country around the world, and Singer instruction manuals have been published in more than 50 languages. In the early 1960s, however, Singer began to grow from a one-item company into a diversified conglomerate. By 1986, with a strong electronics and defense business, Singer spun off its original sewing machine business. Then in 1988 Singer was taken over in a leveraged buyout by corporate raider Paul Bilzerian, who quickly moved to sell off most of the once-proud company.

Isaac Merritt Singer was born in Pittstown, New York in 1811, and ran away from his immigrant parents at the age of 12 to join a troupe of traveling actors. Singer remained an actor until 1835. During the following years he worked at various jobs while he invented things on the side. By 1850, Singer had gone to Boston with a patented device for carving wood-block type he hoped to sell to type manufacturers.

In Boston, Singer became interested in a prospective client's sewing machine–repair business. The first patent for a sewing machine had been granted in England in 1790, but because of their unreliability none of the machines since then had been commercially successful. The first sewing machine with an eye-pointed needle, invented in 1846 by Elias Howe, seemed on the verge of capturing the public interest, but it, too, required frequent repairs. Singer quickly set to work to invent a reliable machine.

Singer finished his machine in 1850 and was granted a patent for it in 1851, the same year that I. M. Singer and Company was established. The machine was an immediate success, prompting Howe to file suit against Singer for patent infringement. In 1854 Singer hired a young lawyer named Edward Clark to defend him; Clark agreed to take the case in exchange for a third of Singer's business, and eventually the two men became equal partners in the company, Singer running the manufacturing side and Clark the financial and sales side.

Clark stymied the lawsuits brought against Singer and then brought the manufacturers together to pool their patents by creating the Singer Machine Combination, the first patent pool in America. The combination, which lasted until 1877, when the last patent ran out, licensed 24 sewing machine manufacturers to make the machines for $15 a machine, with Singer and Howe receiving $5 each for every machine sold domestically.

With Clark supervising the day-to-day operations, I. M. Singer and Company began to grow rapidly. Until the late 1850s the price of a sewing machine limited its market to commercial interests like professional tailors and harness manufacturers. But at that time, Clark introduced the first consumer installment payment plan. This plan, combined with an aggressive marketing strategy, enabled the young company to survive the business panic of 1857 and gave Singer the decisive lead in sewing machines for more than a century.

In 1863, Clark and Singer dissolved their partnership and the company was incorporated as the Singer Manufacturing Company after Singer's rather sordid personal life (which eventually resulted in 24 children by four women) came to light. Both Clark and Singer retained some stock in the company but sold the rest to their employees. Clark continued as president of the company until his death in 1882; Isaac Singer, who had fled to Europe, died in England in 1875.

For the next 70 years, Singer was led by three men: F. G. Bourne, who was president from 1873 to 1905; Douglas Alexander, who led the company from 1906 to 1949; and Milton Lightner, who served from 1949 to 1958. These men increased Singer's role as America's first multinational company. Singer had begun manufacturing in Scotland in 1867 and in Canada in 1873. By the 1880s, the company's extensive European operations were exporting sewing machines to Africa and soon after the turn of the century, Singer was selling its product in the South Pacific. The one setback during this growth and expansion occurred in 1917, when the company's Russian holdings were seized during the Bolshevik Revolution. In 1918 Singer acquired the Diehl Manufacturing Company to make sewing machine motors.

Throughout the 1920s and 1930s, Singer's profits rose steadily as it convinced more and more people around the world that a Singer sewing machine was indispensable. By the end of World War II, however, the sewing machine market had matured in the United States. To make matters worse, within a few years European manufacturers offering zig-zag machines (which Singer had decided in the 1930s wouldn't find a market in the United States) and suddenly highly competitive Japanese manufacturers began to flood the market. In the United States alone,

Singer's market share had halved, to only one-third, by the late 1950s.

Singer had hired a lawyer, Donald P. Kircher, to supervise the company's legal affairs in 1948. In 1955, Kircher was appointed Lightner's assistant, and in 1958 he was made president. Hired to help turn Singer around, Kircher began a complete reorganization of the company: plants were modernized, manufacturing procedures automated, products upgraded, and merchandising improved. By 1963 Singer's share in the U.S. sewing machine market had increased to 40%.

Under Kircher's direction, Singer also began an ambitious overseas construction program. Besides spending large amounts of money to revamp company facilities in Scotland, Brazil, France, West Germany, and Italy, Kircher also started building new factories in Australia, Mexico, and the Philippines. In addition, Kircher reaffirmed the strategy of looking towards underdeveloped regions of the world for the company's largest markets.

Kircher also began a domestic diversification program. One of his first decisions was to purchase Haller, Raymond & Brown, Inc., a leading electronics research firm and Singer's first step into the electronics industry. He also bought three companies in 1960 and 1961: two knitting-machine makers and a carpet-tufting-machinery maker. Initially, this diversification strategy was also successful. Between 1958 and 1963, Singer's sales almost doubled, to $1.2 billion (between 1952 and 1956 they had risen only 12%, from $325 million to $364 million). In 1963, Singer dropped the "Manufacturing" from its name to better reflect the nature of its business.

Kircher's plan also included a more aggressive acquisition-and-diversification policy. The first important purchase, in 1963, was of Friden, Inc., a manufacturer of office equipment and calculators. The second one, of General Precision Equipment Corporation, was made in 1968. General Precision gave Singer access to three markets: industrial products (such as gas meters), defense electronics, and aerospace. But GPE and Friden were only part of Kircher's grand plan. Altogether, Kircher bought 22 manufacturing firms with products ranging from audio to aerospace equipment.

In 1958, 90% of Singer's total sales came from sewing machines; by 1970, this portion was reduced to 35%, and Kircher's diversification strategy seemed to work. Singer's sales exceeded $1.9 billion, 40% from business abroad.

But Kircher, described by subordinates as autocratic and imperious, had overreached himself. Although the company reported $2.6 billion in sales for 1974, one Wall Street analyst estimated that Singer's debt had reached $1.1 billion—a staggering price for its acquisition program. Combined with a collapse in the aerospace market and a glut in office equipment in the late 1960s, it is not surprising that Singer reported a $10.1 million loss in 1974. The single bright spot that year was Singer's original sewing machine operation, which accounted for 54% of company sales.

While Kircher was confined to a hospital bed in 1975, the board of directors looked for someone to replace him. They hired Joseph Flavin, who had worked at IBM and at Xerox, where he was an executive vice-president. Forty-seven years old when he became Singer's president, Flavin immediately took a $411 million write-off to eliminate the company's money-losing ventures, including a home-building concern, a printing operation, a telecommunications firm, an Italian household-appliance plant, and a West German mail-order house. This write-off was the largest of its time and reduced Singer's book value by 50%. Flavin then planned to revitalize the company's sewing machine operation and develop its power-tool and aerospace businesses.

Over the next few years, Singer also concentrated on developing high-technology electric components including air conditioning and heating systems, gas meters, thermostats, electrical switches, dishwashers, and auto dashboards. The company made the guidance system for the Trident missile and navigation equipment for airplanes and ships, while Singer electrical instruments played an important role in NASA's Apollo lunar modules.

Flavin managed to reduce the company's $1.1 billion debt by 55% after he became president, but in 1979 he took a $130 million write-off on the sewing machine business, which in North America and Europe had fallen off drastically. This move involved the restructuring of Singer's North American and European operations; its oldest factory in Europe, near Clydebank, Scotland, was one of the casualties. Flavin also replaced 80 of his top 200 managers. All these changes were made in the middle of a headquarters move from New York City to Stamford, Connecticut.

In 1980, Singer's aerospace and marine divisions' operating profits increased by 34%, to $36 million, due in large part to Singer's role as the nation's leading manufacturer of aircraft simulators, including the one used to train space shuttle astronauts. In addition, this division won a large contract for helicopters from the Defense Department in 1981. Encouraged by these results, management decided to create SimuFlite, a new venture that provided ground-school and flight-simulation training for corporate pilots.

Foreign manufacturers like Bernina, Pfaff, and Viking, along with inexpensive imports from Japan, began to cut deeply into what little was left of Singer's sewing machine market during the early 1980s. That and the belief among top officials at Singer that the sewing industry in the United States was finally drying up led the company to abandon its century-old core business. In 1986, Singer spun off its sewing machine division as a separate company called SSMC Inc.—"Singer" sewing machines are now made by SSMC, not Singer. Singer also got rid of all 1,600 company-owned stores and service centers, either by closing them or making them independent.

Although Singer had become a $2 billion-a-year defense conglomerate, it was beset by endless problems and an enormous debt. Its stock price was driven down by the announcement of a $20 million loss in July, 1987, which it attributed to development costs for several new aerospace products. Then that fall, Chairman Joseph Flavin died unexpectedly. And so, to no one's surprise, Singer became a prime takeover candidate. The buyer was a surprise, however: Paul Bilzerian, a somewhat obscure corporate raider best known as a greenmailer. For $50 a share—some

$15 below what Singer's investment banker, Goldman Sachs, had expected it to sell for—Bilzerian walked away with Singer.

Despite a staggering debt load, Bilzerian at first promised not to strip Singer of its most productive assets, planning only to sell off its defense electronics business. But only months later, prime assets began to go. Between July and October, 1988, Bilzerian sold eight of Singer's 12 divisions, for about $2 billion, which tidily covered his debt.

But in December, 1988, Bilzerian was indicted—for non-Singer-related activities—and in May, 1989, he was convicted of nine counts of securities and tax violations, which he will appeal. More troublesome for the company itself, however, will be the multitude of suits filed against Singer since mid-1988 by former employees regarding pension benefits; stockholders disillusioned by Bilzerian's dealings; buyers of divisions who claim they were overcharged; and the federal government, which seeks treble damages of $231 million for Defense Department overcharges dating back to 1980. Even under a new name, the future of America's first multinational looks grim indeed.

Principal Subsidiaries: Singer Link-Miles Ltd.; Librascope Corporation; Simuflight Training International; Singer Link-Miles Simulation; Singer Link-Miles Corporation.

Further Reading: Cooper, Grace Rogers. *The Sewing Machine: Its Invention and Development*, Washington, D.C., Smithsonian Institution, 1976; Brandfon, Ruth. *Singer and the Sewing Machine: A Capitalist Romance*, London, Barrie & Jenkins, 1977.

COMPAGNIE GÉNÉRALE D'ÉLECTRICITÉ

54, rue La Boétie
75382 Paris Cedex 08
France
(1) 563–1414

Public Company
Incorporated: 1898
Employees: 204,100
Sales: FFr127.96 billion (US$21.12 billion)
Stock Index: Paris

Compagnie Générale d'Électricité, or CGE, as it is more commonly known, is one of France's largest industrial combines. With interests in energy, telecommunications, construction, and manufacturing, CGE may be considered a strategic resource, like Britain's GEC, America's GE, or Germany's AEG.

Much of the attention CGE has attracted during the 1980s had to do with its telecommunications subsidiary Alcatel. As world markets have become more dependent on information, demands on telecommunications technologies have grown more acute and complex. Through Alcatel, CGE has set out to exploit the tremendous business opportunities that exist in telecommunications.

Another matter of attention—and for many, a source of confusion—has been the company's recent experience as a state-owned corporation. After a brief and unsuccessful socialist "experiment," CGE was returned to the private sector in 1986.

For the greater part of its history, CGE was involved almost exclusively in the fields of electric-power generation and distribution. As one of the first companies in Europe to begin commercial production of electricity, CGE developed leading positions in the engineering, design, and manufacture of generators, substations, and distribution devices.

Although capitalized initially with private funds, CGE received generous financial assistance and support from the French government. As a result, it was often obliged to follow state-directed development programs and serve French political interests—particularly as they applied to domestic industrialization and job creation.

CGE experienced strong growth during the interwar period. By 1938 CGE had expanded well beyond its traditional base in industrial eastern France and grown to more than 1.2 million customers, from 2,000 in 1990. The company remained under the managerial domination of several families until the Popular Front government of Leon Blum came to power in 1936. When that government fell in 1938, however, many of these family interests regained influence within the company.

In the years before World War II, CGE purchased construction and civil-engineering interests which further strengthened the company's position in power resources. Because CGE was the leading French utility and a primary industrial resource, and therefore a crucial strategic resource, the company was nationalized and placed under government control. With an increasing threat from Germany, French military strategists had little time to prepare for the defense of the company's resources.

The German invasion of Poland in 1939 prompted France to declare war on Germany, but no major battles were fought for several months. France was ill-prepared for the German invasion which followed in 1940, and eastern and northern France—where CGE was most heavily concentrated—fell quickly. The rest of France came under the control of a rival French government under Marshal Henri Petain, who signed an armistice with Germany. Like many French industrial resources, CGE was taken over by German functionaries and dedicated to the German war effort.

Soon after the United States entered the war in 1942, CGE plants became targets for Allied bombings and sabotage. Many sites, however, were spared in anticipation of the establishment of an Allied beachhead in Western Europe. When that beachhead was established in 1944, CGE facilities were taken back by Allied forces and used to support action against the Germans.

After the war ended in 1945, CGE undertook a massive development program in support of the French government's efforts to re-establish France as a leading military and industrial power. Investigating new commercial markets, CGE expanded in small manufacturing ventures such as batteries, wire, light bulbs, and switches.

Throughout the 1950s, the company's growth was closely tied to the stop-and-go performance of the French economy. By the early 1960s, however, CGE, with over 200 subsidiaries, had become weighed down by bureaucracy and stagnant market growth.

The company undertook a general reorganization and diversification program in 1965. Three years later, CGE was reorganized into several large market groups, including power generation, engineering, telecommunications, cable and wire, raw materials, and nuclear, naval, and electromechanical products. It was at this juncture that Alsthom, another French electromechanical engineering company, became involved with CGE. While both remained separate companies, their ownership was pooled in order to concentrate and rationalize capital and human resources. CGE was converted into a large state-owned holding company with leading interests in virtually every sector of the European electric, telecommunications, and construction industries.

Alsthom was founded at approximately the same time as

CGE, but remained principally an electrical-engineering company, manufacturing power-generation equipment and building power plants. In 1976, Alsthom merged with the French shipbuilding company Les Chantiers de l'Atlantique. The new company, Alsthom-Atlantique, later acquired various other industrial units including the power-turbine generator unit of the Swiss company BBC Brown Boveri, and expanded its activities in power resources, shipbuilding, railway equipment, and switchgear.

CGE, meanwhile, endured numerous restructurings at the behest of the French government. Intended as "fine tuning" to make the company more competitive, frequent changes in management, finance, and organization left CGE an ill-focused and confused institution. As a primary force behind French industry, CGE was slow to respond to national imperatives necessitated by the energy crisis in 1973 and, later, the turbulent downfall of the OPEC oil cartel following the Iranian revolution of 1979.

In 1981 the French elected a Socialist government led by President Francois Mitterand. Mitterand pledged to nationalize many of France's largest industrial combines, including CGE. The nationalization was carried out in 1982, but CGE, which already had endured years of government direction, was barely changed. In fact, many of its nonconsolidated subsidiaries remained under the control of private investors.

Converted into a de facto sub-ministry for energy, CGE was forced to dilute market-based business decisions with French political initiatives. Far from destroying the company, however, nationalization benefited CGE in several ways. As it profited from the opening of several export markets and pan-European trade agreements and remained a major supplier of turnkey projects in areas politically sensitive to Western interests, CGE became the third largest exporter in France, after Renault and Peugeot, earning 40% of its income from exports.

Another result of the nationalization was the government's decision to restructure the French electronics industry by assigning certain operations to specific companies. In 1983 CGE and Thomson-Brandt exchanged various assets so that CGE could assume primary responsibility for telecommunications (while retaining the Thomson product name), and Thomson-Brandt could concentrate on consumer electronics and military equipment.

With the reorganization of the U.S. telephone system, the American company ITT announced divestiture of its foreign telecommunications interests. Originally created as a counterpart to AT&T for foreign telecommunications operations, ITT sought to bolster its performance by concentrating instead on the financial-services industry.

During 1986, CGE negotiated the purchase of 63% of ITT's telecommunications interests—including Standard Electrik Lorenz of West Germany, Bell Telephone Manufacturing of Belgium, Standard Electrica of Spain, Standard Telefon of Norway, Standard Radio and Telefon of Sweden, and Standard Telephone and Radio of Switzerland—for $1.1 billion. CGE merged its existing telecommunications operations with those of ITT, and consolidated the operations under an existing subsidiary called Alcatel, incorporated in the Netherlands but headquartered in Brussels.

The French experiment with socialism produced few positive results for the French economy and had become a growing liability for President Mitterand. While extolling many of the accomplishments of his nationalization program, Mitterand endorsed the privatization of many companies the state had taken over. Accordingly, government control of CGE—what CGE Chairman Pierre Suard has called a "dark period"—ended in 1986.

While CGE has returned to private-sector control, it remains as important to the French economy as ever, and so must occasionally bow to the demands of the government. The company has, however, managed to invigorate its operations with newer, more efficient planning and marketing procedures. With a new and powerful standing in telecommunications, it has set out to overrun AT&T as the world's leading telecommunications company—a goal which, with the advantages of an open European market in 1992, may be within its reach.

Principal Subsidiaries: CGEE Alsthom; CEAc (73.2%); Saft (67%); Alcatel NV (The Netherlands) (61.5%); GEC Alsthom NV (The Netherlands) (50%); Framatome (40%).

COOPER INDUSTRIES, INC.

First City Tower, Suite 4000
Post Office Box 4446
Houston, Texas 77210
U.S.A.
(713) 739–5400

Public Company
Incorporated: 1895 as the C. & G. Cooper Company
Employees: 46,300
Sales: $4.3 billion
Stock Index: New York Pacific

Cooper Industries is a diversified, international manufacturing company divided into three main segments: electrical and electronic products, commercial and industrial products, and compression and drilling products. To protect itself from the highly cyclical nature of the energy industry, Cooper embarked in the mid-1960s on an aggressive program of acquiring manufacturing companies with high growth potential and reputations for high quality. While the company has proved itself expert at acquiring and managing low-technology companies, it does not hesitate to use high-technology equipment and production methods as well as sophisticated accounting, inventory, and quality-control techniques to streamline operations and maximize earnings.

Brothers Charles and Elias Cooper built a foundry in their hometown of Mount Vernon, Ohio and called it the Mt. Vernon Iron Works. Soon better known as C. & E. Cooper Company, their first products were plows, maple syrup kettles, hog troughs, sorghum grinders, and wagon boxes. Charles Cooper was the stronger leader. Aggressively anti-slavery and a dedicated prohibitionist, he became a respected community leader, even though many of his views differed greatly from those of his neighbors. When Elias Cooper died in 1848, Charles Cooper took a succession of partners, and with each the company name changed accordingly.

Mount Vernon was linked to the rest of the nation by the railroad in 1851 and the following year Cooper was able to ship its first steam-powered compressors for blast furnaces. Cooper's relationship with the railroad had its difficulties, however. When the Sandusky, Mansfield, and Newark Railway was delinquent in paying for wood-burning locomotives from the company, Charles Cooper was driven to chain the wheels of a locomotive to the track, padlock it, and stand sentry until he was paid in full.

By the time of the Civil War, Cooper products included wood-burning steam locomotives and steam-powered blowing machines for charcoal blast furnaces. After Charles Gray Cooper, son of Elias, served in the Union army and attended Rensselaer Institute, he became a partner with his uncle.

In 1869 Cooper became the first company in what was then the West to produce the new, highly efficient Corliss engine. Six years later, it offered the Cooper traction engine, America's first farm tractor. Throughout the rest of the century, the Corliss engine was Cooper's principal product.

The company was incorporated as the C. & G. Cooper Company in 1895, and Frank L. Fairchild, a respected salesman of the Cooper-Corliss engine, was named its first president. Fairchild so enjoyed selling that throughout his 17-year presidency he continued to serve as sales manager.

By 1900 gas was being discovered in new fields and shipped more than 100 miles through primitive pipelines. At the same time, the oil industry was also beginning to develop. Not long after Charles Cooper's death in 1901, it became clear that steam turbine engines were destined to replace the Corliss engine. Cooper management recognized the necessity of focusing on a small segment of the market, and in 1908 it wisely chose to make a gradual change to natural-gas internal-combustion engines, which were being used successfully at the compression stage of pipeline transmission.

Fairchild died suddenly in 1912 and Charles Gray (C.G.) Cooper, took his place. One story describes C.G.'s famous bluntness particularly well: C.G. once visited a procrastinating client and without any preliminary niceties asked, "Do you want to buy a steam engine?" The man said he didn't want one just then. "All right, then you can go to hell," C.G. said and stormed out abruptly.

During World War I, Cooper built high-speed steam-hydraulic forging presses for government arsenals, munitions plants, and shipyards, as well as giant gas engines and compressors and triple-expansion marine engines. The company's wartime production demands slowed its transformation from a producer of steam to gas engines, since steam engines were needed for the war effort. But after the war, it became clear that the company had chosen its direction wisely when it set its sights on developing gas internal-combustion engines. The old Corliss was quickly becoming outmoded by competition from steam turbines and gas-powered engines.

In 1919 C.G. Cooper became chairman and Desault B. Kirk, the company's treasurer, became president. Just a year later, Cooper began a long-range program for growth, and the directors elected Beatty B. Williams president. Although he'd married the boss's daughter, few credited Williams's rise to simply marrying into the family. Serving as vice president and general manager during the war years, Williams was single-minded in his dedication to the company's success and directed Cooper (and subsequently Cooper-Bessemer) with great energy and and foresight for 22 years. Always mindful of what he called "an aloofness" that could develop between office and factory workers, Williams held conferences in which factory workers were invited to air their views and offered evening courses in production and management in which any employee could enroll.

Natural gas was gaining growing importance in the manufacture of steel and glass and in the emerging petrochemical industry. Cooper field service engineers were often on hand for months at a time to oversee the installation of huge four-cycle Cooper engines and compressors in compressor stations as new pipelines were routed through West Virginia, Louisiana, Arkansas, Oklahoma, and Texas.

Within just a few years, Cooper became the country's leading producer of pipeline compression engines. Although Cooper also produced smaller two-cylinder engines used in natural-gas fields to extract gas as it came from the well, the Bessemer Gas Engine Company of Grove City, Pennsylvania, dominated that field.

Founded in 1897, Bessemer had produced oil-pumping engines for most of its existence and had invested heavily in diesel engine development during the 1920s. While Cooper and Bessemer had some product overlap, their major strengths were in different areas.

By 1929 Cooper needed additional production facilities to meet the mounting orders for large natural-gas engine compressor units. Bessemer, after its lengthy period of diesel development, badly needed new capital. Both companies had posted nearly identical average earnings for the previous three years. The companies negotiated a merger for several months, and the Cooper-Bessemer Corporation came into being in April, 1929. The merger made the company the largest builder of gas engines and compressors in the United States. Soon afterward it was listed on the American Stock Exchange.

Cooper-Bessemer's business boom was brief. The company continued the Bessemer line of diesel marine engines, and since most ships were built or converted on the East Coast, Cooper-Bessemer soon decided to open a sales office in New York. The office was opened on October 23, 1929, however, at the very beginning of the Great Depression.

Two years later, annual sales had dropped more than 90%, reflecting the almost total halt of construction on long-distance pipelines and in American shipyards. Half of all sales that year were for repair parts. Along with thousands of other American companies, Cooper-Bessemer was forced to lay off workers.

Cooper-Bessemer slowly revived in the middle and late 1930s by continuing to improve products and by entering new markets. The company was convinced that the diesel would replace steam-powered railroad engines and it developed one for the new market.

Charles B. Jahnke was elected president in 1940 and Williams moved to chairman of the board, but Jahnke died a year later and Williams returned to the presidency for two more years. Only when Cooper-Bessemer embarked on a wartime production schedule in 1941 did its sales figures surpass their predepression level. The company had sold engines to several branches of the military before the war and was thus in a favored position to receive large orders during World War II. It became a major producer of diesel engines for military vessels of all kinds and also increased production of locomotive engines. At the peak of its wartime production, Cooper-Bessemer had 4,337 employees working in round-the-clock shifts.

In 1941 Cooper-Bessemer's net sales jumped to an all-time high, and just two years later they had more than tripled. The company was listed for the first time on the New York Stock Exchange in 1944.

Gordon Lefebvre was elected company president in 1943. He had previously served as vice-president and general manager. Formerly the head of General Motors's Pontiac division, he had a background in engineering and was energetic, likeable, and a tough negotiator.

After World War II, Cooper-Bessemer became increasingly interested in selling its products worldwide. It formed an international sales office and announced its first sales-service branch outside the United States, in Caracas, Venezuela, in 1945. Later in the decade, it expanded warehouse facilities in Canada and established a subsidiary sales unit, Cooper-Bessemer of Canada, with three offices, and received its first postwar orders from the Soviet Union.

Cooper-Bessemer had developed its innovative "turbo flow" high-compression gas-diesel engine in 1945, and two years later it introduced the GMW engine, which delivered 2,500 horsepower and could be shipped in one assembled unit. In these postwar years Cooper officials began to discuss diversification, which Lefebvre defined as "finding new markets for old products and new products for old markets, rather than moving into fields with which we are not familiar."

In 1951 Cooper-Bessemer's sales of $52 million surpassed its wartime high by nearly $10 million. Business that year was boosted by the Korean War; company shipments were almost solely to markets supported by the war effort, such as the petroleum, aluminum, chemical, and railroad industries.

In 1954 a combination of internal and external circumstances in 1954 led to a startling 38% decrease in net sales and Cooper-Bessemer's first net loss since 1938. The company's problems included a seven-week strike at the Grove City plant and a nationwide recession, but the main difficulty was the U.S. Supreme Court's decision in the Phillips Petroleum case, which ruled that producers selling gas to interstate pipelines had to submit to the Federal Power Commission's jurisdiction. This decision produced upheaval and uncertainty among pipeline operators, and therefore for Cooper-Bessemer.

While the company was rebuffing a 1955 takeover attempt by a private investor named Robert New, Lefebvre resigned unexpectedly, and Lawrence Williams, Beatty Williams's son, became president. He served beside his father, who was chairman of the board. Lawrence Williams had already served the company in many capacities and had taken early retirement to pursue other interests; he considered his return a temporary one. The takeover attempt had shaken management. In an attempt to bring an infusion of young talent to the company, Williams made a number of top management changes, including elevating Eugene L. Miller to chief operating officer. Due to revitalized demand, sales bounced back in 1956 to a record high of $61.2 million, but it was becoming increasingly clear that

Cooper-Bessemer needed to diversify in order to avoid the cyclical pitfalls of energy-related manufacturing.

In 1957 Gene Miller was elected president. At 38, he was the youngest man to hold the position since the company's original founder. Miller had begun at Cooper-Bessemer in 1946. A year after he became president, the company acquired Rotor Tool Company of Cleveland, the makers of pneumatic and high-cycle electric portable tools.

Over the next few years Cooper-Bessemer struggled to develop an engine to meet the challenge of General Electric's new combustion gas turbine engine, which threatened to supplant several of Cooper's engines in the pipeline transmission market. Its efforts resulted in the world's first industrial jet-powered gas turbine, introduced in 1960.

Under Miller's leadership, the distinction between Cooper-Bessemer administrative and operational management grew more pronounced, as was happening in companies throughout the country. Innovations such as computerization, fluctuations in worldwide monetary exchanges, increased government controls, and changing tax structures had made operating a large business increasingly complicated. In recognition of this, Miller moved the corporate offices from the Mount Vernon plant to offices on the city square to "establish a corporate group capable of administering many relatively independent divisions."

Meanwhile, Cooper-Bessemer's international division was also growing. By the end of the 1950s Cooper had sales agents in ten countries, licensees in three, and franchises in two. In 1964 it opened an office in Beirut and also formed a wholly owned British subsidiary, Cooper-Bessemer (U.K.), Ltd.

Cooper-Bessemer was no exception to the trend toward large conglomerates during the 1960s, but it did try to limit its acquisitions to those that could be mutually beneficial. In the early 1960s, it acquired Kline Manufacturing, a producer of high-pressure hydraulic pumps; Ajax Iron Works, which built gas engine compressors and a water flood vertical pump for oil and gas production; and the Pennsylvania Pump and Compressor Company. Between 1960 and 1965, the company's sales grew from $68 million to $117 million.

Cooper had grown into a large, diverse company. To better reflect its nature, it changed its name to Cooper Industries, Inc. in December, 1965. Two years later it moved its corporate headquarters to Houston, to be more in the geographic mainstream of American business.

Cooper acquired Lufkin Rule Company of Saginaw, Michigan, in 1967. It was the first of many acquisitions for what Lufkin president William G. Rector called a "tool basket"—a high-quality hand tools manufacturing group. Subsequent hand tool-related acquisitions included Crescent Niagara Corporation (wrenches) in 1968, Weller Electric Corporation (soldering tools) in 1970, Nicholson File Company (rasps and files) in 1972, Xcelite (small tools for the electronics industry) in 1973, J. Wiss & Sons Company (scissors) in 1976, McDonough Company's Plumb Tool subsidiary (striking tools) in 1980, and Kirsch Company (drapery hardware) in 1981.

Charles Cooper, the last Cooper family member to be associated with the company, retired in 1968. The grandson of Elias, he had served as a vice-president and board member.

The company branched out into aircraft services in 1970 by acquiring Dallas Airmotive, and later acquired Southwest Airmotive Company in 1973 and Standard Aircraft Equipment in 1975. While these acquisitions performed satisfactorily, the company sold its airmotive segment to Aviation Power Supply in 1981 because it did not see much potential for further growth.

The 1973 oil embargo threw many industrialized nations into an uproar. Cooper's Ajax division struggled to keep up with orders from domestic crude-oil producers and Cooper received a large order for its Coberra gas turbines for the Alaskan pipeline.

After having served as president and chief operating officer since 1973, Robert Cizik was named chief executive officer in 1975. Lured to the company from Standard Oil New Jersey (now Exxon) in 1961, Cizik started his career at Cooper as executive assistant for corporate development.

Cizik stepped up the company's acquisition program. After satisfying a Justice Department challenge, Cooper acquired the White Superior engine division, a heavy-duty engine maker, from the White Motor Company in 1976, and in 1979 Cooper realized a dream of acquiring the Dallas-based Gardner-Denver Company, a company roughly the same size as Cooper. Although *Forbes* described Gardner-Denver as "a company notorious for lack of planning or cost controls," Cooper was confident the company's three energy-related business segments could be successfully merged into its own energy-related manufacturing operations. *Forbes* reported at the time that the merger was one of the ten largest in U.S. history. That year the company passed the $1 billion sales milestone, only three years after it had reached a half a billion dollars in sales.

Cooper has been criticized for handling acquisitions cold-heartedly. After acquiring Gardner-Denver, it closed the company's corporate headquarters, decentralized it, reduced employment, and cut benefits. But many analysts defended these actions, noting that Gardner-Denver had been full of operational problems and very poorly managed.

Cooper is known for its manufacturing efficiency and willingness to make capital investments to improve production or market position. For instance, when the last domestic producer of the very hard steel needed to manufacture files stopped making it, Cooper developed a process for making its own steel that was different from the traditional method but still suitable for making files, at half the cost.

In 1981, Cooper acquired the highly respected Crouse-Hinds Company of Syracuse, New York, makers of electrical products, after a long battle in which Cooper played white knight, rescuing Crouse-Hinds from Inter-North Corporation. Cooper also acquired the Belden Corporation, a wire and cable manufacturer that Crouse-Hinds had been in the process of purchasing. This acquisition expanded Cooper's size by 50%. Shortly after the merger, Cizik explained to *Business Week* that he had entered the electrical components business because "we needed to be in a business that looked beyond the 1980s and even the year 2000 for growth." When demand for gas and oil began to slump in 1981, Cooper's diversification paid off. Sales of the company's energy-related products dropped by 60% but its other two divisions were hurt far less.

Cizik continued to look for new acquisitions. Cooper's next bold move was a 1985 merger with McGraw-Edison Company, a manufacturer of electrical energy-related products for industrial, commercial, and utility use. The merger nearly doubled Cooper's size and made the company one of the largest lighting manufacturers in the world. Cooper's 1985 sales passed $3 billion.

Since the McGraw-Edison acquisition, most Cooper acquisitions have been on a somewhat smaller scale. In 1987 they included the molded rubber products division and the petroleum equipment and products group from Joy Technologies. In 1988, Cooper acquired RTE Corporation, a Wisconsin-based manufacturer of electrical distribution equipment, and Beswick, a manufacturer of fuses and related products in the United Kingdom. But in 1989, Cooper made yet another major acquisition, of the Champion Spark Plug Company, the world's leading manufacturer of spark plugs for combustion engines. Champion, based in Toledo, Ohio, is also a major producer of windshield-wiper blades. And in late November, 1989, Cooper also acquired Cameron Iron Works, a Houston-based company with annual sales of $611 million. Cameron is a maker of oil tools, ball valves, and forged products.

Cooper manufactures more than a million products in 145 plants, 41 of them in foreign countries. Its annual revenues exceed $4 billion. Through its roughly 50 strategic acquisitions, Cooper has proudly remained a manufacturing company noted for excellent management, lean operations, and a willingness to seize opportunities when they arise. While some industry observers question the manageability of Cooper as it continues to expand, all admire its ability to weather fluctuations in individual markets.

Principal Subsidiaries: Cooper Industries Foundation; Cooper Securities, Inc.; Cooper Industries (Canada) Inc.; Gardner-Denver Company; COMTRA Internacional S.A. de C.V. (Mexico); Cooper-Bessemer, S.A. (Switzerland); Cooper Energy Services International, Inc.; Cooper Energy Services (Nigeria) Limited (60%); Cooper Energy Services (UK) Ltd.; Cooper Petroleum Equipment Group, Inc.; Cooper Rolls Inc. (50%); Cooper-Vulkan Kompressoren, GmbH (West Germany) (50%); Gardner-Denver (Aust.) Pty. Ltd. (Australia); Gardner-Denver (France) S.a.r.l.; Gardner-Denver do Brasil Industria e Comercio Limitada; Cooper (U.K.) Ltd.; Gardner-Denver International, C.A. (Venezuela); Gardner-Denver (N.Z.) Ltd. (New Zealand); Gardner-Denver (U.K.) Ltd.; Gardner-Denver Western Hemisphere Co.; Martin-Decker Co. (S) Private Ltd. (Singapore); Martin-Decker B.V. (Netherlands); Martin-Decker Overseas Corp.; Servicios Energeticos Cooper, S.A. de C.V. (Mexico) (49%); Cooper Tools, S.p.A. (Italy); Cooper Tools Ltd., (Great Britain); Deutsche Gardner-Denver GmbH (West Germany); Empresa Andina de Herramientas, S.A. (Colombia) (49%); Kirsch Co.; Lufkin Europa, B.V. (Netherlands); Nicholson Mexicana, S.A. de C.V. (Mexico) (49%); The Cooper Group, B.V. (Netherlands); The Cooper Group Deutschland, GmbH (West Germany); The Cooper Group, Inc.; Arrow-Hart, S.A. de C.V. (Mexico); Componentes de Iluminacion, S.A. de C.V. (Mexico); Componentes e Interruptores, S.A. de C.V. (Mexico); Crouse-Hinds de Venezuela, C.A.; Crouse-Hinds Domex, S.A. de C.V. (Mexico); Crouse-Hinds (Europe) Ltd. (Great Britain); Crouse-Hinds of Europe, S.p.A. (Italy); Hubbard Electric Co.; Carlton Santee Corp.; CI Divest Corp.; Cooper Industries Foreign Sales Company, Ltd. (Barbados); Cooper (U.K.) Limited; McGraw-Edison Export Corporation; Worthington Pump Corporation; Belden Electronics, GmbH (West Germany); Belden Electronics, S.a.r.l. (France); Cooper Power Systems, Inc.; Alco Products, Inc.; Cooper Industries GmbH Beteiligungen (West Germany); C.Y. Lin Trading Company (40%); Farloc Argentina S.A.I.C.Y.F. (23.9%) (Argentina); Frenos Hidraulicos Automotrices S.A. (49%) (Mexico); Taleres Villar, S.A. (33.25%) (Spain); Carson Machine & Supply Co.; Equipos Petroleros Cooper W-K-M Limitada (Chile); I.C. Group Inc.; Joy Manufacturing Co. A/S (Norway); W-K-M (Singapore) Limited.

Further Reading: Keller, David N. *Cooper Industries: 1833–1983*, Athens, Ohio, Ohio University Press, 1983.

EMERSON ELECTRIC CO.

8000 West Florissant Avenue
St. Louis, Missouri 63136
U.S.A.
(314) 553–2000

Public Company
Incorporated: 1890 as Emerson Electric Manufacturing Company
Employees: 69,000
Sales: $6.65 billion
Stock Index: New York Midwest

Emerson Electric Co. stands today as one of America's most admired business success stories. Emerson has quietly grown from a regional maker of electric motors and fans into a highly diversified international firm. One of only a handful of U.S. companies to enjoy a Triple-A rating from both Moody's and Standard & Poor's, it has compiled a remarkable record of sustained growth dating back to the late 1950s.

The company traces its roots back to the dawn of the electrical age in America. Founded in St. Louis on September 24, 1890, the firm was named for a Missouri judge, John Wesley Emerson, a descendant of the New England family of literary fame. Emerson was impressed by the ingenuity shown by a pair of brothers, Alexander W. and Charles R. Meston, in finding applications for the newly developed alternating current electric motor. In addition to lending his name, he provided the financing and became the president of the new company. The fledgling enterprise enjoyed modest success in its first three years, primarily producing small electrical and mechanical products.

In 1892, Herbert L. Parker, a Chicago railroad man, recognized the company's potential and bought Judge Emerson's controlling interest. Parker became president and general manager of Emerson, supervising the company's steady expansion until his death in 1924. During Parker's tenure, electric products developed into household and business necessities, and Emerson became a pioneer in the industry. The company produced a steady stream of innovative products by adapting its electric motors for such items as sewing machines, dental equipment, and water pumps. As electricity became an important factor in mechanized industry, Emerson supplied electric motors for office, factory and farm equipment as well.

In 1920, Parker was elected chairman of the board and T.M. Meston, the founders' younger brother, became president. During the 1920s, electric fans represented 40% of sales. Small electric motors for appliances and general household uses, however, were the dominant business.

Emerson was hit hard by the Depression. The company paid a stock dividend in 1930, but did not do so again for ten years. In 1933, Joseph Newman took control of the company after a career as an executive at Lesser-Goldman, a St. Louis-based cotton and agricultural-products broker. Lesser-Goldman owned an interest in Emerson and was concerned about the company's financial performance during the Depression. Newman streamlined operations, focusing on lowering costs, developing new products, and broadening the company's line of fans.

While sales were uncertain, labor relations between the company and its employees were positively dismal. Convinced that the Wagner Act of 1935, which reaffirmed the right of workers to form unions, was unconstitutional, Newman refused to recognize the United Electrical, Radio and Machine Workers, C.I.O. The union called a sitdown strike in 1937 that lasted 53 days, seven days short of a record. It was 68 days before the employees went back to work, however; Newman settled only after the Supreme Court upheld the Wagner Act.

The settlement came too late for Newman. His bankers had agreed to make a new stock issue just before the strike, but the issue failed. The failure was due partly to the strike, but the company's generally poor financial picture is what ultimately led the board of directors to form a committee to seek new management.

In 1938, William Stuart Symington III was named president of Emerson Electric. A member of a prominent eastern family, Symington arrived in St. Louis facing a daunting array of problems. The company suffered a loss of $138,000 in fiscal 1938. Inventory and overhead were up, while sales had fallen substantially. Symington immediately began cleaning house, firing most of the old top management.

The new management undertook a vigorous campaign to secure new business, and landed Sears, Roebuck & Company as a promising new motor customer. Symington was willing to take risks: he bought an arc-welding business sight unseen and later took Emerson into the delicate business of manufacturing hermetically sealed motors for refrigerators.

Once Emerson was back on its feet, Symington turned his attention to solving the company's long-standing labor problems. The new president, who would later go on to a distinguished career in the United States Senate, faced a union deeply distrustful of management, believing the contract it had so bitterly won was not being honored in good faith. Symington was a realist and decided to work with the fledgling union. The ensuing agreements between Emerson Electric and the United Electrical, Radio and Machine Workers were viewed as landmark achievements for Emerson and followed the example of labor agreements in the newly unionized automobile, steel, and packing industries.

Symington also undertook a major effort to modernize Emerson's manufacturing facilities. At the time the company was housed in five separate buildings in St. Louis. Rents and taxes were high, the multi-storied structures were unsuitable for modern production methods, and none was located near a railroad siding. The company clearly had to relocate to more efficient quarters if it was to compete successfully.

The city of Evansville, Indiana made a pitch to be the company's new home, offering a plant site and $100,000 to facilitate the move. Public officials in St. Louis declined to match the offer, fearing that it would set a precedent they would have to match for other businesses. Indicative of the changed labor atmosphere, however, the union offered to raise a similar sum through a system of wage cuts. Symington declined the union's offer, arranged independent financing, and relocated the company to a suitable location in St. Louis County.

With the advent of World War II, the company joined the war effort and manufactured a variety of war-related items. Emerson's largest contract was for the development and manufacture of the gun turrets used on Air Force bombers such as the B-17, B-25, and B-26, the major weapons in the U.S. bomber force. At the height of production during the war, the company was doing $100 million worth of defense work annually.

Emerson fell upon hard times again after the war, as defense contracts fell drastically, slipping to a low of $1.5 million in 1947. The company had been a leader in its field for most of its life, but in the postwar years large competitors like General Electric and Westinghouse saw potential in Emerson's markets. They moved quickly, building plants in low-wage areas and squeezing the company in its traditional strongholds. In 1945 Symington left the company to pursue a career in politics, boosted in no small part by the reputation he had gained as head of Emerson during the war. When his successor, a long-time company executive, died suddenly, Emerson was once again in the midst of a leadership crisis.

In December 1953, Wallace R. "Buck" Persons was named president. At the time Emerson had sales of only $45 million and a host of problems that had been building for years. But Persons, who came to Emerson from Lincoln Electric, a company known for its cost-effective management, was equal to the task. He instituted an extensive reorganization of the company's commercial product line to exploit Emerson's old-line electric motor business and bring in new customers outside the household appliance market. Products were redesigned using standardized parts to allow for mass production, rather than the company's traditional job-shop lots, producing immediate and dramatic results.

Persons placed heavy emphasis on upgrading Emerson's engineering capabilities. In his first couple of years at the helm he doubled the size of the engineering staff, making a major effort to recruit top-notch engineers and develop the new Electronics-Avionics Division, which worked on fire control systems for jet bombers. He also got tough with labor. Emerson's labor costs were higher than its major competitors, who had relocated to low-wage areas. The company suffered several strikes but eventually succeeded in restructuring its labor agreements to conform with industry standards. However, Persons also emphasized planning, budgetary discipline, and a policy of open communication with employees inncluding annual employee opinion surveys.

Emerson also redoubled its efforts to secure defense contracts, concentrating on the engineering and development of electronics and avionics rather than on armaments production. The modernization of the Air Force's bomber fleet provided a windfall for the company's rebuilding program. By 1956 military sales accounted for 30% of Emerson's total sales.

While Persons' short range plans called for rebuilding Emerson's existing product lines, his long range goal was to expand into new products. To assist with this effort, Persons called in a host of management consultants. One of the first firms hired, Lester B. Knight & Associates, eventually produced Persons's successor, Charles F. Knight.

Beginning in 1958, Emerson embarked on an acquisition program, aiming for quality producers with strong marketing skills. Through merger or acquisition, more than ten companies were added to Emerson during the 1960s, including Day Brite Lighting, U.S. Electrical Motors, Ridge Tool Company, Therm-o-Disc, White-Rodgers, Browning Manufacturing, and In-Sink-Erator. Emerson's industrial and consumer markets expanded significantly, lessening the company's dependence on uncertain defense contracts. When production of B-52 and B-58 air force bombers, for which Emerson was manufacturing tail turrets and fire control systems, was abruptly canceled in 1962, the move away from defense contracting was accelerated. The financial impact of the cancellation was minimized, since Emerson had already heeded the advice of its military consulting experts and concentrated its defense business in helicopters and other "limited war" hardware, but it convinced Persons that defense would not be a consistent growth market and gave added impetus to the company's efforts to expand in commercial markets.

The wisdom of this move was underscored in 1969 when, with almost no warning, the defense department canceled Lockheed Aircraft's huge Cheyenne helicopter program, for which Emerson was the largest subcontractor. The company's defense sales skidded from $70 million to between $35 and $40 million in one day. Following the company's stringent budgetary procedures, and as a result of continued growth through acquisition, Emerson was able to avoid a loss for the year by drastically cutting expenses, but the message was clear. Emerson remained in the military market, but Persons set a cap on military business at 15% of total sales.

By the time the Cheyenne contract was canceled, Emerson had acquired more than a dozen companies manufacturing a wide range of commercial and industrial products. The firm's household products included lighting fixtures, kitchen waste disposers, door chimes, intercom units, power tools, heating and air conditioning controls, and high fidelity equipment. On the industrial side,

Emerson was producing power transfer equipment, industrial test equipment, and industrial tools.

By the early 1970s, Buck Persons had turned Emerson, a troubled maker of small electric motors and fans, into a company capable of competing with the industry giants. But he had no clear successor inside the company, and the time was coming for him to move on. Persons undertook an exhaustive two-year search for the right man, reviewing 150 potential candidates. The final choice was Charles F. (Chuck) Knight, Lester Knight's 37-year-old son and the lead consultant involved in helping find Person's successor. He was named Emerson's vice chairman and CEO in 1973, and chairman the following year.

Knight proved an excellent choice for the job. He knew the company intimately at the highest level, since he had been an Emerson consultant for ten years and a board member of Emerson Motor Division, the company's largest division, for four years. Persons had wanted someone who would accept the company's organization and provide a sense of continuity. Knight had helped set up Emerson's management structure, and shared Persons's commitment to continued strong sales and earnings growth. Knight also had international experience, having overseen his father's European operations before becoming an Emerson consultant. Emerson had been late getting into overseas markets and now faced entrenched competition. One of Knight's main goals was to expand the company's international sales, spearheaded by specialties like its Ridgid tool line.

Knight's management philosophy keeps as much decision-making responsibility as possible at the operational level; each division operates like a separate company in many respects. Managers negotiate wages and benefits according to community standards and are responsible for determining what steps must be taken at the divisional level to respond to market conditions. Emerson avoids the huge manufacturing facilities favored by some of its competitors, keeping a plant size of no more than 800 workers at most locations, and most of its plants are non-union. All these are components of what Emerson calls its "best cost producer" strategy, through which it strives to manufacture the highest-quality products at their lowest relevant global cost.

Emerson frequently enters new markets by the acquisition of an existing market leader or high-quality producer. The company entered the electric-utility supply business for the first time in 1975 with the purchase of A.B. Chance Company. Similarly, Emerson made a strong entry into industrial measurement and process control business in 1976 by buying Rosemount, Inc.

Emerson's strategy of diversification and acquisition continued in the 1980s. Emerson acquired Copeland Corporation, the world's largest manufacturer of compressors for air conditioners and commercial refrigeration applications, in October, 1986. In December 1986, the company purchased Hazeltine, Inc., a leader in state-of-the-art defense electronics components and systems. (In 1988, two officials at the newly acquired Hazeltine unit were indicted on charges of fraud. Emerson and Hazeltine cooperated with authorities, and in early 1989 Hazeltine pleaded guilty to the felony charge.) In March 1987 Emerson acquired Liebert Corporation, a maker of computer support products.

Emerson seeks companies that provide not only immediate sales and profits gains, but growth potential for years to come, and prefers to buy private firms to avoid paying the large premiums over book value that public companies demand.

Emerson Electric today is a highly diversified company able to withstand setbacks in any of its markets. In 1988, the company posted its 31st consecutive year of earnings growth, a record that makes the company a perennial Wall Street favorite. Emerson's quiet, steady growth throughout the 1980s shows no signs of faltering. Its biggest customers are now commercial and industrial buyers of a broad array of factory automation and process control equipment, but no one segment of the business dominates to the point of vulnerability.

In September, 1988, James F. Hardymon was named president of Emerson. C.F. Knight remained chairman and CEO. The company continues to expand in both domestic and international markets as it becomes a global manufacturer. Emerson's challenge will be to continue the impressive record of growth the company has compiled since the late 1950s. Many of Emerson's core businesses are in mature industries, where high growth rates are difficult to achieve. But Emerson has in the past relied on acquisitions to spur growth, and indications are that this philosophy will continue to guide the company in the future.

Principal Subsidiaries: Appleton Electric Co.; Automatic Switch Co.; Beckman Industrial Corporation; Beckman Components GmbH; Beckman Composants S.a.r.l.; Bicomp S.A. de C.V.; Branson International Plasma Corporation; Branson Sonic Power S.A.; Branson Ultrasonics Corporation; Camco Corporation; Chromalox, S.A.; Compania do Motores Domesticos; Computer Power Systems Corporation; Copeland Corp.; Electronic Speed Control Development Corp.; Emerex S.A. de C.V.; Emerson Contract Division, Inc.; Emerson Electric (Asia) Ltd.; Emerson Electric C.A.; Emerson Electric Foreign Sales Corp. FSC; Emerson Electric (France) S.A.; Emerson Electric Industrial Controls, S.A. (France); Emerson Electric Nederland B.V.; Emerson Electric Overseas Finance Corp.; Emerson Electric Puerto Rico, Inc.; Emerson Electric, S.A. (Belgium); Emerson Electric Systems Corp.; Emerson Electric (U.S.) Holding Corp.; Emerson Finance Co.; Emerson Pacific Pte. Ltd.; Emerson Power Transmission Corporation; Eitrex S.A.; Fusite Corp.; Harris Calorific France, S.a.r.l.; Harris Europa, S.p.A.; Emerson Italia S.P.A.; Hazeltine Corporation; Inno Ven 111 Corporation; Kiowa Corporation; Krautkramer Branson Incorporated; Krautkramer GmbH; Liebert Corporation; Liebert Ireland; Load Management Development Corporation; Metaloy, Inc.; Micro Motion, Inc.; Midwest Components, Inc.; Ridge Tool Co.; Ridge Tool GmbH; Ridge Tool Europe, S.A.; Ridgid Ferramentas E Maquinas, Ltda.; Rosemount Inc.; Rosemount Instruments (Belgium); Skil Corporation;

Southwest Mobile Systems Corp.; SWECO, Inc.; Therm-o-Disc, Inc.; Vacco Industries; Western Forge Corporation; Xomox Corporation.

Further Reading: Dyer, Davis and Cruikshank, Jeffrey. *Emerson Electric Co.: 100 Years of Manufacturing*, St. Louis, Emerson Electric Co., 1990.

FUJI ELECTRIC CO., LTD.

12–1, Yuraku-cho 1-chome
Chiyoda-ku
Tokyo 100
Japan
(03) 211–7111

Public Company
Incorporated: 1923
Employees: 12,260
Sales: Y479.18 billion (US$3.83 billion)
Stock Index: Tokyo Osaka Nagoya

Fuji Electric is a manufacturer of electric machinery, components, and appliances. Most of its customers are other manufacturers who either use Fuji products or incorporate them into their own products. Because Fuji does not make television sets or stereos, it is virtually unknown outside of Japan.

But what Fuji lacks in public recognition, it makes up for in technological contributions. It is a major builder of integrated power plants and factories, as well as of power distribution systems, production control systems, and factory automation networks. It maintains close ties to several other leading industrial electronics companies, including Siemens, Demag, General Electric, and Westinghouse Electric.

Fuji Electric was founded in 1923 as a joint venture to facilitate technological cooperation between Furukawa Electric, of Japan, and Siemens, of Germany. Nearly a year and a half after its founding, Fuji Electric began production at a new factory in Kawasaki, near Tokyo. The company manufactured a variety of electrical components as well as telephones. In 1930 Fuji began making mercury-arc rectifiers, and in 1933 it added porcelain expansion-type circuit breakers to its product line. As the joint research between Furukawa and Siemens led Fuji further into the heavy machinery sector, Fuji decided that its telephone division would be better off as a separate company, and in 1935 that division was incorporated as Fujitsu, Ltd.

A second technical agreement, between Fuji and the German company Voith, led to a production agreement for that company's 4850-horsepower Francis turbines. As electric power came into widespread use in Japan, particularly in industry, Fuji began production of small and industrial watt-hour meters and larger, more advanced circuit breakers.

As militarists consolidated their hold on the Japanese government during the 1930s, they promoted a rapid economic and military mobilization. As Japan marched toward World War II, Fuji came under a greater degree of central control, leading it to cooperate more closely with other manufacturing interests related to Furukawa Electric. As a result, new factories at Matsumoto, Fukiage, Tokyo, and Mie were completed between 1942 and 1944 and immediately brought on line to manufacture a variety of products for the war effort. These factories were heavily bombed in the last year of the war, effectively crippling the company.

When the war ended in 1945, Fuji Electric was placed in government custody until military investigations were carried out and the company could be rehabilitated. Fuji began production again in stages, as factories were repaired and markets recovered.

In 1952 Fuji Electric helped to establish the heavy engine manufacturer Fuji Diesel, and the following year Fuji concluded another technical agreement, with the West German company Demag, to license technology for the production of magnetic motor starters, which it began to produce in 1954.

To a country so poor in natural resources, atomic power held tremendous potential in the 1950s. Accordingly, Fuji Electric joined the Daiichi Atomic Power Industry Group. Founded in 1956, this consortium of 22 companies built the first nuclear power plant in Japan through a combination of technology development and licensing. The 166-megawatt Tokai Nuclear Power plant went on line in 1960.

Fuji developed in two directions during the 1960s. It engineered larger and more powerful heavy machinery, such as transformers and propulsion equipment, and at the same time pioneered new diode and miniature circuit technologies. Fuji's strengths in research and development were greatly enhanced by the establishment in 1964 of its Central Research Laboratory.

During this period Fuji built new factories in Chiba, Kobe, and Suzuka to manufacture heavy transformers, control systems, switchgears, and motors. The company also made a technical agreement with Seeburg, of the United States, to purchase vending machine technology. The machines, produced at the Mie factory, became very profitable. Fuji's manufacturing capacity was expanded further in 1968 when it took over the operations of its smaller rival, Kawasaki Denki Seizo.

By 1970 Fuji Electric began to recognize that its spectacular growth had left weaknesses in its organization. Rival manufacturers had emerged with stronger positions in several markets. The company took measures to strengthen the Furukawa group, but it also set up a second, more specialized 15-company group specifically for heavy industrial projects.

Fuji Electric opened its eighth factory, to manufacture circuit breakers and control systems, in Ohtawara in 1974. The company also introduced a variety of new products and processes, including large-capacity steel furnaces, process computers, and robots during the early 1970s.

Fuji survived the oil crisis of 1973 without great strain, and in the mid-1970s started to benefit from the dovetailing of research efforts carried out with Fuji group members, primarily Fujitsu. This effort resulted in the development of several improved-technology items in control systems and computers, as well as more efficient generators and larger transformers.

By the late 1970s, Fuji had greatly strengthened its position as a leader in industrial electronics and had forged a close relationship with Fujitsu, which had emerged as Japan's leading computer software developer. Fuji made a major committment to technology in 1980 when it established a special corporate research and development subsidiary to concentrate attention on new technologies, previously developed by different divisions, in one place.

Fuji became involved in numerous foreign turnkey projects, many of them power plants. During 1980 and 1981 Fuji completed a geothermal power station and a 495-megawatt hydroelectric plant. Projects like these have given Fuji an international reputation for superior power-generating technology and engineering.

This reputation for quality was established over many years, but was first achieved with smaller devices. Fuji's strength in this market continued into the 1980s and even led the company to expand its capacity by opening a ninth plant in Kobe in 1983. Electronic products, which currently account for about 30% of sales, are expected to increase to 50% by 1993.

The company is divided into five groups. The electric machinery group is responsible for plants and heavy machinery. The systems group covers instrumentation, information systems, and mechatronics, including robots and data processing equipment. The standard machinery and apparatus group manufactures programmable controllers, heavy motors, and magnetic devices. The electronics group produces large diodes, transistors and circuits, as well as computer components and measuring equipment. The vending machine and appliance group manufactures vending machines and large refrigerator display units like those found in grocery stores.

Fuji Electric is unique among Japanese electronics firms because it has no in-house computer development. Instead, it manufactures semiconductors, hard disks, and other components for its affiliate Fujitsu. Fuji Electric and Fujitsu maintain a substantial cross-ownership of stock.

Known for attracting some of the most talented engineers, and with hundreds of monuments to its accomplishments in Japan and abroad, Fuji Electric is bound to remain a world leader in industrial electronics. Fuji is also in an excellent position, with its strong research organization, to develop leadership in new areas.

Principal Subsidiaries: Fuji Electric Corp. of America; U.S. Fuji Electric, Inc.; Fuji Electric GmbH; Hong Kong Fujidenki Co., Ltd.; Fuji Electric do Brasil Industria e Commercio Ltda.

THE GENERAL ELECTRIC COMPANY, PLC

1 Stanhope Gate
London W1A EH
United Kingdom
(01) 493-8484

Public Company
Incorporated: 1900 as General Electric Co. Ltd.
Employees: 145,029
Sales: £6.45 billion (US$11.66 billion)
Stock Index: London Glasgow Birmingham Manchester

The General Electric Company, PLC (GEC) is entirely separate from the General Electric Company in the United States, although the companies do share several European joint ventures. Both companies, however, have played similar roles in the development of their respective countries' electrical production and consumption. In fact, both were central to electrification programs and were ideally placed to supply the consumer electrical appliances that increased demand for their machines for generating electricity. GEC's stature today as an industrial giant is due in large part to that ability to both create and supply a tremendous demand for electricity over the past 100 years.

GEC was formed in 1886, when two enterprising young men, Hugo Hirst and Gustav Byng, teamed up in London to form a company. They originally acted as wholesalers of electrical products made by other companies. GEC's first catalog was issued that year and became a guide to popular uses of electricity. However, both men were so enamored of electricity's potential that they yearned to expand its applications beyond its early use as an alternative to gas illumination. (The lighting system in the House of Commons had been electrified in the early 1880s and the electrification of several other prominent London buildings soon followed.) Hirst had had experience with several other applications of electrical power—he had driven an electrically powered boat on the River Thames, ridden on an electric cycle, and even developed an electric-powered dog cart for an Indian rajah. His ambition was to become a manufacturer of electric products, and so within three years of the founding of their company Hirst and Byng opened a factory in Manchester.

From the start GEC manufactured devices for both consumer and industrial customers: telephones, electrically activated bells, ceiling roses, switches, and fittings. One of GEC's first successes in developing new electrification technology was the use of china as an insulating material in switches. Light bulbs were added to the product line in 1893. GEC catalogs began to include instructions for customers wanting to wire and equip their own homes for electricity.

Applications of the new technology abounded in industry. GEC installed its first commercial alternating-current (AC) motor in 1896 at a grain warehouse in Liverpool. Three years later the company won its first contract for a power-generating station, putting GEC in an enviable position as a provider to both consumers and producers of electricity. This first contract was for the Fulham Power Station and included the provision of arc lamps for surrounding streets.

GEC embarked on international expansion at the turn of the century. The company set up agencies throughout Europe and in Japan, Australia, South Africa, and India, and exported heavily to South America—an additional factory had to be built in order to accommodate the export-stimulated increase in production.

Between 1907 and 1912 the number of factories using electricity in Britain doubled, and GEC was well positioned to take advantage of this tremendous increase in demand. The company provided the Portsmouth Dockyard and London subway system with over 300 electric motors each.

Along with this expansion of industrial electrical needs was a growth in the demand for telephone systems. GEC's business in telephones and telephone equipment was so great that in 1910 a subsidiary operation devoted exclusively to this technology was created. Called the Peel-Conner Telephone Works, its first big job was the Central Telephone Exchange for the city of Glasgow. It was also during this period that GEC introduced its first metal-filament light bulb.

During World War I GEC's consumer items took a back seat as the company concentrated on war production—carbon filaments for arc lamps, wireless radios, signaling lamps, motors, and wiring. By the end of the war, more than 90% of GEC's business was for the military and its work force had swollen to over 15,000.

The major change at GEC to come out of the war experience was the establishment in 1919 of a separate research center, headed by Sir J. J. Thompson, a Nobel Prize–winning physicist.

By 1920, electric lighting was universally accepted and the demand for electrical appliances was beginning to grow as new uses for electricity were being discovered constantly. During the 1920s work started on Britain's National Grid, a network of power-generation stations built to meet the growing industrial and residential demand for electric power. GEC played a significant role in this project by supplying electrical equipment to the Central Electricity Board. GEC was also heavily involved in the expansion of radio in Britain since its research center was at the forefront of radio development. Two other triumphs during this period were the use of GEC transmitting valves in the transatlantic telephone system and in the BBC longwave transmitter at Droitwich.

International projects continued during the 1920s and 1930s, and included the installation of hydroelectric equipment in the palace of the Dalai Lama in Tibet. GEC undertook other major projects in countries such as Malaya, Canada, and Argentina to provide electric tramways, diesel-powered alternators, electric-propulsion units for ships, and of course lighting.

Perhaps the most important development at GEC in the 1930s was in television. In 1935, GEC opened a laboratory to study television technology, and production work on receivers started at the end of the decade.

War put another halt to the development of consumer devices. During World War II, GEC again contributed primarily in the fields of communication and electrical-power production. But its most important contribution to the war effort was the production of radar. The demand for radar was so great that part of the space in the research laboratory was converted to a "pre-production" area for the radars.

After the war, production on commercial projects resumed with an emphasis on several major lighting contracts. Notable among these was the illumination of the House of Commons and of the Grand Mosque in Mecca. GEC also began marketing fluorescent-tube lighting and airport-lighting equipment during the late 1940s, and its work in television also progressed rapidly—by 1949 the company had achieved a relay-link of television picture and sound. Throughout the postwar period, GEC was also involved in the production of nuclear energy, semiconductors, and computers.

GEC grew exponentially during the 1960s through several major acquisitions. The company was merged with Radio & Allied Industries, which had been created by Michael Sobell and Arnold Weinstock. The merger was intended to strengthen the electronics industry in Britain and was noteworthy in that Weinstock soon after became head of GEC. In 1967 GEC acquired the Associated Electrical Industries, Ltd. in a hostile bid. In the following year, GEC merged with English Electric which included Elliott-Automation and, most importantly, the Marconi Company, a major pioneer in the radio and electronics fields. Following these mergers and acquisitions, total employment at GEC surpassed 150,000 and GEC was manufacturing everything electrical—from power generation (both nuclear and nonnuclear) to consumer appliances to satellites.

By the end of the decade, GEC was the top electronics and appliance company in the United Kingdom; revenues in 1978 were £2.3 billion. Even so, Weinstock hoped to double GEC's size, primarily through expansion into U.S. markets. This led GEC into another series of acquisitions, this time of American companies, including White Industrial Power, AB Dick Company, Cincinnati Electronics Corporation, Picker International, and Cilbarco. However, this venture into American markets was mostly into industrial markets. By 1986 sales had surpassed £5 billion, with about 20% of that coming from the Americas; total income from the Americas was almost double that from Europe. GEC had become Britain's largest manufacturing company and one of its leading exporters.

But Weinstock was still not content. In the mid-1980s, GEC attempted to take over Plessey, another major British aerospace and electronics firm. The GEC offer involved both cash and new GEC securities, but placed the value of Plessey shares at less than their stock market price. Plessey flatly rejected the offer, calling it "unwelcome and palpably inadequate in form and substance." GEC was undeterred by this response, but at this point the Monopolies and Mergers Commission stepped in to investigate. Plessey waged a fierce public-relations campaign to bolster its image as a high-technology giant and argued the necessity for domestic competition. GEC argued that size was needed to compete internationally. Near the end of 1986, the government, stating that a combined Plessey-GEC firm would monopolize the defense-electronics and telecommunications-equipment markets in the United Kingdom, finally vetoed the merger. But, since both companies felt a need for greater size to compete in the international telephone-switching equipment market, the government did encourage the companies to combine their switching operations.

GEC was always heavily involved in defense projects during wartime, but production of military electronics did not end with World War II. Since then, in fact, GEC has won large contracts from all the NATO countries to provide equipment ranging from military satellites for NATO to air-data computers for United States Air Force and Navy aircraft. The company has also supplied electronic components for the American Minuteman, Titan, and MX missiles (all part of the nuclear arsenal) and was awarded three major contracts for the American Strategic Defense Initiative. However, GEC was recently set back in its defense business when the British government canceled an order for an airborne early-warning radar device. GEC claimed that the cancellation reduced profits by £24 million and necessitated the relocation of 1,000 employees within the company.

As research and development costs skyrocketed in the late 1980s, GEC sought joint ventures with a number of foreign electronics firms. In 1987, the company tried unsuccessfully to combine its medical electronics unit with that of the Dutch company Philips. In November, 1988, GEC joined forces with West Germany's Siemens to renew its takeover attempt of the Plessey Company. This deal was put on hold until mid-1989, when the government approved the proposed takeover as long as British national security secrets were not sent overseas. Shortly thereafter, GEC and Siemens gained control of Plessey.

In early 1989, GEC entered into an agreement with France's Compagnie Generale d'Electricite to combine their power-generating equipment into a £4 billion joint venture.

GEC is heavily involved in operations outside the United Kingdom, deriving only slightly less than half of its revenues from its overseas business. Not all of that revenue, of course, is derived from exporting products manufactured in the United Kingdom. For instance, only about 25% of GEC revenues from the

United States come from United Kingdom–manufactured exports. GEC has won several major export contracts recently from the Soviet Union, including orders for car-painting robots, offshore oil technologies, ship-positioning systems, programmable-logic industrial controls, and railway signaling equipment.

Research and development continues apace at GEC. Its laboratories employ 2,500 people, of whom 1,400 are degree-holders, and GEC recently spent £12 million to update capital equipment at these labs. Current research focuses on superconducting materials, industrial applications of artificial intelligence, radar, satellites, integrated circuits, and optical telecommunications.

In general, electronics makes up more than a third of GEC's business activities, while telecommunications and business systems together account for less than half of that amount. GE also produces automation and robotics, medical equipment, and power-generation equipment as well as consumer electric products. The company differs from its American counterpart not only in size, but also in its range of business. GEC is also more heavily involved outside its home country than GE.

GEC's future looks very bright, since its high-tech products continue to see significant growth. More joint ventures are likely as they keep development costs low and build strength in the face of the relaxation of European trade barriers.

Principal Subsidiaries: The English Electric Company, Ltd.; Associated Electrical Industries Ltd.; The Marconi Company Ltd.; GEC–Elliott Automation Ltd.; GEC-Marconi Ltd.; GEC Australia Ltd.; Marconi Electronic Devices Ltd.; EEV Inc. (US); EEV Canada Ltd.; Salford Electric Instruments Ltd.; AB Dick Company, USA; GEC New Zealand Ltd.; GEC Electrical Projects Ltd.; GEC Industrial Controls Ltd.; GEC Measurements Ltd.; Satchwell Control Systems Ltd.; GEC Marine & Industrial Gears Ltd.; GEC Composants SA (France); Picker International Inc. (US); GEC Turbine Generators Ltd.; Ruston Gas Turbines Ltd.; The General Electric Company of India Ltd. (66.7%); The English Electric Company of India Ltd. (66.7%); Wire & Cables Group; GEC-General Signal Ltd. (50%); GEC Large Machines Ltd.; The Express Lift Co. Ltd.; Woods of Colchester Ltd.; GEC Engineering (Accrington) Ltd.; GEC Reinforced Plastics Ltd.; GEC Foundries Ltd.; A.G. Hackney & Co. Ltd.; Hotpoint Ltd.; OSRAM-GEC Ltd. (51%); Walsall Conduits Ltd.; The English Electric Corporation (US); The General Electric Company of Bangladesh Ltd. (60%); GEC Canada Ltd.; The General Electric Company of Hong Kong Ltd.; The General Electric Company of Singapore Private Ltd.; GEC Zambia Ltd.; GEC Zimbabwe (Pvt) Ltd.; GEC Power Systems Ltd.; GEC Energy Systems Ltd.; GEC Electro-motors Ltd.; Mechanical Engineering Laboratories; GEC Switchgear Ltd.; GEC Transformers Ltd.; GEC Transmission and Distribution Projects Ltd.; Vacuum Interrupters Ltd.; GEC Automation Projects Inc. (US); GEC Installation Equipment Ltd.; The Micanite & Insulators Co. Ltd.; Engineering Research Centre (Stafford); Vynckier NV (Belgium); NNC Ltd.; GEC Transportation Projects Ltd.; GEC Electronic Metrology Systems Ltd.; Marconi Circuit Technology Corporation (US); EEV Ltd.; Salplex Ltd. (60%).

GENERAL ELECTRIC COMPANY

3135 Easton Turnpike
Fairfield, Connecticut 06431
U.S.A.
(203) 373–2211

Public Company
Incorporated: 1892
Employees: 298,000
Sales: $50.09 billion
Stock Index: New York Boston London Tokyo

The history of General Electric is a significant part of the history of technology in America. GE has evolved from Thomas Edison's home laboratory into one of the largest companies in the world, following the evolution of electrical technology from the simplest early applications into the high-tech wizardry of the late 20th century.

Thomas Edison established himself in the 1870s as an inventor after devising, at the age of 23, an improved stock ticker. He subsequently began research on an electric light as a replacement for gas light, the standard method of illumination at the time. In 1876 Edison moved into a laboratory in Menlo Park, New Jersey. Two years later, in 1878, Edison established, with the help of his friend Grosvenor Lowry, the Edison Electric Light Company with a capitalization of $300,000. Edison received half of the new company's shares on the agreement that he work on developing an incandescent lighting system. The major problem Edison and his team of specialists faced was finding an easy-to-produce filament that would resist the passage of electrical current in the bulb for a long time. He triumphed only a year after beginning research when he discovered that common sewing thread, once carbonized, worked in the laboratory. For practical applications, however, he switched to carbonized bamboo.

Developing an electrical lighting system for a whole community involved more than merely developing an electric bulb; the devices that generated, transmitted, and controlled electric power also had to be invented. Accordingly, Edison organized research into all of these areas and in 1879, the same year that he produced an electric bulb, he also constructed the first dynamo, or direct-current generator.

The first application of electric lighting was on the steam ship *Columbia* in 1880. In that same year, Edison constructed a three-mile-long trial electric railroad at his Menlo Park laboratory. The first individual system of electric lighting came in 1881, in a printing plant. However, the first full-scale public application of the Edison lighting system was actually made in London, at the Holborn Viaduct. The first system in the United States came soon after when Pearl Street Station was opened in New York City. Components of the system were manufactured by different companies, some of which were organized by Edison; lamps came from the parent company, dynamos from the Edison Machine Works, and switches from Bergmann & Company of New York. In 1886, the Edison Machine Works was moved from New Jersey to Schenectady, New York.

While these developments unfolded at Edison's company, the Thomson-Houston Company was formed from the American Electric Company, founded by Elihu Thomson and Edwin Houston, who held several patents for their development of arc lighting. Some of their electrical systems differed from Edison's through the use of alternating-current (AC) equipment, since AC systems can transmit over longer distances than DC systems. By the early 1890s the spread of electrification was threatened by the conflict between the two technologies and by patent deadlocks, which prevented further developments because of patent-infringement problems.

By 1889, Edison had consolidated all of his companies under the name of the Edison General Electric Company. Three years later, in 1892, this company was merged with the Thomson-Houston Electric Company to form the General Electric Company. Although this merger was the turning point in the electrification of the United States, it resulted in Edison's resignation from GE. He had been appointed to the board of directors but he attended only one board meeting, the year the company was founded, and sold all of his shares in 1894, although he remained a consultant to General Electric and continued to collect royalties on his patents. The president of the new company was Charles A. Coffin, a former shoe manufacturer who had been the leading figure at Thomson-Houston. Coffin remained president of General Electric until 1913, and chairman thereafter until 1922.

In 1884, Frank Julian Sprague, an engineer who had worked on electric systems with Edison, resigned and formed the Sprague Electric Railway and Motor Company, which built the first large-scale electric streetcar system in the United States, in Richmond, Virginia. In 1889 Sprague's company was purchased by Edison's. In the meantime, the two other major electric-railway companies in the United States had merged with Thomson-Houston, so that by the time General Electric was formed, it was the major supplier of electrified railway systems in the United States.

One year after the formation of General Electric, the company won a bid for the construction of large AC motors in a textile mill in South Carolina. The motors were the largest manufactured by General Electric at the time and were so successful that orders soon began to flow in from other industries like cement, paper, and steel. In that same year, General Electric began its first venture into the field of power transmission with the opening of the Redlands–Mill Creek power line in California, and in 1894 the company constructed a massive power-transmission line at Niagara Falls.

Meanwhile the company's electric-railroad ventures produced an elevated electric train surrounding the fairgrounds of the Chicago World's Fair in 1893. Electrification of existing rail lines began two years later.

By the turn of the century General Electric was manufacturing everything involved in the electrification of the United States: generators to produce electricity, transmission equipment to carry power, industrial electric motors, electric light bulbs, and electric locomotives. It is important to any understanding of the evolution of GE to realize that though it was diverse from the beginning, all of its enterprises centered around the electrification program. It is also worth noting that it operated in the virtual absence of competition. General Electric and the Westinghouse Electric Company had been competitors, but the companies entered into a patent pool in 1896.

In 1900 GE established the first industrial laboratory in the United States. Up to that point, research had been carried out in universities or in private laboratories similar to Edison's Menlo Park laboratory. Initially, the lab was set up in a barn behind the house of one of the researchers, but the lab was moved in 1900 to Schenectady, New York, after it was destroyed in a fire. The head of the research division was a professor from the Massachusetts Institute of Technology. The importance of research at General Electric cannot be underestimated—GE has been awarded more patents over the years than any other company in the United States.

During the early decades of the 20th century General Electric made further progress in its established fields, and also made its first major diversification. In 1903 General Electric bought the Stanley Electric Manufacturing Company of Pittsfield, Massachusetts, a manufacturer of transformers. Its founder, William Stanley, was the developer of the transformer.

By this time GE's first light bulbs were in obvious need of improvement. Edison's bamboo filament was replaced in 1904 by metalized carbon developed by the company's research lab. That filament, in turn, was replaced several years later by a tungsten-filament light bulb when William Coolidge, a GE researcher, discovered a process to render the durable metal more pliable. This light bulb was so rugged and well suited for use in automobiles, railroad cars, and street cars that it is still in use today. In 1913, two other innovations came out of the GE labs: Irving Langmuir discovered that gas-filled bulbs were more efficient and reduced bulb blackening. To this day virtually all bulbs over 40 watts are gas filled.

The first high-vacuum, hot-cathode X-ray tube, known as the "Coolidge tube," was also developed in 1913. Coolidge's research into tungsten had played an important role in the development of the X-ray tube. The device, which combined a vacuum with a heated tungsten filament and tungsten target, is the foundation of virtually all X-ray tubes produced ever since, and its development laid the foundation for medical technology operations at General Electric.

Perhaps GE's most important development in the early part of this century was its participation in the development of the high-speed steam turbine in conjunction with English, Swedish, and other inventors. Until this invention, all electricity (except hydroelectric) had been produced by generators that turned at no more than 100 rpm, which limited the amount of electricity a single unit could produce. An independent inventor had come up with a design for a very-high-speed steam turbine before the turn of the century, but it took five years of research before GE could construct a working model. By 1901, however, a 500-kilowatt, 1,200-rpm turbine generator was operating. Orders for the turbines followed almost immediately, and by 1903 a 5,000-kilowatt turbine was in use at Chicago's Commonwealth Edison power company.

Such rapid progress led to rapid obsolescence as well—the Chicago units were replaced within six years. As a result, GE shops in Schenectady were soon overflowing with business. By 1910 the volume of the company's trade in turbine generators had tripled and GE had sold almost one million kilowatts of power capacity.

At the same time, General Electric scientists were also researching the gas turbine. Their investigations eventually resulted in the first flight of an airplane equipped with a turbine-powered supercharger.

In the early days of electric power, electricity was produced only during evening hours, since electric lighting was not needed during the day and there were no other products to use electricity. GE, as the producer of both electricity-generating equipment and electricity-consuming devices, naturally sought to expand both ends of its markets. The first major expansion of the General Electric product line was made in the first decade of the 20th century. Before the turn of the century, light bulbs and electric fans were GE's only consumer product. One of the first household appliances GE began to market was a toaster in 1905. The following year the company attempted to market an electric range. The unwieldy device consisted of a wooden table top equipped with electric griddles, pans, toasters, waffle irons, pots, and a coffee maker, each with its own retractable cord to go into any one of 30 plugs. The range was followed by a commercial electric refrigerator in 1911 and by an experimental household refrigerator six years later.

At the same time two other companies in the United States were producing electric devices for the home. The Pacific Electric Heating Company produced the first electric appliance to be readily accepted by the public: the Hotpoint iron. The Hughes Electric Heating Company produced and marketed an electric range. In 1918 all three companies were prospering, but to avoid competition with one another, they agreed upon a merger. The new company combined GE's heating-device section with Hughes and Pacific to form the Edison Electric Appliance Company, whose products bore either the GE or the Hotpoint label.

GE's first diversification outside electricity came with its establishment of a research staff to investigate plastics. This occurred primarily at the prompting of Charles P.

Steinmetz, a brilliant mathematician who had been with the company since the 1890s. All of the initial work by this group was devoted to coatings, varnishes, insulation, and other products related to electrical wiring, so that even this diversification was tied in to electrification.

A more radical branching of GE's activities occurred in 1912, when Ernst Alexanderson, a GE employee, was approached by a radio pioneer looking for a way to expand the range of wireless sets into higher frequencies. Alexanderson worked for almost a decade on the project before he succeeded in creating electromagnetic waves that could span continents, instead of the short distances to which radios had been limited. In 1922, General Electric introduced its own radio station, WGY, in Schenectady. In 1919, at the request of the government, GE formed the Radio Corporation of America (RCA) to develop radio technology. GE withdrew from the venture in 1930, when antitrust considerations came to the fore. General Electric also operated two experimental shortwave stations that had a global range.

Other developments at General Electric contributed to the progress of the radio. Irving Langmuir had developed the electron tube. This tube, necessary for amplifying the signals in Alexanderson's radio unit, was capable of operating at very high power. Other important developments by scientists at General Electric included the world's first practical loudspeaker and a method for recording complex sound on film that is still in use today.

Developments continued apace at GE in the electric-motor field. In 1913, the United States Navy commissioned General Electric to build the first ship to be powered by turbine motors rather than steam. In 1915 the first turbine-propelled battleship sailed forth, and within a few years, all of the navy's large ships were equipped with electric power.

General Electric also owned several utility companies that generated electrical power, but in 1924 GE left the utilities business when the federal government brought antitrust action against the company.

During the Depression the company introduced a variety of consumer items like mixers, vacuum cleaners, air conditioners, and washing machines. GE also introduced the first affordable electric refrigerator in the late 1920s. It was designed by a Danish toolmaker, Christian Steenstrup, who later supervised mechanical research at the GE plant in Schenectady. And GE introduced its first electric dishwasher in 1932, the same year that consumer financing of personal appliances was introduced.

Also in 1932 the first Nobel Prize ever awarded to a scientist not affiliated with a university went to Irving Langmuir for his work at GE on surface chemistry, research that had grown out of his earlier work on electron tubes. The years that followed witnessed a steady stream of innovation in electronics from the GE labs. These included the photoelectric-relay principle, rectifier tubes that eliminated batteries from home receivers, the cathode-ray tube, and glass-to-metal seals for vacuum tubes. Many of these developments in electronics were crucial to the growth of radio broadcasting.

The broadcasting division of General Electric achieved a breakthrough in the late 1930s. The company had been developing a mode of transmission known as frequency modulation (FM) as an alternative to the prevailing amplitude modulation (AM). In 1939 a demonstration conducted for the Federal Communications Commission proved that FM had less static and noise. GE began broadcasting in FM the following year.

Of course, the light bulb was not forgotten in this broadening of research activity at General Electric. The world's first mercury-vapor lamp was introduced in 1934, followed four years later by the fluorescent lamp. The latter produced light using half the power of incandescent bulbs, with about twice the life span. Less than a year after the introduction of the fluorescent light, General Electric introduced the sealed-beam automotive headlight.

Even though production of convenience items for the consumer halted during World War II, the war proved profitable for General Electric, whose revenues quadrupled during the war. The president of General Electric at the time, Charles Wilson, joined the War Production Board in 1942. GE produced more than 50 different types of radar for the armed forces and over 1,500 marine power plants for the navy and merchant marine. The company, using technology developed by the Englishman Frank Whittle, also conducted research on jet engines for aircraft. The Bell XP-59, the first American jet aircraft, flew in 1942 powered by General Electric engines. By the end of the war this technology helped General Electric develop the nation's first turboprop engine.

When production of consumer goods resumed immediately after the war, GE promptly found itself in another antitrust battle. The government discovered that GE controlled 85% of the light bulb industry—55% through its own output and the other 30% through licensees. In 1949 the court forced GE to release its patents to other companies.

In this period the first true product diversifications came out of GE's research labs. In the 1940s a GE scientist discovered a way to produce large quantities of silicone, a material GE had been investigating for a long time. In 1947 GE opened a plant to produce silicones, which allowed the introduction of many products using silicone as a sealant or lubricant.

Meanwhile, as research innovation blossomed and postwar business boomed, the company began an employee relations policy known as "Boulwarism," from Lemuel Boulware, the manager who established the policy. The policy, which eliminated much of the bargaining involved in labor–management relations, included the extension by GE to union leaders of a non-negotiable contract offer.

During the late 1940s General Electric embarked on a study of nuclear power and constructed a laboratory specifically for the task. Company scientists involved in an earlier attempt to separate U-235 from natural uranium were developing nuclear power plants for naval propulsion by 1946. In 1955 the navy launched the submarine *Seawolf*, the world's first nuclear-powered vessel, with a reactor developed by General Electric. And in 1957 the company received a license from the Atomic Energy Commission to operate a nuclear-power reactor, the first license granted in the United States for a privately owned generating station.

That same year GE's consumer-appliance operations got a big boost when an enormous manufacturing site, Appliance Park, in Louisville, Kentucky was completed. The flow of new GE products—hair dryers, skillets, electronic ovens, self-cleaning ovens, electric knives—continued.

Other innovations to come from GE labs during the 1950s included an automatic pilot for jet aircraft, Lexan polycarbonate resin, the first all-transistor radio, turbine engines for jet aircraft, gas turbines for electrical power generation, and a technique for fabricating diamonds.

Antitrust problems continued to vex the company throughout the postwar years. In 1961 the Justice Department indicted 29 companies, of which GE was the biggest, for price fixing on electrical equipment. All the defendants pleaded guilty. GE's fine was almost half a million dollars, damages it paid to utilities who had purchased price-fixed equipment came to at least $50 million, and three GE managers received jail sentences and several others were forced to leave the company.

During the 1960s and 1970s GE grew in all fields. In 1961 it opened a research center for aerospace projects, and by the end of the decade had more than 6,000 employees involved in 37 projects related to the moon landing. In the 1950s General Electric entered the computer business. This venture, however, proved to be such a drain on the company's profits that GE sold its computer business to Honeywell in 1971.

By the late 1960s, GE's management began to feel that the company had become too large for its existing structures to accommodate. Accordingly, the company instituted a massive organizational restructuring. Under this restructuring program, the number of distinct operating units within the company was cut from more than 200 to 43. Each new section operated in a particular market and was headed by a manager who reported to management just beneath the corporate policy board. The sections were classified into one of three categories—growth, stability, or no-growth—to facilitate divestment of unprofitable units.

When this reorganization was complete, General Electric made what was at the time the largest corporate purchase ever. In December, 1976 GE paid $2.2. billion for Utah International, a major coal, copper, uranium, and iron miner and a producer of natural gas and oil. The company did 80% of its business in foreign countries. Within a year Utah International was contributing 18% of GE's total earnings.

The divestiture of its computer business had left GE without any capacity for manufacturing integrated circuits and the high-technology products in which they are used. In 1975 a study of the company's status concluded that GE, one of the first American electrical companies, had fallen far behind in electronics. As a result, GE spent some $385 million to acquire firms in the field: Intersil, a semiconductor manufacturer; Calma, a producer of computer-graphics equipment; and four software producers. The company also spent more than $100 million to expand its microelectronics facilities.

Other fields in which GE excelled were in trouble by the mid-1970s, most notably nuclear power. As plant construction costs skyrocketed and environmental concerns grew, the company's nuclear-power division began to lose money. GE's management, however, was convinced that the problem was temporary and that sales would pick up in the future. When, by 1980, General Electric had received no new orders for plants in five years, nuclear power began to look more and more like a prime candidate for divestment. GE eventually pulled out of all aspects of the nuclear-power business except for providing service and fuel to existing plants and conducting research on nuclear energy.

Though General Electric's growth was tremendous during the 1970s (earnings tripled between 1971 and 1981), the company's stock performance was mediocre. GE had become so large and was involved in so many activities that some regarded its fortunes as capable only of following the fortunes of the country as a whole.

GE's economic problems were mirrored by its managerial reshuffling. When John F. (Jack) Welch Jr. became president in 1981, General Electric entered a period of radical change. GE bought 338 businesses and product lines for $11.1 billion and sold 232 for $5.9 billion. But Welch's first order of business was to return much of the control of the company to the periphery. Although he decentralized management, he retained predecessor Reginald Jones's system of classifying divisions according to their performance. His goal was to make GE number one or two in every field of operation.

One branch of GE's operations that came into its own during this period was the General Electric Credit Corporation, founded in 1943. Between 1979 and 1984, its assets doubled, to $16 billion, due primarily to expansion into such markets as the leasing and selling of heavy industrial goods, inventories, real estate, and insurance. In addition, the leasing operations provided the parent company with tax shelters from accelerated depreciation on equipment developed by GE and then leased by the credit corporation.

Factory automation became a major activity at GE during the early 1980s. GE's acquisitions of Calma and Intersil were essential to this program. In addition, GE entered into an agreement with Japan's Hitachi to manufacture and market Hitachi's industrial robots in the United States. GE itself spent $300 million to robotize its locomotive plant in Erie, Pennsylvania. Two years later GE's aircraft-engine business also participated in an air force plant-modernization program—GE manufactured the engines for the controversial B-1B bomber.

In 1984 GE sold Utah International to the Broken Hill Proprietary Company of Australia, keeping the company's Ladd Petroleum Corporation affiliate. Ladd provides more than 50% of the natural gas GE's plants consume in the United States.

In 1986 General Electric made several extremely important purchases. The largest was $6.4 billion for the Radio Corporation of American (RCA), the company GE had helped to found in 1919. RCA's National Broadcasting Company (NBC), the leading American television network, brought GE into the broadcasting business in full force. Although both RCA and GE were heavily involved in consumer electronics, the match was regarded by industry analysts as beneficial, since GE had been shifting from manufacturing into service and high technology. After the merger, almost 80% of GE's earnings came from services and high technology, compared to 50% six years earlier. GE divested itself of RCA's famous David Sarnoff Research Center, since GE's labs made it redundant. In 1987 GE also sold its own and RCA's television-manufacturing businesses to the French company Thomson, in exchange for Thomson's medical diagnostics business.

GE justified the merger by citing the need for size to compete effectively with large Japanese conglomerates. Critics, however, claimed that GE was running from foreign competition by increasing its defense contracts (to almost 20% of its total business) and its service business, both areas that are insulated from foreign competition.

In 1986 GE also purchased the Employers Reinsurance Corporation, a financial-services company, from Texaco, for $1.1 billion, and an 80% interest in Kidder Peabody and Company, an investment-banking firm, for $600 million, greatly broadening its financial services division. Although Employer's Reinsurance has contributed steadily to GE's bottom line since its purchase, Kidder Peabody lost $48 million in 1987, in part due to the settlement of insider trading charges. Kidder Peabody did come back in 1988 to contribute $46 million in earnings, but the acquisition still troubles some analysts.

General Electric's operations are now divided into three groups: technology businesses, service businesses, and core manufacturing businesses; because of the restructuring, core manufacturing now accounts for only one-third of the company's earnings. But research and development is still of such importance that in 1988 GE spent $1.2 billion of its own funds on it, and another $2.4 billion in customer-provided research funding. Many current research projects are in energy conservation—more efficient light bulbs, jet engines, and electrical power transmission methods, for example.

In early 1989 GE made a major move to prepare for Europe's unified market in 1992 when it agreed to buy 50% of the European appliance business of Britain's General Electric Company (GEC). The two companies also made agreements in their medical, power systems, and electrical distribution businesses. Welch has said that his aim is to make GE the nation's largest company. Achieving such a goal would entail more massive acquisitions, since GE cannot hope to grow expotentially by itself. Whatever comes of this ambition, however, GE's sheer size gives it a measure of stability and the power to keep a tenacious grasp on its markets.

Principal Subsidiaries: GE Fanuc Automation; Kidder Peabody Inc.; Employers Reinsurance; National Broadcasting Company; Ladd Petroleum.

Further Reading: Hammond, John Winthrop. *Men and Volts*, Lippincott, 1941, Philadelphia; Schatz, Ronald W. *The Electrical Workers: A History of Labor at General Electric and Westinghouse*, Urbana, University of Illinois Press, 1983; Wise, George W. R. *Whitney, General Electric and the Origins of U.S. Industrial Research*, New York, Columbia University Press, 1985.

GM HUGHES ELECTRONICS CORPORATION

3044 West Grand Boulevard
Detroit, Michigan 48202
U.S.A.
(313) 556–2025

Wholly-owned subsidiary of General Motors
Incorporated: 1985
Employees: 97,000
Sales: $11.2 billion

GM Hughes Electronics was established in 1985 when General Motors (GM) purchased the Hughes Aircraft Company. At that time, GM reorganized its Delco Electronics subsidiary, and together Hughes and Delco became GM Hughes Electronics (GMHE). GMHE's business is the business of its two subsidiaries, which are still independently managed.

HUGHES AIRCRAFT COMPANY

Hughes Aircraft is one of America's leading defense-electronics manufacturers. Despite its name, it hasn't built an airplane in over 40 years, but instead has concentrated on developing advanced radar and navigation systems.

The man behind Hughes Aircraft was, of course, Howard Hughes, perhaps the world's best-known billionaire. Hughes inherited a family fortune when he was 19. He dropped out of school and gained control of the Hughes Tool Company, an extremely profitable manufacturer of patented drill bits for the oil industry founded by his father in 1913. Hughes then turned to movie making. His only real achievement in Hollywood was a film about World War I British aviators, called *Hell's Angels*. Dissatisfied with the performance of his stunt pilots—several of whom died in crashes—Hughes performed numerous stunts himself.

Soon bored with filmmaking, Hughes turned to aviation in 1932. It was at this time that his friend, a Los Angeles accountant named Noah Dietrich, set up the Hughes Aircraft Company as a vehicle for Hughes's whims. Hughes, however, was determined to learn the business from the bottom up and took a job as a copilot for American Airways. Six months later, Hughes and Dick Palmer, an engineer who had worked for Douglas and Lockheed, began work on a race plane, the H-1. On September 13, 1935 Hughes set a new speed record; he later broke transcontinental and world speed records. The heroism of his feats, a New York ticker-tape parade, and a whirlwind romance with Katherine Hepburn made Hughes a national celebrity. It was Hughes' money, however, that attracted the interest of Jack Frye, president of TWA.

Fyre invited Hughes to buy into his airline. Hughes viewed the investment as an opportunity to test vigorously the newest aircraft in the hope of designing a superior version of his own for sale to the military. With $1.6 million of Hughes' money, Frye purchased a small fleet of Boeing 307 Stratoliners, which at once made TWA a world-class airline.

Hughes then involved himself in the secret development of the Lockheed Constellation. Before the aircraft could be completed and introduced however, military priority during World War II exposed the project.

At the time, German U-boats were extremely effective in sinking convoys of American supply ships en route to Europe, so the government planned to airlift supplies, using Boeing flying boats. Consolidated Vultee developed an alternative large-cargo airplane—the PB2Y—and then Martin Aircraft entered the field with its mammoth 80-ton Mars. Hughes began work on a much larger marine aircraft, a third larger than a 747. During its development, however, small reconnaissance aircraft equipped with radar became effective antisubmarine weapons, and the greater economy of waterborne transport prevailed. Hughes Aircraft was nonetheless contractually obligated to complete the new flying boat. Made of plywood and powered by eight engines, the *Spruce Goose* became an antique the moment it was completed in 1947—two years after the war ended. Hughes felt obligated to prove it airworthy, but took it only 70 feet into the air before setting it down again. The aircraft was docked in Long Beach, California, and remains there under guard to this day.

Howard Hughes suffered a severe concussion in 1946 when he crashed an experimental airplane into a golf course during a test flight. The crash is believed to have been the cause of a gradual deterioration of Hughes' sanity that rendered the compulsive perfectionist thoroughly disagreeable and irrational. Difficult as he was, he remained in charge of Hughes Aircraft, controlled over 78% of TWA, and continued to make more money than ever from the Hughes Tool Company.

During the war, Hughes Aircraft was managed by Noah Dietrich and its engineer directors and remained free of Hughes' influence. Hughes was preoccupied with another investment: RKO Pictures. But Hughes Aircraft did not emerge from the war with an essential niche in either the civilian or military market. Indeed, it had yet to produce a commercially successful aircraft. Instead, the company's managers emphasized the development of new, advanced avionics and control mechanism. They assembled a team of leading scientists and engineers to lead product development, while still receiving funding from Hughes Tool Company.

When the cold war erupted after World War II, the defense-electronics industry boomed, and Hughes Aircraft led the way. It grew to become one of the nation's largest defense contractors as a supplier of weapons systems, missiles, satellites, and lasers. Housing a greater concentration of technicians than any other company except Bell Labs, Hughes became the primary source of aerial-interception systems for the defense of North America.

Hughes became active at the company again in the early 1950s. He refused, however, to allow any of the directors to buy shares in the company, and used his power as sole owner to override key decisions. As he exerted more influence in the company, directors began to quit. First to resign were Vice-Presidents Dean Wooldridge and Simon Ramo (who later founded TRW) and General Manager Harold George, then Henry Singleton (who founded Teledyne), and Assistant Manager Charles Thornton, and Assistant Controller Roy Ash (who founded Litton). All were leading scientists. Fearing the disintegration of an important strategic resource, Air Force Secretary Harold Talbott flew to California and told Hughes personally, "You've made a hell of a mess of a great property." He then threatened to cancel the company's contracts until Hughes himself restored order.

Hughes attempted to sell the company to Westinghouse, Convair, and Lockheed, but in the end rejected all offers. Instead, he created a charity, the Howard Hughes Medical Institute, and donated all of his shares in the Hughes Aircraft Company as a gift. It was a highly controversial move that won Hughes comparison to Henry Ford for his resourcefulness and determination to save face.

But it also denied Hughes an important source of money two years later when TWA badly needed cash to purchase passenger jets and the Tool Company, the original Hughes money tree, was in the depths of a bottomed-out oil market. Hughes had exhausted his resources and for the first time in his life came up short. He was eventually forced to turn to a group of New York financiers, who denied him voting rights at TWA but did provide funding for jet acquisition.

The Hughes Aircraft Company, meanwhile, had rebuilt its management and research staffs. Hughes personally chose Lawrence Hyland, a former Bendix Aviation executive and co-inventor of radar, to be general manager while Hughes himself retained the title of president. As sole trustee of the Miami-based Medical Institute, Hughes determined what portion of Hughes Aircraft's profits—and they were substantial—would be turned over to the charity. Hughes, perhaps learning a lesson from his harsh treatment of previous executives, gave Hyland, a self-taught engineer like Hughes himself, complete authority over Hughes Aircraft.

Hyland reassembled a top-flight engineering-and-research group and successfully brought down employee turnover. Although Hughes turned his attention to his Las Vegas casino properties, he continued to monitor Hughes Aircraft's performance through regular situation reports and telephone conversations with Hyland. He was in constant contact with Hyland in 1966 when the Surveyor spacecraft, manufactured by Hughes Aircraft, made its successful soft landing on the moon, and he made certain that the company fully exploited the event in institutional advertising.

As Hughes sank into almost total reclusion, Hyland led the company into advanced missile technologies. In 1974, at the insistence of the Internal Revenue Service, Hughes authorized an increase in the company's contributions to the Medical Institute from $2.5 million to $3.5 million. Two years later, Howard Hughes died. Through its association with the Medical Institute, Hughes Aircraft was insulated from the confusion that came in trying to settle Hughes' estate. Hyland remained in control of the company, and a board of Medical Institute trustees was formed to take Hughes' place.

Hyland, however, left Hughes Aircraft in 1978. He was replaced by Allen Puckett, a 30-year company veteran. Under Puckett's leadership, Hughes Aircraft enjoyed 25% annual growth. Much of this growth directly resulted from increased military budgets that began in the last years of the Carter Administration and continued during the Reagan Administration. The company's expansion, however, was poorly managed. Hughes Aircraft overemphasized its small-scale-weapons development at the expense of production. A third factor involved the unmonitored performance of executives entering the company from top-level positions in the Pentagon. By and large, these executive were regarded as deal makers and Washington influence peddlers who had only a minimal commitment to quality or cost control.

Suddenly, early in 1984, the Defense Department, citing a near-complete lapse of quality control and severe cost overruns, refused to take delivery of any more Hughes Aircraft TOW, Phoenix, or Maverick missiles. The air force dispatched a highly effective production auditor named A. Ernest Fitzgerald to investigate Hughes, though a second oversight committee, the Defense Contract Audit Agency, was already on the job. The Audit Agency, which Fitzgerald called a "rubber-toothed, barkless, blind watchdog," was accused of covering up Hughes' deficiencies. It even attempted to prevent Fitzgerald from delivering incriminating testimony to Congress.

Suffering from a public-relations nightmare, Hughes Aircraft began a critical period of introspection and quality control. It was critical because Hughes had reached a point where it could no longer satisfy IRS requirements for contributions to the Medical Institute while maintaining industry-competitive internal research-and-development expenditures. Hughes Aircraft would soon have to be sold, and its reputation as a pariah in the defense industry could only damage the Medical Institute.

After some discussion about taking the company public, the Medical Institute began to entertain the more lucrative possibility of selling the company to an established defense contractor. Interested parties like Boeing, however, became discouraged by antitrust legislation. The Ford Motor Company expressed a desire to fold Hughes into its new aerospace division. But the company that offered the highest bid, $5 billion, was General Motors.

GM formed a new subsidiary, GM Hughes Electronics, to manage the affairs of Hughes Aircraft and its Delco Electronics division. This arrangement, it was hoped, would preserve each company's independence but facilitate a two-way assimilation of advanced technologies.

Hughes continued to win military contracts on the

basis of its technological strengths, but was known to be a non-competitive bidder. As budget pressures fell on the Pentagon, Hughes began to lose vitally important contracts. Worse yet, Hughes' chairman, Albert Wheelon, was forced to resign amid allegations that illegal bribes were paid to the Radiotourismo satellite consortium. Wheelon was replaced by Malcolm Currie, a career Hughes man who had served as under secretary of defense from 1973 to 1977.

In 1988, Hughes Aircraft began to see a turnaround in its business as a three-year plant-modernization program that dramatically improved profitability at the company's Tucson, Arizona missile complex was completed.

Today Hughes Aircraft remains one of America's most important electronics manufacturers and research organizations. It conducts approximately 80% of its business with the Defense Department. But because its broad exposure to the Pentagon may become problematic in the future as the government struggles to bring spending into line, Currie hopes to bring this figure down to 60%. It has successfully applied aerospace technologies to automotive systems, and is a major manufacturer of satellites.

DELCO ELECTRONICS CORPORATION

Delco has been a "captive" manufacturer of car radios and automotive-electronics systems for General Motors for more than 50 years. The company was completely reorganized in 1985, however, when it was nominally merged with Hughes Aircraft, which had recently been acquired by GM. Both companies were made independent divisions of a new company called GM Hughes Electronics.

Delco was originally founded in 1912 by C.F. Kettering as a manufacturer of electronic starters for Cadillacs. The company, located in Kokomo, Indiana, was acquired by General Motors on May 1, 1936, after which it added radios as a new product line. GM had tried once before to establish a radio factory; in 1929 it entered into a joint venture with RCA primarily for home-radio production. The venture failed in 1932, but not before the popularity of car radios was discovered. Since the economy was in severe distress, however, GM decided to wait until demand had recovered to re-enter the radio business.

As America emerged from the Depression, demand for automobiles recovered, and, with it, demand for car radios. The first radios to emerge from Delco were built for Chevrolets. They were strictly "aftermarket" items, installed as dealer options. By 1937 Delco was manufacturing several radio designs for GM, as well as control panels for installing Delco radios in most other American-made cars. By the end of the year, Delco had begun construction on a second plant and added antennae and carburetor production. During this period the company introduced two product innovations: the push-button tuner in 1938, and the elliptical speaker, which improved tone, in 1940.

Clare Swayzee became general manager of Delco in January, 1939. He succeeded Ray Ellis, who had led the division since its inception in 1936.

After four years of often-bitter resistance to organization by labor unions, Delco assented to representation of its employees by a United Auto Workers local in May, 1940. Hostilities in Europe and the sudden declaration of war against Japan, however, turned the company's attention to mobilization for war. Largely through its association with General Motors, Delco was selected to produce a variety of military equipment. With civilian production on hold, Delco manufactured antiradar devices, aircraft and tank radios, ignition testers, oxygen-flow indicators, and the famous two-way field radio.

Delco was awarded the army-navy "E" for excellence in 1943. In great favor with the government, Delco expanded its production by taking over the Malleable Iron Works for a third plant, and later the Continental Can Company facilities in Terre Haute, Indiana. Even after the war ended in 1945, Delco retained a great many military contracts. When civilian production resumed, however, Delco again found rapidly expanding markets in both automotive and home electronics. The company began production of home radios in 1946, but abandoned the market only two years later. By 1948, the company had taken over an RCA facility in Chicago and several naval-air-station buildings in Kokomo, Indiana and had constructed a major new factory adjacent to its original plant.

During the Korean War, Delco developed a lighter-weight field version of the Walkie-Talkie, a Motorola invention. When that conflict ended, in 1953, Delco began production of an antiaircraft-gun-control system called the Skysweeper.

The company's most important development in years, the high-power transistor, came in January, 1956. In its first application, the transistor eliminated radio buzz from the vibrator coil, and later it replaced vacuum tubes. It enabled the development of experimental products including an in-dash portable radio and a 45-rpm automobile record player that, understandably, was never brought to market.

In 1958 Martin J. Caserio replaced Barry Cooper as general manager of Delco. Cooper had been in charge of Delco for 16 years and is credited with overseeing the company's massive wartime expansion. Caserio was a 21-year GM veteran and had managed Delco's AC spark-plug division in Milwaukee.

Delco's ready market for automotive components and radio grew with GM automobile sales. By and large, this remained a stable and profitable source of income. The company's greatest expansion, however, occurred in defense electronics. In October, 1960, Delco was awarded a contract to manufacture components for the Minuteman missile. Delco was singled out by the government for its leading position in solid-state devices.

After seeing Delco into AM/FM stereo-radio production, among other things, Caserio was succeeded as general manager in February, 1964 by Gus Riggs, a former works manager at the Delco Remy facility in Anderson, Indiana. During Riggs' tenure, Delco continued to refine its existing product line and introduced new power and automotive-control systems.

Delco's AC division, with plants in Milwaukee, Wisconsin and Santa Barbara, California, was consolidated with

Delco Radio in 1970 and renamed the Delco Electronics division. The reorganization eliminated redundant managers and provided better production economies. The division also held many government contracts, including one to supply components for the Apollo Mission lunar rovers. In 1973 Delco won a British contract to manufacture inertial navigation systems for the Concorde aircraft. The company became a major INS manufacturer after developing subsequent INS lines as a retrofit item for 747, KC-135, and C-141 aircraft.

Donald J. Atwood, a former director of the GM transportation systems division, became general manager of Delco Electronics in September, 1974. Under his leadership, Delco continued to respond to fads, and marketed an in-dash CB radio. The product was phased out some years later when the public fascination with CB radios ended. Another more successful product, the trip computer (a gadget that, among other things, calculated mileage) was introduced in 1978. In the defense sector, Delco developed a fire-on-the-move control system for the M-1 tank in 1976, and the Magic computer, for use in F-16 fighter jets.

In 1978, in search of less expensive labor and fewer union restrictions, Delco broke ground for a 100,000-square-foot complex in Singapore for manufacturing parts and subassemblies. The plant also gave the company greater access to foreign markets. That same year, Edward Czapor was appointed general manager of Delco. Atwood, like his predecessors, was promoted into GM management. He is best remembered for establishing an enduring cooperation between management and labor.

Delco, whose aluminum-nickel-cobalt speaker magnets had made it the world's largest consumer of cobalt, was forced to develop a ceramic-magnet speaker in 1979 when a world cobalt shortage forced prices up. This became the least of Delco's problems, however, as the following year the combined effects of recession and competition from Japanese companies forced it to lay off thousands of workers. An increase in military budgets that began in 1979, however, bolstered Delco's overall earnings enough to justify recalling several hundred laid-off employees. The company began manufacturing servos and gunsights for the M-48 tank's DIVAD gun system and the nighttime low-altitude navigation-and-targeting LANTIRN system for F-16 and A-10 aircraft.

A second foreign plant was opened at Matamoros, Mexico, just south of Brownsville, Texas, in August, 1980. Three months later, the four-year-old Shreveport, Louisiana plant was closed.

Despite intense competition from Japanese radio manufacturers and upmarket German manufacturers such as Blaupunkt, Delco landed a contract to build an electronically tuned radio, or ETR, for the luxury Opel Senator automobile. Delco, however, was unable to compete with high-end manufacturers, so instead concentrated on traditional markets. Still, Rolls-Royce chose a Delco spark-control system as standard equipment for its new Bentley line.

Robert J. Shultz was named general manager of Delco in November, 1981. Shortly after he took office, Delco furloughed several hundred employees at Kokomo, a result of poor GM sales. Later that year, Delco abandoned its speaker business, choosing instead to tie in with Bose, an established leader in the field. Bose was a well-respected name that did much to improve the marketability of Delco ETRs. Delco also improved its position in European automotive technology by opening a new engineering center in Luxembourg.

Delco's Santa Barbara facility won a lucrative military contract for gun-stabilization units on U.S. Army light armored vehicles. Six months later, in April, 1983, the entire Santa Barbara operation was transferred to GM's new power products and defense operations group. A reorganization was under way at Delco as well that year. Three business units were created, including automotive electronics, semiconductor products, and entertainment and comfort products. The company also inaugurated a $204 million expansion-and-modernization program aimed at bolstering the business of its new operating divisions.

General Motors' acquisition of the Hughes Aircraft Company from the Howard Hughes Medical Institute in 1985 promised to greatly enhance the company's position. Hughes was regarded as a technological powerhouse, with engineering applications for both military and automotive electronics. GM decided that Hughes' vast resources could best be assimilated by grouping the company with Delco under a new GM subsidiary called GM Hughes Electronics. The two companies were to maintain their independence—preserving company loyalty—but GM decided the two companies would be most productive if coordinated.

As a technological resource, GM Hughes Electronics is an essential resource for General Motors (its newly inaugurated Saturn division, for example, is dependent on advanced automotive-electronics systems). This factor, it was hoped, would enable GM to compete more effectively with Japanese manufacturers, against whom it had already lost on labor costs. The extent to which Delco will benefit from Hughes' technologies remains to be seen. Its greatest impact has been in defense-related markets; Hughes' operations increased GM's government business from 1.5% to 7% of sales.

Delco is the largest manufacturer of automotive-electronics systems in the United States. It is a world leader in on-board digital-control computers, and produces a variety of other systems that enable GM automobiles to operate efficiently and safely. And though it is best known for making car radios, Delco remains a major defense contractor. With the backing of GM, Delco promises to maintain a leadership role in both markets.

Principal Subsidiaries: **Hughes Aircraft Company**: Advanced Electronics Systems International; Atlantic Satellites Ltd. (80%) (Ireland); AZ Engineering Co., Inc.; DCC Limited (U.K.); ELBAC Leasing Company; Ensambladores Electronicos de Mexico S.A.; ESAL Company; HESP Company; HNS-Italia, S.r.l.; Hughes Advanced Systems Company; Hughes Aircraft-Alabama; Hughes Aircraft Company (Inc.); Hughes Aircraft International Service Company; Hughes Aircraft Mississippi, Inc.; Hughes Aircraft–South Carolina; Hughes Aircraft Systems

International; Hughes Automation Systems Corporation; Hughes Communications Carrier Services, Inc.; Hughes Communications Galaxy, Inc.; Hughes Communications, Inc.; Hughes Communications International, Inc.; Hughes Communications Japan, Inc.; Hughes Communications Mobile Satellite Services, Inc.; Hughes Communications Satellite Services, Inc.; Hughes Communications Services, Inc.; Hughes do Brasil-Eletronica e Communicacoes Ltda.; Hughes Energy Corporation; Hughes Foreign Sales Corporation (U.S. Virgin Islands); Hughes Georgia, Inc; Hughes Information Systems (The Netherlands); Hughes International Sales Corporation; Hughes International Sales Corporation 2; Hughes Investment Management Company; Hughes Space Defense, Inc.; Hughes Microelectronics Limited (U.K.); Hughes Missiles Electronics, Inc.; Hughes Nadge Corporation; Hughes Network Systems, Inc.; Hughes Optical Products, Incorporated; Hughes Systems Management International; Hughes Technical Services Company; Husint S.A. (Switzerland); Interaz, S.A. de C.V. (Mexico); International Electronics Systems, Inc.; MDP, Ltd.; National Satellite Services, Inc.; Santa Barbara Research Center; Spectrolab, Inc.; Systems Building Corp.; XMC Holdings, Ltd.; XMC Management Company; XMC Properties, Inc.

Delco Electronics Corporation: Delco Electronics Overseas Corporation; Delco Electronics Service Corporation; Delnosa, S.A. de C.V. (Mexico); Deltronicos de Matamoros, S.A. de C.V. (Mexico); GM Singapore Pte. Ltd.

Further Reading: Banner, Glen. *Delco Electronics: A Story of Progress*, Detroit, Michigan, General Motors Corporation, 1983; Drosnin, Michael. *Citizen Hughes*, New York, Rinehart and Winston, 1985.

HARRIS CORPORATION

1025 West NASA Boulevard
Melbourne, Florida 32919
U.S.A.
(407) 727–9100

Incorporated: 1926 as Harris-Seybold-Potter Company
Employees: 35,000
Sales: $3 billion
Stock Index: New York Midwest Pacific Philadelphia Boston

The origin of the Harris Corporation, a leading American electronics company, is actually to be found in the printing business. What began as a minor manufacturer of printing press machinery has evolved during this century into an important developer of cutting-edge electronics technology. In fact, Harris's role in the American electronics industry is so important that the Pentagon recently stepped in to prevent its acquisition by a foreign company.

In 1895 the Harris Automatic Press Company was founded in Cleveland, Ohio. This company manufactured the large multicolor presses that are used to print books and newspapers. In the early decades of the 20th century, the Harris Automatic Press acquired the properties of two other companies involved in the printing business—the Seybold Machine Company of Dayton, Ohio and the Premier & Potter Printing Press Company, Inc. of New York. The name of the company was then changed to Harris-Seybold-Potter Company. In June, 1957 the company merged with the Intertype Corporation of Brooklyn, New York and its name was again changed, this time to Harris-Intertype Corporation. Intertype was a manufacturer of hot metal typesetting machines and operated a plant in England in addition to the plant in New York.

Throughout these acquisitions the company's business remained essentially unchanged: it built and marketed printing and broadcasting machinery. Such machinery included offset lithographic presses, envelope presses, paper cutting machines, and bindery equipment, and at Intertype, hot metal typesetting machines. Later acquisitions, in particular the Gates Radio Company, gave the company the capacity to manufacture broadcasting transmitters and microwave equipment.

The boom in the aerospace industry that began in the 1950s gave rise to many companies that produced components for government projects. One of the earliest of these businesses was Radiation, Inc., established in 1950 by Homer Denius and George Shaw, both of whom were electronics engineers. At first Radiation employed a staff of only 12 and was housed in space rented from the Naval Air Station in Melbourne, Florida. The site was convenient because it was located only a few miles south of the Cape Canaveral (now Kennedy) Space Center. From the start, the company produced miniaturized electronics, tracking, and pulse-code-modulation technologies, all of which are crucial to aerospace programs. Radiation's involvement with the aerospace program included equipment for the Telstar and Courier communication satellites and the Nimbus and Tiros weather satellites. Military systems that relied upon Radiation equipment included the Atlas, Polaris, and Minuteman missiles.

Radiation's initial success was due in part to the high quality of its staff. Many of the highest level managers held advanced degrees in engineering. John Hartley, the current CEO of the firm, joined Radiation after serving on the faculty of Auburn University. Hartley joined the firm in 1956, the same year that Radiation stock was first sold to the public. Another person who left academia to join the staff at Radiation was Joseph Boyd. In the late 1950s and early 1960s Boyd taught electrical engineering at the University of Michigan. At the same time he was also director of the Willow Laboratories, a prestigious science and technology research institute with a staff of more than 1,000 scientists and engineers. Boyd joined Radiation in 1962 and within a year was made president of the firm. His first significant action as president was to set up a microelectronics plant to develop and produce integrated circuits. The following year, Hartley was named as director of this division of Radiation.

During the early 1960s, Radiation devoted itself to improving its market position in the interconnected fields of digital communication, space communication, data management, and computer-based control systems. The company was also successful with satellite tracking systems and alphanumeric data processing. By 1967 the company was one of Florida's largest employers (at 3,000 employees) and sales passed $50 million a year. The company was well-established as a government contractor for both military and non-military projects. But Radiation's management wanted to expand the company's business activity in the commercial sector. To do this, they decided to merge with a commercial company.

At roughly the same time, the Harris-Intertype Corporation was seeking to expand its operations into the electronics field. George Dively, the chairman of Harris-Intertype, had succeeded in building up the company's business from $10 million in annual sales to almost $200 million. But Harris-Intertype's printing machines were still mechanical, and Dively realized that future technological developments would require electronics. Radiation seemed a perfect candidate for acquisition. Dively and Harris-Intertype's president, Richard Tullis, paid $56 million for Radiation. The purchase price was considered quite steep—Harris shares were traded for Radiation's in a ratio that valued Radiation's earnings at twice those of Harris. However, Harris's management wanted Radiation's electronics talent, and not just its earning power. The two companies merged in 1967 under the Harris-Intertype name. Dively remained chairman of the company; Homer Denius, one of the founders of Radiation, became vice-chairman; and Boyd became an executive vice-president for electronics. After the merger, annual sales surpassed the $250 million mark and the combined number of employees exceeded 12,000.

The Harris-Radiation hybrid proved to be a success and innovations began to flow from the company almost immediately. Electronic newsroom technology, for example, was the direct result of a study made by Radiation of how to update Harris's mechanical presses. Most importantly however, the merger gave birth to an essential management strategy known as "technology transfer"—developing commercial applications of technology originally developed for the government.

Two years later, RF Communications, Inc. of Rochester, New York was purchased through an exchange of shares. By the time of its purchase, RF was well established as a manufacturer of point-to-point radio equipment. Even after this rapid expansion, the company's electronics business remained primarily with the government, especially in the aerospace field. Harris-Intertype was responsible for the production and development of the data-handling systems for the preflight check of the Apollo spacecraft and for the digital command-and-control computer of the Gemini spacecraft.

At the beginning of the 1970s, the company made several other major acquisitions. In 1972, Harris-Intertype purchased General Electric's product line of TV broadcasting cameras, transmitters, studio equipment, and antennas for $5.5 million in cash, adding greatly to its original broadcasting product line. In addition, UCC-Communications Systems, Inc. of Dallas, Texas was purchased from the University Computing Company for $20 million in cash. This company was a leading producer of computer terminals and communications subsystems for the data processing industry in general. Two years later, in 1974, Harris-Intertype acquired Datacraft Corporation and also divested itself of its corrugated paper machinery business. Datacraft was a producer of super minicomputers. During the same year the company changed its name to the Harris Corporation.

These acquisitions, made under the leadership of Richard Tullis, were integral to Harris's evolution from a company which was 84% mechanical into a company which was 70% electronic. However, the integration of the purchases and the continual introduction of new product lines took its toll on the company's earnings. From the late 1960s to the late 1970s earnings growth was not outstanding and investors largely ignored the company. But by 1976 things began to change for Harris; over the following three years its stock rose more than 100%. Meanwhile, the acquisitions campaign did not slow down even during the fallow period.

Subsequent acquisitions were all in the field of data processing and handling. Purchases were made every year throughout the remainder of the decade and well into the 1980s. By 1977 Harris's sales were more than $646 million and earnings were greater than $40 million. Boyd was appointed chairman and CEO two years later, in 1979.

That year Harris reached a significant agreement with Matra, a French state-owned electronics company. Under this agreement, which was to provide the French with a factory to manufacture integrated circuits, all of the $40 million funding was supplied by Matra and the French government; Harris provided only technology and management. The French retained 51% of the company, leaving Harris with the remaining 49%.

Since Harris had begun to deal predominantly in electronics, the company found itself in a market with extremely powerful competition. By this time the concept of technology transfer was the central element of the company's management policies. Though defense contracts accounted for only around 20% of Harris's business, military projects were its most advanced production efforts. In general government contracts are for custom products instead of standard items, which helps to push the state of a technological art to its limit. In addition, these projects tend to be motivated more by technology than by cost considerations. Harris's challenge was to translate work on customized, ultra-high technology products into profitable commercial projects. Among the problems Harris faced in doing this was military secrecy—an obstacle which would eventually stymie attempts to take over Harris. In order to overcome problems such as these, Harris instituted managerial policies which made promotion and demotion dependent upon the successful development of commercial products from defense projects. Harris also adopted a more general strategy of competing for government work only in those areas in which the company anticipated the ready development of commercial products. The development of a video terminal for electronic newsrooms, derived from the company's Vietnam-era work on an Army battlefield message sender, was a successful example of this technology-transfer policy.

Throughout Harris's history its acquisitions program has been well-planned. In 1980 Harris made another important purchase, of the Farinon Corporation, a manufacturer of microwave transmitters, electronic switchboards, and other sophisticated telephone products. At the time of its purchase, Farinon was a small company, with sales of only $100 million. Outside observers believed that the purchase price of four million Harris shares, worth around $125 million, was much too high. However, management at Harris justified the price on the grounds that it had to beat out other bids (GTE, RCA, Siemens, and Loral Corporation had all expressed interest in Farinon) and that Harris was buying technology and market position, not earnings or revenues.

Harris passed the billion dollar mark in annual revenues in 1981, and went on to weather the recession of the early 1980s quite well; earnings per share grew roughly 15% a year during this period. New plants were in operation 30 miles south of the Kennedy Space Center in Florida and the company had become the largest industrial employer in Florida. In 1983 Harris marked another turning point in its history. Harris had risen from the sixth largest supplier of printing machines to the number one position in the country, but in the spring of that year, Harris sold its printing business to concentrate exclusively on electronics. In the autumn of that year, Lanier Business Products, Inc. was merged into Harris on a $276 million stock purchase. Lanier was involved primarily in office automation and was noted for its business computers, dictating systems, copying machines, and word processing systems. Lanier brought Harris greater strength in the commercial sector since it boasted 350 sales offices throughout the United States and a sales force of over 2,000 people, 700 of them marketing Lanier's copying machines (which were manufactured by the 3M Corporation).

Later in the year the Federal Communications Commission (FCC) ordered Harris to stop production and marketing of a system that allowed AM radio stations to broadcast in stereo. The FCC also ordered the stations which had already purchased the units to cease broadcasting using the units. According to the FCC, the unit actually marketed by Harris differed significantly from one that the agency had approved the preceding year. Management at Harris claimed that the order had little effect on the company's overall business performance since Harris had a backlog of only $2 million for the system, out of a total of $430 million for the communications sector that year.

But massive layoffs and a major reorganization began in the same year and continued for about three years. The company's government communications systems group was dissolved and employees from that group were reassigned to other divisions in the government systems sector. As other divisions were also consolidated, the workforce at Harris was reduced by several thousand employees.

At the end of this period of adjustment, Harris and 3M entered into a joint venture to market and service copiers and facsimile machines as a result of their earlier connection through Lanier. The new company, named Harris/3M Document Products, Inc., is headquartered in Atlanta, Georgia and owned equally by 3M and Harris.

Harris has had a spate of problems with government contracts. In June, 1987 the company agreed to settle out of court, for $1.3 million, a claim that Harris had overcharged NASA to upgrade the security system for a ground tracking station. Later in the year the company pleaded guilty to making false claims relating to a contract with the United States Army. The settlement in this case came to more than $2 million refunded as excess profits and another $2 million in penalties.

That same year the Pentagon stopped a takeover of Harris by the British communications company Plessey. Plessey, roughly the same size as Harris, is one of Britain's largest electronics manufacturers. The takeover was apparently blocked because of the security-sensitive nature of much of Harris's activities. For instance, the company is the major supplier of electrical components that are hardened against damage from the electromagnetic pulse generated by nuclear weapons. It is reported that Harris also manufactures top-secret equipment for the National Security Agency, which operates the government's spy satellites and communication-interception equipment.

In addition to being well protected against takeover, Harris is well established in custom electronic systems, office automation, communications, and microelectronic products. Company revenues have more than doubled over the last decade, from $850 million to more than $2 billion. The largest growth in both sales and profits came in the semiconductor and government systems sectors. Harris has become the largest U.S. supplier of radio and television broadcasting equipment and dictating equipment, and is the largest producer of low- and medium-capacity microwave radio equipment. It is now the largest supplier of integrated circuits to the U.S. government and the sixth largest producer of integrated circuits in the country. It is also the largest producer of satellite-communications earth stations, a major supplier to NATO armed forces, and sells commercial products in over 100 countries.

The future of the Harris Corporation is difficult to assess. Competition with the Japanese will continue to be fierce, growth is slowing in the communications industry, and office automation has been a more competitive field than Harris anticipated. But cutbacks in personnel and the major reorganization of divisions at Harris streamlined the company. In late 1988 Harris bought GE Solid State, General Electric's semiconductor company, for more than $200 million, and in 1989 Harris purchased 3M's 50% interest in Harris/3M and renamed the company Lanier Worldwide, Inc. after adding Lanier Voice Products to that business. While the competition in semiconductors is cutthroat, Harris's niche in the relatively stable industrial and government markets, balanced by its growing interests in the consumer markets, gives it a solid base.

Principal Subsidiaries: Harris Data Communications Inc.; Harris Data Services Corporation; Harris Far East Ltd.; Harris Installation Corporation; Harris International Sales Corporation; Harris International Telecommunications, Inc.; Harris Investments of Delaware, Inc.; Harris/Intersil, Inc.; Harris Semiconductor, Inc.; Harris Semiconductor (Florida), Inc.; Harris Semiconductor International, Inc.; Harris Semiconductor (New Jersey), Inc.; Harris Semiconductor (Ohio), Inc.; Harris Semiconductor Patents, Inc.; Harris Semiconductor (Pennsylvania), Inc.; Harris Solid State, Inc.; Harris Southwest Properties, Inc.; Harris Space Systems Corporation; Harris Technical Services Corporation; Allied Broadcast Equipment Corporation; Gemco Electronics, Inc.; Lanier Worldwide, Inc.; Harris/3M Document Products Leasing, Inc.

Honeywell

HONEYWELL INC.

Honeywell Plaza
Minneapolis, Minnesota 55408
U.S.A.
(612) 870-5200

Public Company
Incorporated: 1927 as Minneapolis-Honeywell Regulator Co.
Employees: 78,383
Sales: $7.15 billion
Stock Index: New York London Paris Amsterdam Brussels Geneva Zurich Basel

In 1883, when delivery men still toted coal into American basements, Albert Butz created a device to lift a furnace's damper when a home became too cold, letting fresh air fan the flames and warm the house. The "damper flapper," as the device was called, started a business that would become the backbone of Honeywell Inc., a multinational corporation that more than a 100 years later is not only a leading supplier of home, office, and industrial control systems, but is a major defense contractor and an integral part of America's advancement into space.

Honeywell is most familiar to the public for its thermostats. Its most famous thermostat is the "Honeywell Round," Model T86, known in the 1950s for its snap-off plastic cover that could be painted to match the interior of a home.

Thermostats are still a major part of Honeywell's business; today home and commercial accounts together make up a quarter of Honeywell sales. In the commercial arena, Honeywell designs computerized control systems that regulate heat and electricity flow for large buildings, and also manufactures its own switches, electronic parts, and motors for these systems. The company has also ventured into "smart" buildings that regulate themselves with packages that can link together a building's phone lines, control devices, and information systems.

While sales have been on an upward trend in recent years, Honeywell's growth over the century has been far from smooth. The company fell upon hard times more than once in the years following its inception and during the Depression. The longest and most difficult stretch in the company's history was its rocky marriage with the computer industry, one that ended in 1986 when it sold most of its computer assets to two foreign partners, Group Bull of France and Japan's NEC Corporation.

Honeywell today is a powerful force in the public and private sectors. The company has more than 35 divisions and 80 subsidiaries, and offices in all 50 states and around the world. In 1986 the company purchased the Sperry Aerospace Group, now incorporated into Honeywell's aerospace division. Honeywell continues to win military contracts in the millions of dollars, making torpedoes, guidance systems, and ammunition for the nation's defense; meanwhile, sales of its home, building, and industrial controls divisions reached $3 billion in 1987.

By longstanding tradition, Honeywell traces its beginnings back to 1885, the year that Al Butz invented the damper flapper. In 1886, the device was patented and the Butz Thermo-Electric Regulator Company was formed to manufacture it. Butz, from Minneapolis, Minnesota, was more an idea man than a man of business, and the company does not seem to have prospered. In 1888, Butz sold the patent for the damper flapper to his patent attorneys, who founded the Consolidated Temperature Controlling Company in 1888.

During its first years, this company went through financial difficulties, and with these several name changes. It became the Electric Thermostat Company in 1892 and the Electric Heat Regulator Company in 1893. In 1898, William Sweatt, a businessman who had joined the company in 1891, took over the company. He took charge of marketing the damper flapper, increasing advertising and even going door-to-door with his salesmen. This firsthand contact with customers prompted Sweatt to sell the wheelbarrow company he owned at the time and cast his entire future into the Electric Heat Regulator Company.

The damper flappers Sweatt sold remained basically the same until 1907, when a clock was added. Now the thermostat could automatically let a house cool at night and warm it in the morning. The clock also gave the thermostat a new look that would survive well into the 1930s.

When consumers responding to his ads began to request the "Minneapolis" regulator, Sweatt changed the name of his product. He began calling the thermostat "The Minneapolis Regulator" in 1905; in 1909, "The Minneapolis" was put on the face of the thermostats and on the motors, and in 1912 Sweatt officially changed the name of the company to the Minneapolis Heat Regulator Company.

One year later, in 1913, Sweatt's son, Harold R. Sweatt, who had been elected to the board at 18 in 1909, was elected vice-president. At the time, the company had fifty people and a motorcycle, whose engine powered several machines. Sales hit $200,000 in 1914. Sweatt's second son, Charles, joined the company, and was elected to the board in 1916. Sweatt stressed to his sons the importance of manufacturing thermostats, saying that it made no sense competing with their best customers by making furnaces.

As coal furnaces began to be replaced by sometimes dangerous oil burners, Minneapolis Heat Regulator made a circuit that stopped and started the burners. Early attempts failed to eliminate "puffs," as these explosions were called, but modifications on the circuit soon made it possible for the regulator to shut down the burner in case of a malfunction, and the Series 10 was born.

As the home heating market continued to expand, many companies began to manufacture products to compete with the Minneapolis Regulator. In the face of this competition, the company merged with the Wabash, Indiana-based Honeywell Heating Specialties Company in 1927. The two companies had been making complementary and competing products, including oil burner controls, clock thermostats, and regulators, and had even been involved in a legal suit over patents at the time of the merger.

The combination surprised the industry, and even the corporate heads themselves. But the merger made a lot of sense. Minneapolis Heat Regulator doubled its business and became a publicly held company, under yet another name: the Minneapolis-Honeywell Regulator Company.

William Sweatt became chairman of the board in the new Minneapolis headquarters; Mark Honeywell, president; Harold Sweatt, vice president and general manager; and Charles Sweatt, vice president.

The merger gave the business the resources to expand even after the 1929 stock market crash, and marked the start of a decade of acquisition and growth.

In 1931, Minneapolis-Honeywell bought Time-O-Stat Controls Corporation through an exchange of stock. Time-O-Stat was the result of a 1929 merger between four Wisconsin heating controls companies. The purchase brought the company several mercury switch patents and other controls technology.

Minneapolis-Honeywell's next big acquisition marked a move to industrial accounts. In a chance train meeting, Willard Huff, Minneapolis-Honeywell treasurer, and Richard Brown, president of Brown Instrument Company, began discussing the similarities of their businesses. Brown's products measured the high temperatures inside industrial machines, while Minneapolis-Honeywell was a low temperature controls company. Within weeks, the firms were negotiating, and by the end of 1934, Minneapolis-Honeywell had purchased Brown's assets for $2.3 million.

Finally, in 1937, dissatisfied with the high costs of its own pneumatic control devices for larger buildings like schools and offices, Minneapolis-Honeywell bought the only two competing companies in the field: National Regulator Company and Bishop & Babcock Manufacturing Company.

In the ten years since the 1927 merger with Honeywell, Minneapolis-Honeywell had tripled its employee ranks and its sales. Despite the Depression, the company had $16 million in sales and 3,000 employees.

Harold Sweatt had become president in 1934, following Mark Honeywell, who had succeeded William Sweatt. At the start of World War II, Sweatt headed a company with the experience and resources needed to develop precision instruments and controls for the military.

In 1941, the army called upon a group of Minneapolis-Honeywell engineers who had worked on heat regulating systems to develop an automatic bomber pilot that gave precise readings of high-altitude coordinates. The company also produced a turbo regulator and an intricate fire control system during the war; by its end, Minneapolis-Honeywell was well on its way to becoming a major defense contractor.

After the war, Harold Sweatt held fast to his father's rule and kept moving in the direction of controls. He purchased two planes and turned them into flying laboratories for his aviation and research staffs. He also began buying companies related to the manufacture of control instruments.

One such purchase came in 1950, when Harold Sweatt bought the Micro Switch Division of the First Industrial Corporation of Freeport, Illinois. Micro switches are used in vending machines, industrial equipment, and even tanks and guided missile systems. Generally they need a small amount of physical force to activate the electronics. Two years after the purchase, Minneapolis-Honeywell was making 5,000 variations of micro switches.

About this time, Raytheon, a Massachusetts electronics firm, approached Minneapolis-Honeywell about teaming up to enter the computer business. After studying the issue for months, Minneapolis-Honeywell accepted Raytheon's offer in April of 1955. The companies formed Datamatic Corporation, a subsidiary owned jointly by the two companies.

In 1957, the company installed its first line of mainframe computers. The Datamatic 1000 filled several rooms and weighed some 25 tons, and the fist unit sold for $2 million. But Datamatic lacked the customer base that gave competitors like IBM an early edge. Raytheon wanted out, and that year the operation became Minneapolis-Honeywell's Datamatic division.

The company's aerospace divisions were also developing quickly. From its first autopilot in 1941, Minneapolis-Honeywell systems were at the forefront of technology—Honeywell systems were involved in every manned space shot. In 1964, Minneapolis-Honeywell won a bid to make space vehicles designed to carry a variety of NASA equipment. Two were eventually launched, but the company decided expenses were too great to enter into the prime contract field. The company continues to participate in America's space ventures on a smaller scale, supplying digital flight control systems and display and performance monitors for the space shuttle. Also in 1964 the stockholders approved yet another name change, to Honeywell Inc.

While Honeywell ventured further into computers and aerospace technology, its international operations were also expanding. Between 1945 and 1965, Honeywell's overseas business in Great Britain, Canada, Japan, and the Netherlands had grown from almost nothing to account for 23% of sales and 20% of its workforce; these percentages stayed roughly the same into the 1980s. In 1965, Honeywell's overseas operations consisted of 17 subsidiaries with 12,000 employees and revenues of more than $160 million.

Meanwhile, the computer division finally showed a profit in 1967, 12 years after it was established. But research and development costs continued to be enormous. In 1970, Honeywell shocked the business world by purchasing the large systems computer segment of General Electric. The purchase doubled its business and added 25,000 employees in a new subsidiary called Honeywell Information Systems (HIS). The move put Honeywell in second place in computers, behind only IBM. But in the end, the merger only pitted Honeywell against IBM, leading to a long, hard struggle and, eventually, disillusionment.

The early 1970s were a bumpy time for Honeywell. The company received a lot of negative publicity for its involvement with the war in Southeast Asia and for its investments in South Africa. One of the most vocal demonstrators was Charles Pillsbury, a dissident stockholder and heir to the flour empire, who in 1970 shouted the memorable question to Honeywell president James H. Binger, "How does it feel to be the Krupp of Minneapolis?" In 1932, the Pillsbury family had helped Honeywell during the Depression with a contract for flour sifters and water meters. Binger, an outspoken and controversial leader, declared in 1971 that as long as the conflict in Southeast Asia continued, Honeywell would furnish support.

Within the corporation, the 1970s were marked by efforts to streamline business and cut out nonproductive assets. One of the divisions that dwindled during this period was the home smoke alarm business, which was finally cut in 1980. The market had become increasingly competitive; though well known for its fire protection products, the company discontinued its line. Honeywell's entry into microcomputers did turn a profit, doubling sales every year between 1976 and 1980. Unfortunately, however, HIS suffered nearly a 50% decline in operating profits between 1981 and 1982.

At the same time, a new phase of public scrutiny brought protests reminiscent of the early 1970s against the company's South African interests, while in another part of the country, Native Americans claimed that land Honeywell held for defense experiments was sacred, and demanded Honeywell stop all activities there.

In 1982 Honeywell began a major corporate restructuring. James Renier, a Honeywell executive who had climbed the ranks, became president of the computer division. A total of 3,500 jobs were eliminated through layoffs, retirements and transfers, giving Renier the nickname Neutron Jim: "all the buildings were still there," one survivor explained to *The Wall Street Journal*, "it's just the people who were gone." Renier became president and CEO of Honeywell in 1986.

Renier also redefined the corporate attitude toward IBM, resolving to live in an IBM world and begin marketing products that would work along side IBM computers.

With the computer division whipped into some kind of shape, Honeywell decided in 1986 to sell the majority of it to Group Bull of France and Japan's NEC Corporation, creating a three-way joint venture. Honeywell retained 42.5% of the stock, but intends to sell all but 20% to its partners. The divestiture of its computer unit left Honeywell to concentrate on sales of thermostat systems, automation products, and aerospace and defense equipment.

In 1988, Honeywell suffered from a series of unusual charges related to the company's defense unit. Serious cost overruns in a number of contracts, many of them carryovers from the days when Unisys owned the unit, had to be absorbed by the company, resulting in a net loss of $434.9 million for the year. As a general slowdown in defense contracts, combined with the Pentagon's waste-reduction measures, created a tougher business climate for defense contractors, James Renier looked to the company's commercial aerospace business to pick up the slack. By 1989 defense and aerospace accounted for almost half of Honeywell's sales and were contributing significantly to the bottom line. At the same time, automation systems were getting a boost from an upswing in capital investment.

Honeywell has a solid foothold in the automation–systems market and continues to be a leader in heating controls and alarm systems. Prompted in part by takeover threats, the company underwent a major restructuring in a relatively short period of time, but a streamlined and focused Honeywell now looks forward to reaping the rewards of its high-margin units, back in line with William Sweatt's vision at the turn of the century.

Principal Subsidiaries: Honeywell Information Systems Inc.; Honeywell Information Systems De Puerto Rico Inc.; Honeywell Sistemas De Informacion Costa Rica S.A.; Honeywell Information Systems Italia S.p.A.; Honeywell Information Systems Japan Inc.; Honeywell Sistemas De Informacion S.A. de C.V. (Mexico) (98.3%); Disc Instruments, Inc.; Honeywell Sharecom (50%); Digital Datacom, Inc.; Testra Tech, Inc.; ISSC Industrial Solid State Controls, Inc.; Honeywell Optoelectronics Inc.; Honeywell Building Management Services Inc.; Honeywell Communication Services, Inc.; Honeywell Country Club Inc.; Honeywell Electronic Publishing Inc.; Honeywell Disc Inc.; Honeywell Finance Inc.; Honeywell Finance B.V. (Netherlands); Honeywell High-Tech Trading Inc.; Honeywell International Inc.; Honeywell Overseas Finance Co.; Honeywell Realty, Inc.; Honeywell Electronics Corp.; Honeywell Pension Trustees Ltd. (U.K.); Honeywell Export Ltd. (U.K.); Honeywell Leafield Ltd. (U.K.); Honeywell Shield Ltd. (U.K.); Honeywell S.A.I.C. (Argentina); Honeywell Pty. Ltd. (Australia); Honeywell Austria Ges m.b.H. (Austria); Honeywell Europe S.A. (Belgium); Honeywell S.A. (Belgium); Honeywell Assurance Ltd. (Bermuda); Honeywell Controles Ltd. (Brazil); Honeywell Ltd./Honeywell Ltee. (Canada); Honeywell A/S (Denmark); Honeywell Dominicana C. Por A. (Dominican Republic); Honeywell Oy (Finland); Honeywell S.A. (France); Honeywell G.m.b.H. (West Germany); Honeywell Europe S.A. Holding K.G. (West Germany); Honeywell Limited (Hong Kong); Honeywell International Management S.p.A. (Italy); Honeywell S.p.A. (Italy); Yamatake-Honeywell Co., Ltd. (Japan) (50%); Honeywell S.A. de C.V. (Mexico); Honeywell International Finance N.V. (Netherlands Antilles); Honeywell Capital N.V. (Netherlands Antilles); Honeywell Development N.V. (Netherlands Antilles); Honeywell Financiering BV (Netherlands); Honeywell European Distribution Center B.V. (Netherlands); Skinner Europa B.V. (Netherlands);

Honeywell B.V. (Netherlands) (92.6%); Honeywell–Lucifer S.A. (Switzerland); Fema Weber und Freund G.m.b.H. (West Germany) (70%); Honeywell Medical Electronics B.V. (Netherlands); Honeywell (NZ) Ltd. (New Zealand); Honeywell A/S (Norway); Honeywell Turki-Arabia Ltd. (Saudi Arabia) 50%); Honeywell Private Ltd. (Singapore); Honeywell Synertek Pte. Ltd. (Singapore); Honeywell (Proprietary) Ltd. (South Africa); Honeywell S.A. (Spain); Honeywell AB (Sweden); Honeywell AG (Switzerland); Honeywell-Schild AG (Switzerland); Honeywell Synertek (Thai) Co., Ltd. (Thailand); Yamatake-Honeywell Co., Ltd., Taiwan; Honeywell C.A. (Venezuela).

Further Reading: The First 100 Years, Minneapolis, Honeywell Inc., 1985.

INTEL CORPORATION

3065 Bowers Avenue
Santa Clara, California 95051
U.S.A.
(408) 765–1435

Public Company
Incorporated: 1968 as N M Electronics
Employees: 20,800
Sales: \$2.9 billion
Stock Index: New York NASDAQ

Intel has changed the world dramatically since it was founded in 1968: the company invented the microprocessor, the "computer on a chip" that has made everything from the first handheld calculator to today's powerful personal computers possible.

Intel's founders, Robert Noyce and Gordon Moore, were among the eight founders of Fairchild Semiconductor in 1957. Noyce is the co-inventor of the integrated circuit, and Moore made some of the basic discoveries that led to it. In 1968 the two men, feeling frustrated by Fairchild's size, decided to leave to form their own company. They were joined soon after by Andrew Grove, who had been at Fairchild since 1963 and is president and CEO of Intel today.

Noyce and Moore asked Arthur Rock, a venture capitalist who had helped start Fairchild Semiconductor as well as Teledyne and Scientific Data Systems, for help in raising the money to start their company. With a one-page business plan saying simply that they were going into large-scale integrated circuits, they soon had \$3 million in capital. The company was incorporated on July 18, 1968 as N M Electronics (for Noyce Moore), but quickly changed its name to Intel, from the first syllables of "integrated electronics." Intel gathered another \$2 million in capital before going public in 1971.

Despite their scanty business outline, Noyce and Moore had a clear plan for their company. They planned to produce large-scale integrated (LSI) semiconductor memories. At that time, semiconductor memories were ten times more expensive than standard magnetic core memories. But costs were dropping, and Intel's founders felt that with the greater speed and efficiency of LSI technology, semiconductors would soon replace magnetic cores.

Within a few months of its startup, Intel was able to produce the 3101 Schottky bipolar memory, a high-speed random access memory (RAM). The 3101 proved popular enough to sustain the company until the 1101, a metal oxide semiconductor (MOS) chip, was perfected and introduced in 1969.

Intel's next product was the 1103, introduced in 1970: a 1K dynamic RAM, or DRAM, it was the first chip large enough to store a significant amount of information; today DRAMs are indispensable to every computer. With the 1103, Intel finally had a chip that really did begin to replace magnetic cores.

But the company's most dramatic impact on the computer industry didn't come until the introduction of the 4004, the world's first microprocessor. Like many of Intel's innovations, the microprocessor was the by-product of a search for something else. When a Japanese calculator manufacturer asked Intel to design the chips for a series of calculators, an engineer named Ted Hoff was assigned to the project. In his search for cost-effectiveness, he eventually conceived a plan for a central processing unit (CPU) on one chip. The 4004, which crammed 2,300 transistors onto a one-eighth- by one-sixth-inch chip, had the power of the old 3,000-cubic-foot ENIAC computer, which depended on 38,000 vacuum tubes. The microprocessor was born.

Although at first Intel saw the new device as a way to sell more memory, it was soon clear that the microprocessor held great potential for everything from calculators to cash registers and traffic lights. With the 1972 introduction of the 8008, an 8-bit microprocessor developed along with the 4004 but oriented toward data and character (rather than arithmetic) manipulation, microprocessors were off and running. The 8080, introduced in 1974, was the first truly general-purpose microprocessor. For \$360, Intel sold a whole computer, on one chip, when real computers cost thousands of dollars. The response was overwhelming. The 8080 soon became the industry standard and Intel the industry leader in the 8-bit market.

Competitors began to produce 8-bit microprocessors quickly, however. Intel responded with the 8085, a faster chip with more functions. Meanwhile, the company was working on two more advanced projects, the 32-bit 432 and the 16-bit 8086. The 8086 was introduced in 1978, but it took two years for it to catch on. In that time, Motorola produced a competing chip (the 68000) that seemed to catch on faster. Intel responded with a massive sales effort to establish its architecture as the standard. When, among other things, IBM chose the 8088, the 8086's 8-bit cousin, for its personal computer in 1980, Intel's battle over architecture was won.

In the meantime, in 1971 Intel had also developed the erasable programmable read-only memory (EPROM), another revolutionary but unintended research by-product. An Intel physicist named Dov Frohman was working on the reliability problems of the silicon gate used in the MOS process when he realized that the disconnected, or "floating," gates that were causing malfunctions could be used to create a chip that was erasable and reprogrammable.

Standard ROM chips had to be permanently programmed during manufacture; to make a change you had to manufacture a whole new chip. With EPROM, Intel could offer customers chips which could be erased and reprogrammed with ultraviolet light and electricity. At its introduction in 1971, EPROM was a novelty without much of a market. But the microprocessor, invented at the same time, created a demand for memory; the EPROM offered memory that could be conveniently used to test microprocessors. It was a match made in heaven.

Another major development at Intel during the 1970s was peripheral controller chips. Streamlined for specific tasks and stripped of unneeded functions, peripheral chips could greatly increase a computer's abilities without raising software-development costs. One of Intel's most important developments in peripherals was the co-processor, first introduced in 1980. Co-processor chips are an extension of the CPU that can handle specific computer-intensive tasks more efficiently than the CPU itself. Once again, innovation kept Intel ahead of its competition.

Intel's rapid growth, from the 12 employees at its founding in 1968 to 15,000 in 1980, demanded a careful approach to corporate "culture." Since Noyce, Moore, and Grove had left Fairchild because its size had created frustrating bureaucratic bottlenecks, defining a workable management style was important to Intel's founders. Informal weekly lunches with employees kept communication lines open while the company was small, but the system didn't last for long. Instead, a carefully outlined program emphasizing openness, decision making on the lowest levels, discipline, and problem solving rather than paper shuffling has preserved Intel's remarkable ability to innovate. Intel makes no bones about the kind of employees it looks for. In an interview with the *Harvard Business Review* in 1980 Noyce said, "we expect people to work hard. We expect them to be here when they are committed to be here; we measure absolutely everything that we can in terms of performance." Until recently employees who arrived after 8:10 A.M. signed a late list. But this strict attitude is balanced by company commitment. Incentives include options on Intel stock and breakthroughs are celebrated with custom-bottled champagne ("Vintage Intel" marked the first $250 million quarter, in 1983—the year sales reached $1 billion for the first time).

During the 1974 recession, when Intel laid off 30% of its employees, the experience was traumatic enough that when 1981 rolled around, instead of laying off workers, Intel accelerated new product development with the "125% Solution" (asking exempt employees to work two extra hours a day, without pay, for six months), hoping to fight its way through the recession poised to tackle the next upturn. When a brief surge in sales in 1982 didn't last, again, instead of firing, Intel imposed pay cuts of up to 10%. Such measures weren't universally popular, but by June, 1983 all cuts had been restored and retroactive raises had been made. And in December, 1982 IBM paid $250 million for a 12% share of Intel, giving the company not only a strong capital boost, but also strong ties to the undisputed industry leader (IBM eventually increased its stake to 20% before selling its Intel stock in 1987).

During the early 1980s, Intel began to slip in some of its markets. Fierce competition in DRAMS, static RAMS, and EPROMS left Intel concentrating on microprocessors. While competitors claimed that Intel simply gave away its DRAM market, Moore told *Business Week* in 1988 that his company chose microprocessors as the field with the most promise.

The company also struggled during the mid-1980s to overcome its reputation for arrogance in marketing. Customer service, an area Intel had been able to overlook for years as it dominated its markets, became more important as the highly-efficient Japanese and other increasingly innovative competitors challenged Intel's position. In addition, Intel's manufacturing record, strained in years past by undercapacity, needed fixing. Fab 7, Intel's seventh wafer-fabrication plant, opened in 1983 only to face two years of troubled operations before reaching full capacity. Between 1984 and 1988, Intel closed eight old plants, and in 1988 it spent some $450 million on new technology to bring its manufacturing capacity into line with its developmental prowess.

But in the microprocessor market, Intel continued to excel. In 1982, Intel introduced its 80286 microprocessor, the chip that, when IBM came out with the 286-powered PC/AT, quickly came to dominate the upper-end PC market. The 286 was followed in 1985 by Intel's 80386 chip, popularized in 1987 by the Compaq 386, which, despite bugs when it first came out, is one of the most popular chips on the market today. While the 286 brought to the PC a speed and power that gave larger computers their first real challenge, the 386 offered even greater speed and power together with the ability to run more than one program at a time. And in 1989 Intel introduced the 80486, a chip *Business Week* heralded as "a veritable mainframe-on-a-chip."

In designing the i486, Intel resisted an industry trend toward RISC (reduced instruction-set computing), a way of designing chips that eliminates rarely used instructions to gain speed. Intel argued that what RISC chips gained in speed they lost in flexibility—and the ability to run the software already on the market, something Intel feels will secure the 486's position despite whatever speed competitors can offer through non-compatible RISC chips. But a new chip, the 64-bit i860 announced in early 1989, does make use of RISC technology to offer what Intel has claimed will be a "supercomputer on a chip."

Also in 1989 an important lawsuit Intel had filed against NEC in 1984 was decided. Intel had claimed that NEC violated its copyright on the microcode, or embedded software instructions, of Intel's 8086 and 8088 chips, which Intel had licensed NEC to produce, when NEC designed a similar chip of its own. At issue was whether microcode could even be copyrighted. The court ruled that it could be—but that NEC had not violated any copyright in the case at hand.

While Intel faces strong competition both from domestic chipmakers like the giant Motorola and the smaller Sun Microsystems and MIPS Computer Systems, its place at the edge of technology is undisputed. Meanwhile, it has also begun to branch out from chipmaking. The company has begun to build computers of its own, including a parallel processing one. It also has a growing systems business, providing customers with everything they need to build computer systems of their own.

Indeed, it is not technology, but more mundane matters like manufacturing, marketing, and management that are likely to pose challenges for Intel in the 1990s. All three of the company's founders will be looking toward retirement in the next few years, and how the company handles its first leadership transition may make as much difference to its future as the speed of its next chip.

Principal Subsidiaries: Intel Electronics Ltd. (Israel); Intel International; Intel Investment Ltd. (Cayman Islands); Intel Japan K.K.; Intel Puerto Rico, Inc.; Intel Singapore Ltd.; Intel Overseas Corporation.

Further Reading: A Revolution in Progress . . . A History of Intel to Date, Santa Clara, Intel Corporation, 1984.

KOOR INDUSTRIES LTD.

8 Shaul Hamelech Boulevard
P. O. Box 33333
61 232 Tel Aviv
Israel
(03) 250-421

Labor-Union Owned
Incorporated: 1944
Employees: 31,640
Sales: US$2.5 billion

Koor Industries is the largest industrial enterprise in Israel, accounting for 10% of that nation's GNP by itself. Koor derives more than 40% of its income from electronics; the remainder of its income is divided almost evenly among chemicals and rubber, ferrous and non-ferrous metals, and food and consumer products. The company is a major Israeli exporter, providing an often financially chaotic country with an important source of income and industrial growth.

Koor's predecessor is Solel Boneh Construction, founded in British Palestine in 1924 by the Histadrut (the General Federation of Labor) to construct roads and buildings. Through Solel Boneh, the Histadrut provided a livelihood for settlers in an attempt to found a Jewish state in Palestine.

Solel Boneh began planning for independence as early as 1944, when it created an industrial arm called Koor Industries. Koor employed 500 workers at its two plants, Phoenicia Glass and Vulcan Foundries, both in Haifa. Many of Koor's early employees were immigrants who had escaped Europe. After World War II Koor employed many concentration-camp survivors and refugees from Arab nations, providing much-needed job training and employment for these immigrants not just in cities but also in remote villages.

Koor formed Nesher Cement in 1945 as a joint venture with private investors. Koor's first exports, Vulcan car batteries, were sold to Syria in 1947. In 1951, Koor entered the telecommunications field through another joint venture called Telrad, which was located in the town of Lod, near Tel Aviv. From this facility and another built at Ma'alot in 1965, Telrad manufactured telephones, PABX switching terminals, and a variety of other electronic devices.

Shortly after Israeli independence was declared in 1948, the state was attacked by Arab nations. In repelling the attack, Israel took additional land and doubled in size. The war however, left Koor economically isolated within the Middle Eastern region. Without local export markets, the company instead concentrated its sales efforts in Europe, North America, and Africa. But with continuing tensions between Israel and its Arab neighbors came the need for Israel to develop a domestic arms industry. In 1952 Koor, in conjunction with the Finnish company Tampella, established the Soltam artillery-manufacturing plant. Koor's arms manufacturing grew over the years as Israel's Arab neighbors acquired increasingly sophisticated weaponry.

Koor opened the Harsah Ceramics plant in Haifa in 1953, and the following year built a steel-processing complex in partnership with German interests. In conjunction with American interests, Koor established the Alliance Tire and Rubber Company in 1955. Through these ventures, Koor not only contributed significantly to Israeli import-substitution efforts, but generated valuable foreign exchange, too.

By 1958, Koor had grown to 25 plants with 6,000 employees and overshadowed its parent company, Solel Boneh. That year Hevrat Ha'Ovdim, the economic arm of the Histadrut, decided to make Koor a separate entity specializing in industrial products, management and financial services, and foreign trade.

In 1962 Koor created an electronics company called Tadiran, jointly owned by Koor and the Israeli Defense Ministry until 1969. A year after creating Tadiran Koor entered the chemical industry by purchasing Makhteshim. Israel's largest manufacturer of herbicides, pesticides, and insecticides, Makhteshim became an important exporter and source of foreign exchange.

Because it was so closely tied to the Histadrut labor organization, Koor often made business decisions according to workers' welfare rather than profit potential. One of the company's innovations in industrial relations was a joint labor-management committee to discuss production problems. This committee, introduced in 1964 at the Phoenicia Glass plant, raised productivity and minimized labor disputes, and was later copied at other plants.

Israeli borders were expanded again in 1967 after another war with its Arab neighbors. The West Bank, formerly a part of Jordan, the Syrian Golan Heights, and Egypt's vast Sinai Peninsula came under Israeli control. Israeli economic influence spread into these occupied territories with the establishment of communal settlements. The development of these largely agrarian frontier regions represented an expansion of the domestic economy and increased demand for many of Koor's industrial and commercial products.

The Israeli Defense Ministry sold its 50% interest in Tadiran to America's General Telephone and Electronics Corporation (GTE) in 1969. The new ownership gave Koor access to superior technologies developed by GTE and helped Tadiran to become Israel's largest electronics manufacturer and one of its largest employers. In 1970 Koor purchased Hamashbir Lata' asiya, an integrated food manufacturer that produces edible oils and processed, canned, and frozen foods under the Telma brand name. In consumer goods, the company began manufacturing footware, and later added cosmetics, toiletries, cleaning products, and paper goods.

In 1971 Koor took over the government-owned Elda Trading company and renamed it Koortrade. This new subsidiary promoted Koor products in export markets and represented other manufacturers who could not afford to establish their own trade-promotion groups.

Koor also built its international reputation through turnkey projects in developing countries. The first of these was a cotton farm established in Ethiopia in 1972. Additional Koor projects in Nigeria, Togo, and other African nations improved Israeli relations in Africa and elsewhere in the Third World—especially important in light of continued Arab hostility toward Israel.

In 1973, when Israel was attacked by its Arab neighbors, it severely damaged its enemies' air forces in defending itself. Koor now was a more important strategic resource than ever before. The company was called upon to develop new weapons, help increase armament stockpiles, and raise military preparedness. In 1974, as part of an effort to promote more even geographical industrialization, Koor established the Agan Chemical plant in the Negev Desert in southern Israel.

Through peace and war, the company remained highly supportive of its workers, establishing a profit-sharing plan in 1973 and a worker-discount center in 1978. Recognizing the importance of skilled managers, the company also opened a management training school in 1981.

Koor's Telrad subsidiary was awarded the Industrial Development Prize in 1983 for a multiline telephone system it had developed. The award generated greater interest in the system and bolstered both domestic and international sales for the company. Telrad devoted a disproportionately high percentage of earnings to research and development, which led to more sophisticated battle-management systems and communication devices, and "smarter" weapons. In another defense-related project that year, Koor formed a partnership with Pratt & Whitney to build jet-engine parts at Carmel Forge in northern Israel.

Despite a lasting peace agreement with Egypt in 1979, Israel has endured numerous financial crises that have often resulted in a high inflation rate. This in turn has compromised the ability of Israeli exporters to remain competitive in world markets. Indeed, because it is in large part an instrument of Israeli labor, Koor has devoted much of its excess capital to job creation, leaving it few resources to draw upon in times of economic hardship. Worse yet, a 1986 attempt to attract capital in American markets failed, resulting in losses of $253 million during 1987.

A new management team, headed by Benny Gaon, took over in May, 1988 when Gaon's predecessor resigned in protest over interference from the Histadrut. Gaon's first task was to reorganize the company. Several factories were closed and others were combined. Koor's operations were reorganized into five groups, plus one division for international trade. Each group became an individual profit center, placing the burden of performance on individual group heads, while deep cuts were made in management staff. The time had passed when Koor was simply a source of jobs; its survival now depends on its ability to remain competitive and profitable.

But like the economy Koor is so much a part of, the company's difficulties cannot be sorted out overnight. As of 1988, it was saddled with a $1.2 billion debt, a third of which was owed to foreign banks. Many have blamed the government's harsh anti-inflationary policies for Koor's reverses. While these policies brought inflation down from 500% in 1985 to only 20% in 1988, they also cut subsidies and government purchases from Koor.

Others have argued that the company's real problem lies in its inability to be more pragmatic. Hard business decisions, particularly those that involve laying off workers or closing factories, must, they say, be dealt with in purely economic terms. Political interference and meddling by the Histadrut only serve to obscure the company's solutions.

Principal Subsidiaries: Tadiran Ltd.; Telrad Telecommunications & Electronics Industries Ltd.; Telkoor Ltd.; Keren Electronics Ltd.; Koor Communications & Security Ltd.; Clarity Ltd. (71%); Markhteshim Chemical Works Ltd.; Agan Chemical Manufacturers Ltd. (70%); Tambour Ltd. (50%); Rotoplas Ltd.; Caesaria Polymers Ltd. (88%); Gamid Rubber Products & Plastics Ltd. (72%); T.G.L Ltd. (72%); Vulcan Batteries Ltd.; Sefen Ltd.; Shalon Chemicals (50%); 3-H Ltd.; Seffolam Ltd.; Kerem Optronics Ltd. (50%); Unicoor (50%); Alliance Tire & Rubber Co. Ltd. (85%); Nesher Israel Cement Enterprises Ltd. (51%); The Israel Glass Co.; Phoenicia Containers Ltd.; Koor Ceramic Works Ltd.; Barbour; Lapid; Negev 'Hasin-Esh'; Harsa; Naaman; Rami Refractory; Rami-Tech; Shemen Industries Ltd. (87%); Elz-Hazayith Ltd.; Helene Curtis Enterprises Ltd.; Israel Food Products Ltd. (50%); Mata Food Industries Ltd. (50%); H.L.S. Ltd. (74%); Beer-Sheva Flour Mill Ltd. (50%); Rosa of the Galilee Chocolate & Candy Ind. Ltd. (50%); Noon Canning Factory Ltd.; Yona Fishing & Industry Ltd.; Galilee Fruits Ltd.; Jaffa Mor Ltd. (50%); Goldfrost Ltd. (62%); Mega Shoe Ind. Ltd.; Alexander Shoes (51%); Jerusaleum Paper Products Ltd. (74%); Phantom Ltd. (74%); Carmel Plaro Containers-Industries Ltd. (50%); Tri-Wall Containers, Ltd. (50%); Koor Metals Ltd.; Hamat Sanitary Fittings; Hamat Engineering; Vulcan Engineering; Agan Engineering; Simat; Gilmat; Ham-Oz (50%); Ramim Ltd.; Merkavim Metal Works Ltd.; Yuval Gad Ltd.; Project Center; Israel Steel Mills Ltd.; Halom Scrap Metal Center Ltd.; Ma'as Steel Construction Ltd.; Raphael Mitzpe Ramon Ltd.; Kim Manufacturing Ltd. (50%); Alkoor Alloys Ltd. (50%); I. Shinitzky & Co. Ltd.; M.T.L.M. Carmiel Mechanics Ltd.; Hadaikan Metal Works for Spare Parts Ltd.; Hanita Metals Ltd. (50%); Habonim Pipe Products Ltd. (50%); Carmel Forge Ltd. (58%): Explosives Industries Ltd. (74%); Soltam Ltd. (74%); Koortrade Ltd.; Koor Inter-Trade (America) Ltd.; Koor Inter-Trade (Asia) Ltd. (90%); Koor Inter-Trade (Europe) Ltd. (90%); Koor Inter-Trade (Africa) Ltd. (90%); Koor Inter-Trade (Amat) Ltd. (90%): Solcoor Marketing & Purchasing Ltd.;

American Near East Corp. (Israel) Ltd.; Solor Agencies Ltd.; Isra-Tel Telecommunications Systems Ltd.; Hossen Electrical Appliances Co. Ltd.; Ziklag Trade Ltd.; Trade & Maritime Services Ltd. (50%); Middle East Tube Co. Ltd. (92%).

KYOCERA CORPORATION

5–22 Kita-Inouecho, Higashino
Yamashina-ku
Kyoto 607
Japan
(075) 592–3851

Public Company
Incorporated: 1959
Employees: 12,762
Sales: ¥300.4 billion (US$2.4 billion)
Stock Index: Tokyo Osaka Kyoto New York

Kyocera, founded in 1959, was one of the first companies to produce fine ceramic components. It has grown into one of the world's preeminent manufacturers of electronics, optical equipment, and other products that use sophisticated ceramics technology. These products, many of which are manufactured outside of Japan, are sold around the world by the company's own sales force, as well as through a comprehensive network of distributors and dealers.

Ceramic components are used extensively in electronics and electrical equipment, industrial and automotive machinery, and in medical and energy-related fields due to their ability to resist heat and chemicals. They also serve as effective electrical insulators and perform more reliably in environments of extreme temperature change than other materials.

Kyocera produces communication, audio, and business equipment, such as facsimile machines, radio equipment, hard disk drives, calculators, 32-bit personal computers, and cordless telephones. Kyocera is a leading manufacturer of quartz oscillators, which are widely used in such electronic devices as microprocessors and mobile telephones, and has recently developed a compact laser printer.

In addition, Kyocera produces a variety of audio-visual equipment, including single lens reflex (SLR) and 35mm cameras, and video camcorders, through the company's merger with Yashica Company in 1983.

Finally, Kyocera puts its fine ceramics technology to work in a line of consumer-related products including cutting tools, orthopedic and dental implants, jewelry, and solar heating systems.

Kyocera has two research laboratories that serve as repositories for the technological expertise developed since the company's formation. Each division of Kyocera is encouraged to make use of the knowledge and experience of these laboratories throughout the product development process.

The Kagoshima Central Research Laboratory was opened in 1979 to engage in fine ceramics research, particularly in the areas of applied and processing technologies. In 1984, Kyocera established its second research facility in Tokyo to study the areas of electronics, opto-electronics, and other new media.

Although over the years Kyocera has been known more for its individualistic spirit than for a typical Japanese communal character, the company's corporate culture reflects a standard Japanese dedication to the manufacture of superior products. This philosophy was established and carefully cultivated by the company's entrepreneurial founder and current chairman, Kazuo Inamori.

Upon graduation from Kagoshima University, where he studied applied chemistry, Inamori went to work as a ceramics engineer. When he was asked by his employer in 1959 to transfer to Pakistan and become the manager of an insulator factory, Inamori chose instead to take advantage of an opportunity offered by an outside investor to start his own company.

The Kyoto Ceramic Company benefited from creative research ideas and methods that produced discoveries as much through accident as through pure scientific method. For example, during the development of an insulator made of magnesium oxide, a very dry, loose powder, the challenge facing the ceramics industry was to find a way to hold the magnesium oxide together during firing, a problem that leading researchers around the world had been unable to solve.

When Inamori accidentally tripped over a block of paraffin wax as he walked across the lab, it struck him as he removed the wax that had stuck to his shoes that the wax might hold the key to the magnesium oxide problem. Inamori successfully mixed the magnesium oxide and the wax together using what is now humorously referred to in company annals as the "Inamori fried rice powder molding method."

From the very beginning, Inamori instilled a corporate philosophy that emphasized product excellence. To ensure the company's ability to grow without incurring further debt, since Inamori found debt unacceptable, all efforts were directed toward paying off the debt from the company's start-up. The pressure of meeting such ambitious objectives often required salespeople, production staff, and development personnel to work around the clock to fulfill product orders before deadlines.

Kyocera has since grown through a calculated series of mergers and acquisitions to become an international organization of 40 subsidiaries and affiliated companies, 25 of them outside Japan.

In 1969, ten years after Kyocera's birth, Kyocera International, Inc. was established in the United States. Only two years later, this subsidiary entered into an agreement with Fairchild Camera and Instrument of San Diego, California to acquire one of its factories to make ceramic components. On the other side of the ocean, Feldmühle Kyocera Elektronische Bauelemente GmbH was established in the same year as a joint venture with Feldmühle AG of West Germany for manufacturing semiconductor packages and electronic components.

The late 1970s were a time of intense growth and expansion for Kyocera both inside and outside Japan. In 1977, it established Crescent Vert Company, Ltd. to manufacture recrystallized jewels and Kyocera (Hong Kong) Ltd. to supply electronic components and equipment to Southeast Asia. American Feldmühle Corporation and Cybernet Electronics Corporation became affiliates in 1979. The acquisition of Cybernet, a Japanese manufacturer of citizens-band radios and audio equipment, was stimulated to a large extent by Inamori's desire to expand the company's base of business beyond ceramic packaging. Unfortunately, the merger created intense and conflicting company loyalties among the labor union workers inherited from Cybernet and hampered, for a time, the smooth transition Inamori sought.

In 1982, Kyocera Corporation was founded by merging five subsidiaries, including the original Kyoto Ceramic Company.

In 1984, Inamori formed a private telecommunications company called Daini-Denden Kikaku Company, Ltd. to enter into competition with Nippon Telegraph and Telephone (NTT). Funded by Inamori and twenty-four other institutional investors, this venture, NTT's first competitor, was launched in part in retaliation for NTT's successfully blocking an attempt by Kyocera to market its own line of cordless telephones in Japan the year before. NTT had been the only legal supplier. When Kyocera shipped 30,000 of its own units, rated superior to NTT's, NTT lodged an immediate complaint with Japan's Ministry of Ports & Telecommunications and forced Kyocera to recall its product.

Since that time, Daini-Denden, with Inamori as its chairman, has rapidly expanded its business by adding public telecommunications services to its private network and by establishing subsidiaries to institute cellular mobile telephone services in several regions of Japan.

Subsidiary development continued in both North America and Europe during 1985 and 1986, culminating in the 1987 formation of Kyocera America, Inc. and Kyocera Electronics, Inc. to take over for Kyocera International, which became a holding company for seven other U.S. affiliates.

In 1987 Kyocera's Yashica subsidiary successfully introduced the Samurai SLR camera, a breakthrough product integrating advanced technology, ease of use, and reasonable cost. Also in 1987 Kyocera Mexicana, S.A. de C.V. was incorporated, bringing the number of Kyocera's overseas manufacturing facilities to six.

Kyocera's growth has not been free of setbacks. Many have resulted from its chairman's continued resistance to the unspoken tenets of Japanese commerce as, for instance, his duel with NTT in 1984 shows. The following year, Inamori was criticized in the press for ignoring government exportation regulations and directly selling components to a leading U.S. defense manufacturer. A 1980 incident in which Kyocera began marketing a bioceramic medical implant prior to obtaining the official approval of Japan's Ministry of Health returned to haunt Inamori in 1985 when the company was accused of illegal activities by a member of Japan's parliament.

Inamori has often been a target of the Japanese press, which has questioned both his strict managerial style and his judgment in doing things like establishing a company cemetery.

Kyocera's partnership with the California-based Lapine Technology was another deal that brought bad press. In 1986, Kyocera invested more than $10 million to fund the manufacture of 3.5-inch hard disk drives for the Silicon Valley company. This arrangement enabled LaPine to obtain the necessary financing it sought from the Prudential-Bache Trade Corporation. Within months, however, the three-way partnership began to crumble, reducing all three companies to arguments over costs and shipment quantities. As this battle wore on, LaPine customers transferred their orders to other suppliers and employees were laid off in substantial numbers. In the end, Kyocera and Prudential-Bache squared off to fight over what little was left.

Nonetheless, Kyocera has been an active participant in its local and national community. The Inamori Foundation, established in 1984, awards the Kyoto Prize annually for achievements in science, technology, the creative arts, and the humanities. The foundation also funds a number of domestic research projects throughout Japan in a range of technological and cultural specialities.

Kyocera continues to expand its research and marketing activities outside of Japan, while developing new products and technologies. In the future, Kyocera will have to overcome the constraints of increased price competition and the appreciation of the yen, both of which threaten profitability in several areas of the company's activities. In other businesses, such as industrial ceramics, Kyocera's growth may be curbed somewhat until the market achieves more widespread use of the applications that demand these products, or until technological breakthroughs like an all-ceramic diesel engine come.

Although the demand for ceramic and electronic packages appears to remain strong, Kyocera will need to continually monitor the market and enhance its services to overcome increasing competition and keep abreast of the rapid changes in customer needs and the continual demand for cost reductions.

Principal Subsidiaries: Kyocera International, Inc. (U.S.A.); Kyocera America Inc.; Kyocera Feldmühle, Inc.(U.S.A.); Kyocera Northwest, Inc.(U.S.A.); Kyocera Unison, Inc.; Yashica Inc.(U.S.A); Kyocera Electronics, Inc.; Kyocera Canada Inc.; Yashica do Brasil-Industria e Comercio Ltda.; Yashica do Brasil-Exportacao e Industria Ltda.; Feldmühle Kyocera Europa Elektronische Bauelemente GmbH (Germany); Yashica Kyocera GmbH; Kyocera Electronics Europa GmbH; Kyocera (Hong Kong) Ltd.; Universal Optical Industries Ltd. (Hong Kong); Kyocera Electronic Equipment Co., Ltd.; Tomioka Optical Co., Ltd.; Daini-Denden Inc.; Japan New-Media Systems, Co., Ltd.; Kyocera Finance Co., Ltd.; Taito Corp; Kyocera Electronic (U.K.) Co., Ltd.;

Yashica Kyocera GmbH (Germany); Kyocera Mexicana S.A. de C.V.; Kinamed Inc. (USA); Kyocera Building Co., Ltd.; Kyocera Asia Ltd.; Yashica Hong Kong Co., Ltd.; Kyocera Europe GmbH; Yashica A.G.; Yashica Handelsgesellschaft mbH; Kyocera Yashica U.K., Ltd.

LUCKY-GOLDSTAR

20 Yoido-dong
Yongdungpo-gu
Seoul 150-010
Republic of Korea
(02) 787-1114

Public Company
Incorporated: 1947 as Lucky Chemical Company
Employees: 100,000
Sales: US$20 billion

Although Goldstar is one of the newest names in electronics, Goldstar products have existed for many years. A division of one of Korea's largest conglomerates, for many years Goldstar manufactured electronic devices and appliances for sale in the United States under retailers' brand names. Only recently has that conglomerate, Lucky-Goldstar, chosen to meet its Japanese competition head-to-head in several market segments. Goldstar has succeeded in establishing itself in those markets, mainly through competition.

The earliest predecessor of the Lucky Goldstar Group was the Lucky Chemical Company, founded by Koo In-Hwoi in 1947. The company's first product was a line of cosmetic creams. It then expanded into other petroleum products, including caps for the cream jars and other plastic molds.

The business remained small through its early years; Korea suffered severe economic disruption during World War II, and virtual ruin by its partition and subsequent invasion by Soviet-backed armies from North Korea. The American government, however, had a strong interest in seeing both Japan and Korea transformed into large industrial economies in order to check the advance of communism in the East. With substantial foreign aid, industrial programs were created which helped companies such as Lucky to succeed and grow.

Lucky was regarded as a strategic industrial resource; it was Korea's only plastics manufacturer, and held great foreign exchange earnings potential. To that end, Lucky created an export agency in 1953. Observing the success of Japanese consumer goods exporters such as Matsushita and Mitsubishi, Koo decided that Lucky was ready for diversification into electronics.

Lucky created an electrical appliance manufacturer in 1958 called Goldstar Company, Ltd., whose first product was a simple electric fan. The following year, with a new factory located at Pusan, Goldstar introduced the country's first line of domestically-produced radios. These products were unsophisticated and generally unfit for sale abroad. In addition, Goldstar lacked marketing arms in foreign markets. Parallel to Matsushita's experience, Goldstar's products would first satisfy domestic demand (and thereby substitute for more expensive imports) until design changes and improvements could be incorporated. Goldstar would then enter the international market with more thoroughly tested, modern, and competitive products.

Protected from foreign competitors by rigid import restrictions, Lucky Chemical and Goldstar continued to prosper during the early 1960s. Much of the companies' profits were dedicated to the acquisition of new petrochemical technologies and the establishment of a wider market presence. New product development was delayed, hampered by limited engineering resources and expensive patent licensing. Despite these disadvantages, Goldstar managed to successfully market a refrigerator in 1965 and a television a year later. Both were the first domestically manufactured appliances of their kind.

Lucky Chemical established a joint venture with Continental Carbon in August of 1966. The company, called Lucky Continental Carbon, became the largest Korean manufacturer of carbon black, a basic raw material in rubber products. The company entered into a far more significant joint venture the following year when it established the Honam Oil Refinery in conjunction with Caltex Petroleum. Honam was Korea's first privately owned, as well as its largest, refinery. The complex eliminated Korea's dependence on more expensive imported oil products and even permitted substantial export earnings.

When Koo In-Hwoi died in 1969, the chairmanship of Lucky and Goldstar went to his eldest son, Koo Cha-Kyung, who remains chairman today. Nepotism, far from being regarded as dishonorable or unfair, was widely practiced in the company, as in many Asian companies. Members of the Koo and Huh families (the Huhs were close friends who were made business partners) have always occupied top management positions within both companies and their subsidiaries, although as the company has grown, professional managers have come to dominate.

New plant space, meanwhile, was established for the 20 subsidiaries created between 1969 and 1979, mostly in extreme southern Korea, where land is flatter and Korea has more deep-water ports.

Korean industrial organization and government policies were often based on the Japanese experience. The rise of Japan's postwar industry was led primarily by its former *zaibatsu* conglomerates, with substantial direction and cooperation from the Ministry of International Trade and Industry. Korea, too, had such a ministry, and it consciously sought to create *zaibatsu*-type companies out of the nation's leading *chaebol*, or industrial entrepreneurs. Samsung, Daewoo, Hyundai, and Lucky-Goldstar were developed, according to this plan, into economic cornerstones, each involved in a wide range of basic industries.

Park Chung-Hee, a general who had seized power in South Korea in 1962, approached the *chaebol* in an effort to improve living standards in Korea. Since many government officials held financial stakes in the conglomerates (a Lucky-Goldstar director even served in Park's cabinet), the *chaebol* were often afforded special privileges. Lucky-Goldstar proposed that South Korea's export earnings could be increased if the *chaebol* had better engineers. The company asked for, and got, government funds to sponsor students at leading Western universities. It was a heavy investment whose benefits would not be realized for years, but the education scheme was essential to maintaining the company's position.

The government, again using Japan as an example, decided that Korea was ready to begin manufacturing larger and more sophisticated and profitable products. Most notable was Hyundai, whose capabilities in automobile manufacture were greatly enhanced by the government. Lucky and Goldstar were not encouraged to enter new lines of business, but rather to consolidate their positions in textiles, chemicals, and electronics. Consolidation, however, required the development and application of new, proprietary technologies. It was at this stage that the company's foreign-trained engineers became indispensable.

Park, who had eventually been elected as a civilian president, was assassinated in 1979. With his death, much of the government's favoritism was eliminated. All the *chaebol*, including Lucky-Goldstar, had to become more self-reliant, drawing upon their own resources to guarantee markets, seal deals, and cover risks.

These new conditions precipitated an industrial reorganization. Lucky Chemical and Goldstar Electronics were made subsidiaries of a larger parent company, now officially referred to as Lucky-Goldstar. The company maintained a very positive public image, owing to its gentle character and ability to avoid scandal.

The reorganization led to the creation of several joint ventures, with AT & T, Honeywell, Dow Corning, and Englehard. These ventures were intended to help assimilate advanced technologies which could not be developed indigenously. Profits from textiles, an increasingly uncompetitive sector, remained strong and were largely reinvested into the more promising chemical and electronics operations.

Under Koo Cha-Kyung, Lucky-Goldstar adopted a slower, more cautious approach. The company is very proud of its democratic decision-making process, which includes regular strategic meetings at all levels. But many blame this slow approach for Goldstar's sluggish reaction to the market—Goldstar was subsequently overtaken by Samsung. Nonetheless, when both companies entered an unexpectedly soft semiconductor market, Goldstar was able to cut its losses early, while Samsung, which had invested heavily in semiconductors, lost millions of won.

Like its Japanese predecessors, Goldstar established production facilities in its larger markets; it was the first Korean company to do so. The first of these was a television plant at Huntsville, Alabama, opened in 1982.

Lucky-Goldstar had actively pursued technological licensing agreements with leading Western and Japanese companies but had a difficult time coordinating its newly acquired know-how. In 1983 the company began a major research and development effort, aimed specifically at setting the house in order, which included plans to construct a research complex at Anyang, south of Seoul. When Japanese companies later restricted their cooperation with Lucky-Goldstar, fearing that they were only nurturing a fierce competitor, the company responded by placing a higher emphasis on West German and American licensing. But Lucky-Goldstar still relied on Japanese suppliers for between 25% and 40% of its components, which caused problems when these suppliers favored Japanese customers when demand was high.

While the Japanese model of industrial expansion has worked well for South Korea, comparisons between the two economies must be qualified. Perhaps most important, Korea's *chaebol* are neither closely associated with a *zaibatsu*-type industrial "club" nor do they have the benefit of associated banks. In addition to being subject to government regulations, the *chaebol* are largely reliant on government-run banks for financing. Until they fully mature as the international corporations they are intended to become, companies such as Lucky-Goldstar must be considered privately-capitalized instruments of the state.

Principal Subsidiaries: Lucky, Ltd.; Honam Oil Refinery Co., Ltd.; Lucky Petrochemical Co., Ltd.; Lucky Advanced Materials, Inc.; Lucky Polychemical Co., Ltd.; Goldstar Co., Ltd.; Goldstar Electron Co.; Goldstar Semiconductor, Ltd.; Goldstar Telecommunication Co., Ltd.; Goldstar Software, Ltd.; Goldstar Electric Co., Ltd.; Goldstar-Alps Electronics Co., Ltd.; Goldstar Precision Co., Ltd.; Goldstar Electronic Devices Co., Ltd.; Goldstar Industrial Systems Co., Ltd.; Goldstar Instrument & Electric Co., Ltd.; Goldstar Electric Machinery Co., Ltd.; Goldstar-Honeywell Co., Ltd.; Goldstar Cable Co., Ltd.; Lucky Metals Corp.; Lucky–Goldstar International Corp.; Lucky Securities Co., Ltd.; Lucky Insurance Co., Ltd.; Goldstar Investment & Finance Corp.; Pusan Investment & Finance Corp.; LG Credit Card Co., Ltd.; Lucky Development Co., Ltd.; Lucky Engineering Co., Ltd.,; Hee Sung Co., Ltd.; LG Ad, Inc.; Systems Thechnology Management Corp.; Lucky–Goldstar Sports, Ltd.; The Yonam Foundation; The Yonam Educational Institute.

MATSUSHITA ELECTRIC INDUSTRIAL CO., LTD.

1006 Kadoma
Kadoma City, Osaka Prefecture
Japan
(06) 908-1121

Public Company
Incorporated: 1935 as Matsushita Denki Sangyo
Employees: 193,000
Sales: ¥5.5 trillion (US$41.7 billion)
Stock Index: Tokyo Osaka

The Matsushita Electric Industrial Company is the largest consumer electronics firm in the world. While the company's name is virtually unknown outside of Japan, the brand names under which Matsushita sells its products are household words: Panasonic, Technics, Quasar, and National are all manufactured by Matsushita. In Japan, Matsushita is as well-known as its brand names. In recent years, Matsushita has also moved into industrial electronics with great success. The company's founder, Konosuke Matsushita, is regarded as the patriarch of the Japanese consumer electronics industry and a "god of business management."

Konosuke Matsushita was born in 1895, the son of a modest farmer who lost his family's savings speculating on commodity futures when Matsushita was only nine years old. At that age, Matsushita was forced to take a job in a bicycle shop to help his family survive. When he heard some years later that the city of Osaka had installed an electric railway system, Matsushita realized that great opportunities lay ahead for the Japanese electronics industry. He spent a few years working for a light bulb factory in Osaka, and by age 23 had accumulated enough business experience to found his own company to manufacture electric plugs, with his wife and brother-in-law Toshio Iue (who later founded Sanyo Electric).

Although Japan became a major international power during the 1920s, its domestic economy developed unevenly. Matsushita's small company prospered by keeping prices low and by incorporating new technological advances into its products. For this, Matsushita became very popular with consumers. He was also popular with his workers, whom he regarded as important partners with a right to participate in decisions.

After diversifying production to include bicycle lights and electric heaters, Matsushita moved boldly to secure a position as a direct supplier to Japan's large, complex retailing networks, which were historically dominated by larger, more established companies. Matsushita introduced radio sets and dry batteries in 1931 and electric motors in 1934; by creating fierce competition through discounts, the company was able to build large market shares in these selected markets. By 1935 the company had grown to several times its original size. On December 15 of that year, it was incorporated as Matsushita Denki Sangyo (Electrical Industrial).

Japan at this time was undergoing a severe political transformation as a right-wing militarist clique rose to power. The group won support from many industrialists, including Konosuke Matsushita, because it advocated the establishment of a Japanese-led pan-Asian economic community promising great profits for Japanese companies. As a leading manufacturer of electrical devices, Matsushita benefited greatly from the government's massive armament program. It soon gained markets in Japanese-controlled Taiwan, Korea, and Manchuria, and prospered during the beginning of World War II.

After the Battle of Midway, it was clear not only that Japan would lose the war, but also that the Greater East Asia Co-Prosperity Sphere promised by the militarists would never come to pass. Matsushita, locked in an uneasy partnership with the government, saw its fortunes deteriorate with Japan's.

After the war it seemed that the company's greatest task was to maintain sales in a country so thoroughly decimated by the war that the economy relied on barter. But first the company had to deal with the American occupation authority, which not only set price controls but also attacked Konosuke Matsushita for his support of the Japanese war effort and demanded that he resign his chairmanship. The labor unions, which the occupation authority sought to preserve, strongly supported Matsushita and threatened to strike if he resigned. Hoping to avoid wider labor unrest, the authority relented.

In 1951 Matsushita traveled to America for the first time to study the "rich America" he planned to make his most profitable market. An astute businessman, Matsushita recognized that his product lines must first prove themselves in their local market, though. His company successfully introduced washing machines, televisions, and refrigerators in Japan in 1953, and vacuum cleaners the following year. Concerned with maintaining measured and well-planned growth, Matsushita also became the first Japanese businessman to introduce five-year business plans.

When anti-monopoly laws were relaxed after the Korean War, Matsushita was permitted to make its first major corporate acquisition, a 50% share of the financially troubled Japan Victor Company (JVC). It was, for Matsushita, merely an investment; JVC was to remain not only independently managed, but also Matsushita's competitor in several areas.

Matsushita moved "upmarket" early, around 1957, by introducing a line of high-quality FM radio receivers, tape recorders, and a stereo sound system developed by JVC. In 1958 the company succeeded in relaying a color television signal, and soon afterwards entered the television market—an especially important market as Japanese consumers became increasingly prosperous.

Until now, Matsushita had focused on the foreign market in its growth strategies, but the company began actively working to build a solid domestic market share, confident that its sales in Japan would grow with the economy. Using the brand name National, the company established a retail network to sell Matsushita products. With income generated by domestic sales, Matsushita was able to finance an ambitious global strategy independent of the trading houses that controlled the retail system in Japan. As a result, Matsushita brand names became well known in Europe and the United States.

Cheap labor and good labor relations kept Matsushita's costs low, and helped the company to build a strong following in North America. Yet, as the Japanese economy continued to grow, unemployment fell and wages rose. Predicting that rising labor costs would one day compromise its price competitiveness, Matsushita was one of the first companies to set up factories in less developed countries such as Taiwan and Singapore, where wages were lower and the local currency was more stable against the dollar.

In May of 1974 Matsushita purchased the Quasar television division of Motorola for $100 million, hoping to gain U.S. market share by capitalizing on Quasar's well-known name. Quasar had begun to lose market share to more popular imports, so Matsushita made heavy capital investments to improve production efficiency. Efficiency was raised, but market share remained stagnant.

In the early 1970s Matsushita became deeply involved in the development of a commercial home video cassette recording system, or VCR. Matsushita seemed close to an acceptable design when Akio Tanii, then head of the VCR group, saw what he believed was a far superior design under development at JVC. Tanii convinced Matsushita to delay the introduction of a VCR until JVC's Video Home System, or VHS, could be perfected and adopted. This meant allowing Sony, the company's largest competitor, to enjoy a one-year monopoly on the market.

Sony refused to share its Betamax VCR technology with other manufacturers. But Matsushita knew that despite its VCR monopoly, Sony had a limited VCR production capacity. He gambled that there would be enough pent-up demand when JVC and Matsushita entered the market for the two companies to establish VHS as the industry standard. To help this prediction come true, Matsushita made licensing agreements with RCA, General Electric, Philips (which had abandoned its own VCR design), NEC, Toshiba, and Sanyo, all of whom introduced VHS-compatible machines. Sony's Betamax lost so much market share so quickly that Sony's chairman, Akio Morita, was compelled to ask for a compromise. Konosuke Matsushita refused, telling him that such a desperate display was both unacceptable and dishonorable. Eventually even Sony began to manufacture VHS machines.

By the mid-1980s Japan's consumer market was saturated. Tanii, who had been chosen to succeed the company's popular president, Toshihiko Yamashita, advocated entrance into new markets: semiconductors, factory automation, business machines, and audiovisual devices. He noted Matsushita's inability to attract the best engineers graduating from universities and began an effort to build a talented research and development team. He also saw that Matsushita's older, "obsolete" engineers would become under-utilized, and recommended transforming them into expert salesmen capable of selling these new technologies, if not creating them. Finally, he complained that Matsushita's 600 subsidiaries and group companies were too poorly coordinated to work with each other efficiently and decided that contacts within the company should be improved in order to develop technologies more quickly and economically.

In 1989 Konosuke Matsushita died at the age of 94. He had seen his company rise from a small manufacturer of electric sockets to one of the world's premiere consumer goods manufacturers. Matsushita had retired from active management of the company in 1973 and had spent his later years writing books on business philosophy—his basic philosophy, "Peace and Happiness through Prosperity," was the focus of some 50 books.

Matsushita is under contract to manufacture a number of computers for IBM, which is historically weak in the consumer market, and has expressed interest in acquiring Fujitsu, which has traditionally attracted the most talented software engineers. A closer relationship with either company would strengthen Matsushita's sales in the more dynamic and profitable corporate and institutional markets.

Matsushita is sure to remain a major consumer goods manufacturer, protected by its strong presence in the Japanese market both from competition at home and from currency fluctuations and trade protectionism abroad. The company's expansion into industrial electronics has also been highly profitable. In fiscal 1989, industrial electronics represented 35% of sales by Matsushita's major operating units. Tanii's initiatives have positioned the company for several decades of stable growth. He has done much to dispel the notion that Matsushita is merely an imitator of more original companies, but it will take some time to transform the company; its basic strength is still manufacturing.

Principal Subsidiaries: Matsushita Electronics Corporation; Victor Company of Japan, Ltd.; Matsushita Electronic Components Co., Ltd.; Matsushita Battery Industrial Co., Ltd.; Matsushita Seiko Co., Ltd.; Matsushita Kotobuki Electronics Industries, Ltd.; Matsushita Communication Industrial Co., Ltd.; Matsushita Refrigeration Co.; Kyushu Matsushita Electric Co., Ltd.; Matsushita Housing Products Co., Ltd.; Matsushita Industrial Equipment Co., Ltd.; Matsushita Graphic Communication Systems, Inc.; Teichiku Records Co., Ltd.; Matsushita Electric Corporation of America; Matsushita Electric (Taiwan) Co., Ltd.; Matsushita Industrial Corporation Sdn. Bhd.; Matsushita Refrigeration Industries (S) Pte. Ltd.; Matsushita Electric (U.K.) Ltd.; Panasonic España S.A.; Matsushita Electronics (S) Pte. Ltd.

MITSUBISHI ELECTRIC CORPORATION

MITSUBISHI ELECTRIC CORPORATION

2–2–3, Marunouchi
Chiyoda-ku
Tokyo 100
Japan
(03) 218–2111

Public Company
Incorporated: 1921
Employees: 85,723
Sales: ¥2.72 trillion (US$21.76 billion)
Stock Index: Frankfurt Amsterdam Tokyo Osaka Nagoya

Even though it shares a name and common heritage with nearly a dozen of Japan's largest industrial concerns, Mitsubishi Electric is an independent company. Like Mitsubishi Chemical, Mitsubishi Heavy Industries, and the Mitsubishi Bank, Mitsubishi Electric is often confused as a subsidiary of Mitsubishi Shoji, the giant trading company. Although legally and organizationally separate, the Mitsubishi companies do form a group whose partners share market information and often extend preferential terms to each other in business dealings.

The original Mitsubishi company (the name means "three diamonds" in Japanese) was originally founded shortly after the Meiji Restoration in 1868 by Yataro Iwasaki, an enterprising samurai who gained control of shipping in Tosa prefecture in the first years of Japan's industrial expansion. Japan grew into a major economic and military power in the western Pacific, in many ways as a result of Mitsubishi's ambitious maritime activity. The company connected Japan with foreign markets and succeeded in establishing a shipping monopoly, despite a powerful challenge from rival Mitsui.

By the mid 1910s, Mitsubishi was one of the largest companies in Japan, with diversified interests in heavy manufacturing, mining, real estate, banking, and trading. In order to attract investor capital, the Iwasaki family created several independent companies out of Mitsubishi's subsidiaries. Mitsubishi Electric was one of them, created in 1921.

Mitsubishi Electric originated in 1905 in the parent company's Kobe shipyard as a manufacturer of electrical equipment for ships and mining. Five years later, the division constructed a large-capacity induction motor (the first in Japan) and a turbine generator.

As a victor in World War I, Japan gained recognition as a legitimate naval power in the Pacific. In order to preserve and enhance its position, Japan expanded its navy and merchant marine, creating even greater demand for new ships equipped with generators and other electric devices. As the major shipbuilder in Japan, Mitsubishi engineered a merger between the electric-machinery departments of Kobe Shipbuilding & Engine Works and its own Mitsubishi Shipbuilding company. Shares in the new company, Mitsubishi Electric, were sold to investors, and the capital raised was used to acquire new manufacturing space and equipment.

Mitsubishi Electric, however, was unable to develop devices technologically competitive with those manufactured by foreign companies. Like NEC, which had negotiated an extensive cooperative agreement with Western Electric, Mitsubishi Electric became closely associated with another American electronics manufacturer, Westinghouse Electric. Their agreement, concluded in 1923, provided Mitsubishi Electric with Japanese marketing and licensing rights for a number of Westinghouse products and designs. As a result, Mitsubishi Electric successfully built a large 2300-kVA vertical-axis-type hydraulic generator.

Mitsubishi Electric remained the favored supplier of large and small electrical devices to all the various Mitsubishi companies while maintaining its expertise in maritime electronics and gaining new strengths in other fields like communication, power transmission, lighting, and consumer appliances. In 1931 Mitsubishi Electric began commercial production of passenger elevators and started exporting fans to China and Hong Kong. Two years later, reacting to greater domestic demand for home appliances, the company began marketing refrigerators.

The 1930s were a difficult period for Japan's *zaibatsu* conglomerates like Mitsubishi. The 12 major Japanese companies had become inextricably linked to the government through a 50-year industrial modernization program. But the government had recently been taken over by a quasi-fascist element in the military whose aim was to establish absolute Japanese supremacy in eastern Asia. In their effort to modernize and arm Japan for war, the militarists called upon industrial concerns such as Mitsubishi Electric to provide a vast array of equipment.

While Mitsubishi Heavy Industries eventually became the principal manufacturer of warplanes, particularly the notorious *Zero*, Mitsubishi Electric developed radio sets for the *Zero* and other aircraft, and later became deeply involved in additional military projects.

With World War II well under way, Mitsubishi Electric came under increasingly strict control by the government. The company was compelled to follow all military directives and, as a result, in 1944 established a research laboratory whose goal was to develop new instruments for naval and aerial battle management. By August, 1945, however, the war was lost, and Japan's battered industries came under the control of government agencies directed by the occupation authority.

Mitsubishi Electric began the enormous task of

rebuilding its business after the war. Helped by reconstruction loans but impeded by difficult labor regulations, supply shortages, weak domestic demand, and the dissolution of the *zaibatsu*, Mitsubishi Electric struggled to survive. By 1948 the company had resumed production of consumer and some industrial items, including straight-tube fluorescent lamps. Military production, once the primary source of Mitsubishi's profits, had been banned by the occupation authority.

Having reestablished marketing agreements with foreign manufacturers, Mitsubishi Electric began selling televisions in Japan in 1953. After completing several successful industrial projects, Mitsubishi resumed foreign operations in 1954 with the completion of a power substation in India.

As a result of the Korean War, the American government decided to end its extractive, punitive policies toward Japan. Instead, it encouraged the Japanese to build a large and modern industrial infrastructure that would allow Japan to serve as a bulwark against the expansion of communism in the East. Increasingly, in the name of efficient industrial organization, the Japanese government permitted the former *zaibatsu* companies to reestablish ties. The Mitsubishi logo, banned by the occupation authority, was readopted by all the Mitsubishi companies, including Mitsubishi Electric. With the benefit of freer association among the engineering, manufacturing, marketing, and financing wings of the Mitsubishi group, Mitsubishi Electric gained an increased ability to compete in the largely unregulated foreign markets.

The rich American and European markets, however, were already dominated by large electrical-equipment manufacturers like Westinghouse, General Electric, Philips, and GEC. In fact, the Japanese government had passed legislation to protect domestic manufacturers against these companies. Mitsubishi Electric recognized that it could not compete against the large manufacturers until it had first established a stronger base in consumer sales and industrial projects. The increased incomes of Japanese consumers, and the ability of Japanese companies to compete on price in middle-technology projects, provided Mitsubishi Electric with two important ways to achieve that goal.

In 1960 the company became one of the first in Japan to begin production of color televisions, marking a commitment to maintaining market share in the emerging high end of the market. After production of several electric locomotives for the Japanese railway system, Mitsubishi Electric exported its first one, to the government of India, also in 1960.

During the 1960s Japanese products gained a reputation for poor quality and simple technology. In electronics, however, the Japanese Ministry of International Trade and Industry (MITI) assisted companies by coordinating technological developments and protecting certain key markets. One of the earliest to show leadership in technological pursuits, Mitsubishi Electric unveiled a computer prototype in 1960, and the following year began production of its Molectron integrated circuit.

In order to reflect both a corporate reorganization and a more international view, the company's name was changed in 1963 from Mitsubishi Electric Manufacturing to Mitsubishi Electric Corporation, or Melco. The company made its first overseas investment in Thailand in 1964, and two years later concluded a sale of electric locomotives to Spain. In communications, Melco completed the first of several antenna designs for satellite earth stations and placed a remote weather station on the summit of Mount Fuji. Mitsubishi's development of communications technologies later led to its selection for government projects and electronics work with the U.S. Department of Defense.

Melco funded much of its industrial and high-technology research by cross-subsidizing: taking profits from the consumer and business markets and applying them to government and industrial projects with long lead times but large rewards. Among Melco's successes in the low-ticket markets were air conditioners, color televisions, and small office computers. In order to reduce costs in certain areas of research, Melco revived its technical-exchange agreement with Westinghouse in 1966. In later years, Melco began to sell technology to Westinghouse, marking a significant appreciation in Mitsubishi's status.

The increased quality of Japanese products and the continued production-cost advantages enjoyed by Japanese companies led to tremendous demand overseas. It was at this point, around 1970, that Japan's export-led expansion moved into a new phase of feverish growth. In 1972 and 1973 alone, Melco established sales companies in Great Britain, the United States, Brazil, and Argentina, and yet another was opened in Australia in 1975.

Predicting a gradual deterioration in production-cost advantages in Japan relative to other developing Asian nations, Melco began making substantial overseas investments, building a television plant in Singapore in 1974 and another in Thailand three years later.

Until then, Mitsubishi Electric had been primarily a manufacturer of industrial equipment. The oil crisis of 1973–1974, however, critically damaged the company's business in that field and, perhaps more than any other event, convinced Mitsubishi's president, Sadakazu Shindo, that the only way to maintain growth was through expanded consumer sales. One product, aimed directly at the domestic household market, was the futon dryer; 600,000 were sold in 1977 alone.

Melco was one of several companies that elected to develop a home video-recording system based on Matsushita's VHS design. The VHS, although it entered the market a full year after Sony's rival Betamax system, became established as the industry standard. Companies that developed the Beta system—particularly Sony—lost not only a great deal of money in sales but, more important over the longer term, market share. Melco's rising acceptance in the home-video market was complemented by the introduction of such other new products as large-screen projection TVs.

Mitsubishi Electric added sales organizations in West Germany and Spain in 1978, and in Canada in 1980. In order to reduce transportation costs and hedge against rising protectionist sentiment in foreign markets, Melco established television-production facilities in the United States and Britain in 1980, and in Australia in 1982. The following year, Melco opened an integrated-circuit plant in the United States, a cathode-ray-tube plant in Canada, and a VCR plant in Britain. The new plants created thousands of jobs in these countries and revitalized several local economies. By 1985 Mitsubishi Electric's sales had reached ¥2 trillion, double the amount just five years earlier.

Mitsubishi Electric's unusual corporate personality is largely derived from the years Sadakazu Shindo has presided over the company. Later succeeded as president by Nihachiro Katayama and then by Moriya Shiki, Shindo has remained the guiding force at Mitsubishi Electric. Among his strongest legacies are a commitment to frank discussion, honest criticism, and individualism. He was known to have favored the hiring of high school graduates over college graduates, contending that they are only slightly less knowledgeable, but much more willing to ask questions and work in teams.

Mitsubishi Electric is well diversified within the electronics industry, deriving approximately equal amounts of profit from communications, consumer products, heavy machinery, and industrial products. In its effort to overtake competitors such as Hitachi and Toshiba, the company has concentrated its resources on new-product development. The task of selling the products is handled through Mitsubishi Shoji, its former parent trading company, and much of that sales effort is concentrated in the Middle East in an attempt to retrieve what are called oil yen.

Maintaining close relations with both Westinghouse and General Electric, Mitsubishi Electric has bet much of its future success on the integrated microcircuitry that makes possible everything from simple industrial robots to artificial intelligence. Mitsubishi becomes more firmly established as an industry leader as it finds new applications for these technologies in its existing product lines and broadens it product mix in the process.

Principal Subsidiaries: Ryoden Service Co., Ltd.; Ryoden Unyu Co., Ltd.; Mitsubishi Electric Service Engineering Co., Ltd.; Ryoden Estate Co., Ltd.; The Kodensha Co., Ltd.; SPC Electronics Corporation; Toyo Electric Co., Ltd.; Nakayama Kikai Co., Ltd.; Tada Electric Co., Ltd.; Shiga Bolt Co., Ltd.; Melcom Business Machines Co., Ltd.; Ryowa Shoko Co., Ltd.; Ryoden Engineering Co., Ltd.; Ad. Melco Co., Ltd.; Mitsubishi Space Software Co., Ltd.; Ryoden Elevator Construction Co., Ltd.; Ryoreisha Co., Ltd.; Mitsubishi Electric Home Appliance Co., Ltd.; Mitsubishi Electric Credit Co., Ltd.; Ryoden Kasei Co., Ltd.; Mitsubishi Electric America, Inc.; Mitsubishi Electric Sales America, Inc.; Mitsubishi Electronics America, Inc.; Mitsubishi Consumer Electronics America, Inc.; Mitsubishi Semiconductor America, Inc.; Horizon Research Inc. (U.S.); Mitsubishi Electric Manufacturing Cincinnati, Inc.; Mitsubishi Electric Sales Canada Inc.; Mitsubishi Electronics Industries Canada Inc.; Melco do Brazil Com. e Rep. Ltda; MELCO-TEC Rep. Com. e Assessoria Tecnica Ltda.; Melco Argentina S.R.L.; Mitsubishi Electric (U.K.) Ltd.; Mitsubishi Electric Netherlands B.V.; Mitsubishi Electric Europe GmbH; Mitsubishi Electric (Scandinavia) A.B.; Middle East Electric Co. W.L.L. (Kuwait); Melco (Middle East) Ltd. (U.A.E., Iraq and Iran); Mitsubishi Electric Australia Pty. Ltd.; Melco Iberia S.A. (Spain); Mitsubishi Electric Singapore Pte. Ltd.; Melco Sales Singapore Pte. Ltd.; Melco Sales Latin America, S.A. (Panama); Mitsubishi Electric (H.K.) Ltd.

MOTOROLA, INC.

1303 East Algonquin Road
Schaumburg, Illinois 60196
U.S.A.
(708) 397–5000

Public Company
Incorporated: 1928 as Galvin Manufacturing Corporation
Employees: 102,000
Sales: $8.25 billion
Stock Index: New York Midwest London Tokyo

Motorola's story is an American classic. It begins during the 1920s, when a small-town Illinois boy, Paul Galvin, went to Chicago to seek his fortune. His story continues today in a multi-billion dollar corporation with operations throughout the world.

Paul Galvin returned from World War I with an interest in the technological changes of the time. In 1920 he worked for a Chicago storage-battery company, and one year later he opened his own storage-battery company with a hometown friend, Edward Stewart. After two years of rocky operations, the government closed the business for non-payment of excise taxes. The former partners, undaunted by this setback, joined forces again three years later when Galvin bought an interest in Stewart's new storage-battery company. But with the rise of electric power, batteries lost popularity with the public. To keep their business afloat, Stewart created a device that allowed a radio to be plugged into an ordinary wall outlet, aptly named the "battery eliminator." Once again, the storage-battery company failed, though Galvin was able to buy back the eliminators at the company's public auction. Joe Galvin joined his brother Paul this time to peddle the eliminators to various retail distributors like Sears, Roebuck and Company. In 1928 Paul formed the Galvin Manufacturing Corporation, with five employees and $565, and continued making battery eliminators.

During the Great Depression Galvin Manufacturing Corporation found itself burdened by inventory that it couldn't sell because of restricted market conditions and underselling by other manufacturers. To rectify this situation, Galvin began experimenting with the virtually-untouched automobile-radio market. Before this, automobile radios had been deemed impractical because they had very poor reception. The first commercially successful car radio came out of Galvin Manufacturing in 1930 under the brand name Motorola. The name, coined by Galvin, is a hybrid of "motor" and "victrola." The units sold for about $120 including accessories and installation, which compared favorably with the $200–$300 custom-designed units then available.

During the 1930s the company also established its first chain of distributorships (Authorized Motorola Installation Stations), began advertising its products in newspapers and on highway billboards, and started to research radios to receive only police broadcasts. The market for police radios appeared so promising that the company formed a police radio department. In 1937 Galvin Manufacturing entered the home-radio market, introducing push-button tuning at that time.

In 1936 Paul Galvin returned from a tour of Europe with his family, convinced that war was imminent. Knowing that war could provide new opportunities, he directed research into ways his company could be useful to the military. The Handie-Talkie two-way radio and its offspring, the Walkie-Talkie, resulted. Used by the United States Army Signal Corps, these were among the most important pieces of communications equipment used in World War II.

Paul Galvin was always concerned with the welfare of his employees and in 1947 he instituted a very liberal profit-sharing program that was used as a model by other companies. By this time, the company was employing around 5,000 people and had formed a human-relations department. Galvin's son Robert and Daniel Noble, an engineer who would eventually have a tremendous impact on the future of the company, joined Galvin, and in 1947 the company officially changed its name to Motorola.

The first Motorola television was also introduced that same year. It was more compact and less expensive than any of the competitors' models—Motorola charged $180, while its nearest competitor charged more than $300. The Motorola set became so popular that within months of its introduction the company was the fourth-largest seller in the nation.

Later in 1947, Motorola bought Detrola, a failing automobile-radio company that had manufactured car radios for the Ford Motor Company. The purchase was made on the condition that Motorola retain Detrola's contract with Ford. This deal greatly strengthened the company's automobile-radio business. Motorola subsequently supplied 50% of the car radios for Ford and Chrysler as well as all of the radios for American Motors.

The creation of the transistor in 1948 by Bell Laboratories marked a major turning point for Motorola. The company had concentrated on the manufacture of consumer products, and Paul Galvin felt that the company was unequipped to enter the transistor and diode field. However, with his son Robert and Dan Noble advocating the company's expansion into this new market, a semiconductor-development group was formed. The first Motorola product to come out was a three-amp power transistor and later a semiconductor plant was constructed in Arizona. As a result of this expansion Motorola supplied transistors to other companies for use in products that

Motorola also manufactured. In effect, Motorola found itself in the awkward position of supplying its competitors with parts.

During the 1950s, Motorola was involved in the Columbia Broadcasting System's failed entry into the color-television industry. Motorola used the CBS designed and produced color tubes in its color-television sets. After a convoluted struggle for approval from the Federal Communications Commission (FCC), the FCC rejected the CBS system in favor of a system developed by the Radio Corporation of America (RCA). Despite this setback, Motorola pioneered new features in television technology, including a technique for reducing the number of tubes in black-and-white sets from 41 to 19.

By the middle of the decade, Paul Galvin realized that the company had become too large for one man to continue making all the decisions. He granted divisional status to various businesses, giving each its own engineering, purchasing, manufacturing, and marketing departments and regarding each as an individual profit center. This was the beginning of Motorola's famous decentralized-management scheme. As part of this reorganization, Robert Galvin became president and each divisional manager an executive vice-president. Paul Galvin became chairman of the board and CEO, which he remained until his death in 1959.

Beginning in 1958, Motorola became involved in the space program. Virtually every manned and unmanned space flight since that time has been equipped with some piece of Motorola equipment.

Motorola made several acquisitions during the 1960s that left observers baffled. It purchased, and sold almost immediately, Lear Inc.'s Lear Cal Division, which manufactured aircraft radios. This was followed by the purchase and subsequent divestment of the Dalberg Company, a manufacturer of hearing aids. Acquisitions were also considered in the fields of recreation, chemicals, broadcasting, and even funeral homes. This trend continued into the 1970s and constituted a period of real adjustment for Motorola. However, two very important corporate strategies grew out of this floudering.

First, the company began to expand operations outside the United States, building a plant in Mexico and marketing Motorola products in eight countries, including Japan. An office in Japan was opened in 1961, and in 1968 Motorola Semiconductors Japan was formed to design, market, and sell integrated circuits. Second, toward the end of the decade, Motorola gradually began to discontinue its consumer products, a watershed in the company's history.

Motorola's radio and television interests were the first to be disposed of. In 1974 Motorola sold its consumer products division, which included Quasar television to the Matsushita Electric Industrial Company of Japan. Three years later the company acquired Codex Corporation, a data-communications company based in Massachusetts. In 1978 Universal Data Systems was added. At the end of the 1970s Motorola began phasing out its car-radio business. These maneuvers were intended to concentrate Motorola's activities in high technology.

Motorola's largest and most important acquisition came in 1982 with its purchase of Four-Phase Systems, Inc. for $253 million. A California-based manufacturer of computers and terminals, Four-Phase also wrote software for its own machines. The purchase puzzled observers because Four-Phase was in serious trouble at the time. Though Four-Phase did quite well in the 1970s, by the end of that decade its product line was aging, its computer-leasing base had grown too large, and its debt was tied to the rising prime rate. These problems had their origin in the company's insistence upon manufacturing its own semiconductors instead of purchasing commercially available components—an insistence that consumed time and money, and also meant that new product developments at Four-Phase were slow in coming. However, Motorola was looking for a custom-computer manufacturer and was impressed with the sales force at Four-Phase: Motorola's grand strategy was to branch into the new fields of office automation and distributed data processing.

Distributed data processing involves the processing of data through computers that are geographically distributed. The purchases of both Four-Phase and Codex made perfect sense when viewed in light of Motorola's intent to enter this field. The plan was simple: data processing provided by Four-Phase computers would be linked by data-communications equipment provided by Codex, and Motorola proper would provide the semiconductors and much of the communications equipment for the operation. The goal was to create a fully mobile data-processing system that would allow access to mainframe computers from a pocket unit. Motorola also figured that its experience in portable two-way radios and cellular remote telephone systems would prove valuable in this endeavor. Although Motorola was able to turn Four-Phrase around temporarily, Four-Phrase lost more than $200 million between 1985 and 1989.

The cellular remote telephone system was developed by AT&T's Bell Laboratories in the early 1970s. The system functions by dividing an area into units, or cells, each with a low-level transmitter that has 666 channels. As a driver using a phone moves from cell to cell, his call is carried on the transmitter in each successive cell. After he has left a cell, the channel he was using becomes available for another call in that cell. (Earlier remote systems relied on a powerful transmitter covering a large area, which meant that only a few channels were available for the whole area.) Motorola aided in the design and testing of the phones and supplied much of the transmission-switching equipment. Motorola's early estimates of the cellular phone market seemed astronomical—one million users by the early 1990s (in fact, there were more than 4 million users in 1989). However, the system developed major problems. There were massive licensing and construction problems and delays. Added to this were complaints about the quality and reliability of Motorola's phones compared to Japanese-manufactured remote phones. A surplus of phones, coupled with the desire to capture a large market share, soon prompted Japanese companies to cut their prices radically—some by as much as half. Motorola went straight to the United States government to request sanctions against the Japanese companies. In 1986 the commerce department declared that eight Japanese companies were in fact "dumping" (selling at a below-cost price) and were liable to special duties. This has given Motorola a new edge in the cellular-phone market—it is now the world's top supplier of cellular phones—though the competition remains instense.

Motorola's relations with Japanese companies has been checkered. In 1980 it formed a joint venture with Aizu-Toko K. K. to manufacture integrated circuits in Japan. Two years later Motorola acquired the remaining 50% interest in the company from Aizu-Toko and created Nippon Motorola Manufacturing Company, a successful operation run along Japanese lines mostly by Japanese.

Also in 1982, Motorola received a $9 million order for paging devices from Nippon Telegraph & Telephone. These ventures were followed by vigorous pleas from Robert Galvin for the U.S. government to respond in kind to Japan's trade tactics. In fact, Galvin is a founder of the Coalition for International Trade Equity. This organization has lobbied Congress for legislation that would impose tariffs on foreign companies that are subsidized by their governments. Motorola further called for a surcharge on all imports to reduce the U.S. trade deficit. Other major companies in the United States (Boeing and Exxon among them) have rejected these measures on the grounds that they would spark trade wars that would damage the position of U.S. companies doing business with Japan.

In 1986, Motorola made a groundbreaking deal with Japan's Toshiba to share its microprocessor designs in return for Toshiba's expertise in manufacturing DRAMs, or dynamic random access memories, a market the Japanese had driven Motorola, along with nearly every other American semiconductor company, out of with its dumping practices.

In 1988, Motorola took on the Japanese in another way: that year its Boynton Beach, Florida plant began producing the company's Bravo model pocket pager in a fully automated factory. The prototypical facility used 27 small robots directed by computers and overseen by 12 human attendants. The robots can build a Bravo within two hours of the time an order is received at corporate headquarters in Schaumburg, Illinois; the process normally would take three weeks. Through this and other corporate measures focusing on improving quality, Motorola hopes to reduce manufacturing errors to three mistakes per million operations by 1992.

In 1989 Motorola introduced the world's smallest portable telephone, but soon found that its new product was excluded from the Tokyo and Nagoya markets, two cities that together represent more than 60% of the $750 million Japanese cellular phone market. When Motorola cried foul, the Japanese government agreed to allow adapted Motorola phones in Tokyo, but only for use in automobiles. This excluded the 90% of portable phones used on trains. In response to these tactics, Motorola led the push to impose trade sanctions on certain Japanese imports. President George Bush publicly accused Japan of being an unfair trading partner and threatened to take punitive action if the Japanese did not remove barriers to free trade.

The growth of the computer industry has provided new opportunities for Motorola. Throughout the 1980s, the company's most popular 68000 family of microchips powered PCs and workstations built by Apple, Hewlett Packard, Digital Equipment, and Sun Microsystems, among others. Motorola battled Intel, whose chips were the cornerstone of IBM and IBM-compatible PCs, for dominance in the microchip market. In 1988, Motorola unveiled its 88000 microchip series, which through the use of reduced instruction-set computing (RISC) computes twice as fast as Motorola's top-of-the-line conventional chips. But Motorola faces stiff competition in this market, especially from Intel, which introduced an even more powerful chip just after the 88000 series came out.

Motorola is currently divided into six operating units: the Communications Sector, the Semiconductor Products Sector, the General Systems Group, the Information Systems Group, the Automotive and Industrial Electronics Group, and the Government Electronics Group. Aerospace and defense contracts with the government account for about 10% of Motorola's sales and revenues. The automotive group manufactures ignition systems, engine-management controls, and instrumentation.

Future developments at Motorola will include further exploration of robotics, instrumentation, and CAD/CAM (computer-aided design and computer-aided manufacturing). The company hopes its annual sales will top $15 billion in the early 1990s. The steps it has taken during the last decade to provide itself with a related yet diversified group of products and Motorola's campaign for quality, highlighted by its receipt in 1988 of the first annual Malcolm Baldrige National Quality Award, should help it achieve that goal.

Principal Subsidiaries: Codex Corporation; Motorola Credit Corporation; Motorola International Capital Corporation; Motorola International Development Corporation; Universal Data Systems; Motorola Componentes de Puerto Rico, Inc.; Motorola Portatiles de Puerto Rico, Inc.; Motorola Portavoz de Puerto Rico, Inc.; Motorola Telcarro de Puerto Rico, Inc.; Motorola Canada Ltd.; Motorola Data International, Inc. (Canada); Storno, S.A. (Denmark); Motorola Limited (U.K.); Motorola Semiconducteurs S.A. (France); Motorola GmbH (West Germany); Motorola Asia Ltd. (Hong Kong); Motorola Semiconductors Hong Kong Ltd.; Motorola Israel Limited; Motorola Korea, Ltd.; Motorola Malaysia Sdn. Bhd.; Motorola Semiconductor Sdn. Bhd. (Malaysia); Motorola de Mexico, S.A.; Motorola Electronics Pte. Ltd. (Singapore); Motorola Electronics Taiwan, Ltd.

Further Reading: Petrakis, Harry M. *A Founder's Touch: The Life of Paul Galvin of Motorola*, New York, McGraw-Hill, 1965.

NATIONAL SEMICONDUCTOR CORPORATION

2900 Semiconductor Drive
Post Office Box 58090
Santa Clara, California 95052–8090
U.S.A.
(408) 721–5000

Public Company
Incorporated: 1959
Employees: 34,764
Sales: $2.6 billion
Stock Index: New York Pacific

National Semiconductor is an old company in a young industry. The firm was founded by Dr. Bernard Rothlein in 1959, when major advances in semiconductors and other transistor-oriented chips were just being made. Rothlein worked for the Sperry Rand Corporation as a high-level engineer in its semiconductor research unit before leaving to start up his own company.

Rothlein was able to exploit his knowledge of transistorized circuits with great success at first. By 1961 National had reached $3 million a year in sales, and its growth continued to climb rapidly. In 1965, National sold $5.3 million worth of chips, a company record. However, record sales did not correspond to record profits; National's profits slumped to $238,000 in 1965 from $362,000 the year before.

Part of the reason for the drop in profits was the settlement of a suit brought by Rothlein's old employer, Sperry Rand, in 1959 regarding the misuse of Sperry trade secrets. The suit was decided in 1965: National had to pay Sperry $300,000 over five years and agreed not to make certain chips, an outcome that depressed the price of its stock and prevented National from paying dividends to shareholders. Once-soaring National seemed almost lost.

One of National's original investors was Peter Sprague, a highly successful 27-year-old operator of an international food-processing business. When he saw his long-term investment in National becoming extremely short-term, Sprague decided to buy National and see if he couldn't turn it around himself.

Soon after he purchased the company and cleared its legal slate, Sprague went on a talent hunt. It was a search that has shaped National through the rest of its existence. In 1967, Sprague raided the semiconductor division of Fairchild Photographic, one of the world's top three chip makers in what was then a $1 billion industry. He came away with four men, including the number-two man at Fairchild Semiconductor, Charles L. Sporck.

Sprague installed Sporck as president and CEO of National, and Sporck went right to work. In 1968 he moved National's headquarters from Danbury, Connecticut to Santa Clara, California. Sporck, with Sprague's blessing, instituted sharp cost-cutting measures to send the company back towards solvency. "I guess I'm one of the few CEO's who has spent time in the shipping department," reflected Sporck once. "But in that first year, everybody did whatever it took to get products out the door."

The all-hands-on-deck approach succeeded in righting National, thanks in part to another decision made by Sporck and Sprague. The two men decided that National should produce a wide variety of chips instead of just one or two, as many chipmakers its size were doing. Accordingly, National added 30 chips to its product line in 1968. It acted, in other words, like a much larger company—indeed, like the company it has become.

National's wider product line led to a near-100% increase in sales between 1968 and 1969, from $22.9 million to $41.8 million. Sprague's next move was to begin expanding out of National's traditional military and commercial markets into consumer products as well.

In 1970 National moved from its Santa Clara headquarters into a 29-acre research and world headquarters park in Sunnyvale, California. The chip industry in general struggled that year; Fairchild lost $15 million on its chip operations in the first half alone, and Sylvania shut down operations entirely after several consecutive years of losses. National saw sales volume slip slightly, but did not lose money. Sporck told *Business Week* that year, "The only way you can operate securely is to operate very conservatively from the financial standpoint."

The three years between 1970 and 1973, when the oil embargo began, were a period of phenomenal growth for the semiconductor industry. National quintupled in size between 1972 and 1976, when it reached $325 million in sales and added consumer products such as calculators and digital watches to its product line under the name Novus. Stock prices reached a then-all-time high of $55 a share. The company also began to focus its research on three major types of chips: MOS (metal oxide) memory chips, T/L (transistor/logic) logic chips, and linear structured chips.

Behind National's incredible growth in this period was a reputation for high quality and excellent management coupled with the lowest costs in the industry. This combination allowed National to post profit gains in 1975, when the industry as a whole saw sales slacken 30%, one of the worst downturns in computer industry history.

In 1976 National's vaunted management capabilities and manufacturing discipline took a blow. Its venture into consumer products, begun in 1973 to help the company weather typical semiconductor business cycles, had worked well in 1975, when overall sales increased 10% while semiconductor sales fell 25%. But low pricing and the use of Novus consumer products as promotional giveaways worked against National's quality reputation. Consumer products slumped badly in 1976, due to both labor problems and mismanagement.

National was also accused of being slow to enter new markets for memory components and microprocessors. An October, 1976 announcement that it was building its own mainframes to sell in the commercial marketplace did not impress many.

But National weathered this period. By 1978, National's reputation for quality was no longer in question and the company's sales had reached $720 million, a 46% increase over 1977. A new product, an unprecedented 64K chip, led the increase, and National's position as the number-one supplier to cathode-ray terminal-makers also helped.

Still, takeover rumors began to dog the company as Schlumberger acquired Fairchild and United Technologies took over Mostek. National was weak enough in both semiconductors (magnetic bubble memories, high-speed logic chips, and microprocessors) and consumer products to create concern, and its mainframe business had only one customer—ITEL. In addition, it was behind in overseas markets, and the stock price remained low. Analysts eyed its Datachecker subsidiary, which pioneered the supermarket point-of-sale scanner, as an easy spinoff.

In late 1979 National scrapped its mainframe project and purchased troubled ITEL's successful computer-leasing business, bringing the company directly into computer sales and service for the first time in its history. During 1980 National merged its purchase into National Advanced Systems, formerly part of the consumer products group, and continued ITEL's leasing of IBM-compatible mainframes (the machines were made by Hitachi).

After doubling in size between 1978 and 1980 and recording four years of record earnings, National was labeled "the streetfighter of Silicon Valley" for its bottom-of-the-barrel production costs and its management style. Under Sporck's leadership, National cut costs wherever possible. It used sales representatives and distributors for its chips rather than employing a sales force, with its higher overhead. It moved most of its labor-intensive operations to the Pacific Rim, and maintained a spartan office center that lacked such basic amenities as carpeting.

In 1981 sales surpassed $1 billion a year for the first time, and National introduced a rash of new products, including advanced versions of its 32-bit chip, which became commercially available in 1983. Still, the same year saw National abandon bubble memory chips when costs did not decline as expected, making the market for this vital technology small. This move left Intel as the only U.S. chipmaker in bubble memories, an area that subsequently became dominated by lower-cost Japanese producers.

National took a big hit in 1981, despite its $1 billion in sales. The company lost money in the face of an industry recession that was just as severe as the national one. National also suffered a major blow when five top managers left, including Pierre Lamond, National's long-time chief technologist, and Fred Bialek, the trusted troubleshooter who had keyed National's low-cost manufacturing, both of whom had come to National from Fairchild with Sporck.

Sporck came under fire for his highly autocratic, centralized management style, which had created fiercely entrepreneurial product managers and frequent clashes of will. Takeover rumors again surrounded the nation's third-largest chipmaker. At the time, 72% of National's sales came from semiconductors, while its biggest competitors, Motorola and Texas Instruments, each derived less than 40% of their sales from chips. National also carried low long-term debt, making a leveraged buy-out feasible. Despite its troubles, National had several strong product lines, and shared market dominance with Texas Instruments in bipolar logic chips and linear integrated circuits. But no deal materialized, and as what became an 18-month industry slump started to break, National's low-cost production made it the likeliest candidate for a quick recovery.

Besides the difficulties of operating during the recession, international competition, especially from Japanese chipmakers, and the rising U.S. dollar hurt the U.S. semiconductor industry during the early 1980s. Like many U.S. chipmakers, National could best be described as "embattled" during this period. It lost money in both 1982 and 1983.

Research-and-development spending had remained important at National through both the good times and the bad times. Major breakthroughs had come in 1975, with the first commercially available 16-bit chip; in 1979, with the Series 32000 32-bit microprocessor; and in 1982, with Digitalker, a speech-synthesis chip. In response to the challenge from overseas, National nearly doubled its research-and-development budget between 1983 and 1986, to $200 million. Through extensive lay-offs and a new public offering, National was able to eke out near-record earnings in 1984 and 1985. To celebrate, it bought carpeting for its world headquarters.

Successful new products also helped turn the company around. National, not renowned as a leader in new technology, introduced its 32-bit chip in 1984, six months before any competitor had one that was commercially available, and the product sold extremely well. National's line of semicustom chips, which allowed customers to adapt chips to better fit their needs, also sold well.

National restructured in 1986. Sporck, 59 years old in 1986, appointed two executive vice presidents, who are expected to vie for the top position when Sporck steps down. Sporck also directed the company away from Datachecker and National Advanced Systems's sales of Hitachi-made IBM-compatible mainframes, although at one time he felt that these divisions would be National's profit makers for the future. National also established two "core" businesses, the Semiconductor Group and the Information Systems Group. The company's long-term efforts at diversification have met some success; by 1986 only 53% of revenues came from semiconductors and National was manufacturing more than 5,000 types of chips in a wide range of product lines. It also was continuing to produce disk-management systems and computer boards, in addition to its Datachecker operations.

Nonetheless, despite the restructuring, National lost money in both 1986 and 1987. The company made a turn-around in fiscal 1988, posting a $62 million profit. It also acquired troubled Fairchild Semiconductors for $122 million in 1988. Revenues increased to $2.5 billion in 1988 with the acquisition of Fairchild, and National jumped from 11th-largest chipmaker in the world to sixth.

In fiscal 1989 National posted a loss in three of four quarters, and expected a loss for the year. It also sold its National Advanced Systems division to a joint venture of Hitachi and EDS, and sold Datachecker to ICL, a British concern, for a combined total of about $500 million.

Such moves will allow National to concentrate on its core semiconductor business, but the company faces an uphill road in a tough industry.

Principal Subsidiaries: National Advanced Systems; N.S. Electronics Pte., Ltd. (Singapore); National Semiconductor (Hong Kong) Ltd.; National Semiconductor (U.K.) Ltd. (United Kingdom); National Semiconductor S.A.R.L., (France); National Semiconductor GmbH (Germany); Dyna Craft, Inc.; N.S. Distributors (Pty.) Ltd. (Australia) (90%); P.T.N.S. Electronics Bandung (Indonesia); N.S. Electronics do Brasil (Brazil); N.S. International Inc.; N.S. Disco Inc.; N.S. Electronics, Ltd. (Canada); Exsysco, Inc.; National Semiconductor AB (Sweden); N.S. Electronics Phillipines, Inc. (Phil.); N.S. Electronics Ltd. (Thailand).

NEC CORPORATION

5–33–1, Shiba
Minato-ku
Tokyo 108
Japan
(03) 454–1111

Public Company
Incorporated: 1899
Employees: 104,022
Sales: ¥3.08 trillion (US$24.66 billion)
Stock Index: Tokyo Osaka Nagoya Amsterdam Basel Frankfurt Geneva London Zurich

NEC is the largest manufacturer of semiconductors in the world. It is also one of the world's largest suppliers of telecommunications equipment. Like other manufacturers of telephone equipment, NEC has seized the opportunity to combine its background in communications with a new and largely self-achieved position in computer technology. As the world's corporations enter the 21st century, they will rely more than ever on the ability to manage huge amounts of information. NEC is working to ensure that it can provide them with that ability.

The Nippon Electric Company, as NEC was originally known, was first organized in 1898 as a limited partnership between Japanese investors and the Western Electric Company. Western Electric recognized that Japan, which was undergoing an ambitious industrialization, would soon be building a telephone network. With a solid monopoly in North America as the manufacturing arm of the Bell system, Western Electric sought to establish a strong market presence in Japan, as it had done in Europe. NEC went public the following year, with Western Electric a 54% owner. In need of a plant, NEC took over the Miyoshi Electrical Manufacturing Company in central Tokyo.

Under the management of Kunihiko Iwadare and with substantial direction from Western Electric, NEC was at first little more than a distributor of imported telephone equipment from Western Electric and General Electric. Iwadare, however, set NEC to producing magneto-type telephone sets and secured substantial orders from the Ministry of Communications for the government-sponsored telephone-network-expansion program. With steadily increasing, and guaranteed, business from the government, NEC was able to plan further expansion. In September, 1900 NEC purchased from Mitsui a site at Mita Shikokumachi, where a second NEC factory was completed in December, 1902.

In an attempt to heighten NEC's competitiveness with rival Oki Shokai, Iwadare ordered his apprentices at Western Electric to study that company's accounting and production-control systems. Takeshiro Maeda, a former Ministry of Communications official, recommended that NEC emphasize the consumer market, since he regarded the government sales as uncompetitive and limited. Still, government sales were the company's major vehicle for expansion, particularly with Japan's expansion into Manchuria after the 1904–1905 Russo-Japanese War.

Japan's Ministry of Communications engineered an aggressive telecommunications program, linking the islands of Japan with commercial, military, and government offices in Korea and Manchuria. As was Bell in the United States, NEC was permitted a "natural," though imperfect, monopoly over cable communications in Japan and its territories. NEC opened offices in Seoul in 1908, and Port Arthur (now Lüshun), China in 1909.

A serious economic recession in Japan in 1913 forced the government to retrench sponsorship of its second telephone expansion program. Struggling to survive, NEC quickly turned back to importing—this time of household appliances like the electric fan, a device never seen before in Japan. As quickly as it had fallen, the Japanese economy recovered in 1916, and the expansion program was placed back on schedule. Intelligent planning effectively insulated NEC from the effects of a second serious recession in 1922; NEC even continued to grow during that time.

Around this time, Western Electric's international division wanted to create a joint venture with NEC to produce electrical cables. NEC, however, lacked the industrial capacity to be an equal partner, and recommended the inclusion of a third party, Sumitomo Densen Seizosho, the cable-manufacturing division of the Sumitomo group. A three-way agreement was concluded, marking the beginning of an important role for Sumitomo in NEC's operations.

On September 1, 1923 a violent earthquake severely damaged Tokyo and Yokohama, killing 140,000 people and leaving 3.4 million homeless. The Great Kanto Earthquake also destroyed four NEC factories and 80,000 telephone sets. Still, the government maintained its commitment to a modern telephone network and supported NEC's development of automatic switching devices.

NEC began to work on radios and transmitting devices in 1924. As with the telephone project, the Japanese government sponsored the establishment of a radio network, the Nippon Hoso Kyokai, which began operation with Western Electric equipment from NEC. By May, 1930, however, NEC had built its own transmitter, a 500-watt station at Okayama.

In 1925, American Telephone & Telegraph sold International Western Electric to International Telephone & Telegraph, which renamed the division International Standard Electric (ISE). Partially as a result, Yasujiro Niwa, a director who had joined NEC in 1924, felt NEC should lessen its dependence on technologies developed by foreign affiliates. In order to strengthen NEC's research and development, Niwa inaugurated a policy of recruiting the best graduates from top universities. By 1928 NEC engineers had completed their own wirephoto device.

The Japanese economy, which had been in a slump since 1927, fell into crisis after the Wall Street crash of 1929. With a rapidly contracting economy, the government was forced year after year to scale back its telecommunications projects. And while it restricted imports of electrical equipment, the government also encouraged greater competition in the domestic market. Decreased subsidization and a shrinking market share reversed many of NEC's gains during the previous decade.

The deployment of Japanese troops in Machuria in 1931 created a strong wave of nationalism in Japan. Legislation was passed that forced ISE to transfer about 15% of its ownership in NEC to Sumitomo Densen. Under the directorship of Sumitomo's Takesaburo Akiyama (Iwadare had retired in 1929), NEC began to work more closely with the Japanese military. A right-wing officers corps was at the time successfully engineering a rise to power and diverting money to military and industrial projects, particularly after Japan's declaration of war against China in 1937. NEC's sales grew by seven times between 1931 and 1937, and by 1938 the company's Mita and Tamagawa plants had been placed under military control.

Under pressure from the militarists, ISE was obliged to transfer a second block of NEC shares to Sumitomo; by 1941, ISE's stake had fallen to 19.7%. Later that year, however, when Japan went to war against the Allied powers, ISE's remaining share of NEC was confiscated as enemy property.

During the war, NEC worked on microwave communications and radar and sonar systems for the army and navy. The company took control of its prewar Chinese affiliate, China Electric, as well as a Javanese radio-research facility belonging to the Dutch East Indies Post, Telegraph and Telephone Service. In February, 1943, Sumitomo took full control of NEC and renamed it Sumitomo Communication Industries. The newly named company's production centers were removed to 15 different locations to minimize damage from American bombings. Despite this, Sumitomo Communication's major plants at Ueno, Okayama, and Tamagawa were destroyed during the spring of 1945; by the end of the war in August, the company had ceased production altogether.

The Allied occupation authority ordered the dissolution of Japan's giant *zaibatsu* (conglomerate) enterprises such as Sumitomo in November that year. Sumitomo Communications elected to re-adopt the name Nippon Electric, and ownership of the company reverted to a government liquidation corporation. At the same time, the authority ordered a purge of industrialists who had cooperated with the military during the war, and Takeshi Kajii, wartime president of NEC, was removed from the company.

NEC's new president, Toshihide Watanabe, faced the nearly impossible task of rehabilitating a company paralyzed by war damage, with 27,000 employees and no demand for its products. Although it was helped by the mass resignation of 12,000 workers, NEC was soon constrained by new labor legislation sponsored by the occupation authority. This legislation resulted in the formation of a powerful labor union that frequently came into conflict with NEC management. And although NEC was able to open its major factories by January of 1946, workers demanding higher wages went on strike for 45 days only 18 months later.

The Japanese government helped companies like NEC to remain viable through the award of public-works projects. Uneasy about becoming dependent on these programs, however, Watanabe ordered the reapplication of NEC's military technologies for commercial use. Submarine sonar equipment was thus converted into fish detectors, and military two-way radios were redesigned into all-band commercial radio receivers.

Still, NEC fell drastically short of its postwar recovery goals. In April, 1949 the company closed its Ogaki, Seto, and Takasaki plants and its laboratory at Ikuta, and laid off 2,700 employees. The union responded by striking, yielding only after 106 days.

Next on Watanabe's agenda was the establishment of patent protection for NEC's technologies. During the war, all patented designs had become a "common national asset"—in the public domain. Eager to reestablish its link with ISE, NEC needed first to ensure that both companies' technologies would be legally protected. This accomplished, NEC and ISE signed new cooperative agreements in July, 1950.

With Japan's new strategic importance in light of the Korean War, and with the advent of commercial radio broadcasting and subsequent telephone expansions, NEC had several new opportunities for growth. The company made great progress in television and microwave communication technologies and in 1953 created a separate consumer appliance subsidiary called the New Nippon Electric Company. The following year NEC entered the computer field. By 1956 it had diversified so successfully that a major reorganization became necessary and additional plant space in Sagamihara and Fuchu was put on line. NEC also established foreign offices in Taiwan, India, and Thailand in 1961.

Watanabe, believing that NEC should more aggressively establish an international reputation, opened an office in the United States in 1963. In addition, the company's logo was changed, dropping the simple *igeta* diamond and "NEC" for a more distinctive script. In November of the following year, Watanabe resigned as president and became chairman of the board.

The company's new president, Koji Kobayashi, took office with the realization that because the Japanese telephone market would soon become saturated, NEC would have to diversify more aggressively into new and peripheral electronics product lines to maintain its high growth rate. In preparation for this, he introduced modern management methods, including a zero-defects quality-control policy, a concept borrowed from the Martin Aircraft Company. Over the next two years, Kobayashi split NEC's five divisions into 14, paving the way for a more decentralized management system that gave individual division heads greater autonomy and responsibility.

With the continued introduction of more advanced television-broadcasting equipment and telephone switching devices, and taking advantage of the stronger position Watanabe and Kobayashi had created, NEC opened factories in Mexico and Brazil in 1968, Australia in 1969, and Korea in 1970. Affiliates were opened in Iran in 1971 and Malaysia in 1973.

With a diminishing need for technical-assistance programs, NEC moved toward greater independence from ITT. That company's interest in NEC (held through ISE) was reduced to 9.3% by 1970, and eliminated completely by 1978. Similarly, NEC shares retained after the war by Sumitomo-affiliated companies were gradually sold off, an action that reduced the Sumitomo group's interest in NEC from 38% in 1961 to 28% in 1982.

NEC's competitive advantage in labor costs eroded continually from the mid-1960s, when worker scarcity became apparent, until the early 1980s. This, together with President Richard Nixon's decision to remove the U.S. dollar from the gold standard in 1971 and the effects of the Arab oil embargo of 1973, profoundly compromised NEC's competitive standing. The company was forced into a seven-month retrenchment program in 1974, losing precious momentum in its competition with European and American firms.

In an effort to promote Japanese electronics companies, the Japanese government pushed through a series of partnership agreements among the Big Six computer makers: NEC, Fujitsu, Hitachi, Mitsubishi, Oki, and Toshiba. NEC and Toshiba formed a joint venture, which gave both companies an opportunity to pool their resources and eliminate redundant research. However a subsequent attempt by NEC to enter the personal-computer market failed miserably. Still, NEC, choosing to work with Honeywell instead of building IBM compatibles, invested heavily in its computer operations. Confident of its ability to marry its computer technology with communications expertise independently (C&C), NEC aimed to develop state-of-the-art machinery for the 1990s market.

Kobayashi, in the meantime, was promoted to chairman and CEO, and succeeded as president first by Tadao Tanaka in 1976, and then Tadahiro Sekimoto in 1980. Under Kobayashi and Tanaka, NEC tripled its sales volume in the ten years to 1980. A greater proportion of those sales than ever before was derived from foreign markets, and between 1981 and 1983 NEC's stock was listed on several European stock exchanges.

NEC has not yet begun to benefit from its C&C effort, mainly because of the long lead times required to develop multiple, integrated information-processing systems, and then effectively market them to an audience exposed to different equipment from major competitor. Indeed, NEC must introduce a truly revolutionary system capable of winning customers away from IBM and others to realize a return on its risky investment in the future.

Principal Subsidiaries: Ando Electric Company, Limited (50%); ANELVA Corporation (81%); Japan Aviation Electronics Industry, Limited (50.2%); NEC Akita, Ltd.; NEC Engineering, Ltd.; NEC Field Service, Ltd.; NEC Fukui, Ltd.; NEC Fukuoka, Ltd.; NEC Fukushima, Ltd.; NEC Factory Engineering, Ltd.; NEC Gunma, Ltd.; NEC Home Electronics, Ltd.; NEC Hyogo, Ltd.; NEC Ibaraki, Ltd.; NEC Information Service, Ltd.; NEC Kagoshima, Ltd.; NEC Kansai, Ltd.; NEC Kumamoto Ltd.; NEC Kyushu, Ltd.; NEC Software, Ltd.; NEC Miyagi, Ltd.; NEC Nagano, Ltd.; NEC Niigata, Ltd.; NEC Oita, Ltd.; NEC Saitama, Ltd.; NEC San-ei Instruments, Ltd. (95.6%); NEC Shizuoka, Ltd.; NEC System Integration & Construction, Ltd. (58.6%); NEC Tohoku, Ltd.; NEC Toyama, Ltd.; NEC Yamagata, Ltd.; NEC Yamaguchi, Ltd.; NEC Yonezawa, Ltd.; NEC-Toshiba Information Systems Inc. (60%); Nippon Avionics Company, Limited (50.1%); NEC Warehouse and Distribution, Ltd.; NEC Radio & Electronics, Ltd.; NEC Data Terminals Ltd.; NEC America, Inc. (U.S.A.); NEC Australia Pty. Ltd. (Australia); NEC Electronics Singapore Pte. Ltd. (Singapore); NEC Home Electronics (U.S.A.) Inc.; NEC Electronics Inc. (U.S.A.); NEC Electronics (Europe) GmbH (W. Germany); NEC Deutschland GmbH (W. Germany); NEC Industries, Inc. (U.S.A.); NEC Information Systems, Inc. (U.S.A.); NEC Semiconductors Ireland Limited (Ireland); NEC Semiconductors (Malaysia) Sdn. Bhd.; NEC Semiconductors (UK) Limited; NEC (UK) Ltd.

Further Reading: The First 80 Years, Tokyo, NEC, 1984.

NOKIA CORPORATION

Eteläesplanadi 12
P.O. Box 226
SF-00101 Helsinki
Finland
(0) 18–071

Public Company
Incorporated: 1865
Employees: 28,500 1987
Sales: FIM21.82 billion (US$5.25 billion)
Stock Index: Helsinki Stockholm London Paris Frankfurt

Nokia is one of the largest industrial enterprises in Scandinavia and the most important company in its native Finland, as Finland's only multinational and its leading industrial standard bearer.

For many years a diversified conglomerate, Nokia has recently bet its future on success in the high-technology electronics market. In addition, the company has elected to undertake a costly modernization of its marginally-performing forestry, chemicals, and manufacturing units. While this strategy disappoints some investors, it clearly demonstrates Nokia's commitment to long-term growth—a concept which should not be foreign to a 125-year-old company.

Originally a manufacturer of pulp and paper, Nokia was founded in 1865 in a small town of the same name in central Finland. Nokia was a pioneer in the industry, and introduced many new production methods to a country whose only major natural resource was its vast forests. As the industry became increasingly energy-intensive, the company even constructed its own power plants. But for many years, Nokia remained an important yet static firm in a relatively forgotten corner of northern Europe.

The first major changes in Nokia occurred several years after World War II. Despite its proximity to the Soviet Union, Finland has always remained economically connected with Scandinavian and other Western countries, and as Finnish trade expanded Nokia became a leading exporter.

During the early 1960s Nokia began to diversify in an attempt to transform the company into a regional conglomerate with interests beyond Finnish borders. Unable to initiate strong internal growth, Nokia turned its attention to acquisitions. The government, however, hoping to rationalize two under-performing basic industries, favored Nokia's expansion within the country, and encouraged its eventual merger with Finnish Rubber Works and Finnish Cable Works. When the amalgamation was completed in 1966, Nokia was involved in several new industries, including integrated cable operations, electronics, tires, and rubber footwear and had made its first public share offering.

In 1967 Nokia set up a division to develop design and manufacturing capabilities in data processing, industrial automation, and communications systems. The division was later expanded and made into several divisions, which then concentrated on developing information systems, including personal computers and workstations, digital communications systems, and mobile phones. Nokia also gained a strong position in modems and automatic banking systems in Scandinavia.

Nokia continued to operate in a stable but parochial manner until 1973, when it was affected in a unique way by the oil crisis. Years of political accommodation between Finland and the Soviet Union ensured Finnish neutrality in exchange for lucrative trade agreements with the Soviets—mainly Finnish lumber products and machinery in exchange for Soviet oil. By agreement, this trade was kept strictly in balance. But when world oil prices began to rise, the market price for Soviet oil rose with it. Balanced trade began to mean greatly reduced purchasing power for Finnish companies such as Nokia.

While the effects were not catastrophic, the oil crisis did force Nokia to reassess its reliance on Soviet trade (about 12% of sales) as well as its international growth strategies. Several contingency plans were drawn up, but the greatest changes came after the company appointed a new CEO, Kari Kairamo, in 1975.

Kairamo noted the obvious: Nokia was too big for Finland. The company had to expand abroad. He studied the expansion of other Scandinavian companies—particularly Sweden's Electrolux—and, following their example, formulated a strategy of first consolidating its business in Finland, Sweden, Norway, and Denmark, and then moving gradually into the rest of Europe. After the company had improved its product line, established a reputation for quality, and adjusted its production capacity, it would enter the world market.

The most promising market for Nokia was consumer and business electronics. Already a world leader in mobile telephone technologies, the company hoped that further development along this line would contribute to the development of related products as well as new systems.

Meanwhile, Nokia's traditional, lower-technology heavy industries were looking increasingly burdensome. It was feared that trying to become a leader in electronics while maintaining these basic industries would create an unmanageably unfocused company. Kairamo thought briefly about selling off the company's weaker divisions, but decided to retain and modernize them.

He reasoned that, while the modernization of these low-growth industries would be very expensive, it would guarantee Nokia's position in several stable markets, including paper, chemical and machinery production, and electrical generation. In order for the scheme to be practical, each division's modernization would have to be gradual and individually financed. This would prevent the bleeding of funds away from the all-important effort in electronics while preventing the heavy industries from becoming any less profitable.

With each division financing its own modernization, there was little or no drain on capital from other divisions, and Nokia could still sell any group which did not succeed under the new plan. In the end, the plan prompted the machinery division to begin development in robotics and automation, the cables division to begin work on fiber optics, and the forestry division to move into high-grade tissues.

But Nokia's most important focus was development of the electronics sector. The company became the Finnish agent for the French computer firm Bull in 1962. Similarly, Nokia built its expertise in telecommunications by selling switching systems under license from another French company, Alcatel. It then custom designed a digital switching system especially for Finnish telephone companies. Installed in 1982, it was the first digital system in Europe. That same year, Nokia gained 100% control of Mobira, a Finnish mobile phone company.

In late 1984 Nokia acquired Salora, the largest color television manufacturer in Scandinavia, and Luxor, the Swedish state-owned electronics and computer firm. Nokia combined Salora and Luxor into a single division and concentrated on stylish consumer electronic products, since style is a crucial factor in Scandinavian markets. The Salora–Luxor division has also been very successful in satellite and digital television technology.

Nokia, however, although a market leader in Scandinavia, still lacked a degree of competitiveness in the European market, which was dominated by much larger Japanese and German companies. Kairamo therefore decided to follow the example of many Japanese companies during the 1960s (and Korean manufacturers a decade later) and negotiate to become original equipment manufacturer, or OEM, to manufacture products for competitors as a subcontractor.

Nokia manufactured items for Hitachi in France, Ericsson in Sweden, Northern Telecom in Canada, and Granada and IBM in Britain. In doing so it was able to increase its production capacity stably. There were, however, several risks involved, ones inherent in any OEM arrangement. Nokia's sales margins were naturally reduced, but of greater concern, production capacity was built up without a commensurate expansion in the sales network. With little brand identification, Nokia feared it might have a difficult time selling under its own name and become trapped as an OEM.

In 1986 Nokia reorganized its management structure to simplify reporting efforts and improve control by central management. The company's 11 divisions were grouped into four industry segments: electronics; cables and machinery; paper, power, and chemicals; and rubber and flooring. In addition, Nokia won a concession from the Finnish government to allow greater foreign participation in ownership. This substantially reduced Nokia's dependence on the comparatively expensive Finnish lending market. While there was growth throughout the company, Nokia's greatest success was Mobira.

The mobile telephone group received a tremendous boost in the early 1980s when the Scandinavian countries created the Nordic Mobile Telephone (NMT) network. Mobira's regional sales were vastly improved, but Nokia was still limited to OEM production on the international market—Nokia and Tandy Corporation, of the U.S., built a factory in Masan, South Korea to manufacture mobile telephones for sale in the United States.

In 1986, eager to test its ability to compete openly, Nokia chose the mobile telephone to be the first product marketed internationally under the Nokia name; it became Nokia's "make or break" product. The effort, with only a short record so far, has proven moderately successful. Asian competitors began to drive prices down just as Nokia entered the market. Other Nokia products gaining recognition are Mikko computers, Salora televisions, and Luxor satellite dishes, which suffered briefly when subscription programming introduced broadcast scrambling.

Nokia purchased the consumer electronics operations of Standard Elektrik Lorenz A.G. from Alcatel in 1987, further bolstering the company's position in the television market—it is now the third largest manufacturer in Europe. However, the company's expansion, achieved almost exclusively by acquisition, has been expensive. Few Finnish investors other than institutions have had the patience to see Nokia through its long-term plans. Indeed, over half of the new shares issued by Nokia in 1987 went to foreign investors. In early 1988 Nokia acquired the data systems division of the Swedish Ericsson Group, making Nokia the largest Scandinavian information technology business.

Trade with the Soviet Union required neither competitiveness nor a need for innovation; it had been a stagnating influence. As Nokia's dependence on Soviet and East Bloc trade has waned (from 50% of exports to about 6%) the company has gained an improved sense of market trends. Nokia has moved boldly into Western markets, and in 1987 gained a listing on the London exchange.

Nokia's rapid growth was not without a price. In 1988, as revenues soared, the company's profits, under pressure from severe price competition in the consumer electronics markets, tumbled. Chairman Kari Kairamo committed suicide; friends said it was brought on by stress. Simo S. Vuorilehto took over the company's reins and, in spring, 1988 began streamlining operations. Nokia was divided into six business groups: consumer electronics, data, mobile phones, telecommunications, cables and machinery, and basic industries. Vuorilehto continued Kairamo's focus on high-tech divisions, divesting Nokia's $60 million flooring business and entering into joint ventures with companies like Tandy Corporation and Matra of France (two separate agreements to produce mobile phones for the U.S. and French markets). Despite the cut-throat competition in consumer electronics throughout Europe, Nokia remained committed to its high-tech orientation. Vuorilehto emphasized that this area would provide the most growth over the long term. The company is banking on its strength in Scandinavia to anchor its continued thrust into the turbulent world markets. Still, as research and development costs escalate, it remains to be seen whether a company of Nokia's size can survive the changes in high-tech industries.

Principal Subsidiaries: Nokia Cellular Systems Oy; Nokia Data Systems Oy; Nokia Cable Machinery Oy (61%); Nokia Kaapeli Oy; Nokia Matkapuhelimet Oy; Nokia Renkaat Oy (80%); Nokian Paperi Oy; Salora Myynti Oy; Sähköliikkeiden Oy (65.6%); Telenokia Oy; British Tissues Ltd (UK); Graetz Strahlungsmesstechnik GmbH (99.7%) (West Germany); Horda AB (Sweden) (91.1%); Ibervisao-Audiovisao Iberica S.A. (Portugal) (99.7%); Kabmatik AB (Sweden) (61%); Luxor AB (Sweden) (90%); Maillefer S.A. (Switzerland) (61%); Monette Kabel-und Elektrowerk GmbH (West Germany); Nokia A/S (Norway); Nokia Audio Electronics GmbH (West Germany) (99.7%); Nokia Consumer Electronics GmbH (West Germany) (99.7%); Nokia Consumer Electronics Ltd (UK) (99.7%); Nokia Consumer Electronics Italia S.r.l. (Italy) (99.7%); Nokia Data AB (Sweden); Nokia Data A/S (Denmark); Nokia Data A/S (Norway); Nokia Data BV (Netherlands); Nokia Data GmbH (West Germany); Nokia Data Ltd (UK); Nokia Data S.A. (France); Nokia Data S.A. (Spain); Nokia Data Systems AB (Sweden); Nokia Graetz Holzwerke GmbH (West Germany) (99.7%); Nokia Kunststofftechnik GmbH (West Germany) (99.7%); Nokia Ltd (Ireland); Nokia-Mobira AB (Sweden); Nokia-Mobira A/S (Denmark); Nokia Mobira A/S (Norway); Nokia-Mobira Inc. (USA); Nokia-Mobira UK Ltd; Nokia Unterhaltungselektronik (West Germany) (99.7%); Novelectric AG (Switzerland) (99.7%); Oceanic S.A. (France) (99.9%); Salora AB (Sweden); Sodipan-Nokia S.A. (France); Türkkablo A.O. (Turkey) (51%).

OKI

OKI ELECTRIC INDUSTRY COMPANY, LIMITED

7–12, Toranomon 1-chome
Minato-ku, Tokyo 105
Japan
(03) 508–9465

Public Company
Incorporated: 1881 as Meikosha Company
Employees: 18,440
Sales: ¥555.52 billion (US$4.44 billion)
Stock Index: Tokyo Osaka Luxembourg

Oki Electric Industry Company's roots are inextricably tangled up with an American invention. Oki's founder, Kibataro Oki, was an engineer working for Japan's Department of Industry when the first telephones to be imported into the country arrived from the United States in 1877. He participated in the planning and production of Japan's first domestically manufactured telephones, but the Japanese version of the Bell System proved to be a technical failure.

Oki's faith in the future of the telecommunications, however, was not shaken by the experience. Instead, he left government service and founded his own manufacturing company, called Meikosha Company, in 1881 in the Shin-Sakanamachi area of Tokyo. Meikosha started out producing and marketing telephones, electric wires, and bells, and soon added switching equipment, telegraphs, lightning rods, incandescent and arc lamps, and medical equipment to its repertoire. Most of its customers were large institutions—government agencies, private companies, and the Japanese military.

In 1890 telephone exchanges were set up in Tokyo and Yokohama, and Meikosha was among the Japanese companies that manufactured telephones for these systems. It also supplied the nation's first domestically-produced magneto serial repeating switchboard for the Tokyo exchange in 1896. That same year, the company separated its marketing and manufacturing operations, with the former shifting its headquarters to the Kyobashi Ward of Tokyo and changing its name to Oki & Company. The manufacturing plant had changed its name to Oki Electric Plant two years earlier.

Kibataro Oki died in 1906 at the age of 59. The next year, Oki & Company was reorganized as a limited partnership, with a capitalization of ¥600,000. The company underwent further reorganization in 1912, when the manufacturing and marketing operations were again separated from each other. Then in 1917, the two groups were recombined under the name Oki Electric Company, Limited.

During this time, Oki also diversified its product lines. Besides venturing into electric clocks and measuring equipment, it also was a pioneer in the manufacture and sale of radio equipment in Japan. By 1917, it had expanded its facilities to four manufacturing plants, and the company employed nearly 4,000 people.

After the Great Earthquake of 1923 caused severe damage to Tokyo's infrastructure, Japan's telephone exchanges became automated. In 1926 Oki entered into a joint venture with the General Electric Company of the United Kingdom, to manufacture automatic switching equipment. Oki also began to produce electric clocks in 1929.

The political climate in Japan in the 1930s was marked by increasing militarism. In 1931 the Japanese army invaded Manchuria, and in 1937 Japan went to war against China, marking the start of eight years of full-fledged war for Japan. By then, Oki had become one of the nation's leading electrical manufacturers and had built up an overseas sales network that covered China and Southeast Asia. In response to the increasing demand for military hardware, it built two more plants in the late 1930s, one in Shibaura, Tokyo, to produce communications equipment for the army, and another in Shinagawa to build hydrometers for the navy, as well as maritime and aeronautical radios.

After the United States entered World War II in December, 1941, the manufacture of civilian communications equipment came to a standstill as Japan devoted more and more of its resources to the war effort. For the remainder of the war, military orders provided the vast majority of Oki's business. The company underwent significant expansion in the early 1940s, increasing its production of military equipment, such as field telephones, aeronautical radios, and hydrophones. When World War II ended in August, 1945, Oki had 20 plants and nearly 23,000 employees despite the fact that its Shibaura plant had been completely destroyed in an American bombing raid.

Oki radically scaled back its operations after Japan's surrender, trimming itself down to five plants and 4,000 employees. It stopped producing military equipment and restored its remaining manufacturing capacity to civilian uses. Its plant at Warabi had somehow escaped damage during the war, and Oki began turning out automatic telephone switching equipment there. The company produced telephones and radios and, responding to the demand for simple consumer goods in war-ravaged Japan, began making portable cooking stoves and irons as well. Amidst the difficulties of reconstruction, however, Oki also found the time and resources to begin developing the teleprinter, laying the foundation for a business that would become one of its most successful four decades later.

Oki's resurrection was almost cut off in 1948, however, when the American occupation authorities ordered the breakup of large industrial concerns. Similar actions were undertaken in occupied Germany, partly as retribution, but also in the hope that decentralizing the economy would make future remilitarization more difficult. Oki was one of the Japanese companies marked for breakup. Later that year, however, the order was rescinded, and in 1949 the company was incorporated under its current name, Oki Electric Industry Company.

In 1953 Oki's rebuilt Shibaura plant opened and began manufacturing telephones and radios. In 1954 the company entered into a joint venture with Raytheon, a leading American defense electronics contractor, to produce radar equipment. Also during the 1950s, Oki began making semiconductors and entered Japan's fledgling data processing and computer industry. By 1960, it had become one of the Big Six that have since dominated that business in Japan, along with Nippon Electric Company (NEC), Hitachi, Fujitsu, Toshiba, and Mitsubishi.

Beginning in 1962, with the encouragement of the Ministry of International Trade and Industry (MITI), Oki joined other Big Six computer firms in a series of joint research-and-development ventures. The first of these was called FONTAC, and was intended to develop an IBM-compatible mainframe computer to make Japan less vulnerable to mainframe imports from the United States. Fujitsu developed the central processing unit, NEC the electronic peripheral equipment, and Oki the mechanical peripherals, and it resulted in the introduction of Japanese IBM-compatible mainframes in the early 1960s. The remaining Big Six firms were brought into the project in 1966, when work began on the next generation of FONTAC computers. Oki's task was to develop a way to process Kanji, the Japanese alphabet.

In 1963 Oki entered into a joint venture with the American computer company Sperry Rand to manufacture mainframes under the name Oki Univac Kaisha, Ltd. The 1960s also saw a substantial increase in Oki's overseas business, especially in Latin America. It constructed a nationwide communications network in Honduras in 1962 and a regional network in the Bolivian capital of La Paz in 1966. In 1971, Oki developed a microwave radio network in Brazil.

Oki established a new division in 1970 to develop computer software. In 1977 it added a research laboratory to its electronics plant at Hachioji and devoted it to research and development of large-scale integration microcircuits (LSIs), which can pack a relatively substantial number of transistors into a small space. But in this area Oki was somewhat behind because in that year the government initiated a research-and-development program devoted to very large-scale integration (VLSI). VLSI circuits crammed more than 250,000 transistors onto a silicon chip less than one micron wide; they were in common use by the late 1980s. Oki was the only Big Six manufacturer to be left out of the project by MITI, although the company soon began work on VLSI at its Hachioji lab.

Oki was also in a state of severe financial crisis in 1977 and 1978. Sales barely increased between 1975 and 1977, and profits plummeted, to a loss of ¥1.5 billion in 1977. Following an extensive restructuring in 1979, however, the company made a dramatic recovery.

In 1980 Oki built a VLSI plant in Miyazaki. In 1981 it began to produce personal computers, one of the last of the Big Six to do so. And in 1984, Oki responded to increased business opportunities in the United States by merging its five American subsidiaries into one large subsidiary, Oki America, Inc., anticipating that the cost of doing business in America would be lower if its American activities were coordinated in America instead of Japan. In 1985, Oki began manufacturing cellular mobile telephones in the United States since that is where the largest market is. The strong yen also convinced Oki to begin construction of a plant in the United Kingdom for the local production of its popular dot-matrix printers. In the United States, Oki built a major manufacturing facility outside Atlanta in 1988 and an additional factory will open soon in Oregon.

After its financial crisis in the late 1970s, Oki's profits dropped drastically again in 1985 and it lost ¥8.4 billion in 1986, reflecting a profound slump in the semiconductor industry. But Oki, like the industry, bounced back, and today remains one of the world's largest electronics manufacturers and a leading maker of computer peripherals. More than 80 years after Kibataro Oki's death, his legacy still survives.

Principal Subsidiaries: Oki America, Inc.; Oki Electric Europe GmbH (West germany); Okidata GmbH (West Germany); Far Eastern Electric Industry Co., Ltd. (Taiwan); Digiphonic Systems Pte. Ltd (Singapore); Oki Electronics (Hong Kong) Ltd.; Oki (U.K.) Ltd.; Oki Europe Ltd. (U.K.); Oki Electronics (Singapore) Pte. Ltd.; Tohoku Oki Electric Co., Ltd.; Nagano Oki Electric Co., Ltd.; Taiko Electric Works, Ltd.; Nikko Denki Seisakusho Co., Ltd.; Kuwano Electrical Instruments Co., Ltd.; Toho Electronics Co., Ltd.; Shizuoka Oki Electric Co., Ltd.; Oki Ceramic Industry Co., Ltd.; Kinseki, Ltd.; Yamako Electric Manufacture Co., Ltd.; Mikuni Industry Co., Ltd.; Waratoku Steel Co., Ltd.; Oki Electric Cable Co., Ltd.; Miyazaki Oki Electric Co., Ltd.; Miyagi Oki Electric Co., Ltd.; Niigata Oki Electric Co., Ltd.; OF Engineering Co., Ltd.; Oki Unisys Kaisha, Ltd.; Oki Software Co., Ltd.; Oki Telecommunications System Co., Ltd.; Oki Software Kansai Co., Ltd.; Oki Firmware System Co., Ltd.; Oki Software Kyushu Co., Ltd.; Oki Techno Systems Laboratory, Inc.; Oki Information Systems, Co., Ltd.; Oki Micro Design Miyazaki Co., Ltd.; Oki Software Systems Hokkaido Co., Ltd.; Oki FCS Systems Co., Ltd.; Oki Hokuriku Systems Development Co., Ltd.; Oki Software Chugoku Co., Ltd.; Oki Software Okayama Co., Ltd.; Oki Transmission Engineering Co., Ltd.; Oki Medical Systems Co., Ltd.; Oki Seatec Co., Ltd.; Oki Systek Co., Ltd.; Oki System Development Niigata Co., Ltd.; Oki Electric Installation Co., Ltd.; Oki Business Co., Ltd.; Oki Development Co., Ltd.; Oki Welfare Works Co., Ltd.; Oki Engineering Co., Ltd.; Oki Denki Bohsai Co., Ltd.; Oki Logistics Co., Ltd.; Oki Data Machine Service Co., Ltd.; Oki Kanto Service Co., Ltd.; Nichiei Co., Ltd.; Oki Chubu Service Co., Ltd.; Oki Kansai Service Co., Ltd.; Oki Kitakanto Service Co., Ltd.; Oki Kyusyu Service Co., Ltd.; Oki Network Service Co., Ltd.; Oki Supply Center Co., Ltd.; Oki Telecom Co., Ltd.; Oki Alpha Create Inc.

Further Reading: Davidson, William H. *The Amazing Race: Winning the Technorivalry with Japan*, New York, John Wiley & Sons, 1984; Okimoto, Daniel, and Saguno, Takuo, and Weinstein, Franklin, eds. *Competitive Edge: The Semiconductor Industry in the U.S. and Japan*, Stanford, Stanford University Press, 1984; Sobel, Robert. *IBM vs. Japan*, New York, Stein and Day, 1986.

omron

OMRON TATEISI ELECTRONICS COMPANY

10, Hanazono, Tsuchidocho
Ukyo-ku
Kyoto 616
Japan
(075) 463-1161

Public Company
Incorporated: 1948 as Tateisi Electric Manufacturing Company
Employees: 13,851
Sales: ¥72.45 billion (US$2.98 billion)
Stock Index: Kyoto Osaka Tokyo Nagoya Luxembourg Hong Kong Frankfurt

Omron Tateisi Electronics is Japan's largest control equipment manufacturer. Respected in the past for its ability to design and develop new technology, the corporation now emphasizes the coordination of control systems. As a proponent of universal component design, the company continues to invest in research and development even more heavily than the norm for the high-tech industry in order to maintain a prominent market share of control products and influence the electronic universality its founder saw as inevitable.

Kazuma Tateisi, born in 1900, graduated from the electrical engineering department of what is now Kumamoto University. Tateisi worked briefly as an electrical engineer for the government on a Hyogo hydroelectric plant, and then began working for the Inoue Electric Manufacturing Company in 1922.

The New York stock market crash of 1929 triggered the "Great Showa Depression" in Japan. When Tateisi became part of Inoue's reduction in its labor force, he rented a factory and began to manufacture household appliances. Sales on his knife grinder and pant press, items Tateisi developed himself, were low. But in 1932 Tateisi used the knowledge of induction relays he had acquired at Inoue to invent and develop a timing device that limited X-ray exposure to 1/20 of a second. He began production of the timer through a joint venture with Dai Nippon X-ray Inc., using Tateisi Medical Electronics Manufacturing Company as a label.

Early in 1933 Tateisi moved to Osaka to be nearer to Dai Nippon. The Tateisi Electric Manufacturing Company began operations on May 10 that year, the date that is celebrated as the founding anniversary of Omron Tateisi Electronics.

Lack of capital and contractual limitations with Dai Nippon hampered the young company, but in early 1934 Tateisi began to market an induction-type protection relay, which was an essential component of the timer. The component found a large market and successfully raised revenue.

Later that year a typhoon struck Japan's western coast, causing extensive damage to factories there. Hitachi, the chief manufacturer of induction-type protection relays, could not meet the immediate demand, and orders for repair or substitution of relays overwhelmed Tateisi's small factory. The company quickly transferred the manufacturing of its timers to Dai Nippon and concentrated on the relay. The timer would be the last device made by Tateisi for several decades; the transfer marked the beginning of Tateisi's focus on components.

Demand for the relay devices continued after the recovery from the typhoon as Japanese industrial development increased overall, allowing Tateisi to expand his output and facilities. In 1937 Tateisi built a larger factory with offices and a warehouse. He also established a branch office in Tokyo and purchased another factory, where parts from the Osaka plant were assembled.

Research conducted during World War II led to the development of a product line which would become an area of extensive postwar growth for the company. At the request of Tokyo University, Tateisi began to research micro-switches, also known as precision switches, in 1941; in 1944 the company supplied 300 micro-switches to the university.

During World War II, Tateisi produced flap switches for aircraft and acted as a sub-contractor to Mitsubishi Heavy Industries. In 1944 Tateisi converted a movie studio into the Kyoto branch factory. A year later the Tokyo branch office and the main factory were destroyed in air raids, forcing all production to the Kyoto branch, which remained the company's headquarters until 1968.

Since Japan's hydroelectric plants were largely intact after the war, electricity at least was not scarce. The company's initial peacetime production centered on small household consumer appliances under the name Omlon (which later became Omron), an independent subsidiary.

In 1947 the government, seeking to prevent the frequent electrical overloads common at the time, asked appliance manufacturers to develop a current limiter. Production for the government required incorporation, which Tateisi completed on April 14, 1948. Although the company was once again part of the component industry, postwar prosperity was still several years away. In 1949 the allied powers enacted the Dodge Line, requiring the Japanese government to take anti-inflationary action. These measures revoked the funds which had provided the market for Tateisi's limiter.

This action struck a serious blow to Tateisi's 33 employees, who had devoted all production capability to the limiter. Debt forced reductions in operations and reorganization in the company's subsidiaries. Sales dropped 57% that year, to the company's record low.

Efforts to rebuild amid economic instability continued until the intervention of the United Nations in the Korean war stimulated the economy and increased demand for relay devices. This renewed demand allowed Tateisi to reopen the Tokyo branch office and to build a new office in Osaka.

By 1953 the company employed 65 people and Korean wartime demand had boosted the Japanese industrial economy. Kazuma Tateisi had taken an interest in cybernetics—automatic control systems. After a tour of American companies, he felt sure that an automation revolution was at hand in Japan and reorganized the company accordingly.

Development of new products had assumed a rapid pace, and a centralized company could not efficiently administer market-oriented production. Tateisi introduced the "Producer System" (P-system), which delegated individual products to independent companies. Under the P-system, the managers of individual factories and subsidiaries were responsible for production and labor relations while the head office retained all other decision-making. This decentralization allowed a varied product line and profitability on items with slim margins. The company continued to pursue this approach to production, creating separate sales and research subsidiaries in 1955. The P-system is largely intact today in Omron's overseas subsidiaries.

In 1958 Omron became a registered trademark and began to be used on all the company's products. But more importantly, the company developed its first control system, which combined several of its components. The following year a P-system company began production of control systems. With these and other innovations, the company saw sales increase tenfold between 1955 and 1959, to ¥1.3 billion.

With the help of government financing, Tateisi completed his Central Research Institute in 1959, which helped speed the development of new items, especially the contactless switch of 1960. This switch's tremendous success solidified the company's future commitment to research and development and gave it prominence in the area of high-tech research.

In 1961 Tateisi introduced a stress meter, the first of many low-cost cybernetic devices for medicine and biology. Instead of establishing a subsidiary however, health engineering remained part of the parent company as a department. Today, health-related equipment makes up a small but influential part of sales.

Complex vending machines, introduced in 1963, were also a long-term success for the company. Capable of dispensing several different items and accepting a variety of currencies, the machines' currency calculation and detection equipment soon found applications in areas beyond food vending. The device proved to be a major breakthrough for the company, as it offered electronic processing of financial transactions, an enormous area of growth in the decades to come.

During the mid-1960s, international sales grew through long-term export contracts. Tateisi opened a representative office in New York, and began to earn the respect of American buyers as a quality producer of vending machines and other electronically monitored control devices just as market demand for such items intensified.

When the company went public in 1962 it had to consolidate the management and financing of the P-system companies in order to be traded on commodities markets, a process that was completed in 1965. Although this sacrificed many of its cost advantages, Tateisi took advantage of its public status. Thanks in part to a period of national economic growth, the company now had the means to invest more heavily in its structural facilities and established eight new factories, four offices and seven retail branches.

During the eight-year period ending in 1967, annual sales increased almost 10-fold again, to ¥10 billion. In 1968, the company built new headquarters in Kyoto and changed its name to Omron Tateisi in celebration of its 35th anniversary.

Omron established the first Japanese research center in the United States in 1970, benefiting from reduced funding for NASA, which made more technically trained employees available. The research and development center in California met with some hostility from people who saw it as another example of the growing economic threat Japan's booming economy represented. The center eventually helped to develop integrated circuits, large-scale integrated circuits, and liquid crystals, further advancing Omron in the area of electronics research. Such overseas ventures continue to play an important financial and political role amid growing threats of trade restrictions.

The late 1960s and early 1970s were a healthy time for Omron; the company set a five-year sales goal in 1969 of ¥100 billion, and increased its international presence.

The pace of product development grew. During the 1960s, technology advances, including devices pioneered by Omron, created the possibility of universal electronic controls, as opposed to the control devices of the 1950s, which were developed individually as needed. In 1968 Omron introduced a contactless pinboard sequence programmer, which allowed systems flexibility and increased the number of individual tasks to which they could be applied. Four years later, Omron introduced a programmable sequence controller.

The oil crisis in 1973 sparked a period of slow growth nationwide. The mid-1970s were the most stagnant years since the Dodge Line of 1949. Omron was caught expanding its production once again, and was forced to lay off workers and cut production in the P-system companies. In an attempt to build immunity to such fluctuations, the company pruned management and restructured. While many Japanese companies increased their export drive to overcome this economic shock, Omron delayed such efforts until its reorgnization of 1976 was completed.

The reorganization was expensive but successful. Sales decreased and the company reported negative net profits for 1975 to 1976, but after three years it was back on course. In 1978, four years behind its original goal, Omron's sales reached ¥101.1 billion. In 1979, Takao Tateisi succeeded Kazuma Tateisi as president, and a new sales goal of ¥500 billion was set for 1990.

Two years later the goal still looked reasonable. Demand for control systems increased 20% each year and overall sales grew steadily. But the next decade was an unstable one for Omron, and many changes were eventually required.

Growth slowed substantially in 1981 and actually reversed in 1982. Sales slowly increased but it was six years before the company was fully recovered. Although still sensitive to the global economic climate, Omron had satisfactory returns in many areas. Exports had slowed due to yen appreciation, but overall sales of ATMs, switches, relays, office automation equipment, and medical devices increased rapidly, while control systems continued to increase more moderately.

The brisk pace of 1984–1985 hinted at recovery, and the corporation set record net profit levels. But sales of control systems, Omron's largest sector, did not increase and electronic fund transfer systems (EFTS), the second largest sector, actually decreased. Further frustration came from the appreciating yen, which limited export potential.

By 1987 international sales accounted for only 17% of sales, down from 25% at the beginning of the decade. Yet Omron's limited vulnerability to fluctuations in the exchange rate did offer opportunities, and the company mobilized to capitalize on them. The strong yen led many companies in Japan to reinvest in their manufacturing facilities and information systems, which improved Omron's domestic sales. Omron also invested in itself, nearly doubling its long-term debt during the decade to ¥34.8 billion, and lowering its earnings for 1985 and 1986. The exchange rate also allowed the company to increase overseas production and buy more components from Taiwan and South Korea. In 1988 these investments finally improved earnings, which nearly doubled in one year, while sales, only slightly behind schedule, jumped to ¥315 billion.

Omron had also used the slow growth period to restructure. Its most important move was its transition from a component manufacturer to a producer of integrated control systems. As it entered the late 1980s, Omron relied on research and development and its expertise in combining cybernetic technology, advanced controls, computers, and telecommunications technology to position all of its sectors for the next growth period.

Such flexibility in applications is crucial as customers' needs grow more complex. The retail industry, for instance, will increase its demand for faster seller recognition, order placement, and stock control. Other industries interested in EFTS technology include insurance and securities companies wishing to gain rapid access to markets. The company's interest in system development will also make it a good candidate to fill growing demand in North America for network EFTS.

Health-related equipment remains a small portion of sales, but it is easy to produce and generates high profit margins, so Omron is unlikely to leave the market.

Omron's most significant move toward systems development came in 1988, when the company integrated the Control Components (65% of sales) and the EFTS divisions (19%), believing that technical integration of the company's two largest divisions will be vital to future growth. These divisions have been regrouped as Industrial-related Strategic Business Units (SBUs) and Social-related SBUs. The latter will certainly employ the company's Office Automation and Information Systems divisions, which made up 10% of sales in 1988.

The years of the appreciating yen have provided Omron the chance to rediscover its domestic market. Japan itself has become a region of emphasis, along with North America, Europe, and the rest of Asia and the Pacific. The company's structure makes it well-positioned for international growth if the yen declines. Omron projects worldwide growth in factory automation, computer integrated manufacturing, and information systems that support service industries, all areas of Omron expertise.

Principal Subsidiaries: Iida Tateisi Electronics Co.; Nogata Tateisi Electronics Co.; Okayama Tateisi Electronics Co.; Sanyo Tateisi Seiki Co.; Aso Tateisi Electronics Co.; Kurayoshi Tateisi Electronics Co.; Ichinomiya Tateisi Electronics Co.; Tateisi Technical Service Co.; Izumo Tateisi Electronics Co.; Yamaga Tateisi Electronics Co.; Takeo Tateisi Electronics Co.; Tateisi Enterprise Co.; Kumamoto Tateisi Kiko Co.; Tateisi Institute of Life Sciences, Inc.; Omron Systems Co.; Tateisi General Service Co.; Omron Electronics, Inc. (U.S.A.); Omron Electronics G.m.b.H. (West Germany); Omron Electronics B.V. (Netherlands); Omron Singapore (Pte.) Ltd.; Omron Eletronica Do Brasil Ltda.; Omron Canada, Inc.; Omron Geschaftssysteme G.m.b.H. (West Germany); Omron Terminals (UK) Ltd.; Omron Trisak Co., Ltd. (Thailand); Omron Business Systems Singapore (Pte) Ltd.; Omron Business Sistemas Electronicos Da America Tatina Ltda (Brazil); Omron Electronic Ges.m.b.H. (Austria); Omron Electronics S.a.r.l. (France); Omron Electronics S.r.L. (Italy); Omron Electronics S.A. (Spain); Omron Electronics S.A. (Belgium); Omron Electronics A.G. (Switzerland); Omron Electronics A/S (Norway); Omron Electronics O.Y. (Finland); Omron Electronics A.B. (Sweden); Omron Taiwan Electronics Inc.; Omron Electronics Pty. Ltd. (Australia); Omron Malaysia Sdn. Bhd.; Omron Europe G.m.b.H. (West Germany); Omron Electronics Europe B.V. (The Netherlands); Omron Electronics Componentes e Sistemas Electronicos LDA (Portugal); Omron Asia Pacific Trading (Pte) Ltd. (Singapore); Omron Electronics Asia Ltd. (Hong Kong); Omron Korea Co. Ltd.; Omron Taiwan Electronics Inc.; Omron Electronics (U.K.) Ltd.; Omron Manufacturing of America Inc.; Omron Componentes Eletronicos Da Amazonia Ltda. (Brazil); Omron Malaysia Eletronics Sdn. Bhd.; Omron Systems of America, Inc.; Omron Systems of Canada Inc.; Omron Research Institute Inc. (U.S.A.); Omron Finance Netherlands B.V.

Further Reading: Fifty Years of Omron: A Pictoral History, Kyoto, Omron Tateisi Electronics, 1985.

N.V. PHILIPS GLOEILAMPEMFABRIEKEN

Groenewoudseweg 1
5621 BA
Eindhoven
The Netherlands
(040) 757223

Public Company
Incorporated: 1912
Employees: 310,300
Sales: Dfl 56 billion (US$27.9 billion)
Stock Index: Amsterdam

Inspired by the visions and leadership of several generations of the Philips family, Philips Incandescent Lamp Works has grown from a small light bulb maker into one of the largest and most successful electronics firms in the world. Throughout the company's history, the family has sustained a strong commitment to technological innovation, market expansion, and stringent management policies.

The early years of the company were very much a family affair. On May 15, 1891, Gerard Philips, a young engineer who saw commercial potential in newly developing electrical technology, formed Philips & Company, a partnership with his father, Frederik Philips, to manufacture incandescent lamps and other electrical products. The elder Philips, a wealthy tobacco merchant and banker from Zaltbommel, provided the financing while Gerard contributed the technical expertise.

Philips & Company began operations in a small factory in Eindhoven. Production started in 1892, but the fledgling company encountered problems from the very beginning. The firm could not produce as many lamps as Gerard had forecast, nor did the lamps fetch the price he had expected. Father and son had underestimated the strength of international competition in the young industry, especially from the large German manufacturers who had entered the market in the early 1880s and were already well established.

The company suffered heavy financial losses in 1893, and by 1894 the two men decided to sell the business. That might have been the end of the family's venture into the electrical industry had it not been for the fact that the only offer they received was considered unacceptable by Frederik. After negotiations broke down with the prospective buyer, the Philipses decided to risk everything rather than sell at too low a price.

The company was clearly in need of someone with commercial skills and ambition to make it profitable. Frederik was preoccupied with his banking and commercial interests in Zaltbommel, and, while Gerard possessed the technical ability necessary to manufacture electric light bulbs and other innovative products, he was not by nature a businessman. Frederik thus turned to his youngest son, Anton.

Anton Philips, who was 16 years younger than Gerard, joined the firm in early 1895. Anton had left school early to work in London for a brokerage firm. This brief training in business helped; once he assumed control, Anton began winning the company new customers both at home and abroad. In a few years, the company was growing at a healthy rate.

At the turn of the century the company kept pace with constant innovations in the electrical industry by developing a skilled staff of technical and commercial specialists. When the carbon-filament lamp became obsolete after 1907, Philips and other companies pioneered the development of lamps that used tungsten wire, which produced three times as much light for the same amount of electricity. Philips was also at the forefront of revolutionary improvements in the manufacture of filament wire, which gave rise to the production of incandescent lamps of all types and sizes. In 1912 Philips & Company was incorporated as N.V. Philips Gloeilampfabrieken and began offering its shares on the Amsterdam Stock Exchange.

As the company grew, it became increasingly evident to both Gerard and Anton that a strong research-and-development capability would be critical to its survival. Consequently, in 1914 Gerard appointed a young physicist, Gilles Holst, to lead the company's research effort. Dr. Holst and his staff worked as a separate organization, reporting directly to the Philips brothers; this laboratory eventually developed into the Philips Research Laboratories.

The Netherlands remained neutral in World War I, to the company's benefit. Shortages of coal for the production of gas resulted in gas rationing, which in turn stimulated the use of electricity. By 1915, Philips had succeeded in producing a small, economical argon-filled lamp that was immediately in great demand.

When Germany prohibited the export of argon gas, Philips avoided a production breakdown by completing its own argon-production facility. Similarly, the glass bulbs used in manufacturing its lamps, which had been obtained from factories in Germany and Austria before the war, suddenly fell into short supply. The brothers decided in 1915 that the supply problem could be solved only by constructing a glass works of their own. That factory opened in 1916, followed shortly by additional facilities for the production of hydrogen gas and corrugated cardboard. These moves were the first steps toward the vertical integration of the company's production processes.

After the war, Philips began to expand its overseas marketing efforts significantly. Before 1914, Philips had autonomous marketing companies in the United States and France. In 1919, La Lumière Economique was established in Belgium, followed by similar organizations set up in 13 other European countries as well as China, Brazil, and Australia.

Research conducted under the direction of Dr. Holst played a critical role in the development of new products during this time. Fields such as X-ray radiation and radio reception were given high priority, resulting a few years later in product-line additions such as X-ray tubes and radio valves.

In 1920 a holding company, N.V. Gemeenschappelijk Benzit van Aandeelen Philips Gloeilampenfabriken known as N.V. Benzit was formed and assumed ownership of Philips.

Gerard Philips retired in 1922 and was succeeded as company chairman by Anton, who was 48 years old. Under Anton's management, the company began to manufacture complete radio sets; it displayed its first model at the Utrecht Trade Fair in September, 1927. From then on, rather than manufacturing just electrical components, the company started to manufacture complete products whenever possible—a significant change in management strategy.

During the 1920s, the company's headquarters at Eindhoven underwent extensive renovation and expansion, with the construction of additional buildings for new and existing industrial products. Toward the end of the decade, Philips' Lamp Works set up more overseas subsidiaries in Asia and Africa, as well as in Europe.

The worldwide depression of the 1930s, however, stalled the company's robust expansion, forcing employee layoffs and an administrative reorganization. As a result, new budgeting methods and an improved cost-price calculation were introduced to facilitate a faster response to changing market conditions. Research continued with considerable vigor, producing new products such as gas-discharge lamps, X-ray equipment, car radios, telecommunications equipment, welding rods, and electric shavers, all of which ultimately helped alleviate the company's financial difficulties. And, despite its problems, the company opened a number of new offices in South America.

The international trade barriers erected by many national governments during the 1930s in an attempt to protect domestic industries from foreign competition forced a major change in the structure of the company. As a result of the barriers, it became extremely difficult for Philips to supply its overseas marketing companies from its headquarters in Eindhoven. Management responded by establishing local production facilities in foreign countries.

Anton Philips retired in 1939 as president, though he remained active in a supervisory role as "president-commissaris." He was succeeded as president by his son-in-law, Frans Otten, while his son, Frits Philips, was made a director of the company.

The ominous political developments in Europe at the end of the 1930s prompted management to prepare for the worst. The North American Philips Corporation (NAPC) was founded in the United States in anticipation of the possible Nazi occupation of the Netherlands. When the Nazis invaded in May, 1940, Dutch defenses crumbled and the country capitulated within a week. The management of Philips followed the Dutch government into exile in England. Eventually, the top management made its way to the United States, where NAPC managed operations in nonoccupied countries for the duration of the war. Frits Philips, while attempting to maintain as much independence as possible from Nazi authorities, remained behind to manage operations in the Netherlands.

Philips' activities in the Netherlands suffered seriously as the war progressed. In 1942 and 1943 company factories were bombed by the Allies, and in 1944 the Nazis bombed them a final time as they withdrew. Thus the first order of business after the war ended was reconstruction. By the end of 1946, most of the buildings had been restored and production had returned to its prewar level.

The postwar years were a time of worldwide expansion for the company. The existing Eindhoven-centered management structure was revised to allow overseas operations more autonomy. National organizations, responsible for all financial, legal, and administrative matters, were created for each country in which Philips operated. Manufacturing policy, however, remained centralized, with various product divisions in Eindhoven responsible for overall development, production, and global distribution.

The research arm of the company remained a separate entity, expanding in the postwar years into an international organization with eight separate laboratories in Western Europe and the United States. Philips laboratories also made major technological contributions in electronics, including the development of new magnetic materials such as ferroxcube and ferroxdure, and work on transistors and integrated circuits.

The growth of the Common Market, established in 1958, presented the company with new opportunities. While factories had previously manufactured products solely for local markets, larger-scale production units encompassing the entire European Economic Community were now possible. With export to Common Market countries made easier, a new approach to product development was also necessary. Philips' factories were gradually integrated and centralized into International Production Centers—the backbone of its product divisions—as it made the transition from a market-orientated to a product-oriented business.

Frits Philips was named president in 1961 and managed the firm during a very prosperous decade, so that when, in 1971, Henk van Riemsdijk was appointed president, he took over a company riding the crest of 20 years of uninterrupted postwar success. The 1970s, however, were a difficult time, as competition from Asia cut into Philips' markets. Many of its smaller, less-profitable factories were closed as the company created more large-scale, efficient units. The company also continued its innovative efforts in recording, transmitting, and reproducing television pictures. In 1972, for example, the company introduced the first video cassette recorder to the market.

In 1977, Nico Rodenburg became president. Under Rodenburg sales grew steadily for most of the late 1970s and early 1980s, but increased profits did not follow. As Japanese companies, with their large, automated plants, flooded the market with inexpensive consumer electronics, Philips, with factories scattered throughout Europe and rising labor costs, saw its market share continue to decline.

The company's fortunes began to change with the appointment of Wisse Dekker as president and chairman of the board in January, 1982. Dekker initiated an ambitious restructuring program intended to control Philips' unwieldy bureaucracy and increasingly haphazard productivity. After only a few months, Dekker had closed more than a quarter of the company's European plants and had significantly pared down its global workforce.

Dekker also began to seek acquisitions and joint ventures designed to help concentrate the company's resources on its most profitable and fastest-growing product lines. Philips bought the lighting business of the American company Westinghouse outright, and acquired a 24.5% stake in Grundig, the largest West German consumer-electronics firm. In the United States, North American Philips consolidated the operations of its Magnavox consumer-electronics division with the Sylvania and Philco businesses it had already purchased from GTE Corporation, in 1981. Two years later, the company announced a 50-50 joint venture with AT&T to manufacture and market public-telephone equipment outside the United States, a deal it hoped would save millions in research-and-development costs.

When Cornelis van der Klugt assumed the presidency of Philips in 1986, he continued to seek acquisitions and joint ventures to improve the company's market position. Philips' research in solid-state lasers and microelectronics, resulting in advancements in the processing, storage, and transmission of images, sound, and data, has also helped regain part of the market lost to the Japanese. This research has produced innovative items such as the LaserVision optical disc, the compact disc, and optical telecommunications systems.

Van der Klugt reorganized the company, eliminating an entire layer of management and setting policy by committee. Van der Klugt has also made an effort to globalize the company's structure, improving profitability; in 1988 Philips' profits rose 29%. Rationalization of operations has also played a role in this restructuring. In 1987, Philips geared up for a major international push into consumer electronics, and targeted U.S. markets hoping to broaden its market share in TVs, VCRs, and CD players. In response to Japanese competition, van der Klugt began to focus Philips' resources more closely on electronics and to drop unrelated activities. Philips also began to share rising research-and-development costs with other large corporations such as AT&T, GEC, Siemens, and Whirlpool through joint ventures.

As Philips looks toward its centenary in 1991, the future appears especially bright. With a wide range of products in lighting, consumer electronics, domestic appliances, professional systems, and components, the company is poised to gain a larger share in each of these markets. No doubt Philips Laboratories, one of the most highly respected research facilities in the world, will continue to develop the items necessary for the company to maintain its position as a leader in the electronics industry.

Principal Subsidiaries: Nederlandse Philips Bedrijven BV; Philips International BV; Philips Export BV; Bauknecht Holdings BV; North American Philips Corporation.

THE PLESSEY COMPANY, PLC

Vicarage Lane
Ilford, Essex IG1 4AQ
United Kingdom
(01) 478–3040

Public Company
Incorporated: 1925 as the Plessey Co. Ltd.
Employees: 26,216
Sales: £1.65 billion (US$2.98 billion)
Stock Index: London

Plessey is one of Britain's largest electronics manufacturers. Primarily involved in the design and development of communications systems, it has in recent years been an excellent case study in corporate revivals. As late as 1979, Plessey was in such poor shape that it was touted as an industrial garage sale waiting to happen. But after a long search for an effective management strategy, Plessey finally launched an aggressive development program that drastically improved the company's prospects. By 1981, Plessey was growing at a record pace. A strong performance throughout the decade ended in the joint purchase of Plessey by the General Electric Company PLC, Plessey's foremost British rival, and Siemens, the German electronics giant, in the fall of 1989.

The company was founded in Ilford, Essex in 1917 by Allen Clark. Plessey was originally a manufacturer of small electronic components. Clark later transformed Plessey into a "jobbing shop," or secondary manufacturer; Plessey manufactured entire parts and components lines for other companies at a greatly reduced cost. Its products were primarily simple technology items, such as switches, connectors, sockets, relays, and even sheet metal. Clark was meticulous about every aspect of his operation, but because his business depended on spreads, he paid particular attention to minimizing unit costs. In addition, by selling only to other manufacturers, Plessey insulated itself from turbulent consumer markets.

The company prospered as the British electronics industry expanded, and was thrust into a period of high growth by World War II. In order to meet wartime production goals, Plessey maximized use of its plant space and added shifts. Although a small player in the wartime defense industry, the company's work on the development of advanced electronic devices for the war effort was the start of its intimate involvement with the armaments industry.

After the war, Clark was able to use Plessey's cost advantages to win new business and build market share despite Britain's difficult postwar economy. The company also found itself well positioned to build upon its wartime relationship with the government. Anchored by Plessey's traditional job-shop business, Clark was quick to exploit the opportunities that came with the nationalization of major industries by securing government contracts for Plessey.

Clark, who was knighted Sir Allen, died in 1961. He was succeeded by his two sons: John, who became president, and Michael, who took charge of financial affairs. In his last year Sir Allen had placed Plessey on a new course through the purchase of two large telephone electronics manufacturers. The acquisition of Automatic Telephone & Electric and of Ericsson Telephone doubled the company's size and made Plessey a major supplier to the government. But as the company evolved into an end seller, it became necessary to develop long-term planning capabilities—something Plessey had great difficulty achieving.

Plessey continued to grow by acquisition during the 1960s. It purchased the Ducon Group and the Rola Group, both in Australia, in 1963 and 1964, the Telegraph Condenser Company in 1965, and made its first American acquisition, the New Jersey-based Airborne Accessories Corporation, in 1968. In Britain, Plessey acquired the Painton Company (later Plessey Connectors) in 1969. Also that year, at the behest of the British Minister of Technology, Plessey acquired the numerical controls divisions of Airmec-AEI Ltd. and Ferranti Ltd., which were later merged to form Plessey Controls.

With each takeover, however, Plessey lost some of its focus; as it grew more diverse, it became harder to manage. John Clark recognized this problem early on, and oversaw the splitting of the company's operations into four divisions: telecommunications, components, dynamics, and electronics, to better match Plessey's diversified nature.

Continuing its streak of acquisitions, Plessey began buying into International Computers, Ltd. in 1967 in the belief that computer and communications technologies were converging. In 1968 Plessey attempted a takeover of English Electric, but was outbid by GEC. It did, however, succeed in taking over the heavy radar operations of Decca.

Plessey's profits grew 17% annually between 1966 and 1970. But this was mainly due to acquisitions, and cracks in the new management scheme were beginning to show. Decentralized management eroded Plessey's cohesion and left it directionless. John Clark, who had assumed responsibility for long term strategic planning, was frustrated by the company's lack of coordination. Michael Clark, in charge of day-to-day affairs, was overwhelmed as corporate headquarters lost control of line operations. In addition, the tough, hands-on management style both men had adopted from their father was inappropriate for the company at that stage, and resulted in increasingly high employee turnover rates.

In 1974 John Clark abandoned the four-division structure and replaced it with a system in which each of

Plessey's 24 businesses operated as an independent profit center. The 24 businesses were organized into nine divisions, each represented by a manager who reported directly to Michael Clark. This unorthodox rebuilding of the corporate structure from the bottom up bridged the gap between management and operation, and allowed the company to take advantage of unrealized synergies.

Plessey was soon back on the acquisition trail. In 1970 it purchased Alloys Unlimited, an American electronics company particularly strong in semiconductor packaging technologies, for $81 million. This addition reduced the company's reliance on increasingly unstable government business. It also made Plessey the only European company with such broad strength in the growing semiconductor market. Unfortunately, the semiconductor market crashed and Alloys began to lose money. At the same time, Plessey's troubled numerical controls and hydraulics divisions also started to post losses.

Instead of reforming its poorly-performing profit centers, Plessey made more strategic acquisitions. In December of 1970, the company took over Arco Societa Per L'Industria Elettrotecnica, an Italian components manufacturer. In 1971 Plessey, which already owned the stereo manufacturer Garrard Engineering, attempted to buy BSR, a turntable manufacturer. BSR, however, backed out when the monopolies commission began an inquiry. Already established in manufacturing telephone equipment, radar systems, stereos, and other products, Plessey began a major push into postal automation systems.

The reorganization process begun in the late 1960s—what Sir John called "subsidiarization"—was successful in most respects, but failed to distinguish between operations and policy responsibilities. This backed up both product development and marketing efforts and, once again, upper management became bogged down by too many decisions.

To remedy the situation, Plessey began to hire personnel and management experts away from competitors in 1974. The following year, the old product divisions were abandoned in favor of a system of "strategic business units." This system, devised by the American General Electric, created independent subsidiaries divided according to product lines and geography, and forced them to perform on their own merits. Strict budget discipline was enforced, and assets were controlled to prevent individual units from hoarding capital or manpower.

Although the scheme faced strong opposition from the directors of Sir Allen's era—"the Ilford Mafia"—it marked a turnaround at Plessey. Decentralization helped line managers to identify with company interests and stimulated plant and equipment modernization programs. It also identified terminally underperforming units for disposal. In 1979 alone, Plessey sold Garrard, Plessey Controls, a Portuguese subsidiary, and its 25% interest in International Computers, and phased out production on marginal lines such as burglar alarms, test equipment, and power rectifiers.

Plessey cleaned up its books by collecting debts more rigorously, and cut employees from 66,000 in 1976 to 47,000 by 1981. Investors' one remaining concern was Alloys, which never regained its market footing and was too component-oriented to be an asset in Plessey's systems-oriented future.

Lacking the capital to invest in the development of a major new product and unwilling to sell any other operations, Plessey next entered into a joint venture with its chief rival, GEC, with financing from British Telecom. The two companies formed a special group to develop a new digital switching device called System X. The venture was located at Plessey's Edge Lane facility in Liverpool, which had been nearly idle and losing money since 1976.

The first System X was delivered in early 1981. Despite joint development, the two companies manufactured the devices in competition to avoid accusations of monopoly. Initial sales to the Post Office (which runs the British telephone system) guaranteed a stable market for System X in the near term, but both companies expected further profits from exports promoted by British Telecom.

In 1985 GEC expressed an interest in purchasing Plessey. A merger would have eliminated costly dual System X production and created a stronger company by combining Plessey's research capabilities with GEC's development strengths. Roundly opposed as anti-competitive, however, the merger eventually broke down.

Even amid the merger speculation, Plessey was preoccupied with its 1982 acquisition of the American company Stromberg-Carlson, a telecom manufacturer, from United Technologies. Plessey bought Stromberg-Carlson for its access to the American market. The company had been a money-loser, suffering from many of the same problems Plessey had overcome. Plessey was able to apply the lessons it had learned, and by 1985 Stromberg-Carlson was profitable.

In 1988 Plessey agreed to merge its international telecom operations with GEC for better international competitiveness against Siemens, NEC, Ericsson, and a host of American companies. Because the companies maintained their domestic competition, there was no opposition from the British government.

But this comfortable arrangement with GEC was short-lived. Late in 1988 GEC and Siemens jointly bid to take over Plessey for £1.7 billion. Plessey tried to block the bid, arguing that the takeover was in violation of Article 85 of the Treaty of Rome. In addition, the bid violated an earlier agreement made by GEC and Siemens stipulating that neither company would seek to acquire more than 15% of Plessey. But a general lack of sympathy from the European Commission and Britain's Monopolies and Mergers Commission, together with weaknesses in Article 85, made Plessey's defense quite difficult. After a fierce ten-month-long battle, Plessey finally succumbed in September, 1989 to a £2 billion bid from the two companies.

Principal Subsidiaries: Plessey UK Limited; Hoskins Group PLC (94%); Plessey Incorporated (U.S.A.); Plessey Electronic Systems Ltd.; Leigh Instruments Ltd.; Plessey SpA (Italy); Plessey Pacific Pty. Ltd. (Australia); Electronique et Systemes SA (France); Plessey South Africa Limited (74%); Plessey GmbH (West Germany); Hoskyns Group PLC.

RACAL

RACAL ELECTRONICS PLC

Western Road, Bracknell
Berkshire RG12 1RG
United Kingdom
(344) 481-222

Public Company
Incorporated: 1950
Employees: 33,702
Sales: £1.6 billion (US$2.7 billion)
Stock Index: London

Racal Electronics PLC is a multinational manufacturer and service provider in telecommunications, security, data communications, defense radar and avionics, marine and energy electronics, radio communications, and specialized electronics. A conglomerate of some 150 medium-sized, autonomous companies, Racal was named "best-managed company" between 1976 and 1985 by Britain's prestigious *Management Today* magazine.

Racal operates through a network of subsidiaries in England, the United States, Europe, and Asia. Twenty of these subsidiaries are in North America. Overall, sales outside of the United Kingdom account for more than 54% of Racal's annual revenues.

Raymond Brown and Calder Cunningham founded Racal as a two-man consulting firm in 1950. Seven years passed before Racal marketed its first proprietary product: a high-frequency radio receiver. Cunningham died the following year, in 1958, but the company's momentum continued. Racal went public in 1961. Brown guided Racal into the next decade, laying the groundwork for the company's future as a manufacturer of specialized radio equipment. At the time, most military radios were made according to Western specifications. Racal realized that countries with warm climates didn't need radios that could operate in freezing temperature. Company researchers visited equatorial countries, crawled around in trenches, and came up with a lighter, cheaper radio that gave Racal a competitive edge in the international market years before its first major British acquisition. The "Squadcal," a "tactical military man-pack radio," entered production in 1966.

That same year, Brown left his job as chairman to establish a sales department for the Ministry of Defence. Brown passed the company's reins to Ernest Harrison, who started with Racal as an auditor soon after its founding and became its chief accountant on his way to becoming chairman and CEO.

Under Harrison Racal experienced its greatest period of growth and acquisition. In 1969, Harrison orchestrated a merger between Racal and British Communications Corporation, a move that strengthened Racal's tactical radio communications business. That same year, pretax profits exceeded £1 million for the first time.

The late 1960s also marked Racal's entry into the data communications industry. In 1969, Racal entered a partnership with Milgo Electronic Corporation of the United States, creating Racal-Milgo Ltd. and paving the way for a strengthened presence in the U.S.

In the years that followed, the Racal-Milgo partnership prospered. Racal too prospered overall, reaching sales of $140 million in the mid-1970s.

In 1977 Racal found itself in the middle of a bidding war for Milgo. The fight came as a surprise, since Racal's bidding adversary, Applied Digital Data Systems Inc., a manufacturer of computer terminals, was considerably smaller than Racal. In January, 1977 Applied offered one and a half shares of its own common stock for every preferred share of Milgo stock, translating to a bid of $24 a share. Racal countered with a bid of $26.

Belief in the solidity of Applied's stock and its impressive growth record kept bidding going. By mid-February, the bidding hit $37 a share. According to *Business Week* analysts, Racal continually underestimated Applied's exchange offers, believing cash would always outweigh other types of bids. Racal eventually won the closely-contested battle, for an estimated $60 million, in part because it seemed the friendlier suitor.

In the months that followed, however, Racal dragged Milgo through an executive shakeout. Five top Milgo executives resigned, allowing Racal to staff Milgo with its own people.

Next, Racal acquired Vadic Corporation, a maker of low- and medium-speed modems, for $10 million, as a part of its aggressive push into data communications. Racal also set up two American firms on its own.

The Milgo and Vadic purchases increased U.S. sales tremendously, from $5 million to an estimated $355 million between 1976 and 1982.

In 1980, Racal bought the British firm Decca Ltd. Analysts at the time believed that Decca would give Racal too many businesses "irrelevant" to its major activities. But the company pursued Decca for its expertise in radar, microwave frequency radios, and electronic warfare systems. Racal believed it had too many holes in its military offerings to satisfy the many governments, especially in the Third World, who wanted a single supplier for all their needs. With Decca, Racal acquired defense radar, avionics, and marine and survey electronics capabilities.

Another bidding contest, this time with rival British electronics firm General Electric, hiked Decca's sale price from $150 million to $250 million. The purchase, however, was looked upon as a victory because Racal beat the richer, more powerful General Electric. In the summer of the following year, 1981, Harrison was knighted. The company proclaimed the news to its employees by sending parachutists to land in the middle of a company picnic.

The knighting of Harrison was only confirmation of Racal's success: operating profits and sales were growing as fast as 25%. Racal's growth continued until the time of its next big acquisition: the £180 million purchase of Chubb and Son PLC, a security firm with sales in the U.S., Canada, and elsewhere. The purchase of Chubb made security Racal's single largest activity; a year after the purchase, security products accounted for 28% of sales.

In 1985, Racal began to suffer from a shakeout in the information technology industry. A recession in the American data communications industry dealt a severe blow: Racal-Milgo and Racal-Vadic, once accounting for 40% of total revenues, totaled only 27% at mid year. At the time of its greatest slump, Racal took another risk—one that already promises tremendous success.

Racal's gamble was to set up a cellular telephone network in Britain. Start-up costs for Vodafone, as the network is called, cut deeply into profits in 1985, but two years later Racal reported a third of its profits from the cellular network.

Part of Vodafone's success was its market: gadget-minded Britain has more computers and video recorders per household than anywhere else in Europe. The size and population density of Britain were also factors in its success. But a more important reason was the increased competition among equipment suppliers. Japanese and American firms began entering the supply market, and as a result, equipment costs went down. Both Vodafone and its competing British cellular network stepped up development of their operations, to reach 90% of England's population. By mid-1988, Racal had more than 170,000 subscribers calling each other from their cars or briefcases, and new customers were signing on at a rate of 15,000 a month.

The stunning success of Vodafone made the recently struggling electronics firm a turnaround candidate and a prime target for takeover. In the spring of 1988, trading on Racal stock began to increase, signaling an imminent takeover bid.

In response, Racal put 20% of Vodafone up for sale. Racal officials billed the move as a way to raise money for expansion of its other businesses, but it made a very effective takeover hedge, sending Racal shares soaring 35%.

Short of any takeover, Racal's management succession is clear. David Elsbury, one of three deputy managing directors, was appointed deputy chief executive in 1983. Ten years younger than Harrison, Elsbury has been with Racal over 30 years. With him, a new generation of management has moved into senior positions.

"We don't leave things Friday night to do Monday morning," one Racal executive told the *New York Times*. "We will work over the weekend or all night if necessary, and that's very un-British." This successful management style, together with Racal's ability to find and fill unexploited niches, promises to keep the company at the forefront of the electronics industry.

Principal Subsidiaries: UK:- Decca Ltd; Ablex Audio Video Ltd; Decca Radio and Television Ltd; Decca Survey Overseas Ltd; Fibre Form Ltd; Racal-Decca Ltd; Racal Avionics Ltd; Racal-Decca Advanced Development Ltd; Racal-Decca Marine Navigation Ltd; Racal Defence Radar Ltd; Racal Defence Electonics (Radar) Ltd; Racal Defence Radar and Displays Ltd; Racal Marine Group Ltd; Racal Marine Electronics Ltd; Racal-MESL Ltd (Scotland); Racal Marine Systems Ltd; Racal Survey Ltd; Racal Survey China Ltd; Racal Survey (UK) Ltd; Racal-Decca Service Ltd; Weyrad (Electronics) Ltd; Racal-Chubb Ltd; Albert Marston & Co Ltd; Chubb & Son's Lock & Safe Company Ltd; Chubb Security Installations Ltd; Chubb Alarms Ltd; Chubb Wardens Ltd; Chubb Fire Security Ltd; Racal Panorama Ltd; Chubb International Ltd; Chubb (N.I.) Ltd; C E Marshall (Wolverhampton) Ltd; Josiah Parkes & Sons Ltd; Racal-Chubb Security Systems Ltd; Union Locks Ltd; I & F Willenhall Ltd; Racal Acoustics Ltd; Racal Antennas Ltd; Racal Automation Ltd; Racal Communications Ltd; Racal Communications Systems Ltd; Racal-Comsec Ltd; Racal-Dana Instruments Ltd; Racal Engineering Ltd; Racal Finance Ltd; Racal Group Services Ltd; Racal-Guardall (Scotland) Ltd; Racal-Guardall (Sales) Ltd; Racal Imaging Systems Ltd; Racal International Ltd; Racal Management Services Ltd; Racal Microelectronic Systems Ltd; Racal-Milgo Ltd; Racal Oil and Gas Ltd; Racal Properties Ltd; Racal Recorders Ltd; Racal-Redac Ltd; Racal-Redac UK Ltd; Racal Research Ltd; Racal Safety Ltd; Racal-Tacticom Ltd; British Communications Corporation Ltd; Racal-Mobilcal Ltd; Racal-Tacticom Systems Ltd; Racal Telecom PLC; Racal Cellular Ltd; Racal-Vodac Ltd; Racal-Vodafone Ltd; Racal-Vodata Ltd; Racal Training Services Ltd.; H.S. Control Systems Ltd.; Chubb Electronics Ltd.; Chubb Fire Ltd.; Chubb National Foam Ltd.; Racal-Redac Group Ltd.; Racal-Vodapage Ltd.

RAYTHEON COMPANY

141 Spring Street
Lexington, Massachusetts 02173
U.S.A.
(617) 862–6600

Public Company
Incorporated: 1922 as American Appliance Company
Employees: 77,000
Sales: $8.2 billion
Stock Index: New York

Raytheon is one of the largest and most diversified electronics companies in the United States. While it conducts approximately half of its business with the United States government, it also manufactures such consumer items as Amana microwave ovens, Speed Queen washers and dryers, and Caloric cooking ranges. Raytheon's historical area of expertise, however, remains its strongest—radar technology for the military.

Raytheon was founded in 1922 when a civil engineer named Laurence Marshall was introduced to an inventor named Charles G. Smith. Marshall proposed a business partnership with Smith after hearing that he had developed a new method for refrigeration using compressed gases. Marshall raised $25,000 in capital from his former World War I comrades and incorporated the partnership in Cambridge, Massachusetts as the American Appliance Company.

Marshall and Smith never developed their refrigeration technologies for the market but instead shifted their attention to vacuum tubes and other electronic devices. In 1924 Marshall made a three-month tour of the United States to study the pattern of growth in the electronics market. Having concluded that consumer demand for radios was about to increase dramatically, Marshall negotiated the purchase of patents for the S-tube, a gas-filled rectifier that converted alternating current (AC) to the direct current (DC) used in radio sets (Charles Smith himself had developed the S-tube some years earlier while he worked for the American Research and Development Corporation).

In 1925, shortly before S-tube production began, Smith and Marshall decided to change the company's name to Raytheon Incorporated. Contrary to a once widely held idea that *raytheon* is Greek for "god of life", the name in fact has no meaning, but was chosen for its modern sound. By 1926, Raytheon had become a major manufacturer of tube rectifiers and generated $321,000 in profit on sales of $1 million.

Virtually all the tubes produced by Raytheon were used in radio sets whose design patents were held by RCA. In 1927 RCA altered its licensing agreements with radio manufacturers to stipulate that the radios could be built only with new rectifier tubes (called Radiotrons) manufactured by RCA. Raytheon was, in effect, denied access to its markets. The company was forced to switch to the production of radio-receiving tubes, a field in which more than 100 companies were engaged in fierce competition.

Marshall's response to operating in this difficult environment was to diversify. Raytheon acquired Delta Manufacturing, a producer of transformers, power equipment, and electronic auto parts. Profits resulting from new products were immediately put back into research and development to improve products, particularly in industrial electronics and microwave communications.

In 1940 U.S. President Franklin Roosevelt and British Prime Minister Winston Churchill authorized the joint development of new radar technologies by American and British institutions. Through the Radiation Laboratory at the Massachusetts Institute of Technology, Raytheon was chosen to develop the British magnetron, a high-frequency radar power tube. In June, 1941 Raytheon won a contract to deliver 100 radar systems for navy ships and patrol boats. Shortly after the Japanese attack on Pearl Harbor, the U.S. Navy appropriated $2 million for the construction of a large new factory for Raytheon in Waltham, Massachusetts.

Workers produced 100 magnetrons a day until plant manager Percy Spencer discovered a method, using punch presses, to raise production to more than 2,500 a day. By the end of the war, Raytheon magnetrons accounted for about half the one million magnetrons produced during the war. Raytheon also offered complete radar installations, with the help of subcontractors, and developed tubes for the VT radio fuse, a device that detonated fired shells when it sensed they were near solid objects.

Raytheon was fortunate to be involved in a high-growth area of defense industry. When the war ended, companies specializing in high-technology military systems suffered less from cuts in the postwar defense budget than aircraft or heavy-vehicle manufacturers, or shipbuilders. Largely as a result of the war, Raytheon emerged as a profitable and influential, but still financially vulnerable, electronics company.

During the spring of 1945 Raytheon's management formulated plans to acquire several other electronics firms. As part of a strategy to consolidate independent component manufacturers into one company, in April the company purchased Belmont Electronics for $4.6 million. Belmont, located in Chicago, was a major consumer of Raytheon tubes and was developing a television for the commercial market. That October, Raytheon acquired Russell Electronics for $1.1 million and entered merger negotiations with the Submarine Signal Company. Sub-Sig, as the company was known, was founded in Boston in 1901 as a manufacturer of maritime safety equipment, including a depth sounder called the fathometer. Sub-Sig manufactured a variety of sonar equipment during the war and, like Belmont, was a major Raytheon customer. When the two companies agreed to merge on May 31, 1946, it was decided that Sub-Sig would specialize in sonar devices and that Raytheon would continue to develop new radar systems.

Despite Raytheon's strengthened position as a result of the mergers, the company faced severe competition in both the sonar and radar markets from companies like General Electric, RCA, Westinghouse Electric, and Sperry. Belmont, which planned to bring its television to market in late 1948, suffered a crippling strike during the summer and, as a result, lost much of its projected Christmas business. Unstable price conditions the following spring created further losses from which the subsidiary was largely unable to recuperate.

Laurence Marshall, though a superb engineer, was generally regarded as a poor manager. His inability to effect positive changes within the company led him to resign as president in February, 1948. The following December he resigned as CEO, but he remained chairman of the board until May, 1950, when he resigned after failing to gain support for a proposed merger with International Telephone & Telegraph. Percy Spencer and Charles Adams, a former financial advisor who joined Raytheon in 1938, assumed Marshall's responsibilities.

The sudden resumption of military orders after the outbreak of the Korean War in June, 1950 greatly benefited Raytheon, as defense department contracts enabled the company to develop new technologies with initially low profitability. Raytheon's advanced research center, called Lab 16, was designed to develop the Sparrow air-to-air and Hawk surface-to-air, or SAM, missiles. Through Lab 16 (later renamed the missile & radar division), Raytheon became a partner in Selenia, a joint venture with the Italian firms Finmeccanica and Italian Società Edison that was established to develop new SAM technologies. Raytheon's association with Selenia afforded it an opportunity to work with the Italian rocket scientist Carlo Calosi.

Raytheon's Belmont operation was re-formed in 1954, but two years later all radio and television operations were sold to the Admiral Corporation. Raytheon continued, however, to develop new appliances such as the Radarange microwave oven. In 1956 Charles Adams hired Harold S. Geneen, a highly innovative and dynamic manager. Three years later, however, Geneen left Raytheon to become chief executive of ITT. Richard E. Krafve (who once headed the Ford Motor Company's Edsel project) enjoyed only a short tenure as Geneen's successor; he disagreed frequently with Adams and was unable to gain the respect of engineers.

In 1956 and 1957, Raytheon and Minneapolis-Honeywell jointly operated a computer company called Datamatic. Raytheon soon sold its interest to Honeywell when Datamatic failed to compete effectively against IBM. Raytheon's joint-venture projects with Italian companies continued to expand, however, enhancing both the company's expertise and reputation in the field of attack missiles. Dyer Brainerd Holmes, a former director of the American manned-space-flight program, joined Raytheon in 1963 to develop a new SAM missile using phased-array radar guidance. Holmes and a talented engineer named Tom Phillips (who had succeeded Krafve as president) assumed more specialized control over Raytheon's growing missile operations as managers such as Percy Spencer retired.

Raytheon's top managers began to recognize weaknesses in the company's organizational structure perhaps as early as 1962; Raytheon, they decided, had become too dependent on government contracts. So in 1964 Raytheon conceived a careful reorganization that aimed to diversify the company's operations in a series of five-year plans. Raytheon acquired Packard-Bell's computer operations and a number of small electronics firms. In 1965, Raytheon purchased Amana Refrigeration and the memory core division of Philco. By 1967, Raytheon had absorbed a number of educational-services companies including Dage-Bell and D.C. Heath & Company; a geological-survey company called the Seismograph Service Corporation; and the Caloric Corporation, a manufacturer of gas ranges and appliances.

Raytheon's association with Calosi, the director of Selenia, became strained in 1967. Although an excellent engineer, Carlo Calosi, like Laurence Marshall, was a poor manager. Raytheon's directors concluded that its Italian partners were unwilling to reform the operations of Selenia and Elsi (a jointly operated electronics firm). They voted to sell Raytheon's share of the companies to its partners and end their association with Calosi. Nevertheless, the defense department selected Raytheon as the prime contractor for the new SAM-D missile.

Raytheon's diversification continued with the acquisition of two construction-engineering firms: the Badger Company and United Engineers & Constructors. The goal of reducing Raytheon's proportion of sales to the government from 85% to 50% was achieved on schedule in 1970. But, while Raytheon's sales continued to rise, profits began to lag. After a series of heated discussions between Tom Phillips and Charles Adams, it was decided that, with the exception of D.C. Heath, Raytheon should dispense with its marginally performing educational-services units. In 1972, after several more smaller acquisitions, Raytheon purchased Iowa Manufacturing, a producer of road-building equipment.

When Charles Adams retired in 1975, Tom Phillips was named Raytheon's new chairman and Brainerd Holmes was promoted to president. Adams had been Phillips' most vocal (if amicable) opponent within Raytheon. But the five-year plans that were created to promote consensus between the two were retained even after Adams left.

Raytheon's financial performance during the mid-1970s was impressive; from 1973 to 1978 sales and profits grew at annual rates of 15% and 26% respectively. The company's retained earnings were placed in high-yielding money-market accounts until needed to finance acquisitions.

In 1977 Phillips tried to acquire Falcon Seaboard, an energy-resources company involved primarily in strip mining coal, but withdrew the offer when favorable terms could not be reached. Instead, Phillips entered into negotiations to acquire Beech Aircraft, a leading manufacturer of single- and twin-engine aircraft. Raytheon acquired Beech in February of 1980 for $800 million. Shortly before it bought Beech, Raytheon also purchased the laundry products and kitchen appliance divisions of McGraw-Edison, which included the popular Speed Queen brand name.

At this time Raytheon's business with the government consisted mainly of radar systems and the Hawk, Sparrow, Patriot, and Sidewinder missiles, all of which totaled less than 40% of Raytheon's sales. Raytheon was now more widely exposed to commercial computer and consumer markets, but these markets had become unexpectedly competitive, leading Raytheon management to reconsider its trend of moving away from stable military contracts.

Raytheon's Data Systems division, created in 1971 through the merger of the company's information-processing and display units, established a small market by manufacturing terminals for airline reservation systems. Raytheon failed, however, to integrate Data Systems effectively with a word-processing subsidiary called Lexitron, which it acquired in 1978. As the computer-products market expanded, Data Systems found itself unable to compete. After mounting losses, the division was sold to Telex in 1984.

In January, 1986 Raytheon acquired the Yeargin Construction Company, a builder of electrical and chemical plants, and the following October it acquired the Stearns Catalytic World Corporation, an industrial plant maintenance company. As with all of the company's other subsidiaries, Raytheon preserved the independence of Yeargin and Stearns and retained their individual staffs. Raytheon offers its new subsidiaries only the managerial assistance they require and the financial resources necessary for the implementation of new operating strategies.

Raytheon is responsible for a number of radar and microwave technologies, with applications ranging from microwave ovens to the B-1B bomber and the American air traffic–control system. Raytheon also had a substantial role in the construction of the Washington, D.C., Metro, one of the finest and most modern commuter rail systems in the world. Raytheon is thoroughly diversified, and has attained many of the goals it set forth over the years through successive five-year plans.

When Brainerd Holmes retired on May 31, 1986 as he reached the traditional retirement age of 65, he was succeeded as president by R. Gene Shelley, who himself retired in July, 1989 and was replaced by Dennis J. Picard. Tom Phillips remained chairman and chief executive of Raytheon, and Charles Adams continued to serve on the board of directors.The modern complexion of Raytheon is largely to the credit of these two men.

Principal Subsidiaries: Raytheon Marine Co.; Switchcraft, Inc.; Cossor Electronics Ltd. (England); Data Logic Ltd. (England); Electrical Installations Ltd. (England); Raytheon Canada Ltd.; TAG Semiconductors Ltd. (Switzerland); Beech Aircraft Corp.; The Badger Company, Inc.; Seismograph Service Corp.; United Engineers & Constructors, Inc.; Amana Refrigeration, Inc.; Caloric Corp.; Speed Queen Co.; D.C. Heath & Company; Raytheon Service Co.; Cedarapids, Inc.

Further Reading: Scott, Otto J. *The Creative Ordeal: The Story of Raytheon*, New York, Atheneum, 1974.

RCA CORPORATION

General Electric Company
3135 Easton Turnpike
Fairfield, Connecticut 06431
U.S.A.
(203) 373–2211

Incorporated: 1919 as the Radio Corporation of America
Absorbed by the General Electric Company

At the end of World War I, the Marconi Wireless Telegraph Company of America was the only company in the United States that was equipped to operate transatlantic radio and telegraph communications. The United States government found this unacceptable since the Marconi Wireless Company of America was entirely owned by a foreign company—the British Marconi Company. At the prompting of Franklin D. Roosevelt, who was undersecretary of the navy at the time, General Electric (GE) formed a privately owned corporation to acquire the assets of American Marconi from British Marconi. On October 17, 1919, the Radio Corporation of America (RCA) was incorporated and within a month had acquired those assets.

General Electric was the major shareholder of RCA and the two companies cross licensed their patents on long distance transmission equipment. A year later American Telephone & Telegraph (AT&T) bought into RCA and also cross licensed patents with the new company. Transoceanic radio service began that same year with a major station in New Jersey broadcasting to England, France, Germany, Norway, Japan, and Hawaii. The world's first licensed radio station also began transmitting in 1920. This station, KDKA of Pittsburgh, was owned by the Westinghouse Company.

In 1921, Westinghouse, too, joined the ranks of asset holders of RCA; in exchange for selling Westinghouse radio equipment to the public, RCA was permitted access to Westinghouse patents. RCA entered the broadcasting field in 1921 with its transmission of the Dempsey-Carpentier fight in Jersey City, New Jersey. Using a transmitter borrowed from the navy. The company began full-time radio broadcasting shortly afterwards when it became an equal partner with Westinghouse in station WJZ of Newark, New Jersey.

RCA continued to expand its transoceanic communications operations and opened two more broadcasting stations, in New York and Washington, D.C. In 1924 RCA transmitted the first radio-photo, a portrait of Secretary of State Charles Hughes. This transmission was made from New York to London and back to New York, where it was recorded and marked a pioneering development in the history of television. Two years later, in 1926, RCA formed the National Broadcasting Company (NBC). NBC controlled the radio stations owned by RCA, produced radio programs, and marketed these programs to other radio stations, activities which constituted the first radio network. David Sarnoff, the leading figure at RCA during these formative years, had envisioned the radio network as a form of public service, free from advertising, but this proved financially impossible and sponsors were solicited. At this time RCA began selling components manufactured by the Victor Talking Machine Company of Camden, New Jersey.

Product innovation abounded in this era. In 1927 RCA introduced the first Radiotron tube. This radio tube was the first to operate on alternating current, thereby eliminating the need for batteries—a crucial step in the development of mass-produced electric radios. A year later General Electric perfected a system of recording sound on film, which it called the RCA Photophone. This system was superior to a competing system called Vitaphone developed by Western Electric and Warner Brothers, but movie theaters were already adopting the Vitaphone system by the time the RCA product was ready for marketing. The two systems were incompatitble, so RCA's only hope of entering the market was to equip a competing theater chain with the Photophone system. With the aid of Joseph P. Kennedy, RCA Photophone, Inc. was merged into two Kennedy-controlled companies—the Film Booking Office of America (FBO), a movie production company, and the Keith-Albee-Orpheum theater chain. RCA owned a substantial interest in this creation, the Radio-Keith-Orpheum (RKO), which provided an initial market for the RCA Photophone.

In the following year RCA purchased the Victor Talking Machine Company. Sarnoff had always wanted to market a radio and phonograph housed in the same box, but the phonograph companies were suspicious of radio, fearing the loss of their market. So Sarnoff decided to purchase a phonograph company. Several years of negotiation preceded RCA's 1929 purchase of Victor. RCA owned 50% of Victor, General Electric owned 30%, and Westinghouse owned the remainder. RCA formed the RCA-Victor Company (and the RCA Radiotron Company) only after it had acquired tube-manufacturing assets from General Electric and Westinghouse. The trademark of the Victor company, a dog staring at an old phonograph above the caption "His Master's Voice," was also purchased by RCA and became one of the most famous trademarks in marketing history.

David Sarnoff became president of RCA in 1930, the year legal problems concerning the company's monopoly status began. The Justice Department filed an antitrust suit against RCA seeking to strip RCA of all the patents it had gained. The battle ended two years later; RCA retained all of its patents but General Electric, AT&T, and Westinghouse were forced to sell their interests in the company. The General Electric association was remembered in NBC's trademark three-note chime—G,E,C—which stands for General Electric company.

By this time RCA's various businesses included broadcasting, communications, marine radio, manufacturing and merchandising, and a radio school. The year after it became an independent company, RCA moved into its new headquarters—the RCA Building in Rockefeller Center in New York City.

Though the company managed to move during the height of the Depression, this period was as difficult for RCA as it was for any other company. However, while most companies were reducing expenditure across the board, Sarnoff, though he reduced expenditures elsewhere, greatly expanded RCA's high-technology research department during the Depression. Sarnoff believed that for RCA to retain its position in the electronics field, continued technological research was essential.

One of the technological advances RCA investigated during the Depression was television. RCA made the first public television broadcast at the New York World's Fair in 1939, when David Sarnoff dedicated the RCA pavilion before TV cameras, and the world's first public television service was unveiled at the fair. This experimental system only covered the metropolitan area of New York City; the RCA Victor television console manufactured at this time stood over four feet high yet had only a four-inch screen.

The Federal Communications Commission (FCC) approved RCA's television system in the spring of 1941, but World War II halted further development of commercial television. RCA was also affected by a 1941 Federal Communications Commission investigation that decided that NBC, which operated two networks (the red and the blue) was a monopoly. The FCC declared that no company could own more than one network, and RCA was ordered to sell one. Two years later the less-profitable blue network was sold to Edward Noble and became the American Broadcasting Company (ABC).

RCA profited immensely from the World War II, when it began its long association with the Defense Department. Due to the scarcity of raw materials for television development, RCA switched production to military electronic equipment such as tubes for radio, radar, and microwave communications.

After the war, RCA resumed the production of radios and commercial tubes and turned to its television research once again. The NBC radio network expanded into television, and in 1946 the first television network linked NBC facilities in New York City, Washington, Philadelphia, and Schenectady, New York. Television became commercially available that same year when RCA introduced the world's first mass-produced television set, which sold for $375.

The entire electronics industry underwent a fundamental change with the birth of the transistor in 1948. RCA quickly entered the semiconductor field and developed new types of transistors. The company eventually applied this new technology to military and commercial electronic products, data-processing systems, and aerospace production.

The progression from black-and-white to color television occurred swiftly, but color programming did not become available to the public until 1954. RCA developed a color system which was compatible with the existing black-and-white TVs (a color set could receive black-and-white broadcasts and a black-and-white set could receive color broadcasts). The company's main competitor, Columbia Broadcasting System (CBS), also developed a color system. Although the CBS system produced a higher-quality picture, it was not compatible with existing sets. The Federal Communications Commission approved only the CBS system since the relatively small number of television sets in American homes made incompatibility a fairly insignificant consideration. RCA appealed the decision and worked on the quality of its system. In 1953 the FCC reversed its decision, since RCA had greatly improved its picture quality and the number of sets in American homes had increased significantly, making compatibility a more important consideration.

During the late 1950s RCA ventured into satellite equipment. In December, 1957 the first successful satellite radio-relay equipment was launched into space aboard an Atlas missile. RCA produced the radio equipment used in this experimental attempt at global communications. In the following years RCA developed a number of satellites for the National Aeronautics and Space Agency (NASA). One such project, completed in 1962, involved six weather satellites and a ground-based complex for televised observation. The following year the Relay communications satellite was put into orbit. This satellite transmitted TV pictures between the United States and Europe and linked Latin America to the United States by radio.

RCA also planned and coordinated the construction of the Ballistic Missile Early Warning System, a project that involved almost 3,000 subcontracted companies. This radar defense system stretches across the Canadian Arctic and is intended to warn the United States of impending missile attack from the Soviet Union.

During the 1960s, color television became a staple of life in the United States; by 1966 sales of color television sets industrywide rose to $3 billion a year. During this decade RCA continued production of home television sets, and came to dominate camera industry with its best-selling TK-44 camera.

RCA was also involved in the major space projects of the 1960s. The first live pictures to be transmitted from outer space to earth were recorded by a miniature RCA camera carried aboard the Apollo 7 flight, and the first words to be broadcast to the earth from the moon were transmitted by an RCA-manufactured radio backpack carried by Neil Armstrong.

At the end of the decade the Radio Corporation of America officially changed its name to the RCA Corporation. A change in trademark went along with this change in name—the circular logo with lighting bolt was replaced by a simpler three-letter block design.

In 1971 David Sarnoff died. He had been president of RCA since 1930 and chairman since 1947; though he resigned as CEO in 1966, he remained chairman until his death. His reign proved a difficult one to follow.

Sarnoff's son Robert succeeded him as head of the company, remaining until 1975, when the board asked for his resignation. Robert Sarnoff was succeeded by Anthony L. Conrad, who was forced to resign almost immediately when the board learned that he had not filed personal income tax reports. In 1976 Edgar H. Griffiths took over. Described as a "numbers man" who was primarily concerned with quarterly profits, Griffiths began divesting RCA of some of its diverse subsidiaries, which by then included Banquet frozen foods, Hertz rental cars, and the publisher Random House. During the following ten-year period, RCA divested itself of roughly one subsidiary a year. However, under Griffith's direction RCA also purchased CIT Financial, a financial services conglomerate which caused the company to lose its A credit rating. Shortly afterward, in 1981, the board ousted Griffiths and asked RCA board-member Thornton F. Bradshaw, president of the Atlantic Richfield Company, to take over.

Bradshaw made Robert R. Frederick, formerly of General Electric, president of RCA. Both men favored decentralized management and the delegation of authority. By 1985, all of RCA's diversified subsidiaries had been sold, except for Coronet Industries, the carpet manufacturer.

In June of 1986, the giant General Electric Company acquired RCA for $6.4 billion in cash, and the company ceased to exist. The Justice Department, which had forced GE to divest its interest in RCA more than 50 years before, approved the merger with the requirements that GE sell RCA's vidicon tube business and five radio stations controlled by NBC. Since RCA's record company, carpet business, and insurance firm did not fit into GE's long-term business strategy, they were all sold in 1986, for more than $1.3 billion. GE kept the RCA brand name, and made NBC a relatively autonomous division of GE; the rest of RCA's businesses were combined with GE's operations.

Further Reading: Dreher, Carl. *Sarnoff: An American Success*, New York, Quadrangle/New York Times, 1977; *RCA: A Historical Perspective*, Princeton, New Jersey, RCA, 1985.

SANYO ELECTRIC COMPANY, LTD.

2–18, Keihan-Hondori
Moriguchi City
Osaka Prefecture 570
Japan
(06) 991–1181

Public Company
Incorporated: 1950 as Sanyo Electric Works
Employees: 34,000
Sales: ¥987.54 billion (US$7.9 billion)
Stock Index: Tokyo Nagoya Osaka Amsterdam Zurich Frankfurt Basel Geneva Paris

The Sanyo Electric Company was born in the shadow of the giant Matsushita Electric, one of Japan's largest industrial institutions. Sanyo's founder, Toshio Iue, was the brother-in-law of Konosuke Matsushita and an original partner in Matsushita Electric. Shortly after World War II, the occupation authority ordered Matsushita broken up into two smaller companies as part of its industrial decentralization policy. Several of Matsushita's operations were turned over to Iue, who set up his own company to produce and export bicycle lamp generators. Dreaming of one day having 100 factories around the world, Iue called his company Sanyo, a somewhat generic name that means "three oceans." On April 1, 1950, after paying off its unsecured loans, the company was incorporated as the Sanyo Electric Works.

Unlike Sony, NEC, or JVC, Sanyo has traditionally relied heavily on existing technologies in product development, concentrating on marketing and price competitiveness. After entering the American market as a "low end" manufacturer, Sanyo now produces some of the highest quality products coming out of Japan.

The dynamic economic atmosphere in Japan after the Korean War raised personal incomes and stimulated consumer demand. Sanyo grew modestly at first, offering only a limited line of simple electrical appliances. In order to boost its sales through greater name recognition, Iue asked Matsushita for permission to use that company's brand name, National. With only minimal benefit from Matsushita's broad marketing network, Sanyo widened its product line to include radios, tape recorders, and even televisions. The company later began marketing products under its own name through independent retailers.

Toshio Iue believed in a unique management philosophy called the "white paper" method. Similar to the process by which parliamentary governments announce general policy goals and invite criticism or discussion, the white paper system encouraged a consensus approach to management.

As the Japanese economy began to grow even faster during the mid-1950s, consumers, long deprived of even simple amenities, expressed increasing demand for household appliances. Sanyo was well established in the market and had great success in simple-technology items such as washing machines, air conditioners, and improved radios. Iue did not regard other electrical manufacturers as his competition. Instead, he saw consumers—the ones who dictate the market—as competitors. This philosophy generated a very high creative awareness that forced him to anticipate new markets.

Sanyo created a separate affiliate in 1959 called Tokyo Sanyo Electric which, Iue hoped, would make it easier for the company to respond to market demand and to raise capital. Although Sanyo eventually only maintained a 20% interest in Tokyo Sanyo, the two companies frequently engaged in bouts of constructive competition, what Iue himself described as a "friendly rivalry."

In pursuit of his goal of running a world-wide company, Iue began to export Sanyo bike lamps to underdeveloped countries. He reasoned that as these countries developed, Sanyo's sales volume would grow accordingly, much as it had done in Japan. Most of these countries, however, lacked fundamental industrial bases, and while Sanyo outsold its European competitors, the growth he expected in these economies never materialized. In 1961, Sanyo established its first overseas factory in Hong Kong. Sanyo also entered into an agreement to market transistor radios in the United States with the American antenna manufacturer Channel Master in the 1950s. This arrangement was later expanded to include Sanyo televisions, tape recorders, and some home appliances.

In 1962 Sanyo marketed a revolutionary new type of battery called the Cadnica. Named for its cadmium and nickel components, the Cadnica was especially durable and also rechargeable. The battery became very popular at the high end of the market and represented a new and profitable product line.

During the mid-1960s Japan maintained such strong price competitiveness in certain market segments—especially textiles and consumer appliances—that these segments became the primary source of the country's export-led growth. In 1965 Sanyo became a leading exporter, deriving an ever larger percentage of its profits from the United States.

Two years later, at the end of 1967, Toshio Iue relinquished the company presidency to his younger brother Yuro Iue. While the elder Iue continued to serve as chairman, Yuro made some important changes in the company's direction. He led the development of new divisions outside of the traditional consumer products markets, and also placed a greater emphasis on Sanyo's internationalization.

Toshio Iue died in July, 1969, leaving Yuro Iue in a dual role as president and chairman. At the end of 1970, he turned over the presidency to another brother, Kaoru Iue.

Kaoru introduced a new sales plan to Sanyo, known as the "one-third marketing strategy." Under this scheme, Sanyo would attempt to diversify its manufacturing capacity geographically into three equal sectors: domestic manufacture for the domestic market, domestic manufacture for foreign markets, and foreign manufacture for additional foreign markets. Less a means to Toshio's "100 factories" than a method to reduce risks in the international trade structure, Kaoru's "one third" plan nevertheless contributed to the balanced growth of the company on a global basis.

In 1973 the American company Emerson Electric asked Sanyo to help revive its subsidiary, the Fisher Corporation. Fisher, acquired by Emerson in 1965, had moved its manufacturing operations to Hong Kong due to high labor costs, but continued to suffer from quality problems. The cooperation between Emerson and Sanyo continued until May, 1975, when Sanyo, which still had no American manufacturing affiliate, engineered the transfer of several Fisher product lines to Japan and rehabilitated a Fisher speaker plant at Milroy, Pennsylvania. As 50–50 partners, Sanyo and Emerson were unable to resolve numerous differences of opinion in regard to Fisher. Finally, in May, 1977 Emerson agreed to sell its share in Fisher to Sanyo. That year the new, profitable Fisher Corporation moved its headquarters from New York to Los Angeles.

Sanyo realized tremendous growth during the 1970s; sales grew from $71.4 million in 1972 to $855 million in 1978. Subsequent growth, particularly in the video sector, was slowed by the ill-fated decision to adopt Sony's Betamax VCR format instead of Matsushita's VHS. While initially successful, the Betamax has since become all but obsolete. Sanyo avoided further damage by later switching to the VHS format.

During the same decade it became increasingly evident that in order to remain competitive in world electronics, Sanyo would have to move more decisively into high-technology markets. This process was begun in the mid-1970s, but pursued in earnest only in the late 1970s, when a variety of products and integrated systems, ranging from LED televisions to home solar energy systems, were introduced commercially. Several manufacturing facilities and sales organizations were established in Europe and China, and a research institute was inaugurated at Tsukuba.

By 1986, in light of the increased industrial concentration of competitors and the rising value of the yen, the sibling rivalry between Sanyo Electric and Tokyo Sanyo had become uneconomic. It was decided at that time to merge the two companies to form the "New Sanyo Electric." Similarly, the following year, Sanyo's American affiliate merged with Fisher to become Sanyo Fisher (U.S.A.) Corporation. The mergers made the entire organization more efficient, but also resulted in the departure of certain key executives, most notably Howard Ladd, a Fisher executive who first introduced the Sanyo name to America in the early 1970s.

Kaoru Iue resigned suddenly in 1986 as a demonstration of responsibility for the deaths of customers who died using faulty Sanyo kerosene heaters. He was succeeded by Toshio Iue's son, Satoshi Iue, and subsequently died two years later.

Sanyo's new president promised to expand the company's overseas production capacity. Already the largest Japanese manufacturer outside of Japan, Sanyo builds refrigerators in Kenya, portable stereos in Zimbabwe, air conditioners in Singapore, and operates a television factory in Argentina's desolate Tierra del Fuego. Despite labor problems at a large plant in Arkansas, Sanyo intends to expand in the United States. To that end, in 1988 Sanyo created Sanyo North America Corporation, with 24 subsidiaries and affiliates.

Somewhat behind its competitors in the high-technology field, Sanyo nevertheless remains highly profitable in consumer electronics. Its current restructuring, intended to improve the company's standing in high-technology areas, will not be completed for several years. A more immediate high-growth area will likely come in office automation products, a market where Sanyo's strong consumer sales network may be deployed easily and quickly.

Principal Subsidiaries: Sanyo Electric Trading Co., Ltd.; Sanyo Electric Credit Co., Ltd.; Sanyo Electric Tokki Co., Ltd.; Tottori Sanyo Electric Co., Ltd.; Sanyo Manufacturing Corporation; Sanyo Fisher (USA) Corporation.

SCHNEIDER S.A.

4, rue de Longchamp
75116 Paris
France
(1) 4505–7800

Public Company
Incorporated: 1966
Employees: 75,000
Sales: Ffr40.49 billion (US$6.68 billion)
Stock Index: Paris

The consolidation of industries in France has taken two general forms: those by government decree, and those by management initiative. In the 1950s and 1960s, basic industries like oil, steel, and aircraft production were concentrated at government behest to preserve them as strategic assets. Indeed, many of these industries were owned by the state. The French electronics industry has recently undergone similar rationalization programs, but in the 1980s such programs have increasingly been effected by private managements.

Schneider, one of France's oldest firms, is also one of the most important members of this industry. As a public company relatively free of government intervention, Schneider is profit oriented and internationally competitive.

Schneider was originally founded in 1782 to manufacture industrial machinery at Le Creusot. The company was taken over by two Schneider brothers in 1836, at the dawn of the industrial age in France. By 1838 Schneider had built the first French steam locomotive and it later expanded into building other large, complex mechanical devices. By the late 1800s it had become involved in a wide variety of heavy industries, including steel manufacture.

Schneider gained recognition as a major French company during World War I. It survived nationalization efforts during France's three-year popular-front government of 1936–1939 and was called upon to help mobilize French forces in the months before World War II. Overrun during the war by German troops, Schneider's factories were either closed or redirected to support the German war effort.

By the time the war ended in 1945, many of Schneider's factories had been bombed or were obsolete. Charles Schneider undertook a recovery effort in which the company was reorganized into a holding company. In 1949 Schneider's industrial interests were transferred to three operating subsidiaries in civil and electrical engineering, manufacturing, and construction.

With the benefit of government direction and regulation, Schneider entered the 1960s fully recovered from war damage and well established in its various operations. In 1963, however, another family industrial group called Empain acquired a large financial stake in Schneider. Empain, founded in 1881 by Edouard Empain, was a pioneer in rail transit. The company installed the Paris Metro system in 1900 and later formed a successful rail-construction firm called Electrorail.

While the Empain and Schneider operating companies remained largely separate, the holding company conducted a series of further acquisitions that greatly expanded the subsidiaries' involvement in basic industries. The two operating companies grew increasingly close between 1966 and 1969, when they were merged into single group called Empain-Schneider.

The new company's assets remained divided between Schneider S.A. (incorporated in France) and Electrorail (incorporated in Belgium), but they shared the same management structure and president, Baron Edouard Empain. By 1971 Empain-Schneider had become one of the most important industrial groups in the world, with interests in virtually every sector of heavy industry and infrastructure.

In 1972 Empain-Schneider took over the civil- and electrical-engineering group Spie-Batignolles. With interests in nuclear power, construction, and oil platforms, Spie-Batignolles was formed in 1968 by the merger of the Societe de Construction des Batignolles (founded in 1846) and the Societe Parisienne pour l'Industrie Electrique (founded in 1900).

Three years later Empain-Schneider acquired control of another vital French company, the industrial electrical products supplier Merlin Gerin. Founded in Grenoble in 1920 by Paul-Louis Merlin and Gaston Gerin, the company was a leader in industrial circuit breakers and switching gear.

A third major industrial group controlled by Empain-Schneider was Creusot-Loire, a heavy-equipment and special-steels manufacturer. It was also a leading builder of nuclear power stations through its subsidiaries Framatome and Novatome, and was heavily involved in turnkey projects abroad. By the late 1970s Empain-Schneider had developed a fourth major subsidiary, an energy and communications products group called Jeumont-Schneider. This company consisted of existing Schneider enterprises and several others controlled by the Jeumont-Industrie industrial group.

In 1980, however, the Empain family divested itself of its interest in Empain-Schneider, forcing the reorganization of the company and reducing Empain's involvement in the group from 45% to about 5% of turnover. A more serious restructuring took place the following year when a Socialist government under President Francois Mitterand came to power.

The government sought to nationalize major companies in an effort to better coordinate industry with its national objectives. Under the new program the first sector to be nationalized was banking; the state took control of all banks with more than $220 million in assets. This included Schneider's banking subsidiary, the Banque de l'Union Européenne.

Between 1981 and 1986 Schneider undertook a restructuring program whose objective was to transform the company from a complex family financial trust with many diverse interests into a leading international industrial group. As part of this effort, Schneider divested its machine-tool, heavy-equipment, shipbuilding, and steel operations, and later sold its lower-margin rail transport, nuclear-power, and private-telecommunications businesses.

The sectors that remained under the new simplified structure included construction of electric-power plants and power-distribution systems, building and civil-engineering projects, industrial infrastructure, and a wide variety of industrial electronics systems. Schneider's primary operating subsidiaries remained Spie-Batignolles, with 55% of total revenue; Merlin Gerin, with 31%; and Jeumont-Schneider, with 14% in 1987. Reflecting Schneider's position in international markets, 41% of the company's revenues were generated through foreign projects.

During the difficult restructuring process, the company's chairman, Didier Pineau-Valencienne, gained a reputation for waging controversial corporate battles. In 1984 he failed to win government support for his plan to restructure Schneider's troubled capital-goods subsidiary, Creusot-Loire. After declaring the subsidiary bankrupt, Pineau-Valencienne was roundly accused of mismanagement and incompetence.

Undaunted, Pineau-Valencienne carried out the remainder of his restructuring plan and sold off those parts of the company he considered unrelated to Schneider's core operations. In the process, Schneider accumulated a large cash reserve that Pineau-Valencienne earmarked for strategic acquisitions.

The first of those was for the industrial-automation company Telemecanique, which Pineau-Valencienne had hoped to merge with Merlin-Gerin. The takeover battle, launched in February, 1988, involved many bitter and complicated legal and labor disputes, and finally government intervention. By July Schneider had won permission to acquire Telemecanique, but in the process had inspired a national debate on hostile takeovers.

Pineau-Valencienne has successfully remolded Schneider into a more efficient and responsive industrial group and given the company new credibility as an equal player with competitors such as Westinghouse, Rockwell, and Mitsubishi. But though the groundwork has been laid, Schneider's ability to compete over the long run has not been proven.

Nonetheless, Schneider is in an excellent position to realize strong growth and progressive consolidation of its chosen markets. The company is now neither so large nor so diverse as to detract from its ability to undertake more-efficient, coordinated strategies. Schneider is sure to benefit from improved focus and mobility and, given its interest in foreign markets, remain a world leader in industrial electronics and construction and in civil projects.

Principal Subsidiaries: Spie Batignolles (62.6%); Merlin Gerin (50.1%); Jeumont Schneider; La Chaleassiere; Paramer.

SHARP

SHARP CORPORATION

22–22, Nagaike-cho
Abeno-ku
Osaka 545
Japan
(06) 621–1221

Public Company
Incorporated: 1935 as Hayakawa Metal Industrial Laboratory
Employees: 60,000
Sales: ¥992.67 billion (US$7.94 billion)
Stock Index: Tokyo Osaka Nagoya Paris Luxembourg Zurich Basel Geneva

The Sharp Corporation is one of the largest and oldest Japanese consumer goods manufacturers. Founded on a business creed reminiscent of the ancient trading houses—"Sincerity and Creativity"—and built largely on the hard work and determination of one man, Sharp is in many ways Japan's most "traditional" modern electronics manufacturer. Despite its decidedly Japanese character, Sharp remains an outward-looking, international corporation, as dedicated in each of its foreign markets to assimilation as to success.

The company was founded as a small metal works in Osaka in 1912 by an inventor and tinkerer named Tokuji Hayakawa. After three years in business, earning a modest income from gadgets and repair jobs, Hayakawa engineered a mechanical pencil he called the "Ever-Sharp." Consisting of a retractable graphite lead in a metal rod, the Ever-Sharp pencil won patents in Japan, and even the United States. Demand for this simple and durable instrument was immense. To facilitate greater production, Hayakawa first adopted an assembly line and later moved to a larger factory.

Hayakawa's business, as well as his life, were ruined on September 1, 1923. On that day, the Great Kanto Earthquake caused a fire which destroyed his factory and took the lives of his wife and children. Hayakawa endured severe depression; it was a year before he re-established his factory. The Hayakawa Metal Industrial Laboratory, as the company was called, resumed production of the Ever-Sharp pencil, but Hayakawa became interested in manufacturing a new product: radios.

The first crystal radio sets were imported into Japan from the United States in the early 1920s. Hearing one for the first time, Hayakama immediately became convinced of its potential. With little understanding of radios, or even electricity, he set out to develop Japan's first domestically-produced crystal radio. After only three months of study and experimentation, Hayakawa succeeded in receiving a signal from the broadcasting service which had begun programming—to a very small audience—only a few months before, in 1925.

The radio entered mass production shortly afterward, and sold so well that facilities had to be expanded. Crystal radios, however, are passive receivers whose range is limited. Hayakawa felt that powered radios, capable of amplifying signals, should be the subject of further development. While competitors continued to develop better crystal sets, Hayakawa began work on an AC vacuum tube model. When the company introduced a commercial model, the Sharp Dyne, in 1929, Sharp was firmly established as Japan's leading radio manufacturer. The company expanded greatly in the following years, necessitating its reorganization into a corporation in 1935.

The laboratory, for all its success, was not a leader in a wide range of technologies; it led only in a narrow section of the market. In addition, the company did not have the benefit of financial backing from the *zaibatsu* conglomerates or the government. It was, in the realm of the national modernization effort, an outsider. This may have been its saving grace, however, as the government had become dominated by a group of right-wing imperialists within the military. Whatever their political opinions, the leaders of Japan's largest corporations were compelled to cooperate with the militarists in their quest to establish Japanese supremacy in Asia. Hayakawa, on the other hand, was for the most part left alone.

During World War II, Hayakawa and his company were forced to produce devices for the military, and even to restructure, as new industrial laws intended to concentrate industrial capacity were passed. Renamed Hayakawa Electrical Industries in 1942, the company emerged from the war damaged but not destroyed. While other industrialists were purged from public life for their support of the militarists, Hayakawa was permitted to remain in business. His biggest concerns were rebuilding his company and surviving Japan's postwar recession.

By 1950 more than 80 of Hayakawa's competitors were bankrupt. But Hayakawa's officials personally guaranteed the company's liabilities when the company suffered a critical drop in sales, and Hayakawa Electric was able to obtain the cooperation of major underwriters until the first major expansion in the Japanese economy occurred in 1952.

Hayakawa considered television, a field that had not yet proved commercially successful, a highly promising new area. The company began development of an experimental TV set in 1951, even before plans had been made to begin broadcasting in Japan. Two years later, when television broadcasting started, Hayakawa Electric introduced its first commercial television set under the brand name "Sharp," in honor of the pencil. Hayakawa's good timing was essential in allowing the company to establish and maintain a significant and profitable market share.

The company started development of a color television

in the mid-1950s. In 1960, with the advent of color broadcasting in Japan, Hayakawa introduced a line of color sets. This was followed in 1962 by a commercial microwave oven, and in 1964 by a desk-top calculator. The Compet calculator, which looked like an adding machine, was the first in the world to use transistors. In 1966 the microwave oven received a rotating plate and calculators shrank with the use of integrated circuits.

Hayakawa recognized the great sales potential of the United States; a sales subsidiary was established in 1962. It served the dual purpose of facilitating sales and observing the market. By the late 1960s, the Sharp brand name had become well-established in North America. Sales in the United States provided the company with a large and increasing portion of its income. In addition, subsidiaries were established in West Germany in 1968 and Britain in 1969.

Hayakawa Electric made two major breakthroughs in 1969. That year the company introduced the Extra Large Scale Integration calculator, a device now reduced to the size of a paperback book. The other new product was the gallium arsenide light-emitting diode (LED)—in effect, a tiny computer light. Like the radio and television before them, improved versions of both the calculator and LED were subsequently introduced in future years.

Tokuji Hayakawa retired from the day-to-day operations of his company in 1970, assuming the title of chairman. He was replaced as president by Akira Saeki, a former executive director. Saeki oversaw an important reorganization of the company intended to establish a new corporate identity and unify product development efforts. That year, Hayakawa Electric Industries also adopted its new name: Sharp Corporation.

Saeki, who witnessed the Apollo moon landing while in America, decided that the company's future efforts should center on the development of semiconductors, the electronic components which had made the lunar mission possible. He initiated construction of a massive research complex called the Advanced Development and Planning Center. The project was a significant investment for Sharp, since its budget was already seriously strained by the construction of an exhibit for Expo '70. Nevertheless construction was begun on a 55-acre research complex in Tenri, Nara Prefecture.

During the 1970s, Sharp consolidated its position in consumer goods by broadening its product line to include refrigerators, washers, portable stereos, copiers, desk-top computers, video equipment, and "Walkman"-type headsets. Profit generated from consumer goods sales was largely invested in the Tenri facility. When completed, the research complex cost ¥7.5 billion, representing about 70% of Sharp's capitalization.

Perhaps the most important product to come out of the Tenri research facility was the Very Large Scale Integration (VLSI) factory automation system. Building upon existing integration technologies, VLSI production lines enabled manufacturers to reduce defects and raise productivity through the use of industrial robots and other mechanical apparatus.

In an effort to head off impending protectionist trade legislation, Sharp built new factories in its largest overseas markets, principally the United States. The company's decision to build a plant in Memphis, Tennessee was criticized at first. RCA had closed a plant in Memphis in 1966, favoring production in Taiwan. Sharp maintained that RCA had merely suffered from inept management and went ahead with the plant. By pushing its American suppliers for parts with zero defects and incorporating the Japanese concept of full worker involvement, the Memphis plant proved highly successful.

President Saeki retired in 1986, continuing to serve the company as an advisor. He was succeeded by Haruo Tsuji, a "numbers man" with an exemplary record in middle and upper management.

Sharp operates 12 research laboratories and 34 plants in 27 countries. Its employees are equally divided between Japan and foreign countries. Through its 18 divisions, Sharp has diversified into a wide range of consumer products and established itself as an originator of new industrial technologies. Indeed, Sharp has placed great emphasis on the development of artificial intelligence. In consumer electronics and appliances, the company has engaged in a measured effort to move upmarket, offering more expensive, but higher-quality, products. On this strong base, Sharp is in an excellent position to maintain its current place as a major force in world electronics for many years.

Principal Subsidiaries: Sharp Electronics Corporation (United States); Sharp Manufacturing Company of America; Sharp Microelectronics Technology Inc. (United States); Hycom Inc. (United States); Sharp Electronics of Canada Ltd.; Sharp Electronics (Europe) GmbH (West Germany); Sharp Electronics (Svenska) AB (Sweden); Sharp Electronics (U.K.) Ltd.; Sharp Precision Manufacturing (U.K.) Ltd.; Sharp Electronics GmbH (Austria); Sharp Electronics (Schweiz) AG (Switzerland); Sharp Electronica Espana (S.A.); Sharp Corporation of Australia Pty. Ltd.; Sharp Manufacturing France S.A.; Sharp-Roxy Sales (Singapore) Pte. Ltd.; Sharp Electronics (Singapore) Pte. Ltd.; Sharp Electronics (Taiwan) Company Ltd.; Sharp Appliances (Thailand) Ltd.; Sharp-Roxy (Hong Kong) Ltd.

SIEMENS

SIEMENS A.G.

Wittelsbacherplatz 2
D-8000 Munich 2
Federal Republic of Germany
(89) 2 34 0

Public Company
Incorporated: 1966
Employees: 365,000
Sales: DM61.2 billion (US$34.51 billion)
Stock Index: Berlin Hamburg Dusseldorf Munich Brussels Paris Zurich Basel Geneva Amsterdam Vienna

Siemens A.G. is an electrical manufacturing giant and West Germany's leading technology concern. George Williamson of *Fortune* once wrote that "second is best" might as well be its motto, referring to the company's history of achieving success through well-engineered refinements of other people's inventions. But opportunism is not the only interesting facet of Siemen's history, which is also a story of a long family tradition and intimate involvement with some of the most important events of the 19th and 20th centuries.

Siemens & Halske was founded in Berlin in 1847 by Werner Siemens and J. G. Halske to manufacture and install telegraphic systems. Siemens, a former artillery officer in the Prussian army and an engineer who already owned a profitable patent for electroplating, was the driving force behind the company and remained so for the rest of his life. The company received its first major commission in 1848, when it contracted to build a telegraph link between Berlin and Frankfurt.

Construction of telegraph systems boomed in the mid-19th century and Siemens & Halske was well equipped to take advantage of the situation. In 1853, it received a commission to build an extensive telegraph system in Russia. Upon its completion, the company opened an office in St. Petersburg under the direction of Werner Siemens' brother Carl Siemens. In 1857 Siemens & Halske helped develop the first successful deep-sea telegraphic cable. This led to the tansformation of the London office into an independent company under the direction of Wilhelm Siemens, another of Werner's brothers, the next year. By 1865 the company's English operations had become substantial. Its name was changed to Siemens Brothers, still under the direction of Wilhelm, who was eventually knighted as Sir William Siemens.

In 1867 Siemens Brothers received a contract for an 11,000-kilometer telegraph line from London to Calcutta, which it completed in 1870. In 1871 it linked London and Teheran by telegraph. In 1874 Siemens Brothers launched its own cable-laying ship, the *Faraday*, which William Siemens codesigned. The next year, it laid the first direct transatlantic cable from Ireland to the United States.

In 1877 Alexander Graham Bell's new telephones reached Berlin for the first time. Immediately grasping their worth, Werner Siemens quickly patented an improved version of the device and began production. In the next decade, Siemens & Halske also developed and began manufacturing electrical-lighting and power-generating equipment after Werner Siemens discovered the dynamo-electric principle in 1866..

In 1888 Werner Siemens was ennobled by the Germ kaiser for his achievements. Two years later he retire and his company became a limited partnership share by his sons Arnold and Wilhelm and his brother Carl. Werner Siemens died in 1892. But the House of Siemens continued to prosper. That same year, Siemens & Halske built a power station at Erding in Bavaria and founded an American subsidiary, Siemens & Halske Electric Company, in Chicago. The latter, however, closed in 1904. In 1895 Wilhelm Conrad Roentgen discovered the X-ray, and the very next year Siemens & Halske owned the first patent for an X-ray tube. In 1897 Siemens & Halske decided to go public and reorganized with Carl Heinrich, now Carl von Siemens after being ennobled by the Russian czar in 1895, as chairman of the supervisory board. He retired after seven years in that post and was succeeded by his nephew Arnold.

Siemens & Halske remained busy as the 19th century gave way to the 20th. In 1903 it established Siemens-Schuckertwerke GmbH, a subsidiary devoted to electric power engineering. In 1909 Siemens & Halske developed an automatic telephone exchange serving 2,500 customers in Munich. But when World War I broke out, orders for civilian electrical equipment slowed considerably and the company began production of communications devices for the military. Siemens & Halske also produced explosives, gun locks for rifles, and, later in the war, aircraft engines.

But perhaps the company's most successful contribution to the German war effort was the fire control system it produced for the navy's battlecruisers, which proved its worth at the Battle of Jutland in 1916. There, the battlecruiser squadron of the High Seas Fleet met its British counterpart for the only time during the war. While the main fleets fought to a draw, the German battlecruisers used their superior gunnery equipment to batter their opponents, sinking two British ships and severely damaging several others. It was a highlight for the German navy in a battle from which it otherwise won no advantage.

On the balance, however, the war hurt Siemens & Halske badly. The Bolshevik government that seized power in Russia in 1917 also seized the assets of the company's St. Petersburg subsidiary, which were worth about 50 million rubles. Siemens Brothers was taken over by the British government in 1915 and sold to British interests the next year. The company was not returned to the Siemens family after the armistice, although it retained their name for business purposes. Siemens Brothers eventually re-established links to its old parent and its general manager, Dr. Henry Wright, even became a member of the Siemens & Halske supervisory board in 1929. But Carl Friedrich von Siemens, a son of Werner's who had headed the British subsidiary for six years and had many English friends, was shocked by these events. "They have stolen our name," he was wont to lament.

Arnold von Siemens died in 1918, before the end of the war. He was succeeded by his brother Wilhelm, who died the next year. Carl Friedrich then became chairman. Despite the precarious state of the German economy in the 1920s and a bias among foreign customers against doing business with a German company, the company continued to make its mark in electrical manufacturing. In 1923 it started producing radio receivers for the consumer market. In the same year, recognizing the growing importance of Japan as an industrial power and not wishing to concede that market to General Electric and Westinghouse, Siemens & Halske set up a Tokyo subsidiary, Fusi Denk, later known as Fuji Electric. In 1925 Siemens began construction of a power station on the Shannon River in Ireland, and in 1927 the company began work on another hydroelectric power station for the Soviet government, near Zaporozhe. Back home in Germany, Siemens & Halske financed and produced a railway network in suburban Berlin that began operation in 1928. By the end of the decade, the company was accounting for one-third of the German electrical manufacturing industry's production and nearly the same proportion of its employees.

Siemens & Halske was bloodied by the Great Depression, but it survived. It was forced to halve its dividend in the early 1930s and lay off employees in large numbers, but remained on relatively sound financial footing until the Nazi government's rearmament project helped revive its fortunes in 1935. During the remainder of the decade, Siemens & Halske manufactured a wide range of equipment for all of Germany's armed services. One of its most significant technical contributions at this time, the development of an automatic-pilot system for airplanes, was the result of a project initiated for the Luftwaffe.

The company's activities during this time are difficult to evaluate. One the one hand, according to family historian Georg Siemens, Carl Friedrich von Siemens was repelled by the Nazis' anti-Semitism from the start and only grew more disgusted with their goals and methods as time went on. Just before his death in 1941, he wrote to an assistant: ". . . my work no longer brings me satisfaction or joy. Those who were once proud that their work was devoted to the task of serving progress and humanity, can now only be sad that the results of their work merely serve the evil of destruction. Whenever I start to think, 'why,' I should prefer to creep into a corner, so as not to see or hear any more." And yet there is no question that Siemens & Halske benefited from German rearmament during the late 1930s. Certainly the company did little or nothing to hinder Nazi militarism.

Carl Friedrich went into partial retirement in 1940 and appointed Hermann von Siemens, Arnold's eldest son, to succeed him. By this time, Siemens & Halske was devoting virtually all of its manufacturing capacity to military orders and would do so for the duration of the war. In 1944 it helped develop and manufacture the V-2 rocket. Its factories also suffered substantial damage from Allied bombing raids. And after the Soviet army conquered Berlin in 1945, Russian occupation authorities completely dismantled the Siemensstadt factory works and corporate headquarters.

In 1945 Hermann von Siemens, who had also been a director of Deutsche Bank, was arrested by American occupation authorities and interned for two years. There is also no question that the company employed slave labor during the war. Georg Siemens points out that every major German industrial concern used forced labor because of manpower shortages caused by the war, and asserts that Siemens & Halske treated its laborers better than most companies. But in 1947, allegations surfaced that three of the firm's directors had been active in importing slave laborers from occupied countries. In addition, testimony from death camp survivors also surfaced at this time that Siemans had supplied gas chamber equipment to the concentration camps. These allegations were never proven, however, and the company denies them both.

Hermann von Siemens resumed the chairmanship upon his release in 1948. The company had been devastated by the war and required years of rebuilding to get back on its feet. Its corporate headquarters were relocated to Munich in 1949. By the early 1950s, Siemens & Halske was once again producing railroad, medical, telephone, and power-generating equipment, as well as consumer-electronics products. In 1954 it established an American subsidiary in New York, Siemens Inc. Its first product sold to the American market was an electron microscope. In the mid-1950s Siemens & Halske entered the burgeoning fields of data processing and nuclear power. It introduced its first mainframe computer in 1955 and its first nuclear reactor went into service in 1959 at Munich-Garching.

Hermann von Siemens retired in 1956 and was succeeded by Ernst von Siemens, Carl Friedrich's only son. In the mid-1960s, Siemens & Halske technology went to Mars after the company developed a disc-seal triode that was used in the transmitter of the American space probe Mariner IV. In 1965 it scored another coup when its 03 high-speed passenger train went into service with the German Federal Railway. And in 1968, it began constructing a nuclear power station at Atucha, Argentina, the first such facility in South America.

The company underwent a major reorganization in 1966, bringing all of its subsidiaries directly under control of the parent company and reincorporating as Siemens A.G. By the end of the decade, worldwide sales had reached DM10 billion; in 1970 they reached DM12.6 billion. In 1971 Ernst von Siemens retired and his cousin Peter succeeded him as chairman.

The 1970s were prosperous years for Siemens. Despite

a slower worldwide economy that cut into customer orders in some areas and forced the company to cut its workforce, sales grew to DM20.7 billion and net profits to DM606 million in 1976. When the summer Olympic Games came to Munich in 1972, Siemens was its first official supplier of telecommunications and data-processing equipment. In 1977 the company entered into a joint venture with the American engineering firm Allis-Chalmers, called Siemens-Allis Inc., to market turbine generators in the United States. In fact, Siemens' status as an electrical manufacturer rose to the point that *Fortune* wrote in 1978 that it had "replaced Westinghouse in General Electric's demonology." Siemens had replaced Westinghouse as the world's number-two electrical manufacturing concern, ranking "as GE's major worldwide competitor in everything from motors and switchgear to generators and nuclear reactors." It had also raised its share of the West German mainframe computer market to 21%, cutting sharply into IBM's position as the Bundesrepublik's leading mainframe supplier.

In the late 1970s, Siemens stumbled when it initiated a research-and-development effort in microcircuit technology, against the advice of a consulting firm employed by the West German government to counsel the nation's industrial companies. It was thought that Siemens' slow and methodical practices would render it unable to keep up with the small, quick Silicon Valley firms that were breaking ground in this area. Nonetheless, Siemens A.G., with its research-and-development budget of $1 billion (one-eight of all the money spent by West German industry on research at the time), eventually entered into a joint venture with Dutch rival Philips to develop advanced microcircuits. None of the company's efforts on this front have been successful, however. Its components division lost money through 1987 and Siemens was forced to buy chips from Toshiba to meet its commitments until its own became available in early 1988.

In 1981 Peter von Siemens retired and was succeeded by Bernhard Plettner. For the first time, the Siemens family relinquished day-to-day control over the company it had founded over a century ago. But the 67-year-old Plettner had worked for Siemens for all of his adult life, and Peter von Siemens felt that his own son, at the age of 44, was still too young and inexperienced for the top job.

Under Plettner and new CEO Karlheinz Kaske, Siemens embarked on an expensive and ambitious program of acquisitions and research and development to try to make itself into a world leader in high-technology. Its effort to develop its own microchips was a part of that effort. So was the acquisition of IBM's struggling Rolm Systems subsidiary in 1988. That deal cost Siemens $844 million, but gave control of the third-largest supplier of PBX telephone switching equipment in North America. Siemens' strategy during the 1980s was designed to pay off over the long term and produced few tangible benefits in the short run. The company spent $24 billion on both research-and-development and acquisitions between 1983 and 1988, and the tremendous cash drain produced both a significant drop in earnings and a cut in the dividend in 1988. As one analyst told *Business Week* in 1988, "Siemens will be an interesting story in the 1990s." And Heribald Närger, who succeeded the retiring Bernhard Plettner as chairman in 1988, will have to see that the company actually writes that story.

It appears that direct control of Siemens A.G. has finally slipped away from the family whose name it bears. The only family member who appears in the 1988 annual report is Ernst von Siemens, Werner's 84-year-old grandson, whose place on the supervisory board is purely honorary. But the history of Siemens is still essentially that of the Siemens family. Werner von Siemens, scion of a family that made a marginal living farming wheat on the slopes of the Harz mountains, once wrote in a letter to his brother Carl Heinrich: "From my young days it has always been my ambition to found a business of international repute." In this he certainly succeeded.

Principal Subidiaries: Osram GmbH; Dr.-Ing. Rudolf Hell GmbH; Vacuumschmelze GmbH; Reaktor-Brennelement Union GmbH, (60%); Interatom GmbH; Heimann GmbH; Rofin-Sinar Laser GmbH; NRG Nuklearrohr-Gesellschaft mbH; Siemens Finanzierungsgesellschaft für Informationstechnik mbH; Sietec Siemens-Systemtechnik und Portfolio GmbH & Co. OHG; Siemensstadt-Grundstücksverwaltung GmbH & Co. OHG; Siemens Beteiligungen AG, (Switzerland); Siemens S.A., (Brussels); ATEA N.V., Herentals (Belgium) (80%); Siemens A/S, Ballerup (Denmark); Siemens Osakeyhtiö, (Finland); Siemens S.A.,St. Denis (France); Bendix Electronics S.A., (France); Siemens A.E., Elektrotechnische Projekte und Erzeugnisse, (Greece); Siemens Ltd., Sunbury-on-Thames (U.K.); Siemens Ltd., (Ireland); Siemens Telecomunicazioni S.p.A., Cologno Monzese (Italy) (65%); Siemens S.p.A., (Italy); Siemens Nederland N.V., (the Netherlands); Siemens A/S, (Norway); Siemens AG Österreich, (Austria) (74%); Siemens S.A., (Portugal); Siemens-Elema AB, Solna (Sweden); Siemens AB, (Sweden); Siemens-Albis AG, (Switzerland) (78%); Siemens S.A., (Spain) (93%); Etmas-Elektrik Tesisat ve Mühendislik A.S., (Turkey) (51%); Türk Siemens Kablo ve Elektrik Sanayii A.S., (Turkey) (55%); Osram S.A., Molsheim (France); Osram Società Riunite Osram Edison-Clerici S.p.A., (Italy); Osram S.A., (Spain) (90%); Siemens Corporation (USA); Siemens-Bendix Automotive Electronics L.P. (USA); Siemens-Bendix Automotive Electronics Ltd. (Canada); Siemens Electric Ltd., Pointe Claire (Canada); Equitel S.A., (Argentina); Siemens S.A.I.C.F.l.yM. (Argentina); Siemens S.A., (Brazil) (84%); Siemens S.A. (Colombia) (79%); Siemens S.A. de C.V. (Mexico); Siemens S.A. (Venezuela); Osram Argentina S.A.C.I. (66%); Osram do Brasil-Companhia de lâmpadas Elétrocas S.A. (Brazil); Osram S.A. de C.V., Naucalpan (Mexico);Siemens Western Finance N.V.,Willemstad (Curacao); Siemens Ltd. (India) (51%); Siemens K.K. (Japan) (83%); Siemens Components (Advanced Technology) Sdn. Bhd. (Malaysia); Siemens Pakistan Engineering Co.Ltd. (Pakistan) (64%); Siemens Components (Pte) Ltd. (Singapore); Taicom Systems Ltd. (Taiwan) (55%); Siemens Ltd. (South Africa) (52%); Siemens Ltd. (Australia).

Further Reading: Siemens, Georg (trans. A. F. Rodger and Lawrence N. Hole). *History of the House of Siemens*, Munich, Karl Alber, 1957; Scott J.D. *Siemens Brothers, 1858–1958*, Weidenfeld and Nicolson, 1959; Siemens, Werner von. *Inventor and Entrepreneur: Recollections of Werner von Siemens*, London, Lund Humphries, 1966.

SONY CORPORATION

6–7–35, Kita-Shinagawa
Shinagawa-ku
Tokyo 141
Japan
(03) 448–2111

Public Company
Incorporated: 1946 as Tokyo Tsushin Kogyo K.K.
Employees: 44,908
Sales: ¥1.03 trillion
Stock Index: Tokyo Osaka Nagoya New York London Amsterdam Pacific Hong Kong Paris Frankfurt Zurich

The Sony Corporation is one of the best-known names in consumer electronics. Since it was established shortly after World War II, Sony has introduced a stream of revolutionary products, including the transistor radio, the Trinitron television, the Betamax VCR, and the Walkman portable cassette player.

Sony was founded by a former naval lieutenant named Akio Morita and a defense contractor named Masaru Ibuka. Morita, a weapons researcher, first met Ibuka during World War II while developing a heat-seeking missile-guidance system and a night-vision gun scope. After the war Ibuka worked as a radio repairman for a bomb-damaged Tokyo department store. Morita found him again when he read in a newspaper that Ibuka had invented a shortwave converter. In May of 1946 the two men established a partnership with $500 in borrowed capital, and registered their company as the Tokyo Tsushin Kogyo (Tokyo Telecommunications Engineering Corporation, or TTK). Morita and Ibuka moved their company to a crude facility on a hill in southern Tokyo, where they developed its first consumer product: a rice cooker, which failed commercially. In its first year TTK registered a profit of $300 on sales of less than $7,000.

But as the Japanese economy grew stronger, demand for consumer goods increased. Morita and Ibuka abandoned the home-appliance market and, with injections of capital from Morita's father, concentrated on developing new electronic goods. Ibuka developed a tape recorder fashioned after an American model he had seen at the Japan Broadcasting Corporation. Demand for the machine remained low until Ibuka accidentally discovered a U.S. military booklet titled *Nine Hundred and Ninety-Nine Uses of the Tape Recorder*. Translated into Japanese, the booklet became an effective marketing tool. Once acquainted with its many uses, customers such as the Academy of Art in Tokyo purchased so many tape recorders that TTK was soon forced to move to a larger building in Shinagawa.

Norio Ohga, a student at the academy, wrote several letters to TTK criticizing the sound quality of its recorder. Impressed by the detail and constructive tone of the criticisms, Morita invited Ohga to participate in the development of a new recorder as a consultant. Ohga accepted, and subsequent models were vastly improved.

Constantly searching for new technological advances, Masaru Ibuka heard of a tiny new capacitor called a transistor in 1952. The transistor, developed by Bell Laboratories, could be used in place of larger, less-durable vacuum tubes. Western Electric purchased the technology in order to manufacture transistorized hearing aids. Ibuka acquired a patent license from Western Electric for $25,000 with the intention of developing a small tubeless radio.

TTK began mass production of transistor radios in 1954, only a few months after they were introduced by a small American firm called Regency Electronics. The TTK radio was named Sony, from *sonus*, Latin for "sound." The Sony radio had tremendous sales potential, not only in the limited Japanese market, but also in the United States, whose economy was much stronger.

Traditionally, international sales by Japanese companies were conducted through trading houses such as Mitsui, Mitsubishi, and Sumitomo. Although these trading companies were well represented in the United States, Morita chose not to do business with them because they were unfamiliar with his company's products and did not share his business philosophy. Morita traveled to New York, where he met with representatives from several large retail firms. Morita refused an order from Bulova for 100,000 radios when that company required that each carry the Bulova name. Morita pledged that his company would not manufacture products for other companies and eventually secured a number of more modest orders that assured his company's growth at a measured pace.

The rising popularity of the Sony name led Morita and Ibuka to change the name of their company to Sony Kabushiki Kaisha (Corporation) in January of 1958. The following year Sony announced that it had developed a transistorized television. In 1960, after a business dispute with Delmonico International, the company Morita had appointed to handle international sales, Sony established a trade office in New York City and another in Switzerland called Sony Overseas.

A subsidiary called Sony Chemicals was created in 1962 to produce adhesives and plastics to reduce the company's dependence on outside suppliers. And in 1965 a joint venture with Tektronix was established to produce oscilloscopes in Japan.

During the early 1960s Sony engineers continued to introduce new, miniaturized products based on the transistor, including an AM/FM radio and a videotape recorder. By 1968 Sony engineers had developed new color-television technology. Using one electron gun, for more-accurate beam alignment, and one lens, for better focus, the Sony Trinitron produced a clearer image than conventional three-gun, three-lens sets. In what has been described as its biggest gamble, Sony, confident that technology alone would create new markets, invested a large amount of capital in the Trinitron.

Also in 1968, Sony Overseas established a trading office in England, and entered into a joint venture with CBS to produce phonograph records. The venture was under the direction of Norio Ohga, the art student who had complained about Sony's early tape recorder, whom Morita had persuaded in 1959 to give up opera and join Sony. The company, called CBS/Sony, later became the largest record manufacturer in Japan. In 1970 Sony Overseas established a subsidiary in West Germany to handle sales in that country.

After a decade of experience in videotape technology, Sony introduced the U-matic three-quarter-inch videocassette recorder (VCR) in 1971. Intended for institutions such as television stations, the U-matic received an Emmy Award for engineering excellence from the National Academy of Television Arts and Sciences. In 1973, the year Sony Overseas created a French subsidiary, the academy honored the Trinitron series with another Emmy.

Sony developed its first VCR for the consumer market, the Betamax, in 1975. The following year the Walt Disney Company and Universal Pictures filed a lawsuit against Sony, complaining that the new machine would enable widespread copyright infringement of television programs. A judgment in favor of Sony in 1979 was reversed two years later. Litigation continued, but by the time the matter reached the U.S. Supreme Court the plaintiffs' original case had been severely undermined by the proliferation of VCRs, making any legal restriction on copying television programs for private use nearly impossible to enforce.

During the mid 1970s, competitors, such as the American RCA and Zenith and the Japanese Toshiba and Victor Company of Japan (JVC), effectively adopted and improved upon technologies developed by Sony. For the first time, Sony began to lose significant market share, often in lines that it had pioneered. Strong competition, however, was only one factor that caused Sony's sales growth to fall (after growing 166% between 1970 and 1974, it grew only 35% between 1974 and 1978).

Like many Sony officials, Akio Morita lacked formal management training. Instead, he relied on his personal persuasive skills and his unusual ability to anticipate or create markets for new products. In typical fashion, Sony introduced the Betamax VCR well before its competitors, in effect creating a market in which it would enjoy a short-term monopoly. At this stage, however, Morita failed to establish the Betamax format as the industry standard by inviting the participation of other companies.

Matsushita Electric (which owns half of JVC) developed a separate VCR format called VHS (video home system), which permitted as many as three additional hours of playing time on a tape, but which was incompatible with Sony's Betamax. When the VHS was introduced in 1977, Morita was reported to have felt betrayed that Sony's competitors did not adopt the Betamax format. He appealed to 81-year-old Konosuke Matsushita, in many ways a patriarch of Japanese industry, to discontinue the VHS format in favor of Betamax. When Matsushita refused, many believed it was because he felt insulted by Morita's failure to offer earlier collaboration.

Matsushita launched a vigorous marketing campaign to convince customers and other manufacturers not only that VHS was superior, but that Betamax would soon be obsolete. The marketing war between Matsushita and Sony was neither constructive nor profitable; both companies were forced to lower prices so much that profits were greatly depressed. Although Betamax was generally considered a technically superior product, the VHS format grew in popularity and gradually displaced Betamax as a standard format. Despite its falling market share (from 13% in 1982 to 5% in 1987), Sony refused to introduce a VHS line until the late 1980s.

In 1979 Morita personally oversaw the development of a compact cassette tape player called the Walkman. Inspired by Norio Ohga's desire to listen to music while walking, Morita ordered the development of a small, high-fidelity tape player, to be paired with small, lightweight headphones that were already under development. The entire program took only five months from start to finish, and the product's success is now legendary—Walkman even became the generic term for similar devices produced by Sony's competitors.

During the 1970s, Masaru Ibuka, 12 years Morita's senior, gradually relinquished many of his duties to younger managers such as Norio Ohga, who was named president of Sony in 1982. Ohga became president shortly after a corporate reorganization that split Sony into five operating groups (marketing and sales, manufacturing, service, engineering, and diversified operations). While not classically trained in business, Ohga nonetheless understood that Sony was too dependent on an unstable consumer-electronics market. In one of his first acts, he inaugurated the 50-50 program to increase sales in institutional markets from 15% to 50% by 1990.

Sony's research-and-development budget consumes approximately 9% of sales (Matsushita budgets only 4%). Another groundbreaking result of Sony's commitment to research and development was a machine that uses a laser to reproduce music recorded digitally on a small plastic disk. The compact disk (or CD) player eliminates much of the noise common to conventional, analog phonograph records. Sony developed the CD in association with the Dutch electronics firm Philips, partly in an effort to ensure broad format standardization. Philips, which had developed the most advanced laser technology, was an ideal partner for Sony, which led in the pulse-code technology that makes digital sound reproduction possible. The CD format has been adopted by competing manufacturers, and is expected largely to replace phonograph systems by the mid-1990s.

In addition to the CD player, Sony has introduced a new video camera that is lighter, less expensive, and more portable than VHS cameras, but that uses 8mm videotape, and is therefore incompatible with both Betamax and VHS machines. The 8mm video system has also been developed by competitors such as Fuji, Canon, Kodak, and Pioneer, on the premise that it will gain wider acceptance by tourists as a convenient travel camera.

In May, 1984 Sony purchased Apple Computer's hard-disk-technology operations. Hard disks store more information and are more durable than floppy disks, and are a very popular computer storage medium. As a result of this acquisition, Sony may be better placed to introduce a line of personal-computer systems for business, thus helping to increase the proportion of its sales derived from institutional customers.

On November 29, 1985 the Sony Corporation of America, which operates several assembly plants in the United States, purchased the Digital Audio Disk Corporation from its affiliate CBS/Sony. Two years later, Sony purchased CBS Records for $2 billion. CBS Records, whose labels include Epic and Columbia, is the largest producer of records and tapes in the world.

Sony's motivation for the somewhat expensive purchase was the coupling of its own hardware expertise with CBS Records' premium "software" talent. Sony had learned through its Betamax experience that a superior product alone doesn't insure market dominance—had Sony been able to flood the market with exclusively Beta-formatted movies, the VCR battle might have turned out differently. Looking towards the future development of audio equipment, including digital audio tape (DAT), Sony bought the record manufacturer with an eye toward guaranteeing compatible "software" in whatever new formats it developed. The acquisition marked less of a diversification for Sony than an evolution toward dominance in a specific market.

Sony sought further diversification in U.S. entertainment companies. In 1988, the company considered an acquisition of MGM/UA Communications Corporation, but decided the price was too high. Then in 1989 Sony made headlines around the world when it bought Columbia Pictures Entertainment Group from Coca-Cola for $3.4 billion.

In the late 1980s, Sony also pushed hard for the introduction of high-definition television (HDTV) to consumer markets, and hoped to market the new product by the early 1990s.

Sony maintains a number of joint ventures, including one with Union Carbide to manufacture Eveready batteries in Japan. Sony also operates a life-insurance company in association with the Prudential Life Insurance Corporation and, with Pepsico, runs a company that imports and markets Wilson sports equipment. Sony has also established a joint venture with the Chinese government to produce television sets in the People's Republic of China.

Akio Morita told *Business Week* that he regards the Sony Corporation as only a "venture business" for the Morita family, which has produced several generations of mayors and whose primary business remains the 300-year-old Morita & Company. Under the direction of Akio Morita's younger brother Kuzuaki, Morita & Company produces sake, soy sauce, and Ninohimatsu brand rice wine in Nagoya. The company, whose initial $500 investment in TTK is now worth $430 million, owns a 9.4% share of Sony.

Sony's rise to preeminence in the world consumer-electronics market is almost entirely self-achieved; Sony has outperformed not only its Japanese rivals, among them associates of the former *zaibatsu* (conglomerate) companies, but also larger American firms, which today have all but abandoned the consumer-electronics market. The company's success is a direct result of the wisdom of its founders, who had the talent to anticipate the demands of consumers and to develop products to meet those demands.

Principal Subsidiaries: Sony Ichinomiya Corp.; Matsushin Denki Corp.; Sony Kohda Corp.; Sony Magnetic Products Inc.; Sony Kisarazu Corp.; Sony Kokubu Semiconductor Corp.; Sony Minokamo Corp.; Sony Shiroshi Semiconductor Inc.; Sound System Corp.; Tohkai Electronics Corp.; Sony Inazawa Corp.; Sony Asco Inc.; Sony Denshi Corp.; Sony Haneda Corp.; Motomiya Denshi Corp.; Sony Chemicals Corp.; Sony Mizunami Corp.; Sony Warehouse Corp.; Sony Audio Inc.; Sony Service Co., Ltd.; Bonson Electronics Inc.; Sony Enterprise Co., Ltd.; Taron Corp.; Sony Trading Corp.; Sony Tsukuba Corp.; Sony Shoji Corp.; Toyo Electronics Corp.; Sony Finance International Inc.; Sony Corporation of America (USA); Sony Overseas S.A. (Switzerland); Sony Corporation of Hong Kong Ltd.; Sony (Australia) Pty., Ltd.; Sony Corporation of Panama S.A.; Sony CSA, S.A.

Further Reading: Lyons, Nick. *The Sony Vision*, New York, Crown, 1976; Morita, Akio. *Made in Japan, Akio Morita and Sony*, New York, Dutton, 1986.

SUMITOMO ELECTRIC

SUMITOMO ELECTRIC INDUSTRIES, LTD.

4–5–33, Kitahama
Chuo-ku
Osaka 541
Japan
(06) 220–4141

Public Company
Incorporated: 1920
Employees: 12,721
Sales: ¥605 billion (US$4.8 billion)
Stock Index: Tokyo Osaka Nagoya Luxembourg

Sumitomo Electric is one of the major companies associated with the giant Japanese Sumitomo group. Sumitomo was founded during the 17th century as a copper refinery, and grew to become one of the country's largest industrial corporations. Its involvement in copper refining brought it to mining and milling, and later to the production of wires and cable. Sumitomo Electric ultimately took over production of wires and cable as an independent corporation, and today is one of the world's leading manufacturers in this sector.

The restoration of the Meiji Emperor in 1868 marked the beginning of Japan's industrialization. Many large industrial concerns, called *zaibatsu*, were formed during this period; Sumitomo became one of the largest. As the nation's leading mining and metals company, Sumitomo possessed the most advanced technologies. It also had the capital and expertise to develop new methods for extracting, refining, and manufacturing finished products.

Industrialization ushered in an era of automation and telecommunication that was totally dependent on copper and other non-ferrous metal products. This demand for power cables and wire naturally led Sumitomo into the cable and wire industry. In 1897 the company purchased a factory at Ajigawa, near Osaka, from the Japan Copper Manufacturing Company. The facility was retooled to produce cable and wire, and was renamed the Sumitomo Copper Rolling Works. The Rolling Works was one of Sumitomo's main enterprises, manufacturing a variety of finished products with copper from the company's rich Besshi mine.

The Ajigawa plant was expanded in 1908. Three years later the cable and wire operations were separated from the Rolling Works. The Sumitomo Electric Wire and Cable Works remained in the same facility but maintained separate books and management, under the control of Sumitomo Shoji, until Sumitomo Electric was incorporated in 1920. Minority blocks of its shares were distributed among other companies controlled by Sumitomo Shoji.

As Japan began to build large electrical generating plants, there was a great demand for heavy cable to carry the power to where it was needed. Sumitomo Electric rose to the task, manufacturing many hundreds of miles of wire and cable a week. Its most spectacular display of achievement was laying what was then the world's longest underwater power cable across the 20-kilometer Seto Inland Sea between the islands of Honshu and Shikoku in southern Japan in 1922.

In order to maintain its technological edge (or, at least, to minimize its disadvantage) over foreign cable and wire manufacturers, Sumitomo Electric established a research laboratory in 1923, which eventually developed improved casing methods and discovered more efficient metal alloys for conducting electricity.

Sumitomo Electric also worked closely with Sumitomo Steel and with it began production of special steel wires in the 1930s. This relationship continued even after the Rolling Works and Sumitomo Steel merged in 1935 to form Sumitomo Metal Industries. The next new product Sumitomo Electric manufactured was piano wire, introduced in 1938.

Sumitomo Electric also had, and still maintains, a very close working relationship with the Nippon Electric Company (NEC). In fact, NEC came under Sumitomo Electric's control in 1932, and until 1942 operated as its electronics division.

Sumitomo Electric's name was changed to Sumitomo Electric Industries in 1939. In 1941, it established a second works at Itami. Later that year, of course, Japan went to war with the United States and Britain, and Sumitomo Electric was pressed into service. While many of the company's regular products were in high demand, it was also assigned to produce several other new products, including rubber vibration absorbers and aircraft fuel tanks. To handle the increased demand, an additional facility was opened in Nagoya in 1943.

Because of its involvement in the war effort, Sumitomo Electric's facilities became air raid targets. By the end of the war in 1945, Sumitomo Electric had been virtually destroyed. However, the company was recognized as an important basic industry by the occupation authority and rehabilitated under a reconstruction program.

During the occupation, *zaibatsu* industrial groups were completely dissolved by anti-monopoly laws. Sumitomo Electric, like all of Sumitomo's other divisions, was made an independent company and prohibited from reestablishing ties with other former Sumitomo companies.

When the anti-monopoly laws were relaxed to permit limited contact between former Sumitomo companies, Sumitomo Electric shares were gradually bought up by affiliates such as the Sumitomo Bank, Sumitomo Life Insurance, and Sumitomo Trust & Banking. It resumed dovetailed marketing and sales strategies with the former head Sumitomo company, the Shoji, and quickly regained its position as the country's leading cable and wire producer.

In order to reduce its reliance on subcontractors and expand its product line, Sumitomo Electric began to manufacture plastics in 1961 to replace rubber on wire casings and for use on a variety of molded intermediate products such as terminals. The company also opened a new plant in Yokohama that year.

Although Sumitomo Electric was the leading Japanese cable manufacturer, it felt an urgent need to formalize its research and development effort to avoid falling behind American and European competitors. The company's Kumatori research lab, opened in 1963, became a center for extra-high voltage transmission research, while alloy research and new product development are conducted at the Itami Works.

The automotive industry offered Sumitomo an important opportunity to diversify. By exploiting its expertise with alloys, the company became a leading parts supplier. It began production of disk brakes and related products in 1963, an activity which eventually grew to account for 10% of Sumitomo Electric's total sales.

A second field for diversification, also a result of its metal technology, was production of refined metallurgical powders. These were sold to specialty manufacturers in the electronics industry, and also came to represent about 10% of the company's sales.

Cables and wire products, however, continued to represent over half the company's total income. Included in this sector were standard insulated wires, magnetic cables (used in traffic control), bare wires, and wires made of aluminum. Gaining importance, however, were Sumitomo's special steel and alloy wires, used in construction, musical instruments, and for many other purposes.

As Japan's cable and wire market became saturated, Sumitomo Electric had to find additional markets to maintain its high growth levels. Here, the company's association with the Sumitomo group resulted in better foreign representation and greater foreign sales, which now account for about 7% of turnover. The Kanto works, completed in 1971, helped the company maintain the growth in productive capacity necessary to reach its goals.

During the early 1980s, Sumitomo decided to begin full-scale development of a new, more efficient product for telecommunications: optical fiber cables. These cables transmit pulses of light, rather than current, and are capable of handling hundreds of times more information per second. The company has also recently developed strong capabilities in integrated circuits and synthetic diamond crystals. Sumitomo's committment to research and to exploiting the full potential of its technologies promise continued growth and leadership in the wire and cable industry.

Principal Subsidiaries: Tokai Rubber Industries, Ltd.; Sumitomo Wiring Systems, Ltd.; Sumitomo Densetsu Co., Ltd.; Osaka Diamond Industrial Co., Ltd.; Tokyo Tungsten Co., Ltd.; Meguro Telecommunications Construction Co., Ltd.; Okayama Sumiden Seimitsu Ltd.; Hokkaido Sumiden Precision Industries, Ltd.; Asahi Metal Industries, Ltd.; Nankai Senshu Steel Wire & Rope Company, Limited; Kyushu Sumiden Precision Industries, Ltd.; Sumiden Shoji Co., Ltd.; Sumiden Fine Conductors Co., Ltd.; Tokai Chemical Industries, Ltd.; Sumiden Cable Co., Ltd.; Toyokuni Electric Cable Co., Ltd.; Sumitomo Electric U.S.A., Inc.; Sumitomo Electric Europe S.A. (U.K.); Sumitomo Electric Asia, Ltd. (Hong Kong); Sumitomo Electric Carbide, Inc. (U.S.A.); Sumitomo Electric Interconnect Products Inc. (U.S.A.); SEMIA, Inc.; O&S California, Inc. (U.S.A.); Sumitomo Electric Hartmetall GmbH (West Germany); Sumitomo Electric Hardmetal Ltd.; PDTL Trading Co., Ltd. (Thailand); Sumitomo Electric Thailand Ltd.; Igetalloy-Kirby (Pty.), Ltd. (Australia); Cocesa Ingenieria Y Construccion S.A. (Chile); Thai Sumiden Engineering and Construction Co., Ltd.; Sumitomo Electric Communications Engineering (Thailand), Ltd.; Uniphone Ushasama Sdn. Bhd. (Malaysia); Optix Australia Ltd.; Sumi-Pac Electronic-Chemical Corporation (Taiwan); Sumi-Pac Construction Co., Ltd. (Taiwan); The SAAD Japanese Electric Development Co., Ltd. (Saudi Arabia); SEI Nigeria Ltd.; Optical Networks Pty. Ltd. (Australia); Sumiden Wire Products Corp.; Sumitomo Electric Fiber Optics Corp. (U.S.A.); LITESPEC, Inc. (U.S.A.); Sumitomo Electric Wiring Systems, Inc. (U.S.A.); Alcan-Sumitomo Electric, Inc. (U.S.A.); Lucas Sumitomo Brakes Inc. (U.S.A.); Judd Wire, Inc. (U.S.A.); Engineered Sintered Components Inc. (U.S.A.); Sumiden Tikai Do Brazil Industrias Electricas Ltda.; Sumitomo Electric Insulated Wire, Inc. (U.S.A.); Alambres Y Cables Venezolanos C.A. (Venezuela); Electronic Harnesses (U.K.) Ltd.; Sumitomo Electric Hartmetallfabrik GmbH (West Germany); Nigerian Wire and Cable Co., Ltd.; Phelps Dodge Thailand Ltd.; Siam Electric Industries Co., Ltd. (Thailand); Thai Copper Rod Co., Ltd. (Thailand); Sumitomo Electric (Singapore) Pte. Ltd.; Sumitomo Electric Interconnect Products (Singapore) Pte., Ltd.; Sumitomo Electric Interconnect Products (M) Sdn. Bhd. (Malaysia); Sumitomo Electric Magnet Wire (M) Sdn. Bhd. (Malaysia); Korloy Inc. (Korea); Korea Sintered Metal Co., Ltd.; Walsin Lihwa Electric Wire & Cable Corporation (Taiwan); Pacific Electric Wire & Cable Co., Ltd. (Taiwan); Wha-Yo Electronic Materials Corporation (Taiwan).

TANDY CORPORATION

1800 One Tandy Center
Fort Worth, Texas 76102
U.S.A.
(817) 390–3700

Public Company
Incorporated: 1960
Employees: 37,000
Sales: $3.8 billion
Stock Index: New York

How does a small family-owned leather store become one of the world's leading computer and electronics retailers and manufacturers? The transformation of Tandy is due to the two strong CEOs who have been in charge since the company was incorporated in 1960. Charles Tandy made the company a giant in electronic retailing. His successor, John Roach, spearheaded a move to make the corporation a force to be reckoned with in the personal computer industry.

Charles Tandy's talent for marketing became evident when he took over the leather store his family had operated since 1919. He began to expand into the hobby market. Subsidiary locations had to be found as mail order and direct sales increased. In 1960, as Scouts and campers all over America made moccasins and coin purses from Tandy leathercraft and hobby kits, the Tandy Corporation began trading on the New York Stock Exchange.

As good as business was, it couldn't satisfy Tandy's passion for retailing. By the early 1960s, he began looking for a way to diversify. In 1963, Tandy purchased Radio Shack, a virtually bankrupt chain of electronics stores in Boston. Within two years, Tandy was making a profit on a company that had nearly $800,000 in uncollectibles when he took over. Ten years after starting with nine Boston outlets, the Tandy Corporation was opening two Radio Shack stores every working day. By 1988, there were more than 7,000 Radio Shack stores. According to Tandy estimates, one out of every three Americans is now a Tandy customer.

By all accounts, Charles Tandy was a Fort Worth "good old boy" who stayed in his original office and answered his own phone to the day he died. His CB radio monicker was "Mr. Lucky." However, analysts don't think it was just luck that made Tandy Corporation grow. They give much more credit to three key marketing strategies that Charles Tandy developed and implemented.

First, Tandy stressed the importance of gross profit margins. Popular wisdom said a chain store's profits lay in cutting prices to yield a high sales volume. Tandy thought differently. As far as he was concerned, cutting the profit margin cut the profit. So he maintained market prices but reduced Radio Shack's 20,000 item inventory to the 2,500 best-selling items.

Second, Tandy kept Radio Shack prices competitive. He eliminated a whole spectrum of middleman costs by limiting stock to private label items. At first, the company established exclusive contracts with manufacturers, but as Radio Shack grew, more and more items were designed and manufactured by associates or subdivisions of the Tandy Corporation. Today, Tandy still manufactures about half of the products sold in its Radio Shack stores. Twenty-five North American and six overseas manufacturing plants produce everything from simple wire to sophisticated microchips, and Radio Shack's "Realistic" brand name has achieved nationwide recognition.

Charles Tandy's strategy of pairing high profit margin with high turnover and of in-house marketing and distribution has more than proved itself. The gross profit margin on sales for Radio Shack division has been consistently above 50%.

Even as he consolidated his inventory, Tandy was keenly aware that buyers must know you are in the market. "If you want to catch a mouse," Tandy was fond of saying, "You have to make a noise like a cheese." So another Tandy strategy was to go all out on advertising. Especially in the early years, as much as 9% of the corporation's gross profits went straight back into advertising. For years, Radio Shack's newspaper ads and flyers were not only frequent but also flamboyant. Bold type and huge letters proclaimed a never-ending series of "super sales." In more recent times, as Radio Shack and Tandy work on strengthening their *Fortune* 500 image, the ads have been toned down.

The third arm of Charles Tandy's strategy was, in the words of one company official, to "institutionalize entrepreneurship." Tandy Corporation and Radio Shack employees were living testimony that hard work and impressive sales earn their own rewards. Store managers, division vice presidents, and Charles Tandy himself regularly earned eight or ten times their relatively modest salaries through bonuses based on a percentage of the profits they had a direct hand in creating; this policy has spawned some 60 home-grown millionaires.

As Radio Shack's electronic line grew increasingly central to Tandy, the family leather business became more and more of an anomaly. Finally, in 1975, the leather line and a related wall and floor-covering business were spun off into separate companies.

When Charles Tandy died suddenly in 1978, at the age of 60, pundits and insiders alike wondered if the corporation could survive without its workaholic director and his individualistic marketing philosophy. Philip North, a director of the company and Tandy's administrative assistant and boyhood friend, stepped in as interim president and CEO of Tandy Corporation.

By his own admission, North knew virtually nothing about the technical side of Radio Shack's product line. "All I know about electronics is that the funny end of the battery goes into the flashlight first," he told *Fortune* magazine. However, North knew plenty about his late friend's retailing style. Analysts credit him with keeping the corporation's strong management team together during the adjustment period after Tandy's death.

During these years, North called more and more on the expertise of John Roach, a man whose scientific and computer background had already attracted Charles Tandy's attention. Within a few years of hiring him as the manager of Tandy Data Processing, Tandy had made Roach vice president of distribution for Radio Shack. Two years later, in 1975, he rotated him to vice president of manufacturing. Roach was then appointed Radio Shack's executive vice president immediately after Tandy died, became the Radio Shack division's president and chief operating officer in 1980, and CEO in 1981. When North retired in July of 1982, Roach became chairman as well.

Roach's major contribution has been masterminding Tandy's entry into the computer market. Before Charles Tandy's death, Roach had talked him into venturing into the preassembled computer market. The sale of 100,000 computers between September 1, 1977 and June 1, 1979 kept Radio Shack comfortably in the black even as the bottom dropped out of the citizens-band radio market.

As Roach moved up the corporate structure, he intensified investment in computers. In 1982, less than a year after becoming CEO, Roach was singled out as "the best of the best" by *Financial World*, which lauded Roach as "the driving force at "the front-running company in the red-hot personal computer race."

Within a short time, however, there were rumblings that the driving force in this hot race might have been burned. By 1984, Radio Shack's impressive 19% market share had plummeted to under 9%.

One of Tandy's problems was an outgrowth of Charles Tandy's policy limiting Radio Shack to private label items, preferably manufactured by one of Tandy's subsidiary divisions. As software and applications software poured out for Apple and IBM-compatible systems, fewer and fewer serious computer users were willing to limit themselves to software designed exclusively for Radio Shack's TRS-80, or "Trash-80", as some sneeringly referred to it. In fact, Tandy found that even a superior machine couldn't overcome the software handicap. Officials at the company were shaken to find they simply couldn't sell their 1983 Model 2000, even though it was three times as fast as IBM's own P.C, because it couldn't run half of the available IBM software.

In addition, Radio Shack's marketing strategies had a vulnerable side. Company policy was to let other retailers test the waters with items like stereos, CB radios and "fuzz buster" radar detectors. Then Tandy would take over a significant part of the market by introducing a house brand it advertised intensively. However, it's not always possible to know what will boom when, and when Radio Shack simply did not have stock on hand when the VCR market exploded in the mid-1980s—the same time the computer market was drying up—both sales and revenues fell at an alarming rate.

That crisis lead Tandy to modify its policy. In 1984, the company introduced two new computers that were fully IBM-compatible, and exchanged the TRS label for Tandy. Radio Shack management then set about underselling its Big Blue competitor. Such price competition was a departure from previous marketing strategy, but because Tandy's own in-house manufacturing divisions still produce virtually all the components, from wire to plastic boards to microchips, Tandy has been able to keep profits up.

While it has never regained its initial share of the PC market, Tandy has consistently held first place among IBM-compatibles since it entered the field in 1985. Tandy regained its place in the computer market by offering the buyer significant savings over IBM and other compatibles. At the same time, Roach also oversaw a wholesale revamping of the company's image. Ordinary Radio Shack stores were given a face-lift. To overcome the reluctance of serious business customers to take a computer shelved next to a CB or electronic toy seriously, Roach established a series of specialized Radio Shack Computer Centers, providing a level of support and service that earned a "Hall of Fame" award from *Consumer's Digest* in 1985.

Tandy continues to pour money into research and development to assure that they won't be left behind again by new developments in the computer field. Its 1988 acquisition of GRiD Systems Corporation is a good example of current policy. GRiD's ability to manufacture and market field automation systems using laptop computers opens a whole new area of expansion into government and *Fortune* 1000 marketing companies.

Tandy has also continued to maintain a high profile in the consumer electronics market outside of computers. The company is putting special emphasis on becoming a major force in both manufacturing and retailing cellular telephones, which it sees as a major consumer product of the 1990s. Another Tandy project—the development of an erasable and recordable compact disc—is also commanding a great deal of interest in the consumer electronics industry.

In many ways, today's Tandy Corporation is simply an expansion of what it was at Charles Tandy's death. It centers its manufacturing and marketing firmly around computers and consumer electronics which it retails primarily through its Radio Shack outlets.

Nonetheless, there have been some significant deviations from Charles Tandy's heritage recently. In 1985 the company entered the name brand retail market with the acquisitions of Scott-McDuff and Videoconcepts, two electronic equipment chain stores. The 290 stores in the Tandy Brand Name Retail Group do not follow the Radio Shack policy of selling exclusively private label brands. Other subsidiaries in the Tandy Marketing Companies also have developed much broader distribution channels. Memtek products, which include Memorex brand audio and video tape products and related accessories, are available virtually everywhere such products are sold.

Tandy has also made a recent push to sell its computers outside of Radio Shack stores. In 1985, the company edged into broader markets by offering its computers on college campuses, military bases, and through special offers to American Express cardholders. In 1988, Tandy test-marketed selling its 100SX computer line through 50 Wal-Mart stores. The company also announced plans to develop new computers with Digital Equipment and to resell the finished product under the DEC name and to supply personal computers to Panasonic to be sold under the Panasonic name.

Some dealers see broadening computer distribution outside Radio Shack stores as a potentially lethal threat. Many Radio Shack stores depend on their computer business for a significant portion of sales and doubt whether they can survive if customers begin to shop around, looking for the same Tandy products for less elsewhere. In August of 1988, a small group of dealers formed the Radio Shack Dealers Association and began considering a class action suit against Tandy. While the company hopes to work out these issues, Tandy Corporation remains firmly committed to broadening its distribution channels.

Tandy's foundation is and will continue to be its Radio Shack retail outlets, but beyond remodeling its 7,000 stores and refining their retail strategies, Tandy's own success has left little room for growth. The company's future lies in its commitment to finding new distribution channels for the products it manufactures and to retailing brand name, discount electronics. As both of these ventures are new to Tandy's whole corporate philosophy, success will depend on Tandy's traditionally strong management team. No one can say how Charles Tandy would regard the changes his company has seen or the challenges it faces, but it seems fair to guess that he would have no quarrel with the outcome so far.

Principal Subsidiaries: Tandy Credit Corp.; O'Sullivan Industries, Inc.; Tandy Electronics, Inc.; A & A International, Inc.

TDK CORPORATION

1–13–1, Nihonbashi
Chuo-ku
Tokyo 103
Japan
(03) 278–5111

Public Company
Incorporated: 1935 as TDK Electronics Corporation Ltd.
Employees: 19,646
Sales. ¥418 billion (US$3.34 billion)
Stock Index: Tokyo Osaka Paris New York London

TDK is most often associated with high quality audio and video tape, and for good reason—the company is the world's largest manufacturer of these products, and recording media have been critical to the company's phenomenal growth. Beyond the view of the average consumer's eye, however, is a company that is a world leader in a number of other product markets as well. TDK's research and development department has been responsible for many discoveries in the application of magnetic materials over the years, and the company continues to drive the cutting edge of this technology today. In addition to TDK's imposing presence in magnetic recording media markets, the company's sales are increasingly made up of electronic components such as ferrite cores and magnets; coil and assembled components including electric convertors and hybrid integrated circuits; ceramic components; and high-tech assembly systems capable of the exceptional precision necessary in the manufacture of circuit boards and other delicate components.

The success of TDK (the initials stand for Tokyo Denki Kogaku Kogyo) parallels the commercial development of a remarkably versatile material known as ferrite, a magnetic material with ceramic properties. It is composed of ferric oxide and any of a number of other metallic oxides, but usually zinc. Ferrite can be produced in several variations, each with somewhat different properties, and it can be categorized in two groups: hard and soft. Hard ferrite can be easily and permanently magnetized. Soft ferrite, on the other hand, does not stay magnetized for any great length of time, but has other properties that make it suitable for many electronics applications. Today TDK supplies about half of the world's ferrite.

Ferrite was invented in 1933 by two Japanese scientists, Dr. Yogoro Kato and Dr. Takeshi Takei, at the Tokyo Institute of Technology. Two years later a man named Kenzo Saito founded the TDK Corporation to market their discovery. Saito had been searching for a manufacturing business that he could establish in his home town, which was wholly dependent on agriculture. When Kato and Saito met by chance, each was impressed by the other, and soon Kato granted Saito the use of the ferrite technology he and Takei had developed.

TDK's first application was a soft ferrite product, marketed as an "oxide core" and employed in transformers and coils. The demand for ferrite was very limited at this time, however, and TDK's first years were hard. But as the number of electrical appliances in the world increased, demand for TDK's ferrite cores also increased dramatically. Early on TDK made research and development a priority by exploring the dimensions of ferrite and finding new ways to employ it. Soon, the use of ferrite cores became widespread in consumer electronic products like radios and televisions, markets that grew considerably during the 1940s and 1950s. Saito left TDK in 1946 and later became a member of the Diet.

Eventually TDK branched into the manufacture of materials other than ferrite. In 1951 the company began to produce ceramic capacitors. These components are used to store electrical energy, inhibit the flow of direct current, or facilitate the flow of alternate current, and are widely used in the production of electronic devices. The Japanese electronics industry would explode before long, and TDK established itself as a key components manufacturer early on.

In 1952 TDK introduced its first magnetic recording tape. TDK's line of recording tape eventually became the industry standard: at one point it accounted for half of the company's sales. In Japan TDK led the development of recording tape, becoming the first domestic manufacturer of audiocassettes in 1966. Two years later the company defied skeptics when it produced the world's first high-fidelity cassettes, marketed by TDK as Super Dynamic (SD) tape. Meanwhile, a TDK researcher named Yasuo Imaoka was looking for a material which could be used to replace chromium dioxide in video and audiotapes. Chromium dioxide, while offering excellent sound quality, is rare and expensive. Imaoka and his team came up with a process that combined ferric oxide with metal cobalt. The resulting material was named Avilyn, and it had a greater coercivity—a measure of magnetic substances—than chromium dioxide. Avilyn videotapes hit the market in 1973. The formula was soon improved by using cobalt hydroxide instead of metal cobalt, and the resulting Super Avilyn audiotapes revolutionized the industry when TDK unveiled its SA line, the first non-chrome high-bias tape, in 1975. (In 1985 the Japanese Council of Industrial Patents named Avilyn as one of the country's top 53 inventions of the century.)

As TDK developed technological innovations, its marketing strength also improved. The company entered foreign markets as early as 1959, when a representative office was opened in New York City. A second American office was opened four years later in Los Angeles. TDK's international operations grew extensively during the late 1960s and the 1970s. In 1968, TDK set up a subsidiary in Taiwan to manufacture ferrite cores, ceramic capacitors, and coil components. Over the course of the next ten years, TDK established subsidiaries in West Germany, Hong Kong, Great Britain, Brazil, Korea, Mexico, the United States, Singapore, and Australia. Manufacturing facilities were set up in many of the countries TDK operated in to ease trade imbalances and to insulate the company from currency fluctuations. TDK or its subsidiaries began producing magnetic heads in the United States in 1972, followed by audiotape a year later; ferrite cores in Korea in 1973; ferrite magnets in Mexico in 1974; ferrite cores in Brazil in 1979; and videotape in the United States in 1980. By the mid-1980s nearly half of TDK's business was generated outside of Japan.

In the mid-1970s TDK's already impressive growth rate took off for a number of reasons. Technological developments in consumer electronics created new demand for the company's expertise in ferrite and other materials. More sensitive audio equipment created strong demand for TDK's SA tapes, and the introduction of videotape recorders to the consumer market created new demand for both the software (videotapes) and hardware (magnetic tapeheads and other components) that TDK was capable of producing. The company's sales went through the roof as the videocassette market expanded 60% a year in the late 1970s.

Videocassettes and audiocassettes made up half of TDK's sales in the early 1980s. In 1983, however, an oversupply of videotapes sent prices into a downward spiral. While TDK's audiotapes sales continued to improve, revenue from videotape declined even though total volume increased. Just as the videotape crunch was at its worst, Yutaka Otoshi, the former chief of the tapes division, took over as TDK president and CEO. Otoshi increased TDK's research and development budget from 3.4% to 5% of sales to ensure the company's technological edge. New products such as the compact 8mm camcorders and players and recordable optical videodiscs were expected to give a boost to the market. Nonetheless, Otoshi focused on expanding TDK's non-tape business. As he told *Business Week* in 1983, "we have never thought it was a good idea to concentrate too much on one product."

In 1984 TDK launched its Components Engineering Laboratory (CEL) in Los Angeles. At this lab TDK's researchers worked with marketing personnel to develop custom prototypes of transformers, microwave products, and other components for use by American customers. In addition to customization, the new lab reduced the time required to go from product development to full-scale production. TDK's research efforts also resulted in the development of a number of new products in the 1980s. The company made breakthroughs in the development of thin-film heads for increased recording sensitivity, in multilayer hybrid circuits that allow equalization in headphone cassette players to be performed in one-third the usual space, and in sensor technology.

Another area in which TDK excelled in the 1980s is the field of anechoic chambers—rooms lined with a material that absorbs radiowaves. Anechoic chambers are used to measure the electro-magnetic emission of electronic products and also a product's vulnerability to interference from such emissions. TDK's success with anechoic chambers grew out of its experience with microwave absorption. The company first began research in that field in 1964 and by 1968 had marketed its first ferrite-based microwave absorbers. The popularity of microwave ovens, which use a ferrite and rubber compound to keep the cooking process inside the oven, bolstered TDK's bottom line. In 1975 the company applied its expertise in microwave absorption to anechoic chambers, and in the 1980s, as demand for these facilities grew on the back of a booming electronics industry, TDK became a major force in the field.

In 1987 the company embarked on a joint venture with the Allen-Bradley Company, of the United States, to produce motor magnets for the automobile industry. Allen-Bradley/TDK Magnetics began production at a plant in Oklahoma in April of that year. TDK benefited from its partner's long-standing relationship with American auto makers, and Allen-Bradley benefited from TDK's magnetics expertise.

The late 1980s also saw the miniaturization of and increased demand for higher-density circuits and components. Manufacturers of these products required extremely precise equipment for their production facilities. TDK's Avimount and Avisert automated assembly equipment was in greater demand as a result. Sales in 1988 were up 25% over the previous year and were expected to continue to rise.

TDK's focus on broadening its non-tape products was successful; by 1988 the non-tape sector accounted for 64% of the company's total sales. But TDK didn't neglect its recording-media development. TDK's floppy discs garnered a respectable market share partly based on the company's excellent reputation in audio and video recording media. In 1987 the company introduced digital audio tape (DAT)—tapes able to play and record music digitally, like compact disks—in Japan and prepared to enter foreign markets as soon as copyright problems were settled. In 1988, it introduced a top-of-the-line videotape called Super Strong, a new product that allowed TDK to raise prices and still maintain market share.

TDK continued to grow on its own and make acquisitions when appropriate. In 1988 the company acquired Display Components Inc. (Discom), of Westford, Massachusetts. The purchase allowed Discom access to TDK's advanced production techniques while TDK received Discom's state-of-the-art magnetic field technology. In 1989 TDK purchased a large American manufacturer of mixed-signal integrated circuits, Silicon Systems Inc., for $200 million, further diversifying its range of products.

As it enters the 1990s, TDK is well positioned in a large number of electronics-orientated markets. The company, which was built largely around the merits of one material—ferrite—has become a diverse, broad-based high-tech company. As technology continues to race ahead, TDK, with its experience and dedication to creativity, can be expected to remain an industry leader.

Principal Subsidiaries: Iida TDK Co., Ltd; Tsuruoka TDK Co., Ltd.; Yuza TDK Co., Ltd.; Kisagata TDK Co., Ltd.; Yashima TDK Co., Ltd.; Ujo TDK Co., Ltd.; TDK Service Co., Ltd.; TDK Design Core Co., Ltd.; TDK-MCC Co., Ltd.; Iwaki Kogyo Co., Ltd.; Yuri TDK Co., Ltd.; Konoura TDK Co., Ltd.; TDK Core Co., Ltd.; Ouchi TDK Co., Ltd.; TDK Distributor Co., Ltd.; Sakata TDK Co., Ltd.; Honjo TDK Co., Ltd.; Kofu TDK Co., Ltd.; Yuzawa TDK Co., Ltd.; Toso TDK Co., Ltd.; TDK Taiwan Corp. (80.24%); Korea TDK Co., Ltd.; TDK Hongkong Co., Ltd.; TDK Manufacturing (Hong Kong) Co., Ltd.; SAE Magnetics (H.K.) Co., Ltd.; TDK Electronics Europe GmbH; TDK Recording Media Europe GmbH; TDK U.K. Ltd.; TDK U.S.A. Corp.; TDK Corp. of America; TDK Electronics Corp.; TDK Magnetic Tape Corp.; TDK Components U.S.A., Inc.; Saki Magnetics, Inc.; TDK Ferrites Corporation; TDK de Mexico S.A. de C.V.; TDK do Brasil Ind. e Com. Ltda.; TDK Singapore (Pte) Ltd.; TDK (Australia) Pty. Ltd.

TEXAS INSTRUMENTS INCORPORATED

13500 North Central Expressway
Dallas, Texas 75243
U.S.A.
(214) 995–2011

Public Company
Incorporated: 1930 as Geophysical Service
Employees: 75,685
Sales: $6.3 billion
Stock Exchange: New York London Switzerland

The history of Texas Instruments (TI) is the history of the American electronics industry. TI was one of the first companies to manufacture transistors, and it introduced the first commercial silicon transistors. It was a TI engineer who developed the first semiconductor integrated circuit in 1958, and TI's semiconductor chips helped fuel the modern electronics revolution.

Texas Instruments traces it roots to Geophysical Service, a petroleum-exploration firm founded in 1930 by Dr. J. Clarence Karcher and Eugene McDermott. Headquartered in Dallas, Geophysical Service used a technique for oil exploration developed by Karcher. The technique, reflection seismology, used underground sound waves to find and map those areas most likely to yield oil. When Karcher and McDermott opened a research and equipment manufacturing office in Newark, New Jersey—to keep their research and their seismography equipment operations out of view of competitors— they hired J. Erik Jonsson, a mechanical engineer, to head it.

Toward the end of the 1930s, Geophysical Service began to change its business focus because of the erratic nature of the oil exploration business. The company was reorganized: an oil company, Coronado Corporation, was established as the parent company and a geophysical company called Geophysical Service, Inc. (GSI), was formed as a subsidiary. McDermott and Jonsson, along with two other GSI employees, purchased GSI from Coronado in 1941. During World War II, oil exploration continued, and the company also looked for other business opportunities. The skills GSI acquired producing seismic devices were put to use in the development and manufacture of electronic equipment for the armed services. This experience revealed marked similarities in design and performance requirements for the two kinds of equipment. Jonsson, encouraged by GSI's expansion during the war, helped make military manufacturing a major company focus. By 1942 GSI was working on military contracts for the U.S. Navy and the Army Signals Corps. This was the beginning of the company's diversification into electronics unrelated to petroleum exploration.

After the war, Jonsson coaxed a young naval officer named Patrick E. Haggerty, a man of exceptional vision, to join GSI. At a time when many defense contractors had shifted their focus from military manufacturing to civilian markets, Haggerty and Jonsson firmly believed that defense contracts would help them establish GSI as a leading-edge electronics company. They won contracts to produce such military equipment as airborne magnometers and complete radar systems. Haggerty, who was general manager of the Laboratory and Manufacturing (L & M) division, also set about turning GSI into a major electronics manufacturer. He and Jonsson soon won approval from the board of directors to build a new plant to consolidate scattered operations into one unit. The new building opened in 1947.

By 1951 the L & M division was growing faster than GSI's Geophysical division. The company was reorganized again and renamed General Instruments Inc. Because its new name was already in use by another company, however, General Instruments became Texas Instruments that same year. Geophysical Service Inc. became a subsidiary of Texas Instruments in the reorganization, remaining as a subsidiary of TI until early 1988, when most of the company was sold to the Halliburton Company.

The next major change came late in 1953 when Texas Instruments went public by merging with the almost-dormant Intercontinental Rubber Company The merger brough TI new working capital and a listing on the New York Stock Exchange, and helped fuel the company's subsequent growth.

Indeed, the 1950s were a heady time for Texas Instruments. In 1953 alone, TI acquired seven new companies. Sales skyrocketed from $6.4 million in 1949 to $20 million in 1952 to $92 million in 1958, establishing TI as a major electronics manufacturer.

A major factor in TI's astronomical growth in the 1950s was the transistor. In 1952, TI paid $25,000 to Western Electric for a license to manufacture its newly patented germanium transistor. Within two years, TI was mass-producing high-frequency germanium transistors and had introduced the first commercial silicon transistor. The silicon transistor was based on research conducted by Gordon Teal, who had been hired from Bell Labs to head TI's research laboratories.

Teal and his research team had developed a way to make transistors out of silicon rather than germanium in 1954. Silicon had many advantages over germanium, not least of which was it's resistance to high temperatures. The silicon transistor was a critical breakthrough.

It was Pat Haggerty who was convinced that there was a huge market for consumer products that used inexpensive transistors. In 1954 TI, together with the Regency division of Industrial Engineering Associates, Inc., developed the world's first small, inexpensive, portable radio using the germanium transistors TI had developed. The new

Regency Radio was introduced in late 1954, and became the hot gift item of the 1954 Christmas season. The transistor soon usurped the place of vacuum tubes forever.

During all this, Haggerty and Mark Shepherd Jr., then manager of TI's Semiconductor-Components division and later chairman of TI, had been trying, with little success, to persuade IBM to make TI a supplier of transistors for its computers. But Thomas Watson Jr., president and founder of IBM, was impressed with the Regency Radio, and in 1957, IBM signed an agreement that made TI a major component supplier for IBM computers. In 1958, Patrick Haggerty was named to succeed Jonsson as president.

From 1956 to 1958, Texas Instruments' annual sales more than doubled, from $46 million to $92 million. In 1957 TI opened its first manufacturing facility outside the United States—a plant in Bedford, England to supply semiconductors to Britain and Western Europe. And in 1959, TI's merger with Metals and Controls Corporation—a maker of clad metals, control instruments, and nuclear fuel components and instrument cores—gave TI two American plants as well as facilities in Mexico, Argentina, Italy, Holland, and Australia.

One of Texas Instruments' most important breakthroughs occurred in 1958 when a newly hired employee, Jack S. Kilby, came up with the idea for the first integrated circuit. The integrated circuit was a pivotal innovation. Made of a single semiconductor material, it eliminated the need to solder components together. Without wiring and soldering, components could be miniaturized, which allowed for more compact circuitry and also meant huge numbers of components could be crowded onto a single chip.

To be sure, there were manufacturing problems to be overcome. The chips had to be produced in an entirely dust-free environment; an error-free method of "printing" the circuits onto the silicon chips had to be devised; and miniaturization itself made manufacturing difficult. But Texas Instruments realized the chip's potential and, after two years of development, the company's first commercial integrated circuits were made available in 1960. Although the electronics industry initially greeted the chip with skepticism, integrated circuits became the foundation of modern microelectronics. Smaller, lighter, faster, more dependable, and more powerful than its predecessors, the chip had many advantages, but it was expensive—$100 for small quantities in 1962. But integrated circuits were ideally suited for use in computers, and together, chips and computers experienced explosive growth.

Semiconductors quickly became a key element in space technology, too, and early interest by the military and the U.S. space program gave TI and its competitors the impetus to improve their semiconductor chips and refine their production techniques. Under Jack Kilby, TI built the first computer to use silicon integrated circuits, for the air force. Demonstrated in 1961, this ten-ounce, 600-part computer proved that integrated circuits were practical.

Chip prices fell to an average price of $8 apiece by 1965, making the circuits affordable enough to use in consumer products. Another importantant breakthrough came in 1969, when IBM began using integrated circuits in all its computers. Soon the government was no longer TI's main customer, although defense electronics remained an important part of Texas Instruments' business. Within ten years of Kilby's discovery, semiconductors had become a multi-billion-dollar industry.

Early on, TI's management anticipated a huge world demand for semiconductors, and in the 1960s the company built manufacturing plants in Europe, Latin America, and Asia. TI's early start in these markets gave the company an edge over its competitors.

In 1966 Haggerty was elected chairman of TI's board when Jonsson left to become mayor of Dallas. He had already challenged a team of engineers to develop a new product: the portable, pocket-sized calculator, to show that integrated circuits had a place in the consumer market. In 1967, TI engineers invented a prototype hand-held calculator, which weighed 45 ounces. It was four years before the hand-held calculator hit the stores, but once it did it made history. Within a few years, the once-ubiquitous slide rule was obsolete.

In 1970 TI invented the single-chip microprocessor, or microcomputer, which was introduced commercially the next year. It is this break-through chip that paved the way not only for small, inexpensive calculators but also for today's ubiquitous computer-controlled appliances and devices.

TI formally entered the consumer-electronic calculator market in 1972 with the introduction of a four-ounce portable calculator and two desktop models, which ranged in price from $85 to $120. Sales of calculators soared from about 3 million units in 1971 to 17 million in 1973, 28 million in 1974, and 45 million in 1975.

Despite this early success, TI was to learn many bitter lessons about marketing to the American consumer. Even early success was hard won. Bowmar Instruments had been selling a calculator that used TI-made chips since 1971. In 1972, when TI entered the calculator market and tried to undercut Bowmar's price, Bowmar quickly matched TI and a price war ensured. TI subscribed to learning-curve pricing: keep prices low (and profits small) in the early stages to build market share and develop manufacturing efficiencies; competitors who want to enter the market later will find it difficult or impossible to compete.

But after a few years, competitors did begin to make inroads into TI's business; by 1975, as increased competition in the market led to plummeting prices, the calculator market softened, leading to a $16 million loss for TI in the second quarter of 1975.

But TI rebounded and again sent shock waves through the consumer-electronics world in 1976 when it introduced an inexpensive, reliable electronic digital watch for a mere $19.95. Almost overnight, TI's watches grabbed a large share of the electronic watch market at the expense of long-established watch manufacturers. A little more than a year later, TI cut the price of a digital watch to $9.95.

When low-cost Asian imports flooded the market in 1978, however, Texas Instruments began to lose its dominant position. TI also failed to capitalize on LCD (liquid crystal display) technology, for which it held the basic patent. It had not anticipated strong consumer demand for LCD watches, which displayed the time continuously rather than requiring the user to push a button for a readout. When sales of LCD watches exploded, TI couldn't begin mass-production quickly enough. The company's digital-watch sales dropped dramatically in 1979, by the end of 1981 TI had left the digital watch business.

Meanwhile, in TI's mainstay business, semiconductor manufacturing, orders for chips became backlogged—Texas instruments had spread its resources thinly in order to compete in both the consumer and industrial markets, and worldwide chip demand had soared at the same time.

Despite these problems, TI grew at a rapid rate during the 1970s. Defense electronics continued to be highly profitable and semiconductor demand remained strong, buoyed by the worldwide growth in consumer-electronics manufacturing. The company reached $1 billion in sales in 1973, $2 billion in 1977, and $3 billion in 1979.

Mark Shepherd was named chairman of the board upon Patrick Haggerty's retirement in 1976, and J. Fred Bucy, who had worked in almost all of TI's major business areas, was named president and remained chief operating officer. Haggerty continued as general director and honorary chairman until his death in 1980.

In 1978, Texas Instruments introduced Speak & Spell, an educational device that used TI's new speech-synthesis technology, which proved quite popular. That same year, TI was held up as *Business Week's* model for American companies in the 1980s for its lead in innovation, productivity gains, and phenomenal growth and earnings records.

In mid-1979 TI announced the introduction of a home computer, which reached the market that December. Priced at about $1,400, the machine sold more slowly at first than TI had predicted. In 1981 sales began to pick up, though, and a rebate program in 1982 kept sales—and sales predictions—very strong. In April, 1983, TI shipped its one millionth home computer.

Then suddenly sales of the TI-99/4A fell off dramatically. By October, TI's overconfident projections and failure to predict the price competitiveness of the market had driven the company out of the home computer business altogether. By the time the 99/4A was withdrawn from the market, TI's usual competitive-pricing strategy had reduced the computer's retail price below the company's production cost, causing TI's first-ever loss, of $145 million, in 1983.

Of course, TI's consumer electronics never had been a consistent money-maker. The company has often been accused of arrogance—of trying to find mass markets for new TI inventions rather than adapting its product lines to accommodate customers' needs—and TI's aggressive price-cutting was often insensitive to dealers and customers alike. In addition, TI's pursuit of both consumer and industrial markets often caused shortages of components resulting in backlogged or reduced shipments.

After experiencing its first loss, TI found regaining its former footing difficult. A slump in semiconductor demand during the recession of the early 1980s made TI's heavy losses in home computers particularly painful. Cost-cutting became a high priority, and TI trimmed its work force by 10,000 employees between 1980 and 1982. In addition, management decided that its matrix management structure was strangling the company and so began to modify the system to revive innovation. Although the company's engineers continued to lead the semiconductor field in innovations, increased competition both in the United States and overseas meant that technological superiority was no longer a guarantee of success.

TI President Fred Bucy was roundly criticized for being abrasive and autocratic, and the disappointments of the early 1980s hastened his demise. In May, 1985 Bucy abruptly retired and Jerry Junkins was elected president and CEO. Junkins, a lifetime TI employee with a much cooler and more conciliatory management style, has proved a popular chief executive. Junkins continued a campaign started by Bucy to refocus TI on its forte, semiconductor development, as part of his strategy to place less emphasis on market dominance and concentrate more on margins. In addition, Junkins recognized that TI needed to improve relations with its customers and eliminate the company's reputation for arrogance.

A recent development has been TI's aggressive defense of its rights to its intellectual property—the patented technological developments of its employees. In 1986 TI filed suit with the International Trade Commission against eight Japanese and one Korean semiconductor manufacturers who were selling dynamic random-access memories (DRAMs) in the United States without obtaining licenses to use technology that belongs to TI. TI reached out-of-court settlements with most of the companies but, more importantly, demonstrated that infringements on its patents would not be tolerated.

In late 1988 Texas Instruments announced plans to join Japan's Hitachi, Ltd. in developing 16-megabit DRAM technology. Although this decision came as quite a surprise to the electronics industry given TI's successful Japanese subsidiary and its manufacturing plant there, TI explained that the move was necessary to spread the mounting risks and costs involved in producing such an advanced chip.

In 1977, TI boldly set itself a sales goal of $10 billion by 1989; not long after, it upped the ante to $15 billion by 1990. The TI that entered the 1990s some $9 billion short of that extraordinary goal has decided to refocus on its original chip business, putting its once-heralded consumer-products operations on the back burner. As the only U.S. chipmaker to have stayed in the DRAM business in the face of Japanese competition in the 1980s, TI is in a strong position in that industry. And TI's defense electronics business remains strong, buoyed by a large contract in late 1989 to build 1,600 HARM missiles. While it still has quite a way to go to reach that $15 billion goal, TI, with very modern manufacturing and design facilities already located throughout the United States, Europe, Latin America, and Asia and more under construction, plans to capitalize on anticipated heavy demand for chips. With a very difficult decade behind it, TI looks ready to shine in the 1990s.

Principal Subsidiaries: Texas Instruments Australia Limited; Texas Instrumentos Eletronicos do Brasil Limitada; Texas Instruments Canada Limited; Texas Instruments Limited; Texas Instruments Deutschland G.m.b.H.; Texas Instruments Holland B.V.; Texas Instruments (India) Private Limited; Texas Instruments Italia S.p.A.; Texas Instruments Japan Limited; Texas Instruments Korea Limited; Texas Instruments Malaysia Sdn. Bhd.; Texas Instruments de Mexico, S.A. de C.V.; Texas Instruments France S.A.; Texas Instruments (Philippines) Incorporated; Texas Instruments Equipamento Electronico (Portugal) Lta.; Texas Instruments Singapore (Pte) Limited; Texas Instruments Taiwan Limited.

THOMSON S.A.

51, Esplanade du Général de Gaulle
La Défense
10 Puteaux
Cedex 67
92045 Paris La Défense
France
(1) 49 07 90 00

Public Company
Incorporated: 1893 as Compagnie Francaise Thomson-Houston
Employees: 104,500
Sales: FFr75 billion (US$12.38 billion)
Stock Index: Paris

Thomson S.A. and its subsidiary, Thomson-CSF, make up one of France's largest industrial combinations. With interests in consumer electronics, television, electronic components, semiconductors, medical equipment, and aircraft and military electronics, Thomson is a major European source of scientific and communications research. The company has developed and maintained a francocentric, somewhat highbrow corporate image, despite years of mismanagement followed by nationalization. Under the leadership of the celebrated Alain Gomez, Thomson has been transformed into a competitive, forward-looking industrial powerhouse.

Thomson was originally founded as the French subsidiary of the Thomson-Houston Electric Corporation, an American tramway-equipment manufacturer with considerable resources in patented machinery for the electric-power industry. The company, called Compagnie Francaise Thomson-Houston, was established in 1893, and operated largely as a sales and administrative office. Ten years later, the parent company was acquired by the American General Electric Company, and General Electric sold the Compagnie Francaise Thomson-Houston to a group of French investors.

The new owners, who retained the name of the company's American founders, were faced with the difficult task of building a strong group of engineers and project managers. For many years, the company maintained a licensing relationship with General Electric. In search of greater managerial and creative freedom, Thomson-Houston began a diversification program in 1921 which led the company into a variety of new marketing segments, including General Electric's emerging specialty: the consumer market.

Thomson-Houston grew slowly during the 1920s and 1930s. Changes in the government resulted in inconsistent industrial policy, which, on occasion, led to adverse economic conditions. Unwilling to invest heavily in new plants and equipment, Thomson-Houston saw no major growth until the eve of World War II, when the government hastily drew up an industrialization plan which, it hoped, would discourage German military adventurism in Europe. Thomson-Houston scarcely had time to begin planning production schedules before its facilities were overrun by German troops.

During the occupation, Thomson-Houston's facilities were either converted to meet the needs of the German war effort or idled. As in virtually every sector throughout French industry, consumer-product manufacturing ceased entirely, leading to a shortage of switches, motors, and lights.

At the end of the war, Thomson-Houston was reorganized to facilitate recovery. At the request of the government, the company first devoted production efforts to rebuilding French infrastructure and industry, but the demand for consumer products remained high for several years as well.

Political discord between France and the United States eventually led many French companies to end associations with American companies. For Thomson, however (the name Houston was dropped during this period), several other factors contributed to the company's decision in 1953 to end its 50-year cooperative agreement with General Electric. Thomson had emerged as an important industrial supplier and strategic military resource. Sensitivity to the security of new French technologies and the French nuclear effort, in addition to Thomson's ability to remain commercially successful on its own, all necessitated independence.

At the same time, Thomson benefited from a government militarization program to support French colonial interests. This provided the company with sufficient capital for a steady and broad internal expansion which continued until 1966. That year, Thomson acquired Hotchkiss-Brandt, a profitable French consumer-products company with substantial interests in automotive and military products. The acquisition marked the beginning of a phase of rapid expansion by acquisition for Thomson.

In 1968 Thomson-Brandt, as the new company was now called, merged its electronics division with the French communications manufacturer Compagnie Generale de Telegraphie Sans Fils. The new subsidiary, Thomson-CSF, became France's primary manufacturer of high-technology professional electronics. Looking beyond its borders, Thomson-Brandt acquired several smaller companies throughout Europe. by the mid-1970s, the company's interests extended to Asia, Africa, and North America.

Thomson-Brandt gradually lost the ability to efficiently manage shortcomings in development, production, and, ultimately, profitability. Overburdened by a bureaucracy which included two autonomous chief executives, Thomson-Brandt had no effective central-planning capability and no real budget control. These problems were exacerbated by a steady diet of government business; because liquidity could be guaranteed through sales volume, Thomson-Brandt continued to sink deeper into financial chaos. The company made numerous attempts to build new markets, including several joint ventures with companies like Xerox, Contel, and later the Italian electronics company SGS.

During this period, industrial mismanagement became a political issue for French Socialists, who promised nationalization of large industries. In 1981, the year the Socialists came to power, the government took over management of Thomson-Brandt. Alain Gomez, a Harvard-educated manager who had worked several years for Saint Gobain, succeeded Jean Pierre Bouyssonnie as chairman. Administrators appointed by the government found the company in such poor shape that it required a massive reorganization. While production continued unhindered, management's three-year shake-up ended in 1981, when Christian Aubin was appointed to overhaul the company's financial-reporting system. New reporting methods enabled Gomez to identify losing and underperforming assets and recommend divisions for divestiture.

The year-long reorganization began in September, 1982 and resulted in the creation of a new holding company called Thomson S.A., which superseded the old Thomson-Brandt organization.

In one of his first moves toward revitalizing Thomson, Gomez participated in a plan led by Industry Minister Laurent Fabius to rationalize French electronics production. Under the agreement, concluded in 1983, Thomson transferred most of its interests in telecommunications equipment and cable manufacturing to French electronics giant Cie Générale d'Electricité (CGE), participating only through a minority interest in a subsidiary managed by CGE. In return, Thomson took over a portion of CGE's interests in consumer electronics, electronic components, and defense electronics. The pact drew much criticism, particularly for Gomez, a visibly frustrated entrepreneur and reluctant government servant. Gomez nevertheless defended the agreement, citing it as an essential step in positioning Thomson for greater competitive innovation.

In a separate move more in keeping with his ambitions, Gomez attempted to acquire the West German electronics company Grundig in 1984. Rebuffed by German antitrust law and the defiance of the company's founder Max Grundig, Gomez turned his attention to an easier target: the somewhat smaller firm Telefunken. Thomson, while successful in this effort, was widely denounced in West Germany, where the nationalization of French industry was perceived, in Gomez's words, "as something between archaic and obnoxious." Thomson's greatest benefit from the takeover was not Telefunken's product line, but instead the ability to circumvent German import restrictions and use Telefunken's marketing network. The company was later criticized for streamlining Telefunken's operations and laying off workers in Germany.

As Thomson's position in world markets continued to recover, mounting opposition to the nationalization program led the Socialist government to reassess its experiment and declare that several companies would be returned to the private sector. On top of this, in 1986, Socialist President Francois Mitterand was forced to share power with a conservative element under Jacques Chirac, a strong proponent of privatization. And so during 1987, several companies were returned to the public ownership, including Thomson. Gomez, who had become chairman of Thomson as a left-wing functionary, had become a proven turn-around artist, widely admired by conservative industrialists.

In July, 1987 Thomson engineered another operations swap. Only one month after acquiring the consumer-electronics unit of Thorn-EMI, Thomson took over the American General Electric Company's entire consumer-electronics line—most of which GE had acquired in its 1986 takeover of RCA—in exchange for its Compagnie Generale de Radiologie medical-equipment unit and some cash. As with Telefunken, Thomson saw nominal value in the products themselves, but sought to take advantage of an established marketing network.

This strategy of acquiring product lines for their marketing networks is not likely to pay off for several years. Meanwhile Thomson struggles to revamp its product lines and create a consolidated brand identity. The strategy carries great risk because it increases Thomson's exposure to the volatile consumer-electronics business, which is dominated by companies such as Philips (which succeeded in acquiring Grundig), Matsushita, and Sony. It is, however, a necessary risk if Thomson is to reduce its dependence on profitable but unpredictable military contracts.

Thomson has been successful in raising quality at its new U.S. operations, and has raised its expenditures on research and development. In anticipation of the creation of a common economic community in Europe in 1992, Thomson entered into an agreement with Philips to jointly develop high-definition television in competition with Japanese consortiums.

Gomez's restructuring efforts have continued unabated, earning record profits. Seeking to end Thomson's staid reputation, Gomez recently moved the company's headquarters out of its posh estate on Boulevard Haussmann and into an industrial development in a Paris suburb. Continued efforts to reduce Thomson's labor force have generated opposition to Gomez's management from left-wing political circles. Despite this, Gomez is determined to make Thomson succeed, an effort he freely admits may yet take many years.

Principal Subsidiaries: Thomson Grand Public (97%); Thomson Consumer Electronics (U.S.A.) (80.1%); Thomson-CSF (60%).

VICTOR COMPANY OF JAPAN, LTD.

4–8–14, Nihonbashi-Honcho
Chuo-ku
Tokyo 103
Japan
(03) 241–7811

Public Company
Incorporated: 1927
Employees: 19,560
Sales: ¥820.91 billion (US$6.57)
Stock Index: Tokyo Osaka

JVC is one of several Japanese companies that has evolved to dominate the international consumer-electronics market. The company has achieved its current position not only through effective marketing but also by consistently developing new products that establish standards within the industry. Like Matsushita and Sony, JVC was strongly influenced by a single dominant personality; as the man most responsible for the success of JVC, Kenjiro Takayanagi is also considered one of Japan's most important inventors.

JVC was founded in 1927, as the wholly owned subsidiary of the Victor Talking Machine Company of the United States, to manufacture and market phonographs in Japan. Victor, however, was purchased in 1929 by the Radio Corporation of America and renamed RCA Victor. As part of an effort to enlist the marketing and sales expertise of well-established Japanese conglomerates, minority shares of the Japanese Victor Company (JVC) were sold to the Mitsubishi and Sumitomo financial groups. JVC was thereafter operated as an American-Japanese joint venture.

In 1930 JVC built a large phonograph-and-record plant in Yokohama, at the time the largest in Asia. Japan, however, soon came under the domination of ultra-right-wing militarists who in 1937 launched Japan into a war with China. The war soon led to hostility with other nations and caused many American interests to reassess their investments in Japan. RCA Victor sold a majority of its shares in JVC to Nihon Sangyo (later the Nissan Motor Company), which assumed managerial control of the company. In an unrelated moved, JVC shares held by Mitsubishi and Sumitomo were transferred to the Dai-Ichi Mutual Life Insurance Company.

RCA Victor sold its minority interest in JVC to Tokyo Shibaura Electric (now Toshiba) and Nihon Denko in 1938, making the company an entirely Japanese enterprise. The following year JVC successfully produced the first television set manufactured entirely from Japanese-made components. The television never entered mass production, but it did establish JVC's reputation as a leading electronics company.

The television was developed by an electrical engineer named Kenjiro Takayanagi. Takayanagi began work on the first Japanese-made television at the Hamamatsu Technical College in 1924, and succeeded in projecting images two years later. Takayanagi developed improved designs and was later awarded a full professorship. He was appointed to a number of positions with the Japan Broadcasting Corporation, where he led the development of television technologies, often in cooperation with companies such as JVC.

World War II had a dramatic impact on JVC, as it did on nearly every Japanese company. In 1943, as part of a government-imposed industrial reorganization, JVC's name was changed to Nippon Onkyo (Japan Acoustics), and in April, 1945 its Yokohama plant was destroyed by aerial bombings. The facility was rebuilt shortly after the war ended, when the company also returned to its former name.

Kenjiro Takayanagi joined JVC as head of the television-research department in July, 1946. The company resumed full production of radios, phonographs, and speakers in 1950, and introduced televisions in 1953, the year that Takayanagi was promoted to managing director of JVC.

As a result of the anti-monopoly laws imposed by the American military occupation authority, Tokyo Shibaura (the primary owner of JVC) was forced to sell its interest in the company. For the next several years JVC endured labor problems and persistent financial instability. Japan's anti-monopoly legislation was relaxed in stages, so that by 1953 the Matsushita Electric Industrial Company was permitted to purchase a 50% interest in the nearly bankrupt JVC.

Konosuke Matsushita, who had founded Matsushita Electric in 1918, decided to maintain JVC's operational autonomy, offering only managerial direction and capital infusions. Initially JVC was considered a good investment for Matsushita because the two companies competed in relatively few areas. But as it evolved, the relationship between JVC and Matsushita became one of competitive cooperation. Matsushita permitted JVC's managers great latitude in making decisions about investments in research and development, joint production, and licensing agreements. One of the ideas JVC developed was a video tape recorder.

In the field of audio technology, JVC developed the 45–45 system, one of the first systems to enable phonographs to reproduce sound in stereo. In conventional monaural systems, a small needle runs through a V-shaped groove that varies in depth, and the vibration of the needle is amplified to produce sounds. The 45–45 system required that depths vary on both sides of the groove. Two separate mechanisms measured the vibration of the needle in perpendicular directions. These vibrations were then amplified independently to produce two sounds simultaneously, or in stereo.

JVC introduced 45–45-system stereo phonographs in 1957, and the following year developed a color video tape recorder. The company began commercial production of color television sets in 1960, at a new plant in Iwai. Color television broadcasting began that same year and greatly increased demand for JVC televisions. In order to take better advantage of the company's growth, JVC shares were listed on the Tokyo and Osaka stock exchanges, and capital raised through subsequent share issues enabled the company to increase production capacity. Favorable economic conditions and low production costs allowed JVC to gain substantial markets shares in foreign countries, particularly in the United States. In 1968, in an ironic reversal of 1927, JVC established a wholly owned American subsidiary called JVC America, and three years later the company created a West German subsidiary called Nippon Victor (Europe) GmbH.

Kenjiro Takayanagi assumed a more influential role in the management of JVC during the 1960s, further diminishing the company's system of consensus management. Trained as an engineer, however, Takayanagi was not able to avoid the prolonged drop in profits that lasted from 1970 to 1976. The management of Matsushita continued to provide the guidance and support necessary to keep JVC from encountering more serious financial difficulty.

During those six years, JVC devoted considerable resources to the development of a commercial video cassette system. As part of a reorganization program in 1973, the company's management separated the music division from JVC and established it as a subsidiary called Victor Musical Industries. During the mid-1970s JVC established additional subsidiaries in Great Britain, Canada, and the United States.

A few months before his 76th birthday, in 1974, Kenjiro Takayanagi retired from JVC, but continued to serve the company as an advisor. The video division, which was largely his creation, introduced the video home system (VHS) format video cassette recorder in 1976. The system was introduced after Sony's Betamax VCR, but was superior in several ways. Matsushita Electric, which had been independently developing a third format, was so impressed with the VHS that it abandoned its project and arranged for cross-licensing of the JVC technology.

Matsushita and its allied brands, Quasar and Panasonic, adopted the VHS format and, with JVC, worked diligently to establish VHS as the industry standard. Their efforts succeded and, despite a full year of monopoly, the Sony Betamax was superseded by the VHS; Sony's market share rapidly diminished.

With the tremendous success of VHS, JVC's profits had risen by a factor of ten by 1982. The video division, which had accounted for 6% of total sales in 1976, accounted for 69% in 1982. JVC established several additional subsidiaries, particularly in Europe, to handle sales of VHS video recorders and other products.

JVC engineers developed a laser-operated video-disc system in 1978. Although the technology gained favor among consumers, the product's inability to record television broadcasts was such a drawback that it curtailed its further development. A subsequent compact disc (CD) format developed by Sony and Philips, however, has proven highly successful for audio reproduction. JVC applied certain video-disc technologies to the CD and developed a VHD videodisc system that is interchangeable with conventional CD players. JVC introduced the VHD to Japan in April, 1983, and has licensed VHD technology to 13 other Japanese manufacturers in addition to Thorn EMI, AEG-Telefunken, and America's General Electric.

Although JVC introduced a line of personal computers and peripheral products in 1983, the company's future product development will be directed toward improved audio and video systems.

While Kenjiro Takayanagi continued to advise the company from retirement, JVC returned to a more democratic form of management, greatly influenced by directors tenured at Matsushita. However, Ichiro Shinji, the first man in 25 years to gain promotion to the company presidency from within JVC ranks, has since been named chairman of JVC. The company's relative autonomy within the Matsushita group continues, and its relationship of constructive competition with Matsushita has proven to be most profitable as well.

Principal Subsidiaries: Victor Musical Industries, Inc.; Victor Family Club Co., Ltd.; Nippon AVC Co., Ltd.; Hokkaido Victor Co., Ltd.; Ou Victor Co., Ltd.; Tohoku Victor Co., Ltd.; Kanto Victor Co., Ltd.; Tokyo-Higashi Victor Co., Ltd.; Tokyo-Nishi Victor Co., Ltd.; Chiba Victor Co., Ltd.; Shinetsu Victor Co., Ltd.; Kanagawa Victor Co., Ltd.; Shizuoka Victor Co., Ltd.; Tokai Victor Co., Ltd.; Hokuriku Victor Co., Ltd.; Keiji Victor Co., Ltd.; Kobe Victor Co., Ltd.; Chugoku Victor Co., Ltd.; Shikoku Victor Co., Ltd.; Kyushu Victor Co., Ltd.; JVC Magnetics of Japan Co., Ltd.; Victor Service & Engineering Co., Ltd.; Sanin Victor Sales Co. Ltd.; Okinawa Victor Sales Co. Ltd.; Victor Finance Co., Ltd.; Nippon VMR Co. Ltd.; U.S. JVC Corp.; JVC Canada Inc.; JVC (U.K.) Ltd.; JVC Video France S.A.; JVC Magnetics Europe GmbH (West Germany); JVC America, Inc.; JVC Electronics Singapore Pte., Ltd.; JVC Deutschland GmbH; JVC Finance B.V.

Westinghouse

WESTINGHOUSE ELECTRIC CORPORATION

Westinghouse Building
Gateway Center
Pittsburgh, Pennsylvania 15222
U.S.A.
(412) 244–2000
Public Company
Incorporated: 1886
Employees: 120,000
Sales: $12.5 billion
Stock Index: New York Midwest Boston Philadelphia Pacific Cincinnati

George Westinghouse, who invented the air-brake as a 22 year-old engineer with little formal education, founded the Westinghouse Electric Company in Pittsburgh in 1886 as a way of entering the infant electrical industry. He began by trying to develop an economical system of transmission using alternating current (AC). At that time direct current (DC), championed by Thomas Edison, was the only form of electrical power in common use. Edison and his Edison General Electric Company responded to the challenge by sponsoring a smear campaign aimed at convincing the public that AC was unsafe. Despite this effort, Westinghouse Electric installed the nation's first AC power system in 1891 in Telluride, Colorado, and scored two major victories in 1893 when it provided the generating system that powered the World's Fair in Chicago and won a contract to provide generators for the new hydroelectric power station at Niagara Falls.

During these years both Edison General Electric and Westinghouse both spent small fortunes accumulating patents, with the result that neither company could market new products without fear of patent infringement litigation. After a series of expensive legal battles in the early 1890s, the two companies called a truce in 1896 and set up a patent control board to avoid all such disputes (in fact, they established a virtual duopoly in electric railway equipment during the 1890s). It marked the beginning of the odd relationship between the two largest electrical companies in the United States, a relationship that has ranged over the years from illegal collusion to fierce competition. The infancy of the electrical industry was dominated by inventor-entrepreneurs like George Westinghouse and Thomas Edison, but their professional rivalry would continue long after both men had died and the Edison General Electric Company had dropped its founder's name.

Westinghouse's association with the company that he founded ended in 1910. After years of expansion, Westinghouse Electric found itself unable to produce the necessary cash to pay $14 million worth of debt that was about to come due because a stock panic had depressed the financial markets and made it impossible to raise money through them. The company was placed in receivership and the bankers who reorganized it appointed a new board of directors. From January, 1909 to July, 1910, when he was ousted, Westinghouse continued as president, with limited authority. He died in 1914 at the age of 67.

But if Westinghouse Electric missed the guiding hand of its founder, it didn't show it. During the 1910s the company accumulated patents in the area of wireless communication. In 1919 and 1920, it joined RCA, General Electric, United Fruit, AT&T, and Wireless Specialty Company in a series of cross-licensing agreements that paved the way for the commercial introduction of radio. Under these agreements, Westinghouse and GE carved up the exclusive right to manufacture radio receivers between them, with RCA as the selling organization.

Westinghouse had also become a pioneer in radio broadcasting when it realized that continuous service would help receiver sales. In 1920 it set up radio station KDKA, which broadcast from the roof of the Westinghouse plant in East Pittsburgh. Over the next five years it opened several more stations across the country, and broadcasting has remained a substantial part of Westinghouse's business ever since.

Westinghouse, however, missed a chance to get in on the ground floor of television manufacturing. Vladimir Zworykin, the inventor of the electronic picture tube, began his research at Westinghouse in the early 1920s. But his superiors showed indifference to his work, and when RCA acquired the manufacturing and sales rights for radio and TV receivers and tubes, David Sarnoff was able to woo him to RCA. While at RCA, Zworykin filed the patent that would form the basis for the modern television set.

The first electrical appliances for consumers were also introduced in the 1920s and Westinghouse was in the forefront. The company offered a variety of products, from electric ranges to smaller household appliances. It introduced a line of electric refrigerators in 1930 and later added washing machines to its repertoire. It also entered the elevator business in 1927 when it acquired Kaestner & Hecht Company.

Westinghouse did not expand very much during the 1930s, as the Depression cast a pall over American industry. All of that changed, however, in 1941, when Westinghouse entered the military electronics business. It became one of the leading contractors for radar, which was invented before World War II. In fact, Westinghouse radar had provided a warning signal of the advance of Japanese planes on Pearl Harbor, but it was assumed that the planes were American. During the war years, Westinghouse grew at a frenetic pace and its defense business became so large that CEO A. W. Robertson hired banker Gwilym

Price in 1943 just to handle financial negotiations on military contracts. Price succeeded Robertson as CEO in 1946.

Westinghouse's performance during the postwar economic boom shows a mixture of successes and difficulties. On the one hand, its longtime connections with electrical utilities enabled it to move quickly into the burgeoning field of nuclear power, and the company has remained a leading producer of nuclear-generating equipment ever since. It also became the leading supplier of reactors for the U.S. Navy's nuclear submarine fleet. And during the Korean War, it scored what *Fortune* called "a brilliant coup" by developing the axial-flow jet engine, which became the prototype for jet engines for the rest of the decade. But following a change in weight specifications for navy airplanes the navy canceled millions of dollars worth of contracts for Westinghouse's J-40 and J-46 engines.

Westinghouse also moved slowly in targeting other branches of the armed forces, with the result that from 1955 to 1957 it ranked only 25th in sales among defense contractors. Rival GE, by comparison, ranked third. Adding to its troubles, poor marketing plagued its consumer-appliance operations and it all but conceded the foremost place in this business to GE. Beginning in October, 1955 Westinghouse suffered through a five-month electrical-workers strike, the longest walkout against an American corporation since the Depression. And in the early 1950s, the three principal manufacturers of heavy electrical machinery—Westinghouse, GE, and Allis-Chalmers—waged a devastating price war that cut into revenues.

As a result of that price war those three companies, along with 26 smaller manufacturers who did business with electrical utilities, entered into a bid-rigging scheme in 1955 in hopes of securing their profit margins. Under the plan, each of the participants agreed beforehand on the amount of each bid and on who would win the contract. In the area of power switchgear, for instance, it was agreed that Westinghouse would win 35% of the contracts, GE 39%, I-T-E Circuit Breaker 11%, Allis-Chalmers 8% and Federal Pacific Electric 7%. In 1957 the Justice Department began to investigate possible violations of the Sherman Antitrust Act, and two years later a grand jury was called into session after the Tennessee Valley Authority complained of collusion among the manufacturers. Forty-five executives from 29 companies were indicted and all pleaded guilty. In the wake of the scandal Mark Cresap, who had succeeded Gwilym Price as CEO in 1958, announced that a section of the company's legal department would devote itself solely to compliance with antitrust laws.

Cresap resigned in 1963 because of ill health and died later that year. He left a Westinghouse that had, according to *Fortune*, "reached a low ebb in its corporate life." Still reeling from the bid-rigging scandal, the company was also plagued by stagnant sales, eroding prices, and declining profits. Into this unenviable position stepped engineer Donald Burnham. It was said of the affable and unpretentious Burnham that when he wanted to rearrange the paintings in the CEO's office, he asked his secretary for a hammer and started pounding nails into the wall himself.

One of Burnham's top priorities as chief executive was to reorganize the corporate chain of command, decentralizing authority and giving individual division heads more freedom. Along with shaking up the bureaucracy, he sought ways to cut costs and use incentives to improve managerial performance. Westinghouse also embarked on a remarkable program of diversification under Burnham, buying into businesses as divorced from its core operations as soft-drink bottling, car rental, motels, transport refrigeration, land development, and mail-order record clubs. One of its most unusual ventures was Urban Systems Development Corporation, which Westinghouse set up in 1968 to respond to the need for low-cost housing by building pre-fabricated residential units. It was a venture consistent with Burnham's belief that social responsibility and corporate profitability were not necessarily incompatible.

In 1964 Westinghouse recorded record sales of $2.1 billion, but profits were sharply lower than in the previous year because of continued depressed prices in its major product lines. In 1966, however, profits reached $119.7 million, nearly a threefold increase from 1963. By the late 1960s the company's financial outlook had brightened considerably, and Burnham was hailed as a hero of corporate America.

But by the time he retired in 1974, Westinghouse was once again in trouble. Decentralization of corporate authority had allowed overzealous division managers to stretch the company's resources to the breaking point. As vice chairman Marshall Evans told *Fortune* in 1976, "we learned to our horror that these companies had gone totally hog-wild in committing the corporation to very substantial projects that were costly to complete." A prime example of this was Urban Systems Development. Although Robert Kirby, Burnham's successor, blamed its failure on lack of cooperation from the federal government, Urban Systems also expanded far too quickly for its own good and wound up posting after-tax losses of $45 million from 1972–1975. And although some of the unfamiliar businesses into which Westinghouse diversified turned a profit, like the Seven-Up Bottling Company of Los Angeles (purchased in 1969), many others did not. The acquisition of Longines-Wittenauer Watch Company, undertaken in 1970 mainly for its mail-order record operations, turned sour immediately, as discount record shops began to give mail-order businesses unwelcome competition. By the time Westinghouse divested its mail-order business in 1975 it had lost $65 million after taxes.

Westinghouse was also hurt by the continued lackluster performance of its consumer-appliance business and the high inflation of the early 1970s, which reduced revenues from fixed-price heavy-equipment contracts that it had signed years earlier. Wall Street analysts continued to downgrade the company, despite the fact that in April, 1974 it received an order for twelve nuclear power systems from France's state-run nuclear power agency, with options for four more units—the largest single order for nuclear equipment in history. One analyst told the *New York Times* that Burnham's decision to continue manufacturing appliances was "greeted with horror."

Later that year Westinghouse stock dropped to $8 a share, from a high of $55 several years earlier. In late 1974, it sold its appliance business to White Consolidated Industries, leaving a field it had helped to pioneer, although White continued to market its products under the name White-Westinghouse.

When Robert Kirby became CEO he immediately declared that Westinghouse would get back to basics and in 1975 the company began to spin off its other unprofitable businesses. But the major event of the first half of Kirby's watch came about as a consequence of Westinghouse's decision in the early 1960s to become a uranium supplier. It had agreed to supply utilities that purchased its reactors with a total of 65 million pounds of uranium concentrate over a period of 20 years, at an average of $9.50 a pound. In 1973, however, the price of uranium skyrocketed, eventually exceeding $40 a pound. Westinghouse was caught with scanty reserves and found itself unable to buy enough uranium to meet its commitments. The 27 utilities with which it had uranium contracts sued to force Westinghouse to live up to those contracts. This would have cost the company $2 billion, the entire worth of its shareholder assets at the time. Westinghouse settled the last of these lawsuits in 1980, having paid a total of $950 million in damages, and managed to recoup some of those losses by suing a number of foreign and domestic uranium producers, charging that they had formed a cartel to drive up uranium prices unfairly. Some of these lawsuits were thrown out of court, but others were eventually settled for cash damages.

With its uranium problems mostly out of the way as it entered the 1980s, Westinghouse once again gave thought to expansion. As early as 1980 it had declared its intention to enter the field of robotics. In 1982 it acquired Unimation, a leading robot manufacturer. Westinghouse Broadcasting also expanded its cable television operations, acquiring cable giant Teleprompter Corporation in 1981 in the largest merger between communications companies in U. S. history. In 1982, a proposed joint cable venture with the Walt Disney Company fell through, but Westinghouse did join with NLT Corporation, a Nashville-based entertainment concern, to form The Nashville Network.

Reduced demand and utility overcapacity in the late 1970s and growing anxiety in the 1980s over the safety of nuclear power hurt Westinghouse's nuclear-equipment business, but the Reagan administration's massive military buildup added life to its defense operations. During the 1980s, Westinghouse received major contracts on such weapons as the F-16 and F-4E fighters, the B-52 and B-1B strategic bombers, the AWACS radar plane, the Mk 48 torpedo, the Trident nuclear submarine, and the MX missile. In 1985 the *Wall Street Journal* ranked Westinghouse as the nation's 13th-largest defense contractor. And in 1988 Westinghouse's electronic systems business, which is comprised almost entirely of military projects, accounted for roughly one-fifth of sales.

Douglas Danforth succeeded Robert Kirby as CEO in 1983. Also in that year, Westinghouse Broadcasting sold its Satellite News Channel to rival Cable News Network after the two had exchanged antitrust and unfair-competition lawsuits. Westinghouse sold its cable television operations in 1986 to a consortium of cable companies for $1.7 billion as part of a major restructuring progam.

The mid- and late 1980s were marked by a number of divestitures of small- and medium-sized companies. Westinghouse also entered a series of joint ventures with foreign firms, most of them reflecting the growing dominance of Japanese companies in the electronics industry. In 1982 and 1985, it joined with Mitsubishi Electric to produce and market circuit breakers. In 1984 it formed a joint venture, subsequently dissolved, with Toshiba to manufacture high-resolution color picture tubes for computers and televisions. It also formed a joint venture with the Korean company Hyundai in 1984 to manufacture elevators and escalators, and with Siemens of West Germany to manufacture automation products in 1988.

In early 1989, Westinghouse also sold off two of its businesses to Swiss concerns. It sold its elevator operations to Schindler Holdings and, after several years of disappointing performance, Unimation to Staubli International.

Although Westinghouse no longer manufactures much of anything for the consumer, and there isn't much visibility in making turbines for power generators or even radar for the F-16, the company is still very much alive. Indeed, Westinghouse claims to be more financially sound now than at any other time in its history. Despite problems such as the wane of the nuclear power industry and a complicated dispute over a nuclear power plant with the Philippine government, Westinghouse has been successful in streamlining its operations during the 1980s. Between 1985 and 1987 Danforth sold 70 less-profitable businesses, replacing them with 55 acquisitions that complement existing Westinghouse spheres of operation. Westinghouse hopes that this diversity will minimize its exposure to recessions and enhance its growth in the future.

Principal Subsidiaries: Fortin Industries, Inc.; Longines-Wittnauer, Inc.; Thermo King Corp.; Tyree Industries Limited (Australia) (69%); Westinghouse Beverage Group, Inc.; Westinghouse Broadcasting Company, Inc.; Westinghouse Canada Inc. (95%); Westinghouse Communities, Inc.; Westinghouse Financial Services, Inc.; Westinghouse de Puerto Rico, Inc.; Westinghouse Electric, S.A. (Switzerland); Hittman Nuclear & Development Corp.; Gladwin Corp.; Hydro Nuclear Service Inc.; TSC, Inc.; Ottermill, Ltd. (U.K.); TCOM Corp.; Westinghouse Foreign Sales Corp. (Barbados); Westinghouse Foreign Sales Corp. (Virgin Islands); Westinghouse Fanal Schaltgerate GmbH (West Germany); Westinghouse International Technology Corp.; Westinghouse Nuclear International, Inc.; Westinghouse Overseas Service Corp.; Westinghouse Thermo King, S.A. (Belgium); Xetron Corp.

Further Reading: Passer, Harold C. *The Electrical Manufacturers 1875–1900*, Cambridge, Harvard University Press, 1953.

ZENITH ELECTRONICS CORPORATION

1000 Milwaukee Avenue
Glenview, Illinois 60025
U.S.A.
(708) 391–7000

Public Company
Incorporated: 1923 as Zenith Radio Corporation
Sales: $1.5 billion
Employees: 35,000
Stock Index: New York

Zenith Electronics Corporation is recognized primarily as a manufacturer of high-quality consumer electronics products. From its start Zenith advertised that its reputation would be built and sustained by the superior workmanship, reliability, and innovation of all products bearing the Zenith name. The company became a huge American success as a top producer first in the radio industry and later in television. However, low-priced imports from Asia began to rock Zenith in the mid- to late 1970s. After major reorganizations, diversification into the personal computer market, initiation of production in other countries, and years of major financial losses despite constantly increasing sales, Zenith seems ready to make a comeback in the 1990s.

Zenith's beginnings were very modest. Two ham radio operators, Karl E. Hassel and R.H.G. Mathews, began manufacturing radio equipment at a kitchen table in 1918. Hassel ran an amateur radio station with the call letters 9ZN, which were the basis for the name Zenith. These two men were joined by Commander Eugene F. McDonald Jr. in 1921. McDonald, already a self-made millionaire when he joined the company, was pivotal to Zenith's growth. He was much more than a financial backer. McDonald's flamboyant style was echoed in the company's dramatic advertising methods and this style, coupled with innovative genius and an ability to sense changes in public tastes, meant that for more than three decades, in the public perception McDonald *was* Zenith.

McDonald was counterbalanced by Hugh Robertson, who joined the company as treasurer in 1923. Robertson's financial expertise and careful planning led Zenith through many difficulties, including the Great Depression. 1923 was significant in many other ways. The company was incorporated as Zenith Radio Corporation that year, and 30,000 shares of stock were issued at $10 par, with the largest single block going to McDonald. At that time, Zenith Radio Corporation took over sales and marketing for the Chicago Radio Laboratory, a maker of radio equipment. Zenith later acquired all of Chicago Radio Laboratory's assets and continued to manufacture under its own name.

Soon McDonald, who preferrred to be addressed as "The Commander" (as a lieutenant commander in the Navy during World War I he was entitled to the name), began to show his flair for drama. He persuaded Admiral Donald B. MacMillan to take a shortwave radio with him on his Arctic expedition. MacMillan's transmissions proved to be exciting demonstrations of the efficiency of shortwave communication. In addition to his advertising schemes, Commander McDonald organized and became president of the National Association of Broadcasters in 1923.

Meanwhile, Zenith's inventors and technicians were developing landmark products. In 1924 Zenith introduced the world's first portable radio. Then in 1925, McDonald helped MacMillan organize another exhibition, this time to the North Pole. McDonald was part of the expedition as a ship commander, but went only as far as Greenland. His shortwave radio broadcasts of Eskimos singing into the microphone was a great success, and Zenith's advertising always reminded the public that Zenith was the choice of the Arctic explorers.

More innovations followed. In 1926 Zenith introduced the first home radio receiver that operated directly from regular AC electric current, and automatic push-button tuning came in 1927. By the late 1920s Zenith was in twelfth place in a $400 million industry.

But when the Great Depression hit after the stock market crash of 1929, the radio industry was thrown into chaos. Zenith's sales went from $10 million in 1929 to less than $2 million in 1932. Although the company suffered five successive years of losses, Treasurer Hugh Robertson managed to get the company through without borrowing until profitability returned.

McDonald, even during those times, did not give up his attempts to get Zenith technology into new areas. In 1934, he sent a wire to all U.S. oil and tire companies: "Watch absence of people on streets between eleven and eleven-thirty during presidential talk." After the talk, he sent letters urging them to become Zenith auto-radio dealers and get rich.

One of McDonald's most popular ideas during the 1930s was the "big black dial" for radios. Its large clock-style numbers were designed to be read from a distance or without glasses. McDonald also promoted portable shortwave radios for $75, an idea that was ridiculed at the time but was extremely successful in the end.

Zenith management valued and encouraged worker loyalty. Therefore, when the company began to be profitable again in 1936 for the first time in five years, Zenith paid its workers, rather than its stockholders, a dividend, in appreciation for sticking out the tough times of little money. Net sales of $8.5 million in 1936 resulted in net income of $1.2 million. By 1937 sales were up to almost $17 million, and net income was nearly $2 million.

By the late 1930s, Zenith was exporting to 96 countries, and was a pioneer in television and FM broadcasting. In 1939 Zenith's station W9XZV, the first all-electronic television station, went on the air. This was followed the next year by W9XEN, one of the first FM stations in the United States. By 1941 Zenith had risen to second place in a $600 million industry, behind only RCA.

Although World War II meant a decline in normal consumer business, this decline was more than offset by war production. Zenith manufactured radar, communications equipment, and high-sensitivity frequency meters. Net sales were $23.8 million in 1941, and $34.2 million in 1942, with $1.4 million in net income that year.

Zenith's major product outside of war-related materials during World War II was a highly successful hearing aid that retailed for $40. A miniature adaptation of a radio receiving set, it made hearing assistance affordable for many thousands of people. Zenith became the largest marketer of hearing aids in the world, outselling all other companies combined.

Once it was able to resume civilian research and production, Zenith concentrated on improving television, even though McDonald had resisted television for almost a decade. The company introduced its first line of black-and-white television receivers in 1948. Also in 1948, in order to meet an immediate increased demand, Zenith purchased the Rauland Corporation, a noted Chicago manufacturer of television picture tubes. One year after this purchase, the combined talents of the Zenith and Rauland researchers produced the non-reflective "black-tube."

While Zenith continued research and development on color television throughout the early 1950s, and even participated in the development of industry standards for a compatible color television system, it still did not get into the color-TV market. McDonald was even more adamant about color television than he had been about black and white, saying "someday, the technical and service problems of color TV will be solved. When that day comes, we will offer you a line of outstanding color sets. In the meantime, we will not try to make an experimental laboratory of dealers and the public. We will keep color in our laboratories until it is ready." Zenith continued to work on its black-and-white televisions, inventing the first wireless remote control in 1956, and held the leading position in black and white television from 1959 on.

The color television breakthrough came in 1961, when Zenith introduced a 10-receiver line of color sets. Demand for these sets grew so quickly that it had to expand its facilities. Also that year Zenith's experimental stereophonic FM broadcasting system was approved by the FCC as the national standard.

Color television improvements continued steadily. In 1969 Zenith introduced the patented Chromacolor picture tube, which set the standard for brightness in the color-TV industry for many years. In 1970, the company received awards from the American Association for the Advancement of Science in recognition of its years of technological achievements. By 1972, the year it introduced a line of 25-inch television, Zenith was number one in production of color television sets.

Enormous profitability led to expansion. In 1971 Zenith acquired a 93% interest in Movado-Zenith-Mondia Holding, a watch manufacturer. It also acquired a one-third interest in a Venezuelan television company in 1974, and significantly increased its U.S. product distributors. Zenith was able to maintain the leading position in the fiercely competitive U.S. color-television market between 1972 and 1978, but was overtaken by RCA in 1979.

Domestic competition, however, did not prove to be Zenith's greatest problem. Manufacturers in Japan, Taiwan, and Korea began selling great numbers of electronic consumer goods in the United States at prices below what American companies could afford to offer. Zenith's then-chairman, John Nevin, filed suits against the Japanese and testified in Congress, accusing the Japanese of dumping goods on the American market at below-cost prices. Nevin's demand that the federal government enforce its 1971 anti-dumping laws was finally met, but not before significant damage had been done.

In 1977, Zenith sold most of its domestic hearing aid instrumentation operation. Also in 1977, Zenith found itself contracting with Japan's Sony Corporation, to market Sony's Betamax home video television recorder in the United States under the Zenith label. By 1978, Zenith had sold most of its Movado watch assets and laid off 25% of its American workers when Zenith established plants in Mexico and Taiwan.

Zenith President and CEO Revone Kluckman realized that action outside Washington was needed to combat the pricing crisis. Kluckman is credited with refocusing Zenith's competitive energies from legal battles to the factory floor by implementing cost-cutting measures and improved manufacturing procedures.

A sweeping reorganization also began in 1978. The corporate structure was rebuilt along product lines, with each group receiving a charter to move aggressively into new businesses. Jerry Pearlman, then a senior Zenith finance executive, now chairman and president, was instrumental in pushing for one business in particular: computers. In 1979, Zenith acquired the Heath Company, a long-time maker of do-it-yourself electronic kits. The shrewd and inexpensive ($64.5 million) purchase occurred right after Heath announced its first personal computer kit and only months after Apple introduced its first personal computer.

Zenith Data Systems, a wholly owned subsidiary, was born after the Heath acquisition. The parent company required that any new business tap at least two of three Zenith capabilities: technology, manufacturing, and distribution. Zenith Data Systems was a perfect match on all three counts. The first Zenith computer, the Z-100, was introduced in 1981; 35,000 Z-100s were shipped that first year.

In addition to complete computers, Zenith began to sell video terminals that were compatible with virtually all personal computers on the market. These became very successful, as were the components Zenith sold to other computer companies. Zenith also entered the market for convertors for the growing cable TV market.

Nevertheless, the early success of Zenith Data Systems was not enough to offset the impact of foreign competition. The company suffered a net loss of $24 million on revenues of $1.2 billion in 1982 and did not pay a dividend that year for the first time in almost half a century.

Zenith continued to push for cost reductions. These were achieved through the use of robotics and other improvements in design and manufacturing, which led to a higher sales volume to offset lower prices. By 1983, although it lacked the advertising dollars to mount the campaigns of other industry manufacturers, Zenith Data Systems boasted an installed base of 95,000 microcomputers. Computer sales mounted to $135 million that year, and Zenith was profitable. It also celebrated a victory in an antitrust suit against Japan that year.

Zenith worked to win large contracts with educational institutions and the federal government, greatly broadening its impact on the personal computer market. It also held a virtual monopoly on the do-it-yourself computer market through more than 70 Heathkit Electronic Centers. Whereas overall computer sales accounted for 1.4% of Zenith sales in 1979 (exclusively Heath), they were up to 15% in 1984. Also in 1984, the electronics industry adopted the Zenith-developed system for MTS stereo TV broadcast and reception. It was another profitable year, marked by a name change from the long outdated Zenith Radio Corporation to Zenith Electronics Corporation.

The roller coaster went down again for Zenith in 1985. Although computer-products sales rose from $249 in 1984 to $352 million in 1985, computer sales did not offset the $125 million loss in consumer electronics. The company was nearly $8 million in the red at year's end.

In 1986 Zenith introduced more new products than at any time in its history, especially in the home entertainment and computer improvement areas. Record numbers of video cassette recorders were shipped, up 34%, and cable operations were up 16%. Foreign operations brought in 13% of overall revenues. Computer systems and components were up 56% to $548 million, accounting for 29% of total sales (consumer electronics figured at 64%, and components at 7% made up the rest). Nevertheless, 1986 was another overall loss—of $10 million—due to pricing pressures and lower profit margins. Japanese, Taiwanese, and Korean prices in the United States were 10% lower in 1986 than in 1985. Zenith chief Jerry Pearlman eventually asked the federal government once again to monitor foreign manufacturers' illegal dumping of inexpensive TV sets on the American market. His request did little good, and as Zenith continued to lose money, pressure from investors to sell its consumer electronics unit mounted. Pearlman, however, resisted, hoping that high definition television (HDTV) would inject new life into the consumer electronics division. In 1988, Zenith entered into an agreement with AT&T Microelectronics. Zenith has developed techology for HDTV broadcasts which it hopes will become the industry standard, and AT&T Microelectronics and Zenith are jointly developing an HDTV receiver for market in the mid-1990s.

In 1988 Zenith reported a modest $12 million profit, ending a four-year streak of losses. But the company was saddled with heavy debt (incurred primarily to finance the growth of its computer business), and competition in both the consumer electronics and computer industries was heating up.

It was becoming increasingly evident to Pearlman that Zenith's continued participation in two tough business areas was hurting the company's competitiveness; while both were over $1 billion in sales by 1988, neither was highly profitable.

In 1989 Pearlman suddenly decided to sell Zenith's computer business to Paris-based Groupe Bull. Zenith used the $500 million it received from Bull to pay off its short-term debt and some of its long term obligations as well.

Zenith management hopes this trimming will improve its ability to compete in consumer electronics in the 1990s. Zenith also continues to make cable products and electronic components, and the company has held onto its computer-monitor business, which, along with its flat tension mask high-resolution TVs, should play some role in the development of Zenith's HDTV receiver.

Zenith's slogan since 1927, "The Quality Goes In Before The Name Goes On," exemplifies its philosophy. The company is focusing on the strength of its reputation and its continued market innovations. With over 30 subsidiaries, Zenith hopes its increasing mix of products will lead to permanent stability despite a highly unpredictable marketplace.

Principal Subsidiaries: Zenith Distributing Corporation; Zenith Electronics Corporation of Arizona; Zenith Electronics Corporation of Texas; Zenith Electronics (Ireland) Limited; Zenith/Inteq, Inc.; Zenith International Sales Corporation; Zenith Microcircuits Corporation; Zenith Radio Canada Ltd./Zenith Radio Canada Ltee.; Zenith Taiwan Corporation; Zenith Video Products Corporation; Zenith Video Tech Corporation; Zentrans, Inc.; Cableproductos de Chihuahua, S.A. de C.V. (Mexico); Electro Partes de Matamoros, S.A. de C.V. (Mexico); Interocean Advertising Corporation; Productos Magneticos de Chihuahua, S.A. de C.V. (Mexico); Partes de Television de Reynosa, S.A. de C.V. (Mexico); Teleson de Mexico, S.A. de C.V.; Televisores Venezolanos S.A. (Televensa); Zenco de Chihuahua, S.A. de C.V. (Mexico).

Further Reading: "Zenith: Highlights of the First 60 Years," Zenith Radio Corporation, Glenview, Illinois, 1978.

ENTERTAINMENT & LEISURE

CAPITAL CITIES/ABC INC.
CBS INC.
COLUMBIA PICTURES ENTERTAINMENT, INC.
GRANADA GROUP PLC
LADBROKE GROUP PLC
MCA INC.
MGM/UA COMMUNICATIONS COMPANY
NATIONAL BROADCASTING COMPANY INC.
PARAMOUNT PICTURES CORPORATION
RANK ORGANISATION PLC
TELE-COMMUNICATIONS, INC.
TOURISTIK UNION INTERNATIONAL GMBH. AND COMPANY K.G.
TURNER BROADCASTING SYSTEM, INC.
TWENTIETH CENTURY FOX FILM CORPORATION
WALT DISNEY COMPANY
WARNER COMMUNICATIONS INC.

CAPITAL CITIES/ABC INC.

77 West 66th Street
New York, New York 10023
U.S.A.
(212) 456–7777

Public Company
Incorporated: 1985
Sales: $4.77 billion
Employees: 13,700
Stock Index: New York

Of three major networks in the United States, ABC is the youngest. The first broadcasting company in the United States was the National Broadcasting Company (NBC), founded by the Radio Corporation of America (RCA) in 1926. By 1928 NBC had grown so large that RCA divided the company into two networks, the red and the blue, and it is in the blue network that ABC's origins lie. The Federal Communications Commission (FCC), worried by the monopolistic tendencies in the broadcasting industry, decided in 1941 that no single company could own more than one network, and ordered NBC to divest itself of one of its two. Accordingly, in 1943 NBC sold the less profitable blue network to Edward J. Noble, who had made his fortune at the head of Life Savers Inc. Noble dubbed his network the American Broadcasting Company.

At first ABC was only a radio broadcaster. NBC and CBS had been involved in experimental television production and transmission for over a decade by the time ABC was created, and the new network found the transition to television difficult, a reputation that dogged ABC for years. It was not until 1953, when ABC merged with United Paramount Theatres, that ABC emerged as a third network of full stature.

United Paramount Theatres had been the movie theater arm of Paramount Pictures until the company was forced by antitrust legislation to divest itself of its theater chain. In the merger, Leonard Goldenson, Paramount's president, became president of the new American Broadcasting-Paramount Theatres, Inc. (AB-PT), the owner now of 708 movie theaters, a radio network with 355 affiliates, a television network with 14 affiliates, and television and radio stations in five major cities.

More importantly, the merger brought ABC cash. Goldenson's first major expenditure as head of AB-PT went to Walt Disney: in return for a $4.5 million loan from the network to complete the construction of Disneyland, Disney agreed to provide a television show for ABC. This deal was the first time that a movie company produced a show for a TV network. AB-PT also acquired a 35% interest in the amusement park, presaging later purchases of similar parks.

The broadcasting division of AB-PT expanded its television programming in that same year from 21 to 35 hours a week. In addition to producing already popular shows like "The Adventures of Ozzie and Harriet," "Make Room for Daddy," and "The Lone Ranger," the network introduced two innovative dramatic series in 1954: "The U.S. Steel Hour" and "Kraft Television Theatre." AB-PT also broadcast 186 hours of the hearings involving the United States Army and Senator Joseph McCarthy. The network was able to broadcast the interrogations live without preempting any of its own programs because AB-PT did not yet have a regular daytime schedule.

A year later Warner Brothers, a major motion picture studio, agreed to begin producing shows for the network, eventually providing AB-PT with "Lawman," "Maverick," "Colt .45," and others. Meanwhile Disney studios provided a program called "The Mickey Mouse Club Show." "The Lawrence Welk Show" also debuted in 1955 and became so popular, especially among senior citizens, that it became ABC's longest-running prime-time series ever.

By 1957, the broadcasting division of AB-PT had passed the theater division as the largest revenue producer for the company—in part because the theater division had, by government order, been reduced to a chain of 537 theaters.

Meanwhile, Am-Par Records, founded in 1954, released its first record to sell a million copies, in 1957: "A Rose and a Baby Ruth" by the singer George Hamilton IV. In 1957 Am-Par also asked a Philadelphia disc jockey, Dick Clark, to come to AB-PT to help promote its records. Clark proposed that he host a TV show devoted to music appreciation for teen-agers; "American Bandstand" has been on the air ever since.

By the end of the decade, ABC had finally entered regular daytime programming. The company also entered another field, buying stock in the Prairie Farmer Publishing Company in order to gain full ownership of WLS radio station in Chicago. Soon afterward AB-PT also bought the Weeki Wachee Spring, a 600-acre scenic attraction near Tampa, Florida, prompted by the tremendous success of Disneyland.

The 1960s brought important changes to AB-PT. Everett Erlick joined the company in 1961 after leaving the advertising firm of Young & Rubicam. He was to play a major role in shaping the network in the coming decades, remaining with ABC for more than 25 years.

Later in 1961 AB-PT expanded Am-Par Records through the acquisition of the Westminster classical music label (Beverly Sills was among its artists) and the introduction of the Impulse jazz label (Duke Ellington was its major star).

ABC had entered sports broadcasting in 1960, when it won the television rights to NCAA college football and basketball games. ABC Sports was founded in 1961, and made a ground-breaking contribution that Thanksgiving during its broadcast of the Texas–Texas A&M football game when it offered TV viewers their first "instant replay." Three years later, ABC Sports began its long association with the Olympic Games when it presented the Winter Games from Innsbruck, Austria. Although ABC ranked third, well behind CBS and NBC, the network was number one in the sports-broadcasting business from early on.

By the middle of the decade, the company had started looking for financing to cover the massive costs of conversion to color broadcasting (which had been in limited use since 1962) and help it bid competitively for feature-film packages. In 1965 the company announced plans to merge with International Telephone and Telegraph, Inc. (ITT), a company with enormous financial resources. The FCC approved the merger and hopes were high at ABC (its name was shortened that year to American Broadcasting Companies). However, the Justice Department's anti-trust division appealed the approval, delaying the merger so long that ITT finally exercised its right to opt out of the deal. ITT did loan ABC $25 million, however, to help the network convert to color broadcasting, and within a year, the entire prime-time schedule was in color.

After the ITT deal fell through, eccentric billionaire Howard Hughes attempted to gain control of ABC through a tender offer for 43% of the company's stock. The management at ABC fought vigorously against Hughes, however, and he dropped his bid two weeks after his initial proposal.

In 1968 ABC was divided into three separate divisions, each to provide the ABC television network with programming: entertainment, news, and sports. The other two networks followed ABC's lead in this restructuring.

The 1960s were a trying time for ABC. Despite an influx of financial support, the network lost more than $120 million between 1961 and 1971. The company was sustained during this time primarily by revenues from its theater chain, its record company, and the television stations that it owned. Radio broadcasting also contributed to its survival—in fact, the network had 500 affiliate radio stations by the end of the decade. Like the television network, ABC organized its radio network into several divisions: American contemporary, American information, American entertainment, and American FM networks.

In 1971 the FCC limited the number of hours of prime-time programming a network could schedule. This proved to be a blessing for ABC since the network had been unable to fill the time anyway, and in the following year, the network became profitable for the first time in a decade: revenues passed the $800 million mark and net earnings were over $35 million. But just as things were looking up, in 1972 the Justice Department filed an antitrust suit against all three networks. The suit aimed to bar the networks from carrying network-produced entertainment programs, including feature films, and charged the networks with monopolizing prime-time television entertainment programming. ABC claimed that documents from the White House, the Justice Department, and the Watergate prosecution would prove that the government's antitrust suit was intended to suppress the three networks, presumably in retaliation for press "harassment" of the president. Though the suit was dismissed without prejudice in November, 1974, the matter was not fully resolved until six years later.

In the meantime, ABC was engaged in the further divestiture of its movie theaters and an expansion of its record business. Anchor Records was established in 1973 to develop European talent for the company.

One of the most famous mass-media programmers in the United States joined ABC in 1975. ABC tempted Fred Silverman (christened by *Time* "the man with the golden gut") away from CBS with an offer of a $300,000 salary, a $1 million life insurance policy, stock options, and homes on both coasts of the United States. Despite such extravagances, the day he joined ABC its stock went up two points on the exchange. Under Silverman's guidance, ABC introduced hits like "Laverne and Shirley" and "The Love Boat" and expanded its soap operas to hour-length features that were not afraid to touch controversial topics, greatly boosting ABC's daytime ratings.

Within a year, ABC had moved into first place in prime-time ratings. In the same year the network created a stir by offering Barbara Walters, then the co-host of NBC's "Today Show," a $5 million contract to co-anchor "ABC Evening News." Walters accepted and became the first full-time female news anchor on any network. Unfortunately, the show flopped. Roone Arledge, the former head of ABC Sports who was now head of ABC News, moved in to salvage things. He changed the format of "ABC Evening News," renaming it "ABC World News Tonight" and using three anchormen, in London, Washington, and Chicago, connected by satellite. By the following year ABC had surpassed CBS as the world's largest advertising medium, and within another year, ABC also led in daytime programming.

In 1978 Silverman was lured from ABC by NBC, not quite three years after he was hired. Silverman's tenure, although brief, benefited the company tremendously: between 1975 and 1978 broadcasting profits rose from $82 million to $311 million. His departure marked the beginning of a period of streamlining for ABC as the company finished selling its theaters and sold its record business in order to concentrate on broadcasting and publishing (it retained its farming journals).

During the Iranian hostage crisis in 1979, ABC aired daily special reports on their condition. These reports were so popular that when the hostage crisis ended, ABC continued to broadcast a special news report in the same time slot, and "Nightline" was born.

The broadcasting industry has never been particularly stable, however, and ABC's fortunes soon changed. Scandal clouded the success of the popular "Charlie's Angels" when a reporter for *The New York Times* uncovered numerous accounting oddities in connection with the show, the show's producers, and Elton Rule, the president of ABC. Some of these oddities, based on informal oral understandings, ran into the millions of dollars. This was followed by an agreement to a consent decree in connection with the antitrust suit the Justice Department had brought in the early 1970s, in which ABC agreed to place ceilings on the number of shows it produced in-house for network broadcast and to give actors, producers, and writers involved in its prime-time schedule greater freedom to leave ABC for other networks. It was a poor start to the 1980s.

By the middle of the decade ABC had once again fallen behind both CBS and NBC in ratings. Despite this poor showing, however, ABC was more profitable than either of the other two networks. This led, as many had predicted, to ABC's takeover.

In 1985 Capital Cities Communications, Inc., a communications company with a one-quarter of ABC's sales, bought ABC for $3.5 billion. The name of the combined operation was changed to Capital Cities/ABC Inc. The business community reacted quite favorably to the announcement: not only did ABC's stock rise as soon as the deal was announced but, unusually, Capital Cities' did too.

Capital Cities owned seven TV stations and 12 radio stations and had annual sales of slightly less than $1 billion before the takover. In addition, the company controlled several publishing interests, including the *Kansas City Star* and several medical journals—a mix that reproduced ABC's on a smaller scale. Capital Cities had long held a reputation for being extremely efficient and many at ABC feared for their jobs. Thomas S. Murphy and Daniel Burke, the chairman and president of Capital Cities, placed Frederick Pierce in charge of ABC. Pierce had been second to Leonard Goldenson for several years before the takeover.

The broadcast industry went through a period of rapid change in the second half of the 1980s as competition from cable television and VCRs reduced network viewing audiences. ABC was in last place among the three networks in 1986 and recorded a substantial loss that year. In order to cut costs, the company trimmed the budget of its nonprogramming-related expenditures. In addition, the company lowered the amount it pays affiliates to carry its programs by about 4% and announced that it would not pay any clearance fees for special events such as mini-series and the Academy Awards. This move touched off a struggle between the network and its affiliate stations, who became less inclined to grant clearances for shows with poor ratings. This tension continued even when ABC's ratings edged past CBS's to take second place in 1987. The network still trailed far behind first-place NBC, however.

In the late 1980s ABC's epic mini-series programs, once a network strength, lost the viewing public. "Amerika," aired in 1987, led the week's ratings, but was hardly a smash success. A year later "War and Remembrance" lost $20 million for the network. ABC had pioneered the mini-series back in the late 1970s with "Roots," but the appeal of the format seemed to have worn out.

ABC's coverage of the 1988 Olympic Games gave the network a big ratings boost, but still resulted in a $65 million loss. On the other hand, ABC's news division was doing well late in the decade with "ABC World News Tonight," "20/20," and "Nightline." In addition, while the network struggled to cope with a changing industry, Capital Cities/ABC's owned-and-operated stations did very well on an individual basis.

The mix of holdings is beginning to diversify. Capital Cities/ABC recently acquired a professional expositions management company and a trade show exhibition company. In addition, ABC has an 80% interest in ESPN, the cable sports channel, and smaller interests in the Lifetime and Arts and Entertainment cable channels, which are all prospering, and the company's publishing interests are also doing well. Meanwhile, innovations in network programming will continue as the battle for ratings and advertiser revenues rages on.

Principal Subsidiaries: Cablecom-General, Inc.,; Capital Cities Entertainment Systems, Inc.; Capital Cities of Illinois, Inc.; Capital Cities of Kansas, Inc.; Capital Cities Media, Inc.; Legal Com of Delaware, Inc.; Securities Data Company, Inc.; Institutional Investor, Inc.; Sutton Industries, Inc.; Tele Hi-Fi Company; Texas Media Holding Company, Inc.; The Kansas City Star Company; The Oakland Press Company; CCC Properties, Inc.; Wilson Publishing Company; CC Finance Holding Corporation; ABC Holding Company Inc. (76.2%); ABC Video Enterprises, Inc.; Ambro Land Holdings, Inc.; Ambroad, Inc.; COMPUTE Publications, Inc.; Farm Progress Companies, Inc.; Hitchcock Publishing Company; Los Angeles Magazine, Inc.; The Miller Publishing Company, Inc.; NILS Publishing Company; R.L. White Company, Inc.; TNC Company, Inc.; WLS, Inc.; WMAL, Inc.; WXYZ, Inc.; Word, Incorporated.

Further Reading: Qinlan, Sterling. *Inside ABC: American Broadcasting Company's Rise to Power*, New York, Hastings House, 1979.

CBS INC.

51 West 52nd Street
New York, New York 10019
U.S.A.
(212) 975–4321
Public Company
Incorporated: 1927 as United Independent Broadcasters, Inc.
Sales: $2.78 billion
Employees: 6,500
Stock Index: New York Pacific

CBS, the world's second-oldest broadcasting network, has a strong tradition of innovative programming and technological contributions. The company's reputation was built on the pioneering work done by CBS's news division and on the stable of celebrities the company acquired over the years. In recent decades, however, the network has de-emphasized news, and programming has suffered from cost-cutting measures and attempts to lure less-mature viewers.

In the late 1920s, Arthur Judson, the impresario of the Philadelphia and New York Philharmonic orchestras, approached the Radio Corporation of America's National Broadcasting Company (NBC), then the only radio broadcaster in the United States, with an idea to promote classical music by broadcasting orchestra performances. NBC declined. Undaunted, in 1927 Judson founded his own broadcasting company, which he called United Independent Broadcasters, Inc., or UIB.

Lacking the strong capital base NBC had in its parent, RCA, UIB struggled to stay afloat for several months. That summer, however, Judson found a rich partner in Columbia Phonograph, a leader in the phonograph record business. For $163,000 Columbia Phonograph bought UIB's operating rights. The new company was named the Columbia Phonograph Broadcasting System.

Columbia Phonograph sold UIB's operating rights back to the broadcasting company in 1928 however, apparently because the phonograph company was frustrated by a lack of advertiser loyalty. The broadcasting company's name was then shortened to the Columbia Broadcasting System (CBS) and its finances were greatly enhanced that year when William Paley invested $400,000 in its stock.

Paley was the son of a Russian immigrant who owned a cigar company. It was assumed that Paley would take over his father's business, but he was drawn to the broadcasting business. Quite early in its history CBS began to earn a reputation as the network with class—a reputation often attributed to Paley's influence.

At the time of Paley's CBS stock purchase, the company consisted of only 16 affiliated radio stations and possessed no stations of it own. Paley, who was quickly elected president of the company, tripled earnings in his first year. This success was accomplished by offering prospective affiliates the network's entire unsponsored schedule at no cost, in contrast to NBC, which charged affiliates for all programs. In return for free programs, affiliates gave CBS airtime for sponsored broadcasts, allowing CBS to assure contracted sponsors that airtime would be available. Within a decade, CBS added almost 100 stations to its network. Since the number of affiliates a network has determines the number of people it can reach, which in turn determines what a sponsor is charged, CBS was soon on firm financial footing. By 1930, CBS had 300 employees and total sales of $7.2 million.

Although CBS fared well, NBC continued to dominate the entertainment-oriented broadcasting industry. Paley therefore decided to explore the potential for network news. Paley viewed news and public affairs as a quick way for CBS to gain respectability. In 1930 he hired Ed Klauber to establish a news and public affairs section and in 1933 the Columbia News Service, the first radio network news operation, was formed. By 1935 CBS had become the largest radio network in the United States.

In 1938 Edward R. Murrow began his career at CBS as head of the network's European division. The first international radio news broadcast was established later that year with Murrow reporting from Vienna, William L. Shirer reporting from London, and others reporting from Paris, Berlin, and Rome. With these broadcasts CBS began the practice of preempting regular programming. These interruptions were planned for prime listening time—8:55 to 9:00 P.M.—and were intended to give the network a "statesmanlike" image.

CBS entered the record business in 1938 with the purchase of the American Record Corporation. Later called the Columbia Recording Corporation, it soon became an industry powerhouse.

By the beginning of World War II CBS employed more than 2,000 people, had annual sales of some $36 million, and had more than 100 affiliate stations throughout the United States. In 1940 the world's first experimental color-television broadcast was made from a CBS transmitter atop the Chrysler Building in New York City and received in the CBS Building at 485 Madison Avenue. And in 1941 CBS began weekly broadcasts of black-and-white television programs. That year the government also ordered NBC to divest itself of one of its two networks, which eventually gave rise to the American Broadcasting Company (ABC).

After the war CBS embarked on a raid of NBC stars. Though CBS continued to expand, NBC was still the industry leader. Under Paley's direction, CBS lured stars away from NBC by devising a plan in which the stars could be taxed as companies rather than as individuals, greatly reducing their taxes. Jack Benny was the first major star to leave NBC for CBS; soon Edgar Bergen and Charlie McCarthy, Amos 'n Andy, Red Skelton, and George Burns and Gracie Allen followed. Within a year CBS took the lead from NBC in programming, advertising revenues, and profits—a lead it maintained as the two networks expanded into television.

In 1946 CBS submitted its color-television broadcasting system to the Federal Communications Commission (FCC) for approval. CBS was confident that its color system would be approved, even though existing black-and-white sets could not receive CBS's color CBS broadcasts, because there were fewer than 25,000 TV sets in the United States. The FCC, however, did not approve the system, calling it "premature." In the meantime, RCA had developed a color system that was compatible with existing television sets. The CBS system produced a better picture, however, and in 1950, when both CBS and RCA submitted their systems to the FCC for approval, only the CBS system was approved. But RCA appealed the decision, preventing CBS from marketing its system and gaining time to improve the quality of its own system. In 1953 the FCC reversed and ruled in favor of the RCA system since more than 12 million black-and-white TV sets had been sold by that time, making compatibility a more important issue.

During the 1950s censorship became an issue in the broadcasting industry. The networks have always been sensitive to censorship pressure because the FCC can revoke a station's license if it does not serve the "public interest responsibly." In addition, advertisers may refuse to sponsor a program which they find offensive, and network affiliates can pressure the network into discontinuing a controversial program. Censorship surfaced at all the networks during the early 1950s as Senator Joseph McCarthy's anticommunist campaign pressured networks and sponsors to blacklist certain actors and writers who were suspected of having left-wing associations. Though CBS was considered the most liberal of the networks, it required 2,500 employees to sign a "loyalty oath" which stated that they "neither belonged to nor sympathized with" any communist organization. In 1954 two CBS News commentators began to expose McCarthy's unethical behavior on the television show "See It Now." These broadcasts helped to discredit the communist paranoia, but proved so controversial themselves that CBS eventually canceled the program.

By this time there were 32 million television sets in the United States, and television had become the biggest advertising medium in the world. The period was marred, however, by a 1956 TV quiz scandal in which CBS's "$64,000 Question" was shown to be rigged.

In late 1950s Paley hired James Aubrey as president of CBS. Aubrey, who purportedly thought that television programming had become too "highbrow," introduced such shows as "The Beverly Hillbillies," "Mr. Ed," and "The Munsters." These shows were extremely popular; in his first two years with CBS, Aubrey doubled the network's profits.

During the early 1960s, CBS embarked on a diverse acquisitions campaign. Before 1964 CBS had made only two acquisitions in its history, but from that year on, the company made acquisitions almost every year. In 1964 the network purchased an 80% interest in the New York Yankees baseball team, which it sold ten years later. Acquisitions in the fields of musical instruments, book publishing, and children's toys were made throughout the 1960s.

By the end of the decade CBS had 22,000 employees and net profits of over $64 million. The network's most notable programming innovation of the decade came in 1968 with the debut of "60 Minutes," a television news magazine. The 1970s were a period of innovative prime-time programming. In 1971 "All In The Family" debuted on CBS and in 1972 both "M*A*S*H" and "The Waltons" debuted. But it was a decade of managerial turmoil.

In 1971 Charles T. Ireland became the president of CBS. He was replaced a year later by Arthur Taylor, who held the position for four years. Taylor was relieved of his duties when the network placed second in the Nielsen ratings for the first time in 21 years, and was replaced by John D. Backe, who had been president of the CBS publishing division since 1973.

Meanwhile, in 1976 CBS relieved reporter Daniel Schorr of all duties after he leaked a secret House Intelligence Committee report on the Central Intelligence Agency to the *Village Voice*. He resigned from CBS several months later. And in April, 1979 in a case involving CBS and two employees—correspondent Mike Wallace and producer Barry Lando—the Supreme Court ruled that journalists accused of libel may be forced to answer questions about their "state of mind" or about conversations with colleagues during the editorial process. The ruling was a victory for former Lieutenant Colonel Anthony E. Herbert, who contended that he was libeled in a "60 Minutes" broadcast that aired in 1973.

In 1979 CBS finally began to divest itself of some of its diverse holdings, selling at least one business every year for the next few years. A year later CBS regained dominance in the prime-time TV ratings, a position held by ABC since 1976. However, one week after CBS took this lead President Backe was forced to resign. He was replaced by Thomas H. Wyman, who had been a vice president at Pillsbury.

CBS went to court again in 1982 after it aired the documentary "The Uncounted Enemy: A Vietnam Deception," which began a long-running battle with retired army General William Westmoreland, who filed a $120 million libel suit against the network. This fight ended several years later when Westmoreland withdrew his suit on a promise from CBS that the network would publicly attempt to restore his character.

By the early 1980s CBS operations fell into six main divisions: the broadcast group, which was concerned with programming and production of shows for the network, theaters, home video, and cable TV; the records group; the publishing group; the toys division; the technology center, which was responsible for research and development of new technologies; and various corporate joint ventures, including CBS/FOX Company, a joint venture with Twentieth Century Fox to manufacture and distribute videocassettes and videodiscs. In 1986 CBS sold its book-publishing business to Harcourt Brace Jovanovich,

Inc. for $500 million, and that same year the company sold all of its toy businesses.

In 1983 CBS, Columbia Pictures, and Home Box Office joined forces to form Tri-Star Pictures, a motion picture production and distribution company. By 1984 Tri-Star had released 17 full-length motion pictures, nine of its own production. But in 1985 CBS sold its interest in Tri-Star Pictures. Another experiment was Trintex, a commercial electronic service that allowed people access to news, weather, and sports information; financial and educational data; and home shopping and banking from a personal computer terminal. This service, initiated in 1984, was the combined effort of CBS, IBM, and Sears, Roebuck. Yet again, CBS withdrew from the venture, in 1986.

In 1985 Ted Turner, owner of Turner Broadcasting System, announced his intention to take over CBS. In order to prevent this CBS swallowed a $954.8 million poison pill by purchasing 21% of its own outstanding stock.

In September, 1986 Larry Tisch replaced Tom Wyman as CEO of CBS. Tisch was the chairman of Loew's Corporation, which owned about 25% of CBS stock at the time. Following a power struggle between Tisch and Wyman, who had remained as president, William S. Paley returned as chairman of the board and Wyman was forced to resign.

Although Tisch was originally to serve only as interim CEO, within four months it was clear that the job was his. He immediately began cutting costs at the network. Tisch cut $30 million from the news division budget, tried to reduce programming costs, cut hundreds of jobs, and sold a number of CBS publishing concerns. He also sold CBS Records to the Sony Corporation in 1987 for $2 billion, even though the subsidiary, which boasted top stars like Michael Jackson and Bruce Springsteen, had been a perennial money-maker for the company.

Tisch was roundly criticized for selling the number-one record company in the industry when the music business appeared to be healthy, and for trying to cut television-programming costs at a time when cable TV and other pay services were seducing viewers by offering a broader and higher-quality selection. CBS's prime-time hits were getting old; in 1987 the network came in last in the Nielsen ratings. To make matters worse, CBS viewers tended to be older than the heavy-spending audience advertisers look for.

In 1988 Tisch, under fire from the CBS board and from affiliate stations for lacking any long-term strategy, appointed 38-year-old Kim LeMasters to head the network's entertainment division. LeMasters' task was to find new programming that would appeal to younger audiences.

CBS continues the struggle to turn around its ratings slump. But it remains to be seen whether the network can win back large audiences, or whether it can remain independent in this era of mergers in the entertainment industry.

Principal Subsidiaries: Aspenfair Music Inc.; Cadisco Inc.; CBS/Australia Pty. Limited; CBS Broadcast International of Canada Limited; CBS Columbia C.A. (Venezuela); CBS/Columbia Inernacional, S.A. (Mexico); CBS Dischi S.p.A. (Italy); CBS Discos del Peru S.A.; CBS Epic (Thailand) Limited (60%); CBS FMX Stereo Inc.; CBS/FOX Company (50%); CBS United Kingdom Limited; CBS Urban Renewal Corporation; CJG Productions, Inc.; Columbia Television, Inc.; Discos CBS Industria e Comercio Ltda. (Brazil); Discos CBS International de Puerto Rico Inc.; Discos CBS S.A.I.C.F. (Argentina); Discos CBS, S.A. (Colombia); Filmvision Inc.; Houston Motion Picture Entertainment, Inc.; Mainstream Communications Corp. (50%); Vista Marketing Inc.; Winterland Concessions Company (50%).

Further Reading: Robert Metz. *CBS: Reflections In a Bloodshot Eye*, New York, New American Library, 1975; David Halberstam. *The Powers That be*, New York, Alfred A. Knopf, 1979.

COLUMBIA PICTURES ENTERTAINMENT, INC.

711 Fifth Avenue
New York, New York 10022
U.S.A.
(212) 751–4400

Wholly owned subsidiary of Sony USA Inc.
Incorporated: 1924 as Columbia Pictures Corporation
Employees: 7,095
Sales: $453.4 million

Hollywood in the 1920s was a booming entertainment factory. As the film industry began to realize its vast potential, ornate moviehouses were erected throughout American cities and towns and cinema became the nation's new favorite pastime. Hollywood's production studios grew rapidly and opportunities for filmmakers abounded.

It was in this environment, in 1918, that independent producer Harry Cohn, his brother Jack, and their associate Joe Brandt started the CBC Film Sales Company with a $100,000 loan. By 1924 the little company on Hollywood's Poverty Row had made its presence known. The company changed its name to Columbia Pictures Corporation and began a period of growth that would rank it among the major studios within ten years.

Columbia was ruled somewhat autocratically by its brash founder, Harry Cohn for more than 30 years. Cohn, the son of immigrant parents, began his career in film in 1918 as the secretary to Carl Laemmle, a founder of Universal Studios. By the mid-1920s Cohn had gained a reputation as one of the industry's toughest businessmen. He ran Columbia's Hollywood film production unit while his brother Jack and Joe Brandt handled financial matters in New York. In 1926 Columbia purchased a small lot on Gower Street that had two stages and a small office building; the move improved the company's status among the small motion picture studios.

Cohn slowly built Columbia during the 1920s by enticing talent from other studios to join his operation. He reduced costs in production by refining out-of-sequence shooting, in which scenes with high-priced stars were filmed one after another whether they followed one another in the narrative or not. Under this method, stars were not left idle on the payroll while scenes they were not needed for were shot. By the end of the decade Columbia was considered a major studio, although a lesser one. Hollywood consisted of the Big Five: Warner Brothers, RKO, Twentieth-Century Fox, MGM, and Paramount; and the Little Three: Universal, United Artists, and Columbia.

By the late 1920s a power struggle had begun to develop between the New York and Hollywood operations of the company, culminating in an unsuccessful attempt by Jack Cohn and Joe Brandt to wrest control of the studio from Harry Cohn. In 1932 Joe Brandt resigned as company president and sold his shares in the company, leaving Harry Cohn to become the first executive in Hollywood to serve as production head and president at the same time. Jack Cohn stayed on as vice-president and treasurer, but the feud with his brother was never mended, and gradually Harry became virtually omnipotent at the studio.

In 1929, Columbia produced its first "talkie" feature film, *The Donovan Affair*. The film was directed by Frank Capra, the man who would prove to be Columbia's most valuable asset in the years to come, and met with both critical acclaim and financial success.

The Depression had different effects on different studios. Columbia, which did not have the theater holdings the Big Five had, therefore didn't feel the impact of empty theater seats in the early 1930s. And when theater attendance picked up, Columbia found it had one very special asset—Frank Capra.

Capra's view of the world seemed to strike a nerve with the average theater-goer during the difficult years of the Depression. His films glorified the common man, the unlikely hero who beat the odds. Films like *It Happened One Night*, *Mr. Deeds Goes to Town*, *You Can't Take it With You*, and *Mr. Smith Goes to Washington* firmly established Capra and Columbia Pictures within the Hollywood establishment.

Throughout the late 1930s and the 1940s, Columbia made many "B" movies—lower budget films that often played as the supporting feature at a theater. About 70% of Columbia's annual roster of between 50 and 60 pictures were B movies, including the highly successful *Blondie*, *Boston Blackie*, and *Lone Wolf* series. The so-called "screwball comedy" became Columbia's standard fare during the era.

Columbia continued to pump out motion pictures throughout the war years. Between 1940 and 1946 revenues doubled and profits increased sixfold. After the war, however, cinema in the United States was faced with a serious crisis: television. As the number of small screens in American living rooms increased, the number of paid admissions to the big screens plummeted. Columbia was the first studio to react to the new medium. In 1948 the studio launched a TV subsidiary, Screen Gems, which began to produce TV shows in 1952. In addition to producing new programs like "Rin Tin Tin," "Captain Midnight," and "Father Knows Best," the Screen Gems subsidiary sold the rights to old Columbia films for television broadcast. Meanwhile, gimmicks like Cinemascope, which emphasized the bigness of the theater, were undertaken with limited success. A number of big hits in the 1950s, including *From Here to Eternity*, *The Caine Mutiny*, and *On the Waterfront*, helped Columbia survive.

In 1958 Harry Cohn died. Some 1,300 people attended his funeral, which was held on a Columbia soundstage. Over the years Cohn had become one of the most despised men in Hollywood, and it was quipped that the large congregation at the funeral had come not to bid farewell but to make sure he was actually dead. Cohn had cultivated his image as a tyrant, keeping a riding whip near his desk and occasionally cracking it for emphasis, and Columbia had the greatest creative turnover of any major studio due largely to Cohn's methods. Yet even his enemies acknowledged Cohn's knack for running a profitable studio.

Cohn was succeeded by Abe Schneider, who had come to Columbia in the late 1920s as an accountant. The company, like other Hollywood studios in the early 1960s, struggled to turn a profit. Theater attendance had dropped drastically since the golden era of the 1930s and 1940s, and without the success of the Screen Gems unit, Columbia would have been in serious trouble. Several box office hits in the early 1960s provided even bigger returns with television broadcast—in 1966 the rights to *The Bridge On the River Kwai* alone brought $2 million for two showings on ABC. *Lawrence of Arabia*, *Suddenly Last Summer*, and *The Guns of Navarone* promised big payoffs as well.

In 1966 a takeover attempt threatened Columbia's management. Maurice Clairmont, a well-known corporate raider, attempted to gain a controlling interest in the company; when he failed to do so on his own, he combined forces with the Banque de Paris et de Pays-Bas, which owned 20% of Columbia, to acquire a majority of shares and snatch control of the company from Abe Schneider. But the Communications Act of 1934 prohibited foreign ownership of more than one-fifth of an American company with broadcasting holdings, and Columbia's Screen Gems unit at the time held a number of TV stations. The Federal Communications Commission allowed the French bank to buy more shares but prohibited it from "any action looking toward an assertion of control by it alone or in concert with any other person over Columbia," effectively thwarting Clairmont's efforts to oust Schneider.

Columbia had a string of successes in the late 1960s including *Oliver!*; *Guess Who's Coming to Dinner*; *To Sir, With Love*; *Divorce American Style*; and *In Cold Blood*. In 1969 *Easy Rider*, starring Peter Fonda, Dennis Hopper, and Jack Nicholson, was made for $400,000 and grossed $25 million for the studio.

But the early 1970s were devoid of box office successes. By 1973 the company had to impose strict cost-cutting measures after losses of $82 million in three years. In July, 1973, Alan J. Hirschfield took over as president and CEO of Columbia. Hirschfield had formerly been with the Wall Street investment-banking firm of Allen & Company, which had gained a substantial interest in Columbia.

In August that year former talent agent David Begelman was brought in to head the motion picture division. Begelman oversaw a number of successful projects, including *Funny Lady*, *Shampoo*, *Tommy*, *The Deep*, and *Close Encounters of the Third Kind*. Begelman, however, brought disgrace to himself and embarrassment to Columbia in 1977 when it was discovered that he had misappropriated about $60,000 in corporate funds. His offenses included cashing a $10,000 check made out to actor Cliff Robertson. The board of directors suspended Begelman in July, and then in December reinstated him. Public outcry over his reinstatement compelled him to resign two months later, but not until after he had landed a lucrative three-year contract as an independent producer. Alan Hirschfield temporarily took over as head of the motion picture unit, but it was clear that his talents lay in finance, not motion picture production. By July, 1978 Hirschfield was replaced by Francis T. Vincent, an attorney with no experience in film. The decision to replace Hirschfield was less obvious than the one to remove Begelman, but apparently some board members felt that Hirschfield had not shown appropriate gratitude to Begelman through public support in his moment of crisis; the company had, after all, jumped in net worth from $4 million to $130 million since Begelman joined Columbia (although at least some of the credit belonged to Hirschfield, who secured new forms of financing). Other speculation centered on Hirschfield's desire to merge with the toy manufacturer Mattel, a move which would have diluted the equity of Columbia's major shareholders.

As Columbia entered the 1980s, changes in the entertainment business provided new opportunities as well as new challenges. The early 1980s saw the significant development of cable TV and home videotape recorders. At first seen as a threat to the movies, these new outlets eventually bolstered demand for product.

In 1981 Columbia narrowly escaped a hostile bid from Las Vegas financier Kirk Kerkorian. The federal government frowned on the move because Kerkorian owned a controlling interest in MGM and his acquisition of Columbia would violate antitrust statutes.

But in 1982 Columbia Pictures was purchased, by The Coca-Cola Company, in a stock and cash deal worth some $700 million. With Coca-Cola as a parent, Columbia changed in a number of ways. The studio used even more market research on film ideas than it had before. Columbia also benefited from the greater efficiencies that Coke's volume discounts on advertising could provide.

Also in 1982 Columbia joined CBS and Home Box Office to launch a new motion picture studio called Tri-Star Pictures. For five years the fledgling studio pumped out hits and expanded its holdings. Tri-Star earned hefty sums through the distribution of movies like *Rambo: First Blood Part II*, and *The Natural*. In 1985 the company offered its shares to the public. Although response was at first lukewarm, 43% of Tri-Star was eventually sold to the public. The company began to branch out in late 1986 when it purchased the Loews theater chain for $295 million. It also took over video cassette distribution of its own films.

Management changes at the studio in the mid-1980s seemed to hinder Columbia's performance. The studio had changed leadership four times since Coca-Cola purchased it, and hadn't had a major hit since *Ghostbusters* earned $200 million in 1984. To make matters worse, as president of the motion picture unit during 1986, British producer David Puttnam (best known for the Academy Award–winning *Chariots of Fire*) complained of overpriced talent and inflated egos and tried to buck Hollywood's well-established star system. As a well-intentioned outsider, Puttnam's attempt to inject a bit of reality into the glamour capital of the world proved a miserable failure for Columbia.

In 1987 The Coca-Cola Company board decided to merge Columbia with Tri-Star to form Columbia Pictures Entertainment, Inc. Tri-Star's Victor Kaufman became president and CEO of the new company. Also in 1987, Dawn Steel was brought in from Paramount to replace Puttnam. Steel lured back Hollywood's top talent, but the studio struggled to find a hit. In 1988, Columbia's share of domestic box office receipts fell to a dismal 3.5%. In spite of the Columbia Pictures Television and Merv Griffin Enterprises TV subsidiaries' relatively solid showing, Columbia registered a $104 million loss for 1988.

In 1989, Columbia released the highly successful *When Harry Met Sally. . . .* Prospects looked better, but the company still struggled to find the cash flow to finance more productions.

Also in late 1989 Columbia entered into an agreement with Sony USA, Inc., a subsidiary of Japan's Sony Corporation, for the purchase of all Columbia's outstanding stock. With the completion of that transaction in November, 1989, Columbia joined the ranks of media and entertainment companies throughout the world that have combined to create huge enterprises. Under the leadership of newly appointed co-chairmen Peter Guber and Jon Peters, Columbia will face the challenges of the global media market of the 1990s on firm footing.

Principal Subsidiaries: Columbia Pictures; Tri-Star Pictures; Triumph Releasing Corporation; Columbia Pictures Television; Merv Griffin Enterprises; Loews Theater Management Corp.

Further Reading: Stanley, Robert. *The Celluloid Empire: A History of the American Movie Industry*, New York, Hastings House, 1978; McClintick, David. *Indecent Exposure*, New York, William Morrow, 1982.

GRANADA GROUP PLC

36 Golden Square
London W1R 4AH
United Kingdom
(01) 734–8080

Public Company
Incorporated: 1934 as Granada Theatres Limited
Employees: 28,000
Sales: £1.47 billion (US$2.66 billion)
Stock Index: London

Granada Group PLC has grown from its founding as a small theater operator into a multinational business involved in the television, leisure, communications, and service industries. The company traces its roots to the early 1900s when, shortly after the turn of the century, Alexander Bernstein opened the Edmonton Empire music hall. During the 1920s his sons Sidney and Cecil started up a chain of movie theaters. The Bernstein brothers approached their business with an innovative spirit and a desire to bring their deep appreciation of cinema to larger audiences. They actively promoted many kinds of films, conducted surveys to determine the kinds of films people most wanted to see, and initiated children's matinees.

The theater chain adopted the name Granada in 1930. The name was chosen by the well-traveled Sidney Bernstein, who felt that its exotic connotation fit with the image he wanted for the theaters. Following the formation of Granada Theatres Limited in 1934, which consolidated all activities into one group, the company made its first public stock offering in 1935 on the London Stock Exchange.

Over the next three years, Granada opened a new theater almost every three months, including "super cinemas" with seating capacity for as many as 3,000 patrons. Created by leading architects, artists, and theatrical designers of the period, the super cinemas offered live programming as well as films in elegantly appointed surroundings. As theatergoing habits changed with the times, however, Granada gradually phased out this concept in favor of theaters with either single or multiple screens, and converted others into bingo and social clubs. The firm moved cautiously into this former area, even though it was a lucrative one, maintaining a low profile until the 1968 Gaming Act legalized bingo and permitted the company to feel more comfortable about its business involvement and the longevity of the game's consumer appeal.

By the late 1940s, Granada's attention had gradually turned away from theatrical entertainment toward the fledgling television industry. After requesting a license to operate an independent television station in 1948, the company finally received the contract in 1954 to broadcast five days a week in all of northern England, becoming one of the four founders of Britain's independent television network. Granada subsequently made its first black-and-white transmission on May 3, 1956 with a program called "Meet the People." This development was particularly well timed, since it offered Granada a new growth area to offset continuing declines in its theatrical operation. In November, 1956 the company introduced a new show, "What the Papers Say," which later became the country's longest-running weekly program on current events. Two years later, Granada became the first network to provide live coverage of a local election, despite strong official opposition, and later it pioneered broadcasts of the annual meetings of the country's major political parties and trade unions.

As the first television company in the country to construct its own studio rather than to use existing facilities built for other purposes, Granada also brought widely acclaimed plays to audiences who had never before had such viewing opportunities. Another program, "Coronation Street," whose characters captured the regional flavor of northern England, began production in 1960 and continues as one of the country's longest-running series.

To reflect its evolving change in focus, the company changed its name in 1957 to Granada Group Limited. Management remained under the tight control of the Bernstein family, with Sidney's eye for opportunities and insistence on quality and creativity to drive the company's business operations.

One of Granada's major areas of growth in the early 1960s was the television-rental business. Granada first opened showrooms under the name Red Arrow to handle rentals of televisions and other merchandise such as records, washing machines, refrigerators, and vacuum cleaners. Granada also expanded into book publishing, in 1961, as an extension of its involvement in the visual media. This business was eventually sold to William Collins & Sons in 1983, since it no longer fit the company's business focus.

In 1963, Granada Television introduced "World in Action," a weekly program that broke with broadcasting tradition by addressing the subject of current events without a host or moderator. Later that year, the company expanded its activities into furniture rental with the formation of Black Arrow Leasing, a business that was sold in 1971.

In 1964 Granada began to export television programming through Granada Overseas Limited (known as Granada Television International today). That year Granada also acquired Barranquilla Investments, a real estate developer, and formed Granada Motorway Services to sell food and fuel to highway travelers across Britain. This business stood in marked contrast to Granada's other ventures in the media area and almost folded within its first six years due to high leasing costs and low profits.

Seven years after the introduction of its domestic television-rental business, Granada expanded into the West German market under the name Telerent Europe (now Granada Overseas Holdings). Additional showrooms were opened in France, Spain, Italy, Sweden, Switzerland, and North America as Granada looked to establish a television-rental market in areas where the concept had never before been introduced.

Granada Group Services was also formed in 1968, initially to provide computerized support to the firm's own businesses, but later to develop systems for outside clients as well. In the meantime, Granada Television continued to prosper and grow technologically. Having been awarded a new seven-days-a-week contract for Great Britain's northwest region, the company began broadcasting programming in color for the first time in September, 1969.

The 1970s brought two additional businesses into the Granada fold. Novello and Company, a music publisher founded in 1811, and L'Etoile, a 70-year-old Belgian insurance company, were acquired in 1973 and 1974 respectively, followed by the 1981 purchase of a second Belgian insurance company, Eurobel, which was merged with L'Etoile. The insurance business was sold a decade later after incurring consistent losses; Novello was sold in 1988 because it no longer fit with the company's core businesses.

In 1979, Sidney Bernstein retired as chairman of Granada and turned over leadership of the company to his nephew Alex. Alex Bernstein inherited an organization whose television-rental operation had grown to represent more than 60% of the company's profits by 1979, but was now threatened by a marked decline in business. The company's overall long-range planning system was erratic and informal at best. He gradually instituted a more decentralized management structure to give Granada's subsidiaries greater operating autonomy.

Continued expansion in the motorway-services business in the early 1980s was accompanied by similar success in the television production area. Granada's programming franchise was renewed in 1982 for another eight years—it is the only independent TV contractor in Great Britain to have held onto its license. Its critically acclaimed dramatic series, "Brideshead Revisited," was broadcast with resounding success in the United States, and Granada Cable and Satellite was formed in 1983 to capitalize on new broadcasting technology.

The firm also embarked upon another new venture in 1983, Granada Microcomputer Sevices, to market computer hardware to businesses through retail outlets. Granada Microcomputer Services began with a single store and from the start met heavy competition from a number of other retailers, making the undertaking less lucrative than it first promised. Granada decided to reposition its shops as business centers that could package microcomputer hardware and software programs into customized systems for small businesses. This operation, however, was sold in 1987 as Granada reorganized and shifted away from computer retailing toward providing computer maintenance services for businesses through Granada Computer Services.

In 1984, Granada made a major move to consolidate its position in the rental business with the acquisition of Rediffusion, a major rental competitor. Although the television-rental market had been declining for several years, the Rediffusion purchase increased Granada's cash flow, market share, and profits, and also gave it a stronger position in VCR and movie rentals. After the Rediffusion outlets had been consolidated and integrated with its own, Granada made a second major decision: to begin selling TVs and video recorders to offset declines in the rental area. That same year Granada Television scored a major programming success in the production area with the premiere of the award-winning series "The Jewel in the Crown."

In February, 1986 Granada received an unwelcome merger offer from the Rank Organisation, a British company with similar interests in the television, entertainment, and leisure industries. At the time, Granada had recently broken off merger negotiations with the Ladbroke Group due to a difference in opinion over Granada's net worth. The Independent Broadcasting Authority, Britain's regulator of broadcasting licenses, blocked the takeover, much to Granada's relief, by ruling that Rank's offer would illegally shift ownership of Granada's television franchise. Rank withdrew its bid a month later, after exhausting its legal appeals.

This incident appeared to sharpen the company's outlook on the future. Shortly thereafter, Granada began refining its planning systems with an eye toward growing in several directions at the same time. This approach contrasted with the Bernsteins' original managerial style, which had focused on personal pet projects, whether or not they fit with the company's strengths and resources.

The new strategy backfired to a certain degree in July, 1986 when Granada's plan to acquire Comet, an electrical appliance retailer, fell through. This purchase was part of an intricate arrangement in which Dixons Group sought to acquire Woolworth Holdings and then sell Woolworth's Comet subsidiary to Granada. When the Dixons takeover attempt failed, Granada was prevented from making a major move into electrical retailing.

Granada overcame this setback the following year, when it made the largest single acquisition in its history. In November, 1987 Granada launched and successfully completed a $450 million bid for Electronic Rentals Group PLC. This purchase gave Granada a stronger presence in the consumer rental and retail markets in the United Kingdom with two chains, and also served as a springboard for renewed growth in the European rental business. The 1987 acquisitions of NASA in France and Kapy in Spain provided additional retailing strength in those countries. The Granada Hospital Group was also formed during the year to oversee the company's television rentals to hospitals in Canada and the United States.

Granada made another significant purchase in June, 1988, when it bought DPCE, a European-based computer maintenance company. Integrated with the company's existing maintenance businesses under the Granada Computer Services International umbrella, DPCE gave the company a larger customer base and a wider range of services to make it a more competitive player in the industry.

Today, Granada defines its overall business in terms of four major growth areas: rental and retail, television, computer services, and leisure. This latter area encompasses not only the original motorway-services operation and bingo clubs, but also bowling centers, travel and tour activities, and theme parks and holiday villages managed by Park Hall Leisure, a 1986 acquisition. The company's diversification strategy has reduced its vulnerability to downturns in any one of its core businesses or in the industries in which it competes.

Granada does face significant challenges to its television operation, in particular, in the form of rapid technological advances and changing governmental regulations and policies which could intensify competition, alter current regional broadcasting franchise relationships, and force the company into a more commercial orientation. After its successful transitions from film to TV, and TV into the diversified company of today, Granada seems well positioned to meet the challenges and take advantage of the opportunities that will certainly come to its rapidly changing industries.

Principal Subsidiaries: UK Rental & Retail Ltd.; Granada Overseas Holdings Ltd.; Granada Canada Ltd.; Granada Distribution SA (NASA); Telerent Fernseh-Mietservice GmbH & Co. KG; Granada Hospital Group Inc.; Kapy SA; Granada Television Ltd.; Granada Television International Ltd.; Granada Leisure Ltd.; Granada Clubs Ltd.; Granada Entertainments Ltd.; Granada Motorway Services Ltd.; Park Hall Leisure PLC; Granada Travel PLC; Granada Computer Services International Ltd.; Granada Computer Services Ltd.; Granada Computer Services SA; Granada Computer Services GmbH; Granada Information Services Ltd.; Granada Properties Ltd.; Barranquilla Investments PLC.

Further Reading: "Report to Staff: 1934–1984 Special Golden Jubilee Edition," London, Granada Group, 1985.

LADBROKE GROUP PLC

87 Wimpole Street
London W1M 7DB
United Kingdom
(01) 935–2853

Public Company
Incorporated: 1967
Employees: 65,000
Sales: £2.8 billion (US$5.01 billion)
Stock Index: London

Since Ladbroke Group was founded more than one hundred years ago as a small agency to handle the horseracing bets of England's high society, it has grown from a simple partnership between a horse trainer and a friend to become one of the world's leading companies in the hotel and leisure industries. Named for the village where it was first established, Ladbroke today concentrates on real estate development, hotel management, commercial racing and off-track betting, and retailing.

Because its betting activities were illegal under British law but permitted on an unofficial basis, Ladbroke maintained a very low profile for almost 70 years. In 1957 it was acquired by a group of investors led by Cyril Stein, its current chairman. Spurred by the legalization of off-track betting in 1963, the size of Ladbroke's racing subsidiary increased significantly in order to reach beyond the upper classes to all who wanted to try their luck at picking a winner. In 1967 the company went public, offering its shares for sale on the London Stock Exchange, and by 1971, the company owned and operated 660 licensed betting shops in the United Kingdom.

Although its betting operations assured Ladbroke of a fairly steady cash flow, Stein knew that Ladbroke also needed to build strong assets as a base for future growth. Applying the expertise they had gained in the racing business, Stein and his management team embarked upon a diversification strategy that took the company beyond horse betting into the property-development and hotel industries.

Through its 1972 acquisition of the London & Leeds Development Corporation, Ladbroke aggressively entered the real estate market with office projects in the eastern United States as well as in Paris, Amsterdam, and Brussels. Property development activities in the United Kingdom led to the formation of four other subsidiaries: Ladbroke Group Properties, handling commercial and residential projects in and around London; Ladbroke City & County Land Company, to oversee local and out-of-town retail projects; Gable House Properties, the largest operator of retirement and nursing homes in the country, acquired in 1986 to develop commercial, residential, and retail properties; and Ladbroke Retail Parks, for the construction of retailing centers outside of London.

Ladbroke entered the lodging business in 1973, when it opened three moderately priced hotels which quickly grew into a profitable chain throughout the country. The success of this venture and the continuing health of Ladbroke's betting and real estate operations helped the company weather the severe losses it incurred during a short-lived entry into the casino business. Casinos, which Ladbroke had hoped might be a lucrative adjunct to its hotel business, were abandoned in 1979 after the company lost its license in a highly publicized case in which it was found guilty of violating government gaming regulations.

Three years later, Ladbroke capitalized on an opportunity to expand its racing operations into Belgium. With the 1984 acquisition of Le Tierce S.A., a chain of Belgian betting shops, Ladbroke rapidly established itself as a leading force in that country's racing industry. Although a plan to purchase the Arizona-based Turf Paradise racetrack fell through in that same year due to problems with obtaining state regulatory approval, Ladbroke successfully acquired the Detroit Race Course at the beginning of 1985 and took the first step toward making its presence felt in U.S. horseracing.

Further expansion in the European racing market occurred in April, 1986 when Ladbroke was awarded exclusive rights to open off-track betting shops throughout the Netherlands. That year also saw the company pursue a new avenue for growth in the retailing area by purchasing the Home Charm Group PLC, a leading chain of over 100 do-it-yourself stores operating throughout the United Kingdom under the Texas Homecare name.

The company's growth has been marked by expansion and acquisition in some areas balanced by consolidation and divestitures in others. As part of a strategy intended to eliminate involvement in markets in which Ladbroke did not hold a major position, the company sold a number of businesses grouped under its entertainment division in 1986, including Lasky's, a chain of consumer-electronics stores, as well as amusement arcades, bingo halls, and local newspaper-publishing operations, while retaining more profitable ventures in magazine publishing and cable television.

That accomplished, the company turned its attention to establishing a more contemporary and stable image. Ladbroke instituted several measures intended to upgrade the public's perception of off-track betting parlors, such as adding snack bars and live television. Ladbroke also joined with three other major bookmakers in 1986 to form Satellite Information Services (SIS), a television communications company set up to transmit horse and greyhound racing directly to Britain's off-track betting shops.

The bookmakers' involvement in SIS prompted an

investigation by the government's Office of Fair Trading (OFT) into possible conflicts of interest. The government was particularly concerned about the bookmakers' influence on the SIS system and their potential for creating a monopoly, but also about their power to shift attendance away from the racecourses to off-track shops and thus affect the odds determining payouts for winning bets. A second investigation resulted from similar concerns over the bookmakers' power expressed by the National Greyhound Racing Club. Ladbroke's share in SIS, which was larger than those of the other investors, made it a primary target of the investigation.

At the same time, Ladbroke brought a suit before the High Court in which it accused the Extel communications group of starting a series of false rumors about the company which had caused a run on Ladbroke shares, reducing the company's value by £200 million in only two days. Ladbroke argued that Extel, which operated a competitive sports-information service, had sought to sabotage the first public offering of SIS stock by simultaneously releasing several damaging reports, including a rumor that Cyril Stein had resigned and implications of improper relationships between prominent racing individuals. The rumors were never substantiated and the OFT investigations ultimately yielded no evidence of wrongdoing on Ladbroke's part.

Although Ladbroke had become the second-largest operator of hotels within its own country by the late 1980s, it had not yet achieved a worldwide reputation in the lodging industry. If anything, its recent sale of the Parkmount Hospitality Corporation and the Dallas-based Rodeway Inn organization to Ramada, Inc. had reduced the company's reach and influence outside the United Kingdom. That all changed in 1987 when Ladbroke successfully acquired the 91-hotel Hilton International chain for more than $1 billion from Allegis Corporation. Ladbroke's bid for Hilton, which beat out several other heavyweight bidders, represented its second attempt in two years to purchase the hotel chain. The first had fallen short when Hilton's previous owner, Transworld Corporation, turned Ladbroke down in favor of an Allegis bid of higher value. This time, however, Stein used a three-week time limit to pressure Allegis to accept the Ladbroke offer immediately instead of waiting for the other bidders to receive approval from their respective governments.

The Hilton International purchase made Ladbroke one of the largest hotel operators in the world, with a presence in 44 countries, including the U.S., where Hilton's six Vista International hotels joined the Ladbroke fold. It also gave the company a 50% share in Hilton's advanced reservation system, which Ladbroke viewed as an important link to travelers around the world. One year later, Ladbroke upgraded and renamed most of its original hotels in the United Kingdom, reintroducing them as part of the Hilton National chain.

Meanwhile, technological enhancements such as a full-color electronic showboard and new Gold Star shops, with services appealing to a wider range of customers, were introduced to maintain Ladbroke's position as a leader in racing and off-track betting. Its presence as the only British betting company operating in the United States expanded too: Ladbroke obtained a license to conduct off-track betting in Wyoming, acquired The Meadows racetrack in Pittsburgh in 1988, and purchased San Francisco's Golden Gate Fields in 1989. Ladbroke also acquired a major competitor in the U.K., Thomson T-Line and its Vernons pools operation, that same year, increasing its share of the betting business in the United Kingdom.

Today Ladbroke's hotels account for the largest share of the company's business activity. Since the Hilton acquisition, Ladbroke has opened more than 13 new, four-star hotels around the globe and has many others under development. It also operates numerous holiday villages and health and leisure clubs within the United Kingdom, and the Comfort Hotel chain throughout Europe. New properties are planned for commercial-office and retail-shopping projects both in the United Kingdom and in the eastern United States. More than 50 new outlets have been added to the Texas Homecare operation since 1987, which is the second-largest do-it-yourself retailer in the United Kingdom with 200 stores, while Ladbroke's racing business continues strong with 1,800 retail betting shops throughout the United Kingdom.

The company credits its success to both good timing, which has allowed it to capitalize on lucrative opportunities, and a hands-on management style which gives operational responsibility to senior executives. Many business analysts also note Ladbroke's ability to rebound from potentially devastating incidents, such as the 1979 casino scandal, with its reputation largely intact.

Ladbroke may face significant obstacles to growth in the racing industry in the United Kingdom. Domestic concerns over the racing industry's financial health raise the possibility that government-imposed restrictions and additional levies may redirect a greater portion of bookmakers' profits toward racecourse rejuvenation.

Ladbroke management will also be challenged to overcome intensified competition in its other core businesses. It will have to improve productivity and contain costs without sacrificing the quality of its services or the systematic planning which has contributed to its successful development to date.

Principal Subsidiaries: Hilton International Co. (USA); Ladbroke Group Properties Limited; London & Leeds Corporation (USA); London & Leeds Estates Limited (87%); Ladbroke Group Homes Limited (75%); London & Leeds Investments (Belgium) SA (77.5%); London & Bardco Investments (Paris) SA (50%); Ladbroke Racing Limited; Ladbroke Racing Corporation (USA); Tierce Ladbroke SA (Belgium); Ladbroke Racing International BV (Holland); Texas Homecare Limited; Multicolor (Wallpapers) Limited; Retail Parks Limited; Ladbroke Group Finance PLC; Town and County Factors Limited; Ladbroke Hotels Limited; Ladbroke City & County Land Company Limited (90%); Gable House Properties PLC; Gable House Estates Limited (75%); Gable Retirement Homes Limited (85%); Ladbroke & Co. Limited; Ganton House Investments Limited; Home and Law Magazine Limited (87%); CableTel Communications Limited (75%); Ladbroke International SA (Belgium).

MCA INC.

100 Universal City Plaza
Universal City, California 91608
U.S.A.
(818) 777–1000

Public Company
Incorporated: 1958
Employees: 17,700
Sales: $1.5 billion
Stock Index: New York Pacific

MCA, once known in the entertainment industry as "The Octopus," was for many years the largest talent agency in the United States. It controlled over half of the big-name stars in the country and, according to *Fortune*, by 1960 represented 60% of Hollywood's "bankable talent"—actors whose names alone could secure a bank loan to make a movie. MCA's list included such clients as Kirk Douglas, Gregory Peck, Clark Gable, Marilyn Monroe, Jimmy Stewart, Tony Curtis, Jack Benny, Ed Sullivan, Alfred Hitchcock, John Ford, Tennessee Williams, Betty Davis, Marlon Brando, and Tommy Dorsey.

The Music Corporation of America was founded in 1924 by Jules C. Stein. In the early 1920s Stein worked his way through medical school at the University of Chicago by playing violin and saxophone with a band. When Stein's band began to generate more bookings than it could handle, Stein began booking other bands. Booking bands on commission was very profitable and Stein soon made a name for himself. In 1924, with $1,000, Stein and William Goodheart, a pianist he had hired to help with the business, started the Music Corporation of America and Stein gave up his budding career in ophthalmology.

MCA, which grossed more than $30,000 in its first year, began to revolutionize the booking business. At the time MCA was founded, most bands played under their bookers' names rather than their own. In return for exclusive rights to represent a band, Stein began to bill bands under their leaders' names. By 1927 MCA represented about 40 bands. In 1930 the company persuaded Lucky Strike to sponsor a radio program that featured a different MCA band every night. The show caused bands to flock to MCA; by the late 1930s the company had attracted some 65% of the major bands in the country. This predominance in booking bands gave MCA such recognition that it was soon able to begin to book other entertainers as well.

In 1936 Stein hired Lew Wasserman to run the company's advertising and publicity departments in Chicago. Wasserman, though only 22 years old, developed rapidly into MCA's top agent. When Stein decided to move MCA to California in 1937, Wasserman became the first agent to negotiate a percentage of a movie's earnings rather than a straight salary for screen stars. These contracts made millionaires of many actors.

At first the company purchased talent agencies, which brought whole stables of stars under MCA's control. When agencies refused to sell, MCA bought individual contracts. In 1945, MCA made its most important acquisition—the Hayward-Deverich Agency in New York City, for $4 million. Hayward-Deverich was the most prestigious firm in the business, and brought clients such as Henry Fonda, Greta Garbo, and Joseph Cotton to MCA, making it the premier talent agency in the United States.

Goodheart retired in 1943. Three years later Stein appointed Wasserman president of MCA, at the age of 33. Wasserman was, by Stein's account, "the student who surpassed the teacher." Highly regarded as a salesman, Wasserman maintained no interests outside his job. He worked seven days a week, sixteen hours a day and required the same commitment from his top executives. Respected for his integrity, Wasserman was also known as a ruthless negotiator.

Wasserman's appointment was a turning point for MCA. Although Stein still influenced policy, Wasserman ran the company. It was he who decided, in 1949, that MCA should become a producer of television shows. MCA formed a subsidiary to film a show named "Stars over Hollywood." This production in turn would provide jobs for MCA's clients. Wasserman soon realized that the filmed shows would become a TV staple. Initially MCA concentrated on selling shows to major networks, but in 1952 it began selling reruns to local stations across the United States. Then MCA produced its first syndicated show, "Chevron Theatre." Two years later the company purchased United Television Programs, a TV syndicator that owned mostly reruns. For the first time, MCA's agency commissions ($6 million) were exceeded by its income from television film rentals (almost $9 million).

In the late 1950s MCA derived revenues from over 45% of all the network evening shows. It produced and coproduced more series than any competitor, including "Riverboat," "Wagon Train," and "General Electric Theater." MCA also acted as selling agent for about 15 other series, including "Alfred Hitchcock Presents," "Ford Startime," and "Wells Fargo."

In 1958 MCA purchased the TV rights to Paramount's pre-1948 library of 750 feature films for $10 million in cash and an additional $25 million in annual installments of $2 million, and in 1959 MCA paid Universal Studios over $11 million for its 420-acre back lot, complete with facilities and equipment. Wasserman regarded the Universal acquisition as a long-term investment.

MCA first offered its stock for sale to the public in 1959, and that year a new parent company, MCA Inc., was organized to replace Music Corporation of America.

The new organization had 20 subsidiaries or divisions, of which the most important were Revue Productions, the division that made television film series for MCA; MCA Artists, a subsidiary that handled the firm's theatrical talent; MCA TV, a subsidiary that functioned as a sales agent for television films; and Music Corporation of America, a subsidiary that represented nightclub and variety performers.

By then MCA was both the largest employer of show-business talent and the largest show-business agent. As a result, the company often hired its own clients, a practice deplored by other industry members. In 1962, when MCA bought Decca Records, Inc., the company that owned Universal Pictures, Inc., the Justice Department forced it to choose whether to operate as a talent agency or a film-production concern. The company decided to divest itself of its talent agency, concentrate on feature-film production under the Universal Pictures name, and branch out into non-entertainment fields to compensate for the loss in agency revenue. Shortly after that, MCA purchased Columbia Savings & Loan in Denver, Colorado, and in 1968 the company bought Spencer Gifts, a small retail chain and mail-order operation.

Until 1970 MCA depended on television production for much of its profit; the company had been unable to transfer its success from the small screen to major motion pictures. But the release of movies like *Airport*, *The Sting*, and *Jaws*, began a long string of successes. *Jaws* made box office history in 1975 by grossing more than $81 million in less than two months, and in 1979 MCA's *The Deer Hunter* won five Academy Awards. In the mid-1970s, for the first time in company history, film revenues surpassed television revenues, though MCA produced some of the most popular shows on TV, including "Kojak," "Quincy," "The Six Million Dollar Man," "The Incredible Hulk," and "The Rockford Files."

In 1973 Wasserman appointed Sidney J. Sheinberg president and chief operating officer of MCA; Wasserman himself became chairman of the board. Hired in 1959, Sheinberg had worked in the television division until he was noticed by Wasserman and made head of that division in 1968. Although Wasserman continued to make major policy decisions and personally supervised the production of theatrical films, Sheinberg assumed responsibility for the firm's day-to-day operations.

MCA purchased Yosemite Park & Curry Company in 1973 and gained exclusive concession rights in Yosemite National Park. In 1974 the company circulated a brochure describing the park as "nature's eloquent answer to a convention city." Environmental groups such as the Sierra Club were infuriated by MCA's proposal for hotels, tennis courts, and glitzy restaurants. The brochure was withdrawn and by 1978 the Department of the Interior had restricted development in the national parks.

By the mid-1970s MCA had transformed the back lot of Universal Studios into one of America's largest tourist attractions, with over four million visitors a year. The complex includes company offices, a hotel, restaurants, an amphitheater, and the sets and sound stages of Universal City Studios, where much of MCA's filming takes place.

With earnings growing at an annual rate of 46% in the early 1970s, MCA's financial position seemed secure. By 1975 the theatrical films and Universal Television operations reported a combined revenue of $364 million, MCA Records tallied $127 million, MCA Recreation's revenues amounted to $10 million, and MCA Financial took in $44 million. Four years later total revenue had reached $1.1 billion.

Much of MCA's success can be attributed to the company's diversification program. Spencer Gifts brought in about 15% of the company's revenue, while the acquisition of G.P. Putnam's Sons and Grosset & Dunlap, Inc. (both publishing houses), ABC Records, and Jove Publications promised even greater income.

In 1980 MCA had more than 20 films, 11 hours of television a week, 90 record albums, and nearly 700 books scheduled for production. But MCA lost this momentum in the first quarter of 1981, when operating income dropped 37%. Cost overruns on *The Blue Brothers*, and unsuccessful releases such as *The Jerk*, *Flash Gordon*, *The Great Muppet Caper*, *The Four Seasons*, and *Endless Love* led to takeover rumors. In order to avert any such attempt, Wasserman and Sheinberg reduced Universal's film budget by 30% and implemented tighter controls on the firm's television-production operations (whose revenues had fallen 30% in 1980).

Wasserman also saw to it that MCA's by-laws were amended in 1979 to require that 75% of the company's stockholders approve any proposed takeover. Since Wasserman controls about 20% of that stock, he is in a strong position to reject any unwanted bids.

In 1981 MCA also purchased 423 acres of undeveloped land in Orlando, Florida for $173 million, where by the end of the decade the company had built a second studio-tour theme park to compete with the Disney/MGM Studio there.

Besides the income from its tourist attractions, the production of several successful TV series, such as "Murder, She Wrote" and "Magnum, P.I.," along with the release of movies like *ET*, *Mask*, and *Back to the Future* helped set MCA back on firmer ground in the early 1980s. In addition, in 1985 MCA booked more than $750 million in future TV syndication contracts.

The late 1980s, however, brought fewer successes. MCA's TV lineup was aging, and film-division head Frank Price was forced to leave after hatching several costly and disappointing films, including *Moon Over Parador*, *The Milagro Beanfield War*, and the $42 million *Howard the Duck*. Price was replaced in 1986 with entertainment lawyer Thomas Pollock, who brought with him clients like Tom Hanks and directors Steven Spielberg, Ron Howard, and George Lucas.

MCA also began to push to lower production costs. Long considered the most lavish spender in Hollywood, MCA began to limit costly action scenes in shows like "Miami Vice" to one per episode. Universal, which spent an average of $31 million on a film—$5 million more than the industry average—vowed to cut expenses in half. More than 30% of the unit's full-time staff was eliminated by 1988 and technical departments were cut or eliminated in favor of outside contractors.

Meanwhile, MCA continued to add to its assets. In

1986 the company acquired 50% of Cineplex Odeon Corporation, a fast-growing chain of movie theaters; in 1987 the company bought New York television station WWOR for $387 million; and in 1988 it purchased a substantial share in Motown Records.

Notwithstanding MCA's attempts to lower costs, the company was still performing below expectations at the end of the decade, and Chairman Wasserman was even reported to be seeking potential buyers. A number of companies showed some interest in various parts of MCA, following the trend in the entertainment industry toward consolidation and reorganization. But a few TV or film successes could easily put the company back on track. Quick turnarounds are not uncommon in the volatile entertainment business, as MCA itself has proven before.

Principal Subsidiaries: Universal Films Exchanges, Inc.; Universal International Films, Inc.; MCA Records, Inc.; MCA Distribution Corp.; Merchandising Corp. of America; Universal City Studios, Inc.; MCA Television Ltd.; Yosemite Park & Curry Co.; MCA Home Video, Inc.; Spencer Gifts, Inc.; MCA Videodisc Inc.; Putnam Publishing Group, Inc.; Berkley Publishing Corp.; Coward-McCann Inc.; Richard Marek Publishers, Inc.; Grosset & Dunlap, Inc.; MCA Charter Communications, Inc.; Duchess Music Corp.; Leeds Music Corp.; MCA Cable Services, Inc.; MCA Concerts, Inc.; MCA Corporate Films, Inc.; MCA Whitney Recording Studio, Inc.; L.J.N. Toys, Ltd.; Universal City Consultants, Ltd.; Universal City Property Management Co.; Universal Pay Television, Inc.; Walter Lantz Productions, Inc.; Womp's Restaurant Bar & Grill; Universal Station; Jove Publications, Inc; Disco-Vision Assn. (50%).

Further Reading: Fitzgerald, Michael G. *Universal Pictures: A Panoramic History in Words, Pictures, and Filmographies*, New Rochelle, New York, Arlington House, 1976; Edmonds, I.G. *Big U: Universal in the Silent Days*, New York, A.S. Barnes, 1977; Fitzgerald, Michael G. *Universal Pictures*, New Rochelle, New York, Arlington House, 1977.

MGM/UA COMMUNICATIONS COMPANY

450 North Roxbury Drive
Beverly Hills, California 90210
U.S.A.
(213) 281–4000

Public Company
Incorporated: 1986
Employees: 770
Sales: $674.9 million
Stock Index: New York

In 1981 Metro-Goldwyn-Mayer and United Artists, two of the greatest names in the history of motion pictures, became the MGM/UA Entertainment Company. The histories of MGM and United Artists read like the history of motion picture itself. At the time of the merger, each had survived the many changes the motion picture industry had undergone, and each was uncertain of its own future. But neither company could have suspected the complications that would follow over the course of the next decade. In 1981 the entertainment industry was transformed with astonishing speed. During the 1980s, MGM/UA went through so many corporate changes that it was hard to tell what was left of the original studios. Nevertheless today's MGM/UA Communications Company and its subsidiaries continue to produce quality entertainment for the silver screen and television.

UNITED ARTISTS

United Artists Corporation began in 1919 as a partnership between Mary Pickford, Charlie Chaplin, Douglas Fairbanks, and D.W. Griffith, four of the biggest names in motion pictures at the time. With the widespread disillusionment that followed World War I, motion pictures became a welcome source of escapist entertainment. America's fascination with movie stars had begun, movie houses sprouted up all over the country, and movies became big business. United Artists was created by these artists to wrest creative control over their own projects from the powerful Hollywood magnates.

The new company could hardly keep up with America's voracious appetite for movies. UA was essentially a cooperative distributor of individual productions. The company did not operate a studio or have stars or directors under contract. Each producer at UA was required to finance his project himself and each kept his own profits. United Artists received a percentage of each film's revenues as the distributor.

Despite the resounding success of UA's first picture, *His Majesty, the American*, starring Douglas Fairbanks, financing new productions was difficult at times during the early years. Conventional bank loans were almost unheard of for such a risky investment as films. While other motion picture companies offered stock to the public to finance expansion, UA remained private in order to retain control. Some assistance came in the form of advances from theater owners, who pre-paid for upcoming features in weekly installments. In its first five years, United Artists scored a number of hits, but the studio's schedule was slow, producing an average of only eight films a year until 1924.

In that year, Joseph Schenck became president of UA and reorganized the company. He brought in stars like Buster Keaton, Norma Talmadge, and Gloria Swanson, as well as producer Sam Goldwyn. By the late 1920s, Schenck had added a number of producers to the company's roster, and United Artists' production schedule had improved considerably. In 1927, a Howard Hughes film, *Two Arabian Knights*, garnered United Artists its first Academy Award. That same year, with the release of Warner Brothers' *The Jazz Singer*, sound came to motion pictures.

The introduction of sound revolutionized the motion picture industry and brought the downfall of many silent-screen stars who were unwilling or unable to adjust to the new technology. Millions had to be spent to upgrade film production facilities and to buy new equipment for movie houses, many of which were affiliated with major studios. The sound revolution took place over a very brief span of time—by 1930, almost no silent films were being produced. The notable exception to this rule was Charlie Chaplin, who continued to produce silent films successfully until 1940.

UA's performance had been inconsistent in its first decade, showing a loss six out of ten years between 1920 and 1930, and the early 1930s were no better. The Depression took its toll on movie attendance in 1931 and 1932, and the five big Hollywood studios—MGM, Warner Brothers, Fox, Paramount, and RKO—dominated what market remained. UA struggled to survive, and did so largely due to the talents of Joseph Schenck. Schenck decided that UA would help finance film productions and take a percentage of the revenue. Schenck also formed an independent production company, Twentieth Century Pictures, with former Warner Brothers production head Darryl Zanuck. That company's success contributed greatly to UA's own profits in the early 1930s. Despite the fact that Twentieth Century Pictures accounted for almost half of UA's films, Fairbanks, Pickford, and Chaplin (Griffith sold his shares in 1933) would not give the production company a slice of their pie. In 1935 Schenck and Zanuck left and merged Twentieth Century Pictures with the Fox Film Corporation. Al Lichtman replaced Schenck as president of United Artists.

Throughout the 1930s many of Hollywood's greatest

independent producers worked through United Artists, among them Walt Disney, Alexander Korda, Sam Goldwyn, Hal Roach, Walter Wanger, and David O. Selznick. The company, however, was plagued by low production, resulting in financial difficulties throughout the 1930s. Though film attendance was healthy, competing with the major studios was an uphill battle. United Artists earned a profit through the late 1930s, but did not keep pace with other film distributors. Internal conflicts disrupted the studio as well. Producer Sam Goldwyn, who had produced almost half of UA's pictures in the late 1930s, felt he wasn't being adequately compensated for his efforts. Disputes between Goldwyn and Pickford, Fairbanks, and Chaplin led to a number of lawsuits, and eventually to Goldwyn's leaving United Artists in 1940. In the 14 years Goldwyn had been associated with UA he had made 50 motion pictures.

Although distribution to foreign markets was severely curtailed during World War II, movie audiences increased during the war in the United States and Canada. While some film companies benefited from this increase in attendance, UA struggled to remain profitable. The chronic problem of an insufficient number of films for distribution compelled UA to lower production standards, and the company's reputation as a provider of high-quality motion pictures faltered.

After the war, independent production became more popular as the big studios struggled to reduce overhead and tax breaks encouraged producers to go it alone. But again, United Artists failed to capitalize on this trend. Independent filmmakers were lured elsewhere. Movie attendance dropped off drastically once America returned to a peacetime economy. In 1946 David O. Selznick, who had produced a number of big hits, including the MGM-released *Gone With the Wind*, left United Artists. Chaplin and Pickford (Fairbanks had died in 1939) had accused Selznick of breaching his UA contract by distributing a number of films through RKO, while Selznick accused UA of doing a sloppy job of distribution. The producer went on to form his own distribution company, and United Artists lost a key contributor. By the end of the 1940s, plagued by poor-quality pictures and shrinking cinema audiences, United Artists was bleeding red ink.

A drastic reorganization was needed, but Pickford and Chaplin dragged their feet. In July of 1950, the owners announced a change in management of the company. Paul V. McNutt, former governor of Indiana, became chairman of UA, and Frank L. McNamee took over as president. McNutt, however, did not have the expertise to solve UA's financial woes. Within a few months he turned over the reins to a group headed by Arthur Krim and Robert Benjamin. Krim had been president of Eagle-Lion Films, and Benjamin had headed the American operations of Arthur Rank Organisation, a British filmmaker. The two made a deal with Pickford and Chaplin which gave Krim and Benjamin control of the company for ten years and guaranteed them half the company if they could turn the debt-ridden distributor around. Krim and Benjamin secured a $3 million loan from Fox Films president Spyros Skouras. United Artists scored two big box office hits with *High Noon* and *The African Queen*. Within a year the company was showing a profit, and Krim and Benjamin had begun a 20-year reign.

As television began to steal the nation's movie audience, Hollywood sought new ways to get people into theaters. Cinemascope, Cinerama, VistaVision, and a number of other devices were introduced to make the "big" nature of motion pictures even bigger. Other gimmicks, like 3-D movies, were equally novel, if less spectacular. United Artists released the first 3-D picture, *Bwana Devil*, in 1953.

Movie budgets skyrocketed as the industry turned to musicals to entice viewers. Racy themes also began to slink their way onto the silver screen. During the mid-1950s, UA's roster filled with names like John Wayne, Bob Hope, and Otto Preminger. In 1955 Chaplin sold his UA shares, which amounted to 25% of the company, to Krim and Benjamin for $1.1 million. A year later, Mary Pickford also sold her shares, for $3 million, giving full ownership to the Krim and Benjamin group. By the end of the decade the company that had once been chronically short of movies was turning out 50 pictures a year. In 1957, United Artists went public with a $17 million stock and debenture offering. The company ended the 1950s solidly in the black and with its reputation for quality restored.

In the 1960s, the trend toward independent production grew even stronger. The major studios underwent a number of changes. Paramount was bought by Gulf and Western, MGM diversified into real estate, and Warner Brothers merged with a television company, Seven Arts Limited. United Artists, meanwhile, was having one of its most successful decades, winning 11 Academy Awards, five of them for best picture. In 1963, Eon Productions released *Dr. No*, the first James Bond movie, through United Artists, beginning what would prove to be the longest-running series in cinema history and a sure money-maker for United Artists.

In 1967 the Transamerica Corporation bought 98% of UA's stock. In 1969, David Picker and his brother Arnold took over as president and chairman, respectively, of the company. But when UA lost $35 million in 1970, Transamerica chairman John Beckett brought back Arthur Krim as chairman and Robert Benjamin as vice-chairman. The early 1970s was a slow period for United Artists, as other studios were scoring the big hits. In 1973, UA purchased the domestic distribution rights to all of MGM's pictures for ten years, after MGM decided to cut back on production and invest in the $120 million MGM Grand Hotel in Las Vegas. High budgets and unpredictable audiences combined to make film production more risky than ever. Finally in 1975, United Artists released *One Flew Over the Cuckoo's Nest*. The film was a smash, cleaning up at the Oscars, and earning more than $56 million. A year later UA's *Rocky* won the Oscar for Best Picture, and in 1977 Woody Allen's *Annie Hall* captured the same honor for United Artists for the third year in a row. In 1978, Arthur Krim split from United Artists after a dispute with Transamerica chief John Beckett. Krim, Benjamin, Eric Pleskow (UA's president), and a number of other key executives formed Orion Pictures. An era had ended at United Artists.

After the departure of Krim and Benjamin, United

Artists struggled to find effective leadership. Andy Albeck, a former vice president of the company and assistant to Krim, was installed as president. Transamerica's James Harvey became chairman. In 1979, hits like *Rocky II*, *Manhattan*, *Moonraker*, and *The Black Stallion* gave UA its most successful season ever. A year later, the studio released director Michael Cimino's western *Heaven's Gate*. Cimino's previous movies, *Thunderbolt and Lightfoot* and *The Deer Hunter*, had been hits. *Heaven's Gate*, however, had grossly exceeded its budget, finally tallying $44 million. Critics panned the film, and the public concurred. Cimino's film recovered only $1.5 million at the domestic box office.

In the wake of *Heaven's Gate*, Albeck resigned as president. Norbert Auerbach, the former senior vice president of foreign distribution, took his place. In May, 1981 at the Cannes Film Festival, Auerbach announced that United Artists had been purchased by MGM. The MGM/UA Entertainment Corporation was born.

MGM

Unlike United Artists, MGM was a complete production studio from the start, with actors, writers, directors, and production coordinators all under long-term contract. MGM rarely had trouble finding financing, producing enough movies, or attracting audiences. MGM, symbolized by Leo the Lion's roar, was for years the king of the Hollywood jungle.

In 1924, three motion picture studios, Metro Pictures, the Goldwyn Picture Corporation, and Louis B. Mayer Pictures, began to operate together under the corporate control of Loew's, Inc., one of the nation's largest theater chains. Marcus Loew had purchased Metro Pictures in 1919 to help fill his theaters with a steady flow of quality motion pictures. Demand for movies was much greater than the supply at that time. By 1924, Loew found that the films coming out of his Metro Pictures unit were lacking in both quality and quantity. At the same time, Lee Shubert, of Shubert Theater fame, approached Loew with the idea of merging Goldwyn Pictures with Metro. Goldwyn Pictures had been plagued by personality conflicts, resulting in the departure of Sam Goldwyn in 1922. Meanwhile, filmmaker Louis B. Mayer, who had a successful production company of his own, heard of the pending merger and flew to New York to negotiate with Loew. A deal was struck merging the Metro, Goldwyn, and Louis B. Mayer studios as a subsidiary of Loew's. Mayer was chosen to head the new studio.

Mayer brought with him the 24-year-old Irving Thalberg, who oversaw the company's production. Prodigiously talented, Thalberg was known as the "boy wonder" of Hollywood. Under the leadership of Mayer and Thalberg, the new company produced more than 100 feature films in its first two years. In 1925, MGM released the extravagant *Ben Hur*, which was a huge success, and MGM-Loew's recorded a $4.7 million profit in its first full year. Throughout the 1920s, movie audiences were strong. In 1927, sound gave the industry a boost, and by the end of the decade, movie-going was a habit for many Americans.

The Depression began to take its toll on the film industry in 1931. The novelty of "talkies" had worn off, and hard times kept people preoccupied with things other than entertainment. Despite these troubles, throughout the 1930s, MGM was the most successful studio in Hollywood. MGM's long list of stars under contract and its reputation for excellence helped it survive the Depression, when theater attendance dropped to half of what it had been between 1927 and 1930. The guaranteed purchase of productions by Loew's theater chain also gave the studio much-needed stability, and Irving Thalberg's penchant for excellence earned for the studio the viewing public's highest regard.

By 1933, attendance began to rise again. In addition to MGM's fine feature films, the studio also distributed quality shorts like the Hal Roach's "Our Gang," "Laurel and Hardy," and the "Patsy Kelly" series, and William Hanna and Joe Barbera contributed animated films, including the well-known "Tom and Jerry" cartoons. In 1936, Irving Thalberg died at the age of 36. With his death, MGM productions turned away from literary toward purely escapist entertainment, but it continued to pursue excellence, including such hits as *The Wizard of Oz* and *Boys Town*.

The year 1939 is often considered the peak of the motion picture industry's glory. That year the industry released such classics as *Stagecoach*, *Mr. Smith Goes to Washington*, *Wuthering Heights*, *Of Mice and Men*, *Gunga Din*, *Jesse James*, *Dark Victory*, and *Intermezzo*, to name just a few. The big hit was, of course, *Gone With the Wind*. Starring Clark Gable and Vivien Leigh, the film became one of the top money makers of all time. Interestingly, the movie was actually a David Selznick production and should by rights have been released through United Artists, as his other films were. Selznick, however, was determined that Clark Gable play the lead role of Rhett Butler. Gable was under contract to MGM, and in order to use him (and acquire a $1.5 million loan from his father-in-law Louis B. Mayer), Selznick had to release the picture through MGM and give the studio half the profits. The film set attendance records worldwide and snatched up ten Academy Awards.

MGM's reign over the industry continued into the 1940s. The introduction of Technicolor, together with the desire for entertainment during the dreary years of World War II, kept audiences in the theaters and profits healthy. After the war, however, the "bigness" that once made MGM prosper became a costly burden. The baby boom and the introduction of television kept audiences at home. MGM's high overhead weighed heavily on the company as it tried to adjust to the changes in the industry. By the late 1940s, film executives were running scared. Loew's president Nicholas Schenck (brother of UA's Joseph Schenck) told Mayer to find a new "boy wonder" to snap the company's production back into shape. Mayer hired Dore Schary, formerly of RKO, as the new production head. Schary pointed MGM in the direction of spectacular musicals to give audiences what they couldn't get anywhere else. It proved to be a wise move. In the late 1940s and early 1950s, MGM released such hits as *Easter Parade*, *Annie Get Your Gun*, *Show Boat*, *Singin' in the Rain*, *An American in Paris*, and *Seven Brides for Seven Brothers*.

In 1952, the major studios were ordered to divest themselves of their theater holdings. Loew's held out for some time, but finally was forced to split from MGM. The industry would never be the same. Without a guaranteed market for the major studios, filmmaking became a risky business. In 1955, theater attendance dropped to its lowest since 1923. The public still came out to see the big hits, but it was getting harder for the studios to predict which films would make money. A large budget was no guarantee. In 1957, MGM lost money for the first time. It bounced back with a profit in 1958, though, despite the general decline in the industry, and relative to other film studios at the time, MGM was doing well.

In the early 1960s, MGM's profits were on-again-off-again. Advertising began to play a key role in any motion picture's success. At the same time, the public's tastes were changing as audiences became younger. By the middle of the 1960s, the major studios began to cater to their younger patrons: movies began to explore controversial topics and sex and violence became more acceptable. By the end of the decade, MGM was no longer at the top of the industry. Independent production had become the standard, and major studios were being bought up by larger corporations.

In 1970, Las Vegas investor Kirk Kerkorian took control of MGM. Kerkorian appointed James Aubrey, a former television executive, as president. The company sold many of its assets, including a number of theaters owned overseas, the MGM record company, and parts of the company's Culver City lot. In 1973, MGM got out of the distribution business altogether by turning over domestic distribution of its films to United Artists. Foreign distribution was licensed to the Cinema International Corporation (CIC). In the mid-1970s, Frank Rosenfelt replaced Aubrey as president of MGM and Kerkorian himself became the chief executive officer.

In general, the 1970s showed improved revenues for the film industry. MGM, however, was focusing on other activities. By the end of the decade the MGM Grand Hotels in Las Vegas and Reno were bringing in more money that the film production unit. No longer a primary force in the film industry, MGM hoped that its 1981 acquisition of United Artists would give it new life.

The new MGM/UA Entertainment Company was established at a time when the entertainment industry was going through many changes. Pay television and videotape players offered new avenues for marketing old movies. Suddenly, MGM/UA's movie library was a vital asset. At the same time, theater audiences were growing. In 1983, the company launched a number of subsidiaries: the MGM/UA Home Entertainment Group, MGM/UA Classics, and the MGM/UA Television Group. Also in 1983, majority stockholder Kirk Kerkorian bid $665 million for the MGM/UA shares he didn't already hold. The bid caused an uproar (and a lawsuit), which convinced Kerkorian to drop the idea of taking the company private, at least for the time being. MGM/UA scored a number of hits at the box office in the early 1980s, including *War Games* and *Octopussy*, but profits didn't keep up with Kerkorian's expectations. In the mid-1980s, the Las Vegas financier instigated a number of deals which eventually led to the formation of a different company with some of the same assets, and nearly the same name. The MGM/UA Communications Company was incorporated in 1986, but the complicated story of its formation began a year earlier.

In 1985, the MGM and UA production units of MGM/UA Entertainment were separated under a general corporate restructuring. Alan Ladd Jr. and Frank Yablans, who until then had run the combined studios together, were put in charge of one unit each. Analysts speculated that Kerkorian was preparing to sell one of the studios, probably UA, in order to raise cash to take MGM private. That theory went out the window, however, when Yablans was fired shortly after the restructuring and Ladd was put in charge of both studios' production units. In August 1985, cable television magnate Ted Turner began negotiations with Kerkorian to buy MGM/UA Entertainment for $1.5 billion. Turner's key interest in the company was its 3,000-title MGM film library, which would provide an excellent source of programming for Turner's superstation WTBS. By January 1986, Turner's buyout, at $20 per share and one new preferred share of Turner Broadcasting System stock, went through. At the same time, Turner sold the United Artists assets back to Kirk Kerkorian for $480 million. The MGM/UA Entertainment Company was now a subsidiary of the Turner Bradcasting System, but United Artists was a separate company.

In June 1986, United Artists, under Kerkorian's control, bought back many of the original MGM assets for $300 million, including the production and distribution units, the Home Entertainment Group, and the UA film library. Turner kept the MGM library, and sold the original MGM Studios real estate in Culver City to Lorimar Telepictures for $190 million. United Artists changed its name to MGM/UA Communications Company, and again restructured its operations.

The "new" company grouped the two television production units together, but kept the film units separate. Alan Ladd headed the MGM group, while Anthony Thomopoulous took over at UA, and David Gerber at the combined TV unit. The company began to come back during the next year. In 1987, *Spaceballs*, *The Living Daylights*, and *Moonstruck* were big hits for the studio. But despite these successful films, MGM/UA recorded an $88 million loss for 1987. In April 1988, frustrated by the company's performance, Kerkorian began shopping for potential buyers for his 82% holding in MGM/UA. By July, he was planning to split the two companies again. Kerkorian struck a deal with investor Burt Sugarman and producers Jon Peters and Peter Guber to sell a 25% interest in MGM. The agreement fell through, however, and top MGM/UA executives, confounded by Kerkorian's unpredictable maneuvers, began to abandon ship. Chairman Lee Rich was the first to go, followed shortly by Ladd and Thomopoulous. At the zenith of this corporate crisis during the summer of 1988, production on many of the company's film projects was canceled.

Stephen Silbert briefly took Lee Rich's place as MGM/UA's chief executive in July 1988. By October, he had stepped aside to let former Merrill Lynch executive Jeffrey Barbakow take the reins. Barbakow was experienced in packaging limited partnerships to finance film ventures. He set out to nurse the ailing studio back to health. In fiscal 1988, MGM/UA lost $48.7 million, considerably less than in 1987. *Rain Man's* success (it won the 1988 Oscar for best picture as well as three other Oscars) promised improvement, but MGM/UA was debt-ridden and had only a handful of films in production.

In 1989 the media company Qintex Australia Limited agreed to acquire MGM/UA, but the deal fell through in October of that year. While Kerkorian continues to look for a buyer, many wonder how MGM/UA will continue to fund the production of movies and TV shows. Nonetheless, despite its present troubles, MGM/UA faces the 1990s still firmly associated with quality entertainment.

Principal Subsidiaries: MGM/UA Film Group; MGM/UA Television Production Group, Inc.; MGM/UA Telecommunications, Inc.; MGM/UA Licensing and Merchandising.

Further Reading: Eames, John D. *The MGM Story: The Complete History of Fifty Roaring Years*, New York, Crown, 1975; Balio, T. *United Artists: The Company Built by the Stars*, Madison, University of Wisconsin Press, 1976; Easton, Carol. *The Search for Sam Goldwyn: A Biography*, New York, William Morrow, 1976; Marx, Arthur. *Goldwyn: A Biography of the Man Behind the Myth*, New York, Norton, 1976; Bergan, Ronald. *The United Artists Story*, New York, Crown, 1986; Berg, Scott. *Goldwyn: A Biography*, New York, Knopf, 1989.

NATIONAL BROADCASTING COMPANY INC.

30 Rockefeller Plaza
New York, New York 10020
U.S.A.
(212) 586–0610

Wholly-owned subsidiary of General Electric Company
Incorporated: 1926 as National Broadcasting Company
Employees: 6,000
Sales: $3.64 billion

The National Broadcasting Company (NBC) was the first permanent, full-service radio network in the U.S. The company provides network television services to affiliated TV stations, produces TV and radio programs, and operates seven TV stations. The NBC Network is one of several competing major national commercial broadcasting television networks and serves more than 200 affiliated stations within the United States.

The original owner of NBC was the Radio Corporation of America (RCA). RCA was formed after World War I by several large American companies in order to keep "wireless" (radio) technology in American hands. At the time, it was the leading manufacturer of radio receivers in the world.

RCA's goal in forming NBC was to be able to provide a large number of quality radio programs so that, as one of its newspaper ads said, "every event of national importance may be broadcast widely throughout the United States." General Electric and Westinghouse also had ownership interests in NBC, but RCA bought them out in January, 1930 and remained the sole owner until 1986, when General Electric acquired RCA for $6.3 billion. NBC is now a wholly-owned operating subsidiary of General Electric.

NBC's first radio broadcast, on November 15, 1926, was a four-and-a-half hour presentation of the leading musical and comedy talent of the day. It was broadcast from New York over a network of 25 stations, as far west as Kansas City; close to half of the country's five million radio homes tuned in. The first coast-to-coast broadcast soon followed, on New Year's Day, 1927, when NBC covered the annual Rose Bowl football game in California.

The demand for a network service among local stations was mounting so rapidly that less than two months after its first national broadcast, NBC split its programming into two separate networks, called the "red" and the "blue" networks, to give listeners a choice of different program formats. By 1941, these two networks blanketed the country; there were 103 blue subscribing stations, 76 red, and 64 supplementary stations using NBC programs. The blue network provided mostly cultural offerings: music, drama, and commentary. The red featured comedy and similar types of entertainment. There were regular radio programs for children, and soap operas and religious programs. When the Federal Communications Commission declared in 1941 that no organization could own more than one network, NBC sold the blue complex, which became the American Broadcasting Company.

Early radio provided a forum for the popular vaudeville entertainers of the day: NBC hired many of them—Rudy Vallee, Fred Allen, Jack Benny, Ed Wynn, Eddie Cantor, Al Johnson, Groucho Marx, Bob Hope, Jimmy Durante, Bing Crosby, Red Skelton, Edgar Bergen and Charlie McCarthy, and George Burns and Gracie Allen, to name a few. These performers had their own shows and appeared on each others' as well.

From the first coast-to-coast broadcast of the Rose Bowl in 1927, sporting events were a radio mainstay. That same year, the red and blue networks tied in with a number of independent stations to broadcast the second Tunney-Dempsey fight from Soldier Field in Chicago. Two years later NBC broadcast the Kentucky Derby. During the 1920s and 1930s, the network featured the World Series many times. It also covered major football games, golf tournaments, and the Olympics in Los Angeles in 1932.

NBC's first special-events broadcast was Charles A. Lindbergh's arrival in Washington on June 11, 1927 after his historic trans-Atlantic flight. In 1928, the network began coverage of national political events, covering the Republican and Democratic national conventions in 1928; the inaugurations of presidents Herbert Hoover in 1929 and Franklin D. Roosevelt in 1933; the opening of the 73rd Congress on March 9, 1933; and Roosevelt's first "Fireside Chat" on March 12 of that year. "NBC News" was officially created in 1933.

The first international NBC broadcast was also in 1928, when the network carried a pick-up of President Calvin Coolidge opening a Pan-American conference in Havana.

In 1923 David Sarnoff, the founder of NBC, wrote a memorandum to the board of directors of RCA about something he called "television," or "the art of distant seeing." "Television," he said, "will make it possible for those at home to see as well as hear what is going on at the broadcast station." The groundwork for his vision had been laid by the invention of the cathode-ray tube in 1906—the forerunner of the modern television picture tube.

RCA engineers began actively conducting television experiments in 1925, but it was not until 1939 that NBC began what is considered the first regular television service, with a telecast of President Roosevelt opening the New York World's Fair. The first television network broadcast occurred on January 11, 1940 when programming was transmitted from RCA's WNBT-TV New York City to General Electric's WRGT-TV Schenectady, New York, via automatic radio relays.

In 1941, NBC obtained a commercial television station license from the Federal Communication Commission for WNBT-TV and officially became the world's first commercial television station.

Television programming was limited by World War II to four hours a day. In 1942 NBC Radio began featuring "The Army Hour," an official weekly broadcast that provided on-the-scene reports from military bases and battle zones. On D-Day, June 6, 1944, the network cancelled all commercial broadcasts to provide continuous news coverage of the invasion of Normandy. Although World War II slowed the growth of television, NBC continued to experiment with new broadcasting concepts, including color television. During the mid-1940s NBC began to build a television empire the same way it had built its radio network. Its first television network consisted of four stations that covered New York City, Philadelphia, Schenectady, New York, and Washington, D.C.

After the war television began to expand news coverage, create new weekly variety and drama programs, and adapt popular radio shows to the screen. "Meet the Press," a program featuring a panel of journalists interviewing important public figures of the day, debuted on NBC Radio in 1945. It switched to NBC Television in 1947, destined to become the longest-running show on television.

By this time, two more stations had joined the NBC-TV network. In 1947 there were only 14,000 television homes; at the start of 1948 this number had swelled to 175,000, and by the end of the year, nearly a million sets had been sold. During this time the number of operating television stations had mushroomed from 19 to 47.

By 1951 NBC had installed regular coast-to-coast network television service. Its first venture was covering the signing of the Japanese peace treaty in San Francisco on September 4, 1951. Popular early coast-to-coast programs included the "All Star Revue" with Jack Carson and "The Colgate Comedy Hour" with Eddie Cantor.

As the 1950s progressed, NBC Radio focused on news, sports, and public affairs programming while NBC Television implemented new programming formats, expanding its schedule from the late-afternoon and evening formats prevalent at the time to include a new kind of show, the early-morning weekly series. The "Today Show," which began in 1952, was the pioneer among such programming, offering news, features, interviews, and entertainment in a two-hour, magazine-type format.

In 1953, NBC presented the first coast-to-coast transmission of a color broadcast; later that year, the Federal Communications Commission approved the RCA-backed National Television System Committee's standards for color compatibility, which removed CBS's rival color system from competition. This new technology made it possible for viewers who did not own a color television set to receive all network programs on their old black-and-white sets, even if the program was broadcast in color.

Television programming continued to expand. As equipment was improved and miniaturized, it became easier for television teams to cover fast-action news in the field. In 1956 NBC aired the first videotape, and in 1962 the launching of the "Telstar" communications satellite made it possible to relay live video sequences from continent to continent almost instantaneously.

By the 1960s television was big business, and NBC continued to expand its programming with popular programs like "The Virginian," "Rowan and Martin's Laugh-In," "The Man From U.N.C.L.E.," and "Star Trek." The network also initiated and presented the 1960 presidential debates between John Kennedy and Richard Nixon. In 1964 it presented the first made-for-TV movie, establishing a new television format.

During the 1970s, though TV programming was swelling to an all-time peak, radio was sagging. NBC tried, unsuccessfully, to buoy radio sales by introducing several new programs. In 1975 NBC Radio introduced an ambitious 24-hour radio news network, the National News and Information Service (NNIS), but it was discontinued two years later for lack of audience and station clearance.

NBC was so disheartened by its lack of success in the radio arena that, in the early 1970s, it developed a plan to sell all of its radio stations and get out of the business. It never followed through, however, and by December, 1983 the network had completed the conversion of its radio transmissions from landlines to satellite. In 1985 NBC established a radio-programming distribution arm called NBC Radio entertainment, allowing it to get involved with a variety of programs such as country and jazz. With these changes, NBC's radio business became profitable again, but in 1988 NBC did finally decide to leave the business, and that year sold seven of its eight radio stations.

The mid-1980s were a hard time for NBC Television. In 1983, none of NBC's nine new shows were renewed and the network received low consumer ratings for the third year in a row. Some sources attributed this decline to poor management and a mishandled budget. The network quickly replaced low-rated programming and managed to bring its ratings up to second place by the 1984–85 season, and to number one by 1985.

In 1986, NBC facilitated the exchange of news between NBC-TV affiliates by launching the "Skycom" domestic and international satellite system. It became the only network to use satellites as its sole method of distribution. In the same year, General Electric Company acquired RCA for $6.3 billion and became NBC's parent company.

Since the late 1970s, television delivery technology has continually challenged the whole TV industry. NBC has been at the forefront in exploring the possibilities of new technology, investing in such successful vehicles as music video shows like "Friday Night Videos" and cable television. Some of its current projects include the development of wide-screen and high-definition television, and the production of theatrical films.

As TV enters a new age, one in which traditional network broadcasting has a decreasing importance, NBC's future will hinge on its ability to make the most of new technology and stay ahead of its competition.

Principal Subsidiaries: Living Music Enterprises; NBC Educational Enterprises; NBC Europe, Inc.; NBC News

Bureaus, Inc.; NBC News Worldwide, Inc.; NBC Productions, Inc.; NBC Television Co., Inc.; Spectacular Music, Inc.

Further Reading: Campbell, Robert. *The Golden Years of Broadcasting: A Celebration of the First 50 Years of Radio and Television on NBC*, New York, Charles Scribner's Sons, 1976; Gorowitz, Bernard (Ed). *On the Shoulders of Giants: 1924 to 1946—The GE Story*, Schenectady, New York, Elfun Society, Territorial Council, 1979; Schatz, Ronald W. *The Electrical Workers: A History of Labor at General Electric and Westinghouse, 1923–60*, Urbana, University of Illinois Press, 1983.

PARAMOUNT PICTURES CORPORATION

5555 Melrose Avenue
Los Angeles, California 90038
U.S.A.
(213) 468-5000

Wholly owned subsidiary of Paramount Communications, Inc. (formerly Gulf & Western)
Incorporated: 1916 as Famous Players-Lasky Corp.
Employees: 2,500
Sales: $1.86 billion

Adolph Zukor, the founder of Paramount Pictures, spent most of his life establishing and supervising one of the largest and most successful motion picture companies in the history of the entertainment industry. Zukor was born in Hungary in 1873, but emigrated to the United States at age 15. He arrived in New York with $40 hidden inside his waistcoat, and got a job sweeping floors in an East Side fur store. By the turn of the century, he was the owner of a prosperous fur business in Chicago.

Eventually Zukor returned to New York in search of new investment opportunities. There he met Mitchell Mark, an owner of penny arcades. These arcades, where customers paid pennies to see a short moving picture, were both popular and profitable. Zukor and Mark soon formed the Automatic Vaudeville Arcades Company with Zukor's friend Marcus Loew. A short time later, they were operating their own separate companies as owners of nickelodeons, where for a nickel customers could see a short movie.

It was a short step from nickelodeons to full-scale variety shows for Zukor and Loew. Combining movies and vaudeville acts, the men pooled their resources and established Loew's Consolidated Enterprises in 1910 with Loew as president and Zukor as treasurer. By 1912 they controlled a growing number of theaters, including New York's Crystal Hall on 14th Street. But Zukor became intrigued by the possibilities of film production, particularly for longer shows (until that time, films had been arbitrarily kept to one reel, or ten minutes, by a consortium of the largest film distributors and licensers). He sold his interest back to Loew for a handsome profit and bought the American distribution rights to a four-reel French production of *Queen Elizabeth*, starring Sarah Bernhardt.

After a tremendously successful opening of *Queen Elizabeth* at New York's Lyceum Theatre, Zukor founded a new company, Famous Players in Famous Plays (later shortened to just Famous Players), to begin producing movies. The company's first four releases—*The Count of Monte Cristo*, *The Prisoner of Zenda*, *His Neighbor's Wife*, and *Tess of the d'Urbervilles*—were moderately successful, but it was not until Zukor signed Mary Pickford that Famous Players started producing hits and making money. By 1913, his firm had increased its production to 30 pictures a year.

In 1914, Zukor met Jesse Lasky. Lasky had established the Jesse L. Lasky Feature Play Company in 1913 with himself as president and Cecil B. DeMille as director general. The firm's first production effort was *The Squaw Man*, directed by DeMille, and was soon followed by *Rose of the Rancho* and *The Virginian*. In its second year, the company released 36 pictures. When Zukor offered a 50–50 partnership in a joint Famous Players–Lasky company in 1916, Lasky didn't hesitate to accept the opportunity. Flattered by the offer and foreseeing a lucrative future for the combine, Lasky allowed Zukor to appoint himself president; Lasky, vice president in charge of production; and Cecil DeMille, director general. Samuel Goldfish (later Goldwyn) was made chairman of the board.

Two months later, Zukor bought a majority of the Paramount Company, the film-distribution company that both Zukor and Lasky had signed with in 1914. Meanwhile, the creative tempo was so great at Famous Players–Lasky that an average of more than two pictures emerged every week between 1916 and 1921. The awkward name of Zukor's firm was soon replaced with Paramount, the distribution company's name and trademark. One of the most familiar slogans in the film industry—"If it's a Paramount Picture it's the Best Show in Town"—was created soon after.

Paramount's large organization began to expand rapidly in the early and mid-1920s. At first Zukor began to build a large theater chain by buying or building showplaces for the company. In 1924 he went overseas and opened the Paris Paramount and the London Plaza. At the same time, Paramount developed a worldwide distribution network and opened studios in London, Berlin, and Bombay, in addition to its American ones.

The studio reached its peak in the field of silent-film making with DeMille's blockbuster *The Ten Commandments* in 1923. Yet scandal cast a shadow over Paramount and the movie industry in general when one of its stars, Fatty Arbuckle, was accused of rape and manslaughter and then acquitted in a much-publicized trial. This and several other events caused a public outcry against immorality in the movies, and DeMille's spectacular productions came under criticism. After an argument with Zukor over artistic differences and rising production costs, DeMille left the company.

Even though Paramount was making more money—a steady $5 million a year—than Warner, Fox, and Universal, Zukor was obsessed with maintaining his company's supremacy in the industry. He began a theater-buying campaign that amassed single houses and entire circuits, paying for many of the acquisitions with Paramount stock. By 1930, the firm's movie-house division had grown to include almost 2,000 units and was named Publix Theaters; that year the company's name was changed to Paramount-Publix.

The significance of the Warner Brother's 1927 movie *The Jazz Singer*, with its brief sequences of song and dialogue, was not lost on Paramount. Warner Brothers had used the Vitaphone sound system for this movie, but Zukor decided to go with Fox's new development, sound-on-film Movietone, which was more technically reliable and easier to handle. Paramount used it in *Wings* and won the first Oscar for best picture, in 1929.

In 1930 the company's stable of stars was one of the most impressive in Hollywood; it included Fredric March, Claudette Colbert, Maurice Chevalier, Kay Francis, Walter Huston, Gary Cooper, William Powell, Carole Lombard, Harold Lloyd, W. C. Fields, and the Marx Brothers. Over the next few years, Paramount also contracted Tallulah Bankhead, Marlene Dietrich, and the inimitable Mae West.

Prosperity and success at Paramount did not last long, however. In 1930 the firm recorded a profit of $18 million, but by 1932 the Depression was at its height and the studio ran a deficit of slightly more than $15 million. The main problem was the Publix theater chain. Many deals during its growth were made by paying owners of theaters Paramount stock, fully redeemable at a fixed price and fixed date. But too many redemption dates came in the middle of the Depression, and the company could not pay. Hundreds of company employees were forced to leave, while others accepted huge salary cuts. Paramount-Publix went into receivership in 1933. When in 1935 it emerged from bankruptcy as Paramount Pictures Inc., John Otterson assumed the position of president, Emanuel Cohen was named studio chief, and Adolph Zukor became chairman of the board. The one bright spot during these years was the return of DeMille.

Sustained by Bing Crosby musicals, DeMille spectacles, and sexy Mae West comedies, Paramount announced a $3 million profit in 1936, a profit of $6 million the following year, and $12 million the next. Despite this turnaround, both Otterson and Cohen were drummed out of the company; Barney Balaban became president in 1936 and Y. Frank Freeman took over as vice president in charge of production in 1938. They lasted until 1966 and 1959, respectively.

The stability that Balaban and Freeman gave Paramount led to a $13 million profit in 1941; by the end of the war, its profits had topped $15 million. The hits of Crosby, DeMille, and West in the 1930s had given way to the more sophisticated and elegant comedies of Ernst Lubitsch, Mitchell Leisen, and Preston Sturges. The number of Paramount releases also dropped, from 71 in 1936 to 19 in 1946 as the studio concentrated on quality over quantity. Leo McCarthy's *Going My Way* won the Oscar for best picture in 1944—the company's first win since *Wings*—and Billy Wilder's *Lost Weekend* won it in 1945. These successes led to a phenomenal $39 million profit for 1946.

In 1948 Paramount, along with all the other major film companies, was found guilty of antitrust-law violations and ordered by the U.S. government to divest itself of all its theater holdings. Within a year, the company had sold the properties that Zukor had collected—and profits dropped from $20 million in 1949 to $6 million in 1950.

By this time, the company was feeling the effects of a growing television audience. The entire movie industry tried to fight back with visual inventions that the smaller screen couldn't duplicate. Three-dimensional effects, Cinerama's huge concave screen, and Twentieth Century Fox's CinemaScope were some of the developments used to help increase box office receipts. Paramount came up with its own panoramic big-screen system, Vista-Vision, which was acknowledged to be a significant improvement over previous systems. But these technical innovations failed to increase revenues. Even though Paramount reported a $12.5 million profit in 1958 (the largest since 1949), it continued to suffer from a decline in theater attendance through the 1960s.

In 1965 George Weltner, the executive vice president of Paramount, led a group of dissident executives in a proxy battle to unseat the old management. (Freeman had retired in 1959, but Balaban had become chairman of the board in 1964.) While both sides were planning their strategies, Gulf & Western Industries (now Paramount Communications) offered to purchase the company at $83 a share, nearly $10 more than the market price. The offer was accepted at the annual stockholders meeting, and on October 19, 1966 Paramount became the first major film company to be owned by a conglomerate.

Paramount was incorporated into Gulf & Western's leisure-time group. Charles Bluhdorn, the founder of Gulf & Western, appointed himself chairman of the board at his newest subsidiary, and Paramount began to produce hits like *True Grit*, *The Odd Couple*, *Romeo and Juliet*, *Love Story*, *Rosemary's Baby*, and *Goodbye, Columbus*.

In 1970 a deal of far-reaching significance between Paramount and Universal studios was made. Bluhdorn and Lew Wasserman, chairman of MCA, agreed to combine their companies' distribution outlets everywhere but in the United States. That new firm was enlarged ten years later when MGM became a joint owner. Since MGM had bought United Artists, foreign countries that had been served by four distribution networks were now served by one, United International Pictures.

In 1974 Bluhdorn relinquished his position as chairman of the board at Paramount to Barry Diller, a change in leadership that in no way diminished the company's good fortune. The *Godfather* movies, each an Academy Award winner, were joined by *The Conversation*, *Chinatown*, *Nashville*, and *Grease* in audience popularity. It was also during this time that Gulf & Western added publisher Simon & Schuster and New York's Madison Square Garden to its leisure-time group. When Adolph Zukor died in 1976 at the age of 103, after having been chairman emeritus for 12 years, he had lived to see the rebirth of his company.

A 1980 Oscar winner for Paramount, *Ordinary People*, was critical as well as a popular success. In 1981, the new champion of box office profits, *Raiders of the Lost Ark*, raked in worldwide rentals totaling approximately $200 million. *Raiders* had been turned down by four other studios by the time Paramount president Michael Eisner decided to take the risk. The film's success was a tribute to his and chairman Barry Diller's instincts. Eisner told *Business Week* in 1984 that unlike other studios, Paramount did not believe in market research. "Everyone thinks they can find a magic wand. But I would rather fail on my own judgment than on the judgment of some man in Columbus, Ohio," he said. "I think about what I like not what the public likes. If I ask Miss Middle America if she wants to see a movie about religion she'll say yes. If I say 'Do you want to see a movie about sex,' she'll say no. But she'll be lying." Eisner and Diller had worked together for several years, first at the ABC television network, then at Paramount. Their instincts had brought the studio a consistent string of big successes.

In 1984, after the unexpected death of Gulf & Western Chairman Charles Bluhdorn, Martin S. Davis took the helm at the holding company. Davis clashed with Paramount chairman Diller, and in late 1984 Diller left to head Twentieth Century Fox. A day later Michael Eisner resigned to head Walt Disney Company. Half of the company's top executives followed them, leaving Paramount with a serious management crisis. Frank Mancuso, the former head of the marketing department, who had been with the company for 24 years, became Paramount's new chairman.

After a brief but severe slump in earnings (in 1985 the motion picture group took the biggest write-off in its history) the soft-spoken Mancuso rebuilt the company's upper echelon and Paramount began churning out blockbusters once again. Hits like *Beverly Hills Cop II* and *The Untouchables* helped Paramount account for 22% of all box office receipts in 1986.

Paramount's television division did extremely well in the later 1980s as well. "Entertainment Tonight" was a huge success breaking into the first-run syndication market for the company and was followed by "Star Trek: The Next Generation," "War of the Worlds," "Friday the 13th," "The Arsenio Hall Show," and "Hard Copy." While a fourth network run by Rupert Murdoch's Fox Broadcasting Company provided a new outlet for Paramount's TV division, the company's network fare included such hits as "Family Ties," "Cheers," "MacGyver," and "Dear John."

By the end of the decade Paramount was making consistently hefty profits on its TV and motion picture operations. Nonetheless, like many entertainment companies, Paramount was unsettled by the merger-mania which seemed to be sweeping the entertainment industry late in the decade. When Time Inc. announced its intention to merge with Warner Communications to create the world's largest media company, Paramount made its own bid for Time. Paramount's bid was rejected by Time, and after a brief court battle Time Warner was created.

Although competition is growing stiffer as Hollywood studios become larger and better diversified, Paramount is well positioned for further growth in the 1990s. The company that struggled to produce a hit in the 1970s held nearly 15% of the domestic film market at the end of the 1980s and was a close second to industry leader Disney. With its television and motion picture teams firmly entrenched, Paramount looks forward to a bright future.

Principal Subsidiaries: Paramount Home Video Inc.; Parmount Television.

Further Reading: Edmonds, J.G., and Mimura, Reiko. *Paramount Pictures and the People Who Made Them*, New York, A.S. Barnes, 1980; Eames, John Douglas. *The Paramount Story*, New York, Crown, 1985.

RANK ORGANISATION PLC

6 Connaught Place
London W2 2EZ
United Kingdom
(01) 629–7454

Public Company
Incorporated: 1937 as Odeon Theatres Holdings Ltd.
Employees: 20,000
Sales: £824 million (US$1.49 billion)
Stock Index: London Toronto Amsterdam Frankfurt Brussels NASDAQ

A browse through the Rank Organisation's recent financial reports seems to indicate a well balanced and widely diversified group of holdings centered around the development of leisure properties—holiday travel, amusement parks, hotels, and resorts. Rank owns a charter airline, condominiums in the Pocono Mountains, a sizable number of Odeon cinema houses, bingo clubs in Bristol, trailer parks in France, and a sprinkling of Texacana Wild-West style restaurants. But the strength of its high-technology subsidiaries, including makers of wide-angle camera lenses, "ultra-precision machining systems for the production of aspheric surfaces," and Pinewood Studios, offering state-of-the-art film-processing services, is puzzling. And so is the report's brief bland note about a joint venture with a company called Xerox. This apparently insignificant division contributed a modest 55% to Rank's 1988 pretax profit of £255 million.

The overall picture of Rank remains rather confusing until one understands that it history falls into two very distinct parts. When J. Arthur (later Lord) Rank founded the conglomerate in 1935, he quickly assembled the dominant motion picture combine in Great Britain, with interests in everything from the manufacture of cameras to Lawrence Olivier's interpretation of *Henry V*. Twenty years later, the film business was suffering and Rank made a deal with a little-known American company to market his film company's product everywhere outside of the western hemisphere. That company was Xerox, and since then the only real task for the managers at Rank has been to decide how to use intelligently the endless profits generated by its partnership. Continually seeking to diversify in order to lessen its fiscal dependence on Rank Xerox, the Rank Organisation has followed a wobbly course of expansion into a variety of areas without managing to correct its fundamental, though hardly fatal, imbalance.

The story of Rank's emergence as the leading film magnate in Great Britain is complex and closely bound up with the history of British film as a whole. Joseph Arthur Rank was born in 1888, the son of a wealthy Yorkshire flour miller who was a founder of today's Ranks Hovis McDougall, one of Britain's leading food companies. He first became interested in film as a means to spread the truths of the Methodist religion, to which he was deeply devoted. Working with a group called the Religious Film Society, he paid for the 1934 production of *Mastership,* and shortly thereafter joined a like-minded millionaire, Lady Yule, in founding Pinewood Studios. Rank soon decided to leave religion in the pulpit, and taking advantage of his growing connections in the film world he began to produce and distribute popular entertainment. The board of directors of Pinewood included members from the boards of the British and Dominion Film Corporation and British National Films Ltd., two of the country's leading production houses. British and Dominion also had an agreement with the American film company, United Artists (UA), whereby the latter distributed Dominion films in Great Britain. From this nucleus of financiers and filmmakers would grown one-third of Rank's empire, the production division.

In March, 1936, Rank and four other men formed the General Cinema Finance Company (GCFC), with enough capital to allow its subsequent acquisition of General Film Distributors Ltd. (GFD), the basis of Rank's future distributing business. GFD's board included members of the British and Dominion board, which formed an important link between GFD and United Artists (as will become apparent, J. Arthur Rank was a lover of intricate corporate strategy). Also in 1936, Rank and a group of American and British investors brought a controlling interest in one of the American "majors," Universal Pictures. As a result, GFD became the distributing arm of Universal in Britain. Another thread in Rank's densely woven corporate cable was represented by A.H. Giannini, a member of the new Universal board of directors who also happened to be the president and chairman of United Artists. In this way, Rank tightened his links with the critically important Hollywood industry and its vast American market.

Having solidified his interests in production and distribution, Rank needed only a circuit of theaters to complete a vertically integrated film combine. As of 1936, the two leading circuits in Great Britain were Gaumont-British and ABPC (Associated British Pictures Corporation), but Odeon Theatres Ltd. was a rising power. In May, 1937, Odeon had purchased a rival company's theaters to secure its position as the third major circuit, with some 250 cinemas in the country. Odeon was already half owned by United Artists, making it a kind of second cousin to Rank's growing interests. Also closely allied to UA was the important London Film Productions Ltd., managed by Alexander Korda and the owner of large new studios at Denham. Toward the end of 1938, Rank began putting together these many pieces. In December, he merged his Pinewood Studios with the extensive complex at Denham (creating D & P Studios), and in the following year GCFC added to its production capacity with the purchase of the Amalgamated studios at Elstree. Finally, and most significantly, Rank acquired an interest in Odeon Theatres by subscribing (via GCFC) to its issue of debentures.

Odeon Theatres was soon in grave financial difficulties. The holding company which controlled it, Odeon Cinema Holdings Ltd., turned to Rank for assistance, and he soon became a 50% owner, along with United Artists (due to certain peculiarities in the company's rules, Rank was able to outvote his partner despite their equal stakes). At about the same time, GCFC was able to buy the holding company which ran the Gaumont-British theaters, giving Rank effective control over approximately 619 cinemas, or one-fifth of the total in Britain. Through a complicated series of holding companies, all of the above-named entities and some 80 subsidiaries were ultimately owned by Manorfield Investments Ltd., a private corporation in turn owned by Arthur Rank and his wife. This tidy arrangement allowed Rank to exert personal control over a vast segment of the British film industry, with commanding positions in all three of the industry's basic components—production, distribution, and exhibition. His dominance is perhaps best illustrated by the fact that of 63 new films made in Britain in 1948, more than half were produced by the Rank empire.

Many of these acquisitions were made possible by the slump that overtook the business in 1938. Inspired by the success of Alexander Korda's 1933 hit, *The Private Life of Henry VIII,* English producers convinced themselves that they could compete with Hollywood in the high-budget blockbuster market. They were wrong, and the failure of numerous costly films during the next few years drove many companies to the brink of bankruptcy. Rank took advantage of the buyer's market to complete the integrated group of holdings outlined above, purchasing for about £1.7 million assets later estimated to have had a normal market value of £50 million.

Such conspicuous success attracted its share of resistance, of course. After its 1941 buyout of Gaumont-British the Rank Organisation had grown sufficiently large to merit the accusation of monopoly. In 1944, the government's Palache Report made several recommendations about how best to curb the growth of the combines while encouraging a healthy degree of independent production. Rank agreed to seek government approval before he bought more theaters, but as he already held a commanding lead over his nearest rivals, the agreement did little to change the industry's excessive concentration.

The government did, however, manage indirectly to bring about the decline of Rank's power. In an effort to redress the growing imbalance in U.S.–British trade, the Labor government instituted in 1947 the so-called Dalton duty, a prohibitively high tax on all foreign films distributed in the country. In retaliation Hollywood refused to release any films at all in Great Britain, at which point the latter's film industry, led by the highly patriotic Rank, offered to step up production to fill the gap. The year 1948 marked the zenith of British production, with Rank showing the way. But in March the government abruptly reversed itself and lifted the duty, precipitating an avalanche of high-quality American imports. The hastily made British films were destroyed at the box office, none more so than Rank's. For the fiscal year ending June, 1949, the group lost a painful £3.35 million.

In retrospect, it is clear that 1948 signaled the beginning of a long decline for the British film industry in general and Rank in particular. Despite his still-dominant position in all three aspects of the business, Rank could hardly continue to suffer the huge losses incurred after the 1948 debacle. But even after cutting his production drastically, Rank faced a complex of more formidable problems. The war years had actually boosted theater attendance, as war-weary British citizens sought escape. By 1950, however, relative prosperity encouraged a raft of new leisure resources, none more important than the automobile and the emerging television industry. The cumulative effect of these and other changes was a fall in theater attendance during the postwar years from 1.6 billion tickets sold in 1946 to only 400 million in 1963. The golden age of cinema had passed, and those producers who survived did so by moving quickly into other fields. Rank and his managing director, John Davis, proceeded to do just that, searching for allied industries in which to make use of the company's expertise and financial muscle. They really found only one such nugget in 20 years of prospecting, but it turned out to be a big one.

Rank's search for alternatives to the film business led him and Davis in two distinct directions, accounting for the oddly bifurcated nature of Rank's portfolio today. On the one hand, Davis tried to exploit the enemy, as it were, by expanding Rank interests into competing leisure and entertainment fields. He first closed down many of the large Odeon theaters; total Rank holdings fell from a postwar peak of 507 cinemas to around 350 by the end of the 1950s. The vacant theaters were either used as real estate for development by one of Rank's newly formed construction companies or were converted into bowling alleys, dance halls, and bingo parlors. The company also took a stab at the burgeoning record business in the late 1950s, and began investing in the new American-style motels and service areas needed alongside Britain's equally new system of highways. Most promising of all, Rank bought a piece of the television industry, taking a 37.5% interest in the Southern Television Corporation, which served several million homes by the end of the decade.

But none of these project proved more than briefly successful. Bowling alleys and large dance halls were largely passé by the early 1960s; the Rank record business failed utterly; Rank's motels and restaurants were not well situated; and even the television station failed to take off as Rank and Davis had expected. Rank had better luck in the other half of its diversification drive, into precision industries and electronics.

Always involved in film producing and processing, Rank was well positioned to expand into new applications of similar technology. Among other companies, it acquired Taylor Hobson, a manufacturer of lenses and precision measuring instruments, and Cintel, an image processing concern. Soon thereafter, Rank began to make and sell television sets in its own retail outlets. The electronics program was much more successful than Rank's leisure ventures, but the company's future did not fully reveal itself until Rank Xerox began its spectacular rise in the early 1960s.

The connection between the two companies dates back ten years earlier, when Rank began making lenses for a new American manufacturer of copying machines called the Haloid Company. Its president, Joseph Wilson, had bought the rights to a dry-copy technique that could be used with nearly any type of paper—a great improvement over the current generation of copiers, which required specially treated paper and liquid toner. To take advantage of his find, called "xerography," Wilson needed a large amount of money and worldwide marketing strength. The Rank Organisation had both, and in 1956 John Davis signed an agreement whereby Rank undertook to manufacture and sell (or lease) xerographic machines everywhere except in the Americas. A new company was formed, eventually to be called Rank Xerox (RX), of which Rank owned 49% of the equity but only one-third of the profit above a certain minimum. Xerox controlled and managed the joint venture while Rank supplied some cash, the manufacturing facilities, and a distribution network. In 1956, it was far from certain that this venture would turn into anything more than another good idea, and Davis in particular must be credited with the foresight and courage needed to make the initial investment. Two other leaders in the field, IBM and Gestettner, had already declined to put their money on the line.

By the early 1960s, Rank had entered the era of Rank Xerox: RX's sales soared from $7 million in 1962 to $276 million in 1969. Its success was so great that the Rank Organisation's other activities became of "academic interest only," as one financial analyst commented at the time. In 1965 the two divisions contributed equally to total Rank profit; three years later RX profits were four times those generated by the rest of Rank (£33 million to £8.4 million). This treadmill continued to spin for quite a few years. While Rank muddled its way in and out of investments in both the leisure and technology fields, making a few pounds here and there but essentially drifting, its Xerox associate churned out profits as if they too could be duplicated at the press of a button. By 1982, this tail-wags-dog situation had reached the point where the rest of Rank's many businesses contributed only 7% to the company's overall profit, while RX brought in 93%. Davis, Rank CEO from 1962 to 1977, seemed somewhat embarrassed by the reduction of his once-mighty empire to the role of coupon-clipper, and for that reason strove ever harder to establish the company in other areas. The results were not good: in 1971, Rank made $17 million on non-Xerox assets of about $204 million; 11 years later, it garnered only $7 million on assets worth twice that much. While RX forged ahead, Rank fell behind.

In the meantime, the world copier market caught up with Xerox. By the end of the 1970s, heavy Japanese competition cut into RX's profit and its market share. The combination of ineffective Rank management and a cooling RX sent investors into a panic. In 1976, institutional investors with large holdings in Rank pushed through a rules change enabling them to exercise closer control over the troubled company; by 1983, brokers were speculating that the organization might be taken over by corporate raiders and its substantial assets sold off piecemeal to those who could manage them more profitably.

Since that year, however, Rank seems to have rebounded under the management of its new CEO, Michael Gifford. All but one of its divisions reported a healthy increase in profits in 1988, and the balance of earnings between Rank and RX is closer to a 50-50 split. Although the company no longer makes any feature films, it does substantial business in educational and training films, continues to work in film effects and processing, and has maintained its position in Odeon Theatres. The holidays and recreation division is now the company's largest, and its collection of resorts and travel interests netted a robust £58 million on sales of £276 million in 1988. Rank's precision industries are less spectacular but remain solid, and the future corporate leader may well be its rapidly growing assortment of large-scale leisure projects in Britain and the U.S. The hotel and catering division is expanding more slowly, but contributed some £18 million to Rank's total 1988 profit of £255 million.

It appears that Rank has weathered the storms of a painful diversification. It remains to be seen whether its newly won positions can be held and expanded, but the picture today looks bright.

Principal Subsidiaries: Wings Ltd.; Haven Leisure Ltd.; Rank Amusements Ltd.; Rank Precision Industries Inc. (U.S.A.); Strand Lighting Inc.; Strand Lighting Ltd.; Rank Development Inc. (U.S.A.); Butlins Ltd.; A. Kershaw & Sons, PLC (78%); Pinewood Studios Ltd.; Rank Audio Visual Ltd.; Rank Advertising Films Ltd.; Rank Film Distributors Ltd.; Rank Film Laboratories Ltd.; Rank Holdings (U.K.) Ltd.; Rank Hotels Ltd.; Rank Industries Australia Ltd.; Rank Motorway Services Ltd.; Rank Overseas Holdings Ltd.; Rank Precision Industries Ltd.; Rank Precision Industries (Holdings) Ltd. (92%); Rank RX Holdings Ltd. (96%); Showboat Holdings Ltd.; Rank Theatres Ltd.; Rank Video Services Ltd.; Top Rank Ltd.; Rank Xerox Ltd. (48.8%); Rank Xerox Holding B.V. (Holland) (48%); Rank Xerox Investments Ltd. (Bermuda) (49%); R-X Holdings Ltd. (Bermuda) (33.3%); Cal Air International Ltd. (50%);

Further Reading: Political and Economic Planning (PEP). *The British Film Industry*, London, 1952; Armes, Roy. *A Critical History of the British Cinema*, New York, Oxford University Press, 1978.

TCI TELE-COMMUNICATIONS, INC.

TELE-COMMUNICATIONS, INC.

4643 South Ulster Street
Denver, Colorado 80237
U.S.A.
(313) 721–5500

Public Company
Incorporated: 1968
Employees: 22,000
Sales: $1.7 billion
Stock Index: NASDAQ

Cable television began as an antenna reception service for communities television signals didn't reach. It has developed into a nationwide distributor of information and entertainment. Fueling the growth and quietly capitalizing on the opportunities offered by this rapidly expanding industry is Tele-Communications, Inc., the largest multiple system operator in the country.

TCI was founded in 1965 by Bob Magness, a former Texas rancher, who built his first cable television system in Memphis, Texas in the late 1950s. Raising the money to start his fledgling company through the sale of some cattle, Magness eventually based his operation in Denver to serve rural towns in Montana, Utah, Nevada, and Colorado.

As the company struggled to get on its feet in the early 1970s, it encountered the traumatic times which affected the whole cable industry. TCI, a small company with a largely rural base and an abundance of floating-rate debt, was in a major construction phase when interest rates suddenly soared. When Magness decided to sell stock to raise the money to pay off some of the debt, the stock market collapsed.

Magness hired John Malone, formerly the head of General Instrument Corporation's cable equipment supply division, to help pull TCI through the crisis. A man with a tough, no-nonsense reputation, Malone used his steadfast negotiating skills and shrewd business acumen to put the company back on track, and earned the title "king of cable television."

With Malone as president (and Magness as chairman) TCI began to make powerful statements about the way it wanted to conduct its business and with whom. In a typical move, when the city council of Vail, Colorado clamored for more services but refused to approve higher rates, Malone cut off all programming for one weekend, broadcasting only the names and telephone numbers of the mayor and the city manager. The city quickly surrendered and TCI resumed broadcasting as before.

For the next two years, TCI fought with city cable regulators throughout the country and negotiated with bankers to keep the company afloat. By 1977, the company was showing a positive cash flow, enabling it to obtain a $77 million loan to refinance its debt and turn itself loose on the cable television industry. John Malone's formidable deal-making tactics had created an organization with ambitious goals and plenty of money to achieve them.

In the late 1970s, the development of communications satellites and the willingness of cable customers to pay for supplemental programming, together with changes in the copyright laws, set off a big-city cable construction boom. But while TCI's competitors waged fierce bidding wars for the right to wire America's urban areas, TCI quietly focused on acquisitions in the suburban and rural areas. Within a few years, many other operators found that, amid mounting losses, they could not fulfill the bloated promises they had made to secure these hard-fought urban contracts and sold them willingly to a cash-rich TCI. In 1984, the company bought the money-losing Pittsburgh franchise from Warner-Amex for only $93 million. By instituting a series of cost reductions and system cutbacks, TCI had a positive cash flow in Pittsburgh only four years later. The company then used the same formula in Washington, St. Louis, and Chicago franchises.

The Cable Communications Policy Act of 1984 effectively deregulated the cable television industry and set the stage for an intense period of consolidation and acquisition among marginal cable operators, much to TCI's benefit. Buffalo, Dallas, and Miami were added to the TCI fold. Through its District Cablevision system, TCI provided the first cable television service to the White House.

The next major expansion of the company occurred toward the end of 1986, when TCI acquired a controlling interest in United Artists Communications after a three-year courtship. Principally engaged in the construction, acquisition, ownership, and operation of motion picture theaters but also owner of the eleventh largest cable television system in the U.S., United Artists provided TCI with access to one of the nation's largest theatrical exhibition circuits and to 23 cable systems serving 750,000 basic programming subscribers. Two years later, United Artists and the United Cable Television Corporation, a 49-system organization serving 17 states, became wholly-owned subsidiaries of a new company, United Artists Entertainment Company, a majority of which was owned by TCI.

Since 1985, Malone has spent more than $3 billion acquiring interests in more than 150 cable companies, representing three million subscribers. In 1987, TCI entered into a merger with Heritage Communications, a cable operator based in Des Moines, Iowa, with a similar reputation for independence, managerial aggressiveness, and risk-taking.

Heritage was formed in 1971 by two long-time, hometown friends, James Hoak Jr. and James Cownie. They had virtually no experience in operating a cable television system but were encouraged by the support of Hoak's father, the founder of a local construction materials company. Hoak and Cownie launched a bid for the Des Moines cable television franchise under the name Hawkeye Cablevision. Hawkeye suffered a temporary setback when the Des Moines City Council recommended awarding the contract to a rival applicant. Iowa law required an election to officially award the franchise, however, and Hoak and Cownie blitzed the media with the rallying cry, "Des Moines has its own experts," winning the election by a landslide.

The victory was short-lived. A lack of original programming to attract subscribers, combined with technical problems, including two natural disasters—a tornado destroyed the plant and a lightning storm interrupted service on launch night—severely damaged whatever interest and loyalty the company had developed.

Desperate but not defeated, Hoak and Cownie persevered. They were quick learners, and by the early 1980s, they had renamed their company Heritage and expanded its influence beyond Iowa's borders, concentrating in farm belt and oil patch areas where reception, rather than programming, was the key to winning contracts. As a result, Heritage, like TCI, was relatively unaffected by the problems of other operators who had oversold and overstated their services to obtain urban franchises.

In 1985 the company entered the big-city market when it spent $110 million for Warner-Amex's failing Dallas franchise, a system plagued by unreliable service and low customer demand. Convinced that its operations prowess would turn the franchise around, Heritage invested another $50 million in a back-to-basics approach—replacing equipment and making other technical improvements, increasing customer service training, and improving programming—in an attempt to increase the number of subscribers and restore consumer confidence in the concept of cable television.

Heritage then made two other major deals: the $43 million purchase of 51% of Gill Industries, in San Jose, and the $630 million purchase of Rollins Communications. The Rollins deal, in particular, expanded Heritage TV holdings from five to 11 stations in areas outside the economically depressed Midwest and prompted diversification into radio and outdoor advertising. Soon TCI was interested in taking over Heritage, which it did in 1987, adding 500,000 subscribers to its stable.

Until now, TCI had been a program distributor able to obtain services at highly-discounted prices due to the sheer size of its system. Since it was virtually impossible for a network to make money without TCI's subscribers, even producers of established cable programs were unwilling to risk losing access to so many viewers and charged Malone's systems only what he was willing to pay since they faced threats of Malone-initiated competition if they balked. But as desirable programming services, just like systems operators, became concentrated in fewer hands through mergers and acquisitions, Malone recognized the dangers a large operator faced at the hands of just three or four program suppliers. Since the proliferation of cable television hook-ups across the country had reduced the need to allocate substantial funds for capital expenditures, Malone turned his company's attention toward exerting its financial clout and the leverage of eight million subscribers on program suppliers.

Malone's goals were straightforward: to strengthen the supply of original cable programming and to compete effectively with the major networks for national advertising dollars. TCI began investing in programmers like the Cable Value Network, Black Entertainment Television, The Discovery Channel, and X*Press Information Services, a service providing news, entertainment, and financial data to home computer users via cable. In most cases, the investments were made with other cable operators to assure the continuing success of the programming effort for the benefit of all cable television customers.

Key to Malone's diversification strategy was TCI's investment, with 28 other cable industry operators, in bailing-out the flamboyant Ted Turner and his Turner Broadcasting System. Turner's assumption of $1.5 billion in debt to secure the MGM library of classic films had placed the survival of TBS in imminent danger. Malone saw TBS, which owned SuperStation WTBS, the Cable News Network, and MGM/UA Entertainment Company, as an attractive launching pad for developing a twenty-four-hour channel offering entertainment, news, and information to challenge the three major television networks. Rather than watch Turner's system fall under the control of a rival organization, Malone engineered a bold rescue plan and put up half of the needed $560 million.

Malone also invested in QVC Network, a home shopping channel, and the American Movie Classics Company, a source of 40 years' worth of Hollywood's most popular films. In 1988 he formed Think Entertainment, a new company dedicated to the actual production and distribution of quality programming exclusively for the cable television market.

Twenty years after its tumultuous start-up, TCI is a major force in U.S. cable television. After its most recent acquisition of Storer Communications, the fourth largest cable television operator, the company leads its closest competitor, Time's American Television and Communications, by almost five million subscribers. The company's wholly-owned and affiliate operations presently include cable television systems in 47 states. TCI also is turning toward other areas of the entertainment business through its recent investment in Blockbuster Video, a chain of video rental stores.

Decentralized in 1986 to facilitate restructuring, if and when it becomes necessary, TCI is currently organized into six divisions, each with its own marketing, accounting, and engineering departments. Ten senior executives run the day-to-day business, sharing the responsibility of supervising a total of only 250 corporate employees.

As TCI and John Malone led the cable television industry into the 1990s, perhaps the most serious threat facing the company was that of reregulation. TCI has reached its number one position through numerous mergers, acquisitions, and partnerships; it is no longer anonymous. Consumer complaints about rate increases and service problems and governmental concerns about the size and undue influence of companies like TCI may prompt the government to impose controls over its activity; a 1988 report from the U.S. Department of Commerce did conclude that the concentration within the cable industry warrants further investigation and possible action.

The company may also face serious challenges from technology, especially direct satellite transmission. However, in anticipation of growth in the television-receive-only marketplace, TCI recently acquired TEMPO Enterprises, a satellite communications company.

The cable industry also faces the potential threat of new rival, delivery systems from utility and telephone companies, which could lease their lines to new operators. And while TCI has based its growth on maintaining a highly leveraged financial position, the size of the company's debt makes it vulnerable to a rise in interest rates or to a recession, which could jeopardize pay cable revenues.

In the meantime, TCI will continue to strengthen and protect the supply of cable programming while also aggressively pursuing growth by adhering to the strategic formula and long-range business orientation that has carried it to the top of the cable television mountain.

Principal Subsidiaries: Alda Communications Corp. of Pa.; All Channel T.V., Inc.; American Microwave & Communications, Inc.; American Movie Classics Co.; Athena Realty, Inc.; Atlantic American Holdings, Inc.; Bob Magness, Inc.; Brookside Antenna Co.; Cabletime, Inc.; Caguas/Humacao Cable Systems; Central CATV, Inc.; Communications Capital Corp.; Communications Services Inc.; Community Realty, Inc.; Complete Channel TV, Inc.; Crest Communications, Inc.; ECP Holdings, Inc.; GWC 106, Inc.; GWC 73, Inc.; Heritage Communications, Inc.; International Telemeter Corp.; JAL CATV Corp.; Kingston CATV, Inc.; LaSalle Telecommunications, Inc.; Liberty Broadcasting, Inc.; Liberty Florida, Inc.; Liberty Investments, Inc.; Liberty Michigan, Inc.; Liberty of Northern Indiana, Inc.; Liberty-CSI, Inc.; Madison Communications, Inc.; Micro-Relay, Inc.; Netlink USA; Orcable Ltd.; PCNH, Inc.; Plains-Indiana, Inc.; Robert Fulk, Ltd.; Rockland Information Systems, Inc.; Satellite Services, Inc.; SEE TV Co.; Silver Spur Land and Cattle Co.; Southwest Video Corp.; SSI 2, Inc.; Screenplay Video; Tele-Ception of Winchester, Inc.; United Artists Communications, Inc.; Upper Valley Telecable Co., Inc.; Wasatch Community TV, Inc.; Wayne County CATV, Inc.; Western Satellite 2, Inc.; X*PRESS Information Services; Telenois, Inc.; Texcom, Inc.; Trans-Muskingum, Inc.; Ulster County CATV, Inc.; TCIP, Inc.

TOURISTIK UNION INTERNATIONAL GMBH. AND COMPANY K.G.

Karl Wiechert Allee 23
3000 Hannover 61
Federal Republic of Germany
(511) 567-0

Private Company
Incorporated: 1968
Employees: 2,185
Sales: DM3.25 billion (US$1.83 billion)

Touristik Union International (TUI) is not only West Germany's foremost tourist travel company, but also one of the largest leisure travel groups in Europe. The company is actually a holding company for eight tour-operating agencies. Each has a distinctive character and history and a specific segment of the travel and tourism market.

TUI was founded in 1968 by four tourist travel companies. Touropa, Scharnow, Hummel, and Dr. Tigges-Fahrten were all highly successful, reputable tour operators that sought to broaden their scope and potential by pooling resources and organizing into a single entity.

At the time of TUI's founding, Dr. Tigges-Fahrten had been in business 45 years. When Dr. Hubert Tigges and his wife Maria first began organizing educational tours in 1928, conditions for starting a new business were far from ideal. The Tigges' tours began modestly, guiding groups of students through Germany, the Netherlands, and Belgium from their base in the Ruhr Valley.

The optimism of the 28-year-old professor and his wife turned out to be well founded as their guided tours, offering in-depth historical and cultural information, began to attract a wider audience. In the first year they led five spring and summer tours and two winter ones. From April through August, and during the week between Christmas and the New Year, they conducted tours by train or bus. By 1932 they had added sites in France, Italy, and Switzerland. By 1933 England, Scandinavia, North Africa, and Spain were included, and in 1934 they led their first trip to Majorca. In 1935 Maria's brother, Alois Fischer, joined the company (he became a partner in 1948).

The travel business came to a standstill during World War II. But after the formation of the Federal Republic of Germany in 1949, the first postwar Tigges travel brochure appeared, advertising a 14-day tour of Cologne and other German cities. The price included bed and board, as well as transportation, and the brochure assured participants of "abundant food and running water."

Gradually, educational tours were resumed, and in 1950 new sites were added: Rome, Lourdes, and Fatima. The first airborne tour was conducted in 1953—a 16-day trip through Spain. The following year, the first chartered flights were made, to London, Barcelona, and the Canary Islands, and the first formal business agreements with hotels as part of the tour packages were arranged. The 1950s included many other first-time events for the company: the first cruise (to Greece and Istanbul), tours to the Middle East and India, and the first round trip to Iceland and Ireland.

By 1961, Reinhold Tigges and Jürgen Fischer, the sons of the founders, had joined the company and helped widen the scope and market for the tours. Two years later, the first world tour was conducted. A few years later a tour group scheduled to visit China was canceled because of the Cultural Revolution.

As Dr. Tigges-Fahrten grew, a rival travel business was formed. Touropa was the result of a 1948 merger of four travel agencies whose businesses had also come to a halt during the war years: Reisebüro Dr. Degener, headed by Dr. Carl Degener; Deutsches Reisebüro DER, headed by Emil Kipfmuller; and Amtliches Bayerisches Reisebüro, headed by Karl Fuss. Carl Degener was placed in charge of the new company.

The first Touropa train excursion went from Hamburg to Ruhpoldig at Christmas, 1948 with 1,200 travelers aboard. The holiday celebrants of 1948 pronounced the ride a resounding success, and many more tours were scheduled, venturing further within Germany. In 1951, the tours became international. A color film advertised the delights of travel via the special Touropa train, and by the end of 1952 the year's participants totaled 194,000.

In 1953, Touropa began offering tours by air—the first, on Air France, was to Algeria. Travelers to Majorca in 1954 went by a combination of railway, bus, and ship. The first Touropa cruise was launched the following year: a trip to Spain, North Africa, and Corsica. A cruise in 1957 was the first postwar one to use a German ship, and in 1964 Touropa sent its first chartered flight to Kenya.

Of the eight TUI companies, Touropa is one of the three high-volume agencies, attracting close to 600,000 tourists in a year. In contrast to the more scholarly intent of Dr. Tigges' tours, Touropa emphasizes carefree vacation jaunts. Today Touropa specializes in lengthy vacations. Many of these tours incorporate a stay at one of the Robinson Clubs, vacation villages inaugurated in 1971. Robinson Clubs (originally the Robinson Hotels) have a variety of athletic facilities and also offer team sports.

The other two companies that formed the original TUI group, Scharnow and Hummel, both started in 1953. Hummel, the smaller of the two, got its start on March 1 that year with the merger of Reisebüro Luhrs, the Original Wassertragers Hummel, and Hummel-Hummel. Letterheads and brochures displayed the name of the new firm, Hummel-Reise, along with combined trademarks of the original companies. The success of Hummel-Reise's first tour, a train trip to the Black Forest, created a demand for additional package tours of picturesque areas in Europe, from the North Sea to the southern Tyrolean mountains. The trips were relatively short—up to 14 days—and by the end of the first year, had attracted 1,500 travelers. These package vacations, many incorporating guided tours of European towns and cities, became Hummel's specialty. Today, those tours attract close to 200,000 vacationers a year.

Scharnow was the largest of the four founding companies and is third-largest in the current TUI group, with over 570,000 clients. Its origins can be traced to a meeting in Hanover on July 2, 1953; four well-established travel groups sent representatives to discuss a merger. Reisebüro Bangemann of Hanover, Essener Reisebüro of Essen, Ferienreise GmbH. of Bielefeld, and Reisebüro Scharnow of Bremen came to an agreement that resulted in the founding of Scharnow-Reisen GmbH. K.G. in November. Wilhelm Scharnow was chosen to head the new company.

Early in 1954 the Scharnow organization took what it termed "a plunge into cold water" with the publication of its first catalog—actually an eight-page brochure—advertising its first tours to the North Sea and Baltic Sea areas. That summer it issued a 24-page catalog showing beautiful vacation spots on other tours in Germany, Italy, Switzerland, and Yugoslavia. One of the seaside towns pictured even made Willy Scharnow an honorary citizen for the influx of tourists the catalog attracted. Altogether, in Scharnow's first full year of operation, 112,000 travelers chose its tours.

The histories of the founding companies intertwined as early as 1956, when Touropa, Hummel, and Scharnow conducted a tour together by air to Majorca and Italy. Another 15-day tour itinerary was added, to Denmark, Sweden, and Holland. Then they organized a 35-day tour of southwest Africa. The three-way collaboration on air tours—called *Deutsche Flugtouristik*—expanded its program to include both nearby and distant sites throughout the continent. In 1962, they began offering chartered flights, which were also popular.

After collaborating on numerous such successful travel projects, Scharnow, Hummel, Touropa, and Dr. Tigges-Fahrten joined forces on December 1, 1968 to form TUI. Willy Scharnow was chosen to head the first supervisory board, and Herbert Degener, Hans-Albrecht Seiffert and Dr. Walter Vogel served on its first board of directors.

Together these leaders mapped out a strategy for marketing the services of the four companies. Each had a well-developed area of specialization, which would be preserved. Dr. Tigges-Fahrten's study tours had a relatively small but stable following. Hummel had built a reputation for an immense variety of vacations in beautiful areas: forest, mountainous, and seaside sites. Also, Hummel was known for its shorter vacations and city tours. Lengthy trips, in some cases with stopovers at spas and fitness clubs, were Touropa's specialty; its tours always involved top-quality facilities in superior vacation areas. To complement but not infringe on these specialties, Scharnow narrowed its focus, becoming a specialist in vacations offering private bungalows or apartments in choice areas. Scharnow began its vacation-home program in 1960, with residential facilities in Germany, Finland, France, Italy, Spain, and Denmark. By the end of a year, it had filled 100 such places; in four years it had filled 3,000.

With the market segments of each company clearly defined, the business grew rapidly. Twen-Tours International, launched originally by Hummel-Reise, became an independent company and joined TUI in 1970. Twen-Tours addressed still another market segment: travelers under 30. Package tours to many countries feature trekking, backpacking, and hiking, with language courses along the way.

In 1972 TUI acquired TransEuropa, today the largest of the TUI brands. Founded in Munich by Dieter von Langen in 1955, Trans-Europa got off to a fast start by conducting very successful air tours at a low cost to travelers. Emphasizing quality and economy has attracted a large number of travelers, making even lower-priced and higher-quality packages. In 1967, for example, TransEuropa tourists were traveling on Condor airplanes. From 218,000 clients in 1971, the company grew to attract more than 650,000 in the late 1980s. TransEuropa now features many long-distance destinations, as well as Mediterranean and Black Sea tours that are popular with families and groups.

Airtours International GmbH. and Company K.G. was founded in 1967 in Frankfurt, uniting several German travel companies that specialized in air travel. The company became part of TUI three years later, with a distinct emphasis on air travel. Airtours specializes in vacations using scheduled airlines, and continues to serve over 200,000 clients yearly.

Hit is TUI's latest acquisition. Hit caters to travelers who like to design their own tours or vacation itineraries. Clients choose the parts of package tours that they prefer, and Hit combines them for efficient travel to the desired destinations. In 1989, TUI also acquired a 40% interest in ARKE, Holland's leading tour operator, and a controlling interest in Robinson Club.

Although TUI is composed of very diverse travel companies, the strategy of assigning each a separate segment of the travel market has worked well. The company's business has increased steadily; TUI today operates close to 3,000 agencies in West Germany alone and about 150 in other countries.

Although each of the component companies has appeals for its own market segment, the executive board and supervisory board provide central control to maintain a unity of purpose. The TUI formula for attracting all parts of the travel market through specialized services has so far been a highly successful strategy.

Principal Subsidiaries: Seetours International GmbH & Co. KG (75%); Dr. Degener Reisen GmbH (Austria); Ultramar Express S.A. (Spain) (77%); Airtour Greece Ltd. (90%); Pollman's Tours and Safaris Ltd. Mombasa (Kenya) (51%); Tantur Ltd. (Turkey) (50%);

Promotel International S.A. (Luxembourg); Promotora S.A. (Iberotel), Palma de Mallorca (60%); Robinson Club GmbH; Gecotel S.A. Rethymnon/Kreta (50%); TUI-Software GmbH; Touristik Marketing GmbH; Touristik Finanz AG (Switzerland) (50%).

TURNER BROADCASTING SYSTEM, INC.

One CNN Center
100 International Boulevard
Atlanta, Georgia 30318
U.S.A.
(404) 827–1500

Public Company
incorporated: 1965
Employees: 3,187
Sales: $806.6 million
Stock Index: American

The history of Turner Broadcasting System is closely tied to the personal history of its flamboyant founder, chairman, and president, Robert Edward "Ted" Turner III. Alternately seeking and shunning media attention, Turner has accumulated colorful nicknames ("Captain Outrageous," "the Mouth of the South," "Terrible Ted") and a reputation for daredevil tactics. Turner's free-wheeling entrepreneurial style is reflected in the strategic and financial risks that the company has taken under his direction and control.

Turner became president and chief operating officer of a $1 million billboard company, Turner Advertising Company, upon his father's suicide in 1963, shortly after concluding an agreement to sell the firm's recently acquired Atlanta division. Turner offered the buyers $200,000 to rescind the deal, and persuaded them to accept his offer by shifting employees and contracts to another division, threatening to destroy financial records, and similar tactics.

In 1970, Turner's company merged with Rice Broadcasting Company, Inc., a small Atlanta UHF TV station. The transaction took the resulting company public, with Turner as majority stockholder, under the new name Turner Communications Corporation.

Turner Communications bought the right to broadcast the Atlanta Braves major league baseball games, then bought the team itself in 1976. The team was said to be losing money at the time and about to leave town; Turner's acquisition kept popular broadcasts on the air and provided diversification for his growing company.

After reading that Home Box Office was transmitting programs nationwide via satellite, Turner saw an opportunity to expand his station's audience enormously and to make it more attractive to advertisers by beaming its signal via satellite to cable TV systems around the country. The resulting "superstation," begun in December, 1976, became, in effect, another TV network. But start-up costs were substantial, cable operators who signed up tended to have questionable credit records, and advertisers were skeptical and reluctant to invest. In the course of a few years, however, the concept proved viable as WTBS-TV became fractionally and then tremendously profitable.

Meanwhile, in January 1977, Turner increased his sports presence by acquiring the National Basketball Association's Atlanta Hawks.

After 21 years at CBS, Robert J. Wussler joined Turner Broadcasting System in April, 1980 as executive vice president, an office he held for several years. At CBS, Wussler had been instrumental in the expansion of satellite usage in news coverage as early as 1962, and in the development of the minicam for on-the-spot news coverage. His career included positions as president of the CBS Television Network and of the CBS sports division.

In its early years, Turner's "superstation" aired primarily reruns and sports. But, in June 1980, Turner created the Cable News Network (CNN) subsidiary to broadcast live news on a 24-hour basis. News bureaus were established in major cities across the United States and around the world. The live, 24-hour format encouraged a more direct and unedited presentation of the news than the networks provided, as well as instant availability at viewers' convenience. The minimal editing and absence of star anchors sparked both positive and negative reactions: some felt the approach lacked polish and professionalism, but others felt it brought viewers closer to the news items at hand. In January, 1981, shortly after CNN began operation, another subsidiary, Turner Program Services, was created to serve as the syndication arm of Turner Broadcasting System.

In January 1982, Turner formed a second all-news television network. Officially named Headline News, the network aired a sequence of half-hour segments edited from the live material shown on CNN. If CNN was conceived as "a newspaper you can watch," in Turner's words then, Headline News permitted a quick scan of the top stories at any time. Just months later, in April, 1982, CNN Radio began operations, offering a 24-hour all-news format on a network basis in the radio market.

By this time the overall broadcast market was becoming increasingly competitive. Turner Broadcasting System benefited as cable became available to an increasing portion of U.S. households. CNN's success pressured the three established networks to acknowledge the audience CNN had uncovered and to provide late-night and early-morning news broadcasts for this group. In addition, Satellite News Channels (SNC) opened direct competition in 1982, as a second 24-hour cable news headline service, promising financial incentives to combat the loyalty of CNN's cable operators and viewers.

In January 1985, Turner Broadcasting System purchased a 75% interest in an Atlanta real estate complex which contained approximately 470 hotel rooms and 775,000 square feet of office and retail space for $60 million. By 1987, Turner Broadcasting had acquired the remaining

25% of the facility, which was renamed CNN Center and housed the corporate offices as well as the Atlanta headquarters for CNN, Headline News, and CNN Radio.

In 1982, CBS had declined to comment on industry rumors that it wished to buy CNN. It wasn't as quiet in April, 1985 when the Turner Broadcasting Company filed a preliminary exchange offer with the Securities and Exchange Commission for CBS. CBS immediately bought back about six million shares of its common stock (amounting to almost $1 billion), forcing Turner to withdraw his offer in August. The aborted bid cost Turner Broadcasting about $20 million in underwriting, legal, and accounting fees, but Turner argued that the action, by forcing CBS into significant borrowing to finance its buyback and absorbing CBS management time and attention, at least hindered CBS as a competitor.

In later years, Turner defended his bid for CBS as an attempt to protect his own company's vulnerability. In addition to the three major networks there were, by this time, more than 25 independent ones, including Fox, Tribune, HBO, USA, Viacom, Time, and Showtime. Turner worried that networks, as the distributors of TV programming, could be held at the mercy of program producers and described his attempt to gain control of CBS as an attempt to strengthen his bargaining position with them.

In a smaller way, Turner also ventured into the production business himself. He helped found the Better World Society in 1985, a nonprofit organization that produced documentaries on ecological and environmental issues. Turner's global consciousness was also behind his company's contribution to the Goodwill Games with the U.S.S.R. These games, patterned after the Olympic Games, were staged as a way to bring U.S. and Soviet athletes away from recent political boycotts of the Olympics and back into sporting competition. Conceived and organized in 1985, they were first held in Moscow in July, 1986. Turner Broadcasting's production costs associated with the Goodwill Games amounted to more than $25 million, a sum not completely recovered through increased revenues as a result of the broadcast syndication of the games.

These ventures into original programming were dwarfed, however, by Turner's acquisition of the film company MGM/UA in 1986. Turner dealt with Kirk Kerkorian, the 50.1% owner of MGM/UA, which was losing money and valued by Wall Street at about $825 million in August, 1985. Kerkorian was represented by Drexel Burnham Lambert, an investment-banking firm famed for dealing in high-risk "junk bonds." In an unusual move, and with the consent of all parties, the bankers switched sides and represented Turner when it became apparent that he needed their expertise to finance the deal that was being discussed.

In the deal's final structure, Turner Broadcasting bought MGM/UA Entertainment for $1.4 billion in March, 1986, immediately sold the United Artists portion back to Kerkorian for $480 million, and assumed $700 million of MGM debt, for a net purchase price of more than $1.6 billion. At almost twice the street price, Drexel Burnham Lambert was at first unable to create securities acceptable to Turner and to potential investors. After Kerkorian was persuaded to accept about $475 million less in cash in return for a new issue of Turner Broadcasting preferred stock, financing for the remainder could be secured. When critics questioned the purchase price, Turner cited the enduring merit of the classic films in MGM's library, the programming security he sought from this entertainment base, his fear of being outbid by another buyer, and, characteristically, his disinclination to haggle.

The new issue of preferred stock carried two provisions. The first was a required payment of $600 million of notes in September, 1986. To meet this requirement, Turner was forced to sell all MGM assets but the film library, many back to Kerkorian himself, just before the September deadline. The second provision involved dividend requirements that threatened corporate control, depending upon market performance.

The entire MGM deal also weighed heavily on the company's financial statements. As Turner conceded in his 1986 report to shareholders, "The financial representation of 1986 is what it is—a net loss of approximately $187 million on revenue of more than $556 million" (in 1985, Turner Broadcasting earned a net income of $1 million on $352 million in revenues). Interest payments, together with amortization of the MGM purchase price, would lead to what Turner described as "substantial accounting losses in the foreseeable future."

In 1987, Turner called on the support of the cable industry to deal with the preferred stock problem created in the MGM deal. A group of 31 cable operators (the companies that provide local cable service—and choose what cable networks subscribers can get) headed by Tele-Communications Inc. (TCI), paid some $565 million for 37% of Turner Broadcasting System. This capital secured Turner's control of voting stock (just), and introduced new directors to Turner operations, including John Malone, president of TCI; Michael Fuchs, chairman of HBO; and Jim Gray, chairman of Warner Cable. While the backing of the cable industry virtually guarantees the success of the Turner networks, the presence of major cable operators on Turner's board also poses certain problems. Since cable operators like TCI purchase programming from Turner, Ted Turner told the *New York Times*, the operators "don't have much incentive to see us make healthy profits." But the rescue deal kept Turner afloat.

Although Turner's MGM purchase was roundly criticized for putting TBS in nearly unmanageable debt, within two years the company's prospects were looking up. TBS's new TNT channel, which is based on the MGM film library but also offers original programming, has done exceptionally well. With eight of 15 places on Turner's board in the hands of the cable consortium, Turner Broadcasting is moving more slowly and deliberately than in the past. Turner himself points to the completion of cable wiring for metropolitan areas as critical to his industry's growth, noting that major events can't very well be covered by cable while cable remains unavailable to large blocks of viewers.

In 1989 Turner Broadcasting made several important moves, including a $1.6 billion refinancing of its debt. The company also launced Turner Pictures, a film-making division, and Turner Publishing, a subsidiary that develops TBS properties for book publication. Meanwhile, Cable News Network is a steady profit maker, and TNT has made a promising start. As the company rebounded, speculation about a takeover—or Turner selling out—surfaced again. Turner's own stake in TBS was reduced from 80% to 43% after the cable-industry bail-out, and Time Inc. already owns 13% of the company. The Time-Warner merger, of course, may well distract Time from buying any more of Turner, but it has said it would like to. Ted Turner's unpredictability makes speculation on the future ownership of TBS futile, but whatever the future holds, Turner Broadcasting seems certain to remain a major force in the communications industry.

Principal Subsidiaries: Atlanta Hawks, Inc.; Atlanta National League Baseball Club, Inc.; Cable News Network, Inc.; Turner Broadcasting Sales, Inc.; Superstation, Inc.; Cable News International, Inc.; Stadium Club, Inc.; TBS Productions, Inc.; Turner Reciprocal Advertising Corp.; Turner Teleport, Inc.; Turner Entertainment, Co.; Omni Ventures; Turner Network Television; Turner Program Services, Inc.; TBS Superstation; Turner Pictures; Turner Publishing; World Championship Wrestling, Inc.; Turner Home Entertainment.

Further Reading: Williams, Christian. *Lead, Follow, or Get Out of the Way: The Story of Ted Turner*, New York, Times Books, 1981.

TWENTIETH CENTURY FOX FILM CORPORATION

10201 West Pico Boulevard
Los Angeles, California 90035
U.S.A.
(213) 277-2211

Wholly owned subsidiary of The News Corporation
Incorporated: 1915 as Fox Film Corporation
Employees: 2,200
Sales: $850 million

Twentieth Century Fox has had its up and downs. Over the years, this venerable Hollywood institution has saved itself from bankruptcy twice by producing blockbuster movies (*The Sound of Music* and *Star Wars*, two of the biggest box-office hits ever). After a fairly tumultuous 1980s, the company today is owned by Rupert Murdoch's News Corporation, the Australian media conglomerate.

In 1904 William Fox, a 25-year-old Hungarian immigrant, bought his first nickelodeon in New York City. Within a few years Fox and two partners, B.S. Moss and Sol Brill, had parlayed their success into a chain of 25 nickelodeons.

The partners soon opened the Greater New York Film Rental Company. Then in 1913, concerned that the demand for movies had begun to outstrip supply, they organized the Box Office Attraction Company to begin producing their own movies. In 1915 Fox founded the Fox Film Corporation to produce, distribute, and exhibit movies and moved his operation to California, whose temperate climate was better suited to film production.

In 1925 Fox Films relocated to its fourth California location when Fox purchased the 250 acres of land in Hollywood which was to be the company's permanent home. In 1929 Fox Films bought 55% of Loew's Inc., then the parent company of MGM, but was later forced by the government to sell that interest.

After several years of steady growth, the company experienced a series of shake-ups beginning in 1927, and in 1930 a group of stockholders ousted William Fox. Fox was replaced by Sidney R. Kent in 1932, and in 1935, Fox Film Corporation merged with Twentieth Century Pictures.

In 1933 Darryl F. Zanuck, head of production at Warner Brothers, had joined Joseph M. Schenck, head of United Artists, in forming the Twentieth Century Company. With Schenck as the administrator and Zanuck head of production, the Twentieth Century Company made 18 films in 18 months, including *The House of Rothschild*, *The Affairs of Cellini*, and *Les Miserables*. Only one film was unsuccessful. During this time, Twentieth Century began making movies out of current news events, with releases like *Little Ceasar* and *Public Enemy*. When the company merged with Fox Film Corporation in 1935, Zanuck became vice president in charge of production of the new Twentieth Century Fox Film Corporation.

Before America entered World War II, Twentieth Century Fox produced two Academy Award–winning films, *The Grapes of Wrath* in 1940, and *How Green Was My Valley* in 1941. During the war, Zanuck served as a lieutenant colonel, making training and combat documentary films. He was awarded the Legion of Merit for his wartime services.

After the war, Twentieth Century Fox produced such hits as *The Snows of Kilimanjaro*, *Winged Victory*, *Twelve O'Clock High*, *The Razor's Edge*, and *All About Eve*. Zanuck also attacked controversial issues in several financially successful movies, proving that audiences did not shy away from issues like mental illness, race relations, and anti-Semitism with *The Snake Pit*, *Pinky*, and *Gentleman's Agreement*.

But by the early 1950s Hollywood's heyday was over. With the advent of television, attendance at movies declined sharply, and film production declined along with it. Studios like Twentieth Century Fox could no longer afford to maintain exclusive contracts with directors and film stars. In 1953 Zanuck began producing all the studio's films in wide-screen CinemaScope. But the attraction of this system did not compensate for the lack of box office hits. Frustrated, Zanuck left the company in 1956 to become an independent film producer in Paris.

The company replaced Zanuck with Spyros Skouras, a well-known Greek theater owner. Between 1959 and 1961, Twentieth Century Fox lost $48.5 million; in 1962 it lost $39.8 million on revenues of $96.4 million.

The immediate source of trouble was the production of *Cleopatra*. From an estimated cost of approximately $7 million in 1961, the film's total expenditures ballooned to $41.5 million. The company poured money into the production, even selling 334 acres of land in Los Angeles's Fox Hills section to help finance it. But it still wasn't enough.

In 1962 Zanuck, still one of the company's largest stockholders, persuaded his fellow-stockholders not to liquidate the business and returned to replace Skouras as president. Zanuck's stability and professionalism soon bolstered the company's waning image. More importantly, however, Zanuck brought in quick cash. *The Longest Day*, made by his own production company in Europe, was released through Twentieth Century Fox. A smash hit, it brought in enough revenue to allow the company to begin making movies again in 1963.

That same year Zanuck made his son Richard vice president in charge of production. Only 28 years old, the younger Zanuck began making pictures with modest budgets, producing 20 movies in 14 months. Once revenues from these films began to accumulate, the company started more expensive productions.

Unlike other movie makers, the Zanucks continued to

produce big, expensive extravaganzas. Forgetting the failure of *Cleopatra*, the two men planned to release as many big pictures in as short a time as they could, hoping for a hit to keep the company solvent. This "blockbuster" strategy was one most other studios had abandoned because of the risk involved.

But the release of *The Sound of Music* in 1964 appeared to vindicate the Zanucks' strategy. The film became one of the top ten box office hits ever, bringing Twentieth Century Fox more than $79 million in revenues. Only a year and a half after its release, the movie had already outgrossed *Gone With the Wind*, the box office champion for nearly 27 years.

By the mid-1960s, Twentieth Century Fox had also grown into one of the largest TV producers. During the 1966–1967 season, Twentieth Century Fox Television placed 12 shows on network TV. The firm also began to distribute its feature films to television. In one of the largest deals of the time, Fox leased 17 pictures to ABC for $19 million, including *Cleopatra*, *The Longest Day*, *The Agony and the Ecstasy*, and *Those Magnificent Men in Their Flying Machines*.

With revenues garnered from television and *The Sound of Music*, the Zanucks went on to produce lavish, big-budget movies like *Hello, Dolly!*, *Dr. Dolittle*, and *Tora! Tora! Tora!* The success of *The Sound of Music* and less expensive hits like *M*A*S*H* and *Patton* fueled the Zanucks' belief that expensive spectaculars were the best way to make money in the industry. In 1969 Darryl Zanuck appointed his son president of Twentieth Century Fox while he remained CEO.

Dr. Dolittle and *Tora! Tora! Tora!* were two of the biggest box office losers in the history of Hollywood; in 1969 Twentieth Century Fox's operating losses amounted to $36 million, and for the first nine months of the following year they came to nearly $21 million.

Following a proxy fight in 1970, in which Richard Zanuck and his mother opposed Darryl Zanuck, Richard was forced to resign. The Zanucks had quarreled over responsibility for the studio's financial difficulties and over some creative matters. Richard was supported by such prominent shareholders as Broadway director David Merrick. Four months later, Darryl Zanuck himself stepped down as chairman. William T. Gossett, an active boardmember and Detroit lawyer, became chairman. Richard Zanuck went on to produce several blockbuster movies, including *Jaws* and *The Sting*, for MCA's Universal Studios.

In 1971 Dennis C. Stanfill, a Twentieth Century Fox vice president and a former Rhodes scholar, was named chairman and CEO, and later assumed the position of president. With a hands-on approach, Stanfill began a wide-ranging diversification program into the record business, broadcasting, film processing, and theme parks. Twentieth Century Fox's most important acquisitions during this time included a string of theaters in Australia and New Zealand, along with the addition of one NBC and two ABC affiliates to its chain of television stations across the United States.

In 1973 Stanfill hired Alan Ladd Jr. to head the company's film division. Under Ladd's direction, Twentieth Century Fox produced a number of very successful movies, including *The Poseidon Adventure*, *Young Frankenstein*, and *The Towering Inferno*, a joint release with Warner. Ladd also invested $10 million to produce a script that other large studios had turned down. In 1977 *Star Wars* became the biggest box office hit in film history and made over $200 million by the end of its first year. During the next five years, company profits quadrupled and its movies were nominated for 33 Academy Awards.

With the money from *Star Wars*, Stanfill accelerated his diversification program, buying Coca-Cola Bottling Midwest for $27 million; Aspen Skiing, the largest ski-resort operator in the United States, for $48 million; and Pebble Beach Corporation, the owner of a resort on the Monterey Peninsula in California, for $72 million. These acquisitions were meant to allow the company to reduce its reliance on film revenues.

Because of differences with Stanfill, Ladd left Twentieth Century Fox in 1979. In January, 1980 Sherry Lansing was hired to replace him, becoming the first female to head the production office of a major motion picture studio. She had previously supervised the production of both *The China Syndrome* and *Kramer vs. Kramer* at Columbia Pictures. Two weeks before her appointment, Darryl Zanuck died in Palm Springs, California.

The release of movies like *Norma Rae*, *Breaking Away*, *Alien*, and *The Empire Strikes Back* made money for the company. But these hits were offset by losers like *The Rose* and *I Ought To Be in Pictures*. In 1980 operating income dropped 10% and entertainment profits (which accounted for 56% of operating income) declined by 18%. In late 1980, when outside groups began to purchase large amounts of company stock, Stanfill initiated a management-led leveraged buyout to prevent a hostile takeover attempt.

In early 1981 Stanfill's plan collapsed. In a move that took the film industry by surprise, oil magnate Marvin Davis and silent partner Marc Rich hastily formed a company called TCF Holdings, Inc., which bid $722 million for Twentieth Century Fox. Borrowing heavily, Davis put up only $55 million of his own money. The purchase was completed in June of the same year. Complaining of interference, Stanfill retired in July, and sued Twentieth Century Fox for breach of contract. The $22 million suit was settled for $4 million. Vice chairman Alan Hirschfield replaced Stanfill as chairman.

In the early 1980s Twentieth Century Fox's financial position deteriorated rapidly. Several movies, including *Modern Problems*, *Six Pack*, and *Quest for Fire*, never recouped their production costs. Davis burdened the company with $650 million in debt to help pay back the loans TCI had secured to buy Twentieth Century Fox. To reduce this debt, Davis sold the soft drink–bottling subsidiary and the Australian theater chain. He also arranged a joint venture with Aetna Life & Casualty to develop Twentieth Century Fox's real estate properties.

But in 1982, the situation went from bad to worse. Sherry Lansing and a number of other top-level officials left the company, reportedly due to Davis's interference in the creative process and his abrupt management style. Disagreements between Davis and Hirschfield also began to increase in intensity. Moreover, Aetna terminated its interest in the joint venture and sued Davis after a deal between Davis and Aetna (and unrelated to Twentieth Century Fox) soured.

In October, 1984, Davis bought the other 50% of TCF from Marc Rich, who had fled to Switzerland following his indictment for tax evasion and fraud. Davis paid $116 million for Rich's share of the company.

Also in late 1984 Davis hired Barry Diller from Paramount to replace Hirschfield as chairman, guaranteeing him $3 million salary and a 25% interest in the company. Diller's expertise quickly began to turn the company around, despite the trouble the company was in (it was so bad, in fact, that Diller threatened to sue Davis, claiming that he misrepresented the studio's difficulties to him when he was hired). Nonetheless, Diller mounted a program to increase film production and sought financing from a variety of different sources. Then, in March, 1985, Australian media mogul Rupert Murdoch advanced Twentieth Century Fox $88 million after buying a half interest in the company for $132 million.

Murdoch assumed an active role at the company from the beginning. He acquired seven television stations from Metromedia, Inc. for $2 billion with the intention of drawing on Twentieth Century Fox's movie library and TV shows. When Davis expressed concerns about the company's film operation being tied too closely to a television network, Murdoch offered to buy him out. And so, in September 1985, Davis agreed to sell his interest for $325 million, keeping some of Twentieth Century Fox's valuable real estate.

Murdoch and Diller turned Twentieth Century Fox around. In late 1987 Diller oversaw the release of two big hits—*Broadcast News* and *Wall Street*—and his involvement with the studio has lured back top talent which had defected elsewhere during the Davis years. A continuing string of successful films like *Big* and *Working Girl* have boosted the company's earnings by 35%. Now that Twentieth Century Fox, under Diller's keen eye, has begun to turn a profit again, it appears that the company is back on track and ready for the future.

Principal Subsidiaries: Amcoho Co. (50%); Aspen Skiing Co. (50%); National Wiz. Co. (60%); Studio Properties Co. (50%); Pebble Beach Co. (50%); CinemaScope Products, Inc.; Twentieth Century-Fox Theatre Productions, Inc.; Twentieth Century-Fox Video Inc. (50%); Twentieth Century-Fox Film (East) Ltd. (Singapore); Twentieth Century-Fox Film (S.A.) (Pty.) Ltd. (South Africa); Hispano Fox Films S.A.E. (Spain); Aktiebolaget Fox Film (Sweden); Twentieth Century-Fox Film Corp. S.d. 'E.P. la S. (Switzerland); Twentieth Century-Fox Film del Uruguay, Ltd.; Twentieth Century-Fox Trinidad, Ltd.; Zambia Film Services Ltd.

Further Reading: Dunne, John Gregory. *The Studio*, New York, Straus & Giroux, 1969; Thomas, Tony, and Solomon, Aubrey. *The Films of 20th Century-Fox: A Pictorial History*, Secaucus, New Jersey, Citadel Press, 1985.

WALT DISNEY COMPANY

500 South Buena Vista Street
Burbank, California 91521
U.S.A.
(818) 560–1000

Public Company
Incorporated: 1938 as Walt Disney Productions
Employees: 39,000
Sales: $3.44 billion
Stock Index: New York Pacific Midwest Tokyo

The Walt Disney Company is one of the most creative and successful forces in the entertainment industry. The company is best known for bringing decades of fantasy to families through its motion pictures, television series, and amusement parks. In the early 1980s Disney expanded beyond the family-film market with the creation of Touchstone Films, which was responsible for the release of some of the most popular motion pictures of the 1980s.

The company's founder, of course, was Walt Disney. Born in Chicago in 1901, Disney's father, Elias Disney, moved his family throughout the Midwest seeking employment. Disney grew up in a household where hard work was prized; feeding the five Disney children left little pocket change for amusement. Walt Disney began working at age nine as a newspaper delivery boy. Elias Disney instructed his children in the teachings of the Congregational Church and socialism. Later, Walt Disney's appeal to greater America was said to have roots in his middle-class, Midwestern upbringing.

Drawing provided an escape for Disney, and at age 14 he took his work on the road and enrolled at the Kansas City Art Institute. Disney's art was temporarily put on hold when he joined the Red Cross at age 16 to serve as an ambulance driver at the end of World War I. In 1919 Disney returned to the United States and found work as a commercial artist. Together with Ub Iwerks, another artist at the studio, Disney soon formed an animated cartoon company.

In 1923, following the bankruptcy of this Kansas City company, Disney joined his brother Roy in Hollywood. By the time he arrived on the West Coast, word came from New York that a company wanted to purchase the rights to a series of Disney's live-action cartoon reels—the one which would later be called *Alice Comedies*. A distributor named M. J. Winkler offered $1,500 per reel and Disney joined her as a production partner.

A series of animated films followed on *Alice's* heels. In 1927 Disney started a series called "Oswald the Lucky Rabbit" which met public acclaim. Winkler, however, had the character copyrighted in her own name, so Disney earned only a few hundred dollars. It was while pondering the unfairness of this situation on a California-bound train that Disney first thought of creating a mouse character named Mortimer. He shortened the name to Mickey, drew up some simple sketches, and went on to make several Mickey Mouse films with his brother Roy, using their own money.

On the third Mickey Mouse film, Disney decided to take a bold step and add sound to what later became *Steamboat Willie*. The cartoon was synchronized with a simple musical background. The process provided some of the first technical steps in film continuity: music was played at two beats a second and the film was marked every 12 frames as a guide to the animator, and later an orchestra.

Film distributors laughed at Disney's ideas. Finally one, Pat Powers, released *Steamboat Willie*, which was met by highly favorable reviews. Audiences loved what they saw and heard, and suddenly he was a hit in the animation business. In 1935, *The New York Times* called Mickey Mouse "the best known and most popular international figure of his day." Meanwhile Disney personally suffered from largely unfair press treatment pointing out that he was not a great cartoonist and that Ub Iwerks was responsible for the design of Mickey Mouse and the other characters. He was, however, given credit for his ability to conceptualize characters and stories.

The Mickey Mouse projects brought in enough cash to allow Walt Disney to develop other projects, including several full-length motion pictures and advances in Technicolor film. Disney's first full-length motion picture was called *Snow White and the Seven Dwarfs*. The movie opened in 1937 to impressive crowds and led to a string of Disney hits, including *Pinocchio* and *Fantasia* in 1940, *Dumbo* in 1941, *Bambi* in 1942, and *Saludos Amigos* in 1943.

In mid-1940 Disney decided to tackle live-action films, first in *The Reluctant Dragon* and to a greater extent in 1946's *Song of the South*. Meanwhile, during World War II, Disney lent his characters to the war effort, making shorts, including one in which Minnie Mouse showed American housewives the importance of saving fats. After the war, Walt Disney Productions was back in business with live-action features including *20,000 Leagues Under the Sea*. *The Living Desert* was released in the early 1950s by Disney's new distribution company, Buena Vista, to tremendous box office success.

During the 1950s, as America became content to stay home and be entertained in front of the TV, Disney's studio took full advantage of the television revolution. In 1954, the "Disneyland" television series premiered. The show included an introduction by Walt Disney, and incorporated film clips from Disney productions, live action, and coverage of Disneyland. Some four million people tuned in each week. Disney also made a national hero out of Davy Crockett when he made the folk hero the subject of a three-part program. Within a matter of weeks, American boys could not live without coonskin caps and other Crockett merchandise, all of which earned Disney a fortune. Crockett's popularity led to the era of the Disney live-action adventures that included the late 1950s hits *The Great Locomotive Chase*, *Westward Ho*, *Old Yeller*, and *The Light in the Forest*.

In October, 1955 "The Mickey Mouse Club" debuted on the ABC television network. The daily hour-long show aired at 5 P.M. and made television history. In 1961 Walt Disney switched from ABC to NBC, where his hour-long show, as one of the first color shows, was renamed "Walt Disney's Wonderful World of Color" (later changed to "The Wonderful World of Disney"). Aired at 7:30 P.M. on Sunday nights, the show ran for 20 years. At the same time, Disney was making movie stars out of Fred MacMurray, Hayley Mills, and Dean Jones in movies like *The Shaggy Dog*, *The Absent-Minded Professor*, *Polly-anna*, and *The Parent Trap*. In 1964, Disney's *Mary Poppins* was one of the top-grossing films of the year.

At the same time, Disney had his hand in diverse projects, including Audio-Animatronics (automatically controlled robots) and a Florida amusement complex which eventually became Walt Disney World, to complement California's Disneyland, which had become a vacation hot spot.

Disney required professionalism of his staff and demanded the highest-quality Technicolor available. His return was live-action films that topped competitors' in both creativity and technical standards.

On December 15, 1966 Walt Disney died of lung cancer. Shortly after Disney's death, his brother Roy issued an optimistic statement to the effect that Walt Disney's philosophy and genius would be carried on by his employees.

But no one could match Walt Disney's keen story sense or enthusiasm, and the studio floundered through most of the 1970s despite several strong CEOs, including E. Cardon "Card" Walker, who had joined the company as a traffic boy in 1938. Not that there weren't any successes. *Blackbeard's Ghost*, with Dean Jones and Suzanne Pleshette, was released in 1968. In 1969 Disney released *The Love Bug*, which became the year's biggest box office hit and the second-highest grossing film in Disney history, after *Mary Poppins*. Three sequels and a short-run television series followed. Other popular releases of the late 1960s and the 1970s included *The Jungle Book*, *The Aristocats*, *Bedknobs and Broomsticks*, and several live-action features.

But a run of box office disappointments followed, including mid-1970s James Garner releases like *One Little Indian* and *Castaway Cowboy*. *Robin Hood*, distributed at the end of 1973, was a minor flop; *The Small One* was released around Christmas, 1976 and was labeled "too saccharine." Finally, *The Rescuers* proved successful. A mildly-successful effort called *Pete's Dragon* followed, combining human and animated characters.

Progress was slow for the Disney studio in the late 1970s and early 1980s. The studio released three new live-action movies: *The World's Greatest Athlete*, *Gus*, and *The Shaggy D.A.* Mediocre films like *Return from Witch Mountain* and *The Black Hole*, a $20 million film that was lost in the amazing success of *Star Wars*, followed.

New CEO Ron Miller brought in new directors and younger writers who produced unremarkable films including *Watcher in the Woods*, *Fox and the Hound*, and even *Tron*, a computer-generated film that was one of Disney's most daring efforts in years.

In 1983, beginning with the release of *Mickey's Christmas Carol*, Disney's fortunes finally began to look up. A string of successful movies followed, including *Never Cry Wolf* and the semi-successful horror movie *Something Wicked This Way Comes*, a Ray Bradbury tale. In 1983 the company also began marketing a pay-TV channel, the Disney Channel, which offers family-oriented programming and quickly became the fastest-growing pay-TV channel.

In 1984 corporate raider Saul Steinberg attempted a hostile takeover of the company. Disney ultimately bought Steinberg's 11.1% holding in the company for $325.4 million. A number of greenmail suits were filed by shareholders against both Disney and Steinberg's Reliance Group Holdings, charging that Disney's managers had attempted to secure their positions and had lowered the value of the stock. The suits were settled in 1989 when the two companies jointly agreed to pay shareholders $45 million.

Shortly after their purchase of 18.7% of Disney's stock, the Bass family of Texas hired Michael Eisner from Paramount Pictures to be Disney's new CEO and Frank Wells to be president. And in 1985 Disney lured Gary Wilson from the Marriott Corporation and made him chief financial officer. Eisner's creative instinct and Wilson's negotiating savvy were crucial to making Disney the success it is today.

Eisner immediately began to emphasize Touchstone Films, a subsidiary whose purpose is to attract adult movie audiences. *Splash*, starring Daryl Hannah, Tom Hanks, and John Candy and directed by Ron Howard had had the biggest opening weekend business in the company's history just six months before Eisner took over.

Eisner, like Walt Disney, has had the ability to predict and deliver the movies people want to see. Films like the 1985 release *Down and Out in Beverly Hills* helped Touchstone build momentum. Touchstone followed up with *Outrageous Fortune*, *Tin Men*, *Ruthless People*, and many other hits. In Eisner's first four years as CEO, Disney surged from last place to first among the eight major studios.

Eisner also set out to take fuller advantage of expanding markets such as cable television and home video. Disney signed a long-term deal with Showtime Networks, Inc., giving the cable service exclusive rights to Touchstone and other Disney releases through 1996. In addition, Eisner bought KHJ, an independent Los Angeles TV station; sought new markets for old Disney productions through television syndication; and began to distribute TV shows like "Golden Girls" and "Win, Lose or Draw."

Certain Disney classics, like *Lady and the Tramp* and *Cinderella*, were released on video cassette during the late 1980s. Eisner protected the value of the films by limiting the availability of the tapes. He also scheduled the re-release of many other films for the late 1980s and early

1990s, by which time a new generation of children would be ready to see the films in the theater once again. Disney's revenues soon began to increase, averaging around a 20% annual improvement during the second half of the 1980s.

Disney also airs a two-hour show each Saturday on French television. Marketing and promotion of Disney videos and tie-in merchandise in other parts of western Europe are increasing. The theme parks continue to flourish. In 1989 Disney/MGM Studios theme park opened near Orlando, Florida, on the grounds of Walt Disney World. Despite its name, the park is not a collaboration between the two studios; Disney purchased the rights to include attractions based on MGM films. Euro-Disneyland, of which Disney owns 49%, will open outside of Paris in 1992; and Tokyo Disneyland, although it is not owned by the Walt Disney Company and profits the company very little, draws phenomenal crowds. In the United States, visitors to each of the original theme parks exceed ten million a year and are expected to continue to increase. Technical developments at the parks remain a major concern to the company. Between 1987 and the summer of 1989 Disney spent more than $1 billion constructing new park attractions.

In the early 1980s the parks were responsible for about 70% of the company's revenue. Carrying a very low debt, and with $315 million in ready cash, Disney hopes to be equally fruitful abroad. Future plans include introducing more Disney books, videos, and tie-in merchandise to the Japanese market. In China, a half-hour Mickey and Donald show is a smash success, with 40 million viewers. Eisner is also exploring the possibility of Disney projects in Korea, Taiwan, Singapore, and South America.

Meanwhile, Touchstone remains healthy. Hollywood Pictures, Disney's newest film-producing arm, began making more films in the late 1980s. Disney's Silver Screen Partners, which arranges financing for films through limited partnerships, seems to have the golden touch. The studio continued to score hits with *Three Men and a Baby*, *Good Morning Vietnam*, *Who Framed Roger Rabbit*, and others. In addition, production costs run around $12 million per movie while the industry average is $16.5 million.

The ability of a motion picture studio to churn out hits consistently is rare. Disney's film subsidiaries did exceptionally well in the 1980s; whether they can continue their success remains to be seen. The theme parks, however, are a very stable high-margin business, and growth for all of Disney's businesses overseas looks quite promising as well. At home, the 200 companies licenced to make Disney products generated $1 billion in 1988. Michael Eisner seems to have found the formula for success in the entertainment business, nearly tripling turnover in his first four years, and Disney is reaping the rewards.

Principal Subsidiaries: Buena Vista Pictures Distribution Inc.; Buena Vista International, Inc.; Disneyland International; Lake Buena Vista Communities, Inc.; Reedy Creek Services Inc.; Walt Disney Travel Co., Inc.; Walt Disney World Co.; The Disney Channel; Disney Development Co.; Buena Vista Home Video; Buena Vista Television; Childcraft Education Corp.; Childcraft Inc.; Disney Educational Productions; The Disney Store, Inc.; Euro Disneyland Corporation; KHJ-TV, Inc.; The Walt Disney Catalog, Inc.; Walt Disney Imagineering; Walt Disney Pictures and Television; WCO Hotels, Inc.; WCO Port Properties, Ltd.

Further Reading: Thomas, Bob. *Walt Disney, an American Original,* New York, Simon & Schuster, 1976; Leebron, Elizabeth. *Walt Disney: A Guide to References and Resources,* Boston, G.K. Hall, 1979; Abrams, Harry. *Walt Disney's Epcot,* New York, Abrams, 1982; Maltin, Leonard. *The Disney Films* New York, Crown, 1984; Birnbaum, Steve. *The Best of Disneyland,* Boston, Houghton Mifflin, 1987; Taylor, John. *Storming the Magic Kingdom: Wall Street, the Raiders, and the Battle for Disney*, New York, Knopf, 1987; Holliss, Richard. *The Disney Studio Story*, New York, Crown, 1988.

WARNER COMMUNICATIONS INC.

75 Rockefeller Plaza
New York, New York 10019
U.S.A.
(212) 484–8000

Wholly owned subsidiary of Time Warner Inc.
Incorporated: 1923 as Warner Brothers
Employees: 15,000
Sales: $4.2 billion

The Warner brothers—Jack, Albert (Abe), Harry, and Sam—were sons of Polish immigrants who arrived in the United States in the late 19th century. Their father, Benjamin Warner, made a living in the United States as an itinerant merchant. The family eventually settled in Youngstown, Ohio, where Sam Warner got a job operating a movie projector at a nickelodeon. When the nickelodeon went out of business, Sam persuaded his father to buy the projector, and the family started a traveling show. The brothers soon rented space in New Castle, Pennsylvania and opened a theater—with chairs borrowed from a funeral parlor.

The Warners' success in the theater business soon led them into producing and distributing motion pictures. With an ever-expanding base of operations, the men decided to establish a permanent headquarters in New York City. But they were unable to make as many films as they wanted because of a lack of space and the poor weather there, so they decided to move the company's production facilities to Los Angeles. Harry was president and Abe was treasurer, while Jack and Sam assumed responsibility for running the studio in Burbank, California and making films. By 1917, the Warners were producing a string of slapstick comedies.

But Warner Brothers also earned a reputation for making films that confronted social and political problems. Two of its earliest releases were *Open Your Eyes*, a semidocumentary on syphilis made in 1919, and another called *Why Girls Leave Home*. Other movies were made in the same vein, and each of them increased the reputation of the Warner Brothers as moviemakers.

When Warner Brothers released *The Jazz Singer* in 1927, it made movie history. Though the film was not the very first to use dialogue, it has gone down in history as the first "talkie," since it was the first talking film to reach a wide audience. Sam Warner had conceived the Vitaphone sound system used in the film, but he did not live to see the fruits of his labor; he died of a stroke 24 hours before *The Jazz Singer* premiered, but talkies were soon the rage across the country.

With Sam gone, Jack assumed complete control of the studio's production facilities and put Warner Brothers at the forefront of the movie industry during Hollywood's golden age, in the 1930s and 1940s. The company was one of the five big film studios of the time (along with MGM, 20th Century Fox, Paramount, and RKO) turning out some 50 movies a year for distribution it its own theaters.

By 1930, the company owned nearly a fourth of all the movie theaters in the United States. During the 1930s, revenues from films began to skyrocket as Warner Brothers introduced Rin-Tin-Tin and Bugs Bunny along with film biographies of prominent figures like Louis Pasteur and Florence Nightingale. Errol Flynn, too, became a household name during this time as a star in Warner movies like *The Adventures of Robin Hood* and *Captain Blood*.

Warner Brothers became known as the quintessential "factory" studio from the mid-1930s through the late 1940s. Remakes were an important part of the assembly line approach to the production and distribution of movies. Successful plots, characters, and incidents were used again and again, sometimes transposed from one genre to another—and sometimes not.

But despite this factory approach, many film historians maintain that Warner Brothers was the preeminent film studio in Hollywood during the 1940s. The company was showing some of the best movies ever made in its expanding chain of theaters. Humphrey Bogart classics like *Casablanca*, *The Maltese Falcon*, *The Big Sleep*, and *The Treasure of the Sierra Madre* were all Warner releases of the period. The company also maintained a prestigious stable of movie stars and directors, including Bette Davis, Edward G. Robinson, Olivia de Havilland, Claude Rains, John Barrymore, Lauren Bacall, James Cagney, Doris Day, Al Jolson, Frank Capra, John Huston, and Ernst Lubitsch.

The production of *A Streetcar Named Desire* in 1950 was a harbinger of the coming bad times for Warner. Neither Elia Kazan, the director, nor the stars, Vivien Leigh and Marlon Brando, were on standing contract with the company. Even worse, the photography director, the art director, the costume designer, and the composer were not Warner employees either. All were hired from outside the studio for that one film. As the assembly line, in which films were designed as vehicles for stars and executed by full-time employees, gave way in the 1950s to films crafted one by one, Warners began to suffer.

The company was affected not only by the rise of independent productions, but also by the advent of television and new postwar recreational patterns. Movie attendance dropped as the number of TVs in the United States rose dramatically. In addition, in 1949 a government antitrust action forced Warner Brothers, like all the other big film companies, to give up its theater chain. As a result, Warner suffered a severe financial and artistic decline throughout the 1950s.

Harry Warner died in July, 1958 at the age of 76; his death seemed to symbolize the final passing of Warner Brothers' greatness. From that time onward, Jack ruled the company. But the company continued its downhill slide. In the early 1960s, Jack produced *Whatever Happened to Baby Jane?* starring Joan Crawford and Bette Davis, both former Warner stars, in what Michael Freeland described in *The Warner Brothers* as "a magnum opus of bitchiness." Later, in 1966, Jack seemed to recapture some of the Warner Brothers' knack for hit movies with Elizabeth Taylor and Richard Burton in *Who's Afraid of Virginia Woolf?*

But in 1966, Jack decided it was time for him to leave the company. He sold all his shares in the company to Seven Arts Productions, Ltd., for $32 million. The new management asked him to stay on as an independent producer, and he was given the honorary title of vice chairman of the board. But Seven Arts was not very interested in producing new movies; it was more interested in the money that lay in selling the television rights to Warner's movie library. Frustrated by his lack of control and saddened by the death of his brother Abe in 1967, Jack Warner left the company's Burbank studios in 1969. He died in 1978.

By 1969, Seven Arts movie production had virtually come to a standstill. The single bright spot for the company during this time was the purchase of Atlantic Records for $17 million in stock. Atlantic's creator and president, Ahmet Ertegun, was responsible for encouraging the proliferation of rhythm and blues in the mid-1950s with his recordings of LaVern Baker and Clyde McPhatter. These artists, in turn, influenced the development of rock and roll.

A short time later, Warner Brothers–Seven Arts was bought by Steven Ross. Ross had spent the late 1950s and 1960s assembling a conglomerate that included a funeral business, a parking lot operation, a car-rental agency, and a building-maintenance company. When he purchased National Cleaning Contractors, Ross decided to name his firm Kinney National Services, and so Kinney became the parent company of Warner Brothers. But by 1971 Ross had sold most of its holdings; that year he changed the company's name to Warner Communications.

Under Ross's direction, Warner's fortunes were revived. *Woodstock* was the company's first big hit in years, and was quickly followed by a popular John Wayne movie, *Chisum*. These films provided Ross with the money he needed to produce two of the box-office smashes of the 1970s: *All the President's Men* and *The Exorcist*. Ross then initiated a diversification program of acquisitions in the entertainment industry, including a toy company, a cable-television business, record companies, a paperback-book publisher, and a magazine-distribution system. The company finished the 1970s with the two most successful movies of 1979, *Superman* and *Every Which Way But Loose*. By 1980, Warner's revenues had reached $2 billion.

The good times, however, did not last long. Warner had purchased Atari, the video-game and computer firm, in 1976 for the bargain price of $28 million. By 1980 Atari's revenues reached $900 million and provided Warner with a large percentage of its earnings. But the video-game market plummeted unexpectedly three years later. The resulting decline in Warner's stock price prompted a takeover attempt by an Australian media tycoon Rupert Murdoch.

Ross appealed to Herbert J. Siegel, chairman of Chris-Craft Industries, for assistance in warding off Murdoch's attempt. In 1983 Siegel agreed to buy a 19% share in Warner, and soon increased it to 29%. But as Siegel became a member of the board of directors as his holdings increased, he and Ross began to disagree about the timing of asset sales and about what Siegel regarded as excessive overhead. Nevertheless, Atari was sold in the summer of 1984 for $240 million and the publishing division, which produces DC Comics and *Mad Magazine*, reached $16 million in operating profits by the end of 1984. But the company was still hurting from the Atari episode: in 1983 and 1984 Warner lost over a billion dollars after taxes and debt piled up to $841 million.

For the next two years, Warner underwent an extensive restructuring program. By 1986, the result was clear—company revenues had climbed to $2.8 billion. The turnaround was sparked by box office successes such as *The Color Purple* and *Pale Rider*, the company's five-year licensing pact with Time Inc.'s Home Box Office (which gave HBO exclusive rights to all new Warner films and some library titles), recorded-music operations (with releases from Madonna, Paul Simon, Van Halen, Genesis, and other artists), and its cable-TV business, America's sixth largest.

But the Ross-Siegel feud had become a familiar story to shareholders and media analysts. By the late 1980s the two communicated primarily through their attorneys. A particularly heated disagreement came in February, 1987 when the Warner board of directors gave Steven Ross a ten-year contract with a potential salary-and-bonus package of about $14 million a year. A furious Herb Siegel argued that no CEO was worth that kind of money; Ross's flamboyant style aggravated the cost-conscious Siegel as well. Rumors that Ross planned to take the company private to rid himself of Siegel, which had begun to circulate soon after the Ross-Siegel rift had first occurred, became more widespread. While the company continued its glorious comeback, however, the soured alliance remained intact.

In contrast to Ross's flashiness, Warner Communications maintained some of the most conservative business practices in the media industry. Chief Financial Officer Bert Wasserman maintained tight control over Warner's books. Unlike other large entertainment companies, Warner set aside reserves on its motion pictures prior to release. The company did not predict syndication on its television programs, but tried to recoup the entire cost of production through network licensing fees; if a program did achieve syndication, the resulting revenues transferred quickly to the bottom line. Wasserman's conservative practices gave Warner a degree of breathing room to execute its high-risk operations.

In February, 1986 the company bought the other half of Warner Amex Cable from American Express for $393 million. Within two years, largely as a result of deregulation in the cable industry, the subsidiary was valued at between $2.5 billion and $3 billion; it had been an incredible buy. Box office hits such as *Goonies*, *The Color Purple*, *National Lampoon's European Vacation*, and two of the *Police Academy* movies gave the motion picture unit a solid performance. The expansion of ancillary markets like syndication and cable also provided strong earnings.

The Warner Records unit became the biggest label in the United States in the mid-1980s with stars like Prince, Madonna, Genesis, and Van Halen bringing in huge sums. Although CBS Records was still number one in total sales worldwide, Warner had the "hottest" stars—a crucial factor in the image-conscious music business. Strong music sales continued throughout the later 1980s and in 1989 Warner's record group became the world's largest.

In 1988 Warner began negotiations that culminated in its January, 1989 purchase of Lorimar Telepictures for $600 million in stock. Itself the result of a 1986 merger, Lorimar Telepictures was one of Hollywood's most successful producers of television programming. Lorimar had produced such hits as "The Waltons," "Eight is Enough," "Dallas," and its spinoffs "Falcon Crest" and "Knots Landing," among others, and Telepictures was responsible for the immensely popular "People's Court," and a number of animated programs, including "Thundercats." After the 1986 merger of Lorimar and Telepictures, the new Lorimar Telepictures had gone on a buying spree, purchasing a diverse group of enterprises including ad agencies, publishing businesses, and TV stations. In 1986, the company bought the 44-acre lot of the legendary MGM Studios in Culver City, California from Ted Turner for $118 million and renamed the studio Lorimar Studios.

While the company's television production unit was at the top of the industry, Lorimar's film production and distribution unit was not as successful—it had yet to score a hit by 1989. Warner's acquisition gave Lorimar Telepictures much needed liquidity. The deal was typical of the mergers sweeping Hollywood in the late 1980s as entertainment companies looked for strength in increased size.

Although the Lorimar acquisition was big, it paled in comparison to Warner's next move. In March, 1989, Warner proposed a merger with the publishing and cable-TV giant Time Inc. to create the world's largest media conglomerate, sending shock waves through the industry. The two companies planned at first to merge by swapping stock. But in June, 1989, Paramount Communications Inc. (formerly Gulf & Western) threw a wrench into these plans when it bid $10.7 billion ($175 per share) for Time. Time rejected the bid and agreed to purchase Warner for $14 billion ($70 per share). Paramount sweetened its bid to $200 per share and took Time to court to keep it from buying Warner. But in July, 1989 a Delaware court put an end to Paramount's ambitions when it approved Time's purchase of Warner.

The new Time Warner is a colossal entity. Once integrated, the new company will be the nation's number-two cable TV operator in addition to controlling the largest pay service, HBO; the company's publishing group will include magazines as diverse as *Mad* and *Time* in addition to several major book publishing concerns; and Warner Brothers Pictures and the Warner record group, both leaders in their fields.

As media companies throughout the world grow larger, the Time Warner merger offers the opportunity for secure growth; the companies' operations are indeed complementary. As the largest media company in the United States and the world, Time Warner's future looks bright.

Principal Subsidiaries: Warner Bros. Inc.; W Cinemas Holdings Inc.; WCI/GFI Inc.; Warner Bros. Records Inc.; WEA International Inc.; Warner Special Products Inc.; WEA Manufacturing Inc.; Warner/Chappell Music, Inc.; Warner Cable Operating Inc.; Warner Cable Communications Inc.; Warner Publishing Inc.; Warner Communications (UK) Holdings; Warner Communications Investors, Inc.; WCI Commercial Corp.; WCI Entertainment Pioneer Inc.; WCI—FMC Venture Corp.; WCI Theater Inc., WNM Ventures Inc.

Further Reading. Highham, Charles. *Warner Brothers*, New York, Scribners, 1975; Freedland, Michael, *The Warner Brothers*, London, Harrap, 1983; Behlmer, Rudy. *Inside Warner Bros. (1935–1951)*, New York, Viking, 1985.

FINANCIAL SERVICES: BANKS

H.F. AHMANSON & COMPANY
ALGEMENE BANK NEDERLAND N.V.
AMSTERDAM-ROTTERDAM BANK N.V.
AUSTRALIA AND NEW ZEALAND BANKING GROUP LTD.
BANCA COMMERCIALE ITALIANA SPA
BANCO BILBAO VIZCAYA, S.A.
BANCO CENTRAL
BANCO DO BRASIL S.A.
BANK BRUSSELS LAMBERT
BANK HAPOALIM B.M.
BANK OF BOSTON CORPORATION
BANK OF MONTREAL
BANK OF NEW ENGLAND CORPORATION
THE BANK OF NEW YORK COMPANY, INC.
THE BANK OF NOVA SCOTIA
BANK OF TOKYO, LTD.
BANKAMERICA CORPORATION
BANKERS TRUST NEW YORK CORPORATION
BANQUE NATIONALE DE PARIS S.A.
BARCLAYS PLC
BAYERISCHE HYPOTHEKEN- UND WECHSEL-BANK AG
BAYERISCHE VEREINSBANK A.G.
CANADIAN IMPERIAL BANK OF COMMERCE
THE CHASE MANHATTAN CORPORATION
CHEMICAL BANKING CORPORATION
CITICORP
COMMERZBANK A.G.
COMPAGNIE FINANCIERE DE PARIBAS
CONTINENTAL BANK CORPORATION
CRÉDIT AGRICOLE
CREDIT SUISSE
CREDITO ITALIANO
THE DAI-ICHI KANGYO BANK LTD.
THE DAIWA BANK, LTD.
DEUTSCHE BANK A.G.
DRESDNER BANK A.G.
FIRST CHICAGO CORPORATION
FIRST INTERSTATE BANCORP
THE FUJI BANK, LTD.
GENERALE BANK
THE HONGKONG AND SHANGHAI BANKING CORPORATION LIMITED
THE INDUSTRIAL BANK OF JAPAN, LTD.
KANSALLIS-OSAKE-PANKKI
KREDIETBANK N.V.
LLOYDS BANK PLC
LONG-TERM CREDIT BANK OF JAPAN, LTD.
MANUFACTURERS HANOVER CORPORATION
MELLON BANK CORPORATION
MIDLAND BANK PLC
THE MITSUBISHI BANK, LTD.
THE MITSUBISHI TRUST & BANKING CORPORATION
THE MITSUI BANK, LTD.
THE MITSUI TRUST & BANKING COMPANY, LTD.
J.P. MORGAN & CO. INCORPORATED
NATIONAL WESTMINSTER BANK PLC
NCNB CORPORATION
NIPPON CREDIT BANK
NORINCHUKIN BANK
PNC FINANCIAL CORPORATION
THE ROYAL BANK OF CANADA
THE SANWA BANK, LTD.
SECURITY PACIFIC CORPORATION
SKANDINAVISKA ENSKILDA BANKEN
SOCIÉTÉ GÉNÉRALE
STANDARD CHARTERED PLC
THE SUMITOMO BANK, LTD.
THE SUMITOMO TRUST & BANKING COMPANY, LTD.
SVENSKA HANDELSBANKEN
SWISS BANK CORPORATION
THE TAIYO KOBE BANK, LTD.
THE TOKAI BANK, LTD.
THE TORONTO-DOMINION BANK
UNION BANK OF SWITZERLAND
WELLS FARGO & COMPANY
WESTDEUTSCHE LANDESBANK GIROZENTRALE
WESTPAC BANKING CORPORATION
THE YASUDA TRUST AND BANKING COMPANY, LTD.

H.F. AHMANSON & COMPANY

660 South Figueroa Street
Los Angeles, California 90017
U.S.A.
(213) 955–4200

Public Company
Incorporated: 1928 as the H.F. Ahmanson Company
Employees: 11,819 (1989)
Assets: $44.50 billion (1989)
Stock Index: New York Pacific London

H.F. Ahmanson & Company is the largest savings and loan institution in the United States. A traditional savings bank and mortgage lender, Ahmanson is the bank more Americans borrow money from to buy a home than any other. Its deposit base, the largest of any savings institution in the country, is made up entirely of individual, rather than institutional, accounts.

Howard Fieldstead Ahmanson, the company's founder, was born in 1906. Considered by his father to be a genius by the age of five, H.F. Ahmanson founded the company that bears his name in 1927, even before graduating from the University of Southern California that year at the age of 22. Ahmanson's company specialized in casualty insurance and quickly became the largest underwriter in California. During the Depression, the company prospered by dealing with foreclosures. Ahmanson once remarked that he felt like an undertaker: "the worse it got, the better it was for me." In 1943 Ahmanson bought control of the North American Insurance Company, the company his father had owned but which the family had been ousted from after his father's death in 1925.

After World War II, the housing market took off. Nowhere was this more evident than in California. In 1947, Ahmanson purchased Home Savings of America, a savings and loan association with assets of less than $1 million, for $162,000. Founded in 1889, Home Savings is today the cornerstone of its parent company, H.F. Ahmanson. In the decade that followed, Ahmanson acquired 18 additional institutions, merged them under the name Home Savings, and turned the group into a financial giant. So meteoric was its growth, in fact, that the Department of Justice's antitrust division launched an investigation in the mid-1950s, but the inquiry was dropped soon afterward.

While involved in this burgeoning savings and loan association, H.F. Ahmanson also formed the Ahmanson Bank and Trust Company in 1957, the National American Title Insurance Company in 1958, and the National American Life Insurance Company of California in 1961.

The company continued to grow at a furious pace until the 1960s, when the housing market began to falter and the federal government began to pass legislation designed to regulate the savings and loan industry. In 1965, the Ahmanson Company wisely shifted its mortgage emphasis from tract housing to apartment buildings and was able to avoid most of the problems that other savings institutions faced. Howard Ahmanson viewed the collapse as good for the industry because homes were being built too quickly. In his characteristically pithy way, he said "it was like a good laxative that cleaned out the system when it could afford to be cleaned."

In the early years, the Ahmanson name cropped up several times in the realm of politics. The first incidence was in the investigation of Bobby Baker, the former Senate Democratic secretary, who was charged with misusing campaign funds. Although Howard's nephew, William A. Ahmanson, testified at the trial that he had given $33,000 to Baker, Howard later denied that it was his money. A few years later, the advertising agency hired by Home Savings was investigated by the Internal Revenue Service for possible "blind" campaign contributions. Actually, Howard Ahmanson was known to have more than a passing interest in California politics. In fact, in 1954 he had managed Lieutenant Governor Goodwin J. Knight's successful campaign for governor.

In 1968, while traveling in Belgium with his wife and son, Howard Ahmanson suffered a heart attack and died. *Fortune* estimated Ahmanson's financial worth at the time at between $200 and $300 million, most of it controlled by trust funds and foundations. The Ahmanson company is decidedly close-mouthed about its operations and it is not clear who succeeded Ahmanson as head of the then-private corporation. However, the executives that Ahmanson left in charge of his empire were carefully chosen, and even after his death, the company's reputation for aggressive and shrewd management continued, as did its ability to weather downswings in the economy.

The late 1960s and early 1970s were lean years for the savings and loan industry. A frantic building spree had led to many foreclosures in California and money was tight. Out-of-state money had poured into California because interest rates there were much higher than in the rest of the nation, but as other states began to match California's rates, the money was withdrawn.

By the latter part of the 1970s, investors were beginning to put their money in California institutions again, but the savers of this generation were not like their parents and tended to spend more and save less. Savings and loans began to look for alternative ways to make money, through consumer lending (such as appliance financing) and loans on properties other than single-family homes. Always ahead of the industry, Ahmanson had been making loans on apartment buildings since 1965 as a cushion against the failing mortgage market. But Ahmanson did not diversify to the point that would cause the failure of many thrift institutions in the years to come, and today it still makes no auto or consumer loans, leases, or unsecured commercial loans.

Several federal regulations passed during this period proved advantageous to H.F. Ahmanson. A 1968 law ended a nine-year freeze on takeovers by holding companies, and a 1971 rule allowed financial institutions to make loans within 200 miles of each branch office—the old rule had restricted lending to within 200 miles of an institution's headquarters only. Spurred by the easing of restrictions, the Home Savings network soon covered the whole state of California, as four offices were acquired in northern California.

In the 1960s, there was intense competition among savings and loan associations centered around sky-high interest rates and offers of expensive premium items for customers who opened new accounts. In 1966, legislation ended the so-called "rates wars," leaving institutions to rely on their advertising budgets to attract new customers. Not surprisingly, the larger institutions with more advertising dollars to spend prospered and the giants, including Home Savings, gained the power to set loan rates.

The Tax Reform Act of 1969, which called for a reduction of concentrated holdings by foundations, resulted in several stock offerings by H.F. Ahmanson, but the company's financial base was so solid that the sales made barely a dent. A $100 million stock offering in 1972 was a record for the time, yet it only represented 6.4% of the firm's $4.4 billion in assets. After the Bank Holding Company Act of 1970, it was necessary for Ahmanson to sell the Ahmanson Bank, which it did in 1976 to private Philippine investors. However, Ahmanson was able to retain its trust operations as a subsidiary, Ahmanson Trust Company.

Ahmanson's insurance operations, the original business of the company, continued to grow, as Stuyvesant Insurance Group was acquired from GAC Corporation in 1974 and Bankers National Life Insurance Company was purchased in 1981.

Having saturated the California savings and loan market, Ahmanson began to merge out-of-state institutions into the Home Savings network under the name Savings of America. In December of 1981, three mergers were completed in Florida and Missouri; six more in Texas and Illinois followed in 1982. A New York merger was completed in 1984. Subsequent mergers included institutions in Ohio (1985), Arizona (1987), and Washington (1987). At the end of 1987, Home Savings reported $27 billion in assets.

These forays outside California often included expensive, and very successful, direct-mail campaigns. One promotion in Texas reportedly brought in $60 million in one month. But Ahmanson's interstate mergers have also generated some opposition. When Savings of America announced plans to open an office in Berywn, Illinois, a community known for its proliferation of financial institutions, critics in the industry questioned Ahmanson's motives. An earlier protest to the Federal Home Loan Bank by Illinois officials had been dropped after the company convinced the protesters that Illinois money would not be used for California investments. In any event, as one official said, protests rarely affect regulatory approvals, and the Savings of America branches continue to attract savers by offering interest rates as much as 2% higher than local competitors.

Further penetration outside California continued when, in January of 1988, Ahmanson acquired the Bowery Savings Bank, an institution that was established in 1934 in New York. The 25 Bowery offices continue to operate under their original name.

Ahmanson also strengthened its loan operations in the 1980s by opening lending offices under the name of Ahmanson Mortgage Company in Colorado, Connecticut, Georgia, Maryland, Washington, D.C., Massachusetts, Minnesota, North Carolina, Oregon, Tennessee, and Virginia. Two regional loan-service centers, in California and North Carolina, provide support for the offices.

Richard H. Deihl became chairman and CEO of H.F. Ahmanson in 1983. A company veteran, he joined Home Savings as a loan agent in 1960 and was elected CEO of the subsidiary in 1967. Despite the company's move into 27 states, it remains a quiet giant. The catastrophes that hit many thrift institutions in the 1980s have not touched Home Savings or Savings of America. Rather than faltering, the company expanded considerably during the decade. With the opportunities for acquisition and expansion that the savings and loan crisis of the late 1980s offers a healthy giant like Ahmanson, its continuing role as a leader in the industry seems assured.

Principal Subsidiaries: Home Savings of America; Savings of America; Ahmanson Mortgage Company; The Bowery Savings Bank; Ahmanson Commercial Development Company; Ahmanson Developments, Inc.; Ahmanson Marketing, Inc.; Griffin Financial Services; Travel of America.

ALGEMENE BANK NEDERLAND N.V.

32, Vijzelstraat
Post Office Box 669
1000 E.G. Amsterdam
The Netherlands
(020) 299-111

Public Company
Incorporated: 1964
Employees: 29,314
Assets: Dfl 150.9 billion (US$84.9 billion) (1987)
Stock Index: Amsterdam Basel Brussels Dusseldorf Frankfurt Geneva Hamburg Lausanne London Paris Singapore Zurich

Algemene Bank Nederland (ABN) has historically been Holland's most internationally oriented bank, as well as an important player in the Dutch domestic banking industry. Often considered a conservative organization in a conservative industry, ABN has at times struggled with its stodgy image. At other times its caution has served it well. Incorporated in 1964 as the result of a merger between two of the Big Four Dutch banks, the Twentsche Bank and the Nederlansche Handel-Maatshappij (Netherlands Trading Society), ABN traces its origins to the golden age of the Dutch Empire.

In 1824, King William I organized the Netherlands Trading Society to help finance commercial ventures in the Dutch colonies in Southeast Asia. The company began its operations from an office in Batavia (now Jakarta), Netherlands East Indies. In its early years it encouraged commercial trade between Holland and its colonies. Toward the middle of the 19th century, the Netherlands Trading Society became increasingly involved in agricultural financing. Dutch banks traditionally specialized either in agricultural or commercial banking, not both. For this reason the Netherlands Trading Society was unique through the end of the 19th century.

At the dawn of the 20th century, the Netherlands Trading Society began to expand by acquiring several small provincial banks in Holland. In 1916, in cooperation with a number of other Dutch banks, the society set up the Netherland Bank for Russian Trade, but the Russian Revolution, one year later, put an abrupt end to the venture.

Throughout World War I, growth was slow but steady. After the war, Amsterdam became the most important financial center on the European continent, keeping the bank's earnings strong through the 1920s. The stock market crash of 1929 and the global depression that followed shook the banking community worldwide, but the Netherlands Trading Society, broadly diversified throughout the Dutch Empire, was able to survive the crisis.

By 1939, Europe was at war again. In May 1940, Nazi troops marched into Holland. As Dutch industry was required to produce goods for the occupying forces and trade regulations were made to favor Germany overwhelmingly, it was estimated that the Nazis drained Dutch national wealth more than 10% a year.

As the Nazis wrought havoc on the Dutch economy at home, the Japanese disrupted activities in the Netherlands East Indies. In 1942, the invaders announced their plans to liquidate a number of British and Dutch bank branches in the territories they occupied, among them the Netherlands Trading Society. After the war Indonesian nationalists assumed power as the Japanese retreated. The Dutch government struggled to return the territories to their political and economic state before the war, and Dutch merchants and bankers returned alongside the government. But after a few years of fighting Indonesian nationalists, the Dutch pulled out. Dutch bank branches were nationalized by the new independent Indonesian government under President Sukarno.

The Netherlands Trading Society suffered considerably from the dismantling of the Dutch empire. Competition with banks from other nations became fierce in areas it had dominated before. Although the bank grew both domestically and internationally throughout the 1950s and early 1960s, it found its influence overshadowed by larger foreign banks. In an effort to remain competitive, it merged with the Twentsche Bank in 1964.

The Twentsche Bank had a more domestic orientation than the Netherlands Trading Society. Established in 1861, the bank at first concentrated on financing exports from Twente, a cotton-producing region in Holland, to the Netherlands East Indies. The bank was prosperous in this enterprise and other export financing for the first 40 years of its operation. Encouraged by its success, it acquired a number of smaller banks in the Netherlands. The Twentsche Bank grew steadily throughout the first two decades of the 20th century. The bank faced hard times during the Depression, but it pulled through because of its cautious policies. During World War II, the bank's domestic network carried on its business under the severe economic disruption Holland suffered during German occupation.

Like the Netherlands Trading Society, the Twentsche Bank grew after the war, but not fast enough to keep up with world economic growth. The bank sometimes had to pool resources with other banks to meet the needs of its largest customers. The appearance of large foreign banks in Holland made the Twentsche Bank uneasy. In 1964, it agreed to join together with the Netherlands Trading Society. On October 3, the two banks merged under the name Algemene Bank Nederland N.V. (it is interesting to note that the other two of the Dutch "big four" banks, the Amsterdam Bank and the Rotterdam

Bank, announced their own merger one week later; the Amsterdam-Rotterdam Bank (Amro) remains ABN's chief rival today.)

The Algemene Bank Nederland was better equipped to deal with the heavy competition in the Dutch banking market. ABN began to grow almost immediately. In 1968, the bank acquired the Hollandsche Bank-Unie, giving it a strong footing in Latin America and making it the largest bank in Holland. Four years later the bank acquired the Antillaase Bank-Unie N.V. in the Netherlands Antilles. Assets and earnings continued to grow steadily in the 1970s, although more slowly than competitors': in the early 1970s, Amro passed ABN to become the largest Dutch bank. But in 1975, ABN once again became the largest when it purchased the bank Mees & Hope, Holland's biggest merchant bank.

Throughout the 1970s, ABN showed a consistent preference for operating independently of other banks. As more and more European banks financed specific projects jointly, Algemene Bank Nederland kept to itself. ABN is a member of the Associated Banks of Europe Corporation (ABECOR), but unlike other banking consortiums, particularly the European Banks' International Company, ABECOR is not a particularly tight affiliation and ABN has only participated in some projects.

In 1979, ABN purchased the LaSalle National Bank in Chicago, giving it a stronghold in the United States. Throughout the 1980s, with domestic competition as fierce as ever, ABN has looked overseas for growth opportunities. In 1981, the bank opened a representative office in New York to promote capital market activities in North America.

ABN experienced steady but slow growth during the early 1980s. The bank's cautious managing board resisted inevitable changes: ABN was slow to install electronic banking systems on a bankwide level. Although slightly ahead of other Dutch banks, it lagged behind the international trend in the use of automated-teller machines. ABN was also sluggish in responding to the growing use of credit cards.

In 1986, the Dutch government deregulated the Dutch capital markets. Dutch banks were able to add floating-rate notes, certificates of deposit, bullet bonds, and commercial paper to their capital investment arsenal. In 1988, medium-term notes and zero coupons were allowed. ABN tried to be aggressive in these markets, but Dutch investors were hesitant to take advantage of the new and unfamiliar investment instruments, although the response was better from abroad.

ABN's caution was an asset in 1987 when Brazil declared indefinite suspension of interest payments on its loans from international banks. This action, combined with political instability in other Third World countries, forced many banks to increase their loan-loss provisions substantially. Many banks showed large net losses during 1987 as a result. ABN, however, because of its low exposure to Third World debt, was not significantly affected by the crisis.

In 1992, the European Common Market countries will remove their trade boundaries, creating one integrated European market. European banks will have to adjust accordingly. The bank's international network, like its loan portfolio, is well diversified. The bank is represented in all the Common-Market countries except Portugal, something which should help if the integration of markets proves more unsettling then ABN expects. Meanwhile, Algemene Bank Nederland's management stresses its plan to continue growth from within on an independent basis.

Principal Subsidiaries: Hollandsche Bank-Unie N.V.; Bank Mees & Hope N.V.; ABN Australia Ltd.; Algemene Bank Nederland (Belgie) N.V.; ABN Bank Canada; Banque de Neuflize, Schlumberger, Mallet; Algemene Bank Nederland (Deutschland) AG; Algemene Bank Gibralter Ltd.; Algemene Bank Nederland (Ireland) Ltd.; Algemene Bank Marokko; Albank Alsaudi Alhollandi; De Surinaamsche Bank N.V.; LaSalle National Bank.

AMSTERDAM–ROTTERDAM BANK N.V.

Foppingadreef 22
Post Office Box 283
1000 EA Amsterdam
The Netherlands
(020) 289393

Public Company
Incorporated: 1964
Employees: 23,198
Assets: Dfl 168 billion (US$83.67 billion)
Stock Index: Amsterdam

The Amsterdam-Rotterdam Bank (Amro) was incorporated in 1964 when the Amsterdam Bank and the Rotterdam Bank, Holland's first and third largest commercial banks, merged. Since then, Amro's assets have grown from Dfl 6 billion to Dfl 168 billion; the bank leads the Dutch domestic market today. Amro currently has 766 branches in the Netherlands and 88 branches overseas.

Before the Amsterdam Bank and the Rotterdam Bank joined forces they were competitors. The Rotterdam Bank was the older bank, established in 1863. In its first decade the Rotterdam Bank operated offices in Singapore and Batavia (Jakarta), but in 1872 it withdrew from the Dutch colonies and concentrated on financing ventures in Rotterdam, which as a seaport was very active during this period. It was the primary link between the developing industry of the Rhine Valley and the rest of the world, and at the same time served the heavy shipping needs of the Dutch Empire. As harbor traffic increased and the city's trade prospered, the Rotterdam Bank grew.

After the turn of the century, the Rotterdam Bank found its own resources inadequate to meet the financing demands of local industry. In 1911, it made the first of several mergers, with the Deposito and Administratie Bank. Other Dutch banks followed suit in a spate of bank acquisitions. The Rotterdam Bank was soon busy outside of the city. It was the first to develop branch banking in Holland, sponsoring the Zuid Nederlandsche Handelsbank and the Nationale Bank Vereeniging in the Dutch provinces.

During World War I the Rotterdam Bank participated in establishing banking ventures overseas, but a number of these failed after the war due to generally poor economic conditions around the globe. This postwar depression took a heavy toll on the Rotterdam Bank: its capital stock fell by a third between 1922 and 1926. The Dutch central bank helped the Rotterdam Bank get back on its feet, and by the late 1920s prosperity had returned, only to face the Great Depression of the 1930s. By the time the Rotterdam Bank began to recover from this depression, Europe was again embroiled in war.

In May, 1940, the Nazis invaded Holland. The occupying force imposed highly unfavorable trade conditions on Holland and slowly drained the country's wealth.

After the war, the Rotterdam Bank helped to finance reconstruction as Holland adjusted to the independence of its colonies and the loss of its preferred trading position with them.

The Rotterdam Bank branched out aggressively in the ten years following the war. Although the bank grew substantially throughout the 1950s and early 1960s, it faced competition from the growing number of foreign banks appearing on Dutch soil. In 1964, the Rotterdam Bank merged with the Amsterdam Bank to keep ahead of these foreign banks.

The Amsterdam Bank was founded in 1871 by several German and Dutch banks, to bring together German and Dutch money market activities. The bank remained small for its first 20 years, and then began to expand rapidly. The Amsterdam Bank was less inclined to acquire existing banks than the Rotterdam Bank, preferring instead to open new branches of its own.

After World War I, the bank prospered despite the postwar economic crunch because of its prudent lending policies. Amsterdam was the most active financial center in Europe at that time, and the bank was busy financing commercial ventures throughout the 1920s and 1930s.

During World War II, the bank coped with the disruption of the Dutch economy as best it could. After the war, the bank expanded at a frantic pace. In 1948, the Amsterdam Bank entered into an operating agreement with the Incasso Bank and fully merged with it after a short time. This merger made the Amsterdam Bank Holland's largest commercial bank. The bank continued to grow throughout the 1950s, but, like the Rotterdam Bank, was anxious about the growing competition from foreign banks.

The merger of the two banks formed the Amsterdam-Rotterdam Bank (Amro). Amro was better equipped to deal with the needs of its customers than either of its predecessors had been, and with a broader network and increased resources, earnings grew. In 1968, Amro's chief rival, the Algemene Bank Nederland (ABN), acquired another large Dutch bank, the Hollandsche Bank-Unie, pushing Amro into second place among Dutch commercial banks. But Amro stayed on ABN's heels throughout the early 1970s. In 1974, a worldwide recession slowed the bank's growth, but Amro did not suffer the losses that many foreign banks its size did. In 1975, Amro acquired the large Dutch merchant bank Pierson, Heldring, and Pierson, improving its network abroad.

Unlike its chief competitor, ABN, the bulk of Amro's business has traditionally been within Holland. When Amro's customers needed international services, Amro relied on its membership in the European Banks'

International Company (EBIC), a group of seven European banks established to strengthen each member's ability to compete with larger international banks. Amro has been a loyal player on the EBIC team, faithfully participating in its joint ventures.

Although earnings continued to grow in the late 1970s, Amro was slow to react to banking trends. The bank relied heavily on its relationships with key Dutch companies and on the EBIC group for its success. In 1979, the Amro board elected Onno Vogelenzang its chairman. Vogelenzang began to expand Amro's international branch network independent of its EBIC connections and to reduce its dependence on corporate customers, launching Amro in a more aggressive direction. By the time Vogelenzang retired in 1983, Amro was a much more dynamic institution than it had been four years earlier.

Vogelenzang was replaced by Roelef Nelissen, who continued Amro's energetic shift in policy. Amro placed greater emphasis on project finance in the mid-1980s, playing a central role in the financing of oil and natural gas exploration in the Dutch sector of the North Sea and participating in the English Channel tunnel project.

Amro added to its capital market strength by acquiring the European Banking Company in late 1985. EBC Amro Ltd., as the London bank was renamed, strengthened Amro's position in the European capital markets considerably. EBC's experience in foreign exchange and in Euro-equities complemented Amro's already strong bond market activity.

In 1986, the Dutch Finance Ministry liberalized the nation's capital market, freeing new investment instruments from regulation by the Dutch central bank. Banks introduced floating rate notes, certificates of deposit, commercial paper, bullet bonds, and later zero coupons and medium-term notes. While Dutch response to these new investment vehicles was sluggish, foreign investors showed more interest.

Despite the stock market crash of 1987, Amro's earnings that year increased 3.5%. The crash put an understandable dent in Amro's securities brokerage activities (Dutch banks offer a full range of financial services to their customers), but the bank was not as shaken as other institutions.

As part of Amro's effort to keep its operations up to date, the bank moved its headquarters across Amsterdam to a more efficient building in 1987. It also improved its electronic banking systems, ahead of its Dutch competitors.

Amro has been the most aggressive of Dutch commercial banks in the past ten years. As Europe prepares to become one integrated market in 1992, competition in financial markets will undoubtedly increase and Amro will have to continue to act boldly to maintain its edge.

Principal Subsidiaries: Amro Australia Ltd., Amro Bank (Asia) Ltd.; Amro Bank und Finance A.G.; Amro Bank Overseas N.V.; Amro Effectenbewaarbeerijif N.V.; Amro (Finance and Securities) Ltd.; Amro Handelsbank A.G.; Auto Lease Holland B.V.; Beheer-en Administratiemaatschappij Lafico B.V.; Bicker Caarten and Obreen N.V.; N.V. Consultants and Assistants "Consultass"; International Factors Nederland B.V.; Maatschappij tot Finaniering van Bedrijifspanden N.V.; Nationale Bank voor Middelang Krediet N.V.; Nationale Trust Maatschappij N.V.; Particuliere Participatie Maatschappij Amro B.V.; Pierson, Heldring and Pierson N.V.; B.V. Projektonwikkelingsmaatschappij Amro.

ANZ Group

AUSTRALIA AND NEW ZEALAND BANKING GROUP LTD.

55 Collins Street
Melbourne 3000
Victoria, Australia
(03) 658–2955

Public Company
Incorporated: 1835 as Bank of Australasia
Employees: 47,009
Assets: A$84.72 billion (US$66.92 billion) (1989)
Stock Index: Australia London New Zealand

The Australia and New Zealand Banking Group Ltd. was formed when the Australia and New Zealand Bank Ltd. (ANZ) merged with the English, Scottish and Australian Bank Ltd. in 1970. ANZ was the result of a merger in 1951 between the Bank of Australasia and the Union Bank of Australia. Today the Group is made up of more than 50 different businesses interacting to give customers access to a wide range of financial services through more than 2,000 offices in some 40 countries around the globe.

The Bank of Australasia (Asia) is believed to have been the idea of Thomas Potter Macqueen, a wealthy colonist who proposed a joint bank and whaling enterprise to some London investors, who liked his idea well enough to become the bank's first provisional directors. Macqueen, however, was caught promoting the rival Commercial Banking Company of Sydney behind the directors' backs, and the Bank of Australasia opened in 1835 without him.

The Union Bank of Australia was founded in a similar fashion. This time a struggling Australian bank, the Tamar Bank in Tasmania, went to London in search of capital and found a group of investors prepared to back a bank in the colony. They founded the Union, which took over the Tamar Bank and opened for business in 1837.

These two groups of investors based their hopes for the Asia and the Union on Australia's potential to meet the large demand for wool by English textile mills. Although some colonial banks already existed, none of these local institutions could match the financial resources of London-based, private trading banks like the Asia or the Union. Moreover, because these colonial banks were unable to tap the British capital market for another 30 years (except for the Commercial Banking Company of Sydney, which did give the British banks some competition), not one of them survived five years. In contrast, the Asia and the Union were immediately successful—the Asia quadrupled its loans between 1836 and the end of the decade.

In 1838 the New Zealand Company, a colonizing enterprise, approached both the Asia and the Union about opening a branch in the firm's new settlement. The Asia hesitated because it had reservations about the New Zealand Company. The Union agreed, however, and became the first bank to do business in New Zealand.

Between 1838 and 1841 the Australian sheep-farming boom reached new and feverish heights. During this period both the Asia and the Union consolidated their positions and built up businesses secure enough to withstand the severe depression that began in late 1841. Both banks had the financial strength to take advantage of colonial banks decimated by the depression: in 1840 the Union absorbed the Bathurst Bank, in 1841 the Asia acquired the Bank of Western Australia, and, in 1844, at the height of the depression, the Union merged with Archers Gilles & Company.

With the discovery of copper and lead deposits north of Adelaide in 1844, the colonies began moving out of the depression. The discovery of gold near Bathurst, New South Wales, in 1851 soon produced a general boom. In these new economic circumstances, gold and foreign-exchange dealing became significant banking services, and branch-banking programs flourished with the influx of new mining customers eager for mortgages.

During the "golden decade" of the 1850s, new banks formed to challenge the foreign-exchange primacy of the Asia and the Union, among them the English, Scottish and Australian Bank (ES&A). Although the ES&A's presence concerned the Asia and the Union, an even greater threat came from the new colonial banks that burgeoned in the country at mid-century. To better compete with English banks, these colonial institutions established London offices of their own, while they also acquired enough colonial investment resources, mainly gold, to provide their own international banking. Thus, from this time on, the Asia and the Union had to share their international role both with new London-controlled banks and with strong colonial competitors.

Between 1860 and 1890 Australia saw prolonged and rapid economic development. But the conservative Asia and Union banks began to prepare for the inevitable downturn in the late 1880s; this letter from the secretary of the Asia, Prideaux Selby, to his superintendent, John Sawers, in July 1888 gives the flavor of the time:

> Lower rates . . . . Let really sound customers feel that they do better by borrowing from us than by looking outside. Keep up rates to those we would rather be without and to those who can only give ordinary security. Sell dead securities while the boom lasts. Shake off speculators and doubtful customers. Do not look for immediate results. Give the seed time to germinate before looking to the harvest, and remember that unless the seed be sown and for the time lost to use, there never can be a harvest at all.

Both the Asia and the Union had steadily built cash reserves up to 20% of all liabilities to the public and remitted heavily to London rather than permit colonial loans to expand. Moreover, both banks had large floating advances to the money market and extensive and varied holdings of gilt-edged stocks from which they could draw in an emergency. Beyond this, they also had many informal connections with other financial institutions. Thus, during the great bank crash of 1893, both the Asia and the Union had a number of sources to turn to for help, including the Bank of England.

In the 35 years after 1853, 28 colonial banks began operations in Australia. Only six of these colonial banks reached the end of the century without temporary or final failure, and of the eight private trading banks that existed in 1850, only the Asia, the Union, and three others survived.

Many of the post-1850 banks failed because they were governed by over-optimism and an avid search for business without enough concern for security. They opened branch banks in small towns without assessing the costs closely, and they attempted to increase their loan portfolios quickly by minimizing risk factors. The Asia and Union never deviated from their conservative policies, but were cautious about opening new offices and circumspect in approving loans.

With the passing of the banking crisis, both the Asia and the Union attempted to increase their lowered earnings. Salaries were reduced and marginal branch banks were closed, except in western Australia, where gold discoveries promised great opportunities. But, more important than branch policy, both banks tried to restrain the unprofitable accumulation of deposits by cutting interest rates, which they believed would decrease the cost of funds and earn the banks more fees through the marketing of cheaper loans to customers. In 1895 both banks agreed to cut interest rates everywhere in the colonies to 3%, even though other banks did not follow.

Despite these measures to preserve profits, the Asia and the Union realized losses in loans to customers who had been devastated in the banking crisis. Although neither bank had missed a dividend payment at any time in its history, stockholders voiced concerns when rates of return fell markedly short of their expectations. Though these dividend results were similar for both banks, the Asia's board maintained confidence in Superintendent John Sawers and his staff, while the Union's board resolved that General Manager David Finlayson should retire.

By 1900, the Asia held 12.7% of all deposits and 9.3% of all advances, and the Union held 12.1% of all deposits and 10.6% of all advances in Australia, and both were members of Australian banking's Big Four banks (the Bank of New South Wales and the Commercial Banking Company of Sydney were the other two). The other seventeen banks in the country were substantially smaller and confined to one or two colonies. Thus, at the beginning of the 19th century the Asia and the Union enjoyed relative strength and prestige throughout the Australian Commonwealth.

In the first decade of the new century, a stable economy prompted both the Asia and the Union to pursue policies of "complacent growth" through branch bank expansion. Between 1900 and the outbreak of World War I, the Asia opened 73 branches and the Union opened 100. Their competitors, still suffering from the banking crash and the depression, had to worry about reconstruction obligations; their relatively small and weak condition dictated a strategy of mergers and absorption rather than branch banking in the battle for market share.

One major issue for both the Asia and the Union in the early 1900s was their relationship with their head offices in London. Better communications and new personalities in London caused a marked shift in formal executive authority from Australia to Britain. London executives began demanding more intimate details and more informed advice than the general commentaries from Melbourne that they had drawn on for broad policy directives during the 19th century. Understandably, Melbourne executives resented their newly subordinate positions. In the end, the transfer of total executive power to the London offices was facilitated by a new policy of elevating older, more conservative executives to the top ranks in Melbourne.

With the inauguration of Australia as a commonwealth in January, 1901, pressure intensified for a government bank. After much debate and discussion, the Commonwealth Bank opened in January, 1913. It offered savings accounts, government banking, public debt management, and rural credit, but it could not issue notes and did not have central bank control. Top executives at both the Asia and the Union were highly critical of and hostile to the Commonwealth Bank. But executives in London took a more balanced view, and both boards refused to contribute to campaigns against the government's bank, although several colonial banks had done so. Further, they directed their chief executives to accept the situation and cultivate amicable relations with the Commonwealth's president.

World War I crystallized the banking structures existing in 1914. However, after the war, rivals of the Asia and the Union began to merge to make themselves more competitive. In 1917, the Royal Bank of Queensland and the Bank of New Queensland merged to form the Bank of Queensland; by 1932, when the Bank of New South Wales absorbed the Australian Bank of Commerce, 11 amalgamations had occurred, reducing the number of Australian trading banks from 20 to nine. During this period the ES&A merged with three other banks: the Commercial Bank of Tasmania in 1921, the London Chartered Bank of Australia in 1921, and the Royal Bank of Australia in 1927.

The Asia and the Union continued to expand their branch banking in an attempt to offset their competitors' growing advantages. Between 1918 and 1929 the Asia opened 49 new branches and the Union opened 41. Although both banks could have benefited from mergers with banks in areas like Tasmania, where they were not strong, both kept to the conservative policies that had been in place since the turn of the century until well into the 1920s.

In London, executives of both the Asia and the Union were aware that their banks had to change strategy if they wanted to rise in rank. Unfortunately, between the Great Depression and World War II, immediate problems took precedence over long-term rebuilding. There was some discussion about a merger between the Asia and the Union during the 1930s, but it wasn't until 1943 that serious interest in the project revived. At that time, both the Asia and the Union were approached by other Australian banks as possible partners. But each thought of the other as the most natural candidate for a merger.

On its own, each bank was less than half the size of the Bank of New South Wales, the largest bank in the country. They both agreed that a merger would make them more competitive, and also would restore lost stature and prestige. Moreover, if they didn't act, it seemed likely that they would be left behind as their smaller competitors did merge.

In addition, both were English corporations, with London head offices and a majority of English shareholders, and their scales and styles of business were quite similar. The Union's strength in pastoral business complemented the commercial and industrial emphasis of the Asia. Only 70 out of 420 branches overlapped. Friendly cooperation within competition had characterized the relationship between the two banks for more than a century.

In 1946 lawyers began work on the details of a merger in which the Asia took over the business of the Union. However, while a government threat to nationalize non-government banks delayed any action, it was decided that the original merger proposal was too costly. In addition, a group of key Union executives, feeling that the banks were equals and should join accordingly, began to resist being absorbed by the Asia. The solution was to create a new company, the Australia and New Zealand Bank Ltd. to subsume both the Asia and the Union. ANZ began business on October 1, 1951.

The merger of the Asia and Union catapulted ANZ to the top tier of banks in Australia and New Zealand. Unfortunately, being bigger failed to make ANZ more profitable. A tight government liquidity requirement forced the bank to cut lending in order to build liquid assets to the prescribed level. To offset the lost loan business, ANZ began looking for new programs to raise profits and reduce expenses. A savings bank subsidiary, which could use existing skills and facilities and be funded within the governments' constraints, was established in 1955. The Australia and New Zealand Savings Bank Ltd. proved very successful.

While ANZ's administrative hierarchy became more efficient in the early 1960s, General Manager Sir Roger Darval decided that emphasizing the bank's domestic business would boost profits. He began an accelerated expansion of branch banking. ANZ opened 127 branches in six years; of these 112 were in central business districts, signaling ANZ's intent to move away from rural business.

ANZ had wooed the English, Scottish, and Australian Bank four times since 1955. ES&A's conservative controls over lending and liquidity, its highly successful hire-purchase subsidiary, Esanda, and its profit-oriented administration all appealed strongly to the ANZ Board, and ES&A came from the same private trade banking tradition as both the Asia and Union. But most of all, the directors thought that a bigger bank would command more resources than either organization could raise itself. In addition, some feared that foreign banks would move in on ANZ's corporate and international business, possibly by using ES&A as a host for entry.

And so in 1970 the merger finally took place. The resulting Australia and New Zealand Banking Group became the third-largest bank in the commonwealth, double the size of the fourth-place bank. Unfortunately, despite its expanded presence in the market place, the Group's profits fell and its expenses rose during its first years, primarily because of a lax administration and unexpectedly high merger costs.

Both ES&A's and ANZ's staffs had opposed the merger, each side fearing it would lose out on the distribution of the higher posts in the new bank. Angered by this situation, the board hired an American management consultant firm in 1973 to help its executives redesign the Group's organizational structure. A modern formalized planning system specifying long- and short-range goals emerged, creating an effective and efficient environment at last. At the same time, the consultants replaced traditional profit goals with goals tied to rates of return on assets. The Group's executives felt that this change required a large amount of capital immediately. When London objected to the exportation of British capital, the Group's board realized it would be in the best interests of the bank to change its domicile. After 141 years, the headquarters of the Group were transferred from London to Melbourne on February 2, 1976, and two years later, the Group moved into the newly constructed ANZ Tower, a symbol of the total transformation in structure, philosophy, and character the bank had undergone.

During the early 1980s monetary authorities in Australia and New Zealand gradually began to relax the controls that had limited banking operations since the 1950s. This, together with a strenuous program of cost cutting, led to a substantial increase in profits. But deregulation of the industry also opened Australia and New Zealand to foreign banking. In response to this foreign competition, as well as increased domestic competition, the Group decided to try to buy strength and diversity. In 1979 it merged with the Bank of Adelaide. In 1981, the Group talked to the Commercial Banking Company of Sydney and then the Commercial Bank of Australia about merging, but neither deal worked out. In 1983 and 1984 the Group did succeed in acquiring or buying half equity in the Development Finance Corporation; the Trustees, Executors and Agency Company Ltd.; McCaughan Dyson and Company, a stockbroker; and Grindlays Bank, of England.

The acquisition of Grindlays, with representation in 40 countries, greatly strengthened the Group's international operations, compelling it to redesign its organizational structure. The bank's hierarchical arrangement of authority was replaced with a horizontal structure of more than 50 business units worldwide. These independent business units brought an entrepreneurial spirit of creativity and ambition as well as increased profits.

Although the bank's most recent acquisitions, including the 1989 purchase of New Zealand's PostBank, which made the ANZ Group the largest banking group in New Zealand, have made it a major international financial player, the Group is still largely a regional organization; in 1989, 77% of its profits came from operations in Australia and New Zealand. However, to remain competitive domestically and internationally, the Group may have to resort to more acquisitions or mergers in order to preserve the profitability of its recent years.

Principal Subsidiaries: Australia and New Zealand Banking Group Limited; ANZ Funds Pty Ltd.; ANZ Holdings (UK) plc; ANZ Life Assurance Company Ltd.; ANZ McCaughan Ltd.; Australia and New Zealand Savings Bank Ltd.; Development Finance Corporation Ltd.; Esanda Finance Corporation Ltd.; McCaughan Dyson Holdings Ltd.; Melbourne Safe Deposit Pty Ltd.

Further Reading: Butlin, S. J. *Australia and New Zealand Bank*, Longmans, 1961; *ANZ Bank: An Official History*, Sydney, Allen & Unwin Australia, 1985.

BANCA COMMERCIALE ITALIANA

BANCA COMMERCIALE ITALIANA SpA

Piazza della Scala, 6
20121 Milan
Italy
(02) 88501

Public Company
Incorporated: 1894
Employees: 21,220
Assets: L81.87 trillion (US$62.67 billion)
Stock Index: Milan Genoa Rome Turin

Banca Commerciale Italiana (BCI) is one of the largest banks in Italy. Most of its branches are concentrated near the northern industrial cities of Milan, Turin, and Genoa, but BCI also has a significant foreign presence, with branches or business operations in 45 nations. The bank is basically a short-term credit institution, and it has traditionally specialized in lending to business. BCI is listed on the Italian stock exchanges, but its major shareholder is the Istituto per la Ricostruzione Industriale (IRI), a state holding company, which owns 59% of the bank (it also controls two other major banks, Credito Italiano and Banco di Roma).

BCI's predecessor, Società Generale di Credito Mobiliare, was founded in 1862. In the newly unified Italy, this institution soon became successful as a lender to the iron and steel industry. During the Italian banking crisis of 1893–1894, however, Credito Mobiliare went under. On October 10, 1894 Credito Mobiliare was re-established as a private joint-stock bank under the name Banca Commerciale Italiana with capital from several German and Austrian banks, including Bleichröder, Deutsche Bank, and Dresdner Bank. BCI was originally modeled along the lines of German banks, making both short- and long-term loans. The young BCI continued to specialize in loans to industry, especially to companies in shipping, textiles, and electricity.

Italy suffered another depression in 1906–1907. During this crisis, the iron and steel obligations that BCI had assumed from Credito Mobiliare put the bank in a dire financial situation. In order to prevent disaster, the Bank of Italy formed a consortium of banks to lend aid to the steel and iron industry.

Prosperity soon returned. In 1911 BCI opened its first foreign branch, in London. The bank's expansion continued until 1913, when inflation finally caused business to slow.

World War I helped many companies to grow rapidly, but by 1918 overexpansion of the war industries had left several large firms failing and weighed heavily on the banks that had made loans to them. In response to this situation, BCI, Credito Italiano, Banco di Roma, and Banca Italiana di Sconto formed a cartel to coordinate the granting of capital to industry, an action that was widely criticized. Observers saw the leaders of big industry and the big banks becoming too intimate and using their collective power to sway the whole financial system.

One of the companies BCI was heavily involved with was Ansaldo, the large steel concern. At one point Ansaldo's management tried to buy up BCI's shares to gain control of the bank and save themselves from bankruptcy, but ultimately they failed to do so.

In 1918 BCI opened its second foreign branch, in New York. Growth was slow but steady during the 1920s until the stock market crash of 1929.

By 1933, BCI, like many Italian banks, was in deep trouble. That year, the government created Istituto per la Ricostruzione (IRI), a public agency, to reorganize not only the banks but also several industries. IRI became the owner of the previously private BCI, as well of Credito Italiano and Banco di Roma. It also acquired the banks' industrial holdings, thus removing them from direct involvement in these companies.

Although IRI was created as a temporary measure and had sold most of its assets by 1936 to private investors, as it had intended, the agency still retained ownership of the banks. In 1936 BCI became primarily a short-term lender when a law was passed that drew a strict line between banks that issued short-term loans and those that issued medium- and long-term loans, in an effort to mitigate some of the worst effects of mixed banking.

In 1937 BCI, Credito Italiano, and Banco di Roma were declared "banks of national interest," a designation that was applied only to banks with branches in at least 30 provinces.

During World War II much of Italian industry and agriculture was destroyed. In the years following the war, the Allied Control Commission took control of IRI and investigated its companies for wartime criminal acts, but they were eventually cleared of any blame. Once again, the plan to break IRI up and sell its parts to private investors was put off, as Italy's capital markets were still too weak.

In 1946, BCI, Credito Italiano, and Banco di Roma founded Mediobanca, a medium-term credit institution that today is a powerful force in the banking industry.

After the war, Italy managed a remarkable economic recovery as it re-entered world markets. BCI became especially active in financing imports and exports. The bank expanded its domestic business to include loans to agriculture and retained its position as the leading domestic lender. BCI also created subsidiaries for mortgage financing, leasing, and factoring.

Italy's stable and long-term growth during the 1950s and 1960s was mainly due to the growth of exports. Banking activity improved, particularly in terms of domestic bank networks, but Italy's internal economic recovery did not push banks toward international expansion. Consequently, the opening of foreign branches slowed.

BCI and the other banks of national interest were chronically lacking in capital. To remedy this, the banks were first allowed to sell shares to the public in 1969, but IRI retained the vast majority of shares. During the 1980s, IRI's ownership of BCI decreased by stages to its current 59%.

In the early 1970s, the oil crisis hurt the Italian economy, especially in the South, and the chemical and metal industries required a great deal of emergency aid from the government through the state-controlled banks. As a result, these banks found their resources concentrated in only a few enterprises.

In 1972, despite the low demand for credit and an overall rise in bank costs, with shrewd management, BCI's net profits rose substantially. But while deposits rose 19%, lending increased only 16%, an indication of the overliquidity in the banking system at that time.

Between 1973 and 1983, the Bank of Italy regulated the money supply through the institution of strict credit ceilings, which fostered competition among the banks but hampered their opportunities for growth. By the end of the 1970s, the Bank of Italy was also restricting international expansion because banks were opening subsidiaries and branches abroad and using them to get around domestic restrictions.

In July, 1981 the Bank of Italy issued guidelines for commercial banks like BCI that curbed freedom in nonbanking areas and tightened control of international ventures. At the same time, it eliminated many of the differences in the regulation of state and private banks.

In June, 1982 BCI's proposed acquisition of Litco Bancorporation, the holding company of Long Island Trust Company in New York, was approved by the United States Federal Reserve Board. By then, BCI was the second-largest commercial bank in Italy, and had branches in New York, Chicago, and Los Angeles. BCI paid $93 million for Litco and agreed to invest $20 million in the company within six months. In accordance with U.S. banking law, BCI also agreed to sell some of its interest in Lehman Brothers Kuhn Loeb Inc., an investment-banking and brokerage firm.

In 1983 the Bank of Italy lifted credit ceilings, prompting increased competition among the banks, and forcing the banks of national interest to re-examine themselves. The system was badly in need of restructuring. It was overstaffed and underproductive, in part because in Italy it was difficult to fire workers in bureaucratic posts. As a result, Italy's banks had very high operational costs by European standards; in its fragmented system of 1,200 banks, it could take up to a month for a check to clear. In addition, Italy's conservative restrictions were preventing Italian banks from achieving modernization at the level of other European banks.

In 1983, BCI and Assicurazioni Generali SpA, a large Italian insurance company, together formed GenerComit Gestione SpA, an investment management company. That year, BCI also established BCI (Suisse) and sold 35% of its interest in the Swiss Banca della Svizzera Italiano.

Throughout the 1980s, BCI continued to be active in financing imports and exports; in 1986, it accounted for 12.3% of the nation's import-export financing. But from January to June, 1986, the Bank of Italy reimposed credit ceilings on banks in an effort to control inflation. Consequently, lending slowed significantly during those six months. In December, the Bank of Italy announced its approvals for new branches, but gave the banks of national interest permission to expand only 3%, much less than had been expected.

In 1987, BCI was the largest Italian bank in terms of lending. That year the bank sold North American Bancorp (formerly Litco Bancorporation) to the Bank of New York. The bank also acquired Finservizi SpA and merged it into the company, taking advantage of the tax deductions attached to its outstanding losses. And that same year BCI created Fin. Comit SpA, a financial-services subsidiary, and opened offices in Munich and Shanghai.

In 1988, BCI transformed its Frankfurt office into a full branch, opened an office in Bombay, and added a representative offrice to its Tokyo branch. The bank also founded the BCI Funding Corporation in Delaware. Although BCI had traditionally held more deposits from companies than households, it began to extend into smaller commercial centers that year to acquire more business from household accounts. BCI established Banca Internazionale Lombarda with the help of Banque Paribas, a French bank, and the Italian insurance company Assicurazioni Generali in order to devise more innovative financial services in Italy and overseas. BCI also planned to reorganize all of its nonbanking activities under one holding company.

In April, 1988, in an effort to strengthen its American business, BCI made a $755 million bid for 51% of the Irving Bank Corporation in New York while Irving was fending off a hostile takeover bid from the Bank of New York. BCI was forced to drop its bid in August, however, because of requirements the United States Federal Reserve Board.

The Bank of Italy began to take measures in 1988 to reform its banking system before the unification of the European market in 1992. Credit controls were abolished and currency exchange controls were to be phased out. In line with this, BCI planned to double its 450 branches by 1991 by pushing into towns where it has been under-represented. In addition, in late 1989 BCI acquired a 2% stake in Compagnie Financiere de Paribas, the French banking group.

Throughout its history, BCI has played an important role in Italian banking, but the future shape of the industry is somewhat uncertain. As Italian banks vie for a place in the unified European market, it is possible that BCI will become entirely publicly owned, or even merge with another institution. In any case, it has a solid chance at securing a leading position, especially in light of its already existing international connections.

Principal Subsidiaries: Banca di Legnano S.p.A. (53.05%); Banco di Chiavari e della Riviera Ligure S.p.A. (69.62%); Comit Factoring S.p.A.; Comit Leasing S.p.A.; Fin.

Comit S.p.A.; Immobiliare Besana S.p.A. (98.43%); Banca Commerciale Italiana of Canada; Banca Commerciale Italiana (Suisse); BCI Limited (70%); BCI Nominees Limited; Societe Europeenne de Banque S.A. (55%); La Gardanella S.r.l.; S.I.R.E.F Societa Italiana di Revisione e Fiduciaria S.p.A. (60%); SATA Sociedade de Assessoria Tecnica e Administrativa S.A.; Servita S.A.; GenerComit Distribuzione S.p.A. (50%); GenerComit Gestione S.p.A. (50%); I.L.S.A. Idroelettrica Ligure S.r.l. (80%); Societa Trezza S.p.A. (76.65%); North American Bancorp, Inc. (74%); Comit Finance (Jersey).

BANCO BILBAO VIZCAYA, S.A.

Gran Via 12
Bilbao, Vizcaya 48001
Spain
(341) 582-6000

Public Company
Incorporated: 1988
Employees: 33,000
Assets: Pts 6.2 trillion (US$54.72 billion) (1987)
Stock Index: Madrid London Frankfurt

In January 1988 Banco de Bilbao and Banco de Vizcaya shocked the financial world by merging to become Spain's largest bank. Both banks had grown from their bases in Bilbao, where they financed the railroad, mining, steel, and shipping industries. And both banks had weathered Spain's repeated financial crises and the major economic disruptions of its brutal civil war to emerge as strong, well-managed financial institutions.

When they merged in 1988, they did so to assure continued profitability after the integration of the European Economic Community in 1992. The merger positioned Banco Bilbao Vizcaya to compete effectively, both domestically and internationally, under the new banking rules that go with EEC membership.

Banco de Bilbao was the older of the two banks. After laws were passed in 1856 allowing the creation of banks and thrift institutions, the Trade Association of Bilbao, a group of businessmen in the developing Basque area, established an office on the Calle de la Estufa in Bilbao to provide financial assistance to businesses. The new bank took over functions formerly filled by the Bilbao consular office, which closed. The Trade Association was also authorized to issue bank notes.

The Trade Association of Bilbao, soon known as Banco de Bilbao, continued to issue notes and business loans until 1878, when the Bank of Spain was named the sole issuer of bank notes for the country. Banco de Bilbao didn't acquiesce quietly, but its lobbying efforts against the change failed. As a result, the bank reorganized. Banco de Bilbao continued to specialize in business loans, but in a step unique to Spanish banking, it also established the first savings bank in Spain, the savings association Sociedad Bilbaina General de Credito.

Those new financial activities made Banco de Bilbao a major backer of the industrial development in the north, which turned Bilbao and the neighboring Vizcaya into Spain's industrial center in the last decades of the 19th century and produced the highest per capita income in the country. Banco de Bilbao helped finance the construction of the Port of Bilbao as well as the development of railroad transport and the mining and steel industries.

Banco de Bilbao was able to become involved in these projects because it was virtually the only game in town until the end of the century. Branches of the Bank of Spain, the Caja General de Depositos, and the Banco de Castilla were established in Bilbao, but as the only independent local financial entity, Banco de Bilbao was able to take a leading position in financing heavy industry.

Because of this role in industry, the bank was able not only to weather financial storms that shook Spain in the last half of the 19th century, including the panic of 1896 that caused much of the Spanish banking system to fail, but even to remain profitable.

Banco de Bilbao built on its position of strength with a two-part strategy of expansion—domestic and international—as the new century opened. The bank began its international expansion by establishing a Paris branch in 1902, becoming the first Spanish bank to have a foreign presence. At home, Banco de Bilbao merged with the Banco de Comercio to extend its industrial financing activities.

World War I meant disruption for the Spanish economy and operating problems for Banco de Bilbao's branches in other European centers such as Paris and London. But because of Banco de Bilbao's continued investments in emerging industries and capital improvements, the war in fact promoted the bank's expansion. It formed subsidiary companies and entered into joint ventures to finance major industrialization projects. The institution was not alone in this enviable financial situation; Banco de Vizcaya and Banco de Bilbao worked together in these years, promoting and financing industrial ventures. Other banks in the north that financed industrialization also emerged from the war in good shape.

The postwar years were marked by economic nationalism in Spain, a policy entrenched under the Second Republic. Under that policy Banco de Bilbao's emphasis on underwriting nascent industrialization again led to profits.

The stockmarket crash of 1929 had a major impact in Spain. The financial crisis led to insolvency for such major Spanish financial institutions as Banco de Barcelona and Credito de la Union Minera.

On the heels of the Depression came the Spanish Civil War. The ideological battle between the Loyalists, who were faithful to the liberal constitution of the republic that replaced the monarchy in 1931, and the Nationalists, who campaigned for Spain's identification as a Catholic nation, devastated a country that was still considered underdeveloped and even backward by the standards of the rest of Europe. When Francisco Franco came to power in 1939, the country faced huge material losses at home. Land, neglected during the conflict, was not immediately productive again. Industries found it difficult to obtain raw materials, equipment, and fuel. Then came the isolation imposed by the Allies during World War II. Spaniards called the 1940s "the years of hunger."

Franco's government attempted to meet these economic problems with tight new regulations on banking. Franco's Ministerial Order of May 17, 1940 established a policy of adhering to the banking status quo. To meet this new form of government intervention, Banco de Bilbao expanded into other parts of Spain through acquisition (between 1941 and 1943, it acquired 16 banks), reorganized its internal structure to operate effectively at a national level, and expanded its international presence. The bank gave its London and Paris offices a greater role in company operations, and in 1945 it established a branch specifically to form contacts for cooperative ventures in the United States and South America. While the bank continued to emphasize industrial development, more important after World War II than ever, it also developed commercial activities and provided personal financial services.

The first centennial of the Banco de Bilbao in 1957 coincided with another event that would have a major impact on its future. That was the year the European Economic Community was formed, the first step toward an international economy. While not immediately ready to integrate its economy into the European economy, Spain became a member of the International Monetary Fund, the International Bank for Reconstruction and Development, and the Organization for European Economic Cooperation (OEEC) in 1958 and 1959.

Spain's immediate task was to halt the country's financial decline. Franco's government passed a stabilization plan in 1959 that devalued the peseta, placed a ceiling on government spending and on credit for government agencies (which had been fueling inflation), limited private credit expansion, improved tax collection, abolished price controls, froze wages, established higher bank rates, and encouraged foreign investment. With the stabilization plan and full membership in the OEEC came foreign assistance in redevelopment. The U.S. government, a group of U.S. banks, the OEEC, and the International Monetary Fund jointly pledged $5.75 million in assistance, with promises of more to come.

By 1962, a new government department was created to plan and coordinate economic development, and the Law of Banking and Credit institutionalized the preeminent position of the major Spanish banks. As a result of the changes, Banco de Bilbao reorganized again, becoming a multi-purpose bank at home and creating a subsidiary, the Banco Industrial de Bilbao, to continue its emphasis on developing new industrial companies.

By the end of the 1960s, analysts were talking of a Spanish economic miracle. Centers of industrialization such as Bilbao experienced relative prosperity as factories created jobs and acceptable standards of living for the working class, produced opportunities for commerce for the middle class, and increased the wealth of the owners. The so-called miracle was again profitable for Banco de Bilbao.

In the 1970s Banco de Bilbao continued to develop into a diversified financial group and into a consumer bank as well. In 1970 the bank began a campaign to attract female customers, in 1971 it began to issue credit cards, and in 1972 it offered "instant credit" to attract customers.

The inflationary pressures of the decade, due especially to skyrocketing oil costs, led to laws that again strengthened the position of the big Spanish banks. A program to combat inflation adopted in 1974 raised the bank rate 1% to make it comparable to international rates. The program also extended access to credit, making business investments easier. And it allowed banks more flexibility by eliminating differences between industrial and commercial banks. The revamping of the banking system encouraged Banco de Bilbao's development into commercial services. The bank was also able to absorb six Spanish banks that weren't able to adapt as successfully.

Diversification and expansion continued into the 1980s after Franco's death and the return of the monarchy. By this time Banco de Bilbao had become a major financial group with 16 banks in Spain and abroad and 50 companies providing banking-related financial services.

Spain's entry into the European Economic Community (EEC) in 1986, with its promise of full integration into the European economy by 1992 and fewer restrictions on competition throughout the European market, prompted Banco de Bilbao to look for the opportunity to grow still larger. Despite the long-term trend toward aggregation of financial services, Spain still had more banks per capita than other European countries, and analysts suggested that the Spanish banking system would be more competitive if it had fewer stronger banks.

To remain competitive by becoming larger, Banco de Bilbao took an unprecedented step in 1987 when it made a hostile takeover bid for its rival, Banco Español de Credito, known as Banesto. Banesto was ranked as Spain's number-two bank while Banco de Bilbao was ranked number three, but a tradition of feuding among the families on Banesto's board made it a takeover target. Banco de Bilbao had to drop its bid when three of the four Spanish stock exchanges that must approve a takeover bid announced they would not allow the takeover—only the Bilbao exchange had been in favor of Banco de Bilbao's bid. Jose Angel Sanchez Asiain, the bank's chairman, told the *New York Times*, "One day someone will have the answer for this historic failure, which halts the modernization of Spain."

Despite the failure of its bid for Banesto, Banco de Bilbao still wanted to grow to meet the new economic realities. And so, on January 27, 1988, Banco de Bilbao merged with its local rival, Banco de Vizcaya. Both banks were considered well-managed organizations in very much the same market. It was "the concern by both banks for efficiency and the capacity to generate income, which made it possible to easily overcome the resistance to losing one's individuality," Asiain said of the merger.

In a speech on the merger, Banco de Vizcaya's chairman, Pedro Toledo Ugarte, alluded to the historical tendency of businessmen in Bilbao to unite to form larger corporations in order to face changes they could not face with their own resources. He saw Spain's entry into the EEC as one of those challenges. "Given the importance of the financial sector, every country wants some of the institutions which compete worldwide to be made up of and managed by its own people," he said. "We all know that this requires management, technologies and, without doubt, a minimum size."

Banco de Vizcaya had a history very similar to that of its new partner. Founded in 1901 to serve Bilbao merchants, Banco de Vizcaya made commercial loans and took business deposits. From this start, the bank expanded throughout the Basque country and then into the rest of Spain.

Banco de Vizcaya began its expansion by absorbing Banco Vascongado in 1903 and Banca Jacquet e Hijos in 1915. In 1918 it earned a national presence when it absorbed the Banca Luis Roy Sobrino in Madrid and made it into Banco de Vizcaya's first branch in the capital. By the 1920s, its expansion policy had resulted in new branches in San Sebastian, Barcelona, and Valencia. The end of the decade saw a strong network of Banco de Vizcaya branches throughout Spain and the beginnings of a presence in France, with its investment in the Banque Française et Espagnol en Paris.

With such a network in place, Banco de Vizcaya became involved in the same sort of industrial financing in which Banco de Bilbao was specializing at the same time. This emphasis meant that even when the crash of 1929 hit the Spanish economy hard, Banco de Vizcaya generated profits and was still able to pay its shareholders dividends.

By 1935 the bank had 200 offices. Despite the 1940 restrictions on banking, Banco de Vizcaya continued to grow, primarily through acquisitions of banks that were in weaker positions. The bank aggressively promoted business through the next 20 years, especially chemicals, textiles, paper, construction, and real estate.

Besides expanding through absorptions and new branches, Banco de Vizcaya became a more diversified financial-services group in the 1960s. It founded Induban in 1964 as its industrial-banking arm, Finsa in 1965 as its real estate-property investment company, Gesbancaya in 1970 as a personal-investment management company, and Liscaya in 1971 as a leasing company for major corporations. Banco de Vizcaya also developed an insurance company when it became part of Plus-Ultra in 1972. At the same time, the bank expanded internationally into Mexico City, New York, Amsterdam, and London, and became heavily involved in the Eurocurrency markets. And the bank rationalized its own operations by completely automating its services. In 1967 the bank set up regional administration centers with direct links to a central electronic data-processing center.

In 1970 Banco de Vizcaya also began to move in another direction, consumer services. The bank was a pioneer in the introduction of credit cards, automated teller machines, gasoline checks, and other consumer products.

The liberalization of banking regulations in 1974 led to further expansion for Banco de Vizcaya. The bank's 305 offices in 1970 had grown to 904 offices by 1980. And in 1979 managers took a step that was not yet common among Spanish banks: calling upon an independent auditing firm to publicly document its position, a move that has had an impact upon Spanish banking ever since.

Banco de Bilbao and Banco Vizcaya were both established to serve business; both financed industrial development in Spain, weathered changing economic conditions by being adaptable to new ways of doing business, and took every opportunity to expand. The two banks are profitable. Together, they should have the scale to continue that profitability in an economic climate that once again means dramatic changes as Spain is incorporated into the European Economic Community.

Principal Subsidiaries: Banco Vizcaya S.A.; Banca Catalana; Banca Mas Mas Sarda; Banco de Crédito Canario, S.A.; Banco de Crédito y Ahorro, S.S.; Banco de Extremadora, S.A.; Banco de Financiacion Industrial, S.A.; Banco de Promoción de Negocios, S.A.; Banco del Comercio, S.A.; Banco del Oeste, S.A.; Banco Industrial del Sur, S.A.; Banco Meridional, S.A.; Banco Occidental, S.A.; Bilbao Merchant Bank, S.A.; Banco Bilbao Vizcaya (Deutschland), A.G. (West Germany); Banco Bilbao Vizcaya (Panama), S.A.; Banco Commercial de Mayaguez, S.A.; Banco de Bilbao (Gibraltar), Ltd.; Banco de Bilbao (Suisse), S.A. (Switzerland); Banque de Gestión Financiere, S.A.; Bilbao Vizcaya Bank (Jersey), Ltd. (U.K.); Ahorro Intercontinental, S.A.; Asgard Estates, Ltd.; Europea de Arrendanuentos, S.A.; Cestión Contratación y Promocion Inmobiliaria, S.A.; Inmobiliaria Bernardo, S.A.; Inmobiliaria Estrella Polar, S.A.; Immobiliaria Guadaira, S.A.; Inversiones Katzen, S.A.; Mobe, S.A.; Prevensey, Inc.; Promociones Inmobiliarias Bancaya, S.A.; Administradora de Patrimonios, S.A.; Bilbao Hambros Asset Management (Guernsey), Ltd. (U.K.); Bilbao Vizcaya Holding, S.A.; Catalana de Estudies Economicos, S.A.; Catalana de Pensiones, S.A.; Enuidad Gestura de Fondos de Pensiones; Celacove C.N., S.A.; Dynamic Management Services, Ltd.; Gescatalana U.S.A.; Gescatalana, S.A.; Gescaya, S.A.; Gestinova, S.A.; Gestion de Patrimonios Bancaya, S.A.; Sogescaya, S.A.

Further Reading: "Banco Bilbao Vizcaya," Banco Bilbao Vizcaya, Bilbao, Spain, 1988.

BANCO CENTRAL

49 Alcala
Madrid 28014
Spain
532 8810

Public Company
Incorporated: 1919
Employees: 23,711
Assets: Pts4.90 trillion (US$43.25 billion)
Stock Index: Madrid Barcelona Bilbao Valencia London Paris Frankfurt New York Toronto

Banco Central was founded in Madrid on December 6, 1919 by the Marquis of Aldama, the Count of Los Gaitanes, and Juan Nũnez Anchustegui. These businessmen realized that the economic growth of the post–World War I era would require financing—and could lead to profits. Banco Central quickly became a major actor in emerging industries, especially coal, iron and steel, shipping, and papermaking. In 1921, the bank made its first major acquisition, of Banco de Albacete, and by 1922, it had established 18 branches. Banco Central was on its way to meeting its goals of promoting industrial development and establishing a presence throughout the country.

Postwar economic nationalism led to similar expansion throughout the banking industry during the 1920s, but not all the expansion could be supported by Spain's underdeveloped industrial base. When the U.S. stock market crash in 1929 led to a worldwide depression, Spanish banks were hard hit. Banco Central's investments in heavy industry gave it a strong position, however, and it was able to continue its policy of growth through merger and acquisition by taking over some of its ailing peers.

Government measures passed in 1931 to meet the crisis in Spanish banking consolidated Banco Central's position. Under the new laws, the Bank of Spain was made responsible for centralized banking functions and would no longer serve the public. This opened a new share of the market for other banks, and Banco Central moved aggressively to fill it.

Following the Depression came a new crisis for Spain. The Spanish Civil War pitted Loyalists faithful to the liberal constitution of the republic (which had replaced the monarchy in 1931) against Nationalists, who stood for Spain's traditional identification as an autocratic Catholic country. The conflict devastated nascent industrial development and set back Spaniards' hopes for a better standard of living. When Francisco Franco came to power in 1939, he faced neglected land that could no longer feed the people and severe shortages of raw materials, including fuel.

Many of Banco Central's branches were located in the republican zone, subject to nationalist blockade. But under the bank's new chairman of the board, Ignacio Villalonga, the bank consolidated its position to become one of the Big Five of Spanish banking after the war.

One reason for Banco Central's growth was that its policy of acquiring or merging with other banking institutions was compatible with the tight new regulations on banking that Franco instituted in an attempt to put Spain back on its feet. in May 1940, Franco passed restrictions preventing banks from entering new areas of business. The only way for banks to grow under these restrictions was to acquire the existing operations of other banks, and Banco Central's business investments gave it the ready money to do so.

The devastation left by the war presented the bank with many opportunities. Like other major Spanish banks, Banco Central created industries from the ground up, providing not only capital but also managerial expertise to run the new firms. The bank often gained seats on the boards of directors of the companies it financed. This close relationship between banks and industry led to a high rate of postwar industrialization, although Spain remained underdeveloped compared to the rest of Europe. It also solidified Banco Central's position in the business world.

In 1958 and 1959 the Franco government took steps to improve the country's depressed economic condition, joining the International Monetary Fund, the International Bank for Reconstruction and Development, and the Organization for European Economic Cooperation (OEEC). In 1959, with the help of these international organizations, the government set up a financial stabilization plan. The plan's provisions included devaluing the peseta; limiting government spending; limiting both government and private credit, which had fueled inflation; improving tax collection; abolishing price controls; freezing wages; establishing higher bank rates; and encouraging foreign investment. In addition, the International Monetary Fund, the OEEC, the U.S. government, and a group of U.S. banks came up with $5.75 million in assistance.

In 1962 the reforms continued with the establishment of a new government department to plan and coordinate economic development, and laws reforming Spanish banking were passed in April and June that year. These laws nationalized and reorganized the Bank of Spain and gave all authority over currency and credit to the government. In effect, the reforms institutionalized the positions of the major Spanish banks.

In the new financial environment, Banco Central continued to concentrate on developing industries that could meet rising consumer expectations. During the 1960s, Banco Central created Saltos del Sil, a hydroelectric development in Galicia; Compania Espanola de Petroleos S.A., the first privately owned petroleum company in the country; and Dragados y Construcciones S.A., a leader in the construction industry. To comply with the new banking regulations, Banco Central also formed Banco de Fomento in 1963 to compete in the newly established industrial bank category.

By the end of the 1960s, analysts abroad referred to a Spanish "economic miracle." A rising standard of living and increased opportunities for middle-class business ventures led Banco Central to offer more consumer services, such as credit and checking accounts.

Even so, by the beginning of the 1970s, Spanish banks were known for their conservative approach to doing business, the legacy of Franco's restrictive measures. In comparison to other European banking systems, there were too many Spanish banks in proportion to the population. Spanish banks also had too many branches and their staffs were too large. Those weaknesses were demonstrated all too well when rising oil prices in the 1970s led to raging inflation and the collapse of many firms—along with the banks that had lent them money. To combat inflation, the government raised the bank rate to make it comparable to international rates, extended business access to credit, and eliminated legal restrictions between industrial and commercial banks.

Banco Central concentrated on "saving" other financial entities during this period by buying them up as they failed and making them part of the Banco Central chain. The bank doubled its number of operating offices between 1970 and 1975, bringing its total to over 1,000 offices. Banco Central also followed a strategy of financially supporting Spanish industrial capacity, which increased the bank's influence in industry.

By the 1980s, Banco Central was the largest Spanish bank, but it was not considered flexible enough to compete effectively in the liberalized and internationalized Spanish economy of the post-Franco era since its longtime chairman, Alfonso Escamez (known as "the dean of Spanish banking") refused to reduce his operating costs to become more competitive.

If Escamez refused to modernize, the Spanish banking community was not immune to the forces of change. As the gentlemanly traditions of the financial world crumbled in the face of the new need to compete effectively, cousins Alberto Alcocer and Alberto Cortina (*los Albertos* to the popular press) put their business acumen to work to challenge Escamez. From their base as operators of their wives' construction company Construcciones y Contratas (Conycon) and executors of family money, the cousins began to buy Banco Central stock in 1988, eventually joining forces with the Kuwait Investment Office (KIO) for about a 12% stake. The cousins then demanded a managerial role in the bank and received five of the 24 seats on the bank's board. They were determined to streamline operations and make it an international player. "We knew that the management of Banco Central was antiquated but we trusted our instincts, our people and management capabilities to improve it," Cortina told the *Financial Times*.

Escamez, however, was furious, and determined not to allow control to be wrested from him by young businessmen with foreign money. He offered to buy them out. Failing that, he turned to another tactic, merger with Banco Espanol de Credito (Banesto) and its friendly chairman, the young Mario Conde, to offset the influence of his challengers. The new unit was to be named Banco Espanol Central de Credito, and with consolidated assets of over Pts7 trillion (about $60 billion) it would have become one of the top 25 banks in Europe.

Forty-year-old Conde was new to his position (he became chairman in December 1987). *Newsweek* had described his appointment as "a changing of the guard . . . in Spain's financial community." But Banesto, Spain's second-largest bank, still represented old-line financial conservatism and family-oriented elite control, just as Banco Central did. Conde had taken over from 78-year-old Pablo Granica, who had followed his father in controlling Banesto. Both banks were seen as cumbersome and old-fashioned, without the flexibility to compete effectively in the new market that EEC membership would mean.

The planned merger also failed to stop the original impetus for it: the Albertos began to buy up Banesto stock so they would continue to have a voice in management of the new merged unit.

When the Albertos assured Conde that they would sell out of Banesto if the merger were called off, the nine-month-old plan came to an inglorious end. The Kuwait Investment Office sold its Spanish banking interests (and then invested in other Spanish industries). Cortina resigned from his seat on the board of Conycon in the wake of a scandal about an extramarital affair and was replaced by his wife. Conde was left to bring Banesto back to financial viability on his own, and Escamez was left back in control at Banco Central, with no successor in sight.

Banco Central has a long history of financing the development of Spanish industry and its name is one of the most prestigious names in Spanish banking. With a network of branches in 23 countries, especially Latin America, where it has traditional ties, it also has a strong international presence. But as full membership in the EEC looms, its history and size alone are not enough to ensure success. It will also have to take some difficult steps toward a more streamlined operation.

Principal Subsidiaries: Banco Popular Argentino; Banco de Valencia; Banco de Fomento; Banco Central of New York (U.S.); Banco Central Corp. (Puerto Rico); Banco de Asunción (Paraguay); Banco Central of Canada; Centrobanco (Panama); Banco de Granada; Banco Internacional de Comercio; Banco Gallego.

Further Reading: "Banco Central History," Madrid, Spain, Banco Central S.A., 1988.

BANCO DO BRASIL S.A.

SBS Edificio
Sede III
21st Floor
70073 Brasilia-DF
Brazil
(61) 212-24-90

Public Company
Incorporated: 1808
Employees: 135,425
Assets: Cz61.38 trillion (US$81.54 billion)
Stock Index: Brazil

The history of Banco do Brasil intertwines with that of Brazil itself. A Portuguese colony since 1500, Brazil was for centuries held under tight commercial restraint, forbidden any industry except for shipbuilding and sugar manufacturing. Even salt, in this coastal country, was imported from Portugal.

But restrictions were relaxed in the early part of the 19th century as Portugal faced war after ignoring Napoleon's demand that all European ports be closed to the British. With no prospect of fighting off Napoleon, Portugal's prince regent, Dom João, his family, and 15,000 subjects fled across the Atlantic Ocean to Brazil. João established a monarchy in Rio de Janeiro and improved trade relations between Brazil and Europe. He created the Banco do Brasil on October 12, 1808, before Portugal had its own bank, as the bank for the Portuguese Court. It was Portugal's principal depository for years.

The bank built schools and hospitals, investing heavily in the country well into the late 1800s. Banco do Brasil also equipped Brazil's navy in its battles for independence from Portugal in the 1820s. When Brazil became a republic in 1889, the bank was a major player in restoring stability to the country's economy. Brazil had been left in shambles after the Portuguese conflict, which caused the fall of the monarchy.

During the period of rebuilding, Banco do Brasil became the country's main bank, the government's financial agent, and both a commercial and development bank focusing on rural areas, exports, and domestic business.

In the last decades of the 19th century, there was another switch in the country's structure, when Brazil's slaves became wage earners. In 1888 Banco do Brasil signed an agreement with the government to ensure the availability of credit for agriculture. The new financing encouraged immigrant settlement in rural areas and was the beginning of an organized push to develop agriculture. The bank opened a branch in 1908 in Manaus, the heart of the Amazon region, to stimulate rubber production. Financial incentives brought people from all over the world, but especially from Italy, to Brazil's rich and plentiful coffee plantations. The flood of immigrants continued past the turn of the century.

Internally, Banco do Brasil was tightening its house. The bank began giving public exams to new employees. So rigid were the tests that in 1909, ten out of the 35 candidates couldn't even complete the exam; of the remainder, only nine passed.

In 1937, the bank created its Agricultural and Industrial Credit Division (CREAI). The division provided the country with a credit program to encourage and support agricultural and industrial development. With CREAI's assistance, Companhia Siderúrgica Nacional, Brazil's first steel mill, was built in the 1940s.

CREAI was involved in almost every aspect of Brazilian agriculture, from rice, cashew nuts, and fruit to sugar cane and coffee. CREAI's agricultural activities eventually turned Banco do Brasil into one of the world's largest agricultural banks.

In 1941, Banco do Brasil laid the foundation for foreign trade support, opening a branch office in Asunción, Paraguay, and then later that same year opening its export and import division.

During World War II, Banco do Brasil provided the troops' payroll as well as war reparations and money transfers to the Brazilian Expeditionary Force. To help operations, three offices were opened in Italy and mobile units were sent to the front lines. The bank also set up a special system through which soldiers could withdraw or deposit cash using passbook entries.

Banco do Brasil's foreign activities continued long after the war, and in 1953, it established a foreign trade division. But it was in 1969, with the opening of its branch in New York, that the bank really became international.

The 1960s were a time of upheaval for all Brazilian banks. In 1964, the government, with increasing inflation on its hands, faced the deficiencies of the country's financial institutions. At the time, short-term lending was the business of commercial banks, which gave them dominance over other financial institutions. Long-term financing was carried out by state institutions, but with growing inflation, these loans were no better than "donations," wrote Oswaldo R. Colin, chairman of the board for Banco do Brasil, in *American Banker*.

The 1964 Banking Reform Law totally restructured the banking system. New types of securities became available, special credit services were offered, and medium- and long-term investments were favored. Banks began to compete by offering increased services such as guaranteed overdraft checking rights and credit cards, and competition, especially among commercial banks, heated up.

The reform law and resolutions that followed initiated a move away from small, specialized banks toward larger institutions offering a variety of services. In 1950, for example, Brazil had 404 banks; by 1972, there were only

128. During the same period in the late 1960s and 1970s the number of branches grew from about 4,000 to 11,000.

In 1975, Banco do Brasil created a fund for scientific research, backing many health and agricultural projects such as the manufacture of artifical arteries, vaccines against measles, hydroelectric turbines suited for rural areas, and better methods for extracting sugar from cane.

Supporting Brazil's business community, especially small businesses, had become a major concern for the bank by the end of the 1970s, and in 1979, the bank created a program that provided financial assistance and technical guidance to small businesses. In 1982 the bank offered a fund to increase agricultural activity, diversify crops, and foster cottage industries. Other projects included building dams, schools, health centers, and small hospitals.

Banco do Brasil entered the credit card business in 1987, signing with Visa International and announcing plans to issue one million cards that first year. Prior to Visa, the bank offered no credit card and up until the mid-1980s handled most of its business through deposits. "Brazil is the largest country in Latin America, with 140 million people, and despite its recent economic problems it has the potential to be a very big consumer credit market," James F. Partridge, Visa's chief general manager for Latin America, told *American Banker* at the time.

In 1988, a new finance minister, Mailson Ferreira da Nobrega, came into power and Banco do Brasil's president, Camilo Calazans, was replaced by the finance ministry's general secretary, Mario Berard. The move came on the heels of the forced resignation of Brazil's central bank president.

Looking ahead to the 1990s, Banco do Brasil intends to diversify activities, increase private sector assistance, moderate interest rates, and play a stabilizing role in Brazil's financial system.

Principal Subsidiaries: Acesita Energética S.A.; BB-Financeira S.A.; BB-Leasing S.A.; BB-Corretora de Seguros e Administradora de Bens S.A.; BB-Administradora de Cartões de Crédito S.A.

BANK BRUSSELS LAMBERT

24 Avenue Marnix
1050 Brussels
Belgium
(02) 517–21–11

Public Company
Incorporated: 1975
Employees: 16,883
Assets: BFr1.8 trillion (US$48.4 billion)
Stock Index: Brussels Antwerp Ghent Liege

Belgium's second largest commercial bank, Bank Brussels Lambert (BBL) was created in 1975 by the merger of Banque de Bruxelles and Banque Lambert. Separately, each bank had survived more than a century of Belgium's often chaotic and war-torn history, and together they now face the more orderly but equally challenging unification of the European market and the intensified competition it will bring. An international orientation is nothing new for Belgian banks, however; situated at the economic crossroads of Europe, Belgium has of necessity always depended on foreign trade, for that reason developing a group of unusually cosmopolitan banks and bankers. Neither Banque de Bruxelles (BB) nor Banque Lambert (BL), for example, was founded by Belgian natives, and throughout their history both were actively involved in the often-byzantine windings of international monetary exchange. From the funding of the rubber trade in Belgian Congo to the day when all of Europe uses one currency, BBL will have maintained a consistently internationalist approach to its task of providing both the Belgian government and private industry with a reliable source of capital.

The precursor to Banque Lambert was founded in Brussels shortly after Belgium won independence in 1831. At that time, the enterprising Rothschild family opened its first Belgian office, adding, within a few years, a second bank in Antwerp under the direction of Samuel Lambert, a Frenchman born in Lyon in 1811. When the head of the main Rothschild branch in Brussels died, Lambert was named as the Rothschild's manager for all of Belgium. Samuel was succeeded by his son Léon Lambert, who moved the bank offices to the elegant former residence of the Marquis d'Ennetières in 1883 and solidified his ties to the Rothschilds by marrying a woman from the French side of that family. Léon furthered his aristocratic aspirations by working closely with the king of Belgium, Léopold II, in financing the king's venture into what became the Belgian Congo. For his help in this colonial experiment, Lambert was made a baron, a title inherited by his son Henri when the latter assumed command of the bank after World War I. Baron Henri Lambert took advantage of the booming economy of the mid-1920s to split away from the Rothschilds and form his own company, Banque Lambert. His first customers were friends of the family, and the bank remained a selective and largely aristocratic institution during its first decades.

When the Nazis occupied Belgium, the Lamberts were forced to flee to England and the United States, and it was not until 1949 that a second Léon Lambert, Henri's son, took control of the bank which bore his name. With the 1953 acquisition of la Banque de Reports et de Depots, BL entered a phase of more aggressive expansion, especially into foreign trade and stock exchange funds. In 1972, a young associate manager at BL named Jacques Thierry steered the company to a merger with Brufina, the large industrial investment holding company formerly a part of Banque de Bruxelles. Thus introduced, the two banks quickly realized that they themselves could benefit from a merger, and in 1975 BBL was formed, with Thierry as president. Fourteen years later, Thierry remains chairman of the combined board of directors.

Banque Lambert's new partner had been in business since 1871. In that year, a young Venetian with the appropriately pan-European name of Jacques Errera-Oppenheim took advantage of Belgium's central location and relatively open economy by founding a large new bank in Brussels. With a group of German and Dutch financiers, he created the Banque de Bruxelles, capitalized with the unusually large sum of BFr50 million. The bank sold government bonds and lent to both private business and the government, but after a few profitable years it was caught in the slump of 1875–1876 and rapidly lost the confidence of its largely German investors. BB was forced to liquidate and reform itself as a smaller entity with the same name, after which it proceeded to grow quickly. BB was a "mixed" bank, active as both a depository for the savings of businesses and individuals and as an equity investor in the industrial sphere—since a large percentage of Belgian assets were still tied up in land, banks had to scramble for the relatively small amount of capital in circulating form.

After weathering the worldwide recession of 1890–1893, BB accelerated its investments in heavy industry, taking significant positions in the steel, coal, transportation, and electric power industries. Its total assets grew at a tremendous pace during the decades leading up to World War I—from BFr39 million in 1877 to BFr628 million just before the war. Many of these assets were tied up in foreign and colonial investments, since BB also took an active role in Belgium's imperial ambitions.

World War I required of BB a greatly increased involvement in the public sector, as it joined the other Belgian banks in trying to keep up with the payment of war indemnities and the floating of interprovincial loans. In a remarkable demonstration of the international nature of modern capital, in 1916 BB took over the Banque

Internationale de Bruxelles, an institution owned by Germans, the power that then occupied Belgium. BB also helped to form the new Banque de Louvain, and in general came through the war in excellent financial condition, its assets nearly doubling to BFr1.2 billion.

In 1919, Maurice Despret became the new chairman of BB, bringing with him an ambitious plan for expansion. Despret first created a widespread network of retail branches throughout Belgium and in the Congo, gradually bringing these under the centralized administration of five geographical groups. The chairman also pursued further investments in heavy industry, setting up six new corporations that were later collected into two holding companies, Electrobel and Companie Belge pour l'industie. Finally, Despret tried to improve BB's overseas connections, working hard to organize the bank's holdings in the Congo as well as seeking new business in Europe and America. In the excellent business climate of the 1920s, these steps were extremely successful, and total assets and profits both rose rapidly despite a number of minor setbacks. At the close of the decade, BB's assets were nearly ten times what they had been at the end of the war, inspiring the confidence and over-speculation which came to an abrupt halt in October of 1929.

The Belgian economy muddled through the first few years of the Depression with some success, but by 1934 the country was nearing a general panic and the van Zeeland government was forced to take action. Since the public at large felt that banks were responsible for the Depression, van Zeeland and his finance minister, Max-Leo Gérard, set out to reform the country's antiquated banking system. One part of their reform was aimed at mixed banks like BB. To satisfy critics who suspected, quite reasonably, that companies owned by banks received undue consideration from their parents, it was declared that all banks would have to restrict themselves either to investment banking or to the deposits and loan business. On December 28, 1934, therefore, the Banque de Bruxelles' investment portfolio became Brufina, a new corporation, while its deposits-and-loan business was taken up by a newly formed Banque de Bruxelles. The companies are required by law to remain separate entitles, but over the years they have continued in close association.

Though these reforms may have helped the banking industry, they did little to solve the basic weakness of the economy, which continued unchanged until World War II erupted in 1939. As in the first war, Belgium spent years under foreign occupation, suffering the combined problems of massive deflation and German demands for equally massive war indemnity payments. BB tried to help the government make these payments, but the period up to and following liberation in 1944 was at best precarious. BB was aided during this bleak struggle by the leadership of former Finance Minister Gérard, who became the bank's chairman in 1939 and remained in that capacity until 1952. Gérard steered the bank through the difficulties of war and the equally challenging task of postwar monetary reform, when Belgium's currency was completely revamped and various other economic reforms were enacted.

Banking in Belgium had evolved into quite a different business than it had been before the reforms of 1934. These, and, to a lesser degree, reforms enacted immediately after the war, made banking into what a later chairman of BB would call "*presque public*"—almost a part of the public sector economy. Reacting to the chaos of the private sector during the Depression, the government decreed that all banks had to keep 65% of their deposits available for loans to the state, which was busily setting up nationalized industrial combines. This program, though stringent by American standards, was readily accepted by Gérard and BB as the Belgian economy accustomed itself to the idea of close cooperation between state and industry. As the repository of capital needed by both partners, the banks became part of a comprehensive planned economy rather than remaining independent agents. The mixed economy thus evolved seems to have worked well for all concerned, and not least the banks. To hold up its end of the bargain with government and industry, BB was forced to raise its capital sharply, from BFr200 million in 1945 to BFr700 million in 1951 and to BFr2.5 billion by 1964; profits have also increased, if not quite proportionately, at least in a continuous upward spiral.

Overseeing the postwar expansion was Louis Camu, chairman since Gérard's retirement in 1952. To take advantage of the greatly increased deposits made by a more prosperous public, Camu designed a program of expansion in both the national and overseas markets. Though prohibited by the reforms of 1934 from holding equity in other companies, BB furthered its expertise in the analysis and management of business affairs, seeking in that way to become more useful to its private borrowers. In 1953, BB introduced its first certified deposits, part of an effort to win a greater share of the retail-banking business across the country. BB has been in the vanguard of the electronic revolution in banking, offering its first automated teller machine as early as 1969 and continuing to upgrade its extensive computer facilities as a matter of course. On the international side, BB participated in the ever-expanding foreign investment and monetary exchange of the Belgian banks. In the mid-1960s, BB entered into special cooperation agreements with two of the world's largest banks, Barclays of London and Chase Manhattan in New York; and in 1971 it was asked to join the influential European banking syndicate, Société Financiére Européenne. In a world growing ever more complex and interdependent, BB has positioned itself to take advantage of the coming changes.

Most important, of course, was the 1975 merger with Banque Lambert. By combining the assets and experience of two of the country's leading banks, BBL strengthened its chances of surviving the gradual economic unification of Europe. With trade barriers gone, European bankers will soon be pressed by rivals from across the continent as well as by their traditional local competitors, and the battle for deposit-and-loan dollars will no doubt be prolonged and bitter. In anticipation of this struggle, Chairman Thierry has reorganized the bank according to five market segments—households, private investors, the Belgian corporate sector, multinationals, and institutional investors. In making this change, however, Thierry has emphasized that the bank is preparing not merely for the

1992 opening of the European market, important as that will be. The chairman is thinking mainly of the date, as yet unknown, yet all but certain, when all of Europe will convert to a single currency—an event which, if nothing else, will be certain to keep BBL and the rest of the European banking community more than a little busy.

Principal Subsidiaries: Locabel-Fininvest (50%); Banco di Roma (Belgio) (50%); Lanson Industries Plant II (90.1%); BBL Capital Management Corp.; Ciabel (99.8%); Sogerfin; Banque Bruxelles Lambert (Switzerland); Banque Louis-Dreyfus (France); BBL Australia; Williams de Broe Hill Ltd. (61.8%) (U.K.); Finanziaria ICCRI-BBL (50%) (Italy); Credit Europeen Luxembourg; BBL Finance Ireland; BBL Curran Mullens Ltd. (95%) (Australia).

BANK HAPOALIM B.M.

50 Rothschild Boulevard
Tel Aviv 65124
Israel
(03) 673–333

Public Company
Incorporated: 1921 as Bank Hapoalim
Employees: 7,500
Assets: US$31.27 billion
Stock Index: Tel Aviv

Bank Hapoalim was founded by the labor movement in Palestine in the early 1920s and set as its task to "assist, adopt, further and grant financial or any other assistance to all branches of activity of the institutions, federations or groups organized by the workers for the purpose of improving the conditions of their members in accordance with cooperative principles." Bank Hapoalim's dedication to the Jewish workers' cooperative development in Palestine continued, albeit without its original zeal, well into the late 1960s. In 1969, however, the bank changed its image, placing emphasis on becoming the international banking institution that it is today. With a high international profile and a focus on corporate profits came broadened responsibility and national influence, and their accompanying challenges and problems. Today Bank Hapoalim is the largest of Israel's commercial banks, with 340 offices in 14 countries around the world.

The political and social environment of Palestine after World War I has had a lasting influence on business ventures in Israel. Political and social tensions were rapidly heating up when the Jewish labor movement began to organize itself in 1920. At that time Palestine was governed by a British mandatory government, established after World War I in the wake of years of neglectful Ottoman rule. The British government's goal was to facilitate the development of both the Jewish National Home and the indigenous Arab population so that the two factions would join cooperatively in self-government.

Anti-Semitism in Poland and Hitler's steady rise to power sent Jewish immigration to Palestine soaring from the early 1920s well into the 1930s. The Jewish labor movement was part and parcel of this immigration, as was the Histadrut, the Israeli federation of labor unions. Because the Anglo-Palestine Company, the Jewish commercial bank at the time, would not grant credit to the Histadrut, labor and Zionist leaders alike saw the need for a bank specifically designed to support the Jewish workers' efforts. On November 20, 1921 Bank Hapoalim was born as the official financial branch of the Histadrut.

From its beginning, Bank Hapoalim took a conservative approach. The bank was dedicated to providing capital to the Histadrut's agricultural, industrial, and marketing cooperatives. However, it gave loans selectively, and rarely supported any one endeavor completely.

The Zionist Organization in Palestine gave vital financial and managerial support to Bank Hapoalim at its start, and Zionists as well as labor leaders looked forward to selling shares at home and abroad. Three representatives of the Jewish labor movement in Palestine arrived in New York City in November, 1921 hoping to sell shares in their newly opened bank. But Jewish laborers in the U.S. were not very interested in Zionism, while the wealthy American Jews who supported Zionism did not support the labor movement. In the end, the group, which had hoped to raise a quarter of a million dollars, managed to sell only $35,000 worth of shares.

The American Friends of the Histadrut was one of the groups that did invest, and with its help the bank separated amicably from the Zionist Organization in 1925. The labor leaders associated with Bank Hapoalim thought that it was important to supply their own bank managers, who would be concerned primarily with the labor movement. They chose Joseph Ahronovitz, editor of the labor publication *Hapoel Hatzair*, to be the bank's managing director.

In 1930, when the Great Depression was making itself felt in other parts of the world, Palestine was booming. One of the primary reasons for this economic upsurge was the increase in the number of Jewish immigrants and the capital they brought. The Jewish population in Palestine rose from 13% in 1922 to 30% in 1936; the sharpest increase came between 1930 and 1936. During this latter period many small new banks sprang up to serve the personal banking needs of the new immigrants. Bank Hapoalim, however, continued to do business mainly with the organizations of the Histadrut.

From September to November, 1935, there was a run on the Palestinian banks when Italy's invasion of Ethiopia provoked widespread fear of war. Many of the small banks folded, but with workers' trust in their bank and the help of Barclays and the Anglo-Palestine Bank, Bank Hapoalim survived.

Unfortunately, soon after this financial crisis had passed, the social and political situation in Palestine worsened dramatically. The difference in standards of living between Arabs and Jews increased in the mid-1930s. After attempted negotiations with the mandatory government to stop the influx of Jewish immigrants and then bouts of violence aimed against the government, the Arab rebellion began in April, 1936. The leaders of the five Arab political parties went on strike, demanding that Jewish immigration be suspended. Highly organized bands of Arab guerrilla fighters maintained by the Arab villagers attacked Jews throughout the country.

In May, 1939 the mandatory government published a White Paper that curbed the number of Jewish immigrants for the following five years. The White Paper also strictly limited the transfer of land from Arab to Jewish hands, to protect poor Arab villagers from being bought out by the Jewish immigrants. An outburst of Jewish violence followed, and social, economic, and political chaos continued until the start of World War II.

During this chaotic time, Bank Hapoalim's major business was to provide credit to the increasing number of agricultural cooperatives, or kibbutzim, being founded. In 1937 the bank's directors chose Avraham Dickenstein, a passionate believer in the potential of the Palestinian economy, to go on a fund-raising mission to the United States.He was driven not so much by ideology as by a keen business sense. Dickenstein knew he needed a key supporter to get started, and decided on U.S. Supreme Court Justice Louis Brandeis. Brandeis was interested in supporting the development of Palestine, but had disagreed with the starry-eyed approach that the first crew of fund raisers took in the 1920s. When Dickenstein arrived advancing rather conservative financial plans for development, Brandeis lent his support generously and influenced others to do the same. Dickenstein left the United States after ten months with 140,000 Egyptian pounds' worth of investments in Bank Hapoalim.

Ironically, it was World War II that brought Palestine out of its slump into a period of relative economic independence and stability. Trade routes in and out of the Middle East were largely cut off, calling for more self-reliance on the part of Palestinian manufacturers. Varied new industries cropped up, agricultural production increased, and British and Allied forces in the area turned to Palestine for a wide range of goods. Diamond production, an all-Jewish industry, replaced citrus fruits as the country's most valuable export. The Arab standard of living also improved due to greater prosperity, particularly better medical facilities.

The directors of the bank decided in 1941 to initiate a new corporation, independent of specific Zionist and labor concerns, to raise funds for investments in Palestinian industry and commerce. Avraham Dickenstein went back to the United States to start Bank Hapoalim's new subsidiary, the American-Palestine Trading Corporation (AMPAL). He arrived on a most inauspicious day: December 7, 1941, the day of the Japanese attack on Pearl Harbor. With the German army steadily advancing toward the Middle East, Dickenstein nevertheless managed to secure US$50,000 for AMPAL. With the momentum he stirred up, by 1946 AMPAL's capital reached US$2 million.

On May 14, 1948 the State of Israel was officially declared. The new government instituted an austerity campaign to deal with the huge influx of immigrants and the economic hardships brought on by the Jewish War of Independence, which lasted until June, 1949. Dickenstein, then director of AMPAL, told *The New York Times* in September, 1949 that this campaign had lowered the cost of living by 7.5% and eradicated the black market in just six months.

AMPAL and the Histadrut, and Bank Hapoalim through its association with these groups, were major contributors to Israel's fledgling economy. AMPAL was busy securing investments in Israeli industry and raising capital for use in general municipal development. In 1948 it began leasing ships to carry badly needed supplies and goods to manufacturers in Israel, and an independent shipping line, the American-Israel Line, soon evolved from these efforts. The Histadrut was a driving force in the Israeli economy, from construction to agriculture to industry, and continued to rely on Bank Hapoalim to finance its many operations.

In 1950 Bank Hapoalim merged with the Tel Aviv workers' savings and loan society, making it one of the three largest banks in Israel. In 1957 the bank merged with the rest of the savings and loan societies in Israel, except the one in Jerusalem, which merged in 1961. These mergers brought the majority of the workers' financial business to Bank Hapoalim, which could manage their money more skillfully than the small, often irregularly organized societies.

Merging with the savings and loan societies also meant that the bank operated on a more individualized basis than before. It began to open new branches rapidly, and offered a range of credit and personal savings plans, such as one to save for high school, which was not free at the time in Israel. These individualized plans in turn provided funds for areas of national development that the bank supported.

Steep inflation was the price of Israel's rapid economic expansion. To combat inflation, the government devalued the currency and did away with export and import regulations, causing a surge in foreign trade. Bank Hapoalim increased its foreign dealings by opening experimental offices in Switzerland and Latin America and participated in raising funds abroad for investment in Israel. Expansion continued until 1966, when inflation won out, pushing Israel into an economic depression that climaxed in early 1967. Following the Six Day War that year, when Israeli troops moved into and occupied the Sinai Peninsula, the West Bank, and Golan Heights, there was a short period of economic improvement. But by 1969 the Bank of Israel had to restrain the commercial banks to handle the shortened supply of capital.

The year 1969 was a turning point for Bank Hapoalim. Until then the bank's primary purpose had been to serve the domestic labor economy. But a new management team resolved that year to transform the bank into a modern international giant. Bank Hapoalim opened its first operating foreign branch in 1971 in London, distinguished from the representative branches of the mid-1960s. It continued to expand abroad and now operates branches in much of Europe, North America, and Latin America.

Unbeknownst to all but a few of the directors during this time, in 1972 Bank Hapoalim joined Bank Leumi, Bank Mizrahi, and the Discount Bank in buying and selling its own shares to falsely inflate their worth. Specifically, Bank Hapoalim bought and sold large amounts of AMPAL stock. It is natural enough for businesses to nudge their share values by doing this, but the banks' exaggerated trading, especially after 1979, increased their shares' values even above the 191% inflation rate for 1983. To raise capital for an intensive push abroad, the banks had all been competing for investors' money by offering artificially high yields and promising to buy back shares whenever shareholders presented them. By 1983 bank stock prices were listed at over three times the banks' adjusted capital. This was an economic crisis just waiting to happen, since bank stocks had remained ahead of inflation for a long time and, as such a sound investment, made up more than half of the total stocks traded in Tel Aviv.

In July, 1983 the government vowed to take decisive steps toward reducing Israel's inflationary cycle. One of these steps was rumored to be a drastic devaluation of the Israeli shekel. In the first week of October, investors, fearful of the imminent devaluation, rushed to sell their bank shares so they could buy dollars. Bank share prices collapsed. On October 6 banks were forced to buy back more than $1 billion worth of shares. Bank Hapoalim was at the time Israel's second largest bank, and lost the most in the collapse. On October 9 the government closed the market to prevent a complete crash, and on October 11, it devalued the shekel by 23%.

The Israeli government stepped in to save the banks and reopened stock trading on October 20, on the understanding that the banks would not buy and sell their own shares, and that the government would maintain the prices of the shares by guaranteeing to buy back investors' shares at set points in the future at their October 6, 1983 U.S. dollar value. By early 1989 this program had cost Israeli taxpayers $7 billion and left the government as owner of most of the shares.

In January, 1985 the Israeli cabinet formed an investigative commission to study the price collapse. In 1986 this commission's report recommended that the four heads of the commercial banks resign or be dismissed, and that major changes be made in Israel's stock market. The commission cited the banks' stock manipulation as the cause of the crash, but also called for the director of the Bank of Israel to resign because he was aware of the banks' activity but did not report it.

The banks claimed that they had been under immense pressure and competition from the government and other businesses to remain attractive to investors abroad. They saw regulating their stock prices as an integral part of maintaining a profitable international business for themselves and the country as a whole. Nonetheless, Giora Gazit, director of Bank Hapoalim in 1986, announced his resignation the day after the commission released its report, and Ephraim Reiner, president of AMPAL in 1986 and chairman of Bank Hapoalim in 1983, resigned two months later.

Since this crisis, Bank Hapoalim has been streamlining operations in Israel and looking for lucrative, reliable business abroad. The bank offered the Israeli public its first credit card, installed automatic teller machines in many areas to expedite personal transactions, cut down on office personnel, and closed branches in Israel.

In early 1989 the banks, nominally owned by the government since it had to buy most of their shares in its 1983 shareholder rescue plan, were trying to convince the government to return ownership to them. Since the government's shares are of a type that has no voting rights, Bank Hapoalim is controlled by the Histadrut even though the Histadrut owns only .11% of the bank's shares. In May, 1989 the government equalized voting rights for all shares, much to the distress of the banks, to make them more saleable. It plans to sell them to the highest bidder, but limit foreign ownership to 30% of each bank.

Meanwhile, the current management team is creating an impressive international niche for Bank Hapoalim as lender to small and mid-sized foreign companies. The bank will continue to trim its operations to a profitable level and mend its damaged image. Political, social, and economic conditions are unstable in Israel, as they have been for decades, yet prosperity and technological innovation are on the rise in many areas. Whatever the outcome of the government's sale, Bank Hapoalim will continue to be shaped by the influence of the government and Israel's social and political environment.

Principal Subsidiaries: Bank Otsar Hahayal Ltd. (50.1%); American Israel Bank Ltd.; Bank "Yahav" for Government Employees Ltd. (50.1%); Bank Massad Ltd. (51%); Israel Continental Bank Ltd. (62%); Bank Hapoalim (Cayman) Ltd. (68.6%); Bank Hapoalim (Switzerland) Ltd. (99.7%); Hapoalim (Latin America) Casa Bancaria S.A. (Uruguay) (68.6%); Bank Hapoalim (Canada); Israel-Ampal Industrial Development Bank Ltd. (36%); Industrial Bank Limited. (36%); Mishkan-Hapoalim Mortage Bank Ltd. (69%); Igrot Hevra Lehanpackot Shel Bank Hapoalim Ltd.; Bitzur Ltd.; Hapoalim Hanpackot Ltd.; Mit'ar Hevra Lehanpackot Ltd.; Tmura Heura Lehanpackot Shel Bank Hapoalim Ltd.; Te'uda Hevra Lehanpackot Ltd.; Tashtit Hanpackot Ltd.; Revadim Properties Ltd.; Investment Company of Bank Hapoalim Ltd. (43.5%); Hapoalim Leasing Ltd. (43.5%); Isracard Ltd. (43.5%); Eurocard (Israel) Ltd. (43.5%); Ampal-American Israel Corporation (36.0%); Ampal (Israel) Ltd. (36.0%); Nir Ltd. (36%); Hapoalim International N.V., Netherlands Antilles; Amot Investments Ltd. (34.2%); Diur B.P. Ltd. (80%); Clal (Israel) Ltd. (34.2%); "Delek" Israel Fuel Corp. Ltd. (30.9%); "Gmul" Investment Co. Ltd. (46.7%).

Further Reading: Meir, Heth. *Banking Institutions in Israel*, Jerusalem, Israel University Press, 1966; "From Cooperatives to Corporations—The Story of Bank Hapoalim," Bank Hapoalim, Tel Aviv, 1988.

BANK OF BOSTON CORPORATION

100 Federal Street
Boston, Massachusetts 02110
U.S.A.
(617) 434–2200

Public Company
Incorporated: 1970
Employees: 20,200
Assets: $34.12 billion
Stock Index: New York Boston

The Bank of Boston's history is older than that of the Constitution of the United States, and its story is a long and distinctive one. From uneasy beginnings in post-Revolutionary America, it has become a super-regional bank that is currently challenging the traditional dominance of New York's money center banks.

Bank of Boston traces its roots back to the Massachusetts Bank, which was founded in 1784. Its progenitors were Boston import-export merchants who were tired of having to deal with British banks when sending money to distant places. The bank was the first bank in the city of Boston and, indeed, the only one until 1792, when the Union Bank was founded and Alexander Hamilton's Bank of the United States opened a branch in Boston.

From the start, the Massachusetts Bank's strict lending policies and conservative ways made it no friends among consumers, who had few alternatives in seeking credit. It not only didn't pay interest on customer deposits, but it even charged a fee for keeping them at one point. But times were uncertain at best during the early years of the Republic; a complete overhaul of the federal government, Shay's Rebellion, the War of 1812, and the ensuing two-year depression all happened within 30 years of the bank's founding. The Massachusetts Bank weathered each of these crises, however, and in 1838 its assets amounted to more than $1 million.

When the Civil War broke out in 1861, the Massachusetts Bank was part of a consortium of Boston banks that extended nearly $35 million in credit to the Union government. It also supported the Union war effort by buying $50,000 worth of treasury bonds. A more important development that occurred during the war was the advent of a national banking system, which Congress created in 1864 to make war financing easier through the establishment and circulation of a national currency. True to the Massachusetts Bank's conservative tradition, President John James Dixwell expressed suspicion about the new system, but saw that if his bank didn't join, it would fall behind its competition. In 1864 the bank renamed itself the Massachusetts National Bank of Boston.

By 1884, there were 59 banks in Boston besides Massachusetts National, and the competition was so fierce that it could not afford to maintain its cautious ways and expect to survive. And yet the bank did just that. As a result, however, its annual profit declined from a record $250,038 in 1873 to $70,000 by the end of the century.

Near the end of the 19th century, Boston's banking industry also underwent a wave of mergers, the most important of them engineered by the Shawmut National Bank and the investment banker Kidder, Peabody & Company. In reaction to this development, Massachusetts National decided to merge with the First National Bank of Boston, which had openly defied Shawmut National's power play, in 1903. First National had been founded in 1859 as Safety Fund Bank, changing its name in 1864 when it joined the national bank system. The new institution bore the First National name, and although Massachusetts National President Daniel Wing stayed on as president, First National President John Carr became chairman of the board.

The First National Bank of Boston prospered under the guidance of Daniel Wing. When World War I broke out in 1914, the bank took little notice—the United States was still a nonbelligerent and Europe seemed far away. The big event of 1914 for the bank was its participation in the new Federal Reserve system; it purchased 6,000 shares of the Federal Reserve bank's capital stock and purged its own board of directors of members involved in securities dealing and investment banking, in compliance with the Federal Reserve Act. In 1915 the bank extended $1 million worth of credit to the British government and made a $5 million loan to Russia the next year. Early in 1917, despite the fact that the distant clash of war was getting closer,the Bank of Boston opened its first overseas office, in Buenos Aires. Once the United States formally entered the war later that year, the bank did its part by purchasing a large quantity of war bonds from the U.S. Treasury.

To say that the Bank of Boston grew and prospered during the boom years of the 1920s would be an understatement. The bank made its first substantial plunge into retail banking in 1923, when it acquired the International Trust Company. By 1924, the bank had grown to many times the size it had been before World War I. It employed 1,657 people, compared to 152 in 1908; its capital stood at $15 million, compared to $2 million; and its loan volume had grown to $222 million, from $28 million.

Despite the October stock market crash that threw the financial community into a panic, 1929 was a prosperous year for the Bank of Boston. Either the directors did not recognize the severity of the crisis right away or they were confident that the bank would withstand it, because they authorized the acquisition of Old Colony Trust Company late that year. And in 1931, the bank bought out the Jamaica Plain Trust Company. Bank of Boston survived the Depression in relatively strong condition, although it cut its dividend continually until 1937. It was also forced to divest its investment-banking arm, the First Boston Corporation, after the passage of the Glass-Steagall Act in 1933, which prohibited commercial banks from engaging in investment banking and securities dealing.

Rumors of war once again emanated from Europe at the end of the 1930s. As in 1914, the Bank of Boston took little notice except regarding the matter of outstanding loans to German interests. As the Nazi government in Germany prepared for hostilities, concerns arose that the bank would not be able to collect from its German borrowers. W. Latimer Gray, head of Bank of Boston's foreign operations, went to Germany himself in the summer of 1939 to secure repayment. Gray had met many prominent Germans in the course of his business dealings, but found himself trailed by Gestapo agents during his trip. He and his wife left the country just before the invasion of Poland, carrying with them a draft on Britain's Midland Bank for $500,000, enough to cover the Bank of Boston's loans.

During World War II employees left to join the military and the bank extended emergency credit to the federal government to help finance military orders, but these things were a matter of course for every major American bank during the war. In 1945, with the end of the war in sight, the Bank of Boston acquired the First National Bank in Revere, Massachusetts. Once the war ended the bank went about expanding as before, opening a branch office in Rio de Janeiro in 1947.

By 1950, Bank of Boston's assets totalled more than $1.5 billion. The bank continued to prosper during the decade and its foreign business expanded. Factoring—the practice of buying accounts payable from merchants and assuming responsibility for their collection—also became a substantial part of the Bank of Boston's business during this time. In 1959 the bank posted record revenues of $20.4 million. It was also one of the few American banks to withdraw its assets from Cuba before Fidel Castro nationalized that nation's banks.

In the early 1960s, the Bank of Boston internationalized its factoring operations. In 1961 the bank's newly formed subsidiary, Boston Overseas Financial Corporation, joined with British merchant bankers M. Samuel & Company and Tozer, Kemsley & Millbourn to form International Factors, Limited. The next year, Boston Overseas Financial expanded its factoring business to the Netherlands, Switzerland, Australia, and South Africa. The Bank of Boston increased its international presence even further in 1964 when it opened a branch office in London.

The First National Bank of Boston continued to prosper through the 1960s, although its financial performance suffered somewhat late in the decade when high interest rates, caused by inflation and increased demand for credit, caused it to take losses on its bond holdings. By 1970, it had acquired a reputation as a creative lender that was always willing to find unconventional solutions to problems of finance. Serge Semenenko, the flamboyant Russian-born head of the semi-autonomous special industries department, contributed substantially to this image. Hilton Hotels, International Paper, *The Saturday Evening Post*, and Warner Brothers Studios were among his many clients.

In 1970 the Bank of Boston reorganized under the name First National Boston Corporation. From there, the bank embarked on a string of acquisitions of Massachusetts banks in an effort to become a regional powerhouse. In 1982, reflecting the new prominence that large regional banks would soon have in the national banking arena, the bank renamed itself Bank of Boston National Association. In 1985 Bank of Boston moved to solidify its grip on New England with the acquisition of Waterbury, Connecticut–based Colonial Bancorp, and followed in 1987 with the purchase of BankVermont Corporation. Its aggressive lending policies also helped spark Massachusetts' much-heralded economic revival in the 1980s, when the bank made substantial loans to high-technology concerns like Wang Laboratories and Data General Corporation. And it did a good job of dodging the Third World debt crisis in 1987 by writing off nearly two-thirds of its loans at the first sign of trouble.

At the same time, however, the Bank of Boston developed a reputation for aloofness, even arrogance, during the 1970s and 1980s. One incident that contributed to this perception occurred in the mid-1970s, when the city of Boston underwent its worst fiscal crisis since the Great Depression and turned to the bank for help. Although the Bank of Boston eventually bought the city's notes as requested, many city officials bristled at the bank's demands, including an unsuccessful insistence that the state guarantee certain city debts. For several years thereafter, Boston City Hall pointedly chose Morgan Guaranty Trust, a New York investment bank, as its underwriter. The Bank of Boston was also known for its unwillingness to discuss its lending practices and local affairs with community activists. "They just project an elitist, uncaring attitude," a spokesman for a rival bank told *Business Week* in 1985.

But the worst public relations disaster of all for the bank came in 1985, when the Justice Department charged that the Bank of Boston had processed more than $1.2 billion worth of cash transactions between 1980 and 1984 without reporting them to the Treasury Department as required by a federal law designed to prevent money laundering. The accusations stemmed from an investigation of Gennaro J. Angiulo, the alleged head of New England's largest organized-crime family. Federal investigators found that Angiulo and his associates had made a habit of walking into a Bank of Boston branch in Boston's North End with paper bags full of cash and exchanging them for cashier's checks. They also found that the bank had not reported large shipments of American currency to and from Swiss banks. At first, Bank of Boston denied any wrongdoing in the Angiulo affair and CEO William Brown charged that it was the victim of misrepresentation in the press. Later, once the evidence came out, Brown was forced to admit to "poor judgment" on the part of lower-level employees; the bank pleaded guilty to the Justice Department's charges and paid a $500,000 fine.

The Bank of Boston seems to have recovered from the Angiulo affair, but the fiasco raised serious questions about the way the bank was run under William Brown and his predecessor, Richard Hill. It will be up to Ira Stepanian, who succeeded Brown as chairman and CEO in 1989, to repair any remaining cracks in the Bank of Boston—such as a $300 million loss in the last quarter of 1989, due in large part to bad property loans—and keep it on track as one of the powerful new breed of super-regional banks in the 1990s.

Principal Subsidiaries: First National Bank of Boston; Bank of Boston International—New York; Bank of Boston International—Los Angeles; Bank of Boston International South—Miami; Bank of Boston Trust Company (Bahamas) Ltd.; Bank of Boston, S.A. (Luxembourg); Boston Overseas Financial Corp.; Mortgage Corp. of the South; First National Bank of Boston (Guernsey) Ltd.; Bank of Boston—Barnstable, N.A.; Bank of Boston—Connecticut; Bank of Boston—Berkshire, N.A.; Bank of Bristol, N.A.; Bank of Boston—Middlesex; Bank of Boston—Norfolk; Bank of Boston—Western Massachusetts, N.A.; Bank of Boston—Worcester, N.A.; Bank of Boston Trust—Arizona; Bank of Boston Trust—Southwest Florida; Bank of Boston Trust—Southeast Florida; Old Colony Trust—South Carolina; Boston Financial Ltd.; FNBC Acceptance Corp.; FNB Financial Co.; FNB Services, Inc.; Firstbank Financial Corp.; Randolph Computer Corp.; First of Boston Mortgage Corp.; First Capital Corp. of Boston; First Venture Capital Corp. of Boston; First National Boston (Hong Kong) Ltd.; First National Boston Clearance Corp.; Boston Trust & Savings Ltd.; Boston Investment & Financial Services S.A. (Switzerland); Nigerian-American Merchant Bank Ltd.; Boston Location, S.A. (France); Boston Credit-Bail, S.A. (France); Boston Bank Cameroon; Banco de Boston Dominicano, S.A.; Casco-Northern Corp.; FBC, Inc.; First National Boston Mortgage Corp.; First of Boston Information Services Inc.; Sociedad Anonima de Servicios e Inversiones: World Trade Group, Inc.; Bank of Boston Canada; Boston Factors of Canada, Inc.; Bank of Boston Trust Co. (Cayman Islands) Ltd.; Corporation Internacional de Boston S.A. (Costa Rica); Boston Leasing Italia S.p.A. (Italy); Boston International Finance Corp. N.V. (Netherland Antilles); Boston Leasing Ltd. (U.K.); First National Boston Ltd. (U.K.); International Banking Facility—Boston; Great Atlantic Trust Co. Boston, S.A.; First Leasing & Finance, Ltd.; First Capital Corp.; RIHT Financing Corp.; Stockton, Whatley, Davin & Co.; FSC Corp.; FNBC Realty.

Further Reading: Williams, Ben Ames, Jr. *Bank of Boston 200*, Boston, Houghton Mifflin, 1984.

BANK OF MONTREAL

129 St. James Street
Place d'Armes
Montreal, Quebec H2Y 3S8
Canada
(514) 877–7110

Public Company
Incorporated: 1822
Employees: 34,482
Assets: C$84.2 billion (US$70.58 billion)
Stock Index: Montreal Toronto Winnipeg Alberta Vancouver London

Until very recently, Canada's banks were stodgy, sheltered, and highly regulated institutions, and the Bank of Montreal was among the fustiest and most traditional of them all. But two singular events in the last two decades—the arrival of an aggressive new CEO in 1975 and the deregulation of the Canadian banking industry in 1985—have shaken up this old bank and forced it to deal with the increasing complexity and internationalization of the financial world.

If any bank had a right to be stodgy and traditional, it was certainly the Bank of Montreal, whose roots stretch back to the early 19th century. It first opened for business in 1817 on St. Paul Street, in the heart of Montreal's business district, as the Montreal Bank. It did so without an official charter and was forced to rely on American investors for nearly half of its initial capital. But within five years the new bank had proven its worth to the community, and it was granted a charter in 1822 as the Bank of Montreal. By then, all but 15% of its capital stock had been repatriated.

During its early years, the bank engaged in bullion and foreign-currency trading in addition to its lending activities. In 1827 and 1828, it was forced to omit its dividend for the first and last time after the bulk of Quebec's fur-trading activity shifted to the Hudson Bay, depressing the local economy and causing a number of loan defaults. During this time, however, the Bank of Montreal also began its long financial and managerial association with the expansion of Canada's canal and railway systems. In the late 1830s, it prospered despite political upheaval. The Bank of Montreal acquired the Toronto-based Bank of the People at that time, so when Upper and Lower Canada were united into the Province of Canada in 1841, its total assets exceeded C$4 million.

During the early 1860s, the Bank of Upper Canada, which was then the Canadian government's official banker, slid inexorably toward failure, and in 1864 the Bank of Montreal was appointed to take its place. It continued in this capacity until the establishment of the Bank of Canada in 1935. The bank also began to expand its branch network when Canada achieved full political unity in 1867, opening two offices in New Brunswick. It opened a branch in Winnipeg, Manitoba in 1877 and followed the Canadian Pacific Railway westward as railroad construction opened up the prairie for settlement. Bank of Montreal branches appeared in Regina, Saskatchewan in 1883, Calgary, Alberta in 1886, and Vancouver, British Columbia in 1887.

The bank already had two foreign offices by this point; it had opened one in New York in 1859 and another in London in 1870. The Bank of Montreal used its foreign representation to expand into investment banking in the late 1870s. It joined a syndicate of London bankers in underwriting loans to the province of Quebec and the city of Montreal. In 1879 it underwrote a Quebec securities issue and floated it on the New York market. And in 1892, it became the Canadian government's official banker in London, underwriting all of the national government's bond issues on the London market.

At the turn of the century, the Bank of Montreal embarked on an acquisition spree that would make it Canada's largest bank by the outbreak of World War I. It improved its position in the Maritime Provinces and northern Quebec by acquiring the Exchange Bank of Yarmouth, the People's Bank of Halifax, and the People's Bank of New Brunswick. And in 1906, it bought out the bankrupt Bank of Ontario.

In 1914 the Bank of Montreal had C$260 million in assets, 179 offices, and 1,650 employees. Nearly half of its mostly male workforce enlisted in the military at the outbreak of war, but the hiring of women in large numbers made up for the loss. In fact, the war had a rather salutary effect on the bank's finances due to the sale of war bonds, which were quite popular. World War I also marked the end the London market's role as the Canadian government's main source of external financing, as the London securities markets were closed to foreign issues from 1914 to 1918 and the Bank of Montreal and the government began to float their bond issues in New York.

An economic crash in 1920 followed a short postwar boom, and the crisis forced Canadian banks to consolidate. The Bank of Montreal had already acquired the British Bank of North America in 1918; it bought the Merchants Bank of Canada in 1922 and the Montreal-based Molsons Bank in 1925. These acquisitions increased its branch network to 617 offices, more than three times what it had been during the war.

The depression that struck Canada in the 1920s, however, was not as serious as the Great Depression of the 1930s. In 1933 Canada's gross national product was almost half of what it had been in 1928, and the number of unemployed increased nearly thirteenfold. Bank of Montreal's assets were worth nearly C$1 billion in 1929, then dropped below C$800,000 for five consecutive years. The Depression finally ended with the outbreak of World War II, during which the Bank of Montreal, just as it did during the previous war, lost large numbers of employees to the armed services and also made money from the sale of war bonds.

The years after World War II brought prosperity and rapid economic development to Canada. Canadian banks also prospered, but in a regulated and noncompetitive atmosphere. "It was sort of a clubby affair," Bank of Montreal executive vice president Stanley Davison told *Fortune* in 1979. Canadian law limited the interest banks could charge on their loans to 6%, and power in the banking industry was concentrated in a group of five major banks, of which the Bank of Montreal was one. During this time, however, the Bank of Montreal also earned itself a reputation for stodginess and an unwillingness to adapt to change. In the mid-1960s its earning performance began to weaken. Then, in 1967, an amendment to the Canadian Bank Act eliminated the interest-rate ceiling, opening up new opportunities in the area of consumer and small-business lending. The Bank of Montreal was caught unprepared to keep pace with its competitors.

Its financial performance was further eroded by a costly but necessary computerization program. The Bank of Montreal's accounting procedures seemed not to have changed much since the age of the quill pen; when CEO Fred McNeil assumed his post in 1968, he asked a personnel department executive for a copy of the departmental budget and the executive replied: "budget? No one has ever asked us to prepare one." But computerizing the bank swallowed up more and more money. Its projected cost in 1969 was C$80 million, and the figure was repeatedly revised upward for several years thereafter. In 1972 the bank started a credit card proram, and the start-up costs added even more financial liability. But the Bank of Montreal was also the last of Canada's five major banks to bring out a credit card.

Into this state of affairs stepped William Mulholland, who was named CEO in 1975, when McNeil became chairman. Mulholland was an American. Formerly a partner at the prominent investment bank Morgan Stanley, in 1969 he was named president of Brinco Limited, a Canadian mining company. After taking the top job at the Bank of Montreal, he dodged the controversy over an American heading up one of Canada's largest banks by promising to consider adopting Canadian citizenship.

Mulholland's aggressive and uncompromising management style was once described as "chewing through underlings with a chainsaw" by *Canadian Business* magazine, and a number of senior executives have left the bank during his tenure. But the bank's condition also improved immediately after he took office. Mulholland closed down 50 unprofitable branches during his first five years in office, revised the Bank of Montreal's internal pricing system to reflect the cost of funds more accurately, and modernized procedures for asset and liability management. He has also been unafraid to bring in outside help, as he did when he recruited IBM executive Barry Hull to get the computerization program on track. The bank opened its first computerized branch office in 1975, and all 1,240 of its branches were plugged into the computer system by 1979.

The Bank of Montreal has also sought to internationalize under Mulholland, joining a trend in which just about every one of the world's major financial institutions has participated since the late 1960s. In 1978 it purchased a 25.1% interest in Allgemeine Deutsche Creditanstalt, a medium-sized West German bank. Also in 1978, the Bank of Montreal tried to expand into the American retail banking market when it began negotiating the acquisition of 89 branch offices from Bankers Trust Company. Mulholland forged ahead with the deal despite analysts' misgivings, but negotiations broke down in 1979 and the deal was never consummated.

The Bank of Montreal suffered in the early 1980s under the strain of loans to Latin America and to oil and real estate interests in western Canada that went sour. But in 1984, it finally obtained entry into the American retail market when it acquired Harris Bankcorp, the third-largest bank in Chicago, for US$547 million. As with the Bankers Trust bid, banking analysts expressed their doubts over the deal; the Bank of Montreal paid US$82 per share for Harris stock, or nearly twice its previous price. But two years later, the analysts had changed their opinion entirely. The Harris acquisition made the Bank of Montreal one of the leading foreign institutions involved in U.S. commercial and industrial lending and enhanced its foreign exchange capabilities. The strong performance of regional bank stocks in 1985 and 1986 also made the deal seem like a bargain in retrospect.

In 1985 the Progressive Conservative government of Prime Minister Brian Mulroney decided to deregulate Canada's financial system, a move that blurred the traditional lines between insurance, banking, and securities brokerage. Companies that had been restricted to one business were allowed to diversify into others, increasing competition among individual firms but also the power of holding companies seeking to build financial-service empires. One immediate consequence of deregulation was a surge in merger-and-acquisition activity involving Canadian securities firms. Growing foreign investment in North America helped accelerate this trend, as did an increasing demand for stocks among domestic small investors (one brokerage executive told *Barron's* "It wasn't too long ago that the average Canadian's idea of a balanced portfolio was a savings bond and a lottery ticket"). The Bank of Montreal responded by acquiring Nesbitt Thomson, Canada's fourth-largest brokerage firm, in 1987.

It is perhaps too early to assess the Bank of Montreal's long-term prospects, given the fact that it has had loans outstanding in several problem areas—the crack in the oil market has not healed completely, keeping real estate prices in western Canada depressed; the Third World debt crisis has yet to resolve itself; and it bought a large securities firm just months before the 1987 stock market crash. But if anyone seems fit to guide the bank through the 1990s, it is William Mulholland, the hard-driving Yankee maverick who has openly admitted that he enjoys tweaking his establishment rivals. The Bank of Montreal has endured for more than 170 years through political instability, depression, and war; it has seen worse times than the present.

Principal Subsidiaries: Bank of Montreal Leasing Corp.; Bank of Montreal Mortgage Corp.; Bank of Montreal Realty Finance Ltd.; Bank of Montreal Realty Inc.; Bank of Montreal Asia Ltd. (Singapore); Bank of Montreal (California) (U.S.A.); Bank of Montreal International Ltd. (Bahamas); Bank of Montreal Trust Co. (U.S.A.); Bank of Montreal Trust Corp. Cayman Ltd. (Bahamas); Empresa Tecnica de Organizacao e Participacoes S.A. (Brazil); First Canadian Assessoria e Servicos Ltda. (Brazil); First Canadian Financial Corp. B.V. (Netherlands); First Canadian Financial Services (U.K.) Ltd.; Harris Bankcorp, Inc.

Further Reading: Denison, Merrill. *Canada's First Bank: A History of the Bank of Montreal*, McClelland and Stewart, 1967.

BANK OF NEW ENGLAND CORPORATION

28 State Street
Boston, Massachusetts 12109
U.S.A.
(617) 742–4000

Public Company
Incorporated: 1985
Employees: 17,299
Assets: $33 billion
Stock Index: New York

The Bank of New England is America's first interstate regional bank holding company. It was created in 1985 by the merger of the Bank of New England Corporation and CBT Corporation, another bank holding company, from Connecticut. BNE owns nine banks (with 470 branches) and 17 other companies that provide various financial services, chiefly consumer banking, wholesale banking, and operational services such as payroll, mutual funds, and data processing.

The Bank of New England and the Connecticut Bank and Trust Company both originated as state banks in the early days of America's efforts at creating a workable banking system. The older of the two is CBT, which was incorporated in 1792 as Union Bank of New London. Merchants Bank, the Bank of New England's earliest predecessor, was granted a state charter in Massachusetts in 1831.

In 1863 Congress passed the National Banking Act. Two separate centralized bank-charter systems, the First Bank of the United States in 1781 and the Second Bank of the United States in 1816, had failed to rationalize the nation's financial activities, leaving banking in America unsophisticated and unstable. Without a central organization and with unlimited (and frequently counterfeit) types of currency in circulation, the money supply was constantly fluctuating. The National Banking Act created a uniform currency and, more importantly, set the framework for a federally chartered system of privately owned national banks. Merchants Bank's successor, the Merchants National Bank of Boston, was one of the first of these, chartered in 1864.

Not long after, in 1868 and 1871 respectively, the Hartford Trust Company and the Connecticut Trust and Safe Deposit Company were founded (one of them as a successor to the Union Bank of New London, although the path is unclear). These two predecessors of the Connecticut Bank and Trust Company busily and quietly conducted their traditional banking businesses and, together with the Merchants National Bank of Boston, survived the postwar chaos and a series of panics which hit over the next 50 years.

Connecticut Trust and Safe Deposit Company and Hartford Trust Company were consolidated in 1919 as the Hartford-Connecticut Trust Company, still providing traditional banking, safe deposit, and trust services. Between 1921 and 1934 Hartford-Connecticut Trust Company's history shows quite a few stock offerings and splits; in 1927 it had a grand total of 142 employees as it entered the Great Depression. The Merchants National Bank of Boston, little changed since it was chartered in 1864, was a bit larger in size and scope during this period; with 166 employees in 1928 it provided transfer, foreign-credit, and tax services as well. However, it did not go through any expansion until 1956, while Hartford-Connecticut Trust Company, through acquisitions and mergers of four entities between 1939 and 1953, was able to make a major move in 1954 when it merged with Phoenix State Bank and Trust Company to become Connecticut Bank and Trust Company.

Between 1929 and 1932, approximately 11,000 American banks failed and $2 billion in deposits disappeared. The failure of several important European banks as well in 1931 created an international monetary crisis. In 1933 newly elected President Franklin D. Roosevelt immediately declared a mandatory bank holiday until every bank in the country could be examined. Hartford-Connecticut Trust Company and the Merchants National Bank of Boston both passed inspection.

World War II finally brought economic relief. After America's entry into the war, in 1941, unemployment fell significantly. In the autumn of 1941 the Federal Reserve froze interest rates at Depression levels, where they remained until 1947. It also asked the banks to cooperate in reducing nonessential private borrowing so there would be more money available to the government.

In the mid-1950s the Merchants National Bank of Boston began to grow. It merged with one bank in 1956 and acquired another in 1958, finally merging on December 31, 1960 into New England National Bank of Boston (originally incorporated in 1869 as New England Trust Company and converted in 1960 to its national bank status) through a share-for-share trade to become New England Merchants National Bank, the fourth-largest bank in the Boston area. The Connecticut Bank and Trust Company was even more active, merging with five banks between 1958 and 1963. One of these mergers, with Wallingford Bank and Trust Company in 1962, was almost not allowed because it eliminated one of the few banks in a small town, and made Connecticut Bank and Trust the second-largest bank in the state.

The 1966 Douglas Amendment to the Bank Holding Act, which had authorized the formation of bank holding companies, in 1956, prohibited interstate banking unless it was authorized by the particular states involved. Massachusetts and Connecticut already had reciprocal arrangements with each other, as well as with Maine, New Hampshire, Rhode Island, and Vermont. In 1970 both Connecticut Bank and Trust Company and New England Merchants National Bank approved the formation of holding companies to acquire their assets: CBT Corporation and New England Merchants Company, Inc., respectively. (The latter was not actually incorporated until 1971.) New England Merchants Company continued to grow throughout the next 15 years, merging with or acquiring seven banks and financial companies. It changed its name in 1982 to the Bank of New England Corporation, and renamed its core bank Bank of New England, or BNE. CBT Corporation was equally active, adding seven banks to its portfolio during that time.

The eventual merger of these two large bank holding companies in 1985 was historic. But before the merger could be completed the banks had to wrestle with the conflict between state and federal powers. The state of Connecticut had a statute on its books allowing only banks from reciprocal New England states to acquire its banks; it was generally acknowledged that the reason for this (and similar statutes in other New England states) was fear of losing its regional identity and becoming absorbed by the major banking centers of New York, Chicago, and California. Although approval for the merger had been obtained from federal agencies in 1984, New York–based Citicorp, one of the nation's largest banking conglomerates, contested the approval on the premise that it represented an "illegal compact between states" and was a violation of the Constitution. The two holding companies took the position that the Douglas Amendment to the Bank Holding Act allowed the states to make their own interstate banking laws. While this matter was being reviewed by the Federal Appeals Court, the merger was effectively in limbo.

Meanwhile, the Senate Banking Committee approved proposed federal legislation creating regional interstate banking zones. New England was the first zone to receive legal attention; the BNE case would affect the formation of other zones, especially in the Southeast, where several holding company actions were pending. In August, 1984 the Federal Appeals Court affirmed Connecticut and Massachusetts laws allowing interstate banking only in the New England states, thereby giving the green light to the planned merger. But Citicorp appealed to the Supreme Court, and another stay was enacted.

On June 11, 1985 the Supreme Court unanimously upheld the decision, declaring it a "historical fact that our country traditionally has favored widely dispersed control of banking." And on June 14 the Bank of New England Corporation and CBT Corporation merged to form the first interstate regional bank holding company, the "new" Bank of New England Corporation (BNE Corporation). As a result, interstate mergers became routine and new banking regions were quickly formed.

The Federal Reserve board also allowed bank holding companies to buy savings banks, opening the door for BNE Corporation to acquire ten more banks, savings and loans, and other financial-service companies throughout New England in just two years and laying the groundwork for its 1987 acquisition of the Conifer Group, a group of six community banks in Massachusetts. During this period BNE added nine banks to its ranks and Connecticut Bank and Trust added two. BNE Corporation's assets by the end of 1987 had grown to $30 billion, from $23 billion in 1986. In April, 1988 BNE Corporation was listed on the New York Stock Exchange as NEB.

Three men—all lifelong New Englanders—were particularly important to the formation and development of BNE Corporation: Walter J. Connolly Jr., Gordon I. Ulmer, and Peter H. McCormick. Working his way up the corporate ladder, Connolly became the Connecticut Bank and Trust's president in 1970, its CEO in 1977, and its chairman as well as chairman of CBT Corporation in 1980. A key player in the merger of BNE and CBT, he was named chairman of the newly formed Bank of New England Corporation in 1985.

Ulmer assumed Connecticut Bank and Trust's presidency in 1980. When Connolly moved to BNE Corporation, Ulmer became chairman and CEO of Connecticut Bank and Trust as well as a vice chairman of BNE Corporation and the president of CBT Corporation.

McCormick became president of BNE in 1978, in 1981 CEO, and in 1985 chairman as well. In 1978 he was also named president of the BNE Corporation, retaining the title throughout the transitional years until his retirement in 1988, when Ulmer became BNE Corporation's president.

In October, 1985 the Bank of New England and three of its employees were indicted on 43 counts related to an alleged money laundering scheme in conjunction with a customer who had previously been convicted of gambling and loansharking. BNE was charged with failure to file large cash transaction reports as required by the Bank Secrecy Act. BNE was only one of several large banks involved in the investigation. In February, 1986 BNE was convicted on 31 of the counts and fined accordingly, although all three employees and the customer were acquitted—a decision which didn't make much sense to BNE management and which didn't affect the bank's business to any noticeable degree. It did, however, make BNE very cautious about its compliance with regulations; the bank volunteered information on accidental violations of the same type in 1987 and was fined $125,000.

Customer service became BNE's focal point in 1988 as competition increased and growth slowed in the New England banking industry. Coming out of a time of high regional unemployment, its goal was to keep virtually all employees it had gained through acquisitions and mergers while keeping its profit at an acceptable level. Since expansion had increased both employee and customer ranks, more efficient use of employees, instead of reductions in staff, meant the bank could offer improved customer service.

But by late 1989 it had become clear that BNE could not afford the luxury of devoting itself to customer service. Uncontrolled growth and unwise acquisitions had obliterated BNE's profits. Although assets doubled between 1985 and early 1990, the company's profits began to plummet. *Business Week* estimated fourth-quarter 1989 losses at as high as $1.2 billion, down from a $74 million profit the previous year.

In its zeal to grow and to capitalize on the booming real estate market in the late 1980s, BNE bought too many banks that proved to be too hard to digest. Connolly also encouraged subsidiaries and branches to enlarge their loan portfolios at such a rate that many loans were approved without adequate security. These problems were exacerbated by an unwieldy management style and sloppy bookkeeping.

BNE entered the 1990s with about $2.3 billion in nonperforming real estate loans and with about 448 branches throughout New England, most of which were losing disenchanted customers. In January, 1990, following a stormy board meeting, Connolly agreed to resign as soon as a successor could be found. BNE's future will rest on the ability of its new managers to restructure and streamline the lumbering regional giant.

Principal Subsidiaries: The Connecticut Bank & Trust Company; Bank of New England (Boston); Bank of New England-Essex; Bank of New England-North; Bank of New England-South, N.A.; Bank of New England-West; Bank of New England-Worcester; Maine National Bank; Bank of New England-Old Colony; New England Commercial Finance Corp.; Bank New England Leasing Group; BNE Vehicle Leasing; McCullagh Leasing Inc.; McCullagh Leasing, Ltd.; New England Capital Corp.; Bank of New England International; BNE Realty Credit Corp.; Constitution Capital Management Co.; BNE Associates, Inc.; Bank of New England Trust Co.; BNE Mortgage Corp.; New England Discount Brokerage, Inc.; BNE Data Services Corp.; BNE Asset Sales, Inc.; BNE Capital Markets, Inc.

THE BANK OF NEW YORK COMPANY, INC.

THE BANK OF NEW YORK COMPANY, INC.

48 Wall Street
New York, New York 10286
U.S.A.
(212) 495–1784

Public Company
Incorporated: 1968
Employees: 14,500
Assets: $47.4 billion
Stock Index: New York

Certain corporations come to bear the impress of a single, dominant individual, and for more than 200 years the Bank of New York has exemplified the fiscal policies, character, and even the temperament of its chief founder, Alexander Hamilton. The patrician lawyer was famous for his brilliant theories of finance, for his personal elegance, and for his staunch conservatism; his bank must be said to share all three characteristics. The Bank of New York has remained a pillar of strength during this country's many panics and depressions, able to weather the financial storms that have sunk so many more aggressive institutions by preserving a conservative lending policy and high liquidity. Indeed, so blue-blooded is the bank's history that one is tempted to ascribe its long-established, understated strength less to sound fiscal strategy than to what its founder would have called "good taste."

There are simply certain things the Bank of New York does not do, has never done, and will never permit—or would not have, that is, until the year 1982, when its new chairman, J. Carter Bacot, began a program of acquisition and restructuring designed to pull his aristocratic bank into the decidedly plebeian 20th century. Bacot appears to be succeeding; the bank is rated the tenth-largest financial institution in the United States and has acquired a very modern reputation for iron competitiveness. Whether the Hamiltons, Roosevelts, and Rikers whose names grace the list of past bank directors would be entirely pleased with these changes it open to some doubt, but their approval is probably not of much interest to Mr. Bacot and his new generation of leaders.

The period immediately following the Revolutionary War was a time of fiscal chaos for the newly-independent states. Incredibly enough, at that point there was only one bank in all of North America, which had opened its doors in Philadelphia in 1781. The colonies had long depended for their medium of exchange on a haphazard mix of barter, wampum, foreign coins, and a vast array of colonial currencies, none of them of much value beyond the immediate vicinity of their printing. In such a confused climate it was difficult to transact business, and in 1784 a group of men in New York decided to create a bank that would help stabilize the precarious situation, in a profitable manner. The leader of this group of citizens was Alexander Hamilton, the distinguished former congressman, revolutionary colonel, and co-author of the *Federalist Papers*. Though only 27 years old, Hamilton was already looked upon as a brilliant statesman with special expertise in the areas of economics and banking. At a time when the country lacked not only banks but also banking laws, Hamilton devised the constitution for what would soon be called the Bank of New York, insisting on a host of policies that were soon adopted as standard practice for all modern banks. In particular, he and the other directors agreed that the bank would sell its original stock for specie only—that is, its capital would consist of gold and silver instead of the land mortgages then backing most of the shaky colonial currencies. Having quickly raised $500,000 in capital, the bank's 13 directors elected General Alexander MacDougall as president and opened its doors at 159 Queen Street on June 9, 1784. New York City finally had its first bank.

The original bank directors included many of the city's leading businessmen: Isaac Roosevelt had made a fortune refining sugar, creating the wealth which later would help raise two of his descendents to the presidency of the United States; MacDougall was not only a successful merchant but had risen to the rank of major general during the war; and Comfort Sands was one of the city's most prominent shippers and importers. The list of shareholders was equally impressive, leading one early social scientist to note that of the 15 New York families reputed to keep carriages in 1804, four of them were at some time represented on the bank's board of directors. From the beginning, the bank's aristocratic heritage helped it gain the confidence of the city's business community.

Prospering immediately, the bank began a string of consecutive dividend payments never to be broken. It was also helpful that its young founder, Hamilton, became the secretary of the treasury of the United States in 1789, fostering a long intimacy between the bank and both state and national governments. Hamilton relied on "his bank" to perform services useful to the new and struggling government, such as loaning it $200,000 in 1789, and two years later buying up large quantities of government bonds to keep their price from falling sharply. In return, as secretary of the treasury, Hamilton did his best to protect the bank during difficult times, fighting to keep government funds in the bank even after the new Bank of the United States (also his creation) established a branch in New York. In this he was ultimately not successful, but it is clear that the bank enjoyed what would now be considered unethical treatment at the hands of its founder.

In 1789, the bank moved to its present location at the corner of Wall and William Streets. By that time, the American banking system had begun to evolve and stabilize its financial markets, and by 1800 the bank had its first competitor in New York, Aaron Burr's Manhattan Company. The city was growing at a frantic pace, however, and there was plenty of business for the plethora of banks soon to follow. The Bank of New York always had the advantage over its rivals of being the first and most prestigious of the New York banks, enabling it to adopt a posture somewhat above the fray of the marketplace. At a time when the young country was being rapidly populated with a variety of shaky frontier banks, the Bank of New York was able to further its reputation for prudence by moving slowly and thoughtfully toward a portfolio of well-secured, stable loans. In 1822, the bank significantly increased its resources and strengthened its image overseas by borrowing $250,000 from two London banks. Already it was known in Europe not only as the largest bank in New York, but also as the safest bank in the United States.

In 1830, a number of the bank's directors helped to found the New York Life Insurance and Trust Company, a similarly patrician corporation which 100 years later would merge with the bank. The 1830s were marked by continued economic growth, often fueled by excessive speculation in the newly created banks and industrial companies. The pyramiding of securities reached such a point that when the Bank of England shut off all credit to the United States, it sparked the national panic of 1837, one of the worst in American history. In what would become its typical fashion, the bank rode out the storm easily, having never indulged in dubious loans and always keeping a larger-than-normal amount of cash on hand. It therefore had fewer nonperforming loans than many other banks, as well as liquid capital to allay the anxieties of its depositors, thus avoiding both prongs of the panic. Such conservative banking policies, which often earned for the bank adjectives like "stodgy" or even "inert," became considerably more appealing in times of panic and depression, and largely account for the bank's continued existence over the past 200 years.

In 1853, New York banks took an important step when they formed the New York Clearing House Association, an instrument through which the banks could settle their daily accounts with each other in a single, secure location. But the clearing house soon took on another, more important function: bringing together all banks and pooling a part of their assets became a line of defense against the danger of massive deposit withdrawal during panics. Any bank facing a grave depletion of funds could receive a loan from the clearing house to keep it afloat until the crisis had passed. Unfortunately, it required another panic to illustrate this potential of the clearing house. As it did 20 years before, the Bank of New York came through the panic of 1857 without suffering any real damage.

The greatest challenge was yet to come, however. By the late 1850s it was clear that civil war was inevitable and for New York banks this was particularly ominous. Over the years, New York had become the center of the booming cotton and clothing trade between England and the southern states, with shipments in each direction stopping at the port of New York and often changing hands there. At the time of the outbreak of the Civil War in 1861, southern planters owed various northern banks an estimated $300 million, making the banks' attitude toward the war more complicated than geography might imply. Furthermore, in 1861 as today, New York banks dominated finance in all of the United States: some $92 million of the country's $126 million in total deposits rested in the vaults of Manhattan banks. The support of the New York bankers was therefore crucial to the success of the Union cause.

Despite the huge losses involved, the financiers threw themselves behind the North without reservation. In August, 1861, Secretary of the Treasury Salmon Chase asked a group of banks for a $150 million loan to equip the Union army, which he quickly got; the Bank of New York eventually held about $3 million in government paper. Unfortunately, Chase insisted on receiving specie for the government notes, assuming that the gold would circulate through the economy and back to the banks. It is no surprise, however, that the gold was promptly snatched up and held by a populace faced with the uncertainties of war, leaving to the various state currencies the role of basic fiscal exchange. Since these were of little use beyond the borders of their issuing states, the federal government was soon forced to print its first "greenbacks" in 1862. To ensure that these were accepted as sound currency, congress passed the National Banking Act the following year. This important measure for the first time regulated all subscribing banks under a federal code, stipulating that if a bank left one-third of its capital with the government, it could loan up to 90% of that amount in the form of the new federal currency or other securities. The danger posed by grossly undercapitalized banks was thus reduced, and in July, 1865 the Bank of New York joined the rapidly growing system, becoming the Bank of New York, N.B.A.

The bank came through the war with its usual health intact, actually raising dividends from 3% to 5% by 1865. The postwar years followed a pattern of frenzied boom period leading to overspeculation, panic, and depression. Though severe, the panic of 1873 and the lean years afterward also had little effect on the bank's overall strength; once again, its conservative loan philosophy spared it the worst effects of typical boom-and-bust cycles. Both in 1873 and in the less acute crash of 1884, the other New York banks looked to the Bank of New York as a haven, relying on its cash reserves for critical loans and on its overall leadership for guidance and support. Toward the close of the 19th century, the bank was, as it had been a hundred years before, New York's largest and most respected financial institution, its list of shareholders a veritable roll call of the city's most famous families. In a time of stupendous economic growth, however, it was not long before the bank lost its claim to being the city's largest, settling instead, as the 20th century began, for the title of most elegant.

The turn of the century saw the bank's increasing involvement in foreign-exchange banking, especially in Latin America. Herbert Griggs, who in 1901 began what would become the longest tenure as president in the bank's history, brought to the position much expertise and interest in the foreign-exchange business, further accelerating the bank's expansion in that area. Even though the bank was no longer New York's largest, the early decades of this century were highly profitable ones for the company as World War I became something of a bonanza for the American economy in general and banks in particular. From a net income of about $400 million in 1900, profits rose to some $820 million in 1917, the year of America's maximum war effort. All of the important New York banks worked closely with the government to finance the war; the Bank of New York by itself loaned about $38 million, and also offered various other services to Washington. The loans were highly profitable, and by the end of the war the bank was more than ready for the 1920s.

Along with the rest of the nation, the bank was soon doing more business than ever. In the heady atmosphere of that decade, even the staid Bank of New York began to hunger for a dramatic increase in its capital—for a way to recoup some of the ground it had lost to younger and more aggressive rivals. In 1922, the bank announced its merger with the New York Life Insurance and Trust Company. The merger was a natural fit, and with little strain the two companies became the Bank of New York and Trust Company, relocating in 1928 to a new 32-story building immediately adjacent to the old bank headquarters. Deposits at the new bank, now once again chartered under state (as opposed to national) banking law, totaled $78 million and continued to climb during the bountiful years leading up to October, 1929.

As its history might predict, the bank sailed through the great panic of that year with little damage. Even the worst of all modern depressions could not upset the carefully managed portfolio at the Bank of New York, which actually increased its total deposits during the slump's most dangerous early years. While 4,600 banks across the country closed their doors, the Bank of New York took an asset depreciation of $6 million without breaking stride, continuing to rack up profits every year and paying its normal, healthy dividends on time and without anxiety. The bank actively supported President Roosevelt's radical attempts to halt the economy's slide. Later the Bank of New York worked along with the nation's other financial institutions in funding the enormous war effort from 1941–1945. In times of crisis such as these, the bank's long and stable history gave to it a special importance in the eyes of the business world.

Since World War II the Bank of New York has undergone a gradually accelerating transformation into a more modern financial institution, most obviously in the form of a series of mergers and acquisitions. In 1948, the bank merged for the second time, joining forces with the Fifth Avenue Bank of mid-town Manhattan; in the mid-1960s it added Empire Trust Company. In 1968 the bank was incorporated as the Bank of New York, Inc., and the next year added the "Company" now in its name when it absorbed six subsidiaries. Between 1969 and 1974, the bank acquired four more small banks. Its next large acquisition came in 1980, when it bought the Empire National Bank and in 1987, it bought the Long Island Trust Company. More significant than any of these moves, however, was the 1982 elevation of J. Carter Bacot from president to chairman of the bank. It has been Bacot's vigorous leadership that has, in the words of one financial analyst, "dragged BONY into the 20th century." A relatively young 49 when he took over, Bacot has shown little patience with the bank's traditional posture of high-toned inertia.

Bacot's changes have been in four basic areas. He sold off the bank's upstate retail branches, concentrating all of its retail business in the greater New York metropolitan area, especially in more affluent Long Island and in the counties north of New York City. Second, Bacot was far more daring in his loan philosophy, dealing more quickly and in larger amounts than the bank had usually allowed. Loans of up to $60 million have become common as the bank has focused its portfolio in the areas of commercial industry, Wall Street securities firms, utilities, and the oil and gas industries. Third, the chairman ended the bank's long ambivalence about the role it wanted to play in the financial world, giving up all pretensions to investment banking and the capital markets to concentrate on becoming a large regional bank. Much of the bank's income is now generated by processing the daily transactions of securities brokers, an activity which, strictly speaking, is not even in the banking field.

Finally, in 1987, Bacot confirmed the bank's place in the rough and tumble of modern business when he initiated a year-long hostile takeover bid for S.B. Irving Trust Bank Corporation, a Wall Street neighbor whose $24 billion in assets were slightly larger than those of the purchaser. When the dust had settled, and Irving Trust was merged with the Bank of New York on December 30, 1988, Bacot had created the nation's tenth-largest bank holding company, one well-positioned for further expansion. The takeover was universally praised by financial analysts (except those at Irving, which fought the takeover), who felt that the two banks' similar interests would mesh together quite well. All in all, a very tidy merger, and not one anyone would have expected of the bank before its recent sea change. No doubt the frankly aristocratic traditions of the Bank of New York will linger on in one form or another, but Bacot seems convinced that even blue blood can be made to circulate faster than was once thought seemly.

Principal Subsidiaries: The Bank of New York; The Bank of New York Trust Co.; The Bank of New York Trust Co. of Florida, N.A.; The Bank of New York Life Insurance Co., Inc.; ARCS Mortgage, Inc.; Beacon Capital Management Company, Inc.; The Bank of New York Commercial Corp.; B.N.Y. Holdings (Delaware) Corporation; The Bank of New York International, Inc.; BNY International Investments, Inc.; BNY Leasing, Inc.; BNY Financial Corporation; BNY Personal Brokerage, Inc.; Wall Street Data Services; Wall Street Trust Co.-California; The Bank of New York Consumer Leasing Corp.; The Bank of New York Overseas Finance N.V.; BNY Australia Limited.

Further Reading: Nevins, Allan. *History of the Bank of New York and Trust Company*, New York, Bank of New York, 1934; Streeter, Edward. *Window on America*, New York, The Bank of New York, 1959.

Scotiabank

THE BANK OF NOVA SCOTIA

44 King Street West
Toronto, Ontario
M5H 1H1
Canada
(416) 866-6161

Public Company
Incorporated: 1832
Employees: 26,187
Assets: C$71.43 billion (US$59.87 billion) (1987)
Stock Index: Alberta London Montreal Toronto Vancouver Winnipeg

The Bank of Nova Scotia, the second oldest bank in Canada, has more than 1,000 domestic offices as well as offices in 45 foreign countries. Scotiabank, as it is usually called, conducts its activities through four major divisions: retail banking and operations, Canadian commercial banking, North American corporate and investment banking, and international.

The first public financial institution in the colonial port city of Halifax, the Bank of Nova Scotia was formed on March 30, 1832 to handle the economic activity associated with the area's lumbering, fishing, farming, and foreign trade. None of the members of the first board of directors had any practical banking experience, but this did not deter them from setting up the necessary operations and appointing James Forman, a prominent citizen of Halifax, to serve as the first cashier (as the general manager was called then).

The bank officially opened in August, 1832, a time of unfavorable economic conditions because of massive crop failures and a cholera outbreak. Early development, therefore, focused on establishing a foreign exchange business with agents in New York, London, and Boston, while local agencies and the main office in Halifax concentrated on making domestic loans.

Over the next 30 years, the bank grew slowly in the face of increased competition from existing institutions, such as the Halifax Banking Company and the Bank of British North America, as well as from new banks opening throughout Nova Scotia. It was not until the early 1870s that the staff also determined that growth had been stunted by Mr. Forman's embezzlement of $315,000 since 1844.

The bank gradually recovered from these losses through the efforts of Forman's successor, William C. Menzies, who guided an expansion program that increased total assets to $3.5 million by 1875. Though local industry was declining, growth continued throughout the decade as the bank found opportunities in financing coal mining, iron, and steel businesses serving the railway and steamship lines. These improvements in transportation stimulated manufacturing throughout Canada, which also served to fuel the bank's development.

The Bank of Nova Scotia expanded outside the maritime provinces in 1882, when it opened a branch in Winnipeg to take advantage of opportunities created by a real estate boom in the area. The boom collapsed within six months, however, saddling the bank with enormous losses and forcing the branch to close three years later.

In 1883, the Bank of Nova Scotia acquired the Union Bank of Price Edward Island. This bank had sought a larger, stronger institution to help it weather hard times that had already forced the liquidation of one local bank and were seriously affecting others in the area. By the end of that year, the Bank of Nova Scotia was operating 23 branches in Prince Edward Island, New Brunswick, and Nova Scotia.

Although a depression in Canada in the early 1880s caused heavy losses stemming from the failure of several businesses, the bank had rebounded enough by 1885 to consider further expansion, this time in the United States. Minneapolis was chosen, because of its strong grain and manufacturing industries, to be the initial site for a direct lending and foreign exchange business. This office closed seven years later when the local environment became less favorable and other cities, such as Chicago, showed more potential.

In 1888, the bank opened an office in Montreal in a second attempt to establish a domestic presence outside of the maritime provinces. This office was followed a year later by an office in Kingston, Jamaica, the first time a Canadian bank had expanded outside North America or the United Kingdom. The next new branch opened in St. John's, Newfoundland in 1894 to handle the business of two local institutions that had dissolved suddenly. Credit for this vigorous expansion goes to Thomas Fyshe, who became cashier in 1876 and resigned in 1897 after 21 years with the bank.

In March, 1900 the bank moved its headquarters to Toronto, to be better able to take advantage of opportunities offered by the Klondike Gold Rush and the completion of the Canadian Pacific Railway, as well as to be closer to its other branches in Canada and the United States. Its move into western Canada was only somewhat successful, however; several unprofitable branches closed soon after they opened, while others in Edmonton, Calgary, and Vancouver were slow to make a profit. Nonetheless, the bank considered expansion a necessary part of its overall strategic plan to achieve national growth and avoid takeover by another institution. Development in the East was more successful; 19 new branches opened in Nova Scotia and New Brunswick, 16 opened in Ontario, and four opened in Quebec between 1897 and 1909.

Beginning in 1901, Henry C. McLeod, who served as general manager from 1897 to 1910, waged a campaign to require all Canadian banks to undergo external inspection by the Canadian Department of Finance. This effort, prompted by the large number of bank failures that had occurred since 1895, was intended to win the public's confidence in its financial institutions. None of the other Canadian banks supported him, so, impatient with the government's inactivity on the issue, McLeod subjected the Bank of Nova Scotia to examination by two Scottish accountants, making his the first Canadian chartered bank to be verified by an independent, external audit. McLeod didn't win his battle until 1913, when the Bank Act was revised and such inspection became compulsory.

Between 1910 and 1920 the bank embarked upon a series of major acquisitions that significantly altered its size and the scope of its operations. After two years of informal discussions, the bank officially merged with the oldest Canadian chartered bank, the Bank of New Brunswick, on December 11, 1912. The Bank of New Brunswick was a relatively small institution, confined to 31 branches in a single region and lacking the resources to expand due to its traditional practice of returning capital to shareholders. In 1914, with the acquisition of the 12-year-old Toronto-based Metropolitan Bank, the Bank of Nova Scotia became the fourth largest financial institution in Canada. Five years later, the Bank of Nova Scotia acquired the Bank of Ottawa, allowing it to expand westward again without having to establish new branches.

Joining other Canadian financial institutions in the war effort during World War I, Scotiabank experienced only minor disruptions in operations and staffing and returned to normal upon the war's end.

During the early 1920s, the bank slowed the pace of external growth to focus its attention on consolidating the operations of the three prewar acquisitions and reorganizing its departments for greater efficiency. An Investment Department was also formed to handle securities transactions, which represented a significant amount of the bank's business in Toronto, Montreal, and New York.

The strong postwar recovery brought healthy earnings throughout most of the decade, until the 1929 stock market crash and subsequent depression. Between 1933 and 1935, the bank closed 19 domestic branches as profits dropped by half a million dollars, to C$1.8 million. Business conditions in Newfoundland deteriorated, the radical Social Credit Party rose to power in Alberta and enacted troublesome legislation there, and political difficulties in Cuba and Puerto Rico pressured international activities.

Economic recovery went up and down between 1936 and 1939 as the positive effects of the growing Canadian mining industry were offset by a drought in the West. The bank's asset base continued to grow, but not without some managerial concern—it consisted largely of loans to the government for relief funds, rather than higher-yielding commercial transactions.

World War II increased the demand for banking services, particularly by the government for financing the war. By the end of the war the bank's assets had surpassed $600 million, but federal government securities represented 50% of the total.

In 1945, the new general manager, Horace L. Enman, renewed prewar efforts to explore new business opportunities and improve shareholders' returns. Buoyed by heavy immigration to Canada and the nation's need for capital, the bank's commercial loan activity increased after the war to restore a more favorable balance between lending to business concerns and to the government. In 1949, Enman became president and C. Sydney Frost became general manager. By this time the bank's rapid growth and extensive reach demanded greater decentralization. Regional offices gradually assumed responsibility for staffing and maintaining branch activities and credit supervision. By 1950, the bank had opened 90 new branches, half in British Columbia and Alberta.

The 1950s were a period of economic prosperity throughout Canada. Resource development and improvements in transportation increased immigration levels in major Canadian cities and provided a stimulus to growth. The change from a fixed to a floating official exchange rate allowed the bank to take advantage of the open market for the Canadian dollar and enhance its exchange-trading skills. When the National Housing Act was passed in 1954, the bank established a mortgage department, and it later developed a secondary mortgage market among pension funds to offset decreased lending activity. The bank also introduced an insured savings plan that brought in a substantial amount of new business, and more importantly, gave the bank a competitive advantage in selling banking services.

A change in the Bank Act in 1954 permitted banks to make automobile and household loans, prompting the bank to introduce a consumer credit program in 1958. In order for the bank to observe the 6% interest rate ceiling mandated by the Bank Act yet successfully operate in the consumer lending area on a large-scale basis, these loans required customers to deposit payments every month into a bank account that would pay off the loan by the due date and return a higher rate of interest to the bank over the life of the loan. By its second year, this plan had generated $100 million in loans and become a major contributor to the bank's overall earnings. When, in 1959, a money squeeze threatened its lending activity volume, the bank introduced a one-to-six-year term note that allowed it to compete successfully with finance and trust companies.

The bank continued its international expansion during this period, particularly in Jamaica, Trinidad, and Barbados, although the nationalization of Cuban banks in 1961 forced it, regretfully, to close the eight branches it had established there at the beginning of the century.

In 1958, the bank joined with British financial interests to form the Bank of Nova Scotia Trust Company to engage in offshore and trust operations which were off-limits to foreign banks. A year later, the Bank of Nova Scotia Trust Company of New York was established.

Beginning in 1960, the bank aggressively pursued a strategy to increase its volume of deposits by resuming the establishment of new branches in Canada as well as abroad. This inflow of funds was required to support the bank's consumer credit operations while also meeting the demand for mortgages and short-term commercial loans. More than 60% of these new branches were in convenient suburban locations to attract new customers in and around Toronto, Montreal, Edmonton, and Calgary.

Coupled with new products like term notes, certificates of deposit, and six-year certificates, this campaign increased the volume of personal savings deposits by 50% between 1960 and 1965.

This increased activity also enabled the bank to maintain its presence in the financial services industry despite the ceiling on lending rates, which had virtually eliminated the bank from competing effectively against trust and finance companies in all areas except for personal loans. During this time, the bank also increased its mortgage involvement by joining with two other partners to form three new ventures: Markborough Properties, a real estate company; the Mortgage Insurance Company of Canada; and Central Covenants, a mortgage financing company.

In 1963, the bank underwent a major internal reorganization, and a new profit planning system was introduced which required each branch and region to submit annual loan and deposit forecasts to be incorporated into the bank's overall plan. This system allowed the bank to further decentralize operations, to encourage competition among branches, and to better identify the services its customers wanted.

Meanwhile, business in the Caribbean continued to grow, despite losses in Cuba. Much of this growth was hotel and resort financing in areas like Jamaica and Puerto Rico, where tourism was becoming big business. The bank also opened branches in London, Glasgow, Amsterdam, Munich, Beirut, and Tokyo. Its international division became a major player in the Eurodollar market at this time.

During the early 1960s, the bank also worked to establish a stronger presence in the United States, particularly in Los Angeles and Houston, by offering financing and deposit opportunities for U.S. corporations in addition to international tax services. These efforts fueled the bank's accelerated growth in the second half of the decade.

At home, the early 1970s saw strong personal and small business lending activity, leading the bank to launch a number of new services, including automobile financing and a farm program to meet credit needs in the agricultural sector. Lending activity shifted significantly toward commercial concerns, particularly retail accounts, later that decade as inflation increased daily operational costs for Canadian businesses.

Actively involved in the precious metals market since 1958, the bank expanded this business throughout the 1970s by buying two-thirds of the country's annual production and then selling actual bullion and bullion certificates. It was also during this period that the rising expenses of branch development caused the bank to refocus its emphasis from opening new offices within Canada to improving existing operations and relocating branches to more lucrative areas.

In 1972, the bank was sued by VK Mason Construction Ltd. for negligent misrepresentation related to the building of an office and shopping complex. The contractor had required assurance from the bank that the developer, Courtot Investments, had sufficient financing to finish the construction before it would agree to take on the job, and Scotiabank had informed Mason that interim financing was available to Courtot if needed. When the project was completed, Mason was paid C$1 million less than had been agreed and found that, rather than helping the developer pay its creditors, the bank called in its own loan and sold the complex when Courtot defaulted.

The Supreme Court of Canada found against the bank, though it affirmed the bank's right of first claim on the developer's assets as the mortgagee. Mason was permitted to collect damages by placing a lien on the bank's assets without having to compete with other Courtot creditors.

Organizational changes at the general office were made in the second half of the 1970s which created separate departments for each of the bank's three main customer categories: individual, commercial, and large corporate. In 1980 an operations department was formed to consolidate many of the branch, regional, and head office functions into one area, a move which signaled a shift away from decentralization toward more direct headquarters control.

The bank's total assets reached C$50 billion by the end of 1981, with international business growing twice as fast as domestic operations and at a higher rate than that of any other Canadian bank. This growth was attributed to many factors, including the bank's established European and American presence, its expansion into Asia and the Pacific, and the development of a worldwide foreign exchange and banking system that operated around the clock. The year also saw the historic opening of the first and only Canadian banking branch in China.

Although a downturn in the economy during 1983 forced the bank to temporarily curtail expansion, its focus on smaller companies saved it from the large-scale losses other Canadian banks suffered from loans made to failing firms like Dome Petroleum and Massey-Ferguson, and to Mexico, Brazil, and Poland.

This focus on smaller companies and individuals did create image problems in the corporate and commercial areas. To counter the perception that the bank was not fully committed to businesses, Scotiabank embarked upon an extensive, innovative advertising campaign in 1986 using customers' case histories and games of visual illusion to show the various ways that the bank had helped companies.

During the first half of the 1980s, the bank was accused of wrongdoing in a series of cases stemming from its activities both at home and abroad. In March, 1983, the bank was asked by a Miami court to release records from its Cayman Islands branch concerning certain customers under investigation for narcotics and tax violations. Although the bank was protected under Cayman Island law from such releases, a Florida judge ruled that the bank stood in contempt of court and fined it $25,000 a day, retroactive to November 1983, for each day it did not produce the records. In order to end a stalemate which could have forced the bank into bankruptcy, the Cayman Islands Governor-in-Council intervened to authorize the bank to supply the required information, but not before the fine had reached US$1.8 million. The bank lost its appeal to the U.S. Supreme Court in January, 1985.

In 1984 the bank, along with four other Canadian banks, was the subject of a one-year investigation by the Royal Commission of the Bahamas into drug dealing and money laundering by Bahamian Prime Minister Pindling and his wife. Scotiabank had lent more than $1 million to Pindling between 1977 and 1983 and had also accepted deposits from the couple totalling $114,000 from an unidentified source. Although the investigation was inconclusive, it cast a cloud on a 1985 case alleging that the bank had committed fraud against the Investment Dealers Association of Canada in its involvement in the failure of Atlantic Securities Ltd. in 1981. Although this case generated much controversy, the Nova Scotia County Court acquitted the bank.

In 1987 Scotiabank further penetrated the financial services market with the formation of Scotia Securities. This new subsidiary, providing discount brokerage and security underwriting services, allowed the bank to compete more effectively with investment banking firms.

Presently, the Bank of Nova Scotia is pursuing a strategy of global operations to assure profitability regardless of any fluctuations in individual markets. Competing successfully with both domestic and foreign banks will require greater investment in new services to attract new accounts, as well as improved efficiency to continue to deliver personalized attention to the bank's current customers. Although Scotiabank shares the dilemmas of other financial institutions in coping with the problems of outstanding Third World debt, and also faces the continuing challenge of inflation at home, the bank and its current chairman, Cedric E. Ritchie, look forward to the coming decades with the enthusiasm and confidence that have characterized its development over the past 150 years.

Principal Subsidiaries: BNS Australia Pty. Ltd.; BNS International (Hong Kong) Ltd.; The Bank of Nova Scotia International (Curacao) N.V.; The Bank of Nova Scotia Asia Ltd.; The Bank of Nova Scotia Channel Islands Ltd.; The Bank of Nova Scotia International Ltd.; The Bank of Nova Scotia Jamaica Ltd.; The Bank of Nova Scotia Properties Inc.; The Bank of Nova Scotia Trinidad and Tobago Ltd.; The Bank of Nova Scotia Trust Company (Bahamas) Ltd.; The Bank of Nova Scotia Trust Company of New York; BNS International (Ireland) Ltd.; BNS International (United Kingdom) Ltd.; Scotiabank (U.K.) Ltd.; Brunswick Square Ltd.; Calgary Centre Holdings Ltd.; Chargex Ltd.; Empire Realty (Cayman) Ltd.; Export Finance Corporation of Canada, Ltd.; First Southern Bank Ltd.; Fredericton Developments Ltd.; JPM, Inc.; Maduro & Curiel's Bank N.V.; MHM Property Ltd.; The Nova Scotia Corp.; Scotia Centre Ltd.; Scotia Leasing Ltd.; Scotia Mortgage Corporation; Scotia Realty Antilles N.V.; Scotia Realty Ltd.; Scotia Securities Inc.; Scotiabank de Puerto Rico; Scotia Export Finance Corp.; Scotia Factors (1985) Ltd.; Scotia Futures Ltd.; WBM, Inc.; The West India Company of Merchant Bankers Ltd.

Further Reading: Schull, Joseph and Gibson, J. Douglas. *The Scotiabank Story: A History of the Bank of Nova Scotia, 1832–1982*, Toronto, Macmillan of Canada, 1982.

BANK OF TOKYO, LTD.

6–3, Nihonbashi Hongokucho 1-chome
Chuo-ku
Tokyo 103
Japan
(03) 245–1111

Public Company
Incorporated: 1880 as Yokohama Specie Bank
Employees: 7,900
Assets: ¥23 trillion
Stock Index: Tokyo Osaka

The Bank of Tokyo is Japan's leading forex, or foreign exchange, bank. It acquired and has maintained that distinction mainly by government fiat, as the Japanese government has found it advantageous to designate certain private institutions to perform official functions. After 30 years of strong economic growth, both government and industry have effectively drawn the line between where competition may and may not occur. As a result, a certain interdependency has evolved in which the Bank of Tokyo has a well-established and protected niche.

Many of Japan's major banks were created shortly after 1868, when with the Meiji restoration the government sponsored a rapid modernization program. The sudden expansion of commerce and industry precipitated a need for banks to serve the *zaibatsu*, or large conglomerates, as well as entrepreneurs and individual depositors. These early banks were usually capitalized by those they served. But Japan's imperial family provided 40% of the capital for the Yokohama Specie Bank, the Bank of Tokyo's predecessor. Far from simply serving the family's interests, however, the bank was primarily conerned with foreign exchange, trade, and short-term financing. It was named after the specie, a silver coin used as international currency for settling payment between traders.

Established in 1880 in the busy port of Yokohama, the bank gained special status as a foreign-exchange institution in 1887. After acquiring the authority to sell bonds on behalf of the government, it raised ¥10 million from its first issue in 1889.

The Yokohama Specie Bank actively participated in financing Japanese ventures in Taiwan, Korea, and China. Under the protection of government regulations, the bank was largely sheltered from competition with the powerful *zaibatsu*-affiliated banks as well as the rapidly growing city banks. With such a strong interest in the bank's functions, the Japanese government began to exercise greater influence over its policies and decisions.

By World War I, the bank's network of representative offices covered every major trading center in the Pacific and the financial capitals of the world. Japan's role in Asia, greatly expanded by postwar agreements, contributed further to trade and commerce, and to the foreign-exchange business. No longer dealing only in silver, Yokohama Specie held substantial dollar and sterling reserves.

As militarists gained power in the government during the 1930s, Japanese development of the Asian mainland became increasingly belligerent. As Japan's war against China, which formally began in 1937, led into World War II, the international trade and industrial finance upon which Yokohama Specie depended were thoroughly disrupted. By the end of the war, Japan had suffered severe damage to its basic industries.

The occupation authority decreed an entirely new set of industrial laws in 1945. The legislation extended to the banking industry, where large banks were divided into smaller ones and forbidden to re-establish preferential relationships with commercial interests. This would have been the case for Yokohama Specie had it not been singled out by General Douglas MacArthur himself to be punished for its role in the Japanese war effort.

With its international assets frozen, Yokohama Specie was forced to rebuild its business completely. It was ordered to change its name—it became the Bank of Tokyo—and, denied access to foreign-exchange business, it started over as a commercial city bank in 1946. The staff, with years of accumulated experience in world currency markets and finance, was clearly frustrated and unenthusiastic about the bank's new role.

As Japanese trade recovered during the early 1950s, however, there was again a need for a specialized foreign-exchange bank. In 1954, the Diet passed the Foreign Exchange Bank Law, which was specifically intended to reinstate the Bank of Tokyo as the nation's primary forex dealer. In fairness to competitors, though, the same law restricted the bank's domestic activities.

In this way the Bank of Tokyo resumed its close relationship with the government's Ministry of Finance. As an important component of national economic management, the bank was frequently given preferential treatment by the government. It met fewer obstacles when applying to open additional foreign offices and was permitted to lend higher percentages of total capital to single countries than either city banks or long-term credit banks.

Starting in 1955, Japanese economic growth was mainly led by exports. Industrial deregulation permitted many of the former *zaibatsu* trading companies to re-establish links with their banks. As these banks became more sophisticated, general trading companies such as Sumitomo, Mitsui, and Mitsubishi increasingly worked through their affiliated banks. The Bank of Tokyo, forced into an increasingly narrow role, concentrated on its one field of expertise: foreign exchange.

There were few incentives for the Bank of Tokyo to

become a "universal" bank, offering a full complement of banking services. Certain operations, in fact, were restricted by law. Instead, the bank used the profits from forex dealing to fund a new campaign to win back business that had been siphoned off by competitors. As an institution intimately involved in both domestic economic management and international finance, the Bank of Tokyo emphasized its multinational character by increasing its hiring of local talent at its various overseas offices.

The Bank of Tokyo was jolted during the oil crisis of 1973–1974, but was actually hurt more by aftereffects suffered by its clients—many of them foreign national banks. As the world economy struggled to regain its balance, many indebted Third World nations encountered financial crises. Chief among them was Brazil, to which the Bank of Tokyo had lent substantial sums. Rather than writing off losses there, however, the bank negotiated a rescheduling and took an active role in strengthening its client's financial position. The bank thus established itself as a trustworthy partner, despite severe losses.

The combined effects of deregulation, competition, and basic changes in the Japanese economy led many Japanese banks to become more resourceful and diverse. Bank of Tokyo, however, first attempted to further consolidate its position in foreign exchange. When even that traditional strength became squeezed, the bank then attempted to raise competitiveness by increasing efficiency and emphasizing more profitable operations such as securities, international ventures, and fee services, gradually converting itself into an investment bank.

The Bank of Tokyo financed industrial resource projects in Canada, Australia, Burma, and the Arctic, and served as an advisor on projects in Singapore and Thailand. In the process, it developed a specialty in railway finance. A long-standing avoidance of business with Taiwanese interests paid off in the early 1980s when the bank was chosen to participate in projects in mainland China.

Still, the unique character and organization of the Bank of Tokyo allowed it to corner the market in long-dated forward deals, in which it surpassed even the long-term credit banks. The bank's strength in this area derives not just from its tremendous capital resources, but also from its ability to manage the foreign-exchange play that often occurs in such deals. The bank has also begun to take on trust banks and securities houses by issuing various kinds of bank debentures.

The bank's greatest strengths of late, however, are attributable to the importance it places on intelligence in local markets. A major player in international finance, the Bank of Tokyo has 104 branches, offices, and affiliates worldwide (not including its California subsidiary's 142 branches), but only 32 branches in Japan. It employs more foreigners than Japanese, by a ratio of seven to five. Given the extraordinary pace of internationalization among Japanese companies and Japan's growing presence in the world economy, the Bank of Tokyo seems poised for success.

Principal Subsidiaries: California First Bank; The Bank of Tokyo Trust Company; The Chicago-Tokyo Bank; Tokyo Bancorp International (Houston) Inc.; Bank of Tokyo International; The Bank of Tokyo Canada; The Bank of Tokyo (Panama), S.A.; Banco de Tokyo S/A; Bank of Tokyo (Curacao) Holding N.V.; Bank of Tokyo (Switzerland) Ltd.; The Bank of Tokyo (Holland) N.V.; Banque Européenne de Tokyo S.A.; The Bank of Tokyo (Luxembourg) S.A.; Bank of Tokyo (Deutschland) AG; BOT Lease (Deutscheland) GmbH; BOT Finanziaria Italiana S.p.A. (Milano); Bank of Tokyo International Limited; Saudi International Bank; The Bangkok Tokyo Finance and Securities Co., Ltd.; Bangkok Tohgin Holding Co., Ltd.; BOT International (Singapore) Ltd.; BOT International (H.K.) Ltd.; BOT Finance (H.K.) Ltd.; Kincheng-Tokyo Finance Co., Ltd.; Bank of Tokyo Australia Ltd.; BOT Securities Inc.; BOT Futures (Singapore) Pte. Ltd.

BANKAMERICA CORPORATION

555 California Street
San Francisco, California 94104
(415) 622–3456

Public Company
Incorporated: 1904 as the Bank of Italy
Employees: 61,020
Assets: $94.65 billion
Stock Index: New York Pacific Midwest

The Bank of America was founded in 1904 as the Bank of Italy. Its credo was radical at the time: to serve "the little fellows." From its humble beginnings in a former tavern, the Bank of America grew to become the world's largest bank and a force that revolutionized U.S. banking. With degregulation, however, its traditional emphasis on the general consumer created problems for the bank.

Amadeo Peter Giannini, the founder of today's BankAmerica, became one of the most important figures in 20th-century American banking. Giannini, an Italian immigrant, was seven when his father died. By age 21, he had earned half ownership of his stepfather's produce business. He married into a wealthy family, and profits from the produce business, combined with shrewd real estate investments in San Francisco, enabled him to retire at age 31.

His retirement was brief. When his father-in-law died, he left a sizable estate, including a directorship of a small San Francisco savings bank. When Giannini failed to convince the board of this bank that the poor but hardworking people who had recently come to the West Coast were good loan risks, he resigned his position and set out to start his own bank—a bank for "people who had never used one."

The year, 1904, was an inauspicious one; an up-and-down economy and the financial irresponsibility of many banks during this period gave banking such a bad name that the government was eventually prompted to create the Federal Reserve system, in 1917. But Giannini's bank was atypical. His policy of lending money to the average citizen was unheard of in the early 1900s, when most banks lent only on a wholesale basis to commercial clients or wealthy individuals.

Giannini raised capital for his new bank, called the Bank of Italy, by selling 3,000 shares of stock, mostly to small investors, none of whom were allowed to own more than 100 shares. Although Giannini never held a dominant share of stock, the extreme loyalty of these and subsequent stockholders allowed him to rule the bank as though it were closely held. His innovative policies made the Bank of Italy and its successor, the Bank of America, the most controversial bank in the United States. The nation watched with wary eyes as he created a system of branch banking that made the Bank of America the world's largest bank in a mere 41 years.

During the famous San Francisco earthquake of 1906 Giannini rescued $80,000 in cash before the bank building burned by hiding it in a wagon full of oranges and bringing it to his house for safekeeping. With this money he reopened his bank days before any other bank and began making loans from a plank-and-barrel counter on the waterfront, urging demoralized San Franciscans to rebuild an even better city.

Giannini's original vision led naturally to branch banking. Expense made it difficult for small depositors to travel long distances to a bank, so Giannini decided his bank would go to them, with numerous well-placed branches. Accordingly, the Bank of Italy bought its first branch, a struggling San Jose bank, in 1909.

Giannini made up the rules as he went; he was not a banker, and his was the first attempt ever at branch banking. Going his own way included loudly denouncing the "big interests," and he repeatedly offended influential members of the financial community, including local bankers, major Californian bankers, and many state and federal regulators, who were already uncertain about how to handle an entirely new kind of banking.

Some did support Giannini's vision though, including William Williams, an early California superintendent of banks, and the Crocker National Bank, which lent money to a subsidiary of the Bank of Italy expressly for acquiring branch banks.

The bank grew rapidly; in 1910 it had assets of $6.5 million. By 1920, assets totaled $157 million, far outstripping the growth of any other California bank and dwarfing its onetime benefactor, Crocker National. Further expansion was stymied, however, by the state of California and by the new Federal Reserve system, which did not allow member banks to open new branches. Giannini shrewdly sidestepped this regulation by establishing separate state banks for southern and northern California (in addition to the Bank of Italy) as well as another national bank, and putting them all under the control of a new holding company, BancItaly. Finally, in 1927 California regulations were changed to permit branch banking, and Giannini consolidated his four banks into the Bank of America of California.

With California conquered, Giannini turned to the national scene. He believed that a few large regional and national banks would come to dominate American banking by using branches, and he intended to blaze the trail. He already owned New York's Bowery and East River National Bank (as well as a chain of banks in Italy); next he established Bank of America branches in Washington, Oregon, Nevada, and Arizona, again before branch banking was explicitly permitted.

Federal regulators, objecting to Giannini's attempts to

dictate the law, took exception to some of his practices. In response, Giannini created another holding company in 1928, to supplant BancItaly. The new company was called Transamerica, to symbolize what Giannini hoped to accomplish in banking.

Giannini knew he needed a Wall Street insider to help him realize his dream of nationwide branch banking, and he thought Elisha Walker, the head of Blair and Company, and old-line Wall Street investment-banking firm, was just the man. So, in 1929, the year Bank of America passed the $1 billion mark in assets, Transamerica bought Blair.

A year later, Giannini consolidated his two banking systems into the Bank of America National Trust and Savings Association, under the control of Transamerica. Sixty years old and in poor health, he relinquished the presidency to Walker, retired for the second time, and went to Europe to recuperate. It was again a short retirement. His stay ended abruptly in 1931, when he received news that Walker was trying to liquidate Transamerica.

Giannini headed straight for California, where three-quarters of the bank's stockholders remained. What followed was one of the most dramatic proxy fights in U.S. history. Giannini crisscrossed California, holding stockholder meetings in town hall, gymnasiums, courthouses, and other public spaces. A poor public speaker, he hired orators to drive home the message that Walker and eastern interests, the dreaded "big guys" Giannini had battled against for years, were trying to ruin the bank. The campaign succeeded and the stockholders returned control of the Bank of America to Giannini.

The bank had suffered, though. By the end of 1932, deposits had shrunk to $876 million, from a high of $1.16 billion in 1930. No dividend was paid that year, for the first time since 1905, and the battle had cost Giannini his New York banks. Depositor confidence had to be rebuilt.

Giannini's presence seemed to be just the right thing. By 1936 Bank of America was the fourth-largest banking institution in the U.S. (and the second-largest savings bank) and assets had grown to $2.1 billion. The bank continued to innovate, instituting a series of new loans called Timeplan installment loans. Timeplan included real estate loans, new and used car financing, personal credit loans from $50 to $1,000, home appliance financing, and home-improvement loans, all industry firsts.

As the Bank of America became more influential, Giannini took on bigger and bigger foes, among them the Federal Reserve, Wall Street, the Treasury Department, the Securities and Exchange Commission, Hans Morgenthau, and J.P. Morgan Jr. Eventually, the enmity Giannini aroused in his war against the Establishment cost the bank its chance for nationwide branch banking. The beginning of the end came in 1937, when the Federal Reserve made its first attempt to force Transamerica and Bank of America to separate.

World War II brought tremendous growth to the Bank of America. As people and businesses flocked to California during the war, the bank more than doubled in size: in 1945, with assets of $5 billion, it passed Chase Manhattan to become the world's largest bank.

As California began to rival New York as the most populous state, Bank of America continued to expand. Giannini continued to battle, and win, against the big interests, until his death in 1949. From radical outsider to the leader of what *Business Week* called the "new orthodoxy" of banking—the trend toward serving average consumers—Giannini's was one of the most innovative careers in 20th-century banking.

He was succeeded as president of Transamerica by his son, Lawrence Mario, long a top official at the bank. L.M. continued in his father's tradition, but for only three years; he succumbed to lifelong health problems in 1952.

Following the deaths of the Gianninis, Bank of America slowly made itself over. New chief Clark Beise moved to decentralize operations, encouraging branch managers to assume more responsibility for their branches. This approach paid off with tremendous growth; by 1960, assets totaled $11.9 billion. The bank continued to innovate. In 1959, it was the first bank to fund a small-business investment company. It was also the first U.S. bank to adopt electronic and computerized recordkeeping; by 1961, operations were completely computerized. Other new programs included student loans, an employee loan-and-deposit plan that let workers transact bank business through their offices (a response to increased competition from credit unions), and the first successful credit card, BankAmericard, the predecessor of Visa.

In addition, Bank of America stepped up its international presence, becoming one of only four U.S. banks with significant impact on international lending. It also began to pursue wholesale accounts, to supplement its traditional retail base. Finally, in 1957, the Federal Reserve forced Transamerica to separate from Bank of America, an event the two institutions had anticipated.

Bank of America's efforts to become a "department store of finance" in the late 1950s and early 1960s marked the last significant period of innovation in the bank's history until the 1980s. It was a time when the bank strove to sell the widest variety of banking services to the widest possible market. Beise felt there was more room for innovation, saying in 1959 "there are new frontiers to develop," but warning that "we are constantly fighting against the attitude of entrenched success." It was a battle that the Bank of America lost, as it eventually became a conservative, stodgy, and inflexible institution.

In 1968, BankAmerica Corporation was created as a holding company to hold the assets of Bank of America N.T. & S.A. and to help the bank expand and better challenge its archrival, Citibank. This came just before banking deregulation, which affected Bank of America more adversely than was predicted. Bank of America's branch banking system was a major problem, since it gave the bank the highest overhead in the banking industry.

Through this period the retail division provided 50% of the bank's profits. It was not until interest rates exploded in the 1970s that the bank's bulk of low-interest-bearing mortgages became damaging, as it was for many savings and loans.

As the largest bank in the world, the Bank of America was a natural target for groups with statements to make during the 1960s. It became the first major employer in California to sign a statement of racial equality in hiring. At the time, the Bank of America had more than 3,500 minority employees—more than 10% of its workforce—and of its 640 black employees, none were menial laborers. The bank also responded to complaints from women's groups, in 1974, by creating a $3.8 million fund for training female employees, and set itself the goal of a 40%-female workforce.

By 1970, Bank of America had established a $100 million loan fund for housing in poverty-stricken areas, and purchased municipal bonds that other California banks wouldn't touch, in keeping with the tradition Giannini had established when he bought rural school bonds and bonds for the Golden Gate Bridge at a time when no other bank would buy such issues.

A.W. ("Tom") Clausen succeeded Rudy Peterson as CEO in 1971. He presided over Bank of America's last tremendous growth spurt—assets jumped 50% (to $60 billion) just between 1973 and 1975. Bank of America was the only one of the 20 largest U.S. banks to average 15% growth between 1971 and 1978; its seemingly unstoppable growth earned its management great praise during the 1970s.

When Clausen left Bank of America in 1981 to head the World Bank, Bank of America had $112.9 billion in assets. Clausen was replaced by 40-year-old Samuel Armacost. Soon the Bank of America began to fall apart. Energy loans, shipping loans, farming loans (Bank of America was the largest agricultural lender in the world) and loans to Third World countries all started to go bad. Bank of America, whose large deposit base had traditionally made it exceptionally liquid but had also given it trouble in maintaining proper capital reserves, was ill prepared to meet the crisis. Suddenly, the biggest bank in the world had no money. It could not even raise capital in the stock market because its stock price had plummeted at a time when most bank stocks were rising.

Armacost started a general campaign to cut costs. The bank dropped a third of its 3,000 corporate clients, sold subsidiaries and its headquarters building, closed 187 branches, and began to lay off employees, something it had never done before. In 1986, the wounded BankAmerica became the target of a takeover bid from a company half its size. First Interstate Bancorp offered $2.78 billion for the nation's second-largest banking group. A few days after this bid was made public in early October, Armacost resigned and was replaced by none other than Tom Clausen, the man many blamed for BankAmerica's troubles in the first place. Clausen resisted the takeover, but Joe Pinola, Interstate's chairman, was determined, and by the end of October had sweetened the deal to $3.4 billion. Clausen was equally determined to prevent BankAmerica's takeover. He rejected First Interstate's bid and battened down the hatches for a hostile assault. In the end, Clausen was able to rally shareholders behind him and thwart First Interstates' plans.

In 1987, BankAmerica set about restructuring its operations. Clausen sold nonessential assets—including the Charles Schwab discount securities brokerage and Bank of America's Italian subsidiary—and refocused the bank's attention on the domestic market. New services, including advanced automated teller machines and extended banking hours, lured Californian customers back. In addition, the bank went after the corporate business it had neglected in the early 1980s. Clausen cut back substantially on staff, cleaned up the nonperforming loans in Bank of America's portfolio, and hired a number of exceptional managers to execute BankAmerica's new directives. By the end of 1988, the bank was in the black again. Though still plagued by a good deal of exposure to Third World debt, BankAmerica was able to record a profit of $726 million, its first in three years.

As the BankAmerica Corporation entered the final decade of the 20th century, it appeared to be on its way to restoring the proud reputation it has enjoyed throughout most of its history. With its rejuvenated strength in the California market and the continued health of its Washington state subsidiary, SeaFirst Corporation, BankAmerica may soon be the West Coast's premier bank holding company. And following the trend toward international banking, BankAmerica is focusing its overseas initiative on the Pacific Rim—on bringing Japanese investment to the U.S. and financing Asian trade. While the bank that A.P. Giannini built struggled through the 1980s, the banking industry, both domestic and international, also struggled with the challenges of deregulation. A revitalized BankAmerica seems to be looking forward to the new opportunities.

Principal Subsidiaries: BA Agency, Inc. (dba BA Insurance Agency, Inc.); BA Cheque Corporation; BA Futures, Inc.; BA Insurance Holding Co.; BA Mortgage and International Realty Corp.; BancAmerica Commercial Corp.; BancAmerica Lease Holding, Inc.; BankAmerica Capital Corp.; BankAmerica Capital Investments, Inc.; BankAmerica Overseas Finance Corp. N.V.; BankAmerica Sutter Mortgage Corp.; BankAmerica Trust Co. of New York; BankAmerica World Trade Corp.; Bank of America NT&SA; Overseas Asset Holdings Inc.; SeaFirst Corp.

Further Reading: James, Marquis and James, Bessie R. *Biography of a Bank: The Story of Bank of America, N.T. & S.A.*, New York, Harper, 1954; Hector, Gary. *Breaking the Bank: The Decline of BankAmerica,* Boston, Little, Brown, 1988.

Bankers Trust
New York
Corporation

BANKERS TRUST NEW YORK CORPORATION

280 Park Avenue
New York, New York 10017
U.S.A.
(212) 250–2500
Public Company
Incorporated: 1903 as Bankers Trust Company
Employees: 12,751
Assets: $57.94 billion
Stock Index: New York London

Bankers Trust New York Corporation, a multibillion-dollar bank holding company, is one of the largest commercial banks in the United States. The nature of the company's business has changed repeatedly since it was founded in 1903. It was first a bankers trust company; by the end of the 1920s it was a wholesale financial-services provider; next it was a retail banking supermarket in the 1960s, with nearly disastrous results; and finally it became a wholesale banker again. Thanks to former Chairman Alfred Brittain III and his successor, Charles S. Sanford, Bankers Trust is now a strong international merchant bank, providing a variety of wholesale banking services to governments, institutions, corporations, and wealthy individuals in the United States and abroad.

In the 1890s and early 1900s, national banks were at a competitive disadvantage to state-chartered trust companies and other financial institutions. The United States was industrializing rapidly and credit needs of growing companies offered the financial-services industry many opportunities for profit and growth. National banks, however, were regulated so stringently that they could not take full advantage of these opportunities. Unlike trust companies, national banks had to satisfy strict capital and reserve requirements, could not branch nationally or overseas, and had no trust powers.

In 1903 a group of New York national banks decided to fight the trust companies on their own ground. The banks formed a trust company, Bankers Trust, to provide trust services to customers of state and national banks throughout the country. Banks could safely refer their fiduciary business to Bankers Trust because the new company would not compete with them for interest-bearing deposits as other trust companies did.

Bankers Trust Company was incorporated on March 24, 1903, with an initial capital of $1.5 million. Legendary financier J. P. Morgan held a controlling interest, and Edmund C. Converse, a very successful steel manufacturer turned financier and then president of Liberty National Bank, was chosen to serve as Bankers Trust's first president.

Bankers Trust opened its doors at 143 Liberty Street on March 30, 1903. Within three months it had deposits totalling $5.75 million; within four months it had outgrown its original premises and moved to Wall Street.

Bankers Trust's stability during the March, 1907 money panic bolstered the company's reputation. A year after that panic, Converse decided to diversify the company's services. Accordingly, in 1908, Bankers Trust established a foreign department to process transactions with correspondent banks. The following year, the company promoted and distributed traveler's checks for the American Bankers Association. The traveler's checks were successful in the United States and abroad, and the company's capital grew to $7.5 million.

Two years later, Bankers Trust made its first merger. Merger prospects were plentiful at the time because the New York State Assembly had recently enacted antitrust legislation requiring insurance companies to divest their banking and trust interests. In August, 1911 Bankers Trust acquired the Mercantile Trust Company, and in March, 1912 it acquired the Manhattan Trust Company. These mergers raised the company's capital to $20 million and its deposit base to over $134 million. Within nine years its deposits reached $168 million and its capital and surplus had increased to $25 million.

In January, 1914 Converse resigned to become president of Astor Trust Company, another Morgan company. Benjamin Strong Jr., Converse's son-in-law, succeeded him. Strong served as president for less than a year, leaving Bankers Trust to become the first governor of the Federal Reserve Bank of New York after helping to establish the Federal Reserve system. Seward Prosser was elected to succeed him.

In the early years of his leadership, Prosser faced a crucial challenge. State institutions had been granted the right to perform trust functions and national banks expected to receive this privilege shortly; such a restricted-purpose organization was no longer needed. In addition, the Federal Reserve banks increasingly held the reserve deposits of national and state banks, a service that Bankers Trust had provided for years.

Prosser transformed Bankers Trust from a single-purpose organization into a full-service commercial bank. In April, 1917 Bankers Trust acquired the Astor Trust Company, still headed by Converse. Prosser made Astor Trust into Bankers Trust's first retail branch. In October, 1917 the organization became a member of the Federal Reserve system.

Bankers Trust was now a commercial bank and Prosser, who became the company's first chairman in 1923 and was succeeded as president by A. A. Tilney, turned his attention to diversifying services. In 1919 the three year old securities department was expanded and developed into a bond department. In March of that year, a special wire office was opened in Chicago to facilitate nationwide distribution of the bond department's offerings. Wire offices were soon opened in 11 more U.S. cities. In 1928 the bank formed the Bankers Company, a wholly owned subsidiary, to replace the bond department and take over the business of underwriting and distributing securities.

The postwar boom in foreign travel and business encouraged Prosser to establish a Paris office in 1920. Two years later an agency was opened in London for the convenience of American customers traveling in England. The agency was so successful that a permanent office was opened in 1924. By 1928 Bankers Trust was one of the leading U.S. banks in Europe.

Bankers Trust was also a pioneer in the field of pension management. The company had established a pension plan for its own employees in 1913. Gradually, it started a similar service for its corporate customers. In the 1920s, the trust division began packaging pension and other employee-benefit plans for companies like the Bell System. These plans soon made up a major part of the company's trust business.

In 1929 Tilney became the first vice chairman and Henry J. Cochran was made president. Cochran was replaced in 1931 by S. Sloan Colt, who also became CEO. Cochran succeeded Tilney, and Tilney succeeded Prosser as chairman. Prosser became the first chairman of the managing committee.

Following this shuffling of the bank's executives, Bankers Trust undertook a major retrenchment program to combat the effects of the Depression. The Bankers Company was discontinued (a move that was necessary to meet the requirements of the Glass-Steagall Act, which mandated the separation of investment and commercial banking activities). In addition, the bank's Paris branch was closed in 1931, and the bank stopped issuing traveler's checks.

Despite the overall retrenchment, the trust department was allowed to continue growing. Bankers Trust had built its name on its fiduciary business, and that department added employees in the mortgage, real estate, and trust investment groups in order to protect its trusts throughout the Depression.

Bankers Trust emerged from the Depression lean but healthy and, in 1935, began making loans to help businesses rebuild. Also in 1935, the bank's assets exceeded $1 billion for the first time.

Foreseeing U.S. involvement in World War II, the bank closed its recently established Paris and Berlin representative offices in 1939. On a Saturday in 1944 its London office was bombed. No one was injured; the debris was cleared on Sunday, and on Monday the office was open for business.

Following the war Bankers Trust extended credit to increasing numbers of small- and medium-sized businesses and to individuals, and broadened the services available to its retail-banking customers. A metropolitan division was organized to attract small and large accounts throughout New York City; consumer checking accounts and Christmas club accounts were offered, and loans to individuals and small businesses were made with minimal security.

In 1948 Alex H. Ardrey was elected executive vice president and in 1949 Francis S. Baer was made senior vice president. In 1950 Bankers Trust, under the leadership of president William H. Moore, executed the first of several mergers which would transform the bank from a provider of specialized services into a diversified wholesale and retail operation. That year Bankers Trust merged with Lawyers Trust Company and acquired the banking businesses of Title Guarantee & Trust Company and Flushing National Bank. During the next two years the bank merged with Commercial National Bank & Trust Company and Bayside National Bank. In 1955 the company merged with Fidelity Trust Company and acquired Public National Bank, a retail bank with the fourth-largest branch network in New York City.

Federal and state regulators unexpectedly opposed Bankers Trust's more ambitious merger plans. In 1959, the company announced a possible merger with Manufacturers Trust Company. Had the merger been accomplished Bankers would have become the fourth-largest bank in the United States. Representative Emanuel Celler of the House Judiciary Committee, however, urged the New York State Banking Commission and the Federal Reserve board to block the merger. As a result, Bankers Trust abandoned its plans.

In late 1960, Bankers Trust agreed to form a bank holding company with the County Trust Company of Westchester County, New York, the largest commercial bank in the county, with 39 branches and assets of over $380 billion. Bankers Trust found the affiliation with County Trust particularly desirable because its established deposit base would allow Bankers Trust to enter the profitable suburban market quickly. The previous March, the state legislature had passed a banking bill that allowed New York City financial institutions to expand into the suburbs under certain conditions, which the proposed merger met. The state banking board, however, vetoed the plan, citing the threat such a merger would pose to independent suburban banks.

In 1965 Moore, now chairman, decided to try a different tactic. Following the lead of Citibank, Moore incorporated a bank holding company, BT New York Corporation (later Bankers Trust New York Corporation) in preparation for expansion into a number of financial-services fields. Bankers Trust Company and three upstate New York banks became BT New York's principal subsidiaries. At the same time Alfred Brittain III became president of the bank.

During the late 1960s and early 1970s Moore initiated an aggressive policy of diversification and expansion. Before this Bankers Trust was mainly a wholesale bank catering to large corporations and wealthy individuals. During this period, Bankers Trust acquired a number of upstate New York retail banks, doubling the number of its retail branches, to 169 between 1966 and 1972. The company also expanded aggressively into international, real estate, and construction, and middle-market lending. In 1968 Bankers Trust acquired Coleman & Company, a factoring company. In 1969 it formed BT Credit Company. This subsidiary was formed to operate a BankAmericard (later Visa) plan. The company also acquired a mortgage bank and an equipment-leasing company in the late 1960s.

During this period Bankers Trust also became more

aggressive in challenging existing banking legislation. In 1973 Bankers Trust challenged the constitutionality of two Florida laws. The first prohibited out-of-state banks and bank holding companies from acquiring or controlling Florida trust and investment companies. The second restricted the provision of trust services in the state to Florida banks and trust companies. In 1980 the Supreme Court unanimously struck down the laws as violations of the interstate commerce clause of the Constitution.

In 1974 Brittain became chairman of the holding company when Moore retired. Charles S. Sanford became vice chairman and John W. Hannon became president of the trust company. The new management team's first challenge was to survive the recession brought on by the oil crisis. Bankers Trust was particularly hard hit by this recession, experiencing some of the worst loan losses in the country, especially in its real estate loan portfolio. In late 1976 the Federal Reserve board turned down the company's proposal to acquire First National Bank of Mexico, New York. The Federal Reserve board uncharacteristically announced that the proposal was denied because Bankers Trust was experiencing financial difficulties. Although the board later issued another statement saying that the company was sound, the damage was done—public confidence in Bankers Trust was not fully restored until the mid-1980s. By the end of 1978 Bankers Trust was the least profitable major U.S. bank.

In 1979 Bankers Trust experienced a turnaround that is largely attributable to Brittain and Sanford. The two men looked at the company's strengths and weaknesses and decided to return to wholesale banking. In their view, retail banking was expensive and risky and the company could not hope to compete with New York's commercial-banking giants. Brittain and Sanford began turning Bankers Trust into a merchant bank, selling 89 retail branches in the metropolitan New York area to the Bank of Montreal. By 1981 all of the company's retail operations had been divested, except for branches in Binghamton, New York, which were sold in late 1984. Proceeds from the sale of retail operations were used to develop the company's four core businesses: commercial banking, money and securities markets, corporate financial services, and fiduciary services.

This merchant-bank strategy required a major restructuring of the company. In 1985 they established PROFITCo., a division that consolidated the company's payments system, securities processing, investment management, and private client businesses. Next they created a financial services division which combined the company's financing, intermediary, and trading and funding activities.

In 1988 Bankers Trust had a record profit of $647.7 million (its 1987 profit was $1.2 million). The company's system of assigning risk factors to loan capital allows the bank to determine how much capital to allot to ventures in certain risk categories and has become the industry standard for controlling loan risks. RAROC (risk-adjusted return on capital) and other improvements have helped Bankers Trust substantially improve its capital position and its return on capital in the late 1980s.

Banker Trust's goal in the 1990s is to become a global leader in the increasingly competitive field of wholesale merchant banking. To that end, the board, led by current-Chairman Sanford, has identified certain short-term goals whose purpose is to help the bank achieve its ultimate end. In the 1990s, Bankers Trust will try to increase its capital base further; to enhance its global presence; and to improve the quality and liquidity of its assets in order to react to opportunities more quickly. These short-term goals should made the bank a healthier and stronger bank than it has been in decades, regardless of whether it achieves it ultimate goal of becoming an international leader in wholesale banking.

Principal Subsidiaries: Bankers Trust Company; BT Futures Corporation; BT Securities Corporation; Bankers Trust International.

Further Reading: Twenty-Five Years of Bankers Trust Company, 1902–1928, New York, Bankers Trust Company, 1928; Lamont, Thomas W. *Henry P. Davison: The Record of a Useful Life*, New York, Harper & Brothers, 1933; Redlich, Fritz. *The Molding of American Banking*, New York, Johnson Reprint Corporation, 1968; *The Changing Times of Bankers Trust Company*, New York, Bankers Trust Company, 1978.

BANQUE NATIONALE DE PARIS S.A.

16 Boulevard des Italiens
Paris 75009
France
(4) 014–4546

State-Owned Company
Incorporated: 1966
Employees: 58,000
Assets: FFr1.19 trillion (US$ 196.95 billion)

Banque Nationale de Paris (BNP) was formed in 1966 by a merger between two long-established French banks, the Comptoir National d'Escompte de Paris (CNEP) and the Banque Nationale Pour le Commerce et l'Industrie (BNCI). Today, it is one of the largest financial institutions in France.

The Comptoir d'Escompte was founded in 1848, primarily to rescue Paris businesses from difficulties in obtaining financing. In 1854, after the crisis had passed and the bank no longer had a special mission, it became a commercial institution, greatly increasing its capital and range of activities. Although it continued to concentrate on commerce in Paris instead of expanding by establishing local branches, the Comptoir d'Escompte did establish itself in French colonies and foreign countries, becoming seriously involved in copper speculation. The bank was very active in the wool trade, and for many years was the only foreign bank in Australia. It was also one of the leading banks in India, and had a significant business presence in London and Brussels. Unfortunately, the bank soon spread itself too thin, and by the late 1880s, its liabilities were of such gigantic proportions that the president, Denfert Rochereau, was incited to commit suicide. The Bank of France and others in the banking community came to Comptoir d'Escompte's aid, meeting its liabilities and repaying its loans. Out of these ruins, a new deposit bank called Comptoir National d'Escompte de Paris arose in 1889.

Not much time passed before the bank had recovered its health. Although it kept its interests abroad, its growth now focused on the French provinces. By 1920, it had opened 223 branches, and had twice that many by the end of the decade. During the Depression, expansion slowed, and things improved little during World War II. In 1946, along with the Bank of France and three other major deposit banks (including BNCI, with which it would later merge) CNEP was nationalized as part of the government's postwar recovery plan. This plan also included legislation requiring banks to identify themselves as investment or deposit (commercial) banks. Altogether the plan created a more specialized and concentrated banking system and gave the government better control over the distribution of credit. The nationalized banks kept the same personnel, characters, and administrative autonomy that they possessed before nationalization, but representatives of state agencies joined their boards of directors. With nationalization, CNEP was assured a central position in the French financial system, and this helped it grow at a strong pace, especially during France's boom years in the 1960s. Nonetheless, throughout the 1950s and 1960s, CNEP remained smaller than the other nationalized banks.

BNCI began as the Banque Nationale de Crédit in 1913, founded by a deposit bank, the Comptoir d'Escompte de Mulhouse (which was founded at the same time as CNEP and for the same reason) and an investment bank, the Banque Francaise pour le Commerce et l'Industrie. By absorbing several smaller banks and opening new branches, it grew geographically at a rapid pace. At the end of World War I, it was the fourth-largest French bank. In the 1920s, Banque Nationale de Crédit merged with the Banque Francaise pour le Commerce et l'Industrie. But the connection was badly timed, since the investment bank was heavily involved in long-term lending to industry, and the economic chaos of 1930 precipitated its ruin. Eventually the minister of finance guaranteed the bank's deposits through the state in order to prevent a panic. In April 1932, with the help of several larger banks, the Banque Nationale de Crédit was resurrected as the Banque Nationale pour le Commerce et l'Industrie, strictly a deposit bank.

Because the economic chaos of the early 1930s hit local and regional banks especially severely, BNCI was able to grow quickly by absorbing them. In 1940, BNCI established an affiliate, the Banque Nationale pour le Commerce et l'Industrie (Afrique).

In 1946, under the same postwar recovery plan that nationalized CNEP, BNCI came under state control. The bank continued to grow internationally, and by the 1950s, it had branches in London, Madagascar, the West Indies, and Latin America. After World War II, London was an especially important financial center, and England and France were eager to help each other recover economically. In 1947, BNCI transformed its London branch into a separate subsidiary called the British and French Bank, with shares held by BNCI and two British investment firms, S.G. Warburg and Company and Robert Benson and Company. The British and French Bank continued to grow in international territory and assets, and BNCI itself grew much faster than the other three nationalized banks.

In the mid-1960s, along with an imposition of strict lending ceilings to shrink the money supply, the government began to talk about rationalizing banks and insurance companies in an effort to better concentrate the financial sector. In 1966, this led to the merger of CNEP and

BNCI and the formation of Banque Nationale de Paris. Henry Bizot was president of the new bank. Since CNEP had retained its strength in Paris and BNCI its strength overseas (it had the widest foreign territory of any French bank), the two banks complemented each other neatly. As a result of the merger, the British and French Bank subsidiary took in the operations of CNEP's London branch.

BNP's first year was a productive one. The new bank offered customers several new account options and also lent a large amount of money for equipment and operations in foreign countries. In addition, the bank established the Societé de garantie des Crédits à court terme to provide financing for small- and medium-sized firms. BNP's subsidiary, Intercomi, helped back the plan for the construction of an underground system in Mexico City that year also, and BNP formed, along with four other major European banks, a new financial organization called Societé Financière Européenne to promote international business through material and strategic support.

In 1968, BNP was one of the first institutions to become involved with Eurocurrency, and its international operations continued to strengthen and grow. By 1970, the bank had re-entered the investment-banking business with the creation of its capital arm, Banexi.

From the time of the imposition of frugal credit limits on the French financial system in the mid-1960s, many French banks had been seeking financial expansion outside the country, where the limits did not apply. Since BNP was already heavily involved in international operations, the credit ceilings hurt it less than they did other banks. Throughout the 1970s, BNP continued to be a leader in international dealings, and France's export strength in the 1960s and 1970s helped the overseas market even more.

In 1972, BNP was one of the first foreign banks allowed to open a branch in Tokyo. In America, the Federal Reserve Board gave BNP permission to establish itself in San Francisco with a new institution, the French Bank of California. By then, BNP was the second-largest bank in Europe, controlling $9.2 billion in deposits.

In 1974, BNP opened a branch in Chicago, and in 1975 and 1976, it opened branches in Seoul; Manila; Cairo; Los Angeles; Newport Beach, California; Houston; Toronto; Vancouver; Moscow; and Teheran. In 1977, it opened branches in Düsseldorf, Stockholm, and Amsterdam.

In 1977, BNP followed several other French banks when it opened a trading company in a joint venture with Inchcape and Company, a British trading firm. The new organization was called Compex, and its founders hoped to attract clients from BNP's branches in 65 countries and from Inchcape's 450 subsidiaries and affiliates.

In 1979, Jacques Calvet, who had been BNP's general manager since 1975, was named president of the bank. He had been a member of Cour des Comptes, a distinguished part of the financial bureaucracy that had been in existence since before the French Revolution. Because of the government's stance on credit ceilings Calvet continued to fortify BNP's status as the most internationally oriented of the nationalized banks. The next year, BNP opened banks in Yugoslavia and Niger and planned to open more branches in South America. Soon after that, BNP gained approval to acquire the Bank of the West, based in San Jose, California.

By the 1980s, the nationalized deposit banks were creeping back into investment banking, since government regulations had limited the growth potential of domestic commercial banking. They had been criticized in the 1970s for practicing so much caution that it hindered their growth. By international standards, the state-owned banks were low in capital and high in loans, and investment banking was one way to remedy this. Again, BNP was a leader among the nationalized banks, with its Banexi capital arm for investment already in operation for more than ten years. In 1985, BNP focused on acquiring stakes in small companies, making mergers and acquisitions, and providing advice to business managers. Banexi examined around 150 entrepreneurs' dossiers that year, and by September it had made 15 investment decisions. In November, BNP introduced a new approach to acquiring a "backup" line of credit. In selling $600 million in notes, the bank offered backup lenders a listed security that they could sell if desired. Before, the backup credit that banks offered each other was non-transferable and didn't appear on balance sheets until drawn upon.

In 1986, BNP's profits rose 52%. The new conservative government that came to power that year implemented a privatization program, selling several state-owned companies. One of the first slated for denationalization was Societé Générale, one of BNP's main competitors. Although now the privatization of BNP was also possible, as the largest bank in France it was expected to be the last one sold. In the meantime, the privatization of some 65 companies in 1987 required FFr300 billion, making it a busy time for banks.

By 1987, Socialists were loudly contesting the government's sale of nationalized companies, claiming the businesses were sold too cheaply and that the sales favored the government's political allies. Edouard Balladur, the finance minister, reacted to these attacks by rushing ahead with his denationalization program to be sure to complete several sales before the next presidential election. BNP's privatization began to look more likely.

In July, 1987, in anticipation of a law expected to be passed shortly to allow banks to buy into investment firms, BNP acquired a 54% controlling interest in the Du Bouzet stockbrokerage firm in Paris. BNP also organized its own investment company, which appeared on the Paris stock exchange as Compagnie d'Investissements de Paris.

In October, BNP acquired Ark Securities Company, of London, to gain entry into the European equity market. Ark had already gained a secure foothold in European stock markets and was beginning to do business in the Far East. This was the first of several moves BNP made over the next two years to strengthen its ties with England.

Despite its active expansion in 1987, the bank's profits fell because of a rise in general operating costs together with the dollar's decline and the stock market crash. The crash also slowed the government's privatization program and BNP's turn was pushed further back.

In 1988, the Socialists regained power in the government, and BNP's chances for privatization were wiped out. The bank faced the problem of finding new ways to increase its capital under the restrictions of the state. To this end, the bank announced plans to issue $400 million in perpetual capital notes and non-voting certificates of investment. The plans were later dropped when it seemed that such an issue would not meet international criteria for increasing its capital-adequacy ratio.

In 1989, BNP opened an office in Budapest in an effort to help joint projects between Hungary and France as well as the businesses of Hungarian state trading companies. That year BNP also took measures to improve its international base in areas other than deposits, focusing mainly on England. It moved its capital markets operations from Paris to London and bought Chemical Bank Home Loans Ltd., a British mortgage operation. BNP increased its involvement in insurance as it had been planning since 1988. Its NATIOVIE life insurance subsidiary had been a major insurer since the 1970s, and in 1989 BNP forged an alliance with the largest insurer in France, Union des Assurance de Paris, also a nationalized company. The agreement would make the two companies one of France's strongest financial groups.

Throughout its history, BNP has worked on developing its international range. In the 1980s, that strategy was modified to build the bank into a forceful competitor in global finance by the time the European Economic Community achieves its unified internal market in 1992. But BNP's future will depend on how fast it can increase its capital and how much freedom the government allows the bank to adapt to the changes coming to its industry worldwide.

Principal Subsidiaries: Cie du Crédit Universal (87.95%); BNP Intercontinentale (52.53%); Banque pour l'Expansion Industrielle-BANEXI (90%); Sté Auxiliaire de Participation et de Gestion-SAPEG (80%); Banque Natiotrésorerie (85.17%); BNP BAIL (53.68%); S.A. Charge du Bouzet (50.04%); BNP Espana (Spain) (74.26%); BNP OHG Frankfurt (West Germany) (99.9%); BNP Canada (89.51%); BNP International Managed Fund (75%); BNP UK Holding Ltd.; BNP Norge (Norway) (75%);BNP International Financial Services (Singapore); BNP International Financial Services Switzerland; BNP Ireland Ltd.; BNP International Financial Services Ltd. (Hong Kong); BNP Luxembourg (54.5%); BNP Sverige (Sweden); Bank of the West (U.S.A.); BNP Suisse (Switzerland) (54.99%);

BARCLAYS PLC

54 Lombard Street
London EC3P 3AH
United Kingdom
(01) 283–8989

Public Company
Incorporated: 1896 as Barclay & Company, Ltd.
Employees: 110,000
Assets: £87.79 billion (US$158.78 billion)
Stock Index: London New York Tokyo

Barclays PLC, a one bank holding company with an enormous network of domestic and international branches, has it origins in the 17th century. Although located in the heart of London's commercial district, the bank became identified with the agricultural and fishing industries through mergers, an identification it retained through much of the 20th century. For years Barclays, steeped in tradition, has been Great Britain's foremost banker.

Barclays takes it symbol, the spread eagle, from the Quaker goldsmithing and banking firm founded by John Freame in 1728. In 1736, James Barclay, Freame's brother-in-law, became a partner in the Black Spread Eagle. When two more of Barclay's relatives joined the firm—Silvanus Bevan in 1767 and John Henton Tritton in 1782—the banking firm took the name by which it would be known for more than a century: Barclays, Bevan & Tritton. While fledgling joint-stock banks outside London struggled to establish themselves in the late 18th and early 19th centuries, Barclays, Bevan & Tritton was still occupied with the well-established and highly lucrative commercial life of London.

A series of legislative changes completed in the late 19th century created a new banking climate that threatened the existence of private banks like Barclays. First, the Bank Charter Act of 1826 allowed banks with more than six partners to be formed only outside London. In 1833 the geographical restriction was removed. Stockholders of new joint-stock companies were granted limited liability for the first time in 1854. Finally, in 1879, existing joint-stock associations were allowed to convert to a limited-liability structure.

As a result of these legislative changes, provincial limited-liability joint-stock companies started picking off private banks. After lengthy negotiations, three of the largest Quaker-run banking firms—Barclays (which had become Barclays, Tritton, Ransom, Bouverie & Company after a merger in 1888), Jonathan Backhouse & Company, and Gurneys, Birkbeck, Barclay & Buxton—and 17 smaller Quaker-run banks agreed to merge and form a bank large enough to resist takeover attempts. Barclays took its modern form in 1896 when the 20 private banks merged to form Barclay and Company, Ltd., a joint-stock association with deposits totaling an impressive £26 million. This marked the beginning of Barclays' tradition of service to farmers and fishermen.

Francis Augustus Bevan, grandson of Silvanus Bevan, served as the new bank's first chairman for 20 years. The company's structure and course, however, were directed for its first 40 years by Frederick Crauford Goodenough, as first secretary until 1917, and then as chairman after Bevan's retirement until his own death in 1934. Goodenough was the only chairman recruited from outside the original founding families until 1987. Recruited from the Union Bank of London, Goodenough remained aloof from family controversies and quickly proved his merit.

Goodenough's first task was to meld the constituent banks into a single enterprise. He took a decentralized approach that was to be Barclays' hallmark for most of the 20th century. Each member bank was independently operated under the control of its own board of directors. Senior partners of the constituent banks were given a seat on the Barclays board. In this way, long-standing relationships between each member bank and its customers were maintained, and the new company took advantage of the knowledge and experience of its leaders.

At the same time, Goodenough initiated a series of mergers which eventually made Barclays one of the largest banks in Great Britain. In its first 20 years, Barclays acquired 17 private banks throughout England, including Woods and Company of Newcastle upon Tyne in 1897, Bolitho Bank in Cornwall, and United County Banks, its first joint-stock bank acquisition, in 1916. The bank's merger with the London, Provincial and South Western Bank in 1918 made it one of the Big Five British banks. During this period, Barclays merged with 45 British banks and its deposit base grew to £328 million.

This era of banking amalgamations came to an end in 1919, when the Colwyn Committee recommended, and banking authorities unofficially adopted, limitations on previously unregulated bank mergers. The committee suggested that thenceforth the Bank of England and the treasury approve only those mergers that provided important new facilities to customers or secured significant territorial gains for larger banks. Mergers were no longer approved if they resulted in a significant overlap in the areas served by constituent banks without countervailing benefits to customers or if they would result in "undue prominence" for a larger bank. After the Colwyn Committee report, mergers were increasingly difficult to justify, and the consensus was that mergers among the Big Five would not be approved.

After Barclays' expansionist phase ended, Goodenough

turned his attention to international banking operations. Barclays' first international venture took place in 1914 when it established its French subsidiary, Cox & Company. Goodenough had a vision of a network of Barclays banks spanning the globe to the greater glory of the British Empire. As early as 1916, he started preparations for worldwide banking by acquiring the shares of the Colonial Bank, established in 1836 to provide banking services in the West Indies and British Guiana. The Colonial Bank's charter was extended by special legislation to British West Africa in 1916 and then worldwide in 1917.

Immediately after World War I, Goodenough began negotiations with the National Bank of South Africa Ltd. and the Anglo-Egyptian D.C.O., operating in the Mediterranean. Despite the opposition from the Bank of England, which feared Barclays would become overextended, Goodenough engineered the 1925 merger of the two banks with the Colonial to form Barclays Bank (Dominion, Colonial & Overseas), later renamed Barclays Bank (D.C.O.). Although Goodenough never realized his dream of establishing banks throughout the British Empire, for decades Barclays was the only British bank to combine domestic business with a widely dispersed international branch network.

A contemporary of Goodenough's speculated that the chairman became interested in expanding Barclays' international operations because domestic growth was very limited. Despite this stagnation and later the Depression, Goodenough's plan did not result in a disastrous overextension of the bank's assets.

Barclays survived the Depression relatively intact to take its place as a leading wartime financier. Goodenough died in 1934 and was replaced by William Favill Tuke, who was in turn replaced in 1936 by Edwin Fisher. Fisher saw Barclays through the boom years of World War II. When Fisher died in 1947, he was replaced by William Macnamara Goodenough.

In 1951, Anthony William Tuke, the son of William Favill Tuke, became chairman following William Goodenough's retirement that year. A.W. Tuke was essentially conservative but encouraged innovations, even those he personally disliked, which were potentially beneficial to the bank. Under Tuke's leadership, Barclays became Britain's largest bank, surpassing the Midland Bank in the late 1950s. Barclays was also a leader in introducing new banking technology: Barclays was the first British bank to use a computer in its branch accounting, in 1959; introduced the world's first automatic cash-dispensing machine; and started a plastic revolution in Britain by introducing the Barclaycard in 1966.

In the late 1960s and early 1970s, when most competitors were struggling to establish international operations, Barclays enjoyed an enormous headstart, since its operations in former British colonies in Africa and the Caribbean were well established. The economies of many of these countries, however, were precarious. To offset its high exposure in developing countries, Barclays decided to enter the U.S. market. It first established Barclays Bank of California in 1965, and then in 1971 formed Barclays Bank of New York. Together these two banks gave Barclays the unique advantage of having retail banking operations on both U.S. coasts. Another advantage Barclays enjoyed was an exemption from 1978 legislation barring foreign banks from operating branches in more than one state.

In 1967 British banking authorities clarified their position on domestic mergers. The National Board for Prices and Incomes stated that mergers would be allowed to rationalize existing networks and that further reduction in the number of independent banks would not be viewed as inherently anticompetitive. Barclays quickly took advantage of the change in policy by merging with the venerable Martins Bank, in November, 1968. Martins Bank began as the Bank of Liverpool in 1831 and had merged with more than 30 smaller banks by the time it was acquired by Barclays. The most important of these mergers was with Martin's Bank of London, founded by Sir Thomas Gresham, chief financial adviser to Elizabeth I and founder of the Royal Exchange. The merger with Martins Bank, the sixth-largest in the country, brought Barclays more than 700 branches, mostly in northern England.

In 1973 A.W. Tuke was succeeded as chairman by Anthony Favill Tuke, William F. Tuke's grandson. A. F. Tuke served until 1981, when he left Barclays to operate a British mining company. His tenure was most notable for Barclays' expansion in North America. In May, 1974 Barclays Bank International acquired the First Westchester National Bank of New Rochelle, New York. In the late 1970s, Barclays opened a series of branches and agencies in major U.S. cities. By 1986, North American operations had extended to 37 states. In the early 1980s Barclays Bank International diversified into commercial credit, acquiring the American Credit Corporation, renamed Barclays American Corporation (BAC), in May, 1980. Later that year BAC acquired 138 offices from subsidiaries of Beneficial Finance and the operations of Aetna Business Credit Inc.

In June, 1981 Timothy Bevan became chairman of Barclays and immediately, with the assistance of United Kingdom Chairman Deryk Weyer, set about restructuring domestic operations. The system of local control initiated by F. C. Goodenough had become outdated as the bank expanded and diversified. Senior managers' responsibilities were not clearly defined, and, although technically higher in authority than regional bank directors, in practice the senior managers were subject to the regional officials' control as board members. Moreover, the original structure of the company tended to produce dynasties. Weyer's strategy was to establish three basic divisions to represent Barclays' most important markets—the large corporate market, the middle market of small- to medium-sized businesses, and the traditional individual-customer and mass-consumer market. Bevan and Weyer moved cautiously, however, avoiding wholesale reorganization of the company so that the relationships of local managers with large customers were not disrupted.

Further changes in the structure of the company followed. Barclays had converted from a joint-stock bank to a public limited company in 1981, and it assumed its present name in 1984. In 1985 Barclays became a holding company and all of its assets were transferred, in exchange for stock, to its operating subsidiary, Barclays Bank International Ltd., which was simultaneously converted to a public limited company and renamed Barclays Bank PLC.

In 1986 Barclay's acquired Visa's traveler's check operation, becoming the third-largest issuer in the world with 14% of the market. That same year, in preparation for the deregulation of the British securities market, Barclays Merchant Bank Ltd. de Zoete and Bevan and Wedd Durlacher Morduant & Company merged to form Barclays de Zoete Wedd, a new investment-banking enterprise.

Barclays and Chairman John Quintin, appointed May, 1987 faced a number of challenges in the late 1980s. Domestic banking, now a 3,000-branch network, has always been Barclays strength. The bank is likely to continue to lead Britain's domestic banks but faces increasing competition. National Westminster Bank has edged out Barclays in assets. The building societies, by offering high interest on savings, have threatened the banks' traditional deposit base. Finally, American and Japanese banks have entered the commercial-lending market and pose a threat to British banks. Barclays is fighting back with two formidable money-generating enterprises, Mercantile Credit and the Barclaycard, which generates about 20% of Barclays' domestic profits. It also continues to rationalize its branches to better serve the three major banking-service markets. In addition, Barclays planned to spend more than £500 million on technological advances, including the introduction of the first electronic debit card in the United Kingdom.

Barclays' future in international banking is less certain. It was dealt a number of setbacks in the late 1980s. In 1986 Barclays divested its 148-year-old, wholly owned South African subsidiary, Barclays National Bank (Barat) in response to a disastrous drop in the subsidiary's earnings from 1984 to 1986 and to losses in the lucrative student market in Britain as Barclays' presence in South Africa became more unpopular at home. Also, the steady deterioration of African economies poses a hazard because the bank's African involvement is so heavy. Barclays has decreased its African investments where possible, but has had difficulties in removing profits and proceeds from Africa. In addition, Barclays' Hong Kong and Italian operations both suffered large losses in the 1980s, and the performance of Barclays' American operations has been consistently disappointing. In the early 1980s, Barclays expanded very rapidly and tried to build earnings quickly through an aggressive lending policy. As a result, branches picked up a large volume of low-quality loans. Bad-debt ratios were very high, costs have only recently come under control, and American operations only started to show a profit in the late 1980s (only 4% of Barclays' profits were from U.S. operations, while 15% of the bank's assets were invested there). As a result, Barclays began offering specialized services in the United States in an attempt to improve its position there. After years of trying to make it profitable, Barclays sold its California banking subsidiary in 1988.

Barclays' investment-banking operations also show promise. Barclays De Zoete Wedd expanded its operations by purchasing 50% of Mears and Phillips, an Australian brokerage firm. Barclays also formed a new bank in Geneva, Barclays Bank S.A., to develop capital markets with Barclays De Zoete Wedd. The investment-banking division, however, has had problems. The division is far from integrated with the rest of Barclays' operations, and is competing in an unstable, highly competitive market.

Barclays is widely regarded as the last bastion of traditional British banking. Perhaps its besetting weakness has been overreliance on the Barclays name and an unquestioning acceptance of tradition. Barclays' challenge in the 1990s will be to adopt operating methods responsive to the current competitive environment.

Principle Subsidiary: Barclays Bank PLC.

Further Reading: Tuke, Anthony, and Matthew, P.W. *History of Barclays Bank Limited*, London, Blades, East & Blades Ltd., 1926; Tuke, Anthony, and R.J.H. Gillman. *Barclays Bank Limited*, London, Barclays Bank, 1972; Great Britain Commission on Industrial Relations. *Barclays Bank International, Ltd.*, London, HMSO, 1974; Bailey, Martin. *Barclays and South Africa*, Birmingham, Haslemere Group, 1975; Crossley Julian. *The DCO Story: A History of Banking in Many Countries 1925–71*, London, Barclays Bank, 1975; Green, Edwin. *Debtors to their Profession: A History of the Institute of Bankers 1879–1979*, New York, Methuen, 1979; Watkins, Leslie. *Barclays: A Story of Money and Banking*, London, Barclays Bank, 1982.

BAYERISCHE HYPOTHEKEN-UND WECHSEL-BANK AG

Theatinerstrasse 11
Munich
Federal Republic of Germany
(89) 2–36–61

Public Company
Incorporated: 1835
Employees: 13,649
Assets: DM135.2 billion (US$76.23 billion)
Stock Index: Munich Frankfurt Düsseldorf Hannover Hamburg Stuttgart Berlin Bremen Basel Lausanne Geneva Zurich Vienna

Bayerische Hypotheken- und Wechsel-Bank, better known as Hypo-Bank, was founded in 1835 by decree of King Ludwig I of Bavaria, who believed that his nation needed a new bank to increase the availability of credit and to stimulate the economy. His economic advisers decided that the new bank should be formed as a private company and accordingly, Hypo-Bank's first share offering was made in December, 1834. Hypo-Bank opened in October, 1835 in the Preysing Palace in Munich, and two years later, it opened its first branch office, in the Bavarian city of Augsburg.

At its inception, Hypo-Bank's activities fell into three principal categories: mortgage banking, commercial banking, and insurance. Deposits were not an important part of its business; they were, in fact, regarded as a potential capital drain. The bank's founding charter prohibited all forms of speculation, merchant banking, or investing in foreign securities. As the national bank of Bavaria, it had the exclusive privilege of issuing paper currency, but abandoned this practice in 1875 when the new Imperial Bank Law placed severe restrictions on issuing banks. The mortgage business was the bank's most popular activity from the outset. The introduction of mortgage bonds in 1864 added another popular and profitable dimension to its operations.

As an important part of the Bavarian economy, Hypo-Bank was vulnerable to the force of larger events. The political upheavals of 1848–1849 threatened its securities business and prompted the bank to stop paying interest on its few deposits. However, it prospered as a result of the Franco-Prussian War of 1870–1871. It placed three million Gulden worth of war bonds at the outbreak of hostilities to support the imperial government's financial needs, and its commercial operations prospered during the economic boom that followed the German victory.

Hypo-Bank entered underwriting and securities trading in 1879 when it syndicated a Bavarian railroad bond worth 60 million Reichsmarks. It also began underwriting and dealing in foreign securities, although its 1879 annual report sought to reassure shareholders by emphasizing that the bank would only touch blue-chip issues. At first, it marketed only Austro-Hungarian, Russian, Romanian, and Bulgarian issues, but in 1889 it began marketing Asian, American, and Latin American securities in small quantities as well.

These latter developments came at a time when large German commercial banks were rapidly expanding their international operations. While Hypo-Bank was already a leading mortgage bank, its commercial banking deartment remained small compared to the Berlin-based *Grossbanken*. Nonetheless, it joined the big banks in founding the Deutsch-Asiatische Bank in Shanghai in 1889. It was also part of the *Asiatische Konsortium*, a famous group of German banks that cooperated with each other in loaning money to Asian nations.

Hypo-Bank began to outgrow its facilities in the Preysing Palace 50 years after its founding. During the 1880s the bank began purchasing houses around Munich and converting them into headquarters for its various divisions. A project converting its property on Theatinerstrasse into a new headquarters for the entire bank was proposed in 1893 and finished in 1898; this building was destroyed in World War II but Hypo-Bank's headquarters were rebuilt on the same site.

Hypo-Bank became Germany's leading mortgage banker when its volume of mortgage loans topped one billion Reichsmarks in 1908 and its total of mortgage bonds reached that level in 1909. But new imperial laws passed in 1906 regulating the insurance industry forced Hypo-Bank to spin off its insurance operations. The new insurance bank, which was named the Bayerische Versicherungsbank, nonetheless remained a wholly-owned subsidiary of Hypo-Bank and inherited the Preysing Palace offices.

Despite its new stature, Hypo-Bank remained a regional bank into the 20th century, while the *Grossbanken* grew ever larger and more powerful. As a result of this increasing centralization in the German banking industry, many smaller institutions were forced into alliances with the largest banks, surrendering their independence in exchange for the security that went with size. Hypo-Bank allied itself with both Dresdner Bank and Discontogesellschaft, but broke away in 1921 by entering a "community of interest" agreement with Barmer Bankverein and Allgemeine Deutsche Creditanstalt of Leipzig. Under the terms of the agreement, which was typical of provincial banks in the 1920s, the three institutions exchanged representatives from their boards of directors and agreed to coordinate their operations.

Of the years 1914–1948, Hypo-Bank's official history says, "Business was at best difficult. . . . Success was measured simply in the ability to survive and assure long-term viablity." After the outbreak of World War

I, the bank's mortgage business benefited from money that flowed into agriculture from military purchases, but it suffered as the war hastened a crack in the urban real estate market. The bank continued to suffer as building activity, and with it the demand for mortgages, slackened during the war. Governmental decree also closed the stock market at the beginning of hostilities, limiting activity in the commercial sector. But the war did not stop Hypo-Bank's expansion; it purchased the Munich bank Fränkel & Selz in 1915, and in 1916 it bought the 50% of Nuremberg's Bayerische Disconto- und Wechsel-Bank it did not already own. It also expanded its branch network throughout Bavaria.

Hypo-Bank floundered along with the rest of the nation in the economic crises of the 1920s. Radical currency devaluation and skyrocketing inflation in 1922 and 1923 forced the bank to virtually shut down its mortgage business, as loans made under more favorable economic conditions were paid back in increasingly worthless paper currency. The Weimar government undertook currency reform in 1923, and the next year Hypo-Bank began to rebuild its mortgage business from scratch. Bank employees had to convert 73,000 old mortgages and 1.2 million mortgage bonds into the new currency, and the bank introduced gold-backed mortgages and bonds. Also in 1923, the bank suddenly sold all of its shares in its insurance subsidiary to the insurance concerns Münchner Rückversicherungsgesellschaft and Allianz Versicherung.

The economic crisis of 1928–1929 that presaged the Great Depression in Germany hurt the bank's commercial department as rising deposits and declining demand for loans coupled to strain its resources. Economic conditions worsened in 1930 and all forms of commercial business declined significantly. In 1931, public panic reached its peak with a run on the nation's financial institutions, culminating in the closing of all banks and stock exchanges on July 14. As a result of the crisis, the bank was forced to reduce its annual dividends by 50% in 1933 and 1934. Nevertheless, its fortunes began to improve slightly in 1934. Although demand for credit was low, government rearmament and war financing stimulated the economy.

Hypo-Bank's official history is largely mute about the war years, saying only that the bank's mortgage business "continued to develop satisfactorily" until the economy collapsed in 1944, while deposits increased and commercial lending declined. The Allied occupation authorities investigating the German banking industry after the war turned up evidence of possible war crimes principally among the *Grossbanken*; smaller institutions like Hypo-Bank were seldom, if ever, mentioned in American newspaper accounts of the investigation. The years immediately following the war also proved painful for Hypo-Bank, as it had to write off mortgages on German property destroyed by the fighting, as well as those in Alsace-Lorraine and Soviet-occupied eastern Germany.

All of that began to change, however, on June 20, 1948, when the West German government enacted radical currency reform and began to rebuild its shattered economy. Aided by the Marshall Plan, economic conditions in the Bundesrepublik gradually approached a state of normalcy during the early years of the Cold War, and Hypo-Bank, riding the tide of increasing prosperity, could report in 1953 that its assets had reached DM1 billion.

The 1950s for Hypo-Bank were marked by expansion and fundamental strengthening of its financial position. Its capital stock increased from DM27 million in 1948 to DM100 million in 1960, and its reserves went from nothing to DM155 million in the same period. The bank's mortgage sector, its traditional mainstay, remained strong, but was surpassed in business volume by its general banking division. Hypo-Bank's work force more than doubled, from 2,603 employees in 1948 to nearly 5,600 ten years later. It also began expanding beyond its geographic base in Bavaria, making business contacts in other German states as well as abroad. Nonetheless, *Euromoney* characterized Hypo-Bank's philosophy during these years as adhering to the old Bavarian proverb: "*Bleib im Land und nähre dich redlich*"—stay at home and live off the fat of the land.

Hypo-Bank continued to prosper and expand through the 1960s. In 1967, *Barron's* described it as one of three West German regional banks with more than $1 billion worth of assets, along with Bank für Gemeinwirtschaft and long-time Bavarian rival Bayerische Vereinsbank. In 1969 it began to negotiate a merger with Bayerische Vereinsbank that would have produced an institution large enough to rival the nation's Big Three commercial banks (Deutsche Bank, Dresdner Bank, and Commerzbank), but it broke off talks in 1971 when the Bavarian state government insisted that Bayerische Staatsbank be included. Also in 1969, it officially joined the trend among financial institutions worldwide by declaring that it would expand and diversify in order to keep up with its major competitors. Hypo-Bank opened 100 new branches between 1969 and 1975, including 37 outside Bavaria. It also internationalized its securities operations, entered the currency trading business, and loaned more money overseas. In 1972, it joined with Banque de Bruxelles, Algemene Bank Nederland, and Dresdner Bank to form ABD Securities Corporation in New York, offering securities and investment-banking services to European investors interested in the United States.

This penchant for limiting risks through joint ventures also marked two of Hypo-Bank's other major enterprises during the 1970s. In 1972, it joined ABECOR (Associated Banks of Europe Corporation) along with its ABD Securities partners; Banque Nationale de Paris, Banca Nazionale de Lavoro, Barclays Bank, Banque Internationale à Luxembourg, and Österreichische Länderbank later joined them. Despite early doubts from some observers, by 1983 ABECOR had 12,000 branches and $440 billion worth of assets. Hypo-Bank also joined 11 other European and Latin American banks to form the Euro-Latin-American Bank in 1974.

Acquisitions and portfolio expansion also marked the bank's activities during this time. In 1971 Hypo-Bank purchased Westfalenbank of Bochum, and between 1968 and 1973, its stock holdings constituting a 10% or larger stake in a company increased from DM148 million to DM995 million. It made its most famous purchases in the brewery industry, including minority interests in

Dortmunder-Union-Brauerei in 1969 and Löwenbräu 1973. In the late 1970s, the bank began to sell off its industrial holdings amid mounting public concern over the power that West German banks were able to wield through their extensive stock portfolios and numerous company directorships. In 1982 Hypo-Bank began to concentrate instead on acquisition and expansion in finance, both foreign and domestic. In 1987 it bought a 15% interest in Italy's Banco Trento & Bolanzo.

Throughout its long history, the Bayerische Hypotheken- und Wechsel-Bank has never quite shed its image as a regional bank. It has never rivaled the very largest commercial banks in size or influence, and in fact, Bayerische Vereinsbank surpassed it in the early 1980s as West Germany's fourth-largest bank. But having survived the most catastrophic events of a turbulent century, its standing as the fifth-largest bank in one of the most prosperous nations in the world is tribute enough to the way in which it has done business.

Principal Subsidiaries: Hypobank International S.A. (Luxembourg); Salzburger Kredit- und Wechsel-Bank A.G. (Austria); Hypo Trade Finance Ltd. (U.K.); Hypo Property Finance (Ireland); Bayernhypo Finance N.V. (the Nethelands).

Further Reading: Whale, P. Barrett. *Joint Stock Banking in Germany*, London, Frank Cass & Company, 1930; *A History of the Bayerische Hypotheken- und Wechsel-Bank, 1835–1985*, Munich, Bayerische Hypotheken- und Wechsel-Bank, 1985.

BAYERISCHE VEREINSBANK A.G.

Kardinal-Faulhaber-Strasse 1
P.O. Box 1
D-8000 Munich 100101
Federal Republic of Germany
(089) 21 32 1

Public Company
Incorporated: 1971
Employees: 12,965
Assets: DM162.58 billion (US$91.67 billion)
Stock Index: Berlin Bremen Hamburg Stuttgart Zurich Geneva Basel Vienna Paris Frankfurt Munich Düsseldorf Hanover

Bayerische Vereinsbank traces its origins to 1869, when King Ludwig II of Bavaria granted a license to a consortium of private bankers to found a bank that would serve the needs of the growing Bavarian economy. Ludwig II is better known as a patron of Richard Wagner and as the eccentric sovereign who dotted the Bavarian landscape with a series of fairy tale–like castles, so the bank is not his most colorful legacy. But over the decades Bayerische Vereinsbank has gained a reputation for a solid, sensible conservatism that not only saw it through Germany's many crises in the first half of the 20th century, but also allowed it to pursue a course of steady growth in more recent years, when major West German banks have sometimes lacked a steadying hand.

Bayerische Vereinsbank was founded in Munich as a commercial bank. In 1869, trade licenses and compulsory guild memberships were eliminated in Germany, opening up new entrepreneurial opportunities, and the bank's initial mission was to encourage economic expansion. In 1870, it loaned money to the Bavarian Railway, and in 1871 it was granted the right to operate as a mortgage bank, issuing real estate loans and mortgage bonds. This last development made Bayerische Vereinsbank into an institution remarkably similar to Bayerische Hypotheken- und Wechsel Bank (commonly known as Hypo-Bank), a mortgage bank established in 1835 by decree of Ludwig I of Bavaria. The rivalry between these two Bavarian banks intensified in 1899 when the Mortgage Banking Act forbade the further establishment of banks offering both mortgages and commercial loans, and it has endured to the present day.

Bayerische Vereinsbank did not participate to any substantial degree in the German foreign banking boom of the late 19th century. It did loan money to the Austrian railway and underwrite securities issued by the Turkish government, but international business was left mostly to the large, Berlin-based *Grossbanken* that have always dominated the German banking industry.

Indeed, the bank remained a relatively small institution into the 20th century. Although it had 15 branch offices at the beginning of World War I, the size of a bank's branch network was not the only measure of its importance. If the *Grossbanken*, such as Deutsche Bank and Dresdner Bank, occupied the first tier of German banking, then Bayerische Vereinsbank ranked in the middle of the second tier, with other large provincial banks like Hypo-Bank and Barmer Bank. German finance had been moving toward ever greater centralization since the nation was united under Bismarck, with the *Grossbanken* wielding considerable power from their bases in Berlin. This trend continued through the economic crises that characterized the years following Germany's defeat in 1918, as struggling banks found that size often determined whether they survived or not.

Both during and after the war, the second-tier banks responded to this trend by joining each other in "community of interest" agreements, exchanging representatives from their boards of directors and operating in accord with each other. These agreements allowed the provincials to fend off takeovers from Berlin and preserve their independence. In the early 1920s, Bayerische Vereinsbank sought to consolidate its position by acquiring an interest in the small Berlin bank E. S. Friedman & Company and by allying itself with Bayerische Handelsbank. In 1922 it entered into a community of interest agreement with Mendelssohn & Company, a prestigious banking house based in Berlin and Amsterdam. Mendelssohn acquired an interest in Bayerische Vereinsbank and representation on its board of directors; Bayerische Vereinsbank justified the deal on the grounds that it would gain a valuable friend in Berlin without sacrificing autonomy.

Bayerische Vereinsbank prospered during the late 1920s; its capital grew from 21 million Reichsmarks in 1927 to 31.1 million in 1930, and its reserves grew from 9.3 million Reichsmarks to 13.8 million. Nonetheless, it remained somewhat smaller than rival Hypo-Bank in 1930 and considerably smaller than any of the *Grossbanken*.

Its lack of size and power relative to the *Grossbanken* should also be taken into account when considering the years of National Socialist rule. Virtually every major bank helped finance Germany's war effort to some degree until the German economy collapsed in 1944. When Allied occupation authorities investigated the extent to which the German business community had aided the Nazis, they found culpability among the *Grossbanken*, in part because their size and influence made their complete innocence inconceivable, but the investigation did not indicate that any of the second-tier banks were suspected of war crimes. Accordingly, in 1947, the occupation authorities decreed that the *Grossbanken* who survived the war should be broken up into smaller institutions, but smaller banks like Bayerische Vereinsbank were not punished.

The bank emerged from the war with 52 branches. From there, it embarked on a course of expansion and internationalization that has ensured it a position of prominence among West Germany's regional banks. In the 1950s, Bayerische Vereinsbank began to expand beyond its traditional base in Bavaria and to internationalize its business. It did so largely without opening foreign branches; it opened its first overseas representative office in Beirut in 1958, but eventually closed it. The bank didn't venture abroad again until 1970, when offices were opened in Tokyo and Rio de Janeiro. It established a presence in the United States when its New York office opened on Madison Avenue in 1971; offices in Chicago, Los Angeles, Cleveland, and Atlanta appeared over the course of the decade. It has also opened offices in Tehran (1971), Paris (1973), Johannesburg (1974), London (1976), Bahrain (1979), Hong Kong (1979), and Beijing (1986).

After the end of World War II, Bayerische Vereinsbank CEO Baron Hans Christof Freiherr von Tucher publicly suggested that his bank should merge with Hypo-Bank. The three surviving *Grossbanken*—Deutsche Bank, Dresdner Bank, and Commerzbank—had re-formed in 1958, just as large and influential as ever, to become West Germany's Big Three commmercial banks. It was von Tucher's idea to merge Bavaria's two largest banks into an institution that could compete with them. Nothing came of his original proposal, but in 1969 Bayerische Vereinsbank and Hypo-Bank did begin merger talks. Negotiations continued for two years, then broke up when Hypo-Bank balked at the Bavarian state government's insistence the Bayerische Staatsbank, Bavaria's third-largest bank, be included in the merger. In the aftermath of the failed merger, Bayerische Vereinsbank agreed to acquire Bayerische Staatsbank for DM40 million—a bargain, since the latter's assets were valued at DM5 billion.

In addition to its international expansion, Bayerische Vereinsbank produced a record of steady asset growth throughout the 1970s. In 1982 Wolfgang Graebner, a managing partner of Berliner Handels- und Frankfurter Bank, told *Euromoney*, "The BV bank is a conservative bank, and that's a genuine compliment . . . They've achieved balance sheet growth instead of dramatic headlines; a smooth ride through troubled waters. That's what I call banking." In the late 1970s and early 1980s, an economic downturn and crises, like the collapse of Bankhaus IG Herstatt and a sharp drop in Commerzbank's profits after a bad hunch on the direction of interest rates, sent shudders through the West German banking industry. But Bayerische Vereinsbank, thanks to what *Euromoney* called its "pushy but conservative style," gained ground on Hypo-Bank and the Big Three. Depending on what statistical measure one used, Bayerische Vereinsbank either was very close to overtaking or had already overtaken Hypo-Bank as West Germany's fourth-largest bank by 1982.

A contemporary trend in which Bayerische Vereinsbank did take part was the divestiture of business holdings. Public concern mounted during the 1970s over the influence that Germany's banks wielded in the commercial and industrial sectors through stock holdings and corporate directorships. To head off possible calls for nationalization, the banks began to sell off their portfolios. In 1982 Bayerische Vereinsbank sold its 36% interest in Hacker-Pschorr Brau, a Munich brewery, to local construction magnate Joseph Schoerghuber.

In 1985, however, the bank made a substantial investment in West Germany's defense industry. It bought a 5% interest in Messerschmidt-Boelkhow-Bloehm, becoming the first bank to ever hold an interest in the nation's premier aerospace concern. It then joined Messerschmidt and Dresdner Bank in a takeover bid for Krauss Maffei, which manufactures the Leopard 2 main battle tank.

In the late 1980s Bayerische Vereinsbank continued to expand its international presence. In 1988 it acquired First National Bank of Chicago's branch offices in Milan and Rome. And in May, 1989, it concluded a historic agreement with four other European banks—Italy's Banca Commerciale, Austria's Creditanstalt-Bankverein, France's Credit Lyonnais, and the Finnish bank Kansallis-Osake-Pankki—and the Soviet banks Vnesheconobank, Promstroybank, and Sberbank to form the International Bank Of Moscow. The proposed bank will constitute the first joint banking venture between Western and Soviet institutions since the Revolution of 1917 and is intended to finance foreign trade and provide financial advice.

Throughout its history, Bayerische Vereinsbank has seldom, if ever, emerged from the shadows when the spotlight has shone on the German banking industry. It has expanded and diversified enough to ensure its continued prosperity, but in recent times it has kept a low profile as well. Even more importantly, it has also stayed healthy at times when some West German banks seemed less than robust.

Principal Subsidiaries: ADIG Allgemeine Deutsche Investment-Gesellschaft mbH (35.5%); Bayerisch-Bulgarische Handelsbank GmbH (51%); Bankhaus Gebruder Bethmann; Bayerische Handelsbank AG (76.4%); Bayerische Kapitalanlagegesellschaft mbH; Bayerische Wertpapiersammelbank AG (24%); Franken WKV Bank GmbH; Internationales Immobilien-Institut AG (50%); Schwaebische Bank AG (25.1%); Simonbank AG (97.4%); Sueddeutsche Bodencreditbank AG (54.2%); Vereins- und Westbank AG (25.4%); Vereinsbank in Nuernberg AG (50.4%); Bayerische Vereinsbank S.A. (BV France) (Paris); Bavarian Finance Company B.V. (Netherlands); BV Overseas Finance N.V. (Curacao); Bayerische Vereinsbank International S.A. (Luxembourg); BV Capital Inc. (U.S.); BV Capital Management Inc. (U.S.); BV Capital Markets, Inc. (U.S.); BV Capital Markets (Asia) Ltd. (Hong Kong) (50%); Wirtschafts- und Privatbank (Switzerland) (50%); Akkurat Grundstuecks-GmbH & Co. Betriebs KG; Aktienbrauerei Kaufbeuren AG, (75.7%); Allgaeuer Brauhaus AG (32.1%); Altius-Alpha Fund Inc. (U.S.) (31.8%); Aufbaugesellschaft Bayern GmbH (48.2%); Bavaria Filmkunst GmbH (32%); Bayerische Immobilien-Leasing GmbH mit Objektgesellschaften; Bayerische Vereinsbank Financial Management GmbH (95%); BD Industrie Beteiligungsgesellschaft mbh (50%); BEWAG (25.4%); Bethmann

Liegenschafts KG (50%); Duesseldorf-Muenchener Beteiligungs-gesellschaft mbH; Grundstuecksgesellschaft Simon bh KG; HAWA Grundstuecks GmbH & Co. OHG Hotelverwaltung Mietfinanz GmbH (23%); Nebelhornbahn AG (26.8%); Neue-Baumwoll-Spinnerei und Weberei Hof AG (40.3%); Pferse Kolbermoor AG, Augsburg (36%); Salvatorplatz Grundstuecksgesellschaft mbH & Co. OHG Verwaltungszentrum; Vermietungsgesellschaft SUDWEST fur SEL Kommunikationsanlagen mbH, Stuttgart (50%); TIG Technologie-Investitions GmbH & Co. KG (30%); TIVOLI Handels-und Grundstuecks AG (99.2%); Verba Verwaltungsgesellschaft mbH (64.3%); Vogtlandische Baumwollspinnerei AG (37.6%).

Further Reading: Whale, P. Barrett. *Joint Stock Banking in Germany*, London, Fred Cass & Company, 1930.

CANADIAN IMPERIAL BANK OF COMMERCE

Commerce Court
Toronto, Ontario M5L 1A2
Canada
(416) 980-2211

Public Company
Incorporated: 1961
Employees: 33,874
Assets: C$88.38 billion (US$67.18 billion)
Stock Index: Toronto Montreal Winnipeg Alberta Vancouver Tokyo London

The Canadian Imperial Bank of Commerce (CIBC) is Canada's second largest bank. The result of a 1961 merger between the Imperial Bank of Canada and the Canadian Bank of Commerce, CIBC today is headquartered in Toronto and operates 1,486 branches in Canada and 108 offices overseas. The bank has been innovative in meeting the needs of an international marketplace that is growing in complexity. Recently split into three units—Individual, Corporate, and Investment banks—CIBC's specialized service has made it a competitive player among Canadian banks.

The older of CIBC's two predecessors, the Canadian Bank of Commerce, was founded in 1867, the same year as Canada's confederation. While Canadian statesmen discussed the advantages of uniting the British North American Colonies under one parliament, a prominent Toronto businessman, William McMaster, was busy acquiring a bank charter from a group of financiers who had been unable to raise the necessary capital to put it to use. McMaster opened the Canadian Bank of Commerce on May 15, 1867 and under his leadership, the bank grew at a tremendous rate. The bank's paid-up capital swelled from $400,000 to $6 million in its first seven years and it soon had offices in New York and Montreal as well as throughout Ontario. Canada was in the midst of an industrial revolution at this time, and the Bank of Commerce was instrumental in financing a number of large capital projects. For its first 20 years, the bank's prosperity fluctuated with economic conditions, but in general it grew and was profitable.

In May of 1893, the bank joined the Canadian push westward by establishing a branch in Winnipeg. In 1898 branches were established in Dawson City, Yukon Territory; Vancouver, British Columbia; and Skagway, Alaska. In 1900, the bank acquired the Bank of British Columbia, strengthening its position on the Pacific Coast. During the next ten years the Canadian Bank of Commerce acquired several other financial institutions; at the start of World War I, it had 379 branches.

During the 1920s, the bank nearly doubled its branch network by acquiring the Bank of Hamilton and later the Standard Bank of Canada. The general prosperity of the 1920s was reflected in the bank's growth. At the time of the stock market crash in 1929, the Canadian Bank of Commerce's assets were C$801 million. The Depression that followed, however, took a heavy toll on the bank, and its assets did not return to their pre-Depression high until 1940.

World War II finally brought economic recovery to Canada. The Canadian Bank of Commerce was active in the war effort, leading victory loan drives among other things. After the war, the bank grew steadily. By 1956, assets had reached C$2.5 billion, and by 1960, they had passed C$3 billion. Despite this success, however, the bank felt pressured by increasing competition and in 1961 agreed to a merger with the Imperial Bank of Canada.

The Imperial Bank of Canada was established in 1875. Its first president, Henry Stark Howland, had been the vice president of the Canadian Bank of Commerce. The bank's first office actually had no vault—overnight deposits were stored at another bank—yet in its first year of operation, the Imperial Bank made a profit of C$103,637. Reluctant to open too many branches too soon, the Imperial Bank's growth was somewhat slower than that of the Bank of Commerce during the same period. By 1880, however, the Imperial Bank had frontier fever. That year it opened a branch in Winnipeg, and the next year it branched out to Brandon and Calgary. By 1900, the Imperial Bank had 32 branches spread across the continent.

Between the turn of the century and World War I, Canada began to tap its mineral resources with amazing speed. The Imperial Bank of Canada earned the nickname the "Mining Bank" because of its ties to that industry.

After the war, the bank opened about 50 branches within just a few years, but not all of them survived the volatile economic conditions that followed the war. In the 1920s, deposits reached record levels, but the stock market crash in 1929 caused severe problems for the bank. Many of its loans went bad, and a number of branches were closed. The bank struggled to recuperate during the late 1930s and by the end of the decade it was making headway once again.

During World War II costs of operation rose faster than earnings, leading to lower dividends during the war years. About one-third of the Imperial Bank's 1,800 employees enlisted in the various services, and 53 died.

After the war, Canada entered a period of widespread prosperity and the Imperial Bank grew rapidly. In 1956, it acquired Barclays Bank (Canada) and increased assets by nearly C$40 million; by 1961, the Imperial Bank had assets of more than C$1 billion and 343 branches.

The amalgamation of the Canadian Bank of Commerce

and the Imperial Bank of Canada in 1961 created the largest bank in Canada at the time. The new Canadian Imperial Bank of Commerce had at its helm L.S. Mackersy, of the Imperial Bank, as chairman and N. J. McKinnon, of the Bank of Commerce, as president and CEO. Altogether the new bank accounted for about one quarter of the assets of all Canadian banks combined.

In 1962, McKinnon became chairman of CIBC's board of directors and steered the bank's course from that position until 1972. The 1960s were a prosperous time for Canada, and the nation's economy grew strongly. The Canadian Imperial Bank of Commerce's net earnings increased substantially each year throughout the decade. The bank also strengthened its foreign operations. At the end of the decade, Canada relaxed some of its restrictions on the banking industry. Notably, interest rates on loans were no longer limited to 6%. In this liberalized banking climate, Canadian banks did very well. In 1969, CIBC added 46 new branches while expanding its work force by only 5%. By 1970, annual profits had risen to C$43 million, more than twice what they had been at the time of amalgamation.

In the early 1970s, Canada began to invest heavily in energy development and agriculture, and the Canadian Imperial Bank of Commerce helped with the financing. Throughout the decade the bank had a close relationship with Canadian oil companies. That relationship would eventually cause the bank problems, but in the early 1970s, when oil prices were skyrocketing, investment in petroleum-related industries seemed like a gold mine.

In 1973, J. P. Wadsworth replaced McKinnon as chairman of CIBC, and remained in office until 1975. Late 1973 brought worldwide recession. Although Canadian domestic demand was adequate, overseas demand was low. This spelled trouble for Canada, whose economy was heavily dependent on exports. Nonetheless, CIBC continued to improve its earnings each year.

In 1976, Russell E. Harrison succeeded Wadsworth as chairman and CEO of CIBC. Harrison tended to run the bank in an autocratic manner. Top executives were not always given real power to make key decisions. In the late 1970s and early 1980s Canadian industry grew very quickly, and CIBC made large loans to many expanding firms.

In 1980, however, this policy began to falter. Massey-Ferguson, the Canadian tractor manufacturer, was in danger of collapsing, and the Canadian Imperial Bank of Commerce was Massey's biggest lender. The Canadian government worked with Massey's creditors to try to bail the company out by allowing it to raise new capital, but it didn't work. Massey lost US$240 million in 1981, and US$413 million in 1982, leaving CIBC with a substantial amount of bad debt.

The Dome Petroleum Company was another of CIBC's large corporate debtors in deep trouble in the early 1980s. When oil prices dropped sharply in 1982, Dome lost more than C$100 million; CIBC had loaned Dome more than C$1 billion. The failing company was eventually bought by Amoco Canada, but again CIBC was left with a pile of bad debt. Between 1979 an 1984, CIBC had the lowest average return on assets of the five largest Canadian banks.

In May, 1984 R. Donald Fullerton took over as CEO and set about restructuring the bank's operations. Fullerton eliminated branches to cut costs and service overlap and injected new blood into the bank's senior management. He also attacked the bank's bad debt, slowly eliminating bad loans from the bank's portfolio.

In 1985, a record number of farm failures caused mild concern among Canadian bankers. Canadian Imperial estimated that about 10% of its agricultural loans were in jeopardy. The problem was not nearly as severe in Canada as it was in the United States, however, where thousands of farmers defaulted on loans.

Under Fullerton's leadership, the bank bounced back from the troubles of the early 1980s to set a new earnings record in 1985. An aggressive new advertising campaign was launched in the United States as part of the bank's thrust internationally. In 1986, Fullerton announced that CIBC would split its operations into three separate units: the Individual Bank, the Corporate Bank, and the Investment Bank.

Each unit was to deal with a specific group of customers. The Individual Bank was CIBC's largest unit, employing three-quarters of the bank's workers to serve individuals and independent business people. The Corporate Bank was intended to provide standard financial services to a variety of Canadian and foreign companies. The Investment Bank was intended to take advantage of the upcoming liberalization of capital and other investment markets in Canada. It oversaw the operations of CIBC's brokerage firms and merchant banks overseas, and then domestically after June 1987, when Canada removed the regulations barring commercial banks from conducting investment banking activities. CIBC Securities Inc. was established in 1987 to offer stockbroker services. The bank also participated in a merchant bank, the Gordon Investment Corporation, with the Gordon Capital Corporation—each was an equal partner in the new bank. In Europe, CIBC operated CIBC Securities Europe Ltd.(formerly Grenfell and Colegrave Ltd.), and a stock brokerage for its overseas customers.

In 1987, Brazil announced that it would suspend interest payments on its foreign loans indefinitely. This action shocked the international banking community, which feared that other Third World countries would follow suit. In August, 1987, the Canadian government issued a guideline that required banks to set aside a large sum to protect against possible losses on loans to Third World countries. CIBC set aside $451 million, resulting in a net loss of $63 million for 1987, though assets increased by almost C$8 billion.

Worldwide deregulation and liberalization of financial markets has made banking more complex as well as potentially more profitable. During the mid- and late-1980s, CIBC responded innovatively to a changing marketplace. The bank regained the lost ground of the early 1980s and made a greater effort to expand overseas than any other Canadian bank. But CIBC still holds a significant portfolio of doubtful loans, a problem it will have to solve if the bank is to thrive. CIBC will have to walk the tightrope between aggressiveness, to keep it competitive, and caution, to keep its deposits safe.

Principal Subsidiaries: Canadian Imperial Bank of Commerce (New York); Canadian Imperial Bank of Commerce (California); CIBC Inc.; CIBC Leasing Inc.; CIBC Mortgages PLC; CIBC Leasing UK Ltd.; CIBC Investment Management Ltd.; CIBC Securities Europe Ltd.; CIBC Ltd.; Canadian Imperial Bank of Commerce (Deutschland) A.G.; Canadian Imperial Bank of Commerce (International) S.A.; Canadian Imperial Bank of Commerce (Suisse) S.A.; CIBC Finanziaria S.p.A.; CIBC Bank and Trust Company (Channel Islands) Ltd.; Canadian Eastern Finance Ltd.; CEF Capital Ltd.; CIBC (Hong Kong) Ltd.; CIBC Asia Ltd.; Bank of Commerce Jamaica Ltd.; CIBC Servicos Ltda.; Canadian Imperial Fund Managers (Cayman) Ltd.; Canadian Imperial Bank of Commerce Trust Company (Bahamas) Ltd.; Bank of Commerce Trust Company Barbados Ltd.; CIBC Bank and Trust Company (Cayman) Ltd.; Bank of Commerce Trust Ltd.; CIBC Australia Ltd.; D & D—Tolhurst Ltd.; CIBC New Zealand Ltd.

THE CHASE MANHATTAN CORPORATION

1 Chase Manhattan Plaza
New York, New York 10081
U.S.A.
(212) 552–2222

Public Company
Incorpored: 1969
Employees: 42,000
Assets: $97.46 billion
Stock Index: New York London Paris Tokyo Düsseldorf Frankfurt

In the 1931 movie *Monkey Business*, Groucho Marx's character asks Alky Briggs, his gangster nemesis, "What's the capital of South Dakota? What's the capital of Chase Manhattan Bank?" Then, as now, Chase Manhattan's capital happened to be quite a lot; today it is the second largest bank in the United States. It offers a wide range of financial services, its subsidiaries and branch offices ring the globe, and it has been a major player on Wall Street for more than 70 years. Groucho didn't have to worry about whether or not his audience would recognize the reference, even during the Great Depression. In good times and bad, people have always recognized the Chase Manhattan name.

Chase Manhattan's earliest predecessor, The Manhattan Company, was formed in 1799, ostensibly to supply New York with clean water to fight a yellow fever epidemic. However, its real purpose was to establish a bank. Organized by Aaron Burr to challenge the supremacy of the Bank of New York and the Bank of the United States, Burr had surreptitiously inserted a clause into the company's charter authorizing it to engage in other businesses with any leftover capital. To no one's surprise, the company soon discovered that the water-supply operation would not require all of its resources, and so the Bank of Manhattan Company was opened in 1799 at 40 Wall Street. The bank's first president was Daniel Ludlow.

In 1808, the year Daniel Ludlow resigned, the company was allowed to sell the water operation to the City of New York and devote its energy to banking. From that time onward, the Bank of Manhattan flourished. The bank introduced several innovative banking practices, including the shady method by which it gained a charter. Its example spawned further corruption among other groups who sought incorporation; the construction of canals during the 1820s and 1830s or the building of railroads in the 1850s and 1860s often became the pretext for procuring a bank charter that might not otherwise have been granted.

Since the bank had virtually no restrictions in its charter, it was able to loan money to all kinds of people. The bank dealt with tradesmen, land speculators, and manufacturers as well as the New York state government. This open banking policy provided a great impetus for westward expansion in the United States during the mid- and late-19th century. By the turn of the century the Bank of Manhattan had established itself as one of the largest holders of individual depositor accounts. Its policy of providing personal banking services worked so well that, at the time of its merger with Chase in 1955, the Bank of Manhattan operated 67 branches throughout New York City and was widely regarded as one of the most successful and prestigious regional banks in America.

The other part of Chase Manhattan, the Chase National Bank, was established in New York in 1877 and named after Salmon P. Chase, secretary of the treasury under Abraham Lincoln. It was not until 1911, however, when Albert Henry Wiggin took over the leadership of the bank, that Chase developed into a power on Wall Street. In 1905, at the age of 36, Wiggin became the youngest vice president in the company's history; by 1911 he was president of the bank and by 1917 the chairman of its board of directors.

Chase was a relatively small bank when Wiggin took over, but he soon began to transform it into one of the largest in the world. Wiggin did this by expanding the bank's list of corporate accounts through the offer of more banking services, especially trust services. He helped to found Mercantile Trust in 1917, and in the same year organized Chase Securities Corporation to distribute and underwrite stocks and bonds. This affiliate soon became a major force in the equities markets. In addition, Wiggin established strong ties to big business by recruiting the bank's directors from the most influential companies in the United States.

Wiggin's greatest contribution to the bank was his arrangement of a series of mergers during the 1920s and early 1930s in which Chase absorbed seven major banks in New York City. The largest of those, the Equitable Trust Company, had more than $1 billion in resources when it was acquired in 1930. The eighth-largest bank in the United States at the time, it was owned by John D. Rockefeller and led by Rockefeller's brother-in-law Winthrop Aldrich. Not long after the merger, Wiggin assumed the chairmanship of what was then the largest bank in the world.

In 1932, however, the leadership at Chase changed dramatically. Wiggin had used not only his own funds, but also those of the bank to engage in stock speculation, and that year was forced to resign. In the following years, Wiggin and a number of his close associates were disgraced by a congressional investigation that uncovered, among other transgressions, the use of affiliated companies to circumvent the laws restricting stock market transactions and the fact that, during the stock market crash Wiggin had made $4 million selling Chase stock short—using bank funds to do so.

Winthrop Aldrich directed the bank's operations from the mid-1930s to the end of World War II, a period when Chase continued to expand and develop, becoming the first bank to open branches in both Germany and Japan after World War II. However, Aldrich knew that Chase was hampered in its domestic development because all of its consumer branches were located in Manhattan. The bank had always concentrated on corporate and foreign business and ignored innovations such as branch banking, leaving it in a weak position to capitalize on the prosperity of middle-class Americans during the postwar boom. And so in 1955, Aldrich arranged a merger between Chase and the Bank of Manhattan, at the time the nation's 15th-largest bank, but more importantly one with an extensive branch network throughout New York City.

From the time of the merger between Chase and the Bank of Manhattan, there was a new driving force behind the bank's activities: David Rockefeller. Rockefeller had joined Chase as the assistant manager of its foreign department after the war, becoming vice president by 1949. In the early 1950s, he was head of the bank's metropolitan department; it was actually Rockefeller who advised Aldrich on the benefits of the merger with the Bank of Manhattan. With the merger complete, he was named executive vice president and given the responsibility for developing the largest bank in New York City. At the same time he was also appointed vice chairman of the executive committee. In 1969, he became chairman of the board of directors, the same year the Chase Manhattan Corporation was incorporated and the Chase Manhattan Bank N.A. became is wholly owned subsidiary.

As the head of Chase Manhattan, David Rockefeller soon became a major international power-broker. Never really interested in the day-to-day operations of the bank, he began to travel constantly, meeting with political and business leaders around the world. This high international profile led Rockefeller to use the bank in the service of what he thought was desirable American foreign policy; by becoming one of the pillars of the U.S. foreign-policy establishment, his influence on the Council of Foreign Relations and Trilateral Commission was very strong.

This close association between Chase and the prevailing U.S. political establishment inevitably drew the bank into controversy. In 1965, Chase's decision to purchase a major share in the second-largest bank in South Africa provoked an intense campaign by civil rights groups to persuade institutions and individuals to withdraw their money from a firm that clearly supported the apartheid regime. And, in 1966, widespread protests were directed against the bank because of Rockefeller's decision to open a Chase branch in Saigon. A strong supporter of American involvement in the Vietnam War, Rockefeller traveled to the southern capital of Vietnam to open the building personally; a sandstone fortress, it was designed to withstand mortar attacks and mine explosions.

David Rockefeller and Chase's foreign controversies continued into the 1970s. The shah of Iran had been the bank's best customer in the Middle East; Iran's $2.5 billion in deposits from oil profits amounted to approximately 8% of Chase's total deposits in 1975. When the shah fell from power in 1979, it was Rockefeller who, with Henry Kissinger, at that time the chairman of the firm's international advisory committee, persuaded the Carter administration to allow him into the United States. When Iran tried to retaliate by removing its deposits from Chase to other banks, Rockefeller succeeded in convincing the government to freeze all Iranian assets in U.S. banks, the move that led to the seizure of hostages at the American Embassy in Teheran.

Despite Chase Manhattan's power and influence in international finance, the 1970s were a difficult time for the bank. Chase lost significant domestic business as regional banks lessened their dependence on Chase Manhattan for their own growth and expansion; their burgeoning resources made it less important that they go to the "banker's banker" for loans. In addition, Chase lost millions of dollars in bad loans to Latin American countries, which resulted in its being placed on the Federal Reserve's list of "problem banks" that needed constant supervision. Although the company's foreign income increased from one-half to two-thirds of its total income during this time—to nearly $4 billion—the bank had a hard time competing with Citibank's aggressive strategy. Notwithstanding these problems, Chase remained the country's third-largest bank, with 226 branches in New York City and 105 branches and 34 subsidiaries around the globe.

The 1980s ushered in a period of significant acquisitions for Chase. In 1984, the bank purchased Nederlandse Credietbank N.V., a Dutch bank headquartered in Amsterdam; in the same year it also purchased the Lincoln First Bank in Rochester, New York; in 1985, the bank bought six Ohio savings-and-loan institutions; and in 1986, Chase acquired Continental Bancor.

In 1981, David Rockefeller retired from his position at Chase. Willard C. Butcher, his hand-picked replacement, had been president and CEO of Chase, and succeeded him as chairman of the board. Butcher took up where his predecessor left off; Chase maintains a very high profile in international finance and still likes to see itself as a power-broker there.

But the most important problem for Chase Manhattan in the 1980s was a series of bad loans that had no equal in quantity or in magnitude in the bank's history. It started in 1982, when Penn Square Bank collapsed after billions of dollars in unsecured loans that it had made to oil and natural gas interests in Oklahoma went sour. Chase purchased some of those loans, but moved quickly to write off many of them to prevent further financial damage. Chase has also been one of the most heavily exposed banks loaning money to Third World countries. On February 20, 1987 Brazil announced that it would suspend payment on its foreign debt and threw the money-center banks into a panic. In May, Chase added a whopping $1.6 billion to its loan loss reserves. As a result, it posted a loss of $894.5 million for 1987—the worst year for American banking since the Great Depression.

Battered by the Third World debt crisis and faced with strong competition from insurgent regional banks, Chase

Manhattan has been sagging against the ropes in the late 1980s. Between 1986 and 1988, it reduced its workforce by 10%, or about 6,000 employees. In 1988 *The New York Times* speculated that the venerable banking giant might be a takeover candidate because of its depressed stock price and prestigious name. But "prestigious" is the word most worth keeping in mind here. Even in bad times, people recognize the Chase Manhattan name.

Principal Subsidiaries: Saudi Investment Bank; Chase AMP Bank Ltd. (Australia); Chase Manhattan Asia Limited (Hong Kong); Chase Manhattan Trust Company (Hong Kong) Ltd.; Chase Manhattan Investment Services (Hong Kong) Ltd.; Chase Manhattan Trust and Banking Co. (Japan) Ltd.; Chase Leasing (Japan) Ltd.; Amanah Merchant Bank Berhad (Malaysia); Chase Investment Bank (Singapore) Limited; Chase Manhattan Futures (U.K.) Ltd.; Chase Manhattan Capital Markets (U.K.) Ltd.; Chase Leasing Ltd. (United Kingdom); P.T. Chase Leasing Indonesia; Chase Manhattan Bank (Austria), A.G.; Chase Bank and Trust Co. (C.I.) Ltd. (Channel Islands); Chase Invest A/S (Denmark); Chase Manhattan S.A. (France); Chase Manhattan Bank Luxembourg, S.A.; Chase Manhattan Bank (Norway) A.S.; Chase Bank (Ireland) PLC; Chase Manhattan Bank Espana S.A.; Chase Manhattan Securities, S.A. (Spain); Chase Manhattan Bank (Switzerland); Chase Investment Bank Ltd. (United Kingdom); Chase Manhattan Milbank Ltd. (United Kingdom); Chase Manhattan Futures (U.K.) Ltd.; Chase Manhattan Gilts Ltd. (United Kingdom); Chase Manhattan Market Makers Ltd. (United Kingdom); Chase Manhattan Service Management Ltd. (United Kingdom); Libra Bank Plc. (United Kingdom); Financiere d'Investissements et de Construction Immobiliere, (F.I.C.I.) (France); Chasefin-Chase Finanziaria, S.p.A. (Italy); Chase Investmenti Mobiliari S.p.A. (Italy); Chase Leasing S.A. (Spain); Chase Tade Finance Ltd. (United Kingdom); Chase Manhattan Trading, S.A. (Argentina); The Chase Manhattan Trust Corporation Limited (Bahamas); Banco Chase Manhattan, S.A.(Brazil); The Chase Manhattan Bank of Canada; Chase Manhattan Trust Cayman Ltd.; Inversiones Chase Manhattan Limitad (Chile); Chase Investment Bank (Panama) S.A.; Chase Manhattan Capital Markets Corp. of Puerto Rico; Chase Manhattan, S.A. Credito Financiamento Investimento (Brazil); Chase Bank AG (Germany); Chase Manhattan Overseas Finance Corp. N.V. (St. Maarten); Chase Manhattan Investment (Uruguay) S.A.; Chase Manhattan Leasing Canada, Ltd.; Chase Securities, Inc.; Chase Commercial Corp.; Chase Home Mortgage Corporation; Chase Investors Management Corp. New York; Chase Manhattan of California Thrift Corp.; Chase Manhattan Bank, N.A.; Chase Manhattan of Utah; Chase Bank of Ohio; Chase Manhattan Capital Markets Corp.; Chase Manhattan Financial Services, Inc.; Chase Bank of Maryland; Chase Manhattan Overseas Banking Corp.; Chase Manhattan Service Corp.; Chase Manhattan Leasing Company; Chase National Corporate Services, Inc.; Chase Lincoln First Bank, N.A.; Chase Trans-Info, Inc.; Chase Bank of Arizona; Chase Bank of Florida; Chase Bank International; Chase Manhattan Investment Holdings, Inc.; The Chase Manhattan Bank (USA), N.A.; Chase Trade, Inc.; Chase Auto Leasing Corp.; Chase Manhattan Financial Center, Inc.; Chase Manhattan Futures Corp.; Chase Manhattan Trust Co. of California, N.A.; Chase Access Services Corp.; Chase Automated Clearing House, Inc.; Chase Manhattan Thailand, Ltd.; Information and Services of Puerto Rico, Inc.; Chase/Clark Credit Company; Saudi Investment Bank.

Further Reading: Wilson, John Donald. *The Chase: The Chase Manhattan Bank, N.A., 1945–1985*, Boston, Harvard Business School Press, 1986.

CHEMICAL BANKING CORPORATION

277 Park Avenue
New York, New York 10172
U.S.A.
(212) 310–6161

Public Company
Incorporated: 1968
Employees: 27,225
Assets: $67.35 billion
Stock Index: New York London

The Chemical Banking Corporation, a multibillion dollar bank holding company, began as a division of a New York City chemical manufacturer during the early 19th century. Although the company has grown steadily, its image had been somewhat dull and its performance less than spectacular. Recently, however, Chemical's management has breathed new life into the bank, with several acquisitions meant to boost sagging earnings.

In the early 1820s, a state-chartered bank in New York could not open its doors unless the New York State Assembly approved its charter. In those days, the legislature was hostile to banks and obtaining a state charter could be rather difficult. Legislators were somewhat more inclined to grant charters to banks that were part of another business. When three New York City merchants—Balthazar P. Melick, Mark Spenser, and Geradus Post—decided to form a bank in 1823, they used a proven tactic to obtain their charter. On February 24, 1823, Melick, Spenser, and three other merchants incorporated the New York Chemical Manufacturing Company, headquartered in New York, to produce a variety of chemicals. The following year they successfully petitioned the New York State Assembly to allow the chemical company to amend its charter to permit the company to conduct banking activities. Chemical Bank was thus formed as a division of the New York Chemical Manufacturing Company on April 24, 1824, with Melick as its first president.

The bank initially served New York's mercantile community. At the time there were only 12 banks in New York City. Chemical Bank flourished in this relatively open market and soon offered older banks, like City Bank of New York (later Citibank), stiff competition. By 1829, Chemical had more than $216,000 in deposits, $20,000 reserved in specie, and retained earnings of more than $4,000. The chemical-manufacturing division was also profitable, earning $50,000 a year by 1832.

In 1831 John Mason was selected to be the bank's second president. Mason, one of the wealthiest land owners in the city, was also president of the New York Harlem Railroad Company. In 1839 Isaac Jones became the third president of Chemical Bank on Mason's death.

In 1844 John Quinton Jones became the fourth president of Chemical Bank. Jones started working for the company as an agent of the chemical division and eventually became cashier of the bank—the equivalent of general manager—during the presidency of his cousin, Isaac Jones. John Q. Jones is noted for developing the weakened bank into a very strong institution.

Also in 1844, when New York Chemical Manufacturing Company's original charter expired, the chemical company was liquidated and the company was reincorporated as a bank only, in accordance with more liberal banking laws passed in 1838. By 1851, the directors had sold all of the chemical division's inventories and real estate holdings and distributed the proceeds as dividends to shareholders.

In 1853 Chemical became a founding member of the New York Clearing House, an association of banks formed to help members clear banking transactions. During the recession of 1857 many banks newly incorporated under the banking act of 1838 were hard hit. Eighteen New York City banks closed in a single day; some 985 banks throughout the country closed during a six-month period. Chemical Bank earned the nickname "Old Bullion" during the crisis by continuing to redeem bank notes in specie for several days after all other financial institutions had started issuing paper loan certificates.

While Chemical Bank earned a reputation for soundness and foresight among grateful corporate and individual customers during the crisis, it earned another reputation among its peers. Other banks regarded Chemical as ruthless and uncooperative—for a time, the bank was even suspended from the New York Clearing House. Chemical had agreed in principle that clearing house members ought to band together to protect weaker banks during times of crisis, but refused to pool its specie reserves to soften the effects of the recession (some historians speculate that Chemical Bank was able to continue to distribute specie after the general suspension only because its largest customers had privately agreed not to withdraw their deposits).

During the Civil War, the country experienced two more recessions, one in 1861 and another in 1863, which were followed by more bank closings. Because of Chemical's reputation for stability, its deposits increased dramatically with each of these later crises. By 1871, its deposits had climbed to $6.08 million.

In 1865 the bank acquired a national charter under the National Bank Act of 1865 as the Chemical National Bank of New York. Chemical began issuing government-backed national bank notes, the forerunner of paper money. The bank gained two further advantages from its national charter: it became a depository of federal funds and the required reserves of other national banks, and its reputation for soundness was enhanced by the higher liquidity and solvency requirements set by the federal government.

In 1878, George J. Williams became president following Jones's death. Williams, who like Jones had served as president of the New York Clearing House Association, was arguably the most successful banker in the United States. Chemical grew rapidly under Williams's leadership during the turbulent decades at the end of the century. In the face of fierce competition, he made Chemical a major correspondent banker and built it into one of the largest and strongest banks in North America.

In 1903, Williams died and was replaced as president by Joseph B. Martindale. By 1907, the bank had lost its competitive advantage and was losing accounts at a rate of about 100 a year. When Martindale died in 1917, the bank was no longer among even the top 100 in the country. It had faltered in part because Martindale was extremely conservative at a time when other major New York banks were aggressively diversifying into securities and international markets.

On Martindale's death, Chemical's board of directors made Herbert K. Twitchell president. Percy H. Johnston, a young Kentucky banker, became vice president in 1917. Johnston turned the company around very quickly. First the bank stopped losing customers. Then, between September and December, 1917, deposits rose from $35 million to $63 million. By 1919, Chemical's stock had increased from a dangerous low to almost $200 a share.

Johnston was made president in 1920, and took the long-overdue step of diversifying the bank's services. He set up a trust department and engineered Chemical's first merger, in 1920, with Citizens National Bank, a small but wealthy New York commercial bank. As a result of the merger, Chemical's assets rose to $200 million, its capital to $4.5 million, and its deposits to $140 million. In 1923 Chemical established its first branch bank. Also in the early 1920s, Johnston recruited a new management team. These managers—Frank Houston, Harold Helm, and N. Baxter Johnson—guided the company through the mid-1960s.

In the late 1920s, Johnston decided to expand the company's trust business. The bank was reincorporated as a state bank in 1929 under the name Chemical Bank & Trust Company because New York State granted broader trust powers than were available to national banks. By then Chemical had 12 branches in Brooklyn and Manhattan, and in 1929 it opened its first overseas office, in London.

Later that year, Chemical merged with the United States Mortgage & Trust Company. After the merger, Johnston became Chemical's first chairman and John W. Platten, formerly president of United States Mortgage, replaced him as president.

Also in 1929, Johnston established two affiliates. The first, Chemical National Company, Inc., bought, sold, and underwrote securities. The second, Chemical National Association, Inc., was formed as a holding company. During the Depression, Johnston was able to maintain a strong capital position by merging the two affiliates into the bank and managing their assets carefully. During the early 1930s, when about 8,000 banks failed and many others struggled to remain solvent, Chemical Bank's deposits actually rose by 40%. Deposits continued to grow during the late 1930s and early 1940s, reaching the $1 billion mark in 1941.

In 1946, Johnston retired. The following year, Chairman Baxter Johnson and President Harold Helm brought about a merger with Continental Bank and Trust Company. This merger was the first in a series that helped increase the bank's assets from $1.35 billion in 1946 to $15 billion by 1972. The most important of these unions was Chemical's 1954 merger with the Corn Exchange Bank Trust Company to form Chemical Corn Exchange Bank. The merger brought Chemical 98 additional branches throughout New York City.

In the late 1950s, under Chairman Helm and President Isaac Grainger, Chemical began expanding its international operations. In 1958 its first international subsidiaries were formed and in 1959 the company's first full-service international branch opened in London. Also in 1959, Chemical merged with New York Trust Company, which had a large trust and wholesale-banking business. In the early 1960s, Chemical began to expand into New York's suburbs, opening branches on Long Island and in wealthy Westchester and Nassau counties.

In 1968, Helm and President William S. Renschard, appointed in 1960, followed a trend started by Citibank. They formed a bank holding company, Chemical New York Corporation, to facilitate expansion into other financial areas. In 1971, the company was internally restructured to decentralize the activities of the bank and clearly mark out areas of responsibility.

Chemical's international operations grew significantly in the late 1960s and early 1970s under the leadership of Donald C. Platten (the grandson of former president John W. Platten). Platten became president in 1972 and chairman of the company in 1973. His strategy was not to build a large network of international branches, which would make the company vulnerable to fluctuations in foreign economies, but to concentrate on establishing branches in key international money centers. Chemical established offices in the Bahamas and Frankfurt in 1969; in Zurich, Brussels, and Paris in 1971; and in Tokyo in 1972. By 1977 Chemical had added branches in Milan, Singapore, and Taiwan. It also expanded its international operations by purchasing a 30% interest in a London merchant bank in 1977 and participating in several ventures with financial institutions in Austria, the Philippines, and other countries.

From 1972 through 1977, Chemical again experienced a period of consistent growth. The bank not only increased the number of operations it controlled, but also diversified the services it offered to both corporate and individual customers. One of Chemical's main objectives was to develop a broad base of fee-generating services that would be unaffected by interest-rate fluctuations. Another was to earn a reputation as a progressive, result-oriented bank. Acquisitions continued during this period. In 1975 Chemical acquired Security National Bank, with its large Long Island branch network. Other important acquisitions at this time included several rural New York banks, a finance company with branches in 11 states, two investment-advisory firms, and a mortgage company. The company also formed a real estate–financing subsidiary, Chemical Realty Company, during this period and a wholesale bank in Delaware. One of Chemical's most popular innovations was "ChemLink," a computerized system that enabled corporations to transfer funds anywhere and to have instant access to their funds worldwide.

In 1980 Platten and Chemical President Norborne Berkeley began restructuring the company's non-consumer banking operations. Independent divisions were set up to operate the company's three largest sectors: multinational corporations, large domestic corporations, and middle-market businesses. This effort to streamline operations and cut out marginal businesses was necessary because, although Chemical had grown steadily over the past 30 years, it had failed to establish a niche in the industry and its overall performance had been unspectacular. What Chemical needed was to create a corporate image to distinguish it from other New York banks.

In 1982 Chemical made its first move to establish a corporate image. The company announced an agreement to merge with Florida National Banks of Florida, Inc. once interstate banking between the two states was permitted. Platten and Chemical President W.V. Shipley were immediately embroiled in a bloody battle with Southeast Banking Corporation, a major competitor of Florida National Banks that wanted to make its own takeover bid. Following law suits, countersuits, and stockholder actions, the combat ended in a draw; Southeast would get the Florida National Bank branches and Chemical got the remainder of the company's business, giving it a foothold in the lucrative Florida market. This deal helped Chemical gain a reputation as a daring and slightly unconventional player in the financial world.

In 1982 the bank introduced Pronto, an electronic home banking system for consumers and small businesses. And in 1985 Chemical, AT&T, Bank of America, and Time, Inc. formed a joint venture called Covidea to provide electronic services.

In 1986, Chemical celebrated its tenth consecutive year of earnings growth by announcing another merger agreement, again with a company whose market is outside Chemical's traditional sphere of operations. This time the merger partner was a New Jersey bank holding company, Horizon Bancorp. Again, the actual merger had to wait until interstate banking between New York and New Jersey was allowed. The merger finally took place in January, 1989, and Horizon was renamed Chemical Bank New Jersey.

Meanwhile, Chemical turned to the acquisition of Texas Commerce Bankshares. This merger, effective in May, 1987, was the largest interstate banking merger in U.S. history and allowed Chemical to expand into yet another major banking market. Texas Commerce was one of the largest bank holding companies in the Southwest, had the largest affiliate system in Texas, and was certainly the best capitalized of the major Texas banks.

Chairman Walter V. Shipley hopes to make Chemical the best-performing money-center bank. His short-range goals are to improve wholesale lending worldwide and to expand commercial-banking activities to other regions of the United States. The company has a number of strengths that will help it meet these goals, including an aggressive and imaginative management.

Principal Subsidiaries: Chemical Bank; Texas Commerce Bancshares, Inc.; Chemical Realty, Corp.; Chemical Business Credit Corp.; Chemical New York N.V.; Chemical Mortgage Company; Chemical Financial Services, Corp. Ltd.; Van Deventer & Hoch; Investment & Capital Management Corp.; Chemical New York Corporation—USA; Chemical Bank & Trust Company of Florida, N.A.; Chemical Bank, N.A.; Brown & Co. Securities Corp.; Alexander, Scriver & Assoc.; Chemical First State Corporation; Chemical Technologies Corp.; Chemical New Jersey Corporation; Chemical Investment Management, Inc.; The Portfolio Group, Inc.; Chemical Futures, Inc.; Chemical Equity, Inc.; Chatham Ventures, Inc.; Quantum Investment Management, Inc.; Chemical Mortgage Securities, Inc.; Chemical Securities, Inc.; Chemical Bank (Delaware); Chemsel, Inc.; Chemical New Jersey Bank.

Further Reading: History of the Chemical Bank 1823–1913, New York, Chemical Bank, 1913; N. Baxter Jackson. *"Old Bullion": One Hundred and Twenty Five Years on Broadway* New York, Newcomen Society, 1949; *Chemical Bank, 1823–1983*, New York, Chemical Bank, 1983.

CITICORP

CITICORP

399 Park Avenue
New York, NY 10043
U.S.A.
(212) 559–1000
Public Company
Incorporated: 1812 as the City Bank of New York
Employees: 89,000
Assets: $207.67 billion
Stock Index: New York Midwest Pacific London Amsterdam Tokyo Zurich Geneva Basel Toronto Düsseldorf Frankfurt

Citicorp, a holding company and the parent of Citibank, is one of the largest financial companies in the world. Often compared to the Bank of America, Citicorp has consistently outperformed Bank of America and others, and is regarded as America's leading bank. At a time when the U.S. budget deficit has led to the transfer of enormous amounts of American capital to foreign banks—particularly Japanese ones—Citicorp has remained highly competitive, even in international markets.

A bank almost as old as the country itself, Citicorp has its origin in the First Bank of the United States, founded in 1791. Colonel Samuel Osgood, the nation's first postmaster general and treasury commissioner, took over the New York branch of the failing First Bank and reorganized it as the City Bank of New York in 1812. Only two days after the bank received its charter, on June 16, 1812, war was declared with Britain. The war notwithstanding, the City Bank was for all intents and purposes a private treasury for a group of merchants. It conducted most of its business as a credit union and as a dealer in cotton, sugar, metals, and coal, and later acted as a shipping agent.

Following the financial panic of 1837, the bank came under the control of Moses Taylor, a merchant and industrialist who essentially turned it into his own personal bank. Nonetheless, under Taylor, City Bank established a comprehensive financial approach to business and adopted a strategy of maintaining a high proportion of liquid assets. Elected president of the bank in 1856, Taylor converted the bank's charter from a state one to a national one on July 17, 1865, at the close of the Civil War. Taking the name National City Bank of New York (NCB), the bank was thereafter permitted to perform certain official duties on behalf of the U.S. Treasury; it distributed the new uniform national currency and served as an agent for government bond sales.

Taylor was the treasurer of the company that laid the first transatlantic cable, which made international trade much more feasible. It was at this early stage that NCB adopted the eight-letter wire code address "Citibank." Taylor died in 1882. He was replaced as president by his son-in-law, Percy R. Pyne. Pyne, who never distinguished himself as a visionary leader, died nine years later, and was himself replaced by James Stillman, who became president in 1891.

Stillman believed that big businesses deserved a big bank capable of providing numerous special services as a professional business partner. After the panic of 1893, NCB, with assets $29.7 million, emerged as the largest bank in New York City and the following year, became the largest bank in the United States. It accomplished this mainly through conservative banking practices, emphasizing low-risk lending in well-secured projects. The company's reputation for safety spread, attracting business from America's largest corporations. The flood of new business permitted NCB to expand; in 1897 it purchased the Third National Bank of New York, bringing its assets to $113.8 million in 1898. Also in 1897 it became the first big American bank to open a foreign department.

Far from retiring or diminishing his influence within NCB, Stillman nonetheless began to prepare Frank A. Vanderlip to take over senior management duties. Stillman and Vanderlip, who was elected president of the bank in 1909, introduced many innovations in banking, including traveler's checks and investment services through a separate but affiliated subsidiary (federal laws prevented banks from engaging in direct investment, but made no provision for subsidiaries).

Beginning in the late 1800s, many American businessmen began to invest heavily in agricultural and natural-resource projects in the relatively underdeveloped nations of South and Central America. But government regulations prevented federally chartered banks such as NCB from conducting business out of foreign branches. Vanderlip worked long and hard to change the government's policy, and eventually won in 1913, when Congress passed the Federal Reserve Act. NCB established a branch office in Buenos Aires in 1914 and in 1915 gained an entire international-banking network from London to Singapore when it purchased a controlling interest in the International Banking Corporation (it acquired it completely in 1918).

In 1919 Frank Vanderlip resigned in frustration over his inability to secure a controlling interest in the company and James A. Stillman, the son of the previous Stillman, became president. NCB's assets reached $1 billion, the first American bank to do so. Charles E. Mitchell, Stillman's successor in 1921, completed much of what Vanderlip had begun, creating the nation's first full-service bank. Until this time national banks catered almost exclusively to the needs of corporations and institutions, while savings banks handled the needs of individuals. But competition from other banks, and even corporate clients themselves, forced commercial banks to look elsewhere for sources of growth. Sensing an untapped wealth of business in personal banking, in 1921 NCB became the first major bank to offer interest on savings accounts, which it allowed individual customers to open with as little as a dollar. And in 1928 Citibank began to offer personal consumer loans.

The bank also expanded during the 1920s, acquiring the Commercial Exchange Bank and the Second National Bank in 1921, and the People's Trust Company of Brooklyn in 1926, and merging with the Farmers' Loan and Trust Company in 1929. By the end of the decade, the "Citibank" was the largest bank in the country, and through its affiliates, the National City Company and the City Bank Farmers' Trust Company, was also one of the largest securities and trust firms.

In October, 1929 the stock market crash that led to the Great Depression caused an immediate liquidity crisis in the banking industry. In the ensuing months, thousands of banks were forced to close. NCB remained in business, however, mainly by virtue of its size and organization. But in 1933, at the height of the Depression, Congress passed the Glass-Steagall Act, which restricted the activities of banks by requiring the separation of investment and commercial banking. NCB was compelled to liquidate its securities affiliate and curtail its line of special financial products, eliminating many of the gains the bank had made in establishing itself as a flexible and competitive full-service bank.

James H. Perkins, who succeeded Mitchell as chairman in 1933, had the difficult task of rebuilding the bank's reputation and its business (it had fallen to number three). He instituted a defensive strategy, pledging to keep all domestic and foreign branches open and to eliminate as few staff as possible. Perkins died in 1940, but his defensive policies were continued by his successor, Gordon Rentschler.

As a major American bank, NCB was in many ways a resource for the government, which depended on private savings and bond sales to finance World War II. The bank followed its defensive strategy throughout the war, amassed a large government bond portfolio, and continued to stress its relationship with corporate clients. Unlike its competitors, NCB was so well placed in so many markets by the end of the war that it could devote its energy to winning new clients rather than entering new markets. Sixteen years after Black Tuesday, NCB had finally regained its momentum in the banking industry.

The bank changed direction after the death of Gordon Rentschler, in 1948, moving aggressively into corporate lending. In 1955, with assets of $6.8 billion, NCB acquired the First National Bank of New York and changed its name to the First National City Bank of New York (FNCB), or Citibank for short.

Citibank used its bond portfolio to finance its expansion in corporate lending, selling off bonds to make new loans. By 1957, however, the bank had just about depleted its bond reserve. Prevented by New Deal legislation from expanding its business in private savings beyond New York City, Citibank had nowhere to turn to for more funding. The squeeze on funds only became more acute until 1961, when the bank introduced a new and ingenious product: the negotiable certificate of deposit.

The "CD," as it was called, gave large depositors higher returns on their savings in return for restricted liquidity, and was intended to win business from higher-interest government bonds and commercial paper. The CD changed not only Citibank, but the entire banking industry, which soon followed suit in offering CDs. The CD gave Citibank a way to expand its assets—but at the same time required it to streamline operations and manage risk more efficiently, since it had to pay a higher rate of interest to CD holders for the use of their funds.

The man behind the CD was not FNCB's president, George Moore, nor its chairman, James Rockefeller, but Walter B. Wriston, a bright and highly unconventional vice president. Wriston, a product of Wesleyan University and the Fletcher School, had worked himself through the company's ranks since joining the bank in 1946. Having made a name for himself with the CD, Wriston was later given responsibility for revamping the company's management structure to eliminate the strains of Citibank's expansion. Like Vanderlip more than 50 years before him, Wriston advocated a general decentralization of power to permit top executives to concentrate on longer-term strategic considerations.

In an attempt to circumvent federal regulations restricting a bank's activities, in 1968 Citibank created a one-bank holding company (a type of company the Bank Holding Company Act of 1956 had overlooked) to own the bank but also engage in lines of business the bank could not. Within six months, Bank of America, Chase Manhattan, Manufacturers Hanover, Morgan Guaranty, and Chemical Bank had also created holding companies.

Citicorp made no secret of its intention to expand—both operationally and geographically. In 1970 Congress, recognizing its error and concerned that one-bank holding companies would become too powerful, revised the Bank Holding Company Act of 1956 to prevent these companies from diversifying into traditionally "non-banking" activities.

Wriston, who was promoted to president in 1967 and to chairman in 1970, continued to press for the relaxation of banking laws. He oversaw Citibank's entry into the credit card business, and later directed a massive offer of Visa and MasterCharge cards to 26 million people across the nation. This move greatly upset other banks that also issued the cards, but succeeded in bringing Citibank millions of customers from outside New York state. The bank failed, however, to properly assess the risk involved. Of the five million people who responded to the offer enough later defaulted to cost Citicorp an estimated $200 million.

In an effort to gain wider consumer recognition, the holding company formally adopted "Citicorp" as its legal name in 1974, and in 1976 First National City Bank officially changed its name to "Citibank." The "Citi" prefix was later added to a number of generic product names; Citicorp offered CitiCards, CitiOne unified statement accounts, CitiTeller automatic teller machines, and a host of other Citi-things.

Citicorp performed very well during the early 1970s,

weathering the failure of the Penn Central railroad, the energy crisis, and a recession without serious setback. In 1975, however, the company's fortunes fell dramatically. Profits were erratic due to rapidly eroding economic conditions in Third World countries. Citicorp, awash in petrodollars in the 1970s, had lent heavily to these countries in the belief that they would experience high growth and faced the possibility of heavy defaults resulting from poor growth rates. In addition, its Argentine deposits were nationalized in 1973, its interests in Nigeria had to be scaled back in 1976, and political agitation in Poland and Iran in 1979 precipitated unfavorable debt rescheduling in those countries. Shareholders soon became concerned that Citicorp, which conducted two-thirds of its business abroad, might face serious losses.

In its domestic operations, Citicorp suffered from a decision made during the early 1970s to expand in low-yielding consumer-banking activities. Although New York usury laws placed a 12% ceiling on consumer loans, Citibank bet that interest rates would drop, leaving plenty of room to make a profit. But the oil shock following the revolution in Iran sent interest rates soaring in the opposite direction; Citicorp lost $150 million in 1980 alone. To add insult to injury, Citibank purchased $3 billion in government bonds at 11%, in the belief that interest rates would continue a decline begun during the summer of 1980. Again, the opposite happened. Interest on the money Citibank borrowed to purchase the bonds rose as high as 21%, and the bank lost another $50 million or more.

One investment that didn't go awry, however, was the company's decision to invest $500 million on an elaborate automated teller network. Installed throughout its branches by 1978, the ATMs permitted depositors to withdraw money at any hour from any one of hundreds of automatic tellers. Not only were labor costs reduced drastically, but, by being first again, Citibank gained thousands of new customers attracted by the convenience of ATMs.

Citicorp raised the profitability of its commercial-banking operations by de-emphasizing interest-rate-based income in favor of income from fees for services. Successful debt negotiations with developing countries cut losses on debts which would otherwise have gone into default. And as a result of the 1967 Edge Act, and special accommodations made by various states, Citicorp, until then an international giant known domestically only in New York state, was able to expand into several states during the 1980s. Beginning with mortgages and its credit card business, then savings and loans, and then banks, Citicorp established a presence in 39 states and the District of Columbia. And internationally, the company expanded its business into more than 90 countries. Some of this expansion was accomplished by purchasing existing banks outright.

Wriston, after 14 years as chairman of Citicorp, retired in 1984, shortly after the announcement that Citicorp would enter two new businesses: insurance and information. He was succeeded by John S. Reed, who had distinguished himself by returning the "individual" banking division to profitability.

In May, 1987 Citibank finally admitted that its Third World loans could spell trouble and announced that it was setting aside a $3 billion reserve fund. Losses for 1987 totaled $1.2 billion, but future earnings were much more secure. Citibank's move forced its competitors to follow suit, something few of them were able to do as easily—Bank of America, for example, wound up selling assets to cover its reserve fund.

Under Reed, Citicorp continues to dominate the banking industry not just in the United States but around the world. Although it has been passed by several Japanese banks in total assets, Citicorp's more than 3,000 offices worldwide give it a presence matched by none. Surprisingly, the bank's size has not created a stodgy, slow-reacting behemoth; Citibank has been able to preserve its slightly nontraditional approach to banking and remain the pioneer of the industry it continues to dominate.

Principal Subsidiaries: AMBAC; Citicorp Diners Club; Quotron Systems; Transaction Technology, Inc.; CapMac (Capital Markets Assurance Corp.); KKB Bank A.G.; Citicorp Mortgage Inc.; Citibank Canada; Citibank Espana; Citibank Italia; Citibank Belgium; Citicorp International Trading Co.; Citibank (Maryland), N.A.; Citibank (Nevada), N.A.; Citibank (South Dakota), N.A.; Citibank (Florida), N.A.; Citibank (New York State); Citibank (Arizona); Citibank (Utah); Citibank (Maine), N.A.; Citibank Delaware; and others too numerous to list.

Further Reading: Leindorf, David and Etra, Donald. *Ralph Nader's Study Group Report on First National City Bank*, New York, Grossman Publishers, 1973; *Citibank, Nader and the Facts*, New York, Citibank, 1974; Cleveland, Harold van B. and Huertas, Thomas F. *Citibank 1812–1970*, Cambridge, Massachusetts, Harvard University Press, 1985; Hutchison, Robert A. *Off the Books*, New York, William Morrow and Company, 1986.

COMMERZBANK

COMMERZBANK A.G.

Neue Mainzer Strasse 32–36
D-6000 Frankfurt
Federal Republic of Germany
(069) 1 36 20

Public Company
Incorporated: 1958
Employees: 25,783
Assets: DM180.4 billion (US$101.72 billion)
Stock Index: Frankfurt Düsseldorf Hamburg Munich Berlin Stuttgart Bremen Hanover Antwerp Brussels Paris Tokyo Luxembourg Amsterdam Basel Bern Geneva Lausanne Zurich London Vienna

Commerzbank has long been one of Germany's leading commercial banks, one of the small number of large and powerful institutions that has dominated Germany's highly stratified banking industry. Although its size and strength nearly led to its demise after World War II, those qualities also allowed Commerzbank to bounce back quickly and take part in West Germany's astounding economic recovery.

Commerzbank began in 1870 in the port city of Hamburg under the name Commerz- und Discontobank. Founded by a group of bankers and Hanseatic merchants, its primary purpose was to finance foreign trade. The years 1870–1872 were boom years for German banking; during this time many commercial banks were founded to take advantage of the business opportunities afforded by the recent unification of Germany and the prosperity that followed its victory in the Franco-Prussian War. Many of these banks were short-lived, springing into existence to profit from the speculative frenzy of the moment, but Commerzbank, along with Deutsche Bank and Dresdner Bank, survived to become one of the three largest banks in West Germany today.

During its early years, however, Commerzbank remained relatively small. Although it became a major shareholder in the London and Hanseatic Bank when that bank was founded in 1872, in order to obtain representation in the world's financial capital, Commerzbank did not participate much in the rapid expansion of German overseas banking during the 1880s and 1890s. Its larger Berlin-based rivals took the lead in German ventures into South American and foreign European markets. Despite its specialization in foreign trade, Commerzbank's name is also notably absent from the list of major participants in the Deutsche-Asiatische Bank, which was founded in Shanghai in 1889 and firmly established German financial presence in the Far East.

Commerzbank took a step up in 1892, when it opened a branch office in Berlin. Following the political centralization inherent in the establishment of the Second Reich, many German banks had gravitated to Berlin, making it the nation's financial capital. All of Germany's major banks were based there, and Commerzbank completed its bid to join their ranks in 1904 when it acquired Berliner Bank. Its Berlin operations quickly came to supercede those in Hamburg in importance. At that time, German banking was dominated by nine Berlin-based institutions which became known as the *Berliner Grossbanken*.

The influence of the *Grossbanken* grew substantially during World War I and again in the years immediately following the armistice, though for vastly different reasons. From 1914–1918, public borrowing to finance the war effort supplanted private-sector loans as the banks' main source of business, and the government naturally chose firms with large capitalization to supply the sums of money that it required. This forced the banks to consolidate; large institutions absorbed smaller ones and smaller banks reached "community of interest" agreements with each other.

The inflation crises of the early 1920s, on the other hand, so threatened the German banking industry that the badly weakened banks were forced to merge with each other merely to survive. In 1920, Commerz- und Discontobank merged with Mittledeutsche Privatbank of Magdeburg, which was then one of Germany's most important regional banks and had long been active in building up a branch network. This new institution changed its name to Commerz- und Privatbank, and later that year acquired Vereinsbank Wismar. In 1924, Commerzbank had 246 branch offices, compared to only eight in 1913, a staggering rate of growth that well outpaced the other *Grossbanken* during this time.

Commerzbank enjoyed a period of relative prosperity in the latter half of the decade, increasing its capital from 42 million Reichsmarks in 1924 to 60 million in 1928, and its reserves from 21 million Reichsmarks to 35.6 million. In 1929 it acquired another Berlin bank, Mittledeutsche Creditbank. It also helped facilitate American investment in Germany during this time. In 1927 it negotiated a loan of $20 million from Chase National Bank and re-lent the money to German firms. Such moves were regarded with some suspicion, as they blurred the traditional line between banks and investment companies. Commerzbank helped solve this public relations problem in 1928 by joining with Chase National to form General Mortgage and Credit Corporation for the sole purpose of increasing foreign investment in Germany.

Commerzbank changed its name to its current form, Commerzbank Aktiengesellschaft, in 1940. During the years of Nationalist Socialist rule, the *Grossbanken*, now numbering six, continued to dominate German banking. In 1944, their assets totalled over 28 billion marks, more than all of Germany's other banks combined. And not only did they play a substantial role in financing the Nazi war effort, but thanks to Germany's universal banking system they were able to hold major interests in and place their executives on the boards of directors of the industrial concerns, like Krupp, Siemens, and IG Farben, that supplied hardware to the German military.

After World War II ended in Europe in April, 1945, Allied occupation authorities began investigating the German banking industry as part of their effort to punish war criminals. They found that not only had the *Grossbanken* provided financial support to the ruling Nazis, but that they had helped plunder the assets of financial instituions in occupied countries and that companies under their control had employed slave labor. Although Commerzbank's sins were not the most grevious to be discovered, the occupation authorities decreed that all the *Grossbanken* would be broken up into a total of 30 smaller institutions. The Allied authorities also hoped that decentralizing the German banking industry would limit its ability to finance future military buildups and that it would encourage American-style competition. As an American diplomat told *The Wall Street Journal* in 1955, "it wasn't merely vengeance we sought. We hoped that by modelling the German banking system after ours, where banks are usually confined to a single state, we'd be able to do a service to the competitive system. . . ."

The new West German government resisted this decree, but eventually gave in under severe political pressure. In 1952, the surviving *Grossbanken*—Commerzbank, Deutsche Bank and Dresdner Bank—were each dissolved into three smaller banks. Commerzbank was broken up into Commerzbank Bankverein, Commerz- und Credit-Bank, and Commerz- und Disconto-Bank. In addition, Chancellor Konrad Adenauer promised that the banks would not be re-amalgamated for at least three years.

In 1955, Chancellor Adenauer's promise expired and plans were laid for the reconstitution of what would become known as West Germany's Big Three. On July 1, 1958, Commerzbank resumed business, now headquartered in Düsseldorf (during the 1970s, it would gradually shift its operations to Frankfurt). Thanks to the size and strength of its constituent banks, Commerzbank was quickly able to regain the position of eminence that it had held 15 years earlier. The survival of Germany's universal banking system also helped; as one German bank official told *Time* in 1962, an American equivalent of a Big Three bank would be like "a combination of Chase Manhattan, First Boston and Merrill Lynch."

In the late 1960s, Commerzbank joined the worldwide trend among financial institutions toward internationalizing its business. In 1967 it joined with Irving Trust Company, First National Bank of Chicago, Westminster Bank, and Hongkong & Shanghai Banking Corporation to form the International Commercial Bank in London. In 1970, it entered into a semi-merger with Credit Lyonnais, France's second-largest bank, and Italy's Banco di Roma in order to both counter increased competition from large American banks and meet the needs of European companies that had expanded their business overseas. The resulting institution had $18 billion in deposits and 3,000 branches, making it the largest banking organization in Europe and the fourth-largest in the world. Differences in national banking laws and traditions prevented the three banks from effecting a full-fledged merger, but they did agree to coordinate management practices and integrate all competing operations outside their home countries. Commerzbank also formed an investment advising company in Tokyo in 1973 and the Financial Corporation of Indonesia in 1974.

At home, the Big Three continued to wield considerable influence in German business through shareholding and corporate directorships, just as they had before the end of World War II. Commerzbank owned substantial interests in breweries, department store chains, and construction companies. In the 1970s, however, the Social Democratic Party's rise to power and widespread anxiety over the scope of the Big Three's influence convinced the banks to divest themselves of their holdings to prevent possible nationalization.

But the public and politicians did a quick about-face in the mid-1970s, when the oil boom generated fears that Middle Eastern interests would use their petrodollars to muscle into strategic German industries. In January, 1975 Commerzbank purchased a sizable stake in GHH, a machinery concern, to help ward off a possible Arab takeover, by acquiring a 25% interest in Regina Verwaltungsgesellschaft, a holding company owning 25% of GHH. The move also helped Commerzbank move into the insurance business through Regina's links with Allianz Insurance Gruppe. And in December of that year, it joined Dresdner Bank, Bayerische Landesbank, and five other partners to buy a 25% stake in Daimler-Benz from Deutsche Bank, which had purchased the shares at the urging of Chancellor Helmut Schmidt to keep them out of the hands of an Iranian concern. Once the panic had passed, Commerzbank resumed its policy of selling off its business holdings. In 1980, it sold a 32% stake in Kaufhof, Germany's second-largest retailer, to the Union Bank of Switzerland and Metro-Verwegensverwaltung, a German-owned Swiss supermarket concern.

But the Kaufhof sale was also a way of raising cash at a time when Commerzbank was struggling badly. German banks in general fared poorly at the beginning of the new decade compared with their British, American, and Japanese counterparts, but Commerzbank suffered in particular from overexpansion in the late 1970s and heavy investments in fixed-interest securities, which turned sour when interest rates did not decline as predicted. The bank's profits shrank to virtually nothing, and in 1980 it failed to pay a dividend for the first time in its history. Chairman Robert Dohm resigned late that year after suffering a heart attack.

Paul Lichtenberg, Dohm's predecessor, became interim chairman and immediately began searching for a permanent replacement. He was able to woo Walter Seipp, vice chairman of Westdeutsche Landesbank, who assumed the chairmanship in 1981. A lawyer by trade, Seipp had worked for Deutsche Bank from 1951 to 1974 before joining Westdeutsche Landesbank and had built a strong reputation for himseslf in both international and domestic banking circles. Under his direction, Commerzbank increased its loan loss provisions in 1982 when faced with the possible default of US$250 million worth of loans to Poland. The bank did not pay out another dividend until 1983, but by 1984 it had returned to financial health.

From there, Commerzbank resumed its ambitious ways. In 1984, it continued to divest its nonbank holdings by selling its stake in the Kempinski luxury hotel group to Saudi Arabian interests. But it also joined Westdeutsche Landesbank, Bayerische Landsebank, and its Big Three rivals to form Deutsche Wagnisfinanzierung, a venture-capital company. In 1986, responding to a new trend among West German companies toward raising money through the securities markets rather than by borrowing from banks, it raised $200 million in fresh capital through a floating-rate note issue. Commerzbank chose a propitious moment to float the new offering, doing so at a time when the market for floating-rate bonds denominated in European currencies was strong.

In 1988, Commerzbank sold its stake in Deutsche Wagnisfinanzierung to Deutsche Bank. That same year it also purchased a 40% stake in Leonberger Bausparkasse, West Germany's fourth-largest savings and loan, from the Stuttgart insurer Allgemeine Rentenstalt Lebens- und Rentenversicherung. And Commerzbank put the crowning touches on its international investment-banking network by opening offices in Tokyo in 1987 and New York in 1988. By 1988, its commercial banking network had branches in Brussels, Antwerp, Paris, Madrid, Barcelona, London, Hong Kong, Tokyo, Osaka, New York, Chicago, Atlanta, and Los Angeles.

Commerzbank has always been the smallest of the Big Three banks, but the very fact that it is one of those select three counts for a great deal in the West German banking industry, where the drop from the first tier to the second is steep. Historically, Commerzbank was a latecomer, joining the major league of German banking long after its rivals had done so. When the European economy becomes fully integrated at the end of 1992, it will present West German financial institutions with a whole new set of challenges. Commerzbank will have to be quick to adapt to change this time.

Princapal Subsidiaries: Berliner Commerzbank AG.; Rheinhyp Rheinische Hypothekenbank AG.; Commerz-Credit-Bank Aktiengesellschaft Europartner; Von Der Heydt-Kersten & Sohne; Ilseder Bank, Sandow & Co,; Commerz-und International Capital Management GmbH; Commerzbank Investment Management Gesellschaft MBH; Commerzbank International S.A. (Luxembourg); Commerzbank (Nederland) N.V.; Commerzbank (South East Asia) Ltd.; Commerzbank (Switzerland) Ltd.; Commerzbank (Geneva) (Switzerland); Commerzbank Capital Markets Corporation N.Y. (U.S.A.); Commerzbank Securities Company Ltd. (Japan); CB Finance Company B.V.; Commerzbank U.S. Finance, Inc. (U.S.A.); S.W.I.F.T. Society for Worldwide Interbank Financial Telecommunications s.c. (Belgium); Unibanco-Banco de Investimento do Brasil S.A. (B.I.B.); Misr International Bank S.A.E. (Egypt); Jean de Cholet-Gilles Dupont S.A. (France); P.T. Finconesia Financial Corporation of Indonesia; EuroPartners Holdings S.A. (Luxembourg); Handelsgest S.A.R.L. (Luxembourg); Indugest S.A.R.L. (Luxembourg); Societe de Gestion du Rominvest International Fund S.A. (Luxembourg); UBAE Arab German Bank S.A. (Luxembourg); Banque Marocaine de Commerce Exterieur (Morocco); Banque Nationale pour de Developpement Economique (Morocco); The Development Bank of Singapore Ltd.; Korea International Merchant Bank; Banco Hispano Americano S.A. (Spain); Corporacion Financiera Hispamer S.A. (Spain); Finance Company VIKING (Switzerland); Mithai Europartners Finance and Securities Company Ltd. (Thailand); International Commercial Bank PLC (UK); Commerzbank U.S. Finance Inc.; EuroPartners Securities Corporation (U.S.A.); Commerzbank Capital Markets Corporation (U.S.A.).

COMPAGNIE FINANCIERE DE PARIBAS

3, rue d'Antin
75002 Paris
France
(33) 1 4298 1234
Public Company
Incorporated: 1872
Employees: 26,000
Assets: Ffr818 billion (US$135 billion)
Stock Index: Paris

The French banking conglomerate Paribas has been one of the most important financial institutions in Europe for more than 100 years. It has played a major role in the development of the French economy, as well as the economies of the Netherlands, Belgium, and Luxembourg. Unrestricted in its scope of activities (France has nothing like America's Glass-Steagall Act, separating commercial and investment banking), Paribas is at once a leading industrial, commercial, and foreign-exchange bank, a securities underwriter and dealer, and a stock broker.

Paribas was formed in 1872 through the merger of the French Banque de Paris and the Banque de Credit et de Depot des Pays Bas, incorporated in the Netherlands. The new company, the Banque de Paris et des Pays-Bas—called Paribas for short—was headquartered in Paris and had branches in the Benelux countries and Switzerland. Its primary backers and customers were large industrial concerns in the manufacturing industries. As a result, the bank was closely associated with many industrial ventures in France and its colonies. Several of these ventures involved production of steel and heavy machinery, as well as oil exploration in North Africa and southwest Asia. Paribas participated in the formation of Compagnie des Francais Petroles in 1924, and became a major competitor of the Banque de l'Indochine et de Suez, France's leading colonial bank.

World War II interrupted much of the bank's international activity. Paribas remained open for business through the German occupation, but stagnated. Under German control, Paribas' major clients faced risks such as the constant threat of RAF bombing. In addition, the bank's managing board was compelled to follow directions from the occupation authority and the Vichy government.

Once again in control of its business after liberation in 1944, Paribas devoted much of its attention to rehabilitating bomb-damaged factories and supporting the war effort. With the fall of Germany in May, 1945, Paribas was again able to concentrate on its international investments. Although pressure from the United Nations precipitated the eventual downfall of the colonial system, France, with numerous interests in Indochina, Algeria, West Africa, and the Western Pacific, was slow to relinquish its empire.

Insurrections in Vietnam and Algeria during the 1950s led to military engagements that seriously damaged French investments, many of which were underwritten by Paribas. While the Americans inherited the Vietnamese War, the conflict in Algeria escalated into a costly war that ended in Algerian independence in 1962. Still, in places where France had relinquished its colonial presence, there remained a strong tie to French culture and a deep dependence on French development aid, in which Paribas played a leading role.

Paribas wound down much of its Latin American lending in the years following World War II. The bank also curtailed activity in the French Western Pacific, an area which, since it offered France little economic benefit, was used increasingly for military projects.

In an effort to expand its presence in major financial markets during the early 1960s, Paribas opened a branch in London and, in conjunction with Lehman Brothers, attempted to start an investment bank in New York, but failed. However, Claude de Kemoularia, a former adviser to the United Nations, made significant inroads for the bank in the Third World, while serving as Paribas' traveling ambassador. As a result of his efforts, Paribas regained its leading position in the Middle East during the early 1970s.

The bank restructured in 1968 and, adopting a holding-company structure under the name Compagnie Financiere de Paris et des Pay-Bas, tried once again to achieve a greater international presence. Paribas opened an office in Tokyo in 1972, and in 1974, with S. G. Warburg and A. G. Becker, formed an investment bank called Becker Warburg Paribas. In 1978 the bank opened a branch in New York and an office in Hong Kong and also purchased 5% of Japan's Orient Leasing. A year later, it increased its holding in France's Compagnie Bancaire, a finance firm, to 45%.

Internationalization became especially important to Paribas during the French elections of 1977. Paribas' board, fearing nationalization by a new left-wing government, set up several new ventures in Spain, Italy, West Germany, and England as part of an effort to transfer as much of the bank's capital as possible out of French jurisdiction. The elections, however, returned the conservative government to power.

In 1981 the threat of nationalization loomed once again for Paribas. With a Socialist, Francois Mitterand, favored to win the presidency, Paribas Chairman Pierre Moussa sold controlling interest in the bank's Swiss and Belgian subsidiaries to prevent the Socialist government from gaining control over those assets. When Mitterand and the Socialists won the election, they pledged to nationalize many of France's largest industries and all of its leading banks. Paribas in particular was vilified as an arrogant and abusive institution preoccupied with self-interest and profit. Even the company's headquarters, the mansion where Napoleon Bonaparte married Josephine in 1796, became an issue.

Although Paribas was taken over by the government in February, 1982, Moussa's plan succeeded in cutting the bank's losses. In November, 1981, Laurent Fabius, Mitterand's budget minister, complained of Moussa's defensive actions. He filed suit against the chairman and several of Paribas' top aides in January, and a month later won their resignations. Moussa was acquitted in 1984, but three of his top officers were convicted, sentenced to prison, and heavily fined. Two sentences were suspended; the third was given to a fugitive. Jean-Yves Haberer, a career civil servant, was appointed to succeed Moussa as chairman of the nationalized Paribas.

While Paribas was run by the government, it adopted Banque Paribas as its official name. In 1983 it terminated its association with Warburg by divesting itself of its Warburg shares and taking control of A. G. Becker, which it later sold to Merill Lynch and Company in 1984. The bank's broad interests in French industries, however, were left largely intact.

The socialist experiment in France did not work as planned. Parliamentary elections in 1986 forced President Mitterand to share power with a conservative prime minister, Jacques Chirac, who had the power and legislative support to return several nationalized companies to private and institutional shareholders. Paribas was second among these.

Haberer, however, had run Paribas with such a heavy hand that he had virtually disenfranchised the bank's top managers and left many employees feeling that they had been reduced to public servants. Indeed, Paribas frequently had come under pressure to aid financially troubled companies—regardless of their viability—as if it were a government rescue bank.

With the new political circumstances, Haberer was dismissed in 1986 and replaced by Michel Francois-Poncet, a 26-year veteran of the bank handpicked by Chirac himself. Francois-Poncet immediately began the difficult task of rebuilding morale by returning responsibilities to managers.

Next, taking American investment banks as a model, Francois-Poncet expanded the bank's involvement in institutional investment markets. He adopted a strategy aimed at preserving the bank's existing customer base by offering a wider range of services. Paribas took over the French sharebroker Courcoux-Bouvet, and Quilter Goodison, a London-based investment bank. In 1987 Paribas managed the partial privatization of Elf Aquitaine and British Gas's French interests and initiated a new campaign to win business from small- and medium-sized firms in search of fee-based income from its consulting services.

Early in 1988 Paribas regained full ownership of Credit du Nord, a recently reprivatized retail bank. Credit du Nord, however, has remained a doggedly expensive operation due to French laws that restrict banks from closing branches.

As a result, Paribas is likely to de-emphasize the retail-banking business of Credit du Nord and other subsidiaries in favor of the more promising investment-banking sector. Paribas also seems to have recognized the small growth potential of its insurance operations, a costly sector that appears peripheral to the company's long-term focus.

Francois-Poncet's greatest achievements are the successful reorientation of the company to sounder operating strategies and the restoration of Paribas' prestigious reputation. Nationalization, if it accomplished nothing else, removed the bank's old-boy-network image. As one of France's premier financial institutions, it intends, Francois-Poncet has said, to become "among the 15 that count in the world," particularly after 1992, when European trade barriers are to be eliminated.

Principal Subsidiaries: Compagnie Financiere De Paribas; Banque Paribas (91.1%); Omnium De Participations Bancaires De Paribas (85%); Banque Pour la Construction Et L'Equipement 'CGIB'; Compagnie Centrale de Financement Cocefi'; Conseil Investissement; Banque Paribas Pacifique (90.0%); Societe Generale de Financement Intercontinentale 'Sogefi'; Societe Anonyme De Transactions Internationales; Societe Nouvelle De Banque Europe: SNB-E; Banque Paribas Polynesie (70%); Credit Du Nord; Union Bancaire Du Nord (61.1%); Banque Tarneaud Freres Et Compagnie (79.1%); Banque Arnaud Gaidan; Caisse Generale Des Depots Et D'Avancees 'Cageda' (99.4%); Banque Nicolet Lanfranechere Et De L'Isere (97.2%); Societe Immobiliere D'Investissement Et De Coordination (99%); Compangnie Bancaire (48.4%); Union De Credit Pour Le Batiment (36.8%); 'Locabail' Compagnie Pour La Location D'Equipements Professionels; Union Francaise De Banques; Fonciere De La Compagnie Bancaire (90.2%); Credit D'Equipement Des Menages 'Cetelem' (75.6%); 'Locobail Immobilier' (40.3%); Compagnie Francaise D'Epargne Et De Credit 'CFEC'; Compagnie Pour Le Financement De L'Industrie, Du Commerce Et De L'Agriculture 'Cofica'; Parit; Banque Financiere Cardif; Kleber Portefeuille; Compagnie Financiere Kleber (99.4%); Cofibail; Banque Paribas Belgique (75%); Banque Paribas Luxembourg (99.4%); Banque Paribas Suisse (90.7%); Banque Paribas N.V.; Banque Paribas Gabon (57.3%); Eural Spaarbank NV (79.7%); Financiere Gabonaise De Developpement Immobilier (67.8%); Paribas Bank International (Texas) Inc.; Banque Paribas Canada; Paribas Suisse (Bahamas) Ltd.; Paribas Finance Inc.; Paribas Quilter Goodison Holding (99.9%); Banque Paribas Deutschland; Paribas North America; Paribas South East Asia; Paribas Finanziari; Paribas Limited; Paribas Finance Texas Inc.; Banque Paribas Cote-D'Ivoire (82.9%); Banque Paribas Norge; Banque Paribas Bienne; Novolease N.V.; Paribas UK Holding; Credit Nord Belge.

CONTINENTAL BANK CORPORATION

231 South LaSalle Street
Chicago, Illinois 60697
U. S. A.
(312) 828–2345

Public Company
Incorporated: 1932 as the Continental Illinois National Bank and Trust Company of Chicago
Employees: 9,624
Assets: $30.58 billion
Stock Index: New York Midwest Pacific Cincinnati London

Today's Continental Bank, known as Continental Illinois until late 1988, is the product of countless mergers, but the bank can trace its roots to two main institutions: the Illinois Merchants Trust Company and the Continental National Bank and Trust Company.

The Illinois Merchants Trust Company's earliest origins lie in the Merchants' Savings, Loan and Trust Company, founded by a group of Chicago businessmen in 1857. Merchants' survived the great Chicago fire of 1871 quite well; though all its records were burned, its valuables survived, and the bank lost only $55,000 in taking the word of its depositors about their accounts.

As Chicago became a major industrial center in the early 20th century, banks with larger lending capacities were needed to meet the increased demand for credit. In 1923 Merchants' Loan and Trust (the word "Savings" was dropped in 1881) merged with the Illinois Trust and Savings Bank. In 1924 they were joined by the Corn Exchange National Bank to form Illinois Merchants Trust Company.

The Continental National Bank and Trust Company was the eventual product of a 1910 merger between the Commercial National Bank and the Continental National Bank. The Commercial had been organized in 1864, while the Continental was chartered in 1883.

In 1898 the Continental absorbed the International Bank and the Globe National Bank, bringing its deposits to $20 million. By 1905 Continental's deposits had topped $50 million, giving it the strength not just to survive the panic of 1907 but to offer help to other banks.

In 1909 the Commercial, which had grown steadily on its own, merged with the Bankers National Bank, another prominent Chicago bank. That same year Continental took over the commercial business of the American Trust and Savings Bank.

But the thriving city of Chicago demanded ever-larger banks, and in 1910 the Continental and the Commercial decided to merge, becoming the Continental and Commercial National Bank. With a total capitalization of $33 million and deposits of $175 million, the bank was Chicago's largest.

In 1918, the Hibernian Banking Association, established in 1861 as Chicago's first savings bank under the name Merchants' Association, was merged into Continental and Commercial.

In 1927 the Continental and Commercial Trust and Savings Bank, which had evolved from the American Trust and Savings Bank, merged with Continental and Commercial National; the resulting bank was the Continental National Bank and Trust Company.

In 1929 Illinois Merchants Trust merged with Continental National Bank and Trust Company to become the Continental Illinois Bank and Trust Company. This bank then became Continental Illinois National Bank and Trust Company of Chicago in 1932, when it was granted a national charter.

This new bank had total resources of more than $1 billion, but Continental's size was of little comfort during the Great Depression, when it had to borrow $50 million from the federal government's Reconstruction Finance Corporation in 1934. At the same time, Continental got a new chairman, Walter J. Cummings, the former head of the Federal Deposit Insurance Corporation.

During World War II and immediately after, Continental remained a cautious, low-profile bank. Its lending policies were unadventurous and it relied heavily on its large bond portfolio for revenue. Such conservatism was appropriate during depression and war, but the American economy boomed during the 1950s, and Continental's financial performance sagged as the bank sat on its hands.

In 1959 Cummings retired and was replaced by David M. Kennedy. As *The New York Times* put it, Kennedy "transformed a hidebound, hyperconservative bank into one of the most dynamic and progressive forces in American banking." Under Kennedy, Continental expanded its international activities significantly, opening a branch in London in 1962 and acquiring branches in Tokyo and Osaka from a Dutch bank. By 1967, Continental had a presence in much of Europe and Latin America. Because of Illinois laws prohibiting branch banking, Continental had never made retail banking an important part of its activities, concentrating instead on business lending. Kennedy pushed Continental into the retail business too. But most of all, Kennedy encouraged his loan officers to think more about growth and less about risk. However, his expansionist policies, as practiced by his successors, also set the stage for Continental's downfall in the 1980s.

In 1969 Kennedy left Continental to become secretary of the treasury in President Richard Nixon's first administration, and D. M. Graham took his place. Under Graham, Continental continued its pursuit of big corporate borrowers. It also reorganized in 1969, creating Conill Corporation, a one-bank holding company, as many large banks did at the time. In 1972 it adopted the name Continental Illinois Corporation. By the mid-1970s Continental was the nation's eighth-largest bank and had acquired a reputation as one of the best-managed and most secure banks in the world.

In 1973 Roger Anderson became chairman. Anderson, a career Continental employee, was a zealous believer in the bank's high-growth strategy. In 1976 he publicly declared that he intended to make Continental the nation's premier commercial lender. Between 1977 and 1982, the bank more than doubled its loan portfolio, outperforming its rivals by a wide margin. By the late 1970s, it had achieved Anderson's goal.

Its areas of highest growth, however, were energy and real estate, and when oil prices collapsed in the early 1980s and American industry reeled under the weight of recession and increased global competition, Continental found itself badly overextended. Its worst loans included $200 million to American Harvester, another $200 million to Dome Petroleum, $173 million to Nucorp Energy, $100 million to the Mexican Grupo Industrial Alfa, and $41 million to Wickes Corporation, all companies in serious trouble.

But Continental's worst problem was the Oklahoma City–based Penn Square Bank. During the heady days of the late 1970s, when energy prices reached an all-time high, Penn Square loaned billions of dollars to oil and natural gas interests in Oklahoma. Many of these loans, however, were either unsecured or secured by dubious collateral. Continental, true to its ways, had been anxious to get as much of the Oklahoma energy market as it could, but had found that the oilmen there had grown imperious as well as prosperous and required a hard sell. Impressed by Penn Square's connections in the area, Continental wound up purchasing more than $1 billion worth of loans from Penn Square.

In 1981 Continental discovered that its Penn Square investment was fundamentally unsound, but expressed no alarm over it. At a shareholder's meeting in April, 1982, Anderson declared that Continental's credit quality was "very high." But that June plummeting energy prices toppled Penn Square's house-of-cards financing scheme and that bank was declared insolvent. Despite shareholder concerns, Continental classified only 15% of its Penn Square loans as nonperforming. Chase Manhattan Bank, another bank caught up in Penn Square's implosion, wrote off 35% of its loans by comparison. Continental suddenly had a $61 million loss for the second quarter of 1982. By the end of the year, nonperforming loans totaled nearly $2 billion.

Some financial observers and perturbed shareholders suspected a cover-up on the bank's part, but author Mark Singer suggests that Continental officials may simply have disregarded all the danger signs. "Among bankers there is an inbred tendency to react to a fiscal humiliation as if one had spilled gravy on a tablecloth or neglected to send a hostess a thank-you note," he writes in *Funny Money*, his account of the Penn Square fiasco.

In February, 1984 Richard Anderson was forced to retire and David Taylor succeeded him. In March, the bank sold its profitable credit card operations, to raise cash. But much of the money went to pay its dividend to shareholders, not to shore up its financial condition. That May Continental suffered a run of monumental proportions.

Seemingly started by a false rumor that Continental was about to declare bankruptcy, the run cost Continental $1 billion in deposits on May 9 and another $3.6 billion on May 11. On the 14th, Continental announced that a consortium of 16 banks, led by Morgan Guaranty, had pledged a $4.5 billion line of credit to Continental. The run kept going. On May 17, the Federal Deposit Insurance Corporation (FDIC) joined 28 banks in pledging another $7.5 billion in assistance, stabilizing, but not stopping, the run.

By mid-July Continental had lost more than $14 billion in deposits. Since no bank had come forward to rescue Continental by means of a merger, that month the FDIC stepped forward to arrange a bailout of Continental itself.

In a very complicated arrangement, that September the FDIC essentially bought 80% of Continental's shares for $1 billion, and paid another $3.5 billion for some $5 billion worth of Continental's shakiest loans. The FDIC also installed John Swearingen, a former chairman of the Standard Oil Company of Indiana, as chairman and CEO.

Under Swearingen, Continental immediately set about selling more assets and cutting costs. The bank's lending operations gained the discipline that they formerly lacked, and loan-loss reserves were strengthened. In 1985 Continental posted a profit of more than $100 million for the year. But over the next several years, it still lacked a coherent strategy for returning to its former greatness. In 1986 the FDIC made its first public offering of part of its stake in Continental, reducing its holding from 80% to about 69%, but at a disappointing price.

In July, 1987 Thomas Theobald, the former head of Citicorp's investment-banking division, took over as chairman and CEO of Continental. Under Theobald, Continental finally decided on a distinctive strategy: to concentrate on providing financial services to business customers. Continental sold its retail-banking business, trimmed its international operations, and focused on services like financial risk management for small and mid-sized companies.

So far, the strategy appears to be successful. In 1988, its first full year as a banker to businesses only, Continental reported record profits. In December of 1988 the bank changed its name, dropping the "Illinois" to officially become the Continental Bank Corporation, in an effort to position itself to business customers nationwide. That same month, the FDIC reduced its stake in the company to just over 40%.

Although the bank still faces stiff competition and several challenges—among them returning to full public ownership—Continental has put the 1980s firmly behind it and enters the 1990s with a strong position in a growing market niche.

Principal Subsidiaries: Continental Bank International; Continental Bank S.A./N.V. (Belgium); Continental Brokerage Services, Inc.; Continental Illinois Venture Corporation; Continental International Finance Corporation; Continental Illinois Limited London; Continental Illinois Servicios LTDA (Brazil); Continental Illinois Finanziaria S.p.A. (Italy); Continental Illinois Leasing S.A. (Spain); First Options of Chicago, Inc.; Continental Futures and Options Corporation; LaSalle Holdings, Ltd. (Canada); CIC Trading, S.A.; Continental International Finance, S.A. (Luxembourg); Societe Anonyme Financiere D'administration et de Gestion (Belgium); First Options of Chicago, Ltd.; Continental Illinois Securities Limited (Hong Kong); Continental Consulting Company, Ltd. (London);Continental Illinois (Asia) Limited (Hong Kong); Securities Settlement Corporation.

Further Reading: Welton, Arthur D. *The Making of a Modern Bank*, Chicago, The Continental and Commercial Banks, 1923; Singer, Mark. *Funny Money*, New York, Alfred Knopf, 1985; McCollom, James P. *The Continental Affair: The Rise and Fall of The Continental Illinois Bank*, New York, Dodd, Mead, 1987.

CRÉDIT AGRICOLE

91–93 Boulevard Pasteur
75015 Paris
France
(1) 43–23–52–02

Cooperative
Incorporated: 1988
Employees: 73,700
Assets: FFr1.02 trillion

France's "green bank" was nicknamed for its roots in agriculture. Crédit Agricole, composed of the Caisse Nationale de Crédit Agricole and 90 regional banks, which together own 90% of the Caisse Nationale, is a unique cooperative organization and one of the most important banking groups in France.

In the mid-1800s, it became clear that there was a need for agricultural credit in France, especially after a crop failure in 1856, which left rural areas in dire straits. One of the main causes of low production was a lack of sufficient credit for farmers, who often could not meet banks' normal credit requirements. In 1861, the government attempted to remedy this problem, asking Crédit Foncier to establish a department expressly for agriculture. But the newly formed Societé de Crédit Agricole accomplished little. By 1866, though some steps towards improvement had been suggested, the outbreak of the Franco-Prussian War prevented their implementation. The society folded in 1876.

Later, several financial cooperatives sprang up independently among farmers, operating in rural towns on a system of mutual credit. In 1885, the first society for agricultural credit was founded at Salins-les-Bains in the Jura; the maximum amount of credit a farmer could get was FFr500, the price of a yoke of oxen. By the end of the century, when talk of modernizing France's agricultural economy became more urgent, it was decided that this system of localized credit was more suitable for the rural population than credit emanating from a big central bank.

In 1894, the Chamber of Deputies proposed a law to organize personal or short-term rural credit, based on the methods of the small credit societies already in existence. The law formalized the requirements for the societies' formation, made them exempt from taxes, and gave them a monopoly on state-subsidized loans to farmers. In 1897, the Bank of France made funds available to the banks through the minister of agriculture, and in 1899, a law was passed to create regional banks to act as intermediaries between the local societies and the minister of agriculture. The local cooperatives were self-governing societies with limited liability. Their members were mostly individual farmers. Each local cooperative was affiliated with a regional bank, where it transferred all deposits and obtained funds for loans. The local banks elected a committee to control the regional banks, which were mainly responsible for medium- and long-term loans. Thus, the hierarchy of Crédit Agricole was established.

One of the reasons Crédit Agricole was so successful was its reliance on individual farmers. In the mid-1800s most of France's agricultural produce came from small farms rather than large estates, and the French government wanted to preserve the small family farm for several social and economic reasons. For instance, it was widely believed that small farmers cultivated the soil most intensively and so made better use of it. It was also thought to be better to have many small family farms than to create a 'proletariat' to work on large farms. Nevertheless, France's agricultural methods were in need of modernization, and Crédit Agricole helped small farmers buy new equipment and supplies to improve production.

In 1910, a law established long-term personal credit for the purchase of land to encourage young men to farm. Only small holdings could acquire these loans, which could not exceed $1,600, and only young farmers were eligible; their characters were the basis for their credit.

When World War I broke out in 1914, the European banking system was under severe duress due to difficulties with the gold exchange. However, gold was still in circulation in France and the Bank of France was able to increase its issue of notes, restoring some financial order. Throughout the war, agricultural production was at a minimum, and Crédit Agricole, still a young institution, was able to survive only through continued support from the government. Agricultural output did not regain its prewar level until 1930.

In 1920, a law was passed to organize the Office National du Crédit Agricole, a national society run by civil servants and the elected representatives of the regional banks but controlled by the government—the minister of agriculture would name its director. Office National du Crédit Agricole also became responsible for the distribution of treasury loan funds and for rediscounting the short-term loans of local and regional societies. In 1926, the name was changed to Caisse Nationale de Crédit Agricole (CNCA).

As Crédit Agricole grew in resources and capacity, it began to help not only individual farmers but also the cooperative trade movement gaining ground among agricultural groups. These new agricultural cooperatives, which organized industries in a way similar to unions, could often not raise the money to organize, and they needed Crédit Agricole's support. In turn, the cooperatives helped France's recovery after the war.

World War II hurt agriculture less than the first war had, and after the war, there was a period of rapid growth, spurred on by Crédit Agricole's loans. Between 1941 and 1945, under the Vichy government, a Bank Control Commission was established and attempts were made to prevent the creation of new banks or branches. After 1945, however, the Bank of France and the other main banks were nationalized. A hierarchy was born, with the Ministry of Finance and the Bank of France at the top, giving the government the ability to sway the distribution of credit. In this sense, it won even more power to help further Crédit Agricole.

After the war, agriculture underwent a massive modernization plan. Crédit Agricole played a major part by supplying capital for fertilizer, equipment, electrification, and improved water supplies. Since agricultural credit was subsidized by the government, and due to the quality of Crédit Agricole's decentralized commercial network, agricultural institutions had the most rapid expansion rate of all the banks. Between 1938 and 1946, the capital funds of the regional societies increased from FFr1.6 billion to FFr28 billion. Crédit Agricole extended its medium- and long-term loan operations and the government established special loans for farm equipment, causing a big increase in the number of farmers driving tractors.

Financing for small farms continued; as late as 1958, cooperatives were favored over large farms. But France's farm productivity was below that of most other European countries, and some blamed the low productivity partially on the credit advantages given to small farms, which kept competition at bay. Earnings did not improve and the industry remained dependent on loans.

About this time, the government began to apply stringent lending ceilings to the whole financial system to restrain the money supply and hold down inflation. This led many banks to diversify into overseas business and the Eurodollar market. A boom in French exports also created a demand for French banking expertise in the export markets. Crédit Agricole, however, held back at first from international expansion, while growing rapidly with the French economy.

In 1966, the state decided to allow Crédit Agricole to widen its operations to become more flexible than a bank strictly for farmers. Under the new reform, Crédit Agricole was allowed to make loans to individuals and organizations not specifically connected with agriculture. It was also allowed to create subsidiaries. One of the most important subsidiaries it created was the Union d'Etudes et d'Investissements, which used its resources to finance individual investments.

In 1967, the government announced that all resources collected by Crédit Agricole's regional and local banks, previously deposited in the French Treasury, would now be deposited with the Caisse Nationale de Crédit Agricole.

In 1971, the Union d'Etudes et d'Investissements, with an eye on important developments in the food processing business, created another subsidiary, L'Union pour le Developpement Régional, which was mainly to provide loans to agricultural and food processing industries or other similar operations in regions where they would create jobs.

In July of the next year, the minister of finance, Giscard d'Estaing, warned Crédit Agricole about its diversification, pointing out that its purpose must stay mainly agricultural and its activities balance financial and social profit, a recurring political theme in Crédit Agricole's development. Other large banks complained about Crédit Agricole's monopoly on farm credit and its tax-free status, which had allowed it to grow into one of the largest banks in France, while those concerned about farm aid worried that the bank's purpose would be diffused. Critics blamed Crédit Agricole's expansion on the other banks' inertia and politicians' reluctance to attack Crédit Agricole for fear of losing the support of farmers. By 1975, Crédit Agricole had begun its international activities, focusing mainly on foreign agricultural loans and export companies.

In 1977, when the U.S. dollar was low, Crédit Agricole ranked briefly as the biggest bank in the world. In 1978, Crédit Agricole's profit of FFr400 million was more than the other three main French banks combined. The bank had begun to finance housing (it is now the leading mortgage lender in France), silo construction, and exports, and had also become a money market lender. After other French banks campaigned for several months against Crédit Agricole's advantages, the government finally curtailed those privileges. Crédit Agricole's surpluses began to be taxed as profits, and for three years, the bank was prohibited from opening new branches in towns where it had no official purpose and competed unfairly with other banks.

The compensation the government offered may have added more to Crédit Agricole's growth than the privileges that were taken away. Before the new rules, the bank could only make direct loans in communities of 7,500 people or fewer, but under the new restrictions that limit was extended to 12,000.

Crédit Agricole continued to push forward with international expansion. In 1979, it opened its first international branch, in Chicago; London soon followed, and a New York City branch opened in 1984. By then, Crédit Agricole was also extremely active in funding development in rural areas for roads, telephones, and airports, and the government was encouraging the bank to help out small industry.

By 1981, Crédit Agricole had several strong subsidiaries: Segespar, which headed the investment-and-deposit service group; Voyage Conseil, a French travel agency; Eurocard France, a payment-card company; Soravie, an insurance company for sales in local branches; Unimat (now Ucabail) and Unicomi, which financed equipment and industrial and commercial building; Unicredit, which provided loans for businesses; and Union d'Etudes et d'Investissements, now heavily involved with rural development.

In January, 1981, Crédit Agricole's charter was changed again to allow the bank to provide loans to companies with fewer than 100 employees, whether or not they were connected with agriculture. The government also eased its credit limits for farmers and stockbreeders, and Crédit Agricole was no longer limited to lending in towns with fewer than 12,000 inhabitants.

However, this wider range was balanced by new limits. Crédit Agricole's tax bill was put in line with those of other corporations, at 50% of its profits. In addition, some of the bank's earlier surplus earnings had to be channeled back into the government's loan subsidies.

In May, 1981, the Socialists won the national election. Soon all major French banks that weren't already nationalized became state controlled, and over the next few years, the government imposed a domestic policy of economic austerity in an attempt to reduce inflation, renew industry, and balance its foreign trade account.

The next year, Crédit Agricole's foreign assets rose by almost 60%. By 1982, only one-third of its funds went to agriculture. Crédit Agricole had already acquired significant experience in the euroloan market, and at the beginning of 1983, it ranked among the most prominent banks in Europe in this area. By 1984, Crédit Agricole had opened foreign branches in North America, Europe, Asia, Latin America, Africa, and the Middle East.

Some Crédit Agricole members were upset by the bank's strengthening international force. In 1984 an official of a farmer's union told *Business Week* that "given the dramatic situation of hundreds of thousands of farmers, Crédit Agricole has better things to do in France." Nonetheless, Crédit Agricole management insisted that international business could only strengthen the company's ability to help farmers in France.

In 1985, Crédit Agricole established a subsidiary called Predica to enter the life insurance market. Capitalizing on Crédit Agricole's extensive branch network, Predica had become the second-largest life insurer in France by 1988.

As the French economy improved, the government began to ease regulations and remove limitations on capital markets. In 1986, a new conservative government came into power, and several Socialist officials were replaced almost immediately, including Jean Paul Huchon, Crédit Agricole's general director. A plan to remove CNCA from state control had been brewing for some time; many other banks were in the process of becoming denationalized. Huchon had opposed this plan for Crédit Agricole vehemently enough to cause his dismissal. His successor was Bernard Auberger, a former director of Societé Générale with ties to the Gaullist Party, which had campaigned to rid CNCA of state control.

The new government also created easier bourse membership rules that allowed outside interests to buy into investment brokers. Following the trend of many banks after this deregulation, in 1988 Crédit Agricole purchased controlling stakes in two Paris stockbrokers, Bertrand Michel and Yves Soulié.

Finally, in 1987, the government began to take steps towards freeing CNCA from state control. On February 1, 1988, the state sold 90% of CNCA's common stock to its regional banks and the company was incorporated with FFr4.5 billion in capital stock. Most of the rest of its stock went to employees, and the government holds a small stake.

Soon after the mutualization, the newly private Crédit Agricole began merging the Caisses Régionales to eliminate redundancies. By January, 1990 the number of district banks had been reduced from 94 to 90 and this number is expected to shrink substantially before the rationalization is over.

The transition to private ownership was not completely smooth, though. A boardroom struggle in 1988 led to the exit of Bernard Auberger. Philippe Jaffré, who was the finance ministry's representative on CNCA's board of directors, was Auberger's surprise replacement.

In 1989 Crédit Agricole ceased to have a monopoly on the shrinking number of subsidized loans to farmers. In losing this monopoly, Crédit Agricole lost an important, captive customer group. The bank should be able to compensate for this loss, however, with the new business it expects to pick up as a result of the lifting of restrictions on its business. When Crédit Agricole lost its monopoly on subsidized farm loans, it was also freed of the unusual government restrictions on its business. Now Crédit Agricole operates in much the same way as any other French bank, and it expects its business to improve rather than suffer as a result of this status.

Under Jaffré, Crédit Agricole, like all European enterprises, faces the challenges that the 1992 unification of the European Economic Community will bring. The bank has already made a successful transition from a purely agricultural bank into a full-service bank. Privatization should give Crédit Agricole the freedom and flexibility it will need to face these challenges, but it will have to struggle with its slightly awkward structure—the 90 regional banks that control parent CNCA diffuse central decision-making power—and tackle operating costs that are much higher than its competitors'. If it can surmount those obstacles and capitalize on its tremendous domestic branch network, Crédit Agricole will be an even more formidable European competitor than it already is.

Principal Subsidiaries: Union d'Études et d'Investissements; Unicredit (98.7%); Sopagri (52.8%); Unimmo France (99.6%); Unidev; Sofipar (52.6%); Ucabail; Segespar; Segespar-Titres (50%); Predica (48%); Unibanque; Sogequip; Cedicam (50%).

CREDIT SUISSE

Paradeplatz 8
CH–8001
Zurich, Switzerland
(01) 333–1111

Public Company
Incorporated: 1856
Employees: 15,055
Assets: SFr113.38 billion
Stock Index: Frankfurt Zurich Tokyo

Credit Suisse began as a commercial bank in 1856, at a time when Switzerland was first embracing the industrial revolution. Today Credit Suisse is one of the Big Three powerhouses of the Swiss banking industry, along with the Union Bank of Switzerland and the Swiss Bank Corporation. In that role alone, the bank ranks among the major players in the world financial arena.

Credit Suisse is further enhanced through its longstanding though often volatile partnership with the American investment bank First Boston, which dates to the mid-1970s and was substantially reorganized in 1988. But despite Credit Suisse's high profile in the investment-banking community, its heart and soul remain its full-service banking activities in Switzerland.

In 1856, Switzerland's federal constitution was only eight years old and there was little industry in the country as the shift from an agricultural to an industrial economy had just begun. Alfred Escher, a young Zurich politician from a prominent local family, was making slow progress in his talks with foreign banks about ways to finance a proposed north-eastern railway, so he decided to set up an independent bank in Zurich, putting SFr3 million worth of shares on public offer. The response was overwhelming: he received SFr218 million in subscriptions within three days, and Credit Suisse opened for business on July 16.

The American Civil War had a great impact on the emerging textile industry in Switzerland, which suffered when cotton prices collapsed after the war ended. CS posted its first and only loss ever in 1867.

The growth of other industries in Switzerland and the continued expansion of the railroads provided ample opportunities for Credit Suisse to grow, however. The bank helped develop the Swiss monetary system and, by the end of the Franco-Prussian War in 1871, Credit Suisse was the largest bank in Switzerland.

The next 40 years, to the beginning of World War I, came to be known as the belle epoque for both the continent and for Credit Suisse. A number of significant changes occurred during this period, including the revision of the federal constitution in 1874 and the resulting political changes that eventually led to proportional representation in local and federal government; an increase in savings, which enabled the country to become an exporter of capital by the mid-1880s and reduce its reliance on foreign capital; and the introduction of electricity, the telephone, and the telegraph, all of which required large infusions of capital for construction of factories, power plants, and phone systems.

The founding of the Swiss National Bank in 1907 and the growth in foreign investment by Swiss banks sowed the seeds for Switzerland's eventual role as the banking capital of the world. Credit Suisse also branched out from Zurich during this period and had 13 different locations in Switzerland by the beginning of World War I.

With the outbreak of World War I, foreign investment stopped completely. As investors in hostile countries returned Swiss securities, Credit Suisse played a crucial role in placing them on the Swiss market. CS also had to defend the interests of Swiss investors abroad, a delicate matter during such a chaotic period.

After World War I, Credit Suisse continued financing the electrification of the country and, in response to a coal shortage, helped finance the national railroad's conversion to electricity in 1924. Foreign investment expanded rapidly during the 1920s, a period that came to a devastating end with the stock market crash in 1929.

The Depression led to cataclysmic changes in Europe, including the rise of nationalist thinking, the imposition of a range of trade barriers like protective tariffs and import quotas, and other developments that resulted in lower production levels, less investment, and economic decline.

Increasing tensions in Europe led to Credit Suisse's emphasis on English-speaking companies, which resulted in the establishment of the Swiss-American Corporation in 1939 to focus on the securities business and the opening of Credit Suisse's first foreign branch in New York in 1940.

During World War II Credit Suisse extended large amounts of credit to Swiss authorities, who were owed more than SFr1.7 billion by Germany by the end of the war. Despite the loss of almost half of the company's employees to war-related service, Credit Suisse emerged from the conflagration financially sound and poised to capitalize on the impending economic upturn.

After the end of World War II, as normal banking activities resumed, reconstruction of the war-torn continent got under way and Credit Suisse again took up issuing paper for foreign debtors. At the same time, Credit Suisse expanded its services to its regular customers by developing new and different types of savings accounts and broadening into activities that were formerly handled by subsidiaries, such as issuing credit cards and providing consumer credit.

During the 1960s the bank also set up a farsighted business arrangement with White Weld, a leading American investment bank in Europe, which would eventually establish Credit Suisse's leading role in the Eurobond-issuing market and would ultimately lead to its relationship with First Boston.

Foreign-exchange dealings assumed greater importance during this time, along with the precious metals markets. With the emergence of a free gold market in 1968, Credit Suisse became a major gold-trading house and, through its acquisition of the precious metals refinery Valcambi S.A., in Ticino, a manufacturer of ingots and coins. By the turn of the decade, Credit Suisse had offices on every continent except Antarctica.

The 1970s brought the introduction of floating exchange rates and the subsequent devaluation of the dollar, a loss of investor confidence in the American market, and the oil crisis of 1973. The bank also experienced a major scandal in 1977 when authorities began investigating a fraudulent banking and foreign exchange trading scheme at the company's Chiasso branch involving more than $1.2 billion. The losses resulted in the resignation of the several top executives and left the current chairman, Rainer Gut, second in line following the retirement of Chairman Otto Aeppli in 1983.

Gut, who is Swiss born but trained in the United States, has brought a measure of stateside savvy and aggressiveness to Credit Suisse. A former partner in New York's Lazard Freres, Gut has shifted the company's focus from traditional Swiss banking practices, which emphasize security and caution, to world investment banking and money management.

By 1986 the bank's assets were $46 billion, and somewhere between $75 and $150 billion more were under active management by the bank—well ahead of the estimated $50 billion under the management of the leading American bank in the field, Citicorp. Under Gut, Credit Suisse was the first Swiss bank to acquire a bank in West Germany, Effectenbank, and it is among only a handful of foreign operations doing trust banking in Japan.

In 1978 Credit Suisse First Boston (CSFB), a joint venture with the New York investment bank First Boston, was formed after White Weld was purchased by Merrill Lynch. The terms under which CSFB was established caused the defection of CSFB Chairman and Chief Executive John Craven, who was replaced by Michael von Clemm.

Although he is consistently pilloried as a bad manager and was eventually replaced as chief executive by Hans Ulrich Doerig from Credit Suisse, von Clemm is widely credited with helping the company achieve its undisputed dominance of the Eurobond market with innovative financing deals. However, he also oversaw one of the greatest financial disasters in the company's history, a $150 million issue bought by the company in 1980. The deal eventually cost CSFB between $20 and $40 million, and the three years during which von Clemm managed the company were its least successful.

Four years later six executives, including three executive directors, left Credit Suisse First Boston. The exodus coincided with the appointment of Jack Hennessey, formerly of First Boston, as chief executive to replace Doerig, who returned to Credit Suisse. A former assistant secretary of the treasury, Hennessey was brought in to reduce the friction and to assume management duties. Von Clemm remained as chairman. The problems were not over, however.

At the beginning of 1984, three CSFB executives defected to Merrill Lynch, taking seven others with them. Published accounts of the brouhaha suggested that the expansion of Deputy Chairman Hans-Joerg Rudloff's power base within the company offended a number of the executives, many of whom were accustomed to operating in a wide-open entrepreneurial environment.

But the company was growing too large, and as senior executives tried to figure out how to manage CSFB, the infighting grew nastier, and Rudloff was considered the consummate corporate infighter.

The final defection came in 1986, when von Clemm resigned quietly after 16 years with the company to devote more time to outside interests. Hennessey took over as chairman and chief executive.

At about the same time, full-service investment-banking companies like Salomon Brothers and Goldman Sachs, as well as Japanese and German concerns, started pushing their way into the Eurobond market. That forced CSFB to diversify into mergers and acquisitions, equity sales, and other specialties, as CSFB's share of the Eurobond market dropped from more than 16% to just over 11%.

Also, CSFB was encountering competition from, of all places, its own two parent companies, Credit Suisse and First Boston. As the need for better cooperation between family members became apparent, CSFB moved one of its New York executives to London to establish better relations. For a while things seemed to be working. One of the first joint ventures among the three companies involved a $4 billion bond floated by General Motors Acceptance Corporation. While First Boston was lead manager, Credit Suisse provided a letter of credit to back the notes and CSFB placed $400 million of the bonds in Europe.

The true survivor of CSFB remains Rudloff, who took the company into Amsterdam with a bank acquisition there in 1986, and then became a director and officer of Credit Suisse itself in early 1987. Rudloff's return to Switzerland was viewed by the staid Swiss banking establishment as a harbinger that the cozy days of gentlemanly Swiss banking had come to a close.

One result of the newly deregulated and ever-fluctuating markets of the 1980s is that the relationship among Switzerland's three major banks, collectively known as "the syndicate," can no longer be so friendly. Once a fairly tightly knit trio, they have recently adopted new guidelines giving each other flexibility to withdraw from deals the others are involved in if they have doubts about the borrower and even to return up to 60% of their allocation of bonds after a deal is done.

Credit Suisse has been characterized in the financial press as a lone wolf rather than a pack hunter sharing the spoils of its deals with other members of the syndicate, conduct that further indicates the end of an era in the Swiss banking industry. And although Switzerland currently has some of the highest commission fees for investment-banking deals anywhere in the world, the breakdown of the syndicate could make the market more competitive and, consequently, the fees lower.

Some of the first signs of the new conditions came when restrictions on gray market trading (trading before the valuation date) were relaxed. Credit Suisse moved aggressively into this area of finance, one it had previously shunned. The other two major Swiss banks sat back and waited and watched. There were also reports in mid-1988 that the syndicate was opening its ranks to smaller, more flexible banking houses in an effort to broaden its market share of new issues, which is up around 70%.

Since that time there have been two other significant developments in Credit Suisse's history. The company has been tainted by charges of laundering drug money from Turkey and Bulgaria. Although the company has denied the charges and, technically, money laundering is not illegal unless the money is used to buy drugs, the stain remains.

Also, Credit Suisse and First Boston restructured their troublesome marriage under a new company, CS First Boston, a move that has been described as a virtual takeover of First Boston by Credit Suisse. The move followed a bad 1988 for CSFB, including an estimated $15 million loss on a debt swap with Italy in 1987.

As one of Switzerland's biggest banks, Credit Suisse has had a strong international orientation since its founding. With its recent aggressive posture in the domestic market and the reformation of its partnership with First Boston, Credit Suisse seems poised to capitalize on the rapid pace of internationalization in the financial industry.

Principal Subsidiaries: Affida Bank; Societe anonyme de participations a des enterprises privees (88.8%); Bank for Commerce and Securities (75%); Bank Hofmann Ltd.; Bank in Luzern; Bank Neumunster (92.3%); City Bank (81.8%); CS Leasing Ltd.; Finanz AG Zurich; Krefina Bank AG; Credit Hypothecaire Suisse pour la Navigation SA; Swiss-Kuwaiti Bank (70%); Credit Suisse Canada; Credit Suisse (Bahamas) Ltd.; Credit Suisse Finance Ltd.; Credit Suisse (Luxembourg) S.A.; Credit Suisse France; Credit Suisse Finance (Panama) SA; Credit Suisse (Guernsey) Ltd.; Credit Suisse Trust & Banking Co., Ltd., (95%); Credit Suisse Buckmaster & Moore Ltd. (United Kingdom) (85%); Schweizeriche Kreditanstalt (Deutschland) AG (80%); Gibraltar Trust Bank Ltd. (95%); Swiss American Securities Inc. (80%); Electrowatt Ltd.; Fides Holding Co.; Premex AG; Savoy Hotel Baur en Ville AG; Societe Internationale de Placements; Credit Suisse Asset Management International Inc.; Valcambi S.A.; Zurich Bonded Warehouse Co., Ltd.; CS Real Estate Leasing Ltd.; CS Auto Leasing Ltd.; Credit Suisse Finance Services; Credit Suisse Finance (Guernsey) Ltd.; Credit Suisse Finance (Gibraltar) Ltd.

Further Reading: 125th Anniversary of Credit Suisse: An Historical Survey, Zurich, Credit Suisse, 1981.

CREDITO ITALIANO

Piazza Cordusio
20123 Milan
Italy
(02) 88621

Public Company
Incorporated: 1870 as Banca di Genova
Employees: 16,636
Assets: L71.75 trillion (US$54.92 billion)
Stock Index: Milan

Credito Italiano is one of Italy's three "banks of national interest." Its principal shareholder is the state holding company, Istituto per la Ricostruzione Industriale (IRI). The bank has over 500 branches within Italy and seven overseas.

Its predecessor, Banca di Genova, was founded in 1870, just after the unification of Italy. By 1872, it had become the first Italian bank to do business in Buenos Aires, Argentina.

At the time Banca di Genova was founded, however, the Italian banking system was inefficient and poorly organized. An agricultural depression in the south, which banks tried to relieve, and an exaggerated amount of building in Rome, which banks helped finance, further aggravated the situation. All of this, plus a worldwide business depression, culminated in the banking crisis of 1893–1894, which caused the failure of several large Italian banks. In the subsequent massive reorganization of banks in 1895, Banca di Genova became Credito Italiano, largely capitalized by German banks.

For its first twenty years, Credito Italiano grew more quickly than other Italian banks. Between 1895 and 1914, its deposits doubled. In 1898, Caisse Commerciale de Bruxelles, Crédit Liégiois, and Comptoir National d'Escompte de Paris acquired equity in Credito Italiano. The bank maintained its relationship with prominent European businessmen through the turn of the century, with representatives of Robert Warschauer and Company, Banque Commerciale-Basle, and National Bank für Deutschland on its board of directors.

In 1907, Credito Italiano increased its capital with the financial support of Banque Française pour le Commerce et l'Industrie and Banque de l'Union Parisienne. Three years later, Credito Italiano helped Société Generale de Belgique to found Banca Brasiliana Italo-Belga.

In 1911, the Italian-Turkish War had a substantial effect on the nation's economy. Government expenditures, financed by an inordinately large issue of five-year treasury bonds, increased inflation. Credito Italiano, however, continued to prosper, and became the first Italian bank to organize an office in London that year. Credito Italiano was also named Correspondent of the Royal Treasury in 1911.

The bank continued to expand, so that by 1914 it had nine main branches, three regular branches, and 52 offices. The close interdependence of European banks at this time heightened some of the conflict leading into World War I. At the war's outbreak, a panic rippled among depositors, and a moratorium was issued in Italy until the banks that issued notes could help other banks meet depositors' demands.

Through its existing international relationship, Credito Italiano helped the war effort by facilitating imports of grain, raw materials, and other necessities in a tense international situation when cash was usually the only payment accepted.

During the war, banks were pushed even more to participate in industry, especially wartime industry. Before the war, the four largest banks, including Credito Italiano, were sharply competitive, but during the war, the increased pressure for credit from both business and government decreased competition among the banks. Finally, in June 1918, the large banks formed a cartel to establish common policies and coordinate the rationing of credit. This group came under much criticism for its close ties to industry leaders.

The ill-planned and rampant growth of wartime industry could not sustain itself in peacetime. After the war, a depression began, and by 1921 businesses had begun to fail in large numbers. Credito Italiano's expansion was less rapid during the war years and the decade following. Its main developments were in merchant banking: setting up new companies, issuing bonds, and increasing capital for businesses. It conducted merchant banking in Egypt, Albania, and Switzerland.

The bank's foreign activity continued. In 1917, a representative office opened in New York, where 700,000 Italian immigrants were potential customers. The bank also increased its interest in Banco Italo-Belga, in Antwerp. In 1919, the bank founded Banca Unione di Credito in Lugano and bought an interest in Banque Génerale des Pays Roumains and in several Austrian and Czechoslovakian banks. A year later, working with the Minister of Financial Affairs and several Chinese backers, Credito Italiano founded Banca Italo-Cinese. It also established Banca Italo-Viennese and Tiroler Hauptbank that year. In 1921, Credito Italiano opened offices in Paris and Berlin.

In 1926, the government announced that all joint-stock banks like Credito Italiano would have to gain the Minister of Finance's consent before amalgamating branches or opening any new ones. But there was still a tight connection between big banks and big business which made some officials nervous.

Credito Italiano continued to extend its reach overseas even after the 1929 stockmarket crash. In 1930, when the bank absorbed Banca Nazionale di Credito, it acquired three foreign affiliates: Banque Italo-Francaise de Crédit, Banca Coloniale di Credito, and Banca Dalmata di Sconto.

Nonetheless, the crash did take its toll. Because of a severe decline in the value of some of its industrial securities, Credito Italiano faced a major cash-flow problem. In the 1930s, many of the companies with which Credito Italiano had done business were going bankrupt and weren't able to pay their debts. Credito Italiano, of course, was by no means the only bank affected.

In 1933, the government stepped in to rescue the banking system by creating IRI, a government holding company to buy the medium and long-term assets of the main commercial banks, including Banco di Roma, Banca Commerciale Italiana, and Credito Italiano. IRI became the banks' main shareholder. IRI was intended at first to be only a temporary organization.

In 1936, the Banking Law was passed. This law, which is still the main legislation governing banks, declared that the three banks under IRI control were "banks of national interest." They were no longer allowed to engage in investment banking, but only in short-term commercial banking.

As Benito Mussolini's lack of economic strategy and policies of expansion during World War II wreaked havoc on the Italian economy, Credito Italiano lost essentially all of its overseas business, and after the war was in need of major restoration.

Between 1945 and 1948, IRI was in such a state of chaos that it could not even be dismembered and privitized, which had been the original postwar plan. The Allied Control commission investigated IRI's businesses for war crimes, but they were cleared of all charges. Although the new government was opposed to many of the controls that had been imposed by the Fascists, it was not feasible to abolish the controls on bank competition.

Soon after the war, Credito Italiano resumed its connections with Banco Italo-Belga and Banco Italo-Egiziano. Its representative office in Zurich remained open, and its London branch was temporarily changed into a representative office. In addition, Credito Italiano's New York and Paris offices were reopened and new offices were opened in Frankfurt, Buenos Aires, and São Paulo. In 1946 Credito Italiano was one of the founders, with Banca Commerciale Italiana and Banco di Roma, of Mediobanca Banca di Credito Finanziario SpA, a medium-term credit bank that today is a powerful merchant bank.

For most of the postwar period, however, energies were spent on the domestic reorganization that came with the growth of exports in the 1950s and 1960s. For the first time in many years, Italy enjoyed sustained, long-term growth. The country's return to world markets helped nourish bank activity, strengthening the existing networks. But this attention to domestic business slowed international expansion.

In 1969, when the United States Federal Reserve Board began a policy of monetary restraint, a huge amount of funds flowed into the United States. This hurt the economies of many European countries, including Italy, as they were forced to adjust to high U.S. interest rates. When domestic growth began to slow in Italy, banks became more active again overseas, although they were somewhat curtailed by the Bank of Italy, Italy's central bank.

The three IRI banks applied to the government in 1969 for permission to increase their capital, which they got. For the first time, the state-owned banks were allowed to offer significant public shares. Until then, the IRI had never held less than 90% of the assets of any of the banks. Credito Italiano and the other two banks were listed on the Italian bourse.

By the 1970s, many domestic clients needed banking services abroad, and Credito Italiano continued to expand by opening a branch in London in 1972, a branch in New York the following year, and a branch in Los Angeles in 1977. It also opened representative offices in Chicago in 1973, Moscow in 1975, Hong Kong in 1978, and Houston, Texas in 1979.

Credito Italiano also acquired much foreign equity interest during the 1970s. In 1973, it acquired stock in Libra Bank Limited of London, and in 1974 it acquired a percentage of Banque Transatlantique in Paris and Orion Bank Limited in Canada.

In 1972, Credito Italiano bought a 50% holding in a British factoring operation in Italy, Credit Factoring International SpA. The low level of domestic investment continued in 1972, coupled with a three-month strike by bank employees and an overall rise in bank costs. Nonetheless, Credito Italiano's profits rose considerably.

The oil crisis that began in 1973 was a severe blow to the Italian economy. It gave rise to high inflation, a growing public deficit, and a skewed balance of payments which jeopardized currency reserves. As a result, in 1976, the lira plummeted against the dollar. To add to Italy's instability, many people feared that the strengthening Communist party might topple the long-standing Christian Democrats in the general election that year. Credito Italiano stayed steady amidst these crises; its profits rose from L7 million in 1974 to L14 billion in 1978.

In the late 1970s, the banks of national interest were put in an awkward position when they were called upon to rescue some of Italy's failing industrial groups, especially those under state control. The banks were concerned that they would have to absorb the companies' losses, and Credito Italiano, in its annual report, made its philosophy on this point clear: "Banking has always meant and always will mean, one simple thing: granting appropriate credit to creditworthy companies."

In 1982, the state-owned companies' losses were even worse and IRI decided to raise money partially by issuing convertible bonds through its three banks and partially by strengthening its relationship with the private sector. Banks were then allowed to raise up to 41% of their capital, so long as IRI retained the majority.

The Italian economy was much stronger by the early 1980s, and the Bank of Italy was gradually able to relax some constraints on the banking industry, allowing more domestic competition and loosening exchange controls. The ceilings on bank lending were removed in 1983 and the Bank of Italy began to liberalize the opening of new bank branches. For example, Credito Italiano was finally granted permission to open a branch in Carpi, a small industrial town near Bologna it had been waiting 20 years to enter.

During the 1980s, Credito Italiano expanded even more in foreign territories, opening branches in the Cayman Islands in 1981, Tokyo in 1982, and Madrid in 1988 and representative offices in Amsterdam and Cairo in 1980 and Beijing in 1987. In 1984, Credito Italiano organized a wholly-owned subsidiary in London, Credito Italiano International Limited, a merchant bank. Also that year, the bank planned to increase its capital from L320 billion to L500 billion through scrip and rights issues.

Between 1984 and 1987, the decline of the U.S. dollar and the collapse of oil prices helped boost the Italian economy. In 1987, the Bank of Italy re-imposed credit ceilings between October and March in an effort to control the money supply, which had grown too fast as the economy surged. That year the securities department at Credito Italiano doubled, from 300 to 600 people as the stock exchange rose to record heights on the dramatic profits companies were making. This expansion sparked a heated debate about how to reform the stock exchange and what role banks should play in the market as Italy faces the challenges of the coming single European market. Nevertheless, the October, 1987 stock market crash was reflected at Credito Italiano in a 33% drop in profits that year.

In 1989, Credito Italiano bought a 4% share in Banca Nazionale dell'Agricoltura (BNA), Italy's largest private bank, and a 20% share in Bonifiche Siele, a holding company that was BNA's largest shareholder. The L227 billion deal was an important move toward rationalizing Italian banking. Credito Italiano and BNA had complementary branches; combined they would form the most important bank in Italy.

In June, 1989, Credito Italiano, in an unusual move for a large Italian firm, closed a distribution deal with a foreign composite insurer, Commercial Union of Britain. This move reflected the trend in Europe for banks and insurers to join together in an effort to broaden the range of bank services. At the end of 1989, Credito Italiano acquired a 35% stake in the Bank CIC-Union Européenne A.G., headquartered in Frankfurt, and in early 1990 the bank acquired a 5% stake in the Banque Commerciale du Maroc.

Credito Italiano prides itself on its high asset quality and its strong capitalization. With its recent acquisitions, which have strengthened it both domestically and internationally, Credito Italiano has begun to take the necessary steps to preserve its place in the coming global financial market.

Principal Subsidiaries: Credit Holding Italia S.p.A.; Credit Factoring International S.p.A. Società per il Factoring Internazionale; Credit Leasing Società per il Leasing Finanziario S.p.A.; Fincor Merchant Credit S.p.A.; Credito Italiano Delaware Incorporated (United States); Credito Italiano Finance Corporation Limited (Nassau); Credito Italiano International Limited (London); Banca Creditwest e dei Comuni Vesuviani S.p.A. (68%); Gesticredit S.p.A. (70%); Credito Italiano Nominees Limited (London); Cordusio Società Fiduciaria Per Azioni (47%); Mediofin S.p.A. (90%).

THE DAI-ICHI KANGYO BANK, LIMITED

THE DAI-ICHI KANGYO BANK LTD.

1–5, Uchi-Saiwaicho 1-chome
Chiyoda-ku
Tokyo 100
(03) 596–1111

Public Company
Incorporated: 1971
Employees: 18,411
Assets: ¥54.28 trillion (US$434.31 billion)
Stock Index: Tokyo Osaka Amsterdam London Paris Zurich Geneva Basel

The Dai-Ichi Kangyo Bank, or DKB, is the largest commercial bank in the world. A traditionally conservative bank deeply rooted in the domestic economy, DKB was largely unprepared for its rapid rise to leadership in international banking during the 1970s.

DKB is the product of a relatively recent merger between two established hundred-year-old banks. The Nippon Kangyo Bank was established in 1867 as a "special bank," which raised capital by issuing debentures. The Dai-Ichi Kokuritsu Ginko, or First National Bank, was founded in 1873 by the industrialist Eiichi Shibusawa. In addition to its regular business, Dai-Ichi issued currency on behalf of the government treasury as a central bank. It was removed from this role when its national banking charter expired in 1896. Dai-Ichi, re-incorporated as an ordinary commercial bank, was headed by Shibusawa until his retirement in 1916. Nippon Kangyo, meanwhile, was incorporated in 1896 to issue long-term and low-interest government bonds for agriculture and industry.

The two banks developed in different directions, particularly during the period between 1910 and 1930, as Japanese industry matured on a large scale. Nippon Kangyo was evenly represented throughout Kanto prefecture and remained closely associated with rural industries. It continued to broaden the scope of its business, adding real estate financing in 1911. Dai-Ichi's business, on the other hand, was concentrated in Tokyo, the industrial center of the prefecture and capital of Japan.

At this time, virtually all these banks had in common was their location and competition against the larger *zaibatsu* banks, namely, Mitsubishi, Mitsui, Sumitomo, and Yasuda. Not really banks as much as outgrowths of enormous industrial combines, the *zaibatsu* banks permeated virtually every sector of Japanese industry and society, providing both high finance and individual banking services. The *zaibatsu* collectively squeezed smaller banks such as Nippon Kangyo and Dai-Ichi out of many high-growth industrial ventures simply by financing themselves.

As the industrial backbone of Japan, the *zaibatsu* naturally wielded great political influence in Japan—influence which perpetuated their strength. During the 1930s, however, a militant right-wing officers corps gained power over the Japanese government. The militarists had hoped to deconcentrate industrial power, but their imperialist adventurism in Asia required the opposite action. In the end, the government encouraged small and medium-sized enterprises to amalgamate into larger companies.

Despite a rash of consolidations, Nippon Kangyo maintained its independence throughout the war, although it was ordered by the government to issue war bonds in 1937. Dai-Ichi, however, was merged with the Mitsui Bank in 1943 and renamed Teikoku Bank.

When World War II ended in 1945, the occupation authority purged Japanese industry of war criminals and enacted laws to divide the *zaibatsu* and other large companies into smaller entities. These laws separated the Dai-Ichi Bank from Teikoku in 1948.

Nippon Kangyo's role in the postwar economy, meanwhile, had yet to be decided upon. It was awarded an exclusive license in 1945 to handle the national lottery for local public agencies. Five years later, the bank gave up its special status and became a general deposit bank. In 1952, following passage of the Long-Term Trust Bank Law, Nippon Kangyo abandoned its original business of issuing bonds.

Both banks provided funding for (in essence, invested in) a number of Japanese industries in their infancy. As the basic groundwork was laid for a modern, export-led economy, Japanese banks in general began to experience a strong and relatively steady expansion. Nippon Kangyo and Dai-Ichi each developed an impressive list of clients who wished to remain independent of the *zaibatsu* groups. Nippon Kangyo's customers included Nippon Express, Shiseido cosmetics, and Seibu Department Stores. Dai-Ichi's list included the more vigorous Hitachi, Kawasaki Heavy Industries, and C. Itoh.

The first indication of reform in the postwar Japanese banking regime came in the late 1960s, when American banks, distinguished by huge capitalizations, moved into Japan and gradually gained control of an ever increasing share of the Japanese lending market. Unwilling to enact protectionist banking legislation, the government's Ministry of Finance advocated consolidations in the belief that larger banks would redistribute their branches and more efficiently tap new sources of capital.

The first consolidation proposal, forwarded in 1969, would have merged Dai-Ichi with the larger Mitsubishi Bank. This proposal failed, in part because Dai-Ichi's "lesser *zaibatsu*" clients, the Furukawa and Kawasaki industrial groups, feared subjugation by their competitors in the Mitsubishi group. Another source of anxiety for Dai-Ichi board members was that because of the uneven size of the two banks, the merger appeared to be a Mitsubishi takeover.

Wishing to preserve the bank's organizational independence and pursue a true merger, Dai-Ichi began to investigate the feasibility of a merger with the Nippon Kangyo Bank during 1970.

Dai-Ichi, Japan's sixth largest city bank at the time, appeared in every respect to be perfectly matched with Nippon Kangyo, then ranked eighth. The greatest benefit the banks would gain from a merger was a more efficient geographical redistribution of branch networks. Dai-Ichi was a metropolitan bank whose business was centered in Tokyo and Osaka. Nippon Kangyo, on the other hand, maintained a nation-wide branch network with offices in every one of Japan's 46 prefectures.

Still, of almost 300 branches, about 50 were in the same location. In order to achieve better geographical coverage, redundant offices belonging to Dai-Ichi were relocated to more promising sites in suburban areas. Another problem with the merger was that Nippon Kangyo's computer system was IBM-based, while Dai-Ichi used Fujitsu equipment. This problem, while not unresolvable, took years to overcome.

The merger was completed in October of 1971. The new bank, called Dai-Ichi Kangyo, immediately became Japan's largest city bank. In order to start with a new, more positive public image, DKB adopted a red heart on a white background as its logo. The gargantuan "bank with a heart" redoubled efforts to gain more business in the individual banking sector by offering new financial products. Among these were the *oyako*, a 50-year parent-child mortgage, created as a way to deal with skyrocketing land values. The new sales effort also gave rise to an army of bicycle-riding door-to-door salesmen, whose mission it was to canvass every home in Japan in search of business.

Troubles with the bank's amalgamation were obscured somewhat by the oil crisis of 1973–1974. But soon afterwards, it was apparent that the merger was not progressing as smoothly as had been anticipated. Dai-Ichi, traditionally government-oriented in its business, was a conservative institution, while the agriculture-oriented Nippon Kangyo adhered to a more progressive philosophy. A dual administrative structure was created that maintained strict parity between "D" men and "K" men in the boardroom and at every level of management. Even in personnel affairs, three centers were created: one for Dai-Ichi people, one for Kangyo people, and one for new recruits.

When Saseba Heavy Industries, a shipbuilder and former Nippon Kangyo client, fell on hard times, the "D" men advocated writing off the account. "K" men appealed for time to set up a government rescue plan. Saseba was saved, but the impatience of the "D" men was clearly not appreciated by the "K" men.

Since the merger, however DKB had experienced very strong growth. It was powerful in both commercial and individual banking, and conducted a number of rather off-beat financial services, including the national lottery. But more importantly, Dai-Ichi Kangyo became the head of a fifth *keiretsu* (the name given to *zaibatsu* groups after the war, which means "banking conglomerate"). Like Mitsui, Mitsubishi, Sumitomo, and Fuyo, the *Sankin Kai*, or Dai-Ichi Kangyo group, had interests in every high-growth sector of Japanese industry. Its clients list included Kawasaki Steel, Kawasaki Heavy Industries, the "KKK" shipping line, Fujitsu, Nippon Kangyo Kakumara Securities, Shiseido, Kobe Steel, Ishikawajima-Harima Heavy Industries, Hitachi, and Isuzu Motors.

Shuzo Muramoto was named president of Dai-Ichi Kangyo in 1976. A career Dai-Ichi man, Muramoto was promoted, in part, to maintain the bank's balance between "D" men and "K" men. He was in many ways a symbol of the bank's first achievement in consensus management. Muramoto was a highly respected advisor to the government on such matters as industrial strategy, the economy, and trade issues. He tempered factional rivalry in the boardroom and focused the bank's attention on setting and attaining goals.

DKB also adhered more closely to the progressive philosophy of Kangyo under Muramoto. DKB's competitors avoided setting up offices in Taiwan in an effort to win favor with the mainland Chinese. DKB, however, actively expanded its presence on the island in the belief that dual contacts would become a great asset as Chinese reunification efforts developed. The bank also began a controversial effort to assist new foreign competitors in Japanese markets. Far from accelerating the loss of domestic business to foreign firms, this policy actually created greater harmony.

After 20 years of export-led growth, Japan's largest banks were very wealthy. The fear that these banks would exhaust Japan's supply of investment opportunities and that competition for what remained would become increasingly acute precipitated a general rationalization and restructuring effort in Japanese banking.

Strict finance laws prevented Dai-Ichi Kangyo and other banks from diversifying into many new areas. Clearly, the best prospects for new growth were overseas. While many of DKB's competitors simply purchased foreign banks, DKB preferred to start its overseas operations from scratch, believing that existing operations often came with unwanted obligations. The one major exception to that rule came in 1980, when DKB purchased the Japan-California Bank (renamed Dai-Ichi Kangyo Bank of California).

Nobuya Hagura, who became president of DKB in 1982, pressed hard for the repeal of Japan's restrictive finance laws—particularly Article 65 of the Securities Exchange Law. This law, comparable to the American Glass-Steagall Act, prevents banks from engaging in the securities business. Hagura and other bankers insisted that this law was obsolete. In the mean time, many banks simply purchased foreign dealers. After waiting some time, Dai-Ichi Kangyo finally entered the New York market in 1986, when it started its own company, the Dai-Ichi Kangyo Trust Company, by purchasing $215 million in business loans from the U.S. Trust Company of New York.

Ten years after the merger, the bank was still dealing with its after effects. Its dynamism was constrained by commitments to clients in the troubled steel and shipbuilding sectors, as well as by overstaffing; Sumitomo, a smaller but more profitable competitor, maintained several thousand fewer employees. In an effort to diversify, to eliminate underperforming accounts, and to reduce employee rolls, the bank initiated two major reorganizations in five years.

Most of the bank's goals were met, but the most important change to take place involved the introduction of electronic information services on capital markets. With a 10% market share in dealing government bonds, the DKB was gearing up for entry into investment banking.

At this time the United States government dramatically increased its borrowing. This led to a sharp decrease in the value of the dollar. As a result, DKB, with the bulk of its assets in yen, surpassed Citicorp to become the largest bank in the world in 1986. Much of the bank's growth, however, must be attributed to lower interest rates, which increased income from spread lending. By 1987, many of the bank's investments in foreign operations were beginning to pay off. Most notable were the New York securities subsidiary, a DKB-controlled bank in Hong Kong, and an investment consultancy in London. Still, the company's greatest assets remain its branch network and prime corporate accounts.

For Dai-Ichi Kangyo, growth begets further growth. It is now one of Japan's most important companies and, with its strong entry into international markets, has become a primary clearing house for large-scale corporate finance.

Despite renewed efforts to dissolve a compartmental mentality, the Dai-Ichi Kangyo Bank suffers from this dualality. Without a powerful figurehead, the DKB remains a largely faceless institution, in strong contrast with its intended character as a "people's bank." But however it is viewed by the public, the Dai-Ichi Kangyo Bank is not only the world's largest bank, but one of its most important institutions.

*Principal Subsidiaries:*Dai-Ichi Kangyo Trust Company of New York (U.S.A.); Dai-Ichi Kangyo Bank of California (U.S.A.); Dai-Ichi Kangyo Bank (Canada); Dai-Ichi Kangyo Bank Nederland N.V. (Netherlands); Dai-Ichi Kangyo Bank (Schweiz) A.F. (Switzerland); Dai-Ichi Kangyo Bank (Luxembourg) S.A.; DKB International Ltd. (England); DKB Investment Management International Limited (England); DKB Asia Limited (Hong Kong); Chekiang First Bank Ltd. (Hong Kong); DKB Futures (Singapore) Pte. Ltd.; Dai-Ichi Kangyo Australia Ltd.; DKB Credit Corporation (United States); DKB Securities Corporation (United States); Dai-Ichi Kangyo Bank (Deutschland) AG.

THE DAIWA BANK, LTD.

1–8 Bingo-machi 2-chome
Chuo-ku
Osaka 541
Japan
(06) 271–1221

Public Company
Incorporated: 1918 as Osaka Nomura Bank
Employees: 8,688
Assets: ¥16.54 trillion (US$132.34 billion)
Stock Index: Osaka Tokyo

The Daiwa Bank is unique among Japanese financial institutions in that it is licensed to conduct both trust and regular banking operations. Daiwa is therefore able to offer a wider range of in-house services and to emphasize a greater number of diverse and more profitable operations as market conditions change. In an environment such as Japan, where a bank's fortunes are normally tied to a narrow range of financial products, Daiwa clearly enjoys greater mobility and flexibility.

The Daiwa Bank was founded in Osaka, Japan's first major industrial and commercial center, by Tokushichi Nomura, a shrewd entrepreneur and talented venture capitalist. Daiwa came into existence in 1918 as the Osaka Nomura Bank. It was created largely to take advantage of the new capital Japan had amassed from foreign commercial ventures and domestic industrialization. In many cases, the Osaka Nomura Bank arranged financing that enabled small but promising companies to expand and prosper under often-difficult economic conditions.

One of the bank's operations, the securities division, experienced such growth both in volume and in profits that it was run almost as a separate entity. Finally, in 1926, the division was spun off to create Nomura Securities, today Japan's leading securities company. The following year "Osaka" was dropped from the bank's name to give it a closer identification with Nomura Securities and to dispel the impression that its business was limited to Osaka.

Daiwa has always maintained a close relationship with Nomura Securities, which is still the bank's only underwriter. (Daiwa Securities, a competitor of Nomura, is in no way related to the Daiwa Bank.) Nomura is a major shareholder of the Daiwa Bank, and, though Daiwa divested itself of its interests in Nomura, the two companies maintain many parallel interests through an informal arrangement.

But while the Nomura Bank had developed interests all across Japan, in 1929 it was appointed the sole banking agent of the Osaka prefectural government. It continued, therefore, to be associated with the Osaka establishment, leading it to be viewed with some suspicion in the more dynamic rival commercial center of Tokyo.

Japanese industry grew spectacularly during the 1930s as Japan began to mature as an industrial power. But one of the most important factors in Japan's industrialization was the rise to power of militarists who favored the creation of larger, centrally directed firms. During World War II these militarists permitted, or directed, the Nomura Bank to absorb the operations of its affiliate, the Nomura Trust Company, in 1944. It was as a result of this somewhat awkward centralization scheme, coming at a time when the war was placing increasing hardships on the Japanese economy, that the bank began to operate both trust and regular banking services.

After the war, the Allied occupation forces enacted a variety of laws aimed at decentralizing Japanese industry. Many companies were divided into smaller ones, and many were forbidden to use their prewar names. Unlike some competitors, the Nomura Bank was not split up. It was also permitted to continue both trust and regular banking services, though it was forced to change its name. In 1948 it became Daiwa Bank (*Daiwa* means "great harmony" in Japanese).

In addition to expanding its domestic network, Daiwa established a foreign department in 1948, and the following year was authorized as a foreign-exchange bank. It took Daiwa several years to open overseas offices. Unlike its competitors Mitsubishi and Sanwa, which had merely to reopen their American and European offices, Daiwa entered these markets with Japanese clients who were attempting to expand overseas. Daiwa opened representative offices in New York in 1956 and in London in 1958.

The bank gained a stronger presence in the Tokyo market in 1954 when it took over seven offices there that had been operated by the Bank of Tokyo. It was an important acquisition for Daiwa, as Tokyo had become the center of Japanese commerce.

Daiwa began pension-trust banking in 1962. It was the first Japanese bank to manage pensions, a business that later proved both stable and profitable. Daiwa was also the only bank allowed to maintain branch offices inside the Diet—the Japanese parliament. The bank established a second office there in 1962, creating one for the Upper House and one for the Lower House. This presence gave Daiwa an intimate knowledge of government activities and a more privileged role in government finance.

Japan experienced a powerful export-led economic expansion during the late 1950s and the 1960s. Daiwa experienced similarly rapid growth as a banker and financial agent for Japanese exporters. But it was from the pension market that Daiwa experienced the bulk of its growth. The Japanese, without a social security program, had a great propensity to save, and their employers generally maintained conservative pension and insurance practices.

During the following decade, the bank opened more overseas offices, in Los Angeles in 1970, Frankfurt in 1971, Hong Kong in 1976, and Singapore in 1979. Although shaken by the Arab oil embargo in 1973 and 1974 and the Iranian Revolution in 1979, Daiwa avoided serious reverses. Some losses were incurred and, predictably, growth slowed. But by 1980 the bank's pension trust surpassed ¥1 trillion and only four years later, the fund exceeded ¥2 trillion.

Beginning in 1952 the gradual deregulation of Japanese financial institutions caused occasional shocks in the banking community. One trend, however, that became especially acute in the 1980s was the narrowing spread between lending and deposits—as a result of increased competition. The Japanese banking community in general began to promote fee-based services. Daiwa took the matter a step further, attempting to cover all the bank's expenses with revenues from fee income alone. In the event that spread-based operations became unprofitable, the bank could more easily maintain growth.

Daiwa established a new trust headquarters in 1985 to reinforce its position in trust banking, promote fee income, and demonstrate its ability to accommodate the increasingly diverse needs of Japanese society. As an example, Daiwa became involved in land trusts, a type of real estate–asset management. The bank's most important land trust is the Chuokan project, operated on behalf of the Osaka prefectural government.

The man most responsible for Daiwa's successful exploitation of fee-based services was Sumio Abekawa, who was named president in 1984. He replaced Ichiro Ikeda who, despite tremendous personal sacrifice, had been unable to shake Daiwa out of a period of stagnation. Daiwa resumed a higher rate of growth during the mid-1980s, and began to prepare for the ensuing decades as a more aggressive and confident institution.

Principal Subsidiaries: Daiwa Bank, Canada; Daiwa Bank Trust Company (U.S.A.); Daiwa Bank (Capital Management) Ltd. (U.K.); Daiwa Overseas Finance Ltd. (Hong Kong); Daiwa Fiananz AG (Switzerland); Daiwa BK Financial Futures Singapore Pte. Ltd.; Daiwa Finance Australia Ltd.

DEUTSCHE BANK A.G.

Taunusanlage 12
P.O. Box 1000601
D-6000 Frankfurt am Main
Federal Republic of Germany
(0211) 71500

Public Company
Incorporated: 1870
Employees: 54,769
Assets: DM305.3 billion (US$172.15 billion)
Stock Index: Berlin Bremen Düsseldorf Frankfurt Hamburg Hanover Munich Stuttgart Vienna Antwerp Brussels Paris Luxembourg Amsterdam Basel Geneva Zurich London Tokyo NASDAQ

Deutsche Bank has weathered two world wars and three depressions to become one of the world's leading financial institutions. Many German citizens regard the bank as the champion of individual and small business interests—and one of the safest places in Europe to store money.

Deutsche Bank was founded in Berlin on March 10, 1870 with the approval of the king of Prussia. The company opened its doors for business a month later under the directorship of Georg von Siemens, with five million thalers in capital.

The company's creation coincided with the unification of Germany. After Germany's victory in the Franco-German War, France was required to pay an indemnity of FFr 5 billion, which greatly stimulated German industry, trade, and consumption. Deutsche Bank naturally assumed a position of leadership in the country's expanding economy. The founding of the Second German Reich in 1871 led to another important development: the thaler was replaced by the mark, a new currency based on gold.

Within two years, the bank had established domestic branches in Bremen and Hamburg and expanded into eastern Asia with offices in Shanghai and Yokohama. In 1872 it opened a London branch, and capital stood at 15 million thalers.

Many joint-stock banks, including Deutsche Bank, had been created in the wake of the liberalization of requirements for starting new companies, but many failed within a few years. During the financial crisis of 1873–1875 it appeared that the entire economic system was on the verge of collapse; small shareholders as well as wealthy businessmen were ruined, and in Berlin alone nearly 50 banks filed for bankruptcy.

But Deutsche Bank, due to its concentration on foreign operations, was largely unscathed by the financial panic. With its assets intact, the young bank began to make significant acquisitions, including Deutsche Union-Bank and the Berliner Bankverein. These purchases transformed Deutsche Bank into one of Germany's largest and most-prestigious banks.

In 1877 Deutsche Bank joined a syndicate of leading private banks popularly known as the "Prussian consortium." The bank was also employed by the government for the issue of state loans, and it grew rapidly in both influence and assets. By 1899 it was able to offer to float, without help from other financial institutions, a 125 million mark loan for Prussia and, at the same time, a 75 million mark loan for the German Reich.

Throughout the 1880s and 1890s, Deutsche Bank was a leader in electrical development. It helped to form finance and holding companies and issued bonded loans and shares for the construction of dynamos, power plants, electric railways, tramways, and municipal lighting systems. By 1897, there were 750 power plants located across Germany. The bank also invested in the Edison General Electric Company in the United States and began to build a power plant in Argentina.

During the same period, the bank was also a driving force behind railway development. In 1888, Deutsche Bank obtained a concession to build an east-west railway to open up Asiatic Turkey. A decade later, 642 miles of the Anatolian railway were in operation in Turkey, from Constantinople through Eskisehir to Ankara, and from Eskisehir to Konya. At the same time, in the United States the bank participated in the financial reorganization of Northern Pacific Railroad. All of this, of course, was done in addition to contributing significantly to the development of Germany's own extensive network of surface and underground railways.

The continuity of bank operations was uninterrupted when von Siemens died in October, 1901. At Deutsche Bank, like most other German banks, all decisions are made by the board of directors, and the board customarily takes credit for the company's successes. The firm has no official chairman, but selects one board member to act as "spokesman." Thus the absence of von Siemens had little effect on the bank, since management by consensus is the bank's guiding principle.

By the early years of the 20th century, the company had acquired the Bergische-Markische Bank, the Schlesischer Bankverein, and interests in the Hannoversche Bank, the Oberrheinische Bank, and the Rheinische Creditbank, and in Italy, participation in the founding of Banca Commerciale Italiana. The bank's capital was now more than six times the amount it was founded with.

The bank then entered a period of consolidation and growth: it built up its sub-branches; improved and extended customer services; paid particular attention to the deposit business; and promoted checks for personal use. In association with numerous regional banks, Deutsche Bank also became involved in a wide range of business activities, including transportation, coal, steel, and oil, as well as railways and electrification. Shortly before World War I, with 200 million marks in capital backed by a 112.5 million mark reserve and deposits and borrowed funds of 1.58 billion marks, the *Frankfurter Zeitung* called it the world's leading bank.

Deutsche Bank weathered the many economic problems during World War I; at the end of the conflict, the bank had offices at 182 locations throughout Germany, and a staff of nearly 14,000. However, with the war lost, the German empire gone, and the transition from monarchy to democracy threatened by revolution, Allied demands for reparations totalling 132 billion gold marks pushed the German banking system to the brink of ruin. By 1923, one gold mark was worth 1 trillion paper marks.

In 1929, as financial chaos loomed, Deutsche Bank merged with its 20-year rival, the Disconto-Gesellschaft. At the time of their merger the banks were the two largest in Germany; combined, their capital, reserves, and deposits were each at least twice as large as that of any competitor. The merger, designed to cut administrative costs by closing competing operations, was very successful, and the resulting bank had enough capital and reserves to withstand the economic crisis. Before the collapse, Deutsche Bank and Disconto-Gesellschaft had handled about 50% of all business conducted by Berlin banks. By 1931, the bank was relying heavily on its undisclosed reserves and had twice reduced capital, but it remained solvent and required no government aid.

Under orders from the National Socialist government that came to power in 1933, unemployed workers were put to work under a "re-employment" plan. At first, the government only concentrated on projects that were meant to counteract the high unemployment rate; the autobahns were the chief showpiece of this strategy. But by 1936, a significant percentage of industrial production had been switched to the manufacture of weapons and munitions and "re-employment" had become "re-armament." Deutsche Bank supported the program through the purchase of government securities.

During World War II, the government financed its budget deficit by printing new money, a misguided practice that quickly led to spiraling inflation. The problem was artificially suppressed by questionable banking measures; more treasury paper began to appear among the bank's assets. Deutsche Bank's enormous losses were made known only when Germany surrendered to the Allies in April, 1945.

After the war, Allied occupation authorities investigating possible war crimes committed by German banks found that Deutsche Bank and its rival Dresdner Bank bore substantial responsibility for the war through their lending to the Nazi government, their purchase of government securities, and the influence that they exerted over large industrial concerns through their shareholdings and corporate directorships. Both banks also had close ties to SS chief Heinrich Himmler and other Nazi officials, had exploited conquered nations through seizing the assets of their financial institutions, and had helped disenfranchise Jews in Germany. Four directors (including one Nazi Party member) and two executives of Deutsche Bank were arrested by the Allied authorities, but were never tried.

After lengthy negotiations with the occupying forces, Deutsche Bank's ten regional institutions were formed into three banks: Norddeutsche Bank A.G., Rheinisch-Westfalische Bank A.G., and Suddeutsche Bank A.G. served the northern, central, and southern areas of West Germany respectively. In 1957, these three banks were again reorganized, this time to form a single Deutsche Bank A.G. with corporate headquarters in Frankfurt. At the time of its reunification, the bank employed over 16,000 people and its assets totaled DM8.4 billion. Hermann J. Abs, the strategist behind the reorganization of the bank and one of the key figures in West Germany's financial recovery, became its spokesman.

In the 1960s, Deutsche Bank concentrated on improving services for its smaller depositors. The bank launched programs for personal loans of up to DM2,000 and medium-sized loans up to DM6,000 for specific purchases, as well as an overdraft facility of up to DM1,000 for consumers. Other services included personal mortgage loans, improvements in savings facilities, and the establishment of a eurocheque system. By the end of the decade, the bank had become the largest provider of consumer credit in West Germany.

Under the direction of Abs, Deutsche Bank began to re-establish its international operations (it had lost all of its worldwide holdings after the war). It first reopened offices in Buenos Aires, Sao Paulo, and Rosario, Argentina, and then in Tokyo, Istanbul, Cairo, Beirut, and Teheran. In 1968, Deutsche Bank joined the Netherlands' Amsterdam-Rotterdam Bank, Britain's Midland Bank, and Belgium's Societe Generale de Banque in founding the European-American Bank & Trust Company in New York, and in 1972 Deutsche Bank founded Eurasbank (European Asian Bank) with members of the same consortium.

When Hermann Abs retired in 1967, his place as spokesman was taken by Karl Klusen and Franz Heinrich Ulrich, who became co-spokesmen. Abs had wielded such a great concentration of economic and financial power that a special law limiting such influence was named after him—"Lex Abs" reduced the number of supervisory-board seats a single person could hold simultaneously in West Germany.

During the 1970s Deutsche Bank became the dominant financial institution in West Germany. Under the guidelines of the "universal banking" system in place in Germany for more than a century, commercial banks are allowed to hold unlimited interests in industrial companies, underwrite and trade securities on their own, and play the foreign currency markets, in addition to providing credit and accepting deposits. Deutsche Bank took advantage of this rule during the 1960s and 1970s by investing in a wide range of industrial companies. In 1979, the bank held seats on the supervisory boards of about 140 companies, among them Daimler-Benz, Volkswagen, Siemens, AEG, Thyssen, Bayer, Nixdorf, Allianz, and Philipp Holzmann.

But the bank's extraordinary influence in West Germany aroused concern about the extent of the bank's instruments in other companies. As a result of these concerns,

Deutsche Bank began to reduce its industrial holdings in the 1970s. This trend, however, was briefly interrupted in 1975 when the possible takeover of key German industries by Middle Eastern concerns flush with petrodollars supplanted the big banks as a source of public worry. At the request of Chancellor Helmut Schmidt, Deutsche Bank purchased a 29% interest in Daimler-Benz from industrialist Friederich Flick to insure that it would stay in German hands, with the understanding that the bank would resell the shares once the crisis had passed. Deutsche Bank already owned 25% of the famed automaker. In December of that year, it resold the shares to a consortium that included Commerzbank, Dresdner Bank, and Bayerische Landesbank.

During the 1980s, Deutsche Bank made major expansions in its foreign operations, both in commercial banking and investment banking. It opened its first U.S. branch office in New York in 1979, and by 1987 had bought out all its partners in the Eurasbank consortium and renamed it Deutsche Bank (Asia), providing 14 more branches in 12 Asian countries. At nearly the same time, the company's capital-markets branch began operating and trading in Japanese, British, and American securities. By the end of 1988, the bank had approximately 7.2 million customers at 1,530 offices, more than 200 of them outside of West Germany.

In 1980–1981 Deutsche Bank was the only one of the West German Big Three banks to turn a healthy profit. Unlike Commerzbank and Dresdner Bank, the other two of the Big Three, Deutsche Bank did not overexpand, but remained cautious in the face of high interest rates and continued recession. In 1984 it acquired a 4.9% stake in Morgan Grenfell, the British securities firm; in 1985 it bought scandal-plagued industrial giant Flick Industrieverwaltung from Friederich Flick, with the intention of taking it public; in 1986 it acquired Banca d'America e d'Italia from the Bank of America; and in 1988 it acquired a 2.5% interest in the automaker Fiat. Another sign of Deutsche Bank's aggressive pursuit of foreign markets is the fact that in the wake of the stock market crash in October, 1987, at a time when massive layoffs were taking place in the securities industry, its American securities affiliate, Deutsche Bank Capital Corporation, expanded its workforce. In 1988 Deutsche Bank entered the treasury securities market at a time when many foreign firms were leaving.

At home, Deutsche Bank took a large and controversial step toward becoming a one-stop financial service center in 1989 when it created it own insurance subsidiary to complement its commercial and investment-banking businesses. Immediately, it was considered a strong rival for the Allianz group, the West German–based company that is Europe's largest insurer.

Wilhelm Christians and Alfred Herrhausen became Deutsche Bank's new co-spokesmen in 1985. When Christians retired in early 1988, Herrhausen was appointed sole spokesman for the bank. Following Herrhausen's assassination on November 30, 1989, Hilmar Kopper became sole spokesman. Kopper is sure to continue the strategy that Deutsche Bank has pursued both at home and abroad during the late 1980s—an expansionist strategy designed to solidify its position at the top of West Germany's banking industry and take it to the top of the world as well.

Principal Subsidiaries: Banca d'America e d'Italia S.p.A.; Deutsche Bank Luxembourg S.A.; Europäische Hypothekenbank der Deutschen Bank (Luxembourg); H. Albert de Bary & Co. N.V. (the Netherlands); MDM Sociedade de Investimento S.A. (Portugal); Banco Comercial Transatlántico (Spain); Deutsche Bank (Suisse) S.A.; Deutsche Bank Capital Markets Ltd. (U.K.); Deutsche Bank (Canada); McLean McCarthy Ltd. (Canada); Deutsche Bank Capital Corporation (U.S.); Deutsche Credit Corporation (U.S.); DB Capital Markets (Asia) Ltd.; PT Euras Buana Leasing Indonesia; DB Capital Markets (Asia) Ltd. (Japan); Bain & Company Ltd. (Australia); Deutsche Bank Australia Ltd.

Further Reading: Seidenzahl, Fritz. *100 Jahre Deutsche Bank*, Frankfurt, Deutschen Bank, 1970.

Dresdner Bank 

DRESDNER BANK A.G.

Jurgen-Ponto-Platz 1
Post Office Box 1100661
6000 Frankfurt am Main 11
Federal Republic of Germany
(069) 2630

Public Company
Incorporated: 1872
Employees: 38,116
Assets: DM207 billion (US$116.72 billion)
Stock Index: Frankfurt Munich Hamburg Düsseldorf Bremen Hanover Stuttgart Berlin Amsterdam Antwerp Basel Brussels Geneva Luxembourg Paris Vienna Zurich Tokyo

When Carl Freiherr von Kaskel, Felix Freiherr, and Eugene Gutman opened the doors of the Dresden Bankhaus for business in Dresden on December 1, 1872, the time was ripe for new banks in Germany. Before its victory over France in 1871 organized Germany as a modern nation-state, there had not even been standardized units of currency, weight, or measurement. The opportunity for economic growth was enormous, and the management team of Dresdner Bank seized it with a vengeance.

As a universal bank, Dresdner Bank was formulated to serve all of the economic needs of its community. The role of the big banks in Germany is closely related to developing industries and expanding commercial opportunities. Accordingly, Dresdner Bank expanded rapidly in its first decade through a series of acquisitions, liquidations, and absorptions of smaller institutions. Though sometimes criticized for being unusually willing to assume risks, the management team of Dresdner Bank, led especially by Eugene Gutman, quickly made Dresdner the number-two financial institution in Germany, behind only Deutsche Bank, a position which the bank still holds today.

In 1884 Dresdner Bank moved its headquarters from Dresden to Berlin and then spent the rest of the decade expanding even more vigorously. Seeing the potential for growth in foreign markets, Dresdner began opening interests in Asia and Italy. This eye for expansion would continue to make Dresdner grow until its foreign interests were lost after World War I. Dresdner's huge credit reserve, like that of the other large German banks, also helped Germany transform itself from a capital importing to a capital exporting economy during the 1880s.

Dresdner opened new branches in Hamburg in 1892 and in Bremen and London in 1895. The London branch was especially significant for the bank because London was the financial center of the world at that time; it gave the company 19 highly profitable years before the onset of World War I.

At this time Dresdner developed close relations with the electro-technical, rail, and oil industries, which allowed it to build, with Deutsche Bank, a railroad line from Constantinople to Ankara, then an important line of transportation. The foundation of the Central Bank for Railway Securities by Dresdner in 1898 further cemented the relationship between the bank and the railroad industry.

In the early years of the 20th century Dresdner's continuous expansion made it a true giant of German industry. Dresdner achieved unprecedented success in the deposit business between 1896 and 1908 largely through innovative marketing techniques and the bold move of offering higher interest rates to deposit customers to draw a profitable volume of business.

In the first decade of this century, Dresdner formed a community of interest with Schaffhausenschor Bankverein in 1903, opened stock companies to start trade with Asia and South America, formed 27 branches through absorption of smaller banks, and formed an alliance with the American bank J.P. Morgan and Company to engage in international finance.

Of the four endeavors, the community of interest with Schaffhausenschor increased Dresdner's power the most. As Dresdner had always been a huge success in international business and its partner had long shown a genius for domestic banking, the alliance was a natural one, and the standings of both firms increased greatly as they shared profits and policies.

World War I and its aftermath were a disaster for almost every company in Germany. Dresdner Bank, which had profited by financing the government's astronomical war-time expenses, found that the German economy's unpreparedness for war, coupled with the Allied blockade and the industrial might of the United States, crippled non-military industries. The war dried up all opportunities for continued expansion and placed a tremendous burden on German industry, forcing it to produce the materials necessary for war on an unprecedented scale. This stifled the basic expansionist impulse of the bank and cut off investment revenue.

The short-lived Weimar Republic (1918–1923) was also difficult for Dresdner Bank. The burden of Germany's heavy war reparations stultified the entire economy. This hurt Dresdner even more than the lack of expansion during the war years had. Since one of the primary reasons for a universal bank is to back developing industry, Dresdner, as a major shareholder in many German firms, felt the pinch of the Treaty of Versailles as sharply as the rest of Germany did. On top of this was the Allies' insistence that all Allied countries be given the right to confiscate any German private property abroad. Firms with international interests as extensive as Dresdner's experienced crushing setbacks as they lost vast international securities and capital holdings.

The loss of wealth coupled with the need to pay reparations produced the legendary hyperinflation of the Weimer Republic, further cutting into the German banking business. At the high point of economic chaos, in 1923, Dresdner held assets of 204 trillion marks. Three years later, when the banking industry was stabilized by the introduction of the Rentenmark, Dresdner's share capital and reserves totaled only 100 million Rentenmarks.

Between 1924 and 1929, Dresdner Bank was involved in a lending policy that brought economic chaos to Germany again in 1931. During those five years, Germany began to rebound economically. In 1929, the economy's volume of business was 50% greater than it was before the war. This was due largely to the capital loans that Dresdner and the other leading banks made to new and developing German industries. But the banks were too loyal to their customers and lent out too much money. When the effects of the American stock market crash of 1929 hit Germany in 1931, there was little cash on hand to pay investors. Also, Dresdner and the other big banks carried too much foreign credit. They needed foreign capital coming in to pay the interest. This bank crisis necessitated federal involvement: in 1931 the German government took over 90% of Dresdner.

Dresdner did benefit somewhat, however, from the government's plan to restructure the banks and keep credit rates down by buying up banks and giving them cash. In the year after the crash, Dresdner was able to buy another of the major Berlin banks, Darmstadter, making Dresdner for a time the largest bank in Germany.

When the Nazis assumed power in 1933, the banking crisis was far from over. The Big Three of Berlin (now Dresdner, Deutsche, and Commerzbank) had lost 1.3 billion marks in assets and capital in the previous two years. Ostensibly socialists, the Nazis were inclined to completely nationalize all the German banks under the absolute power of the Third Reich. The domination of the big banks had long fostered a populist resentment, which the Nazis carefully exploited. Dresdner Bank, as the fattest financial goose among the banks, was the chief target for total and irrevocable nationalization.

In the end, the banks were not nationalized, and Dresdner Bank prospered under state-regulated capitalism. In 1937 Dresdner was able to buy itself back from the government. Its size increased in 1939, when Länderbank, the second-largest bank in Austria, merged with Dresdner after the Anschluss in Austria. The Vienna branch of a Czech bank, Zivnostenska, was also annexed.

Dresdner's relationship with the Nazi government led to dire consequences after the conclusion of World War II. As one of the privileges of leadership, Hermann Goering was allowed to have a company of his own, Goering Werke, an iron ore processing works whose products were in heavy demand during the Nazi war buildup. A representative of Dresdner, Karl Rasche, sat on the management board of a subsidiary of Goering Werke. This was not unusual; having representatives on boards and councils, as well as controlling blocks of voting stock shares, are the chief ways that the big German banks exercise economic control. But Karl Rasche's presence on the board of a Goering Werke subsidiary during this time was later considered positive evidence by the Allies that Dresdner had not only escaped being socialized by the Nazis, but that it had maintained a close relationship with the Nazi government.

After World War II, Dresdner and the other large German banks were split up. Once again it lost branches and assets to the war's victors. With the Soviet occupation of East Germany, all of Dresdner's offices east of the Oder-Neisse line were closed permanently. Of Dresdner's total of 327 offices, only about half remained open, and most of those were badly damaged. Dresdner was at first restructured into ten separate institutions. The bank struggled to regain some of its prominence during the early postwar years but then faced another reformation from the Liquidation Commission.

The Liquidation Commission was formed by the occupation forces to study the roles that various companies and industries had played in the war economy of Nazi Germany. Citing the "silent financing" of the German war effort through loans, as well as direct links of the kind previously noted, the Liquidation Commission decided to restructure Dresdner Bank into 11 small banks, each of which could operate only within its own zone of occupation. Yet Dresdner Bank was, like Germany itself, impossible to keep down. In 1952 the 11 regional banks were turned into three successor institutions of Dresdner Bank. Each of the three derivative banks prospered so much as a part of the "economic miracle" of the 1950s that Dresdner was allowed to recombine itself again in 1957 as Dresdner Bank A.G., with its new headquarters in Frankfurt am Main.

Reunification meant more than gaining domestic strength for the new Dresdner Bank: it meant the bank could expand once again. Dresdner immediately took advantage of its situation and became the first German bank to open an office overseas after World War II when it established a representative station in Istanbul in the late 1950s.

Dresdner also expanded through technical innovation, using data processing systems to manage accounts in 1958, the first West German firm to do so. Dresdner also pioneered the way for foreign stock shares to be traded on West German exchanges at about this time.

When the restrictions limiting the three major branches of Dresdner from operating outside of their zones of occupation were lifted in 1963, the domestic business needed to finance foreign expansion was finally available, and the bank started to become the international giant that it is today. Dresdner again pioneered overseas business dealings by becoming the first firm to set up a German bank outside of its own borders, opening the Company Luxemburgeoise de Banque S.A. in Luxembourg in 1967.

Dresdner continued to expand, opening branches in Singapore and New York in 1972. By developing these overseas connections, the bank was able to outgrow its involvement in various consortiums with other banks and became truly international on its own terms again. In the mid-1970s, Dresdner again pioneered in the field of international finance by opening representative offices in London, Tokyo, and even Moscow.

In 1968 Dresdner established German-American Securities—now called ABD Securities Corporation—in New York. Today this investment banking subsidiary is an extremely important part of Dresdner's worldwide securities expertise. As a measure of the subsidiary's, and Dresdner's, American prominence, ABD's chief, Theodor Schmidt-Scheuber, was the first foreigner to be made head of an American stock exchange, in Boston.

Dresdner earned recognition in 1974 for its adroit handling of the sale of the Quandt family's 10% share of Daimler-Benz to Kuwait, the largest deal of the kind at the time.

In 1977 Dresdner and the whole German business community were shocked when Jürgen Ponto, then chief executive of Dresdner, was killed by left-wing terrorists during a kidnapping attempt. The assasination cut short the life of the man who had headed Dresdner since 1969 and helped make it the international business power it is today.

Hans Friderichs, a former economics minister, was Ponto's eventual replacement. In 1978, Dresdner had officially become one of the ten largest banks in the world. But Dresdner didn't prosper under Friderichs for long; his six years in charge were marked by mounting losses and turmoil among executives. Friderichs's tenure ended sadly in February 1985, when he resigned in the wake of charges that he had accepted a bribe for a favorable tax ruling given to the Flick Industrial Group while he was economics minister.

Friderichs's replacement was Wolfgang Röller, a very able member of Dresdner's board whose specialty was the securities business. It was Röller who had established ABD Securities in 1968, and he who had arranged the Kuwaiti sale of Daimler-Benz. Röller had spent most of his career at Dresdner, becoming one of the youngest executives in the German banking industry when he joined Dresdner's management board in 1971 at age 38. Röller's background in securities made him an especially appropriate choice as the banking industry in general, and Germany's in particular, entered an era of decreasing regulation and intensified international competition.

Under Röller, Dresdner began to prosper again. In his first year in charge, earnings rose 18% and assets 8%, to DM189 billion. That year, Dresdner became the first German company to have its shares listed on the Tokyo stock exchange.

In the late 1980s, banks throughout Europe and the world began to gear up for the unification of the European market in 1992. Dresdner set out to build its presence by concentrating on its expertise in securities trading and fund management, anchored by a strong domestic presence and its American subsidiary, ABD Securities. In May, 1988 Dresdner bought a majority interest in Thornton & Company, a leading British asset-management company, to strenthen its presence in that country and also in Asia, where Thornton has a strong position. It also bolstered its U.S. position by purchasing several seats on the New York Stock Exchange.

Dresdner responded quickly to the tumult in Eastern Europe in 1989, rushing to open an office in Warsaw as well as in several East German cities, including Dresden, the city where the bank was founded in 1872.

As Dresdner faces the coming of the unified European market and the tremendous changes reshaping Easten Europe, it seeks to capitalize on and strengthen both its global network and its domestic presence, especially in investment banking services such as asset management and securities trading. As one of the largest banks in Germany for more than a century, Dresdner faces the challenges ahead with the advantage of a long history of overcoming obstacles and adversity.

Principal Subsidiaries: Bankhaus Reuschel & Co.; Deutsch-Südamerikanische Bank AG; Diskont und Kredit AG; Dresdner Bank Berlin AG; Oldenburgische Landesbank AG; KG Aligemeine Leasing GmbH & Co.; Deutsche Hypothekenbank Frankfurt-Bremen AG; Hypothekenbank in Hamburg AG; Norddeutsche Hypotheken- und Wechselbank AG; Pfaizische Hypothekenbank AG; DEGI Deutsche Gesellschaft für Immobilienfonds mbH; Deutscher Investment-Trust; dresdnerbank investment management; Betelligungsgesellschaft für die deutsche Wirtschaft mbH; Unternehmensbetelligungsgesellschaft für die deutsche Wirtschaft AG; ABD Securities Corporation (U.S.); Banque pou l'Europe SA (Luxembourg); Europa Bank AG (Luxembourg); Banque Veuve Morin-Pon's (France); BNP-AK-DRESDNER BANK A.S. (Turkey); Dresdner-ABD Securities Limited (Hong Kong); Dresdner Bank Canada; Dresdner Bank Luxembourg S.A.; Dresdner Bank (Switzerland) Ltd.; Dresdner Fortfaitierungs Aktiengesellschaft (Switzerland); Dresdner (South East Asia) Limited (Singapore); Thornton & Co. Limited (U.K.); United Overseas Bank (Switzerland).

Further Reading: Woolston, Maxine. *The Structure of the Nazi Economy*, Cambridge, Harvard University Press, 1942; Schweitzer, Arthur. *Big Business in the Third Reich*, Bloomington, Indiana University Press, 1964; Stolper, Gustav. *The German Economy: 1870 to the Present*, London, Weidenfield and Nicolson, 1967; Northrop, Mildred, *Control Policies of the Reichsbank 1924–1933*, New York, AMS Press, 1968; Vogl, Frank. *German Business after the Economic Miracle*, New York, John Wiley & Sons, 1973; Riesser, Jacob. *The German Great Banks*, New York, Arno Press, 1977.

FIRST CHICAGO CORPORATION

One First National Plaza
Chicago, Illinois 60670
U.S.A.
(312) 732–4000

Public Company
Incorporated: 1863
Employees: 16,069
Assets: $44.43 billion
Stock Index: Midwest New York Pacific London Tokyo

First Chicago Corporation is a multibank holding company whose principal subsidiary is the First National Bank of Chicago, the oldest and largest national bank still operating under its original name and charter. First Chicago (the First) takes great pride in its long history of dependable and innovative financial products, which it traces back to the Civil War. In 1969 the First was reorganized as a wholly owned subsidiary of First Chicago Corporation to allow it to broaden the scope of its activities worldwide.

In the summer of 1863, Edmund Aiken headed a group of ten investors who wanted to take advantage of the National Banking Act that President Abraham Lincoln had signed into law earlier that year. This act allowed national banks for the first time to exist along with state-chartered institutions. Aiken, a 51-year-old private banker, realized that the demands of financing war-related businesses, together with the industrial and commercial growth of Chicago and the development of Illinois, created a need for a national bank in the Midwest. Aiken's group invested $100,000 to start the First. The bank opened its doors for business on July 1, 1863, the day the Battle of Gettysburg began.

The First was an immediate success. After only 18 months, the board of directors voted to increase its capital stock to $1 million, which was the limit in the bank's Articles of Association. The First moved twice during its first five years, as increasing business forced it into larger quarters.

Although the First was housed in a fireproof structure when the Chicago Fire struck in 1871, its building was seriously damaged. Fortunately, the bank's safes and vaults withstood the flames and nothing of importance was lost. The job of collecting records and monies buried in the ashes fell to Lyman Gage, a young cashier who eventually became president of the bank and then secretary of the treasury in President William McKinley's cabinet. Gage was one of a long line of employees who used his training and experience at the First to serve the federal government.

Three months after the Great Fire, the First reoccupied its charred quarters and began helping Chicagoans rebuild their city. Out of the ruins, the First emerged as one of the most prominent and respected business leaders in the community.

As Chicago prospered, the First expanded and changed with its growing customer base. To motivate employees the First began awarding bonuses for "able and meritorious" effort; in 1881 the bank distributed $20,000 as incentives to employees. The bank began declaring quarterly dividends to customers at mid-year in 1882. That same year, it became the first bank to open a women's banking department, to make ladies more comfortable when conducting business in the male-dominated bank. During the Panic of 1893, the First found an original solution for the currency shortage: it imported gold from its London correspondent bank, a practice that quickly spread to other banks. In 1899 the bank was the first American bank to establish a formal pension plan, a clear indication of its employee-oriented management style.

At the turn of the century, the industrial revolution created an unprecedented demand for credit. The First met this need through mergers. When it joined with the Union National Bank in 1900, the First's assets climbed from $56 million to $76 million. It combined with the Metropolitan National Bank in 1902 and raised its assets to $100 million. In this way the First acquired the resources to serve both the needs of its regular customers, whose businesses were flourishing, and the needs of new customers, who were trying to capitalize on the opportunities of the era.

In 1903 the First opened the First Trust and Savings Bank, a separate corporation to serve the non-commercial members of the community. During its first seven days of operation this bank tallied more than 1,000 savings accounts totaling in excess of $3 million. In two years the First Trust and Savings Bank had more than 10,000 depositors whose balances totaled nearly $18 million.

The First celebrated its 50th anniversary in 1913 by becoming a charter member of the Federal Reserve system. By 1915 the bank was one of the three most active banks in foreign exchange in the country.

During World War I, the First played a major role in helping the country finance the war effort. When local support for Liberty Bonds and government securities weakened, the First and the First Trust and Savings Bank purchased $10 million for their own accounts. This patriotic act, coupled with the First's President James B. Forgan's active promotion, helped inspire Americans to purchase another $12 million worth of government bonds and securities.

During the 1920s the bank grew steadily. A new addition to its headquarters, designed by Daniel Burnham, was completed in 1928 just as the number of depositors reached 20,000. When the Union Trust Company merged with the First Trust and Savings Bank in 1928, to become the First Union Trust and Savings Bank, the First looked optimistically toward the future. But as 1929 passed, this optimism turned into a painful pessimism. As the great crash neared, the First witnessed a stream of large customer withdrawals to cover speculative securities purchases.

During the Depression that followed the 1929 stock market crash, the First's sound financial base kept it from failing as 11,000 weaker banks did. Even in the depths of the Depression, the First never skipped an interest payment on savings deposits. Its strength allowed the First to merge with the Foreman State Banks in early 1931 and accept all of their deposit liabilities. Moreover, during a frenzy to acquire liquidity in early 1933, depositors were able to withdraw $50 million in just three days from the First without severely hampering the bank's operations.

When President Franklin Roosevelt proclaimed a national bank holiday in 1933 to give banks a chance to stabilize, the First was one of the few banks able to open its doors without regulatory delays. Part of the reason for the First's quick reopening was its status as a Federal Reserve member bank, which meant that it accrued advantages that non-member banks did not. Because the First Union Trust and Savings Bank was not a member, the First decided to absorb all of the savings bank's business in order to retain it customers' loyalty.

The establishment of the National Recovery Administration by Congress and the passage of the Banking Act of 1933 (better known as the Glass-Steagall Act), which created the Federal Deposit Insurance Corporation and separated commercial banking from investment banking, strengthened confidence in the First. When the Securities and Exchange Commission was established in 1934, fears of a second crash dissipated.

The First weathered the Depression and continued to grow as Roosevelt's recovery policies took hold. In 1938, on its 75th birthday, the First's assets reached the $1 billion mark, just as the American economy began to accelerate in anticipation of war. Remembering that capital costs skyrocketed during World War I, the First advised businessmen to avoid high prices by borrowing money for investment before any outbreak of fighting.

During World War II a quarter of the First's staff served on active duty. Women were hired to fill war-time vacancies and to staff new positions as business increased rapidly. In the six years after the start of World War II, women helped the First double the value of its assets to $2 billion.

In 1944 President Roosevelt chose the First's president, Edward Eagle Brown, to be the only American banker to serve at the United Nations Monetary and Finance Conference that met at Bretton Woods, New Hampshire, to sketch plans for the World Bank and the International Monetary Fund. Brown pioneered the development of highly specialized lending divisions to respond quickly and innovatively to corporate customers' financial needs.

During the 1950s and 1960s the First enjoyed a period of sustained growth as it continued to build on its reputation as both a specialist and an innovator in business loans. As a result, the First's assets more than doubled and the number of its loans quadrupled during this period. In 1959 the First opened a London office to improve its service to foreign correspondent banks and customers engaged in international trade. Three years later, the First started a Far East office in Tokyo. In 1980 the bank opened a representative office in Beijing, the first American bank to open such an office in China.

As the First approached the end of the 1960s, the bank prepared to expand, as fast as it could, throughout the Midwest and the world. When Homer Livingston passed leadership of the bank to Gaylord Freeman in 1969, an attitude of unrestrained optimism pervaded at the First.

That year the bank was reorganized as the major subsidiary of the new First Chicago Corporation. This reorganization gave the First a way around restrictive banking laws. From the beginning of his tenure, Freeman followed an aggressive program to increase its assets through the acquisition of more loans.

Freeman doubled First Chicago's size in just five years. He accomplished this by recruiting top business-school graduates and quickly promoting them to positions of considerable lending authority. Unfortunately, this program produced one of the worst loan portfolios in the industry: in 1976 the bank's percentage of nonperforming loans reached a high of 11%—twice the national average.

A. Robert Abboud replaced Freeman in 1975 and immediately began dealing with First Chicago's bad loans. Unlike Freeman, who was warm and supportive, Abboud's methods were described as tyrannical and intimidating. Where Freeman favored a decentralized managerial style that bestowed maximum freedom on loan officers to make decisions, Abboud favored a centralized style to check and double-check every loan. In one 18-month period 118 officers left, reducing the bank's executive ranks by 12%. Even after promoting 84 employees from within, Abboud was still 149 officers short of his budget, but he refused to hire recent business school graduates because he feared their lack of experience.

Abboud also drove away established clients with his highly conservative loan policy. His new controls doubled the time it took to approve loans and also left old customers uncertain as to whether their loans would be approved. Abboud raised interest rates on loans and required corporate customers to maintain compensating balances of 15% on an unexercised credit line when his competition required 10%.

Abboud justified his actions by pointing proudly to First Chicago's balance sheet, which showed a 22-to-1 ratio of assets to equity; only one other bank in the country had a better ratio. By 1980 Abboud had brought nonperforming loans down 6%. First Chicago's 5% rate was still double the national average, however.

After three years, Abboud realized that First Chicago was not prospering. Clients were not returning and new customers were repelled by First Chicago's reputation for insensitivity to its customers' needs. In 1975, Continental Illinois, First Chicago's chief rival, was strikingly similar to First Chicago in size and makeup; they both depended heavily on commercial loans for volume and on money markets for funding. Five years later, Continental's loan volume had grown to $23 billion, 50% larger than First Chicago's, and its earnings grew 73% while First Chicago's grew 4%. Abboud decided that First Chicago had to become a risk-taker to catch up.

Abboud chose to gamble in two speculative areas: fixed-rate loans and arbitrage in the Eurodollar market. By mid-1979, with interest rates on the verge of a historic climb, First Chicago found itself with $1 billion in fixed-rate loans that were being funded by short-term money whose cost was quickly rising above the yields of the loans.

In 1978 Abboud more than doubled the bank's Eurodollar commitment, to $6.7 billion, from $3.1 billion the year before. He was hoping for interest rates to fall, but, following the bank's own forecast, they rose in late 1979 and early 1980. The Federal Reserve made the bank's Eurodollar situation worse by tightening up regulations. Thus, First Chicago found itself funding its Eurodollar placements with higher-cost deposits. Although consumer banking doubled in five years under Abboud, his speculative decisions cost the bank dearly.

Barry F. Sullivan, an executive vice president of Chase Manhattan Corporation, succeeded Abboud as chairman and chief executive of First Chicago in July, 1980. He had the "people skills" the autocratic Abboud lacked and experience putting a floundering bank back on its feet. Once in office, Sullivan zeroed in on building a new management team. He recruited 300 officers for product development and corporate accounts, expanded the corporate-planning staff from 3 to 44, and reshuffled the talent he already had.

At the same time, Sullivan created a new organizational structure for First Chicago based on strategic business units (SBUs). Sullivan partitioned operations into 145 SBUs in an attempt to decentralize and place responsibility for strategic planning and marketing on middle management. Sullivan's philosophy and efforts got results: in the first nine months of 1983, earnings jumped 43% and return on assets, which were 0.23% in 1980, reached 0.53%, close to the 0.57% average return on assets at the ten largest money-center banks in the country. First Chicago caught the attention of Wall Street; at the end of 1983, three and a half years after Sullivan became chairman, First Chicago's stock reached $24 a share, double its price when Sullivan took over.

Sullivan's success can be attributed to more than just his managerial style. He instituted a more competitive pricing schedule for corporate loans and marketed it, and the bank's new organization, aggressively. He eliminated a costly mismatch of maturities and rates in funding the bank's loan portfolio. He abandoned the bank's Brussels office and a Visa traveler's check operation because of poor performance. He developed the industrial specializations that First Chicago had once been known for but that had been neglected by Abboud: energy and commercial real estate. Finally, he drew small- and medium-sized companies to First Chicago, a feat he accomplished by purchasing American National Bank and Trust Company, Chicago's fifth-largest bank and an expert in dealing with mid-size and smaller companies.

In October, 1984, the comptroller of the currency examined First Chicago's loan portfolio. Surprisingly, the comptroller judged that First Chicago had failed to acknowledge some bad loans. As a result, First Chicago was pressured to write off $279 million in its third quarter, six times the amount taken in the second quarter. In addition, the comptroller forced Sullivan to recatagorize as nonperforming another $125 million in loans, bringing the total of nonperforming assets for the third quarter to $840 million.

First Chicago had to report a $71.8 million loss for the third quarter. Most outsiders expected that these bad loans came from the bank's foreign-debt portfolio, but most came from First Chicago's domestic-lending group of energy and agriculture businesses. The oil glut had depressed energy prices far below the break-even point for local drillers, and the strong U.S. dollar had cut American farm exports.

A few months later, First Chicago had to establish a $115 million reserve fund to cover losses stemming from a recent investment in a Brazilian bank. By the end of 1985, First Chicago had written off $131.1 million on its Brazilian fiasco.

Nonetheless, earnings increased in 1985 because Sullivan had made some astute decisions. His purchase of American National Corporation added record profits of $42 million to First Chicago's bottom line. The promotion of First Chicago's credit cards produced consumer loan profits that totaled $65 million. A third decision that paid off was First Chicago's venture-capital stock portfolio, which added $121 million in pretax profits in 1985.

The bank's net income in 1986 climbed to $276 million, which represented the strongest financial results in First Chicago's history to date. In the wake of these profits, Moody's Investor Service gave the bank a vote of confidence by raising the rating of First Chicago's securities. More significantly, the office of the comptroller of the currency acknowledged that First Chicago had met all of its requirements for reducing risk on loans well ahead of the targeted dates.

What the banking industry feared most happened in 1987: Third World countries suspended interest payments on their loans. This situation compelled First Chicago to raise its reserves on troubled-country debtors (mostly Brazil) by $1 billion. At the end of the year, First Chicago reported a loss of $571 million, in dramatic contrast with its historic earnings of 1986.

In 1987 First Chicago acquired First United Financial Services Inc., a five-bank holding company with a solid base of business in the growing western and northwestern suburbs. The bank also purchased Beneficial National Bank USA, Wilmington, Delaware, and renamed it FCC National Bank. With this addition, First Chicago became the third largest issuer of bank credit cards in the United States.

As profits rebounded in 1988, First Chicago took another giant step in developing its customer-banking base through the acquisition of Gary-Wheaton Corporation, a four-bank holding company.

The First was founded in a tradition of service and trust that has survived to the present day. Under Sullivan's stewardship, First Chicago has bounced back from serious domestic and foreign loan problems and the challenges of financial-product development and marketing in a volatile and changing world economy. The next decade will tell if Sullivan can complete First Chicago's recovery and transform it into one of the premier banks in the U.S.

Principal Subsidiaries: First Capital Corp. of Chicago; First Chicago Credit Corp.; First Chicago Financial Corp.; First Chicago Investment Corp.; First Chicago Leasing Corp.; First Chicago Lease Holding, Inc.; First Chicago Overseas Finance N.V. (Netherlands Antilles); First Chicago Properties, Inc.; First Chicago Realty Services Corp.; First Chicago Trust Company (Cayman) Ltd. (Cayman Islands); First Chicago Trust Company of Florida, N.A.; First Card Services, Inc.; First Chicago Trading Co.; First Chicago Trust Co. of New York; First Chicago Leasing (Japan) Co. Ltd.; First Chicago Investment Advisors, N.A.; The First National Bank of Chicago; First Chicago Building Corp.; First Chicago Futures, Inc.; First Chicago Neighborhood Development Corp.; FNBC Properties, Inc.; National Safe Deposit Corp.; Rosely Corp.; Senior Properties, Inc.; Triumph Properties, Inc.; ComTrac, Inc.; First Chicago National Processing Corp.; First Chicago Video Services, Inc.; Arrendadora e Inversionista Latina, S.A. de C. V.; First Chicago Australia Ltd.; First Chicago Hong Kong Ltd.; First Chicago International; First Chicago International Finance Corp.; First Chicago Investments (U.K.) Ltd.; First Chicago Kenya Ltd.; First Chicago Ltd. (U.K.); First Chicago Nominees (Ireland) Ltd.; First Chicago Nominees Ltd. (U.K.); First Chicago Panama, S.A.; First Chicago S.A. (Switzerland); First Chicago Servicos, Ltda. (Brazil); First Chicago (Singapore) Nominees Private Ltd.; The First National Bank of Chicago (C.I.) Ltd. (Channel Islands); First Chicago Australia Securities Ltd.; First Chicago Export Finance Ltd. (England); First Chicago Finleasing S.p.A. (Italy); First Chicago Hong Kong (Nominees) Ltd.; First Chicago Leasing Canada Ltd.; The First National Bank of Chicago (Canada); First Chicago Participacoes, Ltda. (Brazil); Banco Arfina, S.A. (Argentina); American National Corp.

Further Reading: Morris, Henry C. *The History of the First National Bank of Chicago*, Chicago, R.R. Donnelley & Sons Company, 1902; *First Chicagoan: 125th Anniversary Issue*. First Chicago Corporation, Chicago, March, 1988.

FIRST INTERSTATE BANCORP

707 Wilshire Boulevard
Los Angeles, California 90017
U.S.A.
(213) 614–3001

Public Company
Incorporated: 1957 as Firstamerica Bancorporation
Employees: 36,980
Assets: $58.2 billion
Stock Index: New York Pacific Boston Midwest Philadelphia Cincinnati Amsterdam Frankfurt

First Interstate Bancorp is one of the largest bank holding companies in the United States. The company's 55 banks collectively operate 1,033 branches in 13 states, giving it the widest geographical coverage of any banking company in the country. First Interstate is a familiar name to literally millions of Americans who bank there. In the 1980s, the company took advantage of banking deregulation to enter a variety of financial services, including discount securities broking, venture capital activities, and mortgage banking.

First Interstate's history parallels the evolution of banking in the United States. Its major restructurings have usually gone hand in hand with governmental restrictions or critical trends in the banking industry. The company known as First Interstate today was once the Western Bancorporation, and before that the Firstamerica Bancorporation, but its roots go deeper still. Firstamerica was a spinoff of the banking interests of the Transamerica Corporation. Transamerica's origins can be traced to 1904, when A.P. Giannini opened the Bank of Italy in San Francisco with $150,000.

Giannini was a unique figure in the history of American banking. Born in San Jose, California in 1870, Giannini spent much of his youth traveling around the state as a produce buyer for his step-father's distributing firm. Giannini's extensive contact with small merchants drew his attention to the need these businessmen had for financing. Banking at that time was primarily a service for big business. Giannini decided to pursue the business of these "little people," a strategy that paid off handsomely. By 1909, Giannini's Bank of Italy had more than $2.5 million at its disposal.

Giannini remained an outsider from the traditional American banking establishment. The financier's somewhat unorthodox methods were viewed as a threat by many established bankers of the day. As a result, when Giannini went to New York to expand his empire into the nation's financial center, he found a number of obstacles placed in his way. In 1918, Giannini and a group of Italian investors pooled $1.5 million to establish the BancItaly Corporation in New York City. Over the next nine years, BancItaly acquired five New York banks, including one called Bank of America. When Giannini tried to consolidate his BancItaly holdings under the Bank of America charter, the Federal Reserve Bank of New York unexpectedly denied his petition unless he and his associates agreed to divest certain holdings within six months. It was the first time the Federal Reserve had placed such a stipulation on any national bank with a clean bill of health. Although it was never proven, suspicion arose that the move was engineered by the powerful eastern banking establishment. Giannini was forced to agree to the conditions imposed by the Federal Reserve: to back out of the consolidation at the eleventh hour might have shaken public confidence in the bank.

In 1928, soon after the Federal Reserve's orders were carried out, Bank of Italy and BancItaly stocks were dumped on Wall Street by Giannini's banking rivals in order to lower the value of the Californian's banks. Giannini organized a holding company, the Transamerica Corporation, to prevent further manipulation of the stocks' prices. Shares in the new company were issued in exchange for Bank of Italy and BancItaly Corporation shares. The new company engaged in both banking and non-banking activities to spread out risk. With $1.1 billion in assets, Transamerica was a major force in banking from the day it began business.

Transamerica set out to build a national banking system. In 1930, Transamerica merged the Bank of America of California and the Bank of Italy, creating the Bank of America National Trust and Savings Association. This new hybrid, with assets of $1 billion, was the fourth largest bank in the country.

Transamerica began to acquire the banks that would eventually form the core of the First Interstate Bancorporation as early as 1930. During the following decade, Transamerica acquired a number of banks and other financial corporations throughout the western United States. By the end of the decade the company had banks in California, Nevada, Oregon, Washington, and Arizona, as well as New York. Giannini's goal was to unite all of the banks under one umbrella, thereby creating a truly national branch banking system as soon as federal regulations would allow it. The Depression, however, brought more stringent banking regulations as the nation's banks were reorganized during Franklin Roosevelt's "bank holiday." Nonetheless, Transamerica continued its banking operations throughout the 1930s and at the same time expanded its nonbanking activities.

In 1937, Transamerica divested a majority of its shares in the Bank of America. The company continued to hold its other banks, and added considerably to its bank holdings throughout the next decade. In 1948, the Federal

Reserve filed a suit against Transamerica charging that the company's interstate banking affiliations constituted a potential monopoly. The case was resolved in 1953, when a U.S. Court of Appeals ruled that Transamerica's holdings did not consitute a monopoly.

A. P. Giannini died in 1949 and was succeeded as Transamerica chairman by Frank N. Belgrano, who continued Giannini's policies of growth. Transamerica had steadily invested in various insurance companies since the 1930s, and by 1950, the company was aimed more in that direction than in the direction of interstate banking. Belgrano, however, refreshed Transamerica's bank acquisition policies. In the next several years, Belgrano took Transamerica on an acquisition spree; by the mid-1950s, the company had significant new holdings in Colorado, Idaho, Montana, New Mexico, Utah, and Wyoming.

The Bank Holding Company Act of 1956 placed new restrictions on companies like Transamerica. As a result of this legislation, Belgrano separated Transamerica's banking from its non-banking holdings. Transamerica pursued its insurance and other operations while ownership of 23 of Transmamerica's banks in 11 western states were transferred to the new Firstamerica Corporation. All of Firstamerica's shares were distributed to Transamerica shareholders in equal proportion to their Transamerica holdings. By 1959 the two organizations were completely separate.

In 1959, Frank King joined Firstamerica with the acquisition of the California Bank. King became chairman of Firstamerica, guiding its growth for the next ten years. In 1961, Firstamerica changed its name to Western Bancorporation. Under King's direction the company expanded steadily throughout the 1960s, both domestically and overseas. The United California Bank, which had been formed when the California Bank and the First Western Bank and Trust Company merged in 1961, was the jewel in Western's crown at this time. By the end of the decade, Western Bancorporation had assets of more than $10 billion.

In 1972, Frank King retired and Clifford Tweter became chairman of Western's board of directors. At the same time Ralph J. Voss became the company's president. These two engineered further expansion of the holding company's financial services network. The Western Bancorporation Mortgage Company was founded in 1974. A year later, Western Bancorporation Data Processing Company was launched to tackle some of the problems related to the explosive growth of Western's banking operations. In order to improve up-to-the-minute information on Western's millions of customer accounts, the data processing company developed the Teller Item Processing Systems (TIPS). By 1985, this system was processing 750,000 transactions per day.

In 1978, United California Bank's president, Joseph J. Pinola, joined Western Bancorporation as chairman and CEO. He inherited a decentralized collection of banks, many of which had their own operating procedures and marketing strategies. Pinola centralized Western's strategic planning, but left day-to-day decisions in the hands of the individual banks. In 1979, the Western Bancorp Venture Capital Company was formed, further diversifying the financial operations of Western Bancorporation.

In June of 1981, the company changed its name to First Interstate Bancorp. About 900 banking offices throughout 11 states, as well as 40 overseas offices, now identified themselves as First Interstate banks. The move was designed to promote greater public recognition and internal consistency.

The 1980s were a time of rapid change in the banking industry. First Interstate Bancorp introduced the nation's first bank franchise program. Franchisees were entitled to use the First Interstate name, advertising, computer services, and other common products while maintaining local control over operations. At the same time the company continued its strategy of growth by acquisition. In 1983, it acquired IntraWest Bank of Denver, which was merged into the First Interstate Bank of Colorado, making it the state's largest, with assets in excess of $2.4 billion.

First Interstate jumped into new financial services as soon as the banking deregulation measures of the 1980s allowed. In 1982, the bank participated with 12 other banks in the creation of the Cirrus automated teller machine (ATM) network. In 1983, the First Interstate Discount Brokerage was set up to provide bank customers with securities and commodities support. Spoor Behrins Campbell and Young, a financial planning company, was also acquired in 1983.

In 1984, First Interstate branched into merchant banking with the purchase of Continental Illinois Ltd.; equipment leasing with the acquisition of the Commercial Alliance Corporation of New York; and broadened its mortgage banking activities by acquiring the Republic Realty Mortgage Corporation. In January, 1985 First Interstate's flagship, the First Interstate Bank of California, split its operations into two separate units. First Interstate Bank of California served individuals and small- and medium-sized businesses, while a new bank, First Interstate Bank Ltd., provided banking services to large corporate customers.

The bank failures of the mid-1980s gave First Interstate the opportunity to acquire a number of banks in need of repair. In 1986 it bought the First National Bank and Trust of Oklahoma City, which had failed because of an unexpected downturn in the energy and real estate industries, and reopened it under the First Interstate name. The company acquired failed banks in three other states as well.

In 1986 and 1987, First Interstate Bancorp made a bold attempt to take over the ailing Bank of America. Bank of America's heavy exposure to Third World debt and to the troubled energy and real estate industries in the U.S. had taken a heavy toll; the bank lost $1.8 billion between 1985 and 1988. Nevertheless, Bank of America fought First Interstate's takeover bid with determination and was ultimately successful.

First Interstate soon had its hands full with its own problems. In 1987, First Interstate Bank of Texas encountered serious problems with bad debt. This subsidiary bank, like many others, had loaned heavily to the energy and real estate industries, and was unprepared for the sudden downturn. The situation in Texas prompted First

Interstate chairman Joe Pinola to take a closer look at his company's operations. He responded by trimming 8% of the workforce and seeking buyers for unprofitable subsidiaries, among them First Interstate's mortgage banking unit.

In 1988, First Interstate recorded substantial losses. In the last two years of the decade, the company focused on rebuilding and rejuvenating its existing operations rather than on acquiring new ones. Continued deregulation of financial service markets will provide new opportunities for First Interstate Bancorp, and the company that was transformed along with the banking industry will undoubtedly continue to adapt to change.

Principal Subsidiaries: First Interstate Bancard Co., N.A.; First Interstate Bank of Arizona; First Interstate Bank of California; First Interstate Bank International; First Interstate Bank of Denver; First Interstate Bank, Ltd.; First Interstate Bank of Nevada, N.A.; First Interstate Bank of Oklahoma, N.A.; First Interstate Bank of Oregon, N.A.; First Interstate Bank of Utah, N.A.; First Interstate Bank of Washington, N.A.; First Interstate Bancard Co.; First Interstate Discount Brokerage Co.; and First Interstate Life Insurance Co.

Further Reading: Koster, George H. *The Transamerica Story*, San Francisco, Transamerica Corp., 1978; *First Interstate Bancorp: A Brief History*, Los Angeles, First Interstate Bancorp, 1986.

THE FUJI BANK, LTD.

5–5, Otemachi 1-chome
Chiyoda-ku
Tokyo 100
Japan
(03) 216–2211

Public Company
Incorporated: 1923
Employees: 15,000
Assets: ¥43.35 trillion (US$346.86 billion)
Stock Index: Tokyo Osaka London Paris

The Fuji Bank was once the core of the Yasuda *zaibatsu*, or industrial conglomerate. Unlike other conglomerates, which entered almost every industry, Yasuda confined its business to banking, insurance, and lending. It built a strong presence in these areas which, through economic disruption and war, persists to this day. While the Yasuda *zaibatsu* no longer exists, the former Yasuda companies have assembled a new industrial organization called the Fuyo group, which includes a number of large manufacturers.

The earliest predecessor of the Fuji Bank was established by Zenjiro Yasuda, a young entrepreneur who moved to Tokyo from his native Toyama in 1856. In 1866 he opened a money exchange in Kobunacho called Yasuda Shoten, which dealt in gold, silver, and copper. During this period Yasuda established ties with the restoration movement, which sought to overthrow the Tokugawa Shogunate. Two years later, when this movement came to power, new laws were enacted to liberalize and modernize the economy.

Yasuda was rewarded for his early support of the new Meiji government in 1874, when he was designated fiscal agent for the Ministry of Justice. The following year he was placed in charge of finances for the Tochigi prefectural government. Yasuda participated in the formation of the Third National Bank in 1876, and in January of 1880 won a charter to form his own bank. Increasingly recognized as a leader in the financial world, Yasuda was appointed as a founding adviser to the Bank of Japan, the country's first central bank.

The Yasuda Bank became a limited partnership in 1893, in accordance with the Commercial Law and Banking Regulations. The bank grew with the Japanese economy, and gained increasing access to large industrial accounts. In 1900 it became an unlimited partnership, and in 1912 was reincorporated with ¥10 million in capital, representing a fifty-fold increase in just over 30 years.

In 1921 Yasuda was murdered by an extortionist at his summer home in Oiso in 1921. He was 82 years old.

As banking became more complex, the Yasuda Bank recognized a need to reinforce its management structure and strengthen its recruitment of talented personnel. In 1922 it began regular recruitment of university graduates and started sending middle managers on training missions in Europe and America.

Between 1890 and 1920, the Japanese economy was frequently thrown into disarray by financial crises born of monetary mismanagement and inadequate regulation. Then in 1923 Japan suffered a massive earthquake which left the economy in recession. That year, the entire Yasuda financial organization was restructured to rescue banks whose business was most heavily concentrated in the devastated Kanto prefecture.

The bank established two specialty insurance companies and participated in the formation of a trust bank, all bearing the Yasuda name. The Yasuda Bank, meanwhile, absorbed 10 smaller banks: Third National, Meiji Commerce, Shinano, Kyoto, One-Hundred Thirtieth National, Japan Commerce, Twenty-Second National, Higo, Nemuro, and Kanagawa. As a result of the amalgamation, Yasuda became one of the largest Japanese financial organizations. The bank subsequently absorbed the Hammamatsu Commerce Bank in 1924 and the Mori Bank in 1928.

A financial panic in April, 1927 caused a massive run on deposits and, until a moratorium was declared, brought many banks to the brink of ruin. Yasuda, however, remained relatively healthy, and participated in the formation of the Showa Bank, a rescue bank capitalized at ¥10 million. Showa underwrote the accounts of many troubled banks, but the combined effects of government deflationary policy and world recession in 1929 proved insurmountable. Yasuda's business also suffered, forcing the bank to adopt emergency consolidation and austerity measures.

During the early 1930s a group of right-wing officers gained power within the Japanese military. Advocating absolute Japanese suzerainty and economic leadership in Asia, this group put great pressure on moderate forces in industry and government, forcing them to adopt more aggressive policies. In preparation for war, they organized a "quasi-wartime" economy—in effect, a five-year preparation for war.

After a series of incidents which led to the fall of the Hirota government's cabinet, these militarists installed their own puppet cabinet under a government led by Senjuro Hayashi. Included in that cabinet was Nariaki Ikeda of Mitsui, who was named governor of the Bank of Japan, and Toyotaro Yuki of Yasuda, who was made Finance Minister.

Yasuda supported the militarists, believing that economic domination of Asia would greatly enrich the company and Japan. During the war with China, Yasuda, like other Japanese banks, provided funding for the effort and helped to establish profitable ventures in an effort to reduce Japan's increasingly cumbersome external trade deficit.

The economic situation deteriorated rapidly after the United States and Britain entered the war against Japan in 1941. The government was compelled to amalgamate hundreds of industries in an effort to raise productivity. In 1943 Yasuda absorbed the Kyoto Ouchi Bank, the Japan Day & Night Bank, and the Japan Trust Bank. The following year it took over the operations of the Showa Bank. When the war ended in 1945, Yasuda was Japan's largest bank, with 202 branches and ¥13.9 million in deposits.

Under American occupation, all bank accounts were frozen, new bank notes were introduced, and emergency economic measures were enforced to control shortages. War criminals were purged from Yasuda and other companies, and new industrual laws were passed which outlawed the powerful *zaibatsu* groups. The Yasuda Bank was substantially reduced in size and refitted to operate as a common city bank. Its holdings in other Yasuda companies were eliminated and all the Yasuda companies were forced to change their names.

The Yasuda Bank emerged from two years of transformation in 1948 under the name Fuji Bank, a name chosen by its employees. While in 1945 the Yasuda family and holding company had controlled 39% of the bank's shares, by 1949 even the largest shareholder accounted for no more than 1%.

Operating under restrictive new laws, the bank was forced to rebuild its operations almost from scratch. It abandoned leadership by a few men in favor of a presidential form of management under Seiji Sako, and adopted a new logo: the bank's three pillars—shareholders, customers, and employees—enclosed by a circle, the symbol of money.

The Reconstruction Finance Bank (which helped to rebuild Japan's economy, but which also contributed to inflation) was dissolved in 1948, leaving new markets open to the city banks. In addition, industrial laws were relaxed in 1949 and again in 1952. Many companies, including former Yasuda companies, reverted to their prewar names. The Fuji Bank kept its new name, but took advantage of the liberalized environment by re-establishing ties with its former affiliates. The bank restored business contacts and cross-ownership of stock with former *zaibatsu* affiliates, including Yasuda Mutual Life and Yasuda Fire & Marine Insurance.

Having regained some of the advantages it enjoyed before the war, Fuji was better placed than many of its rivals to rebuild its banking empire. By taking advantage of the high savings rate in Japan, Fuji recycled capital from individuals into promising export-oriented industries. As Japanese industry matured, Fuji developed a stronger presence in industrial finance, and in some instances wielded enough influence to win seats on the boards of high-growth client companies.

During Japan's first period of industrial growth (1955–1965), Fuji succeeded in winning back much of its prewar influence. It was not Japan's largest or most important bank, but it did gain a reputation as a *keiretsu*, or banking conglomerate, similar to the old *zaibatsu* combines.

Fuji began an aggressive international expansion during the 1950s, mostly by following clients into important export markets. Under the leadership of Toshi Kaneko, who succeeded Sako as president in 1957, Fuji began to assemble a *zaibatsu*-like organization. The Fuyo group, as it later became known, consisted of several companies involved in basic industries including shipping, trading, electronics, and steel and chemical production. The Fuyo group was created largely in order to protect the markets of non-*zaibatsu* companies against former *zaibatsu* that had begun to reassemble as diversified conglomerates. Major threats were Mitsubishi, Mitsui, Sumitomo, and C. Itoh, all of which operated diverse interests through an efficient worldwide trading network.

The Fuyo group developed much of its identity during the 1960s, when Yoshizane Iwasa, who succeeded Kaneko in 1963, was president of Fuji Bank. Some of the group's major members were Hitachi, Nissan, Canon, and Showa Denko, in addition to the new Yasuda companies. All were associated with Marubeni, a general trading company once associated with Yasuda's rival, the Sumitomo *zaibatsu*.

The Fuyo members were major clients of the Fuji Bank. As such, they were also the bank's primary vehicles of investment; their successes (and failures) were often reflected in the bank's financial statements. True to the spirit of Zenjiro Yasuda, the Fuji Bank oversaw costly rescues of troubled firms—a phenomenon virtually unknown outside Japan. The rescues were intended to demonstrate to other clients the bank's dedication to their businesses. But virtually all of the Fuji Bank's customers were highly successful, which helped the bank emerge in the 1970s as one of Japan's most influential financial organizations.

With establishment of the London-based Japan International Bank in 1970, Fuji became directly involved in European money markets. The bank set up subsidiaries in Australia in 1971 and in Switzerland, Hong Kong, and Singapore in 1972.

One area of particular interest for Fuji was investment banking. Japanese financial regulations, however, prevented city banks from performing non-bank activities. In the less-regulated overseas markets, Fuji was free to pursue whatever businesses local laws would allow. Fuji therefore formed Fuji Kleinwort Benson, a joint venture with the British investment bank Kleinwort Benson's Chicago-based securities brokerage, Kleinwort Benson Government Securities, in 1973. In 1977 Fuji increased its interest in this company to 70% and changed its name to Fuji International Finance. Fuji also established Fuji Bank & Trust in New York in 1974 as a way of entering the trust business.

Kunihiko Sasaki, who led the company from 1971 to 1975, is credited with steering the bank through the difficult years of the energy crisis. Because Japan is totally dependent on foreign oil, the country's basic industries, including those within the Fuyo group, were severely affected. But the crisis created similar adversities in export markets, and demand for Japanese products remained high. Production slowed temporarily while markets adjusted to a new economic order. The latter half of the decade was marked by a strong recovery and expansion in the automobile sector, where Nissan was a major manufacturer.

Fuji forecasted a gradual decline in the rate of growth in the domestic economy many years before it occurred. It continued to take advantage of promising opportunities in the international market, thereby protecting itself against overconcentration in one market.

Under Takuji Matsuzawa, promoted from president to chairman in 1981, and Yoshiro Araki, who replaced him as president, Fuji purchased the financial subsidiaries of the Chicago-based Walter E. Heller International Corporation for $425 million in 1983. The acquisition gave Fuji an established client list and demonstrated the bank's growing commitment to American financial markets. It also promised to win Fuji greater participation in syndicated loans, an activity that was virtually monopolized by larger American banks. In 1986 Fuji made an additional $300 million investment in Heller to strengthen the company's business structure.

Araki, an outspoken advocate of financial deregulation in Japan, was promoted to chairman in 1987. He was replaced as president by Tanzo Hashida. Under these two men, Fuji made its first direct challenge to American securities laws when it attempted to take over its joint venture partner Kleinwort Benson Government Securities.

The U.S. Government opposed the takeover because Kleinwort Benson was a primary dealer of treasury securities, and control of such institutions was legally denied to foreign companies. In a compromise, Fuji was allowed to purchase a 24.9% share of Kleinwort Benson for $39.5 million. While it gave Fuji a far smaller stake than it had originally planned, it also discouraged hostile takeovers of Kleinwort Benson until American securities laws were altered and Fuji could complete the acquisition.

Fuji's international division performed outstandingly during the 1980s, and reported consistently increasing rates of growth. Domestic business, while representing a smaller share of total business, remains stable and strong. As a kind of coordinating body for the Fuyo group, Fuji enters the 1990s as a major international bank and leading member of one of Japan's most powerful industrial organizations.

Principal Subsidiaries: The Fuji Bank & Trust Co. (U.S.A.); Fuji Bank International, Inc. (U.S.A.); Heller International Corp. (U.S.A.); Heller Financial, Inc. (U.S.A.); Heller Overseas Corp. (U.S.A.); Fuji Bank Canada (Canada); Fuji Bank (Schweiz) AG (Switzerland); Fuji International Finance Ltd. (U.K.); Fuji Bank (Luxembourg) S.A.; Fuji Leasing (Deutschland) GmbH (Germany); Kwong On Bank, Ltd. (Hong Kong); Fuji International Finance (HK) Ltd. (Hong Kong); The Fuji Futures (Singapore) Pte. Ltd.; Fuji International Finance (Australia) Ltd.

Further Reading: The Fuji Bank, A 100th Anniversary Commemorative, Tokyo, The Fuji Bank, 1980.

GENERALE BANK (Générale de Banque)

Montagne du Parc 3
1000 Brussels
Belgium
(02) 518–21–11

Public Company
Incorpoated: 1934 as Banque de la Société Générale de Belgique
Employees: 16,367
Assets: BFr 2.33 trillion (US$62.42 billion)
Stock Index: Brussels

Generale Bank (known as Générale de Banque in French-speaking countries) is Belgium's largest bank, consisting of over 1,000 branches in Belgium and maintaining operations in 40 countries worldwide. Although the bank in its present form is the product of a 1965 merger between Banque de la Société Générale de Belgique, Société Belge de Banque, and Banque d'Anvers/Bank van Antwerpen, Generale Bank (GB) can trace its origins back to 1822. In that year the Algemeene Nederlandsche Maatschappij ter begunstiging van de Volksvlijt, or the General Company of the Netherlands for National Industry, was created to serve the financial needs of the southern Netherlands, united with Holland by the Congress of Vienna. In addition to being the world's first all-purpose bank, the General Company was the government cashier and the official issuer of banknotes for the Belgian provinces of the United Netherlands. During the 1820s the company established 20 branches throughout the Belgian provinces.

In 1830, upon the proclamation of the independent Kingdom of Belgium, the bank changed its name to Société Générale pour favoriser l'Industrie nationale, continuing its services and adding savings banks in the towns where it had established itself. Also in the 1830s, two subsidiaries were added to the holdings of Société Générale (SG). Although those particular subsidiaries did not survive past 1848, the trend of growth and acquisition was set.

Société Générale continued to be the issuer of banknotes for the Belgian kingdom until the creation of the National Bank of Belgium in 1850. During the 1850s and 1860s SG developed into what is generally considered to be the world's first joint-stock bank and was a forerunner of the modern investment company. SG accomplished this by making the assets of smaller depositors available for investment in large financial ventures. The bank served as a model for French joint-stock companies such as Credit Mobilier, which flourished during Napoleon III's Second Empire, financing much of the rebuilding of Paris of that period. As SG grew in the latter half of the 19th century, to 2,379 accounts in 1899 from 119 in 1866, it invested heavily in Russian mines and railroads as well as the increasing colonial activities of the European powers. In 1902 SG launched its foreign operations with the incorporation of the Banque Sino-Belge, in Shanghai. Shortly thereafter, the Banque Sino-Belge opened branches in Tien Tsin, Beijing, London, Paris, and Cairo. SG also helped establish Banque du Congo Belge (now Banque Belgo-Zairoise) in Belgian Congo and Banque Italo-Belge (now Banque Européenne pour l'Amerique Latine) in South America. In 1905 the name of the bank was officially changed to Société Générale de Belgique. In 1913 Banque Sino-Belge became an official subsidiary of SG, expanding its foreign operations and taking the name Banque Belge pour l'Etranger.

During World War I Société Générale temporarily moved the head office to its London branch because of the German occupation of Belgium. In 1914 the Germans prohibited the National Bank of Belgium from issuing banknotes and SG undertook this function for the duration of the war, issuing approximately two billion Belgian francs. SG ran afoul of the German authorities for refusing to exchange their German marks (which were legal tender in occupied Belgium) for credits with German banks. The Germans threatened to close SG's doors, but instead seized the German money. SG was finally convinced to allow its circulation.

Between wars SG continued its expansion, founding Banque Générale du Luxembourg. Banque Belge pour L'Etranger also grew, opening new branches in New York, Istanbul, and Hong Kong, among other cities. In addition, SG had banking interests in Portugal, Spain, and much of Eastern Europe. The year before its 100th anniversary, in 1922, SG's books showed credits amounting to BFr 4.1 billion and debits of BFr 2.1 billion.

The losses that financial institutions suffered during the Depression led to banking reform in Belgium during the 1930s. Reform was initiated mainly to protect small depositors and investors who during the Depression had often watched helplessly as uninsured assets melted away. In August, 1934 mixed banks were outlawed and had to be separated into financial societies and deposit banks. Thereafter only certain rigidly defined types of institutions were entitled to use the word "bank" in their names. "The name bank," the decree read, "is reserved for those enterprises which usually collect deposits payable on demand or within no more than two years, so as to use them on their own account." Also, banks were enjoined from acquiring stocks or shares of any kind. In practice, however, this prohibition was filled with loopholes and Belgian banks still hold stocks, albeit to a much lesser degree than previously. In 1935 the Belgian Banking Commission was created to oversee the banking industry in Belgium. The commission was placed under the authority of the minister of finance, rendering the banks more accountable to government.

In accordance with the royal decree of August 1934, Société Générale de Belgique was split into a holding company, which retained the same name, and a bank, called Banque de la Société Générale de Belgique (BSGB). Despite the effects of the Depression and the ensuing government regulation, BSGB emerged in good shape and continued to expand during the 1930s, increasing its assets and adding more offices at home and abroad.

The German invasion and occupation in 1939 severely curtailed BSGB's ability to conduct normal operations. No major innovations or developments occured during the six years hiatus imposed by the war. When the war ended in 1945, BSGB numbered 350 offices throughout the world.

After the treaty of Rome in 1957, which initiated the European Economic Community, BSGB forged a cooperative agreement with the Dutch Amsterdamsche Bank (now Amro Bank) and the German Deutsche Bank. The group was called the "Bachelors Club," alluding to the informal nature of the association, whereby each bank retained managerial autonomy. In 1963 this group was joined by the British Midland Bank and was renamed the European Advisory Committee. In 1970 the group was incorporated in Belgium and operated under the name of European Banks International Company, subsequently adding the French bank Société Générale, the Austrian Creditanstalt Bankverein, and the Italian Banca Commerciale Italiana to the fold. The committee also sought transatlantic connections, founding the European-American Banking Corporation in New York in 1968. In the Belgian Congo, the kingdom's colonial jewel, BSGB's affiliate maintained operations after the Congo became independent in 1960, although the company split into two banks, one operating under Belgian law and the other under Congolese. In Egypt, on the other hand, the Banque Belge et Internationale en Egypte was nationalized by the United Arab Republic.

In 1965 BSGB merged with Banque d'Anvers/Bank van Antwerpen and Société Belge de Banque to create Société Générale de Banque. The merger greatly increased the capital resources of the bank as well as adding more facilities and employees. After the merger Société Générale de Banque (SGB) operated 738 offices and employed a staff of almost 11,000.

In the 1970s and 1980s SGB found itself faced with two major challenges: to adapt and prepare itself for the eventual economic integration of Europe, and to solidify and protect its own position in the Belgian banking industry. The trend toward consolidation in Europe placed smaller financial concerns in danger of being swallowed whole, regardless of the protocols drawn up by the Belgian Banking Commission in 1974 to protect the independence of banks whose assets were still partly controlled by holding companies. Société Générale de Belgique, the holding company formerly related to SGB, still controlled 22% of the bank's assets in 1975.

To keep abreast of the technological improvements in banking, SGB modernized and streamlined its services. In 1972 the bank introduced the Eurocheque card, which enabled the holder to perform transactions in Belgium, Luxembourg, and Germany. SGB also joined the Swift network in 1977, which linked the 500 largest banks in 15 countries, and introduced the "Mister Cash" automated teller machine, the first in Belgium. In 1979 SGB also bought shares in Eurocard, making that service available to its customers, and in 1982 the Euro-Traveller's Check was added.

In the mid-1980s SGB displayed a new sensitivity to the banking needs of smaller customers. Commercial banking on a large scale had been the traditional forte of SGB, but the increasing competition and consolidation of the 1980s has made the importance of personal and small-business banking services evident. SGB realized that to remain a competitive force in European banking it would be necessary to take a broader view of its role and cater its services to a more diverse public. This shift in philosophy followed upon the heels of yet another name change in 1985: the bank was thereafter known as Générale de Banque in French-speaking countries and Generale Bank elsewhere.

In 1988 Generale Bank established even closer ties with the Dutch Amsterdam-Rotterdam Bank (Amro), when, following the breakdown of a merger agreement due to technical problems, the two banks agreed to continue to cooperate informally.

Also in 1988 a dramatic year-long takeover battle was waged between Italian financier Carlo de Benedetti and a Franco-Belgian group headed by the French company Financiere de Suez, over Société Générale de Belgique. SGB still held 13.4% of GB and any takeover of SGB would be certain to have an impact on the bank. In the end de Benedetti's hostile bid foundered due to his inability to attract any support from Belgian financial institutions and he agreed to reduce his stake in SGB from 45% to 15%. Financiere de Suez assumed control of the holding company, but Generale Bank maintained its independence. Subsequently GB has sought to increase its capital reserves in order to be in a better position to resist takeover attempts in the future.

GB, as Belgium's largest bank, has a direct role to play in the workings of the country's economy. By the end of 1984 the bank was underwriting nearly a third of Belgium's large public debt. The Belgian government has followed a policy of financing its debt mainly with domestic capital. GB has supported this policy by cooperating in a cartel with the second- and third-largest banks in Belgium, Kredietbank and Bank Bruxelles Lambert, to ensure a supply of domestic capital. GB has also taken a leading role in financing Belgium's exports, a key ingredient in Belgium's continued economic health.

Principal Subsidiaries: Générale de Banque Belge (France); Generale Bank & Co. (West Germany); Belga Finanziaria (Italy); Generale Bank Overseas (Belgium) (Hong Kong); Generale Belgian Finance Company (Hong Kong); Banque Européenne pour l'Amerique Latine; Banque Belo-Zairoise; Generale Investment Banking Corporation (United States); Quin Cope Ltd. (United Kingdom); Compagnie de Gestion et de Banque Gonet (Switzerland); Banque Belge Ltd. (United Kingdom); Banque Belge Trust Company Ltd. (Guernsey); Generale Bank & Trust (Bahamas) Ltd.

THE HONGKONG AND SHANGHAI BANKING CORPORATION LIMITED

1 Queen's Road Central
Hong Kong
(05) 822–1111

Public Company
Incorporated: 1866
Employees: 52,000
Assets: HK$883.7 billion (US$113.16 billion)
Stock Index: Hong Kong London

The Hongkong and Shanghai Banking Corporation, or HonkongBank as it is commonly known, is one of the largest and most successful banks in the world. Hong Kong, under British control since 1842, has grown into the most dynamic commercial center on the Asian mainland. The HongkongBank has taken full advantage of its position as the leading "home-town" bank and as a natural intermediary between economic interests from politically opposed nations in the region. Few other institutions are as influential in the "China market" as the HongkongBank (indeed, the bank's Shanghai office has remained open continually since 1865) and fewer still have as much influence in Hong Kong.

In the early 1860s, Hong Kong began to emerge as a major commercial center on the coast of the impoverished south China plain. Western commercial interests, under the protection of British guns, conducted a highly profitable trade in tea, opium, and silk. The *hongs*, as these interests were called, resented the sudden arrival of India- and London-based opportunists in the mid-19th century.

When the local *taipans* ("big bosses") heard that a group of financiers based in Bombay planned to establish a "Bank of China" in Hong Kong, they were outraged that local interests would only be offered a limited number of shares. In response, Thomas Sutherland, the Hong Kong superintendent of the Peninsular and Oriental Steam Navigation Company, formulated a prospectus for a bank based on "sound Scottish banking principles." He organized a group of local business leaders, and within a matter of days had established a banking cooperative capitalized at HK$5 million. When the "Bank of China" representative arrived in Hong Kong some weeks later, he found no interest in his bank, its shares, or even its directorships.

The Hongkong and Shanghai Banking Company opened for business in Hong Kong on March 3, 1865, in Shanghai April 3, and in London some months later. Members of the cooperative included American, German, Scandinavian, and Parsee Indian merchant houses, as well as representatives from the Bombay-based David Sassoon & Company and Hong Kong–based Dent & Company. The largest companies in Hong Kong, Jardine Matheson and the American firm Russell & Company, were not represented. The highly favorable response to the bank by foreign interests and *compradores* (Chinese business agents), however, led both to reconsider and join.

An international financial crisis in 1865–1866 could have destroyed the bank. Instead, with financial support from its members, the bank took over the operations of failed competitors and hired their staff. Dent, meanwhile, the dominant Hong Kong member of the group, went bankrupt. But instead of hurting the cooperative, Dent's failure allowed broader representation by more diverse local interests.

The directors of the bank began to investigate methods of incorporation in order to limit their liability. The two forms of incorporation then available to the bank were under colonial regulations or the British banking code, but both required that it locate its head office in Great Britain—a move which would have defeated the original purpose of the bank. After substantial lobbying of the British treasury, the HongkongBank received special permission to incorporate locally, under colonial banking laws, in December, 1866.

In addition to its branches in Hong Kong, Shanghai, and London, the bank set up offices in Yokohama in 1866, San Francisco in 1875, New York in 1880, Lyons in 1881, and Hamburg in 1889. By 1900, additional offices had been established in India, the Philippines, Singapore, Burma, Ceylon, Malaya, and Vietnam.

The bank established its official status early by lending money to the colonial government and attempting to revive the Hong Kong Mint. It was also actively involved in foreign exchange transactions. Because the bank performed official functions in Hong Kong, its directors, all prominent businessmen in the community, had easy access to insider information. So, in order to preserve the integrity of the bank as well as their own businesses, they voluntarily relinquished management of the bank to non-executives.

During this period, from 1876 to 1902, the bank was heavily influenced by its chief manager, Thomas Jackson. Jackson had attempted on three occasions to retire. Each time, however, severe problems befell his successors and he was called back. Jackson was regarded as a prudent manager who kept the bank from insolvency under highly volatile conditions by backing sterling operations only with sterling funds, and backing operations in the East with silver, the common currency.

The HongkongBank issued currency for the government (a practice which continues today), and advised on currency reforms in Japan, Thailand, the Philippines, China, Korea, and the Straits Settlements (Penang and

Singapore). Through a powerful *compradore* in China, the bank established contacts with local officials in Tianjin and Beijing. The bank was later asked to issue a public loan on behalf of the Chinese government, and directed several more in ensuing years. While some of these loans financed China's war against Japan (1894–1895) and the enforcement of peace during internal conflicts such as the Boxer Rebellion in 1900, the bulk were used for infrastructural projects such as railroads, coal mines, and shipping lines.

The bank was able to develop a very favorable rapport with the government and business interests in China mainly because it had a widespread presence in China and was incorporated in Hong Kong. By 1910 it was the favored intermediary of the multinational China Consortium, a result of the demonstrated effectiveness of the Bank's London manager, Sir Charles Addis.

World War I deeply divided the bank, still well represented by both Germans and Britons. The German members of its board, identified in the press as "hostile interests," eventually resigned, marking a more or less permanent end to German participation in the company. Still, the bank's Hamburg office remained open for the duration of the war.

The high price of silver after the war led the bank to make a rights issue to finance an expansion. Chief Manager A. G. Stephen presided over the construction of new facilities in Hankow, Bangkok, Manila, and especially Shanghai, where a new office was opened in 1923. An office opened in Vladivostok in 1918 but was forced to close in 1924, when Russian revolutionary forces completed their consolidation of control over Siberia.

The optimism of the early 1920s crashed after 1929 and continued to deteriorate through the 1930s, as Japanese interests moved into China, this time supported by Japanese guns. At first, the Japanese domination of China was limited to the rich hinterlands of Manchuria and consisted mainly of the commercial exploitation of resources. While the bank was permitted to establish offices in the Manchurian cities of Dairen, Mukden, and Harbin, its operations were limited only to foreign trade. Meanwhile, in the rest of China, the bank experienced new competition from an increasingly sophisticated Chinese banking community.

At the same time, the bank was losing business from the Philippine government and was discriminated against in Indonesia and Vietnam by Dutch and French colonial authorities. Despite generous lending and other support tactics for customers involved in rubber and other volatile commodities trades, bank profits continued to deteriorate. In many cases, competitors complained that the bank's extraordinary care "exceeded the limits of prudent lending." The bank was, however, founded on cooperative precepts, and continued to operate on that basis. Still, it was the shareholders who suffered; shareholder's funds fell from £9.1 million in 1918 to £8.6 million in 1940.

The number of Hong Kong dollars in circulation, 80% of which were printed by the Hongkong and Shanghai Bank, increased from HK$50 million in 1927 to HK$200 million in 1940. In effect, the bank backed HK$160 million of the colony's currency—a dangerous exposure to the local economy, despite transferring the currency from a silver to sterling standard. The bank became involved in an even more unmanageable currency-stabilization effort in Shanghai, from which it eventually had to bow out, turning the scheme over to a government board.

The Japanese occupation of China, meanwhile, had become extremely brutal. Terror bombings, invasion, and a Japanese military riot in Nanking stifled commerce in China and isolated Hong Kong from its Chinese hinterland. Sensing imminent danger, the bank's chief manager, Vandeleur Grayburn, authorized the immediate transfer of silver reserves into sterling assets in London. On December 8, 1940, shortly after completing the transfer, Japanese troops stormed through Hong Kong's New Territories, and on Christmas won a surrender.

Bank staff in Manchuria, Japan, and Indochina were repatriated, and those in Burma and Singapore escaped to India. Employees in China, particularly Foochow, managed to reach Chungking, where the bank opened a formal office in 1943. The staff in Hong Kong were much less fortunate; most of them who were of European descent were imprisoned.

Under prearranged orders from Grayburn, the bank's London manager, Arthur Morse, assumed managerial control of the bank. Morse transferred the dollar-denominated assets located in Hong Kong to London, fearing that if the Japanese gained control of them, the assets would be frozen by the U.S. government. In light of the circumstances—the bank's board was interned in Hong Kong—Morse was named both chief manager and chairman. During the occupation, Japanese authorities forced the bank to issue additional currency in order to support the local economy. Grayburn and his designated successor, D. C. Edmonston, meanwhile, died in prison.

The war ended so suddenly in August, 1945 that Hong Kong remained occupied when Japan surrendered. With colonial authorities back in control, the bank began the difficult and costly task of rebuilding. The amortization of banknotes issued under the occupation cost HK$16 million, and new legislation only permitted the bank to collect debts from enemy interests in depreciated occupation currencies.

Despite its weakened condition, the bank played a major role in the reconstruction of Hong Kong, a task Morse began planning well before the war ended. All the company's branches were reopened—with the exception of Hamburg which, again, had remained open during the war—including those in Japan. By 1947, however, new problems arose in China, where the wartime alliance between Chiang Kai-shek's nationalists and Mao Tse-tung's communists had degenerated into a civil war. The immediate effects were severe inflation and increasing public disorder.

By October, 1949 the communists had gained control of the mainland and the nationalists had fled to Taiwan. When an initial plea by the communists for reconstruction in cooperation with capitalists was suddenly reversed in 1950, industrialists fled China—especially Shanghai—for Hong Kong. The bank maintained offices in Shanghai, Beijing, Tianjin, and Shantou until 1955, when all but the Shanghai branch were closed. The Chinese, it seemed, preferred to do all their business through Hong Kong.

After the war, the British government practiced a "non-extractive" economic policy in Hong Kong which, coupled with the entrepreneurial talent of industrialists transplanted from Shanghai and a labor force swelled by thousands of mainland refugees, created a powerful economic base. The bank financed hundreds of new ventures that helped the colony achieve unprecedented export-led growth. The growth of the textile industry in Hong Kong, however, led the bank to fear that it had become overexposed to that one industry.

Under Michael Turner, the HongkongBank adopted a new strategy of expansion using subsidiaries during the mid-1950s. Initially made necessary by American banking legislation, the subsidiary form of organization was first used in 1955 to establish a branch in California—one step toward reducing its dependence on Hong Kong.

Because Britain relinquished much of its empire after the war, British companies were forced to rationalize, by merger, acquisition, or nationalization. Indeed, many went bankrupt. Two such companies, the Mercantile Bank (formerly the Chartered Mercantile Bank of India, London and China) and the British Bank of the Middle East (known as BBME, formerly the Imperial Bank of Persia), were purchased by the Hongkong and Shanghai Bank in 1959. The addition of the Mercantile Bank, with an extensive branch network in India, and the BBME, strongly represented in the Persian Gulf, made the HongkongBank the largest foreign bank in most of the countries from the Far East to southwest Asia.

Having reduced its exposure to Hong Kong, the bank moved next to diversify operationally. In 1960 it created Wayfoong, a consumer financing group whose name translates loosely as "focus of wealth."

A banking crisis in Hong Kong in 1964 led to a serious run on a competitor, the Hang Seng Bank. As the primary financial institution in Hong Kong and de facto central bank, the HongkongBank, while under no statutory duty to do so, acquired a majority interest in Hang Seng in 1965. Hang Seng subsequently recovered, and today is the second-largest bank incorporated in Hong Kong.

The HongkongBank's expansion through subsidiaries began in earnest with the creation in 1972 of Wardley Ltd., a merchant bank, and an insurance company called Carlingford. The bank also made numerous other investments—in Cathay Pacific Airways, the World-Wide shipping group, and the *South China Morning Post*. All these investments proved highly profitable in light of Hong Kong's rapid economic growth. In addition, the BBME benefited greatly from the newly prosperous oil-based economies in the Persian Gulf. In 1978, however, BBME branches in Saudi Arabia were taken over by the Saudi British Bank, a Saudi-controlled bank in which BBME retained management control, but only 40% ownership.

Under the leadership of Michael Sandberg, the HongkongBank re-examined its position in America as part of a wider strategy to gain greater representation in the major Western economies. The Hongkong and Shanghai Bank of California was sold and the bank purchased a 51% share of the Marine Midland Banks, a New York–based bank holding company, in 1980. The HongkongBank bought the outstanding shares of Marine Midland in 1987. This acquisition inspired substantial debate in the U.S. Congress about whether banking laws should be strengthened to prevent foreign companies from gaining control over American banks.

The bank expanded in several ways during 1980. In China, the Shanghai branch was expanded and a representative office was established in Beijing. In addition, the BBME relocated from London to Hong Kong, and the bank gained control of Concord International, a leasing and finance group, and Anthony Gibbs, a British merchant bank. The following year, a Canadian subsidiary, the Hongkong Bank of Canada, was established in Vancouver. In 1986 the Hongkong Bank of Canada acquired the business of the Bank of British Columbia, bringing the number of branches across Canada to 61.

A bidding war over the Royal Bank of Scotland Group between the HongkongBank and Standard & Chartered (which issues Hong Kong's other currency) was halted by the British Monopolies & Mergers Commission in 1981. Meanwhile, the bank succeeded in establishing a presence in Africa in 1981 through the acquisition of a controlling interest in Equator Bank by its merchant bank subsidiary Wardley; in Cyprus in 1982, also primarily through Wardley; and in Australia in 1985, when it established HongkongBank of Australia.

In December, 1987 HongkongBank entered into an association with Midland Bank, one of four major British clearing banks, when it made the friendly acquisition of 14.9% of Midland's stock. HongkongBank has agreed not to increase its stake in Midland until December, 1990, but to date the association has allowed mutual rationalization. Where this partnership will ultimately lead has yet to be determined.

Despite the bank's growth outside of Hong Kong, it still maintains a commanding presence there. With over 260 branches in the colony and an impressive new headquarters building in the financial district, the HongkongBank has demonstrated a commitment to the territory's future—a future that includes the transfer of Hong Kong from British to Chinese control in 1997.

The bank's most worrisome competitor may well be the mainland-incorporated Bank of China, which has erected an even more impressive skyscraper, designed by I. M. Pei, down the street. Regarded by many as a demonstration of China's willingness to maintain the economic dynamism and stability of Hong Kong, the Bank of China's high profile has led the HongkongBank to improve banking services in the territory. In addition to its traditional banking operations, the bank has emphasized growth in international capital markets, centered in London and New York, and has disposed of other peripheral interests, such as that in the *South China Morning Post*.

Having endured virtually every kind of crisis in the most volatile environments, the Hongkong and Shanghai Bank has emerged older, wiser, and stronger. Its excellent relationship with the Chinese government surely places it in a preferred position to lead future investment in Chinese ventures, as well as to play a major role in Hong Kong after 1997.

Principal Subsidiaries: Hang Seng Bank; HongkongBank of Australia; HongkongBank of Canada; James Capel; Marine Midland Bank; The British Bank of the Middle East; Wardley.

Further Reading: Collis, Maurice. *Wayfoong: The Hong Kong and Shanghai Banking Corporation*, London, Faber and Faber, 1965.

THE INDUSTRIAL BANK OF JAPAN, LTD.

1–3–3, Marunouchi
Chiyoda-ku
Tokyo 100
Japan
(03) 214–1111

Public company
Incorporated: 1902
Employees: 5,250
Assets: ¥33.87 trillion (US$271 billion)
Stock Index: Tokyo Osaka

The Industrial Bank of Japan, or IBJ, is almost exclusively a banker to industry. It is regarded by many as a semi-autonomous government agency that acts closely with various ministries to achieve wider national economic goals. It is, in effect, the banker's bank, acting as a primary source of funds and coordinating new bond issues and debentures for government and industry.

The IBJ was created by the Japanese government shortly after the Sino-Japanese War (1894–1895). Only 25 years before, Japan had ended a centuries-old isolation and embarked on an ambitious modernization. But Japanese industry required inexpensive and reliable sources of raw materials. China held great promise, not only for Japan but for several other imperialist powers, because of its vast forestry and mineral resources.

As a result of its war with China, Japan won rights to these resources in addition to substantial war-reparation payments. The Japanese government studied ways to manage these payments most efficiently, and created three development banks. In 1902 it chartered the Kangyo Bank for agricultural finance, the Hokkaido Takushoku Bank for the development of Japan's northernmost island, Hokkaido, and the Industrial Bank of Japan to supply stagnant domestic industries with long-term funding and to develop the bond market.

The Russo-Japanese War (1904–1905) was Japan's first engagement with a European power. Its victory in that war greatly increased Japanese influence in the region, but the mobilization seriously depleted bank capital. With Japanese industries unable to finance further expansion, the IBJ borrowed heavily from European sources to make capital available to Japanese industry for modernization and expansion.

The IBJ grew with Japanese industry throughout the 1920s and 1930s by financing the construction of integrated steel mills and modern shipyards. As an instrument of government, the IBJ was motivated neither by private interest or private profit.

A right-wing militarist element, which by the mid-1930s had gained control of the government, sought to establish Japanese supremacy in Asia. Opposed at first by political moderates and Japanese industrialists, the militarists eventually won power. By the time the government declared a "quasi-wartime economy" in the late 1930s, the *zaibatsu*, or large "money clique" conglomerates, participated in the mobilization—as much for profit as for political survival.

With the *zaibatsu* brought under the same strict central control as agencies like the IBJ, the Japanese economy was forcibly concentrated in order to raise economic efficiency. While commercial businesses concentrated on military production and the development of occupied territories, the IBJ became involved with the increasingly burdensome task of financing the war against China, and later against the United States; during this time the bank's debts increased from ¥2.7 billion to ¥14.6 billion.

The IBJ survived relatively intact. Instead of financing industrial expansion, however, its new task under the occupation was to assist in the reconstruction of Japan. The bank created a special reconstruction-finance department staffed by 96 men. The department was separated from the IBJ in 1947 and named the Nippon Fukokin Kinyu Koku, or Japan Reconstruction Finance Bank and reorganized in 1952 as the Japan Development Bank.

The American occupation authority undertook a massive decentralization of the Japanese economy by breaking up the *zaibatsu* and forcing the government to make state-owned businesses, including the IBJ, private. Under the Long Term Credit Bank Law, the IBJ was sold to private investors in 1950. Its purpose, however, remained the same: to provide long-term funding for stagnant and undercapitalized firms. The bank continued to serve in a semiofficial capacity and maintained its connections in government and its access to key ministries and agencies.

Japan's industrial sector, which the IBJ had concentrated on developing for over 50 years, finally began to mature in the early 1950s. For nearly 20 years the Japanese economy maintained an annual growth rate of 10%, which provided the IBJ and other long-term credit banks with strong and stable development. As the largest issuer of government and corporate bonds, in addition to its own debentures, the IBJ held tremendous sway over the determination of long-term interest rates.

The appearance of IBJ representatives on the boards of its clients became more conspicuous after the securities crisis of 1966. The IBJ appointed presidents to three of the four major securities houses: Yamaichi, Daiwa, and Nikko, and played a major role in the creation of Nippon Steel, the world's largest steel company, through the merger of Yawata Steel and Fuji Steel in 1970.

Japanese industry, which depends heavily on imported raw materials, was dealt a severe blow during the 1973 oil crisis. Many of the IBJ's largest clients were suddenly faced with drastically weakened markets and even bankruptcy. In the recession that followed, capital investment was either scaled down or canceled altogether. As interest rates rose, the bank's clients paid back much of their debt by liquidating assets or arranging their own financing—either taking their business back from the IBJ or seeking financing in less competitive foreign-loan and bond markets. Within Japan, IBJ debentures suffered from the developing *gensaki* bond-repurchase market and an increasingly sophisticated Tokyo stock market.

Threatened with the possibility of its own redundancy in several important markets, IBJ altered its business strategy. The research department sorted IBJ's existing and potential clients into ones that were successful, ones that needed reorganization, and ones that should be abandoned. The IBJ became more active in its clients' industries and, with the full support of the Japanese government, remade several businesses. Not surprisingly, at times the IBJ was resented for the ruthlessness of its reorganization schemes and criticized for the arrogant and presumptuous manner in which its representatives presided over clients' board meetings.

Nevertheless, several troubled companies, including Toyo Soda, Nippon Soda, the Keisei Electric Railway, and Chisso Chemical, were successfully rehabilitated. For that reason many regard a loan from the IBJ as an insurance policy. Competitors made similar industrial rescues, but often lost hundreds of millions of yen in the process. The IBJ, on the other hand, made a profit from saving companies.

One of the largest projects to be underwritten by the IBJ was a $3.2 billion petrochemical complex at Bandar-e-Shapur (later Bandar Khomeini) in Iran. Iranian revolutionaries halted construction on the plant in the early 1980s, when it was 80% finished, because they regarded Japan as too sympathetic to the United States. The plant was later bombed by Iraqi jets, leaving its eventual completion in doubt.

Although a late entrant into international finance—the IBJ received permission to establish overseas branches only in 1971—the IBJ was nevertheless quick to notice a weakening in the Third World lending market. In 1983 the bank refused to lend money to the Philippines in anticipation of a credit crisis, which duly materialized a few months later. The IBJ has not, however, shunned all investment in developing countries; it has simply managed its risk differently. Unlike many of its competitors, it has chosen to participate in specific projects rather than lend outright to government sponsors.

Careful risk management, in addition to a statutory right to finance itself with more stable long-term debentures, earned the IBJ a successful entrance into European financial markets, allowing it to become a major player in the securities industry. The IBJ remained a lead banker to about 180 of Japan's top 200 firms, marketing both yen-dominated bonds and Japanese government securities.

Much of the credit for the IBJ's recovery from the crisis of the 1970s goes to Kisaburo Ikeura. President of the bank from 1974 to 1983, Ikeura was replaced as president by Kaneo Nakamura, but continued to serve as chairman. One question facing Nakamura was whether to expand into the more stable but highly competitive consumer-banking market. Because it suffered from a lack of branches, any growth in this area would have had to come externally—that is, by acquisition. Instead, the IBJ decided to expand in international securities markets.

The IBJ already occupied an important position in European markets with an English subsidiary, IBJ International, and the Industrial Bank of Japan (Switzerland), which conducts both banking and securities services. The IBJ expanded into the United States by purchasing, through subsidiaries, Aubrey G. Lanston Company, an important dealer in U.S. government securities. Although the U.S. government preserved management control of Lanston, the IBJ has still gained a "ringside seat" at the Federal Reserve.

The IBJ's broad exposure to international markets has made it more sensitive to changes in the value of the yen. Its emphasis on long-term credit, however, brings much of that risk to within acceptable margins. While it competes with the Long Term Credit Bank and the Bank of Tokyo, the IBJ has established and (with government help, some say) protected an important niche in the institutional banking and securities markets. In addition, the IBJ must compete in an increasingly less protectionist international environment. This has resulted in a lower, though not altogether unpredictable, squeeze on growth rates and profits.

Principal Subsidiaries: The Industrial Bank of Japan Trust Company; IBJ Schroder Bank & Trust Company; The Industrial Bank of Japan (Canada); IBJ International Limited; Industriebank von Japan (Deutschland) Aktiengesellschaft; The Industrial Bank of Japan (Luxembourg) S.A.; The Industrial Bank of Japan (Switzerland) Limited; IBJ Asia Limited; IBJ Merchant Bank (Singapore) Limited; P.T. Bumi-Daya-IBJ Leasing; IBJ Australia Bank Limited.

KANSALLIS-OSAKE-PANKKI

KANSALLIS-OSAKE-PANKKI

Aleksanterinkatu 42
P.O. Box 10
SF-00101
Helsinki
Finland

Public Company
Incorporated: 1889 as Kansallis Banken
Employees: 9,492
Assets: FIM144.61 billion (US$34.7 billion)
Stock Index: Helsinki Luxembourg

Long known as Finland's largest commercial bank, Kansallis-Osake-Pankki has developed into a multifaceted financial-services organization. As the parent company of the Kansallis Banking group, Kansallis-Osake-Pankki steers the operations of five main sectors, according to a reorganization that took effect in January, 1988: corporate banking, retail and private banking, international banking, investment banking, and domestic and international trading.

In 1889, the year Kansallis was founded, Finland was an autonomous grand duchy of the Russian Empire. It had been part of the Russian Empire for 80 years, and, before that, had been under Swedish rule for more than half a millennium. Yet, despite these centuries of foreign domination, and perhaps partly because of their relative isolation from other cultures, Finns retained a strong sense of national identity and a desire for independence.

In the 1880s, the Finns began to press their claim to a national identity. The power to make those claims a reality, they realized, could only come by developing economic strength.

In early summer, 1889, five men met at the Finnish Club of Helsinki. August Hjelt was an economist, Otto Stenroth was a lawyer, Otto Hjelt was a merchant, and Matti Äyräpää was a professor of medicine. With Lauri Kivekas, a student leader and a lawyer, they decided to create a commercial bank. By June 27, they had raised an amount roughly equivalent to 50 million of today's Finnish marks, and they held a meeting with representatives controlling over 3,400 shares. By September 12, they had a banking license, and in a month, the bank was a reality. The first branch, opened the following February, stood on the site of today's Helsinki-Aleksanterinkatu branch.

Otto Hjelt became Kansallis's first chief general manager. His aggressive marketing techniques got the bank off to a brisk start. Finland's economy was largely dependent on forestry and agriculture, but some new companies were being formed that reflected the European and American trend toward industrialization. Those companies, and others that transferred their accounts to Kansallis in the hope of obtaining better service, constituted the new bank's clientele.

But within a few years, a general slowdown in the economy caused the bank's growth to falter. In the crisis that followed, the directors dismissed Hjelt in 1892.

Hjelt had been a daring banker—he had been the first banker in Finland to resort regularly to central bank credit. His successor, F. K. Nybom, was an experience banker who took a more cautious approach to his responsibilities and reorganized the bank, curtailing lending operations.

Within a few years, despite an approach so conservative that he favored granting credit through bills of exchange, the bank again began to prosper. By 1914, Kansallis's deposits were close to those of its competitors, the Union Bank of Finland and Pohjoismainen Osakepankki (the Nordic Joint Stock Bank). But Nybom incurred the disfavor of the directors by investing large amounts of money in fledgling companies. He resigned in 1914, having led the bank through a growth period that added 40 branch offices. The companies in which he had invested the bank's funds eventually proved the wisdom of his judgment, however—United Paper Mills, Kajaani Oy, and Rauma-Repola, for example, all became successful businesses.

During the Nybom years, radical changes on the political scene had worked, along with economic growth, to strengthen Finland's fervor for nationalism and drive to become independent. Under Russian rule, as under Swedish rule, Finland had been a grand duchy, but with one difference: where Sweden had sent its own staff to Finland to rule what was considered at that time to be a "backward" people, Russia had delegated Finnish rule to local bureaucrats. Burdened by war with Japan and preoccupied by defeat in 1905, the Russian government scarcely appeared to notice when Finland made a fundamental change in local rule in 1906, replacing the Diet of the Four Estates with a unicameral body granting universal and equal voting rights to men and women.

J. K. Paasikivi, an astute businessman, took over the position as chief general manager of Kansallis in 1914 and restructured the organization. The result was unprecedented growth that swelled the number of branches to 120 in a few years and made Kansallis Finland's largest bank.

The Bolshevik Revolution in 1917 created the opportunity Finland had awaited for so many years—to declare itself a free and independent nation, which it did that year. By 1919, Finland was firmly established as a republic. In that same year, Kansallis lost its number-one position in the nation's banking community when its two principal competitors merged.

But Paasikivi's leadership helped Kansallis pursue opportunities for further growth. It took just eight years for Kansallis to regain its number-one position. By the early 1930s, when the worldwide Depression had begun to cause serious disruptions in Finland's economy,

Kansallis was able to absorb one of the nation's largest commercial banks, Maakuntain Pankki (founded through the merger of Tampereen Osake-Pankki, Lansi-Suomen Osake-Pankki, and Maakuntain Keskus-Pankki). In 1933 Luotto-Pankki Oy was added to the Kansallis group.

Just as Paasikivi had been credited with Kansallis's expansion and growth into financial interests far beyond its core commercial-banking structure, he was criticized when businesses hurt by the Depression failed and Kansallis had to foreclose.

At odds with the chairman of Kansallis's supervisory board, Paasikivi resigned in 1934, but his general policies continued to be effective in the hands of his successor, Mauri Honkajuuri, who had worked closely with him as his assistant. These policies served Kansallis well as the economy began to recover in the late 1930s. Even after November, 1939, when the Soviet Union invaded Finland and throughout World War II, Kansallis continued to function, keeping money flowing to the Finnish business community.

There were losses as a result of the war, of course. Most notably, the Karelian Territory, ceded to the Soviet Union in the peace treaties of 1940 and 1947, contained about 20 of Kansallis's branch offices.

A period of revitalization and reconstruction followed the war. In 1948, Mauri Honkajuuri died in office, and Matti Virkkunen, 39, became the chief general manager. Adopting an aggressive growth policy, Virkkunen engineered the acquisition of Pohjolan Osakepankki (the Northern Joint Stock Bank) that year.

An interest-rate agreement that allowed regional banks to offer higher interest rates on deposits hampered Kansallis, as it did other large commercial banks. Virkkunen led a vigorous effort to make the situation more competitive. His success led to the adoption of a uniform interest-rate system in the early 1950s, and enhanced Kansallis's strength.

During the 1950s, Finnish banking habits began to change. Salaries began to be paid by check, individuals established personal accounts, lending to individuals became commonplace, and households became a major market—a market Kansallis was able to attract in increasing numbers as it branch offices proliferated throughout the country.

At the same time, the small industrial and retail companies Kansallis had assisted in funding through their start-up years had grown, in many cases, along with the bank, and Kansallis had attracted a large corporate clientele.

Throughout the 1960s and 1970s, Kansallis established itself as a major international banking organization. The first step was entry into joint Nordic consortium banks. Branches were established in London, New York, the Cayman Islands, and Singapore. Other offices are located in Stockholm, Hong Kong, Moscow, Frankfurt, and Tokyo, and Kansallis operates a worldwide network with a broad range of banking services.

Domestic and foreign expansion promoted steady growth during the 27 years of Virkkunen's leadership, but it also created financial stress that undermined the bank's profits. Finland's economy was also strained by the effects of the worldwide oil crisis in the early 1970s. By the time Veikko Makkonen became Kansallis's chief general manager in 1975, it was apparent that the bank was entering a period of retrenchment in which the highest priority had to be placed on improving profitability. New strategies and new sources of profit were developed. For example, in 1979, Kansallis entered the U. S. commercial paper market. In 1980, it issued its first floating-rate Eurodollar CDs.

Makkonen succeeded so well in restoring a relatively stable level of profitability that at the time that Jaako Lassila took over leadership of Kansallis in 1983, the bank was on solid footing and ready to resume its expansionist programs. International expansion and deregulation worked together to create a lively money market business. However, the structure of the Finnish money market dictated relatively high interest rates on deposits and relatively low rates on loans; together with a low currency exchange rate, these conditions diminished the profitability of money market instruments.

More reliable sources of income over the years have been Kansallis's extensive investment-banking program, its corporate-advisory services—particularly in the rash of mergers and acquisitions during the 1980s—and its comprehensive retail- and private-banking services. Kansallis handles the majority of financial transactions within the nation and the majority of foreign payments. As computerization has speeded these processes, it has also increased the bank's profit margin.

A reorganization that took effect in 1988 created a cluster system for Kansallis's branch banking, streamlining operations and increasing profitability through a profit-center concept. Electronic funds-transfer operations at point of sale for retail businesses and a microcomputer-based information system expanded the bank's services.

Also during 1988, Kansallis entered into an agreement with the Swedish bank Proventus A.B. that resulted in joint ownership of a holding company and the sale of a Kansallis Swedish subsidiary to Götabanken, a move that provided Kansallis with improved opportunities for operating in the Swedish market.

The liberalization of capital movements in the European Common Market that is targeted for 1992 should provide Kansallis with further opportunities for growth and expansion.

Principal Subsidiaries: Kansallis Finance Limited; Kansallis Mortgage Bank Limited; KOP-Rahasto Oy; Kansalliskortti Oy; Kansallis International Bank (Asia-Pacific) Limited (Singapore); Kansallis International Bank S.A. (Luxembourg); Kansallis Overseas Bank Limited (Bahamas); Nordinanz Bank Zurich (Switzerland).

KREDIETBANK N.V.

Arenbergstraat 7
B-1000 Brussels
Belgium
(02) 517 41 11

Public Company
Incorporated: 1935 as the Kredietbank voor Handel en Nijverheid
Employees: 9,617
Assets: BFr1.55 trillion (US$41.52 billion)
Stock Index: Brussels Amsterdam

The Kredietbank was created in 1935 when the Algemeene Bankvereeniging en Volksbank van Leuven, an institution that had absorbed a number of banks dating back to 1889, merged with the Bank voor Handel en Nijverheid. The Kredietbank was the only Belgian financial institution under Flemish control to survive the world economic crises of the early 1930s; today it is one of Belgium's three largest banks.

Although Kredietbank's initial development was hampered by its high ratio of long-term assets to demand deposits, the bank gradually gained the confidence of business and financial circles and almost doubled its deposit volume between 1935 and 1938. This growth came in large part through a business strategy conceived by Fernand Collin, who became president in 1938, which defined the Kredietbank as an independent bank with a decidedly Flemish character whose responsibility it was to further Flemish economic growth. This growth was to be restricted, however, to short-term loans to small- and medium-sized businesses in Belgium's northern and central regions.

To manage this growth more effectively, the bank formed an executive committee of three board members for handling day-to-day administrative operations and strategic decision-making. This committee closed several unprofitable branches, developed a network of business relationships both inside and outside Belgium, and defused the friction stemming from French-speaking banking institutions in Brussels, as well as from disenfranchised groups previously affiliated with the Bank voor Handel en Nijverheid and the Boerenbond, the Farmers' Union which had formed a now-defunct Flemish financial network at the turn of the century.

Another problem in the bank's early history stemmed from a large debt owed to the bank by the Algemeene Maatschappij voor Nijverheidskrediet (Almanij), a holding company that had contributed significantly to the bank's start-up costs in return for a majority of its shares. The debt, incurred as a result of transactions unrelated to the 1935 merger, created a vicious circle: Almanij could pay the interest on its debt to Kredietbank only if Kredietbank issued dividends on the stock Almanij held; however, Kredietbank could not issue dividends to shareholders without the interest payments due from Almanij.

The only feasible solution to this financial dilemma was to clear the Almanij debt. Almanij began to sell the shares it held in other institutions to generate the capital it needed to pay off its debt, a process that was completed in 1945.

In 1940, the advancing German occupation forced the bank to implement a number of emergency measures, including the relocation of part of the head office to Kortrijk and then to unoccupied France. When the French army fell to the Germans, the Kredietbank staff returned to Brussels to manage the bank's relationship with a new Belgian agricultural organization controlled by the Germans and to handle the transfer of funds to Belgium from Belgian workers in Germany.

Wartime prosperity enabled the bank to increase both the volume of its deposits and the number of operating branches throughout the country, largely through cooperation with small local or regional institutions. This growth initiated a major reorganization in 1941, which divided the Brussels head office into two groups, one handling regular banking activity and the other administering the operations of the entire Kredietbank group. This second one was further reorganized into financial, commercial, and administrative divisions. The financial division, in particular, provided the resources for the bank's postwar development of services for savers and investors of all sizes. The bank launched an intensive campaign to secure deposits from the Flemish middle class, to expand corporate services, and to investigate commercial opportunities outside Belgium. Postwar economic recovery allowed Kredietbank, now the third largest bank in Belgium, to increase the number of operating branches in Flanders. It competed effectively with savings banks in rural areas through the introduction of a pass and deposit book system, and became the first Belgian bank to issue medium-term, fixed interest bonds.

The Kredietbank's growth strategy, which after the war emphasized foreign expansion and the development of portfolio-management services for investors, stimulated its successful involvement in public security offerings for the Belgian government as well as for foreign businesses.

The relaxation of restrictions on operations outside of Flanders and Brussels permitted Kredietbank to amass stakes in selected banks located in Wallonia, two of which later merged into a wholly-owned subsidiary, the Crédit Général de Belgique, in 1961. Another subsidiary, the Kredietbank S.A. Luxembourgeoise, was formed in 1949 to coincide with the establishment of Goodyear Tire and Rubber Company's Luxembourg operation. The Luxembourg subsidiary later focused its attention exclusively on international activities and managing investment funds based in that country.

The Belgian Congo was a third area of postwar expansion. Kredietbank established branches to serve colonists in Leopoldville, Bukava, Elizabethville, and Stanleyville. Internal problems associated with the colony's independence, which was granted in 1960, eventually forced the bank to discontinue operations there in 1966.

Throughout the late 1940s and the 1950s, management of daily operations and decision-making continued to be controlled by the executive committee and its president, Fernand Collin. However, in 1959, the bank added another layer of administrative management between the executive level and the three central divisions, which were also reorganized into regional functions. In 1963, when C. Van Soye succeeded Collin as president, a fourth division was created to manage the bank's growing security and bond issues area.

Beginning in 1965, as competition from foreign banks within Belgium increased and domestic institutions diversified their services, Kredietbank began to develop a strategy for asserting its influence as a major bank while still maintaining its independent, Flemish orientation. This strategy called for continued expansion of its branch network and improvement of consumer services, such as bank cards for transactions paid by check, international traveler's checks, and credit cards. Special accounts and savings plans teamed with other services were also developed to attract new customers, while still other services were created for small- and medium-sized commercial clients. Kredietbank, the first bank in Belgium to install an automated-teller machine (in the late 1960s), joined with two other banks under the name Bancontact to develop a variety of automated banking services.

Although the bank's investment activities produced disappointing results during the 1960s largely due to stricter government regulations, reduced returns, and higher taxes, the Kredietbank continued its involvement in government loan issues, actively placing large international loans in the Eurobond market and participating in the European capital market.

To more effectively manage its international presence, the bank began building a foreign-correspondent network in 1966, supplemented by representative offices in areas which received Belgian exports and that had the potential to support international issues or need loans. The first of these offices were in New York and Mexico City, and offices were later opened in many other cities including Johannesburg, Melbourne, Atlanta, Teheran, Tokyo, Madrid, and Los Angeles.

In 1970, the bank joined six other European institutions to establish the Inter-Alpha Group of Banks. Although this strategy was intended to enhance the Kredietbank's worldwide services, it experienced greater international success in opening its own branches in such areas as New York; London; and the Cayman Islands; and forming a subsidiary in Geneva, Kredietbank (Suisse) S.A.

This expansion, coupled with increased domestic activity, created the need for another internal reorganization in 1972. Additional reorganization efforts focused on improving management of the entire group of subsidiaries and companies controlled by the bank through Almanij. The new structure, instituted in 1978, created three pools, one centered around the commercial business of the Kredietbank, another headed by Almanij to provide special financial services, and a third using the Kredietbank S.A. Luxembourgeoise as the focal point for developing an international merchant and investment-banking operation.

Although international growth slowed temporarily in the early 1980s as many financial institutions suffered losses during the worldwide recession, the bank finished 1984 with assets of BFr671 billion and net profit of BFr2 billion.

Between 1987 and 1988, Kredietbank expanded its services to individuals to include investment options in gold and mutual funds, and became the first bank to offer an index fund tied to the Belgian share market. Introduced in 1986, the bank's Tele-KB service was enhanced the following year, linking business customers with the bank's computers to transmit payment transactions and provide access to current economic and financial data.

Kredietbank is ranked as one of Belgium's top three financial institutions. It has more than 760 branches worldwide and a wide network of associated companies which serve customers in areas where government legislation prevents the bank's direct involvement. Led by its current president, Jan Huyghebaert, the bank expects to meet challenges in the future through continual improvements in customer service, the rapid penetration of new markets, and recognition of growth opportunities that have characterized its development to date.

Principal Subsidiaries: Irish Intercontinental Bank Ltd.; IIB Finance Ltd.; KB-Financial Services (Ireland) Ltd.; KB Financial Services (Dublin) Ltd.; Bankverein Bremen AG; Bank Van der Hoop Offers N.V., S.A.; Gestion KB Income Fund, S.A.; Holding Eurinvest; KB Internationale Financierings-Maatschappij N.V.; Kredietfinance (U.K.) Ltd.; Kredietbank International Finance N.V., S.A.; Gestion KB Capital Fund; S.A. ECU Conseil, S.A.; Decarenta Conseil; Kredietbank North American Finance Corp.; KB International (Hong Kong).

Further Reading: Van der Wee, Herman and Van der Wee-Verbreyt, Monique. *People Make History: The Kredietbank and the Economic Rise of Flanders, 1935–1985*, Brussels, Kredietbank, 1985.

LLOYDS BANK PLC

71 Lombard Street
London, EC3P 3BS
United Kingdom
(01) 626–1500

Public Company
Incorporated: 1865 as Lloyds Banking Company Limited
Employees: 83,932
Assets: £51.83 billion (US$93.74)
Stock Index: London

Lloyds Bank PLC is one of the Big Four British clearing banks and Britain's fourth-largest bank. Through the bank and its subsidiary and associated companies, Lloyds offers a wide variety of international banking and financial services. It has almost 2,700 branches throughout the United Kingdom, and its international business is conducted through approximately 500 offices in 47 countries, including the United States, Canada, Japan, Australia, Brazil, and Egypt. Long considered a conservative banking house, Lloyds has grown increasingly innovative since the early 1970s, often taking the lead among the Big Four clearing banks in offering new financial services and products and in developing an international presence.

Sampson Lloyd II worked for 40 years in the family iron trade in Birmingham before founding Taylors and Lloyds in partnership with John Taylor in 1765. Taylor was a wealthy Unitarian who was a maker of buttons and snuff boxes; Lloyd was a prominent Quaker whose father had settled in Birmingham in 1698. Each man's eldest son was also a partner in the bank, and two of Lloyd's other sons eventually joined it as well.

Taylors and Lloyds opened its accounts in June, 1765. Just five years later, the bank's two junior partners set up their own banking house in London with two other businessmen, forming Hanbury, Taylor, Lloyd and Bowman. This bank then served as the Birmingham house's agent. In 1775 the Birmingham bank had 277 customers.

Sampson Lloyd II had apprenticed to a Quaker businessman in Bristol before joining his father's iron firm. He was married twice and had six children. Little is known of his son and partner Sampson III, who was the last Lloyd to be a partner in both the Birmingham and London houses. Sampson III and his wife had 16 children and were known to have entertained James Boswell and Dr. Samuel Johnson. Sampson's half-brother Charles was the more important of the two, best known for his intellect and remarkable memory. In the final years of the 18th century and the early years of the 19th, Charles was the principal figure in the Birmingham bank. Charles tried mightily to mold his eldest son, Charles II, into a banker, but his efforts failed. His second son, James, became a partner in the Birmingham bank in 1802 and was followed in the mid-19th century by his own three sons.

The Bank of England had a monopoly on joint-stock banking until 1826, when Lord Liverpool, the prime minister, sponsored a new law allowing joint-stock banking, except within a 65-mile radius of London. Seven years later, joint-stock banks were allowed within the 65-mile circle, but in 1844 a stricter law virtually stopped further joint-stock banks from being founded. During those brief lenient years, 120 "joint-stocks" were founded in England and Wales and of these, 20 eventually became part of the Lloyds group. By the time they amalgamated with Lloyds, these 20 banks had a total of approximately 350 offices.

John Taylor died just ten years after founding Taylors and Lloyds. His son John Jr. was 27 at the time of the bank's founding and remained a partner in both the Birmingham and London banks until he died in 1814. His oldest son, John, never entered banking and his two other sons, James and William, were the last Taylors involved with the firm. When James died in 1852, his son was offered partnerships in the Birmingham and London houses but turned both down. Thus, the Taylor family's connection to the bank ceased. The Birmingham bank became Lloyds and Company, and the London house became Hanburys and Lloyds. The latter merged with Barnett, Hoares and Company in 1864 to form Barnetts, Hoares, Hanbury and Lloyds. This transaction brought Barnett, Hoares' sign, a black horse, to Lloyds, where it continues to be the bank's symbol.

In 1865 Lloyds and Company, joined by Moilliet and Sons, was incorporated as Lloyds Banking Company Limited. With the Birmingham bank's change to joint-stock ownership, there came an infusion of new blood into the company. The first chairman of Lloyds Banking Company, Timothy Kenrick, was a Unitarian businessman and a director of the Midland Railway Company. Although he had married into a banking family, he had no banking experience, but was widely respected in Birmingham for both his business acumen and philanthropic activities. During Kenrick's term as chairman, the bank absorbed four other banks.

Sampson Samuel Lloyd, a great-great-grandson of Sampson Lloyd III, became chairman in 1869. He oversaw Lloyds' mergers with seven banks, including its two London agents, Bosanquet, Salt and Company and Barnetts, Hoares, Hanbury and Lloyd, both in 1884. After these amalgamations, which gave Lloyds a foothold in London and entrance to the clearinghouse system of clearing checks and settling balances, the bank was known as Lloyds, Barnetts and Bosanquets Bank Limited. Although the bank's branches were all within a 50-mile radius of Birmingham and the head office remained in that city, its center of activity was rapidly shifting to London. Beginning in 1899, Lloyds' board would meet alternately in London and Birmingham, but by 1910, the board met only in London and all head office business was also transferred there.

Two years after the two important London mergers, Sampson Lloyd handed over the chairmanship to Thomas Salt, whose family had been in banking for generations. Salt had been a director of the bank since 1866, when the bank at which he was a junior partner, Stafford Old Bank, was sold to Lloyds. Early in Salt's term, the bank took the title of Lloyds Bank Limited. In Salt's 12 years as chairman, the bank absorbed 15 banks and grew from 61 offices in 1886 to 257 in 1898.

Also deserving of credit for this growth was Howard Lloyd, who served as general manager from 1871 to 1902. A direct descendant of Sampson Lloyd II, Howard Lloyd held many jobs in the bank, gradually working his way up to secretary and finally, general manager. Lloyd successfully oversaw the melding of Lloyds' two London agents into the Lloyds framework, calling those two amalgamations "the most important forward step of the bank's history." At the end of his tenure in 1902, the bank had 267 offices. Lloyd was fond of saying that Lloyds Bank was to be not necessarily the biggest bank, but the best bank. He stands out in the history of Lloyds as a tireless adminstrator who handled an impressive variety of functions.

John Spencer Phillips became chairman in 1898. The eldest son of a rector, Phillips had been a partner in the Shrewsbury and Welshpool Old Bank, which was acquired by Lloyds in 1880. He became a member of Lloyds board and served as deputy chairman for eight years before assuming the chairmanship. Nine years before becoming chairman, Phillips had been instrumental in negotiating the amalgamation of the Birmingham Joint Stock Bank, which had long been considered Lloyds' chief competitor in that city. The last chairman to also act as chief executive, Phillips oversaw 15 amalgamations. An excellent public speaker, he was the first to offer commentary on national economic affairs at the annual meeting.

In June, 1903, Lloyds opened secret merger negotiations with the Manchester and Liverpool District Bank, but public sentiment against the merger was so strong that the idea was dropped. Manchester citizens were particulary outspoken, objecting to their city's losing its separate identity.

After Phillips died in office in 1909, he was succeeded by Richard Vassar-Smith. His 13 years were a period when, for some time, Lloyds was the biggest bank in England. A director of the Worcester City and County Bank, Vassar-Smith was selected to become a director of Lloyds Bank when the smaller bank was absorbed by Lloyds in 1889. Vassar-Smith was heavily involved in governmental discussions about wartime preparations, and served as chairman of the 1917 Treasury Committee on Financial Facilities. In recognition of his contributions to the war effort, he was made a baronet in 1917.

World War I saw the formation of the Big Five, a group of large clearing banks that included Lloyds. Although the banks still called themselves the London clearing banks, they were in fact national banks.

Several key acquisitions and amalgamations marked Vassar-Smith's years as chairman. In 1914 Lloyds absorbed the Wilts and Dorset Banking Company, which had 200 offices, many in areas where Lloyds already had a branch. In 1918 came the merger of two huge banking concerns: Lloyds with its 888 offices merged with the Capital and Counties Bank, which had 473 offices. Although there was substantial overlap of office locations, each did have offices in areas in which the other had little or no representation. Capital and Counties also had attractive foreign connections. It participated in a bank in France as well as in agencies for banks in Canada, Mauritius, and Brazil. The amalgamated bank, whose title remained Lloyds Bank Limited, had a board of directors consisting of the 19 members of Lloyds and seven from the Capital and Counties board. In 1918 Lloyds had just more than 13% of all bank deposits in Britain.

Poet T. S. Eliot joined Lloyds' colonial and foreign department at the head office in 1917, where he worked as a bank clerk. When Eliot's health deteriorated in the fall of 1921, the bank gave him a three-month leave, during which he finished *The Waste Land*. He left Lloyds for a better-paying job at another bank in 1925.

In the year and a half after the end of World War I in November, 1918, there was a sharp upturn in economic actitvity, but it was succeeded by a lengthy recession. The bank's business mirrored these broad swings in the economy. With the end of the war, official restrictions on branch openings were lifted and in 1919, Lloyds opened or reopened 203 offices. The bank also acquired the 34 offices of the West Yorkshire Bank that year.

With the 1921 acquisition of Fox, Fowler & Company, the last country bank to issue its own note, Lloyds added 55 additional branches and agencies in Somerset, Devon, and Cornwall. By 1923, Lloyds had become a banking giant, with 1,626 offices throughout England.

Nationwide, public concern was mounting over the large number of bank amalgamations, which came to a quick halt after the Treasury Committee on Bank Amalgamations issued its report in 1918. The committee's recommendations for minimizing future amalgamations, although never formally made law, became the country's unwritten law. Henceforth, every amalgamtion would require treasury approval. The treasury usually permitted the acquisition of small banks by large concerns, but it was clear that the amalgamation of any two of the Big Five would not be permitted.

Lloyds averted a serious banking crisis with its 1923 takeover of Cox & Company, West End army bankers with branches in India, Burma, and Egypt. Lloyds also took over Henry S. King & Company, which Cox had recently acquired. These amalgamations were made by order of the Bank of England to avoid an expected run on Cox & Company.

After Vassar-Smith's death in 1922, J. W. Beaumont Pease, who had served as deputy chairman throughout Vassar-Smith's tenure, succeeded him. Another direct descendant of Sampson Lloyd II, Pease had been a partner in the established and prosperous private bank of Hodgkin, Barnett, Pease, Spence & Company of Newcastle upon Tyne. When that bank amalgamated with Lloyds in 1903, Pease was elected to Lloyds' board.

During Pease's lengthy term, Lloyds gained a reputation for its conservatism. When Pease retired in 1945, Lloyds had 60 more branches than when he took office. Although the bank had expanded during the 1920s to nearly 1,950 branches in 1931, many had to be closed during the Depression and World War II.

The Depression made its most serious dent in Lloyds' lending business, with a two-fifths loss of income in this area. Total earnings reflected this loss, with a two-fifths reduction in the overall figure. In 1933, gross profits fell to their lowest level since the turn of the century. Economizing measures were instituted, including a renewed dedication to mechanization and the development of a standard formula for determining which branches were to be closed. In the mid-1930s, approximately 20 branches a year were mechanized, using machines that would post entries on an account and strike a balance.

In the late 1930s, elaborate plans were drawn up to keep the bank functioning in case of war. The clearing banks issued a war preparation report stipulating that in case of war, all ordinary competition between banks would cease entirely. Throughout the war, 641 Lloyds offices were damaged and 32 destroyed. Of the latter, the vaults were destroyed in only two. Between 1940 and 1945, 214 offices were closed and seven opened (a number of those closed were reopened after the war). In addition, three Lloyds branches were overrun by enemy troops during the war: in Jersey and Guernsey in the Channel Islands and in Rangoon, Burma.

Throughout World War II, deposits and the total number of accounts increased each year. Deposits doubled between 1939 and 1945, but with prices rising steadily, real growth was considerably less. Lending activity fell, but this was offset by an increase in investments, especially treasury deposit receipts. For the period 1939–1945, gross profits tripled. Lloyds had inherited the army's business from Cox & Company; at one point during the war, the influx of newly commissioned officers forced the army pay department to work seven days a week.

Lord Balfour of Burleigh succeeded Pease as chairman in 1946. A member of an old Scottish family, he had been named chairman of the National Bank of New Zealand in 1938 and also served as a director of other banks and organizations. Lord Balfour, or "B of B" as he was called, started the practice of having regular dinners at which the chairman, a few directors, and small groups of managers could freely exchange ideas.

The immediate postwar years brought an upturn in the economy. Between 1945 and 1951, total loans almost tripled. Deposits, however, increased by only about a third, a considerably slower rate of growth than during the war, and virtually no real growth at all due to inflation.

Sir Oliver Franks, who had served as Britain's ambassador to the United States from 1948 to 1952, succeeded Lord Balfour as chairman in 1954. The former head of an Oxford college, Franks was one of the finest intellects ever to serve the bank as chairman. Due to the essentially conservative nature of the bank and continued governments controls, however, Franks was not able to make as many changes as he would have liked.

In 1958 the government abolished restrictions on bank-lending and the clearing banks did away with their self-imposed limits on competition among themselves. Lloyds continued to expand. Its total number of branches in 1959 was 1,851, compared to 1,711 in 1951, and its employees had increased from 17,690 in 1951 to 20,160 in 1959.

After Oliver Franks' retirement in 1962, Harald Peake, a director since 1941 and a vice chairman since 1947, was elected chairman. Peake had a varied background in business, having served as chairman of a steel company and director of many other companies. He was a key player in negotiating the purchase of property from the Commercial Union Assurance Company, which allowed for expansion of the head office.

During the 1960s Lloyds developed rapidly. In 1963 it set up Lloyds Bank Property Company to conduct property development schemes that would incorporate branch premises, and in 1967 Lloyds acquired Lewis's Bank from Martins Bank. Lewis's had branches in ten Liverpool department stores. Altogether the bank opened 456 new branches, bringing the total at decade's end to 2,307.

Peake is best remembered for a failed attempt at merging Lloyds with Barclays and Martins banks, a move the monopolies commission deemed would be against the public interest. Barclays finally acquired Martins, making Lloyds the smallest of the Big Four London clearing banks rather than the third-largest among the Big Five.

Eric O. Faulkner, who had spent 32 years in banking at Glyn, Mills and Company and was considered something of a radical, was elected chairman of Lloyds in 1969. He provided a new perspective on how the bank should continue to grow.

One of Faulkner's priorities was the development of an international banking group. He created Lloyds Bank International by merging Lloyds Bank Europe with the Bank of London and South America to form the Lloyds and Bolsa International Bank in 1971, in which Lloyds held a 51% interest. Two years later, it became a wholly owned subsidiary, marked by a name change to Lloyds Bank Interntional. Lloyd's expanded its geographic base considerably during the next several years to include West Germany, Switzerland, the Middle East, Australia, Canada, and the United States in its international network. Early in 1986 Lloyds Bank International was merged with the clearing bank to better meet the demands of a worldwide financial market.

To handle its growing volume of transactions, Lloyds became the first British bank to transfer all its branches to a common computer accounting system in October, 1970. This helped immensely as the bank adjusted to the government's introduction of decimal currency in February, 1971.

Competition among banks intensified after the Bank of England radically changed its control of the banks in 1971, when it introduced a new policy that included removal of a maximum ceiling on bank lending. In this newly competitive environment, Faulkner oversaw many new business ventures. An insurance department was established in 1972, and a year later Lloyds Leasing was started.

By 1978 Lloyds Bank International had offices and subsidiaries in 43 countries. By the end of that year, a little more than half of Lloyds Bank Group's consolidated balance was attributable to the bank's many subsidiaries. In a 1971 interview with *The Banker*, Faulkner echoed Harold Lloyd's words of nearly a century ago when he said, "All these objectives for our domestic business amount simply to being not the largest but the best of the clearing banks."

Sir Jeremy Morse succeeded Faulkner as chairman in 1977. At 47, he was one of the youngest chairmen of a clearing bank in recent history. Morse had served as chairman of the deputies of the International Monetary Fund's Committee of Twenty, where he was involved in efforts to reform the world's monetary system. He had served as Lloyds' deputy chairman for 16 months before assuming the chairmanship.

In 1979 Lloyds became the first clearing bank to move into the home-loan market. Seeking to fill a gap in the home-loan services offered by the British building societies, Lloyds announced it would consider loans over £25,000 and up to £150,000. The building societies' maximum home loans were £25,000.

Two years later Lloyds Bank and American Express announced plans to issue a joint sterling traveler's check from their offices and branches around the world. Lloyds Bank further diversified in 1982 with the creation of Blackhorse Agencies, a real estate–agency business that had as its nucleus a Norfolk-based practice acquired by Lloyds. By 1989, Blackhorse had 563 offices.

Competition between the big London banks intensified in the mid-1980s when Lloyds and other clearing banks announced they would begin offering free banking for clients whose current accounts remained in the black.

In 1986 Lloyds Bank PLC offered £1.27 billion in a hostile takeover bid for Standard Chartered PLC, Britain's fifth-largest bank, but was rebuffed after East Asian and Australian investors made last-minute purchases of Standard Chartered shares. Although Standard Chartered's profits had lagged behind other large British banks for some time, Lloyds was sorry to lose the chance to acquire Standard Chartered's many interests in the Far East, especially in Hong Kong.

Just three months after its unsuccessful bid for Standard Chartered, Lloyds announced it would start its own brokerage firm rather than acquire a brokerage firm, as the other Big Four clearing banks had done. That same year, Lloyds formed a new subsidiary, Lloyds Merchant Bank, to handle its capital market and merchant banking operations.

In 1987 Lloyds announced it would move 1,400 head-office staff from London to Bristol, where it would build a two-phase office development in a park-like setting. Due to the impact of Third World loan losses, Lloyds Bank incurred a pre-tax loss in 1987 of some £248 million, compared to profits of £700 million the year before. Lloyds Chairman Jeremy Morse told *The Wall Street Journal* in early 1988 that Lloyds was "refocusing" its international business on more profitable services such as foreign exchange, trade finance, investment management, and private banking and that it was moving away from wholesale lending to countries and large corporate borrowers.

In 1988 Lloyds' profit figures were handsomely turned around, with both pre- and post-tax profits at record levels. The biggest Third World debtor, Brazil, resumed interest payments in 1988 and several other countries began programs to reduce their debts.

That year Lloyds became the second British bank to offer a debit card, a card that is linked directly to a user's bank account and allows transactions to be debited just as if a check has been written. Also in 1988, Lloyds made a bold competitive move when it began offering interest on basic checking accounts. Although the idea is common in the United States, British banks have competed mainly by cutting fees and adding new services. Analysts saw the move as a predictable response to the building societies' chipping away at the bank's dominance in checking accounts. At year's end, Lloyds acquired a controlling interest in Abbey Life Group PLC, a British life insurer, by merging five of its businesses with Abbey Life to create Lloyds Abbey Life. This bold move into a new market is a part of Lloyds' strategy to attract new business and raise earnings by offering customers a wider range of services.

Principal Subsidiaries: Black Horse Agencies Limited; Black Horse Life Assurance Company Limited; Black Horse Relocation Services Ltd.; Alex Lawrie Factors Limited; International Factors Limited; Lloyds Bank Export Finance Limited; Lloyds Bank Finance (Isle of Man) Limited; Lloyds Bank Finance (Jersey) Limited; Lloyds Bank Insurance Services Limited; Lloyds Bank International (Guernsey) Limited; Lloyds Development Capital Limited; Lloyds Bank Stockbrokers Ltd.; Lloyds Bank Trust Company (Channel Islands) Limited; Lloyds Bank Unit Trust Managers Limited; Lloyds Bowmaker Finance Limited; Lloyds Leasing Limited; Lloyds Bank Financial Futures Ltd.; Lloyds Investment Managers Ltd.; Lloyds Merchant Bank Limited; Lloyds Bank (Belgium) SA; Lloyds Bank (France) Limited; Lloyds International Management SA; Schroder, Munchmeyer, Hengst & Co.; Lloyds Bank (BLSA) Ltd.; Lloyds Bank Canada; Lloyds Government Securities Corp.; Lloyds International Corp.; Bank of London & Montreal Limited; LBI Bank & Trust Company (Cayman) Limited; Lloyds Bank International (Bahamas) Limited; LBI Finance (Hong Kong) Limited; Lloyds International Limited; Lloyds International Merchant Bank (SEA) Limited; National Bank of New Zealand Savings Bank Limited; The National Bank of New Zealand Limited; Lloyds Bank NZA Limited; Abbey Life Assurance Company Limited; Abbey Unit Trust Managers Limited; Abbey Life Assurance (Ireland) Limited; Lloyd's IPB SA; Transatlantische Lebensuersicherungs AG; Harcourt Corporation Limited; Lloyds Corporate Advisory Services Pty Limited; Southpac Corporation Limited.

Further Reading: Sayers, R. S. *Lloyds Bank in the History of English Banking*, Oxford, Clarendon Press, 1957; Winton, J. R. *Lloyds Bank: 1918–1969*, Oxford, Oxford University Press, 1982.

LONG-TERM CREDIT BANK OF JAPAN, LTD.

2-4, Otemachi 1-chome
Chiyoda-ku
Tokyo 100
Japan
(03) 211-5111

Public Company
Incorporated: 1952
Employees: 3,500
Assets: ¥24.85 trillion (US$16.59 billion)
Stock Index: Tokyo Osaka

The Long-Term Credit Bank of Japan (LTCB) is one of only three Japanese banks licensed to issue long-term loans to industry. These banks are unique to Japan. They were created expressly to accelerate postwar industrialization by directing investment funds into basic industries, free of competition from the large commercial "city" banks.

The long-term banks (LTCB, Nippon Credit Bank, and Industrial Bank of Japan) have no private customers; their only clients are corporations. But although they are operationally removed from the public, they have affected the lives of all Japanese citizens by financing construction of the factories where they work, underwriting the development of new products, and in many ways making Japan's "economic miracle" possible.

The LTCB was founded in 1952—quite late in the history of Japanese finance. The Japanese government, through the Ministry of Finance, created two (and later a third) such special banks as a provision of the Long-Term Credit Banking Law of 1952. The LTCB was formed from departments of two established state banks, the Kangyo Bank and the Hokkaido Colonial Bank. Initially, half of the LTCB's capital was subscribed for by the government. But as the Japanese economy grew in strength, the government slowly relinquished its ownership to corporations and private investors.

The LTCB and the Industrial Bank of Japan were given exclusive rights to sell three- and five-year debentures; in return, they were not allowed to accept short-term deposits. As a result, the central bank became the LTCB's primary source of capital; the LTCB channeled investment funding from the government directly to expanding basic industries. Companies often secured their loans with large blocks of shares, which brought LTCB representatives onto the boards of major corporations. As these industries matured, they repurchased their shares with cash, increasing the bank's capital base.

Strictly speaking, the long-term credit banks were not capitalist institutions. They performed part of the central bank's function by managing the allocation of funds for industry. Because they were profit-oriented and publicly owned, and there were only two to serve many competitive industries, the long-term credit banks were required to maintain strict neutrality; favoritism toward any of the emerging industrial groups would have invited government intervention. By 1957, however, the LTCB and the IBJ were unable to handle the tremendous volume of business generated by the rapid expansion of the Japanese economy. That year, in an effort to ease the situation and create more competition in long-term credit, the Japanese government chartered a third competitor, the Nippon Credit Bank.

The Japanese economy's broad-based growth brought continued expansion to the LTCB. As one of the few institutions in Japan awash in cash, the LTCB became a popular source of investment capital for companies involved in such basic industries as electricity, shipping, and steel production. LTCB's influence grew as it continued to gain seats on the boards of such companies. And since most of the companies were investment interests as well, the bank also profited directly from their subsequent growth.

During the late 1960s, the LTCB began to emphasize new industrial ventures, primarily in shipbuilding, electronics, automobiles, and petrochemicals. The bank also pioneered long-term financing of land reclamation and housing projects, and participated in a reorganization of Japan's commodity distribution system.

As a semi-official institution, the LTCB was required to maintain lower-risk activities, and indeed, it experienced no mishaps. Its growth closely reflected general trends in the Japanese economy. The bank was largely unaffected by a stock market crash in 1964, although it suffered some setbacks during the oil crisis of 1973–1974 as industries were forced to adjust to entirely new cost structures.

The second oil price rise in 1978–1979, however, meant slower investment and lower demand for loans. During this period, companies found that in many cases they could do without long-term banks and raise funds more cheaply by issuing bonds. An entire lending sector was thus handed over to Japan's growing securities firms. The LTCB tried to pursue this business into new markets, but was prevented by Japanese financial regulations.

In the late 1970s intensive lobbying efforts from the financial sector began to pressure the government to repeal Article 65, the provision that keeps banks and brokerages from entering each other's markets. Traditionally conservative and staid, the LTCB recognized that it would have to change in order to remain competitive.

Like the city banks, the LTCB began to develop an ambitious international consulting capability. In one sweep, the heads of LTCB subsidiaries in England, Belgium, Switzerland, and Hong Kong were replaced in 1985 with new personnel acting under central direction. LTCB also created a global network for its Merchant Banking Group, formed in 1985, by coordinating its offices in Tokyo, London, New York, Hong Kong, Singapore and Los Angeles.

Another change in the bank's strategy was a realignment of its lending activities away from Japanese heavy industries toward service industries and foreign companies. The LTCB claims to have begun this effort as early as 1965, years before its larger competitor, the IBJ. The bank has, indeed, succeeded in reducing its share of domestic assets to lending in the manufacturing sector from 60% to about 15%, while the IBJ remains at about 24%. Still, the LTCB was forced to write off ¥70 billion in 1985 when Sanko Steamship, a major client, failed.

It has been noted that the LTCB is less likely than the IBJ to participate in the unprofitable restructuring of a client. While this inclination has been good for its books, some companies are less likely to do business with the LTCB knowing that the bank may not be there for them in time of dire need, which may be one reason why the IBJ remains larger than the LTCB.

The LTCB also set its sights on the stable and profitable business of dealing in American treasury bonds and Eurobonds, since it wasn't under the jurisdiction of restrictive Japanese legislation in these foreign markets. In 1987, the LTCB tried to buy Greenwich Capital Markets, a U.S. Treasury bond dealer, but was prevented by the Federal Reserve on the grounds that American banks were being denied similar access in Japan. The LTCB had to be content with a passive minority share of Greenwich until the Fed reversed its decision in June of 1988, allowing the LTCB to acquire full control of Greenwich for $144 million.

The bank met with similar hardship in London, where the Ministry of Finance bans Japanese institutions from lead-managing Eurobond issues. In spite of this handicap, the LTCB has been successful in the Eurobond market. Should financial regulations in England be relaxed, the LTCB could very well become one of London's leading international securities firms.

The LTCB's effort to become an "international wholesale bank headquartered in Tokyo" demonstrates the bank's resolve to seize the initiative as world financial markets open up. While many have feared that Japan's four major brokerages stand the most to gain from such a liberalization, the LTCB appears determined to capitalize as well.

Principal Subsidiaries: LTCB Asia Limited (Hong Kong); The Long-Term Credit Bank of Japan Finance N.V. (Curacao); LTCB International Limited (U.K.); LTCB (Schweiz) AG (Switzerland); Greenwich Capital Markets, Inc.; LTCB Australia Ltd.; LTCB Merchant Bank (Singapore) Ltd.; LTCB Futures (Singapore) Pte. Ltd.; LTCB Trust Co. (U.S.A.); The Long-Term Credit Bank of Japan (Europe) S.A.

MANUFACTURERS HANOVER CORPORATION

270 Park Avenue
New York, New York 10017
U.S.A.
(212) 286–6000

Public Company
Incorporated: 1968
Employees: 23,557
Assets: $66.71 billion
Stock Index: New York

The Manufacturers Hanover Corporation, the holding company of Manufacturers Hanover Trust, is one of the world's leading banking and financial institutions. The company has relied on a long series of mergers and acquisitions to boost its influence nationally and worldwide. Manny Hanny, as the bank is nicknamed, is headquartered in New York City, where it was founded. The company's history parallels New York City's transformation from a postcolonial port into the world's most important financial center.

Both the principal constituents of the company, the former Manufacturers Trust and Hanover Bank, are the offspring of mergers and acquisitions of banks that were organized and consolidated in response to the needs of the financial market. Manufacturers Trust's earliest predecessor can be traced to 1812, when the New York Manufacturing Company was founded. Although it was ostensibly a textile company, the New York Manufacturing Company's charter included the authorization to conduct banking activities. in 1817 this company's banking business was acquired by the Phenix Bank, itself recently organized by influential city merchants and bankers. With the passage of Banking Act of 1865, the Phenix Bank became a national bank. The legendary J. P. Morgan was among the bank's original incorporators. In 1851, the Chatham Bank, named after William Pitt, Earl of Chatham, was established by another group of prosperous merchants. One of these merchants, Earl G. Drake, served as the bank's first president.

The creation of the New York Clearing House gave rise to the use of deposit accounts and checks for the settlement of financial transactions, significantly improving the city's financial and banking services. In 1911, the Phenix and Chatham banks merged to form the Chatham and Phenix National Bank of New York. The Chatham and Phenix Bank soon became one of New York's financial giants.

In 1915 Chatham and Phenix merged with the Century Bank, an institution Chatham and Phenix had held an interest in since its 1901 founding. Century brought 11 branches to the partnership, and special arrangements had to be made to retain these since only state banks were allowed to have branches. In the end Chatham and Phenix was the only national bank in New York City allowed to own branches.

The word "Manufacturers" in the name of today's bank comes not from the New York Manufacturing Company of 1812, but from the Manufacturers National Bank of Brooklyn, which was established in 1853. In 1914 this bank merged with the Citizens Trust Company, a bank that opened its doors in 1905 to serve the Jewish businessmen who flocked to Brooklyn from Manhattan's Lower East Side. It is under the Citizens Trust Company's charter that Manufacturers Hanover operates today. After the merger of the Manufacturers National Bank and the Citizens Trust Company the bank became Manufacturers Trust.

This bank first ventured out of Brooklyn and into Manhattan in 1918, when it purchased the West Side Bank there. Shortly afterwards, it established its main office in Manhattan. By 1921 Manufacturers Trust had $40 million in deposits; by 1929 the bank had absorbed 11 other banks, had a total of 47 offices, and a presence in four New York boroughs. This expansion continued; late in 1931 Manufacturers Trust obtained more deposits and offices in the liquidation of five banks. This activity culminated in 1932 with the merger of Manufacturers Trust and the Chatham and Phenix Bank.

The bank continued to expand through more mergers and outright purchases, solidifying its position in the New York banking industry. In 1950 Manufacturers Trust made one of its largest mergers ever when the Brooklyn Trust Company became part of the organization. Chartered in 1866 by contractors William C. Kingly and Judge Alexander McGee, and given solid support by an influential state senator, Henry C. Murphy, Brooklyn Trust undertook the expensive and politically divisive task of physically linking Manhattan and Brooklyn. The total cost of the Brooklyn Bridge—$15 million, an enormous sum at the time—could not have been financed had it not been for Brooklyn Trust's determination. The merger of the two banks in 1950 increased Manufacturers Trust's office branches to 100, the most in New York City at the time.

The corporation's other constituent bank, Hanover Bank, also traces its history back to the early 19th century. The National Bank of the City of New York was chartered in 1829, funded largely by John Jacob Astor. Its first president, Albert Gallatin, had served as secretary of the treasury under Presidents Thomas Jefferson and James Madison and helped negotiate the Louisiana Purchase of 1803. During Gallatin's tenure as the bank's president, the nation experienced a serious economic downswing culminating in the Panic of 1837. Gallatin is credited with guiding the banking system through this crisis and with establishing New York City as the financial hub of the country. In his honor National Bank was renamed Gallatin Bank. This bank merged with Hanover Bank in 1912.

Hanover Bank received its charter in 1851 with an initial working capital of $500,000, a substantial amount at the time. Although the discovery of gold in the West provided the initial impetus behind the bank's inception, Hanover survived the gold bust, unlike the 1,200 other commercial houses that failed in New York City alone. By 1875 Hanover Bank, now a member of the national banking system, held a deposit line of $6 million. Under James T. Woodward, a noted city merchant who became president of the bank in 1876, Hanover Bank took the lead in the redevelopment of the post–Civil War South and provided financial support and banking services to entrepreneurs and companies engaged in the industrial expansion of the American West. By the time of Woodward's death in 1910, Hanover Bank had built up a deposit line of more than $100 million and had total resources of $117 million.

The depression of 1873 forced Union Trust, another institution that became part of Hanover Bank, to close its doors temporarily, following a run on its deposits. The bank survived, however, and in 1918 Union Trust merged with Central Trust Company to form the Central Union Trust Company of New York, which then merged with Hanover Bank in 1929. The merger was conceived as a way to prepare for the foreseen recession, but it also broadened the new institution's market by combining Central Trust's specialization in corporate trust with Hanover's specialization in personal trust.

The constant pursuit of new markets, a trademark of both Hanover and Manufacturers, and intense competition among banking institutions for new accounts—pension funds in particular—led to the merger of these two banks in 1961. With $6 billion in assets and $7.5 billion in the trust and investment-management business, the new Manufacturers Hanover Trust Company (MHT) ranked at the top of the business. Its pension-plan clients included Union Carbide, Chrysler, Texaco, and American Motors.

But the combination of Manufacturers Trust's strength in retail banking and Hanover Bank's strength in wholesale banking created fears of over concentration in the industry. The Justice Department claimed the consolidation violated antitrust laws and moved to break up the company. The merger, however, survived.

Under President Gabriel Hauge MHT expanded into the international market much as Hanover Bank had once expanded into the reconstructing South and developing West. By 1967, 20% of the company's operating income was derived from its international business. By 1972, this share had increased to 40%. In 1968 Manufacturers Hanover, like the other New York money center banks, created a holding company, Manufacturers Hanover Corporation, and MHT became this company's subsidiary.

During the early 1970s conservatism and bureaucratic inertia eroded the bank's ability to adjust to major economic developments. The loan business provided 75% of Manny Hanny's gross income, more than any other major bank. As interest rates plummeted, earnings dropped 8.5%. In response, the bank increased the size of its loan portfolios to offset the impact of declining interest rates. This policy further increased the bank's exposure to economic fluctuations, caused in part by oil price increases. Moreover, the bank's retail-banking operation, traditionally a strong performer, lagged behind other banks. Hauge acted to move Manufacturers Hanover's reliance on loan-denominated cyclical earnings into more stable businesses such as retail operations, personal loans, and mortgage and consumer credit based on fixed interest rates.

Despite these problems, the corporation continued to grow during the decade. Its subsidiaries' assets alone totaled $2.8 billion and by 1973 the corporation was worth $20 billion.

Manufacturers Hanover continued to expand during the 1970s by acquiring several subsidiary banks and opening more branch offices. In 1970 it acquired banks in Brussels and London, laying the groundwork for future benefits that would accrue from euromarkets flush with petrodollars. The bank also opened branches in Tokyo, Singapore, Rio de Janeiro, and Oslo, and, in 1974, a branch in Bucharest, the first such Western banking office in the Soviet bloc. This international activity spurred Manny Hanny's growth; international business accounted for 60% of total earnings by 1977. As loans on more than $30 billion in long-term debt at fixed rates began to mature, earnings rose to $211 million in 1979, up from $85 million in 1970. Manny Hanny by then had 436 offices in 20 states and 78 facilities in 37 countries with a wide range of financing alternatives and noncredit services.

John F. McGillicuddy became president of Manufacturers Hanover in 1973, when Hauge became chairman. It became increasingly clear to McGillicuddy that in order for the bank to remain profitable in the 1980s, it would have to continue developing and diversifying its services as international competition for new markets increased.

By 1979, despite high earnings, it was ominously apparent that Manny Hanny had become overdependent on international loans. Loan-loss reserves were bolstered 25% as debt repayments from Third World borrowers became increasingly uncertain. By mid-1984, when a 31% drop in the company's stock price forced Manny Hanny to publicly acknowledge that it would write off part of Argentina's $1.3 billion debt to the bank, McGillicuddy had already moved to counteract Manufacturers Hanover's overexposure to Latin American debt.

In late 1983 Manny Hanny bought CIT Financial Corporation from RCA for $1.5 billion, at the time the largest sum a bank had ever spent for an acquisition. This bold move increased Manufacturers Hanover's total assets to more than $63 billion and over 1,000 offices. Nonbank subsidiaries then accounted for 20% of earnings. The addition of CIT brought the West Coast, the Southwest, and Atlanta into Manny Hanny's financial orbit.

Critics maintained, however, that Manny Hanny had still failed to make necessary structural adjustments. The following year McGillicuddy announced a major shift in the company's strategic thinking. Market share would no longer serve as the rationale behind growth. The Latin American debt crisis had illustrated the folly of piling up bad debts. Corporate streamlining and decentralization became the new order.

The bank was divided into five sections to place direct responsibility for performance on managers, and 5,000 employees were let go between 1986 and 1988 alone. A new information system in the accounting system helped to more accurately reveal profits and losses incurred by various units. Unprofitable services were discontinued and the bank sought to decrease its reliance on fickle depositors. Less profitable operations like the Belgian subsidiary and the British consumer units were sold off to reduce overhead. The $1.6 billion Manny Hanny raised through this sale of these businesses was used to help raise reserves $2.3 billion. These reserves, in part, offset the $2.1 billion in bad loans the bank wrote off.

Despite strong earnings of $200 million in 1986, troubles continued as the bank's large Third World, energy, and real estate loans continued to plague it. In 1987 Manny Hanny lost $1.14 million. Continuing to sell off smaller, less-profitable operations, the bank earned $966 million in 1988, bolstered by Brazil's payment of $146 million of its debt. The bank's Third World loan exposure fell by $700 million in 1988, aided in part by the conversion of some Brazilian debt into a 17% holding in a Brazilian chemical company.

Manufacturers Hanover still has a way to go in reconciling its bad loans and recovering from its earnings slump. At about 22%, its reserves are below the U.S. average of 25%, which in turn is below international reserves as high as 75%–100%. The bank has, however, begun a strong recovery. Its strategy now depends on the success of its wholesale-banking, regional-banking, and CIT subsidiaries.

Principal Subsidiaries: Manufacturers Hanover Trust Co.; CIT Group Holding, Inc.; Manufacturers Hanover Futures, Inc.; Manufacturers Hanover New Jersey Corp.; Manufacturers Hanover Equity Corp.; Manufacturers Hanover Equity Capital, Inc.; Manufacturers Hanover Capital Corp.; Manufacturers Hanover Leasing International Corp.; Manufacturers Hanover Venture Capital Corp.; Manufacturers Hanover Securities Corp.; Manufacturers Hanover Securities Holding, Inc.; Manufacturers Hanover World Trade Corp.; Manufacturers Hanover Data Services Corp.; Manufacturers Hanover Wheelease, Inc.; Manufactures Hanover Educational Services Corp.; Manufacturers Hanover Financial Corp.; MHC Holding (Delaware) Inc.

Further Reading: Growth of a Bank, New York, Manufacturers Hanover Trust Company, 1970.

MELLON BANK CORPORATION

One Mellon Bank Center
Pittsburgh, Pennsylvania 15258
U.S.A.
(412) 234–5000

Public Company
Incorporated: 1869 as T. Mellon & Sons
Employees: 16,500
Assets: $31.2 billion
Stock Index: New York

In Pittsburgh, the name Mellon has been synonymous with banking for nearly a century and a half. A multi-bank holding company, Mellon Bank Corporation is comprised of banks developed by the descendants of Mellon's founder, Judge Thomas Mellon. The company boasts a particularly successful track record in bonds, data-processing innovation, and personal trust management. Approximately 400 small banks depend on Mellon to fulfill their data-processing needs, while the personal-trust department is one of the largest in the United States. Mellon survived more than its share of corporate crises in the 1980s, but renewed emphasis on such services as trust management, investment, data processing, and cash management have helped bring the corporation back to the successful regional status it enjoyed under Thomas Mellon in its first few decades.

Born on a potato farm in Ireland in 1813, Thomas Mellon decided at an early age that farming was not his life's calling. When he was five years old, his family moved to Pennsylvania, where he could often be found reading a book as he rode a plow across his father's fields. He became a lawyer in 1839, and although his practice did well, his investments in real estate, construction, and mortgages fared even better. In 1869 Judge Thomas Mellon retired from public service and founded T. Mellon and Sons, a private banking house at 145 Smithfield Street in Pittsburgh.

The bank prospered during the postwar years, and a second bank, run by Mellon's sons, opened soon after the first. In the Panic of 1873, when half the banks in Pittsburgh failed, the Mellons never closed either bank. Although Thomas Mellon died in 1908, his sons, Andrew and Richard, were able to build upon their father's foundation to create the giant that would eventually play a key role in fueling industry throughout Pennsylvania and must of the rest of the country.

The Mellons invested their profits from the bank in other enterprises, such as Alcoa (Aluminum Company of America), originally known as the Pittsburgh Reduction Company, and Gulf Oil Corporation, founded by William Larimer, Thomas Mellon's grandson. Gulf Oil grew to become the world's tenth-largest industrial corporation, and Alcoa became the world's largest aluminum manufacturer. The Mellons' monumental success with Mellon Bank and other such ventures is partly responsible for the long-held belief in Allegheny County, Pennsylvania that "nothing moves in Pittsburgh without the Mellons."

Four financial institutions founded in the 19th century have contributed to the growth and history of Mellon Bank. Besides T. Mellon and Sons, they were: the Farmers Bank of Delaware, established in 1807 by Henry Ridgely; the Harrisburg Bank, founded in 1814 by William Wallace, Robert Harris (son of the founder of the city of Harrisburg), and 11 other Pennsylvania businessmen; and the Girard Savings Institution of Philadelphia, established by Benjamin Wood Richards in 1835. This institution, which eventually came to be known as Girard Bank, was named in honor of Stephen Girard, a multi-millionaire who left $7 million to the city of Philadelphia and lent money to the American government during the War of 1812.

After serving as president of T. Mellon and Sons from 1869 to 1882, Thomas Mellon retired and turned the bank over to his son Andrew. Under Andrew's leadership, the bank financed the creation of Union Transfer and Trust Company; joined the national banking system as Mellon National Bank in 1902; formed its first foreign bureau, in 1908, to provide banking services for customer activity outside the United States; and established a long tradition of growth through acquisitions and mergers.

In the late 19th century, goods were often sold with a three- or four-month grace period between delivery and payment due dates. T. Mellon and Sons profited from the common practice of buying at a discount the documents that showed the amount due and holding them until maturity to collect the full value. This business made T. Mellon and Sons the largest private bank between New York and Chicago. The bank soon decided to expand its range of operations, however, to include trust estates and related work, and created the Fidelity Title and Trust Company with the help of other investors. Fidelity was an instant success—so much so that it found itself turning away business in order to avoid conflicts of interest between clients. Consequently, in 1889 it set up its own rival company, the Union Transfer and Trust Company, which became the Union Trust Company not long after.

In an effort to consolidate the Mellons' banking interests, the family decided in 1902 that Mellon National Bank should become an almost wholly owned subsidiary of Union Trust.

In 1921, Andrew Mellon was appointed secretary of the treasury by President Calvin Coolidge. While he served in Washington, D.C., remaining under presidents Warren

Harding and Herbert Hoover, his brother Richard became president of the bank.

Since Mellon National Bank was a federally chartered corporation and Union Trust and Union Savings were state banks, the Mellons were able to take advantage of both banking systems. Together, the banks could finance virtually any enterprise in the country by the 1920s. In 1929, Richard Mellon formed Mellbank Security Company, a bank holding company that helped save numerous smaller banks in western Pennsylvania during the Great Depression. Mellon's knack for giving sound advice to its customers, together with its ability to maintain sufficient liquidity and one of the highest ratios of cash to deposits in the nation, played a major role in the bank's survival through the 1930s. From 1931 to 1932, the combined earnings of Mellon National and Union Trust totaled nearly $12 million. Indeed, since the Mellon name and conservative reputation were well known by the 1920s, many of the panicked customers who withdrew their savings from other banks after the crash flocked to Mellon National. Seeing the crowds team into the bank, Richard Mellon reportedly muttered "I told those damn architects to make more room in the lobby."

After Richard's death in 1933, his son, Richard K. Mellon, took over as president. When Mellon National Bank and Union Trust Company merged in 1946, Richard became chairman of the newly formed Mellon National Bank and Trust Company. Mellon Bank also entered the retail market by expanding its branch network and merging with Mellbank.

By the middle of the 20th century, Mellon began to build a reputation for technological innovation, especially in cash management. The company bought its first computer in 1955, one of the first banks in the nation to do so. In 1958 Mellon established the Mellbank Regional Clearing House, the forerunner of its Datacenter Group, for overnight processing of checks from correspondent banks.

One measure of Mellon's power was the size of its trust assets: in 1967, Mellon Bank controlled a third of all the trust assets in Pennsylvania. That same year "outsiders"—people who were not Mellon descendants—first filled the bank's top two positions. Richard K. Mellon became honorary chairman of the board, John A. Mayer, president since 1959, became chairman, and A. Bruce Bowden was appointed president. As president, Mayer had helped Mellon double its savings deposits, nearly double its mortgages holdings, and issue credit cards to 250,000 people. His success was the fruition of a program begun by Richard K. Mellon to expand Mellon's reach from its traditional base of wealthy individuals to all kinds of banking customers.

In 1972, Mellon National Corporation was created as a one bank holding company to own Mellon National Bank and Trust Company, which officially became Mellon Bank.

By the mid-1970s, Mellon was still one of the most conservative banks in the country, a philosophy that served it well in 1975, when many progressive banks got into trouble with real estate investment trusts, a popular investment item in the 1960s and 1970s. Banks had lent billions of dollars for real estate and construction ventures. With these loans, real estate development companies built so many condominiums, single-family homes, and other buildings that they found themselves short of buyers. Mellon, however, had advised its customers to avoid the real estate investment trusts and was untouched by this crisis.

In 1982, Mellon's assets totaled $19 billion, more than the combined assets of the next three largest banks in Pittsburgh. The company had also become a strong commercial lender with sophisticated credit-accounting techniques, and managed nearly $13 billion in trusts, including many corporate pension and benefit plans. "It was always easy to identify the leadership in Pittsburgh," Joseph Lasala, a former Philadelphia city representative, told *Philadelphia* magazine in 1986. "There's one of everything. One big industry—steel . . . and one big bank—Mellon."

On the whole, however, the 1980s were a difficult time for Mellon Bank. Although it nearly doubled its assets between 1982 and 1987, its quick expansion overseas and into "high growth industries" such as energy and real estate was poorly timed. Under the leadership of Chairman J. David Barnes, Mellon created an energy lending division and a loan production office in Dallas, Texas, in 1982—just after oil prices peaked. Foreign operations, which accounted for nearly one-third of Mellon's profits in 1982, caused some of the worst damage. Like many large banks, Mellon's international expansion was poorly timed. Overexposure in Mexico, Brazil, and other Third World nations resulted in many problem loans. Mellon eventually closed almost half of its 20 foreign branches. The company also realigned its international operations to focus on multinational corporate customers rather than overseas borrowers.

The merger of Mellon and Girard Bank in 1982 also exemplified Mellon's eagerness to expand. Girard had merged with the Corn Exchange Bank in 1951, installed its first computer in 1962, and, over the next ten years, pioneered the development of automated retail services in Philadelphia. Its automated bank system would eventually gain industry recognition as state of the art. Girard also acquired the Farmers Bank of Delaware in 1981, renaming it Girard Bank Delaware. Girard's earnings dropped significantly in October, 1982, but Mellon finalized the merger anyway, in November, 1982. Girard's growth came to a sudden halt after the merger, and in 1984 the bank's shaky balance sheet—which included a vast portfolio of delinquent loans—contributed to a 14% decline in Mellon's earnings for the year. It also prompted Mellon officers to head to Philadelphia to "Mellonize" things. Their take-charge approach made Girard veterans and customers uncomfortable. In addition to firing several Girard executives, Mellon went so far as to rename Girard Bank Mellon Bank (East), while Girard Bank Delaware became Mellon Bank (DE).

In 1985, Mellon, which had adopted the name Mellon Bank Corporation a year earlier, merged with Commonwealth National Financial Corporation, the Harrisburg-based financial-services holding company formed in 1969 by the merger of the Harrisburg National Bank and Trust Company, Conestoga National Bank, and the First National Bank of York. Mellon also enhanced its integrated banking software and financial data-processing systems through the acquisition of Carleton Financial Computations Inc., in South Bend, Indiana. Also that year, Mellon purchased several subsidiaries of the Fidata Corporation that offered securities transfer, securities pricing, and trust accounting services. By the late 1980s, Mellon was selling its data-processing expertise to some 400 small banks across the country.

Mellon entered the high-growth consumer-banking market in Maryland in 1986, when it bought certain assets of Community Savings and Loan, of Bethesda, and created Mellon Bank (MD). It also opened Mellon Securities Ltd., London to serve the investment needs of United States–based customers, and added Triangle Portfolio Associates to its eight investment-management subsidiaries.

In 1987, Mellon recorded the first loss in its history, due to increased reserves for Third World loans and for certain domestic credits. When this first-quarter loss was announced, stock shares plummeted and Chairman Barnes resigned. The Mellon family, which still holds 15% of the bank's stock, chose an acting replacement for the CEO and, after an extensive search, approved the appointment of Frank Cahouet. Formerly president of the Federal National Mortgage Association, Cahouet is best known in the finance industry for reviving San Francisco's Crocker National Corporation, although it was sold before he could complete his mission. Cahouet recruited Anthony P. Terracciano, former vice chairman at Chase Manhattan Corporation, as president and chief operating officer.

Cahouet immediately froze salaries and ordered the 19,500-member staff reduced by 10%, to Wall Street's approval. The following year, in 1988, the company formed Grant Street National Bank, a separate entity created solely to clean Mellon's bad-debt slate by liquidating many of its weak domestic loans. The bank is partly backed by Mellon funds and junk bonds, sold to investors who hope sales of property securing the bad loans will be profitable. If all goes according to plan, the complicated "good bank, bad bank" plan will allow managers to focus on healthier areas.

Cahouet's plan is to return the company to its original position as a regional bank by becoming a more niche-oriented institution. Specifically, Mellon will concentrate on providing loans and other services to medium-sized companies, breaking its pattern of overextension to large, multinational corporations and foreign governments. This long-term goal to become a super-regional bank, however, puts Mellon in direct competition with PNC Financial, the parent company of Pittsburgh National Bank, which has operated very successfully on the middle-market level for years.

Mellon's approach will be to emphasize its service businesses—trust and investment, data processing, and cash management—which show no signs of slowing down. In 1988, the company acquired Backroom Systems Group, which offers personal computer software designed to automate labor-intensive tasks for financial institutions. Determined to maintain its leadership in the data-processing industry, Mellon has also continued to develop BancSource, a data-processing system that will eventually perform all customer loan and deposit processing.

The final decade of the 20th century will mark the first time that Pennsylvania allows true statewide banking; previously, state law governed how many branches a bank could open beyond county borders. The new law will allow banks to offer services where they make sense in terms of market coverage, not physical boundaries. The 1990s will determine whether Mellon can fully exploit the region to become a leader in the super-regional market.

Principal Subsidiaries: Mellon Bank, N.A.; Mellon Bank (DE) National Association; Mellon Bank (FL) National Association; Mellon Bank (MD); Mellon Bank (North) National Association; Mellon Bank (East) National Association; Mellon Bank (Central) National Association; Mellon Financial Services Corporation; The Commonwealth National Bank; Data-Link Systems Inc.; Mellon Bank International; Mellon Securities Trust Company; Mellon InvestData Corporation; Backroom Systems Group; Collection Services Corporation; InvestNet Corporation; Mellon Bank Canada; Mellon Securities Ltd. (England); Mellon-Pictet International Management Ltd. (England).

Further Reading: McCullough, C.H. *One Hundred Years of Banking*, Herbick and Held Printing Company, 1969; Hersh, Burton. *The Mellon Family: A Fortune in History*, New York, William Morrow and Company, 1978; Koskoff, David E. *The Mellons: The Chronicle of America's Richest Family*, New York, Thomas Y. Crowell, 1978.

MIDLAND BANK PLC

Poultry
London EC2P 2BX
United Kingdom
(01) 260–8000

Public Company
Incorporated: 1836
Employees: 59,093
Assets: £55.7 billion (US$100.75 billion)
Stock Index: London

Although it has fallen off somewhat from its heyday in the first half of the 20th century, when it was the largest bank in the world, Midland Bank is an institution with a proud history and is still one of the four largest deposit banks in the United Kingdom.

The Birmingham & Midland Bank was founded in 1836 as a joint-stock company. The leading figure among its founders was Charles Geach, a 28-year-old Bank of England clerk stationed in Birmingham who quit his job to become the new institution's general manager, which he remained until his death in 1854. Midland's starting capital was a very modest £28,000, but the bank quickly proved to be a successful enterprise. It prospered quietly until 1851, when it acquired Bates & Robins, a Stourbridge private bank. In 1862 it added Baker & Crane, another private bank. These two acquisitions marked the beginning of a long series of amalgamations that would turn Midland into a banking powerhouse by the early years of the next century.

Despite its early success, Midland remained a relatively small institution for the next twenty years, its operations limited to Birmingham and the immediate area. But the bank expanded in the 1880s, beginning with the acquisition of Union Bank of Birmingham in 1883. Amalgamation with Coventry Union Banking Company and Leamington Priors & Warwickshire Banking Company followed in 1889, as well as Derby Commercial Bank, Leeds & County Bank, and Exchange & Discount Bank, Leeds in 1890.

Edward Holden became Midland's general manager in 1891, and it was under his guidance that the bank experienced its greatest rise in stature. Perhaps the most momentous decision of his career at the head of Midland was also one of his earliest: In 1891, Midland acquired Central Bank of London. In one leap, the bank transformed itself from a provincial institution with a presence limited to the industrial Midlands to one with nationwide ambitions and a strong presence in the financial capital of the world. Midland moved its headquarters to London that year and renamed itself London & Midland Bank (it would drop the first half of the name in 1923, giving it its current form).

A further wave of acquisitions in the 1890s established Midland's presence throughout England, from the Scottish border in the North to the Channel Islands in the South. By 1898, it had 250 branches in England and Wales, and £32 million in deposits. Holden's expansion policy was nothing if not aggressive; a contemporary cartoon portrayed him as a hunter bagging hares labeled with the names of Midland acquisitions. He would make an unsolicited takeover offer for a bank, and, if it refused, open a Midland branch to compete with it as soon as possible.

Midland's expansion continued into the early years of the 20th century. The acquisition of North & South Wales Bank in 1908 was one of its more important acquisitions, giving Midland stronger Welsh connections. In 1914 it took over Metropolitan Bank, a substantial institution in its own right with deposits of almost £12 million. In that same year, Midland expanded its presence into Northern Ireland with the purchase of a large interest in the Belfast Banking Company. And in 1918, the bank made its largest acquisition to date when it bought out the London Joint-Stock Bank, with more than £60 million worth of deposits.

Midland also took an increased interest in foreign loans and underwriting during this time. After assuming the title of managing director in 1898 and delegating much of his authority to senior executives, Holden travelled to North America and became convinced that his bank ought to do more overseas business. His straightforward manner won him friends in the American banking community, and he once considered opening Midland branches in New York and Chicago. At Holden's instigation, Midland opened a foreign exchange department in 1905, the first British deposit bank to do so. His London colleagues criticized the move as unconventional, but it proved so successful that all of Midland's major competitors eventually followed suit. The bank's traveler's check business and its installation of branch offices on Cunard ocean liners in 1920 both stemmed from this interest in foreign business.

Sir Edward Holden (he had been made a baronet in 1909) died in 1919. He had started out as a bank clerk and worked in the banking business all his life, and it was a sign of the stature that Midland Bank had achieved during his reign that his successor as chairman was a Cambridge graduate who had served as first lord of the admiralty, home secretary, and chancellor of the exchequer in the liberal government of Prime Minister Henry Asquith. The Rt. Hon. Reginald McKenna left politics in 1917 to become Holden's heir apparent, but remained an outspoken authority on economic matters all his life and was a noted ally of John Maynard Keynes.

Under McKenna, Midland stopped its practice of expansion through acquisition, but only because treasury regulations in the 1920s made mergers virtually impossible. The purchase of North of Scotland Bank in 1924 would be Midland's last acquisition for more than 40 years. Despite these difficulties and the political and economic instability of the interwar years, Midland still prospered and expanded through its branch network. By 1939, it had over 2,100 branch offices. By 1934, it had become the largest deposit bank in the world, with more than £457 million in assets.

Reginald McKenna died in 1943. During the 1940s and most of the 1950s, Midland was comparatively dormant, at first because of the disruption and destruction caused by World War II, and after the war had ended, because of tight credit restrictions. Expansion of its branch network stopped.

The government eased credit restrictions in 1958 and expansion resumed, but Midland found that it had fallen behind its major competitors—Barclays, Lloyds, National Provincial, and Westminster formed the Big Five deposit banks along with Midland—in developing its foreign operations, an area in which it had once blazed the trail. To rectify this situation, Midland combined with the Commercial Bank of Australia, Canada's Standard Bank, and the Toronto-Dominion Bank in 1963 to form Midland and International Bank. The new institution was designed to engage in both merchant and development banking activities, and it also marked the first time that a British bank participated in an international banking joint venture.

In 1967 Midland scored another first when it purchased a 33% interest in the merchant bank Samuel Montagu. This marked the first merger in Britain between a merchant bank and a deposit bank, and was taken as a sign that the Bank of England was willing to blur the traditional lines between financial companies. Midland wanted to diversify its activities and also sought Montagu's expertise in international markets, while Montagu felt that it would gain business among Midland customers.

During the late 1960s, as Midland shed its image as a banker's bank and a correspondent bank, it cofounded Bank Européene de Creditâ Moyen Terme and several other consortium banks, with Deutsche Bank, Amsterdam-Rotterdam Bank and Société General de Banque, but later divested itself of these consortium banks.

In 1974 Midland increased its stake in Samuel Montagu to 100%. It also acquired another merchant bank, the Drayton Corporation, and merged it into Montagu. This stronger commitment to merchant banking did not work entirely to Midland's advantage, however; Montagu's financial performance had been solid, but Drayton came with many questionable real estate investments, causing Midland's position in merchant banking to slip somewhat after the acquisition. In 1982 it sold a 40% stake in Montagu to Aetna Life and Casualty, only to buy it back in 1985.

Despite its international ventures, Midland still lagged behind its rivals in establishing an overseas presence in the late 1970s. The problem was that Midland had done all of its foreign business through correspondent banks, consortiums, and joint ventures and had little direct representation abroad. Midland promptly tried to make up for lost time, but with mixed results. In 1979 it acquired 67% of Banque de la Construction et les Travaux Public, a French mortgage and real estate bank. That year it also made a bid for the American financial company Walter E. Heller, but called it off after discovering that Heller held an unusually high number of problem loans in its portfolio. In 1980 Midland purchased 60% of Trinkaus und Burkhardt, West Germany's largest privately owned bank, from Citicorp. And in 1982 it acquired a 69% interest in Handelsfinanz Bank of Geneva from Italy's Banca Commerciale Italiana. These acquisitions gave Midland a substantial expertise in foreign markets.

But the centerpiece of this strategy was an unqualified disaster. In 1981, Midland acquired a 57% stake in Crocker National Bank, the fourth-largest bank in California and twelfth largest in the United States, for $820 million. It was the largest-ever foreign takeover of an American bank. Midland, of course, sought to establish a large direct presence in one of the most prosperous regions in the country through the deal, and Crocker felt that the increase in capital would allow it to expand. Midland, already the third-largest deposit bank in Britain, became the tenth-largest banking organization in the world when the deal was consummated.

But the honeymoon didn't last long. Crocker's financial performance began to falter almost from the moment Midland took it over, and collapsed in 1983 when it posted a loss of $62 million for the fourth quarter. Plagued by bad real estate loans and a substantial share of Latin American debt, it went on to lose $324 million for its parent company in 1984, causing *The Economist* to exclaim in one headline, "What a big hole Crocker is making in Midland's pocket." Nevertheless, Midland stuck by its beleaguered subsidiary, even buying out the rest of Crocker's stock in 1985 after it hit its rock-bottom price of $16.25 per share, down from $90 in 1983. But before long, Midland decided that it had had enough. In 1986 it sold Crocker National to one of its California rivals, Wells Fargo & Company, for $1.1 billion, roughly the same amount of money that Midland had sunk into Crocker.

But the Crocker debacle didn't end there. Five years of nursing a major acquisition had stunted Midland's capital base while its competitors increased theirs. So when Sir Kit McMahon, an Australian-born former deputy-governor of the Bank of England, became chairman and CEO in 1987, his first priority was to bolster Midland's capital by means of a rights issue and by selling assets. Profitable regional subsidiaries in Scotland, Ireland, and Northern Ireland were divested in 1987. In the same year, Midland Montagu was established, combining the group's treasury, global corporate, international, and investment-banking businesses. Midland Montagu was the result of the merger of Samuel Montagu & Company; Greenwell Montagu Gilt-Edged, the leading British government bond primary dealer; and Midland's international corporate banking operations.

Optimism about Midland began to surface again in the securities markets, and its depressed stock looked like a bargain. In 1987 several parties purchased substantial interests in the bank. Hanson Trust acquired 6.5%, tabloid publisher Robert Maxwell acquired 2.5%, and Prudential Insurance Company bought 2%. In 1988 the Kuwaiti Investment Office disclosed that it owned a

5.1% stake in Midland. All of this led to speculation in the financial press that Midland might itself become a takeover target. Midland reacted in late 1987 by agreeing to let the Hongkong and Shanghai Banking Corporation acquire a friendly 14.9% of its stock. Hongkong agreed to hold the stake for a standstill period of three years while the two banks consolidated and rationalized their international businesses, with Hongkong to concentrate on Asia and Midland on Europe in preparation for the single European market in 1992.

Midland Bank entered the late 1980s on the defensive, a possible takeover target needing to bolster its damaged capital base. It appeared to have blundered badly in its attempt to join the trend toward internationalization that had marked the financial industry since the late 1960s. But it still remains one of Britain's Big Four deposit banks (Westminster and National Provincial having merged in the 1970s) and one of the largest banks in the world.

Principal Subsidiaries: Forward Trust Limited; Griffin Factors Limited, Handelsfinanz Midland Bank (Switzerland) (85%); Midland Bank Group International Trade Services Limited; Greenwell Montagu Gilt-Edged; Greenwell Montagu Stockbrokers; Midland Bank SA (France) (76%); Midland Bank (Singapore) Limited; Midland Bank Trust Company Limited; Midland International Australia Ltd.; Midland International Financial Services BV (Netherlands); Midland Bank Insurance Services Ltd.; Midland Bank International Financial Services Ltd.; Midland Montagu Leasing Limited; Midland Montagu Inc. (U.S.); Midland International Financial Services BV; Midland Montagu Securities Inc.; Midland Montagu Leasing Ltd.; Midland Montagu Ventures Ltd.; Midland Stockbrokers; Samuel Montagu & Co. Limited; The Thomas Cook Group Limited; Trinkaus & Burkhardt KGaA (West Germany) (70%).

Further Reading: Ashby, J.F. *The Story of the Banks*, London, Hutchinson & Company, 1934; Green, Edwin and Holmes, A.R. *Midland: Bankers for 150 Years*, London, BT Batsford, 1986.

THE MITSUBISHI BANK, LTD.

7–1, Marunouchi 2-chome
Chiyoda-ku
Tokyo 100
Japan
(03) 240–1111

Public Company
Incorporated: 1919
Employees: 14,300
Assets: ¥43.31 trillion (US$346.54 billion)
Stock Index: Tokyo Osaka Kyoto Sapporo

The Mitsubishi Bank is only one of many companies that originated as a division of the giant Mitsubishi trading conglomerate and were later incorporated as independent companies. Before World War II, the various Mitsubishi companies were allowed to operate in concert as a large vertical monopoly called a *zaibatsu*. Postwar industrial legislation, however, brought about the disintegration of the conglomerate and forced each Mitsubishi company, including the Mitsubishi Bank, to endure success or failure without support from its sister companies. Industrial deregulation eventually allowed the group to re-form, and many now regard the Mitsubishi Bank as the leader or primary coordinator of business among its former *zaibatsu* partners.

The Mitsubishi Bank has its origin in the exchange office of the Mitsubishi Shoji, which was the original Mitsubishi company and one of the largest maritime shipping and warehousing enterprises in Japan. The exchange office added foreign-currency transactions to its business in 1890, and five years later was reorganized into a full-service banking department. By 1917, as the Mitsubishi group continued to grow, it became necessary that it reorganize. Several divisions were spun off into independent companies, including the bank, which became independent in 1919. The following year, the Mitsubishi Bank opened offices in New York and London.

Business for the Mitsubishi group as a whole remained quite strong through the 1920s, largely because of a rapidly expanding economy. As the primary instrument for the group's financial needs, the bank grew accordingly, and from 1919 to 1929 doubled its capitalization, to ¥100 million.

Japan's tumultuous industrialization brought down many banks, even those connected with trading conglomerates. The Mitsubishi group, however, was the strongest group in Japan, and survived calamitites such as the Kanto Earthquake in 1923 and several serious recessions.

Mitsubishi was one of the most active Japanese interests on the Asian mainland, particularly in Manchuria. The bank opened an office at Dairen, Manchuria's main port, in 1933. At this time, a group within the military was rising to power that advocated a neo-mercantilist Japanese domination of Asia. This led to war with China in 1937, and political isolation some years later. On the eve of World War II, Mitsubishi was forced to close its offices in both London and New York.

The war was at first a profitable venture for the Mitsubishi group, Japan's largest arms manufacturer. But after the United States joined the war against Japan, the entire nation's industrial organization had to be changed. In order to increase efficiency, the government ordered a massive centralization, which in 1943 resulted in the merger of the Mitsubishi Bank and the One Hundredth Bank. The following year, the bank opened another office in occupied Shanghai under a directive to assist Japanese commercial and miltary interests.

When the war ended in 1945, the Mitsubishi group had suffered devastating losses in virtually every area of its operation. This, coupled with the collapse of commerce and the currency, left the bank with little but its human capital. What remained of the organization was split into hundreds of smaller companies by the occupation authority. The Mitsubishi Bank, renamed Chiyoda Bank in 1948, was reorganized and its ranks were purged of war criminals.

The Chiyoda Bank, named for the Tokyo financial district in which it was headquartered, started over as a common city bank and was strictly forbidden to re-establish ties with the other former Mitsubishi companies. These regulations, however, were gradually relaxed over time until, in 1953, after reopening its offices in London and New York, the bank readopted the name Mitsubishi.

With the expertise of its remaining staff, the Mitsubishi Bank quickly re-established itself as a powerful trade coordinating entity and rebuilt its ties with the other Mitsubishi companies, particularly the four trading companies that had re-emerged in 1954. The bank doubled its capitalization to ¥5.5 trillion between 1953 and 1956, and again to ¥11 trillion in 1960. Indeed, the bank had grown so spectacularly that its managerial ranks soon failed to keep pace. In an effort to place more experienced workers in the field, in 1957 the bank established a training center.

During the 1960s, the Mitsubishi Bank opened offices in Los Angeles, Paris, and Seoul. As an institution increasingly involved in corporate finance, the bank followed its clients to both export and resource markets. It financed raw-material purchases, helped to build factories that turned out finished products, and participated in the distribution of those products worldwide. As such, the Mitsubishi Bank became an integral contributor to Japan's export-led growth.

Still chartered as a city bank, Mitsubishi was prevented

from engaging in certain foreign-exchange and long-term-financing activities. Individual banking, perhaps Japan's most stable business, was a low priority for Mitsubishi; the bank simply found greater opportunities in corporate business. Much of that opportunity grew from the influence the bank wielded inside the board rooms of its clients.

During the 1970s, the bank established several more offices in Europe, the United States, and Asia. A subsidiary, the Mitsubishi Bank of California, was opened in 1972. Later in the decade, however, as Japan became a capital-surplus nation, the lending market began to dry up as more and more companies elected to conduct their own financing. By the late 1970s, deregulation had narrowed profits on lending even further.

Recognizing the importance of information management, the bank established an information office in 1972, long before such intelligence units were popular. Such an office provided it the expertise with which to establish an investment-banking operation. Also, Mitsubishi experimented in new areas of business, including leasing, asset management, and a number of other quasi-financial ventures.

A very conservative operation, Mitsubishi is a known risk avoider. As a result, it was only minimally exposed to Third World lending and the rescheduling problems that came with that crisis.

Kazuo Ibuki initiated a broad corporate reorganization shortly after he was named president of the Mitsubishi Bank in June, 1986. In an effort to make Mitsubishi a universal, or full-service, international bank, Ibuki divided the company into five groups: international, merchant, corporate, national banking, and capital markets. A number of young, somewhat less stodgy employees have been promoted to management positions, injecting new imagination and enthusiasm into the organization.

The bank also reorganized its New York-based trust and banking subsidiary, formerly affiliated with the Bank of California, which Mitsubishi purchased in 1984 because it held great promise for Mitsubishi's entry into trust banking and securities.

Despite that development, the Mitsubishi Bank has yet to disprove its reputation as an unimaginative follower. But, especially in light of the changes occurring in the industry, this could be a positive quality. And even in a new, more competitive market, Mitsubishi will continue to benefit from its preferred position within the Mitsubishi group.

Principal Subsidiaries: Mitsubishi Bank of California (U.S.A.); Mitsubishi Bank of Canada; Japan International Bank Ltd. (U.K.); Mitsubishi Bank (Europe) S.A. (Belgium); Banco Mitsubishi Brasileiro, S.A. (Brazil); Liu Chong Hing Bank Ltd. (Hong Kong); Diamond Futures (Singapore) Pte. Ltd. (Singapore); Sime Diamond Leasing (Malaysia) Sdn. Bhd.; The Bank of California, N.A. (U.S.A.); Mitsubishi Bank (Panama) S.A.; Mitsubishi Finance (Cayman) Ltd. (Cayman Islands); Mitsubishi Finance (Hong Kong) Ltd.; Mitsubishi Finance International Ltd. (U.K.); Mitsubishi Bank of Australia, Ltd.; Mitsubishi Bank Trust Company of New York (U.S.A); Mitsubishi Bank (Switzerland) Ltd.; Siam Diamond Leasing (Singapore) Pte. Ltd.

THE MITSUBISHI TRUST & BANKING CORPORATION

4-5, Marunouchi 1-chome
Chiyoda-ku
Tokyo 100
Japan
(03) 212–1211

Public Company
Incorporated: 1927
Employees: 6,300
Assets: ¥17.2 trillion (US$137.62 billion)
Stock Index: Tokyo Osaka London

Mitsubishi Trust and Banking Corporation is the leading trust bank in Japan. The Mitsubishi group, originally a shipping and warehousing conglomerate, created a bank in 1919. The Mitsubishi Bank, however, was prevented by banking legislation from conducting trust operations, an increasingly popular and profitable business. In 1927 various members of the Mitsubishi conglomerate, or *zaibatsu*, led by the Mitsubishi Bank, capitalized and incorporated the Mitsubishi Trust & Banking Corporation. Although it was an entirely separate company, Mitsubishi Trust was controlled by other Mitsubishi companies through cross-ownership of stock and board representation.

Mitsubishi Trust spent much of its early existence busily building market share. The company met intense competition from trust operations run by rival *zaibatsu* groups, mainly Yasuda and Mitsui. In 1929 the company opened a branch office in Osaka, Japan's second city and also the headquarters of Sumitomo, another major *zaibatsu* that operated a trust bank.

Political battles within the Japanese government during much of the 1930s slowed the growth of the *zaibatsu* groups somewhat. A group of militarists who opposed the tremendous economic power of the *zaibatsu* came to power. Many of the Mitsubishi companies tried to be inconspicuous, turning their attention to internal consolidation, while the head of the group worked to maintain good relations with the new government.

Mitsubishi Trust opened its third branch, in Nagoya, in 1940, and additional branches in Fukuoka and Yokohama in 1941. Under the quasi-wartime economy, such expansions were officially considered good for economic efficiency. The new branches enabled Mitsubishi Trust to exploit opportunities in a wider area and to establish a more effective financial network.

Mitsubishi Trust served as a capital resource for the Mitsubishi group, which had become intimately involved with government as a military and public projects contractor. In 1942, with the war well under way, Mitsubishi Trust opened two additional branches, in Kyoto and Kobe.

After the war, however, Japan's economy was in ruins and the occupation authority enacted emergency measures to rescue Japan's financial industries. Mitsubishi Trust was effectively closed. While new financial legislation was drafted, the Trust was reorganized into a smaller company, now called Asahi Trust & Banking, and all its connections with other Mitsubishi companies were eliminated, in accordance with the new anti-monopoly law.

The company reopened in 1948, and was authorized to deal in foreign exchange the following year. In an effort to promote reconstruction and diversify its operations, Asahi Trust took over some stock investment trust business from the Yamaichi and Nikko securities houses.

Japanese industrial laws were liberalized in 1952, allowing former *zaibatsu* affiliates to re-establish limited cross-investment and resume use of their prewar names. Asahi Trust changed its name back to Mitsubushi Trust & Banking. In 1958 it opened a stock transfer agency.

During the 1960s Mitsubishi Trust once again became an integral capital resource for the companies of the Mitsubishi group. Mitsubishi Heavy Industries and the Mitsubishi Corporation, a general trading company, built up large minority stakes in the Trust. Like the other Mitsubishi companies, they provided the Trust with a steady stream of business.

While the Mitsubishi group never regained the power it held before the war, Mitsubishi Trust had become more important to the organization than ever before. As it entered the 1970s, it became increasingly involved in a financial combine within the group. This miniature conglomerate, consisting of the Trust, Mitsubishi Bank, Tokio Fire & Marine Insurance, and Meiji Mutual Life Insurance, acted as a major multi-service financial institution. As interlocking but separate companies, they were able to circumvent financial regulations preventing them from engaging in each others' lines of business.

Mitsubishi Trust maintained a somewhat different outlook from its group partners. While the manufacturing and trading companies of the Mitsubishi group were outward-looking and eager to develop foreign markets, Mitsubishi Trust concentrated on domestic business. It differed markedly from the Mitsubishi Bank, which had long ago established overseas offices to support the group's business in foreign markets. As the group companies continued to expand, they created greater demand for trust business and other banking services, which the Trust gladly provided.

During the 1980s lobbying efforts from every sector of Japanese finance sought to strike down the restrictive regulations which kept banks and other institutions specialized and numerous. When by the mid-1980s it was clear that deregulation would come, Mitsubishi Trust finally adopted a more aggressive attitude.

The company devised contingency plans to develop

a wider base of marketable services. The Trust, however, was in no grave danger of losing out, as it was already closely associated with friendly insurance companies, banks, and brokerages in the Mitsubishi group. Still, eager to exploit new opportunities in the United States, Mitsubishi Trust opened a branch office in New York in 1988.

Mitsubishi Trust & Banking is the leading trust bank in Japan. It enjoys excellent coverage in greater Tokyo, and continues to benefit from its association with the Mitsubishi group. Slow at first to respond to the liberalization of Japanese financial laws, it is now a most aggressive innovator. Its emphasis is on longer-term relationships and premium services. The company's growth has been impressive, and it shows no signs of slowing.

Principal Subsidiaries: Mitsubishi Trust & Banking Corporation (Europe) S.A. (Belgium); Mitsubishi Trust & Banking Corp. (U.S.A.); Mitsubishi Trust Australia Ltd.; Mitsubishi Trust International Ltd. (U.K.); Mitsubishi Trust Finance (Switzerland) Ltd.; Mitsubishi Trust Finance (Asia) Ltd.; MTBC Finance Inc. (U.S.A.).

THE MITSUI BANK, LTD.

1–1–2, Yuraku-cho
Chiyoda-ku
Tokyo 100
Japan
(03) 501–1111

Public Company
Incorporated: 1876
Employees: 10,250
Assets: ¥25.9 trillion (US$207.23 billion)
Stock Index: Tokyo Osaka Frankfurt

It is commonly believed that the Mitsui *zaibatsu*, or conglomerate, started its business as a bank. In fact, the company began trading in textiles and entered banking only after Takatoshi Hachirobei, a founder, decided in 1683 that currency would soon replace the barter system. That year Mitsui purchased a money exchange. This exchange began a slow, steady expansion after its appointment as the Tokugawa government's fiscal agent in Osaka. Mitsui's dry-goods business, meanwhile, declined steadily due to poor management.

In the mid-1860s, Mitsui switched its allegiance to rebel Meiji forces from the failing Tokugawa government, which had repeatedly levied costly tax assessments against the company. After the restoration of the Meiji emperor, Mitsui lobbied for and won a highly favored status in government. By the early 1870s, Mitsui held so much money for the government that it was basically a state treasury.

Rizaemon Minomura, the Mitsui director who was the architect of the company's rise to power, strongly advocated moving the firm to Tokyo, the new center of government and commerce. Once there, Mitsui began taking a more active role in underwriting industrial ventures. After an initial failure in international trading, Mitsui built up a domestic trading network and secured several government and military contracts. Reentering international trade some years later, Mitsui established numerous foreign offices, and in 1876 the Mitsui Bank was incorporated as a separate entity.

The Mitsui Bank served as the exclusive finance agent for the Mitsui trading company, called the *Bussan*, which had discovered a new and highly profitable trade in cottons and textiles. But, unhappy with its increasingly costly dependence on rival Mitsubishi for shipping and warehousing services, the Mitsui Bussan created its own shipping company. A tremendous bout of competition between the two companies ensued, and Mitsui eventually lost. As the underwriter for the Mitsui Bussan, the Mitsui Bank emerged financially exhausted.

But the bank benefited greatly from its privileged position in government. In addition, the Mitsui companies experienced unprecedented growth after Hikojiro Nakamigawa, a talented businessman and former president of the Sanyo Railway, joined Mitsui Bussan in 1891. As senior director, Nakamigawa dismissed redundant personnel and launched a concerted effort to develop Mitsui's industrial divisions. He also introduced the motto "people make Mitsui," a clever response to its rival's assertion that "organization makes Mitsubishi."

Mitsui again profited from its involvement in a military conflict, this time the Sino-Japanese War of 1894 to 1895. A recession following that war, however, halted the company's growth. Furthermore, Nakamigawa died in 1901, leaving the directorship to his rival and predecessor, Takashi Masuda. Masuda emerged from years of semi-retirement determined to shake Mitsui out of stagnation. He introduced foreign-exchange services, secured special trading rights for Mitsui in China, and even proposed purchasing Manchuria in 1911. Two years later he established a Chinese subsidiary, Chogoku Kogyo (China Industries Company).

Although it was a separate company, the Mitsui Bank was very broadly influenced by the Mitsui Bussan and its directors; Masuda in many ways retained authority over the bank's director, Shigeaki Ikeda. Ikeda distinguished himself at the bank by providing Masuda and his successor, Takuma Dan, with no surprises.

Mitsui at this time became a focal point for criticism by a right wing military faction that believed the *zaibatsu* should be destroyed because they had become too powerful. As a result of this group's rise to power, Takuma Dan was assassinated in 1932. Masuda designated Ikeda, a more neutral figure, to run the Bussan and Naojiro Kikumoto was named chairman of the bank.

When the militarists came to power, a centralization of power took place in industrial as well as government circles. Ikeda, in effect leader of both the Bussan and the bank, was additionally named governor of the Bank of Japan in 1937, and minister of finance and minister of trade and industry in 1938. He participated in the government's policy of expansion, supporting the colonization of Manchuria and the war against China, and later against the United States. The Mitsui Bank, meanwhile, was renamed the Teikoku Bank in 1943, following its merger with the Dai-Ichi Bank. Teruo Akashi was named chairman of the new bank. The following year, Teikoku absorbed the Jugo Bank, at the time about one-tenth the size of Teikoku.

When World War II ended in 1945, Ikeda was designated a "Class A war criminal" and purged from public life by the occupation authority. He died in 1950 at the age of 84.

Chairman Akashi was replaced by Junshiro Mandai in 1945. Mandai and six others, however resigned in 1946, shortly before the occupation authorities were to purge them as well. Kiichiro Satoh was then elected president of the bank. After the war the occupying authorities imposed a series of new industrial laws that eliminated the *zaibatsu* system by breaking the conglomerates into hundreds of smaller companies. The Dai-Ichi Bank was separated from Teikoku in 1948, and Teikoku was banned from reestablishing ties with former Mitsui companies. Teikoku, however, was designated an authorized foreign-exchange dealer in 1949.

The bank was permitted to establish correspondent agreements with American banks in 1950, which laid the groundwork for the reestablishment of Mitsui's international operations. After reopening offices in London, Bombay, and Bangkok, Mitsui incorporated an IBM punch-card computing system that permitted the bank to centralize more of its operations at its head office.

In 1954, following the relaxation of antimonopoly laws in 1949 and in 1952, Teikoku reverted to its former name, Mitsui Bank. Increasingly the Mitsui Bank began to conduct more business with the former *zaibatsu* companies. With an international network capable of assembling information on foreign markets in place, the *zaibatsu* began to re-form as a more loosely organized *keiretsu*, or banking conglomerate. This recentralization of industry was permitted by the government to encourage faster recovery and industrialization because of a perceived threat from communists on the Asian mainland.

In the meantime, since the bank's ability to grow was restricted by laws that prevented the establishment of more branch offices, Satoh led a campaign to increase deposits at existing branches.

Satoh was made chairman in 1959, and was succeeded as president by Masuo Yanagi, a career Mitsui employee, who in 1961 initiated an effort to control the bank's lending activities more efficiently. The rapid growth of the economy resulted in periods of simultaneous demand for loans and deposits; corporations borrowed as consumers spent. The addition of new consumer lending projects and the reestablishment of international banking activities resulted in greater liquidity and mobility, and made the bank more competitive.

The Mitsui Bank continued to bring itself closer to the public by marketing financial products specifically for private savers. In 1968 it merged with the Toto Bank, a small, consumer-oriented bank whose 16 branches greatly strengthened Mitsui's presence in Tokyo.

Kyubei Tanaka, who succeeded Yanagi in 1965, was himself succeeded in 1968 by Goro Koyama. Koyama presided over the widespread computerization of Mitsui and ordered the improvement of communications between branches to accommodate people who lived in suburbs but worked in the city.

Also in 1968, Mitsui participated with the Sanwa Bank in the creation of a national credit card company, the Japan Credit Bureau. In an effort to circumvent regulations limiting the number of a bank's branches, Mitsui and the Heiwa Sogo Bank concluded an agreement to service each other's customers, an agreement that was subsequently expanded to include other banks. During the early 1970s, the bank introduced automatic teller machines, which allowed depositors to withdraw money at any hour and greatly reduced labor costs for the bank.

The decision to remove the United States from the gold standard and the subsequent revaluation of the British pound had severe impact on the Japanese banking industry. The Mitsui Bank, which had grown heavily involved in international transactions, was forced to reorganize the following year. But, although profits were squeezed, the bank's capital and deposits reached new heights. Despite a second shock created by the OPEC oil embargo of 1974, the bank remained fairly stable, owing to conservative management and successful risk minimization.

Under President Joji Itakura and his successor Kenichi Kamiya, the Mitsui Bank became a much more business-oriented financial institution, participating in the establishment of special capital groups that oversaw the development of emerging companies breaking into expanding markets. One such venture included a 19-company collaboration on new software technologies. Through Bussan-sponsored monthly meetings, the Mitsui Bank coordinates its business with that of the approximately 40 members of the Mitsui Group, including Toshiba, Oji Paper, and Sapporo Breweries.

As Japan entered a period of lower, more stable growth in the early 1980s, the Mitsui Bank restructured in order to emphasize its business in the consumer and corporate fields and develop groups of market specialists. As part of the "Century Ten" plan, the restructuring was designed to make Mitsui a more competitive bank for the 1980s. Part of that strategy included a shift away from sheer volume (which is percentage oriented) toward more stable flat-fee business. The bank also introduced CMS, a cash-management system that linked its newly established continental headquarters in New York, London, and Tokyo.

In response to the Sumitomo Bank purchase of an interest in the American investment bank Goldman Sachs—a move that greatly strengthened that bank's position in international securities markets—the Mitsui Bank established closer relationships with Nomura Securities and Yamatame Securities.

Kamiya was promoted to chairman in June of 1988, and was succeeded as president by Ken-ichi Suematsu. The bank has repeatedly named like-minded men to the presidency. While that contributes to greater stability and continuity in management policies, critics have pointed out that it also created an army of yes-men. Regardless, the Mitsui Bank remains one of Japan's largest financial institutions. In August, 1989 Mitsui Bank and the Taiyo Kobe Bank announced that they would merge in April, 1990 to form Mitsui Kobe Bank, with about ¥40 trillion in assets. The merger, which will create the world's second-largest bank, can only strengthen both banks' positions in the rapidly changing financial world.

Principal Subsidiaries: Mitsui Finance Asia Ltd. (Hong Kong); Mitsui Financial Futures (Singapore) Pte. Ltd.; Mitsui Finance Australia Limited; Mitsui Manufacturers Bank (U.S.A.); Mitsui Bank of Canada; Mitsui Finance

Trust Company of New York (U.S.A.); Mitsui Finance (Switzerland) Limited; Mitsui Finance International Limited (U.K.); Mitsui Finance (Germany) GmbH; Mitsui Bank (Luxembourg) S.A.

Further Reading: The Eighty-Year History of the Mitsui Bank, Tokyo, Mitsui Bank, 1957; Japan Business History Institute, Ed. *The Mitsui Bank: A History of the First 100 Years*, Tokyo, Mitsui Bank, 1976.

THE MITSUI TRUST & BANKING COMPANY, LTD.

1–1, Nihonbashi-Muromachi 2-chome
Chuo-ku
Tokyo 103
Japan
(03) 270–9511

Public Company
Incorporated: 1924
Employees: 6,200
Assets: ¥10.96 trillion (US$87.69 billion)
Stock Index: Tokyo Osaka

The Mitsui Trust & Banking Company is the oldest institution of its kind in Japan. Mitsui Trust is specially chartered to perform trust banking services. Of Japan's seven trust banks, Mitsui ranks third in size.

In 1923 the Mitsui Bank was prevented from managing trusts by new government legislation. When Mitsui Bussan, the large trading conglomerate which created the Mitsui Bank, wanted to exploit new opportunities in trust banking, it was compelled to found an entirely new company. Using staff from the bank, the Bussan helped to create the Mitsui Trust Company in 1924.

Although it was an independent company, Mitsui Trust was controlled by other Mitsui companies. Just as Mitsui Bank was, to a great extent, the private bank of the Mitsui group, Mitsui Trust was the trust management division of the bank, separated from it only by a regulatory technicality.

As a result of its position within the Mitsui group and behind Mitsui Bank, Mitsui Trust was insulated from many of the political difficulties of the Bussan. In 1932 a group of militarists opposed to the domination of Japanese conglomerates assassinated Takuma Dan, the head of Mitsui Bussan. When these militarists gained control of the government, however, they were compelled to reach an accommodation with the conglomerates in order to achieve the military and industrial mobilization they desired. Instead of being broken up, Mitsui became larger and stronger.

As the group expanded, Mitsui Trust's investment portfolios grew as well. But by the end of World War II, Japan was in ruins. Under the occupation authority, the banking and financial system was reorganized and new anti-monopoly laws were passed. These laws forced conglomerates like Mitsui to disband into thousands of smaller, independent companies, none of which were permitted to keep their prewar names.

Mitsui Trust resumed its business in 1948 as the Tokyo Trust & Banking Company. In order to compete better with the larger city banks, the company was also chartered to engage in general banking. In 1952 industrial laws were relaxed, and Tokyo Trust & Banking was permitted to change its name back to Mitsui. Furthermore, the company was allowed to re-establish ties with other Mitsui companies.

During the 1950s and 1960s, Mitsui Trust maintained a low profile in industrial and banking matters. Because it conducted a great majority of its business with other Mitsui group companies, Mitsui Trust's growth was broadly based among several industries, and therefore largely insulated from sectoral recessions. Profits were lightly and only temporarily affected by the oil crisis of 1973–1974.

By 1980 Mitsui Trust was one of the largest trust banks in Japan. Its continuing success was built largely on the strength of Japan's export-led growth and on the increasingly strong position of Mitsui group companies in the domestic economy.

The 1980s, however, marked the beginning of a new era in Japanese finance. There was increased pressure on Japanese legislators to liberalize the system of financial regulation that prevented financial institutions from entering a broader range of services. The prospect of deregulation forced the management of Mitsui Trust to adopt a more aggressive strategy. While it had operated for many years as a *de facto* division of the Mitsui group with a well-protected niche in the trust banking market, it was now faced with increasingly dynamic and versatile competition.

With further domestic opportunities hampered by its association with Mitsui companies, Mitsui Trust turned to international markets, already a traditional strength. It bolstered its network of overseas offices and prepared to make its bold and very successful entry into foreign capital markets.

Mitsui Trust is today the third largest trust bank in Japan. Its international operations are among the strongest in the world (it is the leading Japanese Eurobond dealer in Europe). As it consolidates its position in international finance, Mitsui Trust is likely to become more aggressive and develop a higher public profile.

Principal Subsidiaries: Mitsui Trust Finance (Hong Kong) Ltd.; Mitsui Trust Bank (Europe) S.A.; Mitsui Trust Finance (Switzerland) Ltd.; Mitsui Trust International Ltd.; Mitsui Trust Finance (Australia) Ltd.; Mitsui Trust Bank (U.S.A.); Mitsui Trust Futures (Singapore) Pte. Ltd.

JPMorgan

J.P. MORGAN & CO. INCORPORATED

23 Wall Street
New York, New York 10015
U.S.A.
(212) 483-2323

Public Company
Incorporated: 1940
Employees: 15,350
Assets: $83.92 billion
Stock Index: New York London Swiss Paris Tokyo

J.P. Morgan & Co. Incorporated is a holding company for entities engaged in a wide range of banking activities worldwide, including corporate finance advisory, securities and trading, trust and agency, and other financial services.

J.P. Morgan's clients are principally corporations, governmental bodies, and other financial institutions, although the company also offers a variety of banking and asset management services to wealthy individuals and other organizations.

J.P. Morgan's principal banking subsidiary is Morgan Guaranty Trust Company of New York, the product of the 1959 merger between J.P. Morgan and Guaranty Trust Company of New York. The J.P. Morgan name re-emerged in 1968 as the holding company of Morgan Guaranty and a number of other subsidiaries.

Alternately one of the most admired and most hated men in America, the savior of his country and a robber baron, John Pierpont Morgan, the founder of J.P. Morgan & Company, was a legendary financier who wielded national and international power on a spectacular scale. Morgan did not allow publicity to influence his actions in the slightest degree. Indeed, Morgan's confidence in his own ultimate success and his unapologetic arrogance are two legacies he handed down to the company that bears his name.

Morgan's father, Junius Spencer Morgan, an American, became a partner in the influential London banking firm of George Peabody and Company in 1854, changing the name of the company to J.S. Morgan & Co. when Peabody retired and he took over in 1864. (Today that firm is Morgan Grenfell.) The firm soon became one of the most important links between London and the rapidly developing American financial community. J.P. Morgan entered his father's banking house in 1854 at the age of 17. In 1857 he was sent to work for the firm Duncan, Sherman & Co. in New York, the New York correspondent of his father's firm. In 1860, Morgan left Duncan, Sherman and founded J.P. Morgan and Company to act as agent for his father's company. In 1864 J. P. Morgan asked Charles H. Dabney to be senior partner in a new firm, which became Dabney, Morgan & Co.

Morgan first drew the attention of the business community in 1869, when he successfully battled Jay Gould and James Fisk, two notorious American financial buccaneers, for control of the Albany and Susquehanna Railroad. In 1871 Dabney retired and Anthony J. Drexel, the head of the Philadelphia investment bank Drexel & Co., became Morgan's new senior partner in a firm called Drexel Morgan & Co.

In 1879, Morgan arranged to sell $25 million worth of the Vanderbilt interest in New York Central Railroad through his father's firm in England. Vanderbilt was impressed enough to give Morgan a seat on the board of directors of New York Central. Six years later Morgan used this position to settle a dispute between the New York Central and Pennsylvania railroads over the New York, West Shore and Buffalo Railroad. It was senseless, Morgan argued, for Pennsylvania and New York Central to engage in a rate war. He suggested that the Pennsylvania should allow the Central to buy the West Shore line and that the Central should turn over control of the South Pennsylvania to the Pennsylvania. They quickly agreed.

In 1886 Morgan implemented reorganization plans for both the Philadelphia and Reading Railroad and the Chesapeake and Ohio Railroad. A short time later, he also played a major role in reorganizing the Baltimore and Ohio. After the Interstate Commerce Act was passed in 1887, Morgan helped to convince the country's railroad executives to abide by the law and cooperate with the Interstate Commerce Commission. After the Panic of 1893 Morgan was called upon by the government to reorganize a number of the leading railway systems in the nation, including the Southern, the Erie, the Philadelphia and Reading, and the Northern Pacific. By the end of the century, only two American systems were outside his control.

When Junius Morgan died in 1890, J. P. Morgan became head of the London house. Three years later, in 1893, Anthony Drexel also died, and in 1895 Morgan reorganized the Morgan and Drexel firms. New York–based Drexel Morgan became J.P. Morgan & Co., into which the Philadelphia-based Drexel & Co. was partially merged. At the same time, Drexel, Harjes & Co., Drexel's prominent Paris-based investment banking business, was renamed Morgan, Harjes & Co. At the head now of houses in New York, Philadelphia, London, and Paris, Morgan was a a commanding figure in international finance.

At the time, Morgan was still relatively unknown to most of his fellow Americans, but not for long. In 1895 President Grover Cleveland turned to the international bankers for help in stemming the flow of the treasury's gold reserves that had followed the panic of 1893. Morgan, with his connections to the European banking community, helped supply the government with $56 million in gold, much of it from abroad, and profited handsomely on the transaction. The public protest that followed, fueled among other things by Morgan's refusal to reveal his profits to a congressional investigative committee, contributed to Cleveland's fall from power in 1896.

Although Morgan had now become one of the most vilified men in America, his power was only enhanced by the constant publicity. Having organized the railroads and guided the infant Edison Electric Company through its early years, culminating in its merger with the Thomson-Houston Electric Company to create the General Electric Company in 1891, Morgan next turned to the steel industry. In the late 1890s he helped create the Federal Steel Company, the National Tube Company, and the American Bridge Company. The house of Morgan was also instrumental in arranging the takeover of the giant Carnegie Steel Company to form the U.S. Steel Corporation in 1901. A year later, Morgan financed the consolidation of McCormick Harvesting Machine Company, Deering Company, and three other harvesting-machine companies into the giant International Harvester Company.

Also in 1902 Morgan organized the International Mercantile Marine Company, a combination of British and American shipping concerns, to stabilize the shipping trade as his railroad combinations had done. It was one of his rare failures. At the same time, Morgan's image was also sullied in a fight for control of the North Pacific Railroad.

But during the panic of 1907, government officials and important bankers quickly turned to Morgan for leadership, and the secretary of the treasury deposited substantial government relief funds with J.P. Morgan and its affiliate banks.

As he grew older, Morgan continued to consolidate his influence in a number of fields, particularly banking and insurance. Morgan owned a controlling interest in First National Bank of New York and his bank's future partner, Guaranty Trust Company of New York, and was influential in many other prominent New York banks. He already had a significant voice in the administration of the New York Life Insurance Company when he gained a controlling interest in the Equitable Life Assurance Society in 1909.

It was fear of the power of this "money trust" within the New York banking and insurance community, firmly anchored by Morgan, that instigated a congressional investigation in 1912 by the Pujo Committee. The committee revealed that if all the Morgan partners and the directors of First National, Bankers Trust, and Guaranty Trust were added together, this group of businessmen held 341 directorships in 112 banking, insurance, transportation, public-utility, and trading companies with resources altogether of more than $22 billion.

When J. P. Morgan died in 1913, J. P. Morgan Jr., known as Jack, became the head of the family business. Jack Morgan continued his father's work, dealing with industry, railroads, banks, and other financial institutions, but he also made his own reputation in government financing. As the most important international banking house in America, Morgan became the commercial agent for the French and British governments in the United States during World War I, handling orders for more than $3 billion in war supplies before America entered the war. Morgan also organized a group of more than 2,000 banks to underwrite bonds totaling some $1.5 billion for Great Britain and France.

After the war ended, J.P. Morgan & Co. was more powerful than ever. Before the war, the firm's European connections were crucial in bringing capital to a developing America; in the postwar era, however, the United States became a creditor nation and the most important financial market in the world, and Morgan was its leading banker. Continuing to improve its reputation in government financing and the recapitalization of national debts, between 1917 and 1926 the bank floated bond issues totaling nearly $12 billion for Austria, Cuba, Canada, Germany, Belgium, France, Great Britain, and Italy.

When the stock market crashed on October 22, 1929, J.P. Morgan & Co. was again behind a major attempt to avert financial disaster. Five important bankers met in Jack Morgan's office on October 24, 1929 to create a pool to preserve some order in the stock market and stave off disaster. Not only were they unsuccessful, but, afterwards J.P. Morgan and the other companies involved were kept under close governmental supervision to determine whether they contributed to the stock market crash.

During the 1930s J.P. Morgan underwent drastic changes. The Banking Act of 1933, better known as the Glass-Steagall Act, required a separation of deposit and investment banking. As a result, the following year J.P. Morgan & Co. left the investment-banking business and became a private commercial bank. Three Morgan partners left the bank in 1935 to create a new investment banking firm, Morgan Stanley & Company, to handle the business Morgan had been forced to abandon. Although Jack Morgan continued as head of the commercial bank, by the mid-1930s most of its actual management was left to other partners.

In 1940, J.P. Morgan and Company was incorporated as a state bank under the laws of New York and it began the sale of common stock on the New York exchange. This major change was made because Morgan needed more capital than its distinguished, but not particularly wealthy, partners could provide. With incorporation, Morgan's ties with the still-private Drexel & Co. were severed. (Drexel went on to become the Wall Street phenomenon of the 1980s, Drexel Burnham Lambert.)

As a publicly owned, state-chartered bank, Morgan was now permitted to open a trust department, a business private partnerships were prohibited from entering. Formed by Thomas Lamont, Morgan's new chairman, the trust department managed the money of individuals, estates, and large institutions. This department soon became the new center of Morgan's power, managing the pensions and profit sharing funds of some of the largest firms in the country.

Jack Morgan died on March 13, 1943, and his eldest son, Junius S. Morgan II, assumed his position as a director of the firm. Junius, however, remained a figurehead;

the operations of the bank were supervised by various partners and department heads. During the late 1940s and throughout the 1950s, Morgan concentrated on its trust and wholesale banking activities.

In 1959, the world financial community was surprised by the announcement of a merger between Morgan and Guaranty Trust.

The Guaranty Trust Company of New York traced its roots to two predecessors: the New York Guaranty and Indemnity Company, founded in 1864 and renamed Guaranty Trust Company of New York in 1896, and the National Bank of Commerce, the subsidiary of the Bank of Commerce, which was founded in 1839. New York Guaranty's original business was loaning money against warehouse receipts. It was closely connected with the Mutual Life Insurance Company after 1891, and eventually became a power in financing international trade. It was separated from Mutual Life in 1911, and went on to establish a prominent bond department and to underwrite corporate securities. The National Bank of Commerce was also a commercial bank involved primarily in lending to manufacturers and tradesmen. Both Guaranty and National Commerce had close ties to J.P. Morgan & Co. J. P. Morgan himself was a director of the National Bank of Commerce from 1875 to 1910, while several Morgan partners were on Guaranty's board.

Guaranty and National Commerce merged in 1929 to increase their strength and position themselves to broaden the range of wholesale services they could offer their customers. After the merger, the new bank, which retained the Guaranty name and charter, became New York's most prominent trust bank as well as one of the largest dealers in government obligations.

J.P. Morgan and Guaranty Trust, both preeminent wholesale banks, primarily served large corporate accounts. Their merger was intended to make Morgan Guaranty not only the principal banker for corporate enterprise, but also the major banker for governments, foundations, and institutions both at home and abroad. In addition, the new bank managed $6.5 billion in trusts, the largest trust business in the world. The merger of Morgan and Guaranty meant that, unlike other major wholesale and commercial banks, the new Morgan Guaranty would have no retail business to fall back on, but the banks' gamble, and the merger, worked.

In 1960 Morgan Guaranty established the Morgan Guaranty International Banking Corporation and Morgan Guaranty International Finance Corporation to further its international expansion. The next year, Morgan Guaranty made its first, and last, attempt to enter the retail banking business. Morgan Guaranty proposed an affiliation with six upstate New York banks, but the Federal Reserve rejected the arrangement in 1962, fearing too great a concentration of power. With this rejection, Morgan Guaranty renewed its commitment to international operations. The three foreign branches that the bank had at the time of its merger had jumped to 26 branches and representative offices by 1978.

In 1969, Morgan Guaranty became the wholly owned subsidiary of J.P. Morgan & Co., a new holding company. Nearly every major bank made similar arrangements at the time, following Citibank's lead, to take advantage of a bank holding company's greater freedom to engage in other financial businesses.

At the end of the 1970s, Morgan's total assets amounted to $43.5 billion. The firm was the largest stockholder in America, with more than $15 billion invested in the stock market, and its trust department ranked as one of the top five investors in more than 50 major American corporations such as ITT, Sears, and Citicorp.

The 1980s saw drastic change in banking as major corporations increasingly raised working capital in the securities markets rather than from banks, and the trend towards global banking and universal financial services accelerated. J.P. Morgan began to move back to its origins in investment and merchant banking, including advising clients on corporate restructurings and mergers and acquisitions, and, when possible, securities underwriting and trading. While such securities activities in the United States were severely curtailed by the 1933 Glass Steagall legislation, J.P. Morgan entered the Eurobond market in 1979, and throughout the 1980s, J.P. Morgan Securities Ltd., the firm's London-based securities subsidiary, was among the leading underwriters in that market.

J.P. Morgan continued to call for repeal of Glass Steagall legislation and for deregulation of the products and services that U.S. banks could offer. While Congress continued to postpone action, in 1987, the Federal Reserve Board allowed certain bank units, including J.P. Morgan Securities Inc., the firm's U.S. securities subsidiary and a primary dealer in U.S. government securities, to deal in commercial paper, municipal revenue bonds, and consumer-related receivables. In 1989, the Federal Reserve gave J.P. Morgan Securities permission to underwrite, within a limit of 5% of total revenues, corporate debt securities, and the firm immediately began to trade and deal in corporate bonds. Pending final approval from the Federal Reserve, which is expected in 1990, J.P. Morgan will also begin to deal in equity securities, allowing the firm to add to the range of financial alternatives it can offer clients worldwide.

During the decade, J.P. Morgan achieved notable success in international corporate finance and mergers and acquisitions advisory. The firm's emphasis on fundamental analysis and innovative financial structures won it a substantial number of complex and high-profile mandates, and in 1989, J.P. Morgan was involved in some of the largest cross-border and U.S. transactions of the year, including the mergers of SmithKline Beckman with the Beecham Group and McCaw Cellular Communications with Lin Broadcasting, and the leveraged buyout of Hospital Corporation of America. This success was marred slightly in 1986 when it came to light that Antonio Gebauer, a senior vice president, had diverted $8 million in clients' funds for his own use, a scandal that prompted Morgan to tighten some controls.

Beginning in 1982, J.P. Morgan, like most of the international banking community, was severely affected by the inability of Third World countries to service and repay their growing debt obligations. Throughout the decade both banks and debtors nations were involved in the renegotiation and restructuring of existing debt programs.

The crisis deepened when Brazil suspended payment of interest on its loans in 1987, and J.P. Morgan placed $1.3 billion of Brazilian debt on a non-accrual basis. It became clear that new solutions to the debt crisis had to be found and in 1988, J.P. Morgan and the Government of Mexico offered the first voluntary debt exchange program. However, the environment continued to be highly uncertain, and in September 1989, J.P. Morgan announced that it had added $2 billion to its allowance for loan loss reserves, bringing its reserves to approximately 70% of its Third World debt exposure but causing it to post losses of $1.3 billion for 1989.

J.P. Morgan's capital strength and long-established reputation for high ethical standards will be a valuable advantage as markets around the world become increasingly volatile and competition fiercer. In the past decade, J.P. Morgan has emerged as a leading participant in the world's most active capital markets, adviser to governments and large, international corporations, and provider of innovative products and services.

As it enters the 1990s, Morgan is still the blue blood of American banks. Although its founder, who told the Pujo Committee in 1912: "I do not compete for deposits. . . . They come," might be surprised by the bank's aggressive new posture, its transformation from a traditional commercial bank into an international institution has brought it closer to J. Pierpont Morgan's own firm.

Principal Subsidiaries: Morgan Guaranty Trust Company of New York; Morgan Bank; Morgan Futures Corp.; Morgan Investment Corp.; J.P. Morgan International Finance N.V.; J.P. Morgan International Capital N.V.; Morgan Trust of Florida N.A.; Morgan Trust of the Bahamas Limited; J.P. Morgan Investment Management Inc.; J.P. Morgan Private Finance Corp. of Florida; Morgan Capital Corp.; Morgan Portfolio Corp.; Morgan Realty Corp.; Morgan Securities Services Corp.; Morgan Shareholders Services Trust Co.; Morgan Fonciere Cayman Island Ltd.; Morgan Holdings Corp.; Morgan Christiana Bank; Morgan Community Development Corp.; J.P. Morgan Securities Holdings, Inc.; J.P. Morgan Equities, Inc.; Morgan Christiana Corp.; J.P. Morgan International Holdings Corp.; Morgan Trust Company of the Cayman Islands Ltd.; J.P. Morgan Securities, Inc.

Further Reading: Allen, Frederick Lewis. *The Great Pierpont Morgan*, New York, Harper & Brothers, 1949; Hoyt, Edwin Palmer. *The House of Morgan*, New York, Dodd, Mead, 1966; Carosso, Vincent P. *Investment Banking in America*, Cambridge, Harvard University Press, 1970.

NATIONAL WESTMINSTER BANK PLC

41 Lothbury
London EC2P 2BP
United Kingdom
(071) 726–1000

Public Company
Incorporated: 1968
Employees: 110,000
Assets: £98.64 billion (US$178.4 billion)
Stock Index: London New York Tokyo

National Westminster Bank (NatWest) was created in 1968 by the merger of three major banks all established in the early 19th century: the District Bank, the National Provincial Bank, and the Westminster Bank. By vigorously expanding in size and significantly improving the quality of its customer services since its first business day in 1970, NatWest overtook Barclays to become Britain's largest commercial bank.

The District Bank was first established in 1829 in Manchester as the Manchester and Liverpool District Banking Company, with a starting nominal capital of £3 million. The company planned to create a banking network for northwest England by opening new branches and acquiring smaller banks, and within five years had opened 17 branches.

By 1840, however, District Bank was forced to write off over £500,000 in bad debts—a huge sum at the time—due to management misjudgment, slowing the firm's acquisitions and expansion for the next few years. In addition, the bank was closely associated with England's textile industry; the company suffered during the cotton famine of the 1860s caused by the North's blockade of southern ports during the American Civil War. Judicious acquisitions, however, helped District Bank to weather this particular storm.

At the beginning of 1885, District Bank, recovered from its previous losses, opened an office in London. As customer deposits increased and astute commercial credit policies and management were put to work, the bank began a moderate expansion program that lasted until the outbreak of World War I. After a five-year hiatus, the company was caught up in the postwar boom and opened 130 new branches between 1919 and 1924.

Relatively unscathed by the worldwide Depression of the late 1920s and early 1930s, the bank continued its expansion program, and immediately after World War II decided to create a network of branches throughout the country. In 1935 District Bank merged with the County Bank, a Manchester-based entity, increasing its paid-up capital to almost £3 million and kicking off its nationwide expansion. This strong-growth strategy continued unabated up to and following World War II until District Bank's acquisition by National Provincial Bank in 1962.

National Provincial Bank was organized as a joint-stock company in 1833. At the time, the Bank of England had exclusive statutory power to issue bank notes within a 65-mile radius of London. Although the bank's administrative offices were in London, it decided to open its branches outside the 65-mile radius so that the bank could issue its own notes. From the beginning National Provincial lived up to its name, serving provincial customers throughout England. The bank was without a national competitor for about 60 years.

The first branch of National Provincial bank was opened on January 1, 1834 in Gloucester. Like the District Bank, the company planned to establish new branches and acquire smaller banks, and by 1835 had opened 20 new offices. By the mid-1860s, National Provincial had acquired more than a dozen small banks and had established 122 branches and sub-branches throughout England and Wales. It finally opened a London banking office in 1866, recognizing that a presence in the world's financial capital was worth the sacrifice of its note-issuing privilege.

The bank continued to grow rapidly. At the turn of the century, the company had about 250 offices in England and Wales and approximately £3 million in capital. After World War I, the company began an accelerated acquisition-and-merger strategy. The most important of its mergers during this time was with the Union of London and Smiths Bank, itself the product of the amalgamation of two of the most venerable banking institutions in England, which added 230 branches to National Provincial's growing financial network.

Although National Provincial's growth had been interrupted by World War I, the bank vigorously renewed its acquisition program after the war. Sheffield Banking Company, Northamptonshire Union Bank, Guernsey Banking Company, Bradford District Bank, and Coutts & Company, all acquired between 1919 and 1924, and North Central Finance, acquired in 1958, were a few of the significant purchases made by National Provincial. In 1962, District Bank was bought by National Provincial to create a company with over £1.4 billion in assets and 2,100 branches, although the two banks maintained their separate identities and independent operations.

Westminster Bank was organized in 1834 as the London and Westminster Bank, the first joint-stock bank in London. This firm was the first bank established under the auspices of the Bank Charter Act of 1833, which allowed joint-stock banks to be founded in London. For various reasons, the press, private banking concerns, and the Bank of England were so hostile to the Bank Charter Act that London and Westminster's management was primarily concerned with defending the company's right to exist rather than setting up an extensive branch network. As a result, the bank opened only six London branches in its first three years and no additional offices were established until nearly 20 years later.

London and Westminster made its first acquisition in 1847, when it bought Young & Son. In about 1870 it acquired Unity Joint-Stock Bank, and mergers with Commercial Bank of London and Middlesex Bank had been arranged in 1861 and 1863 respectively. By 1909 London and Westminster had opened or acquired 37 branches in and around London. Yet, despite this expansion effort, the bank felt the effects of competition from provincial banks like Lloyds and Midland. These two banks had already established large regional branch networks and were quickly encroaching upon the London market. In order to meet this challenge, London and Westminster merged with the influential and prestigious London and County Bank in 1909, which had 70 offices citywide and almost 200 in rural counties. The resulting entity was named the London County and Westminster Bank.

In 1913, the bank formed a subsidiary, London County and Westminster Bank (Paris), which opened branches during and after World War I in Bordeaux, Lyons, Marseilles, Nantes, Brussels, and Antwerp. The bank itself also established offices in Barcelona and Madrid during the same time. In 1917, bank officials decided to acquire the Ulster Bank (which continued to operate separately), with 170 branches throughout Ireland, and in 1918 bought Parr's Bank, with over 320 offices throughout England. These purchases made London, County, Westminster & Parrs (which became simply Westminster Bank Ltd. in 1923) the fifth-largest bank in England.

During the economic difficulties of the late 1920s and early 1930s, the bank kept tight centralized control over the continental branch of the business to avoid the dangers of too rapid an expansion in unfamiliar markets, but this policy stunted Westminster's international operations. It did mean that the bank escaped the bad debts and currency fluctuations that plagued many other banks between the world wars, allowing the domestic side of the business to grow steadily. At the time of the merger with National Provincial in 1968, Westminster had 1,400 branches in England alone.

The merger of National Provincial and Westminster Bank, announced in early 1968, shocked the British public and banking community. In the late 1960s, the Bank of England tried to rationalize the banking industry through a policy known as competition and credit control, which aimed to put banks on a more equal and competitive footing and to improve control of the nation's money supply. Although the Bank of England indicated a willingness to allow mergers as part of the rationalization process, no one had seriously believed it would permit mergers among the largest and most influential banks.

The District Bank, National Provincial, and Westminster Bank were fully integrated in the new firm's structure, while Coutts & Company (a 1920 National Provincial acquisition), Ulster Bank, and the non-banking subsidiaries continued as separate operations. Duncan Stirling, chairman of Westminster Bank, became NatWest's first chairman. In 1969 David Robarts, former chairman of National Provincial, assumed Stirling's position. The new company, National Westminster Bank, opened its doors for business on January 1, 1970.

In the late 1970s and early 1980s, following a massive restructuring and rationalization, NatWest began a concerted effort to expand its international operations. In 1975 NatWest expanded into Scotland, opening offices in Edinburgh, Glasgow, and later Aberdeen to support its participation in North Sea fuel projects. Under the direction of Robin Leigh-Pemberton, who became chairman in 1977, the company purchased the National Bank of North America in New York. By 1979, NatWest had extended its bases of operation in France and Belgium, had opened offices in West Germany, and had established overseas representatives in Australia, Bahrain, Canada, Greece, Hong Kong, Japan, Mexico, Singapore, Spain, and the Soviet Union.

Thomas Boardman replaced Robin Leigh-Pemberton as chairman of NatWest in 1983 when the latter was appointed governor of the Bank of England. Boardman and Tom Frost, NatWest's CEO since 1987, continued to transform NatWest from a domestic banking institution into an international financial organization. Part of the plan included forming NatWest Investment Bank through the acquisition of a medium-sized stock exchange jobber and a broker. NatWest also expanded its American subsidiary, NatWest USA, by acquiring First Jersey National Bank in 1987 and Ultra Bancorp, another New Jersey–based bank, in 1989. These acquisitions gave NatWest USA 285 branches throughout the Northeast and $20 billion in assets. Despite its reputation for caution, NatWest remained intent throughout the 1980s on building its American subsidiary into a super-regional bank that might someday challenge the traditional dominance of the New York money-center banks.

The bank lived up to its reputation for caution, however, with its handling of the Third World debt crisis. In June, 1987 it added £246 million to its reserves, becoming the first British bank to follow the lead of the American money-center banks by limiting its exposure to Third World loans.

NatWest's good name was tarnished, however, in December, 1988, when the Department of Trade and Industry (DTI) began to investigate the role played by the bank's investment-banking subsidiary, County NatWest, in an acquisition by the employment agency Blue Arrow. In 1987 County NatWest underwrote a stock offering for Blue Arrow to raise cash for the deal, but the results were disappointing. County NatWest was left with an interest in a 13.5% stake in Blue Arrow. It concealed that substantial interest by dividing the stake between itself, its own market-making arm, County NatWest Securities, and the Union Bank of Switzerland (UBS), to which it granted an indemnity against losses.

These moves were made in secret, however, to spare County NatWest the public embarrassment of a failed offering. But after the October stock market crash opened the Blue Arrow wound even further, its actions could no longer be concealed. In December 1987, County NatWest made a payment to UBS to release the indemnity, purchased County NatWest Securities' holding, and announced that it held a total stake of 9.5% in Blue Arrow.

The DTI released the results of its investigation in July, 1989, sharply criticizing County NatWest's actions. In failing to report its stake in Blue Arrow, it said, County NatWest violated a law requiring any party holding a 5% or greater interest in a company to report that fact in a timely fashion. This served to deceive both regulators and the financial markets about the true value of Blue Arrow stock. Although the DTI report did not criticize him, Lord Boardman announced that he would retire from the bank in September, five months ahead of schedule, and two of NatWest's deputy chief executives and another senior director also resigned. Lord Alexander, the former head of the British government body overseeing corporate takeovers, became chairman on October 1, 1989.

While the Blue Arrow affair certainly damaged NatWest's once-sterling reputation and its budding investment-banking business, the bank's strength and reputation for caution promise a quick recovery and a bright future.

Principal Subsidiaries: Centre-file Ltd.; Coutts & Co.; Credit Factoring International Ltd.; Deutsche Westminster Bank AG; HandelsBank NatWest (87%); Isle of Man Bank Ltd.; Lombard North Central PLC; NatWest Australia Bank Ltd.; NatWest Holdings Inc.; National Westminster Bancorp Inc.; National Westminster Bank USA; NatWest Commercial Services Inc.; National Westminster Bank of Canada; National Westminster Channel Islands (Holdings) Ltd.; National Westminster Financial Futures Ltd.; National Westminster Home Loans Ltd.; National Westminster (Hong Kong) Ltd.; National Westminster Insurance Services Ltd.; NatWest International Trust Holdings Ltd.; NatWest Investment Bank; NatWest Personal Financial Management Ltd.; Ulster Bank Ltd.

Further Reading: Ashby, J. F. *The Story of the Banks*, London, Hutchinson & Company, 1934; Gregory, T. E. *The Westminster Bank Through a Century*, Oxford University Press, 1936; Reed, Richard. *National Westminster Bank: A Short History*, London, National Westminster Bank, 1989.

NCNB CORPORATION

One NCNB Plaza
Charlotte, North Carolina 28255
U.S.A.
(704) 374–8633

Public Company
Incorporated: 1960
Employees: 29,000
Assets: $59.6 billion
Stock Index: New York

Expanding across the southern United States with lightning speed, NCNB Corporation has become known in the last decade for its voracious approach to the banking business. With the 1988 purchase of First Republic Bank of Texas, NCNB Chairman Hugh McColl Jr. quintupled his bank's assets in only five years and elevated if from a regional financial leader to a national powerhouse. NCNB is now in the biggest financial pond of them all, where the other fish await its next attack with more trepidation than they might care to admit. Chairman McColl is an ex-Marine who, according to *Fortune*, once considered adopting as his motto, "crush the sons of bitches and have a nice day." McColl, however, has inspired his employees to make NCNB the American bank to watch over the next decade.

NCNB's history was unremarkable until very recently. Its earliest ancestor was the Commercial National Bank of Charlotte, founded in February, 1874 with paid-in capital of $50,000. Despite Charlotte's tiny population of 2,500, the bank immediately prospered; its first president, Major Clement Dowd, waited only nine months before announcing the first of what would become an unbroken string of dividend payments. Through a combination of relatively conservative fiscal policy, sound analysis, and a helping of plain good luck, Commercial National weathered the banking storms of 1893, 1907, and 1929–1933 with its assets largely intact. When World War II ended in 1945 the bank was in excellent condition, well-poised to take advantage of the postwar economic boom.

Commercial National's future partners were not founded until the early part of this century. The Southern States Trust Company was created in 1901 in Charlotte by two businessmen named George Stephens and Word H. Wood, who changed the bank's name in 1907 to American Trust Company. Security National Bank was formed in Greensboro at the height of the Depression. It not only survived, but later established offices in a number of other North Carolina cities.

All three of these banks prospered in the fertile postwar economic environment, when intensified competition made large-scale mergers at first appealing and then inevitable. Commercial National and American Trust were Charlotte neighbors, the former a largely retail bank, the latter preferring commercial markets. In November of 1957 the two banks agreed to pool their complementary portfolios and become American Commercial Bank, to which the First National Bank of Raleigh was soon added. This flurry of mergers created one of the Carolinas' largest banks and set the stage for still more dramatic changes. No sooner had American's cross-state rival Security National merged with yet another sizable player, Depositors National Bank of Durham, than American and Security began discussing the combination of their recently swollen institutions. On July 1, 1960, the merger was completed and North Carolina National Bank opened the doors of its 40 offices across the state. The new regional bank had assets of $480 million and deposits of approximately the same amount.

In the decades following, NCNB consolidated its position as one of the Southeast's leading financial powers. By means of a long series of minor acquisitions the company quickly grew to include some 91 offices in 27 North Carolina cities and towns, with total deposits reaching more than $1 billion by 1969. In 1973, NCNB had passed its arch rival, the Wachovia Corporation of Winston-Salem, as the leading bank in the entire southeast region.

The following year nearly proved disastrous for the high-flying NCNB, however, when its real estate investment trust suffered large losses, precipitating a general belt tightening and shift in company philosophy—in the direction of still further expansion. Always aggressive, the bank accelerated its program of acquisition and finished the decade with $100 million mergers with the Bank of Asheville and Carolina First National in Lincolnton. With assets of $6 billion and 172 offices across North Carolina, NCNB was forced to look outside the state for its next campaign, even though interstate banking was still prohibited by law in 1979.

The bank began lobbying heavily for an end to restrictions on regional banking, and in 1981 it discovered a loophole in Florida law which would allow it to purchase banks via a subsidiary it had owned in that state since 1972. After a long legal battle, NCNB's position was upheld and its invasion of Florida began. In rapid order, NCNB snapped up First National Bank of Lake City, Gulfstream Banks of Boca Raton, and Ellis Banks of Bradenton, the latter alone holding $1.8 billion in assets and operating 75 branches. NCNB had largely concentrated its Florida purchases along the state's west coast, but in 1985 it charged into the competitive Miami area with the acquisition of Pan American Banks, with $2 billion in assets and 51 offices. By the time the dust had settled in 1987, NCNB National Bank of Florida had become the fourth-largest financial institution in a state whose rapidly growing, affluent population makes it one of the most desirable markets in the banking world.

Meanwhile, the southeastern United States had agreed in 1985 to allow reciprocal interstate banking, launching another spate of takeovers by Chairman McColl and his "hungry tiger," as he sometimes refers to NCNB. On the last day of 1985 the tiger gobbled up Southern National Bankshares of Atlanta, moved next to Bankers Trust Company of South Carolina in 1986, and finished the repast with Prince William Bank of Dumfries, Virginia at the end of that year. The following year, CentraBank of Baltimore fell victim, making NCNB the only bank to operate in six southern states and rounding off its combined assets at a tidy $20 billion. The scope of NCNB's expansion drive becomes clear when one recalls that the corporation has grown fortyfold since it was formed in 1960.

Along the way, NCNB and McColl (chairman since mid-1983) have alienated more than a few southern bankers. One company went so far as to accept a significantly lower takeover bid from a white knight in order to avoid becoming part of the NCNB empire. Some analysts believe that McColl's style has been a handicap for the company, but it is hard to argue with success. In 1988 the chairman pulled off a still-greater coup with the purchase of a bankrupt Texas giant, the $26 billion First RepublicBank.

In a complicated deal, NCNB received from the Federal Deposit Insurance Corporation a five-year option to buy all of First Republic's shares, which it did, plus a cash infusion and IRS tax breaks worth an estimated $5.5 billion. Not only has the carefully planned acquisition catapulted NCNB into the banking big league, with total assets now at around nearly $60 billion, but even the troubled First Republic has already contributed a handsome profit. And McColl shows no signs of slowing down. Most recently, NCNB tried to put together a deal for Citizens and Southern of Atlanta which, had it gone through, would have created the sixth-largest bank in the United States. Citizens was not interested, and McColl quickly withdrew his bid, with NCNB management already stretched thin by the First Republic takeover. With the additional purchase of the London investment firm of Panmure Gordon, NCNB is beginning to focus on the international market as well. As Chairman McColl has said, "I expect the Herculean." So far he has gotten it.

Principal Subsidiaries: NCNB National Bank of North Carolina; NCNB National Bank of Florida; NCNB National Bank of Texas; NCNB South Carolina; NCNB Financial Services, Inc.; Superior Life Insurance Co.; NCNB Virginia; NCNB National Bank of Maryland.

Further Reading: NCNB: A Brief History, Charlotte, NCNB Corporation, 1988.

NIPPON CREDIT BANK

13-10, Kudan-Kita 1-chome
Chiyoda-ku
Tokyo 102
Japan
(03) 263-1111

Public Company
Incorporated: 1957
Employees: 2,200
Assets: ¥16.42 trillion (US$131.38 billion)
Stock Index: Tokyo Osaka

Since 1957 the Nippon Credit Bank has been one of only three banks specially chartered by the government to conduct large-scale long-term credit activity. The last of these banks to be founded, the Nippon Credit bank is generally considered number three in the industry in Japan. It has, nevertheless, striven to build its market share by offering a more diverse mix of services. But as Japan's financial environment becomes more liberalized, the bank increasingly finds itself competing in the same markets as regular city banks, trust banks, brokerage houses, and even insurance companies.

Japan's long-term credit banking system emerged during the 1920s as part of a government effort to aid economic development. The government created the Industrial Bank of Japan to manage and regulate long-term financing for emerging industries.

After the war, the IBJ was preserved, but privatized on the premise that a privately capitalized institution would perform more efficiently. Its role was formalized with the passage in 1952 of the Long-Term Credit Bank Law. Despite the fact that the IBJ was heavily regulated—on a quasi-concessionary basis, like a power utility—the government felt that competition would enhance efficiency in the industry. The new law therefore provided for the creation of a second institution, the Long-Term Credit Bank.

By 1956 the government decided to charter a third long-term credit bank. The institution chosen to fill this role was a former colonial bank, called the Bank of Chosen (*Chosen* is the Japanese name for Korea), which had been under government control since the war.

Korea became a Japanese colony in 1910, and was subject to an ambitious development plan by Japanese industries and the government. In order to assist in this effort, the government established a special development bank, the Bank of Chosen. The bank channelled investment funds from the Japanese mainland to Korea and helped to establish that country's basic manufacturing, mining, and forestry industries.

World War II drastically altered the bank's operating conditions. While not exposed to enemy action or bombing, the bank was severely affected by the collapse of the Japanese economy. At the end of the war, all Japanese banks came under the control of a central authority that reorganized the industry.

The Bank of Chosen remained under government control until 1957, when it was re-established as a public company called the Nippon Fudosan Bank (*Fudosan* means "real estate" in Japanese). As Japan's third long-term credit bank, Nippon Fudosan was licensed to issue three- and five-year debentures, something the city banks could not do. But at the same time, the bank was prevented from accepting short-term deposits from individuals as city banks could do.

Nippon Fudosan's customers were large companies in search of investment capital. The interest they paid on industrial loans increased the bank's pool of capital, making investment funds available for other projects. As a result, long-term banks like Nippon Fudosan made possible the quick development of such basic industries as steel, chemicals, and heavy manufacturing.

During the 1960s, the long-term banks wielded great influence in industry because they were the primary sources of investment capital. It became a common practice for banks to make major investments in client companies and for bank officials to occupy seats on clients' boards of directors. But the banks' influence was strictly limited by the government regulators who had created the oligopoly; long-term banks were prohibited from making unfair use of their power.

Indeed, the neutrality forced upon the long-term banks became a great asset. Nippon Fudosan was free to deal with any of a number of competitors in a given industry simultaneously. Likewise, client companies had no fear that industrial secrets or proprietary strategies would be compromised. As a result, the long-term banks had ready access to and excellent relationships with the largest and fastest growing companies in Japan.

The oil crisis of 1973–1974 profoundly changed the conditions under which the long-term banks operated. Growth in Japanese heavy industry began to slow as energy costs rose. While Nippon Fudosan concentrated mainly on small- and medium-sized firms, the bank's exposure to certain depressed industries slowed its earnings. Gradually, however, more efficient production methods and the implementation of rationalization programs set the bank's growth back on track. In order to better reflect its role in long-term finance, Nippon Fudosan changed its name to Nippon Credit Bank in 1977.

Oil caused a second, more serious shock in 1978–1979. The Iranian Revolution caused a serious rise in energy prices, effectively destroying OPEC and in the process deeply hurting the small- and medium-sized Japanese companies the Nippon Credit Bank depended upon.

As the heavy industrial sector underwent reorganization, including amalgamations, buyouts, and failures, Nippon Credit started to emphasize service industries and foreign companies. In doing this, the bank entered the American and European bond markets in an attempt to become more like brokerage, consultancy, and wholesale banks such as Morgan Guaranty and Bankers Trust. While such multiple roles were prohibited for any one company in Japan (and elsewhere), no laws prevented a company from operating each of its services in a different country.

The economic slowdown that followed the 1979 oil shock caused lowered demand for industrial financing from all sources, particularly the long-term credit banks. Increasingly, companies found it easier and cheaper to raise their own investment capital through bond issues. This marked the beginning of a disturbing trend for the Nippon Credit Bank.

In order to adapt to these new conditions, the bank planned to move more aggressively into securities markets, but could only do so outside of Japan. Meanwhile, the long-term banks began an effort to liberalize Japanese financial regulations—namely Article 65 of the finance code—to allow greater operating latitude. Such a liberalization, long overdue in light of new market conditions, would allow long-term banks to compete with brokerages, city banks, and even trust banks and insurance companies in a wider range of capital markets.

The effort has wide support throughout Japan's finance industry, but has been slowed by lobbyists' attempts to skew the new legislation in favor of certain sectors. The long-term banks, which most need legislative reform, are perhaps most threatened by it. The widening of their historically narrow role in the economy would most certainly come at the expense of greater numbers of other institutions. As a minority within the industry, it is unlikely that the long-term banks will prevail.

Certain that liberalization is inevitable, the Nippon Credit Bank is completing the first phase of its transformation into a "global financial engineer." The process, begun in April, 1985, placed a new emphasis on foreign offices in the world's leading financial centers. In addition to New York, Los Angeles, Singapore, and Hong Kong, the bank maintains offices in London, where in October, 1985 it opened a new subsidiary, Nippon Credit International.

Domestically, the bank remains deeply involved in corporate finance. Its principal business is divided among the manufacturing, real estate, and finance industries, but the bank also provides loans for companies involved in construction, communication, and transportation, and is a leading retail lender. Like other Japanese banks, Nippon Credit is highly supportive of its clients (in 1986 it took over management of Kurushima Dockyard, an unprofitable shipbuilder).

In the future, Nippon Credit is likely to meet intense competition both at home and abroad. However, it maintains a loyal following among small- and medium-sized companies, and bears a significant advantage in overhead costs; the bank maintains only 20 branches—one-tenth as many as most city banks—and just over 2,000 employees.

Principal Subsidiaries: Nippon Credit Bank (Curaçao) Finance N.V. (Netherlands Antilles); Nippon Credit International (HK) Ltd. (Hong Kong); Nippon Credit International Ltd.; Nippon Credit Australia Ltd.; Nippon Credit (Schweiz) AG (Switzerland).

NORINCHUKIN BANK

8–3, Otemachi 1-chome
Chiyoda-ku
Tokyo 100
Japan
(03) 279–0111

Cooperative
Incorporated: 1923
Employees: 3,130
Assets: ¥32.5 trillion (US$260 billion)

The Norinchukin Bank is a unique institution in Japanese banking. It is a cooperative agricultural bank owned by farming, fishing, foresting, and other rural cooperatives. It has ties to virtually all Japanese industries and plays an important role in determining Japanese monetary policy.

The Norinchukin Bank was established by the Japanese government in 1923 specifically to modernize and expand Japan's agricultural industries. The name Norinchukin comes from the Japanese words for agriculture (*no*), forestry (*rin*), cooperative (*chu*), and bank (*kin*).

As a cooperative, Norinchukin is able to offer its members financing at very competitive rates. The bank is also a supporter of a political lobby which opposes agricultural imports and any deterioration in rural living standards, arguing that unlike industry, which is dependent on imported raw materials and fuel, agriculture is one sector in which Japan can and should be more self-sufficient.

During World War II, the Japanese agricultural industry was virtually unaffected by allied military action until late in the war, when bombing destroyed railroads and processing factories and energy resources were exhausted. In an effort to finance the war, the government placed such restrictions on banks that Norinchukin was depleted of investment funds.

At the end of the war, Japan's factories had been destroyed and many of its people were near starvation. Agricultural commodities were the only products that could be produced immediately. The occupation authority undertook land reform and set new commodity prices in its effort to restore a functioning economy. As a primary source of funds, Norinchukin played an important role in this effort. The bank gained a reputation for conservative management and ultra-safe deposits which later helped it grow during the late 1940s and early 1950s.

As the leading agricultural bank, Norinchukin played a semi-official role in state economic organization. Because of its unique position, Norinchukin reported to two government agencies: the Ministry of Agriculture, Forestry and Fisheries and the Ministry of Finance—in that order.

Japanese industry, however, recovered quickly after the war, and as export income grew, it became clear that certain labor-intensive industries weren't economical. The first industry to go was the textile industry, from which the government actively encouraged divestment. Agricultural industries feared they were next. In response, they formed an effective political lobby through the farmer's cooperative organization, or *nokyo*, which did win greater support for agricultural industries in the form of import quotas, subsidy programs, and measures to ensure the viability of agricultural institutions like the Norinchukin Bank.

The bank's success rested on its large savings base. With this money, Norinchukin was able to buy government bonds which yielded 6% to 7%, several points more than the interest it paid, giving the bank a comfortable spread. In return, the bank offered better interest rates than commercial banks and paid dividends. Because its investments are primarily in low-risk government bonds, returns are very stable. As a cooperative, Norinchukin is not profit-motivated, and with strong government support for the industry, the financial integrity of its investor base is well protected.

The bank collects funds through a complicated three-tier system. At the lowest level, the *nokyo* offers savers deposit desks at 16,000 offices (only the postal savings system has more offices). These offices serve 5,612 cooperatives which, with several fishing cooperatives, deposit their savings with 47 prefectural, or county, agricultural banks called *shinnoren*. *Nokyo* offices are entitled to make loans from their deposits, but two-thirds of what remains must be deposited with the *shinnoren*. The *shinnoren* may, in turn, make their own loans, but half of whatever they don't loan must be deposited with Norinchukin.

As Japan began to play a more important role in the world economy, consumers, tired of paying high prices for food, began to pressure politicians to support imports and cut agricultural subsidies. But the agricultural lobby's influence in local elections was strong enough to turn several subsidy opponents out of office.

Norinchukin's traditional profitability in spread lending became compromised by low interest rates during the mid-1980s. At the same time, the government was issuing fewer bonds as Japan began to prosper. Norinchukin was nevertheless required to accept deposits from *shinnoren*, leaving it flush with capital, but squeezed by ever-smaller profit margins and lower demand for loans from agricultural industries. Norinchukin was described by *Euromoney* in 1987 as "a desperate dinosaur."

Regulation and xenophobia kept Norinchukin out of foreign capital markets for almost 60 years, but in 1979 the bank finally set up an international department. This department began to buy foreign government-backed bonds and even some Japanese-backed Eurobonds. As funds began to leave the bank (and the agricultural cooperative system) in the search for higher rates of return, Norinchukin grew more interested in international securities markets. Since it had no experience, it established a relationship with the Bank of Tokyo, exchanging its broader representation (the Bank of Tokyo has only 32 branches) and capital for know-how and a chance to participate in deals.

With help from the Bank of Tokyo, Norinchukin established a representative office in New York in 1982. The office was upgraded to a branch in 1984; a second office was opened in London in 1985; and two years later the bank opened a securities brokerage in London. In 1986 the Japanese government rewrote the bank's charter, effectively allowing Norinchukin to act as a full-service commercial bank. In 1989 the bank established Norinchukin Finanz (Schweiz), a wholly owned subsidiary, in Zurich.

Despite these changes, Norinchukin remains an agricultural cooperative, a bank with a deep commitment to agriculture. Norinchukin will also continue to evolve slowly into a modern international bank. It is, however, often at odds with the *shinnoren*, which favor a speedier realignment and disagree with Norinchukin's penchant for lending to foreign agricultural interests.

While it retains substantial support from its members, the possibility of a decline in agriculture in Japan is almost certain to make Norinchukin act more like a regular city bank. As Japanese banking adjusts to deregulation, Norinchukin may well widen its association with the Bank of Tokyo (which, like Norinchukin, is one of only a few banks chartered to issue debentures). Still, the bank is unlikely to do more than simply de-emphasize agricultural banking. Like every other bank in Japan, Norinchukin recognizes that it must diversify in order to remain competitive.

Principal Subsidiaries: Norinchukin International (U.K.); Norinchukin Finanz (Schweiz) (Switzerland).

PNC FINANCIAL CORP

PNC FINANCIAL CORPORATION

Fifth Avenue and Wood Street
Pittsburgh, Pennsylvania 15265
U.S.A.
(412) 762–2666

Public Company
Incorporated: 1983
Employees: 17,000
Assets: $36.5 billion
Stock Index: New York

In 1983, two Pennsylvania banking concerns, the Pittsburgh National Corporation and the Provident National Corporation, merged to form the PNC Financial Corporation. PNC's relatively brief history is one of stunning growth and outstanding management. The Pittsburgh-based holding company doubled its assets in only five years, going from $16.4 billion in 1983 to more than $36 billion by 1988, and boasts the strongest return on assets and return on equity of any of the 15 largest American banking groups. PNC showed remarkable agility in its response to the banking industry's dramatic changes in the 1980s. As a result it has emerged as one of the nation's most respected, indeed at times envied, banking groups.

PNC Corporation's forerunner, the Pittsburgh National Bank, was incorporated in 1959, but its roots can be traced back to 1852, when steel magnates James Laughlin and B. F. Jones opened the Pittsburgh Trust and Savings in downtown Pittsburgh. PNC's other predecessor, the Provident National Bank, headquartered in Philadelphia, can also be traced to the mid-1800s. In 1847, the Tradesmens National Bank of Philadelphia opened its doors. After more than a century of banking and a series of name changes and acquisitions, it became the Provident National Bank in 1964. The Pittsburgh National Bank and the Provident National Bank combined their extensive banking experience in 1983. At that time, the newly formed bank holding company was no more than a medium-sized regional concern, but it rapidly developed into one of the nation's most powerful super-regional banks.

PNC's first chief executive, Merle Gilliand, had already served as CEO at Pittsburgh National Bank for 11 years by the time PNC was formed in 1983. Gilliand set the tone of PNC's management style, which has been described as "bottom-up management." He surrounded himself with competent senior executives and allowed them to make decisions on their own. This grass roots approach was rare in banking. Gilliand, however, contended that this method provided better service and over the long run a better bank. Under Gilliand's leadership, PNC emphasized quality, not size. Nonetheless, this strategy also proved very conducive to growth in the changing markets of the 1980s.

PNC's chief rival is the Mellon Bank. For years, Mellon controlled the large corporate accounts of Pittsburgh's many companies (the city ranks third in the nation in number of corporate headquarters). As a result, PNC was forced to cater to mid-sized companies, and to businesses outside of Pittsburgh. But, when Pittsburgh's big companies experienced difficulties in the late 1970s and 1980s, PNC was not as exposed to the "rust belt" problems as the Mellon Bank. PNC, under Gilliand, was content to operate on a smaller scale than its rival, but strove to provide all the same services with greater quality.

Banking deregulation allowed, and to some extent encouraged, mergers between banks. As the 1980s wore on, a number of well-run banks found it in their interest to join forces with the PNC group. PNC's acquisition strategy focused on purchasing healthy banks which would add to the corporations' overall strength. In 1984, PNC acquired the Marine Bank of Erie, Pennsylvania. A year later, it acquired the Northeastern Bancorp of Scranton, Pennsylvania. PNC's criteria for acquisitions are strict by industry standards. Acceptable banks were mid-sized, with assets of between $2 and $6 billion, had a solid market share in their operating regions, earned excellent return on equity and on assets, and ideally had expertise in a specific area of financial services which would benefit the entire group. Close attention was also paid to whether or not the bank's management philosophy was compatible with PNC's.

In 1985, Thomas H. O'Brien replaced the retiring Merle Gilliand as CEO at PNC. At 48, O'Brien was the youngest CEO of any major U.S. bank. Ironically, he had started his banking career at PNC's archrival, the Mellon Bank, before earning his MBA at Harvard. O'Brien had risen quickly through the ranks of the Pittsburgh National Bank, eventually heading PNC's merchant banking activities, and finally becoming chairman and chief executive. As the top executive at PNC he continued Gilliand's bottom-up management style. O'Brien would let executives at affiliates implement their own ideas at their own bank without a great deal of interference from the top. As a result of the autonomy PNC gave its affiliated banks, the banking group was an attractive merger partner for exactly the healthy regional banks it wished to acquire. PNC could grow, and the new affiliates could take advantage of the extended services offered by the group. PNC became known for its friendly takeovers of already successful banks.

Under O'Brien's conservative yet aggressive leadership, PNC grew at a tremendous rate. In 1986, the Hershey Bank joined the group. In 1987, with the acquisition of Citizen's Fidelity Corporation of Louisville, PNC grew larger than its rival, the Mellon Bank. In 1988, PNC acquired the Central Bancorp of Cincinnati, and the First Bank and Trust of Mechanicsburg. While acquisitions normally dilute the value of a corporation's stock for some time, PNC's careful planning allowed it to quickly make up for the dilution. By the late 1980s, Wall Street analysts were so confident in PNC's management that acquisition announcements did not seriously reduce the stock's price.

The relaxation of interstate banking regulations in the U.S. created a new kind of bank, the super-regional. Super-regionals operate in a number of states, and have begun to compete with the money center banks for a greater share of large corporate business. As mid-sized companies have needed more services in the international trade arena, the super-regionals have become more and more involved there as well. With its network spread throughout Pennsylvania, Kentucky, Ohio, and Delaware, by 1987 PNC was the premier super-regional in the United States and had become the nation's 12th largest banking group. Its assets had more than doubled since 1983, and its earnings were among the highest in the industry.

Like many banks throughout the world, PNC was forced to set aside huge sums as a provision against bad debt in Third World countries in 1987. Unlike many banks, however, the PNC group still earned a substantial profit that year, despite its $200 million increase in loan loss reserves. While two-thirds of U.S. banks actually showed losses, PNC netted more than $255 million for its shareholders.

The banking group was very conservative in its lending throughout the 1980s. It set limits for the number of loans allowed to any particular industry and enforced stringent credit criteria. At the same time, PNC was energetic in its marketing. The corporation went after trust and money management business as well as corporate lending. PNC affiliates also showed higher than average earnings from fee income.

PNC Financial Corporation's history is one of astounding growth. The corporation's young and aggressive management intend to continue growth while maintaining cautious lending policies, high quality service, and high profitability. As banking in the United States becomes more complex due to deregulation, banks will have to show ingenuity if they hope to remain competitive. PNC has shown great foresight in meeting the changes of the 1980s. If its past success is any indication of its future, PNC has much to look forward to.

Principal Subsidiaries: Citizen Fidelity Corporation; The Hershey Bank; Marine Bank; Northeastern Bank of Pennsylvania; Pittsburgh National Bank; PNC National Bank; Provident National Bank; The Central Bancorporation, Inc.; The First Bank and Trust Company; PNC Investment Company; PNC Merchant Banking Company PNC Trust Company of Florida, N.A.

THE ROYAL BANK OF CANADA

1 Place Ville Marie
Post Office Box 6001
Montreal, Quebec H3C 3A9
Canada
(514) 874–2110

Public Company
Incorporated: 1869 as the Merchants Bank of Halifax
Employees: 46,400
Assets: C$110.05 billion (US$92.31 billion)
Stock Index: Toronto Montreal Vancouver

The Royal Bank of Canada is Canada's largest financial institution. The bank maintains more than 1,500 branches in Canada and conducts business through more than 100 facilities worldwide.

Founded in 1864 by a group of eight businessmen in Halifax, Nova Scotia, the Merchants Bank, as it was then called, began with $200,000 in capital to support local commerce. The bank's establishment coincided with a sharp increase in the area's commercial activity, a result of the American Civil War—Halifax was a thriving center for blockade runners crossing the U.S. border.

The bank made a successful start under these conditions, and was incorporated five years later as the Merchants Bank of Halifax. Thomas C. Kinnear, one of the original founders, was its first president.

During the next few years, the bank expanded conservatively, opening branches in several more maritime towns. But from 1873 to the end of the decade, a business depression hit Nova Scotia's shipbuilding industry hard and kept the bank's growth slow.

When the business environment rebounded for a short time in the early 1880s, the bank resumed its growth plan, and in 1882 opened its first branch outside Canada, in Hamilton, Bermuda—before it had even expanded as far as Ontario domestically. Although this branch closed in 1889, the bank remained committed to international operations, opening several branches in Latin America before it was well established in western Canada.

By 1896, Merchants Bank's assets totaled $10 million. The gold rush in the early 1890s in southern British Columbia gave it the impetus to open agencies there in 1897 and 1898, especially since, with the completion of the Canadian Pacific Railway in 1885, the area seemed ripe for development.

In 1899 two more branches were established in New York and Havana. The bank took a conservative approach in developing its Cuban business and made only a handful of initial loans. But as confidence in Cuba's future grew, particularly with the formation of the Republic in 1902 and the continuing growth of the sugar industry, the bank gradually expanded, opening several branches around the country. (This business upswing came to a temporary halt when the sugar market suffered its first collapse, in 1920.)

In an effort to distinguish the bank from two other institutions with similar names, the bank was renamed the Royal Bank of Canada in 1901.

The dawn of a new century heralded a period of growth and prosperity in Canada, especially in the area between Winnipeg and the Rocky Mountains. The bank grew too, opening more branches and acquiring several smaller institutions. With this growth, the bank decided in 1907 to relocate from Halifax to Montreal, where the general manager was based. The move reflected Montreal's growing importance as a financial center and the relative decline of maritime commerce.

By the following year, the Royal Bank of Canada had 109 branches and $50 million in assets. This strong base provided the foundation for the bank's acquisition, in 1910, of the 54-year-old Union Bank of Halifax. Subsequent acquisitions of the Traders Bank of Canada and the Bank of British Honduras in 1912 more than doubled the number of operating branches and doubled its asset base by the end of the next year.

At the start of World War I, the Canadian real estate market had collapsed and very little capital was flowing into the country from abroad. In this uncertain atmosphere, the bank could not even promise staff who had enlisted reinstatement upon their return. Soon, however, business expanded sharply as wartime industry geared up, and the bank was forced to break with tradition and hire women.

Although the war put pressure on the Royal's day-to-day operations, the bank continued to grow, buying the Quebec Bank in 1917, the Northern Crown Bank in 1918, and two other banks in British Guiana and Nassau. By the end of the war, the Royal was the second largest bank in Canada, with 540 branches, assets of more than $422 million, and a new foreign trade department to handle its growing international presence.

The Royal Bank weathered the period of economic collapse that followed the end of World War I and, by 1925, had resumed its quest for expansion with the purchase of the Bank of Central and South America and the Union Bank of Canada. The Union Bank was the Royal Bank's largest takeover yet, and strengthened its presence in the three prairie provinces.

The bank's solid structure and leading position in the banking industry helped it survive the stock market crash relatively well, but it was not totally immune. Asset and profit levels fell, branches were closed, staff were laid off, and expenditures and the salaries of remaining employees were cut. Yet, while banks in the United States were closing in record numbers, not one Canadian chartered bank failed during this time.

By 1939, total assets were more than $1 billion, for

the second time in ten years, and the bank was ready to take advantage of the opportunities World War II offered. In cooperation with other banking institutions, the Royal actively participated in war measures, and it was instrumental in operating a ration coupon system for food and gasoline. But basically the war meant increased government expenditures for the war effort. The bank's domestic business flourished, though internationally its European branches were constrained under German occupation.

After World War II, the Royal led the way in developing the country's oil, gas, and resource exploration industries by providing banking services in remote locations. It opened an oil and gas department in Calgary in 1951, and also established banking services in cities along the British Columbian route of a massive project undertaken by the Aluminum Company of Canada. The bank continued its international expansion with the establishment of the Royal Bank of Canada Trust Company in New York in 1951 as well.

When Fidel Castro came to power in Cuba in 1959, the Cuban banking system was nationalized. The Royal Bank of Canada and the Bank of Nova Scotia were, alone among banks, permitted to operate independently, but the losses they incurred as nationalized businesses transferred their banking to the nationalized system were too heavy, and the Royal Bank sold its Cuban assets to the Banco Nacional de Cuba in December of 1960.

In 1962, almost 100 years after its founding, The Royal Bank of Canada adopted a new emblem to replace its original coat of arms. The emblem's design incorporated a lion, a crown, and a globe to symbolize the bank's position as a leading force in international banking. That same year, the bank's offices moved into a new, 42-story skyscraper now known as Place Ville Marie. The building's construction set in motion a large-scale urban development plan that turned midtown Montreal into a vital commercial district.

At the same time, the bank sharpened its focus on consumer-oriented financial services by entering the market with a product called TermPlan, a package of credit and insurance benefits. Six years later, in partnership with three other banks, the bank introduced Chargex, a credit card that allowed holders to make purchases within a specified credit limit and obtain cash advances through any of four participating institutions.

The 1967 revision of the Bank Act sparked vigorous competition among Canada's chartered banks, which had long operated under a morass of special restrictions. In removing or easing these constraints, the new act permitted banks to vie for loans, deposits, and conventional mortgages on an equal basis with other lending and borrowing institutions. By 1967 the Royal Bank had written more than half of the residential mortgage loans provided by all of the chartered banks combined.

In the early 1970s, the Royal Bank joined forces with five other banks to form Orion, a London-based merchant banking organization designed to enter the financial services market. Although Canadian law prohibited banks from entering this market domestically, Orion competed successfully in placing international bond issues and securities. Orion became a wholly owned subsidiary of the Royal Bank in 1981, enabling the bank to diversify its operations up to the limits imposed by Canada's banking laws and position itself for the possibility of international banking deregulation.

In 1979 Rowland Frazee, who had been with the bank for 40 years, was appointed chief executive officer. He replaced W. Earle McLaughlin, who became chairman after a popular 18-year reign as CEO.

By 1981, the Royal Bank was the fourth largest bank in North America, with assets of $53 billion. Although one-third of that total was attributed to its international activities, the bank had lost its early advantage in many foreign markets to other institutions. One of Frazee's first orders of business was to strengthen the bank's influence in the United States. He poured new capital into the Royal Bank and Trust Company, in New York, and increased its staff. A second Frazee priority was the development of a Global Energy Group, based in Calgary, to provide technical consultation as well as capital for energy-related projects on an international basis. To manage its newly aggressive stance, the bank reorganized into four groups, two responsible for Canadian retail and commercial business, and two to handle corporate banking and international operations.

In 1986, Allan Taylor became chairman of the Royal Bank. Taylor's rise from junior clerk at the age of 16 to chairman 37 years later has been a remarkable one. His appointment as chairman replaced the bank's traditional conservatism with a more entrepreneurial approach to the challenges the bank faces.

One of the first challenges Taylor met was the relaxation of rules governing the ownership of brokerage firms by banks. The Royal began negotiations with Wood Gundy, a leading Canadian brokerage firm, in the spring of 1987, some months before the law actually changed. That deal fell through, but the Royal went on to acquire Dominion Securities, the largest investment house in Canada, just after the stock market crash in October that year. Although it was one of the last of Canada's big banks to enter the brokerage market, by waiting, the Royal got the best deal of all, saving a significant amount over pre-crash prices.

The Royal has succeeded in reducing its net exposure to Third World debt from 200% of shareholder equity to 75% and hopes to reduce it to 25% in the early 1990s. An even greater challenge, however, will be to formulate longer-term repayment strategies to assist these borrowers in becoming economically viable again.

The Royal Bank has grown from a modest regional bank more than a century ago into a major domestic and international force, with assets over C$110 billion and more than 46,000 employees. Buoyed by its acquisition of Dominion Securities and an increasingly entrepreneurial spirit, the Royal Bank seems well positioned to lead Canadian banks into the twenty-first century.

Principal Subsidiaries: NMRB Limited (Australia) (50%); Finance Corp. of Bahamas Limited (FINCO) (75%); Royal Bank de Puerto Rico; The Royal Bank of

Canada A.G. (Germany); RBC Finance B.V. (Netherlands); Royal Bank of Canada (Bahamas) Limited; RBC Barbados; Banco Royal do Canada (Brasil).

Further Reading: Ince, Clifford. *The Royal Bank of Canada: A Chronology: 1864–1969*, Montreal, The Royal Bank of Canada, 1969.

THE SANWA BANK, LTD.

10, Fushimimachi 4-chome
Higashi-ku
Osaka 541
Japan
(03) 202–2281

Public Company
Incorporated: 1933
Employees: 14,337
Assets: ¥41.04 trillion (US$328.37 billion)
Stock Index: Frankfurt Osaka Tokyo Kyoto London

Unlike many Japanese city banks, the Sanwa Bank places a special emphasis on being the "people's bank." But in an era when domestic banking has become highly competitive and international activities are more profitable, Sanwa has gradually begun to cultivate more corporate business. The success of this effort rests not only on the bank's ability to compete, but on its adaptability. Sanwa's task is to exploit numerous opportunities in the world market while maintaining its base in personal banking.

Few other companies in the world have histories as long as Sanwa's. The product of a merger in 1933, Sanwa's principal predecessor was the Konoike Bank. The Konoike family enterprise began in 1656 and built a considerable fortune brewing sake. This fortune financed a number of other ventures, most notably a shipping operation. Additional capital generated by these businesses was later used to start a money exchange whose principal business was lending.

Although Japan remained isolated from the world for the next two centuries and commerce there remained limited by traditional practices, the Konoike money exchange gained prominence in the Osaka region. After Japan's opening to the world in 1868, the government sponsored an ambitious industrialization campaign that brought about a modernization of the banking industry. The Konoike money exchange was awarded a national banking charter in 1877. Over the next several decades, Konoike profited from an expansion in personal income and from the growth of small- and medium-sized companies.

Konoike was a small city bank, especially compared to banks affiliated with the *zaibatsu* conglomerates. It did not engage in foreign activities, even when Japanese commercial interests were extended to Taiwan, Korea, and Manchuria. And although the bank benefited indirectly from Japan's modernization, it suffered indirectly from financial shocks and recessions caused by government economic mismanagement and uneven industrial development.

In the early 1930s, the bank began to lose ground to the *zaibatsu* banks, which were closely linked to the rapidly expanding heavy-industry sector. In order to remain competitive, the Konoiki Bank merged with the Yamaguchi Bank and the Sanjushi Bank in 1933. After the merger the new entity, based in Osaka and tied to textile production and other light industries, took the name Sanwa (*san* meaning "three," *wa* meaning "harmony.")

The Sanwa Bank had the largest deposits of any Japanese commercial bank. Still, since it was not directly involved in large-scale industrial finance or overseas investments, Sanwa avoided direct confrontation with the militarists who rose to power in the early 1930s. Only after Japan went to war with the United States in 1941 did Sanwa become part of the government's centralization plan: between 1942 and 1945 Sanwa absorbed an affiliated trust company and several more local banks. When the war ended, however, Sanwa was forced to sell many of its operations under terms established by the occupation authority. Several operations were spun off, leaving the original "harmonious three."

Most of the largest Japanese banks after the war were former *zaibatsu* affiliates (although the *zaibatsu* were officially outlawed, the independent companies they were divided into continued to maintain close relationships with each other). These banks provided much of the financing for large industries. Sanwa, however, was never affiliated with any one industrial group, and in many cases was seen as a competitor not just of the *zaibatsu* banks, but also of the large industrial companies they were affiliated with. As a result, the bank continued to concentrate on individual banking and the financing of small businesses, most of which were not involved in war production, and so survived the war relatively undamaged.

In 1953 Sanwa adopted a green clover-like symbol as its logo and opened its first overseas office, in San Francisco, in anticipation of the needs of Japanese exporters.

As a growing city bank with a solid account base, Sanwa had greater success winning large corporate accounts. With loans to companies in steel production, shipbuilding, automobile manufacture, and petrochemicals, Sanwa became directly linked to Japanese heavy industry. Japan's first period of export-led growth, from 1955 to 1965, depended heavily on the development of basic industries. As these industries grew, Sanwa not only recovered its loans, but won further business and, as an investment partner, grew with its clients.

Sanwa redoubled its effort to expand in international banking and, studying the Bank of America as a model, mapped out a strategy for growth in the retail sector. It also moved its center of activity from Osaka to the more dynamic Tokyo. Of the three "Osaka banks" (the others being Sumitomo and Daiwa), Sanwa was most successful in exploiting the growth of the Tokyo market.

In 1959 Sanwa sold its trust operations to the Toyo Trust and Banking Company. The sale was not required by industrial decentralization laws, but was made simply to permit Sanwa to focus its attention on two new financial products: credit cards and leases. It founded the Japan Credit Bureau, or JCB, in 1961, and established Orient Leasing in 1964.

The bank's growth during the 1960s was characterized by conservative management and avoidance of high-risk investments. It also benefited early from computerization and "near-banking" activities. Its one notable loss came from its involvement with financially troubled Maruzen Oil, an industry in which Sanwa had little experience. Overall, Sanwa's expansion paralleled the rapid growth of the Japanese economy.

Sanwa turned its attention to building an international network during the 1970s. With offices in London, Sydney, Singapore, and Hong Kong, the bank served its clients' needs in a new way. Japanese industry had evolved to a position from which it not only traded in goods, but exported production capacity to less expensive operating environments—particularly in textiles.

The bank entered a new phase of development in the United States in 1972 when it established the Sanwa Bank of California. This subsidiary later acquired the Charter Bank and the Golden State Bank, both in southern California, and in 1978 changed its name to Golden State Sanwa Bank. Continuing its expansion in California—the world's sixth-largest economy—the bank acquired the First City Bank of Rosemead in 1981. Sanwa itself, meanwhile, opened offices in New York, Chicago, Atlanta, Dallas, Boston, Los Angeles, Toronto, and Vancouver.

As lending and other traditional banking operations became less profitable during the 1980s, Sanwa moved even further into predominately fee-based near-banking services, acquiring a leasing subsidiary from Continental Illinois Bank in 1984 which it renamed the Sanwa Business Credit Corporation.

Although well represented worldwide, Sanwa is strongly committed to commerce in the Pacific Rim. It maintains an impressive breadth of vision that has allowed it to remain competitive with the more industrial-based former *zaibatsu* banks. The bank's firm grounding in international markets and retail banking should assure its ability to face the challenges of deregulation in the Japanese banking industry successfully.

Principal Subsidiaries: Sanwa Factors Ltd.; The Sanwa Credit Co., Ltd.; Sanwa Card Services Co., Ltd.; Sanwa Systems Development Co., Ltd.; Sanwa Business Finance Co., Ltd.; Sanwa Capital Co., Ltd.; Sanwa Capital Management Co., Ltd.; Sanwa Research Institute Corp.; Sanwa Network Services Corp.; JCB Co., Ltd.

SECURITY PACIFIC CORPORATION

333 South Hope Street
Los Angeles, California 90071
U.S.A.
(213) 345-6211

Public Company
Incorporated: 1871 as The Farmers and Merchants Bank
Employees: 43,300
Assets: $72 billion
Stock Index: New York

In the space of two decades, Security Pacific has grown from a mid-sized regional southern California bank into the nation's sixth-largest bank-holding company and an international player in a range of non-banking financial industries. SecPac has shed the image that gave it the name "Security Pathetic" for its once meager earnings, and has steadily gone about the business of diversifying from traditional banking into the securities and capital markets, venture capital, currency trading, and insurance and commercial leasing in the United States, Europe, and Asia.

Security Pacific began in 1871 as the Farmers and Merchants Bank. Both a consumer and a commercial bank from its start, the Merchants and Farmers, which became the Security First National Bank of Los Angeles in 1929, continued to grow, often by acquisition, to become a major southern Californian bank. By the late 1960s, it was ready to expand beyond California. At that time, the top management team consisted of Chairman and CEO Frederick Larkin Jr., President Carl Hartnack, and head of international and corporate banking Richard Flamson III, a tough, demanding, outspoken executive who once worked repossessing cars before beginning his banking career with SecPac.

These three men believed that deregulation of the banking industry was inevitable and that traditional banking activities could no longer sustain the kind of growth they felt their company needed. They opened offices in New York, Tokyo, London, and Sydney, and they also bought a northern California bank called Pacific National Bank, resulting in a name change to Security Pacific Bank.

When the Bank Holding Company Act was passed and banks were allowed to own non-banking financial subsidiaries, the company reincorporated in 1971 as Security Pacific Corporation. It then set about implementing a diversification strategy that went into high gear when Flamson took over as chairman and CEO in 1978.

Today, the company is divided into three major divisions: Security Pacific Bank, which functions as a retail and commercial bank in California and as a merchant bank in California and in the capital markets around the world; the interstate banking network, which includes consumer and commercial banks in several other western states; and the financial services system, which began as a small consumer finance subsidiary and has expanded nationwide and diversified into international commercial finance, leasing, and venture capital projects in the United States and England. In practice, these divisions function as a loose confederation of independent businesses rather than as an interdependent, synergistic conglomerate.

Although he is routinely described as a gambler and a risk-taker, Richard Flamson has insisted in published interviews that he "never bets the company." While many analysts have questioned SecPac's seemingly inscrutable trail of acquisitions, Flamson maintains that they are carefully chosen and that extensive groundwork precedes every acquisition.

A good example is the company's entry into the consumer finance market in 1974. The bank began by hiring William Ford, an executive from the General Electric Credit Corporation, to set up a consumer finance business. After that turned a profit in its first year, the company bought a small Kansas-based finance company, Bankers Investment. Once they were convinced that consumer finance was a good business to be in, SecPac purchased Maryland-based American Finance Systems, with 390 offices in 39 states. By 1987, the consumer finance division employed 3,500 people in 45 states and netted the company almost $60 million.

SecPac used a similar strategy to gain a seat on the London stock exchange. In July of 1984, the company purchased John Govett & Company, an English investment management company, but it wasn't until 1986 that the bank increased its ownership of the renamed Hoare Govett Ltd. to 83%, giving it greater flexibility in the operation. Other recent international acquisitions include a West German finance company and a Canadian commercial bank. The holding company currently has offices in 23 foreign countries and maintains 24-hour trading rooms in seven different countries. In 1988 it acquired 30% of Burns Fry Ltd., a Toronto broker.

While SecPac has set its sights far afield, it has also kept a close eye on its own backyard, purchasing major banks in Arizona, Washington, Oregon, Alaska, Nevada, and northern California in the late 1980s. These acquisitions have given Security Pacific a very strong retail network, and access to approximately 30% of the nation's mortgage market. In the ten years since Flamson took over as CEO, assets have grown from $22 billion to over $87 billion, and profits have increased by 15% to 17% a year for most of the decade.

That growth came to an abrupt halt in 1987, when the company decided to take action to resolve its exposure to the growing Third World debt crisis. With more than $2 billion at risk, company officials felt they could no longer sit back and hope for a change, and in 1987, they diverted over $900 million toward a special reserve fund for unpaid loans to developing countries. The action followed several years of write-offs totaling hundreds of millions of dollars, and resulted in a net income of only $15.7 million for the year instead of an after-tax profit of $518 million, but the company now has more than half of its non-trade related outstanding loans to Third World countries covered and has eliminated its exposure in five developing countries. More than two-thirds of its extant outstanding loans are to Mexico and Brazil.

This problem was compounded by the October, 1987 crash, which forced the company's securities business to retrench. Flamson told *Business Week* in May, 1988 that acquisitions would slow down because of plummeting profits in the securities subsidiaries. But Flamson remains optimistic about his diversification strategy. He says that Security Pacific will continue to push for further deregulation so that it can compete more heavily in the insurance, securities, and real estate fields. He has also demonstrated his willingness to pay top salaries for talented executives from other companies, prefering to use managers from the appropriate industries to head SecPac's non-banking subsidiaries.

Through the company's merchant banking arm, SecPac acted as the agent in a $1.65 billion refinancing of Allied Stores in 1987. The same subsidiary acted as agent or co-manager in $2 billion worth of additional projects in the entertainment and construction industries, and ended up with almost $100 million in income from the merchant bank alone. The growth of the company's global merchant banking division has led to comparisons with financial giant Citibank, but while Citibank seems to want to be everything to everybody, SecPac officials insist that they are more interested in mining specialty niches.

Security Pacific has also been a leader in the development of automated teller systems and other electronic advancements in the banking industry and maintains a fulltime subsidiary of 5,500 employees for this purpose.

Flamson is credited with much of Security Pacific's success of the past decade. He has a few years left before retirement, and though he has promised to slow down his acquisitions, he has also conceded that he is looking to gain a toehold in the Tokyo market. He is said to have a relaxed collegial style during his weekly meetings with the senior management team, and a loose overview of the whole organization. His philosophy and style were best represented by a statement he made to *Institutional Investor* describing the key to his success: "You don't need a Ph.D., but you do need market sense, street sense and common sense to make a business plan so the pieces go together."

Principal Subsidiaries: Security Pacific National Bank; Hoare Govett Ltd.; Pacific Century Group; Security Pacific Bank Canada; Security Pacific Finance Corp.; Security Pacific Housing Services, Inc.; Security Pacific International Bank; Security Pacific Investment Managers, Inc.; Security Pacific Leasing Corp.; Security Pacific Venture Capital Advisory Corp.; Security Pacific Finance Systems Inc.; Security Pacific State Bank; SPC Securities Services Corp.; Security Pacific Northwest, Inc.; Security Pacific Bank Washington, Inc.; Security Pacific Oregon, Inc.; Security Pacific Bank Alaska, Inc.; Security Pacific Southwest, Inc.; Security Pacific Bank Arizona, Inc,; Security Pacific Bank Nevada; Security Pacific Financial Services System, Inc.

SKANDINAVISKA ENSKILDA BANKEN

Kungsträdgårdsgatan 8
S-106 40 Stockholm
Sweden
(46) 822–1900

Public Company
Incorporated: 1972
Employees: 9,440
Assets: SKr289 billion (US$47.24 billion)
Stock Index: Stockholm

The S-E-Bank Group, the parent of Skandinaviska Enskilda Banken and Scandinavia's largest banking group, continues to move ahead in a highly competitive market by its consistent pursuit of two goals: to expand in widening geographical areas and to add profitable financial instruments and services in response to demand. As government banking policies were gradually liberalized during the past decade or so, some important obstacles to the advancement of such interests for S-E-Banken have been removed. At the same time, however, the number and strength of the bank's competitors has increased.

Sweden's banking regulations, framed and reframed over the years to relieve budget deficits incurred by its "cradle to grave" social welfare system, had grown into a complex web of restraint by 1971. The boards of two of Sweden's leading commercial banks met in September of that year to discuss a remedy: liquidating and transferring their assets and liabilities to a new bank that would be set up differently, able to expand in different markets. Stockholms Enskilda Bank had been in operation since 1856, Skandinaviska Banken since 1864. Both were respected institutions that had grown as much as their boards expected they could under current conditions.

The first privately owned bank in Stockholm, Stockholms Enskilda Bank was started by A. O. Wallenberg. The bank participated actively in the country's booming export economy from the start, using those profits to fund the building of the Swedish industrial infrastructure. When the boom broke, the bank found itself the owner of several businesses and the victim of large loan losses.

When Wallenberg retired, his two sons, K. A. and Marcus, succeeded him. K. A. developed the bank's international business. Marcus took an active role in promoting the industrial development that took place in Sweden during the decades prior to World War I. Stockholms Enskila Bank's development remained routine through the Depression and World War II. A third generation of Wallenbergs took over prior to World War II and continued serving Swedish commercial customers. During the 1960s, however, the industry underwent rapid expansion and larger companies began to demand increased financial resources. At the same time, government regulations made these demands difficult to meet. These circumstances combined with the international trend toward diversification caused Stockholms Enskilda Bank to begin to consider a major merger.

Skandinaviska Banken had been a pioneer in commercial banking since its inception in April, 1864 as Skandinaviska Kredit-Aktiebolaget i Göteborg. The idea of organizing a commercial bank to provide investment capital in Scandinavia dates back to the early 1860s, when C. F. Tietgen, a Danish banker, convinced several Swedish industrialists and bankers to help him create a new bank. The bank was to invest in shares in new industrial companies and later place the shares on the market. A third of the new bank's shares were to be sold in Sweden and the rest in major financial centers in Europe. Unfortunately, a sudden increase in the discount rates on the continent near the end of 1863 doomed this plan.

Nevertheless in 1864 the bank was brought to life by Swedish industrialists and bankers, with Tietgen as the only non-Swedish board member. Theodor Mannheimer, the first managing director of the new bank in Göteborg, and Henrik Davidson, who joined the bank's Stockholm staff when it opened an office there in 1865, had numerous contacts in Europe's financial centers. As their experience had been with private trading firms as well as banks, these two men were able to establish business agreements with major European banks quickly. One of their first transactions was to market an eight million mark government-railway loan for Hamburg Banco, which attracted much attention. Skandinaviska Banken had taken its first step toward becoming one of the largest foreign exchange dealers in the world.

The new bank opened branches in Sweden's major cities but was able to make contacts throughout the provinces without incurring the expense of opening an extensive branch network because it acted as agent for most of Sweden's provincial banks. A mounting tide of industrial activity around the turn of the century greatly increased the volume of business.

In 1910 following the restructuring of the Swedish banking system Skandinaviska merged with Sweden's second-largest bank, Skånes Enskilda Bank, which had a number of provincial branches. A final merger 39 years later joined Skandinaviska with Göteborgs Handelsbank, adding another 40 provincial branches.

Skandinaviska was among the first banks in the country to introduce the check system, which attracted a large volume of new savings. Shortly after 1945, the bank introduced a commercial information service, providing expertise on economic conditions in foreign countries along with information on their markets, customs, laws, and currency. This service led to the publication of books and periodicals to communicate the information on a regular basis.

On December 17, 1971 the Swedish government approved the Articles of Association of the Skandinaviska Enskilda Banken and granted it permission to take over the activities of the two original banks, commencing January 1, 1972. Shareholders in both banks exchanged their shares for shares in the Skandinaviska Enskilda Banken and many of the staff members of the original banks found positions in the new bank.

The investment management business was the new bank's first step outside the original framework of its operations. In 1974 S-E-Banken became the owner of Aktiv Placering A.B. in Stockholm. This wholly owned subsidiary was established to manage the portfolios of individuals, provide legal services for families, and provide advice on taxes and life insurance. As legislation, securities markets, and other factors have changed through the years, this subsidiary has grown and acquired other subsidiaries both in Sweden and overseas. It now manages about 40 mutual funds.

Although for many years Sweden protected its own banks by refusing to allow foreign banking within its borders, competition among Swedish banks for domestic business did not give any of them much potential for growth. Skandinaviska Enskilda Banken took a giant step into a lucrative new market when it went international in 1976.

Its first international acquisition was an interest in Deutsch-Skandinavische Bank in Frankfurt am Main, Germany; today S-E-Banken owns 80% of that business. The next step was the formation of Skandinaviska Enskilda Banken (Luxembourg) S.A. And in 1979 S-E-Banken reached halfway around the world to establish a subsidiary in Singapore to handle southeast Asian business, creating Skandinaviska Enskilda Banken (South East Asia) Limited.

During the late 1970s, as inflation and interest rates scaled new heights, there was a record amount of money in circulation. The Swedish government began to look for alternatives to the restrictive banking regulations in place and decided to pursue a course of gradual deregulation.

The first major step in deregulation was to relieve Swedish banks of the obligation to purchase new issues of the fixed-rate, long-term priority bonds that had been the traditional annual solution to the country's budget deficit. (Life insurance companies and pension fund, however, were still required to invest in them.)

The government next moved to allow Swedish banks to issue certificates of deposit, starting in 1980. These short-term, high-interest instruments became as popular in Sweden as they had become elsewhere and helped attract substantial numbers of new clients, many of whom went on to use additional bank services.

The Swedish savings rate had been sluggish for years, mainly because of Sweden's high income tax, which left households with little discretionary income. In addition, banks were only allowed to offer a relatively low interest rate on conventional savings accounts. The time was right for the introduction of new financial instruments offering better returns.

In the three years that followed introduction of certificates of deposit, the government created several additional avenues for bank profits: Swedish treasury bills, a commercial paper market, and market-rate state bonds. S-E-Banken, already the front-runner in industrial corporation accounts, also led the nation in private business.

Svensk Fastighetskredit A.B. (SFK) had begun offering real estate financing and property management in 1961. Now a wholly owned subsidiary, SFK continues to finance single-family homes and commercial property and has expanded steadily. In addition to conventional long-term, fixed-rate loans, SFK has also made short-term and intermediate credit available for projects in the process of construction. A.B. Arsenalen and A.B. Garnisonen, subsidiaries established in 1965 and 1968 respectively, specialize in property management and related services such as appraisal, estate brokerage, construction management, and architectural services. These subsidiaries do not own property but have become national leaders in property management.

In 1981, S-E-Banken created a new real estate–related subsidiary to fill its own needs for suitable premises for the bank's growing number of branches and subsidiaries: SEB-Fastigheter A.B. This subsidiary protects S-E-Banken's investments in existing properties by maintaining them and renovating them as needed to assure their continuing appreciation. It also invests in properties and constructs new buildings.

The following year, 1982, was a banner year for acquisitions. Deutsch Skandinavische Bank, founded in 1976 in Frankfurt, opened a branch office in Hamburg, and subsidiaries were opened in two major trade centers. Skandinaviska Enskilda Banken Corporation was opened in New York, initially to handle transactions relating to business in Sweden but ultimately to gain a foothold in business involving American companies. With the growth of this business, branch offices have been set up in New York and in the Cayman Islands to facilitate transactions involving such matters as the clearing of currency. And in London S-E-Banken established another wholly owned subsidiary, Enskilda Securities, Skandinaviska Enskilda Limited. Along with facilities such as FinansSkandic (UK), which had been in operation since 1964 and focused on corporate lending, the new subsidiary offered full-service banking to Swedish and international clients.

S-E-Banken had also entered into a partnership in 1969 with Scandinavian Bank, a consortium bank based in London, which was flourishing. The other two main partners were Bergen Bank of Norway and Union Bank of Finland. To outdistance competitors in their respective homelands, the three banks, with Privatbanken of Denmark, formed Scandinavian Banking Partners, an organization that made it possible to facilitate fast money transfers and cash management services for any client in any of the three countries. Sten Westerberg, then senior vice president of S-E-Banken's international division, called the new organization "a cheap way of expanding in terms of costs, and more efficient than opening up subsidiaries."

Longstanding cooperative relationships with other banks throughout the world have been an important factor in S-E-Banken's growth. Currently, it maintains close relationships with more than 2,700 correspondent banks. At the same time, there is intense competition among Sweden's top four banks (Svenska Handelsbanken, PKbanken, and Götabanken are the other three). All four are studying new approaches to retail banking in preparation for deregulation. Electronic banking was one instant success—pioneered by Götabanken, it was quickly emulated by the other leading banks, including S-E-Banken.

The heightened personal-banking activity that came with deregulation did not include a surge of new savings accounts; Sweden's savings rate has continued to be low. But S-E-Banken found that adding new personal banking services and investment instruments resulted in a lucrative and less volatile rate of return than overdependence on the highly competitive money markets with their relatively narrow profit margins. (Within a few years of its inception, the Swedish money market had become the third largest in the world.)

As inflation and interest rates began to decline, the Swedish government took further steps toward deregulation. In 1985 it lifted its ban on foreign banking in its domestic market. Business was brisk, and S-E-Banken expressed no worry about the prospect of additional competition. Within a year, a dozen foreign banks had established facilities in Sweden but posed no immediate threat to any of the Big Four banks.

That same year government controls on interest rates and lending volume were removed—an occasion one banker described as "liberation day." With controls removed and the economy booming, the big banks' profits virtually doubled during 1986.

Also in 1985, S-E-Banken formed a new division, Enskilda Fondkommission, in Stockholm, to conduct investment banking in Sweden in cooperation with Enskilda Securities in London. And in 1987 S-E-Banken opened additional facilities, notably Enskilda S.A., Paris, a subsidiary of London's Enskilda Securities. Additional branches were opened the following year in London, Hong Kong, New York, and Singapore.

S-E-Banken established a new subsidiary in Stockholm at the beginning of 1988, called Kortbetalning Servo A.B., to develop new routines for redeeming credit and charge card bills, according to an agreement the bank had made with PKbanken and the Swedish savings banks. The bank's credit and charge card business conducted by the FinansSkandic A.B. subsidiary underwent a radical change beginning with S-E-Banken's 1987 purchase of the remaining shares in Kortgruppen Eurocard-Köpkort A.B. Eurocard operations remained an independent entity within the FinansSkandic group; the credit card operations were merged with FinansSkandic's existing operation. FinansSkandic, as a group, leads Sweden's credit and charge card market. It is also Sweden's largest leasing company.

S-E-Banken, together with its Enskilda Securities subsidiary, also pioneered a new bond, denominated in Eurokronor. First issued in October, 1988 by the World Bank, the bond sold out immediately.

While Skandinaviska Enskilda Banken's move into international banking has clearly been a success so far, the future poses a real challenge for the bank. In order to maintain its position, S-E Banken must continue to dominate in its domestic market while at the same time battling for a growing share of the European market—a market that will only grow more competitive as the European Economic Community moves toward its ultimate goal of total economic integration.

Principal Subsidiaries: Aktiv Placering AB; Arsenalen AB; FinansSkandic AB; Garnisonen AB; Kortbetalning Servo AB (58%); SEB-Fastigheter AB; Svensk Fastighetskredit AB; Deutsch Skandinavische Bank AG (West Germany) (80%); Skandinaviska Enskilda Banken Corporation (United States); Skandinaviska Enskilda Banken (South East Asia) Ltd. (Singapore); Skandinaviska Enskilda Banken (Luxembourg) SA. (99%); Enskilda Securities, Skandinaviska Enskilda Ltd. (United Kingdom); SEB Funding Limited, Inc. (United States); Fastighets AB Abisko (50%); Bankgirocentralalen BGC AB.

SOCIÉTÉ GÉNÉRALE

SOCIÉTÉ GÉNÉRALE

29 Boulevard Haussmann
75009 Paris
France
(1) 40-98-52-16

Public Company
Incorporated: 1864 as Société Générale pour Favoriser le Développement du Commerce et de l'Industrie en France S.A.
Employees: 33,266
Assets: FFr942.1 billion (US$155.49 billion)
Stock Index: Paris

Société Générale is one of the largest banking groups in France today, and has almost 1,800 offices in 62 countries around the world. The bank's business practices, often called conservative, have nonetheless given it a long history of steady growth.

In 1864, when France was in the midst of its industrial revolution, steel magnate Joseph Schneider along with a group of private Paris bankers formed Société pour Favoriser le Développement du Commerce et de l'Industrie en France S.A. Another Schneider, Eugene, was the first president of the bank. At first, Société Générale was both a deposit bank and an investment bank. It grew rapidly by establishing regional banks all over France and by investing in industry, particularly in metals. For several years, this system worked well, yielding large profits.

The bank opened its first branch in 1864, in Bordeaux. The next year it opened nine more in other cities, including Orleans, Lyons, Tours, and Toulouse. The following year several more branches were opened, among them ones in Lille, Marseilles, Nantes, and Rennes. In 1869 and 1870, Société Générale opened branches in towns important to the metal industries, St. Etienne and Clermont-Ferrand. And in 1871, the bank opened its first foreign branch, in London.

Société Générale established itself in Alsace-Lorraine before the Franco-Prussian War in 1870, in Strasbourg and Mulhouse, and a little later in Colmar. After the war, however, the territory belonged to Germany, and in 1880 Germany's assimilation policy forced the bank to either close the branches or divide them with an Alsatian firm. Thus, Société Générale Alsacienne de Banque was founded by an Alsatian venture partly backed by Société Générale. Progress was slow for the next two decades in that region.

By 1875, there were 71 Société Générale branches in all, but during the 1880s and 1890s growth was much more gradual, due largely to losses from risky investments. Because the bank had not accumulated reserves from profits or acquired fresh capital, it suffered heavy losses at the end of the century.

After 1900 Société Générale built up its capital again, focused more strictly on deposits, and resumed its growth. In 1914, it had 114 branches covering nearly all commercially or industrially significant towns. The bank had also opened 560 ancillary offices, with limited hours and services, by that time.

World War I slowed Société Générale's progress. The Alsatian bank, however, opened branches within Germany and, despite the conflict between Germany and France, relations between the two banks remained close. Although after the war the Treaty of Versailles returned Alsace-Lorraine to France, Société Générale and the Alsatian bank remained separate entities.

Société Générale continued to grow during the 1920s, when an effective economic stabilization policy was implemented throughout the country. Nonetheless, when the Great Depression hit France in 1930, the Bank of France was not able to soften the blow. Several banks failed, but Société Générale survived. During the 1930s, Société Générale entered into an agreement with Crédit Lyonnais, another large deposit bank, to cut back on expansion.

During World War II, under the Vichy government's plan for a "provisional organization for production," banks were discouraged from opening new branches and forbidden to sell any stock or interests they held in other banks.

After the war, the government took on a much greater role in the French banking system. In December, 1945, France's four largest deposit banks, including Société Générale, were nationalized. Société Générale's stockholders were duly bought out by the government, and it became a state-controlled bank. But like all of the nationalized banks, Société Générale retained its essential individuality and autonomy. It also kept its personnel, which helped to quell customers' suspicions of the new structure.

The nationalized banks possessed about half the total assets of all French banks, and as smaller banks were absorbed by larger ones the French financial system became even more concentrated, especially since the government had also passed new laws in 1946 giving the state control over the distribution of credit. As a central part of this system, the nationalized banks experienced three decades of steady growth.

After World War II, there was a trend in banking toward international expansion. Although Société Générale was reluctant to join this movement, by 1955 it had 35 branches spread throughout Algeria and other French colonies and in several foreign countries.

In the 1950s, the National Credit Commission required all banks to reduce the number of their branch offices and to gain its permission before opening more as part of the government's continued attempt to make the financial industry more efficient.

In the early 1960s prospects for domestic expansion were curtailed even more for banks like Société Générale when the government imposed sharply restrictive lending ceilings on the financial system in its effort to reduce inflation. This move forced banks to search for avenues of expansion other than those of traditional deposit banking. Many of them entered the Eurodollar market; others plunged into merchant banking or extensive overseas banking. Société Générale was one of the first to begin dealing in eurocurrencies.

In the 1960s France enjoyed a period of strong economic growth, as it entered the European Economic Community and its exports boomed. By 1968, the state was encouraging banks to diversify their roles, especially in the area of housing construction. That year, Société Générale planned to establish a banking concern in the United States called Sogen International Corporation. In addition, the bank continued to expand internationally with a focus on commercial trading and foreign currency.

In 1973 a new law was passed that allowed Société Générale to sell up to 25% of its equity to its staff and a limited number of institutional investors. Also, Société Générale waas the lead institution behind France's first venture-capital company, Soginnove, which began with FFr60 million.

In 1974, the bank's involvement in euromarket loans put it in the center of an international crisis. Most of the Eurodollar loans were short term and influenced by the flux of world trade. Many companies used the loans only to borrow from the least expensive market, but some were Eurodollar borrowers because they could not qualify for loans in their own countries. Also, several borrowers came from underdeveloped countries, where sufficient capital was not always available. These factors and the fact that average loan terms had suddenly lengthened from five to ten years put the euromarket in a precarious situation, especially in the midst of the oil crisis that began in 1973.

Société Générale was also one of the main lenders in a foreign syndicate that lent Eurodollars to the failing United States National Bank of San Diego (U.S. National) in 1973. When U.S. National did fail, Société Générale lost $7.5 million.

In 1975, Société Générale introduced Agrifan, a food-products trading company to connect French suppliers with foreign food buyers. The trading company was such a success—handling $70 million in deals within two years—that the bank organized two more trading companies in 1977, one for medical supplies and another for food-industry equipment. The three trading companies were controlled by Sogexport, Société Générale's new subsidiary. The government encouraged the bank's moves because they helped the French export industry. Inspired by Société Générale's success, several other large banks formed their own trading companies.

During the mid-1970s, Société Générale handled almost a quarter of the new French security introductions on the Paris stock market and almost half of the new foreign ones.

In 1978, Société Générale began a heavy overseas expansion program. That year the bank opened a branch in New York, and in 1979 it opened branches in Latin America and Asia. In 1979 it also formed a new banking group in a joint effort with the National Bank of Egypt, and continued to look for ways to grow in the Middle East. By that time, the bank had 200 foreign branches in 60 countries.

In 1979, a new law allowed Société Générale to increase its capital without government intervention, although at that time the government still owned 92% of the bank's stock. The next year, Société Générale was the first of the nationalized companies allowed to raise a large part of its capital on the stock market, and by 1980 the government's stake had decreased to 87%.

In 1980, the bank acquired a controlling interest in the London stockbrokers Strauss Turnbull and Company, and also acquired its Eurobond operations. In addition, the bank opened branches in Milan, Bucharest, Manila, Taipei, Athens, and Panama City and formed Société Générale Australia Limited Investment Bank and Société Générale North America to issue high-rated commercial paper.

In 1981 France elected a socialist government again, and the state regained full ownership of Société Générale the following year.

In 1982, Jacques Mayoux was appointed chairman of Société Générale. Mayoux was viewed as one of the few leaders of state-owned banks who would keep his position should there be a right-wing victory in the future. He was prominent in financial circles for having served in the French treasury for 11 years and as general manager of France's agricultural bank, Credit Agricole, for 12 years.

Mayoux began to move Société Générale out of commercial banking and into corporate finance and investment banking. He also began to develop the bank's business with small- and medium-sized companies by expanding its work in consumer credit financing and improving its equity base through issues of nonvoting stock and perpetual bonds. In 1983, Société Générale pour Favoriser le Développement du Commerce et de l'Industrie en France officially shortened its name to Société Générale.

Although the bank was very successful within France, its international operations were floundering, a situation some experts blamed on the bank's late arrival to international corporate banking. In 1984, international operations suffered a $2.4 million loss. However, in 1985 the bank began to refocus its international operations by concentrating more on wholesale and financial activities and specialized financing.

In 1985, Mayoux also sought to reduce the bank's number of employees, then at 33,000, in order to cut operational expenses, which had been driven up by what he told *American Banker* were "atrocious expenses involved in reprogramming software every time the government changes a regulation."

Société Générale, like the other nationalized banks, had long been criticized for its caution, which some said had hindered its progress, but in the mid-1980s it began to strengthen its riskier investment-banking operations. By international standards, the big French banks were undercapitalized, and investment banking was one way to alleviate the condition.

In 1985, the bank organized a new company called Projis, to take stakes in larger companies, and also planned to form its own investment-banking arm with capital of FFr100 million to complement Projis. And Soginnove, its venture-capital company, doubled its capital to FFr120 million. In general, there was increased activity between entrepreneurs and bankers as commercial banks, including Société Générale, stepped up their investment services. Nonetheless, Société Générale did not shrug off its legacy of caution: one spokesman told the *Financial Times* in 1985, "we have to fill the investment banking gap. But we will be doing it with prudence, not a flaming torch."

In 1986 the conservatives regained power in the government and soon began an extensive denationalization program, returning the companies nationalized by the Socialist Party in 1981 to the private sector and also beginning to do the same with banks and insurance companies that had been under state control since just after World War II.

In June, 1987 Société Générale was officially privatized, with FFr21.5 billion in capital. To protect the newly private companies from foreign takeover, the Ministry of Finance arranged for a *noyau dur* (hard core) of stable shareholders to invest in them.

Société Générale's shares remained at depressed levels following the October, 1987 stock market crash. "It was not surprising that the shares seemed attractive to large numbers of buyers," said Marc Vienot, the new chairman of Société Générale. Société Générale, anticipating passage of a law that would change the French stock exchanges, also purchased a controlling stake in the Paris brokerage firm of Delahye Ripault.

After the socialists' election in 1988, Société Générale's shares rose sharply, to FFr550, in late October. About that time, the head of Marceau Investments, George Pébereau, announced that he had a 9.16% stake in the bank. But because Pébereau was backed by at least two state-owned companies, there was a conservative outcry, causing a raid on Société Générale. Vienot combated the raid by persuading five private companies to buy a substantial stake in Société Générale.

In 1988, Société Générale acquired Touche Remnant Holdings Ltd., a British asset-management firm, and in 1989 it acquired Ingwerson and Company, a Dutch brokerage firm. Earnings in 1988 were very strong, up 28%. Continued strong earnings would help build its capital to comply with international capital-adequacy ratios that will come into effect in 1992. But now that the bank is publicly owned, it can also raise capital directly, unlike its nationalized counterparts.

Société Générale has grown at a consistent, if sometimes plodding, rate into one of the world's largest banks. Its future will depend on whether its traditional prudence can be applied successfully to a new market as Société Générale adjusts, with the rest of the banking industry, to the post-1992 banking world.

Principal Subsidiaries: Société Générale Alsacienne de Banque Group (56%); Société Centrale de Banque Group; Génébanque; Societé Générale de Banques aux Antilles; Société Générale Calédonienne de Banque; Banque de Polynésie; Société Générale de Banques en Espagne (Spain); Banco Supervielle Société Générale (52%) (Argentina); Société Générale (Canada); Société Générale Australia Holdings Limited; Société Genérale Elsassiche Bank (78%) (West Germany); Société Générale Bank Stockholm (Sweden); Société Générale Merchant Bank PLC. (United Kingdom); Société Générale Strauss Turnbull Securities Limited (50%) (United Kingdom); Sogen Securities Corporation (50%) (USA); Sogen Securities (North Pacific) Limited (USA); Sogen Asia Limited; Sogen Financial Corporation (USA); Sogen Lease Limited (United Kingdom); Banque Internationale de Placement (50%); Banque de Réescompte et de Placement; Financière des Marchés à Terme (75%); Généfim (53%); Société Générale des Financements Immobiliers par Crédit-Bail; Société Anonyme de Crédit à l'Industrie Francaise; Société Financière pour le Crédit-Bail; Société Auxiliaire de Crédit; Diebold Computer Leasing; Solomateg (90%); Europe Computer Systemes (87%); Crédit Immobilier Général; Groupe du Crédit Général Industriel (64%); Société Générale de Services et de Gestion Group "SG2"; Société Générale d'Exportation (90%); Société Générale d'Affacturage (99%); Sogecap (98%).

Further Reading: Wilson, J.S.G. *French Banking Structure and Credit Policy*, Cambridge, Massachusetts, Harvard University Press, 1957.

Standard Chartered

STANDARD CHARTERED PLC

38 Bishopsgate
London EC2N 4DE
United Kingdom
(01) 280 7500

Public Company
Incorporated: 1969 as The Standard and Chartered Banking Group Ltd.
Employees: 28,850
Assets: £23.7 billion (US$42.86 billion)
Stock Index: London

Standard Chartered PLC is the parent company of a number of banks and financial service companies spread across the world. Its largest subsidiary is Standard Chartered Bank, which accounts for the overwhelming majority of its operations. Standard Chartered is in some ways a relict of the British Empire. Standard Chartered was formed in 1969 as a merger between the Standard Bank, which did business throughout Africa, and the Chartered Bank, which operated branches throughout India, China, and southeastern Asia. Lacking a truly strong domestic network, the banking group's progress has been largely dependent upon Third World economic and political conditions, an unenviable position at times.

Both the Standard Bank and the Chartered Bank had been in operation for more than a century when they combined forces. The Chartered Bank, originally incorporated in 1853 as the Chartered Bank of India, Australia, and China under a charter from Queen Victoria, was influential in the development of British colonial trade throughout Asia. Up until World War II, British trade in Asia flourished, and the Chartered Bank prospered.

The Standard Bank was established in 1862 as the Standard Bank of British South Africa by a schoolmaster named John Paterson. Paterson had eclectic interests, including mining, railroad promotion, and real estate development. He set out to make Standard a large bank, and proceeded to acquire smaller banks throughout southern Africa. For the next century, the bank played a significant role in the banking of the region.

Since both banks were products of the colonial era, with similar structures and experience, they made an excellent match. Their complementary geographic coverage and similar historical backgrounds made for a relatively smooth transition.

The new Standard and Chartered Banking Group took its time integrating the management of the two banks. Throughout 1970 each former unit performed its operations more or less unchanged—indeed, bank branches continued to operate under their old names for a number of years. Each was able to expand independently in its own markets, and there was no need to immediately restructure either bank's operations. But the company slowly began to develop long-term plans for the entire bank.

Standard Chartered's first chairman, Sir Cyril Hawker, came to the group from the Bank of England, where he had served since 1920. His sensitivity to the needs of developing nations made him an excellent choice to guide Standard Chartered in its early years. In 1970, Hawker brought Standard Chartered deeper into the eurocurrency markets. Both the Standard Bank and the Chartered Bank had entered these markets in the 1960s. By 1970, Standard Chartered was using funds generated in the Euromarkets to finance projects throughout the world.

Because of its Third World involvement Standard Chartered has had to deal with more problems than most banks. Unstable political and economic conditions pose a constant threat to the bank. During the 1960s some branches were nationalized by the countries they operated in. In the 1970s, though conditions were generally calmer, Standard Chartered had to be prepared to adapt to the whims of sometimes irrational governments in Africa and Asia. Wars and rebellions were a constant threat. When new regimes came to power, Standard Chartered's branches were at times subject to new regulations, nationalization, or a transfer of ownership to native financiers. In 1970, for example, the African nation of Zambia partially nationalized the Standard Bank operating there. Nationalization was the greatest fear of any overseas bank operating in politically unstable countries. But at the same time, these regions were often very profitable.

In 1971, the Eastern Bank, a Middle Eastern bank Chartered had acquired in 1957, became fully integrated with the Chartered Bank. The Standard Bank's Nigerian branches had a good first year in the reconstruction period after the civil war there ended in 1970. Operations in Hong Kong, Singapore, and Malaysia showed strong results in the early 1970s, although depressed economic conditions in South Africa resulted in a poor performance for the Standard Bank branches operating there. Nevertheless, the bank's dependence on the unreliable conditions of Third World nations induced it to seek a stronger foothold in industrialized nations to add stability to its international network. Throughout the early 1970s, the bank increased operations in European and American capital markets and began to cooperate with other international banks.

In 1973, the banking group diversified heavily. The acquisition of Mocatta and Goldsmid Ltd. brought Standard Chartered into the gold and precious metals markets. The group's computer leasing company, Standard and Charted Leasing, expanded into European markets. The banking group also formed a partnership in a merchant bank.

By 1974, Standard Chartered's gradual integration was complete and the managements of the Standard Bank and of the Chartered Bank came together under one roof. In

August of 1974, Sir Cyril Hawker retired and was replaced by Lord Barber. Barber oversaw the formulation of a long-term strategy for the bank. Standard Chartered would concentrate on what it did best: overseas commercial banking. Unlike a growing number of international banks during this period, Standard Chartered did not intend to branch into other areas of financial services. The bank would continue to strengthen its European position to offset fluctuations in Third World economies, but would not attempt to enter retail banking in Britain. The 17 British branches Standard Chartered already operated focused on import-export financing and banking support services.

In 1974, Standard Chartered's diversity was key in insulating it from a worldwide recession. In October of 1975, the group changed its name to the Standard Chartered Bank Ltd., although subsidiaries throughout the world still operated under their old established names.

The bank grew throughout the late 1970s. Profits improved consistently, and assets continued to grow. In 1979, Standard Chartered made a major acquisition in the United States by purchasing the Union Bancorp of California.

As international banking competition became more intense, Standard Chartered's management began to see weaknesses in the bank's lack of a domestic base. In 1981, the group bid on the Royal Bank of Scotland Group. This bank had the domestic branch network that Standard Chartered wanted and was amenable to a takeover by Standard Chartered. But a rival bid by the Hongkong and Shanghai Bank sent the issue to the British Monopolies Commission, which ruled against both bids. The banking group entered the 1980s heavily reliant on the financial success of underdeveloped nations.

The 1980s were difficult times for many of the countries where Standard Chartered operated. Singapore and Malaysia fell into a serious recession in the mid-1980s. As Hong Kong's shipping industry struggled to survive, a number of large loans went bad, putting Standard Chartered in serious financial straits. By 1986, the Standard Chartered Bank was in a financial mess. The bank's strategy of focusing on commercial banking proved to have been an error, as large customers were choosing international banks that could provide them with a complete line of financial services, including stockbroking and issuing commercial paper. Capital markets and money markets were deregulated in many countries in 1986, leading to increased competition for which Standard Chartered was unprepared.

Standard Chartered's affiliate in South Africa had performed inconsistently in the 1980s, but was for the most part a profitable venture. Growing political pressure to divest South African holdings caused the bank some unrest. Standard Chartered was reluctant to sell its 39% interest in the bank at the unfavorable exchange rate of the time and take a large loss. Finally, in 1987 the bank divested its South African holdings, ending its 125-year presence in that nation. It was the last foreign bank to leave South Africa.

In 1986, London saw an explosion of mergers and acquisitions among banks with the financial deregulation known as the "Big Bang." Standard Chartered became the target of a takeover by Lloyds Bank, which Standard Chartered's chief executive, Michael McWilliam, was determined to prevent. The purchase of 35% of Standard Chartered's shares by three businessmen helped to thwart the Lloyds bid. Standard Chartered received a thrashing in the British press when it became known that one of its white knights, Tan Sri Khoo, had received a large loan from the bank just before he invested in its shares, but the bank called for an investigation to clear its name and was vindicated by the Bank of England a year later.

Although Standard Chartered was successful in warding off the hostile takeover by Lloyds, its troubles were not over. The banking community's dependence on the Third World caught up with it in 1987, when, due to larger loan-loss provisions, Standard Chartered showed a net loss of £274 million. McWilliam tried to restructure the bank's operations and replaced many high-ranking executives. Chairman Sir Peter Graham stated that the bank needed to inject new capital through a rights issue. In 1988, the bank reversed its position on divesting non-core assets to raise capital and sold the United Bank of Arizona to Citibank and later, its profitable Union Banking group to California First, a subsidiary of the Bank of Tokyo.

Standard Chartered's situation began to improve in 1988. A new rights issue in September of 1988 helped repair the bank's capital balance. Profits for the first half of 1988 were £154 million compared to a loss of £222 million during the same period a year before. McWilliam, who had directed the bank's operations during its stormiest year, resigned in early 1988 and Sir Peter Graham, who had been chairman for only two years, retired. Rodney Galpin took over as both chairman and chief executive. Galpin had spent most of his career at the Bank of England and intended to be a "hands-on" chairman.

Standard Chartered has had to adjust its structure and policy to meet a rapidly changing international financial marketplace. The bank still lacks a strong footing in Great Britain or North America, but has made a stronger domestic base a goal. As Standard Chartered strengthens its financial position, it also makes itself a more attractive acquisition target. It remains to be seen whether or not the bank will be able to continue to grow independently or will choose to link up with another bank.

Principal Subsidiaries: Standard Chartered Bank; Standard Chartered Bank Africa PLC (Lesotho); Standard Chartered Bank Australia Ltd.; Standard Chartered Bank (Switzerland) AG; Standard Chartered Bank Botswana Ltd.; Standard Chartered Bank Cameroon S.A.; Standard Chartered Bank (C.I.) Ltd.; Standard Chartered Bank Gambia Ltd.; Standard Chartered Bank Ghana Ltd.; Standard Chartered Bank Ireland Ltd.; Standard Chartered Bank (Isle of Man) Ltd.; Standard Chartered Bank Kenya Ltd.; Standard Chartered Bank of Canada; Standard Chartered Bank Sierra Leone Ltd.; Standard Chartered Bank Swaziland Ltd.; Standard Chartered Bank Uganda Ltd.; Standard Chartered Bank Zambia Ltd.; Standard Chartered Bank Zimbabwe Ltd.; Standard Chartered Acceptances Ltd. (Kenya); Standard Chartered Asia Ltd. (Japan); Standard Chartered Australia Ltd.;

Standard Chartered Finanziaria SpA (Italy); Standard Chartered Merchant Bank Ltd. (Chile); Standard Chartered Merchant Bank Asia Ltd. (Singapore); Standard Chartered Merchant Bank Zimbabwe Ltd.; CEC Finance Ltd.; Chartered Trust PLC; Credit Corporation (Brunei) Berhad; Credit Corporation (Singapore) Ltd.; P.T. Standard Chartered Leasing; Standard Chartered Export Finance Ltd.; Standard Chartered Finance Ltd. (Australia); Standard Chartered Finance Ltd. (Hong Kong); Standard Chartered Finance Ltd. (Singapore); Standard Chartered Finance Uganda Ltd.; Standard Chartered Finance Zimbabwe Ltd.; Standard Chartered Leasing Company Ltd.; Mocatta Commercial Ltd.; Mocatta & Goldsmid Ltd.; Mocatta Hong Kong Ltd.; Mocatta Metals Corporation (U.S.); Scimitar Asset Management Ltd.; Standard Chartered Fund Managers (C.I.) Ltd.; Standard Chartered Bank Hong Kong Trustee Ltd.; Standard Chartered Trustee Singapore Ltd.; Standard Chartered Futures (S) Pte Ltd.; Standard Chartered Trustees AG; Standard Chartered Trust Zimbabwe Ltd.; Standard Chartered International Trustee Ltd.

THE SUMITOMO BANK, LTD.

4–6–5 Kitahama
Chuo-ku
Osaka 541
Japan
(06) 227–2111

Public Company
Incorporated: 1912
Employees: 16,038
Assets: ¥45.08 trillion (US$360.7 billion)
Stock Index: Tokyo Osaka Nagoya Paris London

Once the banking division of one of Japan's largest and oldest *zaibatsu* conglomerates, the Sumitomo Bank today is one of the most-highly valued companies in the world. It is also characterized by an obsession for becoming Japan's largest bank, displacing such formidable competitors as Dai-Ichi Kangyo and the Fuji Bank. Sumitomo is the central coordinating body for the now-independent but former *zaibatsu* members of the Sumitomo group and has assumed the new identity of *keiretsu* (banking conglomerate).

The Sumitomo group of enterprises is one of the oldest surviving business entities in the world, dating to the early 1600s. Sumitomo was originally founded near Kyoto as a medicine and book shop. The discovery by a family member of a new method for copper smelting led the company into the expanding and highly profitable copper trade. The acquisition and development of large copper mines had made Sumitomo one of Japan's largest companies by 1868, when battling clans restored the Meiji emperor to power.

Although Sumitomo supported the losing side in that struggle, the company managed to develop good relations with the new government and later purchased some state enterprises as part of a national modernization campaign. As the company grew, Sumitomo's director general, Teigo Iba, advocated diversification into new fields of business. Flush with money from Sumitomo's copper operation, Iba set up a banking division in 1895 called the Sumitomo Bank.

Acting as the private banker for the ever-expanding Sumitomo enterprises, the Sumitomo Bank experienced smooth and rapid growth. In 1912, in need of further capital, the bank was incorporated and made a share offering. In doing so it became the first Sumitomo division to go public. Between 1916 and 1918 the bank established branch offices in San Francisco, Shanghai, Bombay, New York, and London, and an affiliate, the Sumitomo Bank of Hawaii.

Japan emerged as a major world power following its victory in the Russo-Japanese War in 1905 and, later, after World War I. This new prestige afforded companies like Sumitomo new business opportunities throughout Asia as Japan became a colonial power on par with Great Britain, the United States, the Netherlands, and France. The Sumitomo Bank established an interest everywhere the Sumitomo group went—Korea, Formosa (Taiwan), and China.

The Sumitomo Bank spun off a division of its own in 1923, when its warehousing arm was incorporated as the Sumitomo Warehouse Company. Two years later the Sumitomo group broadened its financial activities by taking over the management of Hinode Life Insurance, which was renamed Sumitomo Life Insurance the following year. Despite the creation of separate Sumitomo corporations—Sumitomo Machinery Works, Sumitomo Fertilizer Works, Sumitomo Mining, and so on—the Sumitomo group remained a closely knit conglomerate called a *zaibatsu* (literally, a "money clique") whose constituent companies owned collective majorities of shares in each other.

The power of the various *zaibatsu* was greatly resented by a quasi-fascist element in the military that rose to power during the 1930s. Advocating Japanese supremacy in Asia as well as a more equitable distribution of wealth, these militarists were bent on the eventual nationalization of the *zaibatsu*. But because the *zaibatsu* made up Japan's military-industrial complex, they were essential to the militarists' plans for conquest.

The *zaibatsu* were uncomfortable in their cooperation with the militarists: they stood to profit from Japan's expansion, but they also faced disintegration if the plan worked. Nonetheless, the Sumitomo Bank helped to finance the military's preparation for combat. Many Japanese considered the war a patriotic cause, seeking to remove western imperialists from Asia. But most Japanese companies, regardless of their reservations, were treated according to their cooperation with the militarists after World War II, and the Sumitomo companies were no exception.

Despite the militarists' desires, the Sumitomo group, having taken over a number of formerly independent or associated companies, became larger and more concentrated as a result of the war. After the war the Allied occupation authority imposed a series of antimonopoly laws that broke the *zaibatsu* into hundreds and even thousands of smaller companies. Each was forbidden to use its prewar name or to engage in cross-ownership of stock. The Sumitomo Bank was reorganized under this plan in 1948 as the Bank of Osaka.

A relaxation in industrial laws in 1949, and again in 1952, permitted the former Sumitomo companies not only to conduct business with each other, but also to resume use of the Sumitomo name and cross-ownership of stock. The *zaibatsu* re-formed, and the Sumitomo Bank became its coordinating entity.

The man placed in charge of the company after the war

was Shozo Hotta, who believed that the bank should differentiate itself from other banks by emphasizing business efficiency. He also personally evaluated business ventures that he felt the Sumitomo Bank should back. As the bank grew during the 1950s, it became better able to support larger industrial ventures such as Matsushita Electric, Toyo Kogyo, and Daishowa Paper. Many of these investments were highly successful, particularly the Matsushita venture. During Japan's first period of export-led growth, from 1955 to 1965, Matsushita grew several times over to become the nation's largest electronics manufacturer.

Adopting the new goal of "quality and quantity," the Sumitomo Bank expanded its corporate business, recognizing the diminishing opportunities for growth from its historical affiliates such as NEC, Matsushita, and other Sumitomo companies. In addition, much of the bank's business was concentrated in the Kansai area around Osaka, leaving Tokyo and Yokohama, both rapidly growing markets, largely unexploited by Sumitomo.

In a separate effort to expand, the Sumitomo Bank merged with the Kawachi Bank in April, 1965. Retaining the Sumitomo name, the banks' combined deposits surpassed those of their competitor, Fuji Bank.

Hotta was named chairman of the bank in 1971, when he was replaced as president by Koji Asai. Asai and his successor, Kyonosuke Ibe, each had a comparatively short tenure, Ibe being replaced by Ichiro Isoda. Although Hotta was removed from the day-to-day administration of the bank, the organization strongly reflected his personality: bureaucratic and authoritarian. Often described as the father of the restoration of the Sumitomo Bank, Hotta had nevertheless created for it a poor public image, which Isoda was determined to change.

Higher earnings permitted the bank to increase lending to Matsushita, Toyo Kogyo, and Daishowa, as well as to companies outside the Sumitomo group like Idemitsu Kosan, Uraga Dock Company, Taisho Pharmaceutical, and Ataka & Company. Again, many of these investments were highly profitable. Those to Ataka, Daishowa, Uraga, and Toyo Kogyo, however, were not. Toyo Kogyo, in particular, was in very serious condition. The manufacturer of Mazda trucks, Toyo Kogyo had bet its future on the success of the Wankel rotary engine, a prewar German design that was supposed to be highly fuel efficient. It proved otherwise, and became a costly problem for Toyo Kogyo, especially in combination with the 1973–1974 oil crisis. Sumitomo nevertheless supported Toyo Kogyo during its reorganization.

More serious, however, was the impending failure of Ataka & Company, a major Japanese trading firm. Because it stood to lose substantial amounts of money if Ataka went bankrupt, the Sumitomo Bank pledged to support Ataka until it could again be made solvent. Hotta entrusted Isoda with responsibility for rehabilitating Ataka. Isoda in turn appointed Yasushi Komatsu, managing director of the bank, to head Ataka. A more outgoing, congenial man than Hotta, Isoda enlisted help from the Ministry of Finance, the Bank of Japan, Ataka's customers, and even competitors of the Sumitomo Bank. Under a coordinated effort, Ataka was completely restructured; its unprofitable and underperforming divisions were sold off and cost-cutting procedures were initiated for those that remained. A year after assuming control over Ataka, the bank arranged a merger with C. Itoh, Japan's largest general trading company.

The Sumitomo Bank's handling of the Toyo Kogyo and Ataka affairs greatly enhanced its image among business and government leaders, as well as with the public. The bank's character changed at a crucial time, as the Japanese economy was entering a period of stable growth. A buyer's market emerged in banking, and with little remaining room for growth, each bank was forced to compete vigorously for market share. Had Isoda tried to cut losses by permitting both companies to go bankrupt, the bank would almost certainly have lost major clients to competitors. Instead, Sumitomo demonstrated an unusual degree of dedication to its customers and won more confidence than any advertising campaign could have hoped to generate.

The company's ability to support its clients through hard economic times was tested in the late 1970s when the industrial base in Kansai began to deteriorate. The textile industry, long in a state of decline in Japan, finally felt the effects of cheaper foreign competition. Within the Sumitomo group, business was down for Sumitomo Light Metals, Sumitomo Cement, Sumitomo Metal, and Sumitomo Chemical.

Still, by this time, the Sumitomo Bank had become Japan's largest bank in terms of deposits. That position was later lost, however, not due to a failure in business, but due to the merger of the Dai-Ichi Bank and the Kangyo Bank. A similar merger between Sumitomo and the Kansai Sogo Bank was cancelled in 1978 because the resulting bank would have been too deeply influenced by the Kansai economy.

In 1979 the Sumitomo Bank carried out a general reorganization on the recommendations of the American consulting firm MacKenzie & Company. The bank was divided into four divisions: business, sales, international, and planning and administration. In addition, greater freedom was given to division heads in order to achieve greater decentralization.

Isoda ordered the expansion of international financial services and the establishment of an in-house securities business. Toward that end, Sumitomo purchased the Swiss Banca de Gottardo in February, 1984, and later became the leading Japanese bank in foreign markets.

Isoda became chairman in 1983, when he was replaced as president by Koh Komatsu, an imaginative manager who had distinguished himself during the 1960s by rehabilitating Sumitomo's operations in California.

In 1986, observing Citicorp's experience with bank competition in the United States, Komatsu decided that Sumitomo needed to diversify its customer base geographically. Having made little progress moving into Tokyo, the bank proposed a merger with an established institution in the region. The partner bank eventually settled upon was the Heiwa Sogo Bank, an institution with about 100 branches that operated until 7:00 P.M.—four hours later than other banks.

Sumitomo, already an established leader in international

banking and finance, announced in December, 1986 that it had made a $430 million, or 25%, investment in the New York–based investment bank Goldman Sachs. The investment, which amounted to a controlling interest, greatly alarmed American banks, which charged that a foreign competitor had been permitted to enter a field the Glass-Steagall Act had barred American banks themselves from. The Federal Reserve later ruled that Sumitomo's investment was legal, but that Sumitomo could not increase its interest, exercise management rights, or expand to other countries.

Trouble came for Komatsu the following year, when reports of friction among bank divisions and depressed earnings led the board of directors to replace him as president with Sotoo Tatsumi. The new president pledged to remove excessive layers of bureaucracy that had recently compromised the bank's reputed speed and efficiency. Emphasizing a new competitive spirit, Tatsumi was charged with consolidating the gains made under Komatsu, to rationalize the company's busy expansion of the previous year.

The bank has relatively few problems that are beyond its control. It is sufficiently diversified, operationally and geographically, both within Japan and internationally, to withstand downturns in specific industry sectors. It not only remains the primary source of funds for the Sumitomo group, but has established itself as a major force in international finance. Deregulation and consolidation of the Japanese banking industry will pose challenges for Sumitomo in the future, but its foundation seems more than sturdy enough to adapt profitably to change.

Principal Subsidiaries: Sumitomo Bank of California (U.S.A.); San Francisco International Banking Division (U.S.A.); Los Angeles International Banking Division (U.S.A.); Banco Sumitomo Brasileiro S.A. (Brazil); Sumitomo Finance Overseas, S.A. (Panama); Central Pacific Bank (U.S.A.); Sumitomo Bank of New York Trust Co. (U.S.A.); Sumitomo Bank Capital Markets (U.S.A.); Sumitomo Bank of Canada; Sumitomo Finance International (U.K.); Sumitomo International Finance A.G. (Switzerland); Banca del Gottardo (Switzerland); Sumitomo Finance (Middle East) E.C. (Bahrain); Sumitomo Bank (Deutschland) GmbH; Japan International Bank Ltd. (U.K.); B.S.F.E.—Banque de la Societe Financiere Europeenne (France); Sumitomo Finance (Asia), Ltd. (Hong Kong); China International Finance Co. Ltd.; Sumitomo International Finance Australia Limited; Sumitomo Financial Futures (Singapore) Pte. Ltd.; P.T. BEII General Leasing Company (Indonesia); P.T. Merchant Investment Corp. (Indonesia); BBMB Leasing Berhad (Malaysia).

THE SUMITOMO TRUST & BANKING COMPANY, LTD.

4-5-33, Kitahama
Chuo-ku
Osaka 541
Japan
(06) 220–2121

Public Company
Incorporated: 1925
Employees: 6,759
Assets: ¥16.58 trillion (US$132.66 billion)
Stock Index: Osaka Tokyo

Sumitomo Trust & Banking is one of many companies that bear the name Sumitomo. Sumitomo, originally a copper producer, was one of Japan's conglomerates. By subsidizing new ventures with existing operations, Sumitomo branched into numerous businesses, including transport and warehousing, insurance, engineering, and banking.

Sumitomo established a successful banking subsidiary in 1912. The Sumitomo Bank was eager to enter trust banking, but was prevented by financial regulations from doing so. Sumitomo circumvented the regulations by creating another subsidiary, the Sumitomo Trust Company.

Established in 1925, the Trust was actually a spinoff of the Sumitomo Bank, staffed at first with bank personnel. Although technically it was an independent corporation, Sumitomo Trust was controlled by other companies in the Sumitomo group. As a "captive" subsidiary, it functioned as the group's private trust bank, becoming an important link in an increasingly complex financial organization that included commercial banking, insurance, and corporate finance.

Sumitomo Trust benefited greatly from Japan's strong industrial growth during the 1930s. But at the same time the government was ruled by a military clique which, threatened by the power of huge industrial groups like Sumitomo, favored their dissolution. This inclination, however, was strongly tempered by the government's reliance on their industrial might for its massive armament program.

During World War II, Sumitomo Trust was forced to obey strict instructions from the government. When the war ended in 1945, the occupation authority ordered a complete breakup of the Sumitomo group. This meant that Sumitomo Trust's ties with other group companies had to be cut completely. Each company was purged of managers who overtly supported the war, and each was forced to change its name.

The Sumitomo Trust returned to business in 1948 as the Fuji Trust & Banking Company. As a result of new financial regulations, primarily the Commercial Banking Law, Fuji Trust was also permitted to engage in limited banking activities. In 1950 the company was authorized to deal in foreign exchange, and the following year started trusteeships for investment trusts.

In 1952 industrial laws were liberalized and the company was allowed to change its name back to Sumitomo. In addition, the former Sumitomo companies were permitted to hold minority shares in each other and to conduct regular strategy meetings.

In an effort to maintain leadership in the industry, Sumitomo Trust consistently pioneered new forms of trust management. In 1952 it introduced loan trusts, and in 1957 began pension-trust management.

The company grew steadily during the 1960s, just as it had in its early years. The Trust had many profitable middle-market clients, but its primary sources of business were affiliated Sumitomo companies; it was again, in many ways, the private trust bank for the Sumitomo group.

In 1973, after setting up foreign offices in New York, London, and Los Angeles, Sumitomo Trust opened an international department to gather intelligence on capital markets. The establishment of this department marked the beginning of Sumitomo Trust's interest in developing a solid international financial network. This was later expanded, with offices in Europe, the Middle East, Australia, and elsewhere in Asia and the Americas.

It was not until the early 1980s, however, that Sumitomo Trust became highly active in international markets, becoming more aggressive in marketing its services to third parties with little or no association with other Sumitomo companies. The Trust's business expanded accordingly, and by 1987 it was the second-largest trust and banking company in Japan.

The company soon outgrew the limited opportunities of its close association with the Sumitomo group, and during the late 1980s it began to forge new relationships with foreign banks and securities dealers. In spite of an impending liberalization of Japanese financial laws, Sumitomo has not yet announced plans to develop any capabilities of its own in securities dealing.

Sumitomo Trust & Banking is bound to remain closely associated with the Sumitomo group (its four largest shareholders are Sumitomo companies). It will, however, take on an increasingly high profile in international finance. Its greatest assets are its highly efficient management structure and membership in the Sumitomo group.

Principal Subsidiaries: Sumitomo Trust International Limited; Sumitomo Ivory & Sime Limited; Sumitomo Trust Finance (Switzerland) Limited; Sumitomo Trust & Banking (Deutschland) AG; Sumitomo Trust & Banking

(Luxembourg) S.A.; The Sumitomo Trust Finance (H.K.) Limited (Hong Kong); STB Financial Futures (Singapore) Pte. Limited; Sumitomo Trust & Banking Co. (U.S.A.); Sumitrust Security Pacific Investment Managers, Inc. (U.S.A.).

SVENSKA HANDELSBANKEN

Kungstragardsgatan 2
S-10670 Stockholm
Sweden
(8) 701 10 00

Public Company
Incorporated: 1919
Employees: 5,564
Assets: SKr238 billion (US$38.9 billion)
Stock Index: Stockholm

In its infancy, Svenska Handelsbanken was a small bank, with operations confined to the city of Stockholm. In the first half of the 20th century, it was the foremost financier of Swedish heavy industry. And in the latter half of this century, it has led Scandinavian banks into the brave new world of international finance.

Svenska Handelsbanken began its life in 1871 under the name Stockholms Handelsbank. Its founders were former directors of Stockholms Enskilda Bank who left that bank after losing an internal power struggle. Their new bank, Stockholms Handelsbank, was one of the nation's first joint-stock banks (along with Skandinaviska Bank) and engaged primarily in small-scale commercial lending.

The bank remained small throughout most of the remainder of the century. Sweden was a poor, mostly agrarian nation with little heavy industry, and the authorities who oversaw the banking system kept it regional in nature, believing that a bank should be able to carve out its own geographical domain. All of this began to change, however, in the 1890s, as Sweden industrialized. Under managing director Louis Fraenckel, who led the bank from 1893 to his death in 1911, Stockholms Handelsbank pursued an aggressive lending policy to take advantage of this development; between 1893 and 1913, its loan volume increased nearly sevenfold, from SKr17 million to SKr114 million. Fraenckel also used his extensive connections with the nation's industrialists to secure underwriting and investment-banking business. Of Sweden's ten largest industrial concerns in 1912, eight of them had done business with Stockholms Handelsbank at some point.

Corresponding changes were taking place in the banking industry as well. Larger industrial undertakings required larger financing packages, which in turn required larger banks to extend the credit. Swedish banks began to amalgamate and the old regional fiefdoms dissolved. Stockholms Handelsbank embarked on a series of mergers in 1914, when it acquired a bank in northern Sweden and along with it, ties to the lumber and paper industry. In 1917 it acquired another northern bank. In 1919 it purchased a bank in the South that was involved in agriculture and the textile industry. The bank exploded in size through these mergers; its branch network expanded from seven offices in 1914, all of them in Stockholm, to more than 250 nationwide. Its assets totalled SKr1.6 billion in 1919, making it the largest bank in the nation. To reflect this, the bank changed its name to its present form, Svenska Handelsbanken, in 1919.

Sweden remained neutral during World War I, so while the hostilities produced much anxiety about the nation's economy, they did little damage to it. Industry continued to prosper and banking power continued to concentrate. By 1924, four institutions, including Svenska Handelsbanken, were accounting for 56% of Sweden's banking activity. The early 1920s, however, were marked by severe depression. In 1922, the bank decided to write off more than Skr100 million in bad loans and additions to its reserves.

The economy began to recover in 1923, and so did Swedish banks. But renewed prosperity also brought with it a dizzying wave of speculation. Before the decade was out, an ambitious Swede named Ivar Kreuger pulled Svenska Handelsbanken into what has been called the largest financial fraud in history. An engineer by training, Kreuger made a small fortune in the construction business in the early 1910s, and he used that stake to start building his own financial empire. His main goal was to turn his family's match business into a worldwide monopoly, but he also involved himself in other ventures, including a corporate-raider-style takeover of telecommunications giant L. M. Ericsson in 1925. Kreuger obtained most of his financing from American sources, but he also borrowed heavily from Swedish banks, including Svenska Handelsbanken. The problem was that he lied extensively and convincingly about his net worth, and offered as security assets that did not exist. His practice of hiring accountants based either on their lack of accounting skill or their vulnerability to blackmail helped him in this regard.

Kreuger killed himself in 1932 when the Great Depression threatened to unravel his pyramid-financing game. An audit undertaken after his death revealed the extent of the fraud he had perpetrated, and Svenska Handelsbanken could not help but be involved in the bankruptcies and restructurings that followed. Not only had Kreuger embezzled $5 million from L. M. Ericsson, but he had endangered its independence by borrowing against his controlling interest in the company. Svenska Handelsbanken, along with rival Stockholms Enskilda Bank, was closely involved in Ericsson's reconstruction. The bank also took control of what remained of Svenska Cellulosa Aktiebolaget (SCA), a Kreuger venture for which it was the major creditor. It formally bought out SCA in 1934 for SKr3 million, and considered itself fortunate when it resold an 83% stake in the company to industrialist Axel Wenner-Gren later that year for Skr10 million.

Sweden's economy fared better than the rest of the world's in the 1930s. Whereas the overvalued kronor in the 1920s encouraged capital flight and banks struggled to keep their deposits, in the 1930s the opposite happened. Undervalued currency kept money at home and banks had to fight to maintain a profitable loan volume. During this time, Svenska Handelsbanken benefited from its geographical diversity; deposit surpluses in areas where economic activity was especially slow could be sloughed off on areas where lending was brisker. The bank also continued its close involvement with heavy industry, despite that sector's growing independence from the big banks in general. In 1935 more than one-third of all money loaned to large Swedish industrial concerns came from Svenska Handelsbanken.

During World War II, Sweden once again remained neutral, but its aloofness failed to keep Swedish banks entirely insulated from the shock of war. Political uncertainty kept deposits high and it became even more difficult to maintain profitable loan volumes than it had been in the 1930s. The government helped alleviate the banks' difficulties by selling them large quantities of securities; Sweden found a large military buildup necessary to protect its neutrality and financed it through war bonds.

For Svenska Handelsbanken in particular, the 1940s were marked by divestiture of its industrial holdings. Banking laws enacted in reaction to the Kreuger crash and the Depression restricted, among other things, the amount of stock that banks could own in other companies. In 1943 the bank organized Industrivärden, a holding company devoted to managing its portfolio. Between 1943 and 1946, it sold Svenska Handelsbanken's entire interest in the steelmaker Fagersta for more than SKr37 million. After years of struggle, SCA gained solid financial footing during World War II and the bank bought out Axel Wenner-Gren in 1947 for nearly SKr18 million, then resold the company in 1950. Also in 1950, the bank sold the agricultural machinery firm Bolinder Munktell to Volvo.

Svenska Handelsbanken then began to re-orient itself toward small- and medium-scale lending. In 1955 it acquired Stockholms Intecknings Garanti, a real estate lender. It also began to expand its branch network after a 1954 study commissioned by the bank found that convenience was of paramount importance to retail customers. By 1968, it had 500 branch offices throughout the nation. It also sold its controlling interest in Reymersholm, a chemical and mining company, to Boliden Mining in 1963.

By the mid-1960s, Svenska Handelsbanken had not only become the largest bank in all of Scandinavia, but it was also a leader among Swedish banks in recognizing the increasing importance of international markets. Major Swedish companies had always conducted much of their business abroad, but the lack of Swedish banking presence in those countries meant that foreign banks wound up supplying their credit needs. In 1964 Svenska Handelsbanken joined with three other Scandinavian banks—Kjøbenhavns Bandelsbank of Denmark, Den norske Creditbank of Norway, and Kansallis-Osake-Pankki of Finland—to establish Nordfinanzbank in Zurich and Banque Nordique du Commerce in Paris. Over the next several years, it also acquired stakes in banks in Greece and Spain to help Swedish companies capitalize on foreign markets.

Svenska Handelsbanken continued to prosper and expand its foreign operations in the 1970s. It took a merger between Stockholms Enskilda Bank and Skandinaviska Bank in 1972 to overtake it as Scandinavia's largest bank. In 1970 Svenska Handelsbanken participated in the formation of Nordic Bank Limited in London, along with Den norske Creditbank and Kansallis-Osake-Pankki. In 1974 it opened a representative office in Moscow, responding to increased trade between Sweden and the Soviet Union. The next year, it established a subsidiary in New York, Nordic American Banking Corporation, devoted largely to import and export financing for North and South American clients doing business with Nordic countries. And in 1978, it set up a subsidiary bank in Luxembourg, Svenska Handelsbanken S.A., Luxembourg.

Svenska Handelsbanken raised a few eyebrows in 1971 when, under the guidance of Chairman Jan Wallander, it abandoned most forms of long-range economic forecasting and planning, deciding to rely instead on shorter-term forecasting and greater flexibility of action. Writing in *Euromoney* ten years later, President Jan Ekman announced that the policy had produced results above the industry average. "Forecasting is an exercise in meaningless impossibilities," he declared, deriding the large margins of error that characterize long-range prognostication.

By the early 1980s, Svenska Handelsbanken had grown to the point where it no longer needed consortium partners to carry out its international business. In 1982 it established its own merchant-banking subsidiary in London, Svenska International. The next year, it sold its interest in Nordic Bank Limited to Den norske Creditbank. In 1984 it formed a subsidiary in Singapore, Svenska Handelsbanken Asia Limited, and sold much of its stake in Nordfinanzbank to Kansallis-Osake-Pankki, giving its Finnish partner a controlling interest. In 1985 it sold its 25% share of Nordic American Banking Corporation to Den norske Creditbank. And in 1988 it established a subsidiary bank in Norway.

The 1980s have also been marked by a decline in the influence of banks over other segments of the Swedish business community as major corporations set up their own in-house financing units. Svenska Handelsbanken is no longer the kingmaker of industry that it once was. But Svenska Handelsbanken has made up for the end of this role by playing its newer one to the hilt. While profiting from the smaller end of the domestic market, it has also led Scandinavian banks into the modern financial world of international, integrated markets. Increasing deregulation of Sweden's banking industry and the advent of a single European financial market in 1992 will present the bank with further challenges, but its past history gives reason to believe that it will meet them successfully.

Principal Subsidiaries: Sigab (95%); Svenska Finans AB (95%); Fastighets AB Blasieholmen; Fastighets AB Filia;

SHB Kapitalplacering AB; Svenska Handelsbanken S.A. (Luxembourg); Svenska Handelsbanken PLC (U.K.); Svenska Handelsbanken Asia Ltd. (Singapore); Svenska Handelsbanken Norgea A/S; Svenska Handelsbanken Inc. (USA); Nordic Monitoring Services Ltd. (U.K.); Oy Rahameklarit AB (50%)(Finland).

Further Reading: Hildebrand, Karl-Gustaf. *Banking in a Growing Economy: Svenska Handelsbanken Since 1871*, Svenska Handelsbanken, Stockholm, 1971; Shaplen, Robert. *Kreuger: Genius and Swindler*, New York, Garland Publishing, 1986.

SWISS BANK CORPORATION

Aeschenplatz 6
CH-4002 Basel
Switzerland
(061) 20-20-20

Public Company
Incorporated: 1872 as the Basler Bankverein
Employees: 17,477
Assets: SFr154.11 billion (US$102.64 billion)
Stock Index: Basel Zurich Geneva Lausanne Berne Neuchatel St. Gall

From its founding by six private bankers in Basel more than a hundred years ago, the Swiss Bank Corporation has grown to become the second-largest bank in Switzerland and one of the largest financial institutions in the world. The bank attributes this success to three major factors: its corporate mission, which emphasizes the development of those business relationships with the greatest profit-making potential; the strength and flexibility with which it conducts its banking activities; and an uncanny sense of opportunity and luck, balanced with traditional Swiss conservatism. Not even the sinking of the Titanic could steer the bank off its steady course; two senior managers who were passengers on that ship survived the disaster.

The bank was first established as the Basler Bank-Verein in 1854 by a group of six private bankers in response to the growing credit needs of Switzerland's railroad and manufacturing industries. The bank's founders initially resisted joint-stock ownership because they wanted to keep the bank small and manageable, but they gradually yielded this position in the early 1870s as a number of new competitors entered the market and as colleagues in Germany and Austria increased pressure to have a large bank headquartered in Basel. And so in 1872 the Basler Bankverein was established as a joint-stock company.

In its first year operation the Basler Bankverein it was nominated the official Swiss bank of issue for the French national loan, for financing the growing textile and metal industries in France. However, beginning in 1873, the bank encountered several major setbacks. The Vienna stock exchange collapse, falling prices, and many bad loans forced the bank to forego issuing dividends to shareholders in favor of establishing a loss reserve. With this reserve, it was able to withstand an economic slowdown and problems in the domestic railway industry which occurred later that decade.

Over the next 20 years, the bank experienced a series of ups and downs which paralleled fluctuations in the Swiss industry and trade. Nevertheless, the bank played a significant, although restrained, role in establishing new industrial companies within Switzerland as well as new banks in Italy and Belgium.

After merging with the Zürcher Bankverein in 1895, the bank changed its name to the Basler and Zürcher Bankverein. Upon acquiring the Schweizerische Unionbank in St. Gall and the Basler Depositen-Bank in 1897, the bank began operating under its present name, Schweizerischer Bankverein, or Swiss Bank Corporation, with offices in St. Gall and Zurich in addition to the headquarters in Basel. Although a new internal structure was set up to offer autonomy to each office through three local board committees managed by one central group, this system proved too difficult to manage on a uniform basis and was later revised so that the central committee was involved more directly in the daily affairs of each office.

As the bank attempted to resolve these operational issues, it continued to grow both through its participation in Switzerland's industrial growth and foreign trade, and through the acquisition of smaller, weaker financial institutions. It also supported the government's efforts to buy back the country's major railroads from foreign investors during the early 1900s.

This activity came to an abrupt halt in 1914 with the advent of World War I as the bank supported neutral Switzerland's wartime economy and aided the country's war effort. Unlike other banks, which incurred major losses abroad during this period, Swiss Bank Corporation survived the war's financial pressures in spite of restricted access to its assets held outside the country. One noticeable effect of the war on the bank, however, was the collapse of several industrial firms in which the bank had held a major interest.

Beginning in 1924, the bank took an active role in rebuilding the international economic system by extending loans to other countries. It also served as a depository of foreign funds for investors threatened by inflation and political instability in their own countries. In 1929 the bank assisted in locating the newly formed Bank for International Settlements in Basel. This body was formed to mediate the payment of war-related reparations.

As the country struggled to overcome the Depression in the aftermath of the stock market crash in New York and the devaluation of the Swiss franc in 1936, the bank was forced to draw upon its already strained resources to help other institutions stay afloat. When it became apparent that the world was about to fall victim to another major war, the bank received a large influx of foreign funds for safekeeping and also rallied its own resources in preparation for the conflict by opening an agency in New York in 1939 to store assets in case of an invasion. As traditional business fell off once the war began, the Swiss government became the bank's largest customer as funds were directed toward the country's defense. This war had a predictable effect on dividend payments and earnings, but Swiss Bank endured as best it could.

Dr. Rudolf Speich became chairman in 1944, soon to face the problems and opportunities of the postwar period. At the end of World War II, Swiss Bank's assets were nearly SFr2 billion. Once postwar finances had been sorted out, the bank turned its attention to financing private rather than state industry and to rebuilding the shattered economies of Europe. By 1947 Swiss Bank was lending money abroad again, and between 1945 and 1948 it contributed some SFr2.5 billion to Switzerland's efforts to help its neighbors rebuild.

By 1958 the bank's assets had doubled, to SFr4 billion, and under Samuel Schweizer, who became chairman in 1961, they had doubled again by 1964. Fueling this growth were a growing number of branches, both domestic and international. In addition to the London banking office, which had opened in 1898, and the New York operation that began in 1939, the bank opened offices all over the world. In the United States, offices were opened in San Francisco in 1965 and Los Angeles in 1968. In 1965 it became one of the first European financial institutions in Tokyo.

During the 1970s, due to heavy competition within Switzerland, the bank focused on the business of multinational corporations based in the United States and Canada, expanding its offices to several other North American cities. In 1972, it formed the Swiss Bank and Trust Corporation Ltd. on Grand Cayman Island, followed by financial services subsidiaries in Hong Kong in 1973, in London in 1974, and in Luxembourg a year later.

A notable exception to this global focus was Swiss Bank's participation in a major restructuring of the Swiss watchmaking industry, which was suffering from competition from technologically superior Japanese companies. Swiss Bank and some of its competitors extended new credit to the nation's watchmakers, enabling them to use quartz technology in watches rather than obsolete mechanical designs.

In 1978, the bank appointed a new chairman, Hans Strasser, to lead it into a new decade. Strasser was the first high-ranking Swiss banking official to come from the working class; he had been an employee of the bank for over 30 years. Strasser was instrumental in shifting some of the overall decision-making responsibility from the bank's central management to its head branches and their respective subsidiaries. At the same time, management worked to establish a better balance between domestic and international banking activity, temporarily restraining the development of new business opportunities by the foreign offices, and, in particular, decreasing the number of less profitable interbank loans until business with private and commercial customers increased at home.

During the 1980s, the bank also played a significant part in protecting Swiss interests in its existing international business affairs. In 1982, the bank formed SBC Portfolio Management International, Inc. in New York. In addition, as one of the world's largest private gold dealers, it joined with the country's two other leading banks, the Union Bank of Switzerland and the Credit Suisse, to form Premex A.G., a brokerage house designed to strengthen Swiss involvement in the international precious metals market, and in particular to reinforce gold bullion trading activity in Zurich, which had recently begun to falter.

Three years later, the three banks were allies once again in refusing to participate in Swiss franc note issues lead-managed by the Swiss subsidiaries of two Japanese banks, the Long-Term Credit Bank of Japan and Industrial Bank of Japan. Basing their protest on claims of unequal treatment of foreign banks by the Japanese government, the Swiss banks argued that since they were not permitted to underwrite securities or join the bond underwriting syndicate in Japan, Japanese banks should face similar restrictions in Switzerland.

Toward the end of 1985, in another minor incident, but one with political ramifications, the Supreme Court of Switzerland ordered the bank to release information to Scotland Yard about an account that had allegedly been used to deposit a \$2.9 million ransom paid in an Irish Republican Army blackmail scheme two years earlier. The bank claimed that providing this information would endanger the customers involved, but the court held that it was in the country's best interests for the bank to cooperate with the British government, although it required that the information supplied by the bank be used only in prosecuting the IRA.

In 1986, the growing problem of international debt facing the world's financial institutions reached a critical juncture. In an attempt to keep Mexico from defaulting on its foreign loans, an international group of bank creditors attempted to negotiate a US\$1.5 million bridge loan to Mexico which would allow the country to fulfill its interest obligations on existing debt until a longer-term financing package was arranged. Alone in its resistance to this plan, Swiss Bank proposed instead that Mexico be permitted to miss upcoming interest payments, which would then be added on to the amount of the present loan. Under pressure from the International Monetary Fund and the other banks involved, Swiss Bank eventually agreed to participate in the original lending plan. Two years later, a more satisfactory agreement enabled the banks to exchange their existing Mexican loans for \$10 billion in new higher-yield 20-year bonds issued by the Mexican government.

At the end of 1986 the bank's investment banking operation added a branch in the Netherlands to its existing network of offices in London, Tokyo, New York, Frankfurt, Melbourne, and Zurich, providing more direct Swiss access to Dutch equities and bonds in the guilder market. This expansion was followed in 1987 by the acquisition of Savory Milln, a London-based securities broker, and Banque Stern, a French investment bank, as well as taking a controlling interest in the Paris brokerage house of Ducatel-Duval. These takeovers were in Swiss Bank Corporation's tradition of international expansion, necessary in a small country with a limited—and crowded—domestic banking market.

Worldwide competition was inevitable and in 1988 the Swiss banking community as a whole attempted to make up ground lost to more aggressive American, Japanese, and British financial rivals. No longer able to remain cautious and grow solely by offering foreign investors the stability of the Swiss economic system and the tax advantages of a Swiss account as it had in the first half of the century, Swiss Bank attempted to further strengthen its international portfolio and solidify its U.S. presence with the purchase of a multiple-story office tower in New York for its North American headquarters.

In 1988 in the midst of these attempts to redefine its business strategy, the bank, along with the Union Bank of Switzerland and Credit Suisse, found itself embroiled in a $1 billion money-laundering scheme operated by a Lebanese-Turkish drug syndicate. While the bank did hold accounts for some of the people involved, it denied that it had acted in violation of Swiss banking laws. And in early 1989, Swiss Bank was excluded from participating in a C$500 million issue of Eurobonds because the Canadian government suspected it of conducting business with South African authorities.

The bank went on the offensive beginning in February, 1989 when, as one of the underwriters of Swiss franc bonds issued by RJR Nabisco, it attempted to force the company to redeem these notes because of an impending buyout by Kohlberg Kravis Roberts and Company. According to the provisions of the original bond issue, the bondholders were entitled to the return of their investment in the event of a corporate reorganization. The lawsuits filed by the bank on behalf of its bondholders were settled over the next two months before the eventual sale of the company.

Today, the Swiss Bank Corporation operates 219 domestic branches and 15 abroad, in addition to its 27 representative offices worldwide, including one in Seoul, which was the first established there by a Swiss bank. With a broad network of European and international offices and visibility on the world's major stock exchanges, the bank, under its current chairman, Franz Galliker, continues to work to remain a leading full-service universal bank.

Principal Subsidiaries: Swiss Deposit and Creditbank; Banque Procrédit S.A.; Bank Finalba Ltd.; Bank Ehinger & Co. Ltd.; Armand Von Ernst & Co. Inc.; SBV Finance Ltd.; Factors Ltd.; Special Financing Ltd.; Indelec Holding Ltd.; Industrie-Leasing AG; IL Immobilien-Leasing AG; Aucreda AG; Schweizerischer Bankverein (Deutschland) AG; Frankfurter Münzhandlung GmbH; Société de Banque Suisse (Luxembourg) S.A.; Banque de Placements et de Crédit (Monte Carlo); Swiss Bank Corporation (Canada); Swiss Bank Corporation (Jersey) Ltd.; Swiss Bank Corporation (Overseas) Ltd. (Nassau); Swiss Bank Corporation (Overseas) S.A. (Panama); Swiss Bank & Trust Corporation Ltd. (Grand Cayman); SBC Finance (Cayman Islands) Ltd.; S.B.C. Australia Ltd.; SBC Portfolio Management International Inc. (New York); SBC Portfolio Management International Ltd. (London); SBC Portfolio Management Ltd. (Zurich); Schweizerischer Bankverein Kapitalanlagegesellschaft mbH (Frankfurt); SBC Investment Services Ltd. (Dublin); SBC Portfolio Management International K.K. (Tokyo); SBCI Futures Inc. (New York); SBCI Swiss Bank Corporation Investment Banking Inc. (New York); SBCI Swiss Banking Corporation Investment Banking N.V. (Amsterdam); SBCI Hong Kong Ltd.; SBCI Holding (Basle); SBCI Securities (Asia) Ltd.; SBC Securities Ltd. (Hong Kong); Métaux Précieux S.A. Metalor; SERIMO Immobiliendienste AG; Société de Constructions de Gérances et de Placements SOCOGEP; Swiss Auditing and Fiduciary Company; Systor AG; Ideal Job conseils en personnel S.A.; TRANSPLAN Ltd. (50%); HIMAC AG für Verwaltung von Anlagefonds; SAGEPCO S.A. de Gérances et de Placements collectifs; INTERFONDS International Investment Trust Company; Société Internationale de Placements, SIP (50%); Swiss Bank Corporation US-Dollar Money Market Fund Management Company.

Further Reading: Bauer, Hans. "The Eventful Hundred Years of the Swiss Bank Corporation," Basel, Swiss Bank Corporation, 1972.

THE TAIYO KOBE BANK, LTD.

56 Naniwa-cho
Chuo-ku
Kobe 650–91
Japan
(078) 331–8101

Public Company
Incorporated: 1973
Employees: 13,000
Assets: ¥21.78 trillion (US$174.27 billion)
Stock index: Tokyo Osaka

The product of a merger between the Bank of Kobe and the Taiyo Bank in 1973, the Taiyo Kobe Bank is unusual in many respects. It has achieved great success as a major commercial, or "city," bank without being directly associated with any of Japan's major trading conglomerates. Instead, its four largest shareholders are unrelated life-insurance companies. Similarly, the bank is equally represented by Japan's four largest securities firms. As one of Japan's most independent companies, the Taiyo Kobe Bank may also be its country's most successful merger.

The Bank of Kobe was established in 1936 as the result of the amalgamation of seven banks in Hyoto Prefecture, the Kobe-Osaka-Kyoto region of western Japan. Osaka, once Japan's financial center, and Kyoto, the pre-Meiji capital of Japan, had by then given way to Tokyo. The Kobe region, however, was still home to many of Japan's large industries, and though the financial community was now focused on Tokyo, many opportunities remained in Kobe. These, however, were not fully exploited until after World War II.

In the years leading up to and during the war, the financial interests of the *zaibatsu* conglomerates dominated banking and industry in Japan. While many smaller banks were absorbed by the *zaibatsu* during the war, the Bank of Kobe remained independently managed and free from outside interference.

After the war, the Bank of Kobe emerged from a general reorganization of the banking industry relatively intact, and in 1945 added trust operations. Its importance in the region was recognized by regulators in 1949, when it was authorized to become a Class A foreign-exchange bank. It was relatively undistinguished in the banking

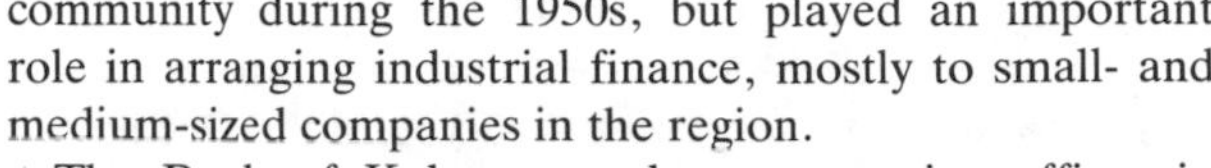

community during the 1950s, but played an important role in arranging industrial finance, mostly to small- and medium-sized companies in the region.

The Bank of Kobe opened representative offices in London in 1956 and in New York in 1958, and made a name for itself in the early 1960s by seizing two great initiatives. Recognizing its own wealth of staff with planning expertise, the bank opened a consulting division in 1961. The following year it acted as an underwriter and international marketer of bond issues for the city of Kobe. The bank's exposure to these markets led it to open branch offices for these divisions in New York in 1963 and London in 1966, and representative offices in Los Angles 1970 and Sydney in 1971.

However, in accordance with financial regulations designed to keep banking specialized, the Bank of Kobe was obliged to turn over its trust operations to Toyo Trust and Banking in 1960. During the late 1960s a series of bank consolidations and expansions, combined with a more competitive atmosphere, led to a gradual deterioration in the bank's position. It was geographically overconcentrated and limited in its ability to win business in high-growth areas. This, in turn, endangered its long-term viability and, to a lesser extent, that of the region.

The bank, its clients, and the government all wanted to strengthen the bank's position. Because it was an otherwise healthy organization, the most logical solution—and one frequently advocated by the government—was to merge the bank with another similarly troubled organization from another region. A merger would provide geographical diversity and immediately create a larger bank that could benefit from economies of scale.

The Taiyo Bank shared a similar history of independence and catering to smaller industries. It also shared similar problems: it was concentrated in the Tokyo region and was unable to promote itself into a larger role in the financial community there.

Like the Bank of Kobe, Taiyo was founded just before the war, by the merger of four small mutual savings and loans, and incorporated in 1940 as the Dai Nippon Mujin. The bank operated under increasingly difficult circumstances during the war, including heavy regulation. It resumed regular business in 1948, having dropped *Dai*, meaning "great," from its name. In 1951 it was rechartered as a mutual bank and its name was changed to the Nippon Sogo (or "Japan Mutual") Bank.

Nippon Sogo undertook a slow expansion, but though it accumulated many branches in the Tokyo area, it failed to establish itself as a major city bank. Eventually, in 1968, Nippon Sogo won permission to conduct foreign-exchange transactions. In order to project a new image as an international bank, the company changed its name to the Taiyo Bank.

The merger of the Bank of Kobe and the Taiyo Bank resulted in a nationwide bank with well over 300 branches, the largest network in Japan. Capitalizing on its new status as a top-20 bank, Taiyo Kobe opened a series of offices overseas during 1974. Branches were opened in Seattle and Hamburg, and representative offices were opened in São Paulo, Singapore, and Brussels.

The bank suffered only minimally from the oil crisis

that began in 1973, since its broad exposure to small- and medium-sized, domestically oriented firms insulated it somewhat from the recessionary period. During the recovery that followed, Taiyo Kobe's growth was driven by the strength of Japan's export-led expansion and high savings rates among its increasingly affluent population. Throughout the 1970s and well into the 1980s, the bank experienced consistently positive growth without any disruptions.

During this period the bank opened a new foreign office about every eight months. Its growth is attributed to the same strategic planning abilities it sells as a business consultant. Under banner names such as "Action IV" and "Innovation V," these management plans have allowed the bank to maintain and increase its competitiveness in the difficult and gradually deregulating Japanese banking industry.

Of Japan's 13 "city banks," Taiyo Kobe still maintains the largest number of branches. In profits per employee or per branch, however, Taiyo Kobe trails its competitors. As it pursues more efficient management policies at home, it is actively working to diversity in the global market. In June, 1987 the bank opened a trust-banking subsidiary in New York that promises to become its most important overseas office.

In August, 1989 Taiyo Kobe and the Mitsui Bank announced that they would merge in April, 1990 to form Mitsui Taiyo Kobe Bank. Taiyo Kobe's strong branch network and domestic savings business are intended to balance Mitsui's stronger corporate and international business. With assets of some ¥40 trillion, it will be the second-largest bank in the world.

Principal Subsidiaries: Taiyo Kobe Bank (Luxembourg) S.A.; Taiyo Kobe Finanz (Schweiz) A.G. (Switzerland); Taiyo Kobe International Limited (U.K.); Taiyo Kobe Finance Hongkong Ltd.; Taiyo Kobe Financial Futures (Singapore) Pte. Ltd.; Taiyo Kobe Australia Ltd.; Taiyo Kobe Bank (Canada).

THE TOKAI BANK, LTD.

21–24, Nishiki 3-chome
Naka-ku
Nagoya 460
Japan
(052) 211–1111

Public Company
Incorporated: 1941
Employees: 11,836
Assets: ¥31.42 trillion (US$251.4 billion)
Stock Index: Nagoya Tokyo Osaka

The Tokai Bank is one of the leading commercial banks in Japan. Based in Nagoya, it is the dominant bank in the Chukyo region of central Japan, where Toyota, among other companies, is based. The product of a wartime amalgamation, Tokai has since survived numerous reorganizations of the banking industry and has successfully established a presence in Japan's leading financial centers, Tokyo and Osaka.

The Tokai Bank was established in 1941, approximately six months before Japan entered World War II but in the midst of Japan's war with China. At that time the Japanese government was dominated by a military group that had ordered the concentration of several industries in an effort to raise economic efficiency. As part of that initiative, three small banks in Nagoya—the Aichi Bank, the Nagoya Bank, and the Ito Bank—were merged. Each had been in existence for many years. The oldest, the Aichi Bank, was founded in 1877 as the Eleventh National Bank.

The three banks were roughly equal in size. Because they all wanted to make a break with their troubled pasts as small local banks, they adopted a different name for the new bank: *Tokai*, Japanese for "East Sea." The East Sea, or Sea of Japan, was at the time a rich source of food and the main conduit between Japan and its colonies and conquests on the Asian mainland.

The Tokai Bank never got an opportunity to participate in any large wartime development projects, however, but instead was forced into defensive measures and spent much of the war issuing debt.

When the war ended in 1945, the occupation authority laid plans for the postwar banking industry and initiated purges of managers suspected of aiding the war effort. The Tokai Bank was deemed the appropriate size for a regional bank, and, because it had not contributed significantly to the war effort, was permitted to keep its management and to retain its name. In 1947 Tokai was awarded a foreign exchange license, greatly improving its clout. The following year, under the Reconstruction and Reorganization Act, it was permitted to increase its capitalization to ¥435 million—a substantial increase in size.

During the 1950s, Tokai was given de facto responsibility for aiding recovery in Chukyo prefecture. Because Japan's Ministry of International Trade and Industry had set broad and ambitious goals, the bank had a great deal of work to do. The completion of large plants required tremendous amounts of capital and long lead times that often exceeded the bank's capacity. Nagoya, however, grew steadily during this period and savings rates remained high. By the mid-1950s, as some of the bank's client projects came on line, margins were greatly improved.

Dedicated to offering the highest degree of service in a relatively unsophisticated market, Tokai inaugurated checking accounts in 1960. The bank had also developed a successful trust business. In 1962, however, Tokai became obligated under financial regulations to separate this business from its regular operations and in the process founded the Chuo Trust & Banking Company. Tokai began loan services in 1963, started the country's first on-line money-order system in 1965, and in 1968 opened a foreign trade information center, whose aim was to assist in marketing financial opportunities overseas.

Once it had successfully expanded its offices in Tokyo and Osaka, Tokai began to look overseas. The bank opened its first overseas branch, in London, in 1963, partially in an effort to assist Japanese export firms in European markets but mostly to gain representation in a major world capital. A New York office, established in 1954, was upgraded to a branch in 1965.

As Japan entered its second period of industrial growth in the mid-1960s, Tokai's location gained greater significance. Situated midway between Tokyo and Osaka, Nagoya had grown into a major industrial region, and Tokai was the only major bank with its head office there. It naturally had the strongest relationships with local government and businesses, and therefore became the most important economic intermediary in the region.

Tokai gained even greater significance in the early 1970s as domestic demand in basic industries began to show the first signs of saturation. Equally important were preparations for an ambitious export drive being made by leading manufacturers and trading companies. In order to maintain its position in the region, Tokai started to emphasize international expansion. Additional offices were opened in Los Angeles, Amsterdam, Hong Kong, Zurich, Sydney, and Singapore, and the foreign-trade information center was upgraded to include investment activities.

Tokai's most important customer during this period was undoubtedly the Toyota Motor Corporation, which became Tokai's largest shareholder. Toyota's tremendous sales, particularly in the United States, created numerous expansion opportunities for both the company and the bank. But, although both companies were closely associated with other firms, they fell short of creating an industrial group similar to the Dai-Ichi Kangyo, Sumitomo, or Mitsubishi groups. Tokai had cultivated important relationships with many companies associated with otherwise rival industrial groups, but it was simply not in its interest to become involved in such an industrial group.

Tokai pursued its expansion in international markets into the 1980s by opening a branch in Chicago and offices in Atlanta; Dallas; Lexington, Kentucky; and other places. As part of its expansion, Tokai established subsidiaries in North America, including the Tokai Bank of California, the Tokai Trust Company of New York, and the Tokai Bank of Canada.

The trust operation in New York allowed Tokai to begin building its expertise in trust banking, an activity it is not chartered to perform in Japan. The rapid liberalization of financial regulations in Japan, however, virtually ensures that one day soon institutions such as Tokai will be permitted to engage in trust banking, insurance, and securities underwriting.

Tokai undertook a reorganization in 1988 that resulted in the creation of a treasury and capital market group and a corporate planning group. These new groups are intended to enhance the bank's ability to manage information in bond and other securities markets and assist client corporations in developing sound business strategies.

While working to develop capabilities in a broader range of activities, Tokai has recently concentrated on consolidating its position with middle-market corporations, offering these companies services that were once available only to large corporations. As a result, the bank has become exceedingly popular in that sector, which makes up a growing share of Tokai's business.

In foreign markets, Tokai has seized an opportunity to work with non-Japanese clients in such areas as leveraged buyouts, corporate restructuring, and large-scale real estate development projects. While these are higher-risk activities than Tokai has been accustomed to undertaking in Japan, they are also normally fee-based, and therefore are somewhat more stable undertakings.

Tokai's immediate goals include consolidating reliable profit centers like retail banking while developing a more complete range of financial services. Because Tokai is already associated with companies involved in these services—including Chiyoda Mutual and Nippon Life Insurance—it stands a good chance of succeeding when Japan's financial markets are fully liberalized.

Principal Subsidiaries: Tokai Bank of California; Tokai Bank Nederland N.V.; Tokai Asia Ltd. (Hong Kong); Tokai International Ltd. (U.K.); Tokai Finance (Switzerland) Ltd.; Tokai Australia Finance Coporation Ltd.; Tokai Financial Futures (Singapore) Pte Ltd.; Tokai Trust Co. of New York; Tokai Bank Canada; Tokai Leasing (Deutschland) GmbH (West Germany); Tokai Credit Corporation; Master Lease Corporation; Tokai Securities, Inc.; P.T. Tokai Lippo Bank.

THE TORONTO-DOMINION BANK

Post Office Box 1
King Street West and Bay Street
Toronto, Ontario M5K 1A2
Canada
(416) 982–8222

Public Company
Incorporated: 1955
Employees: 22,853
Assets: C$58.1 billion (US$48.7 billion)
Stock Index: Toronto Winnipeg Montreal Tokyo Vancouver London Alberta

The Toronto-Dominion Bank's hyphenated name suggests its origins: the amalgamation of the Bank of Toronto and of the Dominion Bank. The Bank of Toronto missed celebrating its centennial by six weeks when the new bank's charter was signed on February 1, 1955. Today, the Toronto-Dominion Bank leads Canada's banks in profits although it is only fifth in assets. Strong leadership has enabled the bank to endure economic contraction and to prosper during expansion.

Founded by flour producers who wanted their own banking facilities, the Bank of Toronto was originally chartered on March 18, 1855. The Millers' Association of Canada West, as Ontario was then known, coordinated its preliminary affairs, and on July 8, 1856, the bank opened its doors to the public.

From its initial service to wheat farmers, millers, and merchants, the Bank of Toronto quickly expanded to the lumber industry and to other agricultural interests, mirroring the expansion of business activities on Canada's frontier as pioneers pushed west. In addition to this expansion, railroad booms both in England and in the United States increased the demand for flour and timber. Unfortunately, both booms collapsed at the same time, sharply curtailing the Canadian economy and with it, the westward growth of railroads and towns. Entire communities that had borrowed heavily to finance the building of rail service to their areas went bankrupt.

Although geographically in the middle of this national crisis, the Bank of Toronto was not as imperiled as many other businesses that had invested in the promise of the railroads because it had been established too late to provide much of the financing to the industry. Nor was it directly affected by the radical swings in real estate prices, dependent on the coming of the railroad, because its first officers did not believe in investing in an asset which fluctuated in value. While the business of the bank did contract, wheat was still grown, milled and shipped.

The Canadian economy rebounded when markets in the United States reopened after the American Civil War in 1865. Fledgling businesses in leather, tanning, and liquor distillation sprang up, but the harvest still formed the backbone of business for native Ontario banks. A good year brought prosperity and a bad one meant hardship.

The Bank of Toronto was not without competition. The Bank of Montreal, older and larger, attempted to have the new bank's status limited to that of a community bank with no authority to establish branches. This debate was settled by Lord Durham's Report of 1850, which established branch banking as the national structure for the industry and guaranteed that successful banks could compete within their provinces and beyond, giving all institutions the opportunity to establish national identities.

The volume of business in Ontario in general and in Toronto specifically encouraged a group of professional men to seek a charter and to found the Dominion Bank, which opened for business on February 1, 1871. The Toronto-Dominion Bank was foreshadowed from the start: stock subscriptions for the Dominion Bank were deposited in the Bank of Toronto. Although originally incorporated to facilitate and promote agricultural and commercial growth, the Dominion Bank stressed the commercial end of banking, investing heavily in railway and construction ventures as well as in the needle trade in Ontario and Montreal.

Over the next several decades, through a series of booms and busts, Canada's economy grew and new industries were established: dairying, textiles, pulpwood, mining, and petroleum. The Canadian frontier advanced through Manitoba, Saskatchewan, Alberta, and British Columbia. Both the Bank of Toronto and the Dominion Bank responded to this expansion with a pioneering spirit. Many a new office shared the counter of a town's one general store, while a one-man staff slept with deposits beneath his mattress and a revolver under his pillow.

The outbreak of World War I brought great demand for Canada's natural resources. Within a year the country had erased its trade deficit and become a creditor nation. A few brief years of prosperity followed Germany's surrender in 1918, but the depression and panic preceding World War II appeared at the Dominion Bank on October 23, 1923. Sometime that Friday morning a foreign customer presented a check that was uncashable due to insufficient funds in the account. The teller attempted to overcome the customer's lack of fluency by raising his voice. "No money in the bank," he said. Those five words began a run that lasted until Tuesday afternoon, when rational voices finally overruled rumors.

Hastily established branches were another symptom of the shaky ground on which growth was built. For example, when three banks, one of them the Bank of Toronto, decided simultaneously to open an office at Cold Lake, Manitoba, the Bank of Toronto's officer rushed to be the first—with the help of Western Canada Airways. Although undocumented, he claimed it was the first bank in the world to open with the help of aviation.

The impact of the 1929 stock market crash in New York was compounded in Canada by the beginning of a seven-year drought. Foreign trade decreased, inventories accumulated, and factories closed. Both banks compensated by closing unprofitable branches, writing off bad debts, and reducing assets. Public criticism abounded. Partly as a response to the outcry but also as an attempt to coordinate the industry, the Bank of Canada was founded in 1934 to issue currency, set interest rates, and formulate national monetary policy. During World War II, the Foreign Exchange Control Board had issued regulations for all foreign transactions. Both banks worked under these restrictions and cooperated with the Bank of Canada to raise C$12.5 billion from Canadian citizens to finance the war effort. In another major contribution, 707 employees of the Dominion Bank and more than 500 of the Bank of Toronto, approximately half of each staff, served with the Canadian forces while their jobs were held for them.

By 1954, both the Bank of Toronto and the Dominion Bank occupied a special position among the nine major banks in Canada. Each had achieved national prominence through its own efforts rather than through merger or acquisition. Each bank, however, realized that to retain its position, it needed to improve its capital base. Only a merger would support the size of industrial loans, which had grown from thousands to millions of dollars. The Minister of Finance approved the merger on November 1, 1954 and it was enacted on the following February 1, the first amalgamation of chartered banks since 1908 and only the third in the nation's history.

On opening day, the Toronto-Dominion Bank operated 450 branches, including offices in New York and London. It controlled assets of $1.1 billion and a loan portfolio of $479 million. During its first 15 years the new bank devoted a great deal of effort to establishing a unified image. In 1967, it moved into the 56-story Toronto-Dominion Bank Tower of the Toronto-Dominion Centre.

During the 1970s, the Toronto-Dominion Bank began to expand internationally. Within three years, it opened branches in such diverse locations as Bangkok, Frankfurt, and Beirut. During the mid-1970s, the Toronto-Dominion issued the $65 million offering for the Toronto Eaton Centre, a 15-acre urban redevelopment project in downtown Toronto.

The past 15 years form one distinct chapter in Toronto-Dominion's history, in the person of Richard Murray Thomson, who has guided the institution as president and, since the end of 1976, as chairman. The bank has consistently outperformed its rivals both in return on assets and in stock performance for the past decade and is one of only two non-regional banks in North America to enjoy an AAA credit rating. Yet Thomson is independent enough to have refused the government's request to provide free services to retail depositors and to have led the opposition against the bailout of two regional banks in Alberta. On the other hand, he willingly stopped the flow of money to Canadian firms for the purchase of foreign oil companies because it was causing a run on the already weak dollar in 1981. Thomson boasts that the Canadian system of banking is the envy of the world. During the current decade the Toronto-Dominion Bank helped solve two major concerns threatening Canadian banks: Third World debt and the debt of Dome Petroleum.

Developing countries offered a financial frontier for large banks during the 1960s and 1970s. By 1987 Brazil's debt alone totaled C$90.4 billion. Of that amount, Brazil owed C$7.1 billion to Canadian creditors, including C$836 million to Toronto-Dominion. In February 1987, Brazil suspended payment on the entire debt. After months of negotiation, a settlement was reached in which several Canadian banks, including Toronto-Dominion, agreed to assist Brazil with a C$2 billion interest payment to the United States by loaning the country an additional C$6 billion. This action protected the U.S. banks from classifying Brazil's loans of C$37 billion as uncollectible and preempted a banking crisis in that country. Internally, Toronto-Dominion reclassified most of its Brazilian loans as non-accruing in the second quarter of 1987. Thomson reduced the risk from all Third World debt further by selling off C$411 million in loans for 66 cents on the dollar.

The other major liability resolved under Thomson's guidance involves Dome Petroleum. Problems began in 1981 when Dome purchased Conoco, Inc. for US$1.7 billion. As oil prices fell, Dome attempted to restructure its debt, but only succeeded in prolonging the inevitable. By early 1987, Dome was entertaining buyout discussions with several different companies. Amoco Canada Petroleum emerged as the early leader among the bidders and signed an agreement with Dome in April. It took eight months and an additional C$400 million for Dome's creditors to approve the largest buyout in Canadian history. The final C$5.5 billion offer provided 95.4 cents on the dollar to each secured creditor.

The outlook for Toronto-Dominion is bright. Overseas operations have been trimmed to eight and U.S. offices to six as Thomson works to capitalize on strengths. It has taken the lead in lending to the cable-television industry and will continue to explore industries in which it can play a leadership role. There is every reason to expect that the little bank of the Big Five will continue to outperform its older, bigger colleagues.

Principal Subsidiaries: Chargex Ltd. (25%); The Edmonton Centre Ltd. (30%); Export Finance Corporation of Canada, Ltd. (11%); Pacific Centre Ltd. (33.3%); Scotia-Toronto Dominion Leasing Ltd. (50%); TD Capital Group Ltd.; Torcred Developments Ltd. (50%); TD Mortgage Corp.; Toronto-Dominion Centre Ltd. (50%); Toronto-Dominion Export Finance Co. Ltd.; Toronto-Dominion Leasing Ltd.; Toronto-Dominion Realty Co. Ltd.; 82195 Canada Ltd. (25%); TD Factors Ltd.; TD Financial Futures Ltd.; TD Forest Investments Ltd.; Green Line Investor Services Inc.; TD Securities, Inc. *Foreign:* Commercial Pacific Trust Co. Ltd. (12.5%); Dominbank Nominees Ltd.; Toronto Dominion Nominees Ltd.; Tordom Nominees (H.K.) Ltd.; Tordom Nominees (Pte) Ltd.; Toronto-Dominion Holdings (U.S.A.), Inc.; Toronto Dominion Investments B.V.; Toronto Dominion

(South East Asia) Ltd.; 3637 Indian Creek Drive Corp.; Toronto Dominion Australia Ltd.

Further Reading: Schull, Joseph. *100 Years of Banking in Canada: A History of the Toronto-Dominion Bank*, Copp Clark, Toronto, 1958.

UNION BANK OF SWITZERLAND

Bahnhofstrasse 45
Zurich 8021
Switzerland
(01) 234 11 11

Public Company
Incorporated: 1912
Employees: 20,872
Assets: SFr160.4 billion (US$106.83 billion)
Stock Index: Zurich Basel Geneva Bern Lausanne Neuchatel St. Gallen Frankfurt Tokyo

Switzerland is a country fond of boasting that it has more banks than dentists, and Union Bank of Switzerland (UBS), along with Credit Suisse and Swiss Bank Corporation, has been one of its three largest banking institutions for five decades now. In fact, it currently ranks as Switzerland's largest bank, and although it has lagged behind its competitors in internationalizing its operations, its domestic operations remain unmatched. It is without doubt a banking kingpin in a nation where banking is one of the most important industries.

UBS was formed in 1912 when Bank of Winterthur and Toggenburger Bank merged. Bank of Winterthur was founded in 1862 and established itself as a business lender with strong international connections. Toggenburger Bank was founded in 1863 and became a general-service regional bank based in eastern Switzerland. In addition to its savings and mortgage banking businesses, it also engaged in securities trading. When the two of them amalgamated, the resulting institution possessed nine branch offices and SFr202 million in assets. But although the two banks seemed like complementary partners—one with an international reputation, the other with a strong domestic base—UBS confined its operations at first to its regional strongholds in the east and northeast of the country.

At first, UBS operated from dual headquarters in the cities of Winterthur and St. Gallen, but it soon became apparent that its Zurich office would be the best place from which to direct its activities. In 1917 UBS built a new corporate headquarters at Bahnhofstrasse 45, and its current headquarters still occupy that site. In the years following World War I, the bank expanded its operations into the cantons of Aaragau, Bern, and Ticino through the opening of new branches and the acquisition of local banks. It continued to prosper through the 1920s, and by the end of the decade it possessed assets worth SFr992 million.

UBS struggled along with the rest of the world during the Great Depression, suffering a decline in its assets. It did not really recover, in fact, until after World War II. Despite Switzerland's famed neutrality, the war hurt the bank by virtually shutting down its international businesses. And while banks in major belligerent countries like the United States and Germany began to recover from the Depression because of wartime economic expansion and their governments' need for emergency financing, UBS's performance continued to lag.

Once the war ended, however, so did the bank's slump. Only a few months after Germany's defeat in 1945, it acquired Eidgenössische Bank, a prominent Zurich financial institution. This acquisition pushed UBS's assets to SFr1 billion and established it as one of Switzerland's largest banks. UBS also established a presence in the United States for the first time when it opened a representative office in New York in 1946. But the bank's strategy during the postwar years concentrated on developing its domestic business. It continued to open branches and acquire smaller institutions within Swiss borders throughout the 1950s. By 1962, UBS's assets had reached SFr7 billion and the bank had 81 branch offices.

In 1965 UBS and other major Swiss banks found themselves unwillingly embroiled in an international controversy when nervous investors sparked a run on the British pound. Swiss banks, through their reputation as the world's safest money havens, had accumulated substantial deposits in pounds sterling, and it was from them that unwanted pounds were withdrawn for sale on the currency markets. The banks themselves sank $80 million into stopping the panic, but the British were not impressed—Labor Party politicians derisively labeled them "the gnomes of Zurich." In response, UBS Chairman Alfred Schaefer complained to *Time*, "These campaigns really wound us. At times it makes one melancholy."

UBS underwent a burst of expansion in the late 1960s funded largely by the 1967 acquisition of Interhandel, a Swiss financial company possessing substantial cash holdings from the sale of its majority stake in GAF, the American chemical concern. In 1968 UBS acquired four small domestic savings-and-mortgage banks, strengthening its mortgage-banking operations. In 1969 it diversified into consumer lending, leasing, and factoring through the acquisition of four more domestic financial companies: Banque Orca, Abri Bank Bern, Aufina Bank, and AKO Bank.

UBS opened its first foreign branch office in 1967 in London. It continued to expand its overseas business in the 1970s, establishing Union Bank of Switzerland Securities Limited in London in 1975 and UBS Securities Incorporated in New York in 1979. Both of these subsidiaries were devoted to gaining a share of foreign underwriting markets.

But UBS has lagged behind its competitors in expanding its foreign operations in the past 20 years, when internationalization has been the watchword of the financial industry all over the world. It was the last of the three largest Swiss banks to establish a branch office in the United States, which it finally did in 1970, in New York. Its foreign securities subsidiaries also remained small compared to those of Swiss Bank Corporation and Credit Suisse. UBS's caution in testing international waters, however, was a longstanding matter of policy. The bank's directors still remembered how the sudden termination of foreign business in World War II had delayed its recovery from the Depression, and concentrated instead on building up its domestic business long after its competitors had begun to internationalize.

As a result, UBS began losing what international business it had in the 1980s because its operations were relatively unsophisticated. It was also faced with the fact that it had just about reached the limits of expansion in the domestic banking arena. So in the middle of the decade, it made a fresh assault on the Eurobond market in an attempt to become a leading European underwriter. In February, 1985, UBS surprised Eurobond underwriters when it brought major bond issues worth a total of $850 million for Nestlé, Rockwell, IBM, and Mobil to market at unusually low yields. The low yields were meant to attract corporate customers who liked the prospect of paying lower interest rates on their issues, but left competing underwriters astonished by UBS's aggressiveness and the high prices that it charged for the bonds. The general manager of a rival bank attributed its approach to the Eurobond market to the influence of the preponderance of Swiss army officers in UBS's hierarchy. "They make immensely careful preparations before making a move, and then they throw all their power into an advance," he told *Euromoney* in 1984.

UBS did not stop there in its late drive to internationalize. Anticipating the 1986 deregulation of Britain's financial markets, it acquired the London brokerage house Phillips & Drew in 1985. In 1986 it bought the West German bank Deutsche Länderbank, which it renamed Schweizerische Bankgesellschaft, and established a Phillips & Drew office in Tokyo. And in 1987, it opened an Australian merchant-banking subsidiary, UBS Australia Limited.

During the summer of 1987, UBS sought to solidify its position in the London markets with a bid to take over the British merchant banker Hill Samuel. The deal fell through, however, when UBS refused to accept Hill Samuel's shipbroking and insurance services in the deal along with its core merchant-banking businesses. Rumors circulated that UBS might then go after Kleinwort Benson, a British merchant bank that was reeling at the time from a slump in the bond market and a series of unfortunate acquisitions. As it turned out, however, UBS was having enough trouble digesting Phillips & Drew. The brokerage subsidiary lost £48 million as a result of the October, 1987 stock market crash, but even before then an inadequate settlement system had cost it £15 million when a rush of bull market–inspired orders proved overwhelming. Between April, 1987 and February, 1988, UBS spent a total of £115 million on Phillips & Drew.

Still, UBS seems prepared to stick it out in the British securities market. And back home, it appears to be in little danger of losing its dominant position as one of Switzerland's three largest banks. The Big Three have a virtual stranglehold on the domestic securities brokerage and underwriting businesses, and they often behave as members of a club rather than competitors. As a syndicate, their power is quite considerable. Despite sentiment emanating from the regulatory Swiss National Bank in 1989 that there should be greater competition in the nation's financial markets, UBS's future position seems quite secure.

Principal Subsidiaries: AKAG Anlage-und Kapital-AG (99%); AKO Bank; Argor-Heraeus S.A. (75%); Aufina Leasing & Factoring AG; Banco di Lugano; Bank Aufina; Bank Cantrade Ltd. (85%); Saudi-Swiss Bank (51%); Bank Rohner Ltd. (80.3%); Cantrade Participation Ltd. (85%); Credit Industriel SA; Eidgenossische Bank Beteilgungs-und Finazgesellschaft (99.9%); Intrag Ltd. NZ (85%); Orca Bank Ltd.; Swiss Mortgage and Commercial Bank (99.5%); "Thesaurus" Continental Securities Corporation (99.9%); UBS Finanzholding AG; UBS Phillips & Drew Ltd. (U.K.); Schweizerische Bankgesellschaft (Deutschland) A.G.; UBS Australia Ltd.; Union Bank of Switzerland (Canada); Union Bank of Switzerland Finance N.V. (Netherlands Antilles); Union de Banques Suisses (Luxembourg) S.A.; Union Bank of Switzerland (Panama) Inc.; UBS Asset Management Ltd. (U.K.); Union Bank of Switzerland (Trust and Banking) Ltd. (Japan); Union Bank of Switzerland (U.K.) Ltd.; Union Bank of Switzerland (Underwriters) Ltd. (Bermuda); UBS Finance Inc. (USA); Phillips & Drew International Ltd. (U.K.) (50%).

WELLS FARGO & COMPANY

420 Montgomery Street
San Francisco, California 94163
U.S.A.
(415) 477-1000

Public Company
Incorporated: 1968
Employees: 19,700
Assets: $46.62 billion
Stock Index: New York Pacific London Frankfurt

Wells Fargo & Company, a multibillion-dollar regional bank holding company, traces its earliest origins to a banking and express business formed in 1852 to exploit the economic opportunities created by the California gold rush. Throughout its colorful history, the company has provided innovative services to its customers and has demonstrated an ability to weather economic conditions that have ruined its competitors.

Soon after gold was discovered in early 1848 at Sutter's Mill near Comona, California, financiers and entrepreneurs from all over North America and the world flocked to California, drawn by the promise of huge profits. Vermont native Henry Wells and New Yorker William G. Fargo watched the California boom economy with keen interest.

Before either Wells or Fargo could pursue opportunities offered in the West, however, they had business to attend to in the East. Wells, founder of Wells and Company, and Fargo, a partner in Livingston, Fargo and Company, were major figures in the young and fiercely competitive express industry. In 1849 a new rival, John Butterfield, founder of Butterfield, Wasson & Company, entered the express business. Butterfield, Wells, and Fargo soon realized that their competition was destructive and wasteful, and in 1850 they decided to join forces to form the American Express Company.

Soon after the new company was formed, Wells, the first president of American Express, and Fargo, its vice president, proposed expanding its business to California. Fearing that American Express's most powerful rival, Adams and Company (later renamed Adams Express Company), would acquire a monopoly in the West, the majority of the American Express Company's directors balked. Undaunted, Wells and Fargo decided to start their own business while continuing to fulfill their responsibilities as officers and directors of American Express.

On March 18, 1852 they organized Wells, Fargo & Company, a joint-stock association with an initial capitalization of $300,000, to provide express and banking services to California. Financier Edwin B. Morgan was appointed Wells Fargo's first president.

The company opened its first office, in San Francisco, in July, 1852. The immediate challenge facing Morgan and Danforth N. Barney, who became president in 1853, was to establish the company in two highly competitive fields under conditions of rapid growth and unpredictable change. At the time, California did not regulate either the banking or the express industry, so both fields were wide open. Anyone with a wagon and team of horses could open an express company and all it took to open a bank was a safe and a room to keep it in. Because of its late entry into the California market, Wells Fargo faced well established competition in both fields.

From the beginning, the fledgling company offered diverse and mutually supportive services: general forwarding and commissions; buying and selling gold dust, bullion, and specie; and freight service between New York and California. Under Morgan's and Barney's direction, express and banking offices were quickly established in key communities bordering the gold fields and a network of freight and messenger routes was soon in place throughout California. Barney's policy of subcontracting express services to established companies, rather than duplicating existing services, was a key factor in Wells Fargo's early success.

In 1855, Wells Fargo faced its first crisis when the California banking system collapsed as a result of overspeculation. A run on Page, Bacon & Company, a San Francisco bank, began when the collapse of its St. Louis, Missouri parent was made public. The run soon spread to other major financial institutions, all of which, including Wells Fargo, were forced to close their doors. The following Tuesday Wells Fargo reopened in sound condition, despite a loss of one-third of its net worth. Wells Fargo was one of the few financial and express companies to survive the panic, partly because it kept sufficient assets on hand to meet customers' demands rather than transferring all its assets to New York.

Surviving the Panic of 1855 gave Wells Fargo two advantages. First, afterward it faced virtually no competition in the banking and express business in California; second, Wells Fargo attained a reputation for dependability and soundness.

From 1855 through 1866, Wells Fargo expanded rapidly, becoming the West's all-purpose business, communications, and transportation agent. Under Barney's direction, the company developed its own stagecoach business, helped start and then took over the Overland Mail Company, and participated in the Pony Express. This period culminated with the "grand consolidation" of 1866 when Wells Fargo consolidated under its own name the ownership and operation of the entire overland mail route from the Missouri River to the Pacific Ocean and many stagecoach lines in the western states.

In its early days, Wells Fargo participated in the staging business to support its banking and express businesses. But the character of Wells Fargo's participation changed when it helped start the Overland Mail Company. Overland Mail was organized in 1857 by men with substantial interests in four of the leading express companies—American Express, United States Express, Adams Express, and Wells Fargo. John Butterfield, the third founder of American Express, was made Overland Mail's president. In 1858, Overland Mail was awarded a government contract to carry the U.S. mail over the southern overland route from St. Louis to California. From the beginning, Wells Fargo was Overland Mail's banker and primary lender.

In 1859 there was a crisis when Congress failed to pass the annual post office appropriation bill and left the post office with no way to pay for the Overland Mail Company's services. As Overland Mail's indebtedness to Wells Fargo climbed, Wells Fargo became increasingly disenchanted with Butterfield's management strategy.

In March, 1860 Wells Fargo threatened to foreclose. As a compromise, Butterfield resigned as president of Overland Mail and control of the company passed to Wells Fargo. Wells Fargo, however, did not acquire ownership of the company until the consolidation of 1866.

Wells Fargo's involvement in Overland Mail led to its participation in the Pony Express in the last six of the express's 18 months of existence. Russell, Majors & Waddell launched the privately owned and operated Pony Express. By the end of 1860, the Pony Express was in deep financial trouble; its fees did not cover its costs and, without government subsidies and lucrative mail contracts, it could not make up the difference. After Overland Mail, by then controlled by Wells Fargo, was awarded a $1 million government contract in early 1861 to provide daily mail service over a central route (the Civil War had forced the discontinuation of the southern line), Wells Fargo took over the western portion of the Pony Express route from Salt Lake City to San Francisco. Russell, Majors & Waddell continued to operate the eastern leg from Salt Lake City to St. Joseph, Missouri under subcontract.

The Pony Express ended when transcontinental telegraph lines were completed in late 1861. Overland mail and express service was continued, however, by the coordinated efforts of several companies. From 1862 to 1865 Wells Fargo operated a private express line between San Francisco and Virginia City, Nevada; Overland Mail stagecoaches covered the route from Carson City, Nevada to Salt Lake City; and Ben Holladay, who had acquired Russell, Majors & Waddell, ran a stagecoach line from Salt Lake City to Missouri.

By 1866, Holladay had built a staging empire with lines in eight western states and was challenging Wells Fargo's supremacy in the West. A showdown between the two transportation giants in late 1866 resulted in Wells Fargo's purchase of Holladay's operations. The "grand consolidation" spawned a new enterprise that operated under the Wells Fargo name and combined the Wells Fargo, Holladay, and Overland Mail lines and became the undisputed stagecoach leader. Barney resigned as president of Wells Fargo to devote more time to his own business, the United States Express Company; Louis McLane, Wells Fargo's general manager in California, replaced him.

The Wells Fargo stagecoach empire was short lived. McLane had reached an agreement with a railroad group that failed. Although the Central Pacific Railroad, already operating over the Sierra Mountains to Reno, Nevada carried Wells Fargo's express, the company did not have an exclusive contract. Moreover, the Union Pacific Railroad was encroaching on the territory served by Wells Fargo stagelines. Ashbel H. Barney, Danforth Barney's brother and cofounder of United States Express Company, replaced McLane as president in 1868. The transcontinental railroad was completed in the following year, causing the stage business to dwindle and Wells Fargo's stock to fall.

Central Pacific promoters, led by Lloyd Tevis, organized the Pacific Express Company to compete with Wells Fargo. The Tevis group also started buying up Wells Fargo stock at its sharply reduced price. In October, 1869 William Fargo, his brother Charles, and Ashbel Barney traveled to Omaha, Nebraska to confer with Tevis and his associates. There Wells Fargo agreed to buy the Pacific Express Company at a much-inflated price and received exclusive express rights for ten years on the Central Pacific Railroad and a much-needed infusion of capital. All of this, however, came at a price: control of Wells Fargo shifted to Tevis.

Ashbel Barney resigned in 1870 and was replaced as president by William Fargo. In 1872 William Fargo also resigned, to devote full time to his duties as president of American Express (he had been appointed its second president on Henry Wells' retirement in 1868). Lloyd Tevis replaced Fargo as president of Wells Fargo.

The company expanded rapidly under Tevis' management. The number of banking and express offices grew from 436 in 1871 to 3,500 at the turn of the century. During this period, Wells Fargo also established the first transcontinental express line, using more than a dozen railroads. The company first gained access to the lucrative East Coast markets beginning in 1888; successfully promoted the use of refrigerated freight cars in California; had opened branch banks in Virginia City, Carson City, and Salt Lake City by 1876; and expanded its express services to Japan, Australia, Hong Kong, South America, Mexico, and Europe. In 1885 Wells Fargo also began selling money orders.

In 1905 Wells Fargo separated its banking and express operations. Edward H. Harriman, a prominent financier and dominant figure in the Southern Pacific and Union Pacific railroads, had gained control of Wells Fargo. Harriman reached an agreement with Isaias W. Hellman, a Los Angeles banker, to merge Wells Fargo's bank with the Nevada National Bank, founded in 1875 by the Nevada silver moguls James G. Fair, James Flood, John Mackay, and William O'Brien to form the Wells Fargo Nevada National Bank.

Wells Fargo & Company Express had moved to New York City in 1904. In 1918 the government forced Wells Fargo Express to consolidate its domestic operations with those of the other major express companies. This wartime measure resulted in the formation of American Railway Express (later Railway Express Agency). Wells Fargo continued some overseas express operations until the 1960s.

The two years following the merger tested the newly reorganized bank's, and Hellman's, capacities. In April, 1906 the San Francisco earthquake and fire destroyed most of the city's business district, including the Wells Fargo Nevada National Bank building. The bank's vaults and credit were left intact, however, and the bank committed its resources to restoring San Francisco. Money flowed into San Francisco from around the country to support rapid reconstruction of the city. As a result, the bank's deposits increased dramatically, from $16 million to $35 million in 18 months.

The Panic of 1907, begun in New York in October, followed on the heels of this frenetic reconstruction period. The stock market had crashed in March. Several New York banks, deeply involved in efforts to manipulate the market after the crash, experienced a run when speculators were unable to pay for stock they had purchased. The run quickly spread to other New York banks, which were forced to suspend payment, and then to Chicago and the rest of the country. Wells Fargo lost $1 million in deposits a week for six weeks in a row. The years following the panic were committed to a slow and painstaking recovery.

In 1920, Hellman was very briefly succeeded as president by his son, I. W. Hellman II, who was followed by Frederick L. Lipman. Lipman's management strategy included both expansion and the conservative banking practices of his predecessors. In late 1923, Wells Fargo Nevada National Bank merged with the Union Trust Company, founded in 1893 by I. W. Hellman, to form the Wells Fargo Bank & Union Trust Company. The bank prospered during the 1920s and Lipman's careful reinvestment of the bank's earnings placed the bank in a good position to survive the Great Depression. Following the collapse of the banking system in 1933, the company was able to extend immediate and substantial help to its troubled correspondents.

The war years were prosperous and uneventful for Wells Fargo. In the 1950s, Wells Fargo President I. W. Hellman III, grandson of Isaias Hellman, began a modest expansion program, acquiring two San Francisco Bay–area banks and opening a small branch network around San Francisco. In 1954 the name of the bank was shortened to Wells Fargo Bank, to capitalize on frontier imagery and in preparation for further expansion.

In 1960, Hellman engineered the merger of Wells Fargo Bank with American Trust Company, a large northern California retail-banking system and the second-oldest financial institution in California, to form the Wells Fargo Bank American Trust Company, renamed Wells Fargo Bank again in 1962. This merger of California's two oldest banks created the eleventh-largest banking institution in the United States.

Following the merger, Wells Fargo's involvement in international banking greatly accelerated. The company opened a Tokyo representative office and, eventually, additional branch offices in Seoul, Hong Kong, and Nassau, as well as representative offices in Mexico City, São Paulo, Caracas, Buenos Aires, and Singapore.

In November, 1966, Wells Fargo's board of directors elected Richard P. Cooley president and CEO. At 42, Cooley was one of the youngest men to head a major bank. Stephen Chase, who planned to retire in January, 1968, became chairman. Cooley's rise to the top had been a quick one. From a branch manager in 1960 he rose to become a senior vice president in 1964, an executive vice president in 1965 and in April, 1966 a director of the company. A year later Cooley enticed Ernest C. Arbuckle, the former dean of Stanford's business school, to join Wells Fargo's board as chairman.

In 1967 Wells Fargo, together with three other California banks, introduced a Master Charge card (now MasterCard) to its customers as part of its plan to challenge Bank of America in the consumer lending business. Initially 30,000 merchants participated in the plan. Credit cards would later prove a particularly profitable operation.

Cooley's early strategic initiatives were in the direction of making Wells Fargo's branch network statewide. The Federal Reserve had blocked the bank's earlier attempts to acquire an established bank in southern California. As a result, Wells Fargo had to build its own branch system. This expansion was costly and depressed the bank's earnings in the later 1960s.

In 1968 Wells Fargo changed from a state to a federal banking charter, in part so that it could set up subsidiaries for business like equipment leasing and credit cards rather than having to create special divisions within the bank. The charter conversion was completed August 15, 1968.

The bank successfully completed a number of acquisitions during 1968 as well. The Bank of Pasadena, First National Bank of Azusa, Azusa Valley Savings Bank, and Sonoma Mortgage Corporation were all integrated into Wells Fargo's operations.

In 1969 Wells Fargo formed a holding company and purchased the rights to its own name from the American Express Corporation. Although the bank always had the right to use the name for banking, American Express had retained the right to use it for other financial services. Wells Fargo could now use its name in any area of financial services it chose (except the armored car trade—those rights had been sold to another company two years earlier).

Between 1970 and 1975 Wells Fargo's domestic profits rose faster than any other U.S. bank's. Wells Fargo's loans to businesses increased dramatically after 1971. To meet the demand for credit, the bank frequently borrowed short-term from the Federal Reserve to lend at higher rates of interest to businesses and individuals.

In 1973 a tighter monetary policy made this arrangement less profitable, but Wells Fargo saw an opportunity in the new interest limits on passbook savings. When the allowable rate increased to 5%, Wells Fargo was the first to begin paying the higher rate. The bank attracted many new customers as a result, and within two years its market share of the retail savings trade increased more than two points—a substantial increase in California's competitive banking climate. With its increased deposits, Wells Fargo was able to reduce its borrowings from the Federal Reserve, and the ½% premium it paid for deposits was more than made up for by the savings in interest payments. In 1975 the rest of the California banks instituted a 5% passbook savings rate, but they failed to recapture their market share.

In 1973, the bank made a number of key policy changes. Wells Fargo decided to go after the medium-sized corporate and consumer loan businesses, where interest rates were higher.

Slowly Wells Fargo eliminated its excess debt, and by 1974 its balance sheet showed a much healthier bank. Under Carl Reichardt, who later became president of the bank, Wells Fargo's real estate lending bolstered the bottom line. The bank focused on California's flourishing home and apartment mortgage business and left risky commercial developments to other banks.

While Wells Fargo's domestic operations were making it the envy of competitors in the early 1970s, its international operations were less secure. The bank's 25% holding in Allgemeine Deutsche Credit-Anstalt, a West German bank, cost Wells Fargo $4 million due to bad real estate loans. Another joint banking venture, the Western American Bank, which was formed in London in 1968 with several other American banks, was hard hit by the recession of 1974 and failed. Unfavorable exchange rates hit Wells Fargo for another $2 million in 1975. In response, the bank slowed its overseas expansion program and concentrated on developing overseas branches of its own rather than tying itself to the fortunes of other banks.

Wells Fargo's investment services became a leader during the late 1970s. According to *Institutional Investor*, Wells Fargo garnered more new accounts from the 350 largest pension funds between 1975 and 1980 than any other money manager. The bank's aggressive marketing of its services included seminars explaining modern portfolio theory. Wells Fargo's early success, particularly with indexing—weighting investments to match the weightings of the Standard and Poor's 500—brought many new clients aboard.

By the end of the 1970s Wells Fargo's overall growth had slowed somewhat. Earnings were only up 12% in 1979 compared with an average of 19% between 1973 and 1978. In 1980 Richard Cooley, now chairman of the holding company, told *Fortune*, "it's time to slow down. The last five years have created too great a strain on our capital, liquidity, and people."

In 1981 the banking community was shocked by the news of a $21.3 million embezzlement scheme by a Wells Fargo employee, one of the largest embezzlements ever. L. Ben Lewis, an operations officer at Wells Fargo's Beverly Drive branch, pleaded guilty to the charges. Lewis had routinely written phony debit and credit receipts to pad the accounts of his cronies and received a $300,000 cut in return.

The early 1980s saw a sharp decline in Wells Fargo's performance. Richard Cooley announced the bank's plan to scale down its operations overseas and concentrate on the California market. In January, 1983 Carl Reichardt became chairman and CEO of the holding company and of Wells Fargo Bank. Cooley, who had led the bank since the late 1960s, left to revive a troubled rival. Reichardt relentlessly attacked costs, eliminating 100 branches and cutting 3,000 jobs. He also closed down the bank's European offices at a time when most banks were expanding their overseas networks.

Rather than taking advantage of banking deregulation, which was enticing other banks into all sorts of new financial ventures, Reichardt and Wells Fargo President Paul Hazen kept things simple and focused on California. Reichardt and Hazen beefed up Wells Fargo's retail network through improved services like an extensive automatic teller machine network, and through active marketing of those services.

In 1986, Wells Fargo purchased its rival, the Crocker National Corporation, from Britain's Midland Bank for about $1.1 billion. The acquisition was touted as a brilliant maneuver for Wells Fargo. Not only did the bank double its branch network in southern California and increase its consumer loan portfolio by 85%, but the bank did it at an unheard of price, paying about 127% of book value at a time when American banks were generally going for 190%. In addition, Midland kept about $3.5 billion in loans of dubious value.

Crocker doubled the strength of Wells Fargo's primary market, making Wells Fargo the tenth-largest bank in the United States.

The integration of Crocker's operations into Wells Fargo's went considerably smoother than expected. In the 18 months after the acquisition, 5,700 jobs were trimmed from the banks' combined staff and costs were cut considerably.

Before and after the acquisition, Reichardt and Hazen had also aggressively cut costs and elminated unprofitable portions of Wells Fargo's business. During the three years before the acquisition, Wells Fargo sold its realty-services subsidiary, its residential-mortgage service operation, and its corporate trust and agency businesses. Over 70 domestic bank branches and 15 foreign branches were also closed during this period.

In 1987, Wells Fargo set aside large reserves to cover potential losses on its Latin American loans, most notably to Brazil and Mexico. This caused its net income to drop sharply, but by mid-1989 the bank had sold or written off all of its medium- and long-term Third World debt.

Concentrating on California has been a very successful strategy for Wells Fargo, but after its acquisition of Barclays Bank of California in May, 1988, few targets remain. One region Wells Fargo may try to expand into is Texas, where it made an unsuccessful bid for Dallas' FirstRepublic Corporation in 1988. In early 1989 Wells Fargo expanded into full-service brokerage and launched a joint venture with the Japanese company Nikko Securities. Also in 1989, Wells Fargo divested itself of its last international offices, further tightening its focus on domestic commercial and consumer banking activities.

Although Wells Fargo's loan portfolio is still loaded with leveraged debt and real estate loans that some consider risky, the bank has vastly improved its loan-loss ratio in recent years. Wells Fargo is unusual among major American banks in its decision not to invest in international banking, but it has shown that it is an able competitor in the consumer and smaller-business market it has targeted.

Principal Subsidiaries: Wells Fargo Bank, N.A.; Crocker Miles Crossing; Crocker Bishop Companies; Wells Fargo Foreign Lending; Montgomery Estates; WFIC Ltd, Cayman; Crocker Holding, Inc.; Crocker Life Insurance Co.; Crocker Pacific Trading Co.; Wells Fargo Credit Corporation; Wells Fargo Insurance Services; Wells Fargo Securities Clearance Corporation; Wells Fargo Ag Credit; Wells Fargo Corporate Services; Wells Fargo Capital Markets, Inc.; Wells Fargo Financing Corporation; Wells Fargo Investment Advisors.

Further Reading: Wilson, Neill C. *Treasure Express: Epic Days of the Wells Fargo*, New York, Macmillan, 1936; Winther, Oscar O. *Via Western Express and Stagecoach*, Stanford, California, Stanford University Press, 1945; Beebe, Lucius M. and Clegg, Charles M. *U.S. West: The Saga of Wells Fargo*, New York, E. P. Dutton, 1949; Hungerford, Edward. *Wells Fargo: Advancing the American Frontier*, New York, Random House, 1949; Moody, Ralph. *Wells Fargo*, Boston, Houghton Mifflin, 1961; Loomis, Noel M. *Wells Fargo—An Illustrated History*, New York, Clarkson N. Potter, 1968; *Wells Fargo Since 1852*, San Francisco, Wells Fargo & Company, 1988.

WestLB

WESTDEUTSCHE LANDESBANK GIROZENTRALE

4000 Düsseldorf
Herzogstrasse 15
Federal Republic of Germany
(211) 826-01

State Owned
Incorporated: 1969
Employees: 9,996
Assets: DM92.1 billion

Westdeutsche Landesbank Girozentrale is the central bank of West Germany's most populous region, North Rhine–Westphalia, and the clearing bank for its 250 savings associations. Because of this, it is a major force in the German economy and a strong competitor of the Big Three German banks. Its strength is in part the result of its structure—joint ownership between the state government, regional banks, and local authorities—a structure that can be traced to its origins in two 17th-century provincial banks.

In 1818 the Swedish government stunned Europe by offering 160,000 taler to the German province of Westphalia as reparation for the damages incurred when Swedish and Dutch soldiers marched through the province during the Napoleonic Wars. This money was decreed the property of all Westphalia by its president, Freiherr von Vincke. The funds were used to develop the region's economy and pay for public-works projects, but some formal policies were needed to distribute the money. In 1832 the Westphalian Provinzialbank-Hülfskasse was founded to accomplish this task. The bank was the first *hilfskasse*, or assistance bank, in Prussia and played a pivotal role in developing the region's economic potential throughout the 19th century.

Frederick William IV, the king of Prussia, was impressed by the advantages the *hilfskasse* offered Westphalia and ordered that a similar bank be created in the Rhineland in 1847. Its government, influenced by the economic success of the Aachener Union already in business within the province, founded the Provinzial-Hülfskasse of the Rhineland in 1854.

The two banks were instrumental in making the Rhine–Westphalia region one of the biggest and most productive industrial areas in Europe by the time World War I began. Both banks became *landesbanks* before the end of 19th century, which greatly increased their range of services, since *hilfskasse* banks had more restricted charters. Their new names were Landesbank für Westfalen Girozentrale, Münster and Rheinsche Girozentrale und Provinzialbank, Düsseldorf.

Both *landesbanks* endured the boom-bust economic cycle of Germany during the military buildup of the World War I years, the hyperinflation of the Weimer Republic, the second buildup as the Nazis assumed power in 1933, and the economic chaos of the immediate postwar years. Finally, with the Marshall Plan and the currency reforms of 1948, Germany's postwar recovery began. At about this time both banks expanded their services to include clearing transactions for savings banks, thus adding the generic term *girozentrale* to their names. With the economic miracle of the 1950s, there was talk of combining the two *landesbank girozentrale* institutions, since the North Rhine and Westphalia provinces had become politically unified under the British occupation. For political reasons, however, this merger was not feasible until the late 1960s.

On January 1, 1969 the two local banks were combined at last, ostensibly to fight the economic domination of the Big Three banks—Deutsche Bank, Dresdner Bank, and Commerzbank. The new institution, based in one of Germany's most populous and wealthy states, could hope to rival the leading international banks and pose a challenge to the Big Three, which exercised overwhelming economic control over West Germany and showed relative insensitivity to regional needs, especially for capital for the large export industries in the region.

Thus the Landesbank für Westfalen Girozentrale, Münster and the Rheinsche Girozentrale und Provinzialbank, Düsseldorf, became a new entity, the Westdeutsche Landesbank Girozentrale, and Ludwig Poullain was named chairman of the management board. He committed the bank to a policy of growth and expansion that would enable it to challenge, and occasionally surpass, the Big Three banks in total assets.

During its first few years WestLB prospered. Because of its unusual flexibility, the bank could, for instance, offer tailor-made long-term loans to customers. Also, because of the increased capital which WestLB controlled, its commercial-loan operations expanded to include larger companies, which meant larger loans and greater profits.

In 1970 WestLB made international news by joining the Chase Manhattan Bank and two other banks in starting up Orion Bank Ltd., an international merchant bank. The bank, in which WestLB held a minority interest, had an initial capitalization of US$24 million.

In 1973 WestLB made news when it posted more than US$150 million in foreign-exchange losses, the result of unauthorized speculative trading by employees who were subsequently fired.

During the mid-1970s WestLB did indeed reach its goal of joining the Big Three banks, becoming Germany's third-largest lending institution in 1976. That year WestLB proposed a merger with the troubled Hessische Landesbank. The resulting firm would have been Europe's largest bank, but the merger eventually fell through for political reasons. But a drawn out scandal soon began to tarnish the bank's image. It began when Ludwig Poullain, the bank's founding chairman, announced his resignation in December, 1977, claiming that his chairmanship was untenable. The WestLB supervisory board refused his resignation and fired him for "gross neglect of his duties." Poullain successfully sued to force the bank to pay his remaining contractual wages of US$230,000 a year for six years.

Over the next several years Poullain was charged with bribery, fraud, and malfeasance regarding a US$465,000 consulting fee he received from Josef Schmidt, a financial broker who himself was charged with embezzlement, tax evasion, breach of trust, and criminal bankruptcy.

Poullain had not fully disclosed to WestLB management the terms of the consulting fee that Schmidt gave him, nor had he informed WestLB that he had granted Schmidt a loan for the coincidental sum of US$465,000 and had neglected to tell the WestLB management board that Schmidt was under investigative arrest when it granted him another loan for US$930,000, again at the behest of Poullain himself. Poullain later claimed that the charges against him were politically motivated because his steering the bank into an international presence had allegedly upset some state politicians. In 1981 he was found not guilty of the charges.

In 1980 the bank reported that it had made huge profits in foreign currency for 1979, in contrast to 1973. Even so, total earnings were down by almost 68% and the bank stopped paying dividends until 1986.

Profits were down by two-thirds for fiscal 1980, and some called for the resignation of Johannes Völling, who had replaced Poullain. WestLB was suffering from a rise in interest rates. The bank was forced to finance fixed-rate long-term loans with higher-cost short-term funds. Since WestLB is North Rhine–Westphalia's central bank and the clearing bank for the area's 159 savings associations, any dip in WestLB's profits affects the region.

Eventually Völling did resign, in July, 1981, stating that the bank's low profits had eroded confidence in his ability. Friedel Neuber, formerly head of the Rhineland Federation of Savings Banks, was appointed the new chairman. The 46-year-old Neuber's appointment drew criticism, as he had never worked at a bank. Neuber's priorities were to restructure, review operations for profitability, and expand the bank's international business.

In late 1981, WestLB sold its stakes in two industrial companies, Philipp Holzmann and Preussag, raising some DM700 million, part of it to cover anticipated losses for the year. In mid-1982, WestLB raised DM1.12 billion in new capital from its shareholders; the North Rhine–Westphalia state government contributed the most, raising its stake in the bank to its present 43%. This capital increase was designed to provide WestLB with capital for future growth and to help mitigate the higher degree of risk involved in its loans to Third World countries. WestLB began to strengthen its loan-loss reserves following Mexico's suspension of debt payments in August, 1981; by 1988, its reserves covered more than 50% of its exposure.

These measures soon paid off; WestLB's earnings rose sharply in 1982—enough to allow it to repurchase a 35% stake in Preussag.

In 1984 WestLB, along with four other German banks, combined forces to create a new venture-capital company. The same year at least one top credit official on the management board resigned because of his role in the bank's involvement with Deutsche Anlagen Leasing GmbH, a lending concern that lost huge amounts of money due to overextension, weak management controls, and devaluation of its assets. Nevertheless, WestLB again experienced high earnings in 1986 and that year was able to resume the payment of dividends.

During 1985–1986 WestLB increased its international business, as Neuber had long planned. In 1985 Owens-Illinois Inc. sold a 58% share of Gerresheimer Glas AG to the bank, which syndicated the glass manufacturer for other German investors. In 1986 WestLB dramatically heightened its international profile by taking part in an arrangement with the Japanese to sell securities on the Tokyo exchange. In exchange for access to the deutsche mark bond Europe market, the Japanese allowed WestLB and three other large German banks to deal securities under certain limited circumstances.

This strong international position allowed WestLB to lead a banking syndicate that bought a one-fourth share in the Deutsche Babcock AG engineering group from the government of Iran in 1987. And the bank again profited from selling the shares to institutional investors after syndicating its interest in the acquired firm.

As part of the improvement of economic and political relations between Eastern and Western Europe, in May, 1988 WestLB joined most of the other major German banks in offering sizable loans to the Soviet Union. WestLB also played a historic role in furthering open trade when a Swiss subsidiary of the bank brought Moscow's first foreign bond issuance since the 1917 revolution to market, in a formal acknowledgment of the close economic ties that exist between the two countries.

WestLB also revived its plan to merge with Hessische Landesbank. Though the proposed merger caused much excitement, the planned merger collapsed in December, 1988 and the state of Hessen, Hessische's home region, plans to sell its 50% stake in Hessische to the Hessen savings banks, which disapproved of the proposal.

Even so, WestLB's future looks bright. The unification of the European Economic Community in 1992 should help the bank, whose presence is mostly in European and other Western markets. In an effort to enhance its business, WestLB has been increasing its representation both abroad and at home. This increase includes a link-up with the British Standard Chartered Bank. WestLB has also benefited from a January, 1987 reorganization designed to strengthen its investment-banking operations.

For the most part, WestLB seems to have overcome the difficulties it experienced during the 1970s and the early 1980s, and is now one of the strongest as well as the fourth-largest West German bank.

Principal Subsidiaries: WestLB International S.A.

(Luxembourg); Banque Franco-Allemande S.A. (France); Bank für Kredit und Aussenhandel AG (Switzerland); WestLB (Schweiz); WestLB Securities Pacific Ltd. (Japan); WestLB UK Ltd.

Further Reading: Pohl, Hans. *Von der Hülfskasse von 1832 zur Landesbank*, Düsseldorf, WestLB, 1982.

WESTPAC BANKING CORPORATION

60 Martin Place
Sydney, New South Wales 2000
Australia
(02) 226 3311

Public Company
Incorporated: 1850 as the Bank of New South Wales
Employees: 46,000
Assets: A$108.6 billion (US$92.75 billion)
Stock Index: Australia New Zealand London Tokyo New York

Westpac Banking Corporation, Australia's largest banking and financial services group, was the first bank to be established in Australia. The bank was founded in 1817 and was incorporated in 1850 as the Bank of New South Wales. In 1982, the bank merged with the Commercial Bank of Australia Limited, founded in the state of Victoria in 1866, and changed its name to Westpac Banking Corporation. Westpac's name is derived from the area which it has historically served—the western Pacific. The bank has shown tremendous growth in recent years and has become a truly international financial services group.

When Australia was settled, in the late 18th century, the colony's economy was based on a system of barter. A variety of foreign coins also circulated, but these usually found their way back overseas in exchange for the many imported goods the colony needed, so Australia had trouble keeping any form of currency in the colony. Governor Laughlan Macquarie was determined to solve his country's monetary problems. To help prevent currency from disappearing overseas, Macquarie had the center cut out of coins, creating a donut-shaped "holey dollar." The center piece, known as a "dump," was worth one quarter of a holey dollar. But currency and exchange problems continued to plague the Australian colonies.

In 1816, Governor Macquarie began to push for the establishment of a colonial bank, and a group of 46 subscribers formed a committee to organize the bank's operations. On April 8, 1817, the Bank of New South Wales opened for business in a house in Macquarie Place. Edward Smith Hall was the cashier/secretary, and Robert Campbell Junior was the head accountant. The bank's first depositor was Sergeant Jeremiah Murphy, who entrusted £50 to the new bank.

The bank of New South Wales operated for five years under its original charter, granted by Governor Macquarie, and then for another five under a renewal issued by Governor Brisbane. In 1828, however, the British authorities declared the Bank's charter invalid, claiming that colonial governors had no authority to issue such charters. The Bank of New South Wales was then reorganized as a joint-stock company.

As trade expanded throughout the Australian colonies, the Bank of New South Wales grew. In 1847, it employed the London Joint Stock Bank as its overseas agent in London. Foreign exchange was a growing area of the bank's activities. In 1850, the bank was incorporated by an act of the New South Wales Parliament and was allowed to establish branches. The first branch opened in the Moreton Bay area of what was soon to become the colony of Queensland. A year later gold fever struck Australia, and the bank soon sent its agents directly to the mining regions. Some branches were no more than a tent; others were built with furnaces to smelt gold right on the premises. In 1853, the bank established an office to handle the colony's growing export trade.

The mid- to late-1800s saw widespread development of the country's resources. Bank branches were established at scattered points across the continent. Travel was difficult and often dangerous, as the story of Robert White, the "terror of the bushrangers" illustrates. In 1863, Robert White, an accountant at the Deniliquin branch of the Bank of New South Wales was held up. Although he put up a fight he found himself bound and gagged and the bankrobbers headed out of town with £3,000 in gold and notes. The accountant managed to free himself, however, and was soon on the bandits' trail. He successfully recovered the £3,000 and the bushrangers landed in jail. On another occasion, White was ambushed in Gympie while carrying a great deal of money. He drew his pistol and charged his adversaries, wounding two of them. After his banking career, White was elected to the New South Wales legislative assembly.

In 1866, the Commercial Bank of Australia opened in Melbourne. CBA focused on suburban and rural areas. In 1870, Henry Gyles Turner became general manager of CBA; Turner directed the bank for the next 30 years. By 1876 the bank was operating 34 offices and agencies throughout the Victoria territory. CBA expanded steadily across the rest of the continent and had offices in Sydney, Perth, Adelaide, and Brisbane by 1890.

In 1893, Australian banks faced a major crisis. Overvaluation of urban real estate and a sharp drop in wool prices precipitated a depression. Depositors panicked and scrambled to withdraw their funds. Fewer than half of the 28 conventional banks were able to continue operations without some interruption, but the Bank of New South Wales was able to. Not until after the turn of the century did the economy fully recover. At that time, both the Bank of New South Wales and the Commercial Bank of Australia branched out further. CBA soon moved to Tasmania and New Zealand; "the Wales," as the Bank of

New South Wales had come to be known, ventured to Fiji, Papua New Guinea, and Samurai Island. Increased trade with the neighboring islands paralleled a general increase in foreign trade.

In 1914, World War I broke out. Many employees of both the Bank of New South Wales and the CBA enlisted in the Australian Imperial Force. Of the 1,112 men from the two banks who volunteered, 186 were killed in action. In 1918, John Russell French, general manager of the Bank of New South Wales, was knighted for his service in helping Australia finance the war effort.

Australia experienced the economic boom of the 1920s along with the rest of the world. In 1929, on the eve of the Depression, the Bank of New South Wales appointed a new general manager. Alfred Charles Davidson took the helm at a time when Australian banking was undergoing many changes. Davidson introduced a travel department, (which later became the largest in the southern hemisphere) and established the British and Foreign Department. The bank stepped up overseas operations in the early 1930s. In 1931, Alfred Davidson was instrumental in the Australian government's decision to devaluate its currency, a move that improved trade conditions for exporters. By the mid-1930s the economy was recovering from the Depression.

World War II brought about strict controls on Australian banking. Bank branches were closed to release manpower for the war effort. The Japanese invasion of the Pacific threatened some of the branches of the CBA and "the Wales." Branches in New Guinea and elsewhere were closed. An air raid on the northern Queensland town of Darwin caused extensive damage to the Bank of New South Wales branch there, and lesser damage to CBA's branch. During the war, the Bank of New South Wales saw 3,330 (65%) of its male staff enlist.

After the war, private Australian trading banks were soon entrenched in another conflict. On August 16, 1947 Prime Minister Ben Chifley announced that the banks would be nationalized. According to Chifley's plan, the Commonwealth Bank (Australia's central bank) would acquire the shares of the private banks and then appoint directors to run them as arms of the central bank. The private banks immediately challenged the constitutionality of nationalization and waged a political war to have the Labour Party ousted and eliminate the threat of other obnoxious legislation. The bankers were successful on both counts. The Australian High Court declared the Bank Act of 1947 unconstitutional because it interfered with the freedom of trade and commerce among the states guaranteed in section 92 of the Australian constitution. In 1949, the Labour Party was overwhelmingly defeated in the general election. It was a major victory for the Bank of New South Wales, the Commercial Bank of Australia, and Australia's other private banks.

Throughout the 1950s, the Australian economy was in an upswing. Savings bank deposits were growing in popularity at this time. Before 1956, savings bank operations were conducted exclusively by the government-owned Commonwealth Bank. The Bank of New South Wales entered the savings bank field in the late 1950s and competed aggressively for savings accounts. In compliance with government regulations, the bank earmarked a certain percentage of its savings bank deposits for housing construction loans. Demand for housing and durable goods was high in the 1950s and 1960s. In 1957, the Bank of New South Wales purchased 40% of Australia's largest finance company, the Australian Guarantee Corporation Ltd. (AGC). AGC made loans to businesses as well as consumers and was active in investment and merchant banking as well as insurance.

In 1966, Australia switched from pounds to dollars. For the next two years, the public traded in its imperial currency—pounds, shillings, and pence—for new Australian dollars and cents. Banks had the difficult task of converting to the new decimal currency. Machinery had to be changed, staffs had to be retrained, and accounting had to be translated.

In the 1970s, the Bank of New South Wales and the Commercial Bank of Australia diversified both their services and their areas of operation. Both banks opened more branches overseas. At the same time each was busy acquiring different financial companies at home to expand upon the services they provided. The Bank of New South Wales's holding in the Australian Guarantee Corporation increased to 54% by the early 1970s, while the Commercial Bank of Australia operated a finance company, General Credit Ltd., as a wholly owned subsidiary. Both banks also became involved in merchant banking. The Bank of New South Wales, for instance, owned a substantial number of shares in Partnership Pacific Ltd., Schroder Darling & Company, and Australian United Corporation. CBA held significant interests in the merchant banks Euro-Pacific Finance and International Pacific Corporation. In 1974, Australian banks entered the credit card field with Bankcard. Banks also got involved in insurance activities in the 1970s.

The mid-1970s saw the Australian continent in a severe recession. During these years the large amount of foreign investment in Australia's raw-commodities industries became a political hot potato. Australians felt that foreign investors had too much say in the allocation and development of their resources, particularly in petroleum and mining operations. The fact remained, however, that Australia lacked the capital to develop industry on its own. A debate over capital market regulations grew louder in the late 1970s. In 1979, growing pressure to deregulate the financial markets led to the appointment of a government committee to investigate the effects deregulation would have on the economy.

The committee, headed by Australian businessman Keith Campbell, reported its findings two years later, and deregulation soon followed. Foreign banks were allowed to set up shop in Australia, and many of the restrictions on the trading banks were removed. By 1982, it had become clear that competition from abroad and at home would be fierce in the future. Anticipating this inevitability, the Bank of New South Wales and the Commercial Bank of Australia decided to join forces to protect their position in the domestic market and strengthen their position overseas.

Westpac was formed in October, 1982 with Robert

White, not to be confused with the 19th-century gun-toting accountant, as general manager. The merger was the largest in Australian history.

Robert White began his banking career at the age of 16 at the Bank of New South Wales. He rose through the ranks, becoming general manager in 1978. White was determined to strengthen Westpac's position in world banking. The bank was a leader in the implementation of technology. Westpac's "handybank" automated teller machine network gave customers instant access to their accounts as early as 1980, and had developed substantially after 1982. In 1984, Westpac began work on its CS90 computerized banking system. Employing an IBM mainframe and computer-aided software engineering designed by the Canadian firm Netron, the bank revolutionized computerized banking. By 1988, Westpac officials were boasting the most advanced system in the world.

Technological innovation was one of Westpac's key goals throughout the 1980s, and diversification was another. The bank stepped up operations in the eurocurrency markets. It also opened new offices or branches in Jersey, Los Angeles, Seoul, Kuala Lumpur, and Taipei. Westpac's thrust was rewarded quickly: between 1982 and 1986, assets more than doubled.

In the late 1980s, Westpac took advantage of the deregulated financial markets around the world. In 1986, it took a greater stake in the gold-bullion markets when it purchased part of the London dealer Johnson Matthey Bankers Ltd. In 1987, the bank acquired U.S. bond dealer William E. Pollock Government Securities. Westpac also continued to improve its branch network throughout the Pacific in the face of growing competition from Japanese banks.

Westpac's aggressive moves in the euromarkets and in technological development and application focused a great deal of attention on the bank. Its low exposure to Third World debt helped keep earnings healthy at a time when bad debt provisions were getting the best of many international banks.

On January 1, 1988, Stuart A. Fowler replaced Robert White as Westpac's managing director and CEO. Fowler continued the aggressive campaign begun by White. In 1988, the bank purchased the remaining shares of the Australian Guarantee Corporation, making it a wholly owned subsidiary. As the 1980s closed, Westpac focused on bringing operating costs down, through automation and elimination of redundant branch services.

Westpac's history is one of continuous growth in assets and earnings. Its position as a world-class bank is gaining strength, and its leadership throughout the 1980s has put it in an excellent position for the future. The bank's domestic footing is solid; Westpac controls 25% of Australia's bank deposits. Whether Westpac chooses to expand through another major merger remains to be seen, but the bank's tradition of success indicates a secure future either way.

Principal Subsidiaries: Westpac Banking Corporation; Westpac Savings Bank Ltd; Westpac Bank PNG Ltd.; Westpac Finance Asia Ltd.; Australian Guarantee Corporation Ltd.; Partnership Pacific Ltd.; Westpac Merchant Finance Ltd.; Westpac Properties Ltd.; BLE Capital Ltd.; Bank of Kiribati Ltd.; International Business Analysis Pty Ltd.; Mase Westpac Limited; Westpac Pollock Inc.; Westpac Travel Limited; Westpac Financial Services Group Ltd.; Westpac Life Ltd.; Ord Minnett Group Limited.

Further Reading: From Holey Dollars to Plastic Cards: The Westpac Story, Sydney, Westpac Banking Corporation, 1987.

THE YASUDA TRUST AND BANKING COMPANY, LTD.

2–1, Yaesu 1-chome
Chuo-ku
Tokyo 103
Japan
(03) 278–8111

Public Company
Incorporated: 1925
Employees: 5358
Assets: ¥10.62 trillion (US$84.97 billion)
Stock Index: Tokyo Osaka

The Yasuda Trust & Banking Company is one of only 16 Japanese financial institutions licensed to engage both in banking and in trust management. The regulatory standards for such trust banks are more stringent, requiring these institutions to maintain higher reserves. Yasuda has been one of the most consistently successful trust banks, and has made significant contributions to the Japanese economy through both trust management and industrial financing.

Yasuda was once one of the most powerful industrial groups—called *zaibatsu*—in Japan. The Yasuda group was built mainly on financial services, including banking, insurance, and lending. Yasuda decided to enter the trust business soon after the passage of the trust banking laws in 1923. In 1925, several financiers, led by Yasuda, established the Kyosai ("mutual aid") Trust Company. Yasuda quickly expanded its interest in the trust bank, and the following year changed its name from Kyosai to Yasuda.

Unlike other *zaibatsu*, which diversified into manufacturing, transportation, and natural resources as well as banking, Yasuda remained solely dedicated to finance. At this point, the Yasuda group consisted of the Yasuda Bank, the Yasuda Fire & Marine Insurance Company, Yasuda Mutual Life Insurance, and the new Yasuda Trust Company.

The 1930s were a tumultuous period for Japanese industry. Government regulation of the economy remained unsophisticated, and because many basic monetary functions were handled by the competing *zaibatsu*, much of the regulation that existed was uncoordinated. But despite frequent—and occasionally serious—recessions, Yasuda and the other *zaibatsu* grew larger and stronger.

This trend was checked, however, when a quasi-national socialist military group rose to power. One of the goals of this group was decreasing the power of the *zaibatsu*. But by 1940, the war-time economy required the concentration of industry, and the *zaibatsu* were once again allowed to absorb smaller companies, in the name of economic efficiency. The Yasuda group, however, and Yasuda Trust in particular, avoided amalgamation throughout the war, although it did take over certain accounts from other institutions. As a powerful financial institution, Yasuda was nonetheless intimately involved in war finance.

When the war ended in 1945, the American occupation authority dissolved the *zaibatsu* into thousands of smaller enterprises. Ties between the Yasuda companies were cut, and each was forced to change its name. The Yasuda Bank, the center of the group, became the Fuji Bank. In 1948, under new trust laws, Yasuda Trust was reincorporated as Chuo Trust & Banking, taking its name from the Chuo, or "central," district of Tokyo, where it was headquartered.

Japan's industrial organization laws were relaxed in 1952, and with the enactment of the Loan Trust Law, Chuo changed its name back to Yasuda. This law enabled Yasuda to tap a new, stable market for long-term beneficiary certificates of variable denominations. In this way, customers, mostly private individuals, provided the bank with additional capital for long-term industrial financing.

Using its trust and long- and short-term finance products, Yasuda forged close relationships with Japan's largest industrial companies, including Hitachi, Nippon Steel, the Nissan Motor Company, and Marubeni, a general trading company once associated with Sumitomo. The companies of the former Yasuda group re-established ties through cross-ownership of stock to form the new postwar Fuyo industrial group.

Yasuda adopted an extremely cautious approach to trust and asset management. Much of this caution was required by law, but Yasuda set out to build a reputation for conservative management. As a primary manager of funds for Japan's largest and fastest growing companies, Yasuda benefitted directly from the rapid expansion of Japan's heavy industries during that country's first period of industrial growth (1955–1970). As the bulk of the company's income was spread-based, rather than fee-based, Yasuda grew at an exponential rate.

Such conservative management, however, made Yasuda a largely faceless institution, distinguished only by its smooth and predictable growth and its affiliation with the influential Fuyo group. Still, many of Yasuda's competitors gained similar reputations.

The entire Japanese economy was profoundly affected by two events in the early 1970s. The first was the Nixon Administration's decision in 1971 to abandon the Bretton-Woods system of currency valuation. This resulted in a sharp appreciation of the yen against the dollar, and slowed Japanese export-led growth. The second was the OPEC oil embargo of 1973, which drastically raised production costs at all levels of the Japanese economy.

While many less conservative financial institutions were seriously jeopardized by the effects of these crises,

Yasuda's growth was merely slowed. Though Yasuda was exposed to contracting sectors such as steel and shipbuilding, its investments were diversified enough that it was able to re-orient itself to the new economic environment quickly. This lesson became institutional policy and was instrumental in avoiding a similar crisis during the second oil crisis, in 1979.

Yasuda recognized many years in advance that financial management opportunities in Japan were becoming saturated. Japan's second period of industrial growth (1970–1985) flooded Japanese financial institutions with capital at the same time it exhausted investment opportunities; Japanese investments were no longer competitive with foreign projects.

In order to effect a stable entry into foreign financial markets, Yasuda had established "intelligence-gathering" offices in major foreign markets as early as the 1960s. Often, these offices were jointly operated with fellow Fuyo members, or even competitors, such as Mitsui, Mitsubishi, and Sumitomo. When its clients began to investigate the establishment of foreign-registered subsidiaries, Yasuda was able to offer good intelligence and management services specifically tailored for Japanese companies in these markets. Today Yasuda operates branches or agencies in Hong Kong, London, Los Angeles, New York, and Singapore, in addition to 13 representative offices on five continents.

A major obstacle to further growth in Yasuda's home market is government regulation. In response to an ongoing effort by the banking, trust, and securities industries, this regulation is gradually being relaxed, and may result in several company consolidations. Much of this activity, however, has been limited to the banking industry. Yasuda has prepared for increased competition in Japan by establishing strengths in six distinct areas of long-term growth potential.

In the area of pension management, Yasuda takes advantage of the trend in which the ratio of employees to pensioners, now five to one, will fall to two and a half to one by the year 2020. With more than ¥2.2 trillion in pension fund assets in 1988, Yasuda has compiled the best investment record of any Japanese trust bank, and is well positioned to maintain its position. In addition, because Japanese business is devoting less money to investment, despite record earnings, Japanese companies enjoy greater liquidity than ever before. Yasuda has responded by creating new corporate cash management services. Yasuda has also established its expertise in real estate development, international finance and market services, and leadership in the Tokyo investment market.

Much of the company's preparation for deregulation and world-wide expansion results from a decidedly consensus-oriented management board. This board is presided over by Yoshio Yamaguchi, chairman, and Fujio Takayama, president and CEO since 1985. In keeping with company's reputation for low-key, thoroughly investigated business decisions, neither may be considered particularly eccentric or revolutionary in style or character. Any deviation from this tradition is highly unlikely. Yasuda, however, must adapt to a new environment requiring maximum efficiency and diversity in investment options. The days when it could simply manage the assets of its spectacularly-performing clients are drawing to an end.

Principal Subsidiaries: Yasuda Trust and Finance (H.K.) Ltd.; Yasuda Trust Europe Ltd.; Yasuda Trust Finance (Switzerland) Ltd.; Yasuuda Trust Australia, Ltd.; YTB Financial Futures (Singapore) Pte. Ltd.; Yasuda Bank and Trust Co. (U.S.A.); Yasuda Trust and Banking (Luxembourg) S.A.

FINANCIAL SERVICES: NON-BANKS

AMERICAN EXPRESS COMPANY
BEAR STEARNS COMPANIES, INC.
CS FIRST BOSTON INC.
DAIWA SECURITIES COMPANY, LIMITED
DREXEL BURNHAM LAMBERT INCORPORATED
FEDERAL NATIONAL MORTGAGE ASSOCIATION
FIDELITY INVESTMENTS
GOLDMAN, SACHS & CO.
HOUSEHOLD INTERNATIONAL, INC.
KLEINWORT BENSON GROUP PLC
MERRILL LYNCH & CO. INC.
MORGAN GRENFELL GROUP PLC
MORGAN STANLEY GROUP INC.
THE NIKKO SECURITIES COMPANY LIMITED
NIPPON SHINPAN COMPANY, LTD.
NOMURA SECURITIES COMPANY, LIMITED
ORIX CORPORATION
PAINEWEBBER GROUP INC.
SALOMON INC.
SHEARSON LEHMAN HUTTON HOLDINGS INC.
STUDENT LOAN MARKETING ASSOCIATION
TRILON FINANCIAL CORPORATION
YAMAICHI SECURITIES COMPANY, LIMITED

AMERICAN EXPRESS COMPANY

American Express Tower
World Financial Center
New York, New York 10285
U.S.A.
(212) 640-2000

Public Company
Incorporated: 1965
Employees: 100,188
Assets: $142.7 billion
Stock Index: New York Boston Midwest Pacific London Zurich Geneva Basel Düsseldorf Frankfurt Paris Amsterdam Toronto Tokyo

The American Express Company, a multi-billion-dollar holding company whose subsidiaries provide travel and financial services worldwide, traces its roots to a New York express business founded by Henry Wells in 1841. Throughout its history, American Express has enjoyed a reputation for innovation, profitability, and integrity. Today, American Express dominates in the premium card and traveler's check markets and is among the leaders in financial services.

Henry Wells began his career as an expressman as an agent for William Harnden, who had founded the first express company in the United States in 1839. Express companies were in the business of transporting money and other valuables safely. Wells was an ambitious man who repeatedly proposed expanding the business westward—to Buffalo, New York, the Midwest, and the far West. When Harnden refused to leave the East Coast, Wells struck out on his own, organizing Wells & Company in 1841.

At first Wells and his associate, Crawford Livingston, served only New York City and Buffalo, then an arduous route by five rickety shortline railroads and wagon or stagecoach for the last 65 miles into or out of Buffalo. A few years later, Wells and William G. Fargo launched an express service from Buffalo to major midwestern cities. Although appreciated by the midwestern business community, the new express service simply did not pay. In 1846, Wells decided to retrench and focus his energies on the growing routes serving New York City, Buffalo, Boston, and Albany, leaving the express business west of Buffalo to Fargo's company, Livingston, Fargo & Company.

In 1849 John Butterfield, a wealthy and experienced transportation mogul, entered the express business with Butterfield, Wasson & Company, a direct competitor to Wells & Company on New York state routes. Later that year, Butterfield proposed that he, Fargo, and Wells eliminate their wasteful competition by joining forces. On March 18, 1850, the three companies consolidated to form the American Express Company, a joint-stock company with initial capital of $150,000. Wells was elected the new company's first president; Fargo became vice president.

Under Wells's leadership American Express was immediately and unexpectedly profitable, expanding rapidly and acquiring small competitors in the Midwest, negotiating contracts with the first railroads, and running packet boats on the Illinois Canal to connect Ohio, Illinois, and Iowa with steamship lines on the Illinois River. In 1851, American Express reached an amicable agreement with its major rival, Adams & Company (reorganized as Adams Express Company in 1854). American Express was to expand north and west of New York while Adams was free to grow south and east. This agreement was kept and renewed over the next 70 years, buying American Express time to establish its business solidly.

Despite their agreement with Adams & Company, Wells and Fargo still distrusted their rival and feared it would gain a monopoly in the California gold fields. When Wells proposed his old dream of a transcontinental express service to the American Express board of directors, they rejected his idea. But in 1852 Wells and Fargo got the board's blessing to launch an independent venture, Wells Fargo & Company, to provide express and banking services in California.

In 1854, trouble developed with the New York, Lake Erie & Western Railroad (American Express's link to the Midwest) when Daniel Drew, the railroad's owner, became outraged that American Express had picked off the Erie's most profitable freight business by shipping light, high-rate freight on the Erie under its express contract. Drew was determined to award the express rights to others. In response, American Express created an affiliate and presented it as a bona fide competitor. American Express loaned the funds to start a new company to Danforth Barney, then president of Wells Fargo. Barney's new company, United States Express Company, then acquired the Erie express rights from Drew and split the lucrative midwestern business with American Express.

American Express's first decade saw two other noteworthy accomplishments. In 1857, American Express launched the Overland Mail Company as a joint venture with Wells Fargo, Adams Express Company and United States Express Company. The Overland Mail (later controlled by Wells Fargo) won the first transcontinental mail contract from the United States Postal Service, which led to its involvement in the Pony Express. Also, James C. Fargo, William's younger brother, proposed the establishment of a fast, bulk-freight express service for merchants. Merchants Dispatch, created in 1858, proved immediately successful.

The Civil War was enormously profitable for American Express, as it was for the express industry generally. American Express shipped supplies to army depots, took election ballots to soldiers, and delivered parcels to parts of the Confederacy taken by Union forces. During this period, American Express distributed huge dividends to its shareholders.

After the war, the express industry attracted the attention of financial raiders. The first raid, by National Bankers Express Company in 1866, was thwarted at relatively low cost. American Express quickly reached an agreement with Adams Express and United States Express to neutralize the threat by giving National Bankers Express shares of the established companies and a seat on the American Express board of directors.

The second raid had much more serious consequences. Late in 1866, a group of New York merchants established Merchants Union Express Company, to both get into the express business and destroy the three largest express lines—Adams, American, and United States. Merchants Union first hired away the older companies' experienced agents, and then invaded their territories. American Express suffered such losses in 1867 that for the first and only time in its history it failed to pay a dividend. On December 21, 1868, the four express companies reached a peace agreement, dividing the express and fast-freight business, and pooling and distributing net earnings. American Express got the worst of the deal; Merchants Union acquired rights on railways that had been its bread-and-butter lines (the Hudson River and New York Central railroads) and lost its supremacy in the express business. In 1868, American Express was forced to merge with Merchants Union to form the American Merchants Union Express Company (shortened in 1873 back to the American Express Company). Also in 1868 Henry Wells retired and was replaced as president by William Fargo.

William Fargo's tenure saw the beginning of two trends that would later prove significant. First, Fargo's brother, James, expanded Merchants Dispatch Express operations to Europe. Soon Merchants Dispatch was transporting more than half the first-class tonnage from New York City to over a dozen European cities, making international operations a lucrative sideline for American Express. Second, high express rates set after the Panic of 1873 created public demand for a government-operated parcel post. In 1874, the U.S. Postal Service began to deliver packages at a new, low rate. The following year, Congress set the parcel rate at a half-cent per ounce, far below cost. This cut deeply into express-company profits. Express-industry lobbying and the post office's substantial operating loss soon persuaded Congress to raise rates to a more reasonable level, but the precedent for governmental involvement in the express business had been established.

William Fargo's death in 1881 and James' succession to the presidency began a new era for American Express. Although James Fargo was often described as autocratic, aloof, and old fashioned, he was also remarkably innovative. During his term of office, American Express first diversified into the financial-services industry with the introduction of two instruments—the American Express Money Order in 1882 and the American Express Travelers Cheque in 1891.

The post office first introduced the postal money order in 1864. This immediately threatened the express industry because it reduced banks' and merchants' demand for the transport of money and other valuables. The postal money order, however, had a serious flaw: its face value could be altered without detection. Although American Express directors had discussed introducing a money order since the end of the Civil War, it took James Fargo to galvanize the company into action. At his direction Marcellus Berry, an American Express employee, designed a safer money order. American Express's money order was an immediate hit; it could be used to settle charges on express shipments, was more readily available than the postal money order, and was simpler, cheaper, and easier to negotiate. Not only did the money order provide a new source of revenue (over 250,000 were issued the first year), but for the first time American Express had a credit balance (or "float"—funds from instruments that had been paid for but were not yet cashed) that could be safely invested to bring in additional income.

The traveler's check filled a similar financial niche. Before 1891, tourists and business travelers could transfer funds from the United States to Europe only via a letter of credit, a time-consuming and cumbersome method: only specified correspondents of the issuing United States bank could negotiate letters of credit, and then only during banking hours and after an appreciable delay. Fargo, annoyed by his own experience with the procedure, again directed Marcellus Berry to find a solution. The American Express Travelers Cheque was a marked improvement over the letter of credit in several respects: its simple signature and counter-signature provision made the instrument very secure; it could easily be converted into foreign currency at any American Express freight office; and, if lost or stolen, American Express would refund the owner's money. The value and convenience of the traveler's check was recognized at once, and its popularity again provided American Express with additional revenues and float.

After the traveler's check was introduced in 1891, travelers began making American Express freight offices their informal headquarters—places to convert funds, to seek information about hotels and travel arrangements, and simply to congregate. American Express officers saw the opportunities offered by the travel industry and urged diversification in that direction. James Fargo, however, was absolutely opposed to the idea. He allowed American Express agents to offer travel information purely as a service to customers, but drew the line there. American Express's official entry into the travel industry, which became one of its best-known and most lucrative businesses, was delayed until after Fargo's retirement in 1914.

After the turn of the century, the express industry came under attack from a number of quarters. The railroads had steadily eroded express profits by raising their rates from 40% of gross receipts to more than 55% by 1910. Also in 1910, long-overdue government regulation of the express industry began with passage of the Mann-Elkins Act, which made express companies common carriers subject to the scrutiny of the Interstate Commerce Commission (ICC). In 1912, New York express-company drivers and their helpers went on strike for higher wages and fewer working hours (they were underpaid and overworked, even in an era of low pay and long hours), exciting highly unfavorable press and public reaction. In 1913, the U.S. Post Office again expanded parcel-delivery services at reduced rates, while the ICC set express rates that the industry feared were prohibitively low.

When George C. Taylor, a longtime American Express employee, was elected the company's fourth president on Fargo's retirement in 1914, the end of the laissez-faire express industry was in sight. Taylor's first actions, to expand foreign remittance operations and to officially inaugurate travel services by opening a travel department in 1915, saved the company when its domestic express division was nationalized in 1918 and became part of the American Railway Express Company as a wartime measure. Another of Taylor's accomplishments was to establish the American Express Company, Inc. This wholly owned subsidiary was created in 1919 primarily to expand international banking operations (which had been conducted sporadically through foreign remittance offices since 1904). Although American Express was slow to gain a foothold in Europe, its international banking operations flourished in Asia during the 1920s and 1930s, especially in Hong Kong and Shanghai.

In the late 1920s, American Express again changed hands. The express industry was targeted for takeovers during this period because most express companies had been organized prior to antitrust legislation, raising the possibility of their exemption from antitrust regulations. American Express was especially attractive because its net income had more than doubled in the six years ending in 1928. In 1927 Albert H. Wiggin, chairman of the Chase National Bank, started buying American Express stock through dummies. By July, Wiggin had acquired two seats on the board and 42% of the stock, at a bargain price. In 1929, Chase Securities Corporation, an affiliate of Chase National, acquired control of American Express in a stock exchange and Wiggin was elected first chairman of the American Express board.

In May, 1930 Chase National merged with the giant Equitable Trust to become the largest bank in the world. John D. Rockefeller supplanted Wiggin as largest shareholder and Winthrop W. Aldrich, Rockefeller's brother-in-law, became chairman of both the Chase Securities and the American Express boards.

This was a difficult time for American Express management, headed by Frederick P. Small (who became president on Taylor's death in 1923). Not only were the directors preoccupied with their power struggles, but the financial climate was steadily worsening. Then the Great Depression hit. Between 1930 and 1932, roughly a third of all American banks failed. In early 1933, President Franklin D. Roosevelt announced a national bank holiday to allow banks to recover from the panic. The bank holiday brought commerce to a virtual standstill. During this period American Express, since it was not a bank and thus not required to close, enjoyed a tremendous advantage: it remained open and redeemed traveler's checks, providing the only financial services available to individuals and merchants while the nation's assets were frozen. The traveler's check business ultimately allowed American Express to remain profitable throughout the Depression and World War II.

In 1944 Ralph T. Reed replaced Small as president. Under Reed's management, the late 1940s and the 1950s were a period of expansion, primarily in the booming travel industry. Within seven years the number of American Express offices increased by 400% and international operations surpassed their prewar level.

When Diners Club introduced the first credit card in the mid-1950s, American Express executives proposed investigating this new line of business. Reed, who thought the company should improve existing business and feared a credit card would threaten its traveler's check business, opposed the proposal. In 1958, Reed reversed himself and the American Express travel-and-entertainment card (the American Express green card) was introduced virtually overnight. The company had 250,000 to 300,000 applications for cards on hand the day the card went on the market, and 500,000 cardmembers within three months. Introduction of the green card began an era of unprecedented growth: earnings rose from $8.4 million in 1959 to $85 million in 1970.

A new era of management began when Howard L. Clark was elected president and CEO on April 26, 1960. Clark transformed American Express from a renowned but fairly small company to a corporate giant with diverse interests. Clark's goal was to establish a balanced earnings base dependent on multiple sources and thus more resistant to economic fluctuations. His strategy was to expand American Express's business within its areas of expertise—travel and financial services.

But before Clark could put his plan in operation, the company had to be streamlined and modernized. Management had long been centralized and the chain of command obscure. Clark gave each division room to innovate and made each directly responsible for its own performance. Also, the company had had no uniform identity. The now-famous "blue box" logo was developed at Clark's direction and adopted by all the divisions.

Next, the company's accounting system had to be overhauled, since the system then in place was obsolete and unable to handle the high volume of charge card transactions. Moreover, the travel division (the glue that held the various divisions together and gave the company its identity) had to improve its profitability. By the time the jet-airline industry made an impact on commercial travel, American Express was ready.

Also, the charge card had yet to show a profit, in large part because American Express had no experience dealing directly with merchants and consumers or with credit controls. Clark brought in George Waters, formerly of IBM and the Colonial Stores supermarket chain, to put the charge card division on a sounder footing. Waters used two simple strategies: first, he raised the card fee and merchant discount; next, he persuaded merchants to think of American Express as their marketing partner by dedicating .05% of gross sales to retail advertising. By the end of 1962 more than 900,000 cards had been issued, and by the end of 1963 the card division had shown a profit.

Finally, marginal operations had to be divested. Ridding the company of one subsidiary, American Express Field Warehousing Company, proved to be a nightmare. When the field warehousing division was sold to Lawrence

Warehouse Company in 1963, Clark withheld the two most profitable accounts, Allied Crude Vegetable Oil Refining Company and Freezer House (both owned by Anthony "Tino" De Angelis), pending an investigation of other field warehousing opportunities. Late that year, Clark decided to sell the two accounts to Lawrence Warehouse. An independent audit conducted prior to closing revealed that about 800 million tons of vegetable oil was missing. Holders of some $150 million in security interests and notes (some forged by De Angelis) were understandably upset. The American Express board realized the company's reputation was at stake and quickly issued a statement to the effect that American Express assumed moral responsibility for the losses caused by its subsidiary. American Express's assurances did little to appease those defrauded. The "salad oil swindle," as it was dubbed by the press, involved American Express in complex and protracted litigation that was settled in 1965 (although a final case lingered until 1970) at a cost to American Express of $60 million, excluding attorneys' fees.

With the salad oil swindle behind it and reorganization of the divisions completed, the late 1960s and early 1970s were good years for American Express. Consolidated net income grew steadily and Clark concentrated on expanding the company's financial services. In 1966, American Express acquired W.H. Mortion & Company, an investment-banking house with an excellent reputation for underwriting municipal and government bonds. And in 1968, American Express made the most important purchase yet in its diversification strategy: the Fireman's Fund Insurance Company, one of the largest property and casualty insurers in the nation.

Even the international monetary crisis of 1971, culminating in the devaluation of the dollar and the suspension of almost all dollar transactions, did not phase American Express. The company honored its traveler's checks at the exchange rate posted before trading was suspended and its card continued to be accepted internationally. American Express extended emergency funds to thousands of tourists caught short abroad and its international-banking subsidiary advised corporate clients on how to protect their foreign assets and import-export payments during the crisis.

During the late 1970s, however, American Express seemed to lose its direction, and its integrity and soundness were challenged on many fronts. In 1975, *The Washington Post* suggested that American Express was successful only because it was not regulated as banks and other financial institutions were. When Visa and MasterCard started competing in the traveler's check market, Citicorp, a major issuer of the bank credit cards, took out a full-page advertisement accusing American Express of false and deceptive advertising of its traveler's checks. American Express also received unfavorable publicity when four acquisition attempts in a row failed.

The last of these attempts, a bid for the McGraw-Hill Publishing Company in 1979, produced the worst repercussions. Roger Morley (who had replaced James D. Robinson III to become American Express's tenth president when Clark resigned in 1977 and Robinson became chairman and CEO) was a member of the McGraw-Hill board at the time. After American Express bid for the publisher, McGraw-Hill sued the company and Morley, accusing them of breach of trust and corporate immorality.

But in 1981 American Express made the big acquisition it had been looking for when it bought Shearson Loeb Rhoades Inc., one of the nation's leading brokerage houses, which became an independently operated subsidiary. Shearson in short order acquired Robinson-Humphrey, an Atlanta-based brokerage firm; Foster & Marshall, a well-respected securities firm; and Balcor, the largest real estate syndicator in the United States.

In 1982, American Express was reorganized under a holding company called American Express Corporation; its travel services became a wholly owned subsidiary, American Express Travel Related Services.

Sanford I. Weill, formerly of Shearson Loeb Rhoades Inc., was elected twelfth president of American Express in early 1983. Under Weill, American Express continued to expand. That same year, American Express acquired Ayco Corporation, a financial-counseling firm, and in 1984 it bought Alleghany Corporation's principal subsidiary, the financial-planning company Investors Diversified Services, Inc. (IDS). Also in 1984, Shearson acquired Lehman Brothers Kuhn Loeb, one of the most respected Wall Street brokerage firms, to form Shearson Lehman Brothers Holdings Inc.

In 1985 American Express announced that it would spin off Fireman's Fund, the property and casualty insurer it had purchased in 1968. Stiff competition in the insurance industry during the early 1980s had led to price wars, and the subsidiary's profits had been declining since 1983. In addition, in 1983 and 1984, American Express had had to spend $430 million strengthening Fireman's reserves. The first public offering of Fireman's Fund stock was made in October, 1985; by December, 1987, American Express retained only 31% of the company. In 1988 its holding was reduced to 20% and American Express formally exited the insurance business.

Also in 1985 the American Express International Banking Corporation, established in 1919 to help American Express expand internationally, became simply American Express Bank, Ltd. Today American Express is a thoroughly international company; its bank, with a presence in more than 40 countries, completes the range of financial services the company offers, focusing on private banking for wealthy individuals.

1987 was a dramatic—and difficult—year at most financial companies, and American Express was no exception. The stock market crash in October shook Shearson Lehman, and fears about Third World debt forced American Express Bank to add nearly $1 billion to its loan-loss reserves. But American Express's core business, Travel Related Services, continued to prosper. That year it introduced its Optima Card, American Express's first credit card (regular American Express cards are charge cards; the balance must be paid in full each month). By late 1989, Optima had garnered some 2.5 million members.

In the 1980s, as competition in the card industry intensified, American Express pursued both an increased customer and increased merchant base. At the beginning of the decade, American Express had 10 million Cardmembers who had roughly 400,000 places to use their cards. By the end of the decade those numbers had grown to 33 million cardholders around the world whose cards were accepted at 2.7 million places. But sheer size was not the objective: American Express emphatically positions its services as "premium"—its card costs much more than credit cards, like Visa and MasterCard, offered by banks, and it charges merchants a higher percentage of the bills charged to the card than its competitors do. These higher fees to merchants are warranted, the company tells them, by the business its generally high-income cardmembers generate; the higher card dues buy better services. Nevertheless, American Express has run into heavy competition, especially abroad, where its greatest hopes for expansion lie.

At the beginning of 1988, Shearson made another dramatic acquisition when it bought E.F. Hutton and became Shearson Lehman Hutton Inc. Such growth in so short a time added up to a second year of decreased earnings—a 5% drop on top of 1987's 70% drop. At the end of 1989 Shearson was still struggling to cut costs and raise profits. American Express announced plans, in December, 1989, to pump an additional $900 million into its ailing subsidiary. The recapitalization included $350 million of American Express's own money. The rest was to come from notes.

Although it is a diversified company, American Express's businesses do retain a common thread that runs back to the company's original express business. From the safe transport of valuables it grew naturally into money orders and traveler's checks; from there its travel-service operations, including its card, also grew naturally, as did the additional financial services American Express offers today, from financial planning through IDS to merger and acquisition advice from Shearson Lehman Hutton. The breadth of the financial services it offers and a ubiquitous international presence dating back a century put the company in a strong position in the increasingly global, and competitive, financial-services industry.

Principal Subsidiaries: American Express Travel Related Services Company, Inc.; IDS Financial Corp.; American Express Bank Ltd.; Shearson Lehman Hutton Inc.

Further Reading: Promises to Pay, New York, American Express Company, 1977; Carrington, Tim. *The Year They Sold Wall Street*, Boston, Houghton Mifflin, 1985.

BEAR STEARNS

BEAR STEARNS COMPANIES, INC.

245 Park Avenue,
New York, New York 10167
U.S.A.
(212) 272–2000

Public Company
Incorporated: 1985
Employees: 6,000
Assets: $32.17 billion
Stock Index: New York

Bear Stearns Companies, the holding company that owns Bear, Stearns & Company, was created on October 29, 1985 as the successor to Bear Stearns & Company and Subsidiaries, a partnership organized in 1957. The partnership, in turn, was the successor to a company founded in 1923 by Joseph Bear, Robert Stearns, and Harold Mayer as an equity trading house. Bear Stearns today is a full service brokerage and investment banking firm.

Throughout its history, Bear Stearns has been characterized as aggressive and opportunistic, willing to forego long-range planning in favor of immediate profits, and willing to take risks where others would not. This approach has certainly paid off: Bear Stearns has not had an unprofitable year since its founding in 1923.

The original company was founded with $500,000 in capital in response to the thriving investment climate of the early 1920s. World War I, with its heavy demand for capital, had encouraged the public to enter the securities markets in mass, and the young Bear Stearns prospered in the frenzied optimism of those markets. The company began trading in government securities, and it is still one of the leading traders in this area.

Trading fell off sharply, of course, when the New York stock market crashed in 1929. Though Bear Stearns suffered setbacks, it had accumulated enough capital to survive quite well: during this crisis it not only avoided any employee lay-offs but continued to pay bonuses. As the country struggled out of the Depression, Bear Stearns entered enthusiastically into the bond market to promote President Franklin Roosevelt's call for renewed development of the nation's infrastructure through the New Deal.

During the period following Roosevelt's reform measures, the nation's banking system had accumulated a large amount of cash, since demand for loans was very low. At the same time, bonds were very cheap. Bear Stearns made its first substantial profits by selling large volumes of these bonds to cash-rich banks around the country.

By 1933 the firm had grown from its original seven employees to 75, had opened is first regional office in Chicago (after buying out the Chicago-based firm of Stein, Brennan), and had accumulated a capital base of $800,000. That year Salim L. "Cy" Lewis, a former runner for Salomon Brothers, was hired to direct Bear Stearns' new institutional bond trading department. Lewis, who became a partner in 1938, a managing partner in the 1950s and then chairman, built Bear Stearns into the large, influential firm it is today. An almost legendary character, Lewis's outspokenness and drive were what gave Bear Stearns the style that makes it stand out on Wall Street to this day.

In 1935, Congress passed the SEC's Public Utilities Holding Company Act, which precipitated a break-up of utility holding companies. As new securities were being issued for the formerly private companies, Bear Stearns positioned itself to take advantage of the opportunity, trading aggressively at what Lewis later called "the most ridiculous prices you ever saw in your life."

Revolutions in the freight and transportation industries beginning in the 1940s offered other opportunities. As auto transportation became more efficient and civil aviation more feasible, the once booming rail industry began to decline. Bear Stearns was quick to see an opportunity, and as most of the nation's railroads went into bankruptcy, Bear Stearns became one of the biggest arbitrators of mergers and acquisitions between railroad companies.

In 1948 Bear Stearns opened an international department, although it was not until 1955 that the firm opened its first international office, in Amsterdam. As its international business prospered, the company opened other foreign offices, in Geneva, Paris, London, Hong Kong, and Tokyo.

In the 1950s, Lewis was one of the originators of block trading, which by the 1960s was the bread and butter of most of Wall Street. Bear Stearns, like other companies, profited nicely from this trading until May 1, 1975, when the SEC's Security Act amendments, which eliminated fixed brokerage commissions went into effect.

Bear Stearns began expanding its retail business operations in the late 1960s, once again ahead of the trend. It opened an office in San Francisco in 1965, and between 1969 and 1973 opened offices in Los Angeles, Dallas, Atlanta, and Boston. The company was very successful at attracting and managing accounts for wealthy individuals. These accounts also laid the foundation for the company's successful margin operations. In margin trading, brokerage houses loan their clients' securities to short sellers, who match the fund with their own capital and use the entire amount to finance trade, paying interest on the amount loaned. Bear Stearns currently manages about 300,000 margin accounts.

In 1975, when New York City was near bankruptcy, Bear Stearns proved again that it was a risk-taker by investing $10 million in the city's securities. Though it came close to losing million of dollars, the firm eventually profited greatly from the gamble.

In May 1978, Alan "Ace" Greenberg became chairman of Bear Stearns, following the death of Cy Lewis. Greenberg had joined the firm as a clerk in 1949. He moved up rapidly within the company; by 1953, at age 25, he was running the risk arbitrage desk and by 1957 he was trading for the firm. By the time he became chairman, Greenberg had earned a reputation as one of the most aggressive traders on Wall Street. Like his predecessor, Greenberg shunned long-range planning in favor of immediate returns. It soon became apparent that Greenberg's abilities equaled and perhaps surpassed those of his predecessor. From the time he took over as chairman until Bear Stearns went public in 1985, the firm's total capital went from $46 million to $517 million; in 1989, it was $1.4 billion.

Bear Stearns' willingness to take risks has pushed it into the forefront of corporate takeover activity. The firm has been described as a "breeding ground" for corporate takeover attempts, and as masterful at disguising takeover maneuvers. In some instances however, Bear Stearns' aggressiveness has earned it an unsavory reputation. The firm as been known to wage proxy battles against its own clients, as it did in 1982 against Global Natural Resources after deciding that Global's management had undervalued its assets and could realize greater profits. In 1986, Bear Stearns developed an option agreement that essentially allowed clients to buy stock under Bear Stearns' name, a tactic that facilitates corporate takeover attempts. The Justice Department and the SEC put an end to such tactics by filing suits against several of Bear Stearns' clients for "parking" stock (all of them settled).

In October 1985, Greenberg and the firm's executive committee announced that Bear Stearns would make a public stock offering in an effort to increase the company's ability to raise capital to finance larger trades. Shortly after the initial 20% offering, Bear Stearns reorganized from a brokerage house into a full-service investment bank. It now maintains divisions in investment banking, institutional equities, fixed income securities, individual investor services, and correspondent clearing.

Much of Bear Stearns' success has been realized through short-term profit making ventures. As the company tries to build an identity as a major investment bank, it will have to attract larger corporate clients who seek long-term financial planning and commitment. Given its historical focus on short-term profits, some critics question the company's ability to succeed in context of the longer term horizons required in investment banking, but so far, Bear Stearns' profits and capital continue to grow.

Principal Subsidiaries: Bear Stearns & Co. Inc; Custodial Trust Co.; Bear Stearns Mortgage Capital Corp.; Bear Stearns Fiduciary Services, Inc.

CS FIRST BOSTON INC.

Park Avenue Plaza
New York, New York 10055
U.S.A.
(212) 909-2000

Private Company
Incorporated: 1934 as First Boston Corporation
Employees: 6,000

CS First Boston was created in 1988 when First Boston Inc., the parent of the old-line American investment bank The First Boston Corporation, went private and merged with Financière Crédit Suisse–First Boston, a European affiliate it had created with the Swiss bank Credit Suisse in 1978. These two operations and a third, newly created one called CS First Boston Pacific, make up CS First Boston Inc., a holding company that is controlled by Credit Suisse, which owns 44.5% of the new investment bank.

First Boston, today a global leader in the investment banking industry, traces its origins to The First of Boston, the underwriting subsidiary of the First National Bank of Boston. In March, 1933, on the eve of President Franklin D. Roosevelt's banking moratorium, this company traded in capital markets around the clock to allow banks to meet depositors' demands.

The Depression spawned a wave of legislation imposing constraints on the private sector. The Banking Act of 1933, better known as the Glass-Steagall Act, required banks to restrict their operations to either commercial or investment banking. In response to the act, Chase National Bank and the First National Bank of Boston spun off their securities underwriting affiliates, Chase Corporation (successor of Chase, Harris, Forbes) and The First of Boston. In June, 1934 the two affiliates merged to create the First Boston Corporation (FBC), with an immediate working capital of $9 million. It was the first publicly held underwriting firm.

First Boston's leaders, from Chase, Harris, Forbes (CHF) and The First of Boston, included Alan M. Pope as president, Harry M. Addinsell as chairman of the executive committee, John R. Macomber as chief executive, and George D. Woods as vice president. These men were able to reap intangible assets from the good will and client contacts of their former companies as well as their own personal prestige on Wall Street. Profits followed quickly. Within its first six months of operation, the company reported a dividend of $1.50 per share. During its first year of operation the company also established the First Boston, London Ltd.

FBC had a strong foothold in utility and railroad underwriting. It managed its first public offering during 1934 for Edison Electric Illuminating Company for $35 million. The following year First Boston raised $165.5 million for Southern California Edison Company. But, despite this strong start, within three years the company reported a loss of nearly $2.5 million, marking the beginning of a lean period in the field of security underwriting which would last until the early 1940s. It was not until World War II began to place heavy demands on industrial manufacturers that companies turned back to the securities market for the capital they needed to expand. In 1946, First Boston Corporation acquired Mellon Securities. The deal brought in an additional $8 million in capital and access to Mellon's industrial accounts, among them Alcoa, Allegheny Ludlum, and Gulf Oil.

While the deal with Mellon offered FBC very favorable opportunities, bleak times were just ahead. In 1947 the federal government named First Boston Corporation, along with 16 other companies, as a defendant in an antitrust suit. The defendants became known as "Club 17." As a member of the club, FBC was charged with the illegal monopolization of securities. The case lasted for six years. By the time it was finally dismissed due to insufficient evidence in 1953, legal fees had come close to $1 million.

In 1954 FBC orchestrated the financing of an oil refinery in Puerto Rico for the Commonwealth Oil Refining Company by arranging for $2 million in bank loans. FBC sold $16 million in debentures and purchased 500,000 shares of common stock in the refinery. This deal soon proved disastrous: by 1956 Commonwealth was losing $600,000 a month.

George Woods, the FBC officer who had negotiated the deal, reorganized the oil-refining company and made himself chairman of the finance committee. For more than a year he devoted most of his time to reshaping the company and recruiting new managers. By 1958 the company broke even, and during the first quarter of 1959 Commonwealth showed a profit.

In the same year, FBC was able to convince the Japanese government of the capital benefits of long-term money markets, resulting in a $30 million bond issue. FBC also managed the public distribution of World Bank bonds and participated with Kuhn, Loeb and Lazard Freres in an underwriting syndicate that placed $85 million in bonds and notes for European Coal and Steel. In the U.S. however, the market cooled in the 1960s as corporate demand slowed and the private sector showed caution in the face of rising labor costs.

FBC President James Coggeshall retired in 1962. Coggeshall had addressed administrative functions and nurtured clients, but he had never held a formal trading or sales position with the company. These skills were supplied by his successor, Emil J. Pattberg. Unlike his predecessor and much of the company's staff, Pattberg held no Ivy League degree but had dropped his college plans to support his family in 1929 and began working with the First of Boston in the "cage." Pattberg was promoted to a sales position in government bonds in 1935. After World War II he returned to the company to head up the bond department; in 1949 he moved into a policy making role, and by 1952 Pattberg held the post of chairman of the executive committee.

Although Pattberg's talents were many, they were no match for slowing markets, and he watched earnings decrease throughout the decade. Between 1968 and 1969, earnings nearly halved and trading volume dropped about 30%. Part of the reason for this was FBC's tendency to rely upon its conservative image and its contacts. FBC failed to pursue new clients aggressively, which impeded the company's ability to compete. The creative talents of its executives went astray under poorly structured management.

Another factor that seemed to hurt FBC's corporate image was the youth of its top corporate-finance officers—their average age was 30. However talented these men were, older clients felt uncomfortable with FBC's lack of gray-haired executives. FBC's rank as the number-one underwriter in the 1960s slipped to number three in the 1970s. Profits plunged from $14.4 million in 1971 to $3 million the following year. The company's conservative financial policies caused it to avoid hostile takeovers and created a weakness in the area of ventures and mergers.

To remedy these deficiencies the firm recruited new talent. Ralph Saul joined the firm in 1971. His role as president of the American Stock Exchange and his seven years with the Securities and Exchange Commission brought FBC expertise in new areas. His recruitment also coincided with FBC's efforts to gain membership on the New York Stock Exchange. The "Big Board" set a historical precedent when it approved membership for the First Boston Corporation on March 25, 1971—it was the first publicly held investment bank to be granted membership.

Concern over short-term debt brought private industry back into the bond market again in the 1970s, and FBC captured a quarter of the overall underwriting market. The firm participated in $380 million in debt financing and set records in every area of selling and trading. Revenues doubled, to $80 million, earnings jumped more than 10%, and capital funds increased significantly. First Boston's distribution network, which by 1971 had 105 salesmen in nine cities, bolstered its success. The firm's strategy was to call on institutional clients in teams, to provide individual expertise on different fields of investment and give the customer many options to choose from.

Recognizing the need to expand in foreign markets, in 1972 Saul recruited Minos Zombanakis to head FBC's international finance operations. Zombanakis had acquired valuable contacts while working for Manufacturers Hanover in London; he focused on revitalizing underwriting and corporate finance in the European and Middle Eastern markets, hiring Guido Carli, former governor of the Central Bank of Italy, as a consultant. The efforts of these men brought the company into new areas of bond underwriting, such as pollution control.

FBC made some decisive internal changes in the mid-1970s. It continued recruiting talent away from competitors and introduced a major restructuring of the company. The firm hired George L. Shinn from Merrill Lynch in 1975 to become chairman and chief executive, and Alexander Tomlinson from Morgan Stanley in 1976 to become chairman of the executive committee. Their combined abilities provided a cohesive management. Shinn initiated major revisions in salary scales to counter the remuneration offered by competitors, doubled the size of the staff, and streamlined the management system.

First Boston focused on domestic distribution by adding two new offices and paid more attention to smaller institutional investors. Competition remained stiff, though, and an aggressive Salomon Brothers captured an increased share of the underwriting market. First Boston countered with a $750 million issue for the World Bank and the Japanese Development Bank. Despite the reorganization of its management, it did not lose its entrepreneurial talent—it managed, for example, to place $100 million of American Telephone & Telegraph Company notes with the Saudi Arabian government, and to entice Inland Steel away from Kuhn, Loeb.

In March, 1976, the First Boston Corporation became a wholly owned subsidiary of First Boston Inc., but the reorganization did not dramatically alter the subsidiary's sphere of business. The company remained strong in underwriting, but had trouble with mergers and acquisitions. When International Paper used First Boston as a consultant in acquiring General Crude Oil, unexpected complications led International Paper to seek advice from Morgan Stanley, costing First Boston the deal. In another noteworthy deal, FBC helped the Bangor Punta Corporation to buy shares in the Piper Aircraft Corporation. Bangor's rival, Chris-Craft Industries, claimed that Bangor violated securities laws and sued the company, and FBC, for $36 million in damages. While FBC was only active in one of the three violations cited, the judgment in favor of Chris-Craft Industries held FBC liable for the whole $36 million if Bangor defaulted. This case changed the way the whole industry looked at the financial liquidity of its clients.

Other deals, however, went considerably better. When Pullman Inc. began to sense unwelcome takeover maneuvers by J. Ray McDermott, FBC was hired to find a suitable investor to purchase Pullman shares. FBC successfully proposed Wheelabrator-Frye, a New Hampshire engineering firm, and FBC earned $6 million in fees.

When Zombanakis left First Boston Corporation in 1978 to chair INA Corporation, however, he took a valuable client, Chrysler Corporation, with him. His departure forced First Boston to look at alternative options in international investment banking. An opportunity appeared when a deal between Credit Suisse and Merrill Lynch to form an investment bank fell through. George Shinn wanted to take advantage of the international leverage Credit Suisse offered, even at the expense of giving up controlling interest. Negotiations began in May, 1977, and in 1978 Financière Crédit-Suisse First Boston (CSFB), a holding company for a diversified group of European financial enterprises, was born. First Boston held a 40% interest in CSFB.

By 1985, FBC had doubled the amount of risk capital it had in block trades and had gained an edge in the market through the use of computer-orchestrated hedging in index futures and options. The company moved into new product lines—money market accounts, mortgage-backed securities, and risk management. It also designed new techniques for dealing in municipal bond index futures and had made a successful thrust into over-the-counter trading by 1985. With its concentration on improving research and sales, FBC was rated the most-improved company in 1986 by *Financial World*.

First Boston's 1978 alliance with Credit Suisse led to a worldwide expansion. Ten years later, on October 10, 1988, First Boston, Inc. announced that it would go private by merging with Financière Crédit Suisse–First Boston to form a new worldwide investment-banking concern—CS First Boston Inc. As part of the deal, Credit Suisse agreed to raise its 24% stake in First Boston Inc. to 44.5%, assuming effective control of First Boston. First Boston continues to operate in the Americas, while Financière Crédit Suisse-First Boston ovesees operations in Europe, the Middle East, and Africa, and CS First Boston Pacific, a new entity still looking for an Asian partner, will cover the Far East and Australasia.

The globalization of private industry makes First Boston's access to international markets an integral element of its operations. The new CS First Boston Inc., organized as it is to cover Europe, America, and Asia, offers First Boston a chance to operate a truly global financial network, but much depends on a smooth relationship with its dominant European partner and on keeping the politics and infighting that have posed problems in the past to a minimum.

Principal Subsidiaries: The First Boston Corp.; Financière Crédit Suisse–First Boston; CS First Boston Pacific.

Further Reading: William, Ben Ames, Jr. *Bank of Boston 200: A History of New England's Leading Bank 1784–1984*, Boston, Houghton Mifflin Co., 1984.

DAIWA SECURITIES COMPANY, LIMITED

6–4, Otemachi 2-chome
Chiyoda-ku
Tokyo 100
Japan
(03) 243–2111

Public Company
Incorporated: 1943
Employees: 9,102
Assets: ¥4.4 trillion (US$30 billion)
Stock Index: Tokyo Osaka Nagoya

Daiwa Securities Company is the second-largest securities broker in the world and has been called the most international of Japan's Big Four securities houses. Daiwa conducts traditional investment banking activities and also operates as a retail brokerage. To a great extent its history parallels Japan's economic prosperity since World War II. In good times, active stock and bond markets produced excellent profits for securities companies. In recessionary periods, commissions and underwriting profits suffered from investor reluctance and lack of volume. Since its incorporation in 1943, Daiwa has seen Japan rise to the forefront of world commerce. It has played a vital role in the development and advancement of Japanese capital markets, and has helped shape personal investment in Japan.

Daiwa Securities Company was incorporated in 1943 as a merger between the Fujimoto Bill Broker & Securities Company and the Nippon Trust Bank. The company's origins date back to 1902, when Sibei Fujimoto entered the bill-brokering business at a time when Japan's securities industry was still in its infancy. In 1907, the company entered the banking business and took the name Fujimoto Bill Broker and Bank, to reflect its expanded services. World War I brought tremendous growth to the Japanese economy. Export demand skyrocketed and stock trading increased, as did the number of corporate and government bond issues. As a result, the Fujimoto organization grew quickly.

After the war and throughout the 1920s, Fujimoto engaged in both banking and securities brokering. Bond trading reached new highs, and as the Japanese economy became more complex, stock trading set records too. But a number of financial catastrophes rocked the economy in the later 1920s. In 1927, a run on the banks sent shock waves through the financial community. Dozens of banks and securities dealers collapsed, but Fujimoto, due to prudent management, survived intact. The Depression which followed the collapse of the New York Stock Exchange in 1929 brought about changes in the laws regarding Japanese financial institutions. Fujimoto was forced to give up the banking business, so in 1933, the Fujimoto Bill Broker & Securities Company was established in compliance with these new government regulations.

The 1930s were a time of great political turmoil in Japan. By the end of the decade, the country was at war with China. Increased demand for war-related goods accelerated economic expansion. The stock market was active, and prices went up. As the Japanese government began to issue bonds to fuel the war, it also exercised greater control over the markets. Nonetheless, Fujimoto continued to profit from its underwriting and brokerage activities. By 1941, Japan had entered World War II. The war had a positive impact on the Japanese economy until 1943, when Japan's military success began to falter. The market responded accordingly, and stock prices plummeted. Fujimoto Bill Broker & Securities Company decided to combine forces with another financial institution. On December 27, 1943, it merged with the Nippon Trust Bank to form a new entity, the Daiwa Securities Company.

After the war, the occupation forces halted all securities trading on the exchanges and restructured the Japanese economy and political system. Daiwa survived by trading non-defense-related industry securities over the counter at its offices until 1949, when the exchanges were reopened.

Throughout the next decade Japan's economy, and Daiwa with it, flourished. The Korean War created tremendous demand for Japanese goods, and the economy began the steady climb which has continued almost uninterrupted to the present day.

In 1951, Daiwa entered the investment trust business. Investment trusts were a very popular savings instrument among the Japanese. Within eight years Daiwa's investment trust activity had grown so large that a separate company had to be set up to handle its business. The Daiwa Investment Trust and Management Company, Ltd. opened its doors in 1959. During the 1950s, Daiwa's underwriting and brokerage activities made it one of Japan's most successful financial companies. Daiwa's innovative philosophy was characterized by its motto, adopted in 1957: "scrupulous as well as daring."

The early 1960s were a period of growth for Daiwa, both at home and abroad. Encountering stiff competition from other securities dealers in Japan, Daiwa began to look overseas for new opportunities. Japanese companies had begun to issues stocks on foreign exchanges, and Daiwa actively pursued the underwriting of these issues. In 1964, Daiwa established an office in London. Later that year, the Japanese stock market experienced the worst panic since before the war. Daiwa Securities was hit hard by the panic, as was the rest of the securities industry. The recession lasted through 1965, and prompted the Ministry of Finance to implement tighter restrictions on securities-company licensing, primarily requiring that companies acquire separate licenses for underwriting and for retailing. It was a technicality that affected small dealers but had little impact on Daiwa's operations.

By the end of 1965, the Japanese economy had bounced back. Daiwa established the Daiwa Securities Research Institute to forecast trends in the economy and analyze specific industries and companies. In 1967, the Japanese government liberalized Japanese capital markets, giving Daiwa an opportunity to solicit more foreign investments. By the early 1970s, considerable capital was flowing both in and out of Japan.

During the early 1970s Daiwa's international sector saw the greatest growth. In 1970, Daiwa Securities (Hong Kong) Ltd. was established, followed by Daiwa Singapore Ltd. and a representative office in Paris in 1972. A year later, Daiwa Europe N.V. was incorporated in Amsterdam. The company also set up a subsidiary to handle asset management services in 1973, the Daiwa International Capital Management Company, Ltd. (DICAM). DICAM worked closely with the Daiwa Securities Research Institute to offer investment advice to its international customers.

During the 1970s, the bond market in Japan exploded. Beginning in 1970, foreign government bonds denominated in yen took the Japanese market by storm. These so-called "samurai bonds" increased in popularity throughout the decade. A secondary market for bonds soon developed, and was accompanied by an influx of Japanese government, particularly municipal, bond issues. Between 1970 and 1975, bond sales in Japan tripled.

In 1978, Daiwa (Switzerland) Ltd. was incorporated. Together with its operations in Great Britain, the Netherlands, France, and West Germany, Daiwa had a firm base on the European continent that proved to be invaluable during the 1980s. The European appetite for Japanese stocks and bonds combined with surplus Japanese capital available for foreign investment made Daiwa a major dealer in the euromarkets by the late 1970s.

Throughout the first half of the 1980s Daiwa's earnings were staggering. The fact that Japan still allowed fixed commissions on security trades made Japanese brokers like Daiwa the most profitable in the world. Many new kinds of bonds appeared in the mid-1980s, when the Japanese Ministry of Finance approved substantial changes in the capital market regulations. Colorful names like "shogun bonds," "sushi bonds," and "geisha bonds" denoted a variety of issues, some in yen, some in foreign currencies. These new investment vehicles were, in effect, completely new product lines for Daiwa Securities.

Under pressure from abroad, mainly the United States, the Japanese continued to deregulate their capital markets. Daiwa was suddenly subject to competition from huge American investment banking firms like Morgan Stanley, First Boston, and Salomon Brothers on their home turf. At the same time, Japanese banks became active in securities trading. But Daiwa, with its close ties to institutional investors, was not as affected by the new competition as were other Japanese dealers who relied heavily on retail activities.

The company saw its future in U.S. markets. By the mid-1980s, Daiwa had become a large dealer in U.S. treasury notes. However, virtually all of its customers were Japanese. The company's American subsidiary, Daiwa Securities America Inc., struggled to build a domestic base in the United States to ensure its success in those markets, but like other Japanese securities companies, had only measured success. Part of the problem was the reluctance of American corporations to develop close ties with foreign investment bankers. Another was that Japanese dealers were sluggish in reacting when American underwriting opportunities did arise; key decisions always had to be cleared with top management in Tokyo.

Daiwa was the first of the large Japanese securities companies to give its American employees authority to make underwriting decisions on the spot. Daiwa Securities America had an American vice chairman. In addition, the subsidiary's American employees outnumbered their Japanese co-workers six to one. These characteristics made Daiwa more attractive to Americans than other Japanese houses, but the company still had trouble competing with American investment bankers.

Daiwa's weak base in the United States was compounded by the stock market crash of October, 1987. Many Japanese investors were scared out of the stock market. In 1988, Daiwa cut its American staff by 7%, but remained determined to position itself in the American market. In the late 1980s, Daiwa diversified its services in the United States, initiating mergers and acquisition services both at home and in America. It was designated a primary dealer in U.S. government securities in 1986. It became increasingly active in commodities futures trading in 1988 and became a member of the Chicago Board of Trade. And by the end of the decade, American attitudes toward Japanese securities firms were changing. The sheer size of Daiwa and other large Japanese dealers had finally attracted the attention of American investors and issuers.

Daiwa Securities' growth in the 1980s was astounding. It is still considerably smaller than its rival Nomura Securities, but Daiwa's progressive attitude regarding its American operations and its historically stronger ties to institutional investors may help it close the gap. Daiwa has the most experience in international markets of any Japanese securities house, an important edge as securities markets become more and more global.

Principal Subsidiaries: Daiwa Securities Research Institute; Daiwa International Capital Management Inc., Ltd.; The Daiwa Investment Trust and Management Co., Ltd.; Nippon Investment & Finance Co., Ltd.; Daiwa Computer Service Co., Ltd.; Daiwa System Service Co., Ltd.; Daiwa Mortgage Co., Ltd.; Daiwa Credit Service Co., Ltd.; The Daiwa Building Co., Ltd.; The Daiwa Real Estate Co., Ltd..

Further Reading: A History of Japan's Postwar Securities Industry, Tokyo, Japanese Securities Research Institute, 1984.

DREXEL BURNHAM LAMBERT INCORPORATED

60 Broad Street
New York, New York 10004
U.S.A.
(212) 480–6000

Private Company
Incorporated: 1976
Employees: 10,000
Assets: $35.9 billion

Since its incorporation in 1976, Drexel Burnham Lambert, once a little-known, second-tier underwriter, has become perhaps the most widely publicized investment bank in U.S. corporate history. Drexel pioneered the "junk bond" craze of the 1980s and played a leading role in many of the decade's best known corporate takeover bids. At its peak in the early 1980s, Drexel had a firm grip on more than 70% of the junk bond market. The company's innovative and aggressive financing strategies made the firm virtually an overnight success, and Drexel became one of Wall Street's most respected, and at times most resented, investment banking houses. But in 1986, the firm became the center of an investigation by the Securities and Exchange Commission involving insider trading and other illegal trading practices. Drexel Burnham Lambert's role in the scandal took its toll on the company. In the late 1980s, its business declined as quickly as it had been built, and in February, 1990 Drexel declared bankruptcy and liquidated its business. It was the end of an era.

Drexel Burnham Lambert's roots can be traced back to 1838, when Francis Martin Drexel went into the banking business. His son Anthony took over Drexel and ran it until the 1890s. During the late 19th and early 20th century, Drexel was the Philadelphia arm of J.P. Morgan and Company, of New York. The company conducted both commercial and investment banking until 1933, when the Glass-Steagall Act precluded commercial banks from underwriting and dealing in securities. Drexel and Company, like Morgan, followed the commercial banking route.

But in 1940 former Drexel partners Edward Hopkinson Jr. and Thomas S. Gates Jr., together with a number of their associates, founded an investment bank. The commercial bank was completely absorbed into the Morgan organization and they acquired the rights to the Drexel name. The new Drexel began with an initial capital investment of $1 million. The firm, although profitable, grew very slowly during its first 15 years, never quite making it to investment banking's first tier. In those days Wall Street played by a strict set of unwritten rules which insured the continued dominance of only a few investment banks. One such practice was "bracketing," which refers to the order of listing participants in the advertisement for an underwriting. The "special bracket firms," such as Morgan Stanley, First Boston, and Merrill Lynch, were listed first, then the "major bracket firms," then "submajors," then "regional firms." This hierarchy clearly indicated to issuers and buyers who the most powerful investment banks were. Drexel held close ties to many of the nation's biggest securities issuers, but it ranked one notch below the special firm bracket and was not one of the dominant forces on Wall Street.

In 1965, Drexel merged with Harriman, Ripley and Company to form Drexel Firestone Inc. That arrangement, however, lasted only two years. With its capital dwindling, Drexel Firestone Inc. merged with the very successful, though relatively unknown, Burnham and Company.

Burnham and Company had been built by I.W. "Tubby" Burnham, who founded the company in 1935. Burnham began with $100,000 in capital, $96,000 of which Tubby had borrowed from his grandfather and the founder of I.W. Harper, a Kentucky distillery. Burnham and Company, though very successful, was still a submajor investment bank. By the late 1960s, Burnham could see that if he wanted to expand much further he would need to link up with the reputation of a major firm. The ailing Drexel Firestone provided the opportunity for such a combination. Drexel provided the "white-shoe" image and Burnham provided the capital.

Burnham's investment bank had grown substantially over the years and by 1973, its capital was $44 million—80% of the new Drexel Burnham and Company. Tubby Burnham served as chairman of the new company. By focusing on underwriting securities issues of small- and medium-sized companies, Drexel Burnham prospered.

In 1976, Drexel Burnham and Company merged with Lambert Brussels Witter, which was controlled by the Belgian Bank Brussels Lambert. The Lamberts were one of Europe's oldest banking families. Baron Leon Lambert served as a director of the new Drexel Burnham Lambert, Inc. while Tubby Burnham continued as chairman. Burnham's protégé, Robert E. Linton, was president and CEO.

From the start, Drexel Burnham Lambert concentrated on the leftovers of Wall Street's bigger investment banks, going after smaller companies with less than perfect credit ratings. The company's high-yield (junk) bond department, which would spearhead its climb to the top of the investment banking heap, had the unique talents of Michael Milken. While working on his MBA at Wharton, Milken had discovered that so-called junk bonds—bonds rated BB or lower by Standard and Poor's—had an only slightly higher rate of default than blue chip issues, while their premiums were considerably higher. Milken found that through careful research and selection, a diversified bond portfolio made up of junk bonds would pay interest rates which more than made up for the higher risk. Milken looked at a number of factors which the rating services ignored and paid more attention to a company's future than its past. It was a very successful formula.

In 1978, Milken moved the high-yield bond department to Beverly Hills, a clear indication of his influence inside Drexel as the king of junk bonds. Before 1977, the junk bond market consisted entirely of "fallen angels"—bonds issued by former blue chip companies which had run into financial difficulty and had fallen from grace. In the late 1970s, however, a number of lower credit companies began to issue their own bonds, rated BB or lower. Milken and Drexel Burnham, with their close ties to the institutional investors who liked junk bonds, controlled this rapidly expanding market. Milken's confidence in his ability to distribute high-yield bonds made Drexel actively seek out low credit issuers. Drexel's first issue was Texas International, followed by Michigan General. As low-credit companies found they could raise capital without having to offer equity shares, the junk bond craze took off. Drexel Burnham Lambert had created a market for first-issue junk bonds.

In the early 1980s Drexel Burnham Lambert continued to tighten its stranglehold on the junk bond market. Investors trusted Milken, who had gathered the most talented group of researchers and traders of any investment bank and paid them well enough to prevent defections. If a company Milken had recommended got into trouble, Milken was on the phone with them getting information and giving advice. Drexel Burnham Lambert was also always willing to make markets for the bonds it underwrote. This built special confidence in the firm, since investors knew they wouldn't get stuck with a bad issue. This, combined with Milken's genius for picking winners, made Drexel the hottest investment bank on Wall Street. Although nobody is perfect—Drexel watched the Flight Transportation Company default on a $25 million issue it had underwritten in 1982—Drexel's record was the best of any investment bank.

In 1982, Tubby Burnham stepped down as chairman and was replaced by president and CEO Robert E. Linton. Linton was one of a handful of investment banking executives who had never attended college; he had joined Burnham and Company after his discharge from the Air Force following World War II. Frederick Joseph, formerly head of the company's corporate finance department, took over as president.

Joseph had joined the old Drexel and Burnham in 1974 and had worked closely with Milken assembling an aggressive team in the corporate finance department. Cultivating Drexel's image as an upstart, Joseph once remarked that his firm was loaded with "fat women and ugly men"—not the typical blue-eyed six-footers most people picture as the classic investment banker. Joseph was described as a diplomat in an aggressive business, and was seen as the man who could best coordinate Drexel's West Coast and New York offices. In 1983, Drexel underwrote its first $1 billion junk bond issue, for MCI Communications. Drexel's share of the junk bond market peaked at about 75% in 1983 and 1984. At that time, other major investment banks, including Merrill Lynch and Morgan Stanley, were lured into these not-quite-respectable but highly lucrative markets. Drexel maintained its overall superiority, but these companies gradually encroached on its market share.

In the early 1980s Drexel also became increasingly active in mergers and acquisitions, specializing in leveraged buyouts financed by junk bonds. A letter from Drexel saying that it was "highly confident" that financing could be arranged was the go-ahead for many hostile bids, and Drexel became associated with the decade's most notorious corporate raiders. It arranged financing for T. Boone Pickens' unsuccessful run at Gulf Oil in 1983; it helped Carl Icahn try to take over Phillips Petroleum; and it financed Saul Steinberg's bid for Disney Studios. One of the largest leveraged buyouts it arranged was Ted Turner's purchase of MGM/UA for a staggering $1.3 billion.

While junk bonds remained its greatest strength, Drexel had been expanding in other areas as well. In 1984, Drexel acquired the Denver firm Kirchner, Moore, and Company, expanding its expertise in municipal bond financing. Drexel also launched a major effort to enter the mortgage-backed securities markets in 1984. By the mid-1980s, Drexel Burnham Lambert ranked solidly among Wall Street's top investment banks.

But at this time Drexel and the junk bond market it had created began to draw some criticism. Critics claimed that many companies were overleveraged, while the media dubbed junk bonds "toxic waste." Although default rates were no higher than before, there was speculation that the collective risk was accumulating and that a major default would soon shake the market. In addition, Drexel Burnham Lambert seemed to be making too much money too fast. Competitors—and the federal government—were inclined to take a closer look at the company.

In May, 1986 the Securities and Exchange Commission charged a Drexel Burnham Lambert managing director, Dennis Levine, with insider trading. When Levine pleaded guilty, a wave of insider charges ensued, including those involving corporate raider Ivan Boesky. Slowly, one of the Wall Street scandals of the century unraveled. The SEC investigated Drexel Burnham Lambert for two years before bringing any charges against the firm, while U.S. Attorney Rudolph Guiliani targeted Michael Milken himself. The investigation itself may not have been directly responsible for Drexel's estimated 79% drop in earnings in 1987, the same year the stock market crashed, but the cloud over Drexel certainly didn't help business. In spite of the negative publicity, Drexel maintained a 49% market share of the junk bond market in 1987, down considerably from the early 1980s but still the biggest single slice of the pie, as junk bonds made up about one-fifth of all new bond issues.

In December, 1988, threatened with racketeering charges that would have allowed seizure of certain Drexel assets and effectively put the firm out of business, Drexel pleaded guilty to six felony charges of illegal trading and paid $650 million in fines. In addition, Drexel agreed to withhold Milken's estimated $200 million compensation for 1988 and remove him from his position as head of the high-yield bond operation.

Milken challenged the actions in court, but finally left Drexel in March, 1989, after he was formally charged with 98 counts of wrongdoing, including securities fraud, racketeering, and tax fraud. Milken pleaded not guilty; his defense was expected to center on the notion that a $175 billion market was obviously too big to be controlled by one man.

In April, 1989, Drexel announced it was going to sell its retail operation. Many Wall Street firms had been suffering since the October 1987 stock market crash undermined public confidence in the markets, and Drexel's investigation by the federal government was a double blow to the investment bank's business. In an effort to brighten its tarnished image, Drexel brought in former SEC chief John Shad as chairman in 1989. Shad vowed he would be an active chairman rather than a "window dressing," but just how he planned to restore Drexel Burnham Lambert in the wake of one of the broadest securities scandal of the century was uncertain. And indeed Drexel, which had risen from semi-obscurity in the mid-1970s to achieve annual revenues of $4 billion in the mid-1980s, survived barely more than a month of the new decade. The junk bond market had collapsed, and Drexel declared bankruptcy on February 13, 1990.

Principal Subsidiaries: Drexel Burnham Lambert American Specialist; Drexel Burnham Lambert Capital Markets Espana S.A.; Drexel Burnham Lambert Commercial Paper Inc.; Drexel Burnham Lambert Finanx A.G.; Drexel Burnham Lambert (France) S.A.; Drexel Burnham Lambert Government Securities Inc.; Drexel Burnham Lambert International Bank N.V.; Drexel Burnham Lambert International Inc.; Drexel Burnham Lambert International Ltd.; Drexel Burnham Lambert Management Corp.; Drexel Burnham Lambert (Netherlands) B.V.; Drexel Burnham Lambert Options Inc.; Drexel Burnham Lambert Puerto Rico Inc.; Drexel Burnham Lambert Securities Ltd.; Drexel Burnham Lambert Trading Corp.; Drexel Burnham Lambert Trading Ltd.; Drexel Management Corp.; Harbor Trust Co.; Kirchner Moore and Co.; The Washington Forum, Inc.

Further Reading: Hoffman, Paul. *The Dealmakers: Inside the World of Investment Banking*, Garden City, New York, Doubleday, 1984; Bruck, Connie. *The Predators' Ball: How the Junk Bond Machine Stalked the Corporate Raiders*, New York, Simon and Schuster, 1988.

FEDERAL NATIONAL MORTGAGE ASSOCIATION

3900 Wisconsin Avenue, NW
Washington, DC 200016–2899
U.S.A.
(202) 537–7000

Public Company
Incorporated: 1938 as the National Mortgage Association of Washington
Employees: 2,500
Assets: $103 billion
Stock Index: New York Boston Pacific Midwest Cincinnati Philadelphia

The Federal National Mortgage Association, better known as Fannie Mae, is worth more than $100 billion, making it the third largest corporation in the United States in terms of assets. The one-time government agency has made a tremendous impact on the home finance industry since it was chartered by Congress in 1938. As a publicly owned company regulated by the federal government, Fannie Mae is an unusual instrument in the American economy.

Fannie Mae was originally designed to help relieve the nation's housing problems during the Depression. Title III of the Federal Housing Act of 1934 provided for the incorporation of private national mortgage associations to create a national secondary mortgage market. But in February, 1938, since no private associations had yet formed, the Federal Housing Administration chartered the National Mortgage Association of Washington to buy and sell mortgages. Its name was changed three months later to the Federal National Mortgage Association, or FNMA, and it has been known as Fannie Mae ever since.

The federal government took an interest in facilitating home mortgages as a way to invigorate the residential construction industry as well as to provide adequate housing for its citizens. The Depression had taken a heavy toll on private lending institutions. Fannie Mae's primary purpose was to establish a secondary mortgage market to rejuvenate original lenders such as mortgage banks, savings and loan associations, and commercial banks by stimulating enough cash flow to allow them to make new loans. Fannie Mae bought mortgages insured by the Federal Housing Administration (FHA) from these private lenders, and either kept them for its own portfolio or sold them to private investors.

The secondary market Fannie Mae created also made private lenders confident about making FHA-insured mortgages, which some had been reluctant to do. Once assured that they could easily turn these mortgages into cash if they needed to, lenders were more inclined to extend mortgage credit. In addition, the secondary mortgage market helped smooth out discrepancies between capital-rich and capital-poor regions of the country. Fannie Mae could buy mortgages from the South or West and sell them to investors in the capital-rich East. In this way a Boston banker could invest in Arizona mortgages while a local lender in Arizona was no longer limited in the number of loans he could make by the cash deposits of his customers. Under Sam Husbands, who presided over the association from 1938 to 1948, Fannie Mae bought 66,947 FHA-insured mortgages and sold 49,048.

In 1949, Fannie Mae expanded its activities to include buying and selling loans guaranteed by the Veterans Administration (VA). As veterans returned from the war and the great American baby boom got under way, Fannie Mae was busier than ever. The association bought 133,032 mortgages in 1950 compared with 6,734 in 1948. Some critics viewed Fannie Mae's growth with alarm, however, charging that the company had brought government too far into the private sector.

In 1954, Congress responded with the Federal National Mortgage Association Charter Act, which turned Fannie Mae into a mixed ownership corporation. The Treasury of the United States was issued non-voting preferred stock, and non-voting common stock was sold to mortgage lenders, who were now required to own stock in order to sell mortgages to Fannie Mae. Fannie Mae was made responsible for special assistance for certain mortgages when the president or Congress requested, and also for the management of mortgages acquired before 1954.

Throughout the 1950s and early 1960s Fannie Mae continued to buy and sell FHA and VA mortgages. But in 1966, primary mortgage lenders found themselves temporarily without the liquid resources to make new mortgages. Fannie Mae, until then a relatively minor player in the secondary market because it was restricted to government-insured (FHA and VA) mortgages, became the largest buyer in the market. The cost of borrowing enough money to purchase all the mortgages was high enough that Fannie Mae's profits dropped significantly that year. Lending eased at the end of 1966, relieving the pressure on Fannie Mae. But when mortgage funds became scarce again a year later, it became clear that major changes were necessary to ensure Fannie Mae's continued prosperity.

In 1968, Fannie Mae began the transition from mixed ownership to a private corporation. The Housing and Urban Development Act of 1968 split the old Fannie Mae into two separate corporations: the new Fannie Mae conducted secondary mortgage market activities just as the old one had done, while a new company called the Government National Mortgage Association (GNMA), or Ginnie Mae, assumed the "special assistance" and "management" functions of the old Fannie Mae, guaranteeing FHA and VA mortgages. The Treasury Department's preferred stock was retired and a schedule was set for non-voting common shares to become voting ones. The Department of Housing and Urban Development (HUD) maintains "regulatory power" over the new Fannie Mae. Any stock, obligation, or other security must be approved by the Secretary of HUD. The secretary may also require that a reasonable number of Fannie Mae purchases are in step with HUD's goal of assuring quality housing for moderate- and low-income families.

On December 2, 1969, President Richard Nixon dismissed Raymond H. Lapin as chief of Fannie Mae. A Democrat, Lapin had been appointed president of the association by President Lyndon Johnson in July of 1967 and had overseen Fannie Mae's transitional period. The ousted chief filed suit in federal court claiming that his removal was politically motivated and that Nixon had failed to show "good cause," but the courts twice refused to reinstate Lapin. In January of 1970, Oakley Hunter took over as president; Fannie Mae's transition to private control was completed on May 21, 1970. The new board of directors had 15 members, ten elected by the stockholders and five appointed by the president.

As a private corporation, Fannie Mae has had to adjust to the growing complexity of the secondary mortgage market. In 1972, the company bought its first conventional mortgages—mortgages not insured by the FHA or guaranteed by the VA—and in 1974, Fannie Mae began buying condominium and planned unit development mortgages. This flexibility kept the company profitable through the first half of the 1970s.

As interest rates began to rise in 1979, Fannie Mae faced the most critical period in its history. Because the company borrows the money it uses to purchase mortgages through debentures and short-term notes, it is especially vulnerable to rising interest rates. The sky-rocketing rates of the early 1980s put Fannie Mae's new chairman, David O. Maxwell, to the test. Maxwell replaced Hunter in 1981, a time when Fannie Mae was losing millions of dollars by borrowing at high interest rates to carry mortgages at lower ones. Maxwell initiated several programs to transfer some of the interest-rate risk to someone else. One of these was to begin buying adjustable-rate mortgages (ARMs), especially since many primary lending institutions were shifting to ARMs. The interest rate on ARMs varies: if interest rates go up, the homeowner pays more per month; if they go down he or she pays less.

Fannie Mae also began selling mortgage-backed securities (MBS) in 1981 to help finance its mortgage purchases and to generate fee income. These securities are attractive investments because they are more liquid than the usual packaged mortgage pools. Fannie Mae's MBS "Swap Program" allows lending institutions to trade loans directly for the more liquid securities. Fannie Mae guarantees the timely payment of interest and principal on the securities. By 1988, Fannie Mae had issued more than $140 billion in mortgage-backed securities.

By 1985, Fannie Mae was profitable again. The company had survived the interest-rate nightmares of the early 1980s and had positioned itself against future interest-rate risk through ARMs and MBSs. That year, Fannie Mae began borrowing money from abroad to finance its purchases, since the 30% withholding tax on foreign investment had been abolished. Continuing to respond to changes in the home finance market, Fannie Mae began marketing real estate mortgage investment conduits (REMICs) in 1987. These securities can be specifically tailored to an investor's needs in terms of maturity dates, allowing Fannie Mae to attract investors not traditionally interested in mortgage-related investment products.

In 1988 Fannie Mae celebrated 50 years of service to the home finance industry with record earnings of $345 million in the first three quarters alone. Of the $400 billion Fannie Mae has pumped into the nation's mortgage industry in the past half century, $300 billion of it came after 1980. Under Chairman David Maxwell's aggressive leadership, Fannie Mae has become more profitable than ever. The secondary mortgage market has changed dramatically since 1938. Fannie Mae has shown remarkable agility in adapting to those changes. As large corporations such as Sears and Citicorp become more active in the secondary mortgage market, Fannie Mae will have to continue to be innovative to remain competitive.

Further Reading: Federal National Mortgage Association: Background and History, Washington, D.C., FNMA, 1975; *Housing America: An Overview of Fannie Mae's Past, Present and Future*, Washington, D.C., FNMA, 1986.

FIDELITY INVESTMENTS

82 Devonshire Street
Boston, Massachusetts 02109
U.S.A.
(617) 570-7000

Private Company
Incorporated: 1946 as Fidelity Management and Research Company
Employees: 5,500
Assets: $85 billion

Fidelity Investments is one of the largest retail investment-services firms in the United States. Fidelity offers its customers one of the widest ranges of mutual funds in the industry, as well as discount brokerage and institutional and trust services. Innovation in particular has played a key role in the company's progress. The investment industry has raised many an eyebrow at the way Fidelity chairmen have led their company through uncharted areas. Fidelity was first, for example, to offer mutual funds with check-writing services; first to offer hourly updates on the net value of a mutual fund; and first to offer same-day trading of fund shares. Fidelity is privately owned and based in Boston, not New York. Although it is set apart from its competitors, the company, with more than three million individual and corporate customers, is one of the largest managers of mutual funds in the country, second only to Merrill Lynch.

The Fidelity Fund was created in 1930, not a booming time for an investment industry reeling from the stock market crash of 1929 and heading into the Great Depression. In 1943 Edward C. Johnson II, a Boston lawyer, bought the fund, which had $3 million in assets under management, and became its president and director. In 1946, Johnson formed Fidelity Management and Research Company, the predecessor of Fidelity Investments, to serve as an investment advisor to the Fidelity Fund. He also established the Puritan Fund, the first income-oriented fund to invest in common stock.

In an era when investment management was dedicated to preserving capital, Johnson's objective was to make money. And make money he did. His strategy was not to buy blue chip stocks but to buy stocks with growth potential.

Johnson believed that the management of a mutual fund should rely on one person's instincts and knowledge instead of on management by committee. He was the first to put an individual in charge of a fund. One of Johnson's earliest, and most successful, fund managers was Gerry Tsai, a young, inexperienced immigrant from Shanghai whom Johnson hired as a stock analyst in the early 1950s. Tsai began running the Fidelity Capital Fund in 1957, buying speculative stocks like Polaroid and Xerox. His performance gained him fame and customers, and in less than ten years he was managing more than $1 billion. Tsai left Fidelity in 1965, when Johnson reportedly told him that he planned to turn the company over to his son.

Edward C. Johnson III (Ned) graduated from Harvard in 1954, served in the army for two years, and worked at a bank before joining his father's company in 1957. Between 1961, when he became manager of the newly established Trend Fund, and 1965, the Trend Fund ranked first among growth funds.

The 1960s were a decade of growth for the American economy and for Fidelity. In 1962 the company established the Magellan Fund, which eventually became the largest mutual fund in the world. The firm also launched FMR Investment Management Service Inc., in 1964, for corporate pension plans; the Fidelity Keogh Plan, a retirement plan for self-employed individuals, in 1967; and, to attract foreign investments, established Fidelity International the following year in Bermuda. In addition, it formed Fidelity Service Company in 1969 to service customer accounts in-house, one of the first fund groups to do so.

Ned Johnson succeeded his father as president of Fidelity Investments in 1972, around the time that the market began to take a turn for the worse and investors began to abandon stocks and equity funds and return to the security of savings accounts. That same year the Johnsons formed FMR Corporation to provide corporate-administration services to other Fidelity companies.

During Johnson's first two years as president of Fidelity Investments the financial market was virtually dormant, and assets shrank by more than 30%, to $3 billion in 1974. Ned Johnson needed a way to reverse the firm's course. He found it in the money market fund. These new funds used investors' deposits to make very-short-term loans. Because the principal is never really at risk and only the interest fluctuates, money market funds turned out to be a great investment, but Johnson knew that unless the new funds offered the same liquidity and service as savings accounts, they would never be truly competitive. Consequently, in 1974 he established Fidelity Daily Income Trust (FIDIT), the first money market fund to offer check writing, a revolutionary—and instantly successful—idea.

While his father had remained devoted to mutual funds, Ned Johnson explored new aspects of the business. In 1973 Johnson began to integrate the company vertically by taking over back-office account-processing functions from banks that handled the job for most mutual funds. He also turned to direct sales, rather than sales through brokers, enabling Fidelity to cut costs. However, this also meant that at a time when Fidelity was low on cash due to a bad market, Fidelity was spending millions on computers, advertising, and telephones.

In the mid-1970s, the company created the Fidelity

Group Individual Retirement Account (IRA), as well as Fidelity Municipal Bond Fund, the first no-load, open-ended fund in the United States to invest in tax-free municipal bonds. In 1977, the year his father retired, Ned Johnson became chairman and CEO of Fidelity and Peter Lynch began managing the Magellan Fund, which now had assets totaling $22 million.

After the United States abolished fixed-rate brokerage commissions in 1975, Fidelity became the nation's first major financial institution to offer discount brokerage services when it formed Fidelity Brokerage Services Inc., in 1978. In 1979, Fidelity Institutional Services was formed to manage relationships with corporate clients.

Like the rest of the United States, Fidelity enjoyed the bull market during the 1980s, a decade of considerable growth for the firm; assets under management grew from $3 billion in 1974 to $13 billion in 1981. Between 1980 and 1983, Fidelity launched several new products: the Tax-Exempt Money Market Trust, the nation's first no-load, tax-free money market fund; Fidelity Money Line, to provide electronic fund-transfer services nationwide; the Ultra Service Account, the only asset-management account offered by a mutual fund organization; and sector funds, which featured separate portfolios specializing in specific industries.

The firm also spun off several subsidiary companies, each run by a president who ultimately reports to Johnson. They include Fidelity Systems Company; Fidelity Management Trust Company; Fidelity Marketing Company; Fidelity National Financial, one of only three publicly owned title insurers in the United States; and Fidelity Investments Southwest, a remote-operations center in Dallas, Texas that is part of a state-of-the-art telephone network. After introducing telephone switching, a service which allowed customers to change funds over the telephone, the company opened another remote-operations center, in 1986, in Salt Lake City, Utah.

The firm also unveiled same-day trading of its 31 Select Portfolio funds, which enabled investors to get quotes on an hourly basis, and redeem or purchase shares between 10 A.M. and 4 P.M., rather than waiting until after 4 P.M. to get a fund's closing net asset value. By 1986, Fidelity had 2,800 employees, 104 mutual funds, $50 billion in assets under management, and more than two million customers—400,000 of them in the $4 billion Magellan Fund. Between 1977, when Peter Lynch first took over Magellan, and 1987, the fund's shares had grown by more than 2,000%, outperforming all other mutual funds and making Lynch the industry's most successful fund manager.

Because Lynch did not invest heavily in conservative stocks and kept very little liquid capital, the Magellan Fund was hard hit by the crash that shook Wall Street on October 19, 1987. Fidelity, caught off guard, was forced to sell shares heavily in a plummeting market to meet redemptions. On that day alone, it sold nearly $1 billion worth of stock. By the end of the week, Fidelity's assets had dropped from $85 to $77 billion. Still, almost all of the firm's equity funds beat the market on Black Monday. In 1988, the year following the crash, Fidelity's revenues were down a quarter and profits were 70% lower.

Although Johnson would prefer to keep Fidelity private, many analysts believe it will eventually go public. Meanwhile, Johnson concentrates on long-term success and strengthening Fidelity's discount brokerage operation —already one of the nation's top three—in an attempt to lure small investors back to the market. Fidelity closed four offices after the crash, but it also opened three new ones and plans to add five to ten annually and to acquire smaller discount brokers. Determined never to suffer another Black Monday, Johnson has also cut personnel by almost a third, from a pre-crash high of 8,100. And Fidelity is sharpening its international presence and beginning to enter the lucrative insurance field. In 1989, with more than $80 billion in assets under management, the firm had more than 9% of the entire mutual fund industry. Not bad for a family that started only 46 years before with one $3 million mutual fund.

Principal Subsidiaries: FMR Corp.; Fidelity Management & Research Company; Fidelity Management Trust Company; Fidelity Investments Institutional Operations Company; Fidelity Investments Institutional Services Company, Inc.; Fidelity Investments Retail Services Company; Fidelity Investor Information Services Company; Fidelity Service Co.; Fidelity Brokerage Services, Inc.; Fidelity Investor Centers; National Financial Institutional Services Company; National Financial Services Corporation; Fidelity Information Services Company; Fidelity Software Development Company; Fidelity Telecommunications; Boston Coach Corp.; Fidelity Investments Life Insurance Company; Fidelity Investments Southwest Company; Fidelity Properties, Inc.; Fidelity Publishing Group; Fidelity Security Services, Inc.; Fidelity Ventures Associates, Inc.; Graphiks Gallery, Inc.; J. Robert Scott, Inc.; TeleSearch, Inc.; Fidelity Institutional Retirement Services Company.

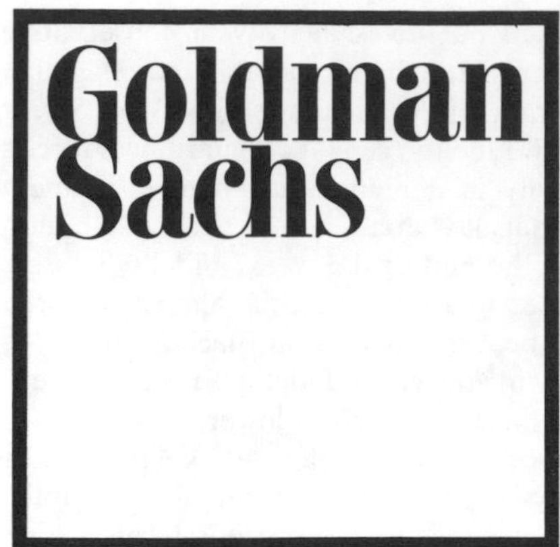

GOLDMAN, SACHS & CO.

85 Broad Street
New York, New York 10004
U.S.A.
(212) 902–1000

Private Company
Established: 1885
Employees: 6,800
Assets: $51.3 billion

Goldman, Sachs has been a respected player in world finance for more than 100 years. Something of a cautious follower in an age of daring leveraged buy-outs and corporate raids, Goldman, Sachs is nevertheless one of the world's leading brokerage and securities businesses. What Goldman lacks in bravado and innovation, it makes up for in prudence and surety.

The company was founded by Marcus Goldman, a Bavarian school teacher who emigrated to the United States in 1848. After supporting himself for some years as a salesman in New Jersey, Goldman moved to Philadelphia, where he operated a small clothing store. After the Civil War he moved to New York City, where he began trading in promissory notes. In the morning, Goldman would purchase securities from jewelers on Maiden Lane, in lower Manhattan, and from leather merchants in an area of the city called "the swamp." Then, in the afternoon, Goldman visited commercial banks, where he sold the notes at a small profit.

Goldman's son-in-law, Samuel Sachs, joined the business in 1882. The firm expanded into a general partnership in 1885 as Goldman, Sachs & Company when Goldman's son Henry and son-in-law Ludwig Dreyfus joined the group.

Henry Goldman led the firm in new directions by soliciting business from a broader range of interests located in Providence, Hartford, Boston, and Philadelphia. In 1887, Goldman, Sachs began a relationship with the British merchant bank Kleinwort Sons, which provided an entrée into international commercial finance, foreign-exchange services, and currency arbitrage.

On the strength of this growing exposure, Goldman, Sachs won business from several midwestern companies, including Sears Roebuck, Cluett Peabody, and Rice-Stix Dry Goods. With the establishment of Goldman, Sachs offices in St. Louis and Chicago, Henry Goldman became responsible for the firm's domestic expansion.

Railroads—indispensable to the opening of the American West—were the preferred investment of Eastern financiers at this time. But Goldman, Sachs, committed to a diversified portfolio, saw great potential in a number of other developing industries. At first difficult to market, these investments became profitable ventures only after Goldman, Sachs persuaded companies to adopt stricter accounting and audit procedures.

In 1896, soon after Samuel Sachs's brother Harry joined the company, Goldman, Sachs joined the New York Stock Exchange. With Harry Sachs in the company and with the New York operations firmly under control, Samuel Sachs took special responsibility for Goldman, Sachs's overseas expansion. Through Kleinwort, he gained important new contacts within the British and European banking establishments.

In 1906, one of the firm's clients, United Cigar Manufacturers, announced its intention to expand. Goldman, Sachs, which had previously provided the company with short-term financing to maintain inventories, advised United Cigar that its capital requirements could best be met by selling shares to the public. Although Goldman, Sachs, had never before managed a share offering, it succeeded in marketing $4.5 million worth of United Cigar stock; within one year United Cigar qualified for trading on the New York Stock Exchange.

On the strength of this success, Goldman, Sachs next comanaged Sears Roebuck's initial public offering that same year. Henry Goldman was subsequently invited to join the boards of directors of both United Cigar and Sears. The practice of maintaining a Goldman partner on the boards of major clients became a tradition which continues today.

During the 1910s, a time of feverish industrial activity, Goldman, Sachs instituted a number of innovative financial practices which today are common, including share buy-back and retirement options. The firm managed public offerings for a number of small companies which, in part due to Goldman, Sachs's activities, later grew into large corporations. Some of the firm's clients at this time included May Department Stores, F.W. Woolworth, Continental Can, B.F. Goodrich, and Merck.

Henry Goldman retired in 1917 and shortly afterward Samuel and Harry Sachs became limited partners. The company was still a family business, and a third generation consisting of Arthur, Henry E., and Howard J. Sachs were promoted to directorships.

World War I depressed financial activity until 1919. In its aftermath, however, came a strong economic expansion. Built primarily on large war-related capital investments, the expansion led many of the firm's clients—H.J. Heinz, Pillsbury, and General Foods among them—to return to Goldman, Sachs for additional financing.

The expansion continued well into the 1920s and created great demand for investment services. Goldman, Sachs, eager to take advantage of this new and promising market, formed an investment subsidiary called the Goldman Sachs Trading Corporation. The new company expanded rapidly. But in the fall of 1929, Goldman Sachs Trading, like many other companies, fell victim to a crisis of confidence which forced the stock market into a devastating crash. By 1933 the investment subsidiary was worth only a fraction of its initial $10 million capitalization.

The company's recovery from the Depression was slow, but by the mid-1930s, the commercial-paper and securities businesses again were highly profitable. During this period Sidney J. Weinberg, an "outsider" in the family business, assumed a leading position within the firm.

Starting out in 1907 as a porter's assistant making $2 per week, Weinberg rose quickly at Goldman, Sachs. In 1927, at the age of 35, Weinberg became only the second outsider to be made a partner. Weinberg was known for his diligence and for his attention to detail.

In the aftermath of the 1929 stock market crash, Congress passed the Securities Act of 1933. This act created the Securities and Exchange Commission, which required that every investment be accompanied by a detailed prospectus, often containing confusing small-print passages. As a conservative and practical securities dealer, Goldman, Sachs worked to reduce investor confusion by providing concise information in common language.

Goldman, Sachs also began a securities-arbitrage business in the 1930s under the direction of Edgar Baruch and, later, Gustave Levy. Meanwhile, the firm continued to expand by taking over other commercial-paper firms in New York, Boston, Chicago, and St. Louis. The firm subsequently engaged in a broad variety of investment activities, including new domestic and international share offerings, private securities sales, corporate mergers and acquisitions, real estate financing and sales, municipal finance, investment research, block trading, equity and fixed-rate investment portfolios, and options trading.

During World War II, Sidney Weinberg was placed on leave to serve on the government's War Production Board. With virtually all American industry under special government supervision, many of Goldman, Sachs's activities were supplanted by government agencies; investment capital was raised through instruments such as war bonds, which were sold to individuals.

Goldman, Sachs did not fully regain its prewar momentum until several years after the war ended. During that time, however, American industry and the economy in general experienced unprecedented growth. Intimately involved in this economic expansion, Goldman, Sachs recruited hundreds of new employees from leading business schools and launched many new activities in finance and investment.

Sidney Weinberg was called into government service again during the Korean War, serving with the Office of Defense Mobilization. His absence, in part, precipitated the creation of a management committee, intended to decentralize the decision-making process. Gus Levy, who later became president of the New York Stock Exchange, was its first chairman.

Goldman, Sachs's most important management of a new share issue occurred in November, 1956, when shares of the Ford Motor Company were sold to the public for the first time. As co-manager, Goldman, Sachs helped market 10.2 million shares, worth $700 million. The firm set another record in October, 1967, when it handled the floor trade of a single block of Alcan Aluminum stock consisting of 1.15 million shares, worth $26.5 million, at the time the largest block trade ever made.

Sidney Weinberg died in November, 1969 and was succeeded as senior partner by Gus Levy. Goldman, Sachs began to attain its current position as a highly influential financial institution during the 1960s, but that position was solidified during the 1970s, as commodities such as oil grew to dominate the economy. Large new investments in domestic petroleum projects placed the company at a critical juncture; to some degree it was able to determine the complexion of the industry by channeling investment funds. Goldman, Sachs's expertise in this area resulted in its management of several large energy-industry share offerings.

John L. Weinberg and John Whitehead were promoted to senior partners upon the death of Gus Levy in 1976. Some years later, Whitehead left the firm to become assistant secretary of state in the Reagan administration and Weinberg became chief partner and chairman of the management committee.

Goldman, Sachs diversified late in 1981 by absorbing the commodities-trading firm of J. Aron & Company, which dealt mainly in precious metals, coffee, and foreign exchange. In May, 1982, the firm took over the London-based merchant bank First Dallas, Ltd., which it later renamed Goldman, Sachs, Ltd.

Beginning in 1984, however, a new craze erupted on Wall Street in which investment companies engineered leveraged buyouts (LBOs) of entire firms. These buy-outs were financed with junk bond debt, which was paid off with operating profits from the purchased firm or from the piecemeal break-up and sale of the firm's assets. At the time, the practice could be highly profitable for firms willing to assume the associated risks.

Goldman, Sachs, however, preferred to stress its transaction work rather than to undertake higher-risk LBOs. But the market crash of October, 1987 reduced the profitability of transaction work. In addition, Goldman, Sachs began to lose clients to more aggressive investment firms.

In early 1989, Goldman, Sachs elected to expand its merchant-banking activities by forming an eight-bank consortium, with Citibank and the Sumitomo Bank, called BroadPark. Goldman, Sachs had begun its relationship with the Sumitomo Bank in 1986, when the bank purchased a 12.5% share of Goldman, Sachs. While entitled to 12.5% of Goldman, Sachs's profits, Sumitomo is prevented by federal law from having any representation within the partnership.

Through BroadPark and other subsidiaries engaged in bridge loans and LBOs, Goldman, Sachs has been transformed into a holding company which, technically, is not subject to the capital requirements of the New York Stock Exchange. While these subsidiaries have bolstered the company's profits, they have also been noted with caution by independent bond-rating agencies such as Moody's and Standard & Poors. Nonetheless, the firm continues to be the leader in its industry.

Principal Subsidiaries: Goldman Sachs International Limited (U.K.); Goldman Sachs (Japan) Corp.; Goldman Sachs (Asia) Limited (Hong Kong); Goldman Sachs (Singapore) Pte. Ltd.; Goldman Sachs (Australia) Limited; Goldman Sachs Canada; Goldman Sachs Finanz A.G. (Switzerland); Goldman Sachs Money Markets Inc.

HOUSEHOLD
INTERNATIONAL

HOUSEHOLD INTERNATIONAL, INC.

2700 Sanders Road
Prospect Heights, Illinois 60070
U.S.A.
(708) 564–3663

Public Company
Incorporated: 1925 as Household Finance Corporation
Employees: 12,000
Assets: $21 billion
Stock Index: New York Midwest

Household International is the oldest, as well as one of the largest, consumer finance companies in the world. It was founded in Minneapolis in 1878 by Frank Mackey. The company has grown almost continuously since its inception and has at the same time led the way in educating consumers about an industry that has frequently been misunderstood and mistrusted. Household has also been an innovator in loan industry operations, from initiating direct-mail advertising to drafting important industry regulations.

Frank Mackey was a man with ambitious business interests in several fields, from selling safes to investing in the mining industry. He moved to Minneapolis in 1878, a time when the town was expanding from a large farming village into a hub for distant logging and farming territories. Its booming population was fertile ground for Mackey's small personal loan venture. He made small loans of $10 to $200 to families for the purchase of household items, farming equipment, emergency medical fees, or anything else that they were temporarily unable to pay for.

Mackey's father died in 1879, leaving him a substantial amount of money. This, along with loans from several uncles, enabled Mackey to keep up with the blossoming demand for his company's loans.

In 1883 Mackey constructed a building in Minneapolis to house his prospering business and opened his first branch office, in St. Paul. He also hired a manager named Thomas Hulbert. An aggressive salesman, Hulbert oversaw the company's expansion, largely through advertising. This was one of the first methods the loan company used to set it self apart from its competitors.

As the company rapidly expanded, Mackey assumed decreasing responsibility for daily operations. He provided capital for expansion, but spent his time overseeing his other businesses, such as precious metals mines and real estate ventures. Despite limited personal contact with his high-level managers, Mackey kept their loyalty through their participation in a profit sharing plan.

Mackey soon appointed Hulbert general manager. Hulbert's first major responsibility was to move the company's headquarters to Chicago. He moved in September 1885 and from there directed the rapid opening of more branch offices. By 1890 he had opened 13 branches in the Midwest and the East, and additional offices had sprouted in Chicago.

The loan business, neither a bank nor a savings and loan, was one of a handful of such firms in the country during the late 19th century. Loans were approved on a case-by-case basis, and were payable in full after three months. For a fee, Mackey offered extensions to those he believed were in genuine need. One of Mackey's first employees, R. L. Read, proposed an "Extension Plan" whereby loans were made for one month only and renewed at the same extension rates that the three month loans had been. Under this plan, fees were collected after the principle had been paid off, and actual fees paid often accumulated beyond a borrower's original understanding, to the distress of many customers. Nonetheless, demand for loans was so high that the company was able to operate in this way past the turn of the century.

Although Hulbert was a strong proponent of this existing monthly extension plan, some branch managers argued in favor of an installment plan. Michael Drennen, manager of the Pittsburgh office, quietly initiated such a plan without Hulbert's consent. His plan included a rebate bonus for early repayment of the loan, correctly anticipating a positive response to such a public relations move. Hulbert was gradually convinced of the merits of the installment system, and all branches were using it by 1905.

In 1896 a second Pittsburgh branch began another significant innovation—soliciting customers for new loans by mail. Solicitation letters were an instant success, and other Mackey branches quickly adopted the approach.

By the turn of the century the demand for non-bank loans had created a burgeoning national industry. As public awareness of the industry grew, so did the number of reports of exorbitant interest rates and heavy-handed collection methods by some less scrupulous lenders. Government efforts to control loan sharks often did more harm than good by making it impossible for legitimate lenders to stay in business. Indeed, in observing the events from 1900 to 1910—the company's loan account decreased between 1900 and 1907; Hulbert retired in 1907, as did his successor a year later; and a number of branches were forced to close—Mackey himself was ready to retire from the field. It took convincing from a handful of his managers that the business could survive, and more importantly, arguments from his attorney that the industry was no less than vital to the economy, to keep Mackey from closing shop.

Mackey agreed to stay in business, but provided little more than emotional support during the crucial phase that followed. The key players were Frank Hubachek, Mackey's counsel; Leslie Harbison, district manager of western branches; and Fred Huettmann, a manager who had opened many new branches in the East. These men recognized both the need for the industry and the reality that without cooperation between it, the government, and the public, the industry would quickly disintegrate. They decided it would be a public relations boost for Mackey's company to lead the way in cleaning up the loan business.

Arthur Ham, a Columbia University graduate student, was given a grant by the Russell Sage Foundation in 1907 to research the small-loan industry. Ham found that there was an enormous demand for small loans; that existing companies couldn't supply this demand; and that most families who needed loans had no way of meeting credit demands for bank loans. He also suggested that while legitimate loan businesses could operate profitably at lower rates than they currently charged, excessive restrictions could put them out of business. By 1913, 25 states had adopted loan legislation limiting interest rates to 6%.

When Pennsylvania passed such an act in 1913, Hubachek challenged the legislation, which failed to say exactly which loans were subject to it, as unconstitutional and won. A similar law that he wrote, void of the questionable sections of Ham's law, was upheld by the Pennsylvania Supreme Court. Thereafter Harbison, Hubachek, and Huettmann worked with Ham directly, along with a handful of others, under the name of the American Association of Small Loan Brokers, to agree upon a set of industry regulations.

The Uniform Small Loan Law was passed in 1916. This law allowed lenders to charge an interest rate of no more than 3.5% per month. The law enhanced the public image of the industry and helped the growth of legitimate loan businesses through World War I. For their part, Harbison and Hubachek began to develop reputations as champions of consumers' concerns.

In 1918, several branches of the Mackey system were banded into Peoples Finance Company, which incorporated as Household Finance Corporation (HFC) in September, 1925. By this time Mackey spent his time almost exclusively in Europe, so Leslie Harbison was the logical choice to become president, a post he held until he died in 1933.

Thomas Hulbert had been an aggressive, expansion-minded manager who at times was blinded to the future by short-term goals. Harbison was equally interested in the growth of Household, but he envisioned this expansion as the natural by-product of customers' satisfaction with the company's activities and style of operation. His eight year term began a growth trend for Household that has hardly skipped a beat since. In 1925 HFC paid a quarterly dividend on its common stock, and it has paid dividends every quarter since. On Harbison's recommendation, Household was the first loan company to offer an interest rate below the legal limit, dropping its monthly rate to 2.5% in 1928. Harbison decided that the increased volume of business would offset decreased revenue per loan and that decreasing the charge would help the industry by staving off more repressive legislation. To capitalize such a substantial reduction in rates, HFC offered 140,000 shares of preferred stock, making it the first loan company to be publicly held. Competitors were not happy with this HFC initiative, but the public expressed its confidence in the company by buying up the entire stock offer almost immediately. The company's preferred stock was granted listing on the New York Stock Exchange in 1928, and its common stock was listed in New York in 1936. In 1929 Household acquired its first subsidiaries, absorbing three smaller lending firms, and with the 1933 acquisition of Central Finance Corporation of Canada—the first chartered loan company in that country—Household entered the international business arena.

The late 1920s was a time of growth for HFC: its loan account was about $6 million in 1925, and $15 million in 1928, then more than doubled to $33 million in 1929. Net earnings rose nearly 50% in 1929 alone. But from 1930 through World War II, HFC toiled to sustain its reputation as sensitive to customers' interests. A handful of lawsuits and government threats to reduce the legal lending rates even further than HFC had done on its own made this a difficult task.

Harbison started a public relations department in 1930, and in 1932 established a separate Department of Consumer Education, which published several pamphlets for customers. The first was "Money Management for Households," in April, 1931. The booklet outlined sample budgets, and presented well-known but not always well-understood information in a clearly written and organized form. Not only was consumer response positive, but the government praised Household for its initiative. *The New York Times* even ran an editorial applauding the booklet.

Despite all of Household's good-will work, the depression had predictably negative effects on the company and the loan industry in general. HFC's loan account dropped 22% between 1931 and 1933, losses and delinquencies ballooned, and the ratio of people who qualified for loans dropped from 70 out of a hundred to 30. The company narrowly averted disaster in 1931 when the banks that had regularly extended credit to HFC became wary of economic conditions and skeptical about the future of the loan business, and froze HFC's credit. Household had to stop making loans for four months during the busiest season of the year—Christmas—so that cash receipts could accumulate sufficiently to pay back the banks. The credit freeze was lifted by June, 1932, and HFC quickly returned to its pattern of growth despite lingering questions about the health of the economy.

Byrd Henderson became president upon Harbison's death in December, 1933. Harbison's stamp on the company had been to educate consumers; Henderson vigorously continued this practice, but he saw it purely as a method to increase business. He directed a period of phenomenal growth for HFC that continued after his retirement in 1951. Despite stringent credit controls and economic rationing by President Franklin Roosevelt, HFC's loan account grew steadily during World War II, then exploded at its end.

Henderson's tactics were aggressive and straightforward. He encouraged many more consumer education publications; he held frequent manager-level meetings to discuss company operations openly; and he instituted an aggressive advertising campaign that included dramatized radio spots, increased direct mailings, and as many solicitations of employers as of consumers.

Many commercial banks entered the personal loan business in 1934. Even though they frequently charged higher rates than HFC and other loan companies, banks had the vital trust of the public. Consequently, loan accounts for banks were 40% higher than that of loan companies by 1946. Nonetheless, Henderson recognized that the increased competition was healthy for the industry, as it created more borrowers.

The war years were difficult ones for the company, primarily because of government regulations restricting consumer credit in order to direct money toward the war effort. Household made the best of the situation, and benefited in the end from the innovations that wartime shortages made necessary: offices learned to run with fewer people and developed more efficient ways to investigate loan prospects.

It was a difficult time for other reasons, too, though. In 1943 several borrowers in New York, claiming ambiguities in loan contracts such that borrowers were not fully aware of their obligations, sued Household and won. But when one couple expanded the scope of this decision and sued Household for all loan payments received in New York during the previous three years, the judge summarily dismissed the case, although he did warn HFC and other loan companies to show restraint in their collection of laggard loan payments, as some companies had begun to practice strongarm collection tactics.

Henderson's successor, Harold MacDonald, was hired as executive vice president in 1948. The first outsider to be hired to direct Household, MacDonald's experience was in standardized chain store methods. Under Henderson, HFC had grown at breakneck speed; under MacDonald, the goal was to centralize control to ensure uniformity of operations and increase efficiency.

MacDonald began the practice of annual meetings at which branch managers were encouraged to suggest changes in operations. At the first conference in 1951, he held daily meetings for a month, tirelessly asking managers from across the country what they saw as company strengths and weaknesses. The result was the "Uniform Operations Manual," which was distributed to all 573 offices. It provided concise directions on all manner of relations with customers and employees and even set guidelines for office layout and organization. He also instituted an employee-training program, the core of which is still in use today.

A second long-lasting company trend MacDonald initiated was diversifying into businesses outside the loan industry. In 1958 HFC began offering credit life insurance to customers, and also created Household Flight Credit Corporation in conjunction with United Airlines. Education Funds, Inc. was created in 1960 to offer help in paying college tuitions.

Household's first major acquisition, in 1961, was Coast-to-Coast Stores, a company that supplies professional services to franchises nationwide. Many other companies were added, eventually becoming the merchandising group: Badger Paint and Hardware Stores, of Milwaukee, was incorporated into Coast-to-Coast in 1963; City Products Corporation, a merchandising conglomerate comprised of furniture and department store chains, in 1965; White Stores, a hard-goods store chain in the southwestern states, in 1966; and Von's Grocery Company, a supermarket chain in southern California, in 1969. With the acquisition of Von's, the merchandising division's net sales exceeded $1 billion for the first time in 1969.

Under Arthur Rasmussen, who became president in 1967, HFC entered the manufacturing field in 1968 with the acquisition of King-Seeley Thermos, a producer of camping and outdoor recreation equipment. In 1969 Household added National Car Rental, the third-largest automobile rental company in the United States, to its purchases.

In 1970, a data-processing system called Orbit was installed at all U.S. branch offices. This network, attached to a main computer at HFC headquarters, saved the corporation money by reducing clerical and related tasks that previously had been done separately at each branch. Orbit became a profitable venture for Household when the company signed a five-year contract in May 1981 to provide services to the General Finance Corporation. Orbit computer services were tailored and marketed to other consumer finance companies throughout the 1970s; again, innovation at HFC led to an industry trend.

Gilbert Ellis became HFC's fifth president in 1972, and he promptly signed a joint venture agreement with J.P. Morgan & Company, a finance company that had long served wealthy individuals and large corporations. The companies formed a jointly owned bank to provide retail banking as well as consumer finance services. This was HFC's first office in England.

In March, 1972 HFC signed a consent agreement with the Justice Department in answer to the agency's charges of employment and lending discrimination. Though HFC never admitted to the accusations of bias, the agreement set guidelines for equal opportunity lending to blacks, Hispanics and American Indians, and for equal opportunity hiring and promoting of women and nonwhite employees. A Household spokesmen told *The Wall Street Journal* that the order was a ". . .continued implementation of longstanding company policy." But the Justice Department's charges, which included the first by the government to charge lending discrimination and the first to win back pay in a case of sex discrimination blemished HFC's public image.

During the mid-1970s it became clear that HFC's diversification outside the loan business had been a strong move. Unforeseen rises in interest rates and the expanding involvement of banks and credit unions in the personal loan industry restricted opportunity for growth in the finance division. HFC's average interest costs rose more than 30% between 1972 and 1974, and this growth in rates was necessarily passed on to borrowers. With widespread uncertainty about whether federal interest rates would ever return to their previous position, and with HFC's large surplus of capital on hand, the challenge of CEO Ellis was to find profitable non-lending financial services while continuing to expand in manufacturing and merchandising.

Ellis's solution was to expand the company's offerings to include personal and commercial banking services. In 1976 HFC acquired Keystone Savings and Loan in California and several commercial banks in Colorado. HFC also began to offer real estate–secured loans.

In 1977 Donald Clark became president. Clark continued to concentrate on HFC's finance operations. He created HFC Leasing, a subsidiary that offered leveraged leasing services, and consolidated all insurance services under the Alexander Hamilton Life Insurance Company, which had been acquired in 1977. Clark also expanded international operations, increasing HFC's Canadian portfolio and opening lending offices in Japan in 1978 and in Australia in 1979. He then restructured the loan business, focusing in areas that were less directly affected by fluctuating interest rates. HFC pursued loans of larger average sizes and in more deregulated areas, and also made a substantial cutback in operating expenses.

In 1977 a New York Supreme Court judge charged that Household unethically solicited former, unpaid borrowers who had since been declared bankrupt. As with the discrimination lawsuit in 1972, HFC denied that it had broken any laws, but agreed to a consent order to restrict its contact with bankrupt former customers. The order stated that if a borrower was given a new loan with a proviso that he must first pay off the unpaid amount of his old loan, HFC had to provide the customer with a statement of his legal rights and a ten-day grace period during which he could cancel the new loan.

In 1979 Household purchased $600 million of accounts receivable from the ailing Chrysler Financial Corporation. It was the largest single transaction HFC had ever made, and although the company had never entered a similar agreement, Household's size and surplus capital made it an attractive deal to both sides. HFC also purchased a 56% share in Wien Air Alaska in 1979; the airline became a wholly owned subsidiary in 1980.

HFC's operations were restructured in 1981 under a holding company named Household International. The merchandising division's sales had topped $4 billion in 1980, and finance's receivables exceeded $4 billion in 1981. Manufacturing operations were nearly tripled in 1981 with the acquisition of Wallace Murray Corporation, a *Fortune* 500 maker of truck engine parts, metal-cutting tools, and plumbing fixtures.

Household continued to expand, acquiring Valley National Bank, of Salinas, California, in 1981, Fidelity Federal Savings and Loan, of Baltimore, Maryland in 1984, and American Heritage Savings, of Bloomingdale, Illinois, in 1984. Meanwhile, however, the company sold several unprofitable merchandising units—White Stores was sold in 1981, and the furniture operations were sold as a unit in 1984.

The latter transactions marked the beginning of an almost drastic turnaround for Household. Its 25-year trend of diversification into other businesses became a new pattern of large-scale divestiture in 1985, when all remaining merchandising units were sold.

Household International also restructured its finance businesses in 1985 by forming Household Commercial Financial Services, consisting of four divisions: capital equipment and property financing; specialty products and services; real estate services; and business equipment financing and services. Household was further trimmed with the 1986 sale of National Car Rental.

The capital raised from these large divestitures was used to strengthen Household's foothold in its two remaining divisions. Between 1985 and 1988 manufacturing acquired the following companies: J.P. Heilwell Industries, of Philadelphia, producer of food service equipment; Lern, Inc., of Schiller Park, Illinois, a producer of commercial refrigeration products; 45% of Booth, Inc., of Dallas, a manufacturer of soft drink dispensers; GlasTec, a producer of bathroom showers and other water equipment, located in Middlebury, Indiana; and Omni Products International, of Fairfield, New Jersey, a producer of leisure furniture. During the same period the Finance division made even more purchases: BGC Finance, a consumer finance company in Australia; Fidelity Savings and Loan Company, of Martins Ferry, Ohio; Brighton Federal Savings and Loan Association in Brighton, Colorado; Century Savings Association of Kansas, in Roeland Park, Kansas; Avco National Bank, a subsidiary of Textron; TSO Financial Corporation, of Horsham, Pennsylvania; the credit card portfolios of Beverly Hills Savings, of Mission Viejo, California, and Great American First Savings Bank of San Diego; and thirteen branches of Diamond Savings & Loan, in Columbus, Ohio.

In January, 1989, Household culminated a return to its core Finance business with the announcement that it would sell or spin off all units in its manufacturing division. Eventually three spinoffs were created as independent companies in which Household International shareholders received common stock. These companies are Eljer Industries, a producer of building products; Schwitzer, a manufacturer of diesel and gasoline performance-enhancing components; and Scotsman Industries, a producer of commercial refrigeration machines and equipment.

Edwin Hoffman, Household International's new president, has ambitious plans for the remaining financial services businesses. Given that Household's strength has always been its financial services, the company's decision to focus all of its energy there bodes well for the future.

Principal Subsidiaries: Household Finance Corp.; Household International (U.K.) Limited; Household Bank, f.s.b.; Household Bank, N.A.; Alexander Hamilton Life Insurance Company of America; Household Retail Services, Inc.; HFC Financial Services, Ltd. (Australia); Household Finance Corp. of Canada/Household Trust Company; HFC Trust and Cavings Ltd./Hamilton Insurance Companies (U.K.); Household Commercial Financial Services, Inc.

Further Reading: Kogan, Herman. *Lending Is Our Business: The Story of Household Finance Corporation*, Chicago, Lakeside Press, 1965.

Kleinwort Benson Group plc

KLEINWORT BENSON GROUP PLC

20 Fenchurch Street
London EC3P 3DB
United Kingdom
(01) 623-8000

Public Company
Incorporated: 1961
Employees: 3,250
Assets: £9.57 billion (US$17.31 billion)
Stock Index: London

During their golden age, there was an air of exoticism and romance surrounding British merchant bankers. Many were foreign merchants who had moved to London to escape the turmoil of the Napoleonic wars, and their fraternity had a distinctly international quality. In time, they diversified into banking and loaned money overseas, providing capital for the expansion of the British Empire. As their descendents assimilated into British society, their banks became decidedly British institutions. But the increasing integration of the world's financial communities over the last 20 years has forced Kleinwort Benson, one of Britain's largest merchant banks, to regain something of the industry's old international flavor by building a network of diverse financial enterprises that stretches from London to New York to Tokyo.

Kleinwort Benson was formed in 1961 when the firm of Kleinwort, Sons & Company merged with Robert Benson, Lonsdale & Company Limited. Both houses were British merchant banks of long standing. Kleinwort could trace its roots to 1838, when a Hamburg shipping clerk named Alexander Kleinwort emigrated to Cuba and joined a Havana trading company run by James Drake. Kleinwort relocated to London in 1855. He quickly became the dominant partner, and by 1883 he and his sons were in sole control of the company and had given it their family name. Kleinwort also shifted its focus from trade to merchant banking during these years.

World War I caused trouble for British merchant banks by disrupting foreign trade, and Kleinwort, which relied considerably on business in Germany, was among the hardest hit. Nonetheless, the firm suffered no permanent damage from the war, and even had slightly more capital in 1918 than it did in 1913. But the merchant banks' traditional business of raising money for foreign ventures never fully recovered after the armistice, due to informal restrictions on foreign trade and increased competition from banks in New York and other up-and-coming financial centers.

In response, Kleinwort joined the industry-wide trend toward raising money for domestic industry in the 1920s. It did so under the guidance of Herman Andrae, Alexander Kleinwort's grand-nephew, who had become a partner in 1907 and whose influence in the firm waxed as that of his aging uncles waned. Kleinwort took on more domestic underwriting business than it had in the past, but it also embarked on unsuccessful forays into shipbuilding, cotton manufacturing, and fire insurance. In the first two cases, the firm found itself with unprofitable investments in failing companies that it was also forced to manage; in the third, it loaned money to insurance entrepreneur Clarence Hatry, only to lose all of it when Hatry was convicted of fraud in 1929. Kleinwort's profitable activities in precious metals and foreign currency trading during this decade helped offset these fiascos.

The Depression proved disastrous for many British merchant banks, slowing foreign trade to a virtual standstill. Even worse for Kleinwort, the German government declared a moratorium on the repayment of foreign loans in the wake of that nation's bank crisis of 1931. In response, foreign bankers with loans outstanding in Germany declared that they would grant no more credit to German interests. Because of its traditional reliance on trade with Germany, Kleinwort was hit harder than most of its competitors by the crisis. But at least Kleinwort survived the Depression, when other merchant banks folded or needed a handout from the Bank of England.

The German debt problem continued to dog Kleinwort after the outbreak of war in 1939. At the time, it had £4.4 million in German, Austrian, and Hungarian bills outstanding. It tried to recover its money through foreign courts, but without success. After 1945, the destruction of the German economy, the loss of prewar loan records, and the fact that Soviet Union did not want to see money repaid to Western bankers from its zone of occupation complicated the matter of settling the debts. In 1951, the West German government and the banks reached an accord whereby the banks would end the credit freeze and German companies would repay their debts, figured at a 4% annual rate from 1939 to 1953. By 1959, Kleinwort had recovered £2 million.

The Benson family came from the Lake District and were of Quaker stock. By the 1780s they had gone into business in Liverpool as cotton merchants. The firm moved to London in 1852 and gradually began to specialize in investment banking. By the end of the century, the Bensons had scored a major prestige coup by providing capital for the railroad construction boom in the American West. In 1948, Robert Benson & Company Limited merged with Lonsdale Investment Trust, whom it had served as bankers, to form Robert Benson Lonsdale.

In 1958, Robert Benson Lonsdale became embroiled in what became known as Britain's Great Aluminium War. The fracas started when Reynolds Metals, in cooperation with the relatively new British investment firm Tube Investments, made an unfriendly bid to take over British Aluminium, which was then considering a friendly offer from Alcoa. A syndicate of 14 old-line merchant banks, which was led by Hambros and Lazard Brothers and included Robert Benson Lonsdale, came to the aid of British Aluminium. But S. A. Warburg, another London banking house of long standing, sided with Reynolds, producing a bitter and divisive rupture in London's merchant-banking fraternity. Reynolds finally won, acquiring 80% of British Aluminium stock by early 1959. The Great Aluminium War altered merchant banking by turning mergers and acquisitions into a high-profile, high-profit business.

When Kleinwort and Robert Benson Lonsdale merged in 1961, *The Economist* described it as "a marriage of essentially complementary partners." Kleinwort had strong overseas connections thanks to its history of involvement in foreign trade, but was weak in corporate finance and investment banking. Robert Benson Lonsdale's strengths lay in corporate finance and underwriting, but it had done little business in more traditional areas of merchant banking. The resulting Kleinwort Benson Lonsdale held assets of £60 million. Its new-found size and strength stood it in good stead for the hectic times to come.

The 1960s and 1970s were years of fierce activity for merchant banks, marked by increased competition both from foreign firms and from domestic rivals spurred on by a 1971 Bank of England policy statement encouraging looser regulation of British financial institutions. As a result, merchant banks had to diversify and shuck their traditional specialist status. By 1977, Kleinwort Benson had become involved in unit and investment trusts, factoring, leasing, insurance brokering, venture capital, tax planning, executor and trustee services, property development, commodity dealing, and bullion brokering and dealing, among other services.

In 1965, Kleinwort Benson entered the oil and gas business when its subisidiary Kleinwort Benson Energy began drilling on the continental shelf. Two years later, Kleinwort Benson entered a consortium with 17 other partners, including Barclays and the Bank of Scotland, to form Airlease International, a company specializing in aircraft leasing. In 1986 it entered the domestic life insurance business by buying Transinternational Life from Transamerica Corporation and, even more importantly, prepared itself for the impending deregulation of the British financial markets known as the Big Bang by acquiring the securities brokerage Grieveson Grant.

Kleinwort Benson's 1984 annual report spoke of the firm forming a "global chain." In fact, its international expansion had actually been underway for over a decade. In 1967, it opened an investment bank in New York, using its strong reputation in the Eurobond market to get underwriting business. In 1970, it opened an office in Tokyo which, combined with its subsidiaries in Thailand and Hong Kong, gave it a stronger presence in Asia than any other British merchant bank.

In 1984, anticipating the new opportunities that the 1986 deregulation of the financial markets would bring and aware of the increasing interdependence of the world's financial markets, Kleinwort Benson redoubled its efforts, making several major acquisitions in the United States. In New York, it bought ACLI Government Securities Incorporated, a U.S. government securities dealer, from the investment bank Donaldson, Lufkin & Jenrette, renaming it Kleinwort Benson Government Securities (KBGS). The deal made Kleinwort Benson the first foreign bank to own a government securities firm that dealt directly with the Federal Reserve Bank of New York. In Chicago, it acquired the institutional and funds operations of Virginia Trading Corporation, a futures brokerage. And in Los Angeles, it purchased the services of a group of brokers specializing in interest-rate swaps and renamed it Kleinwort Benson Cross Financing. Also in that year Kleinwort Benson Australia acquired a 50% interest in Australia Gilt Company Group, a dealer in Australian government securities.

Some of these moves worked well; others didn't. Kleinwort Benson Cross Financing proved to be a consistent moneymaker, while KBGS disappointed its parent's expectations. Kleinwort Benson had made the acquisition in order to acquaint itself with price trends and auction techniques in the American treasuries market. But KBGS seldom participated in auctions, nor was its familiarity with the demand for treasury securities as strong as had been hoped. In 1988, Kleinwort Benson sold a 25% interest in KBGS to Fuji Bank. In addition, Kleinwort Benson's Australian banking and securities operations were sold to Security Pacific in October, 1989.

In 1986, *The Economist* called Kleinwort Benson the "great white hope of British merchant banking," stating that Kleinwort Benson and S. A. Warburg were the only British merchant banks poised to become world-class financial institutions. But as it turned out, the year of the Big Bang was not entirely kind to Kleinwort Benson. The worldwide slump in bond prices, a decrease in mergers and acquisitions activity in Britain, and problems with Kleinwort Benson's settlement system all hurt its financial performance and left it in need of capital. Before the year was out, the house had sold a 4.9% interest to American Can, which sold its shares to Morgan Stanley International several months later. Late in 1987, Kleinwort Benson sold a 1.5% stake to Sumitomo Life Insurance, and Consolidated Gold Fields bought a 50% interest in Kleinwort Benson Energy. In 1988, American International Group acquired a 5.3% interest in Kleinwort Benson.

Thanks to the integration of the world's financial markets, the American stock market crash of 1987 was felt around the world. Nonetheless, Kleinwort Benson survived the crisis in better shape than its competitors. It was one of the few British securities firms that made a profit on equities dealing in late 1987 and early 1988. It also disclosed in its 1987 annual report that its treasury division chalked up "record operating income" due to volatility in the dollar and interest rates.

But Kleinwort Benson did not fare as well in the second half of 1988. Its securities business lost more than £45 million, reducing the bank's overall pre-tax profits to £17.7 million that year as compared to £51.6 million in 1987. Thanks to this poor performance, its stock price neared a four-year low in the spring of 1989. But Kleinwort Benson remained committed to securities. Jonathan Agnew, who succeeded Michael Hawkes as chief executive of the Kleinwort Benson Group in 1989, staked the firm to the prospect of becoming an integrated investment bank based on the conviction that a strong securities business would help market the products generated by the bank's other activities. Such an attitude was not surprising, coming from a man who was elevated to chairman of Kleinwort Grieveson Securities in 1987, following the acquisition of Grieveson, Grant and Company, in an effort to give the former Grieveson Grant younger and more aggressive leadership.

Nonetheless, Kleinwort Benson's share of the British equities market remained at 5% in 1989, not enough to put it in the front ranks of Britain's securities firms. Corporate finance continued to account for a large share of its revenues and according to *The Economist*, it also had "the biggest banking book of any British merchant bank, with some £3 billion of loans outstanding."

With its place in the securities industry somewhat uncertain, the future of Agnew's vision of Kleinwort Benson as a fully integrated investment bank seems equally up in the air. But merchant bankers have always had to live with uncertainty. No matter what its future, Kleinwort Benson still deserves credit for its ambitious program of expansion and diversification in the 1970s and 1980s, which recalls the golden age of the British merchant banks. Back then, the influence of the merchant bankers extended to the far corners of the world as they provided the money that built the empire. Kleinwort Benson recognized early on that the future of merchant banking also lay over the seas. By 1989 it could boast of offices and subsidiaries in ten countries and four continents—a small empire of its own.

Principal Subsidiaries: Kleinwort Grieveson Securities Ltd.; Kleinwort Benson Securities Ltd.; Kleinwort Grieveson Charlesworth Ltd.; Kleinwort Benson International Ltd.; Kleinwort Benson International Inc.; Kleinwort Benson Industrial Finance Ltd.; Robert Benson Lonsdale & Company Ltd.; Fendrake Ltd.; Kleinwort Benson Development Capital Ltd.; Kleinwort Benson Investment Trust Ltd.; Kleinworth Grieveson Investment Management Ltd.; Kleinwort Barrington Ltd.; Kleinwort Benson International Investment Ltd.; Kleinwort Grieveson Financial Services Ltd.; Kleinwort Grieveson Insurance Brokers Ltd.; Kleinwort Benson Trustees Ltd.; Sharps Pixley Ltd.; J.S. Knight & Son Ltd.; Edward Day & Baker Ltd.; Vale & Weetman Ltd.; Harley Mullion & Company Ltd.; Renown Energy Ltd. (50%); Kleinwort Benson (Guernsey) Ltd.; Fenchurch Navigation Corporation (Hong Kong); Kleinwort Benson (Jersey) Ltd.; Kleinwort Benson (Europe) S.A. (Belgium); Banque Kleinwort Benson SA (Switzerland); Fitrust Fiduciaire et Trustee S.A. (Switzerland); Kleinwort Benson Inc. (United States); Kleinwort Benson U.S. Finance Inc.; Sharps Pixley Inc. (United States); Kleinwort Benson Government Securities Inc. (United States); Virginia Trading Corporation (United States); Kleinwort Benson Cross Financing Inc. (United States); Kleinwort Benson Australia Ltd.; Kleinwort Benson (Hong Kong) Ltd.; KGIM Pacific Ltd. (Hong Kong); Kleinwort Benson (Hong Kong) Trustees Ltd.; Kleinwort Grieveson Securities (Asia) Ltd. (Hong Kong); Sharps Pixley Pacific Ltd. (Hong Kong); Rodskog Shipbrokers Ltd. (Hong Kong); Kleinwort Benson Investment Management KK (Japan); Kleinwort Benson (Singapore) Ltd.

Further Reading: Channon, Derek. *British Banking Strategy and the International Challenge*, London, Macmillan Press Ltd., 1977; *A Short History of the Kleinwort Benson Group*, London, Kleinwort Benson Group, 1988.

MERRILL LYNCH & CO., INC.

North Tower
World Financial Center
New York, New York 10281
U.S.A.
(212) 449-1000

Public Company
Incorporated: 1959
Employees: 43,400
Assets: $64.4 billion
Stock Index: New York Midwest Pacific London Paris Tokyo

Merrill Lynch is the largest retail brokerage house in the United States and a leading investment banker as well. Long committed to the needs of the small investor, Merrill's nationwide brokerage force now numbers about 11,800, but in recent years the company has become increasingly active in a variety of other investment fields. In 1988, nearly 60% of Merrill's profits were generated outside the retail business, an indication of how far the company has evolved from its original concentration on what its founder called "people's capitalism."

Merrill Lynch's oldest direct predecessor was the partnership of Burrill & Housman, founded in 1885. In 1890, William Burrill left the firm he had created, and the next year Arthur Housman's brother Clarence joined what was then A. A. Housman & Company. When Arthur Housman died in 1907, he left behind one of Wall Street's leading brokerage houses.

That same year, Charles Merrill and Edmund Lynch arrived in New York, where they met and became friends. The two 22-year-old entrepreneurs had both recently finished college and gravitated to Wall Street to seek their fortune. At that time, the stock market was chiefly the domain of a small number of eastern businessmen, but Merrill quickly realized the vast potential of financial markets funded by a broad spectrum of middle-class Americans. He received his initial training in the bond department of Burr & Company, and then set up his own firm in 1914. The following year he persuaded Edmund Lynch to join him, and Merrill, Lynch & Company was born.

The company prospered and grew quickly, earning a strong reputation in financial circles for financing the newly emerging chain store industry. Merrill himself was a founder of Safeway Stores, and the company underwrote the initial public offering for McCrory Stores. By the late 1920s, Merrill, Lynch was reaping the benefits of that decade's prolonged economic boom, but Charles Merrill gradually became uneasy about the frantic pace of investment. He predicted that bad times were ahead as early as 1928, warning his clients and his own firm to get ready for an economic downturn. When the crash came in 1929, Merrill, Lynch had already streamlined its operations and invested in low-risk concerns. Despite this foresight, in 1930 Merrill and Lynch decided to sell the firm's retail business to E.A. Pierce & Company and concentrate on investment banking.

E.A. Pierce & Company was the direct descendent of A.A. Housman & Company. The company was named for Edward Allen Pierce, who had joined Housman in 1901, become a partner in 1915, and the managing partner in 1921. After World War I, Pierce concentrated on building the firm into a nationwide network of branches connected by telegraph, in order to reach more customers. After a 1926 merger with Gwathmey & Company, the firm was renamed E.A. Pierce & Company the following year.

Like most brokers, Pierce struggled through the depression years, and in 1939 he persuaded Charles Merrill to rejoin him in the retail business. In 1940, Merrill Lynch, E.A. Pierce & Cassatt opened its doors, dropping the comma between Merrill and Lynch for the first time and adding Cassatt, a Philadelphia firm that had sold part of its business to Pierce and part to Merrill, Lynch in 1935.

The new firm was devoted to the radical concept of offering to its investors a "department store of finance." Clients were urged to research their financial options, and Merrill Lynch saw itself as a partner in that process, even providing educational materials. In 1941 the firm merged again; this time it became Merrill Lynch, Pierce, Fenner & Beane when it absorbed Fenner & Beane, a New Orleans company that was the nation's largest commodities house and the second-largest "wire house" (an investment firm that, like E.A. Pierce, depended on its private telegraph wires for a broad-based business).

During World War II the company benefited greatly from the economic turnaround brought by increasing military spending. Throughout the bull market of the postwar period and the 1950s, Merrill Lynch continued to be an innovator and a popularizer of financial information. The firm erected a permanent Investment Information Center in Grand Central Station, distributed educational brochures, ran ads with titles like "What Everybody Ought to Know About this Stock and Bond Business," and even sponsored investment seminars for women. These new ideas made Merrill Lynch the best-known investment firm of the day. Charles Merrill's reputation soared to such heights that shortly before his death in 1956 one Wall Street historian referred to him as "the first authentically great man produced by the financial markets in 50 years."

In 1958 the firm juggled names again. Alpheus Beane Jr. dropped out of the firm, and since Winthrop Smith had taken over as directing partner two years earlier, the firm was renamed Merrill Lynch, Pierce, Fenner & Smith (ML). The next year it became the first large Wall Street firm to incorporate, and earnings reached a record high of $13 million

During the 1960s the company began to diversify and expand internationally. In 1964 Merrill Lynch entered the government-securities business when it acquired C.J. Devine, the nation's largest and most prestigious specialist in that market. Over the course of the decade the firm also entered the fields of real estate financing, asset management, and economic consulting, and added 20 new overseas offices. The company paid special attention to establishing a European presence, which allowed participation in the developing Eurobond market, and by 1964 had succeeded in becoming the first U.S. securities firm in Japan. In that same year ML was named lead underwriter for the $100 million public offering of Comsat, builder of the world's first telecommunications satellite, thus solidifying its position as one of the country's major investment-banking firms. The company underwrote the sale of Howard Hughes's TWA stock in 1965, and in the next ten years added significant new business with firms such as Commonwealth Edison, Fruehauf, and Arco. By the end of the decade Merrill was managing about $2 billion annually in such offerings.

One of these projects, a 1966 debenture issue for Douglas Aircraft, led to an investigation by the Securities and Exchange Commission (SEC) and a substantial rewriting of the regulations governing full-service investment firms like ML. The SEC charged that Merrill had passed on to some of its institutional clients confidential information about Douglas gathered while serving as the latter's investment banker. The company neither admitted nor denied the allegations but did agree to pay some fines, and the SEC took the opportunity to tighten its rules regarding insider trading and the prevention of unwarranted intra-office disclosures.

Net income in 1967 was a handsome $55 million, representing an increase of 300% during the past eight years. In the following year, Donald Regan was named president of Merrill Lynch, and two years later he became chairman and CEO. Regan guided ML in an ambitious program of diversification aimed at making the company a "one-stop investment and estate-planning institution." This included ML's first determined entry into the real estate field with the 1968 acquisition of Hubbard, Westervelt & Motteley, enabling it to offer to customers a range of mortgages, leasebacks, and other options; a major move into the mutual fund markets; and the purchase of Royal Securities Corporation of Canada, significantly strengthening ML's position in that country.

The firm also absorbed the New York Stock Exchange's fifth-largest brokerage house, Goodbody & Company, in 1970 when that company fell victim to Wall Street's so-called "paper crunch disaster." Overextended trading houses were generating more transaction records than their accounting departments could keep up with, resulting, in the case of Goodbody and many others, in massive confusion and eventual collapse. The exchange asked ML to step in and help Goodbody, and ML ended up acquiring the firm at the end of 1970. The bailout cost little and brought ML new expertise in the area of unit trusts and options trading.

In 1971 Merrill Lynch became the second member of the New York Stock Exchange to invite public ownership of its shares, and in July of that year became the first to have its own shares traded there. Shortly thereafter, the company adopted its most recent change of name, forming a holding company called Merrill Lynch & Co., Inc., with Merrill Lynch, Pierce, Fenner & Smith as its principal subsidiary.

Regan's diversification program continued with a 1972 move into international banking. London-based Brown-Shipley Ltd. soon became Merrill Lynch International Bank, and in 1974 ML acquired the Family Life Insurance Company of Seattle, Washington. In 1976 ML formulated a strategy to meet the challenge of the increasingly complex international financial marketplace by offering "a diversified array of securities, insurance, banking, tax, money management, financing, and financial counseling." Formerly clear demarcations between the various money professions were rapidly blurring, as ML demonstrated in 1977 when it announced the creation of the Cash Management Account (CMA). This unique account allowed individual investors to write checks and make Visa charges against their money market funds. Banks did not appreciate this incursion into their territory and mounted a number of legal campaigns to stop it, all to no avail. By 1989, fully half of ML's $304 billion in customer accounts were placed in CMAs, and most of the other leading brokerage houses had developed similar integrated-investment vehicles.

Despite its sustained attempt to achieve a steady level of profit through diversification, ML's earnings have reflected the volatile nature of its core securities business. For example, 1971 profit reached a new high of $70 million, but was followed by the difficult oil-embargo years of 1972–1974; and while 1975's record $100 million was not equaled for several years afterward, 1980 saw record highs of $218 million in profit and $3 billion in revenues. That year also marked the end of the Regan era at ML, as new President Ronald Reagan named Donald T. Regan secretary of the treasury and later made him White House chief of staff.

Roger Birk became the company's new chairman and CEO, followed in 1984 by William A. Schreyer. Schreyer, unhappy with ML's failure to match the earnings of some of its more flamboyant competitors, has made increased profitability his chief goal. To that end, Schreyer reorganized the vast company, strengthened its trading, underwriting, and merger and acquisition departments, and made a $1 billion move into new offices in the World Financial Center. The firm also cut spiraling operating costs and trimmed 2,500 employees from its ranks.

In 1985, ML met a longstanding goal when it became one of the first six foreign companies to join the Tokyo Stock Exchange. The following year, when the firm became a member of the London Exchange, ML was able to offer round-the-clock trading. Later in 1986 ML sold its real estate brokerage unit as part of Schreyer's plan to unload low-profit concerns so that the company could focus more on using its powerful retail divisions to sell the securities its investment-banking department brought in. The strategy worked; profits increased to a record $453 million during that year.

Also in 1986, scandal hit ML when Leslie Roberts, a 23-year-old broker, was arrested by the FBI for mail fraud. Roberts's complex fraud scheme lost huge sums—as much as $10 million from a single investor's account. The Roberts case typified for many the money fever of pre-crash Wall Street, and the incident attracted international attention.

The crash of October, 1987 sent profits reeling and forced ML to freeze salaries, cut bonuses, dismiss employees, and slash commission payouts to its sales force. But profits increased dramatically the next year, reaching a record high of $463 million. During 1988 ML also achieved a long-held goal when it edged out Salomon Brothers to become the largest underwriter in America. The following year ML realized another long-term goal: the firm became the world leader in debt and equity securities, this time besting First Boston Corporation in the race for the top spot. Merrill Lynch remained in the thick of the hot merger-and-acquisition business as well, earning, for example, a tidy $90 million for helping put together the $25 billion leveraged buyout of RJR Nabisco Inc. that year.

With a huge base of loyal customers and its enormous volume of business, Merrill Lynch's future looks very solid. Its traditional commitment to small investors, coupled with it's broad range of financial services, will make Merrill Lynch a dificult target for any competitor that dares to challenge its position at the top.

Principal Subsidiaries: Merrill Lynch, Pierce, Fenner & Smith Inc.; Family Life Insurance Co.; Merrill Lynch Asset Management, Inc.; Merrill Lynch Bank & Trust Co.; Merrill Lynch Capital Partners, Inc.; Merrill Lynch Capital Services, Inc.; Merrill Lynch Fiduciary Service, Inc.; Merrill Lynch Futures, Inc.; Merrill Lynch Government Securities, Inc.; Merrill Lynch Group, Inc.; Merrill Lynch International Inc.; Merrill Lynch Options/Futures Management Inc.; Merrill Lynch Realty, Inc.; Merrill Lynch Specialists, Inc.; Merrill Lynch Trust Co.; Merrill Lynch Trust Services, Inc.

Further Reading: Hecht, Henry, ed. *A Legacy of Leadership: Merrill Lynch 1885–1985*, New York, Merrill Lynch, 1985.

MORGAN GRENFELL GROUP PLC

MORGAN GRENFELL GROUP PLC

23 Great Winchester Street
London EC2P 2AX
United Kingdom
(01) 588 4545

Wholly owned subsidiary of Deutsche Bank A.G.
Incorporated: 1971
Employees: 2,569
Assets: £6 billion (US$10.85 billion)
Stock Index: London Ireland

Morgan Grenfell Group PLC is an investment holding company that offers international merchant banking and investment management services around the world. It has international operations in the Channel Islands, Europe, the United States, Asia, and Australia, and owns Morgan Grenfell Laurie, which provides commerical property services. With assets of nearly £6 billion, it is the second-leading merchant bank in Britain.

At its founding by philanthropist George Peabody in 1838, Morgan Grenfell was known as Peabody, Riggs & Company. The son of a leather worker, Peabody was born in South Danvers, Massachusetts (later renamed Peabody in his honor). After a few years of schooling, he went to work as a country-store clerk at age 11. He became a partner in a Baltimore dry-goods business at 19 and, over the next seven years, helped the business establish branches in New York and Philadelphia. After several visits to London, Peabody, already a rich man by 1838, decided to stay in the city and establish a merchanting firm.

Over the next decade, from his office in London, Peabody imported cotton, textiles, tobacco, and steel for British railways. He financed the operations with a sterling-dollar exchange, which gradually resulted in his shifting from merchanting to merchant banking. Much of Peabody's profit came from backing American securities, which he bought at almost giveaway prices, with his personal funds. In the 1850s, he helped finance the American railway system, by which he profited handsomely. His successful bond sales in London stimulated the American stock market to reinvest in railroads, canals, and exports.

The wealthy banker was also a renowned host, holding lavish banquets for such guests as the Duke of Wellington. It was during one such occasion that he met Junius Spencer Morgan, a partner in a Boston dry goods firm. In 1854, Junius accepted a partnership at George Peabody and Company, which had become Europe's leading American merchant bank. In 1864, the 70-year-old Peabody turned control over to Junius Morgan, who renamed the firm J.S. Morgan and Company. With the end of the Civil War, Morgan eagerly took advantage of the opportunities reconstruction offered for financing public utilities, consumer goods, and of course railroads, which had become the nation's most important investment during the 1860s.

In 1864, under the direction of Junius Morgan, the company began a long tradition of issuing loans to foreign countries, including a £10 million loan to France in 1870 when the Prussians were beseiging Paris. The deal earned £1.5 million, making it the firm's most profitable loan.

In 1862, Junius' 25-year-old son John Pierpoint Morgan founded J.P. Morgan and Company in New York. Initially the firm operated as the American representative for his father's company in London. J.P. Morgan began by marketing United States railroad securities abroad; by the turn of the century, it had become a leader in the consolidation and merger of railroads.

When Junius Morgan died in 1890, however, John Pierpoint Morgan returned to England to become chairman of J.S. Morgan and Company. Under his direction, the House of Morgan, as its American and European offices were collectively referred to, supervised the financial activities in the United States and much of Europe through the 19th and early 20th centuries. In 1905, J.P. Morgan's son Jack returned from a 15-year stay at J.S. Morgan and Company in London to take an active role in the American firm, J.P. Morgan and Company, which had become a key player in the House of Morgan.

J. S. Morgan and Company became Morgan Grenfell and Company in 1910, when Edward Grenfell, a manager with the firm since 1900 and a partner since 1904, was named senior resident partner. Grenfell's cousin, Vivian Hugh Smith, had also become a partner, in 1905. The cousins made Morgan Grenfell the focus of their lives and both eventually became senior managing directors of the merchant bank.

Meanwhile in New York, Jack Morgan continued to finance governments and invest in American securities, as his grandfather had done. During World War I, when Britain turned to the United States for food and industrial supplies, it found J.P. Morgan and Company was the best candidate to serve as purchasing agent in the United States. The company lent more than US$1.5 billion to Britain, France, and Russia and supervised the purchase of American war supplies by its allies. In fact, with the help of Morgan Grenfell, which served as liaison between the British government and J.P. Morgan and Company in the United States, the company loaned more money to European governments than any other institution. Thus Morgan Grenfell, because of its ties to both sides of the Atlantic, played a major role in helping to rebuild Europe after the war by coordinating reconstruction loans to the governments of Belgium, Austria, Italy, and Germany.

In 1925, a move to return England to the gold standard, which was abandoned in 1919, was initiated by Montagu Norman, governor of the Bank of England. In response,

Benjamin Strong, governor of the Federal Reserve Bank of New York, spearheaded the bank's loan of US$200 million to the Bank of England, while J. P. Morgan and Company loaned the British government US$100 million. The loan was a profitable one for Morgan Grenfell as well, which gained £100,000 in commission along with a healthy share of the US$2 million commitment fee.

In the United States, as part of President Herbert Hoover's New Deal, the Banking Act of 1933 required J.P. Morgan and Company to narrow its interests by choosing between investment and commercial banking. Its choice, commerical banking, meant the company could no longer underwrite securities issues, which caused it to lose prestige in Europe, as well as much control of its investments. Because the move also limited J.P. Morgan's relationship with Morgan Grenfell to banking, Morgan Grenfell became an incorporated limited liability company in order to continue its financial business in the United States, thus forming Morgan Grenfell and Company Limited in 1936.

The firm soon found new markets when Vivian Smith succeeded Edward Grenfell as senior managing director after Grenfell's death in 1941. In his new position, Smith spent much time abroad, extending the company's business to Africa, Latin America, and especially India and the East. He remained head of Morgan Grenfell until his death, in 1956.

Lord Catto, son of Sir Thomas Catto, who joined the bank in 1928 and had become its largest individual shareholder by 1933, came on board in 1948. Growing up in his father's shadow gave Catto a unique perspective of Morgan Grenfell as he watched the firm evolve over the century. The future chairman once remarked that the bank remained much the same from the 1920s, when his father joined, until the 1960s. The pace quickened, however, in the 1960s, when the bank increased its involvement in corporate finance, investment management, and Eurobonds. In an effort to prepare for the deregulation of London business, it also expanded its securities operations.

Also throughout the 1960s and 1970s Morgan Grenfell took part in several joint ventures with Morgan Stanley and Morgan Guaranty Trust (the result of the 1958 merger between J.P. Morgan and Guaranty Trust). Morgan Guaranty still owned a third of Morgan Grenfell and most of the British bank's international ventures were undertaken in cooperation with its American cousins.

When Lord Harcourt, a great-grandson of J.S. Morgan and former economic minister at the British Embassy in Washington, became chairman of Morgan Grenfell in 1968, "the really major changes happened," according to Catto. Prior to Harcourt's term as chairman, the company had remained a conservative merchant bank, underwriting more than half of England's fixed-interest loans in the oil, chemical, and steel industries. But industry was changing, and with those changes came a need for banking skills in leasing, export finance, and foreign exchange. In 1967, Harcourt appointed Sir John Stevens, then head of the treasury delegation and economic minister in Washington, as senior director in charge of international business. Stevens, a former executive director at the Bank of England, sparked a period of rapid expansion for Morgan Grenfell when he decided that the firm should become an international bank based in the United Kingdom, rather than a London bank with overseas interests. In 1969 Morgan Grenfell (Overseas) Ltd. was incorporated to support international growth. In 1970, Stevens became executive vice chairman of the bank, which was incorporated in the United Kingdom in 1971 as an investment holding company. But he never saw his strategy come to fruition: Stevens died in October, 1973, leaving the bank's future to Lord Catto, chairman of the executive committee.

Under the guidance of William Mackworth-Young, who succeeded Stevens as chief executive, Morgan Grenfell quickly rose from a bank with 200 employees and £150 million in assets to an international player with a leading reputation in the British takeover arena. By 1975, Morgan Grenfell had opened 20 offices worldwide, compared to one overseas office in 1969 and had established several new international subsidiaries, in profitable markets like Singapore and Switzerland. In addition, it began financing projects for exporters in the United Kingdom and evolved as a key advisor and provider of major loans for industrial companies in many of the Organization for Economic Cooperation and Development (OECD) countries.

Much of the bank's activity in the last few decades of the 20th century has centered around financing expansion projects in countries such as Brazil, Iran, Iraq, Japan, Nigeria, Oman, and the Soviet Union. In 1975, Morgan Grenfell issued several loans to finance what was then the largest overseas project handled by the company—the construction of a major steel mill for Aco Minas in Brazil. Although the project began in a flourishing economy, work eventually came to a halt when recession hit in the late 1970s and early 1980s. As the price of steel dropped, so too did enthusiasm for the steel mill project; the first phase of the project was not completed until 1986.

The Soviet Union also became a key market for Morgan Grenfell's international corporate finance activity. After signing a £25 million line of credit with the country, Morgan Grenfell financed 80% of the business conducted between the United Kingdom and the Soviet Union between 1972 and 1988. In 1977, the firm established an office in Moscow, becoming the first merchant bank to be represented in the Soviet Union.

Another important change in the 1970s was an increase in competition between Morgan Grenfell and its two American cousins. These companies had traditionally cooperated in ventures and avoided competing with each other. As the market became increasingly global and growth was achieved primarily through international expansion, this unofficial policy of cooperation was increasingly set aside. The last ties between Morgan Grenfell and Morgan Guaranty Trust (now J.P. Morgan & Co.) were cut in 1981, when Morgan Guaranty disposed of its 33% shareholding.

The name Morgan Grenfell Group PLC was adopted in 1986, when the firm became a public company. Since going public, however, Morgan Grenfell has faced numerous problems. Several top managers were involved in financial scandals, among them Geoffrey Collier, who was charged with insider trading. In the mid-1980s, the Guinness affair dominated headlines in the United Kingdom. Guinness, a liquor distributor that Morgan was helping to take over Distillers, had allegedly bought some of its own shares in an effort to keep the Guinness price high before the takeover. Although the official investigation, which was directed at Guinness and not Morgan, began in 1989, the team that had helped to build Morgan from the 1970s to the 1980s—including Graham Walsh, former head of corporate finance—resigned when the scandal first came to light in 1986. Chairman Lord Catto also left soon after.

In May, 1987 John Craven took over as head of Morgan Grenfell in the wake of the Guinness scandal. That year was a mixed one for the firm. While Morgan Grenfell celebrated its position as the leading adviser in U.K. public takeovers for the sixth consecutive year, its stock-broking subsidiary, Morgan Grenfell Securities, struggled for market share in the U.K. Also that year, the group merged two of its units in he United States, Cyrus J. Lawrence Inc. and Morgan Grenfell Inc., to form C. J. Lawrence, Morgan Grenfell Inc.

While profits were £41.8 million in 1987 despite the stock market crash, Morgan Grenfell lost £19.2 million after taxes the following year. The loss was due in part to Craven's decision to abandon the securities business in December of that year, which reduced its employee ranks by some 450 and substantially reduced overhead. And indeed, profits began to rise significantly in 1989.

But 1989 brought other complications. That fall, suitors began to dance around Morgan Grenfell. France's Banque Indosuez announced in October that it had acquired a 14.8% stake in the company. When Barclays de Zoete Wedd proved unable to save Morgan Grenfell from Suez, Morgan Grenfell accepted a £950 million bid from Deutsche Bank, West Germany's largest bank, bringing to an end more than 150 years of independence.

Principal Subsidiaries: Morgan Grenfell & Company Ltd.; Morgan Grenfell Securities Holdings Ltd.; Morgan Grenfell Asset Management Ltd.; Morgan Grenfell Laurie Holdings Ltd.; C. J. Lawrence, Morgan Grenfell Inc.

Further Reading: Hoyt, Edwin P., Jr. *The House of Morgan*, New York, Dodd, Mead & Company, 1966; Burk, Kathleen. *Morgan Grenfell 1838–1988: The Biography of a Merchant Bank*, Oxford, England, Oxford University Press, 1989.

MORGAN STANLEY & CO.
Incorporated

MORGAN STANLEY GROUP INC.

1251 Avenue of the Americas
New York, New York 10020
U.S.A.
(212) 703–4000
Public Company
Incorporated: 1935 as Morgan Stanley & Company, Incorporated
Employees: 6,414
Assets: $40.05 billion
Stock Index: New York Boston Pacific Midwest

Morgan Stanley is one of the world's top investment banking firms. It has been underwriting, managing, and distributing corporate and governmental securities issues since 1935. In step with the deregulation of the financial markets during the 1980s, Morgan Stanley diversified its range of financial services. Today, in addition to traditional investment banking services, the company operates an active mergers and acquisition department, provides consulting services, and is active in real estate, futures trading, asset management, commercial paper, municipal finance, and leveraged buyouts. The investment banking field is considerably more complex today than it was in 1935, but Morgan Stanley has kept pace with the changes and remains a leader in the field.

The story of Morgan Stanley begins long before it was incorporated in 1935. The company traces its roots to 1860, when J.P. Morgan founded the world's first international banking concern, Drexel, Morgan & Company. Morgan's financial empire became legendary, as large industrialists turned to Morgan and his colleagues when they wanted to raise capital. By 1895, the firm had become J.P. Morgan and Company, and by the turn of the century Morgan was a premier agent for large quantities of securities, selling them both at home and abroad.

At this time, investment houses began to join together in syndicates to share the responsibilities and risks of financing to better serve the mushrooming capital requirements of American industry. They also affiliated themselves with large, prestigious banking syndicates to provide credibility and value to the issue of borrowers' securities. Syndicates could often broaden the geographic scope of a company's investors—the reason Boston-based American Telephone and Telegraph granted leadership to Morgan's New York firm in 1906 to underwrite $100 million of a $150 million bond issue, although it retained Kidder, Peabody as its principal banker.

As industry depended on the banks for capital, and banks depended on the revenue created by generating that capital, it became very common for bankers and businessmen to serve on each others' boards. These interlocking directorships became a primary concern of the United States House of Representatives Banking and Currency Committee, which decided to investigate. Its findings led to the Federal Reserve Act of 1913 and the Clayton Antitrust Act of 1914, which ended reciprocal directorships.

Regulation of investment banking remained an area of public concern throughout the first few decades of the century. Kansas was the first state to regulate all securities offered for sale to its citizens, a trend which spread across the nation. By 1933 every state but Nevada had enacted legislation to protect investors from fraud.

During World War I, investment bankers coordinated the sale of more than $2.2 billion in French and British bonds and the resale of more than $3 billion in American securities held in Europe. The house of Morgan accounted for more than $2 billion of that total. By serving in this capacity, investment bankers played a vital role in transforming the United States from a debtor to a creditor nation and in making New York the financial capital of the world.

The disastrous business practices of banks during the decade before the stock market crash on October 29, 1929 provided the real impetus for the birth of Morgan Stanley. During these years, commercial banks speculated with their depositors money—borrowed money—and played the market on margin. The frenzy escalated as hundreds of issues, many of them worthless, flooded the market and fueled the speculation. The market's plummet devastated margin players on all levels. Upon taking office, President Franklin D. Roosevelt initiated a number of investigations and Congress enacted legislation to prevent a recurrence of the events that caused the crash.

The Banking Act of 1933, better known as the Glass-Steagall Act, affected the investment banking industry more significantly than any other piece of legislation by requiring the separation of commercial and investment banks. Deposit business went to commercial banks, and underwriting and syndication went to investment banks, thus making the average depositor's money unavailable for speculation. The act became law June 16, 1933, and banks were given 12 months to comply.

J.P. Morgan and Company chose to pursue deposit banking. Within a year and a half of this decision, three of its partners organized Morgan Stanley & Company to enter the investment banking business. The new company was incorporated on September 16, 1935, and claimed some of the most experienced men in investment banking as assets. Harold Stanley, at age 42 one of the youngest J.P. Morgan and Company partners, was president. Henry Morgan, grandson of J.P., was secretary-treasurer. Morgan would play an integral role in the firm for more than 40 years.

The extensive experience of Morgan Stanley's leadership was one key to the company's immediate success. Another was the firm's ties to J.P. Morgan and Company and the corporate connections that came with them. Personal endorsements carried a great deal of influence during this period. Morgan Stanley chose syndicate partners based on "historical affiliations," meaning those that had been in place before Glass-Steagall.

During its first month alone, the new investment bank handled three major underwritings, including $43 million for AT&T—Morgan Stanley was blue chip from the start. It was also one of a select group that managed underwriting syndicates and handled wholesaling. It rarely participated in originations directed by another firm. Morgan Stanley's clients included nearly half of the largest 50 companies in the nation, among them Exxon, General Motors, and General Electric. By the end of its first full year of operations, Morgan Stanley had acquired a 24% market share of negotiated corporate and foreign issues, and by 1938, Morgan Stanley led all New York investment firms in original bond issues.

Throughout the 1930s, investment banking was dominated by a relatively small number of firms, and by the end of the decade, the government had again taken an interest in the affairs of investment houses. Morgan Stanley's quick success made it a particularly visible target. The Temporary National Economic Committee was formed to investigate monopolies in big business. In 1939, the committee called a number of investment bankers to testify in order to determine how much power investment banks held over industry through their control of the access to long-term capital markets. A key issue during the hearings was whether the negotiation of prices between corporations and securities underwriters infringed upon free trade. Many investment bankers, most notably Harold Stuart of the Chicago investment bank Halsey, Stuart & Company, were in favor of the competitive bidding system. Under this system, securities were auctioned off to the the highest bidder. Morgan Stanley, which benefitted immensely from its strong personal connections throughout the business community, was fiercely opposed to mandatory competitive bidding. The government, however, leaned in favor of the sealed bid system.

In 1941, the SEC required all public utilities companies to issue securities by public sealed bidding. Public utilities made up a substantial portion of the domestic market—between 1935 and 1939, they accounted for 13% of all U.S. common stock offerings. In addition, the Federal Communications Commission urged AT&T to use the competitive bidding system for its issues. Many investment banks feared the nature of their business would be drastically changed. In anticipation of the changes, Morgan Stanley decided to branch into the brokerage business. On November 28, 1941, in order to meet the criteria for membership on the New York Stock Exchange, Morgan Stanley & Company liquidated its stock and reorganized as a partnership.

World War II brought the securities business to a virtual halt. Morgan Stanley survived on brokerage commissions, consulting fees, and a small number of private placements. Founding partner Henry Morgan joined the navy, where he served on the Joint Army and Navy Munitions Board and as a Commander attached to the Naval Command Office of Strategic Services. Other high-ranking Morgan Stanley officers also entered the service in various capacities, including partner Perry Hall, who served as Executive Manager of the War Loan Committee of the Second Federal Reserve District. After the war, the company quickly reestablished its business relationships.

Government allegations of monopoly continued to plague Morgan Stanley in the late 1940s. In 1947, the Justice Department filed suit against Morgan Stanley and 16 other investment banking firms accusing them of conspiring to monopolize and restrain the securities industry. In forming syndicates, the government charged, investment bankers practiced both collusion and exclusion. After three years of pretrial hearings, proceedings opened in Circuit Court of New York on November 28, 1950. On September 22, 1953, three years after its introduction in court, six years after the suit was filed, Circuit Judge Harold R. Medina concluded that none of the 17 investment banks named in the suit were guilty of any of the charges brought forth by the government. "What is now taking shape," Medina wrote, "is not a static mosaic of conspiracy but a constantly changing panorama of competition among the 17 defendant firms." The antitrust storm had finally passed.

In 1951, Harold Stanley took a back seat in the operations of the company and Perry Hall, another of Morgan Stanley's founding partners, took his place. Hall remained managing partner until 1961. The 1950s were a prosperous time for Morgan Stanley, and the firm grew steadily throughout the decade. In 1954, Morgan Stanley managed a $300 million bond issue for General Motors. It was at the time the biggest securities issue ever underwritten in the history of investment banking. At the time Perry Hall commented to *The New Yorker*, with the nonchalant confidence typical of Morgan Stanley & Company, "After the G.M. deal was cooked I went down to South Carolina for a week's shooting. Shot two wild turkeys while I was down there. First time I ever got turkey. Generally got quail before. Come to think of it I got quail this time, too—fifteen of them."

As the bull market of the 1950s continued into the 1960s, Morgan Stanley remained a leader in institutional investment banking. The company consistently ranked in the top five firms managing new issues. In its first 30 years Morgan Stanley had managed or co-managed over $30 billion in public offerings and private placements.

In the later 1960s, the firm expanded its base. In 1966, together with the Morgan Guaranty Trust Company, it established a French subsidiary to broaden its international operations. The new Morgan & Cie International S.A. managed and participated in underwritings of foreign securities. In 1967, Morgan Stanley moved its headquarters to 140 Broadway from its old home at 2 Wall Street in deference to the need for more space. In 1969, Morgan Stanley plunged deeper into real estate financing when it bought a controlling interest in Brooks, Harvey & Company, Inc. Brooks, Harvey had been in the business of advising and financing real estate developments for more than 50 years.

The 1970s, however, were a more volatile time for Morgan Stanley. Early in the decade, the company went through a major corporate restructuring, reverting to incorporation from a limited partnership. The trend in investment banking was toward full service. Morgan Stanley, like other large investment banks, entered retail markets, added venture capital units, and aggressively sought foreign customers. In 1971, Morgan Stanley moved its headquarters for the second time in five years, to the Exxon Building in Rockefeller Center, in order to be nearer its corporate clients' midtown headquarters. Samuel Payne was the reorganized company's first president. He was soon followed by Chester Lasell, and in 1973, by Robert Baldwin. The company created a mergers and acquisition department in 1972 to help its clients find and evaluate appropriate acquisition targets and to provide strategic planning to complete the deals. It also broadened its real estate activities with the creation of Morstan Development Company, Inc. In 1973, Morgan Stanley opened a research department and entered the equity markets full-scale. Morgan Stanley's Asset Management Division, which began in 1975, became a strong revenue producer. Morgan Stanley began to offer individual investment services to wealthy individuals and to smaller institutional investors in 1977.

Not only did the substance of Morgan Stanley's business shift during the 1970s, but the tone of its leadership did too. In 1973, Frank Petito became chairman of Morgan Stanley, the year Robert Baldwin became president. Petito, and to an even greater extent Baldwin, represented the new breed of investment bankers. While Morgan Stanley had until now depended heavily on relationships and personal affiliations, the revamped company, following the general trend in big business, concentrated on the bottom line. Under its new leadership, Morgan Stanley grew rapidly. Paid-in capital mushroomed from $7.5 million in 1970 to $118 million in 1980, and the staff swelled from fewer than 200 to 1,700 in the same period.

Growth did not come without pain, however. IBM abandoned its long-term relationship with the firm when Morgan Stanley refused to share managership with Salomon Brothers on a $1 billion note issue. Olincraft, Inc. sued Morgan Stanley for divulging confidential information for use by another client in a hostile takeover, and Occidental Petroleum filed a separate suit on similar grounds that was later dropped.

The court ruled in favor of Morgan Stanley in the Olincraft case, stating, "Olincraft's management placed its confidence in Morgan Stanley not to disclose the information. Morgan Stanley owed no duty to observe that confidence." Not surprisingly, despite winning the suit, Morgan Stanley was subsequently viewed in a different light by corporations and by its competitors. The firm's reputation, commonly referred to as "the franchise," was not as lily-white as it once had been.

In 1981 it came to light that two former employees of Morgan Stanley had passed on inside information during the mid-1970s to a number of outside traders in return for a share of the resulting profits. Information on at least 18 acquisitions was leaked between 1974 and 1978. The incident focused a great deal of attention on insider trading, and the business community called for harsher penalties for violators.

As the firm entered the 1980s, competition in investment banking was as fierce as ever. Although Morgan Stanley continued to grow at a considerable pace, it was outperformed by its rivals. While investment bankers like Salomon Brothers and Goldman, Sachs began trading in commercial paper, mortgage-backed securities, and foreign currencies early in the decade, Morgan Stanley, fearful of overextending itself, dragged its feet in these areas. The company also lagged behind in leveraged buyouts and the explosive municipal bond market.

In 1984, leadership passed to an even more aggressive team. S. Parker Gilbert, the stepson of Harold Stanley, became chairman, and Richard Fisher became president. The company had set out to fill the gaps in its financial services in 1983 by hiring an aggressive staff. By the time the new management team was in place, the firm was making headway in a number of key areas.

Throughout the 1980s, the U.S. government deregulated financial markets, allowing increased competition across the board. Commercial banks began to operate in the capital markets for the first time since the Glass-Steagall Act. Competition, both at home and abroad, increased as financial service companies expanded the range of services they offered. In 1986, in order to meet the demands of the increasingly complex marketplace, Morgan Stanley went public in order to broaden its capital base.

By the end of the 1980s, Morgan Stanley had regained its position. The company was the only New York investment bank to increase its profits in 1987. Its activities in leveraged buyouts were exceptionally profitable—the company's first leveraged buyout fund earned more than 25 times the original investment. By the end of the decade, Morgan Stanley's long-term equity investments were worth more than $7 billion.

Morgan Stanley has withstood many changes since it began in 1935. It continues to adapt to the volatile capital markets. Having correctly assessed that investment banking would become a global business early in the 1980s, Morgan Stanley positioned itself accordingly by establishing new offices throughout the world including two in Australia and one in Japan. It has focused on long-term equity investments, causing stock analysts to recommend Morgan Stanley as a solid investment for the future. Throughout its history, Morgan Stanley & Company has blended tradition with innovation and proven itself a formidable investment banker.

Principal Subsidiaries: Morgan Stanley Asset Management Inc.; Morgan Stanley Canada Ltd.; Morgan Stanley International; Morgan Stanley Ventures Inc.; Brooks Harvey & Co., Inc.; Morgan Stanley Realty Inc.; Morstan Development Company, Inc.; Execution Services Inc.; MS Securities Services Inc.

Further Reading: Carosso, Vincent P. *Investment Banking in America: A History*, Cambridge, Harvard University Press, 1970; Ferris, Paul. *The Master Bankers*, New York, William Morrow, 1984; Hoffman, Paul. *The Dealmakers: Inside the World of Investment Banking*, Garden City, New York, Doubleday, 1984.

NIKKO

THE NIKKO SECURITIES COMPANY LIMITED

3–1, Marunouchi 3-chome
Chiyoda-ku
Tokyo 100
Japan
(03) 283–2255

Public Company
Incorporated: 1944
Employees: 9,448
Assets: ¥3.6 trillion (US$28.8 billion)
Stock Index: Tokyo Osaka Nagoya Düsseldorf Frankfurt Luxembourg Paris

The Nikko Securities Company is one of the largest securities companies in the world. With assets of more than ¥3 trillion, Nikko ranks third among Japanese securities companies. An underwriter and dealer in securities, Nikko is represented in all the major capital and equities markets around the world, and has 116 branch offices in Japan as well as 15 subsidiaries and nine representative offices overseas.

Founded in 1944, Nikko is the youngest of Japan's Big Four securities houses, which collectively transact more than half of the brokering and investment banking in Japan. Nikko was formed as a merger between the Kawashimaya Securities Company and the Nikko Securities Company, which was at that time part of the Industrial Bank of Japan. The new company could count the long experience of its two predecessors among its assets.

In 1918, Genichi Toyama founded the Kawashimaya Shoten to buy and sell stocks and bonds; two years later his company was incorporated as Kawashimaya Shoten Inc., Ltd. Kawashimaya expanded throughout the 1920s and 1930s and in 1939 Toyama set up a separate company, Kawashimaya Securities Company, Ltd., as a bond underwriter. In 1943, the business of Kawashimaya Shoten was assimilated by the Kawashimaya Securities Company.

The Nikko Securities Company grew out of the securities department of the Industrial Bank of Japan. Although Nikko separated from IBJ in 1920 and operated autonomously on a day-to-day basis, it remained under the ultimate control of the bank. In 1943, Nikko strengthened its position in the markets when it acquired the Kyodo Securities Company, Ltd. A year later, in 1944, it merged with Kawashimaya, formally separating itself from IBJ and creating the present-day Nikko Securities Company.

Japan's securities markets were in a chaotic state after World War II as stock prices plummeted. In 1945, all trading on the major exchanges was suspended while the Occupation forces restructured the Japanese economy and political system. Because of the forced disintegration of the huge Japanese cartels known as *zaibatsu*, stock ownership became broadly based. Reconstruction called for extensive borrowing, and this need was met by substantial debenture issues. The new Nikko Securities opened during this chaos with 736 employees in 12 offices. It survived by buying and selling securities over the counter at its offices throughout Japan.

In 1948, Japan's Securities and Exchange Law laid the foundation for the reopening of Japan's principal exchanges, allowing the Tokyo Stock Exchange and the other major markets to reopen in 1949. The economy took off in 1951 as a result of increased export demand from United Nations forces, primarily American troops, engaged in the Korean conflict. This boom pulled the Japanese stock market out of a serious slump and heralded the steady growth of the Japanese economy. Nikko's own growth, for the most part, mirrored that of Japan.

In the postwar period, Nikko, along with the other Japanese securities houses, invested heavily in public relations to educate the Japanese people about equity and capital markets. The investment paid off; nearly half of all Japanese became active investors during the 1950s. Nikko established "public relations libraries" where people could go to keep abreast of the markets. These outreach centers were found in shopping centers, railway stations, even underground on subway concourses. In addition, the company sponsored a television show called "Morning Smiles," which went on the air as the Tokyo Stock Exchange opened and reported trends and developments in the securities markets. Nikko also targeted women in its advertisements and media campaigns, and women became a significant group of investors. "Discussions of the market receive almost as much attention in most Japanese homes as the weather and baseball," Genichi Toyama, the founder of Nikko, said in the early 1960s. Nikko had helped cultivate a nation of avid securities consumers.

Investment trusts became one of the most popular ways for Japanese to invest. Nikko opened the first of its investment trusts in 1951, and by 1957 was managing more than ¥100 billion in subscriptions. The company offered two types of investment trusts. A unit-type trust allowed an investor to purchase a unit for ¥5,000 that would mature in five years. An open-end type resembled the American mutual fund: shares were bought and sold at the market price, which was in turn based on the net asset value at a given time.

With an increasing need for capital in the late 1950s, Nikko established itself abroad to facilitate the flow of foreign capital into Japan. In 1959, Nikko set up an office in New York. This office was primarily a research center until 1965, when it took on new services and was upgraded to subsidiary status. Nikko's main U.S. affiliate in the late

1950s and 1960s was Nikko Kasai Securities Company, a joint venture with Kasai Securities established in 1955 in San Francisco. Nikko Kasai focused on developing an interest in Japanese securities among West Coast investors. Nikko continued to expand into key foreign financial centers in the 1960s, opening an office in London in 1964 and in Zurich in 1969.

In 1961, Nikko Securities went public, offering its shares on the Tokyo, Nagoya, and Osaka exchanges. Japanese securities market activity expanded at an incredible rate until 1964, when the economy slipped into the most severe recession of the postwar era. The Japanese government's newly imposed tight monetary controls combined with U.S. restrictions on foreign investment to put a clamp on growth. The resulting drop in stock prices caused a public loss of confidence in the markets.

Some analysts blamed the securities companies for irresponsible, even unethical, behavior in the months leading up to the crisis. They accused the dealers of overzealously pushing securities on investors to avoid getting stuck with issues they had underwritten. As a result of these and other practices, the Japanese Ministry of Finance called for the complete reorganization of the securities industry. Nikko was reviewed and allowed to obtain the new licenses necessary to operate as a securities underwriter and dealer. Top management underwent major changes: many of the company's managers were replaced by younger executives, nine directors retired, and the 56-year-old Moriatsu Minato, a former director with a strong background in banking, became president. By 1966, the Japanese economy had resumed its extraordinary rate of growth—growth that continued virtually unbroken until the oil crisis of 1973.

When the worldwide oil crisis struck, Japanese industry, heavily dependent on imported oil, suffered a terrible blow. More than 11,000 companies went bankrupt during the recession that followed. When the economy recovered, the stunning growth rates of the 1960s and early 1970s leveled off, and slower (though still impressive) growth characterized the second half of the 1970s. This period also saw the development of a more sophisticated bond market. Large government issues beginning in 1975 brought about changes in the capital markets. Japanese companies were in competition with the government for Japanese capital investment.

Nikko responded to this challenge by establishing new offices and subsidiaries around the world. By 1979, Nikko had offices or subsidiaries in Frankfurt, Luxembourg, Paris, Hong Kong, and Singapore in addition to its London and New York operations. Japanese stocks and bonds became increasingly popular overseas, particularly in Europe, and by 1980, Nikko, riding the wave of Japanese industrial strength, was competitive with Europe's largest securities companies.

As countries relaxed their regulations on financial services in the 1980s, the securities industry became increasingly globalized. Nikko's skyrocketing profits reflected those developments. In fact, Japanese securities companies, Nikko included, were soon ranked among the world's largest financial-services companies. Domestic competition among the Japanese Big Four, (Nomura, Daiwa, Nikko, and Yamaichi) was fierce. Nikko continued to look overseas for new opportunities. Since the United States represented the largest single market in the world, Nikko resolved to establish itself there.

In the mid-1980s, the Ministry of Finance approved substantial changes in Japan's capital market controls. Japanese securities companies found new opportunities in the new varieties of bonds that were now permitted. European issues of Japanese bonds denominated in yen became very popular. As the yen took on greater significance as a benchmark currency, Nikko further solidified its position in the euromarkets. The company's progress in the United States, however, was not as spectacular.

Nikko had difficulty penetrating American markets for a number of reasons. Its primary operations in the United States during the mid-1980s revolved around U.S. treasury bonds. The company was designated a primary dealer in U.S. government securities by the Federal Reserve in 1987, and Japanese investors had a large appetite for U.S. treasury bonds. Since it did not have a base of domestic investors in the United States, Nikko focused on investment-banking services rather than brokering. But virtually all the Japanese securities houses were treated with caution by American investors and corporations issuing debt or equities. Nikko had trouble competing with the investment-banking services of large U.S. companies like Goldman Sachs, First Boston, or Salomon Brothers.

Further, some analysts considered the Japanese style of management poorly suited to the complex world of investment banking. Decisions which needed instantaneous resolution were deferred to top management in Japan, and further held up by the consensus approach characteristic of Japanese business. These problems were compounded in October, 1987 when the New York stock market crashed and Nikko's mainstay—Japanese investors—were scared out of the markets. Although still committed to entering American markets, Nikko needed to regroup and develop a new strategy.

Nikko set out to diversify its services, purchasing 20% of the Blackstone Group in 1988. Blackstone, an American merchant bank, specialized in friendly takeovers, the only kind the Japanese will contemplate. As demand for mergers and acquisition assistance grew in the late 1980s, Nikko's connection with the American company proved an excellent arrangement. Nikko also became heavily involved in swaps, designing an advanced method of valuing swaps called "zero coupon valuation" that was superior in many ways to those used by some of Wall Street's best-known investment banks. Nikko also established a presence in the American commodity futures industry in the late 1980s. Through these new services Nikko hoped to attract U.S. customers and broaden its Japanese base.

Since its incorporation in 1944, Nikko Securities Company has grown into one of the world's largest financial corporations. As world financial markets continue to globalize, Nikko's sheer size will give it the ability to compete with the largest investment banks and brokerages. Nikko has shown an ability to adapt to the chaotic changes of the 1980s. As the nature of financial service companies changes in the future, Nikko will continue to evolve.

Principal Subsidiaries: Nikko Research Center, Ltd.; Nikko Systems Center, Ltd.; Nikko International Capital Management Co., Ltd.; Nikko Investment Trust & Management Co., Ltd.; Nikko Venture Capital Co., Ltd.; Nikko Building Co., Ltd.; Nikko Real Estate Co., Ltd.; Nikko Enterprises, Ltd.; Shin Nikko Shoji, Ltd.; Nikko Kaikan, Ltd.; Koei Enterprises, Ltd.; Nikko Securities Co. International, Inc.; Nikko Securities Co. (Europe) Ltd. (United Kingdom) Ltd.; Nikko (Switzerland) Finance Co., Ltd.; Nikko Securities (Deutschland) GmbH; Nikko (Luxembourg) S.A.; Nikko Securities Co. (Asia) Ltd. (Hong Kong); Nikko Merchant Bank (Singapore) Co., Ltd.; Nikko Securities Co. Canada, Ltd.; Nikko France S.A.; Nikko Nederland N.V.; Nikko Investment Banking (Middle East) E.C. (Bahrain); Nikko Securities (Australia) Ltd.; Nikko DC Card Services Co., Ltd.; Nikko Million Card Services Co., Ltd.; Nikko Business Service Co., Ltd.; Nikko Enterprises, Ltd.; Nikko Computer System House Co., Ltd.; N.B. Investment Technology Co., Ltd.; IBJ-NIKKO Information Systems, Ltd.; Kyodo Mortgage Acceptance Co., Ltd.; Central Capital Ltd.; Nikko Securities Co. International, Inc. (United States); Nikko Bank PLC (United Kingdom).

NIPPON SHINPAN COMPANY, LTD.

33–5, 3-chome Hongo
Bunkyo-ku
Tokyo 113–91
Japan
(03) 811–3111

Public Company
Incorporated: 1951 as Nippon Shinyo Hanbai Company
Employees: 6,369
Assets: ¥4.52 trillion (US$36.18 billion)
Stock Index: Tokyo Osaka Nagoya Frankfurt Luxembourg

When Mitsunari Yamada convinced four Japanese department stores to accept coupons in lieu of cash in 1951, he started what would become Japan's first and largest consumer credit company, one that today handles credit cards, loans, credit guarantees, real estate, financing and leasing.

Yamada pioneered Japan's credit industry during a time of high consumer prices and economic uncertainty. In the years following World War II, Japan faced not only rampant inflation, but a shortage of resources amid a boom in population. This economic plight was ripe ground for Yamada's credit services. With the founding of Nippon Shinpan's forerunner, Nippon Shinyo Hanbai Company, in Tokyo in 1951, Yamada offered consumers a chance to pay for goods on installment. Yamada had negotiated an agreement with four major department stores to accept Nippon Shinyo Hanbai's coupons as payment for goods. In the years to follow, the company, which soon changed its name to Nippon Shinpan, gradually added stores to its network, to make credit payment more convenient and appealing to consumers.

Just five years after launching its credit business, Nippon Shinpan moved into another industry, real estate, marketing Japan's first luxury condominium in 1956. The successful endeavor lead to handling mortgages and selling homes and home sites.

Nippon Shinpan's housing business would prove vital after the Ministry of International Trade and Industry (MITI) in 1959 set restrictive guidelines on credit services. Designed to help small retailers, the MITI guidelines limited coupon use geographically, severely curtailing Nippon Shinpan's credit business.

The company responded by stepping up its housing-related activities. In 1960, Nippon Shinpan became the first company to offer housing loans, with more housing and condominium development to follow. Taking a bold step, the company also began to guarantee unsecured cash loans made by other financial lenders. The move brought new opportunities to consumers and, according to the company, the service grew "phenomenally" after it was initiated.

By 1963, Nippon Shinpan had found a way to sidestep MITI guidelines by offering "shopping loans." These loans involved no coupons and as a result were not covered by the MITI rules. Under the procedure, consumers would apply for credit at member stores. Once credit was approved, Nippon Shinpan would pay the purchase price for goods and consumers would pay the loan back in installments.

Nippon Shinpan began issuing credit cards in 1966, launching what would turn into its largest business. Also during this time, the company made plans for an extended network of offices and branched into loans backed by securities.

The 1970s marked Nippon Shinpan's first ventures abroad. In December 1969, the company struck an agreement with MasterCard International (then Interbank Card Assocation) to make the Nippon Shinpan card accepted internationally. By June of 1973, Nippon Shinpan was issuing MasterCards overseas.

Its ventures overseas prompted the company to establish liaisons with retailers and banks in Hong Kong and Hawaii, two popular Japanese tourist destinations. Leisure had already become an important sideline for Nippon Shinpan. In 1971, the company opened its exclusive U-Topy tennis club in the resort area of Karuizawa.

Foreign bonds became company business in the late 1970s; Nippon Shinpan issues Swiss franc bonds in 1976 and deutsche mark bonds in 1978.

In 1981, Nippon Shinpan entered a joint venture with the BankAmerica Group to set up the International Factoring Corporation, a financing concern targeting small and medium-sized companies. The newly formed company focused on purchasing debt and servicing accounts. Japan's sluggish loan business prompted BankAmerica to pursue the partnership, according to the *Financial Times*.

Though continuing to expand both its financial and real estate businesses, growth in the credit card arena was Nippon Shinpan's signature for the 1980s. During a four-year period between 1984 and 1988, card circulation grew from 10 million to nearly 18 million. Member stores in Japan hit 334,000 in 1988. The company also entered joint-card agreements with Japan's Postal Savings system, a major savings organization, as well as MasterCard and Visa International.

The Visa deal, in 1987, put the Visa logo on the 13 million cards Nippon Shinpan had in circulation in Japan at the time. Most of the cards were private-label cards for companies like Shell Oil and Shiseido, a cosmetics retailer. The remaining cards Nippon Shinpan issued itself.

In 1988, the company established the International Credit Card Business Association, an organization with a goal of promoting MasterCard and Visa credit cards, ensuring that credit cards will continue to be the backbone of Nippon Shinpan's business well into the next decade.

Principal Subsidiaries: International Factoring Corporation; Nippon Shinpan General Finance Company, Ltd.; Nippon Shinpan Money Shop Company, Ltd.; Nisshin Kensetsu Company, Ltd.; Seibu Nippon Shinpan Company, Ltd.; Nippon Shinpan Information Systems, Inc.; Nippon Shinpan (Asia) Ltd.

NOMURA SECURITIES COMPANY, LIMITED

1–9 Nihonbashi 1-chome
Chuo-ku
Tokyo 103
Japan
(03) 211–1811

Public Company
Incorporated: 1925
Employees: 10,200
Assets: ¥4.6 trillion (US$36.81 billion)
Stock Index: Tokyo Osaka Nagoya Amsterdam Luxembourg

The Nomura Securities Company, the largest securities firm in Japan, has long been recognized as an industry pace setter. Since, as *The Economist* has put it, "What Nomura does this morning, the rest of the Japanese securities industry will do after lunch," Nomura has played a key role in the development of the securities industry in Japan. The company has recently made great strides in the international arena as well. It was the first Japanese company to become a member of the New York Stock Exchange, in 1981, and has seen phenomenal success in the Euromarkets. Since it was established in 1925, Nomura has struggled through many economic and cultural changes in Japan, but it has emerged as a powerhouse not only at home but also in the international securities markets.

Nomura was incorporated in 1925, but its story begins much earlier. In 1872, four years after the Meiji Emperor reclaimed the Japanese throne and began an unprecedented reform campaign, Tokushichi Nomura opened the Nomura Shoten in Osaka, Japan. Nomura was a moneychanger. At that time there was no one single currency in Japan. Various gold, silver and copper coins were appraised by merchants like Nomura, and their value was dictated by the current market price. But along with the Meiji Restoration came extensive monetary reforms, and Nomura's business changed rapidly as the Japanese industrial revolution came into full swing.

In 1878, Tokushichi Nomura had a son, Shinnosuke (later called Tokushichi II). In his youth, Shinnosuke Nomura assisted his father in the moneychagning business, but his interests lay in a field which was still quite new to Japan—stock trading. At age 19, after completing his studies at the Osaka Commercial School, Shinnosuke Nomura went to work as an apprentice at a small stock trading shop managed by his brother-in-law. Nomura's apprenticeship was cut short after only a few months when he was conscripted into the Japanese army for three years. When he returned home, however, Nomura resolved to take Nomura Shoten into the stock trading business.

During the 1890s the stock market in Japan was still a somewhat crude affair. Only a few joint-stock companies existed at all. Most shares were held by a handful of rich and powerful businessmen, and government regulation of the exchanges was virtually non-existent. Price rigging and other corrupt practices gave stock brokers a bad reputation. Shinnosuke Nomura believed that through sound, ethical business practices, Nomura Shoten could win the confidence of investors over the long haul. Under his guidance, the stock trading department of Nomura Shoten was a consistent money maker by the turn of the century.

In 30 years Japan had transformed from a feudal to an industrial country. In 1904 and 1905 Japan fought and won a war against Russia. Her victory over a major European power signified that Japan had come of age. The stock markets reflected the optimism which military victory brought and trading volume reached record heights.

In 1906, Nomura Shoten established the first research department at a Japanese financial company. The company also began publishing a daily financial newsletter that year, the *Osaka Nomura Business News*. Nomura's innovations began to attract a great deal of attention. In 1907, Tokushichi Nomura retired, leaving Shinnosuke to run the business, Shinnosuke was known from this time as Tokushichi Nomura II.

In 1908, Tokushichi Nomura II took a five-month tour of the world's financial centers. When he returned he brought with him many new ideas. The research department was split into four separate divisions: research, statistics, editing, and translation. While in the United States, Nomura saw the positive impact publicity could have on profits, so he began investing a good deal of money in advertising his company's services. Nomura also entered the bond trading and underwriting fields. By the beginning of World War I, Nomura Shoten was regularly participating in underwriting syndicates.

World War I brought a boom to the Japanese economy. Exports to belligerent nations increased dramatically. As Japanese heavy industry floated bonds to finance its rapid expansion, Nomura's business picked up accordingly. After the war the bull market subsided, but Nomura continued to expand. In 1917, Nomura Shoten was reorganized as Nomura Shoten Incorporated. One year later, Tokushichi Nomura II fulfilled a life-long dream when he opened the Osaka Nomura Bank (now Daiwa Bank). He also set up a securities department to handle bond sales and underwriting. By 1920, regulations on bond trading were relaxed and bonds were sold at the exchanges. The market for securities had come a long way in 30 years.

In 1922, Nomura and Company was established as a holding company for the entire Nomura group, including the Osaka Nomura Bank and Nomura Shoten Inc. Throughout the early 1920s the bond market became more and more active, and the securities department of the Osaka Nomura Bank was expanding at a tremendous rate. In order to serve its customers better, the department was separated from the bank.

The Nomura Securities Company, Limited was incorporated on December 25, 1925. The company focused on the bond market and left the stock market alone. Otogo Kataoka, the president of the Osaka Nomura Bank and former head of its securities department, was elected president. Tokushichi Nomura II oversaw the entire operation. The firm began business with 84 employees and offices in Osaka, Nagoya, Tokyo, Kyoto, and Kobe.

The later 1920s were a time of economic difficulties for Japan. In 1927, a major panic rocked the financial community and 37 banks were forced to close. In 1929, the collapse of the New York stock market brought a worldwide depression. The economic difficulties were paralleled by the rise of militant nationalists in Japan.

Under the influence of these political groups, the government began to assume control over the economy. In 1931, Japan set up a puppet regime in Manchuria, and hostilities with China escalated until those two countries were fully at war by 1937. To finance the conflict, the government found it necessary to increase its bond issues. Nomura Securities was one of eight houses allowed to underwrite and sell bonds for the government and corporations. Government control of the bond market, however, pushed investors in the direction of stocks. In 1938, Nomura Securities opened a stock department and became an active dealer in both stocks and bonds.

At first, World War II stimulated economic growth in Japan. Stocks and bonds were traded briskly and Nomura, as one of the official dealers, did well. By 1942, Nomura had a 19% market share of the bond market, the largest of any securities house. But a year later it was clear that Japan's military success was coming to an end and the stock market plunged. Nomura, however, through its bond activities and through the newly authorized investment trust business, managed to expand right up until the end of the war.

The investment trust business was introduced in Japan in 1941 as a way of providing additional funds to finance the war. Nomura was the first company to offer the new form of investment. The decision to enter this new field caused some controversy in the company's board room, however. Otogo Kataoka, who was now chairman of Nomura Securities, was against their entry into the investment trust business. Tokushichi Nomura II, on the other hand, was in favor of entering the new business in full force. His long experience in finance and his knowledge of investment trusts overseas convinced him that the new investment vehicle could prove to be very profitable. The company's almost immediate success in the investment trust area proved him right. Nomura enjoyed a 47% market share of the investment trust business between 1941 and 1945. Chairman Kataoka, having been overruled on such a key issue, resigned.

From 1941 to 1947, Seizo Iida was president of Nomura Securities. Iida had been largely responsible for Nomura's entering the investment trust business. He had begun with the Nomura group in 1922 at the Osaka Nomura Bank and joined Nomura Securities at its founding in 1925. He wrote a number of books on economic analysis, and continually stressed the importance of Nomura's Research Department. Iida left the company in 1947, when the occupation authorities mandated retirement of many top corporate officers of the large family-controlled Japanese industrial groups known as *zaibatsu*.

After the war, Japan was devastated. It was estimated that one-fourth of Japan's national wealth was wiped out in 1944. Millions of Japanese were homeless. Jobs were scarce, and with six million returning soldiers, the unemployment rate seemed hopeless. The occupation forces began to reorganize the nation's political and economic structure. The 15 largest *zaibatsu*, of which the Nomura group was one, were broken up to end family control of the Japanese economy. Nomura Securities Company was dissolved and reorganized. Trading on the exchanges was prohibited until 1949. In the meantime, securities companies traded non-defense-related industry securities over-the-counter at their offices. This market was vigorous as people flocked to liquidate their holdings for cash. As industrial reconstruction reached full swing, the bond market picked up. By 1948, Nomura, stressing the individual investor, had captured 10% of the market, the largest share of any investment house.

Throughout the late 1940s, Nomura built its retail network. In addition to its 15 regular offices across Japan, Nomura set up 19 investment consultant centers in shopping malls and other key locations. These centers were an excellent way for the company to develop new customers. By providing basic information on the stock and bond markets, Nomura attracted customers who might not otherwise have been interested in investing.

In mid-1950, the Japanese economy slumped. But the Korean War soon stimulated demand and the economy revived quickly. Japanese exports increased dramatically. The country entered a period of steady growth, and Nomura's profits reflected this trend. In 1951, investment trusts were allowed for the first time since World War II. Nomura focused a great deal of energy on recruiting investors for the trusts and used a number of new techniques for this task. For example, it held a number of "Ladies Savings Investment Seminars" to educate women about the various forms of investing. The company also introduced the "Million Ryo Savings Chest" program, and lent out cash boxes as "piggy banks" which, once full, could be turned in for a share in an investment trust. The idea was to promote securities investment as a form of savings. The program was very successful, and by 1962 more than a million chests had been distributed.

In 1953, Nomura re-established its office in New York, which had been closed since 1936. It also established a Transfer Agency Department, the first in Japan, in 1953. In 1955, Nomura became the first company in Japan to introduce a computer system—a Univac 120. Two years later the company established the Nomura Real Estate Development Company, Ltd. The traditional businesses of Nomura grew as well throughout the decade.

In 1959, Tsunao Okumura was replaced by Minoru Segawa as president of Nomura Securities. Okumura had presided over the company since 1948. He became chairman of the board and remained in that office until 1968. Minoru Segawa had previously served as general manager of the firm. One of Segawa's first important actions was to set up separate companies to handle Nomura's huge investment trust funds. In 1960, the Nomura Investment Trust Management Company and the Nomura Investment Trust Sales Company assumed the management and development duties of Nomura's investment trusts.

Nomura's success continued throughout the early 1960s. In 1961, Nomura passed a milestone when it co-managed the first Japanese stock offering in the United States. The issue of ¥100 million worth of Sony Corporation american depositary receipts (ADRs) sold out in one hour. A year later, Nomura co-managed the first bond issue of a Japanese company in the United States. This $10 million issue for Mitsubishi Heavy Industries was soon followed by $20 million bond issue for Toshiba. Foreign capital poured into Japan, and Nomura cashed in on the increase in investment.

In 1965, Japan was hit by a severe recession, but Nomura's stable position in the marketplace allowed it to weather the storm. Nomura was the only one of the Japanese big four securities houses to record profits for both fiscal 1964 and 1965. Nomura launched one of its most ambitious projects in 1965—the Nomura Research Institute (NRI). Rather than expand its existing research department, Nomura decided to establish an independent research institute which would serve not just Nomura's needs but those of Japan as well. A number of advisors from the Stanford Research Institute in the United States helped Nomura set up the new "think tank." The company's belief that economics and technology would be closely intertwined in the future proved to be correct. NRI remains one of the premier research organizations in Japan.

In 1967, the Japanese government liberalized the capital markets, giving Nomura the opportunity to solicit greater foreign investments. Nomura International (Hong Kong) was established in 1967. In 1968, Kiichiro Kitaura became president. Kitaura was strongly in favor of an international orientation, and under his guidance Nomura continued to strengthen its overseas network. In 1969, Nomura Securities Inc. was incorporated in the United States, and was the first Japanese securities company to become a member of an American stock exchange (Boston).

In 1973, the oil crisis sent shock waves through the Japanese economy. Japanese industry, heavily dependent on imported oil, suffered a major blow and stock prices tumbled. Nonetheless, capital continued to flow into Japan in the 1970s, and as the Japanese government removed further restrictions on foreign investment, began to flow out of the country as well. Nomura established a number of investment trusts based on foreign stocks. By 1973, some half a dozen foreign stocks were listed on the Tokyo Stock Exchange. "Samurai bonds," bonds issued by foreign governments but denominated in yen, became very popular in the first half of the decade. In 1973, Nomura had its own shares listed on the Amsterdam Stock Exchange. Activities in Europe picked up dramatically. Branches in Amsterdam and London were incorporated as a single subsidiary, Nomura Europe N.V. The Frankfurt office became the headquarters of a separate subsidiary, Nomura Europe GmbH.

During the first half of the 1970s the bond market in Japan began to expand at a tremendous rate. The development of a secondary market for bonds was bolstered by an increase in government, particularly municipal, bond issues. In 1975 bond sales were more than three times what they had been in 1970 and Nomura's profits on bond transactions were up 900%. The "bond boom" continued throughout the decade.

In 1978, Setsuya Tabuchi took over as president of Nomura. Tabuchi devoted himself to making Nomura a primary force in the international securities arena, but also stressed the importance of the satisfied customer to the company's continued success. Tabuchi served as president for seven years, and then became chairman of the board. In 1979, the second oil crunch jeopardized economic growth, but unlike the oil crisis of 1973, panic did not set in. High-tech and other export-related companies had growth enough to ensure continued prosperity in the markets. As Nomura entered the 1980s, the Japanese economy was in excellent shape.

In 1981, Nomura's American subsidiary, Nomura Securities International, Inc., became the first Japanese securities company to gain membership on the New York Stock Exchange. As Japan strengthened its position in the world economy, Nomura Securities prepared to do the same. Nomura initiated a "Buy Japan" campaign designed to attract investment from the Middle East, Europe, and the United States and began an intensive, worldwide recruiting campaign to lure the best talent to Nomura's expanding global organization. As new offices and subsidiaries opened in Paris, Sydney, Beijing, Bahrain, Zurich, and Kuala Lumpur, they were staffed by the cream of the crop of local and Japanese personnel. Nomura also maintained its lead in securities-related computer technology. A computerized communications system, COMPASS-III, linked all its international offices by 1985. In 1982, CAPITAL (Computer Aided Portfolio and Investment Total Analysis) began to provide customers with up-to-the-minute market information and analysis. In 1985, the STOCKPORT function of CAPITAL was providing fund managers with quick analyses of the effect certain securities would have on their portfolios.

In the mid-1980s, Japan's Ministry of Finance approved substantial changes in Japan's capital market regulations. The markets were to be less restricted, allowing greater foreign competition and new debt-issuing instruments. Nomura responded by developing new kinds of bonds and by increasing its underwriting activities. Nomura presided over what can best be described as a Euroyen craze. By managing large issues like a ¥50 billion Euroyen bond issue for Dow Chemical and a $100 million forex-indexed issue for IBM Credit Corporation, Nomura established a reputation as a world-class securities house. Its success in the Euromarkets was a highlight of Nomura's growth in the 1980s.

In 1985, Yoshihisa Tabuchi was chosen as Nomura's next president. Setsuya Tabuchi, (no relation), nicknamed "Big Tabuchi" even though he is several inches shorter than his successor, became chairman. One year after taking the helm at Nomura, "Mini-Tabuchi" was named Man of the Year by *Financial World* magazine. In many ways the honor was a recognition of Nomura's ascension to the top of the world's securities industry.

Despite Nomura's success in Japan and Europe, the company, along with other Japanese securities houses, had difficulty establishing itself as a major player in the American market. Nomura Securities International operated more or less as an arm of the parent company. Most of its customers were Japanese. The company found it very difficult to compete with large American firms like Salomon Brothers, Merrill Lynch, Morgan Stanley, First Boston, and others who had long-established ties to institutional fund managers and debt issuers. Some analysts blamed the problem on Nomura's lack of decision-making autonomy: all major decisions had to be approved by the Tokyo office, and although Nomura recruited top-notch managers from other investment firms, many stayed only a short time because of a lack of real power to make decisions. Another problem Nomura faced was the traditional, consensus-oriented style of Japanese management. This lesson was brought home when Nomura missed out on the opportunity to participate in a $300 million issue for J.P. Morgan & Company led by Merrill Lynch in 1986 because it could not obtain approval for the action within fifteen minutes. Nomura was embarrassed to have missed the boat, and has begun to take steps to remedy this weakness.

In the later 1980s, Nomura Securities International in New York fell upon hard times. The stock market crash of October, 1987 wiped out some investors and scared many others out of the market. Bond sales, including U.S. treasury notes, also declined a year later. Although Nomura was the largest and wealthiest securities firm in the world by 1989, it was still having trouble muscling into the U.S. domestic market and was considering acquiring an established American securities firm.

For more than one hundred years, the name Nomura has been associated with the securities industry in Japan. Its sheer size guarantees that it will remain a major player in the world investment markets. President Yoshihisa Tabuchi continues to stress the commitment to each customer's success that Tokushichi Nomura II declared the primary directive of the company in 1925. Nomura has responded positively to the challenges that accompany a transforming industry. It has found opportunities for growth in the changes of the past, and can be expected to do so in the future.

Principal Subsidiaries: Nomura Research Institute (NRI); NRI Life Science; Nomura Investment Management Co., Ltd.; Nimco Europe Ltd.; Nomura Computer Systems Co., Ltd.; Nomura Operation Services Co., Ltd.; Nomura Business Services Co., Ltd.; Nomura Land and Building Co., Ltd.; Nomura Real Estate Development Co., Ltd.; Nomura China Investment Co., Ltd.; The Nomura Securities Investment Trust Management Co., Ltd.; Nomura Tourist Bureau, Inc.; Japan Associated Mortgage Acceptance Co., Ltd.; Nomura Card Services Co., Ltd.; Japan Associated Finance Co., Ltd.; JAFCO American Ventures Inc.; Jafco International (Asia) Ltd.; Jafco Finance Co., Ltd.; Nomura, Babcock, & Brown Co., Ltd.; Nomura Securities International Inc.; Nomura Securities International Ltd.; Nomura International Finance Plc; Nomura Belgium; Nomura Europe N.V.; Nomura Europe GmbH; Nomura (Switzerland) Ltd.; Nomura France; Nomura Investment Banking (Middle East) E.C.; Nomura International (Hong Kong) Ltd.; Singapore Nomura Merchant Banking Ltd.; Nomura Futures (Singapore) Pte Ltd.; Nomura Australia Ltd.; Associated Japanese Bank (International) Ltd.; P.T. Finconesia.

Further Reading: Beyond the Ivied Mountains: The Origin and Growth of a Japanese Securities House, Tokyo, Nomura Securities Company, Ltd., 1986.

ORIX CORPORATION

World Trade Center Building
2–4–1, Hamamatsu-cho
Minato-ku
Tokyo 105
Japan
(03) 435–6641

Public Company
Incorporated: 1964 as Orient Leasing Company, Ltd.
Employees: 4,000
Assets: ¥2.6 trillion (US$20.8 billion)
Stock Index: Tokyo Osaka Nagoya

Orix Corporation is Japan's largest general leasing firm. The company began as a Japanese-American joint venture in the mid-1960s, and helped introduce Japanese business to the idea of leasing its equipment instead of owning it. Now a multinational corporation, Orix leases computers, office equipment, cars, trucks, ships, and jumbo jets to businesses across Asia, Europe, and the United States, and also offers loans, direct financing leases, installment sales, and consumer credit.

In 1964 Nichimen Company (now Nichimen Corporation) and the United States Leasing Corporation established the Orient Leasing Company (OLC) in Osaka. Backed by the Sanwa Bank the company began with an initial capital of ¥100 million. At this time, leasing was very new in Japan. Growth was slow throughout the 1960s as Japanese business adjusted to the idea.

OLC spent much of the 1970s establishing itself throughout Asia, developing a pattern of growth either through ties with well-established local businesses or through heavy investment in local companies.

In 1970, OLC was listed on the second section of the Osaka Stock Exchange; by 1973 it was on the first section in Tokyo, Osaka and Nagoya. The following year, the company established its first wholly-owned subsidiary, Orient Leasing (Asia), in Hong Kong. The subsidiary handles mortgage loans, finances in multiple currencies, and leases major items like ships and planes.

In 1972, OLC established its first major subsidiary in Japan, Orient Leasing Interior Company. That same year, Orient Leasing established the Korea Development Leasing Corporation and Orient Leasing Singapore, which leases vehicles, machinery, furniture, medical and dental equipment, and vessels. In 1973, OLC entered Malaysia; in 1975, Indonesia; in 1977, the Philippines; in 1978, Thailand. OLC also established subsidiaries in South America during the 1970s, entering Brazil in 1973 and Chile in 1977.

Orient Leasing began to lease commercial aircraft in 1978, when the company purchased a DC10 from McDonnell Douglas and two Boeing 747 passenger jets for lease to Korean Air Lines. The company purchased another aircraft in the same deal for lease to Thai Airways International. This deal, part of a joint venture with Nippon Shinpan Company, came at a time when American aircraft manufacturers were complaining that limited export funding was making it difficult for them to compete internationally. According to *The Wall Street Journal*, the purchases were arranged in an effort to show genuine Japanese concern for reducing its trade surplus. Later in 1978, OLC purchased two wide-bodied airbuses with C. Itoh & Company for lease to Greece's Olympic Airways.

While Orient Leasing spent the 1970s establishing itself in Asia, the 1980s were a time of expansion in the United States, Europe, and China, one still untapped Asian market. OLC brought leasing to a developing China in 1981. In partnership with two Chinese companies, China International Trust and Investment Corporation and Beijing Machinery and Equipment Corporation, OLC founded the China Orient Leasing Company. Leasing in China boomed in the following years, as state-owned enterprises demanded machinery for their outdated factories. In 1984, China Orient Leasing Company wrote $40 million in contracts, three times the amount it had written just two years earlier, for equipment as varied as plant machinery, film development equipment, and printing presses.

In 1982 Orient Leasing opened a representative office in Greece, and in 1983 the company established Orient Leasing (U.K.) in London, its first step toward an independent presence in Europe. Growth continued in 1986 with the establishment of Lombard Orient Leasing Ltd., a partnership between OLC and Lombard North Central, the largest finance company in the United Kingdom. In 1988, OLC expanded further into Europe when it made an agreement to form a leasing company in Spain to lease Japanese computers and office equipment.

In America, OLC set up Orient Leasing USA Corporation in 1981 and Orient-U.S. Leasing Corporation in 1982. In the late 1980s, OLC began to diversify, investing in the Hyatt Group, a hotel chain, and Rubloff Inc., a major Chicago real estate company.

With the Hyatt Group, OLC arranged financing for hotels in Chicago, Illinois; Greenwich, Connecticut; and Scottsdale, Arizona. Most of the equity financing came directly from OLC and Hyatt; OLC assembled Japanese investors to cover the rest.

In 1987, Orient Leasing entered the American real estate market when it bought a 23.3% interest in Rubloff. Willard Brown Jr., the chairman of Rubloff, told the *Chicago Tribune*, "(Orient Leasing) has a substantial appetite, and (Rubloff's) job will be to create the right investments for them."

OLC entered the housing loan and mortgage security

loan markets in the early 1980s. OLC also diversified into securities in 1986, surprising the leasing community with the purchase of Akane Securities Company, Ltd., a small Japanese brokerage firm. Though lease-financing is its core business, with this purchase the company announced its intention to initiate "new operations in related, high-potential fields."

As part of its plan to diversify, Orient Leasing renamed itself Orix in 1989, the company's 25th anniversary. According to company officials, Orix is an abbreviation of "original", with the "X" added to symbolize a future of "flexibility and diversity." As part of a campaign to increase recognition of its new name, Orix bought a Japanese baseball team, the Hankyu Braves, and renamed it the Orix Braves.

The leasing business has soared in Japan in the past few years, fueled by heavy capital investments by Japanese industry. It has become such an attractive business, in fact, that many new companies have entered the field, pushing profit margins below 1% even for industry-leader Orix, according to *The Economist*. Orix's name change is just the most visible part of the company's move to broaden the financial services it offers and decrease its reliance on the leasing business.

Principal Subsidiaries: Orient Auto Leasing Co., Ltd.; Orient Leasing Interior Co., Ltd. (80%); Computer Systems Leasing, Ltd. (49%); Y.O. Machinery Leasing Co., Ltd. (81%); Orient Aircraft Co., Ltd.; Osaka Ichioka Co., Ltd. (47%); Orient Instrument Rentals Co., Ltd.; Budget Rent A Car Co., Ltd. (70%); Family Consumer Credit Co., Ltd. (72%); OSR Co., Ltd. (90%); Akane Securities Co., Ltd. (95%); Orient Capital Co., Ltd. (35%); Perseus Shipping Co., Ltd.; Orient Insurance Center Co., Ltd.; Toshiki Co., Ltd. (52%); Orient Leasing (Asia) Ltd.; Orient Leasing (Hong Kong) Ltd.; Korea Development Leasing Corp. (34%); China Orient Leasing Co., Ltd. (50%); Consolidated Orient Leasing and Finance Corp. (Philippines, 40%); Thai Orient Leasing Co., Lt. (49%); United Orient Leasing Co. Bhd. (Malaysia, 45%); Orient Leasing Singapore Ltd. (50%); Orient Car Leasing Private Ltd. (Singapore, 45%); P.T. Orient Bina Usaha Leasing (Indonesia, 49%); Lanka Orient Leasing Co., Ltd. (Sri Lanka, 30%); Orient Leasing Pakistan (Private) Ltd. (40%); S.A. Locabel (Belgium, 25%); Orient Leasing (U.K.) Ltd.; Lombard Orient Leasing Ltd. (50%); Orient Leasing USA Corp.; Orient-U.S. Leasing Corp (50%); Rubloff Inc. (38%); Bradesco Leasing S.A. Arrendamento Mercantil (Brazil, 25%); Leasing Andino S.A. (Chile, 35%); Budget Orient Leasing Ltd. (Australia, 40%).

PaineWebber

PAINEWEBBER GROUP INC.

The Paine Webber Building
1285 Avenue of the Americas
New York, New York 10019
U.S.A.
(212) 713–2000

Public Company
Incorporated: 1970 as Paine, Webber, Jackson & Curtis Inc.
Employees: 12,800
Assets: $17.9 billion
Stock Index: New York Pacific

The PaineWebber Group is one of the largest financial service companies in the world, offering asset management, investment banking, and brokerage activities to both institutional and individual investors. From a tiny partnership founded more than a hundred years ago, PaineWebber has grown into a major international presence.

Paine & Webber was founded in 1880 by William A. Paine and Wallace Webber, formerly clerks at Boston's Blackstone National Bank, who set up shop on Congress Street in Boston. The next year, Webber acquired a seat on the Boston Stock Exchange. The firm admitted Charles Paine as a partner in 1881 and changed its name to Paine, Webber & Company.

From there, Paine Webber embarked on a steady course of expansion that would last well into the next century. In 1890, the firm joined the New York Stock Exchange. It purchased seats on the Chicago Board of Trade in 1909 and the Chicago Stock Exchange in 1916. Paine Webber opened its first branch office in 1899 in the copper mining town of Houghton, Michigan. Nine branches sprang into existence during World War I, including Paine Webber's first in New York City, in 1916. Before this office opened, business in New York had been conducted by wire and through New York brokerage houses. During the feverish years of the late 1920s, five more offices opened and six moved to larger quarters. By its 50th anniversary, in 1930, the firm could boast of 25 branch offices in 22 cities spread throughout the Northeast and upper Midwest, and a position as one of the largest firms on Wall Street.

But the bull market that had fueled this growth came to a shattering end in October, 1929, and the Great Depression that followed brought lean times to the brokerage industry. Paine Webber maintained its standing as a leading Wall Street firm, but did not emerge from the Depression unscathed. By the late 1930s, its presence had shrunk to 19 cities. Not only did the Depression mark the end of the Paine Webber's steady growth, but it had to face this period of crisis without the guidance of its founders. Wallace Webber had retired in 1894, and William A. Paine, who had continued to head the firm, died in September, 1929.

Paine's son Stephen was a partner in the firm by this time, but it was through him that Paine Webber found itself embroiled in one of the major securities fraud cases of the decade. In the Continental Securities Corporation scandal of 1938 to 1939, a group of American and Canadian financiers gained control of six different investment trusts, sold off their portfolios, and filled them up again with unmarketable securities of dubious value, including shares in dummy companies owned by the conspirators themselves. Creditors of these trusts found themselves defrauded of more than $6 million. Paine Webber, through Stephen Paine, loaned the money used in four of the takeovers and sold off the portfolios for the conspirators. The firm itself was ultimately cleared of all wrongdoing and ended its role in the case with damage payments to some of the creditors. But the New York Stock Exchange suspended Stephen Paine and Frank Hope, a fellow partner and former governor of the New York Stock Exchange, for ignoring evidence of the fraudulent nature of these transactions. Paine was also convicted in federal court of mail fraud and served four months in prison.

World War II finally ended America's economic slump, and in 1942 Paine Webber merged with Jackson & Curtis, a fellow old-line Boston house. The resulting conglomeration of Paine, Webber, Jackson & Curtis listed 23 branch offices. For two decades after the merger, Paine Webber remained essentially the same kind of establishment it had been for the first 60 years of its existence: a privately owned brokerage house that made most of its money in the retail trade, buying and selling securities for private customers. Although it had long been one of the largest firms on Wall Street, it was still tiny by today's standards.

In the late 1960s and the 1970s, lower stock market volume combined with two important legislative changes to radically alter the brokerage industry. The first of these, the Employee Retirement Income Security Act of 1974, increased the importance of institutional investors as a revenue source. The second, the abolition of the brokers' fixed-rate commission structure in May, 1975, slashed profit margins by allowing fierce price competition among houses. Together, these factors forced brokerage houses to merge and expand in order to increase their working capital and compensate for reduced profit margins. Conservative companies whose mainstay had always been the retail trade were forced to enter new markets. Paine Webber, although it was often slow to innovate and to this day relies heavily on retail sales, was caught up just like its competitors in the changes in the brokerage industry during these years.

Much of this change broke upon the firm during the watch of a single CEO, James W. Davant. When Davant assumed the post in 1964, Paine Webber had fewer than

40 branch offices, annual revenues of $30 million, and $1 million in capital. When he retired in 1980, Paine Webber's 229 branches earned revenues of $900 million and capital had reached $240 million.

As if to usher in this new era of change and expansion, Paine Webber moved its headquarters in 1963 from genteel Boston to New York City. In 1967 it made the first acquisition in its history. An industry-wide trend had developed in which large, New York–based houses were acquiring regional securities firms in order to increase their presence nationwide, and Paine Webber joined it by buying the brokerage house of Barret Fitch North, based in Kansas City, Missouri. The acquisition also marked a break from the Northeast–upper Midwest area of operation to which Paine Webber had confined itself since the turn of the century.

In 1970, Paine Webber moved into the mid-Atlantic region by acquiring the principal offices of the securities firm Abbott, Proctor & Paine, based in Richmond, Virginia. It also conducted unsuccessful merger talks with Dean Witter & Company, the first of several efforts on its part to merge with another major house to form a brokerage juggernaut.

The firm underwent a major reorganization that year, incorporating and changing its name to Paine, Webber, Jackson & Curtis Inc. This decision was taken for the sake of tax benefits and greater operating flexibility. Once again, Paine Webber was joining a trend rather than starting one. In breaking the news of the pending incorporation, *The New York Times* described the company as "one of the last major brokerage-house partnerships." The transformation of the old New York houses from private partnerships to publicly-held corporations began as a result of the financial setbacks suffered by the securities industry during 1969 and 1970, when lower stock market volume showed up the fragility of the retail trade and forced companies to search for more dependable sources of capital. Paine Webber finally went public in 1972 when it absorbed Abacus Fund, an investment company, and paid Abacus stockholders with Paine Webber shares.

The firm took a great leap in 1973 when it opened its first overseas offices, in London and Tokyo. But the other significant events of the remainder of Davant's stewardship have a more familiar ring to them. In 1973, Paine Webber acquired two more firms: F.S. Smithers and Mitchum, Jones & Templeton. The firm underwent another reorganization in 1974, forming a holding company for Paine Webber called PaineWebber Incorporated. Two more proposed mergers with major houses fell through: the first, with Shearson Hammill & Company in 1972, drew a Justice Department antitrust inquiry and would have formed the nation's second-largest brokerage house behind Merrill Lynch Pierce Fenner & Smith; the second, with Oppenheimer & Company, fell through in 1976. The company also completed more acquisitions, buying four offices from duPont Walston in 1974 to bolster its retail capacity; acquiring the securities research firm of Mitchell Hutchins in 1977; and merging with Blyth Eastman Dillon & Company in January, 1980.

The merger with Blyth Eastman Dillon nearly proved ruinous, however. PaineWebber, caught up in the intricacies of assimilating the investment banking firm, was blindsided by the explosion in stock market volume which presaged the bull market of the 1980s. The company's operating systems were overloaded and many customer orders were left unprocessed or even lost. These orders then had to be tracked down manually, at great expense of time and money, and created further order backlogs. Eventually PaineWebber was forced to suspend some of its businesses, including bond and over-the-counter stock trading. For fiscal year 1980, the firm reported a $6.9 million loss on revenues of $896 million in what should have been an exceptional money-making year.

Davant waited until the Blyth Eastman Dillon crisis had simmered down before passing the baton to Donald Marron in May, 1980. The two men offered something of a contrast with each other. Davant, described by *The Wall Street Journal* as "courtly" and "low-key," spent virtually all of his adult life with PaineWebber, rising through the ranks to CEO. When asked at the press conference announcing his retirement if he would consider returning to the securities industry, he quoted Oscar Wilde in reply: "To win back my youth . . . there is nothing I wouldn't do—except take exercise, get up early or be a useful member of the community."

Marron, on the other hand, charted a more aggressive and entrepreneurial career on Wall Street. He came to PaineWebber through Mitchell Hutchins, an acquisition he had brought about as president of the smaller firm. He had a reputation as a prodigy and a forceful self-promoter—at the age of 25, he was running D. B. Marron & Company, his own investment banking firm, which merged with Mitchell Hutchins in 1965.

Under Marron, PaineWebber continued to diversify. In 1983 it acquired Rotan Mosle Financial Corporation, a southwestern company which still functions under its old name, and First Mid America, headquartered in Nebraska. In 1984, the firm acquired Becker Paribas Futures, a commodity-futures trading firm, to expand its presence in that market and moved into mortgage banking with the purchase of Rouse Real Estate Finance. Also in 1984, a reorganization of the company combined the three subsidiaries, Paine, Webber, Jackson & Curtis; Blyth Eastman Paine Webber; and PaineWebber Mitchell Hutchins, under one name, PaineWebber Incorporated. PaineWebber Group Inc. was established as the parent holding company. In 1985, Marron declared in *Fortune* that he intended to make PaineWebber one of Wall Street's top five investment bankers within four years (it was generally ranked ninth at the time). Pursing its new goals in investment banking, PaineWebber participated in the leveraged buyouts of National Car Rental in 1986 and Greyhound in 1987 and brokered the purchase of Braniff in 1988 by a group of East Coast investors.

In the wake of the October, 1987 stock market crash, most major brokerage houses reported tiny profits or even losses for the fourth quarter of the year. PaineWebber was no exception, citing pre-tax earnings of $35,000, versus figures in the tens of millions for the previous three quarters. The firm streamlined by selling its commercial paper operations to Citicorp in November, 1987 and its venture capital unit to the unit's managers in January, 1988. Also in 1987, the company began to move some of its operations to Lincoln Harbor, New Jersey. PaineWebber also moved to bolster its capital, selling an 18% equity interest to the Japanese insurance giant Yasuda Mutual Life Insurance Company in November, 1987 (the proceeds were earmarked for its merchant banking unit) and acquiring Manufacturers Hanover Investment Corporation in early 1988.

The October, 1987 collapse in stock prices frightened away many small investors and few of them returned to the market over the next year. This lack of interest proved damaging to PaineWebber, reliant as it is on the retail trade. PaineWebber hopes that its new corporate strategy, announced in July, 1987, will help lure back some of these investors. The strategy focuses on four core businesses: investment and merchant banking, capital trading, asset management, and retail and institutional sales. So far this plan seems to be working, with 1989 earnings up about 25% over the year before.

Principal Subsidiaries: PaineWebber International Inc.; PaineWebber Inc.; PaineWebber International Bank Ltd.; PaineWebber International Capital Inc.; PaineWebber Properties.; PaineWebber Capital Inc.; PaineWebber Development Corp.; PaineWebber Mortgage Finance.; Rotan Mosle; Mitchell Hutchins Asset Management, Inc.; Mitchell Hutchins Institutional Investors.

Further Reading: Paine, Webber & Company: A National Institution, Paine, Webber & Company, Boston, 1930.

SALOMON INC.

One New York Plaza
New York, New York 10004
U.S.A.
(212) 747-7000

Public Company
Incorporated: 1981
Employees: 8,400
Assets: $85.26 billion
Stock Index: New York

Salomon Inc. is a diversified financial-services company led by its flagship subsidiary, Salomon Brothers Inc., one of Wall Street's leading securities houses. The parent company also engages in commodities trading and petroleum refining through its subsidiaries Phibro Energy Inc. and Philipp Brothers, Inc. Swiss-based Salomon Commercial Finance AG rounds out Salomon's worldwide financial presence. This slightly unusual combination of businesses is the result of the 1981 purchase of Salomon Brothers, then a private partnership, by the commodities company Phibro Corporation. The resulting company was named Phibro-Salomon until 1986, when the firm assumed the name Salomon Inc.

Salomon Brothers may not be Wall Street's most famous name, but this reflects more than anything else the firm's long and continued absence from the retail end of the securities business. Institutional investors and companies in search of an underwriter don't need pithy advertising slogans to catch their attention. Throughout its history, Salomon has stuck mainly to the two businesses that it knows best—wholesale securities trading and underwriting—and used them to rise from modest beginnings to a position of prominence in the financial community.

Salomon Brothers began in 1910 in New York City when Arthur, Herbert, and Percy Salomon broke away from their father Ferdinand's money-brokerage operation and went into business for themselves. They took with them a $5,000 stake and their father's clerk, Ben Levy, and opened a small office on Broadway near Wall Street. Later that year, they became Salomon Brothers & Hutzler when they brought broker Morton Hutzler into the firm for the sake of his seat on the New York Stock Exchange.

During its infancy, Salomon concentrated on money brokerage, an obscure Wall Street specialty that consisted of arranging loans for securities brokers and trading bonds for institutional clients. The partners branched out into underwriting in 1915 by participating in a $15 million offering of short-term Argentine notes. But expansion of its underwriting activities was limited: underwriting was dominated at the time by a select group of old-line firms. Reputation and connections were essential to building a clientele, and the Salomons had neither.

Salomon Brothers' big break came when the United States entered World War I. The Liberty Loan Act of 1917 unleashed a flood of government securities that needed someone to take them to market, and social connections were not necessary to getting business, so Salomon entered the lucrative government-bond market. The firm's expansion continued through the boom years of the 1920s. By 1930, Salomon had opened branches in Boston, Chicago, Philadelphia, Minneapolis, and Cleveland and employed a staff of more than 30 traders and salesmen.

The 1920s are remembered most for the big bull market in stocks, but Salomon entered the equities business tentatively, even then dealing only wholesale. As a result, the firm made little money in the bull market, but also escaped serious damage in the market crash in 1929. Arthur Salomon, in fact, had decreed in 1927 that all of his company's margin accounts be terminated.

The eldest and most forceful personality among the three Salomons, Arthur was without question the firm's dominant partner. A shrewd player of the financial game and a hard worker who held few interests beyond Wall Street, he became known, according to Salomon historian Robert Sobel, "as one of the very few individuals who could see J.P. Morgan without an appointment." His death in 1928 left a power vacuum that was not filled until his nephew William became managing partner 35 years later.

In addition to coping with the Great Depression, Salomon had to cope with an internal struggle in the 1930s centering around Herbert, who considered himself Arthur's natural heir. Herbert was the youngest brother, but Percy was too retiring by nature to assume leadership. However, Herbert lacked Arthur's *savoir-faire* and failed to earn the confidence of many partners, who found a reluctant leader for their opposition in Ben Levy. The general slump in the bond market increased tensions within the firm, squeezing its profits and forcing it to lay off traders.

The one bright spot in the decade for Salomon came at the end of the capital strike of 1933–1935, when the establishment investment banks protested the Roosevelt administration's formation of the Securities and Exchange Commission by refusing to bring new issues to market. In 1935, both the government and the banks were looking for a face-saving end to the moratorium, but Salomon, still an outsider, decided to end it on its own by underwriting a bond issue for Swift & Company, the meat packer. This was the first new debt issue to come to market under the new SEC rules and, though it brought the Salomon name into the spotlight, it caused resentment among the old-line underwriters that would last into the 1950s.

The firm concentrated on government bonds during World War II but didn't find them as great a boon as in 1917. After the war, Salomon's power vacuum persisted and the firm lacked strategic direction as a result. Nonetheless, individual departments prospered when left to their own devices. In 1951 Herbert died and Rudolf Smutny became the dominant figure in the firm, becoming senior partner in 1955. But Smutny's abrasive manner and questionable business decisions led to his ouster the next year. Percy Salomon's son William, aided by Ben Levy, spearheaded the coup.

William's coming of age in the family business solved the leadership problem that had existed since Arthur's death. William gradually accumulated influence at the firm in the years after Smutny's departure and was named managing partner in 1963. He guided Salomon through a massive expansion marked not by rapid diversification but by an aggressive, no-guts-no-glory approach to fields in which it was already established. According to journalist Paul Hoffman, William once boasted, "We'll bid for almost anything, and we take many baths."

In 1960, the firm moved to shore up a major weakness by starting its own research department, hiring economist Sidney Homer away from Scudder, Stevens & Clark to head it. Two years later, Homer was joined by Henry Kaufman, whose extraordinary ability to forecast interest rates would earn him the nickname "Dr. Gloom" on Wall Street.

In 1962, Salomon pulled a major coup by underwriting an AT&T offering worth $218 million, even though the financial markets were paralyzed at the time by the Cuban Missile Crisis. Also in the autumn of that year, the firm formed, with Blyth, Merrill Lynch, and Lehman Brothers, a group that became known as "the fearsome foursome." This association tried to break the establishment firms' stranglehold on the underwriting business by putting together syndicates that sought to outbid them on major utility-bond issues throughout the decade. Between 1962 and 1964, Salomon more than tripled its underwriting business, from $276 million to $873 million.

Salomon finally began to diversify its activities in the mid-1960s when, aided by the new computer technology on Wall Street, it expanded its block-trading activity on the New York Stock Exchange. In 1965 the firm bought seats on exchanges in Boston, Philadelphia, Washington, and Baltimore and on the Pacific Stock Exchange in Los Angeles. Salomon took advantage of an opportunity created by depressed stock prices in 1969 to expand its merger-and-acquisition activity, forging, among others, the Pepsi-ICI merger and Esmark's acquisition of Playtex. In 1971 the firm opened its first overseas office, in London, and the next year another in Hong Kong; in 1980 it opened a third in Tokyo.

In 1970, the firm finally dropped Morton Hutzler's name (Hutzler had retired in 1929) to mark a new era in Salomon's history. In 1971 the SEC began the process of deregulating brokerage commissions. Fees earned on the largest block trades were the first to be cut loose. Salomon responded by slashing its commission rate 50%. When rate structures ended in April, 1972, Salomon and archrival Goldman, Sachs led the way in conducting the first major block trades. Soon, however, sluggish stock market conditions made block trading less lucrative, and in 1973 Salomon posted its first money-losing year since 1956.

In 1975 the firm participated in one of the year's major stories when New York City found itself unable to meet its financial obligations and appealed to the state and federal governments for aid. William Simon, a former Salomon partner who was treasury secretary in the Ford administration at the time, said that Washington might organize a "punitive" bailout package to discourage other cities from doing the same in the future. New York state, for its part, formed the Municipal Assistance Corporation (MAC) to generate funds for the city. Salomon, along with Morgan Guaranty Trust, led the syndicate that marketed MAC debt offerings. Salomon also helped underwrite two more major bailouts before the decade was through, for the Government Employee Insurance Company in 1976 and Chrysler Corporation in 1979.

Having transformed Salomon into the second-largest underwriter and the largest private brokerage house in the United States, William Salomon retired in 1978 and was succeeded as CEO by John Gutfreund. Described by *Business Week* as "shrewd, supremely intelligent, cosmopolitan yet street-fighter tough" and as a member of Manhattan high society who would "host extravagant parties straight out of *The Great Gatsby*," Gutfreund had studied literature at Oberlin College and considered teaching English before joining Salomon in 1953. He became a partner in 1963 at the age of 34 and became William Salomon's heir apparent when Simon left to join the federal government in 1972.

Under Gutfreund, Salomon participated in the leveraged-buyout boom of the 1980s, including Xerox's acquisition of Crum & Foster, Texaco's controversial acquisition of Getty Oil, and the mergers between Santa Fe Industries and Southern Pacific and Gulf Oil and Standard Oil of California. The firm was also retained as an adviser by AT&T when the telecommunications giant underwent the largest corporate breakup in United States history. But, as it had been for seven decades, the core of Salomon's business remained underwriting and bond trading. By 1985 Salomon's underwriting business generated 22% of all the money raised by American corporations through new issues, while Salomon's high-volume, low-margin approach to the bond business had made it the largest dealer of U.S. government securities.

The most important event in Salomon's recent history occurred in 1981, when the company was acquired by Phibro Corporation, a commodities firm. The new entity was known as Phibro-Salomon Inc. until 1986, when Salomon gained control and changed the name of the parent company to Salomon Inc. The merger gave Phibro the diversification it desired and gave Salomon the operating capital it needed for further expansion. But many partners were not pleased by the prospect of becoming salarymen whose profits would belong to Phibro management and not themselves. William Salomon also expressed displeasure that retired partners received nothing out of the merger deal while general partners like Gutfreund and merger-and-acquisition specialist J. Ira Harris received bonuses of over $10 million. "I would have thought that those of us who had been here 40 years deserved to share in the gain," he told *Business Week*. He and his successor rarely spoke after the merger.

The flight of individual investors that followed the stock market crash of 1987 did not hit Salomon as hard as it did retail-oriented houses like PaineWebber and Merrill Lynch. In fact, it closed out the year as the largest underwriter in the country, and the second-largest in the world after sponsoring $40.3 billion worth of new issues. But Salomon had also announced significant retrenchment plans prior to the crash and laid off 800 employees. Changes in the tax laws and rising interest rates in the first half of 1987 caused a slump in the bond market, seriously affecting Salomon's main business, and competition from Japanese firms further cut into profits. Although the firm could boast of co-lead managing Conrail's $1.7 billion stock offering (the largest initial public stock offering in history), it also lost $79 million in a post-crash underwriting for British Petroleum and was nearly left with a $100 million loss when Southland Corporation decided to postpone a junk-bond offering in November of that year.

To cope with the slow securities markets, many Wall Street firms turned to merchant banking and junk bonds for revenue. Thanks in part to lower stock prices, mergers and acquisitions increased in 1988. But Salomon, which had always specialized in trading and was plagued by weakness in its merchant-banking division (Salomon's reputation was tarnished by its involvement with two leveraged buyout failures—TVX in 1987 and Revco in 1988) was slow to diversify and its financial performance suffered. Its underwriting business also suffered and in 1988 Merrill Lynch overtook Salomon as the nation's top underwriter. Gutfreund came under substantial external and internal criticism for a lack of strategic direction, causing financial journalists to refer to him as "embattled" throughout 1988 and into 1989. Key personnel began to leave, and rumors circulated that Salomon would take itself private or be taken over. One bright spot, however, is its subsidiary in Japan. The leading foreign trader in government bonds there, Salomon Brothers Asia, Ltd. is, according to *Business Week*, "Tokyo's largest and most successful foreign brokerage." Given Japan's notoriously clubby business atmosphere, Salomon's success is particularly impressive.

Despite its recent troubles, Salomon remains a success story. Back in Arthur Salomon's day, Salomon Brothers carried on an ambivalent relationship with the old-line firms that controlled the underwriting market, on the one hand resenting their dominance but on the other needing their indulgence in order to get new business. By the 1980s, it had become widely respected as the most important underwriter in the nation. After decades of fighting the establishment and feeding at the fringes of an industry that is, in the words of Paul Hoffman, "as rigidly hierarchical as the army, the Catholic Church, or the Soviet Presidium," Salomon today is firmly established at the top.

Principal Subsidiaries: Residential Funding Corp.; Residential Funding Mortgage Securities I, Inc.; Salomon Capital Access Corp.; Salomon Capital Access for Savings Institutions, Inc.; PRI Petroleum Inc.; Salomon Forex Inc.; Scanports Shipping, Inc.; Home Mac Government Financial Corp.; Home Mac Government Financial Corp. West; Home Mac Mortgage Securities Corp.; Hill Petroleum Co. (80%); Hill Petroleum Co. A.G.; Salomon Commercial Finance AG; Scanport Shipping Ltd.; Mortgage Corp. Ltd.; Derby & Co., Inc.; Phibro Energy Inc.; Phillip Brothers Inc.

Further Reading: Hoffman, Paul. *The Dealmakers: Inside the World of Investment Banking*, Garden City, New York, Doubleday, 1984; Sobel, Robert. *Salomon Brothers 1910–1985: Advancing to Leadership*, New York, Salomon Brothers Inc., 1986; Lewis, Michael. *Liar's Poker: Rising Through the Wreckage on Wall Street*, New York, W.W. Norton, 1989.

SHEARSON LEHMAN HUTTON HOLDINGS INC.

World Financial Center
American Express Tower
New York, New York 10285
U.S.A.
(212) 298-2000

Public Company:
Incorporated: 1983 as Shearson Lehman Brothers Holding Inc.
Employees: 38,500
Assets: $84.84 billion
Stock Index: New York Pacific

Shearson Lehman Hutton is one of the largest investment-banking firms in the United States. The firm has had a lot of practice in mergers and acquisitions as it took over some 40 firms in its rise to prominence, including old-line firms such as Hayden Stone, Shearson Hammill & Company, Loeb Rhoades, Hornblower & Company, Lehman Brothers Kuhn Loeb, and E.F. Hutton. Today it is a subsidiary of American Express, which owns 61% of the company.

Sanford Weill was Shearson's guiding force through much of its history. Starting out as a runner for Bear Stearns, Weill eventually became president of American Express in 1983. Weill and then his protege, Peter Cohen, led the firm on an aggressive route that has involved some of the most famous deals on Wall Street.

In 1960 Weill helped form the investment firm of Carter, Berlind, Potoma & Weill. With some $215,000 in capital, CBPW was tiny, but Weill's ambition and his genius for melding companies characterized its growth.

The firm made little news during its first five years. In 1965 it evolved into Carter, Berlind, Weill and Levitt, Inc., and Weill became chairman. Two years later, CBWL made its first acquisition, taking over Bernstein Macauley, Inc., a firm that specialized in investment management. This first deal had most of the characteristics of a Weill deal—a long-established, respected firm would run into trouble, and Weill's firm would take it over, merge it smoothly into his operation, usually cutting its back-office employees and keeping its sales representatives. Frequently, the target firm specialized in an area of investment banking in which Weill's firm was weak.

After the takeover of Bernstein Macauley, Weill waited three more years to acquire another firm. This time, the deal was a bizarre and influential merger unlike anything yet seen on Wall Street. On the surface, the facts were straightforward. In 1970, CBWL acquired Hayden Stone, an old-line retail brokerage that had fallen victim to what can only be called an excess of success. Hayden Stone had grossed $113 million in 1968, five times its gross in 1960, earning significant profits. In the late 1960s, though, many Wall Street firms had difficulties with their back-office functions, and Hayden Stone's difficulties were among the worst. Its rapid expansion (the firm had almost tripled, to more than 80 offices within the decade) was too much for it to handle, and it was forced by the New York Stock Exchange to cut back on its trading.

When losses accelerated in 1969 and then worsened in the first months of 1970, Hayden Stone began to look for a merger partner. CBWL, whose gross revenues in 1970 were only $11 million, emerged as the leading candidate when Walston & Company decided, due to Hayden Stone's lack of capital, not to acquire all of the firm but to take just 15 retail offices instead.

Several of Hayden Stone's private investors proved more interested in suing the firm than in selling it, though. These investors felt that they had been duped into investing, and that Hayden Stone, which the New York Stock Exchange (NYSE) allowed to operate despite its being in violation of NYSE capital rules, should be made an example of and allowed to fail (for which the NYSE would have to pick up the tab, since Hayden Stone was a member firm). The NYSE and CBWL engaged in a furious effort to convince investors to agree to the sale—which included a clause prohibiting them from suing. Eventually, after President Richard Nixon's name was invoked, the last investor agreed to the deal and Hayden Stone merged with CBWL. This deal also led to several significant reforms in the operations of the New York Stock Exchange.

This takeover thrust the firm, now called CBWL-Hayden Stone, into Wall Street's limelight. Weill was able to successfully merge the two companies, and his strict control of the back office helped solve Hayden Stone's biggest problem and stemmed losses at the firm.

During the recession of the early 1970s, Wall Street suffered along with U.S. industry. Many firms decided their best chance for survival was to join forces, and CBWL-Hayden Stone took advantage of the difficult days of 1973 to acquire H.L. Hentz, another brokerage, and Saul Lerner & Company. Then came its 1974 acquisition of Shearson Hammill & Company, easily the most ambitious takeover Weill had yet attempted.

Despite its strong retail sales force, Shearson Hammill had become strapped for cash, and in the difficult times of the early 1970s, the firm opted to merge with the smaller, but better-capitalized, CBWL-Hayden Stone. The two firms became known as Shearson Hayden Stone, keeping the Shearson name because the brokerage had been a "major" underwriter, one looked to on the biggest deals, a status Hayden Stone did not have.

Shearson Hayden Stone made two major acquisitions in 1976. One was Faulkner, Dawkins & Sullivan, a regional brokerage with one of the best research divisions in the industry. The other was Lamson Brothers, a well-regarded commodities broker.

By 1977, Shearson's holdings were consolidated, and the result was the seventh-largest investment-banking firm in the country. Its revenues had more than tripled since 1972, to $134 million in 1977, and employees now numbered more than 4,000.

Shearson's growth and success seemed to defy the environment on Wall Street in the mid-1970s. Firms were now legally unable to both advise and underwrite a client on a particular deal. Overall trading volume had dropped significantly, New York Stock Exchange seat prices were down by a factor of ten (by 1976 prices were down to $40,000 a seat), and some were calling for membership requirements to be liberalized. Wall Street also faced increased regulatory pressures from the Securities and Exchange Commission (SEC) and competition in its traditional fields from a variety of sources. Some companies even took to underwriting their own issues (Exxon most prominent among them). Mergers and bankruptcies had driven the number of New York Stock Exchange member firms down from the 1960s high of 681 to 490. Worse, on May 1, 1975 fixed commissions were eliminated. Price cutting ensued, which further increased the pressure on firms to perform well.

Even long-standing, highly successful firms suffered under these pressures. In 1979, Shearson acquired Loeb Rhoades, Hornblower & Company, one of Wall Street's oldest and most successful firms. The takeover of Loeb Rhoades made Shearson number-two in the investment-banking world. Weill's mastery of mergers paid off as he brought the two large firms together. One of the keys to his methods was to ensure that Shearson kept absolute control of back-office functions, which allowed both firms to run smoothly as they joined. Also, Shearson usually incorporated firms very slowly, a kind of patience rarely seen in Wall Street–firm mergers.

In 1981, after Shearson had averaged a 60% yearly increase in profits over the last four years, Weill gambled big—he directed the takeover of the Boston Company, a money-management firm. The $47 million takeover was in direct violation of the Glass-Steagall Act, which separated commercial and investment banking after the stock market crash of 1929.

Many banks protested this violation of Glass-Steagall, but a number of the major money-center banks were in favor of it because this made it more likely that the banks would be allowed to underwrite securities and perform other actions that Glass-Steagall had denied them. Shearson eventually was allowed to keep the Boston Company.

Not long afterwards, Weill approached the American Express Company to suggest that it take over Shearson. Weill wanted the capital that American Express could provide to give Shearson more deal-making power. A well-capitalized partner is also a stabilizing factor in uncertain times. In addition, American Express and Shearson together would be able to offer customers more services. The potential scope of the combined company was much broader than that of any bank.

The $900 million deal had its hitches. Some felt that risk-taking Shearson would lose flexibility when mired in the bureaucracy of a peace-of-mind oriented, $21 billion company like American Express, making it unable to practice its aggressive strategies. There were also those who remembered American Express's previous venture into the investment-banking world, when it bought 25% of Donaldson, Lufkin & Jenrette only to see the firm, and the investment, fizzle.

But Shearson and American Express fit together rather neatly. Within 18 months of the deal, Shearson had acquired four more companies and its capital had more than doubled.

Shearson did not make another major acquisition until 1984. In May of that year, Shearson acquired Lehman Brothers Kuhn Loeb for $360 million. Only ten months before, Lehman Brothers had reported another in a string of exceptionally profitable years. Then, in a stunningly short span, the firm fell apart, due largely to the combined forces of a market downturn in 1984 and an internal power struggle in which Peter Peterson was replaced as chief executive by Lew Glucksman.

Acquiring Lehman Brothers established Shearson as a dominant force on Wall Street. It also marked Peter Cohen's coming of age. Cohen, Weill's longtime personal assistant, had taken over as CEO when Weill became president of American Express in 1983.

Between 1984 and 1987, Shearson rode a lengthy bull market smoothly, surviving the insider-trading scandal of 1986 better than most. The firm had been quiet for longer than usual, but 1987 made up for it. First, in March 1987, American Express sold 13% of Shearson to Nippon Life Insurance, a Japanese company, for $508 million. Later that year Shearson went public, with American Express retaining 61% of the firm. Then came the stock market crash of October 19, 1987.

Shearson suffered along with the rest of Wall Street. For the year, revenues were flat, at $6.7 billion, and earnings dropped 70%, to $101 million. But only two months after the crash, Shearson announced a blockbuster deal: the purchase of E. F. Hutton.

Hutton had been in difficulty for some time; in fact, its top officers had debated heatedly before rejecting an offer from Shearson in October, 1986. Hutton's fortunes plunged after the crash, so when Shearson returned in late 1987 offering $962 million, Hutton accepted. While the timing seemed poor, coming so soon after a tremendous downturn, Shearson had frequently made its acquisitions during troubled times on Wall Street. The key would be whether Cohen could continue Shearson's tradition of smoothly merging disparate corporate cultures.

Hutton was not like Shearson at all. While Shearson's employees were from all sorts of backgrounds, Hutton's were almost all long-term Hutton employees, and from a firm that at the height of Wall Street's takeover craze had boasted that it still had only one name.

After the acquisition, Shearson became Shearson Lehman Hutton and established itself as a retail force second only to Merrill Lynch on Wall Street.

But 1988 brought continued problems. In swallowing Hutton, Shearson Lehman Hutton laid off 6,000 employees and closed or merged 150 offices. It also absorbed charges of $165 million due to the acquisition.

The firm began 1988 with a strong first quarter, but performance declined throughout the year, and dropped sharply when Kohlberg Kravis Roberts & Company beat Shearson's bid for the right to underwrite the RJR Nabisco leveraged buyout, the largest in world financial history.

Losing the deal damaged Shearson's reputation, as did a scandal at its Boston Company subsidiary in 1988. The firm also suffered setbacks in 1989. Three of its top officers left Shearson, due to conflicts of personality and strategy with Cohen. And, in the face of SEC objections, Shearson also had to abandon its attempts to sell a new investment instrument, the unbundled stock unit, after only four months. But Shearson also advised Time, Inc. in its purchase of Warner Communications, one of the year's biggest deals.

In February, 1990, Cohen resigned and was replaced as CEO by American Express's chief financial officer, Howard L. Clark Jr. This change was greeted with relief by many. At the time Clark took over, Shearson was struggling to protect its credit rating, and, following a failed share offering, had hastily announced a rights offering to its common shareholders.

With a plummeting stock price and serious financial and morale problems, Shearson and Clark have their work cut out. But Shearson also has a strong parent company and a capable new leader to shoulder the burden of returning it to profitability.

Principal Subsidiaries: Shearson Lehman Hutton Inc.; Shearson Lehman Brothers International; The Robinson-Humphrey Co., Inc.; Foster & Marshall Inc.; The Boston Co.; The Balcor Co.; Shearson Lehman Mortgage Corp.; Lehman Management Co.; Shearson Asset Management, Inc.; Shearson Lehman Commercial Paper Inc.; Shearson Lehman Money Markets International, Inc.; Bernstein-Macaulay, Inc.; The Ayco Corp.; Shearson Management Inc.; Shearson Equity Management; Shearson Lehman Investment Strategy Advisors, Inc.; Shearson Lehman Global Asset Management Ltd.

SallieMae

STUDENT LOAN MARKETING ASSOCIATION

1050 Thomas Jefferson Street, NW
Washington, D.C. 20007
U.S.A.
(202) 333-8000

Public Company
Incorporated: 1972
Employees: 680
Assets: $28.63 billion
Stock Index: New York

Although the Student Loan Marketing Association, better known as Sallie Mae, was created by Congress, it is a publicly owned, for-profit company. Sallie Mae was created in 1972 to provide a secondary market for the exchange of federally insured, guaranteed student loans. Congress created Sallie Mae to make student loans more liquid, and therefore give lenders a greater incentive to participate in the Guaranteed Student Loan Program (GSLP). Edward A. Fox has been president and CEO of Sallie Mae since its inception. His conservative fiscal policies are given credit for the company's remarkable success.

Sallie Mae's pool of voting stockholders is restricted by Congress: only banks and colleges eligible to participate in its programs can own voting shares in Sallie Mae, although its nonvoting shares are unrestricted. Sallie Mae's board of directors represents the three institutions with which it is involved: financial, educational, and governmental. Financial institutions holding voting stock elect seven directors, as do educational institutions, while the president of the United States appoints seven more and chooses the chairperson.

Sallie Mae began by offering two basic services: loan purchases and warehousing advances (secured loans and lines of credit). By purchasing student loans, Sallie Mae offers lenders liquidity; the knowledge that they can sell the loans and are not required to use the money to make new student loans makes lenders less nervous about tying up money in student loans in the first place. Under its warehousing program Sallie Mae lends financial institutions money to make new student loans by accepting existing loans or other government securities as collateral.

Guaranteed student loans are a special market for several reasons. The Guaranteed Student Loan Program, created in 1965 by the Higher Education Act, was established to supplement the government's grant and work-study programs, which help students finance higher education. Under the GSLP, the federal government assumes the risk for defaulted student loans. Originally, the government guaranteed the loans directly, but now state and nonprofit agencies directly insure the loans, backed up by federal reinsurance.

The GSLP allows qualified students to borrow a certain amount at a special fixed interest rate each year they are in school. While students are in school and for a short grace period after they leave, the federal government pays the interest on their loans, so that a student must pay back only the principal plus the interest accrued after graduation. In addition, the government pays a special allowance to lenders to make up the difference between the low rate of interest students pay and the market rate of return. Today this allowance is set at 3.25% above the 90-day treasury bill rate. The borrowing rate for students is 8%, so, for example, if the treasury bill rate is 10%, lenders get the 2% difference between that rate and the 8% students pay, plus 3.25% on top, adjusted quarterly according to the treasury bill rate.

Since collection procedures make carrying student loans costly once they reach the repayment phase, many lenders sell student loans to Sallie Mae when the student graduates. Student loans are costly not because student default rates are high (defaults are guaranteed by the government anyway) but because they are relatively small loans that require a lot of work. In addition to the federal collection and reporting requirements that must be followed to qualify for the government guarantee in the case of default, student loans are often complicated to keep track of; for example, students must be granted deferments for unemployment, return to school, or any of a host of other reasons.

Sallie Mae's high volume means that the company can administer the collection of loans with greater cost effectiveness—in 1988, Sallie Mae held 24% of all outstanding student loans. Thus, Sallie Mae ensures an adequate supply of credit for educational needs by enabling lenders to hold onto their loans during the lucrative in-school phase, sell the loans when they begin to require more attention, and use the money to make new loans.

But one of the reasons many lenders are willing to lend to students to begin with is that students make a very attractive pool of future customers. Therefore, some banks prefer to hold onto their loans. For them, Sallie Mae also offers services to make processing the loans easier. Its automated portfolio systems, both on site (PortSS) and off site (ExportSS), offer operational support to guide lenders through the life of a loan.

As a federally chartered corporation, Sallie Mae's history has been shaped by legislation. After adjusting the interest rates and special allowances for GSLP borrowers and lenders for several years in its efforts to make enough educational credit available, Congress chartered Sallie Mae in 1972 to create a secondary market for student loans. The company opened for business in 1973 with financing from Washington, D.C. banks, repaying these loans through the sale of federally guaranteed securities the same year. After that, Sallie Mae depended on financing from the Federal Financing Bank, an arm of the Treasury Department, where it could borrow money at very attractive rates. But Congress never intended Sallie Mae to be government supported, and in 1981 Sallie Mae started raising the money it needed on public capital markets. Since then, it has become known for its inventive financing schemes, designed to lock in floating-rate liabilities to match its floating-rate assets.

In 1974, Sallie Mae made its first issue of common stock, raising $24 million in capital. The sale of this stock was restricted to banks or educational institutions, who were required to buy 100 shares in order to participate in Sallie Mae's programs (this requirement was later lowered to 50 shares, and small institutions are exempt).

In 1976, the lender allowance was tied to the 90-day treasury bill rate and its ceiling was raised from 3% to 5%. That year, in an effort to reduce the red tape and inefficiencies that often accompany federal programs, the government transferred responsibility for the GSLP to the states and encouraged them to set up their own guaranteeing agencies. It also authorized Sallie Mae to buy loans originated under a newly created Health Education Assistance Loan Program (HEAL) to help graduate students in the health professions finance their educations.

By 1977, Sallie Mae was able to issue its first dividend. The next year, the Middle Income Assistance Act removed all income restrictions for student borrowers in response to complaints from middle-income families that they were too rich to get assistance but too poor to pay rising education costs, especially if they had more than one child in college at a time. Since students were no longer required to demonstrate financial need to qualify for loans, the program expanded rapidly—from $2 billion in new loans in 1978 to $3 billion in 1979 to $8 billion in 1980. In 1978 Congress also removed the ceiling on the special allowance to lenders, setting the allowance simply at 3.5% above the 90-day treasury bill rate, so that lenders were guaranteed a market rate of return. That and the elimination of the paperwork involved in determining eligibility made student loans more attractive to lenders. Sallie Mae grew accordingly, from assets of $1.6 billion in 1979 to $7.5 billion in 1982.

In 1980, as a prime rate near 20% pushed the cost of the GSLP sky-high, Congress made further amendments to the Higher Education Act. For the first time since 1968, the interest rate charged to student borrowers was raised, from 7% to 9%, for as long as treasury bill rates remained at a certain level (this rate stayed at 9% until 1983, when treasury bill rates fell enough to lower the rate to 8%). The amendments of 1980 also established a new educational lending program called PLUS, for parents of dependent students.

More important to Sallie Mae, however, were changes that increased the company's range of operations and gave it new ways of raising capital, to begin weaning it from federal support. Congress set the expiration of Sallie Mae's authority to issue federally guaranteed obligations for 1984, but gave the secretary of the treasury power to buy as much as $1 billion of nonguaranteed Sallie Mae securities and authorized Sallie Mae to issue nonvoting common stock.

Congress also broadened the services Sallie Mae could offer, giving the company much greater flexibility in making warehousing advances by loosening the restrictions on what Sallie Mae could accept as collateral for them and by liberalizing the requirement that warehousing advances go directly back into student loans. Sallie Mae was also permitted to consolidate or refinance loans for highly indebted students; to make advances to state and other nonprofit agencies for their student loan operations; and to make loans directly to students in areas of the country where there was insufficient credit available.

In 1981, under the new Reagan administration, Congress reinstated a needs test for borrowers with a family income above $30,000 and pushed Sallie Mae to lessen its reliance on federal funds more quickly. Accordingly, expiration of Sallie Mae's authority to issue federally guaranteed obligations was moved up to 1982, and in mid-1981 Sallie Mae made its first public offering, of short-term discount notes.

Congress also continued to broaden Sallie Mae's activities, authorizing the company to deal with educational loans not insured by the GSLP and to buy and sell the obligations of state and nonprofit educational-loan agencies.

During the 1980s, Sallie Mae experimented with ways of raising funds at as low a cost as possible. Since all of its assets—the student loans it has bought and the warehousing advances it has made—earn a floating rate of interest tied to the 90-day treasury bill rate, Sallie Mae prefers to borrow money at a floating rate tied to the same indicator. The company has been very successful at doing this. With both assets and liabilities tied to the treasury bill rate, Sallie Mae is insensitive to changes in the interest rate; as a quasi-governmental agency whose assets (those same student loans) are guaranteed by the federal government, Sallie Mae is able to raise money easily and fairly cheaply. As the cost of education has continued to out distance inflation, student loans have continued to be in heavy demand, so Sallie Mae's assets have grown at a breakneck pace: from $1.6 billion in 1979 to $28.63 billion in 1988, an increase of nearly 1,700%. And to Sallie Mae, which makes its money on the fixed spread between its floating-rate assets and floating-rate liabilities, increased assets mean increased profits.

In April, 1983 Sallie Mae made its first offering of preferred stock, and in September of that year it made its initial offering of nonvoting common stock, thus becoming a publicly owned company. Though the company has lobbied for permission to give voting power to all its common stock, it has so far been unsuccessful.

In 1986, when Congress reauthorized the Higher Education Act of 1965, it again broadened Sallie Mae's range of operations, while requiring a needs test for all loan applicants, even those with family incomes of less than $30,000, and lowering the allowance to lenders to 3.25% above the treasury bill rate. Sallie Mae was given the latitude to deal in loans to educational institutions for physical improvements. Congress also authorized the establishment of the

College Construction Loan Insurance Association (Connie Lee) to provide insurance for loans to academic institutions for facilities. Sallie Mae helped set up Connie Lee, which opened for business in 1988.

Student loans are a high-volume, low-margin business. Sallie Mae's status as the largest (and the only national) secondary market for these loans gives it the volume it needs to maximize that margin and make student loans a viable business. While it will always be subject to legislative regulation and the whims of Congress, the growing recognition of the importance of higher education in maintaining America's competitiveness in world markets and the continually rising costs of that education assures a sound future for Sallie Mae.

TRILON FINANCIAL CORPORATION

Royal Trust Tower
Toronto Dominion Centre
Toronto, Ontario, M5K 1G8
Canada
(416) 363–0061

Public Company
Incorporated: 1982
Employees: 20,000
Assets: C$27.25 billion (US$22.84 billion) (1987)
Stock Exchange: Toronto Montreal Vancouver

Trilon Financial Corporation is a diversified Canadian financial services company that manages trust, insurance, and brokerage operations through three principal subsidiaries. Trilon was formed in 1982 as the financial service company of Brascan, a natural resource recovery and power production company founded in 1899 by Brazilian and Canadian entrepreneurs. Brascan, which owns some 47% of Trilon, was acquired in 1979 by Edper Equities, the Toronto-based holding company of Seagram Company heirs Peter and Edward Bronfam.

At the time of its acquisition by the Edper group, Brascan had completed the sale of its major Brazilian subsidiary, Light-Servicos de Eletricidade S.A., to the Brazilian government for US$380 million. Under the direction of Edper's chief strategist, Trevor Eyton, Brascan made plans to diversify in its three principal areas of strength: consumer goods, natural resources, and financial services. With limited debt and a substantial cash reserve, Brascan planned to create Canada's largest diversified financial services corporation.

Trilon has been at the front of the Canadian trend toward one-stop financial service companies. The trend began with similar diversification in large American financial companies such as Merrill Lynch and Prudential Insurance Company. Restrictive legislation prohibited diversification in Canada until the 1980s, when deregulation permitted companies to enter new markets.

The economic climate was ripe for the formation of diversified financial companies. The Canadian life insurance industry had done poorly in the early 1980s. Inflation had decreased the value of insurance products and, in addition, the industry faced increased competition from products offered by banks, trust companies, and governments, all of which had begun to offer similar products to compete for Canadians' savings.

As a foundation for its operations, Trilon planned to acquire the London Life Insurance Company and the Royal Trust Company, both companies in which Brascan held substantial minority positions. London Life was originally founded in 1874 and had grown to become Canada's largest individual policy insurer. Royal Trust, founded in 1899, is one of Canada's largest trust companies.

Under Canadian legislation, insurance companies were prohibited from directly owning trust companies. However, insurance and trust activities could be coordinated under the direction of a holding company. Upon its formation, under federal charter, Trilon increased its holdings in London Life to 80% and then in February, 1983 to 98%. Shortly thereafter Trilon made a $102 million share offering, the proceeds of which were used to acquire a 42% controlling interest in Royal Trust in July, 1983.

Trilon's management hoped to create a company capable of conducting the entire range of a family's or business's financial needs. The company's strategy was to link trust, insurance, and brokerage operations to take advantage of broadened investment powers which would not be available to each independently. This provided the necessary defense against loss to competition between financial sectors. It also allowed the companies to refer business back and forth between affiliates. Though critics said the formation of Trilon and similar companies presented opportunities for conflict of interest, Trilon argued that the arrangement would bring greater convenience, to the overall benefit of both stockholders and clients.

Trilon's management came primarily from within the ranks of Brascan, Edper, and the companies they had acquired. Allan Lambert, the former chairman of Toronto-Dominion Bank, was appointed chairman, and Melvin Hawkrigg, the former senior vice-president of Brascan, was named president and CEO.

Trilon grew rapidly through a series of acquisitions backed by Brascan's substantial capital base. The company's strategy was to acquire existing companies with the necessary expertise in their respective fields. In its first six months, Trilon became Canada's sixth largest financial institution, behind the country's five largest banks. Trilon's resources were so extensive that it was able to devise a marketing plan to target all of Canada's six million families.

To coordinate and manage the diversification of its operations, Trilon formed intermediate companies corresponding to its respective services. Lonvest Corporation was formed to manage insurance operations and Royal Trustco to manage trust operations. Trilon also formed a corporate financial services division to manage its own investments and to provide brokerage services. In 1986, this division became Trilon Bancorp, an independent subsidiary.

Trilon's trust division, Royal Trust Company, was already one of Canada's largest trust companies when it was acquired. Under Trilon's direction, Royal Trust began to shed its long-held reputation as a conservative financial institution, taking bold measures to compete with Canada's banks. In 1984 Royal Trust expanded into real estate operations through the acquisition of A.E. LePage, merging Canada's largest real estate brokerage with its second largest provider of mortgages. Though the banks had access to greater resources, Royal Trust's smaller size gave its flexibility and the ability to process transactions more rapidly. Recognizing this advantage, the company streamlined operations even further through greater use of computer technology and the elimination of as many as seven layers of management between the chairman and customers. In 1987 Royal Trust introduced several innovative products in the guaranteed investment certificate markets (GICs), including guaranteed market index investments, stock price adjusted rate certificates, and diversified guaranteed investment certificates. These allowed investors to protect their principal while taking advantage of rises in the stock market.

In its insurance operations, Lonvest also reorganized and acquired in an attempt to broaden the range of its services. At the time of its acquisition, London Life, Lonvest's primary component, was trying to regain its place as one of the top five companies in the Canadian life insurance industry. It began revamping traditional whole life policies and introduced new insurance and annuity products, including "savings and accumulation" plans similar to plans being sold by banks and trust companies. In 1985 Lonvest acquired all of the outstanding shares of Fireman's Fund of Canada for C$143 million. Fireman's Fund, subsequently renamed Wellington, had been operating as a general insurer in Canada since 1840. In September, 1986, Lonvest acquired a 59% interest in the Holden Group for C$57 million. The Holden Group is a U.S.-based specialty insurer that provides individual and group benefit plans for educational institutions and public employees. And in 1987 the company acquired a 60% interest in the Optimum Financial Services Limited. The Optimum manages automobile and property insurance for members of professional and alumni associations in Quebec, Ontario, and Alberta.

Like Trustco and Lonvest, Trilon Bancorp also expanded actively. In March, 1985, it formed its leasing division by acquiring a 50.6% interest in CVL Inc., an auto leasing company, for $1.5 million. The following year it changed the name from CVL to Triathlon Leasing. Through the acquisition of City National Leasing in 1986 and Kompro Computer Leasing in 1987, Triathlon also began to lease equipment and computers. Triathlon is Canada's largest leasing operation, with more than 40,000 vehicles under management. In 1986 Trilon Bancorp acquired an 11% interest in the Great Lakes Bankgroup, a banking and hydroelectric energy production company, and also acquired Eurobrokers Investment Corporation, a wholesale money broker. Bancorp expanded into real estate in 1987 by purchasing Trustco's 51% interest in Royal LePage. That year it also formed Trilon Capital Markets and Trivest Insurance Network to conduct merchant banking activities for small- and medium-sized businesses. Trivest Insurance Network is a risk management company which at its formation planned to spend nearly $100 million to acquire minority equity positions in general insurance brokers.

In addition to establishing itself as one of Canada's largest diversified financial institutions, Trilon has also made significant efforts to expand internationally. In 1986 Royal Trustco acquired Dow Financial Services Corporation, Dow Chemical's financial services subsidiary, for C$239 million. Following this purchase, Royal Trust established R.T. Securities and Royal International in Amsterdam and opened an office in Tokyo to promote trade between Japan and Canada.

This international expansion continued through 1987 and 1988, when Trilon opened offices in Geneva, Hong Kong, Luxembourg, Austria, and Singapore. In 1987, Trilon Bancorp also entered into a joint venture with Taiwanese investors, obtaining a $6 million, 49% common equity interest in China Canada Investment and Development Company.

Trilon anticipates increased consolidation of financial companies and intense competition between a small group of globally active institutions. Considering its rapid growth to date, Trilon will undoubtedly contribute to the realization of that vision.

Principal Subsidiaries: Lonvest Corporation; Royal Trustco Ltd; Trilon Bancorp; Trilon Capital Corp.; London Life Insurance Co.; Holden Group Inc. (U.S.A.); Security National Insurance Co.; The Optimum Financial Services Ltd. (60%); Royal LePage Ltd.; Triathalon Leasing, Inc.; Eurobrokers Investment Corp.; Trilon Capital Markets Inc.; Trivest Insurance Network Ltd.; Reed Stenhouse Personnel Insurance Ltd.

YAMAICHI SECURITIES COMPANY, LIMITED

4–1, Yaesu 2-chome
Chuo-ku
Tokyo 104
Japan
(03) 276–3181

Public Company
Incorporated: 1943
Employees: 8,816
Assets: ¥3.3 trillion (US$26.1 billion)
Stock Index: Tokyo Osaka Nagoya Paris

Yamaichi Securities Company, the smallest of Japan's Big Four securities houses, deals in a variety of foreign and domestic securities. As Japanese industry has grown, Yamaichi has profited handsomely from its equity and capital market activities. In recent years, with the deregulation of financial and capital markets worldwide, the company has become a world class investment banker and securities brokerage house.

Although incorporated in its present form in 1943, Yamaichi can claim to be the oldest of the major Japanese securities houses. Its origins date back to 1897, when the Koike Shoten was licensed as a broker on the Tokyo Stock Exchange; the Yamaichi name was adopted 20 years later. At that time, securities trading was very primitive in a country still struggling to industrialize. Nevertheless, Yamaichi grew steadily throughout the 1920s and 1930s, even though securities trading before World War II was limited to a very small segment of the Japanese population. The economy for the most part was dominated by family-controlled industrial groups known as *zaibatsu* (literally "money cliques").

By the time Yamaichi Securities was incorporated in 1943, Japanese military success in the Pacific had already peaked. Prices dropped drastically, and trading remained unpredictable until the end of the war. After the war, Japan was devastated both physically and psychologically. The *zaibatsu* were broken up by the Allied occupation forces, which began the reorganization of Japanese society and the economy. Not only was the trading of defense-related securities prohibited, but all trading on the stock exchanges, which had been suspended near the end of the war, was also prohibited until 1949. Yamaichi survived by buying and selling securities over the counter at its offices. Trading in this manner was relatively profitable since many people wanted to exchange their holdings for cash during the difficult postwar years.

In 1949, the principal securities exchanges were reopened. Yamaichi lead-managed the first Japanese convertible bond issue, for the Tosa Electric Railway Company. The exchanges had been open only a short time when stock prices started to drop: in the 14 months following the Tokyo Stock Exchange's reopening, the Nikkei Stock Average fell from ¥175.21 to ¥85.25. A lack of confidence in the economy further contributed to the market's downslide. However, at the beginning of the Korean War in June, 1950, the production demands of the United Nations Forces began to invigorate the Japanese economy. The resulting corporate expansion dramatically increased the number of stock issues, as well as Yamaichi's underwriting revenue and brokerage commissions.

The stock market boom was followed by an increase in bond issues a few years later, and the Japanese economy was on the road to full recovery. Yamaichi, along with the other large securities houses, began a massive public relations effort designed to encourage the Japanese to invest in securities. Investment trusts became a convenient way for people to invest their savings, and by 1959, Yamaichi's investment trusts were so popular that a separate company, the Yamaichi Investment Trust Management Company Ltd., was set up to manage them.

Throughout the 1960s, the Japanese economy grew at the staggering rate of 10% a year. Yamaichi forged close ties to Japanese companies, and its underwriting business became increasingly profitable—underwriting remains one of Yamaichi's strongest areas today. Bond issues also increased substantially during the early 1960s as companies discovered the advantages of borrowing. Capital in Japan, however, was somewhat scarce, and so foreign investment began to play a more vital role. Bond issues of Japanese companies were well-received on the New York market, but U.S. legislation intended to improve America's balance of trade put an end to the practice in 1963. Japanese companies had to seek capital elsewhere.

At the end of 1963, the Japanese government tried to tighten the money supply. The result was a severe recession the following year. Japanese manufacturing concerns were hit hard; many were forced into receivership. The stock market's plunge prompted the Ministry of Finance to prohibit new stock issues. A group of financial companies, Yamaichi included, joined together to purchase stocks when necessary to help stabilize prices. Nonetheless, stock prices dropped further.

The panic of 1964–1965 hit Yamaichi harder than any other securities house. Because of fierce competition in the securities industry, the company's management used poor judgment in aggressively marketing stocks. The company was accused of keeping certain stock prices artificially high until it could unload the entire issue it had underwritten. Stocks were pushed like "weekly specials" at grocery stores. Yamaichi was certainly not the only securities house to engage in such practices, but it, and the others, did receive a great deal of negative publicity. As the recession worsened, the Japanese Securities and Exchange Commission blamed the securities houses for undermining public confidence in the markets. The Japanese SEC imposed new licensing requirements and called for the reorganization of the securities houses. Yamaichi's president was removed as a result.

As if this was not bad enough, Yamaichi had accumulated a huge debt by expanding too quickly in the late 1950s and early 1960s. The company owed $214 million, primarily to the Fuji Bank, Mitsubishi Bank, and the Industrial Bank of Japan. Only government intervention saved the company from bankruptcy: the Bank of Japan, the central bank, approved unlimited loans to rescue the ailing company, and Yamaichi's three biggest creditors temporarily suspended interest payments. Teru Hidaka was brought in as president to reorganize Yamaichi. Hidaka cut down on staff, trimmed some branches from Yamaichi's domestic network, and sold some of the company's unneeded assets. He also oversaw Yamaichi's implementation of new government regulations. By 1967, Yamaichi was on its feet again.

In the late 1960s, Japan relaxed its barriers to foreign investment somewhat. Yamaichi responded by asserting itself in foreign markets, particularly in Europe. This expansion picked up in the 1970s. In 1973, Yamaichi established a universal bank in Amsterdam, Yamaichi International (Nederland) N.V., and also set up a representative office in Paris. In 1974, Yamaichi International (Deutschland) was established, followed in 1976 by Yamaichi Bank (Switzerland), headquartered in Zurich.

Increased activity in the bond markets paralleled this geographical expansion. Sophisticated new types of bonds allowed almost tailor-made investments, and Euroyen bonds grew in popularity. Yamaichi became a major player in these markets, showing particular strength as an underwriter. By the end of the decade it was clear that capital markets would continue to globalize. Japan's strong export industries had made the country capital-rich. As Japanese investors looked for opportunities in Europe and the United States, Yamaichi was a key intermediary.

By 1980, Yamaichi Securities was firmly established throughout the world. Its London and New York subsidiaries complemented its primary operations, based in Tokyo; in 1986 they became members, respectively, of the London and New York stock exchanges. The changes in the world's financial markets during the 1980s amounted to nothing short of a revolution. Many trade barriers were eliminated, allowing even greater innovation in security issues. New types of bonds found their way into the markets, and foreign listings on the stock exchanges increased.

Japanese tastes for U.S. treasury notes brought Yamaichi deep into that market in the mid-1980s. The company was the last of the Japanese Big Four, however, to be designated a primary dealer by the New York Federal Reserve, in late 1988. By the end of the decade the four Japanese houses accounted for more than 7% of the entire U.S. treasury bond market.

In the mid-1980s, Yamaichi became increasingly active in mergers and acquisitions. As hostile takeovers are virtually nonexistent in Japan, Yamaichi's role had been one of making good corporate matches rather than working out takeover strategies. This style of mergers and acquisitions was foreign to American and European corporations, so Yamaichi's expertise made its services attractive to foreign companies interested in purchasing Japanese firms. Although most deals of this kind were kept secret, the Japanese press reported that Yamaichi assisted Shell Oil in the acquisition of 45% of Showa Oil, and Canon Sales's purchase of a 19% interest in Nippon Typewriter.

In October, 1987 the New York stock market crash wreaked havoc throughout the international financial community. Yamaichi suffered a major setback in its development of the U.S. market since many of its Japanese equities customers were frightened out of the market while at the same time Yamaichi faced intense competition from U.S. securities firms. By 1988, Yamaichi, like the other Japanese securities houses, had cut back on its New York staff instead of expanding as it had hoped to do.

Nonetheless, by 1989 Yamaichi was earning 20% of its profits from its overseas operations. Although it still struggles to become a major dealer in the U.S. market, Yamaichi Securities has come of age. Japan's continued economic prosperity ensures Yamaichi a solid share of the European equity and capital markets, and promises to attract more attention from American investors and security issuers. As financial markets continue to become more complex and competitive, Yamaichi remains flexible and ready to greet the new challenges and opportunities that change will bring.

Principal Subsidiaries: Yamaichi Investment Trust Management Co., Ltd.; Yamaichi Research Institute of Securities and Economics, Inc.; Yamaichi International Capital Management Co., Ltd.; Yamaichi Uni Ven Co., Ltd.; Yamaichi Computer Center Co., Ltd.; Yamaichi Real Estate Inc.; Yamaichi Echo & Co., Ltd.; Yamaichi Enterprise, Inc.; Yamaichi General Finance Co., Ltd.; Yamaichi World Tourist Inc.; Yamaichi Card Services Co., Ltd.; Yamaichi International (America), Inc.; Yamaichi Financial Services, Inc.; Yamaichi International (Canada) Limited/Limitee; Yamaichi International (Europe) Limited; Yamaichi Bank (U.K.) Plc; Yamaichi International (Nederland) N.V.; Yamaichi International (Deutschland) GmbH; Yamaichi France S.A.; Yamaichi Bank (Switzerland); Yamaichi International (Middle East) E.C.; Yamaichi International (Hong Kong) Limited; Yamaichi Merchant Bank (Singapore) Limited; Yamaichi Futures Private Limited.

FOOD PRODUCTS

AJINOMOTO CO., INC.
ASSOCIATED BRITISH FOODS PLC
BEATRICE COMPANY
BORDEN, INC.
BSN GROUPE S.A.
CADBURY SCHWEPPES PLC
CAMPBELL SOUP COMPANY
CANADA PACKERS INC.
CARNATION COMPANY
CASTLE & COOK, INC.
CONAGRA, INC.
CPC INTERNATIONAL INC.
DALGETY, PLC
GENERAL MILLS, INC.
GEORGE A. HORMEL AND COMPANY
H.J. HEINZ COMPANY
HERSHEY FOODS CORPORATION
HILLSDOWN HOLDINGS, PLC
IBP, INC.
ITOHAM FOODS INC.
JACOBS SUCHARD AG
KELLOGG COMPANY
KONINKLIJKE WESSANEN N.V.
KRAFT GENERAL FOODS INC.
LAND O'LAKES, INC.
MEIJI MILK PRODUCTS COMPANY, LIMITED
MEIJI SEIKA KAISHA, LTD.
NABISCO BRANDS, INC.
NESTLÉ S.A.
NIPPON MEAT PACKERS, INC.
NIPPON SUISAN KAISHA, LIMITED
NISSHIN FLOUR MILLING COMPANY, LTD.
PILLSBURY COMPANY
QUAKER OATS COMPANY
RALSTON PURINA COMPANY
RANKS HOVIS MCDOUGALL PLC
RECKITT & COLMAN PLC
ROWNTREE MACKINTOSH
SARA LEE CORPORATION
SNOW BRAND MILK PRODUCTS COMPANY, LIMITED
SODIMA
TAIYO FISHERY COMPANY, LIMITED
TATE & LYLE PLC
TYSON FOODS, INCORPORATED
UNIGATE PLC
UNILEVER
UNITED BISCUITS (HOLDINGS) PLC
UNITED BRANDS COMPANY

AJINOMOTO®

AJINOMOTO CO., INC.

1–5–8, Kyobashi
Chuo-ku
Tokyo 104
Japan
(03) 272–1111

Public Company
Incorporated: 1909
Employees: 9,532
Sales: ¥509.94 billion (US$4.08 billion)
Stock Index: Tokyo Osaka Nagoya

Ajinomoto, the world's first and still-largest producer of monosodium glutamate (MSG), is one of Japan's largest food-processing companies. In addition to seasonings, Ajinomoto produces edible oils, frozen and processed foods, amino acids, pharmaceuticals, and other specialty chemicals. But the company entered the 1990s determined to become one of Japan's leading developers of life-science products and pharmaceuticals. This dramatic shift stems from a strong technological base that extends back to the company's birth. Although Ajinomoto has been manufacturing for the pharmaceutical industry since 1956, it has simultaneously broadened its food-processing operations. By funding costly drug research and development with cash flow from its food products and cashing in on products developed slowly over the last 20 years, the company stands to grow rapidly with the demand for amino acid–based products.

MSG, the company's mainstay for more than 80 years, was discovered in kelp by Kikunae Ikeda at the University of Tokyo in 1908. With help from Ikeda, Saburosuke and Chuji Suzuki—two brothers who had been extracting iodine from seaweed since 1890—formed Ajinomoto to produce the substance commercially. They began marketing it in 1909 as "AJI-NO-MOTO," which translates literally as "essence of taste."

The company has had a focus on international sales and a strong base in chemical development since its inception. A New York office was opened in 1917, and between the wars production and sales offices were opened throughout Asia, giving it a global position decades before other Japanese companies. During this time the company began to produce MSG from soybean protein, which eventually led to the production of cooking oils. World War II halted MSG production, but between 1947 and 1953 AJI-NO-MOTO became available in the United States and Europe, and the company also began to sell cooking oil. In 1954, Ajinomoto opened offices in São Paulo, Paris, Bangkok, and Hong Kong.

Emphasis on chemical research culminated in the creation of the Central Research Laboratories in 1956. Research during the 1950s brought about not only different biological and synthetic methods of MSG production, but an entry into an industry that today is the division most important to management. The development of crystalline essential amino acids, used for intravenous solutions, introduced Ajinomoto to pharmaceuticals. Amino acids were found to have a wide variety of applications, and before the end of the decade they were being used in the company's seasonings and animal-feed additives.

The company took larger strides toward internationalization in the 1960s. Most overseas growth was limited to expanded production of seasonings in Asia and South America. But through joint ventures and licensing agreements with American and European companies, Ajinomoto increased its presence on those continents and at the same time expanded its product line domestically. The first large-scale licensing agreement came in 1962 when it began marketing Kellogg's breakfast cereals in Japan. A similar agreement with CPC International to manufacture and market Knorr soups was reached in 1965. These ventures established the company as a food processor and not just a seasonings producer. After 1965, the company applied its research to the development of new seasonings, soups, margarine, mayonnaise, frozen foods, and flavored edible oils. In 1973, Ajinomoto formed yet another joint venture, with General Foods, to produce coffees, instant coffees, and soft drinks.

The oil crisis led most companies to consolidate in 1973 and 1974, and internal development of food products increased during the 1970s. By 1978 seasonings accounted for only 22% of sales and processed food had boomed to 31% from 3% in 1965. In 1970 the company created Ajinomoto Frozen Foods and also began to collaborate with the NutraSweet Company of the United States that year. A 1979 joint venture with Dannon introduced dairy products for the first time to the company's product line.

Ajinomoto's new focus on products derived from its amino acids research proved well-timed as the company entered the 1980s. Growth in the Japanese food industry slowed significantly. Although MSG sales overseas increased, the domestic market was mature. Food-related products, which made up 80% of the company's sales, could no longer be relied on for large-scale or long-term growth. Management initiated a plan to expand its fine chemicals divisions further while diversifying the food products made by its overseas subsidiaries.

Pharmaceutical-product sales were ¥20 billion in 1980; U.S. medical institutions and pharmaceutical manufacturers purchased half of the company's output. Although the reliance on exports would prove damaging to many Japanese companies as the yen appreciated in the late 1980s, Ajinomoto's extensive research investments in the 1970s gave it prominence in the field and made the division less vulnerable to international cycles.

The diversification into the pharmaceutical business has not been easy. The complexity of the pharmaceutical market calls for completely different marketing techniques as well as lengthy approval processes from various governments. In order to defray these high research-and-development costs, Ajinomoto typically uses other companies to market its drugs or uses licensed companies to produce them.

Ajinomoto's new venture department, established in 1987, will focus on new markets and cooperative producers in the life-sciences area. The department symbolizes the company's commitment to the industry, and earnings show why. In 1988 sales rose only 0.5% but earnings grew 15.4%—due largely to the much higher margins the company can earn on life-science products.

Although the international market for research and development in pharmaceuticals makes Ajinomoto less vulnerable to currency valuation cycles, a strong yen hurts the company nonetheless. In response to a reduced export market, the company turned to domestic food sales in the late 1980s, becoming more active in restaurants and food service and entering the fresh vegetable and fish market for the first time. The food-processing division was the only one in 1988 to show an increase in sales—to 40.6% of the company total—reflecting the influence of the difficult export market. Ajinomoto hopes to increase its overseas food production by taking advantage of the strong yen to acquire companies and diversify the product lines of its foreign subsidiaries.

The company continues to spend a higher percentage (3.3%) of sales on research than most food processors do, reflecting its interest in the fine chemical and pharmaceutical industries. In addition to this money, the Japanese government funds research on problems like AIDS, and in the late 1980s university research became available to commercial developers. Funding from the MIT Cancer Research Institute, for example, will help fund research and provide a wider variety of potential developments.

Nonetheless, Ajinomoto remains one of Japan's largest food companies. As such, it will continue to generate earnings increases despite currency fluctuations. Research conducted ten years ago is just now coming to fruition, and increased sales of its existing amino acids as well as new developments from current research give the company firm ground to stand on to make its ambitious ¥ 15 trillion sales projection for the year 2000.

Principal Subsidiaries: Knorr Foods Co., Ltd.; Toyo Oil Mills Co., Ltd.; Ajinomoto Frozen Foods Co., Ltd.; Sanpuku Co., Ltd.; Tokyo Sanmi Co., Ltd.; Sanpo Unyu Co., Ltd.; Daimi Co., Ltd.; Daimi Butsuryu Co., Ltd.; Kumazawa Seiyu Sangyo Co., Ltd.; Ajinomoto Finance Inc.; Ajinomoto General Foods, Inc. (50%); Charles River Japan, Inc. (50%); Ajinomoto U.S.A., Inc.; Ajinomoto Interamericana Indústria e Comércio Ltda. (Brazil); Ajinomoto del Perú S.A.; Deutsche Ajinomoto GmbH. (Germany); Ajinomoto Co., (Thailand) Ltd.; Ajinomoto (Malaysia) Berhad; A.I.F. Investments Pte. Ltd. (Singapore); Heartland Lysine, Inc. (U.S.A.); Ajinomoto do Brasil Indústria e Comércio Ltda.; Nissin-Ajinomoto Alimentos Ltda. (Brazil); Eurolysine S.A. (France); Ajinomoto Osteuropa Handels-Gesellschaft mbH. (Austria); NutraSweet AG (Switzerland); Union Ajinomoto, Inc. (Philippines); California Manufacturing Co., Inc. (Philippines); P.T. Ajinomoto Indonesia; Ajinomoto Company (Hong Kong) Ltd.; CPC/AJI (Asia) Ltd. (Hong Kong); Corn Products Co. (Hong Kong) Ltd.; Ajinomoto (Singapore) Pte. Ltd.; CPC (Singapore) Pte. Ltd.; Wan Thai Foods Industry Co., Ltd.; CPC Thailand Ltd.; Best Foods Co. (Thailand) Ltd.; CPC (Malaysia) Sdn. Berhad; P.T. Ajinex International (Indonesia); CPC (Taiwan) Ltd.; Best Foods Ltd. (Taiwan); Cheil Frozen Foods Co., Ltd. (Korea); Omnichem S.A. (Belgium).

ASSOCIATED BRITISH FOODS PLC

Weston Centre
Bowater House
68 Knightsbridge
London, SW1X 7LR
United Kingdom
(1) 589-6363

Public Company
Incorporated: 1935
Employees: 54,100
Sales: £2.5 billion (US$4.52 billion)
Stock Index: London

A multibillion-dollar international conglomerate that characterizes itself as a "family of businesses" may seem ironic or unduly modest in calling up so cozy an image, but in some ways it is an appropriate description of Associated British Foods (ABF). ABF subsidiaries, whether self-developed or acquired through merger or acquisition, retain their individuality in name, operations, and clientele, yet maintain strong connections with the parent's central management core. Advertising and marketing of ABF's wide range of products and services—bakeries, supermarkets, restaurants, catering companies, and clothing stores—are geared to the family as consumers. And for more than half a century one family has controlled ABF: the Westons.

The family saga began in Toronto, Canada, in 1882, when George Weston, then 18, bought a bread-delivery route. During the following 36 years, he built a number of successful bakeries in that area. Today George Weston Ltd., a Toronto-based chain of bakeries and supermarkets, consistently ranks among North America's top businesses.

When George Weston's son Garfield took over the bakery business at his father's death in 1924, he had much more in mind than simply maintaining or building up the chain of local bakeries his father had founded—he was determined that it grow into an international business. Eleven years later, in November, 1935, he took a giant step toward that goal by purchasing seven bakeries in England, Scotland, and Wales for his newly formed Food Investments Ltd., quickly renamed Allied Bakeries Limited. All seven are still in operation today, three under their original names.

Within four years, Garfield had 18 bakeries and four biscuit factories throughout the British Isles, beginning decades of expansion into Europe, Africa, Australia, Asia, and North America. The expansion went beyond food products to encompass seed production, milling, canning, retail grocery and clothing outlets, restaurants, vehicle parts, fuel, and basic research.

The expansion has not always been steady. At the onset of World War II, wartime restrictions and shortages of supplies began to slow production, while high taxes and voluntary defense contributions reduced profits.

But expansion picked up again in the postwar period. A postwar excess-profits tax refund was wholly invested in expansion and equipment. In 1948 Garfield's son Garry joined the board of directors. The following year, the company purchased two Australian firms: Gold Crust Bakeries in Adelaide and Gartrell White in Sydney. By the end of the decade, profits had surpassed £2 million a year.

A growth spurt in the 1950s added dozens of new bakeries, tea shops, restaurants, and catering businesses, many of them in newly constructed shopping centers, where, with gas rationing at an end, consumers could drive to one location to purchase may different products. Food stores purchased by the company were refashioned into supermarkets to suit new shopping habits. This diversification led to a name change in 1960, to Associated British Foods. By 1964, the company claimed to be the largest baker in the world and one of the largest millers, in addition to being one of the largest grocers in the United Kingdom.

Rapid growth continued during the 1960s, with the acquisition of A.B. Hemmings, Ltd., a chain of 230 bakery shops in the London area, the entire chain of Fine Fare food shops, and a 51% interest in the South African Premier Milling Company.

In 1970 ABF also opened the largest bakery in western Europe, in Glasgow, Scotland. A year later, ABF's Fine Fare opened its first two "superstores." As the 1970s progressed, the Stewart Cash Stores in Ireland, which ABF had acquired some twenty years before, followed suit, opening their first hypermarket. In 1978, ABF expanded into a new market—frozen foods—by buying an ice cream factory and a pizza bakery.

Garfield died in October 1978 and Garry is now the chairman of ABF. The family no longer seeks the public eye—they have kept a low profile since 1983, when an attempt by six Irish Republican gunmen to kidnap Galen was foiled.

Despite difficulties such as fluctuation of the pound and climatic conditions affecting crops, ABF has continued to expand and prosper. In 1980, a subsidiary, Twinings Tea, opened its first North American factory, in Greensboro, North Carolina, and also opened the Grosvenor Marketing Company in Paramus, New Jersey. Additional bakeries and other businesses have been acquired, and ABF's continual program of monitoring and modernizing keeps products and services up to date and operations efficient.

Some of ABF's subsidiaries are much older than their parent. The Twining Crosfield Group, for example, dates back to a coffee shop purchased by Thomas Twining in 1706, when coffee was the fashionable drink for men. Tea, introduced early in the 17th century, had been popularized as a drink for ladies by Queen Catherine, the wife of Charles II, at mid-century, but men usually drank it for medicinal purposes only (it was widely regarded as a remedy for headaches). When Twining introduced tea as a sideline, he found it was so popular that in 1717 he converted Tom's Coffee House into the Golden Lyon, London's first tea shop.

Twinings tea, exported to 90 countries, may be ABF's best-known brand name. It has won the Queen's Award for export achievement, and consistently dominates its market. The tea is blended in several factories in the British Isles and one in the United States; ABF marketing companies in both countries manage distribution.

The Ryvita Company, purchased by ABF in 1949, has won the Queen's Award for export twice with the crispbread that has long been its principal product—and probably ABF's second-best-known brand name. The steady growth of interest in health foods has made Ryvita and the company's other main product, Crackerbread, popular in many countries. Demand for high-fiber foods and the availability of a new extrusion technology have resulted in the development of Allinson's products, Croustipain, and other extruded breakfast cereals and cereal products.

Allied Bakeries, the group of bakeries Weston purchased at the time of incorporation, still functions as part of ABF's largest subsidiary. It has grown to include some 40 wholesale bakeries and close to 1,200 retail bakery shops and restaurants throughout the British Isles. The addition of in-house bakeries in many supermarkets has put a slight crimp in the wholesale baked-goods business, but Allied Bakeries has added a line of partially baked goods (to be completed at an in-house bakery or by the retail consumer at home) and a line of frozen bakery products to counter this trend.

Cereal Industries, a holding company for six subsidiaries, also works closely with Allied Foods Group. Fishers Agricultural Holdings, one of the six cereal industries subsidiaries, includes Fishers Nutrition, which supplies animal feeds and livestock marketing services, and Fishers Seed and Grain, which produces agricultural seeds. The Allied Grain Group, another of the six, markets seeds and fertilizers. Mardorf, Peach and Company imports and exports cereals. ABR Foods supplies wheat by-products to several types of industry: baking and brewing, food and pharmaceutical manufacturers, animal feed, and packaging products. The Aughton Group, which, with ABR, constitutes the fifth Cereal Industries group, supplies computerized process-control systems to a variety of industries. Westmill Foods, with Alric Packing, is the sixth. Westmill supplies retail grocers and caterers with Allinson's flour, yeast, bran, and wheatgerm, among other products.

ABF's Burton's Gold Medal Biscuits is one of the largest biscuit manufacturers in the United Kingdom; as it has grown, there have been occasional rumors that it plans to take over a competitor, such as United Biscuits. Burton's is pursuing an aggressive program of investment in new and modernized equipment and cost-effective production techniques in order to maintain its leadership in the market.

The Irish retail group is the largest supermarket chain in Ireland (Quinnsworth stores in the Irish Republic and Stewarts and Crazy Prices in Northern Ireland). Many of these stores opened in the 1960s; they continue to do a thriving business. This group also includes retail clothing stores that emphasize fashions for young people: Penneys in Ireland and Primark in the United Kingdom. Business has been brisk enough to warrant plans for further expansion.

AB Ingredients, formed in 1982, and AB Technology, formed in 1987, constitute ABF's newest division. AB Ingredients develops and manufactures new ingredients and additives for Allied Bakeries and for other independent companies. It also develops improved bakery processes. AB Technology specializes in high-tech improvements for several types of industry, including food production.

It takes a strong central management, an efficient reporting system, and vigilant personnel and investment programs to hold together so many relatively independent companies of disparate size and design, in widely separated geographical locations. ABF's continual expansion testifies to its strength, but its structure, marked by an intricate system of holding companies and representation, is difficult to penetrate and analyze.

The lifting of the trade barriers among the 12 countries of the European Common Market in 1992 will offer ABF further opportunities to expand. ABF already has a foothold on the continent through Twinings' Foods International S.A. If the Westons continue to exercise firm control of ABF, further expansion should be expected for a long time to come.

Principal Subsidiaries: Allied Bakeries (N.I.) Ltd.; Sunblest Bakeries Ltd.; Allied Foods Ltd.; ABR Foods Ltd.; Allied Grain Ltd.; Allied Grain (North East) Ltd.; Allied Grain (Scotland) Ltd.; Allied-Love Adhesives Ltd. (89%); Allied Mills Ltd.; Chancelot Mill Ltd.; Cranfield Brothers Ltd.; Fishers Agricultural Holdings Ltd.; James Neill Ltd.; George Weston Foods Ltd. (Australia); N.B. Love Industries Pty. Ltd. (Australia); Allied Foods (N.Z.) Ltd. (New Zealand); R. Twining and Company Ltd.; Namosa Ltd.; Walter Williams & Co. (London) Ltd. (55.6%); Foods International S. A. (France); R. Twining & Co., Ltd.. (USA); Grosvenor Marketing Ltd. (USA); AB Ingredients Ltd. (94%); AB Technology Ltd.; Burton's Gold Medal Biscuits Ltd.; Crazy Prices; C.W.I.I. Ltd.; Eastbow Securities Ltd.; Koters (Liverpool) Ltd.; Lax and Shaw Ltd.; Mardorf, Peach & Co., Ltd.; Mauri Products Ltd. (50.1%); Power Supermarkets Ltd.; Primark Ltd.; Primark Stores Ltd.; The Ryvita Company Ltd.; Stewarts Supermarkets Ltd.; Serpentine Securities Ltd. (Pref. nil); Walmsley Ltd.; Weston Research Ltd.; Wilsdon & Company Ltd.

BEATRICE COMPANY

Two North LaSalle Street
Chicago, Illinois 60602
U.S.A.
(312) 782–3820

Private Company
Incorporated: 1898 as Beatrice Creamery Company of Nebraska
Employees: 19,700
Sales: $4 billion

Beatrice's steady, sometimes spectacular, growth into one of the largest and best-known food companies in America was built upon the foundations of a modest butter manufacturer in Nebraska. A dairy company for half a century, Beatrice began to expand into other food areas after World War II. Decades of dizzying acquisitions came to an end when the company was taken private through a leveraged buyout in April, 1986. Beatrice's new management trimmed the company radically, selling $7.3 billion worth of assets in two years. Beatrice today consists primarily of Beatrice/Hunt-Wesson, a packaged foods producer; Swift-Eckrich, a producer of prepared meats; and Beatrice Cheese.

Beatrice founder George Haskell began his career as a bookkeeper for the Fremont Butter and Egg Company in 1886. When this company went out of business in 1891, Haskell went into partnership with a man named Bosworth and bought Fremont's Beatrice, Nebraska plant. In 1895 he organized the Beatrice Creamery Company with $40,000 in capital, and Beatrice churned its first butter. The company's headquarters were moved to Lincoln, Nebraska in 1898, when the Beatrice Creamery Company of Nebraska was incorporated with $100,000 in capital. That year, Beatrice produced 940,000 pounds of butter.

Beatrice's first decade was a hard one. The company struggled through economic hardship, scarce financing, low prices, and drought. Nonetheless, Beatrice continued to grow, churning and distributing fresh butter directly to grocery stores, restaurants, and hotels. Beatrice soon found itself in the cold storage business as well, a natural adjunct given the refrigeration plants required to manufacture butter. During this time, to sell their cream, farmers had to deliver milk daily to a skimming station, and then haul their skim milk back to the farm for livestock feed. One of Beatrice's first innovations was to help farmers reduce costs and inefficiency by financing their purchase of cream separators.

In 1901 the Beatrice plant in Topeka, Kanasas hired an agency to find a name for its butter. The patent office granted the company the trademark "Meadow Gold" later that year—one of the first trademarks for butter.

Over the next four decades, Beatrice grew steadily, branching into other dairy products and pioneering in many industry innovations. Beatrice was one of the first companies to pasteurize churning cream on a large scale and the first to package butter in sealed cartons. The company opened an ice cream plant in 1907 in Topeka, and ice cream soon became a significant business segment. Beatrice was the first to advertise an ice cream brand nationally, in 1931, as it had been the first to advertise its Meadow Gold butter, in 1912. In 1923 the company opened a fluid milk plant in Denver, Colorado and entered the distribution of milk, cottage cheese, and buttermilk. It was a pioneer in the use of aluminum foil to make milk bottle caps and introduced homogenized milk in 1930 to wide consumer acceptance.

Like businesses everywhere, Beatrice struggled through the Depression. The company reported, for instance, that "the year 1933 was one of the most difficult years . . . in the history of the dairy business . . . by December 14th [the price of butter] declined to 15¢, the lowest level for the month of December in twenty-five years." But Beatrice survived.

World War II brought its hardships—the government demanded a 30% share of all butter and rationed the rest, froze milk prices, limited the use of milk fats and solids in ice cream, and otherwise restricted business—but in general sales were strong, and increased steadily from year to year. In 1941 Beatrice produced 70 million pounds of butter, and in its annual report that year, celebrating the 40th anniversary of the Meadow Gold brand, it declared: "the Company is not trying to be the largest in the business, but we are endeavoring to continue one of the best. . . ."

Despite this sentiment, Beatrice continued to grow. In 1943 the company bought La Choy, a producer of oriental foods, as part of its plan to diversify outside of dairy markets. And in 1946, in keeping with this plan, the Beatrice Creamery Company became the Beatrice Foods Company.

In 1949 Beatrice was able to report its tenth consecutive year of increased net sales and a tripling of total sales—all during what it described as "the extremely unstable market conditions that have prevailed since the end of the war."

In 1952, Clinton Haskell, who had become president in 1928, died. Under Haskell, Beatrice had grown from a regional butter manufacturer into a prominent, national producer and distributor of a variety of foods. Throughout this transformation, and to this day, the company never veered from a determined policy of decentralized management. Its multitude of businesses have always been managed by their own, local managers, whose intimate knowledge of their own conditions, Haskell maintained, would produce the best business decisions. This dedication to decentralized management is perhaps the single strongest thread linking the company of today with its past.

William Karnes replaced Haskell as president. He had been with the company since 1943, and from 1948 was executive vice president. Karnes accelerated the trend toward growth and diversification that had begun in the early 1940s, buying small companies, expanding their markets, and leaving the newly acquired companies on their own, in line with Beatrice's long practice. Under Karnes, whom *Fortune* described as having "a gimlet eye for attractive enterprises," this aggressive acquisition strategy took Beatrice not only into foods as diverse as candy and vegetables, but also into dozens of non-food businesses like luggage, furniture, and chemicals. Until the early 1970s, this expansion produced a string of earnings increases that let Beatrice write its own ticket on Wall Street.

But by the time Karnes retired, in 1976, Wall Street was less interested in growth than in profitability, and Beatrice's relentless acquisitions were beginning to disappoint investors. Karnes named Wallace Rasmussen, a former ice-hauler with a bullying reputation, as a sort of interim president—he would have to retire in three years, when he reached the company's mandatory retirement age of 65. This arrangement led, naturally, to a long power struggle within the upper management. Out of this James Dutt emerged as CEO in 1980.

Dutt had worked his way up through the ranks, joining the local Beatrice plant in his hometown, Topeka, as a college student. Rasmussen hadn't stopped acquiring, despite Wall Street. Of Rasmussen's purchases, which included a candy company and Culligan, the water-softening company, the biggest had been Tropicana Products, an orange juice producer, for $490 million. Dutt faced the daunting task of rationalizing the behemoth he had inherited.

His first move was to analyze Beatrice's operations by return on net assets so that he could jettison those that weren't able to make a 20% return. But he didn't just chop recklessly—he paid attention to the mix of companies and tried to create a coherent whole. To the stockholders' delight, he sold dozens of companies, including Airstream, the trailer producer; Morgan Yacht Corporation; Dannon Company, of yogurt fame; and all domestic soft drink operations, chiefly Royal Crown Cola and Seven-Up franchises.

But another Dutt decision seemed inconsistent with these sales. In 1981, Dutt struck a $580 million deal with Northwest Industries to buy the Coca-Cola Bottling Company of Los Angeles and Buckingham Corporation, the importer of Cutty Sark and other liquors.

Dutt defended his acquisition, arguing that his strategy was to create a bigger, even more profitable Beatrice that was a "premier marketer." He planned to improve corporate marketing both on a regional level, by offering incentives to regional managers, and on a national level. To this end Dutt quintupled Beatrice's advertising and marketing budget, from a paltry $160 million to $800 million a year. And to symbolize the company's new character, Beatrice's name changed again, from Beatrice Foods to Beatrice Companies, in June, 1984.

Convinced that effective marketing and continued growth would transform Beatrice from a group of decentralized, regional operations into a major worldwide marketer, that summer Dutt bought Esmark, a Chicago-based food and consumer products giant, for $2.7 billion. This price, 23 times earnings, added so much debt to Beatrice's balance sheet that Standard and Poor's downgraded Beatrice securities from AA to A.

During these difficult years, *Fortune* reported that Dutt had turned into a "fiery-tempered autocrat" who drove his employees mercilessly and demanded absolute allegiance. Of Beatrice's 58 top officers at the end of 1980, when Dutt took over, 37 had left the company by mid-1985. Over a three-year span La Choy had three presidents, and in a single year, Tropicana Products went through three. Further, Beatrice's merger with Esmark, which Dutt had promised would be exceedingly smooth, caused dozens of firings and resignations among Esmark executives.

By mid-1985, all confidence in Dutt's grand vision of Beatrice had dissipated. Although he had succeeded in making Beatrice larger, his achievements fell far short of his promise to raise return on equity and speed growth in earnings. In August, 1985, Beatrice's board of directors—many of them appointed by Dutt—asked for Dutt's resignation.

William Granger Jr. came out of retirement to replace Dutt, and soon announced his intent to sell assets to reduce Beatrice's $2.5 billion debt load. But before he could accomplish this, Donald Kelly, the former chairman of the board of Esmark, took Beatrice private with the help of Kohlberg Kravis Roberts in a $6.2 billion leveraged buyout. Beatrice was reorganized as the wholly owned subsidiary of BCI Holdings Corporation.

Kelly began selling off assets immediately: only 12 days after taking over, he sold Avis, the number-two car rental company in the U.S., for $250 million. He continued to sell subsidiaries until July, 1987, when he decided to spin off a miscellaneous collection of 15 consumer goods and specialty food companies into a company called E-II Holdings. BCI shareholders received one share of E-II for every three of BCI.

Kelly became chairman and CEO of E-II as well as chairman of BCI. In September, 1987, Kelly changed BCI's name to Beatrice Company to signal his intent to return to the food industry.

Meanwhile, Kelly, in his role as the leader of E-II, launched a raid on American Brands, a tobacco company. The tables soon turned, however, and Kelly agreed to sell E-II to American for $800 million (earning a tidy $50 million himself for his seven months at E-II).

By the fall of 1988, Kelly's steady dismantling of Beatrice had earned about $7.3 billion, more than offsetting the $6.2 billion he had paid for the company. In addition to the E-II deal, some of Kelly's largest sales were: Playtex, for $1.25 billion, to its management; the Los Angeles Coca-Cola Bottler, for $1 billion, to Coca-Cola; International Foods, for $985 million, to the TLC Group; and Tropicana, for $1.2 billion, to Seagram.

But Kelly didn't plan to stop there. He originally planned to sell the remaining Beatrice businesses as a whole to a single buyer. But when he found no such buyer, he stepped down as chairman (though he remains on the board) in October, 1988 and left the running of the remains of Beatrice to Frederick Rentschler, a former Esmark executive who had been president and CEO of Beatrice since mid-1987.

Beatrice began in the dairy business, and for 45 years was content to remain there. During World War II its focus broadened, and in the following decades, Beatrice's growth took it into nearly every aspect of the food business—and beyond food altogether. But decades of acquisition, combined with a determined policy of decentralized management, created an enormous, poorly rationalized company. What remains today, after the frenzied selling that followed the company's leveraged buyout in 1986, are Beatrice's main domestic food operations. So, after nearly half a century of expansion, Beatrice now finds itself trimmed to a more manageable size and tightly focused once again on the food industry.

Principal Subsidiaries: Beatrice/Hunt-Wesson; Swift-Eckrich; Beatrice Cheese.

BORDEN, INC.

180 East Broad Street
Columbus, Ohio 43215
U.S.A.
(614) 225-4000

Public Company
Incorporated: 1899 as Borden Condensed Milk Company
Employees: 45,400
Sales: $7.24 billion
Stock Index: New York Tokyo Basel Geneva Lausanne Zurich

Although Borden is America's largest dairy business and it is still best know among consumers as a milk company, Borden's dairy division today generates the least income of all its divisions. During the 1980s Borden emerged as one of the fiercest buyers and sellers of branded regional food companies, drawing attention to itself once again after several decades of nondescript efforts in industrial chemicals and leaner-margin dairy products. Borden now looks for the largest growth in snacks and pasta, two new areas for the company in which it holds top positions in the market. A parent company to many smaller regional labels for 30 years, Borden combines a low marketing profile with enormous sales volume.

Gail Borden Jr., the company's founder, was born in 1801 in Norwich, New York. When his family migrated west, they stopped in Kentucky and Indiana Territory. Borden then moved to Mississippi before settling in Galveston, Texas. Along the way he worked as a surveyor, school teacher, farmer, and government official. He edited the first permanent newspaper in Texas, the *Telegraph & Texas Register*, and is said to have written the famous headline "Remember the Alamo."

Borden made a hobby of inventing things. Among his creations was the prairie schooner, an awkward, sail-powered wagon. Another Borden device, the lazy Susan, can now be found in households everywhere. He also concocted the unsavory, yet serviceable, "meat biscuit," a lightweight, nonperishable food suited to travelers. Although the meat biscuit was a commercial failure, it was hailed as a scientific breakthrough and in 1851 Borden was invited to London to receive the Great Council Medal from Queen Victoria.

During his passage back from London, Borden saw several children on board ship die after drinking contaminated milk. Because no one yet knew how to keep milk fresh, spoiled and even poisonous milk was not uncommon. Borden knew that the Shakers used vacuum pans to preserve fruit, and he began experimenting with a similar apparatus in search of a way to preserve milk. After much tinkering, he discovered he could prevent milk from souring by evaporating it over a slow heat in the vacuum. Believing that it resisted spoilage because its water content had been removed, he called his revolutionary product "condensed milk." As Louis Pasteur later demonstrated, however, it was the heat Borden used in his evaporation process that kept the milk from spoiling because it killed the bacteria in fresh milk.

Despite the apparent usefulness of condensed milk, the U.S. Patent Office rejected Borden's patent application three times. It was finally accepted on August 19, 1856 after Robert McFarlane, the editor of *Scientific American*, and John H. Currie, head of a research laboratory, convinced the commissioner of patents of the value of condensed milk. Soon afterward, Borden started a small processing operation near a dairy farm in Wolcottville, Connecticut and opened a sales office in New York City. Consumers, however, took little notice of canned milk, and, after only a few months in business, sluggish sales forced Borden to return to Texas in need of more capital. Undaunted, he resumed production in 1857 in Burrville, Connecticut under the name Gail Borden, Jr., and Company.

The second enterprise also struggled financially until Borden met Jeremiah Milbank, a wholesale grocer, banker, and railroad financier. With Milbank's funding they formed a partnership in 1858 known as the New York Condensed Milk Company. Another stroke of fortune came when Borden decided to advertise in an issue of *Leslie's Illustrated Weekly*, which coincidentally contained an article condemning the unsanitary conditions at city dairies and the practice by many unscrupulous dairymen of adding chalk and eggs to enhance their "swill milk," as it was called. Soon after the magazine appeared, the New York Condensed Milk Company was delivering condensed milk throughout lower Manhattan and in Jersey City, New Jersey.

In 1861 the United States government ordered 500 pounds of condensed milk for troops fighting in the Civil War. As the conflict grew, government orders increased, until Borden had to license other manufacturers to keep up with demand. After the war, the New York Condensed Milk Company had a ready-made customer base in both Union and Confederate veterans. To distinguish this product from its new competitors, Borden adopted the American bald eagle as his trademark.

Gail Borden Jr. died in 1874, leaving management of the thriving company to his sons, John Gail and Henry Lee, who presided from 1874 to 1884 and 1884 to 1902, respectively. In 1875 the company diversified by offering delivery of fluid milk in New York and New Jersey. Ten years later, it pioneered the use of glass bottles for milk distribution. In 1892 Borden's fluid-milk business was expanded to Chicago and the company began to manufacture evaporated milk. Seven years later, Henry Lee Borden opened the first foreign branch, in Ontario, Canada, bringing to 18 the number of towns in which the company had facilities. In 1899, as fresh and condensed milk sales generated profits of $2 million, the company was incorporated as the Borden Condensed Milk Company.

William J. Rogers, the company's first president from outside the Borden family, took over in 1902. He was succeeded in 1910 by S. Frederick Taylor. Concentrating on its strongholds in New York, New Jersey, and Illinois, Borden built new evaporation facilities and tin-can factories, as well as pasteurizing and bottling stations. Local dairy farmers often helped finance the construction, and in return Borden brought stability to milk markets, which at that time were subject to sudden fluctuations, by setting prices for six-month periods. Relations with milk suppliers remained generally friendly until the 1930s, when the market was glutted and farmers charged Borden and other distributors with conspiring to depress prices.

Toward the close of World War I, Borden strengthened its board of directors. Albert G. Milbank, a descendant of Jeremiah Milbank and a founding partner in the New York law firm of Milbank, Tweed, Hope & Webb, was named Borden's first chairman of the board in 1917. The following year, directors from outside the dairy industry were appointed for the first time. These changes reflected Borden's expanded business and helped to make possible its explosive growth in the next decade.

Under Arthur W. Milburn, the Borden Company, as it was renamed in 1919, embarked on a buying spree that transformed it into a multinational conglomerate. Between 1927 and 1930, it bought more than 200 companies around the country and became the nation's largest distributor of fluid milk. In the process, it entered five new fields: ice cream, cheese, powdered milk, mincemeat, and adhesives. The J.M. Horton Ice Cream Company and the Reid Ice Cream Corporation, which Borden bought in 1928, were both well established on the East Coast. Ice cream fit logically into Borden's fluid-milk operations, as did cheese, which was added in 1929 when Borden acquired the Monroe Cheese Company, Chateau Cheese Company, Ltd., and several other leading producers. Two slightly more adventurous acquisitions proved instrumental in Borden's subsequent development. In 1927, it acquired the Merrell-Soule Company, whose None Such mincemeat and Klim powdered milk were sold throughout the world. Borden relied on the technology behind Klim when it developed instant coffee, coffee creamer, and other powdered foods during World War II.

In 1929, Borden acquired the Casein Company of America in Bainbridge, New York. This small company, which manufactured a cold-water-soluble, water-resistant adhesive from casein, a byproduct of skim milk, became the foundation of Borden's vast chemical operations.

In 1929 Borden became the holding company for four separate companies: Borden's Food Products Company, Inc.; Borden's Dairy Products Company, Inc.; Borden's Ice Cream and Milk Company, Inc.; and Borden's Cheese & Produce Company, Inc. This structure was discontinued in 1936 and the subsidiaries became divisions.

Earnings plunged when the national economy stalled in the 1930s, but, more significantly, new price regulations on fluid milk irreversibly eroded profit margins. With the approval of the United States Department of Agriculture, many dairy farmers formed cooperatives to establish prices. Some states established milk-control boards to administer price supports to ensure adequate supplies and low cost to the consumer. Distributors like Borden were forced to pay more for milk, but were prevented from passing the increased cost on to the consumer. When distributors tried to compensate for thinning margins by manipulating prices in unregulated regions, vehement, sometimes violent protests from farmers and consumers alike followed. In 1938 a federal grand jury in Chicago indicted Borden and several other competitors for antitrust violations. Although the charges were dropped two years later in a consent decree, price regulations continued and profit margins did not improve. Tax hikes and escalating wages in unionized cities such as Chicago also hurt profits.

Also in the 1930s, a line of "perscription products" was introduced. This line, marketed primarily to doctors, included products like Biolac, an evaporated infant food, and a modified milk sugar called Beta Lactose. Eventually these products led to the establishment of a special products division.

Theodore G. Montague, a former dairy owner and operator from Wisconsin, succeeded Milburn as head of Borden in 1937. In an effort to deal with regulatory policies and employee relations, which varied from one state to the next, Montague decentralized management under a system of checks and balances. He promoted low-volume, high-margin manufactured goods like cheese, mincemeat, condensed milk, and especially ice cream—Borden's most popular product and a leading source of income from the late 1930s through World War II.

As it turned out, Montague's most important decision was to cultivate Borden's small adhesives business. By far the largest buyer of the company's glues was the forest products industry, where casein adhesives were used to coat paper and strengthen plywood. This swelling market prompted Borden to build its second glue plant in Seattle in the 1930s. But no sooner had the Seattle factory come on line than stronger, less expensive synthetics threatened to make casein compounds obsolete. Although adhesives accounted for less than 1% of its gross revenues, Montague embraced this new technology, and Borden developed its own urea and formaldehyde glues. These were followed in the early 1940s by even stronger phenol formaldehyde resins. By the 1950s, Borden had become a leading supplier of bonding agents to the lumber industry.

Borden's entry into the raw-chemical business followed naturally from its success in synthetic glues. It built a formaldehyde plant in Springfield, Oregon to satisfy its own growing demand for this primary ingredient, but soon found that selling formaldehyde to competitors was very profitable. Four additional units were constructed, three in the United States and one in Curitiba, Brazil in collaboration with Incola, S.A. Today, Borden is one of the largest formaldehyde producers in the country.

The man responsible for the expansion of Borden's chemical business was Augustine R. Marusi. Marusi, whose background was in chemical engineering, joined Borden in the early 1950s as a salesman. He was sent to Brazil to oversee the completion of the Curitiba facility, but brought back in 1954 to be made head of the chemical division. He quickly overcame the resistance of the dairymen on the board of directors and steered Borden into printing inks, fertilizers, and the burgeoning new filed of polyvinyl chloride (PVC), which became a mainstay of the chemical division along with adhesives. In 1954 Borden acquired three small thermoplastics firms that produced PVC resins for use in paper packaging and paint. Then, in 1957, the company began making raw PVC at plants in Illinois and Massachusetts for sale mainly to the phonograph-record and floor-covering industries. Within four years, Borden was manufacturing 7% of all domestically produced PVC. Borden also developed acetate packaging films commonly used in supermarkets and acquired companies that made vinyl-coated fabrics and wall coverings.

In 1961, Borden and Uniroyal joined forced to build a huge petrochemical complex in Geismar, Louisiana known as Monochem. Three-quarters of Monochem's output goes to other Borden operations; it supplies methanol for Borden's formaldehyde production, vinyl-chloride monomer for its PVC production, and acetylene for its vinyl-acetate production. Over the years, as Borden has enlarged Monochem's capacities and added new processes, the company has become one of the largest and most integrated chemical companies in the world.

Harold W. Comfort, who became president in 1955 when Montague was made chairman of the board, supported Marusi's activities as a way of freeing the company from dependence on its increasingly less profitable dairy business. Comfort took other measures, too. He made many food acquisitions abroad and promoted foreign sales, especially in South and Central America, where the company faced fewer regulations and competitors than in Europe. While the national supermarket chains that emerged in the 1950s squeezed profits on fluid milk, they created market openings for processed, specialty groceries. Borden developed unique dairy products such as protein-enriched milk, premium-quality ice cream, and, later, diet cheeses, in order to establish supermarket niches. It also began a program of acquiring food manufacturers with well-known or one-of-a-kind items that were successful in the intense competition for supermarket shelf space. Among the companies it took over between 1959 and 1965 were the makers of Snow's seafood chowders (1959); Wyler's bouillon and powdered soft drinks (1961); ReaLemon lemon juice (1962); Cracker Jack candied popcorn and Campfire marshmallows (1964); Wise potato chips (1964); and Bama preserves (1965). In chemicals, too, Borden put new emphasis on its consumer products like Elmer's Glue-All and Krylon spray paints.

Marusi's success with the chemical division earned him a promotion to president in 1967 and the distinction of being Borden's first non-dairy CEO. But disappointing performances in Borden's three major divisions—dairy, food, and chemicals—marked the early years of his reign. In response, Marusi announced a number of painful austerity measures. Borden sold its office building in Manhattan, moved its headquarters to Columbus, Ohio, and closed scores of unprofitable dairy facilities. In 1969 alone it took write-offs totalling $70 million. Marusi also tightened the corporate office's control and greatly improved financial planning. He also doubled the budget for marketing, which had not kept pace with Borden's diversification—although Elsie the Cow had become one of the most widely recognized trademarks in the world since her introduction in 1936, she was of little use in selling PVC. Marusi further enhanced Borden's public relations with a program to contract with minority-owned businesses, an initiative that inspired the National Minority Purchasing Council, which Marusi helped establish.

Throughout this period, Borden's international operations also continued to grow apace. By 1968, the company had acquired or organized chemical interests in Argentina, Mexico, Canada, the Philippines, Colombia, France, Norway, and Nicaragua. Its food interests included companies in Canada, Puerto Rico, Bermuda, Mexico, Venezuela, Ireland, Spain, West Germany, and Sweden. In 1968, Borden organized Borden Inc. International, a division responsible for all international manufacturing and export operations.

The 1970s were a period of slow growth and cost reductions at Borden. In accordance with company policy, Marusi retired at age 65 in 1979. His impatience with product development had evolved into a management philosophy that Borden maintains today. Unlike other food companies that acquire smaller regional brands, Borden keeps its regional brands regional, offering its new subsidiaries steady, cheaper supplies while the subsidiaries provide expertise in penetrating their particular markets. As a result, Borden spends little on national advertising and distribution and has a reduced vulnerability to product failure. Because of this low-profile yet aggressive approach, Marusi's successor, Eugene J. Sullivan, inherited a more efficient company.

Nonetheless, in 1980 Sullivan began a five-year, $1.5 billion restructuring. Intent on increasing shareholders' return on investment, Sullivan consolidated operations by cutting 5,000 employees and selling 48 companies in his six-year tenure.

Yet Borden grew during this period too. Sullivan purchased 33 companies—mostly in the packaged consumer products and specialty chemicals areas, two growth fields for Borden—and redirected the company toward consumer foods. Most of Sullivan's purchases were food businesses, and he built for Borden the second-largest market share for pasta and snack foods, two areas Borden emphasizes heavily because of their potential for growth.

As the second in a line of three CEOs who ascended through the chemical industry, Sullivan still found it difficult to abandon the chemical market altogether. Marusi had kept Borden's chemical businesses but had found it increasingly difficult to keep a giant food company on top of dramatic changes in the chemical industry. Chemical manufacturing has significantly higher margins than food, but a depressed petrochemical market in the mid-1980s forced Sullivan to reevaluate Borden's ability to maintain long-term growth in the industry. As a result, Sullivan strengthened Borden's specialty chemicals and integrated international operations with domestic (both in food and chemicals), hoping to make production and marketing more efficient.

Compared to its competitors, Borden was considered a conservative, even unimaginative, company by analysts when R.J. Ventres took over as CEO in 1986. Its success in managing regional food companies was overlooked because it didn't create national brands. Ventres soon changed Borden's image with a feverish spate of acquisitions, purchasing 62 companies, for a total $1.4 billion, between 1986 and 1989. These were mostly companies like Meadow Gold Dairies, Inc., that dovetailed nicely with existing operations. In 1987 Borden's 18 purchases made it the nation's most active acquirer according to *Mergers & Acquisitions*. Its $180 million purchase of the Prince Company that year made Borden the undisputed leader in U.S. pasta sales, as the owner of nine companies nationwide, representing nearly a third of the market.

Ventres also rediscovered the value of the company's dairy operations, which generate high-volume cash flow with little inventory expense because of rapid turnover. And Borden succeeded in doubling its snack food sales by 1989 through its growing national network of regional brands and its penetration of international markets in snack foods through acquisition.

At the same time, Ventres continued to consolidate. In 1987 the company's stock buy-back program left only 73.7 million shares outstanding, a 22% reduction since Marusi's retirement eight years earlier, while petrochemical and PVC producers were sold to the public, further distancing the company from raw-chemical manufacturing.

Borden's renaissance in food production has rekindled interest in the company, as the magnitude of Ventres's acquisitions and the company's market shares in pasta and snacks have given the company a renewed national prominence. Borden remains a tightly focused company that pays attention to regional market share and return on shareholder investment rather than popular opinion.

Principal Subsidiaries: Anthony Macaroni Co., Inc.; Bayamon Can Corp, Inc. (80%); Borden Inks of Puerto Rico, Inc.; Borden, Interamerica, Inc.; Borden International, Inc.; Borden International (Europe) Ltd.; Borden World Trade, Inc.; Buckeye Potato Chip Co., Inc.; Caribbean Snacks, Inc.; Cheese-Tek Corp.; Coco Lopez Manufacturing Corp. (80%); Fabric Leather Corporation; Guy's Foods, Inc.; Imperial Flavors, Inc.; Industrias La Famosa, Inc.; Marshall Energy, Inc.; Monochem, Inc.; National Food Products, Inc.; Productos Borden, Inc.; Ragsdale Bros., Inc.; Seyfert Foods, Inc.; Sterling Plastics Co.; Superior Dairies, Inc.; T.H.E. Tool Co., Inc.; Viking Engraving Corp., Inc. (77%); Borden S.A. (Panama); Crown Wallcovering Ltd. (U.K.); Demer, S.A. (50%) (Spain); Este, S.A. (50%) (Spain); Naturin, S.A. (50%) (Spain); Productos Quimicas y Alimenticious Borden Chile Ltd. (50%); Wilhelm Weber GmbH (West Germany); H&H Hobby-Und Modellbauprodukte GmbH (West Germany); Klemmc GmbH & Co., K.G. (50%) (West Germany); Borden U.K. Holdings, Ltd.; Borden (Bray) Ltd. (Ireland); Borden Australia Pty. Ltd.; Hong Kong Snack Foods Ltd. (50%); Borden Chemical Co. (France) S.A.; Societe d'Application du Flockage (France); Societe Nouvelle Cellonite (France); Borden Company A/S (Denmark); Borden Company, Limited (Ireland); Borden Company Limited (Canada); Borden Company, S.A. (Panama); Borden Far East Trading Ltd. (Hong Kong); Borden International Philippines, Inc. (98%); Borden Kjemi Norge A/S (Norway); Borden (Pty.) Limited (South Africa); Borden Overseas Capital Corporation, N.V. (Netherlands Antilles); Borden Nederland, B.V. (50%) (Netherlands); Thompack B.V. (70%) (Netherlands); C.O. Mason, Inc. (Puerto Rico); Compania Casco S.A.I.C. (Puerto Rico); Compania Internacional de Ventas, S.A. (Panama); Mason Wholesale, Inc. (Puerto Rico); Cia. Internacional De Ventas, S.A. (Panama); Borden Chemical (M) Sdn. Bhd. (66%) (Malaysia); Fabrica de Productos Borden, S.A. (Panama); Helados Borden S.A. (Panama); Hitachi-Borden Chemical Products, Inc. (50%) (Japan); Meiji-Borden, Inc. (50%) (Japan); Quimica Borden Ecuatoria, S.A. (75%) (Ecuador); Suzy International N.V. (Belgium); Broex, S.A. (Belgium).

BSN GROUPE S.A.

7, Rue de Téhéran
75381 Paris Cedex 08
France
(01) 42–99–10–10

Public Company
Incorporated: 1966 as Boussois Souchon Neuvesel
Employees: 42,234
Sales: FFr42.2 billion (US$6.96 billion)
Stock Index: Paris Zurich Basel Geneva Brussels London

The origins of the BSN Groupe lie in a small bottlemaker called La Verrerie Souchon-Neuvesel, but it grew into the giant it is today by filling the bottles that it made. One of the largest food manufacturers in Europe, BSN makes beverages, dairy products, grocery products, biscuits, and containers including such well-known brands as Evian mineral water, Kronenbourg beer, and Dannon yogurt.

In 1958, 39-year-old Antoine Riboud inherited the glass-making company founded by his great-uncle nearly a century before in Lyons. Riboud had begun his career working in its factory during World War II. Souchon-Neuvesel produced hollow glass, bottles, jars, flasks, and glass tableware. A small company, it recorded only about $10 million in sales that year.

Riboud concentrated on hollow glass–making until 1966, when La Verrerie Souchon-Neuvesel merged with Glaces de Boussois, a maker of flat glass for automobiles and housing. The new company was named Boussois Souchon-Neuvesel, and Riboud was named president.

In 1967, the company boasted FFr1.1 billion in sales and was renamed BSN. It had become a major European maker of glass containers, but was still dwarfed by its competitor and France's largest glassmaker, Compagnie de Saint-Gobain, founded in 1665 by Louis XIV. The next year Riboud made one of the largest French takeover bids ever for this company, with more than ten times as many employees as BSN, using tactics considered radical in France at the time: he proposed to swap BSN convertible bonds for Saint-Gobain stock. Saint-Gobain's board members fended off the offer by claiming that it violated French laws and European Economic Community rules on monopolies. Saint-Gobain also launched a major publicity campaign to rally support from stockholders against BSN's "cheap" bid. *The Wall Street Journal* called it "the David-vs.-Goliath campaign," and Riboud's tactics brought him the admiration of younger businessmen ready for fresh air in the French business establishment. Sadly, in the midst of such publicity, Riboud's apartment in Paris was bombed by a terrorist gang. In the end, shareholders came to Saint-Gobain's rescue, acquiring a 40% holding to BSN's 10%, and BSN dropped the bid.

BSN's defeat led Riboud to diversify into the food industry. "I saw it would be better to fill the bottles rather than just make them," he explained to *Forbes* in 1980. In 1970, BSN acquired Societé des Eaux d'Evian, Societé Européenne de Brasseries, and Brasseries Kronenbourg, becoming a leader in natural spring water and baby food, as well as the largest brewer in France. The next year, in an effort to tap the consumer taste for premium beers, BSN introduced its Kanterbraü beer.

In the meantime, BSN established its first flat-glass manufacturing subsidiary, Flachglass A.G., in West Germany in 1970, and two years later it acquired a controlling interest in Glaverbel, a Belgian flat-glass producer. Together with earlier expansion programs in West Germany, Austria, and the Benelux countries, these acquisitions gave BSN almost half the European market for flat glass.

The establishment of the Common Market at the end of the 1950s forced French companies to be more competitive, and between the early 1960s and 1973 France became the fastest-growing industrialized country after Japan. BSN also experienced rapid growth, culminating in 1973 with a merger between BSN and Gervais Danone, France's largest food company and the leader in yogurt, natural cheese, deserts, and pasta. That year sales for the new BSN-Gervais Danone topped FFr9 billion.

By 1973, however, BSN began to suffer from the impact of the energy crisis, which had severe consequences for the two main markets for flat glass, the construction and automotive industries. For the next five years the profits of many major French companies declined sharply, mainly because of higher costs for energy and raw materials. After a period of growth, the French foreign trade balance fell into deficit. Fortunately BSN had made most of its acquisitions with stock rather than cash, so the company's finances were able to weather the crisis. Riboud tried to help the flat-glass sector recover by building three new glass units in northern France and adding more efficient float glass equipment to BSN plants all over Europe. Nonetheless, beginning in 1974, the company shut down 22 furnaces and reduced its workforce by 30%. In five years of restructuring the company spent FFr2.5 billion. The crisis was a turning point for the company; from now on glass would be primarily a complement to its food and beverage businesses.

BSN acquired a minority interest in Ebamsa (now Font Vella), the leading Spanish bottler of natural spring water in 1973, and between 1974 and 1977 introduced several new products, including Lacmil and Gervillage. In an effort to dominate the European beer market, in 1978 BSN acquired a minority interest in Alken, a large Belgian brewery. A year later it acquired one-third interests in the breweries Mahou in Spain and Wührer in Italy, and a majority interest in Anglo-Belge in Belgium.

BSN next bought four French food manufacturing firms through an exchange of stock interests with Genérale Occidentale, a move encouraged by the French government, which was eager to invigorate the food industry and actually drew up a special incentive agreement for investments in food processing and food exports. In 1980, the company entered Japan's dairy market through a joint venture with Japan's Ajinomoto. BSN also bought two French producers of frozen foods and ice cream and two breweries in Nigeria. As it moved into these new fields, BSN nearly doubled it annual sales in grocery products.

At the same time, BSN was finally leaving the flat-glass industry, prompted in part by the fear that another oil crisis was imminent. In 1980, BSN sold its West German flat-glass ventures to the British company Pilkington Brothers, and by 1981, BSN had sold its flat-glass subsidiaries in Germany, Austria, Belgium, and the Netherlands. The following year, it sold the French Boussois subsidiary, the last of its flat-glass operations, leaving it with only nine glass container factories. Also in 1981 BSN acquired Dannon, the largest American yogurt-maker, from Beatrice for $84.3 million.

In 1983, BSN-Gervais Danone changed its name back to BSN. In an effort to increase efficiency, Riboud installed computerized production lines, which meant that the company had to lay off 1,000 of its 40,000 employees, a move opposed by the unions but encouraged by French President François Mitterand, who praised BSN for its contribution towards modernizing French industry. By 1984, BSN had acquired all shares of the champagne makers Pommery et Greno and Lanson Pere et Fils, and had introduced a number of new yogurt products, as well as the Plastishield plastic-coated bottle. Since 1981, the company's sales had risen sharply, and that year it made a record capital investment totaling FFr2.4 billion. But in July, the European Economic Community imposed fines of about US$3.2 million on BSN and Saint-Gobain for price-fixing in the Benelux glass market.

BSN has continued to grow in the latter half of the 1980s. In 1985 BSN sold its glass-jar and glass-tableware operations to Verreries Champenoises and acquired a minority interest in that company. BSN also bought the pharmaceuticals-maker Bottu, which specializes in pain relievers and artificial sweeteners.

In 1986, the company's twentieth anniversary, sales were 35 times higher than the FFr1.1 billion of its first year. A year later, BSN merged with Genérale Biscuit S.A., the top producer of biscuits and toasted bread in Continental Europe. BSN also merged its Kronenbourg and Societé de Brasseries breweries under the Kronenbourg name. The company acquired Sonnen Basserman in West Germany, and became the world's largest bottler of natural spring water. It also bought a majority interest in Angelo Ghigi, an Italian pasta maker.

In August, 1988, BSN acquired the Belgian Maes Group Breweries, the British H.P. Foods, and the American Lea & Perrins as part of Riboud's strategy to gain a more substantial market in Britain and America for BSN products (64% of BSN's total sales still come from France). Concentrating on growth, Riboud also built several new yogurt plants and bottling facilities in strategic locations, and he spent more than US$ 100 million on European television advertisements for BSN brands.

In 1989 BSN bought the European operations of Nabisco, making it the world's second-largest producer of biscuits. Also in 1989 BSN made several Italian acquisitions and is now the leader in food production in that country.

Since the company's beginning, Antoine Riboud's aggressive and shrewd business sense has transformed BSN from a small glassmaker into one of Europe's largest food companies. But experts say, and Riboud concurs, that BSN must quickly increase in size to avoid getting lost—or broken up—in the fast-paced restructuring going on in the European food industry in preparation for 1992.

Principal Subsidiaries: Gervais Danone France; Laiterie De Villecomtal (50.2%); Stenval S.A.; Gervais Danone A.G. (West Germany); Richter KG; Gervais Danone Austria GmbH; Gervais Danone Belgique (Belgium); Gervais Danone Nederland (the Netherlands); Gervais Danone Italiana (Italy); Dannon Company (U.S.A.); LPC Industrias Alimenticias (55.1%) (Brazil); Danone La Madrague; Rossignol—Generale Traiteur; Stoeffler; de Bellevue; Societe Fonciere et Commerciale du Silo de La Madrague; Ropssignol—Generale Traiteur; Stoeffler; Diepal; Conserves Lenzbourg; Etablissements Lerebourg; Amora; Vandamme-Pie Qui Chante; Mariebel; Segma Liebig Maille; Gallia—H—PH; Panzani Ponte Liebig (Italy); Liebig Benelux (Belgium); Sonnen–Bassermann (West Germany); HP Foods (U.K.); Lea & Perrins (U.S.A.); LU; L'Alsacienne; Heudebert; Generale Biscuit Expansion; Generale Biscuit Glico France; Generale Biscuits Belgie (Belgium); General Biscuits Nederland (the Netherlands); General Biscuits GmbH (West Germany); General Biscuits Osterreich (90%) (Austria); General Biscuits Espana (Spain); Galletas Siro (94.8%) (Spain); Proelga (Spain); Italu (Italy); General Biscuit Brands (U.S.A.); Mothers Cake and Cookie Co. (U.S.A.); Brasseries Kronenbourg; Sofid; Brasseries Alken-Maes (50%) (Belgium); Birra Wuhrer (98.1%) (Italy); Champagne Lanson Pere et Fils (99.9%); Champagne Pommery et Greno (99.4%); Chpl; Sa des Eaux Minerales D'Evian Seat; Font Vella (61.7%) (Spain); Verreries Souchon Neuvesel; Verreres de Masnieres; Seprosy; Vereenigde Glasfabrieken (66%) (the Netherlands); Vidrieria Viella (99.9%) (Spain); Giralt Laporta (Spain); Compagnie Gervais Danone; Generale Biscuit S.A.; Cofinda; BSN Finance; Finalim; BSN Services (Belgium); Cofive (Belgium); Mecaniver (89.3%) (Belgium); Selba Nederland (the Netherlands); BSN Italia (Italy); Sifit (50%) (Italy); BSN UK; BSN Foods Co. (U.S.A.); Generale Biscuits of America; Ajinomoto Danone (50%) (Japan); Danone Espagne (20%) (Spain); SCBK (50%) (Congo); Mahou SA (33.3%) (Spain); Peroni (20.4%) (Italy); Acque E. Terme di Boario (35.2%) (Italy); Ferrarelle Spa (35.2%) (Italy); Sangemini (35.3%) (Italy); Sangemini Finanziaria (35.2%) (Italy); VMC (39%); Ifil Partecipazioni (20%) (Italy).

Cadbury Schweppes

CADBURY SCHWEPPES PLC

1–4 Connaught Place
London W2 EX2
United Kingdom
(01) 262–1212

Public Company
Incorporated: 1969
Employees: 27,000
Sales: £2.38 billion (US$4.3 billion)
Stock Index: London NASDAQ

Cadbury Schweppes PLC is one of the oldest and largest family-run businesses in the world today. Although confectioner Cadbury Limited merged with the carbonated drinks company Schweppes Limited in 1969, Cadbury Schweppes is still run by members of the Cadbury family, which has been represented in Cadbury's top management for more than 170 years. The company is currently one of the world's leading producers of chocolate candy and soft drinks.

The history of Cadbury dates back to 1824, when John Cadbury opened his grocery business in Birmingham. From the start, drinking-cocoa and chocolate were his most popular products, and in 1831 he moved to larger quarters and began manufacturing his own cocoa products. In 1847 he took on his brother Benjamin as a partner. Two years later the Cadbury brothers spun off their retail operations to Richard Cadbury Barrow, a nephew, and concentrated on manufacture and wholesale distribution. In 1853 Cadbury Brothers received a royal warrant as manufacturers to Queen Victoria; the company still holds the distinction of being confectioner to the Crown.

Shortly thereafter, however, business began to decline. The two Cadbury brothers dissolved their partnership in 1860 when Benjamin left the company, and John also retired the very next year. He left the business to his sons Richard and George, who continued to struggle for several years. But in 1866, the new Cadbury brothers introduced an improved process for pressing cocoa butter out of the cocoa bean to produce cocoa essence. This resulted in purer drinking-cocoa and plentiful cocoa butter that could be made into eating chocolate. In 1868, Cadbury Brothers began marketing its own lines of chocolate candy, reviving its fortunes and breaking the stranglehold that French confectioners had on the British market.

Renewed success brought with it renewed expansion. In 1879 Cadbury Brothers began constructing a new factory outside Birmingham. In 1881 the firm received its first export order from a representative in Australia, and by the middle of the decade its overseas business had expanded to New Zealand, South Africa, India, the West Indies, and both North and South America. In 1899 it incorporated as Cadbury Brothers Limited, with George Cadbury as chairman.

In 1906 Cadbury Brothers introduced a new recipe for milk chocolate, marketed under the name Cadbury Dairy Milk, which has remained a mainstay of its product line ever since. After World War I, innovations in industrial technology made the manufacture of chocolate cheap enough to price chocolate candy for a wider market, and the company accordingly retooled its factory for mass production in the late 1920s. Cadbury Brothers opened its first overseas plant in Australia in 1922, and more foreign production ventures followed from its 1919 acquisition of J.S. Fry & Sons. In 1932 Fry's Canadian plant began to manufacture Cadbury products, and the next year Cadbury Fry, now a subsidiary of Cadbury Brothers, opened a factory in Ireland. Cadbury Brothers also began to manufacture in South Africa in 1939 and India in 1947.

Throughout the postwar years, Cadbury maintained its position as the leading chocolate manufacturer in the world's leading per-capita candy-consuming nation. ("They chew through plays and they chew through films and they chew in trains," a theater critic for the *London Daily Mail* once lamented. "They suck lollies through *Macbeth* and *Hamlet*, and they while away Tennessee Williams with the chocolates with the scrumptious centers.") In 1962 Cadbury and Cadbury Fry, along with their competitor Rowntree, accounted for 51% of British candy sales.

In 1964 Cadbury entered the sugar-candy business when it acquired confectioner Pascall Murray. All the while, the company remained a family business. At the time of the merger with Schweppes, its chairman had always been a direct descendent of John Cadbury and the vast majority of its stock belonged to family members or trusts.

The same cannot be said, however, for Schweppes Limited, which has not felt the guiding hand of a Schweppe for almost 200 years. The company bears the name of Jacob Schweppe, a German-born jeweler and amateur chemist who entered into a joint venture in 1790 with pharmacist Henry Gosse, engineer Jacques Paul, and his son Nicholas. Together, they formed Schweppe, Paul & Gosse, which devoted itself to producing artificial mineral water. Schweppe moved to London in 1792 to establish the company's English operations, and when the partnership dissolved the next year he retained the business for himself.

In those days, aerated water was believed to have medicinal value, and Schweppe's brand was popular because it contained a higher degree of carbonation than its competitors. In 1799 Schweppe sold a 75% interest in his business to three men from the island of Jersey and retired. The company, however, continued to use the Schweppe name.

In 1834 Schweppes was bought by William Evill and John

Kemp-Welch, whose descendants would remain associated with the company until 1950. In 1836 the company received its first royal warrant, from the Duchess of Kent and Princess Victoria, soon to become Queen Victoria. Schweppes also gained substantial prestige when it was granted a catering concession for the Great Exhibition of 1851.

The company began to introduce new product lines in the second half of the century. Schweppes started marketing ginger ale in the 1870s. Tonic water, now its most famous product, also appeared at about this time in response to a demand from Britons returning from India who had developed a taste for the solution of quinine, sugar, and water they had drunk there as a malaria preventative. And in 1885, Schweppes introduced a carbonated lemonade. Such was the company's success during the Victorian era that it went public in 1897.

In 1923 Schweppes consolidated its overseas operations into a single British-based subsidiary. This move was intended to facilitate further international expansion. During the interwar years and through World War II, however, the company's fortunes began to wane as sales went soft. It wasn't until Sir Frederick Hooper took over as managing director in 1948 that Schweppes regained its strength through shrewd marketing and a renewed focus on its overseas business. An integral part of that campaign for two decades was the use of Commander Edward Whitehead, who became chairman of Schweppes USA in 1952, as the company's American advertising spokesman. From the early 1950s through the early 1970s, Commander Whitehead, whom *Time* once described as an "engaging walrus," ingratiated himself with Americans as he espoused his products' unique "Schweppervescence." By 1962, foreign operations accounted for one-fifth of the company's net sales.

Schweppes was also forced to diversify as the demand for soft drinks and mixers at home leveled off. In 1960 it acquired three makers of jams and jellies: Hartley's, Moorhouse, and Chivers. These acquisitions required substantial reorganization, however, and did not work out very well; by 1964 only Hartley's was turning a profit for its parent company. Nonetheless, Schweppes prospered under Sir Frederick Hooper's guidance. Its annual profits increased nearly sevenfold between 1953 and 1962, from $756,000 to $4.8 million. Hooper retired in 1964 and was succeeded by Harold Watkinson, a former Conservative defense minister.

In 1968 Schweppes acquired Typhoo Tea to further diversify its product line and strengthen its ties to grocery retailers. But with no growth in its domestic markets, Lord Watkinson realized that overseas expansion was the key to Schweppes's future. Unfortunately, its capital base was tiny compared to that of the American conglomerates with which it would have to compete. That fall, Watkinson met with Cadbury Chairman Adrian Cadbury at a trade show and found that Cadbury had similar concerns about his own company. Schweppes and Cadbury began merger talks soon thereafter and reached an agreement in January, 1969.

Technically, Schweppes came out of the merger as the surviving company. It bought out Cadbury stockholders by replacing their shares with $290 million worth of its own stock. Watkinson became chairman in the new chain of command, with Adrian Cadbury assuming the titles of deputy chairman and co-managing director. But the new company bore the Cadbury name in front of Schweppes's, and the candy business was clearly not to be neglected. Although the two companies consolidated some of their operations, they maintained autonomy in the matter of distribution, since bottling franchisees control local distribution in the soft drink business.

The 1970s were marked by further diversification and attempts to capture international markets. In 1973 Cadbury Schweppes ventured into alcoholic beverages when it acquired Courtney Wines International from LRL International. Also in 1973, Schweppes South Africa merged with Groovy Beverages. A year later, it acquired Pepsi Cola South Africa. But most of Cadbury Schweppes's moves in the early 1970s were small in scale and generally unsuccessful. It also spread itself thin at home by introducing a large number of unprofitable new products.

Adrian Cadbury succeeded Watkinson as chairman in 1974, and under his direction Cadbury Schweppes focused its efforts on gaining a greater share of the lucrative American market. In 1978, aided by a strong pound, it acquired Peter Paul, a Connecticut-based confectioner, for $58 million. This gave Cadbury Schweppes a 10% share of the American candy market in one swoop. In 1982 it bought Duffy-Mott, a producer of fruit juices and other fruit products, from American Brands for $60 million.

Cadbury Schweppes made several other overseas acquisitions in the early 1980s. In 1980 it increased it stake in its French subsidiary, Schweppes France, to 100%. In 1982 it purchased a two-thirds interest in Rioblanco, a Spanish soft drink company that owned the Schweppes franchise in Spain. And in 1984 it acquired Cottees General Foods, General Foods's Australian subsidiary and a producer of coffee products, jams, jellies, and fruit juice cordials. In Britain it ended its 32-year-old franchising agreement with PepsiCo in 1985 to become Coca-Cola's British franchisee, noting Coke's dominant position in the British market.

But Cadbury Schweppes remained focused on the American market throughout the 1980s. In 1985 it acquired Sodastream Holdings, a British company that produced equipment for making carbonated drinks at home, as a way of trying to capture American customers without competing head-on with Coke and Pepsi—Cadbury Schweppes held only 1% of the American market in 1986, while the two native giants controlled roughly three-quarters between them.

But Cadbury Schweppes began to take on Coke and Pepsi with increasing vigor. In 1986 it bought the Canada Dry and Sunkist soft drink lines from RJR Nabisco for $230 million. RJR Nabisco was anxious to leave the soft drink business in the face of increased competition from Coca-Cola and Pepsi, which were growing ever larger. Pepsi had just acquired Seven-Up, and Coca-Cola had agreed to buy Dr. Pepper, a deal which would later fall apart. Sunkist was in danger of losing market share to Coca-Cola's new Minute Maid line and Pepsi's Slice.

But while RJR Nabisco was ready to get out, Cadbury Schweppes was desperate to get into the market. Buying Canada Dry and Sunkist increased its share of U.S. soft drink sales to 5.3%, making it the fourth-largest soft drink company in the nation.

Cadbury Schweppes then spun off Canada Dry's Canadian operations to Coca-Cola for $90 million. It needed the cash to acquire 30% of Dr. Pepper as part of a consortium that included the brokerage house Shearson Lehman Brothers and Dallas-based investment group Hicks & Haas. This group bought the soft drink company from Forstmann Little & Company for $416 million.

Cadbury Schweppes became the subject of takeover speculation in 1987 after General Cinema announced that it had acquired an 8.3% interest in the company. General Cinema, a soft drink bottler which also owns the Neiman Marcus department stores and operates a large movie theater chain, said that it had bought the Cadbury Schweppes shares purely as an investment. But speculation increased later that year when General Cinema raised its stake to 18.2%. And the next year, rumors circulated that Swiss giant Nestlé would try to acquire Cadbury Schweppes. With stock prices depressed in the wake of the October, 1987 stock market crash and Cadbury Schweppes's strong financial performance, it was an attractive takeover candidate.

Amid all this uncertainty, however, Cadbury Schweppes continued to go about its business. In 1987 it acquired Chocolat Poulait, a French confectioner, from Midial for $173.1 million. In 1988 it sold its American confectionery operations to Hershey Foods as a franchise, deciding that its products would benefit from Hershey's superior distribution network in the United States. In 1989 it bought out the British confectioner Bassett Foods to rescue it from a hostile takeover by the Swedish consumer-products concern Procordia. It also continued its pursuit of the American soft drink market by acquiring Crush International from Proctor & Gamble for $220 million. At that point, Cadbury Schweppes controlled a 4.7% market share in the United States and a 15.1% share in Canada.

In a sense, the takeover speculation surrounding Cadbury Schweppes is a tribute to its success over the last decade. In 1979 the company announced that it would refocus on its core businesses and devote itself to cracking the American marketplace. In 1986 it sold off its domestic beverage and foods division, which included the tea and jam businesses that Schweppes had acquired in the 1960s and Cadbury's popular Smash instant-mashed-potato product. All of its other important actions in the 1980s have related to confectionery and soft drinks. These moves have paid off. Cadbury Schweppes has increased its share of American soft drink sales almost fivefold and improved its financial situation significantly.

But perhaps the most interesting aspect of Cadbury Schweppes is the fact that it remains a family-run business even though it has also become a major corporation. Sir Adrian Cadbury (he was knighted in 1977), the great-grandson of John Cadbury, is still chairman. His brother Dominic was appointed CEO in 1983. Many successful companies that pass from generation to generation eventually lose their character and sense of family tradition as they grow older and larger, but after more than 170 years, there seems to be reason to believe that in the years to come Cadbury scions will still be making Cadbury Dairy Milk—and Schweppes tonic water too.

Principal Subsidiaries: Cadbury Schweppes Investment (Jersey) Ltd.; Cadbury Schweppes Investments B.V. (Netherlands); Cadbury Schweppes U.S.A. Inc.; Cadbury Ltd.; Schweppes International Ltd.; Canada Dry Corporation Ltd. (Ireland); Schweppes Ltd.; Cadbury Schweppes Research Ltd.; Cadbury Schweppes Export Ltd.; Cadbury Schweppes Finance Ltd.; Cadbury Schweppes Overseas Ltd.; Cadbury Ireland Ltd.; Cadbury Schweppes GmbH (West Germany); Sodastream Deutschland G.M.B.H. (West Germany); Sodastream Ltd.; Schweppes AG (Austria); Schweppes France S.A.; Cadbury Schweppes de Espana SA (Spain); Schweppes S.A. (Spain) (66%); Cadbury Schweppes Holdings Inc. (U.S.A.); Canada Dry Limited (Canada); Canada Dry Corporation Holdings Inc. (U.S.A.); Sunkist Soft Drinks Inc. (U.S.A.); Cadbury Schweppes (Canada) Inc.; Cadbury Schweppes Australia Ltd. (70%); Cadbury Schweppes (Pty) Ltd. (Australia) (70%); Cottee's General Foods Ltd. (Australia) (70%); Cadbury Schweppes Hudson Ltd. (New Zealand) (70%); Allied Foods Ltd. (Ghana); Cadbury Schweppes Holdings Ltd. (Kenya); Cadbury Schweppes Kenya Ltd.; Cadbury Schweppes (Zambia) Ltd.; Schweppes (Central Africa) Ltd. (Zimbabwe) (69%); Cadbury Schweppes holdings (Pty) Ltd. (South Africa); Cadbury Schweppes (South Africa) Ltd. (53%); Cadbury Confectionery Malaysia S.B.

Further Reading: Williams, Iolo A. *The Firm of Cadbury 1831–1931*, Constable and Co., London, 1931.

Campbell Soup Company

CAMPBELL SOUP COMPANY

Campbell Place
Camden, New Jersey 08103-1799
U.S.A.
(609) 342-4800

Public Company
Incorporated: 1922
Employees: 55,400
Sales: $5.67 billion
Stock Index: New York Philadelphia London Swiss

While Campbell Soup Company is clearly the number-one maker of soups, it is also a leading manufacturer of foods ranging from frozen dinners and entrees to baked goods, fruit juices, pickles, spaghetti sauces, and ready-to-eat salads.

The Campbell Soup Company can be traced back to 1860, when Abraham Anderson opened a small canning factory in Camden, New Jersey. In 1869, Philadelphia produce merchant Joseph Campbell became Anderson's partner, forming Anderson and Campbell. The company canned vegetables, mince meat, jams and jellies, and a variety of soups. In 1876 Anderson and Campbell dissolved their partnership and Campbell bought Anderson's share of the business, changing its name to Joseph Campbell Preserve Company. In 1882 a partnership was formed between Campbell's son-in-law, Walter S. Spackman; Campbell's nephew, Joseph S. Campbell; and Arthur Dorrance, Spackman's personal friend who brought a cash infusion to the partnership. At this time the company was renamed Joseph Campbell Preserving Company. The senior Campbell maintained daily involvement in the company until his death in 1900.

In 1896 the company built a large factory in Camden and expanded its product line to include prepared meats, sauces, canned fruits, ketchup, and plum pudding. The next year Arthur Dorrance hired his nephew, John Thompson Dorrance, a chemical engineer and organic chemist. By 1899 John Dorrance had successfully developed a method of canning condensed soup. This innovation helped Campbell outstrip its two soup-canning competitors. While others were still shipping heavy, uncondensed soup, Campbell was able to ship and sell its product at one-third the cost. As the company began increasing the variety of soups it offered, it began canning less produce. John Dorrance became director of the company in 1900, and sometime not long after the company became the Joseph Campbell Company.

Campbell's soup began finding its way into American kitchens at a time when the prepared-food industry was growing rapidly yet still small. By 1904 the company was selling 16 million cans of soup a year. With 21 varieties of soup by 1905, Campbell began to eye a bigger market, and in 1911 Campbell entered the California market, thus becoming one of the first companies to serve the entire nation.

In 1910 Dorrance was made general manager of the company, and in 1914 he became president. Dorrance immediately discontinued the marginal line of ketchups, preserves, and jams to focus on soup. In 1915, Dorrance became sole owner of Campbell when he bought out his uncle, Arthur Dorrance.

In 1912 Campbell began growing its own produce in an effort to standardize quality. This program was the first of an ongoing series of efforts Campbell has made to grow what it processes. At that time, during the eight summer weeks in which tomatoes were harvested, the Campbell plant devoted its entire effort to the production of tomato soup and tomato juice. During World War I almost half of Campbell's sales were of these two products.

In 1921 Campbell acquired the Franco-American Food Company, and the next year the company was renamed the Campbell Soup Company. In 1923 Arthur C. Dorrance, John Dorrance's brother, became Campbell's general manager. In 1929, Arthur C. Dorrance was made a director and vice president of the board of directors. When John Dorrance died in 1930, Arthur C. Dorrance was elected president.

Throughout this period Campbell continued to grow. In 1929 it opened its second major facility, in Chicago, and in 1930, its first international subsidiary, Campbell Soup Company Ltd., was formed in Canada. This was followed in 1933 by the British subsidiary Campbell's Soups Ltd. In 1936 Campbell began making its own cans and in 1939 its agricultural research department was formed. In 1942 sales topped $100 million for the first time. In 1946 Arthur C. Dorrance died and James McGowen Jr. became president. The following year Campbell began growing its own mushrooms in Prince Crossing, Illinois.

Despite this growth, Campbell was slow to diversify. In 1948 the company acquired V-8 juice, but its first major purchase was not made until 1955, when it bought the Omaha, Nebraska–based C.A. Swanson & Sons, the maker of TV Dinners, the first frozen dinners.

In the midst of this growth, W. B. Murphy was elected president, following McGowan's retirement in 1953. In 1954 Campbell took its stock public, and, in 1957, the company formed an international division to oversee its foreign concerns. In 1958 sales exceeded $500 million for the first time and Campbell established Campbell's Soups, S.p.A. in Italy. This venture was followed, in 1959, by the opening of subsidiaries in Mexico and Australia.

Through the 1960s Campbell was conservatively managed and quite successful. In that decade 11 new plants were opened on three continents, as were two new mushroom-growing facilities. The company's continued growth in this decade underwent a slight shift in emphasis. In the 1960s Campbell's growth began to include regular acquisitions in addition to internal expansion.

In 1961 Campbell acquired Pepperidge Farm, a maker of quality baked goods, and a similar Belgian company, Biscuits Delacre. In 1965 Campbell created a food-service division, and, in 1966, began marketing EfficienC, its own brand of food-service products through that division. Also in 1966, Campbell formed Godiva Chocolatier to distribute the Belgian-made chocolates in the United States; in 1974 the company completed a purchase of the European Godiva company and became its sole owner. Finally, in 1969, Campbell created Champion Valley Farms, a pet food concern.

During the 1970s the company's slow but steady growth continued. Campbell, which had built its fortune on Dorrance's invention of condensed soup, introduced the first in a new line of Chunky ready-to-serve soups, a highly successful enterprise. In 1971 sales for the first time topped $1 billion. In 1972 Murphy retired and was replaced by President Harold A. Shaub. Also in that year Swanson introduced Hungry Man meals, a very successful line of frozen dinners that consisted of nothing more sophisticated than larger portions. In 1973 Campbell acquired Pietro's Pizza Parlors, a chain of restaurants in the Pacific Northwest. This led, in 1974, to the formation of a restaurant division, heralding Campbell's intention to add more restaurants to its growing list of subsidiaries.

In 1978 Campbell made one of its largest acquisitions ever when it purchased Vlasic Foods, a Michigan-based producer of pickles and similar condiments, for about $35 million in capital stock. This acquisition gave Campbell the lead over archrival H.J. Heinz in the pickle-packing business. The Vlasic acquisition was followed in 1979 by the acquisitions of seven small European food-producing companies and three small domestic operations. That same year sales topped $2 billion for the first time. In 1978 Campbell made a brief and unsuccessful foray into the Brazilian soup market.

The diversification movement started by Shaub in the early 1970s has prepared the company for long-term growth. Campbell's debt is very low and the company's new products and acquisitions have provided it with popular brand names in a variety of food-industry sectors. The key to growth in this mature market is diversification, and Campbell is doing just that. Shaub was responsible for changing a long-standing policy on new-product development that required a profit within the first year. Shaub's most notable innovation, however, was his decentralization of marketing for major product lines.

To sustain these growth-oriented policies, Campbell broke with its life-long tradition of relying on internally generated funds to finance its efforts and, for the first time, entered the debt market in June, 1980 with a $100 million, ten-year offering. As a cautious food producer, Campbell's earnings have always been healthy, if uninspiring. Shaub hoped to increase sales and profit margins. A key reason for Shaub's determination to allow Campbell to diversify was the recognition that the market for many of these products had matured and growth had slowed.

In 1980 R. Gorden McGovern succeeded Shaub as president and Campbell made two acquisitions: Swift-Armour S.A. Argentina and a small American poultry-processing plant used by Swanson for its frozen chicken dinners. Campbell's efforts in Argentina have not been entirely fruitful, though much of the difficulty is related to currency-transaction adjustments. Also in 1980, Campbell acquired additional bakery, pasta, and pickle operations.

In 1981 McGovern reorganized management structure, dividing the company into two new divisions—Campbell U.S.A. and Campbell International—and about 50 business groups. This new structure was meant to foster entrepreneurship and heighten management's sensitivity to consumer opinion, long a weakness at Campbell. It also acquired Snow King Frozen Foods, a large producer of uncooked frozen specialty meats, and introduced the wildly successful Prego spaghetti sauce nationally in 1981. In 1982 Campbell acquired Mrs. Paul's Kitchens, a processor of frozen prepared seafood and vegetables. Several of its subsidiaries also made major purchases. Vlasic Foods acquired Win Schuler Foods, a specialty-foods producer, and Pepperidge Farm completed the purchase of an apple juice processor, Costa Apple Products, with markets primarily on the East Coast. Also in 1982, Juice Bowl Products, a fruit juice processor, was acquired.

A variety of other acquisitions in the early 1980s added Annabelle's, a restaurant chain; Triangle, a manufacturer of physical-fitness and sports-medicine products; a fresh-produce distributor; a Puerto Rican canning company; and an Italian manufacturer of premium biscuits.

McGovern further increased emphasis on marketing and new-product development in an effort to shift the company away from its production-oriented focus. McGovern also introduced Total Systems, a worker-oriented system designed to increase quality and efficiency. Total Systems is similar to the successful worker management strategies employed by many Japanese companies.

One of McGovern's primary concerns was turning Campbell into a "market-sensitive food company." After McGovern publicly referred to some of the company's Swanson TV Dinner line as "junk food" in 1982, Campbell initiated Project Fix in an effort to upgrade food quality and improve packaging of its older products. One of the most important facets of McGovern's makeover was his goal of positioning the company with consumers as "somebody who is looking after their well-being," McGovern told *Business Week* in 1983. The 1983 Triangle Manufacturing purchase and 1982 formation of a health-and-fitness unit were both designed to meet that goal. Campbell's involvement in frozen fish, juices, and produce were also part of the new market sensitivity urged by McGovern.

In addition, Campbell has attempted to market products regionally and according to age group. The central marketing department was broken into 20 regions in an effort to allow tailoring of advertising and marketing to fit each region's peculiar demographics. For instance, its nacho cheese soup is spicier in Texas than elsewhere. The company has even begun aiming advertising of its national brands at regional audiences, with spots featuring local celebrities and locally arranged promotions. The company that, in the 1950s, reached half the nation's homes just by sponsoring "Lassie" on TV spent 15% of its advertising budget in regional efforts in 1983. And that figure could eventually reach 50%.

McGovern increased Campbell's sales and earnings significantly in his first few years. His encouragement of new-product development and line extensions—in areas like frozen entrees to compete with Stouffer's, dried soups to challenge Lipton, and name-brand produce such as Farm Fresh mushrooms and tomatoes, complemented by exotic varieties of mushrooms, refrigerated salads and pasta sauces, and juices—was, however, a bit too heated. The company introduced 334 new products in the first half of the 1980s and has made more than a few costly mistakes, like the 1984 failure of Pepperidge Farm's *Star Wars* cookies, which did not fit the brand's high-quality image. Spurred on by successes like Le Menu frozen dinners, McGovern overemphasized marketing and new-product development. In 1985 the company decided to cut back on new-product gambles and McGovern reevaluated his goals and returned the company's focus to product quality and efficiency.

Throughout this period, in which it became increasingly clear that McGovern's plan was destined to fail, acquisitions and group formations continued, but at a pace reminiscent of the old Campbell. A Belgian food producer and 20% of Arnotts Ltd., an Australian biscuit manufacturer, were purchased in 1985. In 1986 the company bought two more American food companies and established Campbell Enterprises to oversee non-grocery products. Meanwhile new products were gradually but steadily introduced.

In 1984 John T. Dorrance Jr., the son of the inventor of condensed soup, retired as chairman of the board and became director of the board's executive committee. He was succeeded by William S. Cashel Jr. Dorrance and other members of his family, however, still controlled 58% of Campbell's stock and showed no interest in selling, keeping the company safe from takeover.

By 1987 Campbell decided that it was better to be safe than sorry. McGovern began selling off some of the company's less-successful ventures. In 1987 the company sold its disappointing pet food, Triangle physical fitness, and Juice Works beverage businesses, and in 1988 the Pietro's pizza and Annabelle's restaurants were also sold, taking Campbell out of the restaurant business entirely.

However, the company also bought several smaller companies in 1987 and 1988 that were more compatible with its traditional lines of business, including a French cookie maker, the Open Pit barbecue sauce line, an American olive producer, and Campbell's largest acquisition to date, Freshbake Foods Group PLC, a British producer of frozen foods. Also in 1988, Robert J. Vlasic, whose Vlasic Foods Campbell had purchased in 1978, became chairman of Campbell.

McGovern left Campbell in late 1989. His final attempt to recoup Campbell's losses, a $343 million restructuring program, earned him little praise. Although sales had doubled during his term, profits had dropped 90% as a result of his aggressive capital commitments. In January, 1990 David W. Johnson was elected president and CEO. Johnson came to Campbell from Gerber Products Company, where he had been successful in streamlining that company's operations. Campbell's directors hope that Johnson's aggressive style will also be effective in improving profitability at their own company.

Although Campbell, with a virtual lock on the soup market (an estimated 80% share) and consistent sales growth, is very well positioned for long-term growth its future is uncertain. Its management crisis was exacerbated by the death, in April, 1989, of John Dorrance. Dorrance's 31% of the company's stock was split between his three children, who have demonstrated an interest in preserving family control of the company. The remaining 27% of the family-owned stock is split among other members of the clan, some of whom (representing about 17.4% of the company's stock) have expressed a desire to sell Campbell. But Chairman Vlasic had loaded the board with family members loyal to the company (six of the 15 board members are family members, including John Dorrance's three children), so a proxy battle seems unlikely. The future of Campbell now appears to rest on CEO Johnson's ability to provide strong leadership and the continued loyalty of the Dorrance heirs.

Principal Subsidiaries: CSC Advertising, Inc.; Campbell Finance Corp.; Campbell Investment Co.; Campbell Sales Co.; Campbell Soup (Texas) Inc.; Casera Foods, Inc.; Domsea Farms, Inc.; Godiva Chocolatier, Inc.; Herider Farms, Inc.; Joseph Campbell Co.; Juice Bowl Products, Inc.; Martino's Bakery, Inc.; Mrs. Paul's Kitchens, Inc.; Pepperidge Farm, Inc.; Pepperidge Farm Mail Order Company, Inc.; Vlasic Foods, Inc.; Swift-Armour Sociedad Anonima Argentina; Campbell's Soups (Aust.) Pty. Ltd. (Australia); N.V. Biscuits Delacre S.A. (Belgium); Campbell Europe Food and Confectionery, S.A. (Belgium); Campbell Soup Company Ltd. (Canada); Campbell Foods P.L.C. (England); Societe Francaise des Biscuits Delacre S.A. (France); Eugen Lacroix GmbH (West Germany); Campbell Soup Far East Limited (Hong Kong); D. Lazzaroni & C. S.p.A. (Italy); Campbell Japan Inc.; Campbell's de Mexico, S.A. de C.V.; Camilar, S.A. de C.V. (Mexico); Sinalopasta, S.A. de C.V. (Mexico); European Biscuit Holding (EBN) B.V. (The Netherlands); Campbell Soup Overseas Finance N.V. (Netherlands Antilles); Compania Envasadora Loreto, S.A. (Spain); ECF Espana, S.A. (Spain); Beeck-Feinkost GmbH (West Germany).

Further Reading: Sim, Mary B. *History of Commercial Canning in New Jersey*, Trenton, New Jersey, New Jersey Agricultural Society, 1951; *A History*, Camden, New Jersey, Campbell Soup Company, 1988.

Canada Packers Inc.

CANADA PACKERS INC.

30 St. Clair Avenue West
Toronto, Ontario M4V 3A2
Canada
(416) 766–4311

Public Company
Incorporated: 1927 as Canada Packers Ltd.
Employees: 12,000
Sales: C$3.2 billion (US$2.68 billion)
Stock Index: Toronto Montreal

Canada Packers was formed in 1927 during a period of consolidation among Canadian meat packers. The decade was a hard one for Canadian meat packers, who were increasingly reliant on exports for expansion. Before the 20th century miners and settlers had provided an expanding market, but the domestic market leveled off with the century's beginning. While worldwide demand soared, so did production, creating a volatile industry susceptible to both agricultural and manufacturing cycles.

Meat production had increased to meet wartime demand, but, in the aftermath of World War I, Canada was cut off from much of the European market by 1920, and the United States imposed a tariff on Canadian beef in 1921. By the mid-1920s Canada faced new competition for the vast American market from Argentina and Australia. Tariffs and cheaper competition have made reliance on the U.S. market impossible for Canadian agricultural producers ever since.

The Canadian domestic market could not absorb the surplus created by these pitfalls, and the number of meat processing-plants dropped from 86 to 76 between 1912 and 1927. For nearly the same period, the number of food producers also decreased, yet employment and value added by the manufacturer grew.

In 1927 the Harris Abattoir Company of Toronto acquired three smaller meat packers. Unlike its competitors, Harris had remained profitable during the 1920s through substantial cuts in personnel. With distribution branches throughout Canada, Harris's earnings easily overshadowed those of the companies it purchased. Gunns Ltd., a Toronto packer, transferred its stock to Harris in February when it found itself unable to attain credit. In June, Harris purchased the much smaller Canadian Packing Company Ltd., and in August Harris merged with William Davies Ltd., Canada's oldest meat packer. The new holding company was named Canada Packers Limited and in its first year it made a profit of more than $1 million.

The four companies remained separate operating units and continued to compete with each other, but by 1929 the Harris Abattoir offices in Toronto had become the central headquarters. The companies could not have survive the postcrash Depression separately. Meat prices were high relative to other commodities following the market collapse, and drought in the western provinces produced higher unemployment and lower consumer demand for meat. Already merging slowly, heavy losses in 1931 forced the closure of the William Davies Toronto plant and the formation of a single company at the beginning of 1932.

By 1933 operating expenses had been drastically cut. Only five of nine plants remained, the work force had been cut by 40%, and total expenses had been reduced by $7 million annually.

During the mid-1930s the company revived. The Ottawa Agreements allowed 280 million pounds of bacon a year to be exported to England, giving Canadian companies entry into a market previously filled by European companies. The agreement increased production at all plants at a crucial point in Canada Packers' development.

Simultaneously, the company's by-product division, which had been selling scraps for fertilizer, began to sell a mixture of scraps as a feed concentrate for animal food, a new venture that proved extremely profitable. Thirty years later the fertilizer business would be sold entirely, but animal feed remains an active and relatively reliable division for the company under the name of Shur-Gain.

In 1936 the company began its first expansion since its formation. It built a meat-processing plant in Alberta and acquired a tannery in Ontario. During the period between world wars this growth continued as British bacon and American beef imports reduced livestock surpluses. In 1938 Canada Packers opened an additional packing house; renovations of other plants brought capital investment between 1935 and 1938 to more than $2.5 million.

During World War II Canada continued to be a major supplier of meat to England—the amount of bacon shipped overseas more than doubled during the course of the war. Demand increases brought about the first labor shortage in Canada's meatpacking history. Canada Packers' work force more than doubled to over 11,000.

Increased postwar demand allowed continual expansion, but improvements in infrastructure and employment for returning soldiers were needed. In response to an anticipated recession, the company stepped up its diversification efforts. The company's work force was nearly as large then as it is now, but overall production constantly expanded in the succeeding decades.

The emphasis on war-time efficiency required the establishment of a research laboratory, leading Canada Packers into synthetic vitamins, gelatin, synthetic detergents, and dairy products by the end of the war. By 1946 the chemical applications of animal by-products being investigated by the research lab would warrant the status of a separate division.

Another war-time development was the creation of union representation. During 1943 and 1944 Canada

Packers agreed to representation by the United Packinghouse Workers of America, later the Canadian Food and Allied Workers Union. It did not take long for this bargaining unit to have a periodic impact on earnings. In 1947 a nationwide strike involving more than 16,000 meatpacking workers occurred. No longer a wartime necessity, food production was once again controlled by the manufacturers. Canada Packers and a competitor negotiated new contracts two months later.

From World War II on, Canada Packers' sales have been greater than its two closest competitors' combined. The anticipated recession never hit the company as population growth and prosperity increased demand for meat and all other food products. The research lab, which had so far worked only on chemical development, began to look for improved production methods. Automated killing operations finally replaced the outdated manual process, and the company kept pace with the industry by applying new technology to the mass production of poultry.

During the decades following the war Canada Packers made its first significant transition to meet new demand. In the 1950s the per capita consumption of poultry doubled and it continued to increase during each following decade. Through timely acquisition, investment, and the development of a new feather-cleaning company, the company began to increase its presence in the poultry industry. The company also entered oil production through acquisition in 1951.

Canada Packers' postwar expansion was rapid and prominent. The 1955 purchase of two packers brought the company into a dispute with the Restrictive Trade Practices Commission. Canada Packers argued successfully that industrywide competition had increased and that the purchase would have no restraining effect.

Late in the 1950s the company reorganized its many businesses into separate divisions, including feed and fertilizer, consumer products, and canned and frozen vegetables. J. S. McLean, president since the company's formation and the man responsible for the company's postwar diversification, retired in 1954, and his son William succeeded him. By 1958 only 55% of sales were from meat.

Canada Packers kept capital investment steady through the 1960s to continue expansion and diversification. To meet perennially increasing poultry demand, the company built two plants, in New Brunswick and Quebec, expanded operations in Ontario and Manitoba, and acquired an Alberta plant. In 1963 only 36% of its assets were devoted to livestock products.

Although sales had increased more than 50% since 1951, the 1960s brought about the most dramatic changes for the food-processing industry to date. As international distribution became more common, production became more specialized. During this period North American beef came to spend more time in transit than any other meat, reflecting the specialized processses of raising cattle and producing meat. As Canada's largest processor, Canada Packers had much to contribute to this changing environment.

During the decade the company created the largest private food-research facility in Canada. Inventories as well as product composition were determined through data processing centers in Toronto, Montreal, Winnipeg, and Edmonton, and new meatpacking technology in areas like packaging and flavoring were implemented in a $10 million Toronto facility.

In addition to these technological advances, Canada Packers expanded internationally during the decade. The company purchased meatpackers in England, West Germany, and Australia and set up trading companies in London and Hamburg. Trading operations with the United States also grew, as did its interest in Southeast Asia. By 1969 exports exceeded $145 million, nearly 16.5% of company sales.

With the sale of the fertilizer sector, feed and fertilizer became the Shur-Gain division and investment in feed mills intensified. In 1966 the United Packinghouse Workers of America led its first strike since 1947. Although the strike was national, it hit Canada Packers hardest. Another strike in 1969 also affected earnings.

Despite inflationary stress and an increasingly competitive climate in the meatpacking industry, the company continued to increase capital spending. Between 1970 and 1977 Canada Packers spent $137 million on expanded facilities. It also increased its overseas presence by purchasing two more Australian meat processors. Even though these subsidiaries did poorly for several years, they were expected to fill the growing Asian demand.

During the 1970s Canada Packers became a more diversified food processor and separated the management of its other food-production groups from meatpacking. The company granted division status to its fruit and vegetable segment in 1970 (York Farms brand), poultry in 1971, and edible oils and dairy in 1975.

The chemical division, created in the late 1960s, became more significant with the establishment of Harris Laboratories, which develops pharmaceuticals for human use, in 1975. The division also created MTC Pharmaceuticals for the veterinary-product industry in response to continual growth in demand for drugs related to foodlot production.

Overseas packers and lean margins continued to plague the company, but its diversification kept earnings at acceptable levels. Nonfood sales contributed 15% of the total; it was the only sector to show significant increases in the early 1970s. Animal feeds did grow steadily, helping to ease the earnings drain caused by meat.

Valentine N. Stock became president of Canada Packers in 1978. As the company entered the 1980s, earnings margins were still lower than expected, less than 1% for the third consecutive year. Sales value had increased, but sales volume remained the same. The increases in product value had benefits, but also added to higher-cost inventories. With relatively low long-term debt, at $34.7 million, the company planned to grow through acquisitions and to earn higher margins through packaged meats. Since consumers continued to demand convenience, meat processing was the only growth area in the company's core business. Stock also planned to increase non-food and international operations, despite disappointing results overseas.

1979 was a bad year for Canadian food processors due

to increased costs for meat and a seven-week labor dispute that closed some facilities. Canada Packers' competitor, McCain Feeds Ltd., of New Brunswick, increased its holding in Canada Packers to 10.3%, fueling takeover rumors. As a precaution, Canada Packers repurchased 3.5% of its shares, but takeover remained unlikely since the McLean family and their associates controlled 34% of the company's shares.

As expected, the company looked to international markets by acquiring Delmar Chemicals Ltd., a supplier to the pharmaceutical industry, for C$18.2 million. Delmar was coupled with the company's existing pharmaceutical division to increase nonfood exports.

The company remained close to its food core and Maple Leaf brand of meats nonetheless, and accepted a $4 million grant from the Ontario government to construct a canola (rapeseed oil) processing plant.

By 1981 profits had soared 50% over their 1979 level, up to a record $30 million. But the cyclical nature of the industry still affected the company as pork operations proved disappointing, carcass prices rose, and a reduction in consumer demand and greater competition among packers continued to erode earnings. Occasional plant closings continued to be the industry norm.

In 1983 the Canadian government began investigations of price fixing involving Canada Packers and four other meat packers. Some of the charges were dropped in 1984, and although the other four companies would eventually plead guilty, Canada Packers was completely exonerated and partially reimbursed for legal expenses in 1986.

Profits plunged to their 1979 level in 1983, even though sales continued to grow. Earnings were affected by the cost of plant closings and poor performances in fresh-meat operations, and foreign subsidiaries proved disappointing. The packing house division, in fact, suffered the worst loss in its history, but processed meat remained profitable. As a result, the company earmarked $50 million for structural improvements in these profitable areas and cut hundreds of jobs in fresh meat. Although its outlook was better, previous profit levels looked unreachable.

Another strike in 1984 involving 3,700 strikers at most of the company's 12 plants eventually cost the company $7.5 million. Although it lasted only five weeks, the strike kept the company's Maple Leaf brand from store shelves and strengthened competitors. As the country's largest meat packer, the strike of the United Food Commercial Worker's Union (UFCW) demonstrated the company's vulnerability to labor disputes. The strike caused a slight earnings decline for 1985.

Nonfood products showed a surprising decrease in profits for 1983, proving that the company could not venture far from its traditional core business—one with fiercely competitive margins but with proven cash flow. Although making up less than half of Canada Packers' profit, meat products still account for two-third of its sales.

Despite setbacks, however, the mid-1980s were prosperous for the company. Increased cash flow allowed a four-year, $200 million revitalization spending plan. Poultry production was enlarged, reflecting the division's profitability and continued long-term potential.

A reorganization, begun in 1984 and completed by 1985, was the largest and most expensive in the company's history. Unprofitable businesses, including an ice cream plant and five slaughterhouses, were sold, and other meat plants and oil refineries were purchased and upgraded. Earnings for the next four years climbed at record rates from $25 million to more than $38 million.

Canada Packers then entered a joint venture with Sea Farm of Norway and began fish farming in New Brunswick. A long-term investment, the company now has production facilities on both coasts of Canada and sees fish farming as its most promising growth industry.

Canada Packers circumvented another strike by reducing the scope of nationwide bargaining in 1986, a record year for earnings. By keeping negotiations on a provincial and single-plant level, the company quickly settled with the UFCW. As the meatpacker with the most employees, Canada Packers' labor relations have a strong influence on the industry as a whole, making national strikes in the future less likely.

At the beginning of 1987 Valentine Stock died and James Hunter was appointed acting CEO. A. Roger Perretti, former vice president of finance, became CEO at the beginning of 1989. During Stock's tenure the company had seen a continued decline in beef demand and completed a ten-year consolidation. The company consistently reduced dependence on fresh meat and turned to areas with higher and more reliable margins, like fish farming, processed foods, salad oils, and pharmaceuticals. After Hunter came to power, the company planned further acquisitions outside the meat industry.

As the company entered the 1990s, earnings dropped to $25.2 million, the same level they were ten years earlier. There were several reasons for the decline, demonstrating the uncertainty of agricultural earnings. Strikes at two Ontario plants in 1987 affected profits and poultry inventories industrywide were excessive, surprisingly, since the year before demand had outstripped supply. Processed meats showed a slight increase from the previous year's decline, but the company took losses in its processed foods sector due to lower margins. Since this was perceived as a long-term growth area, the company also absorbed heavier start-up costs for some of these products. Nonfood profits fell dramatically due to an agricultural subsidy dispute between the United States and the European Economic Community, eliminating large export markets for oil. A North American drought also lowered amounts of available feed.

Once again, the company responded by reorganizing and consolidating its consumer foods division by closing plants and updating existing equipment. The advent of free trade with the United States renewed the company's interest in its southern market. Its British, German, and Japanese subsidiaries also showed promise for long-term gains.

Canada Packers' investment in long-term earnings potential has been its most dramatic change, since the meatpacking industry is historically vulnerable to short-term declines. Despite cyclical earnings, capital investment has continued to exceed $50 million annually through the 1980s. Company officials anticipate the most growth from international markets and the time-intensive process of salmon raising. Poultry will remain an area of emphasis, as consumer consumption patterns continue, as they have for the last forty years, move further away from red meat.

Canada Packers still suffers from lean margins. Reliant on its domestic market for cash flow, the company enjoys a market share of slightly less than half of all Canadian meatpacking—an industry that totaled $8 billion in 1986. In addition, the company has reported a profit for every one of its more than 60 years—a significant achievement given the rocky years at its beginning. Meatpacking remains an industry where profits come from cash flow and turnover rather than long-term holdings or growth. Although Canada Packers has always sought related industries to change this situation, subsidy and tariff disputes make expansion through export unreliable and unlikely.

Canada Packers' first president said in 1963 that the company's "narrow margin on sales is sufficient because base turnover is so rapid. On fresh meat we turn over our money approximately 14 times within a year." This remains true today, and although a diversified Canada Packers expects long-term declines in meat and growth in other areas, the company still relies on its domestic food operations. World wars facilitated the export of food products for the first half of this century and industry consolidation made mass production more profitable. It was these formative years, when the industry changed rapidly and frequently, that gave birth to Canada Packers, but the company succeeded during the second half of the century by continuing to develop new technological applications and by entering new food markets. Long-term investments in more stable food areas promise a steadier path in the future.

Principal Subsidiaries: Federal Cold Storage and Warehousing Company Limited; Hoffman Meats Inc.; Ontario Rendering Company Limited; René Poirier Ltée; P.E.I. Produce Company Limited; Couvoir Désy Ltée; Bazinet & Fils Inc.; Archibald Farms Limited; Canada Packers (USA) Inc.; Canada Packers (UK) Limited; Canada Packers GmbH (West Germany); Canada Packers (Japan) Inc. (more than 50%); Haverhill Meat Products Limited (United Kingdom); Palethorpes Limited (United Kingdom); Sea Farm Canada; Sea Farm Marketing Inc.; Prairie Margarine Inc.

CARNATION COMPANY

5045 Wilshire Boulevard
Los Angeles, California 90036
U.S.A.
(213) 932–6000

Wholly owned subsidiary of Nestlé S.A.
Incorporated: 1916 as Carnation Milk Products Company
Sales: $2.65 billion

The 1984 Nestlé takeover of Carnation was at the time the largest acquisition outside the oil industry. The $3 billion deal allowed Carnation to renew its focus on consumer foods and pet foods and reduced its traditional reliance on its dairy division's cash flow. Carnation once had a reputation for conservative yet effective marketing, capturing small markets before advancing to larger. Today it markets more aggressively, acting like an independent company while sharing risk with its Swiss-based parent. As a unit of Nestlé's U.S. holding company, Carnation focuses on domestic sales.

Elbridge Amos Stuart knew almost nothing about the evaporated-milk business when Thomas E. Yerxa persuaded him to join in the purchase of a bankrupt condensery in Kent, Washington in 1899. Having grown up on a farm in Indiana, however, Stuart was acquainted with dairying, and as the former proprietor of a general store in El Paso, Texas and later a wholesale grocery in Los Angeles, he recognized the value of sanitary milk at a time when fresh milk was neither universally available nor always potable. Although both of his prior ventures in food sales failed, Stuart had developed a knack for marketing and publicity, which proved to be an important factor in the success of the Pacific Coast Condensed Milk Company, as he and Yerxa called their partnership.

They put John B. Meyenberg, the Swiss inventor of evaporated milk, in charge of the condensery, and paid him $25,000 for his patented technology. (Evaporated milk is made by heating fresh milk quickly to kill harmful bacteria and then sealing it in an airtight can. Distinct from condensed milk, which Gail Borden developed in 1856, evaporated milk contains no sugar preservatives and more closely resembles fresh milk.) Before signing on with Yerxa and Stuart, Meyenberg had helped establish the Helvetia Milk Company in St. Louis, Missouri—the maker of the evaporated milk Stuart had stock in his El Paso store. Meyenberg's former employer, later renamed Pet Milk Company, soon faced growing competition from Pacific Coast Condensed Milk.

Stuart chose the name Carnation after a brand of cigars by that name. Despite the memorable name and a bright red-and-white label, consumers were slow to buy Carnation evaporated milk at first, and the company lost $140,000 in its first year, prompting Yerxa to sell his interest to Stuart. After this inauspicious beginning, the company seldom lost money again. Soon it found a sizable market among Alaskan gold prospectors who valued evaporated milk because it was nonperishable and easily transported. As business picked up, a sales office was established in Seattle, another plant was opened in Forest Grove, Oregon, and state-of-the-art canning and homogenizing equipment was installed.

While early newspaper advertisements emphasized that Carnation milk was safe for babies, a product formulated especially for this use called Sanipure was abandoned after a disappointing reception in the marketplace. Stuart expanded distribution cautiously at first, and insisted on capturing a 65% share of existing markets before penetrating new ones. But competition in much of the West was thin, so Pacific Coast Condensed Milk extended its territory systematically. By 1911, condenseries in Wisconsin were supplying the Midwest and East with "milk from contended cows," as the famous slogan introduced in 1907 said. The company had already rejected two purchase offers, including one for $1 million from its much larger competitor, Borden.

In 1909 and 1910, Stuart established Carnation Stock Farms on 750 acres of lush land in Washington's Snoqualmie Valley. He made the farms into a company showpiece by spending lavishly, buying prized Holstein-Friesian cattle and hiring animal husbandry experts. The investment paid off as Carnation cows set numerous records for milk and butterfat production and won the acclaim Stuart sought. In 1915 a second farm was purchased near Oconomowoc, Wisconsin where, a year earlier, the company had located its eastern division offices. The farms did not significantly reduce Carnation's reliance on independent dairymen, but they did contribute to a smooth rapport with suppliers, whose cows were crossbred with Carnation's, thus greatly improving the productivity of their stock.

Relations with the dairy industry were sometimes less friendly. In 1916 the company introduced a lower-cost alternative to condensed milk in which coconut oil was substituted for butterfat. The new product, called Hebe after the Greek goddess of youth, was seen as a threat by dairymen, who lobbied successfully to have it banned in Ohio. Carnation fought the prohibition to the Supreme Court but lost when the Court found that Hebe had been misleadingly sold as pure milk. Subsequently, in 1923, the government passed the Federal Filled Milk Act, which outlawed the shipment of adulterated milk across state lines.

Sales of Carnation evaporated milk were surprisingly brisk in the Midwest and the East, where older companies such as Borden and Pet dominated the market. Reflecting this expansion, the company reincorporated in Maine in 1916 and changed its name to the more geographically neutral Carnation Milk Products Company. To keep pace with its burgeoning eastern business, it opened an office in Chicago, built a can factory in Oconomowoc, and acquired several condenseries, including two in Canada. By 1919 it operated 20 facilities that produced approximately 530 million pounds of evaporated milk annually, up from 16 million pounds in 1915.

Carnation and other American milk companies helped alleviate severe shortages in Europe during World War I by contracting to supply European firms such as Nestlé. But when the war ended, Carnation found itself wallowing in surpluses. Therefore, Carnation took advantage of a loophole in the antitrust laws and opened an overseas affiliate with Pet Milk Company. Branches of American Milk Products Corporation, as the joint venture was called, were opened in Paris and Essen, Germany. When the French imposed prohibitively high tariffs on imported milk in 1923, the partnership converted an old creamery in Carentan, France into an evaporation plant, and thus avoided the new tariffs. Later a condensery was built in Germany to circumvent similar import barriers there. Despite the fact that Pet and Carnation competed domestically, American Milk Products Corporation was an enduring success; in the 1930s and the 1940s it added condensing and canning facilities in the Netherlands, Scotland, South Africa, Peru, and Mexico. The partnership thrived until 1966, when Carnation bought Pet's share for $42 million.

At home, Carnation diversified into related businesses through acquisitions. It brought the Malt-A-Milk Company in Kansas City in 1922, adding Cho-Cho malted milk to its product line. It entered the fresh-milk business in 1926 with the purchase of six dairies in Seattle, and over the next decade Carnation developed its dairy operations as methodically as it had its evaporated milk operations, again securing one market before advancing to another. It acquired dairies in Oregon, California, Texas, Oklahoma, and Iowa in this way.

Carnation's first step outside the dairy business came in 1929, when it bought Albers Brothers Milling Company in Seattle, a well-established manufacturer of cereals and a pioneer in soybean livestock feed. That same year, recognizing that it was no longer just a milk company, officers renamed the company simply Carnation Company.

When Elbridge A. Stuart retired in 1932, he was succeeded by his son, Elbridge Hadley Stuart, who had advanced through the organization since his college graduation. The younger Stuart took over a company on its way to losing more than $660,000—its worst year ever. But by extensive cost cutting he put Carnation into the black the next year, with earnings of more than $1 million. Remarkably, Carnation did not lay off any of its 4,000 employees during the Great Depression, although wages were sharply reduced.

E. H. Stuart shared his father's penchant for publicity. In 1931 Carnation began sponsoring "The Contented Hour" on NBC network. The program was broadcast nationally from 1932 until 1951, when Carnation began sponsoring the "Burns and Allen" television show. Carnation advertising also commanded the public's attention. In 1934, Carnation inaugurated a massive promotional campaign that featured the Dionne quintuplets. Carnation arranged to have the celebrated babies reared on its new vitamin D-enriched evaporated milk and at the same time worked closely with pediatricians to position its product as the formula ingredient for healthy infants.

While Carnation's public relations people were working to gain doctors' endorsements, nutrition specialists from Albers Milling were at Carnation stock farms testing a new livestock feed that increased an animal's consumption and thereby improved its productivity. The feed, known as Calf Manna, was introduced in the early 1930s specifically for dairy cows, but was found to benefit other stock animals as well. By 1936, it had become a staple on farms around the world. Albers research scored another success in 1934 with the introduction of Friskies, the first dry dog food. Marketed under Carnation's familiar strategy, Friskies was first sold in the West and then spread eastward city by city. Its sales got a boost during World War II when many competitors had to limit dog food production because of tin rationing.

Domestic demand for evaporated milk rose substantially during World War II, reaching a peak of 86.8 million cases in 1945. Although Carnation's sales advanced, price ceilings and government rationing held earnings steady. Nevertheless, Carnation enjoyed unparalleled prosperity immediately after the war. In 1946, profits topped $3.2 million, versus less than $2.5 million the year before. By the company's fiftieth anniversary in 1949 profits had climbed to a record $7.76 million—more than double what they were in the first postwar year. Also in 1949 Carnation opened new corporate offices on Wilshire Boulevard in Los Angeles. Before that, Carnation managers had been scattered across the country at the company's general offices in Seattle and Milwaukee; at the evaporated-milk division in Oconomowoc; at the fluid-milk and ice cream operations in Los Angeles; at Albers Milling, in Seattle; and at the vastly expanded overseas collaboration with Pet, now known as General Milk, in New York City.

This consolidation of the executive offices brought more cohesive management and more comprehensive planning. Carnation had long had a reputation for conservative marketing, but in the 1950s it became even more cautious. Before introducing a new product or pushing into a new region, the company invested heavily in market studies. Product development, an area in which Carnation's record had been mixed, became a specialty. In 1953 it opened a new research laboratory in Van Nuys, California and increased that facility's staff over the next two decades from seven to 170. Product development went hand in hand with market analysis; the company focused on new items that could be sold under the well-known Carnation brand name and distributed through existing networks. When Carnation did finally bring out a new product, it did so decisively and with a generous promotion budget. Sometimes several years elapsed before an investment began to pay off, but the returns—sales gains and enhanced consumer recognition—were substantial.

The move into powdered milk illustrates the advantages as well as the pitfalls of Carnation's approach. Consumption of evaporated milk fell dramatically in the United States after World War II. Meanwhile, demand for economical nonfat dry milk soared. Americans bought 2.4 million pounds of powdered milk in 1948 and 94 million pounds in 1953, despite the product's annoying tendency to cake, its thin flavor, and its inability to dissolve easily in water. Reluctant to sell a product with these disagreeable qualities and convinced that they could be eliminated, Carnation lagged behind the other major milk companies in introducing powdered milk, until its reservations became too costly. Finally, Carnation capitulated and began to make its own brand of the same product. It was about to begin distribution when it learned that David Peebles of the Western Condensing Company had patented a powdered milk that had none of the unpleasant characteristics of other brands. Carnation abandoned its plans and formed the Instant Milk Company with Western in 1954 to sell the superior formula under the Carnation name. Carnation spared no expense in advertising and eventually forced Peebles's underfinanced company to bow out of the partnership. Sales were strong from the outset, but because of the heavy start-up costs, the enterprise did not show profits until the 1960s.

Success with dry milk inspired Carnation researchers to develop more powdered foods. Instant cocoa was introduced in 1956, followed in 1961 by Coffeemate, today the leading non-dairy lightener. When a study commissioned by Carnation in the early 1960s revealed the increasing popularity of convenience foods, the company developed Instant Breakfast, a milk fortifier derived from the Peebles technology. A dietetic version called Slender came out in 1966, but had to be reformulated in 1969 when cyclamates were banned. By the mid-1960s, Carnation had converted numerous condenseries to the production of instant foods, which had replaced evaporated milk as the profit generators.

Another lucrative field in the late 1950s and the 1960s was pet foods, which grew with the explosive growth of the pet population in the United States. Again, product development was instrumental in Carnation's success. In 1956 it introduced Friskies cat food to complement its dog food of the same name. Canned versions of Friskies for both dogs and cats came out in 1959, followed by puppy food in 1962. Buffet was introduced in 1967 in response to a Carnation report suggesting that many consumers preferred single-serving, premium-quality cat food. A similar, very profitable product for dogs, Mighty Dog, reached the shelves in 1973.

E. H. Stuart became chairman of the board in 1957 and was replaced as president by A. M. Ghormley, who, like many other Carnation executives, had spent his entire professional life working for the company. Ghormley became vice chairman in 1963, but during his brief tenure was largely responsible for an impressive expansion of Carnation's product line. His successor as president in 1963 was H. Everett Olson, an accountant and another career Carnation man; in 1964 E. H. Stuart's son Dwight became vice president.

Under Olson, Carnation made a number of significant acquisitions. In 1963, it bought Contadina, the California-based processor of canned tomatoes. Trenton Foods, one of the country's biggest suppliers of canned meats and sauces to institutional customers, was purchased in 1966. In the 1970s Carnation acquired Pronto Pacific and the Western Farmers Association processing plant, expanding the line of dry and frozen potatoes it had launched in 1959 with Trio instant mix. Reliable Tool, bought in 1970, fit neatly with Carnation's substantial tin-can business, and the purchase of several firms engaged in genetic research and the artificial insemination of livestock was logical, given the company's experience in breeding.

In 1971 Olson became chairman when E. H. Stuart retired at the age of 83. Stuart died the next year, and in 1973 his son Dwight L. Stuart became president of Carnation. In a stab at diversification reminiscent of food companies a decade earlier, in 1973 Olson purchased Herff Jones, a manufacturer of school rings, graduation garb, and other scholastic products, and announced that Carnation would buy Timpte Industries, a truck-trailer company. When Carnation's stock dropped dramatically in response to these moves, however, the Timpte purchase fell through.

In 1976 the company was the second-largest producer of pet foods. Evaporated milk was an ever-shrinking market, but Carnation's new businesses, especially its instant products, pet food, and international divisions made up for the loss.

Olson's leadership was enigmatic in many respects. Under Stuart, Carnation had maintained a policy of strict corporate secrecy, disclosing little more about the company than what was legally required. This policy began to change after the Timpte announcement and subsequent stock-price crash, but not much. Product development, Carnation's lifeblood in the 1960s, slowed in the 1970s, and in the late 1970s advertising was even cut. There was some speculation that the Stuart family holding company pressured Carnation to squeeze money out of the company rather than invest for the long term. The company's closed-door policy also led to negative governmental action. Carnation was periodically cited during the 1970s with violations like price-fixing, illegal campaign contributions, and illegal payments to foreign governments. But overall, Carnation's sales and earnings hardly suffered—the company's unbroken string of annual earnings increases stretched back 28 years in 1980.

That year Olson also persuaded the Stuart family trust, which controlled nearly half of the company's shares, to dissolve itself, a move which allowed family members to sell their stock if they wished. This done, the pace of product introductions increased noticeably. However, the company's market share in pet foods slipped to fourth by 1981 and a lack of dairy-product introductions hurt its core business cash flow. In 1982 Carnation—in line with Slender, introduced in the mid-1960s, and 2% and nonfat evaporated milk, introduced during the 1970s—opened its first Health & Nutrition Centers, which offered formal diet programs, to a very good response.

Carnation's growing pile of cash, despite increased dividends, increased capital investment, and a share buy-back program to counteract the effect of share sales by the Stuart family began to attract attention. Rumors of a deal with Nestlé surfaced as early as 1980, but nothing came of them. Barring a major acquisition by Carnation, the company looked ripe for takeover.

In 1983 Timm F. Crull succeeded Dwight L. Stuart as president of Carnation. The next year, the long-rumored takeover finally took shape. Formal negotiations with Nestlé began in July, 1984, and by September the two companies had agreed on a $3 billion, $83-per-share friendly takeover. The acquisition formally took place in January, 1985. There was some controversy, however, over Carnation's repeated denials of merger talks even as they were taking place. Carnation settled a shareholder suit for $13 million in 1987, and as a result of Carnation's handling of its deal, the Securities and Exchange Commission issued new rules that required company statements addressing unusual market activity to acknowledge any merger discussions underway.

The deal left Carnation's management largely intact. Nestlé quickly sold Carnation's non-consumer-products divisions and many of its international operations. At the time of the deal, Carnation's sales were $3.7 billion, but Nestlé's cuts brought sales down to $2.1 billion.

Nestlé incorporated Carnation into its U.S. holding company, which includes Stouffer Corporation, Libby McNeil & Libby Inc., and Beech-Nut Corporation. Carnation, however, still reports directly to Switzerland. After spinning off unwanted divisions, the purchase of Carnation increased Nestlé revenue 20% to $13.5 billion, giving the parent company more product lines (pet foods were new to Nestlé) and improved market shares.

In 1985 Olson retired after leading Carnation for 20 years. Crull succeeded him as CEO. Carnation's new status as a subsidiary allows more long-term planning as well as access to Nestlé's extensive research-and-development facilities. Carnation's new areas of emphasis are ice cream novelties and its Contadina fresh pasta and cheese products. Carnation has invested nearly $100 million in Contadina alone, and Nestlé will also stress food sectors like Carnation's food-service and potato-processing lines, and Carnation's emphasis on pet foods will continue.

Carnation today is more heavily involved in higher-margin food processing than it ever was before. The Nestlé purchase makes possible a reversal of prior approaches, in which dairy and nonfood production were emphasized over food-processing lines. Today Carnation is entirely involved in domestic sales of food products and pet food. What was once a conservative, short-term growth company is now a risk-taking one positioned for the long term.

Further Reading: Weaver, John Downing. *Carnation: The First 75 Years, 1899–1974*, Los Angeles, Anderson, Ritchie & Simon, 1974.

CASTLE & COOKE, INC.

CASTLE & COOKE, INC.

10900 Wilshire Boulevard
Los Angeles, California 90024
U.S.A.
(213) 824–1500

Public Company:
Incorporated: 1894
Employees: 42,000
Sales: $2.47 billion
Stock Index: New York

In 1837 Samuel Northrup Castle and Amos Starr Cooke landed on Hawaii, then known as the Sandwich Islands, as part of the Seventh Reinforcement of the American Board of Commissioners for Foreign Missions, to begin their lives as lay missionaries. Castle's assignment was to order, unload, and distribute supplies for the mission depository. Cooke's job was to teach the "natives"—he taught the children of the royal families who then ruled the various islands for many years.

Over the years Castle, who felt Cooke's accounting abilities would help the depository, kept trying to convince his friend to join him. Cooke firmly declined until 1849, when his schooling of the royal children was complete. He needed to make a living since monetary support from Missions headquarters had been discontinued.

That year Castle suggested to Cooke that they set up a partnership to take over the operation of the depository as a private enterprise. Money could be made by trading with the community at large, while mission posts could be supplied at cost. They took up the matter with the Mission Board in Boston, which, after two years, decided to release the partners from the mission and pay each a yearly salary of $500. On June 2, 1851 their partnership began, and a sign reading "Kakela me Kuke" ("Castle & Cooke") was installed at the entrance to the Honolulu depository.

Business began with a bang. In their first year in business, profits came to nearly $2,000. In 1853 a branch store was opened downtown, to be closer to the considerable action the California Gold Rush brought. Also in 1853, Castle and Cooke purchased their first ship, the *Morning Star* to ship produce to California. By 1856, the partners elected to sell the depository, located on the outskirts of Honolulu, to concentrate on their burgeoning downtown business.

In 1858 Castle and Cooke first ventured out of the mercantile business to make an investment in the new sugar industry. In the late 1860s they branched into the shipping business, handling shore-side business for a number of transpacific schooners and several inter-island vessels. Despite these diversifications, however, the mercantile portion of the business continued to provide the bulk of the profits.

As time went on, Joe Atherton, Cooke's son-in-law, handled more and more of the day-to-day business while Castle devoted most of his time to public affairs. On July 14, 1894, ten days after the Republic of Hawaii was proclaimed, Samuel Castle died at the age of 86.

On December 28, 1894, the Castle & Cooke partnership was incorporated and Joe Atherton was elected president. At this time the company was just coming out of a financial slump caused by its 1889 investment in a sugar development called Ewa Plantation on the island of Oahu. To provide the huge amount of money needed to fund the project, Castle & Cooke had sold a large part of its holdings, including its valuable interests in the Haiku and Paia sugar plantations on Maui. The company continued to believe in the profitability of the Ewa Plantation and the risk paid off. By 1898, its production totaled 18,284 tons of sugar; in 1925 it reached 50,000. To add to the abundance, when Congress annexed Hawaii in August, 1898, sugar prices rose.

Also in 1898, the original merchandise business was sold. Diversification did not stop, however. In the ensuing years Castle & Cooke involved itself in an (unsuccessful) automobile company, the Hawaiian Fertilizer Company, and a big but short venture into the sugar refinery business with the Honolulu Sugar Refining Company. Although C & C had been in the shipping business for 50 years, a 1907 agreement with William Matson to be the agent for his Matson Navigation Company greatly increased the business in this area. The agreement endured for 56 years, most of them profitable.

In 1916 Edward Davies Tenney, a Castle nephew, became chairman of Castle & Cooke and a year later president of Matson Navigation upon William Matson's death. He held these posts for more than 30 years, until his death in 1934. Tenney became chairman just as the United States was entering World War I. Hawaii was a long way from the war zone; the only real effect of the war was to drive up the price of sugar, increasing Castle & Cooke's profits. Within a few months after the war, Tenney began to act on his prewar decision to diversify. He acquired for the company an assortment of stocks and bonds, including shares in the Bank of California, Pennsylvania Railroad, California Telephone and Light, Poulsen Wireless, Santa Cruz Portland Cement, and Sterling Oil & Development.

His next big project was the company's entrance into the travel business. In 1925 a group of entrepreneurs decided that the travelers on their luxury cruise lines needed a glamorous place to stay during their trip to Hawaii. As president of the Territorial Hotel Company (almost half of the directors worked for Castle & Cooke) Tenney oversaw the building of the $2 million Royal Hawaiian. In the long run the hotel was a flop, but news of its glamour ranged far.

The company's growth continued when Matson bought

the Los Angeles Steamship Company to ward off its taking over his luxury steamship trade. Castle & Cooke, along with Matson Navigation, was now the largest steamship system in the Pacific.

The Depression was less severe in Hawaii than on the mainland. Although Castle & Cooke never missed a dividend payment, the year-end bonus in 1931 included a warning that it probably wouldn't be repeated. In April, 1932, salaries and pensions were cut. By the time Alexander G. Budge became president in 1935, Castle & Cooke was already making a rapid recovery, in large part due to its 1932 purchase from Jim Dole of a 21% interest in his Hawaiian Pineapple Company. The Waialua Agricultural Company (part of Castle & Cooke) had already acquired a one-third share of Hawaiian Pineapple in a 1922 lease agreement. The purchase caused hard feelings between Dole and Castle & Cooke. After the reorganization, Dole was made chairman of the board, but was immediately sent on a "well-earned rest" from which he was never recalled. When he finally returned in 1933 he found his office moved to a storeroom.

World War II had a much more immediate effect on Castle & Cooke than the first war had. The military requisitioned most of the canned fruit that Hawaiian Pineapple and other companies produced, the cannery was blacked out completely, and chunks of acreage were converted to potatoes and other vegetables to help feed the military and local populations. Equipment and manpower were also commandeered; the labor force was cut in half, and key officials were given war-time jobs. Even so, sugar plantations stayed at close to normal production levels and with careful planning, enough vessels were made available to carry some crops to the mainland.

As life returned to normal after VJ day in 1945, the question of statehood for Hawaii resurfaced. During and just before the war, articles had appeared in the mainland press criticizing what were termed feudal practices in Hawaii, especially by the Big Five companies there, which included Castle & Cooke. Many in Hawaii, especially heads of the bigger corporations, felt that this problem was hindering Hawaii's acceptance into statehood. The heads of fifteen Hawaiian companies employed a New York public relations firm to make a study of the island's industry and social structure and tell them what to do. The report recommended that the leading island companies divest themselves of stock in rivals and foster real competition. Budge had already done this, limiting himself to positions on the boards only of the seven companies in which Castle & Cooke held a large financial stake. The company also disposed of holdings in agencies that were its competitors; Matson followed suit and several big estates were broken up and distributed among the heirs.

The labor movement also picked up again after the war, and Castle & Cooke's operations were involved in several disputes. In late 1946 the International Longshoremen's and Warehousemen's Union (ILWU) led a strike of 28,000 workers on 33 sugar plantations. The strike lasted 79 days; all over the islands irrigated cane dried and lost its sugar-bearing juice, resulting in a loss of some $20 million of sugar. Then in April, 1949 the union called out 2,000 longshoremen, cutting off all of Hawaii's supplies completely: nothing could come into the islands and nothing could be shipped to the mainland. This remarkable strike lasted 179 days and in the end the union lost its major demands, but it gained rank and file solidarity. During the strike, no goods could travel on the Pacific coast, but cargoes could and did use Gulf and Atlantic docks, giving Hawaii's economy links to the Atlantic coast for the first time in almost a century.

As the Hawaiian Pineapple Company suffered losses due to another strike in 1952, Budge kept pushing for diversification to end the firm's dependence on sugar and pineapple. In 1946 Hawaiian Tuna Packers had been purchased for this reason, and in 1948 Castle & Cooke organized the Royal Hawaiian Macadamia Nut Company as well.

Throughout its history, Castle & Cooke had only owned real estate indirectly, as an investor in agricultural businesses. In 1958 that changed: Helemano Company, Ltd. was merged into Castle & Cooke, adding 27,000 acres of land to its holdings.

Finally, in 1959, Hawaii became a state. Also in 1959, Malcolm MacNaughton became the president of C & C. He believed that an entirely new corporate structure was needed to promote the company's growth.

Through the years, Hawaiian Pineapple had been run independently, but in the late 1950s frictions reached a point of no return. Henry White, who had run the company for many years, had made some decisions about diversification that Budge had strongly disagreed with. As Hawaiian's profits fell, White was moved out of his position and in 1961 the company was merged into Castle & Cooke, adding another 15,000 acres t C & C's holdings.

The same year, Columbia River Packers (renamed Bumble Bee Seafoods, Inc.) was merged into Castle & Cooke, making the company an important player in the food industry, along with its shipping, stevedoring, and merchandising businesses.

By this time, Castle & Cooke owned 155,000 acres of land in Hawaii and a ranch in California. To manage and develop this property, Oceanic Properties was formed as a wholly owned subsidiary. The subsidiary's projects have included new towns, golf courses, apartment and medical buildings, and downtown development worldwide.

International development became a reality when Dole Philippines was organized in 1963 to farm 18,000 acres on the island of Mindanao. The decision to farm abroad was made when management felt that costs, especially labor, were too high.

Castle & Cooke then turned to bananas. With cash from the sale of Matson (in 1964) and Honolulu Oil, Castle & Cooke purchased a 55% share of Standard Fruit and Steamship Company of New Orleans; the rest of the stock was purchased in 1968. By 1973 Donald J. Kirchoff, C & C's executive vice president on the project, had made Castle & Cooke the U.S. leader in the banana market.

Consolidations and acquisitions continued during the 1960s. Expansion in the Pacific Basin, begun in Manila, also continued, growing to include Thailand and Malaysia. By the beginning of the 1970s a decision was made to bring the various companies together, tightening the loose-knit corporate structure.

In 1972 a complete corporate revamping took place. Kirchoff, now president, felt that C & C had always just evolved rather than grown according to a plan. Now the company was a group of unrelated businesses, including a 26-store retail chain, a plate glass company in the Philippines, a drainpipe company in Thailand, and a quarry in Malaysia. The first step was to centralize food marketing and corporate financial administration in San Francisco, with headquarters to remain in Honolulu. This move eliminated overlapping assignments and allowed for a 30% reduction in corporate staff. Tight central controls were established over budgets and results reviewed quarterly against performance. All food activities except sugar were brought into a single group, Castle & Cooke Foods. Real estate activities and manufacturing and merchandising were organized into two additional groups. Rather than buying companies, "just because the numbers looked good," Kirchoff used planned diversification, buying companies in fast-growing niches of the food market.

Over the next several years, Kirchoff's plan worked extremely well. Between 1972 and 1978, earnings rose about 20% a year. The bubble burst, however, in 1979. Besides bad luck with the weather, some critics claimed that the expansion program was just too ambitious; for example, C & C's movement into the European banana market ended up causing an oversupply.

C & C's problems persisted into the early 1980s. In July 1982, Kirchoff resigned and Henry Clark assumed interim responsibilities. The company tried moving in directions that would not be as cyclical—regional preparation centers to prepare vegetables for fast food restaurants, for example. When Ian Wilson became president, he concentrated on three main areas—fresh produce, packaged foods, and real estate. In 1983, he purchased the A & W root beer business, and at the same time placed more emphasis on marketing and advertising. Castle & Cooke's current logo for Dole brands was introduced as part of a drive to establish itself as a premier marketer of fruits around the world.

The next few years were turbulent ones for Castle & Cooke. The company was the subject of several takeover bids, by Houston investor Charles Hurwitz in 1984, then by Minneapolis investor Irwin L. Jacobs, and finally by David Murdock, who merged C & C with his Flexi-Van Corporations in July, 1985 to keep the company from going bankrupt.

Murdock, who installed himself as chairman and CEO of his new company, took firm control of Castle & Cooke, reorganizing it into a holding company for three separate operations: Flexi-Van, Dole Food, and Oceanic Properties, and relocating its headquarters to Los Angeles. Prospects began to brighten immediately and kept improving.

Today, Castle & Cooke's Dole Food unit is the world's largest pineapple marketer, ranks second in banana sales, and is a leading purveyor of iceberg lettuce, celery, cauliflower, broccoli, and other vegetables. The company owns vast amounts of land around the world: 28,000 acres in Honduras, 12,000 in Costa Rica, 18,400 in the Philippines and 5,000 in Thailand, as well as approximately 46,000 acres in the United States. Through Oceanic Properties the company also owns 151,000 acres, including virtually the whole Hawaiian island of Lanai, about 89,000 acres and extensive property in Oahu, and 5,200 acres in California. Throughout its history the company has had its ups and downs, and in this era or mergers and acquisitions, one can't be sure what will happen next, but it is safe to say that the two missionaries started a successful venture.

Principal Subsidiaries: Flexi-Van Corp.; Castle & Cooke Fresh Fruit, Inc. (Nev.); Castle & Cooke Fresh Vegetables, Inc. (Cal.); Castle & Cooke Kabushiki Kaisha, Limited (Japan); Castle & Cooke Worldwide Limited (Hong Kong); Intercontinental Transportation Services, Limited (Liberia); Dole Philippines, Inc. (Republic of the Philippines); Dole Thailand, Ltd. (Thailand); Kohala Corporation (Hi.); Oahu Transport Company, Ltd. (Hi.); Oceanic Properties, Inc. (Hi.); Pina Antilana, S.A. (Honduras); Produce Continental, Limited (Bermuda); Produce International A.B. (Sweden); Standard Fruit and Steamship Co. (Del.).

Further Reading: Taylor, Frank J. et al. *From Land and Sea: The Story of Castle & Cooke of Hawaii*, Chronicle Books, San Francisco, 1976.

CONAGRA, INC.

ConAgra Center
One Central Park Plaza
Omaha, Nebraska 68102
U.S.A.
(402) 978–4000

Public Company
Incorporated: 1919 as Nebraska Consolidated Mills Company
Employees: 42,993
Sales: $9.5 billion
Stock Index: New York

In 1919 Alva Kinney brought four grain milling companies in south central Nebraska together to take advantage of increasing grain production in the Midwest, and the Nebraska Consolidated Mills Company was born. Seventy years and a name change later, ConAgra is a diversified international company whose products range from agricultural supplies such as fertilizers, pesticides, and feeds to prepared gourmet dinners for a new age of consumers.

Officially formed on September 29, 1919, the Nebraska Consolidated Mills Company (NCM) was headquartered in Grand Island, Nebraska. At first Kinney concentrated on milling the bumper postwar wheat crops at his four Nebraska locations. But soon, to accommodate his growing business, Kinney added a mill in Omaha, in 1922, and moved the headquarters of the company there. He continued to run a profitable and relatively quiet company solely in Nebraska until he retired as president in 1936.

Kinney was succeeded by R. S. Dickinson. Initially, Dickinson followed his predecessor's simple but successful policy of milling grain in Nebraska. World War II and the postwar boom kept the demand for grain high and the milling business profitable.

During the early 1940s Dickinson began to use the company's profits to expand. Other successful milling operations, such as General Mills and Pillsbury, were expanding both the number of plants and the number of products they offered, and NCM followed the same trend. In 1942 Dickinson opened a flour mill and animal feed mill in Alabama. He also promoted research into new types of prepared foods that used flour, which led to the development of Duncan Hines cake mixes, introduced in the early 1950s.

The Alabama expansion was profitable, but Dickinson found that it was more difficult to gain a foothold in the prepared-foods market. Cake mixes, though only a small proportion of the total flour market, accounted for as much as $140 million a year in retail sales by 1947. But the market was dominated by General Mills's Betty Crocker brand and by Pillsbury, each with one third of the market share, while Duncan Hines controlled only 10–12%. Unable to increase its share of the highly-competitive cake mix market, NCM eventually decided to get out of prepared foods and use the money it raised to expand in basic commodities: grains and feeds. So, in 1956 the company sold its Duncan Hines brand to Proctor & Gamble.

The new president of Nebraska Consolidated Mills, J. Allan Mactier, used the proceeds from the sale to expand aggressively. In 1958, NCM built the first major grain processing plant in Puerto Rico through its subsidiary, Caribe Company. The $3 million plant processed flour, corn meal, and animal feeds at Catano in San Juan harbor. Production at the plant did not compete with the parent company's already-existing concerns; none of the flours and feeds produced there were exported to the mainland.

Caribe's foothold on the island led to further Puerto Rican expansion in new areas. A second subsidiary, Molinos de Puerto Rico, took over Caribe's animal feed business on the island while also developing Puerto Rico's virtually nonexistent beef industry as a market for its products. In Molino's first five years of operation, consumption of animal feeds in Puerto Rico increased from 136,516 tons, of which 100,314 were imported, to 249,267 tons, of which only 46,723 were imported. The company also profited from an increased demand for meat and milk on the island.

Elsewhere, however, flour millers faced shrinking profits as demand leveled off in both domestic and foreign markets. European grain production had recovered from the disruption of World War II, and prosperity at home in the 1950s and 1960s allowed consumers to buy more expensive food items, leading to lower flour consumption.

Large millers turned to diversification to offset declining profitability. Industry leaders General Mills and Pillsbury developed their consumer foods lines and introduced new types of convenience foods, while the third of the "Big Three" in flour milling, International Milling company, Inc., diversified primarily into animal feeds. Nebraska Consolidated Mills, perhaps unwilling to compete again in packaged foods after its experience with Duncan Hines, also developed the animal feed end of its business. Throughout the 1960s and into the 1970s, the company developed mills and distribution centers for feed and flour in the Southeast and Northwest.

NCM also turned to another basic commodity: chicken. It developed poultry growing and processing complexes in Georgia, Louisiana, and Alabama during the 1960s.

In 1965 the company also began to expand into the European market by going into partnership with Bioter-Biona, S.A., a Spanish producer of animal feed and animal health products and breeder of pigs, chickens, and trout.

By 1971 Nebraska Consolidated Mills had outgrown its early base in Nebraska as well as its name. It chose a new name to reflect its new concerns: ConAgra, meaning "in partnership with the land." ConAgra was listed on the New York Stock Exchange in 1973.

The new name, however, did not necessarily mean continuing success. The early 1970s, in fact, brought the company to a low point. Many of its acquisitions during the expansion of the 1960s and early 1970s were only marginally profitable at best. In 1974 the company posted net losses and suspended dividends. Heavy losses in commodity speculations brought ConAgra to the brink of bankruptcy in 1975.

ConAgra's first high-profile chief executive, former Pillsbury executive Charles Harper, was named president in 1975 with a mandate to turn the ailing company around.

Harper first sold nonessential operations to reduce debt. He then began to buy agricultural businesses at the low end of their profit cycles and turn them around. Harper originally intended to stick with ConAgra's emphasis on basic commodities rather than compete with the packaged-food giants. When he purchased Banquet Foods Corporation in 1980, he claimed that the acquisition was not an entry into prepared foods but a way to increase ConAgra's chicken capacity. ConAgra's chicken production did increase by a third, bringing the company from eighth to fifth place among chicken producers. Harper expanded into fish as well as poultry in the 1970s with investments in catfish aquaculture.

Another of Harper's acquisitions put ConAgra in the forefront of its original flour market. In 1982 ConAgra bought the Peavey Company, a Minneapolis-based flour miller and grain trader, giving it 16.3% of the nation's wheat-milling capacity and a system of grain exporting terminals. Political barriers to U.S. grain exports had depressed Peavey's profits, and so far the acquisition has not been the success story that Banquet was for ConAgra. But by 1986, Peavey had shown a $16.4 million profit on sales of $1.2 billion, a promising upward trend.

Harper also kept to a commodity-oriented approach by diversifying into agricultural chemicals. ConAgra expanded into fertilizers, and in 1978 acquired United Agri Products, a distributor of herbicides and pesticides. Higher grain prices, Harper reasoned, would mean increased demand for such chemicals.

But, in an attempt to counter the cyclical profit pattern of basic agricultural commodities, Harper also entered areas that didn't mesh well with the company's traditional orientation: pet accessories, a Mexican restaurant chain, and a fabrics and crafts chain, among others. These acquisitions have yet to be as profitable as anticipated.

In a dramatic change of direction during the 1980s, ConAgra decided on prepared foods as a better way to balance cyclical profits in the food industry. In 1981 the company bought Singleton Seafood, the largest shrimp processor in the country, and Sea-Alaska Products. In 1987 ConAgra bought Trident Seafoods and O'Donnell-Usen Fisheries, the producer of Taste O' Sea frozen seafood products, thus positioning the company to compete against the leading frozen seafood brands, Mrs. Paul's Kitchens, Gorton's, and Van de Kamp's.

In 1982, during a low in the poultry cycle, ConAgra moved to take first place in the chicken industry by forming Country Poultry, Inc. By the next year, Country Poultry was delivering more than a billion pounds of brand-name broilers to markets, making it the biggest poultry producer in the country. In 1986, the company formed ConAgra Turkey Company and in 1987 it acquired another poultry company, Longmont Foods, further strengthening its position in the field. But ConAgra's poultry concerns no longer focused on the basic bird Harper purchased Banquet for: Country Poultry introduced a number of higher-profit convenience poultry products, such as marinated chicken breasts, chicken hot dogs, and processed chicken for fast food restaurants.

ConAgra moved into another area of processed foods in 1983 when the company purchased Armour Food Company, a processor of red meats such as hot dogs, sausage, bacon, ham, and lunch meats. The acquisition also included Armour's line of frozen gourmet entrees, Dinner Classics, which complemented Banquet's line of frozen foods. As with many of his other acquisitions, Harper bought Armour in a down cycle for book value ($182 million). By waiting to complete the deal until Armour closed several plants, Harper painlessly eliminated about 40% of the Armour's major union's members. Some Armour plants still have unions, but without a master contract labor costs were slashed. Harper then reorganized the company, emphasizing new marketing strategies (reintroducing the familiar Armour jingle to take advantage of consumer recognition) and refocusing product lines. The Dinner Classics line has been hurt by price competition and the introduction of new brands of premium frozen dinners. Armour as a whole was still unprofitable in 1988, but the Classics line has increased profits since the purchase.

In 1986, Harper increased ConAgra's presence in frozen foods by purchasing the Morton, Patio, and Chun King brands. And in 1987, the company expanded in red meats with its purchase of E.A. Miller, Inc., a western producer of beef products, and Montfort of Colorado, Inc. Almost a decade earlier, ConAgra had tried to purchase MBPXL Corp., the number-two beef packer in the country, only to be blocked at the last minute by the privately owned Cargill Inc. The Montfort deal, for $365 million in stock, made ConAgra the third-largest U.S. beef producer. Although health-conscious consumers are eating less beef, ConAgra hopes to develop new meat products as it developed new poultry products. Another 1987 acquisition, 50% of Swift Independent Packing Company, a processor of beef, pork, and lamb, made ConAgra a leading meat processor as well. Harper has rounded out his changes at ConAgra to date by developing the company's international trading position and by developing its own financial services subsidiary.

In 70 years, ConAgra changed from a low-profile flour miller into a producer of basic commodities, and then into an acquisition-driven, diversified international food company with interests across the food industry. As such, the company seems well-positioned to balance cyclical trends in foods as well as changing consumer taste. The company's poultry, seafood, and grain concerns appeal to new consumer interests in low-cholesterol eating, while busy families are ringing up profits for ConAgra in its prepared foods division.

Principal Subsidiaries: AgriBasics Fertilizer Co.; Agricol Corp., Inc.; Alliance Grain, Inc.; Molinos de Puerto Rico, Inc.; CAG Co.; Cropmate Co.; Trekker Co.; Atwood Commodities, Inc.; United Agri Products, Inc.; Armour Food Express Co.; Kurt A. Becher GmbH & Co. KG; Bergerco USA; Bergerco (VI), Inc.; Taco Plaza, Inc.; To-Ricos, Inc.; Atwood-Larson Co.; U.S. Tire, Inc.; Canadian Harvest Process (1988) Ltd.; C & L Grain & Feed Co.; Woodward & Dickerson (Japan) Ltd.; Saprogal; Sapropor (75%); Geldermann, Inc.; United Agri Products Financial Services, Inc.; Weld Agricultural Credit, Inc.

CPC INTERNATIONAL INC.

Box 8000
International Plaza
Englewood Cliffs, New Jersey 07632
U.S.A.
(201) 894–4000

Public Company
Incorporated: 1906 as Corn Products Refining Company
Employees: 33,500
Sales: $5.1 billion
Stock Index: New York Midwest Pacific Basel Geneva Lausanne London Paris Zurich Frankfurt

CPC International Inc., one of America's largest food companies, is a leading corn refiner as well as the producer of many of America's best-known and top-selling brands: Mazola corn oil, Argo corn starch, Hellmann's and Best Foods mayonnaise, Mueller's pasta, Knorr soup, Skippy peanut butter, and Thomas' English muffins are all CPC products. But as its name implies, CPC International is also a distinctly international company, producing more than 2,000 food products and several dozen wet-milled corn products at over 100 manufacturing plants located in 47 countries. In 1988 57% of the company's food revenues came from outside the United States, more than any other major American food company. Today CPC traces its roots back to two main predecessors: the Corn Products Refining Company and Best Foods, which merged in 1958 to become the Corn Products Company.

CPC has transformed itself from a grain producer and processor into a major international consumer grocery producer. Consumer foods are now about 80% of total sales, while corn refining has been reduced to 20%. Today the company has five major consumer foods groups—mayonnaise and corn oil; Knorr products; bread spreads and cheese; bakery and pasta; and starches, syrups, and desserts.

But the company's corn-refining division's oils, starches, syrups, sugars, and agricultural feeds are no less familiar to producers of finished goods in more than 60 industries than its consumer products are to shoppers. The most plentiful of the corn-refining products is corn starch. CPC makes it in over 200 varieties for use in the production of goods such as paper products, foods, pharmaceuticals, textiles, chemicals, and adhesive materials.

CPC traces its corn-refining ancestry to the development in 1842 of the first workable method for extracting starch from corn. By the turn of the century, a number of corn refineries were processing corn to obtain its starch and sugar, including the Corn Products Company, a predecessor of Corn Products Refining and the producer of Karo corn syrup.

In 1900 the National Starch Manufacturing Company reached an agreement to cooperate with the United States Glucose Company, which was also a major stockholder in the United States Sugar Refining Company. By 1902, when the three companies officially merged to form the Corn Products Company with C. H. Matthiessen as president, they produced about 84% of all American corn starch.

In 1901 Thomas Edward Bedford, an executive of Standard Oil of New Jersey, organized the New York Glucose Company to compete with the Corn Products Company. In January, 1906, the two companies, together with Warner Sugar Refining Company, merged to form the Corn Products Refining Company and Bedford became president of the new group.

The new company, headquartered in New York City, continued to manufacture products like corn starch, corn syrup, and corn oil. It acquired several other major corn wet milling businesses in subsequent years and soon became the undisputed giant of the industry. In 1906 Corn Products opened sales offices in Germany and the United Kingdom.

By 1916 Corn Products Refining Company (CP) manufactured more than 75% of all American-made glucose, selling roughly 30% of this to the confectionery industry. For some refined corn products it was said to have 90% of the U.S. market.

In the early 1900s the company responded to mounting competition by eliminating obsolete refining plants and replacing them with modern facilities to lower manufacturing costs. One of these plants, the world's largest corn-products manufacturing plant, was begun in 1908 near Summit, Illinois, and, when it was completed, processed about one-third of CP's total output at that time.

Corn Products continued to broaden its product line during its early years. Although by 1912 Karo corn syrup accounted for 80% of its sales, the company introduced Mazola corn oil in 1911, and at that time was also packaging syrups, jams, and both edible and laundry starches. Much of this production was sold to wholesalers for sale under private labels.

In 1913 the federal government brought suit against Corn Products Refining Company and its related companies for violations of the Sherman Antitrust Act. The government charged CP with conspiracy to restrain trade in the corn-refining business by attempting to regulate the production and sale of many corn products, and asked the court to declare CP a combination in restraint of free trade, and therefore, to dissolve it. In 1919, following protracted litigation, the Supreme Court ordered CP to divest itself of several properties, but did not require that the company be dissolved.

The company continued to grow, purchasing its first overseas plant, in Germany, in 1919. In January, 1921 the company purchased several more German production facilities. By the beginning of the 1930s Corn Products owned or licensed operations in Canada, Mexico, Czechoslovakia, England, France, Italy, the Netherlands, Switzerland, Yugoslavia, Argentina, Brazil, the Dominican Republic, and Japan.

The Best Foods, Inc. traces it beginnings to a number of 19th-century flaxseed, cottonseed, and flour-milling businesses. In December, 1898 the company's oldest component, the American Linseed Company, was incorporated in New Jersey. American Linseed began to diversify in 1917, acquiring the Nucoa Butter Company, whose largest subsidiary, The Best Foods, Inc., produced margarine, mayonnaise, and other edible-oil products.

A second antecedent of Best Foods, American Cotton Oil Company, also moved from a basic commodity business to packaged-good marketing around 1920. In June, 1922 American Cotton Oil sold its cottonseed-crushing mills in the South and began to concentrate on its soap-making subsidiary, the N.K. Fairbank Company. Among the subsidiary's products was Gold Dust, a popular brand of soap. The Gold Dust name was applied to the surviving consumer-products company, and the Gold Dust Corporation was incorporated in September, 1923 in New Jersey. Gold Dust then acquired the F.F. Dalley Company's shoe polish lines, including the popular Shinola brand.

The union of American Linseed and Gold Dust occurred in 1928, when Gold Dust bought blocks of American Linseed stock, acquired American Linseed's packaged-goods division, and, in July, 1928, finally bought the rest of the business, selling its flaxseed operations. In January, 1929 the enlarged Gold Dust Corporation bought the Standard Milling Company, the oldest and second-largest American milling company. In 1930 Gold Dust's assets totaled about $41 million; Corn Products' were about twice that amount.

Less than two years after Gold Dust outbid the Postum Company for American Linseed, Gold Dust and Postum (which later became General Foods) entered a joint venture. The Best Foods division of Gold Dust and Postum's Richard Hellmann Company linked up to distribute the margarine, dressings, and spreads they both manufactured.

During the Great Depression the food industry was a relatively stable one. In 1931, Edward T. Bedford died. His successor at CP was George M. Moffett.

In November, 1936 Gold Dust combined its three operating subsidiaries, 2-in-1 Shinola Bixby Corporation, Preserves and Honey, Inc., and Hecker-H-O Company, Inc. into a single corporation, taking the Hecker name for the whole. And in 1939 Hecker President George Morrow sold the Gold Dust soap business to Lever Brothers Company for $2.5 million.

In November, 1942 Hecker paid General Foods $5.5 million for General Foods' 29% interest in the Best Foods–Hellmann shipping operation. The following month Hecker changed its name to The Best Foods, Inc.

Meanwhile, amid continuing prosperity in the 1940s, Corn Products shut down its most visible public symbol: its large Edgewater, New Jersey corn refinery, which was visible from Manhattan across the Hudson River. The plant's mounting obsolescence, together with rising tariffs on Argentine corn, forced CP to ship midwestern corn overland to the plant; the natural solution was to transfer its work to the Midwest.

During World War II the United States mounted an enormous lend-lease assistance program to aid the Allies while struggling to keep its own troops supplied. These wartime demands were felt nowhere more than in the agricultural-products industry. Corn supplies were restricted because of heavy demand and pricing structure. By April, 1944, CP's Kansas City, Missouri and Pekin, Illinois refineries had been closed for lack of corn and the same kind of stoppage threatened its big Argo, Illinois plant. It was not just a simple problem of shortage, however. The government-mandated price for corn was so low that farmers, with a limited amount of the grain, found it more profitable to feed the corn to their hogs than to sell it to refiners. Nonetheless, CP survived the war and soon was expanding again.

In 1955 Best Foods made several important acquisitions. It first bought the Rit Dye Company after a series of transactions begun a decade earlier. Best Foods then acquired the Rosefield Packing Company, of Alameda, California and Good Foods, Inc., of Minneapolis, Minnesota. The purchase of these two companies gave Best Foods ownership of the Skippy peanut butter brand. Best Foods also sold Standard Milling Company that year.

In April, 1958 CP President William Brady announced that the company would acquire C. H. Knorr Company of West Germany, a maker of bouillon, dehydrated soups, and other convenience foods. This acquisition was the last in a long string of postwar acquisitions for the company. By 1958 CP was involved in the producing and processing of feed and grain, corn and chemical refining, banking, construction, and the running of a railroad and a shipping line.

Following complicated preparations begun in September, 1958, Corn Products Refining Company and The Best Foods, Inc. formally merged in May, 1959. The merger was the result of the recognition that CP's future relied on its ability to develop a successful-grocery products business in order to maintain growth.

In 1959 and 1960 CP established new businesses in the Philippines, France, Sweden, and Venezuela. The company continued growing throughout the decade, introducing Mazola margarine in the United States in 1961. In 1963 the company established a Knorr plant in Japan and began manufacturing starch in Pakistan. This growth enabled the company to surpass $1 billion in sales for the first time in 1966.

In April, 1969 the company changed its name to CPC International Inc. Although it continued to add units in its chemicals and packaging divisions and also made a foray into restaurants with the purchase of the Dutch Pantry chain in 1969, CPC had clearly decided to emphasize packaged foods. In 1969 sales of the company's consumer grocery products surpassed those of its wet-milled corn products for the first time.

S. B. Thomas, a baker of English muffins and other specialty breads, was bought in 1970. Ten years later the S. B. Thomas subsidiary bought Sahara brand pita bread. And, in 1983, CPC acquired the C. F. Mueller Company, one of the largest U.S. pasta makers, for $122 million.

During the 1970s Best Foods, as the consumer-foods division is still known, also started its first facility outside the United States, a vegetable oil manufacturing and packaging facility in Puerto Rico. In 1974 CPC's sales topped $2.5 billion, only four years later they surpassed $3 billion, and in 1980 sales were over $4 billion.

In 1981 and 1982 the company opened five new U.S. corn wet milling plants as CPC began a program to reduce costs and improve the productivity and capacity of its corn wet milling operations. Between 1983 and 1985 the company spent more than $400 million in "Investment for Growth" projects. The largest of these was the rebuilding of the company's huge Argo, Illinois factory.

In 1986 CPC successfully fought off a takeover attempt by Ronald O. Perelman, chairman of the Revlon Group. The CPC board authorized a repurchase of over 20% of the company's stock, to be financed by borrowing and then repaying the debt by asset sale. CPC eventually bought back Perelman's 3.68 million shares for $88.5 million.

Freed of Perelman, the company moved ahead with its takeover-prompted restructuring plans, completing the buyback of 20% of its stock in 1988 at a total cost of $836.9 million. Under this restructuring plan the company acquired several new companies and stripped away some of its poor performers. CPC also reduced its workforce by some 17%. In 1988 CPC consolidated its worldwide food operations into one group, a move away from the company's longtime practice of granting autonomy to its international operations.

The first of the company's new acquisitions was Arnold Foods Company, in November, 1986. CPC paid $145 million for the bread company, whose sales were $230 million. Also in 1986 CPC bought the Old London melba toast baking business from Borden, Inc. for about $25 million and combined Old London, Arnold, and S. B. Thomas to form the Best Foods Baking Group. Several other smaller acquisitions brought the total cost of 1986 acquisitions to nearly $193 million. In 1987 and 1988 CPC spent about $200 million on packaged-food companies in Latin America, Brazil, Italy, France, Germany, and Great Britain.

During the same period CPC sold many holdings, including its $600 million European corn-milling operations and its South African unit. The company also sold its 50% interest in a Japanese food business and 50% of its food companies in Hong Kong, Malaysia, the Philippines, Singapore, Taiwan, and Thailand to Ajinomoto, its partner in a Japanese joint venture.

CPC also strengthened its successful food-service operation, which serves institutional customers. This fast-growth business, known as CPC Foodservice in the United States and Caterplan in Europe, Latin America, and Asia, today generates about 10% of the company's grocery-product sales.

After steering CPC through the takeover attempt and restructuring, CEO James R. Eiszner was named chairman in 1987, succeeding Chairman James W. McKee Jr. Eiszner has continued to maximize CPC's international exposure, brand-name products, and healthy financial picture to allow the company to continue to grow worldwide. Today products made under the Knorr brand (a German subsidiary) account for almost a quarter of the company's grocery-product earnings worldwide.

CPC has spent the better part of the 20th century expanding globally and entering new markets, but the company is now trying to strengthen its U.S. growth as well. Although it is still interested in reentering the Japanese market, which it abandoned after the Perelman raid, CPC has begun to focus on U.S. operations in an attempt to increase its size and scope.

Although CPC has had mixed results with new products—light and cholesterol-free mayonnaises have been wildly successful, while Mueller pastas with sauces were less than profitable—new products and some acquisitions are now important elements of CPC's strategy for growth in the U.S. market.

CPC's unorthodox growth should continue for the foreseeable future; it has been, and will continue to be the secret to the company's success. CPC has been well established in the global marketplace for decades with popular brands bought from and run by local people. Its U.S. products are equally popular. CPC looks to accomplish further domestic growth using those same tactics.

Principal Subsidiaries: CPC Europe (Group) Ltd.; Best Foods-Caribbean, Inc.; S.B. Thomas, Inc.; C.F. Mueller Company; Arnold Foods Company; Canada Starch Company Inc.; Knorr Holding Gesellschaft mbH, Wels (Austria); Mais-Monda N.V./S.A. (Belgium); CPC Foods A/S (Denmark); OY Suomen CPC (Finland); Societe des Produits du Mais, S.A. (France); Maizena Gesellschaft mbH (West Germany); Knorr (Hellas) A.B.E.E. (Greece); CPC Benelux B.V. (the Netherlands); CPC (Ireland) Ltd.; CPC Italia S.R.L. (90.19%); CPC Norge A/S (Norway); Knorr Portuguesa Productos Alimentares S.A.R.L. (Portugal); CPC Espana, S.A. (Spain); CPC Foods AB (Sweden); Knorr Zurich AG (Switzerland); CPC (United Kingdom) Ltd.; CPC Kenya Ltd. (95.30%); CPC Maghreb, S.A. (Morocco); Refinerias de Maiz S.A.I.C. (Argentina); Refinacoes de Milho, Brasil Ltda.; Industrias de Maiz y Alimentos S.A. (chile); Masizena, S.A. (Columbia); Productos de Maiz y Alimentos S.A. (Guatemala); Almidones del Istmo, S.A. de C.V. (Honduras); Productos de Maiz, S.A. (Mexico); Alimentos y Productos de Maiz, S.A. (Peru); Industrializadorade Maiz, S.A. (Uruguay); Aliven S.A. (Venezuela); Rafhan Maize Products Company Ltd. (Pakistan) (51%).

DALGETY

DALGETY, PLC.

19 Hanover Square
London W1R 9DA
United Kingdom
(01) 499–7712

Public Company
Incorporated: 1884 as Dalgety and Company, Ltd.
Employees: 24,000
Sales: £4.6 billion (US$8.32 billion)
Stock Index: London

Dalgety has grown from an Australian merchant house connected with the wool trade to become one of the world's largest food and agricultural conglomerates. Today the company has major holdings in England, Canada, the United States, and Australia and is engaged in such varied activities as snack food production, cereal milling, pig breeding, and fast food distribution.

The company was founded by Frederick Dalgety, a Scotsman who emigrated to Australia in 1833 at the age of 16. Dalgety apprenticed with a Sydney merchant until 1840, when he moved to Melbourne and found a job as the manager of a wool trading firm. Dalgety soon secured a partnership in the business, and, when his partners left the firm, he formed his own company in 1846. Dalgety and Company outfitted sheep ranchers with supplies and financed them in anticipation of yearly wool sales. The firm then shipped wool to England, where it was sold to the textile industry.

The Australian wool market collapsed in the late 1840s, and Dalgety would have been hard-pressed to continue had it not been for the discovery of gold in Australia in 1851. Dalgety and Company made a fortune supplying prospectors with food and digging equipment. The company also bought gold from the miners and then sold it abroad for a substantial profit. Although the gold rush brought Frederick Dalgety sudden wealth, he did not abandon his original business. The wool market recovered from its slump and Dalgety expanded his firm's activities throughout the continent and to New Zealand. Dalgety's connections with the wool trade became so pervasive that sheep farmers nicknamed the company and its representatives "Uncle Dal."

In 1854 Dalgety established an office in London to expedite his overseas transactions and thereafter managed his business from England. As Dalgety's firm came to dominate the Australian and New Zealand wool market, it became apparent that incorporation was necessary to supply the needed capital. Thus, in 1884 the business was floated as a public limited company with a capital of £4 million. The share issue was a great success, and Frederick Dalgety acted as the company's first chairman until his death in 1894.

The new company experienced a number of hardships in its early years. In 1893 an Australian banking crisis led to financial contraction on that continent. Then, Australia's agrarian economy was devastated by the Great Drought, from 1895 to 1902. Dalgety's new chairman, Edmund Doxat, saw fit to charter a new course for the company. Dependence on wool had left Dalgety vulnerable to the drought, so Doxat began a policy of diversification.

The new process of refrigeration allowed Dalgety to tap into New Zealand's farming communities. Lamb and mutton as well as butter and cheese could now be transported safely to European markets. Refrigeration gave rise to a New Zealand dairy industry which eventually rivaled Europe's. Entry into the food business helped Dalgety weather the Great Drought, and the company began the 20th century with newfound strengths.

The early years of the new century were a prosperous time for Dalgety. World War I later stimulated wool production, for uniforms, and the postwar economic boom increased the demand for Australian and New Zealand food products. Dalgety benefited greatly from the prosperity of the 1920s, but, like many other businesses, was caught unaware by the stock market crash of 1929. The Depression was a lean time for the company, marked by losses and employee pay cuts. Although the outbreak of World War II in 1939 ended the Depression, wartime price controls and regulations prevented Dalgety from reaping the full benefits of the economic upswing.

The Allied victory in 1945 inaugurated a period of unprecedented growth for Western business generally, but not for Dalgety and the wool trade. In the decade following World War II, the advent of synthetic fibers such as rayon and orlon greatly undermined the wool industry. Because of falling profits during the 1950s, Dalgety attempted to narrow its field of competition by acquiring rival wool firms. The company's amalgamation policy culminated in the 1962 merger with the New Zealand Loan and Mercantile Agency, making Dalgety the largest wool broker in the world. Near monopoly status, however, could not protect the company from seasonal swings in the wool market or fluctuations in the Australian climate.

During the 1960s drought once more wreaked havoc on the Australian wool industry. Dalgety had survived drought in the 1890s through diversification, and the company's management again decided to expand into other fields. From the late 1960s onwards, a series of acquisitions brought Dalgety into a vast range of agricultural and food businesses that eventually resulted in today's multinational conglomerate.

In 1966 Dalgety bought the two Balfour Guthrie companies of North America. This acquisition consisted of a Canadian trading company with a major interest in western Canada's lumber industry, and a poultry business in the United States. Dalgety next acquired two British firms: the feed company, Grossmith Agricultural Industries, in 1969, and a pig-breeding concern called the Pig Improvement Company, in 1970. In 1972 Dalgety purchased Associated British Maltsters, Britain's largest malting firm, for £19 million. With these acquisitions, the company moved away from its original base in Australia and New Zealand so that by 1976, the vast majority of Dalgety's profits came from activities in England, Canada, and the United States.

Dalgety underwent a marked shift of direction into the food business during the 1970s and 1980s. In 1977, food processing and distribution accounted for only 16% of Dalgety's product sales, but by 1981 this sector had risen to 45%, while the company's agri-business sector became less important. The shift toward food began in 1977, when Dalgety initiated a hostile takeover of Spillers, the British flour milling and grocery giant. There was a fierce battle between the two companies, both of which waged heated press campaigns to win the support of Spillers' shareholders. Dalgety finally acquired Spillers in 1979 for £76.5 million, giving the company a leading role in grocery product manufacture. That same year Dalgety purchased the American company Martin-Brower, one of the world's largest distributors of fast food and supplier to MacDonald's restaurants in the United States and Canada. Dalgety once again increased its food product holdings in 1985 with the acquisition of the Anglo-American firm Gill and Duffus, the world's largest trader of cocoa.

During the 1980s Dalgety became a major supplier of ingredients to food manufacturers. In addition to its flour, malt, and cocoa businesses, Dalgety acquired the ingredients firms James Fleming of England and Modern Maid Food Products of America. These companies produce flavorings, coatings, and glazes for baked goods and frozen foods.

In 1987 Dalgety initiated a vigorous rationalization program to reduce company debt from previous acquisitions and concentrate on its core food business. Dalgety therefore sold a number of subsidiaries, including Balfour Guthrie and Associated British Maltsters. By late 1987 the company's asset disposal had raised some £150 million for continued expansion into the food industry.

Dalgety has since moved into the lucrative snack food business, purchasing in 1987 the four Golden Wonder companies of England and Holland, producers of a popular line of potato chips and processed snacks. The following year Dalgety acquired Continental Savouries, a British company that manufactures frozen pizza. The addition of Hunters' Foods in 1989 gave Dalgety the leading role in British snack foods.

Recent acquisitions in the food sector include the British egg distributor, Goldenlay Eggs, and America's largest asparagus distributor, Lee Brands. One of the company's most promising new ventures is Dalgety Inc., an American subsidiary that supplies supermarkets with fresh produce. Dalgety is also much involved in the development of microwave food products.

Dalgety has already established joint ventures in Japan and China, and hopes to expand further into the vast Asian market in the future. Altogether, the company is well placed for continued growth in the food industry.

Principal Subsidiaries: Dalgety Agriculture Ltd.; Dalgety Produce Ltd.; Dalgety Agriculture Ltd.; Dalgety Engineers Ltd.; Dalgety Meat Products Ltd.; Dalgety Farm Eggs Ltd.; Deans Farm Eggs Ltd.; Golden Wonder Ltd.; Golden Wonder (Holland) BV.; Lecureur SA (98% France); Lucas Ingredients Ltd.; Memory Lane Cakes Ltd.; The Pig Improvement Company Ltd.; Pig Improvement Co. Inc.; Homepride Foods Ltd.; Crown Noodle Co. Ltd.; Preservenbedrijf BV. (Holland); Spillers Foods Ltd.; Spillers Milling Ltd.; British Cocoa Mills Ltd.; Gill & Duffus Inc. (USA); Gill & Duffus Ltd.; Gill & Duffus SA (83%) (Switzerland); Joanes Industrial SA (Brazil); Pacol Limited; Usicafe Comissaria & Exportada Ltda (Brazil); Dalgety Farmers Ltd. (69%); Martin-Brower of Canada Ltd.; The Martin-Brower Co. Inc.; Modern Maid Food Products Inc.; Cairns Holdings Ltd. (30%) (Zimbabwe); National Foods Holding Ltd. (17%) (Zimbabwe).

Further Reading: Vaughan-Thomas, Wynford. *Dalgety: The Romance of a Business*, London, Henry Melland, 1984.

GENERAL MILLS, INC.

9200 Wayzata Boulevard
Minneapolis, Minnesota 55440
U.S.A.
(612) 540–2311

Public Company
Incorporated: 1928
Employees: 74,453
Sales: $5.18 billion
Stock Index: New York Midwest

For more than 60 years General Mills has survived as an independent corporation by relying on its flour milling and breakfast cereals. From the 1930s through the 1980s the company attempted to diversify into several industries, but a restructuring in 1985 sent ripples through the company's makeup and earnings, and today it has trimmed itself down to focus exclusively on consumer foods and restaurants.

General Mills was incorporated relatively recently, but its origins go back to 1866, when Cadwallader Washburn opened a flour mill in Minneapolis, Minnesota. His business, which soon became the Washburn Crosby Company, competed with local miller C. A. Pillsbury. In 1869 they joined forces to form the Minneapolis Millers Association. Pillsbury and Washburn both wanted to find a way to make midwestern winter wheat into a higher grade of flour. Eventually, with the help of a French engineer, Washburn not only improved the method but made his product the best flour available in America. When Pillsbury adopted the same technique, Minneapolis became the country's flour-milling center.

In 1878 the Association was reorganized to appease farmers who found its business practices unfair. James S. Bell succeeded Washburn as head of the Washburn Crosby Company, ousting Washburn's heirs, and the mill prospered through the turn of the century. In 1928, the year General Mills was formed, the company had 5,800 employees and annual sales of $123 million. Its strongest products were Gold Medal Flour, Softasilk Cake Flour, and Wheaties, a recently introduced ready-to-eat cereal.

Bell's son, James Ford, was responsible for creating General Mills in 1928 by consolidating the Washburn mill with several other major flour-milling companies around the country, including the Red Star Milling Company, the Sperry Milling Company, and the Larrowe Milling Company. Within five months Ford had collected 27 companies, making General Mills (GM) the largest flour-milling company in the world. As a part of GM, these mills kept their operational independence but left advertising and product development to General Mills headquarters. This consolidation was well timed, as it gave the company the strength to survive and even prosper through the Depression, when earnings grew steadily and stock in the company was stable.

Bell's research emphasis put General Mills in a strong position for the changing demands of increasingly urban consumers. The company soon introduced Bisquick, the first baking mix, and another ready-to-eat cereal, Cheerios, which 50 years later would be the best-selling cereal in America.

Bell's early interest in diversification and technology made mobilization for World War II easier. General Mills' factories were restructured to produce equipment for the navy, medicinal alcohol, and bags to make into sandbags, as well as the expected dehydrated food. In 1942 Donald D. Davis, president of GM since James Bell moved to chairman in 1934, resigned to head the War Production Board.

Henry Bullis, who began at the company as a mill hand after World War I, replaced him. Following Bell's industrial lead, Bullis immediately entered the animal-feed-industry by processing soybeans, a venture which ultimately became GM's chemical division.

Postwar demand for consumer foods allowed the company to de-emphasize industrial activity and to concentrate on the success of its cereals and cake mixes. Consumers demanded less time in the kitchen and continued to buy foods that required less preparation. Ready-to-eat cereals, now the company's staple, grew dramatically, and more brands were introduced.

Throughout the 1920s Bell and his associates had invested heavily in advertising, which was becoming a significant force in selling products to a national market. Betty Crocker, created in 1921, was a legacy from Washburn Crosby. By 1928 Betty Crocker's name, signature, and radio voice had been introduced in connection with General Mills' consumer goods. General Mills also sponsored radio programs and pioneered the use of athlete endorsements on its own radio station, WCCO.

The postwar consumer's interest in convenience complemented General Mills' growing advertising efforts. The company continued to refine its advertising methods after World War II, and promotions like the *Betty Crocker Cookbook* and advertisements on TV, an exciting new medium at the time, helped to increase sales and consumer recognition of the company. Capitalizing on its research and media prominence, the company soon held the second position in breakfast-food sales.

Another career GM man, Charles H. Bell, rose to the presidency in 1952. Since advertising had become the main force in marketing its various brands, centralization had crept into the organization. Bell found it necessary to reassign management decisions closer to operations. In 1958 he moved headquarters out of downtown Minneapolis and into suburban Golden Valley. Still stronger changes were needed, but the company was hesitant. GM's 1940s ventures into electronics and appliances had failed, and the company had recently begun to post losses in animal feeds and flour milling. Consumer foods remained the main moneymaker, but GM's stock value dropped to $1.25 a share in 1962, its lowest point in 12 years.

Bell recruited an outsider, Edwin W. Rawlings, in 1959, and two years later Rawlings was appointed president. Rawlings reevaluated company output and shook up management positions. The family flour market was declining 3% a year, and Rawlings decided consumer preferences had shifted once again. Although the company was then the largest flour miller in the world and flour made up greatest volume of output, Rawlings closed half of GM's mills and renewed the company's commitment to packaged foods by introducing food-service products for restaurants and hotels. He also divested its interests in electronics, appliances, formula feeds, and other smaller operations. These actions caused a short-term, five-year sales decline for the company.

Next he began a series of acquisitions that would alter corporate structure for the next 20 years and provide two decades of continual earnings growth. Snack foods entered the company's portfolio with the purchase of Morton Foods, Inc. in 1964. In 1966 came the Tom Huston Peanut Company, and in 1968 General Mills went abroad with the purchase of Smiths Food Group, Ltd. of England and Belgium. The French Biscuiterie Nantaise soon followed, as did snack-food companies in Latin America and Japan.

Other major acquisitions were Gorton's, a frozen-fish company, and an aggressive move into the toy and game industry with Rainbow Crafts (Play-Doh), Kenner, and Parker Brothers, all in 1968. In ten years international toy operations would comprise one-third of the company's sales, at $482.3 million. General Mills was no longer the world's largest miller, but it was now the world's largest toy manufacturer.

Early in 1969 the Federal Trade Commission issued a consent order blocking General Mills from further acquisitions within the snack-food industry. At the time of purchase, both Morton and Tom Huston were among the top-ten producers of potato and corn chips.

During his seven years as GM chief, Rawlings managed to double the company's earnings and bring consumer foods to 80% of total sales, up from 45%. Although Rawlings wanted another outsider to succeed him, the board of directors chose James P. McFarland in 1969. General Mills was the only company McFarland had ever worked for, and in choosing him the corporation renewed its commitment to balance and stability.

Seeking controlled growth, McFarland slowed, but did not stop, acquisitions. The first of many clothing-company purchases was David Crystal, Inc. (Lacoste clothing) in 1969. Along with the purchase of Monet Jewelry in the same year, the purchase introduced General Mills to specialty retailing. Although the company missed the growth of fast-food opportunities, purchasing and developing the Red Lobster Restaurant chain would eventually make the new restaurant group General Mills' second-largest division.

McFarland, an experienced salesman, involved himself with day-to-day operations and left long-term planning to operating chief James A. Summer. In his first two years as CEO, McFarland saw sales rise from $885 million to $1.1 billion and operating profits from $37.5 million to $44 million. His goal was to reach $2 billion in sales by 1976. Sales that year were actually $2.6 billion, four times the 1969 level, with earnings of more than $100 million. He then announced E. Robert Kinney as his successor.

Like most quickly expanding companies of this time period, however, not all of GM's forays were successful. Between 1950 and 1986, General Mills made 86 acquisitions in new industries; 73% of those made by 1975 had been divested within five years. A profitable core business in consumer foods eased the burden of these failed efforts.

General Mills' advertising budget is typically as large as its earnings. Although spending less than it did in the late 1970s and early 1980s, General Mills still ranks as the thirteenth largest spender in all media, at $572 million a year. Being such a highly visible company has not always provided favorable attention.

In the early 1970s the Federal Trade Commission (FTC) attempted to dismiss GM's 1968 acquisition of Gorton's. The block was lifted in 1973. Later, by allying itself with General Foods, the firm succeeded in blocking a 1977 FTC proposal to forbid advertisements aimed at children. Late in 1980, the FTC again filed a complaint against cereal companies, this time an antitrust suit following a ten-year investigation. It charged that between 1958 and 1972 cereal manufacturers had an average after-tax profit of 19.8%, compared to a general manufacturing average of 8.9% and suggested that Kellogg Company, General Mills, and General Foods Corporation shared a monopoly over the cereal industry. The charges were dismissed in 1981 after the companies had lobbied for and won congressional favor.

By heavily promoting its brands, the company did well in the 1970s, reporting gains in the toy division and the tripling of sales for consumer foods. Between 1973 and 1978, sales increased $1.7 billion. Of this growth, 41% came from new products developed internally, 15% from acquisitions, and 18% from expansion of restaurant and retail centers. General Mills' management system, in which one manager oversees the production, marketing, and sales of each brand, also got credit for some of the increase. After the 1977 sale of the chemical division, General Mills divided its business into food processing, restaurants, games and toys, fashion, and specialty retailing.

In 1981 H. Brewster Atwater Jr. became president. The following year was a solid one for the company, as consumer foods, restaurants, toys, fashion, and retailing reported sales increases of between 12% and 24%. However, retailing profit was half that of its previous year, and although the toy and game division had grown, the toy industry worldwide had decreased 2.9%.

Izod Lacoste also performed well. With $400 million in sales, General Mills intended to develop more items under the label. But by 1985 sales had dropped to $225 million, and the company hoped to cut overhead in order to break even at $180 million by 1986.

In 1985 the largest toymaker in the world divested items representing over 25% of its sales, including toys, fashion, and non-apparel retailing. Former President Kinney became head of the spun-off Kenner Parker Toys Inc. The other spin-off, called The Fashion Company, consisted of Monet jewelry, Izod Lacoste, and Ship 'n Shore. The company kept its furniture group (Pennsylvania House, Kittinger) for future sale. Also kept was Eddie Bauer, despite its reported loss because of excess inventory. General Mills reported a net loss of $72 million due to the restructuring and a 21% increase in advertising expenses.

As expected by analysts, General Mills quickly recovered. Earnings were up to $222 million by 1987. Its core businesses were the Big G cereals, Red Lobster, and Talbot's in its consumer-foods, restaurants, and specialty-retailing divisions.

The consolidation process begun in 1985 continued in the latter half of the 1980s. Pared down somewhat, the company originally planned to expand its remaining retailing operations. But the takeover climate of the late 1980s and a disappointing Christmas in 1987 forced the company to exit retailing altogether by selling Eddie Bauer and Talbot's.

General Mills has divested itself of nearly 50 businesses since 1976, but its surviving businesses have a firm footing in their markets. More than 90% of the company's food sales come from products with a first or second place market share position. Streamlining has also allowed the company to keep up with the rapid pace of new-product development. From 1985 to 1988, 24% to 29% of the food divisions' growth came from new products.

General Mills now focuses on its remaining restaurants, its cereals, and its Betty Crocker brand foods. Food production guarantees a return that can be used in the expensive planning necessary to tap growing demand for restaurants. Keeping its range in the restaurant industry narrow, General Mills finds it growth in sales-per-unit exceeds the industry norm. Red Lobster, for instance, has yet to turn in a decline in average sales-per-unit.

GM has also increased its share in the fast-growing cereal market, boosed by the oat-bran craze of the late 1980s (Cheerios' market share alone climbed 3.1% in one year) and the accompanying breakfast-food boom. General Mills alone among top cereal producers was prepared for these trends. During the 1990s, General Mills should begin to expand into international markets, a sector which rival Kellogg has been exploiting for years.

In 1989 General Mills began showing return for its restructuring efforts. Sluggish since 1983, the company's stock rose 20% toward the end of the decade. Intent on remaining independent despite the acquisition of several of its main competitors, large-scale, tangential acquisitions are unlikely as General Mills faces the 1990s more tightly focused on the food industry than it has been in decades.

Principal Subsidiaries: Alternative Care Capital Corp. (50%); Biscuiterie Nantaise - BN S.A.; General Mills Export Co.; General Mills Europe Co.; General Mills Products Corp.; General Mills Finance, Inc.; General Mills Restaurants, Inc.; GMD Distributing, Inc.; Gold Medal Insurance Co.; Vroman Foods, Inc.; Yoplait USA, Inc.

Further Reading: Kennedy, Gerald S. *Minutes & Moments in the Life of General Mills*, Minneapolis, 1971.

GEORGE A. HORMEL AND COMPANY

501 16th Avenue
Post Office Box 800
Austin, Minnesota 55912
U.S.A.
(507) 437–5611

Public Company
Incorporated: 1901
Employees: 8,000
Sales: $2.3 billion
Stock Index: American

The meat packing industry has always been volatile: profit margins are narrow and companies are heavily dependent on the fluctuating supply and price of livestock. In the 1960s the industry grew even more competitive when new meat packing companies entered the market. By undercutting labor costs, they forced many old-line meat packing companies to disband and forced others to cut wages and streamline their operations. In the 1980s consumers began to eat less meat and meat producers for the first time had to struggle to make their products appealing. Despite these factors, however, George A. Hormel and Company continues to grow and prosper, largely because it is one of the most innovative companies in the meat packing industry.

Hormel looks very different today than it did even ten years ago. It has all but abandoned its participation in the labor-intensive, low-margin slaughtering segment of the meat industry. It has opened a $100 million, state-of-the-art plant in Austin, Minnesota that features robotic technology and automatic ham deboners; it has opened a frozen foods division and has added turkey and fish to its list of products; and most significantly, it has evolved into a market-driven, "total" food company that manufactures value-added foods.

In an 18-month period in the late 1980s, Hormel introduced 134 new products, including Top Shelf, an unfrozen, microwaveable entree with a shelf life of 18 months. CEO Richard L. Knowlton considers this "one of the most important products ever introduced by Hormel. It represents a revolutionary breakthrough in packaging technology and offers consumers a new level of convenience." With new products such as these, Hormel has overcome a period of sluggish sales and earnings between 1979 and 1984 to record net earnings of $60.1 million in 1988, up from $29.4 million in 1984.

Hormel's founder, George A. Hormel, could not have imagined such a future when he borrowed $500 in 1887 to form a retail meat market and pork packing business with his partner, Albrect Friedrich. But he did establish a powerful precedent when he refused to be complacent about their early success and pushed ahead with his plans to set up and operate a packing house. He and Friedrich agreed to disband their partnership in September of 1891, and within a few months Hormel and employee George Petersen had transformed a small, abandoned creamery into a meat packing plant complete with smokehouse and slaughterhouse. In addition, he opened the Hormel Provision Market to sell his products; it quickly became the town's largest and most successful retail meat business.

Faced with low profit margins and competition from large meat packers who could afford state-of-the-art refrigeration facilities, Hormel made expansion his first priority. Within the first few years his two brothers and other members of his family had joined the business, allowing George Hormel to put down his cleaver and devote himself exclusively to management. In 1899 Hormel spent $40,000 to upgrade his facilities, building a new refrigeration facility, new pumps and engines, an electric elevator, smokehouses, and a hog kill. In 1901 the company acquired several acres of adjacent land, and two years later it constructed additional facilities such as a casing processing room and a machine shop. In 1908 it also opened a new office facility, which the company used for more than 60 years.

During this period of expansion Hormel also worked to refine and improve its products. In 1903 it registered its first patent, "Dairy Brand," with the U.S. Patent Office. In 1915 Hormel began to produce several lines of dry sausage, a product that proved particularly popular with ethnic consumers.

In an effort to increase sales volume, Hormel sent salesmen outside of Austin to set up branches and distribution centers. By 1920 the company operated branches in Minneapolis, Duluth, St. Paul, San Antonio, Dallas, Atlanta, Birmingham, and Chicago. In 1905 George Hormel travelled to England to establish the foundation for an export business. Between 1905 and the end of World War I, exports grew to constitute about a third of the company's yearly volume.

The Hormel Company participated fully in America's World War I effort. To control the price and supply of meats, the government regulated the meat packing industry. Hormel expanded its labor force and the hours they worked to help satisfy the increased demand for meat both at home and abroad. With so many American men, including George Hormel's son Jay, away at war, the company employed women for the first time in its history. In addition to producing meat for the war effort, Hormel employees bought Liberty bonds and donated an hour's wages per day to the Red Cross.

When Jay Hormel returned from the war, he rejoined the company and uncovered a scandal that very nearly put Hormel out of business. The company's assistant controller, "Cy" Thomson, had embezzled more than $1 million from the company and had channeled it into several poultry farms. The company had borrowed $3 million that year for operating expenses and hoped to repay the sum at the end of the year. At year end, however, they were unable to do so, and George Hormel had to confront his bankers and convince them to extend the loan.

The embezzlement scandal provided George Hormel with additional incentive to fortify his company. He did so by arranging for more reliable capital management, by dismissing unproductive employees, and by continuing to develop new products. In 1926, after years of research, Hormel introduced "Hormel Flavor-Sealed Ham," America's first canned ham.

In 1929 Jay C. Hormel became the company's second president, and his father, George, became chairman of the board. Under the new president the company continued to expand its product line: some of the company's best-known products—Dinty Moore beef stew (1935), Hormel chili (1936), and SPAM luncheon meat (1937)—entered the market and became extremely popular.

The company survived a bitter labor strike in 1933, during which disgruntled union employees, armed with clubs, physically removed Jay Hormel from the company's general offices and shut off the plant's refrigeration system. The two parties reached a compromise within three days. Soon, the company gained recognition for its innovative labor relations policies. Jay Hormel developed the "Annual Wage Plan," under which employees were paid weekly, their working hours fluctuated according to need, their employment was considered permanent, and they were guaranteed a year's notice before they could be terminated. In addition, the company introduced profit sharing, merit pay, a pension plan, and a joint earnings plan. Under this plan, in 1983 Hormel employees received more than $4 million.

During his tenure Jay Hormel co-founded the Hormel Foundation, which controls the company through holdings of its capital stock, and which serves "religious, charitable, scientific, literary, or educational purposes." This foundation funds the Hormel Institute, a research facility located at the University of Minnesota. Presently this Institute conducts highly respected research on fats and other lipids and how they affect human life.

During World War II, the Hormel Company became a "war facility" and once again increased its meat production. By 1945 Hormel was selling 65% of its total production to the U.S. Government. SPAM, Hormel's canned spiced ham and ground pork product, became the staple of U.S. servicemen throughout the world; in 1941 Hormel was producing 15 million cans a week, and the government was distributing it under the lend-lease program. Overfamiliarity bred substantial contempt and ridicule during and after the war, but the product has demonstrated uncanny resilience: by 1959, Hormel had sold over 1 billion cans of SPAM.

When George Hormel died in 1946, Jay Hormel took his place as chairman of the board of directors and H.H. Corey became Hormel's third president. During the eight years of his presidency, the company continued to renovate and upgrade its existing plants and acquire new facilities. It purchased several new packing operations—in Mitchell, South Dakota; Fort Dodge, Iowa; and Fremont, Nebraska. With the wartime restrictions on tin now lifted and with a tremendous demand for Hormel's canned meat products, the company improved its canning facilities in its Dallas and Houston plants and arranged for independent canning companies to manufacture Hormel products. In addition, Hormel made a concerted effort to make better use of its raw material, and in 1947 the company began to produce gelatin from pork skins.

Hormel's product line expanded along with the company's facilities. Mary Kitchen Roast Beef Hash, Corned Beef Hash, and Spaghetti and Beef in Sauce appeared in 1949, along with a new line of meat spreads.

With its constant expansion, the company had to consider how to dispose of its increased waste material. Hormel Company researchers developed an anaerobic digestive system that removed waste cleanly and efficiently. In 1946 the company financed a $2.25 million sewage system that it shares with the Austin community.

In 1954 Jay Hormel died, and Corey assumed his chair on the board of directors, while R. F. Gray succeeded Corey as president. He held this position for ten years, during which the company continued to pursue quality and efficiency. Hormel added several more slaughtering, processing, and packing facilities throughout the country, and in 1965 it added a new 75,000-square-foot, automated sausage manufacturing building to its Austin plant.

Several new products appeared in this decade as well. In 1960 the company introduced its "Famous Foods of the World" line. The following year Little Sizzlers' sausage entered the market, followed two years later by a fully-cooked sausage product, Brown 'n Serve. The largest success of the decade, however, was the Hormel Cure 81 Ham, a skinless, boneless, trim, cured ham with the shank removed.

After another decade of progressive growth under two different presidents, M. B. Thompson and I. J. Holton, the directors realized that in order to remain competitive in the industry, Hormel needed to undertake a wholesale renovation of its Austin plant. In 1975 the company began planning this new facility, which opened in 1982. At more than a million square feet, it is among the largest and most productive in the industry. Hormel continued to diversify its product lines as well, introducing precooked bacon and three new varieties of Perma Fresh luncheon meats. By 1980 Hormel was producing over 700 different products.

Though this new facility was capable of processing more than two million hogs a year and producing more than 200 million pounds of products annually, the industry began to shrink in the 1980s and Hormel began to feel the effects. With a 40% increase in the price of hogs, Hormel was pinched. It asked employees to accept wage cuts in Austin of more than $2 an hour. In 1985, the union decided to strike. Fifteen hundred workers left their jobs. Under the glare of national publicity, striking workers harassed the 700 nonunion workers whom Hormel hired five months later. In 1986 former employees committed 300 acts of strike-related vandalism. Five hundred union workers eventually returned to work, but the others were either dismissed or were forced into early retirement.

The wounds from this bitter strike were slow to heal,

but the Hormel Company has moved ahead, and under President, Chairman, and CEO Richard L. Knowlton, it is adjusting to a rapidly changing market by moving away from the traditional meat-packing business and its many problems and concentrating on satisfying consumers' appetites for processed foods.

In the late 1980s Hormel focused on the microwaveable-foods market, and by 1989 Top Shelf vacuum-packed unrefrigerated meals were in nationwide distribution. After acquiring Jennie-O Foods, a turkey-processing company, in late 1986, Hormel went on to acquire a small producer of fresh marinated chicken-breast entrees in 1988 and targeted its fish operations for expansion in an effort to exploit the more health-conscious market. Altogether Hormel entered the 1990s well positioned in its new processed-foods niche.

Principal Subsidiaries: Algona Food Equipment Company; Hormel International Corporation; Farm Fresh Catfish Company, Inc; FDL Marketing, Inc., Jennie-O Foods, Inc.; Dold Foods, Inc; Catalogue Marketing, Inc.

Further Reading: Dougherty, Richard. *In Quest of Quality: Hormel's First 75 Years*, Austin, Minnesota, George A. Hormel Company, 1966; *Mill on the Willow*, Lake Mills, Iowa, Graphic Publishing, 1984.

H. J. HEINZ COMPANY

U.S. Steel Building
600 Grant Street
Pittsburgh, Pennsylvania 15219
U.S.A.
(412) 456-5700

Public Company
Incorporated: 1900
Employees: 36,200
Sales: $5.8 billion (1989)
Stock Index: New York Pacific

To most people, ketchup and Heinz go together like pork and beans—another Heinz product. Ketchup is the most ubiquitous condiment in America, and the H.J. Heinz Company has been bottling it for more than a century. But Heinz is far more than ketchup. It manufactures thousands of food products in plants on six continents. The products of its British subsidiary are so well known in that country that many Britons regard Heinz as an English company. In the United States, Heinz ranks number-one in ketchup, vinegar, relish, tuna, and frozen-potato sales and is a major presence in the baby food, canned-bean, and pet-food markets.

This vast food empire sprouted from a Pennsylvania garden when eight-year-old Henry John Heinz began selling produce from his family's plot to nearby neighbors. At ten he used a wheelbarrow, and by the time he was 16 Heinz had several employees and was making three deliveries a week to Pittsburgh grocers. Born in 1844 to German immigrant parents, Heinz was the oldest of nine children. He grew up in Sharpsburg, Pennsylvania, near Pittsburgh, and after graduating from Duff's Business College became the bookkeeper of his father's brickyard. At age 21 he became a partner. (Heinz retained an interest in bricks all his life—he personally supervised the buying and laying of brick for his company's buildings, and his office desk was often piled with brick samples acquired on his travels.)

In 1869, at the age of 25, Heinz and L. C. Noble formed a partnership called Heinz, Noble & Company in Sharpsburg to sell bottled horseradish. Horseradish was soon followed by sauerkraut, vinegar, and pickles.

Following the panic of 1873 and subsequent economic chaos, the business failed in 1875, but Heinz quickly regrouped, and the following year started afresh with the determination to repay his creditors. With his brother John and cousin Frederick as partners and himself as manager, Heinz formed the partnership of F.&J. Heinz to manufacture condiments, pickles, and other prepared food. The business prospered, and Heinz made good on his obligations. In 1888 the partnership was reorganized as the H.J. Heinz Company. Soon Heinz was known throughout the country as the "pickle king."

Small, energetic, and ambitious, the pickle king was a cheerful man with courtly, old-fashioned manners. Heinz exuded enthusiasm, whether for work, family, travel, religious activities, or good horses, and had a passion for involving others in his interests. According to his biographer, Robert C. Alberts, Heinz once installed an 800-pound, 14½-foot, 150-year-old live alligator in a glass tank atop one of his factory buildings so that his employees might enjoy the sight as much as he had in Florida.

In the late 1800s, the typical American diet was bland and monotonous. The Heinz Company set out to spice it up with a multitude of products. The phrase "57 Varieties" was coined in 1892. Tomato soup and beans in tomato sauce were quickly added to the product line. Even as "57 Varieties" became a household slogan, the company already had more than 60 products. At the World's Columbian Exposition in Chicago in 1893, Heinz had the largest exhibit of any American food company.

By 1900, the H.J. Heinz Company occupied a major niche in American business. It was first in the production of ketchup, pickles, mustard, and vinegar and fourth in the packing of olives. Overall the company made more than 200 products. Still, Heinz liked the lilt of his original slogan and in 1900 put it up in lights in New York City's first large electric sign, at Fifth Avenue and 23rd Street. Twelve hundred lights illuminated a 40-foot-long green pickle and its advertising message.

Heinz's clever merchandising won him a reputation as an advertising genius, but he did not allow his ambitions to overcome his religious convictions. During his lifetime, in deference to the Sabbath, Heinz advertisements never ran on Sundays.

Heinz Company factories were considered models in the industry, both in their facilities and their treatment of workers. The company received many awards, and Harry W. Sherman, grand secretary of the National Brotherhood of Electrical Workers of America, remarked after visiting a Heinz plant that it was "a utopia for working men."

Henry Heinz went to England in 1886 carrying a sample case, and came home with orders for seven products. By 1905 the company had opened its first factory in England. In 1906 the Pure Food and Drug Act was vigorously opposed by most food manufacturers, but Heinz, who understood the importance of consumer confidence in the purity of processed foods, was all for it, and even sent his son to Washington, D.C. to campaign for its passage.

By 1919, when Henry Heinz died at age 75, the company's 6,500 employees and 25 branch factories were processing the harvest of some 100,000 acres.

Heinz was succeeded as president of the company by his son, Howard, who began his career with H.J. Heinz as advertising manager in 1905 and became sales manager in 1907. Howard Heinz remained president until his death in 1941. In 1939 *Fortune* estimated total sales for the still privately owned company at $105 million.

By the time Howard's son H. J. Heinz II (known as Jack) became president of the company at his father's death, he had worked in all the company's divisions, from the canning factories to the administrative offices. He chose to launch his career as a pickle-salter for $1 a day in the Plymouth, Indiana plant. Later he became a cleanup man, then a salesman for H.J. Heinz Company, Ltd. in England. In 1935, fresh out of Cambridge University, Jack Heinz was sent by his father to establish a plant in Australia. Heinz-Australia later became that country's biggest food-processing plant.

From 1941, when Jack took over, to 1946, H. J. Heinz's sales nearly doubled. That year Heinz made its first public stock offering and revealed that its net profit was over $4 million. Foreign sales of baked beans and ketchup, particularly in England, contributed substantially to the company's success. During World War II, Jack Heinz was active in food relief and personally made four wartime trips to England to examine food problems there. The company insignia went to war too; the 57th Squadron of the 446th Army Air Force chose for its emblem a winged pickle marked "57."

Jack Heinz's tenure was marked by expansion of the company, both internationally and at home. Subsidiaries were launched in the Netherlands, Venezuela, Japan, Italy, and Portugal. In 1960 and 1961, the H.J. Heinz Company acquired the assets of Reymer & Bros., Inc. and Hachmeister, Inc. Star-Kist Foods was acquired in 1963 and Ore-Ida Foods, Inc. in 1965.

During the 25 years that H. J. Heinz II was chief executive, the food industry changed greatly. The era was marked by the rise of supermarket chains and the development of new distribution and marketing systems. In 1966, H. J. Heinz II stepped down as president and CEO, though he retained his position as chairman of the board until his death in February, 1987.

In 1969, R. Burt Gookin, then CEO of Heinz, made Anthony J. F. O'Reilly president of the company's profitable British subsidiary. O'Reilly, who was managing director of Irish Sugar Company at the time, shook up the company by working 14-hour days and stressing a policy of winning through effort. O'Reilly is an uncommon executive—he has been, among other things, a world-class rugby player.

In 1973 O'Reilly became president of the parent company, and in 1976, CEO. Shortly after the death of H. J. Heinz II, he was also made chairman. From the beginning, O'Reilly stressed the importance of strong financial results. Some sources blamed a pressure-filled atmosphere for the events that led to the revelation in 1979 that managers of several subsidiaries had been misstating quarterly earnings since 1971 to meet their target goals and impress top management.

Overall, O'Reilly's achievements have been impressive, however. The timely acquisition of Hubinger Company in 1975 put Heinz in a position to cash in on the demand for high-fructose corn syrup when the price of sugar soared. In 1978, O'Reilly acquired Weight Watchers International just ahead of the fitness craze that swept America.

At the same time that the company was branching out into new products, O'Reilly was cutting back on traditional businesses. By 1980 Heinz had increased volume but halved its number of plants from 14 to seven and reduced employment by 18%. O'Reilly also gave up the battle with Campbell Soup Company for the retail soup market. And when generic products hit the supermarket shelves, Heinz countered not by producing for the generics industry but by "nickel and diming it," as O'Reilly said. For example, Heinz switched to thinner glass bottles that cut the cost not only of packaging but also of transportation. When imports began to undersell StarKist tuna, StarKist decreased the size of the tuna can, just as Hershey had downsized its chocolate bar when cocoa prices soared. This ploy netted StarKist $7 million in savings. Other nickel-and-dime cost savings have come from eliminating back labels from bottles, reclaiming heat, and reusing water.

O'Reilly's strategy is to pare costs to the bone and to use the savings to beef up marketing, primarily advertising, in an effort to increase market share. At the same time, Heinz is pursuing a cautious acquisition policy. By the mid-1980s, the company had spent $416 million to acquire more than 20 companies. Return on equity increased from 9% in 1972 to 23.3% in 1986.

O'Reilly's cost-cutting war has included a threat to go to contract manufacturers rather than his own plants if the same products could be purchased elsewhere for less. Such tough talk elicited substantial concessions from labor unions in 1986. O'Reilly's hard-nosed, bottom-line strategies won Heinz recognition as one of the country's five best-managed companies in 1986.

In 1988, Heinz bid $200 million for Bumble Bee Seafoods, the third-largest tuna company in the country. The purchase would have given Heinz, whose StarKist brand already ranked number one, more than 50% of the domestic tuna market. Accordingly, the Justice Department prevented the purchase on antitrust grounds. Also in 1988, Heinz reorganized StarKist Foods into StarKist Seafood and Heinz Pet Products in order to strengthen seafood operations for a push abroad. In pet foods, Heinz, already a leading canned cat food producer, strengthened its dog food position through the acquisition of several regional brands.

In overseas markets, Heinz has also begun to expand into the Third World. It became the first foreign investor in Zimbabwe when it acquired a controlling interest in Olivine Industries, Inc. in 1982. Heinz also has joint ventures in Korea and China, and in 1987 the company bought a controlling interest in Win-Chance Foods of Thailand. Win-Chance produces baby food and milk products; Heinz plans to add—what else?—ketchup.

Heinz has already demonstrated a willingness to run lean and to shed unprofitable enterprises. With the rising number of two-income families, consumer demand for convenience food is expected to continue to increase. At the same time, shoppers are demanding quality and good taste. Heinz is well positioned to be there—all around the world—to give them what they want.

Principal Subsidiaries: StarKist Seafood Co.; StarKist Samoa, Inc.; Heinz Pet Products Co.; Hubinger Co.; Caribbean Restaurants, Inc. (80%); Cardio-Fitness Corp.; H.J. Heinz Co. of Canada Ltd.; H.J. Heinz Co. Ltd. (U.K.); W. Darlington & Sons, Ltd. (U.K.); Mastar, Inc.; H.J. Heinz Co. Australia Ltd.; California Home Brands Holding, Inc.; H.J. Heinz Co. Belgium S.A.; H.J. Heinz GmbH (West Germany); H.J. Heinz S.A.R.L. (France); Johma Holding International B.V. (Netherlands); S.A.H.J. Heinz Central Europe N.V. (Belgium); Liven International S.p.A. (Italy); Marie Elizabeth-Productos Alimentares S.A. (Portugal); Pro Pastries, Inc. (Canada); Pro Bakers Ltd.; Scaramellini S.p.A. (Italy); S. Orlando S.A. (Spain); Frutsi Concentrate Co. (Puerto Rico) (80%); Montrose Canned Foods Ltd. (U.K.); Heinz Japan Ltd.; Alimentos Heinz C.A. (Venezuela); Industrias de Alimentaceo Idal, Ltda. (Portugal); Ore-Ida Foods, Inc.; Epicurean Foods & Beverages Pty. Ltd. (Australia); Galco Food Products Ltd. (Canada); Somycel, S.A. (France) (50%); H.J. Heinz B.V. (The Netherlands); Gagliardi Brothers, Inc.; Plasmon Dietetici Alimentari S.p.A. (Italy); Kgalagardi Soap Industries Ltd. (Botswana); Foodways National, Inc.; Weight Watchers International; Nadler-Werke GmbH (West Germany); Ets. Paul Paulet (France) (80%); Fratelli Sperlari S.p.A. (Italy) (80%); Olivine Industries (Private) Ltd. (Zimbabwe) (51%); Heinz-UFE Ltd. (Republic of China) (60%); Seoul-Heinz Ltd. (57%).

Further Reading: Alberts, Robert C. *The Good Provider*, Boston, Houghton Mifflin, 1973.

Hershey Foods

HERSHEY FOODS CORPORATION

100 Mansion Road East
Hershey, Pennsylvania 17033
U.S.A.
(717) 534–4000

Public Company
Incorporated: 1908 as Hershey Chocolate Company
Employees: 12,100
Sales: $2.17 billion
Stock Index: New York

The name Hershey is synonymous with chocolate, yet the company's founder made his first fortune by manufacturing caramel. Today, Hershey makes and markets chocolate and licorice candies, grocery products like cocoa, unsweetened chocolate, chocolate drinks and mixes, and fudge sauce, as well as eight regional pasta brands that account for about 10% of Hershey's sales. Hershey is the largest confectionery company in the United States, the maker of half of the top 20 candy brands in the country. It was pushed to number two in the 1970s by Mars, Inc., but recently won top spot again after its 1988 purchase of the American confectionery business of the British company Cadbury Schweppes.

Milton S. Hershey was born in 1857 in central Pennsylvania. As a young boy Hershey was apprenticed to a Lancaster, Pennsylvania candymaker for four years. When he finished this apprenticeship in 1876, at age 19, Hershey went to Philadelphia to open his own candy shop. After six years, however, the shop failed, and Hershey moved to Denver, Colorado. There he went to work for a caramel manufacturer, where he discovered that caramel made with fresh milk was a decided improvement on the standard recipe. In 1883 Hershey left Denver for Chicago, then New Orleans and New York, until in 1886 he finally returned to Lancaster. There he established the Lancaster Caramel Company to produce "Hershey's Crystal A" caramels that would "melt in your mouth." Hershey had a successful business at last.

In 1893 Hershey went to the Chicago International Exposition, where he was fascinated by some German chocolate-making machinery on display. He soon installed the chocolate equipment in Lancaster and in 1895 began to sell chocolate-covered caramels and other chocolate novelties. At that time, Hershey also began to develop the chocolate bars and other cocoa products that were to make him famous.

In 1900 Hershey decided to concentrate on chocolate, which he felt sure would become a big business. That year he sold his caramel company for $1 million, retaining the chocolate equipment and the rights to manufacture chocolate. He decided to locate his new company in Derry Church, the central Pennsylvania village where he had been born, and where there would be a plentiful milk supply. In 1903 Hershey broke ground for the Hershey chocolate factory, which today is still the largest chocolate-manufacturing plant in the world.

Before this factory was completed, in 1905, Hershey produced a variety of fancy chocolates. But with the new factory, Hershey decided to mass-produce a limited number of products that he could sell at a low price. The famous Hershey's Milk Chocolate Bar, the first mass-produced chocolate product, was born.

In 1906 the village of Derry Church was renamed Hershey. The town was not simply named after the man or the company: it was Milton Hershey's creation, the beneficiary of and heir to his energy and his fortune. Hershey had begun planning a whole community that would fulfill all the needs of its inhabitants at the same time that he planned his factory. A bank, school, recreational park, churches, trolley system, and even a zoo soon followed, and the town was firmly established by its tenth anniversary. One of Hershey's most enduring contributions was the Hershey Industrial School for orphans, which he established in 1909 with his wife Catherine. After Catherine's death in 1915, the childless Hershey in 1918 gave the school Hershey company stock valued at about $60 million. Today the school, which became the Milton Hershey School in 1951, still owns 42% of Hershey Foods Corporation's stock and controls 77% of the company's voting stock.

In 1907 Hershey's Kisses were first produced, and the next year, in 1908, the Hershey Chocolate Company was formally chartered. In 1911, its sales of $5 million were more than eight times the $600,000 made ten years earlier at the company's start.

The Hershey company continued to prosper, producing its milk chocolate bars (with and without almonds), Kisses, cocoa, and baking chocolate. In 1921 sales reached $20 million, and in 1925 Hershey introduced the Mr. Goodbar Chocolate Bar, a chocolate bar with peanuts. In 1927 the company was incorporated as the Hershey Chocolate Company and its stock was listed on the New York Stock Exchange.

By 1931, 30 years after the company was established, Hershey was selling $30 million worth of chocolate a year. As the Great Depression cast its shadow on the town of Hershey, Milton Hershey initiated a "grand building campaign" in the 1930s to provide employment in the area. Between 1933 and 1940, Hershey's projects included a 150-room resort hotel, a museum, a cultural center, a sports arena (where the Ice Capades was founded), a stadium, an exotic rose garden, and a modern, windowless, air-conditioned factory and office building. Hershey liked to boast that no one was laid off from the company during the Depression.

Though Hershey's intentions seem to have been wholly sincere, there was always some suspicion about his "company town." Labor strife came to the company in 1937, when it suffered its first strike. Though bitter, the strike was soon settled, and by 1940 the chocolate plant was unionized.

In 1938, another famous chocolate product was introduced: the Krackel Chocolate Bar, a chocolate bar with crisped rice. The next year Hershey's Miniatures, bite-sized chocolate bars in several varieties, were introduced.

During World War II, Hershey helped by creating the Field Ration D, a four-ounce bar that provided 600 calories and wouldn't melt, for soldiers to carry to sustain them when no other food was available. The chocolate factory was turned over to the war effort and produced 500,000 bars a day. Hershey received the army-navy E award from the quartermaster general at the war's end. He died soon after, on October 13, 1945.

After Milton Hershey's death, the chocolate company continued to prosper and maintain its strong position in the chocolate market. By the 1960s, Hershey was recognized as the number-one chocolate producer in America.

With the growth came expansion. In 1963 Hershey broke ground for the construction of two new chocolate factories, in Oakdale, California and Smiths Falls, Ontario. Expansion for Hershey also meant looking for acquisitions, the first of which was the H.B. Reese Candy Company that same year. Also in 1963, the company's president and chairman, Samuel Hinkle, arranged for the founding of the Milton S. Hershey Medical Center of the Pennsylvania State University in Hershey, Pennsylvania.

While the company played a hand in many developments within Pennsylvania, its main endeavor continued to be the food industry—and for the first time non-confectionery food. Among its acquisitions were two pasta manufacturers, San Giorgio Macaroni Inc., in Lebanon, Pennsylvania and Delmonico Foods Inc., in Louisville, Kentucky, in 1966. In 1967 the Cory Corporation, a Chicago-based food-service company, was acquired. Due to its expansions beyond chocolate, the company changed its name in 1968 to the Hershey Foods Corporation. The name change also marked the passing of an era when in 1969 it raised the price of Hershey's candy bars, which had been 5¢ since 1921, to 10¢.

As the 1970s unfolded, changes in American culture forced Hershey Foods Corporation to change also. Before the 1970s the company, heeding the words of its founder that a quality product was the best advertisement, had refused to advertise. Thousands of people who came to tour the chocolate factory each year had spread the world about Milton Hershey and his chocolate—a visitors bureau had been established as early as 1915 to handle tours of the facilities, and by 1970 almost a million people a year visited Hershey.

Word of mouth had served as a valuable source of advertising for Hershey during most of its existence. But as people became more health conscious and the consumption of candy declined, the influence of advertising became a greater factor in the candy business. By 1970, Mars had deposed Hershey as the leader in candy sales, provoking Hershey to launch a national advertising campaign. On July 19, 1970 Hershey's first consumer advertisement, a full-page ad for Hershey's Syrup, appeared in 114 newspapers. Within months, the corporation was running ads on radio and television as well. Also that year, under an agreement with British candymaker Rowntree Mackintosh, Hershey became the American distributor of the Kit Kat Wafer Bar. Hershey introduced a second Rowntree candy, Rolo Caramels, the next year.

In 1973, Hershey's Chocolate World Visitors Center, was opened to educate people about chocolatemaking, with exhibits about tropical cocoa-tree plantations, Pennsylvania Dutch milk farms, and the various stages of the manufacturing process. The facility was established to replace tours of the actual plant, which were discontinued in 1973 due to an overload of traffic.

The Hershey Foods Corporation imports its cocoa beans from cocoa-producing countries around the world and cleans, roasts, and extracts the meat of the bean for processing inside its two-million-square-foot chocolate factory. To produce milk chocolate, the company purchases milk from over 1,000 nearby farms whose cows supply its daily needs. Hershey also is the largest single user of almonds in the United States.

Under the direction of its chief executive officer, William E. Dearden, Hershey adopted an aggressive marketing plan in 1976 to offset its shrinking market share. Dearden, who had grown up in Milton Hershey's orphanage, joined forces with his chief operating officer, Richard A. Zimmerman, to implement a campaign aimed at customers in grocery stores, where half of all candy is sold. Specialty items such as a wide line of miniatures, holiday assortments, and family packs were marketed. A national ad campaign promoting Hershey's Kisses, and the introduction of the Giant Hershey's Kiss in 1978, tripled sales of the product between 1977 and 1984. The Big Block line of 2.2-ounce bars and premium candies such as the Golden Almond Chocolate Bar were also introduced, as were Reese's Pieces Candy and Whatchamacallit and Skor Candy Bars.

Hershey also made plans to diversify, to lessen the company's vulnerability to unstable cocoa-bean and sugar prices. In 1977, Hershey acquired a 16% interest in A.B. Marabou, a Swedish confectionery company, and bought Y&S Candies Inc., the nation's leading manufacturer of licorice. The following year, it bought the Procino-Rossi Corporation (P&R), and in 1979, it acquired the Skinner Macaroni Company to add to its stable of brand-name pastas. In 1984, Hershey purchased American Beauty, another pasta brand, from Pillsbury and formed the Hershey Pasta Group.

Another 1979 acquisition, the Friendly Ice Cream Corporation, a 750-restaurant chain based in New England, tripled the number of employees on Hershey's payroll. After experiencing major structural changes owing to its 1970s expansion, the company implemented an intensive values study to pinpoint and communicate the principles inherent in its corporate culture and history.

In 1982 Hershey opened another plant, in Stuarts Draft, Virginia. The next year it introduced its own brand of chocolate milk, and in 1984 it introduced Golden Almond

Solitaires (chocolate-covered almonds). In 1986, in addition to introducing two new products, the Golden III Chocolate Bar and the Bar None Wafer Bar, Hershey acquired the Dietrich Corporation, the maker of the 5th Avenue Candy Bar, Luden's throat drops, and Mello Mints. Not content with such a year—the first to top $2 billion in sales—in December Hershey purchased G&R Pasta Company, Inc., whose Pastamania brand became the eighth in Hershey's pasta group.

But the acquisitions did not stop there. In June, 1987 Hershey acquired the Canadian candy and nut operations of Nabisco Brands for its subsidiary Hershey Canada Inc. The three main businesses Hershey acquired were Lowney/Moirs, a Canadian chocolate-manufacturing concern; the Canadian chocolate manufacturer of Life Savers and Breath Savers hard candy; and the Planters snack nut business in Canada.

The biggest acquisition of all came in August, 1988, however, when Hershey made a $300 million deal for Peter Paul/Cadbury, an American subsidiary of the British candy and beverage company Cadbury Schweppes PLC. Hershey purchased the operating assets of the company and the rights to manufacture the company's brands, including Peter Paul Mounds and Almond Joy Candy Bars and York Peppermint Patties, and Cadbury products including Cadbury chocolate bars and Cadbury's Creme Eggs, an easter specialty candy. Hershey's economies of scale and clout with retailers will bring an increased profitability to its newly acquired Cadbury lines. This purchase pushed Hershey's share of the candy market from 35% to 44%, and Hershey to the top of the American candy business. At the same time, Hershey decided to sell the Friendly Ice Cream Corporation to concentrate on its core confectionery businesses. The company was sold to Tennessee Restaurant in September for $374 million.

The decline in candy consumption that began after World War II, as a prosperous America found its waistline expanding uncomfortably, accelerated during the 1970s as the fitness craze began. But in the 1980s, this trend has reversed. Candy consumption increased from 16 pounds per capita in 1980 to 19.5 pounds in 1988. Hershey's highly successful marketing strategy, based on Milton Hershey's contention that a quality product is the best advertising and bolstered by aggressive and successful new product introductions, has put the company in a very strong position to take advantage of this trend.

Principal Subsidiaries: Hershey Canada Inc.; Fifth Avenue Confectionery Co.; Luden's, Inc.; Queen Anne, Inc.

Further Reading: Castner, Charles Schuyler. *One of a Kind*, Hershey, Pennsylvania, Dairy Literary Guild, 1983.

Hillsdown Holdings plc

HILLSDOWN HOLDINGS, PLC

Hillsdown House
32 Hampstead High Street
London NW3 1QD
United Kingdom
(01) 794–0677

Public Company
Incorporated: 1975
Employees: 40,000
Sales: £3 billion (US$5.43 billion)
Stock Index: London

Although Hillsdown Holdings is the United Kingdom's largest egg packer, poultry and meat processor, and producer of canned goods, few Britons have ever heard of the company. Hillsdown Holdings, as its name implies, is a holding company for some 200 independently operated subsidiaries that together stock the shelves of Britain's largest food retailers.

Established in 1975, Hillsdown's growth has been nothing short of phenomenal. The company's founders, Harry Solomon and David Thompson, were a lawyer and a butcher respectively when they met in 1964. Solomon soon became Thompson's legal counsel, advising him as he purchased interests in other companies. In the mid-1970s, they decided to form their own company to manage their investments in such fields as timber, stationery, and securities more efficiently. They named their company Hillsdown, after Thompson's house; rented an office; hired an accountant; and set out to wring value from businesses where others saw none. In so doing, Thompson and Solomon built a company that has had a significant impact on food production in the United Kingdom.

Hillsdown Holdings' acquisitions began in earnest in 1981, when the company made its first big purchase, of Lockwoods Foods Limited, a bankrupt cannery that Hillsdown paid £3.5 million for. By the time Hillsdown purchased the Imperial Group's poultry, egg, and animal-feed businesses for £39 million the following year, its acquisition strategy was already in place. In general, Hillsdown shuns hostile takeovers, preferring instead to make friendly arrangements with the company's present management. The company is committed to capital infusion and refuses to strip assets from newly acquired properties, believing that adding value to commodities is the key to success. Rather than attempt to run their properties themselves, Solomon and Thompson from the start appointed independent managers to run Hillsdown's subsidiary companies as if they owned them. The company strives to limit overhead caused by red tape and bureaucracy, and often streamlines management at the firms it buys—Lockwoods' management was reduced to 40 from 120, and a later purchase, Maple Leaf Mills, saw its central staff shrink from 80 to 11. Hillsdown itself maintains a head office of about 20. Control of day-to-day operations remains in the hands of subsidiaries, who report to directors at economically furnished headquarters in North London. Besides an annual meeting with the Hillsdown director for their industry, subsidiaries are simply required to submit a one- or two-page financial report once a month to Hillsdown.

Hillsdown acquisitions in the same industry have not been merged, but are encouraged to compete—even for the privilege of supplying other Hillsdown subsidiaries with raw materials. In this way, the parent company profits by piecing together its many different companies in the fragmented food-processing field into a vertical whole, allowing it to earn money and control quality at every step. For instance, in the poultry business, Hillsdown companies can provide everything from the breeder hen that lays the egg to the frozen Chicken Kiev dinner it will eventually become.

Despite its dominance in the food industry, Hillsdown eschews flashiness in both personnel and products. Solomon and Thompson are notoriously publicity shy, and there are few products that bear Hillsdown's name. Instead, each product bears the brand of one of Hillsdown's many subsidiaries, or the mark of one of the leading retailers such as Marks & Spencer, Tesco, and Asda with which Hillsdown has developed close and lucrative ties. The company makes a handsome profit on its willingness to work with its customers to provide whatever it is they want.

In 1983, Hillsdown continued to grow by purchasing ailing and undervalued food companies such as TKM Foods and Smedley's canning business, both acquired for a token £1, and FMC, Europe's largest slaughterhouse, for a rock-bottom £4.9 million. The next year, Thompson and Solomon picked up Henry Telfer, a manufacturer of meatpies, again for £1. In its first decade, Hillsdown spent about £50 million making bargain-basement purchases of this sort to become the United Kingdom's fourth-largest food manufacturer, with sales of £1 billion. But these acquisitions, it soon turned out, were mere warm-up exercises.

Hillsdown Holdings went on a marathon buying binge after it put a quarter of its shares on the market in February, 1985. The company made 42 acquisitions in 20 months, stunning London's financial community with the pace of its activity. Newspapers reported that Hillsdown bought a new company every six days. Its acquisitions, scattered as they seemed, all fell into one of five major areas: food, timber, furniture, stationery, and property. Skeptics questioned the point of assembling an empire of such disparate parts, and doubted that one company could sensibly manage such far-flung interests. At the end of its spending spree, Hillsdown was the largest British producer of eggs, poultry, meat, and canned goods, and was second in the timber business. Its profits had grown in proportion to its size.

Throughout this period of enormous growth, Hillsdown stuck, for the most part, to a policy of making friendly bids for small companies. London's financial community waited for what rumormongers called the "big one." In spring of 1986, it came. Hillsdown began its first large contested bid for a company by increasing its stake in S.&.W. Berisford, a commodities-trading firm that had purchased the British Sugar Corporation in 1982. The company was already conducting talks with an Italian food and agricultural group when Hillsdown came on the scene, and soon Tate & Lyle, another British sugar refiner, entered the fray. In April, Hillsdown made its move, offering to buy Berisford for £486 million with the support of the Italian firm. When both bids were referred to the British Monopolies and Mergers Commission in May, however, Hillsdown withdrew, selling its stake in Berisford back to its Italian partner at a handsome profit.

The following year, Hillsdown strengthened its ability to develop small companies by launching the Hillsdown Investment Trust. HIT was set up to provide money and advice to companies with strong potential that were too small or diverse in activity for Hillsdown to buy outright. Also in 1987 Hillsdown began to expand in earnest beyond British shores. In July, it moved into North America with its purchase of Maple Leaf Mills, a Canadian food conglomerate, for £169 million in cash, its largest acquisition yet. At the same time, it launched operations on the European mainland with the formation of Hillsdown International B.V.

Although Maple Leaf Mills appeared to be an excellent match for Hillsdown's interests, the large debt Hillsdown incurred to buy it gave British investors sweaty palms. After making 50 purchases in 1987, Hillsdown found itself with a reputation as a rapacious acquisitor that could only make money through constant buying. To counter this impression, the company began to scale back the pace of its purchases in an attempt to consolidate holdings and reduce its level of debt. Hillsdown restrained itself in 1988, buying only 31 small businesses.

Fighting the perception that the company was "a dead duck in a bear market," as *The Independent* put it, the company strengthened its overseas holdings through further purchases in the Netherlands and North America, and attempted to demonstrate long-term internal growth, rather than short-term acquisitions-fueled growth. Despite lagging performance from its traditionally troubled red-meat companies, Hillsdown largely succeeded in demonstrating that the firm was sound even when it wasn't buying food companies as often as most people buy food. Attempting to widen the margin of profit on the commodities it produced, Hillsdown concentrated on adding value to its products by processing them as far as possible.

Despite its strong performance, Hillsdown's market value remained stagnant in the year following the 1987 stock market crash, in part, again, because the company's far-flung interests made investors nervous. Moving toward a more unified company profile, in September, 1988 Hillsdown sold off a large timber company and purchased Premier Brands Foods for £195 million in May, 1989. Shortly thereafter, it sold off stationery and printing businesses, so that more than 80% of the company's sales were concentrated in the food industry.

Also in early 1989, David Thompson, Hillsdown's co-founder, sold his final 14.5% share in the company, for £154 million. Thompson had first stepped down from an active role in the company in April, 1987, when he sold half his 30% share.

Hillsdown's continued concentration on purchases in industries in which it already has large holdings helped to solidify its identity and standing in the stock market, but not surprisingly, it has also drawn the unwelcome attention of Britain's Monopolies and Mergers Commission (MMC).

In the years since its founding, Hillsdown has experienced phenomenal growth with its somewhat unorthodox pattern of acquisitions and strong management principles. Whether it can build on the assets it now owns and continue to buy wisely in the international market depends on its leaders, who now include just one of the founders, and the skill they use in deploying the somewhat inscrutable Hillsdown philosophy.

Principal Subsidiaries: Beeson Group Limited; Buxted Poultry Limited; Christie-Tyler PLC; Church Farm Turkeys (51%); Classic Ices Limited; Colloids Limited (51%); Culrose Foods Limited; Danegoods (London) Limited; David T. Boyd Limited; Daylay Eggs Limited; J.B. Eastwood Limited; J. Evershed & Son Limited; Farm Kitchen Foods Limited; FMC PLC; Forrest Hodgkinson Holdings Co. Limited; Fresh Country Foods Limited; Vic Hallam PLC; Harvest Poultry Limited; Henry W. Peabody Grain Limited; Henry Telfer Limited; Hermanns Poultry Limited; Hillgas Limited; Hillsdown Limited; Hillsdown Distribution Limited; Hillsdown Insurance Services Limited; Hillsdown International Limited; Hortons Ice Cream Company Limited; I E L Travel Limited (75%); A. S. Juniper & Co., Limited; Lewis Bros. Limited; Ludlam's Catering Butcher Limited; Meadow Farm Produce PLC; Guy Morton & Sons Limited; Needlers PLC; Nitrovit Limited; Northam Food Trading Inc. (Canada) (85%); North Devon Meat Limited; Nutrikem Limited; Perimax Meat Co. Limited; T. J. Poupart Group Limited; Pyke Holdings PLC; Ross Breeders Limited; Rugby Securities Limited; Sterling Wygate Limited; Swan Foods International Limited; Premier Brands (UK) Ltd.; A.J. Mills & Co. Ltd.; Wirral Foods Ltd.; Kana Foods Ltd.; Grain D'Or Bakeries Ltd.; Rowe Manchett & Till Ltd.; Fiesta Foods Ltd.; Harris Pork and Bacon Group; Barker and Heid Ltd.; Buscted Duckling Ltd.; Hillsdown Turkeys Ltd.; Ross Poultry Ltd.; Peter Hand (GB) Ltd. (51%); Formwood Ltd.; Walker and Homer Group PLC; Fairview New Homes PLC; St. Andrews Properties Ltd.; Pinneys of Scotland Ltd.; Hillsdown International (BV) (the Netherlands); Clearwater UK Ltd.; Hillsdown Iberica S.A. (Spain); Abco Holdings Ltd. (Gibralter).

IBP, inc.

IBP Avenue
Box 515
Dakota City, Nebraska 68731
U.S.A.
(402) 494-2061

Public Company
Incorporated: 1960 as Iowa Beef Packers
Employees: 23,000
Sales: $9.1 billion
Stock Index: New York Philadelphia Midwest Pacific

As a company called Iowa Beef Packers, IBP helped to revolutionize the meatpacking industry in the early 1960s. This company's continuing success has also been marked, however, by a long series of legal problems and episodes of labor unrest.

IBP began in 1961 as Iowa Beef Packers, with a single beef slaughtering plant in the western Iowa town of Denison. A.D. Anderson and Currier J. Holman, two meat-industry veterans, founded the company on a simple idea; that the way meat was processed at the time was antiquated. Their goal was equally simple: to revolutionize the industry by creating "meat factories" that could process meat more efficiently and economically.

Traditionally, cattle in the United States had been raised in the country and then brought by train to the vast stockyards of Chicago, Omaha, and Kansas City, where animals were slaughtered in multi-storied packinghouses.

Anderson and Holman located their packing plants in the country, in the center of large cattle producing areas, enabling the company to buy livestock directly from producers. This cut procurement costs by eliminating middlemen and shortening transportation distances. It also minimized the shrinkage and bruising of livestock.

In addition, IBP's plants were built on a simpler and cheaper horizontal, rather than vertical, plan, and made much greater use of automation such as continuous-flow overhead conveyors. Elaborate cooling systems were installed to remedy the common industry problem of shrinkage—moisture loss due to poor refrigeration and packaging methods. IBP also worked to maximize use of beef by-products such as hides and tallow.

From the beginning, Holman and Anderson stressed efficiency and high productivity at a low cost. Managers with meat-industry experience were recruited and all employees were expected to work a six-day week. Cattle buyers drove through the Midwest to buy livestock on the farm rather than wait to buy from middlemen at a stockyard. Inventory was tightly controlled through a two-way radio network that allowed buyers to consult with the main office about immediate demand before any purchase. Once an animal arrived at an IBP plant, the slaughter process was so efficient that it had at most 24 hours to live.

IBP workers, perhaps spurred by the green paint everywhere around them (Anderson selected the color because it was the color of money), were among the most efficient workers in the meatpacking industry, taking just 32 minutes in 1964 to move a steer from plant door to freezer, ready for shipping by rail. Only a few years after the start of operations, IBP had become one of the leading companies in its field.

In creating a labor force to work in its highly automated plants, IBP looked to a non-unionized, unskilled rural populace displaced by increasing mechanization on the farm both to build and to operate its plants. By using sophisticated machinery, IBP "tried to take the skill out of every step" of butchering, as Anderson explained to *Newsweek* in 1965. "We wanted to be able to take boys right off the farm and we've done it." As late as 1964, IBP workers did not belong to a national union, having organized only on the local level.

Along with IBP's strong growth, however, came labor strife. In the spring of 1965, workers at two Iowa plants walked out over issues relating to the right to strike; the conflict became violent before it was settled with the help of Iowa's governor. "We didn't pay enough attention to labor problems, but we don't intend to make that mistake again," one IBP executive told *The Wall Street Journal* in 1966.

In 1967, IBP introduced a further refinement of the meatpacking process at its Dakota City, Nebraska, plant. Instead of shipping beef to customers in whole-carcass form, as the industry had done for years, IBP began to break down the carcass into smaller, vacuum-packed portions which it shipped in boxes. Removing unwanted fat and bone enabled the company to drastically lower shipping costs. It also fit well into the growing trend to market meat not in traditional butcher shops but in large supermarkets, which appreciated the savings on butchering costs that this new process offered. In addition, better packaging improved the meat's shelf life and flavor. *Forbes* described the new process as "a triumph of logic." Over a period of time the process was refined so that meat was broken down into 44 primal cuts, thus further eliminating middlemen and maximizing profit for the packer.

IBP's capacity to efficiently produce boxed beef enabled it to continued its strong growth. In 1969, the company ran eight midwestern beef plants. IBP continued its aggressive growth by taking over Blue Ribbon Beef Pack, Inc., acquiring facilities in LeMars and Mason City, Iowa. In February, 1969, however, a civil antitrust suit successfully contested this acquisition on the grounds that it would threaten competition in the purchasing of cattle in Iowa, Nebraska, Minnesota, and South Dakota. A 1970 consent decree forbid IBP to acquire any more beef slaughtering or processing plants in those four states for ten years, and ordered that the properties acquired from Blue Ribbon be sold. IBP appealed this decision, but sold the smaller of the two plants in 1974.

IBP's policies of innovation and strict control over wages caught up with it in 1969. The Amalgamated Meat Cutters Union (now the United Food and Commercial Workers) saw jobs moving from the urban areas to rural America. Boxed beef also threatened the unions' control over the ultimate carving up of the beef, a job largely restricted to master butchers, who earned high wages and worked limited hours in the backrooms of supermarkets and butcher shops.

The result was friction between IBP and the unions. Most of that friction took place at the company's Dakota City plant, where members of the Untied Food and Commercial Workers union engaged in five labor disputes between 1968 and 1987. On August 24, 1969, 1,200 union members walked off their jobs at the new Dakota City slaughterhouse, leaving the plant to operate at 50% capacity. This was the plant at which IBP had introduced a second level of beef disassembly (called "fabricating"). The union insisted it was striking for higher wages for all IBP employees, and equitable wages for both beef slaughterers and beef fabricators, who were paid less than slaughterers for their allegedly less strenuous work.

Three other IBP plants in Iowa closed in connection with the strike. In October, the company filed a $10 million suit against the union, charging it with sabotage, illegal work stoppages, and walkouts. The union, in turn, filed charges of unfair labor practices against the company with the National Labor Relations Board. IBP was accused of slandering union officials, locking out employees at the three Iowa plants, and failing to bargain in good faith. Before the strike ended on April 13, 1970, there had been one death, 56 bombings, more than 20 shootings, numerous tire slashings, death threats, extensive property damage, and the destruction of fire-bomb of the home of an IBP vice president. In the final settlement, the union gained a salary increase of 20¢ an hour over the wage first offered by IBP, but IBP continued to ignore the "master rate of pay" that other meatpackers paid their employees. In 1977, IBP was finally awarded $2.6 million in damages for union activities during the strike.

Although it appeared that IBP had won significant gains in its showdown with the union, actions taken by Currier J. Holman, one of the company's co-founders, during the period of the strike came back to haunt IBP three years later. Reduced production due to the strike had sharply limited IBP's cash flow, and boxed beef had not yet achieved market acceptance.

Against this background, Holman was desperate to crack the New York market in hopes of saving his company. However, the Amalgamated Meat Cutters and the local butchers were determined to keep IBP beef out of New York because they feared it would cost them jobs. Holman made a deal with a meat broker with underworld ties to obtain contracts with New York supermarket chains, paying the broker a surcharge of nearly $1 million on all beef sold within 125 miles of downtown Manhattan over a period of about 30 months. This surcharge was used to pay off union officials and supermarket executives. In March, 1973, IBP and Holman were indicted on charges of conspiring to bribe supermarket buyers and union officials.

A year and a half later, IBP and Holman were convicted of two charges in a New York state court. However, citing IBP's dire financial straights at the time the arrangement was entered into, the judge refused to fine or punish Holman personally and fined the company the nominal sum of $7,000, saying that Holman had been victimized by the corruption of New York's meat business.

The company, which had changed its name to Iowa Beef Processors in 1970 to better reflect its business, was hit with another lengthy labor stoppage in Dakota City in 1973, again in the name of higher wages. After 27 weeks, the strike was ended through arbitration, and workers were awarded a substantial pay increase.

During the first half of the 1970s, IBP experienced phenomenal growth. By 1974, it had far surpassed all its rivals, becoming the largest beef packer in the world. In November, 1975, the New York deal reared its head again when the company named Walter Bodenstein, the son-in-law of the New York meat broker who had made bribes on IBP's behalf, to a high executive position. When the appointment was announced, the company's financial backers immediately expressed reservations, citing Bodenstein's ties to the mafia, and he resigned amid controversy after a week. The company's standing in the business community was damaged when this and other incidents prompted *The Wall Street Journal* to run a front-page story a year later noting that IBP was now larger than all five of its nearest competitors put together, and denouncing the company as a magnet for "criminals, gangland figures, civil wrongdoers . . . and people engaged in vicious beatings, shootings, and firebombings."

Forbidden by the 1970 consent decree to purchase any new plants in four midwestern states, IBP expanded into Texas in 1975, building facilities near the large commercial feedlot operations in the Southwest, and into the Pacific Northwest in 1976 through the acquisition and expansion of two plants. IBP continued its expansion in 1980, when it completed construction of the world's largest beef slaughtering facility in Finney County, Kansas, and in 1983, when it acquired and expanded its easternmost facility, in Joslin, Illinois.

In May, 1978, the Agriculture Department had dropped an extensive investigation into IBP's suspected attempts to drive other packers out of business after IBP agreed informally not to break the law. But in 1979, Representative Neal Smith of Iowa, a farmer who was chair of a House Small Business Subcommittee, revived the issue by launching an investigation into IBP's allegedly predatory business practices. It was disclosed that the company had violated the Robinson-Patman Act between 1971 and 1975 by offering discounts to customers who bought large quantities of beef. In addition, IBP was convicted a preferential price treatment by a Brooklyn jury in 1981, in connection with price breaks of $10,000 a week given to a New York supermarket chain from 1970 to 1974.

In 1981, IBP was purchased by Occidental Petroleum Corporation, the giant energy conglomerate. During the next six years, as a wholly owned subsidiary of Occidental, IBP increased its revenues 53% and operating income 92%. IBP also added 8,000 employees and operating plants in four additional locations.

In 1982, the company was hit by its second violent strike in five years at its Dakota City plant. In early 1977, 1,800 workers had walked off their jobs, demanding higher wages in a violent 14-month strike that ended when IBP brought in strikebreakers and re-opened the plant. In 1982, the National Guard was brought in to quell violence, and IBP again used open hiring to resume operations, bringing in 1,400 new workers. Yet another strike began in December, 1986. This strike was settled seven months later, as workers successfully resisted company demands for wage concessions. By then, only three of IBP's 14 plants were unionized.

In 1982, IBP moved into the pork industry, and in just six years became a leader in pork packaging. Using the same strategy that had been so successful for IBP's beef-processing operations, IBP's pork division carved out a dominant place in the pork industry. With its expansion into pork, Iowa Beef Processors officially changed its name to IBP, dropping the emphasis on beef. Today IBP is the world's largest producer of fresh pork.

In 1987, Occidental Petroleum moved to sell off 49% of its stock in IBP, reaping a handsome profit. Occidental remains IBP's major shareholder. Although the company was still the world's largest producer of fresh meat, IBP had, by this point, lost much of its reputation as an innovator in the meat-packing business, and the move was seen as a way of fostering the independence necessary for IBP to regain its leading position.

The company also ran afoul of the Occupational Safety and Health Administration, which slapped the company with a record $2.6 million fine for failing to report worker injuries, and after a review of corrected records, assessed additional fines related to a high incidence of carpal tunnel syndrome (a result of repeated, forceful hand motions such as those used in butchering) found among IBP workers. The company eventually paid reduced fines and agreed to set up a study of the disorder.

IBP remains the world's largest producer of fresh meat and the largest U.S. exporter of meat and meat by-products. It operates 16 beef and pork plants, and also produces more than 250 allied products such as pharmaceuticals and hides—IBP has built three chrome hide tanneries since 1984 and is now the largest producer of chrome hides in the world. However, the structure of the meat industry has changed in the 30 years since IBP helped to revolutionize the business, and today the packer faces new challenges, such as the decrease in consumer demand for red meat. The company also faces increased competition from giant agricultural conglomerates such as ConAgra and Cargill.

Despite its checkered past, IBP can point with pride to its tradition of high-quality, low-cost products. Although its marketplace is changing rapidly, the company sees great growth potential in its core meatpacking business. In response to changes, IBP has expanded its nonfood interest significantly in recent years, but the company continues to invest in the meat business; it will open its newest and largest pork plant in 1990. IBP is also exploring a wider variety of products, such as consumer-ready branded meats, in order to maintain its premiere place in the meatpacking industry.

Principal Subsidiaries: IBP International; Transcontinental Cold Storage; Texas Amarillo Systems Company; PBX, Inc.

Further Reading: Skaggs, Jimmy M. *Prime Cut: Livestock Raising and Meatpacking in the United States 1607–1983*, College Station, Texas A & M University Press, 1986.

ITOHAM FOODS INC.

4–27, Takahata-cho
Nishinomiya City
Hyogo 663
Japan
(0798) 66–1231

Public Company
Incorporated: 1948 as Ito Ham Company, Ltd.
Employees: 4,455
Sales: ¥357.59 billion (US$ 2.86 billion)
Stock Index: Tokyo Osaka Nagoya

Itoham Foods is one of Japan's most successful producers of processed meats and sausages, and it has recently joined companies based in Europe and the United States in producing and distributing other food products including edible oils and dairy products. Recognized for its dedication to the promotion of Japanese business in domestic and foreign markets, Itoham plans to expand its investments into biotechnology as a source of long-term stability.

Denzo Ito established a meat-processing company, The Ito Processed Food Company, in Osaka, Japan, in 1928. Two years later this company went bankrupt in response to the worldwide Depression, but it was re-formed in 1932 as Ito Meat Processing Company, in Kobe, Japan. A year later the company first marketed what was called the Pole Wiener, a sausage wrapped in cellophane, a popular base from which the company's product line was to grow in later years.

In 1943 Ito Meat's factory was closed as a result of the emergency conditions brought about by World War II, but Ito Meat's investors were quick to reestablish their company soon after the war. In 1946, the factory in Kobe returned to production, this time as the Ito Food Processing Company. Pressed ham, or yose ham, was one the first products on-line at the Kobe factory. Two years later, the company was reorganized again as the Ito Ham Company Limited, with ¥3 million in capital.

In 1957 Ito Ham Company developed a method of producing hams and sausages which used mutton as well as pork, which was still scarce in Japan. Finding this method a worthwhile money-saver, the company imported 3,000 tons of mutton that year. The company also expanded its production capacity, building a plant in Tokyo in 1959 and one in Nishinomiya the next year.

The business was renamed Ito Ham Provisions Company, Limited, in 1961, and its stock was listed for the first time on the Tokyo and Osaka stock exchanges. The following year Ito Ham built another plant, in Toyohashi. By 1965 Ito Ham was attracting foreign interest. Three years later Ito Ham launched its first ship, to import raw materials from Australia and New Zealand.

In 1967 the company opened yet another plant, this time in Kyushu, and began to produce dairy products, its first nonmeat food prodocts.

Several foreign delegations visited Ito Ham's plants throughout Japan. These included economic delegations from New Zealand, Great Britain, Denmark, Australia, and China. In 1973, Ito Ham began business relations with the United States as the exclusive distributor of Armour Food Company's products in Japan. Then in 1974 Ito Ham acquired Cariani Sausage Company, a sausage maker in San Francisco, California.

Nine years later Ito Ham was again involved with an American company, this time in a joint endeavor with the Carnation Company. In March, 1983 Ito Ham and Carnation agreed to jointly produce cooking oils, chilled foods, sauces and seasoning, milk products, and soft drinks through a venture called Ito Carnation Company. This plan gave Carnation the footing in Japanese manufacturing which it had been seeking and expanded Ito Ham's product range at a time when meat consumption in Japan was slowing.

In September, 1985 Ito Ham entered into an agreement with a French cheese company, Fromageries Bel. Ito Ham agreed to sell three of Bel's natural cheeses in supermarkets throughout Japan, promising initial sales of at least ¥600 million. The companies agreed that when sales of the cheeses exceeded ¥2 billion, Ito Ham would begin to produce the cheese in Japan using Bel's production technology.

Ito Ham again dealt with French food manufacturers in May, 1984, this time hammering out an agreement with Tour d'Argent, a prestigious French restaurant. According to the agreement Ito Ham would distribute the restaurant's specialty food products like tea, coffee, and mustard in department stores and boutiques around Japan.

To insure long-term growth and stability, Ito Ham decided to develop its interest in biotechnology. In August, 1984 it announced plans to commercialize its method of extracting valuable chemical elements from pig blood, particularly an amino acid used for flavoring. The company began building a new laboratory for this and other biotechnical research in December, 1988, and it was during this period that the name Itoham Foods, Inc. was adopted.

Kenichi Ito, Itoham's president, has cited Japan's abundant food supply and the resulting stiff competition in the domestic food market as two of the difficult conditions under which Itoham entered the 1990s. Now that Japan's quantity of food is more than sufficient, Ito has said that Japan's consumers are buying according to taste. Itoham prides itself on its corporate and production flexibility in adapting to changing market trends. Itoham Foods entered the 1990s in a strong position as a leading meat processor and an increasingly integrated food business.

Principal Subsidiaries: Itoham Daily Inc.; Hokkaido Itoham Inc.; Itoham Shokuhin Inc.; Itoham Tokyo Sales Inc.; Okinawa Itoham Inc.; Ariake Meat Packers Inc.; Nippon Farm Inc.; HW Delicatessen Inc.; Sendai Meat Packers Inc.; Toci Meat Packets Inc.; Hoei & Co., Ltd.

JACOBS SUCHARD

JACOBS SUCHARD AG

Seefeldquai 17
8008 Zurich
Switzerland
(01) 385–11 11

Public Company
Incorporated: 1982
Employees: 16,700
Sales: SFr 6.3 billion (US$4.2 billion)
Stock Index: Zurich

Jacobs Suchard has its origins in three spirited entrepreneurs: Philippe Suchard and Johann Jakob Tobler, confectioners; and Johann Jacobs, a coffee merchant. The Suchard and Tobler companies joined forces in 1970 to form Interfood, which Jacobs' coffee company joined 12 years later to form Jacobs Suchard. Today this company is one of the fastest-growing international confectionery corporations in the world, with 12 of the European chocolate market.

Philippe Suchard opened his small confectionery shop in Neuchâtel, Switzerland in 1825. The next year he expanded his business by opening a chocolate factory in Serrières. Before trying the candy business, though, he took part in founding a shipping company on the Rhine River, attempted to raise silkworms to make silk scarves, and tried to establish a Swiss colony in the United States, near Carthage, New York. Later he provided housing for people working in his Serrières factory at a time when they did not have a union to voice their needs and demands. Suchard soon had built his business into the leading Swiss chocolate maker. Four years before his death, the Suchard Company opened its first plant outside Switzerland, in Lörrach, Germany in 1880, the first in a series of international expansion efforts. In 1901 Suchard established the Milka chocolate brand, one of Europe's oldest and most popular brands of milk chocolate.

Suchard's son-in-law, Carl Russ, led the business into other countries, opening another factory in 1888, in Bludenz, Austria, two factories in France in 1903, one in Spain in 1909, one in Italy in 1923, and one in Belgium in 1929. Although the chocolate industry fell on hard times during World War I, by 1931 Suchard had begun to move into sugar confectionery, under the Sugus brand. This venture helped the company weather the Depression. After World War II, Suchard's chocolate business again flourished and the company enjoyed relatively stable success.

The Tobler company, which merged with Suchard in 1970, began in 1867 when Jean Tobler, formally Johann Jakob Tobler, opened a small shop called Confiserie Spécial. A year later, he opened a confection factory in Bern. An avid traveler, Tobler was involved in various ventures while continuing to build his chocolate business, which prospered quickly. In 1908 Jean Tobler's son, Theodor, put the Toblerone chocolate bar on the market. One of the most valuable additions to the Tobler line of chocolates, it is Tobler's hallmark product.

In 1922 Tobler first expanded outside Switzerland, to Paris. It was not until 1951, however, 29 years after moving into France, that Tobler made its second international move, this time into Stuttgart, West Germany. In 1967 Tobler extended into Great Britain. Tobler and Suchard continued to develop their respective chocolates and businesses until 1970, when the companies merged to become Interfood.

The joint effort focused on internationalizing business operations and broadening product lines. In 1980 Interfood acquired Andes Candies, based in the United States, and in 1982 it acquired Callebaut, a well-known Belgian producer of candy coatings and other products.

The Jacobs coffee company, based in Bremen, West Germany, can be traced to Johann Jacobs, born in 1869. This third industrious entrepreneur in Jacobs Suchard's story opened a shop offering chocolates, tea, biscuits, and coffee in 1895. Jacobs opened a roasting plant of his own in 1906, and seven years later registered the Jacobs brand. In 1929 Johann Jacobs handed over the leadership of the company to his son Walther.

Much of Jacobs' subsequent growth is attributed to a vital marketing decision made by Walther Jacobs: the company began delivering freshly roasted coffee directly to retail shops. After World War II, this system of direct delivery was stepped up, along with production and sales, until in the mid-1960s more than 1,000 vehicles delivered Jacobs' fresh-roasted coffee to over 60,000 shops. In 1966 Jacobs began marketing different brand names of its coffee products, beginning with Krönung and growing to include Tradition, Privat, and Edel Mocca.

Klaus Jacobs, Walther's son and the third Jacobs generation to lead the company, took over in 1970. Jacobs had expanded into Austria in 1961 and into Switzerland ten years later. The company, under Klaus's leadership, had plans to expand further into non-German-speaking countries and needed a home office to operate from. In 1973, a management and consulting subsidiary was established in Zurich. Subsequently, Jacobs moved into Denmark, France, and Canada during the 1970s by acquiring roasting and production companies in those countries. Jacobs acquired Jacques Vabre in 1973, and then again set it sights on France and bought Café Grand' Mère, in 1982.

By this time it seemed to Interfood and Jacobs leaders alike that a merger was in order. Both companies had ambitious goals for international expansion. Chocolate and coffee, though hardly the same business, offered some scope for cooperation, and a merger would bring both companies economies of scale. The merger, which created the public company Jacobs Suchard, was accomplished in 1982. Its head office was established in Zurich, since Interfood was determined to stay Swiss, and Klaus Jacobs (whose family controls 55% of the company) was made chairman of the board, since Jacobs was by far the larger of the two companies. In the company's logo, a "J" and an "S" combine to form a "T," for Tobler.

Jacobs Suchard immediately began to cut costs; Jacobs eliminated most of the company's middle management positions, and used capital it raised by selling shares to acquire many established and successful businesses. One of the most prominent of them was the international Monheim Group, which Jacobs Suchard took over in July, 1986. Included among Monheim's subsidiaries was Van Houten, a West German company manufacturing consumer chocolate, cocoa, industrial cocoa butter, and cocoa powder. Another Monheim member was General Chocolate, in Belgium, which marketed specialty sweets under the Meurisse brand. Jacobs Suchard Belgium now handles Van Houten's and General Chocolate's consumer business; its industrial affairs were absorbed into Jacobs Suchard in Zurich.

By the end of 1986 Jacobs Suchard was operating quite successfully with its European additions. On the North American continent, however, save for Andes Candies, the company was doing very little business. So Jacobs Suchard set out to participate more aggressively in the lucrative American candy market.

In December, 1986 Jacobs Suchard completed a takeover of E.J. Brach. The American candy company, in existence more than 80 years, was the third-largest candy company in the United States. Jacobs Suchard saw this acquisition as a profitable enterprise in itself and, perhaps more importantly, as a door through which to introduce its goods to the North American market.

In March, 1987 the company took over the Belgian chocolate company Côte d'Or. The takeover was controversial because the Belgian company was the last of its kind still owned by Belgians. From the late 1960s into the 1980s Belgian candy companies had one by one been bought by foreign interests, including Callebaut's 1982 purchase by Interfood. Nestlé had also bid for control of Côte d'Or, but the families who owned the Belgian "national icon" chose Jacobs Suchard. Jacobs Suchard, vowing to sustain the high quality of Côte d'Or's chocolate, absorbed Côte d'Or into Jacobs Suchard's Belgian operations. Jacobs Suchard has also expanded its product market into Italy and Greece, in preparation for the integration of the European Economic Community in 1992.

In 1988 Jacobs Suchard bid for control of Rowntree, one of the United Kingdom's largest candy companies. In April that year Jacobs Suchard began buying the largest percentage of shares, 29.9%, allowed by British law without placing a bid for the whole company. Nestlé was on the scene again, eager to bid, but Rowntree was not eager to be bought by either Swiss company. Nestlé finally bought the company for about $4.5 billion, topping Jacobs Suchard's offer by $400 million, when Jacobs Suchard decided to stop bidding after a two-month battle and sold its Rowntree holdings to Nestlé for $285 million.

Jacobs Suchard bought a Panamanian bank, Banco Aleman-Panameno, in 1985, and acquired the majority interest in West Germany's Ibero-Amerika Bank in July, 1986. Both have close ties to Latin America's green-coffee business, upon which the company heavily depends. Direct participation in the banks is intended to provide Jacobs Suchard with greater knowledge about the green-coffee business.

Since the 1982 merger that created Jacobs Suchard,the company has seen three phases in its development. In the beginning only key areas, such as personnel and finance management, were integrated, in an effort to bring Interfood and Jacobs together while disturbing their individual operations as little as possible. In 1983 the company reevaluated techniques for marketing its chocolate and coffee products in light of one another and of the various countries in which they were sold and made plans to capitalize on its popular brands and the changing desires of consumers. With consolidation taking a firm hold in management and marketing, in 1986 Jacobs Suchard redefined its business structure to include three business units: core business, finance and trading, and diversification, focused mainly on North America.

Having spent approximately $1 billion in 1987 and 1988 on acquisitions alone, Klaus Jacobs plans to concentrate the company's European production in just six manufacturing centers by the end of 1990 (down from 22 in 1989); to streamline its European product line; and to improve European sales by strengthening its less expensive brands, like Milka.

Jacobs Suchard also hopes to capture a healthy portion of the growing Asian chocolate market. In 1989 the company hired 100 salesmen to push Milka chocolate in the Tokyo area alone. In North America Jacobs plans to cut Brach's array of candies by two-thirds and to spend $70 million to modernize its production facilities to gain better market position.

While looking for other takeover targets in confectionery or other related fields, Klaus Jacobs is focusing on making Jacobs Suchard uncommon among its competitors. It is with a certain refined aggression that he leads Jacobs Suchard into the 1990s.

Principal Subsidiaries: Jacobs Suchard Tobler AG; Ak-P tiengesellschaft Chocolat Tobler; Jacobs Suchard Management & Consulting AG; Taloca AG; Jacobs Suchard GmbH (West Germany); Jacobs Suchard Erzeugnisse GmbH & Co. (West Germany); Jacobs Suchard Berlin GmbH & Co. KG (West Germany); Jacobs Suchard Service GmbH & Co. (West Germany); Jacobs Suchard Manufacturing GmbH & Co. KG (West Germany); Suchard Schokalade Ges.m.b.H. (Austria); Jacobs Kaffee Ges.m.b.H. (Austria); Mirabell Salzburger Confiserie- und Bisquit-Ges.m.b.H. (Austria); Bensdorp Ges.m.b.H. (Austria); Jacobs Suchard France S.A. (France); Café Grand' Mère S.A. (France); Jacobs Suchard S.R.L. (Italy); Jacobs Suchard Kaffe A/S (Denmark); S.A. Jacob Suchard N.V. (Belgium); Koffie Hag N.V. (Belgium); Côte d'Or N.V. (Belgium); Jacobs Suchard/Côte d'Or B.V. (Netherlands); B.V. v/h Fabrieken C.J. Van Houten & Zoon (Netherlands); Jacobs Suchard

Ltd. (U.K.); Jacobs Suchard Espãna S.A. (Spain); Jacobs Suchard Pavlides S.A. (Greece); Jacobs Suchard Inc. (U.S.A.); C.J. Van Houten & Zoon (U.S.A.); Jacobs Suchard Canada Inc.; Comet Confectionery Ltd. (Canada); Suchard Argentina S.A.; Taloca Café S/C Ltda. (Brazil); Casa Exportadora Naumann Gepp S.A. (Brazil); German Merino y Cia, Ltda. (Colombia); Jacobs Suchard (Australia) Pty. Ltd.; Jacobs Suchard Japan Co. Ltd.

Kellogg's®

KELLOGG COMPANY

One Kellogg Square
Battle Creek, Michigan 49016–3599
U.S.A.
(616) 961–2000

Public Company
Incorporated: 1906 as Battle Creek Toasted Corn Flake Company
Employees: 17,461
Sales: $4.65 billion (1989)
Stock Index: New York Boston Cincinnati Midwest Pacific Philadelphia

Will Keith Kellogg once estimated that 42 cereal companies were launched in the breakfast-food boom during the early years of the 20th century. His own venture, chartered as the Battle Creek Toasted Corn Flake Company, was among the last, but it outlasted most of its early competitors and has dominated the ready-to-eat cereal industry every since. The Kellogg Company, as it was ultimately named, followed a straight and profitable path, avoiding takeovers and diversification, relying heavily on advertising and promotion, and posting profits nearly every year of its existence.

By the time Kellogg launched his cereal company in 1906 he had already been in the cereal business for more than ten years, as an employee of his brother's Adventist Battle Creek Sanitarium. Dr. John Harvey Kellogg, a strict vegetarian and the sanitarium's internationally celebrated director, also invented and marketed various health foods. One of the foods sold by Dr. Kellogg's Sanitas Food Company was called *Granose*, a wheat flake the Kellogg brothers had stumbled upon while trying to develop a more digestible form of bread. The wheat flake was produced one night in 1894 following a long series of unsuccessful experiments. The men were running boiled wheat dough through a pair of rollers in the sanitarium basement. The dough had always come out sticky and gummy, until by accident the experiments were interrupted long enough for the boiled dough to dry out. When the dry dough was run through the rollers, it broke into thin flakes, one for each wheat berry, and flaked cereals were born.

Commercial production of the Granose flakes began in 1895 with improvised machinery in a barn on the sanitarium grounds. The factory was soon in continuous production, turning out more than 100,000 pounds of flakes in its first year. A ten-ounce box sold for 15 cents, which meant that the Kelloggs collected $12 for each 60-cent bushel of wheat processed. a feat that did not go unnoticed around Battle Creek, Michigan.

In 1900 production was moved to a new $50,000 facility. When the new factory building was completed, Dr. Kellogg insisted that he had not authorized it, forcing W. K. to pay for it himself.

Meanwhile, other companies were growing quickly, but Dr. Kellogg refused to invest in the company's expansion. Its most notable competitor was the Postum Cereal Company, launched by a former sanitarium patient, C. W. Post. Post added Grape-Nuts to his line in 1898 and by 1900 was netting $3 million a year, an accomplishment that inspired dozens of imitators and turned Battle Creek into the cereal-making capital of the United States.

In 1902 Sanitas improved the corn flake it had first introduced in 1898. The new product had better flavor and a longer shelf life than the unsuccessful 1898 version. By the following year the company was advertising in newspapers and on billboards, sending salesmen into the wholesale market, and introducing an ambitious door-to-door sampling program. By late 1905, Sanitas was producing 150 cases of corn flakes a day with sales of $100,000 a year.

The next year W. K. Kellogg launched the Battle Creek Toasted Corn Flake Company with the help of another enthusiastic former sanitarium patient. Kellogg recognized that advertising and promotion were key to success in a market flooded with look-alike products—the company spent a third of its initial working capital on an ad in *Ladies Home Journal*.

Orders, fueled by early advertising efforts, continually outstripped production, even after the company leased factory space at two additional locations. In 1907 output had reached 2,900 cases a day, with a net profit of about a dollar per case. In May, 1907 the company became the Toasted Corn Flake Company. That July a fire destroyed the main factory building. On the spot, W. K. Kellogg began making plans for a new fireproof factory, and within a week he had purchased land at a site strategically located between two competing railroad lines. Kellogg had the new plant, with a capacity of 4,200 cases a day, in full operation six months after the fire. "That's all the business I ever want," he is said to have told his son, John L. Kellogg, at the time.

By the time of the fire, the company had already spent $300,000 on advertising but the advertising barrage continued. One anonymous campaign told newspaper readers to "wink at your grocer and see what your get." (Winkers got a free sample of *Kellogg's Corn Flakes*.) In New York City, the ad helped boost Corn Flake sales fifteenfold. In 1911 the advertising budget reached $1 million.

By that time, W. K. Kellogg had finally managed to buy out the last of his brother's share of the company, giving him more than 50% of its stock. W. K. Kellogg's company had become the Kellogg Toasted Corn Flake Company in 1909, but Dr. Kellogg's Sanitas Food Company had been renamed the Kellogg Food Company and used similar slogans and packaging. W. K. sued his brother for rights to the family name and was finally successful in 1921.

In 1922 the company reincorporated as the Kellogg Company because it had lost its trademark claim to the name "Toasted Corn Flakes," and had expanded its product line so much that the name no longer accurately described the company. Kellogg introduced *Krumbles* in 1912, followed by *40% Bran Flakes* in 1915 and *All-Bran* in 1916.

Kellogg also made other changes, improving his product, packaging, and processing methods. Many of those developments came from W. K.'s son John L. Kellogg, who began working for the company in its earliest days. J. L. Kellogg developed a malting process to give the corn flakes a more nut-like flavor, saved $250,000 a year by switching from a waxed paper wrapper on the outside of the box to a waxed paper liner inside, and invented All-Bran by adding a malt flavoring to the bran cereal. His father credited him with more than 200 patents and trademarks.

Sales and profits continued to climb, financing several additions to the Battle Creek plant and the addition of a plant in Canada, opened in 1914, as well as an ever-increasing advertising budget. The one exception came just after World War I, when shortages of raw materials and rail cars crippled the once-thriving business. W. K. Kellogg returned from a world tour and canceled advertising contracts and sampling operations, and, for six months, he and his son worked without pay. The company issued $500,000 in gold notes in 1919 and in 1920 posted the only loss in its history. Still, Kellogg rejected a competitor's buyout offer.

At that point the Battle Creek plant had 15 acres of floor space, production capacity of 30,000 cases a day, and a shipping capacity of 50 rail cars a day. Each day it converted 15,000 bushels of white southern corn into Corn Flakes. The company had 20 branch offices and employed as many as 400 salesmen. During the next decade the Kellogg Company more than doubled the floor space at its Battle Creek factory and opened another overseas plant in Sydney, Australia, in 1924.

Also during that period, W. K. Kellogg began looking for a successor since in 1925 he had forced his son, who served briefly as president, out of the company after John Kellogg bought an oat-milling plant and divorced his wife to marry an office girl. W. K. Kellogg objected both to his son's moral lapse and to his preference for oats. Several other presidents followed, but none could manage well enough to keep W. K. Kellogg away. During the Great Depression the company's directors decided to cut advertising, premiums, and other expenses. When Kellogg heard of it, he returned from his California home, called a meeting, and told the officers to press ahead. They voted again, this time adding $1 million to the advertising budget. The company's upward sales curve continued right through the Depression, and profits improved from around $4.3 million a year in the late 1920s to $5.7 million in the early 1930s.

In 1930 W. K. Kellogg established the W. K. Kellogg Foundation to support agricultural, health, and educational institutions. Kellogg eventually gave the foundation his majority interest in Kellogg Company. The company, under W. K.'s control, also did its part to fight unemployment, hiring a crew to landscape a ten-acre park on the Battle Creek plant grounds and introducing a six-hour, four-shift day.

In 1939 Kellogg finally found a permanent president, Watson H. Vanderploeg, who was hired away from a Chicago bank. Vanderploeg led the company from 1939 until his death in 1957.

Vanderploeg expanded Kellogg's successful advertise-and-grow policy, adding new products and taking them into new markets. In 1941 the company began a $1 million modernization program, updating old steam-generation equipment and adding new bins and processing equipment. The company also added new plants in the United States and abroad. Domestic plants were established at Omaha, Nebraska; Lockport, Illinois; San Leandro, California; and Memphis, Tennessee. Additional foreign operations were established in Manchester, England in 1938, followed by plants in South Africa, Mexico, Ireland, Sweden, the Netherlands, Denmark, New Zealand, Norway, Venezuela, Colombia, Brazil, Switzerland, and Finland. During the five years after World War II, Kellogg expanded net fixed assets from $6.6 million to $20.6 million. As always, this expansion was financed entirely out of earnings.

The company also continued to add new products, but it never strayed far from the ready-to-eat cereal business. In 1952 more than 85% of sales came from ten breakfast cereals, although the company also sold a line of dog food, some poultry and animal feeds, and Gold Medal pasta. *Barron's* noted that Kellogg's profit margins, consistently between 6% and 7% of sales, were more than double those of other food companies. The company produced 35% of the nation's ready-to-eat cereal and was the world's largest manufacturer of cold cereal. Kellogg's success came from its emphasis on quality products; high-speed automated equipment, which kept labor costs to about 15% of sales; and substantial foreign earnings that were exempt from the excess-profits tax. Dividends tended to be generous and had been paid every year since 1908; sales, which had been $33 million in 1939, began to top $100 million in 1948. By the early 1950s an estimated one-third of those sales were outside the United States.

In the early 1950s Kellogg's continued success was tied to two outside developments: the postwar baby boom, and television advertising. To appeal to the new younger market, Kellogg and other cereal makers brought out new lines of presweetened cereals and unabashedly made the key ingredient part of the name. Kellogg's entries included *Sugar Frosted Flakes*, *Sugar Smacks*, *Sugar Corn Pops*, *Sugar All-Stars*, and Cocoa Crispies. The company created *Tony the Tiger* and other cartoon pitchmen to sell the products on Saturday-morning television. Sales and profits doubled over the decade. In 1960 Kellogg earned $21.5 million on sales of $256.2 million and boosted its market share to 40%.

The company continued adding new cereals, aiming some at adolescent baby boomers and others, like *Special K* and *Product 19* at their parents. Kellogg's *Corn Flakes* still led the cereal market and got more advertising support than any other cereal on grocers' shelves. Kellogg poured nearly $10 million into Corn Flakes advertising in both 1964 and 1965, putting more than two-thirds of those dollars into television.

In 1969 Kellogg finally made a significant move away from the ready-to-eat breakfast-food business, acquiring Salada Foods, a tea company. The following year Kellogg bought Fearn International, which sold soups, sauces, and desserts to restaurants. Kellogg added Mrs. Smith's Pie Company in 1976 and Pure Packed Foods, a maker of non-dairy frozen foods for institutional customers, in 1977. Kellogg also bought several small foreign food companies.

The diversification may have been motivated in part by increasing attacks on Kellogg's cereal business. Criticism boiled over in 1972 when the Federal Trade Commission (FTC) accused Kellogg and its leading rivals General Mills and General Foods of holding a shared monopoly and overcharging consumers more than $1 billion during the previous 15 years. The FTC said the companies used massive advertising (12% of sales), brand proliferation, and allocation of shelf space to keep out competitors and maintain high prices and profit margins. There was no disputing the profit margins, but the companies argued that the advertising and product proliferation were the result of competition, not monopoly. The cereal companies won their point following a lengthy hearing. During the same period, the industry's presweetened cereals and related advertising also took a beating. The American Dental Association accused the industry of obscuring the sugar content of those cereals and Action for Children's Television lodged a complaint with the FTC, saying that the mostly sugar cereals were equivalent to candy. Kellogg flooded consumer groups and the FTC with data downplaying the sugar content by showing that only 3% of a child's sugar consumption comes from presweetened cereals. This publicity caused sugared-cereal sales to fall 5% in 1978, the first decline since their introduction in the 1950s.

But the biggest threat to Kellogg's continued growth wasn't criticism but the aging of its market. By the end of the 1970s growth slowed dramatically as the baby-boom generation passed from the under-25 group, which consumes an average of 11 pounds of cereal a year, to the 25–50 age group, which eats less than half as much cereal. Cereal-market growth dropped, and Kellogg lost the most. Its market share fell from 43% in 1972 to 37% in 1983.

While Wall Street urged the company to shift its growth targets into anything by the stagnating cereal market, Kellogg continued to put its biggest efforts into its cereal business, emphasizing some of the same nutritional concepts that had given birth to the ready-to-eat breakfast business. And Kellogg was less unwilling to diversify than unable. It made three unsuccessful bids for the Tropicana Products orange juice company and another for Binney & Smith, makers of Crayola Crayons. Despite its problems, Kellogg believed the cereal business still represented its best investment opportunity. "When you average 28% return on equity in your own business, it's pretty hard to find impressive acquisitions," said Chairman William E. LaMothe, a onetime salesman who became CEO in 1979.

In 1984 Kellogg bought about 20% of its own stock back from the W. K. Kellogg Foundation, a move that increased profits and helped defend the company against future takeover attempts while satisfying a legal requirement limiting the holdings of foundations without giving potential raiders access to the stock.

Meanwhile, the company's response to generally sagging markets in the late 1970s was much like Will Kellogg's during the Depression: more advertising. Kellogg also boosted product research and stepped up new-product introductions. In 1979 the company rolled out five new products and had three more in test markets. By 1983 Kellogg's research-and-development budget was $20 million, triple the 1978 allotment. Targeting a more health-conscious market, Kellogg spent $50 million to bring three varieties of *Nutri-Grain* cereal to market in 1982. Kellogg added almost as many products in the next two years as it had in the previous four. And in 1984 Kellogg sparked a fiber fad when it began adding a health message from the National Cancer Institute to its *All-Bran* cereal.

By the mid 1980s the results of Kellogg's renewed assault on the cereal market were mixed. The company's hopes of raising per capita cereal consumption to 12 pounds by 1985 fell flat. But Kellogg did regain much of its lost market share, claiming 40% in 1985. And it continued to outperform itself year after year. In 1986 Kellogg posted its 30th consecutive dividend increase, its 35th consecutive earnings increase, and its 42nd consecutive sales increase.

In 1988 the company sold its U.S. and Canadian tea operations, in a demonstration of Kellogg's renewed commitment to the cereal market. This commitment has taken on new life at Kellogg as a result of the movement in the 1980s away from fatty foods and toward grain-based products. This is a trend Kellogg has helped escalate with the introduction of healthier breakfast foods and advertisements stressing the importance of grains and grain products such as oat bran and other fiber.

Another key facet of Kellogg's strategy continues to be the aggressive marketing and advertising support it gives it products in order to keep them growing in a fairly mature market. Kellogg also routinely spends lavish amounts to expand and modernize its production facilities, keeping actual production costs low and the company's plants well positioned for growth.

Consumer demands for healthier and more convenient food will help Kellogg sustain growth during the 1990s. With an evergrowing U.S. market share, more than double the 20.5% share of closest-competitor General Mills, and an even-faster-growing 50% share of the foreign cereal market, Kellogg should remain in a strong condition even without diversification, but it will continue to look for ways to enlarge its market. More than once Kellogg has averted disaster by use of timely advertisements. It is a good bet that, like W. K. Kellogg himself, the company will continue to foster growth in trying times by the use of aggressive and innovative product development and marketing.

Principal Subsidiaries: Fearn International Inc.; Mrs. Smith's Frozen Foods Co.

Further Reading: Powell, Horace B. *The Original Has This Signature: W. K. Kellogg*, Englewood Cliffs, N.J., Prentice-Hall, 1956; Carson, Gerald. *Cornflake Crusade*, Salem, New Hampshire, Ayer, 1976; *The History of Kellogg Company*, Battle Creek, Michigan, Kellogg Company, 1986.

KONINKLIJKE WESSANEN N.V.

Prof EM Meijerslaan 2
Post Office Box 410
NL-1180 AK Amstelveen
The Netherlands
(31) 20 547 9 547

Public Company
Incorporated: 1913 as N.V. Verenigde Fabrieken Wessanen and Laan
Employees: 6,500
Sales: Dfl3.8 billion (US$1.89 billion)
Stock Index: Amsterdam London Basel Zurich Geneva Frankfurt, Düsseldorf

Koninklijke Wessanen NV (Royal Wessanen) is one of Europe's largest food processors. Founded over two hundred years ago, the company has evolved from a local seed trader into a complex manufacturer of diverse consumer products, bulk specialties such as wheat and wheat derivatives, and semi-manufactured products (like refined oils) for industrial producers of foodstuffs.

Wessanen has broadened its arena of operations steadily over the past decade. The company now makes about 40% of its profits in the United States, where it focuses on the higher-margin edible consumer-products markets. It has also benefited from its many years of experience in both marketing and research. Wessanen was a leader in the development of many products, among them milk replacers for use as an animal feed, and custom semi-manufactured products for food producers. This emphasis on geographic diversification and higher-margin products should strengthen Wessanen as Europe's markets merge by 1992.

On March 22, 1765, cheese merchant Adriaan Wessanen and his 20-year-old nephew Dirk Laan established Wessanen and Laan, with a capital of Dfl 12,000. The company originally traded in a variety of seeds and grains. In 1789, nearly 25 years after the company began, Adriaan Wessanen retired and Dirk Laan took control of the company. The company continued to prosper, eventually becoming active in the milling of various grains.

When Laan himself died in 1791, his son Remmert became head of the company. Remmert Laan faced new challenges. The French under Napoleon dominated the European continent by the early 1800s, and Holland was part of the French Empire, which was at war with the British, among others. Britain's navy was a serious barrier to Dutch ships carrying raw materials to the Netherlands from its colonies and transporting finished goods back to them; as a result, many of Wessanen's trading activities were restricted.

Political changes in Europe after 1814 enabled Wessanen to establish new trading affiliations throughout the continent in cities like Hamburg, Antwerp, and Ghent. Although seed trading remained one of the company's biggest businesses, Wessanen became increasingly active in the trade of wheat, oats, and barley. Before long, encouraged by the Netherlands Trading Company (a company set up in 1824 by King William I to facilitate colonial trade and also a forerunner of the modern-day Algemene Bank Nederland), Wessanen also began trade in milled rice, a staple in the Dutch East Indies. During these years Remmert Laan's sons Jan and Adriaan took an increasing role in the operation of the family business.

In 1839, the company undertook factory-like processing on a major scale when it purchased a facility for the refining of vegetable oils. The purchase of the factory signaled a significant change in the character of the company and in the primary products in which the company dealt, from unprocessed grains and seeds to milled grains and processed oils. Wind was the primary source of power for Wessanen's new plants for some time. By 1865, the year of the company's centennial, Wessanen and Laan was an active cheese broker and producer of flour, vegetable oil, milled rice, barley, and related products, and employed about 100 people.

In 1868 Jan Laan died, leaving his five sons to run the business. That same year the company opened a new steam-powered flour-milling plant, built with the most up-to-date technology to replace a facility that had burned down. Only the plants for milling rice and barley continued to use windmills.

Wessanen and Laan left the cheese, seed, and grain trades at the turn of the century and focused on processed products. The company's biggest commodity was milled rice, now produced in steam-powered factories. The company had been under the direction of the Laans for five generations. Taking into consideration the risks of modern enterprise, in 1913 the family changed the structure of the company to a corporation, with a paid-in-capital of Dfl 7 million. The name N.V. Verenigde Fabrieken Wessanen and Laan was adopted, but was changed in 1916 to Wessanen's Koninklijke Fabrieken N.V. ("Koninklijke" is an honorary title bestowed upon distinguished corporations by the Dutch monarchy.)

During World War I Wessanen continued to trade much as usual, but the company lost a major export market for its finished products and a significant supplier of raw material when the Russian Revolution terminated trade between Russia and the West. Wessanen compensated for this loss by entering rolled-oat production and by starting to produce cocoa and cocoa butter.

During the 1920s, as a favorable trade climate prevailed throughout Europe and in the Americas, Wessanen regularly upgraded its production facilities. The company also sought to build factories abroad to increase productivity, but repeatedly faced stiff opposition from local governments. In 1927, however, the company did open a factory near Krakow, Poland as a joint venture with rival Dutch rice miller Van Schaardenburg. When the Polish rice market collapsed several years later, the venture was abandoned.

Wessanen survived the Great Depression relatively well; food producers are protected from drastic shrinkage of their markets since people must eat even in hard times, and the company had good product diversification. In 1938 Wessanen organized its animal feed unit as a separate division; although these products made up a minor proportion of the company's total sales, their volume was significant.

During World War II Wessanen operated at lower levels of production. Holland was invaded by the Nazis, while the Dutch East Indies were occupied by the Japanese. Raw materials could no longer be imported from, nor finished goods exported to, the colonies. The loss of this trade was a severe blow to Wessanen, and it was compounded by the growing inclination of rice-producing nations to mill their own rice rather than export it for processing. In 1951 Wessanen was forced to shut down its largest rice-milling factory in Holland, but it remained a large miller in the United States.

Throughout the 1950s, economic recovery encouraged Wessanen to enter new product areas. Research in the area of milk replacers—products used to feed calves that are raised away from their mothers—proved extremely profitable for Wessanen. At the end of 1958, the company's paid-in-capital was Dfl 68 million, up from Dfl 7 million in 1913, and in 1959 the Laan family decided to take the firm public.

The transition from private to public corporation was overseen by Wessanen President T. Verspyck and Raymond Laan. In 1962 the last Laan left the company's board of directors, marking the end of nearly two hundred years of direct family control of Wessanen. The Laan family remained its main stockholder for several years, however.

By Wessanen's bicentennial in 1965, the company had about 2,100 employees. The late 1960s brought some unfavorable developments in the company's markets: cocoa-producing countries began refining their products at home, Europe experienced a flour glut, and competition in edible oils put pressure on Wessanen's market share.

In 1971 Gerrit Hendrik van Driel became the managing director of Wessanen and began to formulate a plan to bring the company into new markets. Under van Driel's leadership, the company acquired a number of meat and animal-fat processing facilities and in 1973 laid out a plan for global diversification. Van Driel emphasized decentralized management and conservative handling of the financial risks that accompany broad expansion plans. His strategy included a transition from bulk products to higher-margin consumer products. This led to the acquisition of a cheese factory, a cheese trading company, and a milk-powder factory. The company also looked to the United States as the prime area for geographic diversification and, in the Dutch tradition, planned to grow by relying on its own assets rather than through borrowing. When necessary the company raised capital through new equity issues.

In 1978, Wessanen began to execute its program when it purchased Marigold Foods Inc. of Minneapolis, Minnesota for $20 million. Marigold produced consumer dairy products like milk, yogurt, ice cream, and cottage cheese, as well as fruit juices and drinks. A year later, Wessanen augmented its Marigold acquisition with the purchase of the Clover Leaf Creamery in Minneapolis. The acquisition made Marigold the market leader in many products and increased its coverage throughout Minnesota.

In 1979, Wessanen withdrew from almost all of its milk-replacer activities and sold a 51% interest in Wessanen Cacao to British commodity trader S.&W. Berisford in 1980. A year later it got out of the raw cocoa trade entirely, focusing instead on cheaper cocoa oil substitutes. Wessanen's Friwessa unit distributed these products and other vegetable oils, including palm oil, which was experiencing an increase in demand worldwide.

Profits began to improve for Wessanen after two unsatisfactory years in the late 1970s. By 1982 more than 60% of Wessanen's sales were generated from markets other than the Netherlands. In 1983, Wessanen acquired Crowley Foods, Inc. of Binghamton, New York, for about $16 million. Crowley, like Marigold, was primarily a dairy concern. The acquisition helped Wessanen post record earnings: profits had tripled in the five years since 1979, from Dfl 13 million to Dfl 39 million in fiscal 1983.

The mid-1980s brought Wessanen continued success. Profits increased markedly, as 30% of the company's total turnover came from the higher-margin consumer goods division in the United States. At the end of 1986 Wessanen bought the health food distributor Tree of Life Inc. in St. Augustine, Florida, now a major part of Wessanen's U.S. operations, and announced a joint venture with a cheese factory in Ireland. In 1987 the company purchased Cheshire Wholefoods, a granola producer in the United Kingdom for about £14 million. And in 1988 Wessanen acquired Gourmet Foods of St. Paul, Minnesota, and Award Foods of Dallas, Texas, for an undisclosed amount. Those two companies added about $60 million in sales to Wessanen's sales. Later that year Wessanen also bought Week's Dairy of Concord, New Hampshire and the Ohio Pure Foods group (now American Beverage Corporation) of Verona, Pennsylvania.

Wessanen's acquisitions in the United States were organized under a holding company called Wessanen USA, and benefited from each others' research and product development. For example, the Marigold unit in Minnesota brought a hard-pack frozen yogurt to market in 1987 and its success helped Crowley Foods and Axelrod Foods (another recent East Coast acquisition) to market a similar product in their own markets.

By the end of the 1980s Wessanen was a significantly different company than it had been just 15 years before. In 1989, Gerrit Hendrik van Driel, the architect of the restructuring and now chairman of the managing board, divided Wessanen's operations into three main areas: consumer products, semi-manufactured products, and bulk specialties. Consumer products included the American dairy-related and fruit-juice operations as well as health foods, processed meats, cheeses, mueslis, and chocolate products in Europe; altogether they accounted for more than 64% of group sales by the end of the 1980s. Bulk specialties like wheat, rye, cereal by-products, and animal feeds, once the mainstay of the company, amounted to only about 20% of sales, and semi-manufactures like refined oils and fats, milk powders, and starches (sold primarily to industrial bakers and chocolate manufacturers) made up 16% of revenues at the end of the decade. In late 1989 Wessanen suddenly withdrew completely from the animal-feeds sector by selling its three remaining compound feeds factories in the Netherlands and its last milk-replacers unit in the United States. The decision to withdraw from the animal-feeds sector was made because those operations were no longer aligned with Wessanen's core activities.

Wessanen intends to continue its trend toward greater diversification both in product lines and geography. The company's impressive performance during the 1980s is a tribute to innovative management, a strength that will undoubtedly be an asset when Europe's trade barriers come down after 1992. Wessanen is not only older than its competition, it is actually older than many of the countries in which it operates. Well into its third century in the food industry, Wessanen has proven its ability not only to adapt to industry changes, but also to propel them.

Principal Subsidiaries: Wessanen Nederland BV; Friwessa BV; Delicia BV; Wessanen Deutschland GmbH (West Germany); Baars Kaas BV; Van Heel's Gecondenseerde Melk Maatschappij BV; BV Leeuwarder IJs-en Melkproduktenfabriek; Zuivelonderneming De Vijfheerenlanden BV; Zuivelfabriek Salland BV; De Graaf's Bakkerijen BV; Presco International BV; Latenstein Zetmeel BV; Wessanen Meel BV; Gelerlaender Fleischwarenges mbH; Wessanen USA Inc.; Crowley Foods Inc.; A.M. Axelrod & Son Inc.; Heluva Good Cheese Inc.; Marigold Foods Inc.; Friwessa Inc.; Tree of Life Inc. (U.S.A.); American Beverage Corp. Inc. (U.S.A.).

KRAFT GENERAL FOODS INC.

Kraft Court
Glenview, Illinois 60025
U.S.A.
(708) 998–2000

Wholly owned subsidiary of Philip Morris
Incorporated: 1989
Employees: 94,000
Sales: $23 billion

Kraft General Foods was formed in March, 1989, after Philip Morris's acquisition of Kraft, Inc. in December the year before. The diversified tobacco giant's first major push into the food industry came in 1985, when it acquired the General Foods Corporation. After the Kraft acquisition was completed, Philip Morris combined the two food companies to create one subsidiary called Kraft General Foods, divided into seven major groups: General Foods USA; Kraft USA; Kraft General Foods International; Kraft General Foods Canada; Oscar Mayer; Kraft General Foods Frozen Products; and Kraft General Foods Commercial Products. While the two companies now operate as one under a united name, each has a long and rich history.

GENERAL FOODS

General Foods is in many ways the prototypical American food processor. The company pioneered in the acquisition and assimilation of smaller food companies while building a huge multi-national, multi-product corporation. It has also historically applied leading-edge technology to its product development. For example, it snatched up Clarence Birdseye's company just before he patented the process that made freezing fresh foods feasible. Tang instant breakfast drink, Pop-Rocks carbonated candy, and Cool Whip nondairy dessert topping all originated in the laboratories of General Foods. General Foods is also the largest coffee producer in the world. The company's Maxwell House, Sanka, Brim, Yuban, and General Foods' International Coffees brands make up about 25% of total sales. The company is the nation's number-three manufacturer of breakfast cereals (Post), the leader in powdered drink mixes (Kool Aid, Country Time, Crystal Light, Tang), and the nation's top producer of gelatin dessert products (Jell-O).

It is somewhat ironic that the nation's largest coffee roaster was founded by Charles W. Post, a health fanatic who tried to seduce America's coffee drinkers away from the caffeinated drink with a cereal beverage he called Postum. Post built the company that would become General Foods with a number of promising products and the marvel of modern marketing.

In 1891 Post checked into the Kellogg brothers' renowned sanitarium in Battle Creek, Michigan in hopes of revitalizing his frail health. Post had been ill for several years and was so weak that he was confined to a wheelchair. While at the Kelloggs' sanitarium, Post came up with several ideas which would prove very profitable.

Post later opened the La Vita Inn in Battle Creek, where he experimented with healing by mental suggestion and special diets. A few years later Post began marketing a cereal beverage like the one he had received as a coffee substitute at the Kelloggs'. He began marketing this blend of wheat, bran, and molasses called Postum cereal beverage in 1895. Post incorporated the Postum Cereal Co., Ltd. in 1896 with a paid-in capital of $100,000.

In 1897 Post introduced a new cereal called Grape-Nuts, made from whole wheat and malted barley flour. Grape-Nuts were baked for 20 hours, turning the starch into dextrose and creating a partially pre-digested cereal. In 1904 Post marketed a corn flake cereal under the name "Elijah's Manna." Not immediately successful, the new cereal was renamed "Post Toasties" and subsequently became a big hit with American consumers. Post continued to bring new products to the market, including Post's Bran Flakes, Post's Chocolate Bar, and Post's Wheat Meal.

Within five years of its incorporation, Postum Cereal Company's capital had risen to $5 million. The company's Battle Creek facility was the largest of its kind in the world. Postum employed 2,500 people and its factories covered more than 20 acres. Charles W. Post had meanwhile amassed a considerable personal fortune and spent his money freely to propagate his own views. Post was an outspoken critic of closed shops and labor unions and spent thousands on advertisements attacking organized labor. This crusade against unions caused boycotts of Post products at times and incurred the personal enmity of union organizers throughout the nation. Carroll Post once told an interesting tale about his brother Charles in a letter. One day the two Post brothers sat at a lunchroom counter where two brands of corn flakes—Post Toasties and Krinkle—were for sale. While the two men were eating, a railroad worker came in and asked for corn flakes. When the waitress asked which brand he wanted, the man said, "give me Krinkle. That man Post is always fighting our union." But the Posts had the last laugh: Krinkle was merely another name for Post Toasties, marketed as a reduced-price corn flake.

The Postum Cereal Company did not have trouble with labor in its own factories. It paid the highest wages in the industry, emphasized safe working conditions, and implemented accident and sickness benefit programs. The company also built about 100 homes for its workers which were sold on very favorable terms.

In May, 1914, Charles W. Post committed suicide at his winter home, in Santa Barbara, California. The day-to-day operations of the Postum Cereal Company had been run by a group of managers—C.W.'s "cabinet"—for several years. Upon his death, Post's daughter, Marjorie Merriwether Post, took over the company and launched the expansion which would create the company now known as General Foods.

Marjorie Post was well acquainted with the business when she took it over. She had often accompanied her father on business trips and frequently sat in on meetings. In 1920 she married Edward F. Hutton, the investment broker. Two years later the Postum Cereal Company went public, and Marjorie Post stepped down from active management of the company, leaving her husband, who became chairman of the company in 1923, and Colby M. Chester, who became president in 1924, to run the company's day-to-day operations. She remained a key policymaker, however, and was critical to the company's acquisition strategy and transition into General Foods.

That transition began in 1925 with the acquisition of the Jell-O Company. Jell-O was the premier dessert brand in the days before frozen pies, cakes, and novelties entered the market. In 1926 the company absorbed Swan's Down Cake Flour and Minute Tapioca. Franklin Baker's Coconut, Walter Baker's Chocolate, and Log Cabin Syrup were acquired in 1927. The company also shortened its name to Postum Company that year.

In 1928 Postum Company made a very significant acquisition: Maxwell House Coffee, whose roots date to 1885, when Joel Cheek perfected the coffee blend he served at the famous Maxwell House, in Nashville, Tennessee. President Theodore Roosevelt visited Maxwell House in 1907. When asked if he wanted a second cup of coffee, Roosevelt replied, "Yes, indeed, it's good to the last drop," giving rise to the company's famous slogan.

In 1929 the company made another significant acquisition when it paid $22 million for a controlling interest of the General Foods Company, owned by Clarence Birdseye. Birdseye had developed the first successful technique for freezing vegetables and meat. An adventurer by nature, Birdseye had gotten the idea for his freezing technique while on an expedition to Labrador. Birdseye noted that the Eskimos routinely froze caribou and fish and that it retained its flavor even when stored for months before thawing. He hypothesized that the bitterly cold air had something to do with this, as previous attempts to produce palatable frozen food used much slower freezing. Birdseye returned in 1917 to begin research. Eventually, he perfected a process that could be used commercially, and in 1924 he founded the General Seafoods Corporation in Gloucester, Massachusetts.

Marjorie Merriwether Post had noticed Birdseye's operations in 1926, but it took her three more years to convince Postum executives to acquire the company. The price doubled in that time, but Postum nevertheless happily acquired the company. The enlarged Postum Company also adopted the name General Foods in 1929, and Clarence Birdseye became head of the new General Foods laboratory, where he began work on a food dehydration process.

While the Great Depression affected all parts of the economy, food was a relatively stable industry. After record profits in 1929, General Foods' energy in 1930 went to consolidating its recent acquisitions, and earnings that year dropped slightly. In 1932 the company acquired the remaining 49% of General Foods, which it expanded very quickly, adding six new plants that year to freeze nearly 100 different products. In 1932 General Foods also purchased the Sanka Coffee Corporation, makers of decaffeinated coffee. General Foods had been distributing Sanka since 1927 through an agreement with the company's European owners.

Earnings, which in 1929 had reached $19.4 million, dropped to $10.3 million in 1932. But in 1933 they finally began to rise again as consumer purchasing power began to strengthen. In 1935, E. F. Hutton resigned as chairman of the company and C. M. Chester assumed the post, where he remained until 1946. Marjorie Post returned to the company as a director the next year, a position she retained until 1958.

During World War II, General Foods, like other food companies, achieved record sales, despite food shortages and other wartime exigencies; in 1943, sales of $260 million were more than double 1929's $128 million. During the war, the company's Denver plant produced 10-in-1 rations for the U.S. Army, and General Foods began work on the development of an instant coffee for the army in 1941. In 1943, General Foods acquired the Gaines Dog Food Company, and the next year it added Yuban premium coffee to its already strong coffee line.

General Foods had acquired a soluble coffee with its acquisition of Sanka in 1932, but it delayed the introduction of instant coffee to consumers until it had a better product. Instant Maxwell House coffee was introduced in 1945 as one of the first new consumer foods to come out after the end of the war.

In May, 1953, General Foods acquired the Perkins Products Company of Chicago. Perkins manufactured a powdered beverage mix in a number of flavors to which the consumer added sugar and water for a fruit-flavored drink. Kool-Aid has been a favorite of kids across the nation ever since. Years later General Foods added a number of other products to its beverage division—Tang, Country Time Lemonade, and Sugar Free Crystal Light are all successful products in a market which did not even exist before the 1950s. In 1954 the company entered the salad dressing market with its purchase of the Hollywood manufacturer 4 Seasons, Inc., and in 1960 Open Pit barbecue sauce was acquired.

Large acquisitions of established companies continued as General Foods diversified outside the food industry. In 1957 the company bought the SOS Company, a leading scouring-pad manufacturer, although ten years later the Federal Trade Commission ruled that the acquisition violated antitrust laws, forcing General Foods to sell the company in 1968. That year General Foods entered the fast-food restaurant business with the purchase of the Burger Chef chain for more than $15 million. In December, 1969 General Foods purchased the Viviane Woodard Cosmetic Corporation, a door-to-door operation, for $39 million. And in 1970, Kohner Brothers, a toy company, and the W. Atlee Burpee Company, the nation's largest seed company, were both acquired.

General Foods did not have as much luck with its non-food subsidiaries as it did with food businesses, and most of them were eventually disposed of. Kohner Brothers was sold to Gabriel Industries after just five years; the Viviane Woodard cosmetics business was closed in 1976; Burpee was sold in 1979; and, after consistently losing money, the Burger Chef chain was sold in 1982.

In the late 1950s and early 1960s General Foods aggressively branched out into international markets. In 1956 the company acquired a controlling interest in the La India Company, Venezuela's number-one chocolate company. In 1959 the company's Canadian subsidiary purchased the Hostess snack-food company of Canada; in 1960 it purchased the Kibon ice cream company of Brazil and the French coffee-roaster Etablessements Pierre Lemonnier S.A.; in 1961 it bought Krema Hollywood Chewing Gum Company S.A. of Paris; and General Foods of Mexico S.A. was formed in 1962. Numerous other food processors throughout the world were purchased as well. At the end of the decade General Foods had major subsidiaries operating in Canada, the United Kingdom, Australia, France, Mexico, Brazil, Venezuela, Denmark, Sweden, Spain, the Netherlands, and Italy.

By the mid-1960s General Foods was an established giant in the industry. Chairman C. W. Cook, who took over in 1965, ran a company whose outstanding successes were based on new-product development, sweeping market research, and enormous advertising budgets.

During the 1970s international acquisitions continued at a furious pace, but domestic operations settled down a bit. Frozen foods became more popular as more double-income families had less time to spend on cooking and more money to spend for premium frozen products—the company's Birds Eye frozen-food division also enjoyed a boost in earnings. But not all General Foods units benefited from such favorable demographic changes. Jell-O, for example, suffered as new products such as frozen novelty desserts came to the market. In 1979 the Jell-O unit made a major push to recapture the dessert market, employing an advertising campaign to reverse Jell-O's steady decline and, in the early 1980s, introducing products like Jell-O Pudding Pops—frozen pudding on a stick—to capitalize on its well-known name and expand its share of the market.

Nonetheless, at the end of the 1970s General Foods was not performing up to expectations. The company was overly dependent on coffee for its revenues—its various coffee brands accounted for 39% of General Foods' entire revenues in 1980.

In 1981 General Foods bought the Oscar Mayer company, the leading American hot dog maker, for $470 million, its largest acquisition to date. Oscar Mayer, founded in 1883 by a Bavarian immigrant of that name, was a family-held company until the purchase, and had a reputation for high-quality products. General Foods was trying to reduce its dependence on the cyclical coffee trade, but Wall Street critics charged that with the purchase of Oscar Mayer it was opening itself up to the wildly cyclical, low-margin packaged-meat business. Regardless, the merger did give General Foods access to an extensive refrigerated supply network. In addition, the acquisition gave General Foods a high profile in the refrigerated meat section at the supermarket: Oscar Mayer was the largest national brand of lunchmeats, and its Louis Rich turkey products unit was top in that growing segment of the market.

In 1984 the company agreed to sell its Gaines Pet Food division for $157 million. General Foods' overall performance went down as coffee sales dipped, and the Post Cereals unit, too, began to slide.

In September, 1985 Philip Morris purchased General Foods for $5.6 billion. Philip Morris had long been known as an aggressive marketer. Its chairman, Hamish Maxwell, had plans for turning around the giant food processor and at the same time decreasing Philip Morris's reliance on the shrinking tobacco market. In January, 1987, Philip Smith became CEO of General Foods. Smith began a massive reorganization of General Foods in 1987, splitting its three core product lines—coffees, meats, and assorted groceries—into separate units.

KRAFT

Kraft is one of the oldest and best-known food brands in the world. Many of Kraft USA's products, such as Velveeta pasteurized process cheese spread, Parkay margarine, Miracle Whip salad dressing, and Philadelphia Brand cream cheese, have become integral parts of the American diet, and Kraft products are sold in 130 countries around the world. Such stability seems enviable, yet it has been a mixed blessing. Kraft has long sought a proper balance between the traditional products on which its reputation is based and the development of new endeavors aimed at sustained growth.

One of Kraft, Inc.'s primary predecessor companies was established by James L. Kraft, the son of a Canadian farmer. In 1903 Kraft started a wholesale cheese distribution business in Chicago. Kraft hoped to relieve grocers of the need to travel daily to the cheese market by delivering cheese to their doors. Business was dismal at first and Kraft lost $3,000 as well as his horse the first year.

But the business eventually took hold and James was joined by his four brothers Fred, Charles, Norman, and John. In 1909 the business was incorporated as J.L. Kraft & Bros. Company. New-product development and innovative advertising fueled the company's growth. As early as 1911, Kraft was mailing circulars to retail grocers and advertising on elevated trains and billboards. Later, he was among the first to use color advertisements in national magazines. In 1912 Kraft opened a New York office to begin developing an international business. By 1914 the company sold 31 varieties of cheese throughout the country, and that year it opened its own cheese factory in Stocton, Illinois.

Before the advent of refrigeration, cheese was sold in large wheels, which spoiled quickly after they were cut open. Kraft developed a blended, pasteurized cheese that did not spoil and could be packaged in small tins. Kraft began producing what it called process cheese in 1915, and received a patent in 1916. Six million pounds of this cheese were sold to the U.S. Army during World War I.

In 1919 Kraft placed its first advertisements in national magazines. The next year, Kraft made its first acquisition, of a Canadian cheese company. In 1924, Kraft's name was changed to Kraft Cheese Company and it offered its first shares to the public. That year Kraft also opened its first overseas sales office, in London, which led to the establishment of Kraft Cheese Company Ltd. there in 1927, the same year it moved into Germany by opening a sales office in Hamburg. In 1928, Kraft merged with Phenix Cheese Corporation, the maker of Philadelphia Brand cream cheese. The newly formed Kraft-Phenix Cheese Corporation had captured 40% of the nation's cheese market by 1930 and had operations in Canada, Australia, Britain, and Germany.

The 1920s spawned another growing dairy concern, the National Dairy Products Corporation, whose fortunes were soon to be linked with Kraft-Phenix. National Dairy was the product of a 1923 merger between the Hydrox Corporation of Chicago, an ice cream company established in 1881 and purchased in 1914 by pharmacist Thomas McInnerney, and the Rieck-McJunkin Dairy Company of Pittsburgh. Throughout the remainder of the 1920s, National Dairy acquired other small dairying concerns in the East and Midwest, including the Breyer Ice Cream Company and Breakstone Bros., Inc., the sour cream and cottage cheese company. In 1929, National Dairy set out to acquire Kraft-Phenix; the merger was completed on May 12, 1930. The group of companies assembled by McInnerney prior to the Kraft-Phenix merger eventually formed the core of Kraft's dairy group.

The merger did not radically affect the way the two companies operated. McInnerney's strategy had always been to provide essentially autonomous subsidiaries with the resources needed for growth. Consequently, Kraft functioned independently from New York–based National Dairy, which acted primarily as a holding company.

After the merger, Kraft settled down to introduce many of the brands that now form the heart of its consumer product line; Velveeta pasteurized process cheese spread had been introduced in 1928; Miracle Whip salad dressing and Kraft caramels came in 1933, the famous macaroni and cheese dinner in 1937, and Parkay margarine in 1940. Again, innovative advertising, this time on radio, encouraged quick public acceptance of the new products. In 1933 the company sponsored the "Kraft Musical Review," a two-hour musical variety show. Later the program was shortened to one hour and broadcast weekly as the "Kraft Music Hall," hosted by Bing Crosby. Overseas operations, guided by a policy that mandated local control and products tailored to meet the needs and tastes of foreign consumers, expanded. Meanwhile, in 1935 National Dairy introduced Sealtest ice cream, named after a quality-control system for its dairy products.

Kraft was a major food supplier during World War II. By the end of 1941, four million pounds of cheese a week were being shipped to Britain. Many Kraft products, including field rations of cheese, were produced for the U.S. government. Kraft's labs researched better methods of food production while home economists at Kraft Kitchens, a division established in the home economics department in 1924, developed recipes to make wartime shortages less painful.

In 1945 the Kraft Cheese Company became Kraft Foods Company. In the postwar years, Kraft resumed the formula of new-product development and advertising that had built the company. In 1947, Kraft created and sponsored the first network program on television, the "Kraft Television Theatre." Along with the new advertising vehicle new products, like sliced process cheese in 1950 and Cheez Whiz pasteurized process cheese spread in 1952 were introduced.

In 1951 the postwar economic boom drove National Dairy's sales over the $1 billion mark for the first time. Thomas McInnerney died in 1952 and J. L. Kraft died the following year. Kraft's death marked the end of the Kraft family's leadership of the business. The company began to reorganize along more centralized lines soon after its founders died. The autonomous subsidiaries became divisions of a single operating company in 1956 and 1957. Meanwhile, the company took its first cautious steps toward diversification with the acquisition of Metro Glass, a maker of glass packaging, in 1956.

During the late 1950s and the 1960s, Kraft continued to expand its product line, adding new products like jellies and preserves in 1956, marshmallows in 1959, barbecue sauce in 1960, and individually wrapped cheese slices in 1965. During the 1960s, Kraft also introduced many of its products in foreign markets.

In 1969 National Dairy renamed itself Kraftco and in 1972 it transferred its headquarters from New York to the Chicago suburb of Glenview. The company name was changed again in 1976 to Kraft Inc. to emphasize the company's focus on food processing and to more clearly identify it with the internationally known Kraft trademark. Reorganization accompanied the name change. The movement toward a more centralized structure that had begun in the 1950s was accomplished by partitioning the company into divisions according to specific markets or products.

Kraft manifested a decidedly conservative business strategy during the 1970s. While other major food companies sought acquisitions to shore up sagging profits, Kraft did not. New-product introductions also slowed somewhat; after the introduction of Light n' Lively yogurt and ice milk in 1969, squeezeable Parkay margarine came in 1973 and Breyers yogurt in 1977. The difficult business climate of the 1970s may have encouraged a defensive posture as inflation increased costs and cut into profits.

John M. Richman, who began at Kraft as a lawyer at the National Dairy Products Corporation, became Kraft's chairman and CEO in 1979. Richman's plan was to strengthen the company's position in its traditional markets while diversifying into higher-growth industries. His first move in this direction was truly a bold stoke: a merger with Dart Industries, a Los Angeles–based conglomerate headed by the flamboyant Justin Dart.

Dart Industries was established in 1902 as the United Drug Company. Dart himself began his career in the retail-drug business and built Rexall Drugs into one of the largest chains of drugstores in the country. With

Rexall as his base, Dart began an aggressive acquisition campaign, diversifying into chemicals, plastics, glass, cosmetics, electric appliances, and land development. In 1969, the company name was changed to Dart Industries to reflect this diversity. At the time of the merger, the flagship of Dart Industries was its hugely successful Tupperware subsidiary, which sold plastic food containers through direct sales by independent dealers using a "home party" plan.

The aggressive, innovative, and rapidly growing Dart Industries fit perfectly into Richman's plan; it offered Kraft instant diversification. The merger also offered advantages for Dart and his company. Richman's boldness appealed to Dart, who thought that Kraft would give Dart Industries some stability. Thus, Dart & Kraft was launched on September 25, 1980 with John Richman as its chairman and CEO and Justin Dart as chairman of the executive committee. Kraft and the subsidiaries of Dart—Tupperware, West Bend appliances, Duracell batteries, Wilsonart plastics, and Thatcher glass—continued to operate independently. However, some analysts doubted that such a diverse company would succeed.

As in many restructurings, there were some early rough spots, but major changes in operating procedure were confined to top managers, leaving middle managers in their familiar roles and easing their transition. Altogether, management apparently succeeded in uniting two very different firms with a minimum of friction.

Industry analysts, nonetheless, felt compelled to ask which partner would dominate the merger. Although Kraft was the larger of the two companies, the consensus favored the more aggressive and growth-oriented Dart. Dart was, after all, given preference in the new company's name and it was Kraft's desire to become more like Dart that initially led to the merger. On the first anniversary of the merger, Richman himself commented that "in terms of organization and outlook, we're more a Dart than a Kraft."

Indeed, Dart & Kraft's initial activities bore out this assessment. Soon after the merger, the company bid $460 million for the Hobart Corporation, a manufacturer of food-service equipment; the deal was completed in April, 1981. And even while the Hobart deal was being negotiated, Dart & Kraft announced that it was considering further acquisitions.

Although several smaller acquisitions followed in the next two years, diversification slowed because several subsidiaries experienced managerial problems or proved vulnerable to the recession of the early 1980s. Poor performers included Kraft's European operations and its food-service business, and Dart's plastics unit and its West Bend appliances. Even Hobart was troubled by sagging profits and declining market share in its Kitchen Aid division, which produced top-of-the-line kitchen appliances. Company efforts to get these businesses back on track were beginning to show results when trouble struck Tupperware.

Tupperware had been a phenomenal success; it doubled sales and earnings every five years prior to 1980. But in 1983 sales slipped 7% and profits were down 15%. Tupperware's slide was attributed to attrition among its dealers, as more women took jobs outside the home, leaving fewer to sell, and to buy, Tupperware.

In 1984 the company planned to increase returns from 13.3% to 18%, to place Dart & Kraft in the top fifth of the consumer-products industry. This ambitious goal was to be attained by adding new products, extending existing lines, and using aggressive marketing and advertising.

Michael A. Miles, the man who had revived Kentucky Fried Chicken, was brought into direct the new effort. Miles first cut costs by overhauling the European division. Many of Kraft's brands competed in mature markets. Additions to these lines—for example, bacon and cream cheese-flavored salad dressings—boosted sales. The company also acquired promising new brands that appealed to the upscale consumer. Among these were the import-style cheeses of Churny Company, Inc., Celestial Seasonings herb teas, Lender's bagels, and Frusen Glädjé premium ice cream.

Similar tactics were encouraged in Dart & Kraft's non food businesses, but when by 1986 they continued to lag, the company decided, in effect, to dissolve the six-year-old merger. Hobart, Tupperware, Wilsonart, and West Bend were spun off into a new company called Premark International, Inc. Kraft retained all the product lines it brought with it into the 1980 merger, with the addition of Duracell batteries.

Kraft followed through on its plan to expand its product lines and market them aggressively, a strategy that won visible gains. The company's management seemed to have rediscovered J. L. Kraft's strategy, which combined the stability of well-known brand names with creative marketing and the continuous development of new products aimed at changing American tastes.

Philip Morris's designs on the packaged-foods industry became clear when the company purchased Kraft in October, 1988. In March, 1989 Philip Morris merged the Kraft and General Foods units into one giant entity called Kraft General Foods. At the helm was Kraft's Michael Miles.

There is little doubt that a corporation the size of Kraft General Foods will be able to make a profound impact on the packaged-foods industry. Whether the company will become the well-oiled machine parent Philip Morris hopes it will remains to be seen. Nonetheless, with Michael Miles' experience in corporate turnarounds and the company's strength in so many categories, it is a good bet that Kraft General Foods will succeed.

Principal Operating Units: General Foods USA; Kraft USA; Kraft General Foods International; Kraft General Foods Canada; Oscar Mayer Foods Corporation; Kraft General Foods Frozen Products; Kraft General Foods Commercial Products.

Further Reading: Dudley, Charles Eaves. *Post City, Texas*, Austin, Texas, State Historical Association, 1952; *Kraft, Inc.—Through the Years*, Glenview, Illinois, Kraft, Inc., 1988.

Land O'Lakes, Inc.

LAND O'LAKES, INC.

4401 Lexington Avenue North
Arden Hills, Minnesota 55112
U.S.A.
(612) 481–2222

Cooperative
Incorporated: 1921 as Minnesota Cooperative Creamery Association, Inc.
Employees: 7,000
Sales: $2.3 billion

Land O'Lakes is one of the largest agricultural supply and food marketing cooperatives in the United States, providing both its members and the public with food products and production materials. Best known for its butter and other quality dairy products, the cooperative also manufactures feeds, seeds, fertilizers, and other chemicals to meet the needs of half a million farmers and ranchers.

On June 7, 1921, 350 farmers from all over Minnesota gathered in St. Paul to vote on the organization of a statewide dairy cooperative. With a unanimous vote, the Minnesota Cooperative Creamery Association, forerunner to Land O'Lakes, was born.

Unlike investor-owned corporations, cooperatives work for and answer to their member-patrons, who benefit in direct proportion to the amount of business they do each year with the cooperative—how many products they supply, or how many they buy. Because each member-patron has one vote, cooperatives are democratic enough to have appealed to the independent American farmers who first joined.

Still, as the *St. Paul Pioneer Press* was to write 25 years later, skeptics of farm cooperatives existed everywhere in 1921: "Nobody would ever induce American farmers to work together," they claimed, because a farmer was "too individualistic by nature and too firmly set in his own ways to adapt his operating methods to the machinery of any organization." What they didn't count on was the energy and dedication of the men who had the vision behind Land O'Lakes.

Beginning with a meager financial stake of $1,375, $1,000 of it borrowed from the Farm Bureau, the cooperative's directors launched a statewide membership campaign. Their project was given a boost when in 1922, after a long fight, the U.S. Senate passed the Capper-Volstead bill, which legalized the marketing of farm products through cooperative agencies. The first year's returns showed a slender profit.

John Brandt, one of the original 15 directors elected to run the organization, became president of the association in 1923. He believed that by working together, competing creameries could raise their profits *and* offer a better product to their patrons. He urged cooperation among farmers, engineered joint shipments of butter, and proposed a common standard of quality. Most importantly, he and the other directors of the cooperative decided to concentrate on the quality production and aggressive marketing of "sweet cream" butter, butter made from cream before it soured. Although more costly to make and not as familiar to the public, sweet butter tasted better and kept longer.

In February, 1924 the cooperative announced a contest to capture the public's attention: its high-quality product needed a catchier name than "Minnesota Cooperative Creamery Butter." First prize was $500 in gold. An overwhelming response brought in over 100,000 entries; the contest was tied between two winners who both thought of "Land O'Lakes." Soon thereafter an Indian maiden appeared on the butter's packages, completing the familiar image. The origins of this Indian maiden, however, remain a mystery.

In April, 1924 the cooperative won a contract with the U.S. Navy for 430,000 pounds of the new sweet cream butter and soon thereafter met with a growing demand from American housewives for its conveniently packaged quarter-pound sticks. As Land O'Lakes was already becoming a household name, only two years after the contest, the cooperative changed its name to Land O'Lakes Creameries, Inc. in 1926.

Land O'Lakes first ventured outside of the dairy business two years later, when it organized egg and poultry divisions. This step toward diversification was to prove crucial during the Depression years, when dairy businesses throughout the nation suffered enormous losses. In 1930 dairy production was the lowest it had been in two decades, and by December, 1933 butter prices had declined to 15¢ a pound, the lowest figure for that month in twenty-five years. Excess production and surplus holdings were making it almost impossible for American farmers to get back their cost of production, and dozens of creameries held meetings to decide whether they should continue operating. Although Land O'Lakes suffered setbacks due to these market forces between 1929 and 1940, highly imaginative management and a willingness to fight economic trends cut the cooperative's losses considerably. In fact, for much of the Depression Land O'Lakes sales actually grew because of two central strategies.

The first of these strategies was to seek new markets for its products. Before the Depression Land O'Lakes had dealt mostly with large store chains and other nationwide distributors. But with many of these large accounts retrenching or vanishing altogether in the crunch, Land O'Lakes began to set up smaller sales branches that could sell directly to groceries and other small outlets. Partly as a result of this marketing strategy, and partly because Land O'Lakes Sweet Cream Butter was being advertised nationally for the first time, Land O'Lakes was able to sell a record 100 million pounds of butter in 1930.

The second strategy was to diversify the products the cooperative offered both to its member farmers and to the public. Seeking to spread the risks of operation, Land O'Lakes began an Agricultural Services Division in 1929 to try to reduce member costs for feed, seed, and other farming supplies. In 1934 the cooperative joined three large cheese cooperatives in the operation of 95 cheese factories, and in 1937 Land O'Lakes opened its first milk drying plant, completing a decade of experimentation which pioneered the production of dry milk. As early as 1926, several individual creameries had begun producing powder from buttermilk, previously a waste product. So, when World War II called for milk in a form which didn't require refrigeration and had a fraction of the bulk, Land O'Lakes was prepared. All of these changes were ultimately successful expansions and contributed to Land O'Lakes' relative prosperity in difficult times.

In 1938, workers at the main plant in Minneapolis went on strike for a wage increase and a closed shop policy. The strike was amicably settled when the closed-shop demand was withdrawn and a new wage agreement was approved, but there were $400,000 in losses.

During World War II, Land O'Lakes was required by federal order to set aside 30% of its butter for sale to the government. The cooperative also had a quota of dry milk for the war effort, stepping up production from 22 million pounds in 1941 to 119 million pounds in 1945. By the war's end, Land O'Lakes was producing dried milk and dried eggs in 22 different plants, and eventually became the world's largest manufacturer of dry milk products.

In 1946 Land O'Lakes celebrated its Silver Jubilee under the banner "Pioneers for 25 Years." It prepared for a prosperous future by entering the ice cream and fluid milk markets for the first time, and by developing the world's first successful milk replacement, a dry meal for nursing calves. This meal, a substitute for the skim milk calves were usually fed, overcame opposition to the use of skim milk as a dry milk base.

In 1952 John Brandt, known as "Mr. Land O'Lakes," died after serving as president and general manager for nearly 30 years. Frank Stone became general manager, and M. H. Mauritson became president. Later, a restructuring of the management changed these positions to president and chairman of the board.

To develop its ice cream line, Land O'Lakes acquired Bridgeman Creameries, a chain of soda-grills in Minnesota and Wisconsin, and the operator of fluid milk businesses in North Dakota and Minnesota. The cooperative also expanded three turkey processing plants in 1954.

During the 1960s, the cooperative continued to grow at an astonishing rate. It acquired Terrace Park Dairies of Sioux Falls, South Dakota, a full-line dairy, and H. C. Christians Company, a Chicago manufacturer of butter, and merged with Dairy Maid Products Cooperative of Eau Claire, Wisconsin. In addition, management responded to the broadening scope of Land O'Lakes' interests by making 60 new assignments and by re-structuring the cooperative's internal organization. By the decade's end, Land O'Lakes' sales had reached $400 million and assets totaled nearly $100 million, figures double those of 1960.

Another key merger occurred in 1970, as Land O'Lakes was joined by the Farmers Regional Cooperative, also known as Felco. This move increased Land O'Lakes' capacity to produce and market agricultural production goods (such as fertilizers and insecticides) for its member-patrons, and also brought Ralph Hofstad, Felco's president, to Land O'Lakes, where he is now president. Also in 1970 Land O'Lakes Creameries changed its name to simply Land O'Lakes to better reflect its diverse business.

Expansion and diversification continued at a rapid rate as the 1970s drew to a close. In 1978 the cooperative entered the red meat business for the first time with the acquisition of Spencer Beef, the country's seventeenth largest meatpacker, and in 1980 Land O'Lakes began soybean processing in conjunction with Dawson Mills. The cooperative also produced new products such as "But-R-Cups" and Country Morning Blend, a spread made of 40% sweet cream butter and 60% corn oil margarine, offering more options to American households and food service businesses. Introduced to the food service market in 1975 after ten years of development, "But-R-Cups" were single servings of butter packaged entirely by machine ensuring portion control and standardized freshness. Country Morning Blend appeared in 1981 and was aimed at consumers who preferred the taste of butter but couldn't afford it. It was cleverly designed to make a dent in the margarine market while keeping converts from butter, always Land O'Lakes' mainstay, to a minimum.

In 1981 Land O'Lakes moved into its new corporate offices in Arden Hills, Minnesota, just north of the Twin Cities, with facilities for research, testing, sales, and training.

At the end of the fiscal year 1982, too much supply, too little demand, escalating production costs, and excessive interest rates on existing debts resulted in losses in excess of $19 million. Land O'Lakes had moved too fast and taken on too much in the 1970s and early 1980s, critics said, pointing to the cooperative's ventures in beef, agronomy, petroleum, and soybeans. A merger with Midland Cooperative that year did eventually bring savings in excess of $4 million, and Land O'Lakes' fiscal health was never seriously threatened.

In 1985 a class-action suit brought against Land O'Lakes by 96 turkey farmers claimed that the cooperative had overcharged the farmers for their participation in a marketing pool in 1980. Land O'Lakes eventually settled out of court for approximately $1.5 million.

In recent years Land O'Lakes has shown a continued willingness to expand, while carefully monitoring its less-established commodities. In January, 1987 Land O'Lakes launched an extensive joint venture with Cenex Cooperative to market feed, seed, farm chemicals, and petroleum. Later in the year it embarked on a more limited venture with Mid-America Dairymen (taking advantage of the fact that Mid-America's regional offices and Land O'Lakes' corporate headquarters are both located in Arden Hills) to operate dairy plants together. Land

O'Lakes also left the petroleum resources business in 1987 and has announced plans to sell its turkey and red meat businesses in 1989, reflecting a concern that industry overproduction, widely fluctuating market prices, and increasing operating costs would continue to make their operation unprofitable.

Land O'Lakes will enter the 1990s in a position of considerable strength. Its 1988 margin of $49.4 million from continuing operations before income taxes was the highest in the cooperative's 68-year history. While its research and development will respond to consumers' concerns by featuring lower fat and lower cholesterol items, Land O'Lakes Butter has no challenger threatening its place as the best-selling butter in the United States.

Principal Subsidiaries: Country Lake Foods; Research Seeds; Farmers Marketing Resource; Alex Fries and Brother; Land O'Lakes Finance Company; Cenex/Land O'Lakes Ag, Inc.

Further Reading: Ruble, K.D. *Men to Remember: How 100,000 Neighbors Made History*. Chicago, Lakeside Press, 1947.

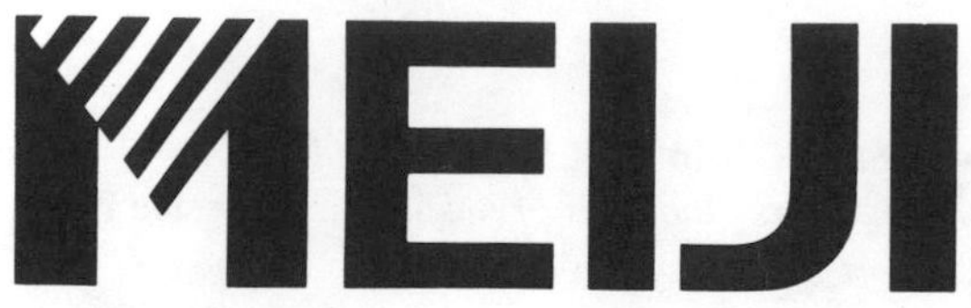

MEIJI MILK PRODUCTS COMPANY, LIMITED

3-6, Kyobashi 2-chome
Chuo-ku
Tokyo 104
Japan
(03) 281-6118

Public Company
Incorporated: 1917 as Boso Condensed Milk
Employees: 5,593
Sales: ¥374.5 billion (US$3 billion)
Stock Index: Tokyo Osaka Nagoya

Meiji Milk Products Company, Limited, the company that introduced condensed milk to Japanese consumers in 1917, is Japan's second-largest producer of fresh and powdered milk. However, the company has gradually changed its marketing thrust over the past several decades and is looking beyond basic dairy products for its future development. Meiji's sales of infant formula and yogurt products now rank highest in the nation, and the company is developing additional products and markets aggressively, to position itself as a leading general food company.

Milk was not a popular beverage in pre-1917 Japan, but a growing awareness of its nutritional value and an appreciation of the storage convenience of unopened cans helped make the launch of condensed milk in Japan feasible.

With the participation of the Meiji Sugar Manufacturing Company, Boso Condensed Milk was founded in the closing months of World War I. Japan had lately risen to the status of a world power, and the resulting increase in contact with Western nations had begun to weaken the resistance of the Japanese public toward departures from traditional dietary customs and habits.

But within months of the launch, a postwar recession began to slow the economy. It took several years for condensed milk to gain general acceptance. Recovery was gradual until the late 1920s, when a period of rapid industrialization took hold. As workers from rural areas flocked to the new factory sites, the mood was again favorable for acceptance of new products and changes in dietary habits.

From the invasion of Manchuria in the early 1930s until the end of World War II, Japan was preoccupied with the production and use of munitions. But despite wartime difficulties in transporting goods, Boso continued to make gains.

When it merged with the Tokyo Confectionery Company in 1940, Boso changed its name to Meiji Milk Products Company, Limited. The company then began to diversify, adding a line of chocolate, candy, gum, snack foods, and other confections, and Meiji grew quickly.

In 1949, Meiji was able to strengthen its position through a merger with Japan Dairy Products and three other companies. The following year, Meiji took over the Imagame factory from the Hokkaido Dairy Farm Association, and also bought the Tokyo Dairy Industry and the Shoman Milk Company. A merger in 1951 brought Asahi Milk Products into the Meiji group.

Although most of the companies Meiji had acquired through these mergers were primarily milk producers, the need for continuing diversification had become a significant factor in planning for the future. The use of condensed milk as a dietary supplement for infants set the stage for development of a line of infant formula and baby food, and the postwar baby boom created a ready market.

In the 1950s, as ice cream became popular, Meiji decided to specialize in a high-grade product and eventually introduced "Lady Borden"—to this day an upscale market leader. Meiji's agreement with the Borden Company, an American food company, was the first of a number of business relationships Meiji has maintained profitably with foreign companies.

The next logical step was to introduce frozen foods, both for individual consumers in the grocery market and in institutional quantities for restaurants, hospitals, and other large organizations. Foods such as pizza, pilaf, frozen rice, and fried entrees have been consistently strong sellers, along with puddings and other desserts, margarine, and creams.

New products are developed in-house, for the most part. Meiji's research-and-development department has explored fermentation processes and worked to develop more efficient technologies for 70 years. One of Meiji's most successful products is Meiji Infant Soft Curd FK-P, an infant formula popular in Japan and many other countries. Another, Meiji Bulgaria Yogurt LB51, is the leading yogurt in Japan.

The growing interest in health foods in the past several decades has not only spurred yogurt sales but also led to the development of other products, such as popular bottled yogurt drinks. Meiji has established a subsidiary, Health Way, Inc., to develop and market new health-related foods.

The market for dairy foods has fluctuated from time to time, with factors such as the rise and fall of the birth rate, but in general the market is a growing one; the market for cheese in particular appears to be rising steadily. Through an agreement with Borden, Meiji imports natural cheese and manufactures and markets processed cheese in Japan.

Branching out into nonfood products and services has also been profitable for Meiji. After manufacturing animal feeds for a number of years, the company has started raising livestock, and it also manufactures veterinary medicines.

One of Meiji's research-and-development sites, the Meiji Institute of Health Science, has been instrumental in adding a line of pharmaceutical products to the company's wares. Among their products are antibiotics, enzymes, and agricultural chemicals. Other products, such as an anticancer drug using lactic acid bacilli, are under development. A Meiji vaccine has proven effective when tested against B-type hepatitis.

Meiji has also capitalized on the time-saving services that have become important to Japanese consumers. Nice Day, Inc., a Meiji subsidiary, operates a shop-at-home service for supplies related to child-rearing. Another specializes in home delivery of foods, and still another provides communication services for users of personal computers. Real estate is another interest the company has developed during the 1980s.

But the main focus of Meiji's efforts continues to be its original interest: the food market. In aspiring to become a major general food manufacturer, the company works with several others overseas. For example, Meiji has an agreement with the England and Wales Milk Marketing Board, a major British dairy organization, to work together to develop new yogurt-related products and technology. Working with the American company Abbott Laboratories provides Meiji with the technology to produce new nutritional products.

In addition to marketing its products to domestic and overseas food outlets, Meiji has also established its own chain of franchised food stores. Meiji's innovation, diversification, and strong marketing are expected to move the company in the direction it has chosen, and it is fast becoming a major, comprehensive food supplier.

Principal Subsidiaries: Meiji Feedstuff Company, Limited; Nippon Canned Foods Company, Limited; Meiji Oils and Fats Company, Limited; Tokyo Gyunyo Unyu Company, Limited; Tokyo Meinyu Hanhai Company, Limited; Tohoku Meihan Company, Limited; Tomei Foods Company, Limited; Chubu Meihan Company, Limited; Kansai Meihan Company, Limited; Kyushu Meinyu Hanbai Company, Limited; Hokkaido Meihan Company, Limited; Chugoku Meihan Company, Limited; Asahi Broiler Company, Limited; Meiji Kenko Ham Company, Limited; Kanto Seiraku Company, Limited; Meiji-Borden, Incorporated; Wako Livestock Company, Limited; Okinawa Meiji Nyugyo Company, Limited; Tokyo Vehicles Co., Ltd.; Meiji Custom Beef Co., Ltd.; Meiji Frozen Desserts Co., Ltd.; Meiji Travel Co., Ltd.; Meiji Techno-Service Inc.; Health Way Co., Ltd.; Nice Day, Inc.; Masternet Inc.; Camp Co., Ltd.; Meiji Sante Ole Co., Ltd..

MEIJI SEIKA KAISHA, LTD.

MEIJI SEIKA KAISHA, LTD

4–16, Kyobashi 2-chome
Chuo-ku
Tokyo 104
Japan
(03) 272–6511

Public Company
Incorporated: 1916
Employees: 5,651
Sales: ¥286.4 billion (US$2.29 billion)
Stock Index: Tokyo Osaka Nagoya

Founded in 1916 as a manufacturer of biscuits and caramels, Meiji Seika Kaisha today is one of Japan's leading producers of chocolate and confectionery products. The company also produces many other foods, as well as pharmaceuticals. Meiji has applied its technological strengths aggressively to enter new markets at home and abroad.

Meiji sought to establish a competitive advantage right from the start by being the first company to introduce chocolate snacks, bars, and candies, all of which quickly became a standard part of the Japanese diet. These products were soon followed by other snack and health-related items.

In 1936, the company diversified into the production of canned vegetables and fruit. The technology used in this expansion was later applied to the manufacture and packaging of a variety of related food products, including cocoa, juices, and carbonated drinks, powdered mixes, and high-protein health foods.

Meiji entered the pharmaceutical market when it began to produce penicillin in 1946. This diversification was a logical outgrowth of the company's experience in using fermentation in food production. Successful introductions of other antibiotic products, geriatric and cancer drugs, and diagnostic reagents provided high levels of return on Meiji's extensive research and manufacturing investments and served as the basis for later development of animal feed additives, germicides, and herbicides both for export and for domestic use. Meiji is one of the largest antibiotic producers in the world; pharmaceuticals currently represent approximately 40% of the company's total sales.

Beginning in the late 1960s, Meiji turned its attention abroad, establishing its first United States subsidiary, Meiji Seika (U.S.A.), for the import and export of food and confectionery products in 1969. Another American subsidiary, Stauffer-Meiji, was established in 1985 and began manufacturing cookies and crackers from its Pennsylvania headquarters in 1986.

Additional marketing and sales affiliates for food and confectionery items were formed in Singapore in 1974, Europe and Colombia in 1984, and Taiwan in 1986. A joint venture with United Biscuits in 1971 brought that British company's McVitie biscuits to Japan in exchange for Meiji's confectionery expertise. The next year Meiji began to import chocolate manufacturing technology from Switzerland's Interfood Ltd. (now Jacobs Suchard A.G.).

In 1973, Meiji established the Dong-Myung Industrial Company Ltd. in Korea to produce and market its pharmaceutical products. These drugs were subsequently introduced in more than 60 countries through affiliates formed in Indonesia in 1974, Thailand in 1979, and Brazil in 1983—the location of another affiliate created nine years earlier to manufacture and sell the company's veterinary products.

By the 1980s, Meiji's confectionery technology was in high demand. Two joint ventures, one in the United States in 1988 and the other with the French-based Beghin Say S.A. in 1989, were established to manufacture and market the artificial sweetener fructooligo saccharide, which Meiji had introduced in Japan in 1984.

Today, under the management of its current chairman, Takeshi Nakagawa, Meiji operates 12 plants, nine research laboratories, 93 branch offices, 45 subsidiaries, three overseas offices, and 102 sales offices worldwide. While continuing to focus on confectionery products, food, and pharmaceuticals, the company has also begun to develop more health-oriented food products, new drugs, enzymes, edible fungi, and agricultural chemicals.

Meiji's skill in applying technological advancements to new product development will be a key factor in its future growth. Swings in the value of the yen, intensified consumer demand and changing tastes, and increasing competition from both domestic and foreign firms challenge the company's major business areas. As the competitive environment, in particular, forces Meiji to reduce product prices in order to hold onto its market share, the company will have to continue to institute operating and production efficiencies and cost reduction measures if it is to match its high level of productivity and performance in the future.

Principal Subsidiaries: Meiji Trading Corp.; Meiji Kosan Co., Ltd.; Meiji Sangyo Co., Ltd.; Meiji Chewing Gum Co., Ltd.; Ronde Corp.; Dohnan Shokuhin Co., Ltd.; Zao Shokuhin Co., Ltd.; Okayamaken Shokuhin Co., Ltd.; Ehime Kanzume Co., Ltd.; Uwajima Canning Co., Ltd.; Taiyo Shokuhin Co., Ltd.; Meiji Shokunhin Co., Ltd.; Yamanashi Jozo Co., Ltd.; Meiji Baking Co., Ltd.; Meiji Frozen Dessert Corp.; Foyer Co., Ltd.; Chocolatier Meiji Co., Ltd.; Meiji Seika Retail Co., Ltd.; Meiji Food Service Co., Ltd.; Fuji Amido Chemical Co., Ltd.; Meiji Food Service Co., Ltd.; Fuji Amido Chemical Co., Ltd.; Nitto Co., Ltd.; Meiji Kaihatsu Co., Ltd.; Meito Warehouse Co., Ltd.; Mayp Co., Ltd.; Suchard

& Tober, Ltd.; Meiji McVitie, Ltd.; Meiji Seika Pharma International, Ltd.; Sanofi-Meiji Pharmaceuticals Co., Ltd.; Meiji Engineering Ltd.; Meiji Information System Center Ltd.; Meiji Jewelery; Meiji Seika (U.S.A.) Inc.; Stauffer-Meiji Co., Inc.

NABISCO BRANDS, INC.

Nabisco Brands Plaza
East Hanover, New Jersey 07936
U.S.A.
(201) 503–2000

Wholly owned subsidiary of RJR Nabisco, Inc.
Incorporated: 1898 as the National Biscuit Company
Employees: 35,000
Sales: $6 billion

For nearly a century, Nabisco has been one of the most widely recognized names in the American food industry. Today the company is among the world's largest manufacturers of cookies and crackers, featuring such famous brands as Oreo, Fig Newtons, and Premium Saltines.

Nabisco Brands was formed in 1981 through a merger of Nabisco and Standard Brands. In 1985 R.J. Reynolds Industries, Inc. acquired Nabisco Brands in one of the largest takeovers in business history. The origins of Nabisco, however, date back to the formation of the National Biscuit Company at the end of the 19th century. In its early years, the company was usually called N.B.C. In 1941 the company adopted Nabisco, already a popular nickname, as the preferred abbreviation, but it was not until 1971 that Nabisco became the official corporate name.

The National Biscuit Company resulted from the 1898 merger of the midwestern American Biscuit Company, itself the result of the merger of 40 midwestern bakeries, and the eastern New York Biscuit Company, formed from eight bakeries and a smaller firm, the United States Baking Company. Thus, N.B.C. represented the culmination of decades of amalgamation within the biscuit industry. With 114 bakeries and a capital of $55 million, the Chicago-based company held a virtual monopoly on cookie and cracker manufacturing in the United States.

The chief architect of the 1898 merger and the first chairman of the new company was Adolphus Green. Green, a Chicago lawyer and shrewd businessman who had negotiated the American Biscuit Company merger, remained the guiding force at N.B.C. during the first 20 years of its existence. It was Green who was responsible for N.B.C.'s legendary emphasis on standardized, brand name products. Every N.B.C. bakery adhered to exact recipes and uniform standards of production, and N.B.C. developed products that could be nationally identified with the company. All of its merchandise was marked with the company's distinctive emblem: an oval topped by a cross with two bars. (Green found the symbol in a catalog of medieval Italian printers' marks, where it was said to represent the triumph of good over evil.)

Green decided to launch the National Biscuit Company by introducing a new line of biscuits. He chose the ordinary soda cracker, but gave N.B.C.'s an unusual octagonal shape and packaged it in a special protective container. Until then, crackers had been sold in bulk from cracker barrels or large crates, which did little to retard sogginess or spoilage. N.B.C. took crackers out of the barrel and put them into small cardboard boxes with the company's patented "In-er-Seal" waxed paper lining to retain freshness.

Novelty packaging was not enough. Green also commissioned the Philadelphia advertising agency N.W. Ayer & Son to come up with a catchy name for the new cracker. The Ayer agency suggested "Uneeda Biscuit," and also helped promote the product with illustrations of a rosy-cheeked boy clutching a box of Uneeda Biscuits. The boy was dressed in a rain coat and galoshes to call attention to the packaging's moisture-proof nature. The Uneeda Boy became one of the world's best-recognized trademarks.

N.B.C. was a pioneer in company advertising, spending an unprecedented $7 million in its first decade to promote its products. Across the country, newspapers, billboards, and posters queried "Do you know Uneeda Biscuit?" By 1900, sales of Uneeda Biscuits surpassed 100 million packages, prompting Green to remark that Uneeda was the most valuable word in the English language.

A host of imitators attempted to cash in on the popularity of Uneeda, and the company's attorneys were kept busy defending N.B.C. trademarks against infringement. The company won injunctions against rival bakeries marketing "Iwanta," "Uwanta," and "Ulika" biscuits. By 1906 N.B.C. had successfully prosecuted 249 cases of copyright infringement.

The National Biscuit Company built its reputation on securing customer loyalty to recognized brands such as Uneeda. In the early years of the 20th century, the company concentrated on expanding its line of cookies and crackers. Older products originally created by Nabisco's precursor bakeries that continued to be successful included Fig Newtons and Premium Saltines. In 1902 N.B.C. introduced Barnum's Animal Crackers in the famous decorative box resembling a circus cage filled with animals. In 1912 both Lorna Doones and Oreos were created, the latter eventually becoming the world's best-selling cookie.

N.B.C. moved its headquarters from Chicago to New York in 1906, where the company's factory on Manhattan's lower west side was the world's largest bakery. Yet Adolphus Green still managed the biscuit conglomerate as if it were a small family business. Green disliked delegating power. He personally inspected every company bakery once or twice a year, and most local managers communicated directly with Green. Green's authoritarian style annoyed many of his colleagues and led to frequent resignations from the board of directors. As a result, when

Green died in 1917, few of the original directors remained and company management was in disarray.

The most pressing task for Green's successor, Roy E. Tomlinson, was reorganizing N.B.C.'s administrative network. Tomlinson had worked his way up the corporate ladder and was sensitive to the various levels of command. He delegated greater authority to other directors and to middle management, and remained company head until the 1940s.

The year Tomlinson took over was the year America entered World War I. During the war N.B.C. produced a special bread ration for soldiers and Tomlinson acted as advisor to the United States Food Administration. Wartime rationing of wheat flour and sugar also meant that cookies were less sweet and crackers were made of corn meal and rye. Company advertisements at the time depicted Uncle Sam holding boxes of N.B.C. products with the patriotic caption "made as he says."

The 1920s were a period of great prosperity for N.B.C. The company built a number of new bakeries and, in 1925, established its first foreign subsidiary, in Canada. N.B.C. also expanded its product line to include pretzels, breakfast cereal, and ice cream cones. Much of this diversification came about through acquisitions of other companies. In 1928 N.B.C. purchased the Shredded Wheat Company for $35 million. That same year N.B.C. acquired the McLaren Consolidated Cone Corporation, the world's largest manufacturer of ice cream cones.

The Depression years slowed company growth, but despite falling profits, N.B.C. managed to maintain and even raise dividend payments through a policy of severe wage reductions. The price of shareholder satisfaction, however, was labor unrest. In the early 1930s serious strikes broke out at Nabisco plants in New York, Philadelphia, and Atlanta, where angry picketers proclaimed "U-Don't-Needa biscuit!"

Some new Nabisco products helped bolster company sales during the Depression. In 1931 Nabisco took over the Bennett Biscuit Company and concentrated on its most popular product line, Milk-Bone Dog Biscuits. Originally marketed as "a dog's dessert," N.B.C. boosted sales by advertising the product's breath-sweetening properties. In 1934 Nabisco met with great success when it launched Ritz Crackers as a new prestige item. Throughout the 1930s, N.B.C. relied heavily on radio advertising, promoting its products on the company-sponsored "Let's Dance" radio program featuring the orchestras of Xavier Cugat and Benny Goodman.

In 1941, the letters "N.B.C." in the official trademark were exchanged for the word "Nabisco," a popular nickname which had first appeared as a possible name for Uneeda Biscuits. The change was made in part to reduce confusion with the recently established National Broadcasting Company.

During World War II the company was again faced with the problem of rationed flour, sugar, butter, and oil. Recipes were altered and substitute ingredients used. Nabisco also developed an emergency field ration for pilots and paratroopers and even supplied the canine corps with dog biscuits.

The immediate postwar years were a troubled time for Nabisco. The company's longtime leadership in the biscuit industry had led to a certain complacency. During the Depression Nabisco had neglected to make capital improvements, and many bakeries were now outdated and in dire need of renovation. In 1945 the Nabisco board elected the young and energetic George Coppers as president. The inertia of the 1930s gave way to an expansive new attitude as Coppers undertook the modernization of Nabisco's antiquated bakeries. Within ten years he had spent more than $150 million renovating old plants and building new ones. The reconstruction program culminated in 1958 with the opening of an ultra-modern bakery and research center in Fair Lawn, New Jersey.

The 1950s also marked the beginning of overseas expansion for Nabisco. In 1950 the company formed a manufacturing partnership with La Favorita Bakery in Venezuela, and in 1953 it established another partnership with the Famosa Bakery in Mexico. From this foothold in Latin America, Nabisco has grown to become a major supplier of baked goods to the region.

In 1960 Lee S. Bickmore succeeded Coppers as president and the company accelerated acquisitions and overseas expansion. In 1961 Nabisco acquired the Cream of Wheat Corporation and the French firm Biscuits Gondolo. The next year, the company purchased the English bakery Frears, as well as New Zealand's largest biscuit firm, Griffin and Sons. In 1963 Nabisco acquired Biscuits Belin of France, the Danish baking concern Oxford Biscuit Fabrik, and the James O. Welch Company, makers of Junior Mints and Sugar Babies. The following year, Nabisco bought Harry Trueller, one of West Germany's largest confectioneries. Overseas acquisitions continued apace in 1965 with the addition of the Italian biscuit company Saiwa and the Spanish bakery Galletas.

By the end of the 1960s, Nabisco was the leading manufacturer of crackers and cookies not only in the United States, but in Canada, France, and the Scandinavian countries and was a major supplier to many other European and South American countries.

The 1970s were a period of continued growth. Nabisco sales reached the $1 billion mark for the first time in 1971, and the $2 billion mark only five years later. In 1970 the company made its first Asian investment by establishing a joint venture with the Yamazaki Baking Company of Japan. Nabisco also upgraded its facilities in 1975 with the construction of a modern flour mill in Toledo, Ohio and a computerized bakery in Richmond, Virginia. That same year the company moved its headquarters to a specially designed complex in East Hanover, New Jersey.

During the 1970s Nabisco made its first acquisitions outside the food industry, buying the toy maker Aurora Products and the drug company J. B. Williams, manufacturer of Geritol and Sominex, in 1971. Here, the company was in unfamiliar territory, and the results were not always satisfactory. Aurora proved largely unprofitable and was sold in 1977. The J.B. Williams unit was frequently at odds with the Federal Trade Commission, and in 1982 Nabisco sold Williams to the Beecham Group for $100 million.

Eventually the inflation and mounting energy costs of the 1970s led Nabisco to consider the possibility of a merger with another large food concern. Early in 1981, Nabisco Chairman Robert Schaeberle and Standard Brands Chairman F. Ross Johnson announced plans for a merger between their companies.

Standard Brands was formed in 1929 when the Fleischmann Company, the maker of products as diverse as yeast and gin; Chase & Sanborn, a coffee roaster; and the Royal Baking Powder Company all merged. The resulting company prospered through the Depression, finding new markets for its products ("Yeast for Health") and expanding existing product lines. Between 1929 and 1981, when Standard Brands merged with Nabisco, Standard Brands acquired several more important businesses, including Planters Nut & Chocolate Co. in 1961 and the Curtiss Candy Company, makers of the Baby Ruth candy bar, in 1964.

Nabisco Brands wasted no time in demonstrating its enhanced potential for growth. In 1981 the company paid $250 million to buy the Life Savers Company. That same year the company bought a controlling interest in the Mexican cookie firm Gamesa for $45 million. In 1982 Nabisco Brands purchased the English biscuit company Huntley and Palmer Foods for $140 million. In 1985 the company formed a partnership with the Yili Food Company in China to produce Ritz Crackers and Premium Saltines for the Chinese market.

The nation's growing health consciousness was a new concern for Nabisco Brands during the 1980s. To this end the company marketed low salt versions of Ritz Crackers, Saltines, and Triscuit Wafers. Nabisco also introduced Wheatsworth Crackers, made with whole wheat flour and containing no artificial flavors or colors.

In a friendly takeover in 1985, Nabisco Brands was purchased by R.J. Reynolds, a worldwide manufacturer and distributor of tobacco, food, and beverage products, for $4.9 billion, creating the nation's largest consumer-products company, with annual sales of more than $19 billion. Nabisco had sought the merger in part to avoid hostile takeover attempts, while Reynolds was interested in diversification. Later in the year R. J. Reynolds changed its name to RJR Nabisco, Inc. F. Ross Johnson, the president of Nabisco and the former chairman of Standard Brands, became RJR Nabisco's new president.

In 1988 Johnson and a management group at RJR Nabisco attempted to take the company private in a $17.6 billion leverage buyout. The buyout was an attempt on Johnson's part to boost stock prices, though he soon lost control of the situation as other firms entered the fray. The brokerage house of Kohlberg Kravis Roberts (KKR) upped the bidding for RJR Nabisco to $20.3 billion. The broker Forstmann Little, along with Procter and Gamble and Ralston Purina, became the third bidder. KKR ultimately won with a record $24.5 billion in cash and debt securities, and replaced Johnson with Louis V. Gerstner Jr., the former president of American Express.

KKR and Gerstner have pledged not to dismember the company but to manage it for the long run. Nonetheless, in order to cover the company's monumental debt, RJR Nabisco does plan some asset sales; the first was its European cookie and cracker business to BSN, France's largest packaged-food group, for $2.5 billion.

Today, as Nabisco Brands tries to maximize profitability, it must face the fact that most Nabisco bakeries are 30 to 35 years old and in need of modernization. Since the major reconstruction phase of the 1950s, the company has neglected capital improvements. On the other hand, Nabisco's famous brand names are a tremendous strength. Ritz, Oreo, Triscuit—few companies can claim so many products that are household words.

Principal Subsidiaries: Nabisco Brands Ltd (Canada); International Nabisco Brands; Nabisco Biscuit Co.; Nabisco Foods Co.

Further Reading: Cahn, William. *Out of the Cracker Barrel: The Nabisco Story from Animal Crackers to Zuzus*, New York, Simon and Schuster, 1969; *42 Million a Day: The Story of Nabisco Brands*, Nabisco Brands, East Hanover, New Jersey, 1986.

NESTLÉ S.A.

CH-1800
Vevey
Switzerland
(021) 510–112

Public Company
Incorporated: 1866 as Anglo-Swiss Condensed Milk Company
Employees: 197,722
Sales: SFr40 billion (US$26.64)
Stock Index: Zurich Geneva Basel Berne Lausanne St. Gall Paris Frankfurt Düsseldorf Amsterdam Vienna

Nestlé is the largest food company in the world. With about 400 manufacturing facilities on five continents, Nestlé has often been called "the most multinational of the multinationals," largely because only 2% of its sales are made in its home country. Nestlé S.A. is a holding company for some 200 operating units that manufacture and sell a wide variety of products, including tea, coffee, dairy products, baby food, frozen foods and ice cream, pet foods, pharmaceutical products, and cosmetics.

While serving as the American consul in Zurich, Charles Page decided that Switzerland, with its abundant milk supply and easy access to the whole European market, was the perfect location for a condensed milk factory. The first canned condensed milk had been produced in the United States by Gail Borden some ten years before, and originally Page planned to produce and sell "Borden Milk" in the European market as a licensee. The plan fell through, however, so in 1866 he established the Anglo-Swiss Condensed Milk Company as a limited company in Cham, Switzerland.

The company's name was meant to flatter the British, to whom Page hoped to sell a great deal of his condensed milk. Anglo-Swiss first expanded its operations beyond Switzerland's borders in 1872, when it opened a factory in Chippenham, England. Condensed milk rapidly became a staple product in European cupboards—the business downturn in 1872 and the depression of 1875 didn't even affect the firm's sales. Charles Page died in 1873, leaving the company in the hands of his brother George and Anglo-Swiss's other investors. The next year, Anglo-Swiss expanded in England again by purchasing the English Condensed Milk Company, in London. By 1876, sales were almost four times their 1872 level.

Meanwhile, in nearby Vevey, in 1867 Henri Nestlé began selling his newly developed cow's-milk food for infants who could not be breast fed. Demand for his Farine Lactée Nestlé soared; between 1871 and 1873, daily production more than doubled, from fewer than 1,000 tins a day to 2,000. Nestlé's goal was to bring his baby food within everyone's reach, and he spared no effort in trying to convince doctors and mothers of its benefits. But while his energy and good intentions were nearly endless, his financial resources were not. By 1873, demand for Nestlé's product exceeded his production capabilities, resulting in missed delivery dates. At 61, Nestlé was running out of energy, and his thoughts turned to retirement. Jules Monnerat, a former member of parliament who lived in Vevey, had long eyed the business, and in 1874 Nestlé accepted Monnerat's offer of SFr1 million. Thus, in 1875, the company became Farine Lactée Henri Nestlé with Monnerat as chairman.

In 1877, Nestlé faced a new competitor when the Anglo-Swiss Condensed Milk Company—already the leading manufacturer of condensed milk in Europe—decided to broaden its product line and manufacture cheese and milk food for babies. Nestlé quickly responded by launching a condensed milk product of its own. George Page tried to buy the competing company outright, but he was firmly told that Nestlé was not for sale. Turning his attention elsewhere, he purchased the Anglo-Swiss Company's first factory in the United States in 1881. The plant, located in Middletown, New York, was built primarily to escape import duties, and it soon was successful enough to challenge Borden's supremacy in the American condensed milk market. It also presented a drawback: George Page spent so much time there that Anglo-Swiss began to lose its hold on Europe—much to the delight of Nestlé. After George Page's death in 1899, the Anglo-Swiss Condensed Milk Company decided to sell its American business to Borden in 1902 so that it could concentrate on regaining market share in Europe.

Until 1898, Nestlé remained determined to manufacture only in Switzerland and export to its markets around the world. But that year the company finally decided to venture outside Switzerland with the purchase of a Norwegian condensed milk company. Two years later, in 1900, Nestlé opened a factory in the United States, and quickly followed this by entering Britain, Germany, and Spain. Early in the 1900s, Nestlé also became involved in chocolate, a logical step for a company based in Vevey, the center of the Swiss chocolate industry. Nestlé became a partner in the Swiss General Chocolate Company, the maker of the Peter and Kohler brands. Under their agreement, the chocolate company produced the first Nestlé brand milk chocolate, while Nestlé concentrated on selling the Peter, Kohler, and Nestlé brands around the world.

In 1905, Nestlé and the Anglo-Swiss Condensed Milk Company finally quelled their fierce competition by merging to create the Nestlé and Anglo-Swiss Milk Company. The new firm would be run by two registered offices, one in Vevey and one in Cham, a practice it continues today. With Emile-Louis Roussy as chairman, the company now included seven factories in Switzerland, six in Great Britain, three in Norway, and one each in the United States, Germany, and Spain.

In response to an increase in import duties in Australia—Nestlé's second-largest export market—the company decided to begin manufacturing there in 1906 by buying a major condensed milk company, the Cressbrook Dairy Company, in Brisbane. In the next few years production, and sales, continued to increase as the company began to replace sales agents with subsidiary companies, particularly in the rapidly growing Asian markets.

But most of its factories were located in Europe, and when World War I broke out in 1914, Nestlé's operations, particularly in warring countries like Britain and Germany, were seriously affected. Although production continued in full force during the early months of the war, business soon grew more difficult. By 1916 fresh milk shortages, especially in Switzerland, meant that Nestlé's factories often sold almost all of their milk supplies to meet the needs of local towns. Shipping obstacles, increased manufacturing and operating costs, and restrictions on the use of production facilities added to Nestlé's wartime difficulties, as did a further decrease in fresh milk supplies due to shortages of cattle.

To deal with these problems and meet the increased demand for its products from governments supplying their troops, Nestlé decided to expand in countries less affected by the war and began purchasing existing factories, particularly in the United States, where it established links with several existing firms. By 1917, Nestlé had 40 factories, and in 1918, its world production was more than double what it was in 1914. Nestlé pursued the same strategy in Australia; by 1920 it had acquired a controlling interest in three companies there. That same year, Nestlé began production in Latin America when it established a factory in Araras, Brazil, the first in a series of Latin American factories. By 1921, the firm had 80 factories and 12 subsidiaries and affiliates. It also introduced a new product that year—powdered milk called Lactogen.

It didn't take long for the effects of such rapid expansion to catch up with the company, however. Nestlé and Anglo-Swiss reported its first loss in 1921, to which the stock market reacted with panic, making matters worse. The company explained that the SFr100 million loss was due to the rising prices of raw materials such as sugar and coal, and a trade depression that had caused a steady fall in consumer purchasing power, coupled with falling exchange rates after the war, which forced the company to raise prices.

To battle the storm, the company decided to reorganize both management and production. In 1922 it brought production in line with actual sales by closing some of its factories in the United States, Britain, Australia, Norway, and Switzerland. It also hired Louis Dapples, a banking expert, to put the company back in order. Dapples directed Nestlé with an iron fist, introducing stringent financial controls and reorganizing its administration. By 1923, signs of improvement were already evident, as Nestlé's outstanding bank loans had dropped from SFr293 million in 1921 to SFr54.5 million in 1923. Meanwhile in France, Belgium, Italy, Germany, and South Africa, production facilities were expanded. By consolidating certain operations and expanding others, Nestlé was also able to widen its traditional range of products.

Overall, the late 1920s were profitable, progressive times. In addition to adding some new products of its own, including malted milk; a powdered beverage called Milo; and Eledon, a powdered buttermilk for babies with digestive disorders, the company bought interests in several manufacturing firms. Among them were butter and cheese companies, as well as Sarotti A.G., a Berlin based chocolate business which began manufacturing Nestlé, Peter, Cailler, and Kohler chocolate. In 1928, under the direction of Chairman Louis Dapples, Nestlé finally merged with Peter, Cailler, Kohler, Chocolats Suisses S.A. (the resulting company of a 1911 merger between the Swiss General Chcolate Company and Cailler, another leading firm) adding 13 chocolate plants in Europe, South America, and Australia to the growing firm.

Nestlé was becoming so strong that it seemed even the Depression would have little effect on its progress. In fact, its U.S. subsidiary, Nestlé's Food Company Inc. of New York, barely felt the stock market crash of 1929. In 1930 Nestlé created new subsidiaries in Argentina and Cuba. In spite of the Depression, Nestlé added more production centers around the world, including a chocolate manufacturer in Copenhagen and a small factory in Moravia, Czechoslovakia to manufacture milk food, Nescao, and evaporated milk. Factories were also opened in Chile and Mexico in the mid-1930s.

Although profits were down 13% in 1930 over the year before, Nestlé faced no major financial problems during the Depression, as its factories generally maintained their output and sales were steady. Although Nestlé's New York–based subsidiary (which had changed its name to Nestlé's Milk Products Company) was more affected than those in other countries, U.S. sales of milk products were steady until 1931 and 1932, when a growing public frugality began to cause trouble for more expensive but established brands like Nestlé's. Profit margins narrowed, prices dropped, and cut-throat competition continued until 1933, when new legislation set minimum prices and conditions of sales.

The markets, like the United States, that were among the first to feel the effects of the Depression were also the first to recover from it. The Depression continued in Switzerland, however. Because currency exchanges to and from Switzerland were especially difficult between the early 1930s, when many major countries devalued their currencies, and 1936, when Switzerland finally did too, Nestlé products manufactured there could no longer compete on international markets. The company decided to streamline production and close several factories, including its two oldest, in Cham and Vevey.

Decentralization efforts begun during the Depression continued to modify the company's structure gradually. By 1936, the industrial and commercial activity of the Nestlé and Anglo-Swiss Condensed Milk Company itself was quite limited in comparison with the considerable interests it had in companies manufacturing and selling its products. More than 20 such companies existed on five continents. In effect, the firm had become a holding company. Consequently, the Nestlé and Anglo-Swiss Condensed Milk Company Limited was established to handle production and marketing on the Swiss market; the parent company officially became a holding firm, called the Nestlé and Anglo-Swiss Holding Company Ltd.; and a second holding company, Unilac Inc., was created in Panama by a number of Nestlé's overseas affiliates.

In 1937, Louis Dapples died and a new management team, whose members had grown up with the organization, took over. It included Chairman Edouard Muller, formerly managing director; Carl J. Abegg, vice chairman of the board; and Maurice Paternot, managing director. In 1938, Nestlé introduced its first non-milk product: Nescafé. The revolutionary instant coffee was the result of eight years of research, which had begun when a representative of the Brazilian Coffee Institute asked Louis Dapples if Nestlé could manufacture "coffee cubes" to help Brazil use its large coffee surplus. Although coffee crystals and liquid extracts had been tried before, none had satisfactorily preserved a coffee taste.

Nestlé's product took the form of a soluble powder rather than cubes, allowing users to control the amount of coffee they used. Although Nestlé originally intended to manufacture Nescafé in Brazil, administrative barriers were too great, so Nescafé was first manufactured in Switzerland. Limited production capacity meant that it was launched without the elaborate marketing tactics usually used for products with such potential.

Nescafé quickly acquired a worldwide reputation, however, after it was launched in 1939 in the United States, where it did exceptionally well. Nestea, a soluble powered tea, also made a successful debut, in the early 1940s.

World War II, not surprisingly, had a dire effect on Nestlé. In 1939, profits plummeted to $6 million, compared to $20 million the year before. As in the last war, the company was plagued by food shortages and insufficient raw material supplies. To wage its own battle against the war, the company decided to split its headquarters at Vevey and transfer part of the management and executive team to an office in Stamford, Connecticut, where it could better supervise distant markets. Nestlé continued under control of dual managements until 1945.

But the war was not all bad for Nestlé. When the United States entered the war in 1941, Nescafé and evaporated and powdered milk were in heavy demand from American armed forces. By the end of the war, Nestlé's total sales had jumped from $100 million before the war to $225 million in 1945, with the greatest increase occurring in North America, where sales went from $14 million to $60 million. With the end of the war, Nestlé's European and American branches were able to discuss future plans without fear of censorship, and the company could begin to face the challenge of rebuilding its war-torn subsidiaries. Nestlé also re-launched Nescafé and baby foods and began to research new products extensively. Researchers focused on the three areas Nestlé considered most likely to affect the food industry's future: an increase in world population, rising standards of living in industrialized countries, and the changing social and economic conditions of raw-material-producing countries.

In 1947, Nestlé merged with Alimentana S.A., the manufacturer of Maggi seasonings, bouillon, and dehydrated soups, and the holding company changed its name to Nestlé Alimentana Company. Edouard Muller became the first chairman of Nestlé Alimentana, but he died in 1948, before the policies he helped formulate would put the company on the road to a new future. Carl Abegg assumed leadership of the board.

In 1950, Nestlé acquired Crosse and Blackwell, a British manufacturer of preserves and canned foods. Nestlé hoped its $24 million investment would serve as a marketing outlet for Maggi products, but the plan was less than successful, primarily because Crosse and Blackwell could not compete in the United Kingdom with H.J. Heinz. Similar setbacks occurred in 1963, when Nestlé acquired Findus frozen foods in Scandinavia for $32 million. Although the company performed well in Sweden, it encountered difficulties in other markets, where the British-Dutch giant Unilever reigned. While parts of the Findus operation eventually became profitable, Nestlé merged its German, Italian, and Australian Findus branches with Unilever. The development of freeze-drying in 1966 led to Taster's Choice, the first freeze-dried coffee, as well as other instant drinks.

In 1971, Nestlé acquired Libby, a maker of fruit juices, in the United States, and in 1973 it bought Stouffer's, which took Nestlé into the hotel and restaurant field and led to the development of Lean Cuisine, a successful line of low-calorie frozen entrees. Nestlé entered the nonfood business for the first time in 1974 by becoming a major shareholder in the French company L'Oreal, today the largest cosmetic company in the world. Nestlé moved further into nonfood fields in 1977, when it acquired Alcon Laboratories, a Forth Worth, Texas pharmaceutical company that specializes in ophthalmic products, as well as Burton, Parsons and Company Inc., an American manufacturer of contact lens products acquired two years later. Also in 1979 the company adopted its present name—Nestlé S.A.

The 1970s saw Nestlé's operations increase considerably in developing countries. Of Nestlé's 303 factories, the 81 factories in developing countries contributed 21% of Nestlé's total production. But in the mid-1970s, the firm faced a new problem as a result of its marketing efforts in developing countries, when a boycott against all Nestlé products was started in the United States in 1977. Activists claimed that Nestlé's aggressive baby food promotions made mothers in developing countries so eager to use Nestlé's formula that they used it any way they could. Due to poverty and illiteracy, this often meant mixing the formula with local, polluted water or trying to make the expensive supplies last longer by using an insufficient amount of formula, eventually starving their infants. Estimate of Nestlé's losses as a result of the boycott, which lasted until the early 1980s, range as high as $40 million.

In 1981 Helmut Maucher became managing direct of Nestlé and made this controversy one of his first projects. He met with boycott supporters and complied with the World Health Organization's demands that Nestlé stop promoting the product through advertising and free samples. His direct confrontation of the issue contrasted with Nestlé's earlier low-profile approach and was quite successful in allaying its critics' fears.

Maucher also reduced overhead by turning over more authority to operating units and reducing headquarters staff. In addition, he spearheaded a series of major acquisitions. In 1984 Nestlé acquired Carnation, a U.S. manufacturer of milk, pet, and culinary products, for $3 billion, at the time one of the largest acquisitions in the history of the food industry. This was followed in 1985 by the acquisition of Hills Brothers Inc., the third-largest American coffee firm, which added ground roast coffee to Nestlé's product line. In the late 1980s, as food companies around the world prepared for the integration of the European Economic Community in 1992, Nestlé continued to make major acquisitions. In 1988 it acquired Rowntree PLC, a leading British chocolate manufacturer, for £2.55 billion, the largest takeover of a British company by a foreign one to date. Also that year it acquired the Italian pasta maker Buitoni SpA.

With factories in 60 countries and sales of SFr40 billion, Nestlé is the undisputed leader in the food industry. Its long history of international operations should stand it in good stead, but the giant will have to stay nimble to maintain its place as trade barriers crumble in Europe and its competition grows large and strong enough to challenge Nestlé around the world.

Principal Subsidiaries: Nestlé Enterprises Ltd. (Canada); Alcon Canada, Inc.; Carnation Foods Company Ltd. (Canada); Nestlé Foods Corp. (U.S.A.); Cain's Coffee Co. (U.S.A.); Stouffer Foods Corporation (U.S.A); Stouffer Restaurant Co. (U.S.A.); Alcon Laboratories, Inc. (U.S.A.); Dermatological Products of Texas Inc. (U.S.A.); Beech-Nut Nutrition Corporation (U.S.A); Nestlé Trading Corporation (U.S.A.); Wine World, Inc. (U.S.A.); Paul F. Beich Co., Inc. (U.S.A.); Hills Bros. Coffee Inc. (U.S.A.); Carnation Company (U.S.A.); Nestlé Beich, Inc. (U.S.A.); Stouffer Hotel Co. (U.S.A.); Pasta & Cheese, Inc. (U.S.A.); L.J. Minor Corp. (U.S.A.); S.A. Nestlé de Productos Alimenticios (Argentina); Companhia Produtora de Alimentos S.A. (Brazil); Alcan Laboratorios do Brasil S.A.; Nestlé Industriale Comercial Ltda. (Brazil); Nestlé Chile, S.A.; Productos Alimenticios Savory S.A.I.C. (Chile); Nestlé de Colombia S.A.; Productos Nestlé (Costa Rica) S.A.; Productos Nestlé (El Salvador) S.A.; Indeca S.A.(El Salvador); Productos Nestlé (Guatemala) S.A.; Nestlé Hondurena S.A.(Honduras); Nestlé Jamaica Ltd.; Compania Nestlé S.A. de C.V. (Mexico); Alimentos Findus S.A. de C.V. (Mexico); Industrias Alimenticias Club S.A. de C.V. (Mexico); Productors Carnation S.A. de C.V. (Mexico); Productos Nestlé (Nicaragua) S.A.; Nestlé Panama S.A.; Nestlé Caribbean, Inc. (Panama); Compania Peruana de Alimentos S.A. (Peru); Nestlé Puerto Rico, Inc.; Sociedad Dominicana de Conservas y Alimentos S.A. (Dominican Republic); Trinidad Food Products Ltd.; Nestlé Venezuela S.A.; Venepastas C.A. (Venezuela); Saudi Food Industries Co. Ltd.; Nestlé Foods Co. Ltd. (South Korea); Nestlé China Ltd. (Hong Kong); Food Specialities Ltd. (India); P.T. Food Specialities Indonesia; Nestlé K.K. (Japan); Alcon Japan Ltd. (Japan); Societe pour l'Exportation des Produits Nestlé S.A. (Lebanon); Nestlé (Malaysia) Sdn. Bhd.; Malaysia Cocoa Manufacturing, Sdn. Bhd.; Nestlé Philippines, Inc.; Nestlé Singapore (Pte) Ltd.; Ceylon Nutritional Foods Ltd. (Sri Lanka); Nestlé Lanka Ltd. (Sri Lanka); Anping Distributors Ltd. (Taiwan); Nestlé (Thailand) Ltd.; Thai Soluble Coffee Company Ltd.; Carnation Manufacturing Co. (Thailand) Ltd.; Food and Nutritional Products (Pty) Ltd. (South Africa); Societe Camerounaise de Produits Alimentaires, Dietetiques et Autres CAMAD-NESTLÉ (Cameroon); Compagnie Africaine de Preparations, Alimentaires CAPRAL-NESTLÉ (Ivory Coast); NOVALIM-NESTLÉ (Ivory Coast); Societe Gabonaise de Produits Alimentaires (SOGAPRAL) (Gabon); Nestlé Ghana Ltd.; Nestlé Foods Kenya Ltd.; Nestlé products (Mauritius) Ltd.; Food Specialities (Nigeria) Ltd.; Nestlé Senegal; Societe Industrielle et de Distribution des Produits Alimentaires et Dietetiques SIDPAD (Tunisia); Nestlé Zimbawe (Pvt.) Ltd.; Nestlé Australia Ltd.; Allen Life Savers Ltd. (Australia); Nestlé New Zealand Ltd.; Nestlé Deutschland A.G. (West Germany); Herta Artland Dorffler GmbH & Co. KG (West Germany); Blaue Quellen Mineral-und, Heibrunnen A.G. (West Germany); Trinks GmbH (West Germany); Heil-und Mineralquellen GmbH (West Germany); Aponti GmbH (West Germany); Dr. Ritter GmbH & Co. (West Germany); Dany Snack GmbH & Co. (West Germany); Alcon Pharma GmbH (West Germany); Alois Dallmayr Kaffee oHG (West Germany); Heimbs & Sohn GmbH & Co. KG (West Germany); Nestlé (Ireland) Ltd.; The Nestlé Co., Ltd. (U.K.); Findus (U.K.) Ltd.; Chambourcy Food Cop. Ltd. (U.K.); Herta (U.K.) Ltd.; Alcon Laboratories (U.K.) Ltd.; AB Findus (Sweden); AB Kaffebonans Rosteri (Sweden); AB Zoegas Kaffe (Sweden); Societe des Produits Nestlé S.A.; Maggi A.G.; Thomi & Franck A.G.; Frisco-Findus A.G.; Dyna S.A.; Leisi A.G. Nahrungsmittelfabrik; Frismat AG; Alcon Pharmaceuticals Ltd.; Nestlé World Trade Corporation; Food Ingredients Specialities S.A.; Prodalim Gida Mamulleri (Turkey); Imalat Ve Pazarlama Anonim (Turkey); Sirketi (Turkey); Osterreichische Nestlé GmbH. (Austria); Nestlé Belgiux S.A. (Belgium); Jacky S.A. (Belgium); Carnex Service Merchandising (Belgium); Herta Belgique S.A. (Belgium); Alcon-Couvreur N.V. (Belgium); N.V. Sanpareil (Belgium); Nestlé Danmark A/S; Sociedad Nestlé AEPA (Spain); Derivados Lacteos y Alimenticios S.A. (Spain); Alcon Iberhis S.A. (Spain); Alimentos Refrigerados S.A. (Spain); Cafes La Estrella S.A. (Spain); Malaga Comercial S.A. (Spain); Productos Brasilia S.A. (Spain); Granja Castello S.A. (Spain); Solis Industrias de Alimentacion S.A. (Spain); Nestlé Findus Oy (Finland); Societe de Produits Alimentaires et Dietetiques, SOPAD-Nestlé S.A. (France); Gloria S.A. (France); Guigoz France S.A. (France); Lait Mont Blanc S.A. (France); France Glaces-Findus S.A. (France); Chambourcy Roche aux Fees & Cie. (France); Laboratoires Alcon S.A. (France); Herta S.A. (France);

Societe Generale des Eauz Minerales de Vittel S.A. (France); Nestlé Hellas S.A.I. (Greece); Carnation Hellas A.E.B.E. (Greece); Loumidis S.A. (Greece); Nestlé Italiana S.p.A. (Italy); Locatelli S.p.A. (Italy); Encia S.p.A. (Italy); Alcon Italia S.p.A. (Italy); A/S Nestlé-Norge (Norway); Nestlé Nederland B.V. (Netherlands); Artland Nederland B.V. (Netherlands); Nestlé Portugal S.A.; TOFA-Torrefaccao de Cafes de Portugal, s.a.r.l. (Portugal); SICAL-Sociedade Importadora de Cafes, Lda. (Portugal).

Further Reading: Heer, Jean. *World Events 1866–1966: The First Hundred Years of Nestlé,* Vevey, Switzerland, Nestlé, 1966.

NIPPON MEAT PACKERS, INC.

47, Minami-Honmachi 4-chome
Higashi-ku
Osaka 541
Japan
(06) 282-3031

Public Company
Incorporated: 1949
Employees: 5,972
Sales: ¥529.29 billion (US$4.23 billion)
Stock Index: Tokyo Osaka Luxembourg Paris

Nippon Meat Packers is one of Japan's leading processors of packaged hams, chicken, seafood, and sausages, marketing popular Japanese brands such as Chicken Nugget, Swift, and Schau Schinken.

In March, 1942, just a few months after the bombing of Pearl Harbor, president and founder of Nippon Meat Packers, Yoshinori Okoso, started in the meat business by establishing the Tokushima Meat Processing Factory in Tokushima. After seven years of producing hams and sausages, Okoso founded the Tokushima Ham Company, the forerunner to Nippon Meat Packers.

Supplies of genuine pork were scarce during World War II and on into the 1950s. As a result, the company often used rabbit and fish meat for their hams and sausages. Despite the hardships of short supply, the company's growth remained steady through the 1950s, marked in 1956 by the construction of the company's Osaka plant.

Pork shortages persisted into the 1960s, when mutton was used as a pork substitute. The company continued to grow, and by 1960, it began offering shares on the Osaka stock exchange. Two years later, the company appeared on the second section of the stock exchange in Tokyo, and in 1967, the company was promoted to the first sections of both the Tokyo and Osaka exchanges.

Growth in the 1960s came through the founding of new companies and links with existing ones. In 1963, the year the company adopted its present name, Nippon Meat Packers, the Torise Ham Company became an affiliate. Five years later, the company founded Nippon Broilers Company, a production and breeding facility for pigs and broiler chickens. The company has since set up similar facilities such as the Japan Farm, Kyushu Farm, Shiretoko Farm, and Tohoku Farm. In 1969, Nippon Meat Packers entered into business with Swift & Company, of the United States, one of the largest meat producers in the world at that time. The association lead to the sale of Swift brand hams and sausages in the Japanese market.

Also in 1969, Nippon Meat Packers established one of its most important product-development tools, the Housewives Directors Group. The group gathers opinions and complaints from women regarding the taste, price, packaging, and advertisement of Nippon Meat Packers' products. The organization helped the company produce big sellers such as Bun-ta-ta sausages, Winny skinless wieners, and Swift Loaf.

The early 1970s were a time of diversification for Nippon Meat Packers. In 1970, the company founded a school known as the Nippon Meat Academy. In 1973, the company entered the food service business with the founding of its John Bull restaurant which it opened as a way of collecting product information and introducing new recipes. It soon opened other restaurants including Berni Inn, a combined pub and steak house; Yashiro, a shabu shabu restaurant; and Schau Essen Haus, a German-style pub.

Besides branching into restaurants, the company entered professional sports with the founding of the Nippon-Ham Fighters baseball club. Investment in the baseball team proved a successful advertising vehicle for both the company and the ham industry in Japan.

In the later 1970s, Nippon Meat Packers began taking global interests. In 1976, the company issued 7.5 million Continental Depositary Receipts on the stock exchange in Luxembourg. The following year, in 1977, the company founded Day-Lee Meats, in Los Angeles. Since then, Nippon Meat Packers has set up affilites in Australia, Singapore, England, and Canada.

The 1980s were marked by continued growth and the introduction of several successful lines of meat. In 1981, the company introduced thin-sliced ham. Only half a millimeter thick, the product became one of the company's biggest sellers in the ham market and even won the *Nihon Keizai Shimbun*'s (Japan's business newspaper) award for "Superior Product of the Year" in 1982.

Growth in production and development continued in 1986, with a new production plant at Shizuoka and a new research center in the Ibaraki plant. The facilities improved the company's technology and processing capabilities. Also in 1986, Nippon Meat Packers introduced its highly successful raw ham products known as Schau Schinken.

Nippon Meat Packers' production extended into western Japan in 1987, with the establishment of the Hyogo Polka plant.

The company continues to grow both by adding processing facilities and introducing new food lines. In 1988 alone, the company introduced three new products: the Essen Burg, Mini Polka, and Lemon Chicken.

Introducing new meats and meat products to the Japanese diet has made Nippon Meat packers one of the country's top food producers and put Nippon Meat

Packers in a strong position to grow with the meat industry in Japan.

Principal Subsidiaries: Day-Lee Meats, Inc. (U.S.A.); Nippon Meat Packers Australia Pty. Ltd.; Nippon Meat Packers Singapore Pte. Ltd.; and Nippon Meat Packers U.K. Ltd.; Nippon Meat Packers Canada Ltd.

NIPPON SUISAN KAISHA, LIMITED

2–6–2 Otemachi
Chiyoda-ku
Tokyo 100
Japan
(03) 244–7000

Public Company
Incorporated: 1911 as Fishery Department of Tamura Kisen Company
Employees: 3,772
Sales: ¥481.1 billion (US$3.85 billion
Stock Index: Tokyo Osaka Nagoya

Japan, home of the world's largest fishing industry, is also the home of Nippon Suisan Kaisha (Nissui), the harvester of Japan's—and the world's—largest fishing haul. Nissui procures fish not only from Japanese waters but from worldwide deep-sea trawling operations and fish farming. The company describes itself as a "vertically integrated marine-based food company," but it also produces, processes, and markets agricultural and livestock products and has developed a line of pharmaceuticals. But unlike Taiyo Fishery, its chief competitor, Nissui seems content to remain primarily a fishing company.

The warm, dark-blue Japan Current runs through cold, pale Pacific waters along Japan's southern and eastern coastlines. Teeming with marine life, the current has always been a major nutritional source for coastal residents. Shoreline farmers who found it difficult to eke out a living from the rocky soil became fishermen, selling their fish further and further inland. But, as individuals, they were limited in the size of the boats they could manage and the size of the nets they could cast. It was not until the early 20th century that improved technology and communications enabled them to work together to begin making the fishing industry a significant part of the Japanese economy.

The first substantial step was taken in May, 1911, when the Tamura Kisan Company established its fishery department. But in August, 1914, Japan entered World War I, declaring war on Germany. Concentration of the nation's resources on the war effort helped raise Japan's status, as one of the victors, to that of a world power, but domestic industries made little progress during the war years.

Renamed Kyodo Gyogyo Kaisha, Limited, the young fishery department made a fresh start in 1919. The success of its operations during the following ten years sparked a bolder venture. On April 6, 1929, the company sent a trawler far beyond Japanese waters to begin fishing operations in the Bering Sea. Six years later, another trawler was sent to Mexico's Gulf of California to begin shrimp fishing, and still another to fish in Argentine waters. By 1937, the company, renamed Nippon Suisan Kaisha, Limited, was the largest company in Japan conducting trawler and factory-ship operations. On factory ships, marine products are processed and canned or packaged right on the ship and then transported directly to distribution centers to be sent to markets worldwide. But Nissui distributes most of its fresh seafood to large "coldchain" wholesale stores with vast refrigeration facilities to be sold in local markets.

In 1938, Nissui launched what was at the time the largest trawler in the world: the 980-ton *Suruga Maru*. But the waters of the Pacific were already churning with Japanese naval maneuvers in preparation for a massive war effort. To an even greater degree than World War I, World War II devastated domestic businesses, particularly fisheries, whose operations depended on venturing beyond the nation's borders. After Japan's defeat, the fisheries lost valuable island bases on four small islands in the Kurile chain north of Hokkaido, whose waters had afforded particularly rich harvests. (Although the waters were technically accessible to Japanese fishing boats, they found the new owners—the Soviets—less than hospitable.)

During nearly seven years of occupation by the Allied forces, profound changes were made in the structure of Japan's government, economy, and businesses. Free enterprise with firm government controls, plus some financial help from the United States, helped many struggling businesses—including Nissui—gain or regain a substantial portion of their markets. By the time the Treaty of San Francisco and the United States–Japan Security Treaty were signed in April, 1952, ending the occupation, Nissui was ready to resume fishing operations in the northern seas. Along with the rapid recovery of the Japanese economy, the fishing industry boomed, and by the end of the decade Nissui had extended trawling operations along the coasts of Africa, Australia, and New Zealand.

The largest trawler built in Japan in 1960 was Nissui's, at 2,500 tons. The company continued to build larger and larger vessels; by 1970 a 5,000-ton trawler and 21,700-ton factory ship had been added to Nissui's fleet. In 1967, the company began trawling operations off the east coast of North America.

The first outpost Nissui built after World War II was in Las Palmas, on the Canary Islands, off the west coast of Africa in 1962. During the following ten years, two more were set up, in Halifax, on the east coast of Canada, and in Seattle, on the west coast of the United States.

In order to broaden the company's line of marine products and reach new markets, Nissui began to enter into joint ventures with companies in foreign countries during the 1970s—the first four were in Indonesia, Spain, Chile, and Argentina. These joint ventures, cooperatives, and overseas trawling operations have added a variety of seafoods from remote waters to the extensive array Nissui harvests in Japan's coastal waters. Nissui also cultivates large fish farms, oyster beds, and edible seaweed in Japanese waters. Seaweed has gained in importance with the growth in popularity of health foods and natural foods during the 1970s and 1980s.

Krill refers to several varieties of small sea creatures that Nissui, like other fisheries, catches in northern waters. Antarctic krill is a tiny variety of shrimp that is rich in protein and easily harvested. Though too bland to appeal to humans, it is highly marketable when harvested and processed into feed for livestock, poultry, and farmed fish.

In 1974, Nissui began sending large trawlers to the Antarctic seas to fish for krill. At that time, the market for krill was undeveloped because of the high cost of transporting krill from Antarctica. During the next decade, many companies tried fishing for krill, but most were unable to make it cost-effective. The problem was particularly acute during and after the OPEC oil embargo of 1973. But Nissui is one of the few fisheries other than Soviet fisheries to persevere and succeed in making money from krill.

In 1976 an international agreement extended the jurisdiction of each coastal nation by 200 miles into its bordering waters. Nissui, like other fisheries that routinely ventured into foreign waters, had to make major changes in the conduct of its business. One solution was to concentrate more on fishing on the open sea. Another was a quota system negotiated by the Japanese government with nations whose waters Japanese fishermen wanted to enter. Still another solution was to purchase seafood from the foreign fisheries entitled to fish within the 200-mile limit. Nissui has done all these, and also has entered into new business relationships with companies overseas, forming a number of new joint ventures.

In 1985 Nissui established a subsidiary in the United States called Great Land Seafoods, Inc. Based in Redmond, Washington, Great Lands manufactures and markets a crab-flavored fish paste.

The following year, the company added another vertical dimension to its operation when it launched a chain of restaurants in Japan; it also launched a state-of-the-art mother ship for the production of surimi (fish paste).

Since the days of Nissui's post–World War I "fresh start," the company has conducted a continuous research program. When it was established in 1920, it was Japan's first private-sector research institution devoted to the study of marine life. In 1987, Nissui's Central Research Laboratory added a new department; the Fine Chemical and Biotechnology Division. Two examples of health foods developed as a result of this research are taurine, an amino acid, and EPA , an unsaturated fatty acid. The pharmaceutical product EPA-E was developed by Nissui's researchers in conjunction with Mochida Pharmaceutical Company, Limited.

Two more joint ventures were started in 1987: A&N Foods Company in Thailand and Dongil Frozen Foods Company in Korea.

Despite its relatively undiversified operations in a rapidly changing industry, Nissui's financial structure is quite solid. Streamlining its fishing operations and taking advantage of the growth of the frozen-food business has kept Nissui's profits at a healthy level; although seafood sales offer a low profit margin, those sales continue to increase. In the future, Nissui will have to face the challenge of growing environmental concerns about the fishing industry and adapt to the new legal restrictions the industry is beginning to face.

Principal Subsidiaries: P.T. West Irian Fishing Industries (Indonesia); P.T. Irian Marine Product Development (Indonesia); New Guinea Marine Products Pty., Ltd., (New Guinea); Empresa de Desarrollo Pesquero de Chile, Ltda., (Chile); Explotacion Pesquera de la Patagonia S.A. (Argentina); Nippon Suisan (U.S.A.), Inc.; Nippon Suisan (Halifax), Ltd. (Canada); Nippon Suisan (Singapore) Pte., Ltd.; UniSea, Inc. (U.S.A.); UniSea Foods, Inc. (U.S.A.); Dutch Harbor Seafood, Ltd., (U.S.A.); Great Land Seafoods, Ltd. (U.S.A.); Intersea Fisheries, Ltd. (U.S.A.); Northern Deep Sea Fishers, Inc. (U.S.A.); Ocean Products, Inc. (U.S.A.); Bangkok Shrimp Cultivation Co., Ltd. (Thailand); K. K. Hosui; Nissui Shipping Corporation; Wakamatsu Zosen K.K.; Nagasaki Zosen K. K.; Tobata Unyu Seikan K. K.; Fuji Seikan K. K.; Sapporo Hinomaru Reizo K. K.; Hakodate Teion Reizo K.K.; K. K. Hachitei; Sendai Hinomaru Reizo K. K.; Tobu Reizo Shokuhin K. K.; Kinki Reizo Shokuhin K.K.; Kita-Kyusha Reizo Shokushin K. K.; Seibu Reizo Shokuhin K. K.; Nippon Shokohin K. K.: Hokkaido Teion Shokoshin K.K.; Mogami Kanzume K. K.; K. K. Chilledy; Kyowa Protein K. K.; K. K. Nishisho; Nippo Sangyo K. K.; K. K. Tosuko; Seafood-Now Inc.; Kyowa Yushi Kogyo K. K.; Nissui Pharmaceutical Co., Ltd.; Nippon Marine Enterprises, Ltd.; Nissui Engineering K. K.; A&N Foods Co., Ltd. (Thailand); Dongil Frozen Foods Co., Ltd. (Korea).

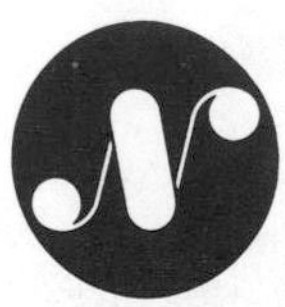

NISSHIN FLOUR MILLING COMPANY, LTD.

19–12 Koami-cho
Nihonbashi, Chuo-ku
Tokyo 103
Japan
(03) 660–3111

Public Company
Incorporated: 1907
Employees: 2,681
Sales: ¥321 billion (US$2.57 billion)
Stock Index: Tokyo Osaka

The Nisshin Flour Milling Company is Japan's largest manufacturer of wheat flour and a leading producer of livestock feed, processed foods, fine chemicals, and engineering technology. Founded in 1900 by Teiichiro Shoda as the Tatebayashi Four Milling Company, Nisshin's initial business operations focused on wheat-flour production, an area which has consistently accounted for over half of the company's total sales. When Tatebayashi merged in 1908 with the new Yokohama-based Nisshin Flour Milling Company, the company incorporated under its present name and moved its head office to Tokyo. A research center was established in 1916 to develop new products, including the world's first synthetic vitamin B6. With construction of the company's largest mill at Tsurumi in 1926, Nisshin's flour milling division expanded its production capacity for Japan's growing export market.

Nisshin's milling plants, damaged during World War II, were rebuilt and expanded between 1945 and 1949 to meet postwar demands for wheat flour. Further modernization occurred in 1957 with the installation of state-of-the-art pneumatic conveying equipment from West Germany and Switzerland.

In the early 1960s Nisshin diversified into areas related to its flour-milling technology and expertise. For example, the feed division was formed in 1961 to take advantage of Japan's increasing meat consumption and the corresponding growth of the livestock industry. The division currently ranks third in Japanese livestock-feed production and has since grown to include the Nisshin Stockfarming Center Company for the commercial breeding and selling of hogs.

In the 1960s, Nisshin moved into the commercial processed-food market. Nisshin Foods Company was established in 1962 to manufacture cake mixes and other flour-based products for the consumer market. Nisshin-DCA Foods was created in 1966 through a joint venture with DCA Food Industries of the United States, to produce doughnut mixes. In 1967 the company purchased Ma. Ma-Macaroni Company, a pasta manufacturer. Nisshin Foods Company was the first food company to improve product quality in response to consumer demand by using imported 100% durum semolina flour, which is better for processing, instead of domestic wheat flour. New products included convenience foods like frozen noodles, frozen dough, and flour mixes for fried food.

In the early 1970s, Nisshin expanded its product line by forming or purchasing subsidiaries to market pet food, ham, and sausages, create stock-breeding operations, and develop restaurant and catering services. The fine chemicals division, part of Nisshin Pharmaceutical Company, markets vitamins and other pharmaceutical products manufactured by another division, the Nisshin Chemicals Company. The company also has several international divisions. Nisshin Seifun do Brasil was formed in 1977 to develop business in Brazil, and Nisshin Badische Company produces and sells feed additives through a joint venture with BASF of West Germany.

In anticipation of its ninetieth anniversary, Nisshin has initiated a company-wide strategy known as "NI-90" to encourage innovation and commitment to continued growth. Led by its current president, Osamu Shoda, Nisshin faces the challenges of international trade, changing consumer tastes, increased foreign competition, and a fluctuating yen. As a member of the powerful Fuyo Group, a leading Japanese industrial group with close ties to Fuji Bank, Nisshin has a solid financial backing for future undertakings.

Principal Subsidiaries: Nisshin Feed Co., Ltd.; Nisshin Stockfarming Center Co., Ltd.; Nisshin Pet Food Co., Ltd.; Nisshin Ham Co., Ltd.; Nisshin-DCA Foods Inc.; Ma. Ma-Macaroni Co., Ltd.; Nisshin Pharmaceutical Co., Ltd.; Nisshin Engineering Co., Ltd.; Fresh Food Service Co., Ltd.

PILLSBURY COMPANY

200 South 6th Street
Minneapolis, Minnesota 55402
U.S.A.
(612) 330–4966

Wholly owned subsidiary of Grand Metropolitan PLC
Incorporated: 1935 as the Pillsbury Flour Mills Company
Employees: 101,000
Sales: $6.2 billion

Pillsbury is one of America's oldest and best-recognized food names. The company began in flour milling, and Pillsbury flour is still a staple on most American grocery shelves, but over the course of more than a century, the company evolved into a broad-based food producer and a major force in the restaurant business. In 1988, Pillsbury was acquired by Grand Metropolitan PLC, a diversified British beverage company.

In 1869, after working in his uncle's hardware supply company in Minneapolis, Minnesota, 27-year-old Charles A. Pillsbury bought one-third of a local flour mill for $10,000 and began the Pillsbury Company. Pillsbury and a competitor, the Washburn Crosby Company, formed the Minneapolis Millers Association that same year.

Pillsbury's improvements in milling machinery included the early incorporation of modern equipment for milling the very hard local wheat. These improvements and the purchase of two additional mills allowed him to produce 2,000 barrels of flour a day by 1872. That year he reorganized the company as C.A. Pillsbury and Company, making his father and uncle partners. In addition, he registered the trademark Pillsbury's Best XXXX in 1872.

During the 1880s the Pillsbury added six more mills, including one that was then the largest flour mill in the world. This mill was equipped with state-of-the-art machinery, which more than tripled the company's output.

Weakened by three mill fires in 1881, Pillsbury Company had just begun to recover, buying grain elevators to cut storage costs, when, in 1889, it sold the Pillsbury mills to an English financial syndicate. The syndicate also purchased competing Minnesota mills, elevators, and bordering water-power rights. Pillsbury remained as managing director of the new company, which was called the Pillsbury-Washburn Flour Mills Company Ltd. The company put its new water-power rights to use, and in 1896 the company passed the 10,000-barrel-per-day mark. Pillsbury-Washburn eventually grew, under Pillsbury's leadership, into the world's largest milling company.

During the 1890s the company focused on vertical integration. It began selling flour directly to retailers and stepped up advertising. Pillsbury-Washburn struggled with freight rates and the depressed agricultural economy during the first few years of the 20th century. In 1907, following a poor harvest, it became impossible for the company to mill profitably. Unmet financial obligations forced it into receivership. Charles S. Pillsbury, Charles A. Pillsbury's son, was one of the three men appointed to reorganize the company, which became the Pillsbury Flour Mills Company.

The new company overhauled the mills and the organization that ran them. In addition Pillsbury became a pioneer in product research by building its own laboratory. The firm rebounded and, on June 27, 1923, the Pillsbury Flour Mills Company purchased all remaining assets from the shareholders of Pillsbury-Washburn.

During the 1920s the Pillsburys opened several new plants and began to diversify. By 1932 Pillsbury had expanded into specialized grain products like cake flour and cereals. Expansion continued through 1940 with deals like the $3 million purchase of the Globe Grain and Milling Company and its various plants. The purchase helped Pillsbury set a new flour-milling record of 40,000 barrels a day. Pillsbury also continued manufacturing Globe's line of pancake mixes, biscuit mixes, and pasta.

In 1944 the company changed its name to Pillsbury Mills, Inc. Throughout this period Pillsbury family members had run the company and in 1940 Philip W. Pillsbury, Charles S. Pillsbury's son, became president. The company limited itself to kitchen staples through the 1940s, but enlarged its market. Pillsbury began to export its flour, introduced products for hotels and restaurants, and manufactured food products for U.S. troops during World War II, developing dry soup mixes in addition to its grains.

In the late 1940s Pillsbury ventured into higher-margin convenience products to meet growing consumer demand. Cake mixes were introduced in 1948, and over the next ten years Pillsbury increased the varieties it offered. The company expanded it product line with yet another acquisition, in 1951, of Ballard & Ballard Company and its line of refrigerated foods.

Pillsbury invested heavily in market research and development during the 1950s, and by the end of the decade had broadened beyond baking-related products. The company also continued its vertical integration efforts during the decade, opening milling plants in Canada and increasing its grain storage capacity. The company grew so quickly in the 1950s that by 1963 the Pillsbury name appeared on 127 different products. As the company's marketing and development continued to accelerate through the decade, so did its interest in a bigger market.

In 1959 Pillsbury began purchasing flour mills abroad, including units in Venezuela, El Salvador, Guatemala, Ghana, the Philippines, and Trinidad. In successive years international operations increased to include food companies in France, Australia, and Germany. Fast growth continued, and in 1960 Pillsbury made its first nonfood purchase, Tidy House Products Company, a manufacturer of household cleaners.

Robert J. Keith, who became president in 1966, brought Pillsbury into a new phase of food production. The postwar convenience era culminated in 1967 with the purchase of Burger King, the fast-food restaurant chain. By 1968 Pillsbury also owned interests in a variety of companies, including a computer time-sharing business, a publications division, and a life insurance company.

At the end of its first 100 years the Pillsbury Company had become highly diversified and decentralized in order to handle the variety of management decisions involved with producing flours and instant foods and running restaurant, computer, and publishing operations. Terrance Hanold, who became president in 1967, planned to continue diversifying and increasing independence for managers in the 1970s.

In 1973 William H. Spoor became CEO and Pillsbury entered an era of increasing sales and earnings. Spoor valued diversification and growth through acquisition, but he limited Pillsbury to the food industry. He quickly stripped the company of housing, computer time-sharing, and flower businesses, as well as other businesses unrelated to food processing.

In following years Spoor purchased Totino's Finer Foods and followed this venture into frozen foods with the 1979 purchase of Green Giant, a packager of frozen vegetables. Steak & Ale, Pillsbury's first full-service restaurant chain, was acquired in 1976; the well-timed purchase of Haagen-Dazs ice cream came in 1983; and Van de Kamp, the seafood company that produced Chicken of the Sea canned tuna followed in 1984. A few weeks after Spoor retired in 1984, Pillsbury announced the purchases of two more restaurant companies: Diversifoods Inc. and QuikWok Inc.

Pillsbury's business boomed during the 1970s, as Spoor solidified Pillsbury's strategy and made several smart purchases. Green Giant and other frozen-food companies gave Pillsbury a much larger share of the food industry and more consistent earnings. Profits in 1976 were divided almost evenly between three groups: consumer foods, agricultural products, and restaurants. By 1984, the agri-products group had shrunk to only 4%, and restaurants provided 53%.

The agri-products group had long been run by Fred C. Pillsbury, Charles S. Pillsbury's brother, who developed cattle feeds from mill by-products before the turn of the century. The division is now responsible for the collection, milling, storage, trading, and distribution of grain and feed ingredients. Pillsbury still provides about 10% of U.S. flour and the division is one of the largest U.S. purchasers of grains and dry beans.

Consumer foods (renamed Pillsbury Foods under Grand Metropolitan), the company's largest division, markets Pillsbury's supermarket products. In addition to its domestic subsidiaries, Pillsbury has sold grocery items through H.J. Green and Hammond's in the United Kingdom, Erasco and Jokisch in West Germany, Gringoir/Brossard and Singapour in France and Belgium and Milani in Venezuela. Pillsbury also owns similar operations in Mexico, Guatemala, Jamaica, and the Philippines. In the United States, Pillsbury's line of refrigerated dough, including products like pastries and cookies, was distributed by Kraft Foods for many years. These products account for about 10% of the company's sales.

Pillsbury owes much of the credit for this extraordinary boom to its restaurants. By expanding Burger King's operations and hiring Donald Smith from McDonald's, it became the second-largest fast-food chain. The purchase of Diversifoods, at $390 million Pillsbury's biggest acquisition, included nearly 400 additional Burger King outlets as well as Godfather's Pizza, Chart House, and Luther's Bar-B-Q. Pillsbury decided to compete with McDonald's not in size but in per-unit sales. As Burger King continued to grow, franchising became more common and only 20% of the restaurants remained company owned.

Like Spoor before him, John M. Stafford inherited a healthy company when he was appointed president in 1984. Each year between 1972 and 1986 the company set records for both sales and earnings. Pillsbury had a reputation for quiet, conservative growth, despite nearly doubling its earnings between 1980 and 1985, from $100 million to $190 million. Pillsbury finally surpassed its chief competitor, General Mills, during Stafford's first full year. Because Stafford, who came to Pillsbury through Green Giant, expected growth through increased demand for products from the agri-products and restaurant groups, company structure remained unchanged.

Pillsbury, however, had dramatically changed its position internationally. The company no longer exported flour, since local mills could produce it more efficiently. Instead, the international division began marketing prepared foods and restaurants overseas. By 1984 Pillsbury sold over 200 products in 55 countries and Burger King had restaurants in 22 countries.

Unchecked growth continued in 1985. Cash dividends increased for the 27th consecutive year. Earnings were up 13%, another record, and over 400% higher than the 1976 level. Pillsbury focused on consumer foods abroad through acquisitions and subsidiary product development.

In 1986 its international subsidiaries reported a 6% increase in sales, and Pillsbury prepared to market its domestic labels, like Haagen-Dazs, in Japan and Europe. International sales increased 18% the next year.

The mid-1980s brought a gradual reversal of the company's progress, however. Sectors of agri-products began to report losses, and the company spent heavily on concept development for its restaurants. The success of its Bennigan's restaurant chain covered its startup costs, but sales for chains like Steak & Ale failed to increase.

Stafford began to shift priorities, albeit conservatively. Bennigan's and Burger King were squeezed to make up for decreasing returns on the smaller restaurant chains. Consumer foods showed a profit gain of 22% between 1985 and 1987, and Stafford planned to continue development of Pillsbury's frozen foods and its microwave line, first introduced in 1979.

The corporation continued to have problems second-guessing the fast-paced restaurant industry. Total sales increased 5%, but earnings declined for the first time in 16 years, down 13%. Consumer foods and agri-products remained strong, but the decline in profits prompted further evaluation.

Although acquisitions overseas and in Canada continued, the company announced early in 1988, after a nine-month review, that it would reduce its restaurant division. While it kept Burger King, Bennigan's, Godfather's, and Steak & Ale, the corporation sought to rid itself of company-run units by selling them to franchisers. It also planned to refurbish 145 Burger King units. These modest reductions disappointed some analysts and takeover rumors began to circulate.

These rumors flourished as the board asked Spoor to return as CEO. Then the chairman of Steak & Ale and the president of the U.S. foods division left the company, creating the perception of a lack of leadership. In 1988 earnings plummeted to $6.9 million, less than half the level of the year before. Management attributed much of this decline to restaurant-related restructuring changes.

Philip L. Smith, formerly of the General Foods Corporation, became CEO in August, 1988. He held the post for five months as he tried to fight off the takeover attempt that began in October, when the British distiller Grand Metropolitan PLC first made a $60-per-share bid for Pillsbury. For nearly three months after Grand Met's initial offer, Pillsbury fought the takeover. The company tried to arrange a poison pill defense and to spin off Burger King, but it was prevented from doing so by court order.

Pillsbury shareholders eventually accepted a $66-per-share offer in late 1988, making the deal worth $5.75 billion. Ian A. Martin was named CEO immediately and restructuring began in March, 1989. Grand Metropolitan reduced Pillsbury's Minneapolis headquarters staff by 23%, and all of Pillsbury's restaurants except Burger King were sold. Grand Met also later sold Van de Kamp and Bumble Bee Seafoods, another tuna-canning company which had been purchased only ten months earlier. Two plants were closed, and the U.S. consumer foods division was renamed Pillsbury Foods. This new division includes all of Pillsbury's branded prepared foods, while the new industrial-foods and food-service division includes the flour-milling and industrial-bakery mixes operations. These divisions, along with separate division for Haagen-Dazs and Burger King, all joined Grand Metropolitan's food sector.

Under Grant Met, Pillsbury today has returned to its proven and profitable core business in consumer foods, a business which, with the famous Pillsbury name, is sure to continue to prosper.

Principal Subsidiaries: Green Giant Company; Pillsbury Holdings (Canada) Ltd.; Pillsbury Grain Export, Inc.; TPC International DISC, Inc.; Renown, Inc.; Lindy Aviation, Inc.; Shamrock Aviation, Inc.; Haagen Dazs Company, Inc.; Haagen Dazs Shoppe, Inc.; TPC Transportation Company; Pillsbury Commodity Services, Inc.; Porr Corporation; Pillsbury U.K. Ltd.; Pillsbury GmbH; F. Vorbeck GmbH; Gringoire S.A. (97%); Pillsbury Japan K.K.; Chemicals Marketing and Transportation Company, Inc. (50%); Snow Brand Pillsbury, Inc. (50%).

QUAKER OATS COMPANY

Quaker Tower
321 North Clark Street
Chicago, Illinois 60604–9001
U.S.A.
(312) 222–7111

Public Company
Incorporated: 1901
Employees: 31,300
Sales: $5.7 billion (1989)
Stock Index: New York Midwest Pacific Toronto London Amsterdam

The product of a rocky union between three 19th-century millers, Quaker Oats has always found success through aggressive marketing. Long considered closed and old-fashioned, Quaker Oats now has one of the most dynamic and respected CEOs in the food industry and maintains a portfolio of strong branded products within and outside the food business. Quaker has also drawn consistent praise for its community involvement and social conscience.

Ferdinand Schumacher undertook an ambitious project in 1856 when he organized his German Mills American Oatmeal Factory in Akron, Ohio. His mission was to introduce steel-cut oats to the American table at a time when oats were considered an inappropriate food for anything but horses. German and Irish immigrants were his original customers, since they were used to the idea of eating oats and unused to the high cost of American meat. Schumacher packed his oats in 180-pound barrels; his newly opened mill could produce 20 of these barrels a day, and by 1886 he was selling 360,000 pounds a day.

Oat milling was a low-cost operation, and competitors quickly appeared as oats gained acceptance as a food. But Schumacher controlled half of the trade, and resulting price wars did not diminish his position.

One competitor with a modern approach to business was located in nearby Ravenna, Ohio. Henry Parsons Crowell purchased the Quaker Mill in Ravenna, gave his oats the Quaker name, and packed them in a sanitary, two-pound paper package with printed cooking directions. He also advertised in newspapers with German, Scottish, and Irish readers, a practice which was at that time associated with disreputable showmen. The Quaker trademark was registered in 1877, the first cereal to do so. Soon Crowell's success carved a significant niche out of Schumacher's business, and urban customers often specified the Quaker name.

Another competitor migrated with his father from Embro, Ontario. Robert Stuart began a mill larger than Crowell's in Cedar Rapids, Iowa in 1873. Eventually he helped finance the building of a new oatmeal mill in Chicago and expanded the original mill. Under the same label the two mills established markets throughout the Midwest, especially in Chicago, Milwaukee, and Detroit, carefully avoiding territories Schumacher or Crowell dominated.

During the price wars of 1885, Crowell and Stuart joined together against Schumacher's larger operation. An attempt to form the Oatmeal Millers Association that year failed when Schumacher refused to join. One year later Schumacher's largest mill burned to the ground; Crowell reacted by immediately raising his prices. Because Schumacher had been uninsured, he finally agreed to join Stuart and Crowell in their venture. Crowell became president of the Consolidated Oatmeal Company, Stuart was vice president, and Schumacher, the former oatmeal king, was treasurer.

Consolidated, however, only made up half of the trade, and the other half was determined to destroy it. Competitors built mills they didn't want, knowing Consolidated would purchase them simply to keep them out of production. Half of Consolidated's earnings were spent this way, and in 1888, under financial and legal pressure, it collapsed.

A third and finally successful attempt at consolidation came that same year, when seven of the largest American oat millers united as the American Cereal Company. Through sheer force of will, Schumacher ended up with a controlling interest, and appointed himself president and Crowell vice president. The company doubled production in two years by condensing production into the two major mills at Cedar Rapids and Akron, Ohio. The concentration of facilities gave them the strength to survive the depression of the 1890s.

Crowell promoted Quaker Oats aggressively during the decade. However, Schumacher insisted that his own brand, F. S. Brand, be sold alongside Quaker, blunting the success of the better-selling Quaker.

As treasurer, Stuart crossed Schumacher by purchasing two food companies at bargain prices and investing in machinery for the Cedar Rapids mill. Opposed to both actions, Schumacher requested and got Stuart's resignation in 1897. The following year the president also voted Crowell out of the organization.

Crowell and Stuart, who together owned 24% of American Cereal, quietly began to buy available shares. In the aftermath of the subsequent proxy fight, in 1899, Schumacher lost control of the company to Stuart and Crowell. Stuart immediately built new facilities and diversified the product line while Crowell increased promotion. Quaker now produced wheat cereals, farina, hominy, corn meal, baby food, and animal feed.

In 1901 American Cereal became the Quaker Oats Company, with sales of $16 million. Twenty years of growth followed, including a wartime peak of $123 million in sales in 1918. With the 1911 acquisition of Mother's

Oats, Quaker owned half of all milling operations east of the Rocky Mountains. (The federal government filed a suit against the purchase, but eventually withdrew its last appeal in 1920, when national interest in trust-busting had faded).

An interest in finding a use for discarded oat hulls led to the establishment of a chemical division in 1921. Although a profitable use for its commercially produced furfural (a chemical produced from oat hulls that has solvent and other properties) would not appear until World War II, postwar sales of the product exceeded oatmeal sales into the 1970s.

Also in 1921 the company weathered a grain-surplus crisis; dealers had been caught with an oversupply and prices fell rapidly, leading that year to the company's first reported loss. Stuart's eldest son John became president of Quaker the following year. John Stuart immediately changed Quaker's retail sales strategy to one of optimum, rather than maximum, sales. The growth of the grocery chains helped to encourage a system of fast turnover rather than bulk purchasing.

Early in the century Crowell and Stuart invested in foreign markets by establishing self-supporting overseas subsidiaries. These subsidiaries operated mills in Europe and sold oats in South America and Asia. Under John Stuart's company reorganization in 1922, foreign operations became a corporate division. Then, as now, approximately 25% of Quaker's sales were abroad.

During John Stuart's 34 years as CEO, the company increased its toehold on the growing market of ready-to-eat cereals with Puffed Wheat and Puffed Rice. Quaker further diversified its product line by purchasing already-established name brands, such as Aunt Jemima pancake flour in 1925. Similarly, the company entered the pet-food industry through the purchase of Ken-L-Ration in 1942. Attempts to develop a cat food failed and culminated in the outright purchase of Puss 'n Boots in 1950.

World War II temporarily severed relations with many European subsidiaries, but 1942 sales reached $90 million. Wartime demand for meat and eggs pumped new life into the sagging animal-feed division as well as the company's grains and prepared mixes. Quaker's furfural became highly valued in the manufacture of synthetic rubber, and during the war Quaker built and ran a bomb-assembly plant for the government.

During the war and in the years that followed, Quaker's sales grew to $277 million and its operations to 200 different products. This broad consumer base needed heavy promotion behind it. John Stuart's younger brother, R. Douglas Stuart, studied under Crowell and assumed control of promotions when John became CEO. After World War II he adopted the then-radical policy of using more than one advertising agency. The Stuart brothers recognized that the grocery industry would continue to expand into pet foods, convenience products, and ready-to-eat cereals, and matched the company's product line and promotions accordingly.

The company's first outside manager, Donald B. Lourie, rose to CEO in 1953. Under Lourie, Quaker retained the atmosphere of a family company with personal leadership. But the company needed outside influence as marketing decisions became more complex. National recognition for the Aunt Jemima brand came at a price of $100,000. The cost of introducing Cap'n Crunch in 1963 was $5 million.

For many food companies, the 1960s were a period of automatic growth as consumer demand for convenience increased and brand recognition grew. For Quaker, however, sales rose just 20% and profits only 10% as long-term development absorbed earnings. Quaker expanded in the industry's fastest-growing areas: pet foods, convenience foods, and ready-to-eat cereals. By the end of the decade growth rates had increased, but not as much as hoped.

Robert D. Stuart Jr. became CEO in 1966. The decade's slow growth and a general corporate trend toward diversification prompted him to make acquisitions outside the food industry, the first since 1942. Many of these acquisitions were eventually sold, but Fisher-Price Toy Company, purchased in 1969, continues to this day to grow beyond expectations. Within ten years, it made up 25% of Quaker's total sales.

Late in 1970 Stuart restructured Quaker's organization around four decentralized businesses: grocery products, which now included cookies and candy; industrial and institutional foods, which contained the newly acquired Magic Pan restaurants; toys and recreational products; and international. Sales in 1968 had been frustratingly low at $500 million, but with Stuart's acquisitions, the company reported $2 billion in sales by 1979.

Hardships during the 1970s kept sales down. A second toy company, Louis Marx Toys, was purchased in 1972. During 1974 and 1975, Marx, which was purchased as a "recession-proof" company, drove earnings per share from $2.04 to $1.45. Magic Pan Restaurant's profits fell for four consecutive years. The chemical division reported a net loss of $7 million when a cheaper substitute for furfural came on to the market. This introduction took the company by surprise, as it expected earnings from that division to climb steadily.

Looking to expand its foreign market in grocery and pet foods, Quaker made seven acquisitions of foreign companies during the decade. But while the company focused on diversification, product development slipped. Between 1970 and 1978, only one new major product, 100% Natural Cereal, was introduced. Shelf space in major grocery chains did not increase. Stuart had successfully lessened the company's dependence on grocery products, but profits also dropped—to a low of $31 million in 1975.

But by the end of the decade a turnaround was in sight. Quaker's least profitable areas were limited to its smallest divisions, and since the entire industrial and restaurant industries had been weakening, the company was already preparing to divest its holdings in that field.

William D. Smithburg replaced Stuart as CEO in late 1979. Smithburg aggressively increased Quaker's sales force and advertising budget, improvements that were badly needed. The company also refocused on its core food business. Quaker had two new successes as the 1980s dawned: Ken-L-Ration's Tender Chunks became the second-best-selling dog food in its first year, and Corn Bran had a commendable 1.2% share of the ready-to-eat cereal market. In addition, Fisher-Price sales had increased tenfold since 1969, to $300 million. Quaker planned to expand the division by building plants in Europe, raising its target age group, and lowering unit selling prices.

By 1979 Quaker had a return on invested capital of 12.3%—higher than the industry average, but well below competitor Kellogg's 19.4%. The company still needed to divest its interests in companies that absorbed profits.

In the first half of the decade, Quaker sold Burry, a cookiemaker; Needlecraft; Magic Pan restaurants; its Mexican toy operations; and its chemical division. During the same period, the company made several acquisitions. Like many food companies at the time, Quaker entered specialty retailing, with purchases like Jos. A. Bank Clothiers, the Brookstone mail order company, and Eyelab, all purchased in 1981. All would be sold in late 1986. By then, Smithburg had decided that the price for retail chains was inflated and that Quaker could get a better return on food. He proved himself right. By 1987 Quaker's return on shareholder equity matched Kellogg's.

Quaker confirmed its new path with its 1983 bid on Stokely-Van Camp, the maker of Gatorade sports drink and Van Camp pork and beans. Quaker's $77 a share surpassed Pillsbury's offer, and critics called the bid extravagant. But by expanding Gatorade's geographic market, Quaker made the drink its top seller in 1987.

Quaker's revival came about through the strong potential of its low-cost acquisitions. Golden Grain Macaroni Company, the maker of Rice-a-Roni, gave the company a base to expand further into prepared foods. Anderson Clayton & Company, purchased in late 1986, gave Quaker a 15% share of the pet-food market with its Gaines brand, effectively challenging Ralston Purina's lead in that market.

With the purchase of Anderson Clayton, financed by the sale of its unwanted divisions, Smithburg managed to strengthen Quaker's position in existing markets and improve its product mix without overloading the company with specialty products. Products with leading market shares made up 75% of 1987 sales, and over half came from brands that Quaker hadn't owned six years earlier.

The late 1980s tempered that success, however. Pet food sales were flat throughout the industry and Quaker took $112 million in charges related to its recently expanded pet division. The corporation was a rumored takeover candidate because of its high volume of shares outstanding and its strong branded products. In response, the company announced in April, 1989 that it would purchase 7 million of its nearly 80 million outstanding shares, and that July, Smithburg reassigned some managerial duties. The company also decreased its advertising and marketing expenses.

Despite these minor setbacks, Quaker entered the 1990s with 14 years of unbroken sales growth. The company now concentrates on three major divisions: American and Canadian grocery products; international grocery products; and Fisher-Price Toys. International sales continue to be a significant percentage of the company's total, and Quaker plans to use its existing base to expand Fisher-Price overseas. Quaker will try to maintain independence through maintaining its market share, keeping pace with new product introductions, and keeping operations consolidated.

Principal Subsidiaries: The Quaker Oats Co. of Canada Ltd.; Quaker Oats Ltd. (U.K.); Quaker Oats, N.V. (Belgium); Quaker Oats, B.V. (the Netherlands); Quaker Produtos Alimenticious Ltda. (Brazil); Quaker France; Fabrica de Chocolates La Azteca (Mexico); OTA A/S (Denmark); Chiari & Forti, S.p.A. (Italy) (97.2%); Elaboradora Argentina de Cereales, S.A.; Quaker Products Australia Ltd.; Herrschners, Inc.

Further Reading: Marquette, Arthur F. *Brands, Trademarks and Good Will: The Story of the Quaker Oats Company*, New York, McGraw-Hill, 1967.

RALSTON PURINA COMPANY

Checkerboard Square
St. Louis, Missouri 63164
U.S.A.
(314) 982-1000

Public Company
Incorporated: 1894 as Robinson-Danforth Commission Company
Employees: 56,219 (1989)
Sales: $6.66 billion (1989)
Stock Index: New York Midwest Pacific

Ralston Purina is largely the result of the vision of one man: William Henry Danforth. Danforth was so extremely hardworking, religious, and philanthropic, he might almost have been a caricature of the Protestant work ethic if he hadn't done so well by it. Today Ralston Purina is the world's largest producer of pet foods and dry cell battery products as well as the largest fresh-product wholesale baker in the United States.

William Henry Danforth was raised and educated in Charleston, Missouri. In 1892 Danforth earned a degree in mechanical engineering from Washington University in St. Louis, Missouri, and the following year he joined two church acquaintances in St. Louis in mixing and selling feed for mules and horses. The blend of oats and corn, billed as "cheaper than oats and safer than corn," sold well among the farmers along the Mississippi River.

In 1894 the company incorporated as the Robinson-Danforth Commission Company and in 1896 Danforth bought control of the company. On the very day after the purchase was completed, the company's new mill—on the site of what is now known as Checkerboard Square, the company's headquarters—was destroyed by a tornado. With the help of a sympathetic banker, Danforth rebuilt, and the company continued to thrive.

In 1898 Danforth discovered a Kansas miller who had found a way to prevent wheat from turning rancid. Danforth introduced the miller's hot breakfast cereal made from cracked wheat. A clever marketing strategist, Danforth persuaded a Dr. Ralston, the head of a string of faddish health clubs, to give the cereal his official sponsorship. The doctor agreed on the condition that it be renamed Ralston Cereal. To advertise the growing success of both the cereal and the feeds—now called Purina to signify purity—Danforth changed the name of his company in 1902 to Ralston Purina and adopted the familiar checkerboard logo, which began to appear on all of Ralston Purina's packages.

The flamboyant Danforth, who wore the ubiquitous checkerboard design even on his jacket and socks, was viewed as a great leader by some but as a tyrant by others. He prohibited smoking anywhere on company premises and rewarded employees who subscribed to his philosophies and went to church regularly. He helped found the American Youth Foundation and the Christmas Carolers Association in St. Louis and served as president of each.

During World War I, Danforth went to France as a representative of the Young Men's Christian Association to give the troops moral support. While there, he observed that soldiers referred to rations as "chow." Returning home, he christened his animal feeds "chows" and, to clinch the custom, fined employees who continued to use the word "feed."

Following the war Danforth visited England, where he was introduced to the concept of compressing feed into cubes. In 1921 he began using this technique in the United States. His pellet-shaped feed revolutionized the industry and is still common today.

Purina chow's main competitor, then and for decades to come, was the individual farmer who had always fed his animals ordinary grain. In 1926 Danforth reluctantly purchased a research farm outside St. Louis at the behest of his son Donald Danforth, who had joined the company in 1920. At this facility new products were tested, including feeds with nongrain ingredients like animal by-products and vitamins. Innovative farm management and sanitation techniques were also tested there. While other feed companies were diversifying, Danforth was pouring his profits into Purina chows, buying up mills nationwide so that he could adapt his mixtures to the climate-related needs of farmers in each region. This tailoring was necessary in order to boost sales, and thus profits, in the low-margin livestock-feed industry.

By 1930 Ralston Purina's sales had reached $60 million. With the advent of the Great Depression, however, farmers could no longer afford commercial feed, and that figure dropped by two-thirds within two years. To compensate for this loss, Danforth persuaded the country's most popular cowboy, Tom Mix, to lend his name to the advertising for Ralston Cereal. Though the inexpensive yet nutritious cereal had long been losing money, it now began to generate a profit.

Meanwhile, Danforth continued to expand the operations of Purina Mills, and after 1933 sales were once again on the rise. Donald Danforth became president in 1932, while the older Danforth split his time between Ralston Purina and the running of the Danforth Foundation. Founded in 1927, the organization built chapels on college campuses and in hospitals and gave generously to the church and to colleges and universities.

During World War II, government regulations fostered tremendous growth in the meat and poultry industries, and farmers increasingly relied on commercially prepared feeds. Ralston Purina's sales more than tripled and, despite price controls, net profits rose nearly 150%.

Realizing that a farmer with disappointing returns was more likely to blame his feed than other contributing factors, the company began training its local salespeople in the basics of farm management, including breeding and sanitation. Thousands of Ralston Purina dealers became sources of valuable free advice.

Will Danforth soon came to be widely recognized as a public relations genius. Through its experimental farm, the company demonstrated to customers that the nutritional balance offered by Purina chows could produce bigger, healthier animals for less money. Groups toured the farm—at their own expense—led by guides who were well versed in the company's overall philosophy and product line. After the tour, visitors attended a show, complete with chorus line, performed by amateurs from the general office in St. Louis. As more sophisticated feed supplements became available, Ralston Purina added them to its chows, while taking care to maintain the homespun image its customers had come to trust.

With the end of the war, the price of grains began to rise sharply. To raise the necessary operating capital, the Danforths reluctantly took their company public. By 1947 sales of Purina chows, milled in 27 plants nationwide, had topped $200 million.

In 1950 Ralston Purina began developing an appealing dog food for sale in grocery stores. Between 1947 and 1957 the nation's canine population soared. Purina, which had been feeding hunting and farm dogs for 24 years, saw the opportunity to use its expertise to capture a high-growth, high profit margin industry. In 1957 Purina Dog Chow entered the market. Within 16 months it had become the market leader, a position Ralston Purina has never relinquished.

William Danforth died in 1955, and Donald Danforth took his place as chairman of the board. New president Raymond E. Rowland led the way in expanding outside the U.S. Under Rowland Ralston Purina became co-owner of feed companies in France, West Germany, and Italy, and bought plants in Mexico, Guatemala, Colombia, Venezuela, and Argentina.

Despite a fire in January, 1962 that destroyed much of the company's St. Louis plant, Ralston Purina continued to grow. Most of this expansion was in the consumer-goods sector. The company increased its penetration of the U.S. supermarket with Chex cereals and Purina Dog Chow. By the mid-1960s feeds represented only half of total sales, down from 90%. In 1963, Ralston Purina made its first major domestic acquisition when it bought the Van Camp Seafood Company, canners of Chicken-of-the-Sea tuna and salmon, for 1.9 million shares of stock.

Donald Danforth retired in 1963 as the company neared $1 billion in sales. The new president, R. Hal Dean, reorganized the chain of command. When Dean became chairman in 1968 he started a program of acquisitions with the purchase of Foodmaker, Inc., a restaurant franchising company. A hockey fan, he bought St. Louis's ailing professional team, the Blues, and renamed their stadium the Checkerdome. Next Ralston Purina purchased Green Thumb, which sold houseplants, for $45 million; a well-known life-sciences testing lab (to be merged with Ralston Purina's own lab) named the WARF Institute; and the Bremner Biscuit Company. New products included Cookie Crisp, which broke records in the children's cereal market. Between 1964 and 1974, the company's sales more than tripled, and in 1976, *Dun's Review* named Ralston Purina "one of the five best-managed companies this year."

By 1979, however, there were signs of trouble. In one 18-month period, the company's dog foods lost a quarter of their market share to competitors. Dean had opened dozens of new fast-food restaurants in the eastern United States only to find the market there already saturated. Houseplants weren't selling, and too much capital had been invested in shrimp farms, tuna boats, a fledgling soy-isolate business, and packaged fresh mushrooms—all enterprises with minimal or unstable profits.

Ralston had acquired a reputation for keeping corporate information private. This secretive policy backfired in November, 1978 at a meeting of stock market analysts, when the company's managers unwisely decided to withhold certain figures and disgruntled analysts went home with Ralston at the top of their sell lists. The company's stock dropped 8% in two days.

Although Dean reorganized again and succeeded in selling off some of the company's less-profitable acquisitions, by 1981 Ralston Purina's earnings were dropping off. As Dean prepared to retire, the company took the unusual step of paying each of three outside directors a substantial sum to assist in finding a new president.

A month after William P. Stiritz was elected, in January, 1981, a Ralston Purina soybean-processing plant in Louisville, Kentucky leaked an explosive solvent into local sewers. The resulting explosion caused few injuries but cost the company over $40 million in reparations, plus an indictment and fine for failing to notify the proper officials of the leak.

With a series of major acquisitions and divestitures, Stiritz began to reshape the company's product lines and priorities. While aggressively buying back the company's own stock (between 1982 and 1988 the company bought back nearly 50 million shares), he started selling less-profitable subsidiaries, including the St. Louis Blues, its fleet of tuna boats, its fresh-mushroom operations, and its soybean-processing business.

At the same time, Stiritz bought up businesses with products complementary to Ralston's own food and consumer items. In 1984 the company bought Continental Baking, makers of Wonder Bread and Hostess Cakes, for $475 million. With the bread industry too intensely competitive to offer much hope of an increase in market share, Purina expanded Continental's line of baked snack products and succeeded in raising profit margins within two years.

In 1985 Ralston Purina shed its restaurant operations, selling Foodmaker for $450 million, and used the cash to help purchase Union Carbide Corporation's battery division for $1.4 billion in June, 1986. Less than two weeks later Ralston Purina purchased Drake Bakeries, an important competitor in baked snacks, for $115 million. An antitrust action persuaded Stiritz to sell Drake in 1987. The company realized an after-tax gain of $43 million on the Drake sale.

With the company focusing increasingly on packaged

consumer products, its U.S. animal-feed division, Purina Mills, was no longer in the mainstream of Ralston Purina's business. In July, 1986 Purina chows found a new home with British Petroleum, which had been looking for a steady earner in the ever-fluctuating U.S. agricultural industry. And in 1988 the company sold its Van Camp Seafood division to a group of investors led by a privately held Indonesian concern for $260 million.

Although Ralston still owns the famous checkerboard logo and the Purina name, the sale of its animal-feeds business virtually severed the company from its origin as a provider of balanced nutrition for farm animals as well as for the farmer's breakfast table. Ralston Purina presently controls 30% of both the dog food and cat food markets and both volume and share continue to rise modestly.

The company's 1984 purchase of Continental Baking has decreased its dependence on pet foods while improving its position as a packaged-consumer-goods company. Ralston Purina now concentrates on human and pet foods like bakery products, dog and cat food, and cereals; other consumer products like batteries; and agricultural products (primarily livestock and poultry feeds outside North America). Today, Ralston's bestseller among its baked products—which combined represent over 30% of total sales—is the Hostess Twinkie snack cake. Continental is also battling damage to its sweet baked-goods business by introducing products meant to appeal to health-conscious consumers.

Chairman and CEO William P. Stiritz's modern management approach is typical of Ralston Purina's tradition of progressive leadership—William Danforth may have delivered a weekly inspirational message to his employees for 40 years, but he also instituted a model benefits program years before such arrangements were standard. Today's decentralized and trim management and staff constantly review and eventually divest underachieving operating units keep the company profitable. Ralston Purina's continued success rests on the continuation of this cautious yet independent approach.

Principal Subsidiaries: Continental Baking Company; Bremner Biscuit Company; Eveready Battery Company, Inc.; Duquesne-Purina, S.A. (France) (68%); Ralston Purina Canada, Ltd.; Ralston Purina Overseas Battery Company, Inc.; Protein Technologies International, Inc.

Further Reading: Danforth, William Henry. *I Dare You!*, St. Louis, Missouri, privately printed, 1969; *Ralston Purina Yesterday*, St. Louis, Ralston Purina Company, 1980.

RANKS HOVIS MCDOUGALL PLC

RHM Centre
Alma Road
Windsor, Berkshire SL4 3ST
United Kingdom
(0753) 857123

Public Company
Incorporated: 1933 as Ranks Limited
Employees: 39,000
Sales: £1.79 billion (US$3.24 billion)
Stock Index: London

Ranks Hovis McDougall PLC manufactures, processes, and distributes food products throughout the United Kingdom, Europe, the United States, Asia, and Australasia. The company's roots can be traced to the flour-milling industry in Victorian England, but through the years it has branched into many other aspects of the food industry, including packaged and prepared foods, bulk chocolate, pasta, and tomato sauce as well as a variety of breads. The company also has invested extensively in research.

Joseph Rank, the founder of the company, began in the milling business in 1875 by renting a small windmill. He lost money at first and had to take a co-tenancy at West's Holderness Corn Mill. But he was soon able to recoup his losses and set enough money aside to expand his business. At this time competition from American and Hungarian flour was an issue for English millers. Rank explored new milling methods to improve his competitive position against these foreign imports. In 1885, he built a mechanically driven flour mill in Hull. By using steel rollers instead of mill stones, the mill was able to produce an impressive six sacks of flour an hour, up from one and a half. In 1888 he built another steel-roller plant in Lincolnshire, and soon after still another even more modern plant. This new plant, equipped with the best technology available, produced 20 sacks of flour an hour and was considered one of the finest flour mills in the country.

At the turn of the century Great Britain was plagued by malnutrition. The poor often lived on little more than bread and tea, and infant mortality was high. In 1901, military recruitment standards had to be lowered to find enough men to enlist for the Boer War: the new minimum height for recruits was reduced to five feet. Since bread was the staple of the country, Joseph Rank was challenged to increase productivity. He installed a plant which produced 30 sacks of flour an hour, and then another plant with a 40-sack-an-hour capacity. He also set up agencies to distribute his flour in parts of England where it previously had not been sold. In May, 1899 Joseph Rank Limited was incorporated, and Joseph Rank became governing director, which he remained until his death in 1943.

In 1902 Rank made his first trip to the United States to see the wheat fields of the Midwest, determined to understand and conquer his competitors. Soon after his trip abroad, the company built mills in London and Cardiff. In 1912 a mill in Birkenhead was built to supply the needs of Ireland and northwestern England. Soon after that, the corporate headquarters was moved from Yorkshire to London.

During World War I, when starvation was a real threat to the people of Great Britain, Joseph Rank was asked to become a member of the Wheat Control Board. Frustrated by the government's inability to warehouse large quantities of wheat—distribution became chaotic as many ships carrying supplies were sunk—he relied much on his own resources and initiative to buy and store quantities of wheat and to increase the production capacity of his London mill. During the war years, the company employed 3,000 workers, many of them women who took on production jobs while men were away fighting the war. Despite his philosophy of personal initiative, Rank and his sons were known for public service, religious faith, and philanthropic work. In 1935 Joseph Rank received the Freedom of the City of Hull (the only public honor he ever accepted) in part because of a trust fund he had set up in Hull to help "poor persons of good character."

During the 1920s, the milling capacity in Great Britain exceeded the demand for flour. Nevertheless, Joseph Rank was able to expand into Scotland and consolidate and expand his operations in Ireland. He perceived the potential of new methods of transportation and communication very early, forming the British Isles Transport Company Limited to provide for the distribution needs of his company in 1920. In 1933, Ranks Limited became a public corporation. By this time, Joseph Rank was in his eighties, but he was still actively involved in the business. His son Rowland was running his own business—the Mark Mayhew mill, which produced animal feed as well as flour, and which, after World War II, would be incorporated into the Rank company. His son James, who after his father's death in 1943 became chairman of the company, was employed during the war as the government's director for cereal imports. Joseph Rank, despite his age, also contributed to the war effort by working as a secret wheat buyer for the government to build up stocks in the year before the outbreak of war.

After World War II, James Rank, the new chairman, was joined by an associate of his government-service days, Cecil Loombe, who became a director. Their challenge was to reconstruct the mills devastated by bombing and to expand the company. A new mill in Gateshead was their first big postwar accomplishment.

In 1952, James Rank was succeeded by his brother Arthur as chairman. Under Arthur Rank, the company explored many new ventures and began to acquire a variety of small, family-owned agriculture and baking businesses. It was also during this period that the company's faith in quality control and research was firmly established. High standards of nutrition were set and maintained for both human and animal foods by testing in every phase of the production process. The legacy of these early efforts is the Research Centre at High Wycombe, staffed by more than 150 scientists who continue to improve the nutritional value of the company's products as well as look for new food sources.

In 1962, still under the leadership of Arthur Rank, Ranks Limited acquired the Hovis-McDougall Company and became Ranks Hovis McDougall, Limited (RHM). In 1968 RHM made another important acquisition: the Cerebos food group, which brought with it a number of popular food brands as well as interests in France, Argentina, New Zealand, Australia, Canada, the United States, and South Africa. By 1969, after transforming the company from a flour mill to an international company with a variety of food interests, Arthur Rank was ready to hand over the chairmanship to his brother's son, whose name, like his grandfather's, was Joseph Rank.

Under Joseph Rank's leadership the company maintained its dedication to research. During the 1970s, research center prospered and undertook projects in crustacea farming, cereal and seed production, wheat hybrids, and protein production from starch. By 1984, research had advanced to the point that the company was ready to undertake a joint venture with ICI, Britain's largest industrial company, to form Marlow Foods, a company dedicated to producing and promoting mycoprotein food—food made by industrial fermentation of wheat-derived products. Mycoprotein food is high in protein and fiber, low in fat, and contains no cholesterol.

By the late 1970s, RHM and its competitor, Associated British Foods, monopolized their industry. Each company was selling over 60% of the flour it milled to its own subsidiaries, thereby offsetting losses in its baking division. Unable to compete or sustain losses, many small independent bakeries closed.

Joseph Rank became president in 1981 and was succeeded as chairman by Sir Peter Reynolds. The company made a number of important acquisitions during the 1980s in the United Kingdom, the United States, and the Far East. The largest acquisition was the purchase, in the United Kingdom, of the Avana Group. After a career with the company that had begun in 1936, Joseph Rank retired in 1988, remaining an honorary president after his retirement.

RHM undertook an unusual advertising campaign in 1986—one designed not for consumers of its products, but rather for the financial press, to increase awareness of the company itself. The ads featured a variety of slogans, all of which emphasized the diversity of the company—"We do not live by bread alone" and "We bakers like to have fingers in many pies."

An innovative accounting practice introduced in 1988 also drew attention to the worth of RHM. In its 1988 annual report, RHM showed the value of all of its brands on its balance sheet. As intangible assets, brands are not usually counted on financial reports as part of a company's assets. Grand Metropolitan was the first company to ever put acquired brands on its balance sheet, in September 1988. RHM went even further by including acquired as well as internally developed brands. Brand accounting is somewhat controversial because procedures for calculation have not yet been standardized.

In 1988 much of RHM's energies were directed to fighting a hostile takeover attempt by Goodman Fielder Wattie Limited, of Australia, which owned 30% of RHM's shares. The financial press saw RHM's move to brand accounting, in part, as a way of discouraging such a takeover.

As it enters its second century, RHM remains dedicated to manufacturing wholesome food products at reasonable prices.

Principal Subsidiaries: Ranks Hovis Limited; RHM Ingredients Limited; Tenstar Products Limited; British Bakeries Limited; Holgran Limited; Inglis & Company, Limited; Manor Bakeries Limited; Société Francaise de Panification et de Pâtisserie-Lyon SA (France); Heinzel (London & Vienna) Limited; RHM Foods Limited; Supreme Salt Company Limited; J.A. Sharwood & Co., Limited; RHM Exports Limited; RHM Foods (Ireland) Limited (Rep. of Ireland); Tiffany Sharwood's Frozen Foods Limited; Chesswood Produce Limited; McDougalls Catering Foods Ltd.; Pasta Foods Ltd.; RGB Coffee Ltd.; RHM Retail Limited; Cerebos Pacific Limited (70% Ord.) (Singapore); Cerebos (Australia) Ltd.; Cerebos Gregg's Ltd. (New Zealand); RHM Computing Limited; RHM Research & Engineering Limited; RHM Holdings (USA) Inc.; Naas Foods, Inc. (U.S.A.); National Preserve Co. (U.S.A.); Pilgrim Farms Inc. (U.S.A.); Red Wing Co., Inc. (U.S.A.); Avana Bakeries Limited; R.F. Brookes Limited; S&A Lesme Limited; O.P. Chocolate Limited; CGPA Peny SA (France).

Further Reading: "RHM: 1875–1975," London, Ranks Hovis McDougall, 1975.

Reckitt & Colman

RECKITT & COLMAN PLC

One Burlington Lane
London W4 2RW
United Kingdom
(01) 994–6464

Public Company
Incorporated: 1954 as Reckitt & Colman Holdings Ltd.
Employees: 21,700
Sales: £1.39 billion (US$2.51 billion)
Stock Index: London

Reckitt & Colman foods, household products, and pharmaceutical goods are familiar to grocery shoppers worldwide. The London-based company specializes in developing novel applications of food technology and creating or acquiring high-quality products, continually extending the range of its wares for a geographically expanding market.

Three sets of roots have given rise to Reckitt & Colman. The company's evolution has been gradual, marked with repeated attempts to graft the stems together. At a watermill in the English countryside near Norwich, Jeremiah Colman began milling flour and mustard in 1814. The business was named J&J Colman nine years later when the childless founder made his nephew James a partner. When they outgrew their first mill at Stoke Holy Cross, Norwich in 1854, the Colmans built the first mustard mill in Britain at Carrow, Norwich. They added mills for wheat flour, starch, and laundry bluing at the same location. Today the same site houses Reckitt & Colman's U.K. food division.

The Colman line continued to flourish, and expanded again in 1903 with the purchase of Keen, Robinson and Company, a food company that had been in business since 1742. Keen, Robinson's products included mustard, spices, and foods for infants and invalids like Robinson's patent barley and groats.

Entry into the starch business had brought the Colmans into rivalry with Isaac Reckitt, a starch manufacturer. Reckitt had started out in business in 1819, milling flour at the Maud Foster Mill in Boston, Lincolnshire. The mill and the flour business were both left behind in 1840 when he bought Middleton's starch works at Dansom Lane, Hull. This business was a success, and he soon made his sons partners and added new products. Washing blue and blacklead for polishing grates were both added in the 1850s, and synthetic ultramarine for bluing was added in 1883.

The Reckitts formed a private company, Reckitt & Sons Ltd., in 1879, and went public in 1888. Reckitt & Sons saw diversification of its product lines as the key to further growth and moved to diversify both through in-house development and through the acquisition of interests in companies with similar products. The introduction of Brasso, a new metal polish, in 1905 led to the acquisition of several polish producers. Reckitt & Sons bought Master Boot Polish Company and the William Berry Company in 1912 and the following year joined Dan and Charles Mason in establishing the Chiswick Polish Company. Reckitt & Sons held equal representation on the board with the Masons as well as a significant share in the company.

Reckitt & Sons continued to add new products related to its original line, even through the difficult years of World War I, and throughout the following decades. In the 1930s, with the addition of a germicide, they began to add pharmaceutical products.

The third branch of Reckitt & Colman began to take shape in 1886, when the Mason family began the Chiswick Soap Company. A producer of soft soap and polishes for metal and furniture, Chiswick received some early complaints about air pollution, but these didn't deter the company. Cherry Blossom shoe polish was added in 1906, and a floor polish called Mansion was added about a year later.

Although the Chiswick shoe polish business did well in Britain, the company had a formidable rival for overseas business: the Nugget Polish Company Limited. When Nugget and Chiswick had to compete for allocations of turpentine during World War I, they decided to pool their efforts. In 1929, they merged to form Chiswick Products. The new company was owned jointly by the Nugget Polish Company and the Chiswick Polish Company—in fact, the success of this merger was a model for the merger of Reckitt & Sons and J&J Colman in 1938.

The merger of Reckitt & Sons and J&J Colman was the culmination of efforts begun many years before. In 1913 the two companies had stopped competing with each other for business in South America by forming a joint company, Atlantis Ltd., to penetrate the South American market. Atlantis was so successful that they decided to unite all of their overseas businesses. Finally, Reckitt & Colman Ltd. was formed in 1938 to hold and manage Reckitt & Sons and J&J Colman, although the two companies still kept separate identities and positions on the London stock exchange.

During World War II, the companies struggled to survive supply shortages, manpower problems, and the damage done by bombings. After the war, efforts began anew to bring them together as a single entity. In 1954, a merger of the Reckitt and Colman companies established Reckitt & Colman Holdings Ltd. Later that same year, Chiswick Products became part of the organization.

The newly organized company began to concentrate its efforts on developing new business in Europe and North America while it also continued to expand its markets in other parts of the world. A major concern in the acquisition and development of new companies and products was the preservation of the high quality that had won Colman's Mustard the Legion of Honor Award in Paris in 1878. Another major aim was to continue strengthening brand-name recognition.

As the company grew throughout the 1960s and 1970s, a number of reorganizations were necessary to accommodate the addition of other types of businesses, notably in the leisure industry. But the company maintained its identity as a manufacturer of brand-name foods, household products, and pharmaceutical items to the world market. At times the rapid changes gave rise to speculation about the direction the company would take. Comments in the press referred to Reckitt & Colman as a "sprawling" company ready for restructuring because of the weaknesses in leadership brought about by the imminent retirement of both its chairman and vice chairman. Although the company's overseas business had grown to more than 70% of its total trade, only one foreign subsidiary, R.T. French, U.S.A., had a representative on the board.

In the 1970s Reckitt & Colman established new divisions to increase production efficiency and improve communication. This reorganization took two years and was described in the press as a period of "abrasive reform," but it succeeded in focusing the company's efforts on a planned expansion program. During the early 1980s Reckitt & Colman embarked upon a carefully executed program which resulted in the expansion and streamlining of the company. This program included the development of innovative products, such as a dual-purpose toothpaste introduced in 1981 to clean both dentures and teeth.

Reckitt & Colman's position in North America was strengthened greatly by its 1984 acquisition of Airwick Industries, a manufacturer best known for its air fresheners, and the 1986 acquisitions of Durkee Famous Foods, a food producer, and Gold Seal, a manufacturer of laundry aids and bath additives like Mr. Bubble. Reckitt & Colman was widely criticized for overpaying for Airwick (its purchase price was almost 40 times earnings), but within the year, Reckitt & Colman had turned the underperforming Airwick around.

Also in the early 1980s, Reckitt & Colman plowed much of its U.S. profit back into household product development following the successful but very costly launch of Bully bathroom cleaner. But the basic products from which the innovative variations have been developed continue to be popular. For example, French's mustard, made by Durkee-French in the North American group, continues to be the best-selling mustard in American grocery stores.

Also as a part of the streamlining program, Reckitt & Colman sold its unprofitable U.S. leisure-industry businesses and, in 1985, it sold its U.S. potato-processing business. And in 1988 the company sold its North American olive, cherry, and caper business. These sales helped channel the company's resources into lucrative areas more closely related to its brand-name products. The one major exception to the company's streamlining strategy, a small group of fine arts, graphics, and pigments companies, has been consistently profitable.

In 1989 Reckitt & Colman continued to expand in the personal-care field, buying Nenuco, a Spanish babycare company. This acquisition also meshed with another of Reckitt & Colman's goals: preparation for the unification of Europe in 1992. In July, 1989 the company became one of the first British companies to announce a major restructuring to accommodate the continent's internal market.

Under the plan, responsibility for production and marketing of certain products will be divided between facilities in the United Kingdom, West Germany, France, and Spain. For instance, all of Reckitt & Colman's metal polishes will be manufactured in Spain when the rationalization is complete in 1991. The reorganization is expected to lead to the discontinuation of a number of lesser brands as the company seeks to establish a unified identity throughout Europe. Innovative development, judicious acquisitions, good management, and consumer responsiveness (many Reckitt & Colman products are the result of extensive consumer research) have allowed Reckitt & Colman to continue growing in a low-growth industry and should contribute to its success in the future.

Principal Subsidiaries: Reckitt & Colman Products Ltd.; Reckitt & Colman (Overseas) Ltd.; Reckitt & Colman Australia Ltd.; Reckitt & Colman South Africa (Pty.) Ltd.; Reckitt & Colman (France); Representacoes Reckitt & Colman Brasil Ltds.; Reckitt & Colman Inc. (U.S.A.).

Further Reading: Reckitt & Colman: A Brief History, London, Reckitt & Colman, 1988.

ROWNTREE MACKINTOSH

York YO1 1XY
United Kingdom
(0904) 653071

Wholly owned subsidiary of Nestlé S.A.
Incorporated: 1969 as Rowntree Mackintosh PLC
Employees: 33,200
Sales: £1.5 billion (US$2.71 billion)

The history of Rowntree Mackintosh before 1969, when Rowntree & Company merged with John Mackintosh and Sons to create Rowntree Mackintosh, has two distinct branches. The Rowntree branch begins with a Quaker woman named Mary Tuke, a grocer in York who dealt in a variety of products but became well known for her coffee and tea. By 1785 she was also selling chocolate and cocoa, and in time the manufacturing of cocoa, chocolate, and chicory became a distinct, although relatively small part, of the Tuke business. When Mary died the business was carried on by her nephew, William, and after William by his sons and grandsons. But by 1862, the Tuke family was ready to disengage itself from various aspects of the business. Their tea business was sold to John Casson and the chocolate business was sold to Henry I. Rowntree, who, like Mary Tuke, was a devout Quaker.

In 1869 Joseph Rowntree joined his brother Henry in the business, eventually becoming the more active and influential of the two brothers. H.I. Rowntree and Company began to experiment with the manufacture of gum sweets, a confectionery more popular at the time in France than in England, and in 1881 started to produce crystallized gums. The experiment was a success and soon led to Rowntree's expansion through the purchase of a facility on North Street.

Henry Isaac Rowntree died in 1883, leaving the business to his brother Joseph (who was later joined by his two sons John Wilhelm and B. Seebohm). At this time the firm manufactured two main cocoa products: Superior Rock Cocoa, a mix of cocoa and sugar compressed into a cake, and a cocoa powder that was ground cocoa with sugar and starch added. But Dutch "cocoa essence"—a pure cocoa powder from which the cocoa butter had been removed—began to gain in popularity. Joseph Rowntree devoted himself to manufacturing a pure cocoa essence using the Dutch method, which he brought out in 1887 and called Rowntree's Elect Cocoa. The success of this product led to even further expansion, and land on the outskirts of York was purchased in 1890. This estate became known as the Haxby Road factory, and by 1922 had grown into a 220-acre complex of factories and other company buildings. In 1897, with over 1,000 employees, the company became a limited liability company called Rowntree and Company, Ltd. That year an electric generator was built to provide power and light for the factories. In 1899, the company began manufacturing its own boxes.

Throughout his long career with the company, Joseph Rowntree spent much of his time and energy building the company's reputation as a good employer. By 1906, Rowntree employed 4,000 workers, who were offered a pension plan, free medical and dental facilities, and education classes. Rowntree even employed seven full-time welfare workers to supervise the young girls working in his factories.

Temperance played an important role in Joseph Rowntree's political thinking; in 1897 he coauthored an important study called *The Temperance Problem and Social Reform.* He also advocated a fairer distribution of wealth and industrial democracy. To a large extent he incorporated his ideas into factory life, forming work councils and becoming one of the first employers to enact a minimum wage. Rowntree also created three influential trusts, one of which was used to finance liberal newspapers and periodicals, including *The New Statesman.* Another of the trusts built a model village with low-income housing, called New Earswick.

Joseph Rowntree's idealism influenced not only employee relations but other aspects of his business life as well. For a long time he refused to advertise his products, putting the company at a commercial disadvantage for a few years. When at one point a local grocer put a promotion label on a packet of Rowntree cocoa powder, Joseph Rowntree reacted angrily to what he felt were outrageous claims: "It is not a pure ground cocoa. It is not produced from the finest Trinidad Nuts. It is not the 'best for family use.' In fact the whole thing is a sham. . . ."

However with time and under the influence of his son John Wilhelm, Joseph Rowntree dropped his objections to advertising. Strong promotion, including full-page advertisements complete with a coupon, helped make Rowntree's Elect Cocoa a success. And during the 1920s and 1930s under the influence of George James Harris, the husband of Henry Rowntree's granddaughter, savvy marketing and consumer research became a hallmark of the company.

In 1923 B. Seebohm Rowntree succeeded his father as chairman, and that year profit sharing for Rowntree's 7,000 employees was established. Seebohm Rowntree also shared his father's work and study on the nature of poverty. He conducted a far-reaching survey of social conditions by interviewing every working-class household in the city of York and published *Poverty, A Study in Town Life* in 1901. He also wrote numerous other books on the subject of poverty.

During the 1920s, the company underwent a period of expansion and acquisition, moving into South Africa,

Canada, Ireland, and Australia, and buying Gray Dunn and Company and W. and M. Duncan.

A number of influential and lasting brands were introduced during the 1930s, including Black Magic chocolates in 1933, Kit Kat and Aero bars in 1935, and Smarties in 1937. Much of the success of these new products can be attributed to the detailed market research conducted by George James Harris.

In 1941 Harris succeeded Seebohm Rowntree as chairman of Rowntree. Although Harris is best remembered for his consumer research and marketing efforts, he continued the company's tradition of community service and employee care. Under his leadership, a company rest house was opened. During World War II, he served as president of the British Cocoa, Chocolate and Confectionery Alliance and after the war he was chairman of the industry's reconstruction committee.

During the 1950s, under the chairmanships of William Wallace and then Lloyd Owen, the company acquired N.M.U. Transport Ltd. and built a new factory in Newcastle. In 1961 the first computer was installed in York. During the 1960s, Rowntree expanded its interests into Germany, Belgium, Holland, and Italy; introduced Jellytots and the After Eight line of chocolate mints; and acquired Valley Transport Company, Creamola Food Products, Maconochie Brothers, Sun-Pat Products, and Stewart Esplen and Greenhough. In 1969, after an attempt by General Foods to take over Rowntree was abandoned, Rowntree merged with John Mackintosh and Sons Ltd. to form Rowntree Mackintosh Limited.

The history of the Mackintosh company began with John Mackintosh, who in 1890 opened a confectionery shop in King Cross Lane, Halifax, which came to specialize in toffee. Mackintosh's innovation was to combine soft American caramel with hard, brittle English toffee, resulting in Mackintosh's Celebrated Toffee. The product was introduced with free samples and much promotion and became quite a success. After four years, Mackintosh sold his shop to concentrate on manufacturing toffee. By 1895, the business had to move to a larger facility, and in 1899 Mackintosh formed a private company, John Mackintosh Ltd. That year he also built a factory in Queens Road. The business prospered; by 1903 Mackintosh toffee was being exported to Italy, Spain, and China, and in 1904 Mackintosh opened a factory in the United States.

In 1909, a year after John Mackintosh's son Harold joined the company, a fire destroyed the factory on Queens Road and business was transferred to the company's present site. Eventually the Queens Road factory was rebuilt and, after Mackintosh began to make chocolate in 1912, it became the center for chocolate manufacturing.

After John Mackintosh's death in 1920, Harold Mackintosh became chairman, and in 1921 the company, with 1,000 employees, changed its name to John Mackintosh and Sons Limited.

Under Harold, the company continued to prosper. A laboratory was opened in 1922, and in 1929 the company formed Anglo-American Chewing Gum Ltd. In 1932 Mackintosh acquired A.J. Caley and Son Ltd. in Norwich. The Caley company had begun in 1880 as a chemist's shop, selling mineral waters as a sideline. From soft drinks Caley branched into cocoa as a way of providing its customers with a winter drink, and from there began making chocolate. By 1898, the firm was also manufacturing Christmas crackers.

The acquisition of Caley expanded Mackintosh's chocolate line considerably. During the 1930s, Mackintosh introduced two important brands: Quality Street, in 1936 and Rolo, in 1937.

During World War II, Mackintosh's Norwich factory was destroyed by bombs, in 1942, halting all production there. But by 1946 Mackintosh was able to begin rebuilding.

In 1950 the Quality Street brand was first exported to the United States, and in 1956 the Norwich factory was reopened. Mackintosh introduced several new brands during the late 1950s and early 1960s, including Munchies in 1957, Caramac in 1959, and Toffee Crisp and Tooty Frooties in 1963.

During the 1960s Mackintosh made a series of acquisitions: Joseph Bellamy and Sons Ltd. in 1964, John Hill and Son in 1965, Gainsborough Craftsmen Ltd. in 1966, and Fox Glacier Mints Ltd. in 1969.

In 1969 Mackintosh merged with Rowntree to become Rowntree Mackintosh Limited. The new company had 28,000 employees at 22 factories making candy exported to 120 countries. During 1969 the new company negotiated an agreement with Hershey Foods Corporation allowing Hershey to market and manufacture some of its products in the United States, and in 1972 an agreement was negotiated with Fujiyi Confectionery Company Ltd. of Tokyo to manufacture selected products for the Japanese market. The new Rowntree Mackintosh also lost no time in making more acquisitions, buying James Stedman Ltd. of Australia and the chocolate confectionery business of Chocolat-Menier S.A. in 1971; Chocolat Ibled S.A. in 1973, and the Dutch Nuts Chocoladefabriek B.V. in 1979.

The 1980s marked continued expansion and acquisitions: by 1986 it had added another 13 companies in the United Kingdom, France, Australia, the United States, and Canada. All of these acquisitions made a reorganization necessary. In 1984 the company was divided into four geographic regions, and in 1987, the company incorporated four new trading subsidiaries in the United Kingdom: Rowntree Mackintosh Confectionery Ltd., Rowntree Mackintosh Distribution, Rowntree Mackintosh Export Ltd., and Rowntree Mackintosh European Exports Ltd. In 1982 the parent company changed its name to Rowntree Mackintosh PLC.

In 1988, two Swiss companies, Nestlé and Jacobs Suchard, began a bidding war for Rowntree. Both companies had chocolate businesses they hoped to strengthen in preparation for the unification of the European Common Market in 1992. On June 25, 1988, after a two-month battle between Nestlé and Jacobs Suchard—neither a welcome suitor—Rowntree was acquired by Nestlé, whose winning £2.5 billion bid made the deal the largest takeover of a British company by a foreign one to date. Nestlé agreed to keep Rowntree's headquarters in York and has created a chocolate, confectionery, and biscuit group based in York responsible for Nestlé's worldwide chocolate and confectionery strategy.

Rowntree may miss the independence it fought so hard to maintain, but Nestlé seems content to let the company continue to do what it has done so well for nearly 200 years. And as a part of a global food giant like Nestlé, Rowntree will have tremendous marketing strength behind it in the battle for dominance of a post-1992 Europe.

Principal Subsidiaries: Nutritional Food Ltd.; Rowntree Mackintosh Confectionery Ltd.; Rowntree Distribution Ltd.; Rowntree Mackintosh Overseas Exports; Multisnack Ltd.

Further Reading: Briggs, Asa. *Social Thought and Social Action, Seebohm Rowntree*, London, Longman, Green & Co., 1961; Vernon, Anne. *A Quaker Business Man*, York, Ebor Press, 1982.

SARA LEE CORPORATION

SARA LEE CORPORATION

Three First National Plaza
Chicago, Illinois 60602
U.S.A.
(312) 726–2600

Public Company
Incorporated: 1941 as C.D. Kenny Company
Employees: 100,000 (1989)
Sales: $11.72 billion (1989)
Stock Index: New York Midwest Pacific London Amsterdam Zurich Geneva Basel

After a decade of restructuring, divestment, and acquisition, the Sara Lee Corporation has emerged as one of America's largest multinational companies. Sara Lee has consolidated its businesses within four areas: U.S. consumer foods, international consumer foods, consumer personal products, and consumer household products.

Formally organized in 1939, what is now the Sara Lee Corporation spent the next three decades under the direction of founder Nathan Cummings. Although he retired from active management of the company in 1968, Cummings remained the largest stockholder until his death in 1985, when Sara Lee bought back 1.8 million common shares from his estate.

Born in Canada in 1896, Cummings began his career in his father's shoe store. By 1917 he had built his own shoe-manufacturing firm. Cummings's enterprise eventually expanded into a successful importer of general merchandise. This venture allowed him to purchase a small biscuit and candy company, which he later sold at a profit.

in 1939, at the age of 43, Cummings borrowed $5.2 million to buy the C.D. Kenny Company, a wholesale distributor of sugar, coffee, and tea established in 1870. The Baltimore-based company represented Cummings's first entry into American markets, and he sought to increase the number of Kenny-label products.

Cummings broadened his geographic scope in 1942 with the purchase of Sprague, Warner & Company, a distributor of canned and packaged food nationwide. Under the established Richelieu label, sales came to $19 million that year, allowing Cummings to begin a significant expansion through acquisition, a strategy the company has consistently pursued.

After several smaller acquisitions, in 1945 Cummings acquired Reid, Murdoch and Company, the producer of the nationally recognized Monarch label. After this acquisition, the C.D. Kenny Company changed its name to the Consolidated Grocers Corporation, and in 1946 Consolidated made its first public stock offering. The Monarch purchase boosted sales to $123 million in 1946.

Smaller food companies struggled through a difficult period in the late 1950s and early 1960s as operational expenses and competition increased—continual development of new products and large promotional budgets were typically the only way to keep shelf space in supermarkets. But small companies offered their already-established brands to a large company like Consolidated, saving the cost of internal development. By 1970, Cummings had supervised the purchase of over 90 companies by pursuing family-owned businesses who consented to mergers.

In 1951 Consolidated consisted of over a dozen companies, and in 1953 sales passed $200 million. They did not remain that high for very long, however. Sales in 1954, the year Consolidated Grocers changed its name to Consolidated Foods, dropped to $133 million. Sales fell another $15 million the following year, when after-tax profits were only slightly over $1 million and earnings per common share fell almost 40%.

Cummings met these losses with further diversification. The Kitchens of Sara Lee, a five-year-old maker of frozen baked goods with annual sales of $9 million, was acquired in 1956 for 164,890 shares—not Consolidated's biggest purchase to date, but eventually a significant one. A slightly larger purchase of 34 Piggly Wiggly supermarkets marked Consolidated's first venture into food retailing. An even larger purchase, of the Omaha Cold Store Company, demonstrated Consolidated's preference for distribution and marketing operations rather than direct-to-consumer sales.

Consolidated continued a rapid acquisition pace into the 1960s with Shasta beverages and the Eagle Supermarket chain in 1961. L.H. Parke Company, Michigan Fruit Canners, and Monarch Food Ltd. of Toronto together added $35 million in sales for 1962. The corporation first went international in 1960 by buying a controlling interest in a Venezuelan vinegar company; a second foreign investment came in 1962, with the purchase of Jonker Fris, a Dutch canner. Although growth was rapid, analysts considered Consolidated stock a risk since dividend increases depended on purchases.

During the 1960s recently acquired Booth Fisheries reported a 16% rise in sales volume for 1962, up to $56.6 million. By following the industry trend toward packaging seafood for the convenience market, Booth Fisheries fought off fish shortages and normally unstable prices, raising division earnings from $2.35 per share to $3.22.

In 1966 Consolidated agreed to a Federal Trade Commission (FTC) order to spin off its supermarket division within three years, principally its Piggly Wiggly and Eagle supermarket chains. This agreement came as a surprise to analysts, because the industry expected leniency from the FTC due to the high cost of small-scale food production and distribution. But Consolidated Foods President William Howlett publicly welcomed the agreement, stating that Consolidated no longer wished to compete at the retail level with its other customers. And Consolidated still kept its convenience retail outlets like Lawson Milk, purchased in 1960.

As Cummings prepared for retirement, Consolidated searched for a larger share of European and American markets. New production facilities were planned for Shasta and Sara Lee in 1964, tripling the latter's output, and sales that year topped $600 million. In 1966, Consolidated made two more important food purchases: Kahn's Meats and Idaho Frozen Foods.

Between 1964 and 1967, Consolidated made eight of its first nonfood acquisitions, including Oxford Chemical Corporation, a maker of cleaning products; Abbey Rents, a home furnishings company; Electrolux vacuum cleaners; and the Fuller Brush Company. Consolidated also entered the apparel industry when it purchased Gant shirts and several other clothing makers during this period. Within five years, nonfood businesses comprised 50% of the company's profits. William Howlett became Cummings's successor in 1968, but Cummings remained a director, and the largest shareholder, until his death. Howlett left two years later due to disagreements with the founding director. Despite the turbulence of the decade, sales tripled and after-tax earnings increased fivefold.

William A. Buzick Jr. became president in 1970, beginning a difficult decade for the corporation: by 1980, the selling price for a common share was almost 40% lower than 1970's purchase price. Although sales continued to rise, as the leader in the trend toward diversification, Consolidated soon discovered the drawbacks of the strategy as well. Consolidated's profits rose only 4% from 1972 to 1973—the year sales hit $2 billion—compared to an industry average of 17%. Sales continued to rise in 1974, but earnings dropped for the first time in 19 years as nonfood business did poorly.

During Buzick's five-year reign, Consolidated sold many of its food-distribution businesses and production facilities. Buzick also increased the company's commitment to nonfood products with the purchase of Max Klein, Inc., a Philadelphia-based clothing company and Erdal (later Intradal), a Dutch personal-care products company.

Nonfood activity peaked in 1975 as durable goods provided almost two-thirds of corporate profits. The diversification was prompted in part by the company's belief that federal restraints on the food industry would continue. In addition, economic constraints made Consolidated's growth goals difficult to achieve as only a food company. Under President Richard Nixon's economic-stabilization program of 1973, for instance, Sara Lee was allowed to raise prices on frozen baked goods only 6.35%; Consolidated had requested a 7.52% hike. Moving into nonfood businesses would make the corporation less dependent on federal decisions and less vulnerable to the antitrust suits that had impeded competitors.

Buzick left in 1975 and John H. Bryan became president. Bryan's family-owned business, Bryan Brothers Packing, was a 1968 Consolidated purchase. Bryan quickly sold more than 50 companies, most of which were smaller acquisitions made in the early 1970s. Fuller Brush and four furniture companies were singled out as problem units and divested. Earnings recovered the following year to $77.5 million, and Consolidated's operating margin returned to 7.6%.

Bryan continued to value nonfood sales, however. For the next ten years, nonfood products continued to make up more than 50% of corporate income but only 30% of total sales. Purchases during the 1980s continued the trend toward solidifying durable-goods production.

Bryan's acquisition portfolio represented a more aggressive stance in all of its markets. Before the 1978 purchase of Douwe Egberts, a Dutch coffee, tea, and tobacco producer, only 11% of Consolidated's income came from abroad; today it makes up nearly 30%. In 1979 Consolidated completed a hostile takeover of the Hanes Corporation, a family-owned undergarment manufacturer.

Despite difficulties—poor performance of some nonfood companies led to earnings losses in 1974 and 1975—Consolidated's performance excelled by the end of the 1970s. Between 1967 and 1973, sales doubled to $2 billion and total assets topped $1 billion. These figures allowed the company to set a goal of doubling sales volume by 1980; the actual amount achieved exceeded $5 billion.

Bryan's initial management goals were to keep the company diversified and decentralized, while keeping the corporate office responsible for financial control and strategic planning. Acquisition targets would be brands with leading market shares in new areas and "integrating acquisitions"—large companies with established brands in Consolidated's markets. Hillshire Farm meats and Chef Pierre pies fell into the latter category, and were purchased in the late 1970s, building on Consolidated's meat and pastry market shares.

The first of two major foreign acquisitions came in 1985 when Nicholas Kiwi Ltd.'s foreign subsidiaries were purchased for $330 million, in addition to 14% of its Australian domestic operations. Kiwi sells a variety of shoe-care products, medicines, cleaners, and cosmetics, and complemented Intradal, Consolidated's Dutch subsidiary. Akzo, a Dutch conglomerate with annual sales of $720 million, was acquired in 1987 for approximately $600 million, the company's largest purchase ever. Another producer of household goods, Akzo was absorbed into Douwe Egberts and Kiwi. By mid-1987, just nine years since its first international venture, Sara Lee was among the largest U.S. multinationals, with foreign revenue reaching almost $2 billion, making up 24.1% of total sales, 26.8% of profit, and 40.5% of total corporate assets.

Although still very active in acquisitions, Bryan also drew praise for stressing internal product development. Return on total investment typically decreases in the wake of large purchases, but Bryan has kept return on equity over 20% since 1985. This is especially unusual for a company whose growth is almost entirely through acquisition—96% of Consolidated's 141 entries into new businesses were through acquisition between 1950 and 1986.

Bryan has been responsible for easing uncertainty of the 1970s, shifting the company's focus to the marketing of consumer products only. He has also improved manufacturing efficiency and product development. In

1986 sales dropped from $8.1 billion to $7.9 billion, yet income increased $17 million. Domestic consumer and institutional food divisions reported the largest sales drop, as Shasta, Idaho Frozen Foods, and Union Sugar were divested and Popsicle was restructured. Bryan has also introduced lower-priced items to complement the corporation's premium Sara Lee and Hanes labels. Bryan hopes, with this tactic, to improve total sales volume as successfully as the meat division has done in the past.

In 1985 Consolidated announced that it would change its name to Sara Lee Corporation. The name was chosen because it was the corporation's most prominent brand name, and as a corporate name would give the company higher visibility and make advertising efforts more cost effective.

Instead of paring back down to a core food business in the 1980s like other American food companies, Sara Lee has continued acquisitions of nonfood producers. The company also used the strong dollar in the mid-1980s to increase it market presence abroad. Nearly one-third of the company's employees and operating profit and more than 40% of assets are from foreign concerns. Bryan believes that nonfood branded products and overseas markets are key to long-term earnings. Although the performance of traditional food products has been improving, the nonfood sectors have historically provided more earnings for Sara Lee relative to sales.

In 1989 the company began the divestiture of its food-service operations, then its poorest-performing division. Although philosophically in favor of future acquisitions, the relatively young Bryan will stress internal development of facilities and products and increasing the company's shares in existing markets. Sara Lee entered the 1990s with the enthusiastic endorsement of stock analysts because of its 1960s-style balance of food and durable-goods operations and a product line which consumers demand in recession as well as in boom times.

Principal Subsidiaries: Aris Isotoner, Inc.; Bali Foundations, Inc.; Bryan Foods, Inc.; Canadelle Intimate Fashions, Inc.; Coach Leatherware Co., Inc.; Green Hill Inc.; Hanes Menswear, Inc.; The Jimmy Dean Meat Co., Inc.; Sara Lee Bakery Co.; Kiwi Brands Inc.; L'eggs Brands, Inc.; Ozark Salad Co.; Peck Foods Corp.; PYA/Monarch, Inc.; Galileo-Capri Salame, Inc.; Bil Mar Foods Inc.; Schloss & Kahn; Sara Lee International Corp.; Seitz Foods, Inc.; Standard Meat Co.; Superior Coffee & Foods, Inc.; Intradal Nederland B.V.; Nicholas Kiwi Australia Ltd. (Australia); Dim S.A. (France); Douwe Egberts (Netherlands); Champion Products; Hygrade Foods; Van Nelle (Netherlands); Hillshire Farm.

Further Reading: Our Corporate History, Chicago, Sara Lee Corporation, 1986.

SNOW BRAND MILK PRODUCTS COMPANY, LIMITED

13, Honshio-cho
Shinjuku-ku
Tokyo 160
Japan
(03) 226–2286

Public Company
Incorporated: 1950
Employees: 8,101
Sales: ¥476.15 billion (US$3.81 billion)
Stock Index: Tokyo Osaka Sapporo

After sparking a revolution in Japanese eating habits, tastes, and nutrition, Snow Brand Milk Products Company, Japan's leading butter and cheese producer, has pursued an expansion program that now includes meat products, convenience foods, wine, and pharmaceutical goods. Snow Brand operates a chain of restaurants, a research-and-development center for new products, and a marketing information network.

Vegetables, rice, and fish had been the traditional Japanese diet for centuries before the late 19th-century move to colonize Hokkaido, the northernmost of Japan's four main islands. Like the others, Hokkaido is bisected by a mountain range, with little flat, arable land. Unlike the rest of Japan, however, Hokkaido's climate is too cold to grow most vegetable crops or rice profitably. But its verdant slopes did offer ample pasture land. Hokkaido's pioneers brought dairy cattle with them and succeeded in producing a fine grade of milk. But for decades the market was too limited for these farmers to do much more than supply their own needs from their herds and small gardens.

The winter of 1920 was particularly severe; storms damaged fodder and frigid weather diminished herds. To add to these troubles, the post–World War I recession reached Japan in the early 1920s. Hardships multiplied until the spring of 1925, when a group of Hokkaido's hard-hit dairy farmers formed a cooperative association and began to formulate a survival plan. On May 17, 1925, the Hokkaido Dairy Cooperative was formed with 629 members.

Torizo Kurosawa, the cooperative's managing director, had noticed the difference milk had made in the nutrition of the local farmers. He spearheaded what was then a daring plan: to produce two heretofore exclusively Western products—butter and cheese—and market them throughout the country. By July, butter was in production, and by October, the butter-marketing program was in full swing. Due in part to the fact that the entire economy had improved and continued to flourish for most of the decade, the plan succeeded.

By the following September, sales were so brisk that a new factory was built in Sapporo; today it is the site of the company's registered office. The Snow Brand trademark was first used in December, 1926.

Two years into butter production, the cooperative dared to introduce another Western product: ice cream. It, too, quickly achieved popularity.

The cooperative finally got around to the production of cheese in 1933, and as different varieties were successfully introduced to the Japanese, additional kinds were made. Today, the company makes more than 60 varieties.

Representatives of the group studied dairy-farming methods in several countries and decided to use Danish dairy farming as a guide. They realized that to keep the cooperative's growing variety of milk products uniform in quality, basic milk production methods also had to be kept uniform. To ensure that all members used the same methods to produce top-quality milk, the cooperative established a training program for young farmers, the Hokkaido Dairy Farming School, in 1934.

By 1935, the cooperative's products had achieved popularity throughout Japan, and a new marketing effort was launched to export them. It began with a butter shipment to London in November, and eventually proved successful for all products.

Japan's government, too, was pursuing expansionist policies. Having created a puppet state in Manchuria in 1931, Japan invaded China in 1937, alienating the Western democracies recently opened as markets by organizations such as the dairy cooperative. With foreign markets limited, the group turned its attention to expanding the variety of its products, and established the Dairy Science Research Institute in 1937.

The Hokkaido Dairy Cooperative had started several new businesses in the next few years: meat processing, margarine production, leather goods, and the manufacture of special farming equipment. The group also went into the land improvement business. Even with the privations and losses of World War II, the group, which was reorganized in June, 1941 as Hokkaido Rakuno Kosha Company, continued to expand.

In the wake of Japan's defeat in World War II, the size of the conglomerate was considered detrimental to the recovery of other Japanese businesses, and in 1948 legal steps were taken to prevent the formation of an economically overpowering cartel. A major reorganization took place, and Snow Brand Milk Products Company, Limited was established to succeed the cooperative in June, 1950. Each of the entities that had formerly made up the conglomerate became an independent subsidiary.

Within the decade, Snow Brand established additional subsidiaries in Tokyo and Osaka to handle the fluid-milk business and took over the milk and milk-products business of local dairy cooperatives in several other locations.

Another reorganization in 1958 rejoined Snow Brand with Clover Milk Products Company (formerly the Hokkaido Butter Company), from which it had separated in 1950. In 1966 Snow Brand's headquarters moved to a new building in Tokyo.

Snow Brand continued to expand, adding new products and new subsidiaries to handle them: frozen foods in 1971, seasonings in 1973, and in 1981 powdered milk for aquatic mammals, a special formula for infants with metabolistic defects, and oat products. The company also began to enter into productive business relationships with other companies both in Japan and abroad. Snow Brand established a joint venture in 1972 with Murray Goulburn Snow in Australia, and began to sell wine in 1974 under contract with companies in five European countries. In 1981, Snow Brand bought Chateau Grower Winery Company and started its own wine production. An additional facility, Snow Brand Belle Foret Winery, has been in operation since 1985. Through a tie-up with Stokely-Van Kamp, the company has been selling Gatorade, a popular sports drink, since 1980. A joint venture with the Pillsbury Company in 1981 resulted in the establishment of Snow Brand Pillsbury, Inc. in Japan. Snow Brand also has agreements with the Quaker Oats Company (U.S.), Melkunie-Holland (Netherlands), Molkerie-Zentrak Sud GmbH. (West Germany), Valio-Finnish Co-operative Dairies' Association (Finland), and Industria Gelati Sammontana (Italy).

In 1983 Snow Brand established the Embryo Transplantation Laboratory, with facilities for cryogenic storage, where bisected high-grade cattle embryos are transplanted and sex is determined through prenatal tests. Further steps to improve herds are made by veterinarians on the dairy farms, which have spread from Hokkaido to the northern portion of the neighboring island of Honshu, as they provide advice on cattle breeding, milk production, and handling. Processing plants are highly mechanized for quality control.

Biotechnology research concerned with gene control, cell fusion, and tissue culture is carried on in Snow Brand's Research Institute of Life Sciences, also established in 1983. Research helps develop new foods, such as varieties of yogurt, as well as pharmaceutical products. A medicine for senile dementia is under development in cooperation with an Israeli biochemical institute, and Snow Brand is currently working on an anticancer drug. The pharmaceutical products planning department, started in 1981, examines technical studies in connection with analyses of market needs.

Snow Brand's health-food line has expanded throughout the 1980s, responding to growing public concern with fitness and nutrition. The company's infant formulas and follow-up formulas, basic to the line, are popular not only throughout Japan but also in southeast Asia and the Middle East. In 1985 the company opened its Health and Nutrition Institute, which publishes dietary advice in a periodical called *Health Digest*.

The company's ongoing concern with nutrition and fitness has led to encouragement and sponsorship of sports activities. In 1960 the first Snow Brand Cup All-Japan Ski-Jumping Competition was held, now an annual event. The Snow Brand ice hockey team was formed in 1979. A year later, the company opened an ice skating center. In 1983 the Snow Brand Field Athletic Cup was established. And each year, the company supports the Snow Brand Cup National Invitational Little League Competition.

The 50th anniversary of the founding of the cooperative dairy group was celebrated with the opening of Snow Brand Historical Museum in Sapporo. The innovative and expansionary policies of the company's early developers are adhered to just as consistently today. Biotechnology and computerization provide new directions for product development and quality control. Snow Brand's General Institute for Dairy Farming, founded in 1976, and its Cheese Research Laboratory, opened in 1979, are just two groups working to provide improvements to tomorrow's cuisine. And the palates they are planning on pleasing aren't limited to Japan—their expansion plans are made in terms of a worldwide market.

Principal Subsidiaries: Hokushin Milk Products Company, Limited; Sendai Snow Ice Company, Limited; Ibaragi Snow Brand Milk Company, Limited; Yatsugatake Snow Brand Milk Company, Limited; Fancy Ice Company, Limited; Showa Milk Company, Limited; Gumma Snow Brand Milk Company, Limited; Snow Brand Rolly Company, Limited; Shizuoka Snow Brand Milk Company, Limited; Sapporo Yukihan Company, Limited; Doto Yukihan Company, Limited; Tokyo Snow Brand Sales Company, Limited; Nagasaki Snow Brand Milk Sales Company, Limited; Saga Snow Brand Milk Sales Company, Limited; Snow Brand Bussan Company, Limited; Nikijima Shoji Company, Limited; Shimaya Shoji Company, Limited; Snow Brand Shoji Company, Limited; Sugino Shoji Company, Limited; Umeya Company, Limited; Snow Brand Seed Company, Limited; Snow Brand Hokumo Transportation Company, Limited; Hokkaido Snow Brand Transportation Company, Limited; Tohoku Snow Brand Transportation Company, Limited; Meisetsu Transportation Company, Limited; Kansai Snow Brand Transportation Company, Limited; Snow Brand Food Company, Limited; Snow Brand Parlor Company, Limited; Kansai Snow Brand Parlor Company, Limited; Snow Brand Snowpia Company, Limited; Research and Development Center for Dairy Farming; Hokkaido Nozai Kogyo Company, Limited; Snow Hall Company, Limited; Snow Brand Children's Farm Company, Limited; Rakumosha Company, Limited; Hokueisha Company, Limited; Chesco Company, Limited; Bull Mart Company, Limited; Japan Milk Products Trade Company, Limited; Snow Brand Belle Foret Company, Limited; Snow Brand Pillsbury, Incorporated; Toyo Reinetsu Company, Limited; Nippon Port Company, Limited; Ueda Oil Refinery Company, Limited; SN Food Research Institute Company, Limited.

SODIMA

170 bis
Boulevard du Montparnasse
75014 Paris
France
(1) 43353720

Cooperative Union
Incorporated: 1964
Employees: 9,400
Sales: FFr13.9 billion (US$2.29 billion)

Although SODIMA is perhaps best known for its Yoplait brand of yogurt, produced and sold in over 37 countries, SODIMA is also one of France's leading producers of other dairy products, such as fromage frais (fresh cheese), creams, and desserts, and, with the Candia brand, is the country's number-one marketer of milk.

Sodima is a cooperative union made up of regional cooperatives. Its Paris headquarters is run by a board of directors made up of representatives from member companies, who try to reach a consensus on policy. The companies act independently in managerial concerns, but they produce and market their products according to SODIMA's national policy.

Dairy cooperatives have existed in France since the 1800s, but it wasn't until the 1960s that local organizations began to organize their production and sales operations on a regional level. At that time, several cooperatives became dissatisfied with the limitations of the regional structure and wanted to organize on a national level. In 1964, six cooperative unions joined forces to create SODIMA (Société de Diffusion de Marques). The cooperatives pooled their resources and knowledge to develop a wide range of fresh dairy products and open the national market in France.

In 1965, SODIMA launched the first national and comprehensive line of dairy products under the Yoplait brand. Through Yoplait's success, SODIMA was able to grow rapidly. Just four years later, Yoplait was introduced outside of France; SODIMA drew up a franchise agreement to give foreign companies the right to use the Yoplait brand name while the union continued to provide marketing, technical, and sales assistance.

In 1971, several member cooperatives also began to market Candia, the first national brand of fluid milk in France. Candia was an attempt to stimulate the milk market by changing milk's image as merely a common household staple. Advertisements depicted milk as more of a luxury beverage, and Candia milk was packaged in brightly colored wrappers instead of the usual white. Like Yoplait, Candia was a success; a year later, the cooperatives introduced Candia skimmed fresh milk.

In 1974, in order to reflect the company's changing interests, SODIMA changed the words behind its acronym to "Société de Développements et d'Innovations des Marchés Agricoles et Alimentaires" (Association for Development and Innovation in the Agricultural and Food Markets).

In 1975, Candia launched Viva, milk with a guaranteed vitamin content, and in 1976, it introduced Candy, a variety of flavored milks. By 1977, Yoplait was being marketed in 22 foreign countries, and the American General Mills Company had acquired the Yoplait franchise to produce and market its yogurt products in the United States. Yoplait soon became a major contender in the U.S. yogurt market. A year later, SODIMA's annual worldwide yogurt sales topped one billion cups.

In 1982, SODIMA created the Yoplait International Institute, an organization to define the guidelines for innovation and research of Yoplait products. Half of the institute's members were from SODIMA member cooperatives and half were from Yoplait's international franchisers. Its chairman, André Gaillard, was also SODIMA's honorary president. SODIMA also organized the André Gaillard International Research Center, to be overseen by the Yoplait International Institute. Located in a suburb of Paris, the center was to coordinate SODIMA's research policies, focusing on biotechnology and the development of new products.

In 1985, SODIMA International S.A. was founded as a subsidiary responsible for Yoplait business outside of France; it is especially concerned with marketing, technical, and sales activities.

Throughout the 1970s and 1980s Candia continued strengthening its position as a leader in the French milk market: pasteurized fresh milk was successfully repositioned and a liquid, ready-to-drink breakfast was introduced. Candia continued to grow in popularity with French consumers; by now, it handled about a third of all packaged milk produced in France.

In 1988, Yoplait began to market Ofilus, a variety of fermented milks with bifidus and acidophilus bacteria, two strains that help balance the digestive and intestinal flora. Ofilus comes in two varieties, one called Ofilus Nature, aimed at health-conscious, regular yogurt eaters, and one called Ofilus Double Douceur, aimed at those who prefer creamy foods. Yoplait had also become a leader in the fresh-cream market, introducing Silhouette, a cream with only a 12% fat content.

In 1988 SODIMA created two more subsidiaries: SODIMA CLB, in Lyons, responsible for Candia marketing and sales; and SODIMA Frais, in Paris, responsible for Yoplait marketing and sales. The sales staff of cooperatives producing Candia and Yoplait were transferred to these two main branches so that each brand would have a single sales force and delivery system.

In 1988, ULPAC, one of the founding cooperatives

of SODIMA, and Centre Lait, another union member, merged into the Alliance Agro-Alimentaires 3A, to collect milk from the central and southwest regions of France and produce both Yoplait and Candia products. The union of these two cooperatives signaled the cooperatives' desire to strengthen the agricultural sector in their regions in preparation for the upcoming single European market in 1992.

In July, 1989 SODIMA announced the creation of SODIAAL (Société de Diffusion Internationale Agro-Alimentaire). Headquartered in Paris, this group economically unites six SODIMA-member cooperatives. Each cooperative is responsible for managing one aspect of SODIAAL, such as milk intake or investments. SODIAAL was formed in anticipation of 1992 and the expected increase in business opportunities. It is now the largest dairy group in Europe.

Also in 1989, Yoplait opened a plant in Tianjin, China, with the larger ambition of developing the modern Chinese dairy industry. International Trust and Investment Corporation, working through Tianjin Agricultural Industry and Commerce Corporation, was SODIMA's main partner in the venture.

Since its organization, SODIMA has continued to diversify its product line according to changing consumer desires and has expanded its territories all over the world. Yoplait and Candia have become leaders in the French market, and SODIMA consumes more than three billion liters of milk a year in manufacturing its products.

With its span of international operations and the strength of its cooperatives within France, SODIMA is well prepared for the economically unified Europe. As consumers become more concerned about health, many milk products, especially yogurt, are increasing in popularity. SODIMA, while not abandoning its desserts and rich creams, has also designed a line of products with less fat and cholesterol. SODIMA's range of products and Yoplait's popularity suggest that the union's organizational flexibility will continue to further its success in France and elsewhere.

Principal Subsidiaries: SODIMA International S.A.; SODIMA Frais; SODIMA CLB; Yoplait S.A.; Cedilac.

TAIYO FISHERY CO., LTD.

TAIYO FISHERY COMPANY, LIMITED

1–1–2, Otemachi
Chiyoda-ku
Tokyo 100
Japan
(3) 216–0821

Public Company
Incorporated: 1943 as Nishi Taiyo Gyogyo Tosei K. K.
Employees: 3,296
Sales: ¥1.05 trillion (US$8.44 billion)
Stock Index: Tokyo Nagoya Osaka

Although the Taiyo Fishery Company has achieved prominence as Japan's second-largest fishery, combined sales of fish and shellfish account for only about 60% of Taiyo's sales. An aggressive new management is steering the company's course toward a future as a giant food conglomerate. The idea of diversification is not new to the Taiyo, however; already the range of its products and services include real estate warehousing, cosmetic ingredients, pharmaceuticals, mink, and pearls.

Taiyo's history goes back to the late 19th century. Ikujiro Nakabe and his father founded Hayashi Kane Shoten in 1880. The business prospered, and they operated markets in several locations. By 1913, the family business had its main store and headquarters in the western port city of Shimonoseki.

By that time the business had survived two wars: Japan had fought China from 1894 to 1895, gaining Taiwan; Russia ten years later, gaining additional territory; and had also annexed Korea in 1910. Fishing boats were venturing farther and farther into Pacific waters. As Japan entered World War I in 1914, the nation was becoming a major sea power; it eventually ousted Germany from its islands in the Pacific, as well as from Shantung.

With the freedom to operate large trawlers in many rich Pacific seabeds, the company grew rapidly during the postwar years. In 1924, the company went public, establishing three corporations: Hayashikane Shoten K.K., Hayashikane Gyogyo K.K., and Hayashikane Reizo K.K., the latter two to process and can foods. However, the corporate structure did not work out as planned. By the following year, the companies were reorganized and a new corporation was formed: Hayashikane Shoten K.K., with ¥10 million in capital. With Ikujiro Nakabe as president, the company began another period of rapid growth.

During the late 1920s and the 1930s, Taiyo expanded into deep-sea operations in the North and South Pacific and developed processing, canning, and packaging technology onshore.

In the 1940s, however, as Japanese losses began to mount in World War II, the domestic economy was shattered. The destruction of Taiyo's physical resources and the depletion of its workforce were severe blows. As major fishing areas had to be abandoned, the company's operations shrank to the point of requiring another reorganization. In the thick of the war, in 1943, the company became a new corporation: Nishi Taiyo Gyogyo Tosei K.K. This name was changed in 1945 to Taiyo Gyogyo K.K., and for the first time the company was referred to as Taiyo Fishery Company, Limited.

Kaneichi Nakabe became president, launching a new period of rapid growth that is now in its fifth decade. In 1949, Taiyo's headquarters was moved to Tokyo, where it remains. From that base of operations, the company carried out a plan to extend its fisheries around the world, using new technology to more fully exploit the waters it fishes.

Mother-ship operations on large trawlers in the Bering Sea, for example, began to carry the equipment to make extensive catches of Alaska pollack and immediately process it into surimi (fish paste), fish meal, and fish oil ready for marketing.

Other trawlers were sent into the South Pacific for merluza, king clip, squid, and Antarctic krill. Because of the distance to Antarctic waters, however, costs cut deeply into profit margins for such expeditions. Operations such as pair trawling in the West China Sea for pomfret, frostfish, and prawns, and salmon fishing in the northern waters of the Pacific were more cost-effective ventures.

In the early 1950s Taiyo used both experimental and traditional fishing methods as it expanded its operations. Surface fishing with purse seines was used to catch tuna, a major product worldwide, and skipjack, a staple of the Japanese diet. And longline fishing for tuna continued to be profitable, with lines extended as much as 140 kilometers into the open sea.

Also in the 1950s, Taiyo began to form international joint ventures, particularly in developing countries, to explore new resources, introduce new technology, and broaden the range of food products it could bring to the market. For example, the joint venture that Taiyo established in the Solomon Islands, sends canned fish to Europe and frozen fish to the United States—and makes up some 40% of the Islands' business. Several joint ventures have been established in the United States as well: Alyeska Seafoods Company, to produce surimi; Trans Ocean Products, to produce crab-flavored fish sticks; and Western Alaska Fisheries, to process herring, sable, flounder, salmon, and roe. In 1985, the China Zhouyang Fishery Company, Limited was formed in the People's Republic of China—Taiyo's 25th joint venture.

Even as early as the late 1950s, the market for seafood showed signs of outdistancing Taiyo's ability to supply it, despite its newly developed resources, and Taiyo began to cultivate a new source that could be continually replenished: fish farming. The research-and-development functions that had been a part of the company's operation since the 1920s took on new importance as aquaculture techniques were developed to farm sea bream, yellowtail flounder, and prawns. By 1985, Taiyo was reputed to be the foremost harvester of cultivated fish in the world, producing 10% of the company's total annual catch through fish farms in 20 locations in Japanese waters.

But even these efforts have not been enough to meet the demand for seafood products. During the past three decades, Taiyo has built up an extensive international network of import operations, bringing seafood from European, African, North Atlantic, and Far Eastern waters to its markets and distribution centers.

Developing new and more efficient methods of maintaining the freshness of its products and speeding them to market has been an important part of Taiyo's function since the first big market expansion of the post–World War I days. Thirteen Taiyo companies operate refrigeration and cold storage facilities, and another ten operate refrigerator ships, oil tankers, and overland shipping vehicles. Automated equipment pioneered in the 1960s and 1970s now contributes to the year-round efficiency of Taiyo's advanced-design pelagic trawlers.

Taiyo began to share this expertise with companies in other countries in 1971, when its company's plant engineers built a cold-storage facility in Kenya, the first of many projects that have created fishing bases, food-processing plants, and factories in Africa, South America, Asia, and the South Pacific islands. The company operates a business consultant service in connection with these projects.

Packaging is another important Taiyo function. Aluminum cans were virtually unknown in Japan when Taiyo introduced them, but they quickly became popular in the late 1940s. Similarly, Taiyo's research-and-development personnel have come up with efficient designs in paper and plastic packaging for freeze-dried and frozen foods, gelatin, and natural seasonings.

Taiyo has diversified over the years from the fishing industry, and the company now includes such diverse entities as agricultural and stock-breeding companies, mink farms and furriers, pearl cultivation centers, real estate warehousing operations, and even a baseball team.

But it is in the area of food products that Taiyo has steadily sought expansion. Western-style and Asian fruits and vegetables were added to their wares decades ago, as was sugar in 1965. Health foods and natural seasonings were added during the 1970s and 1980s. A new margarine, made with sardine oil, was introduced in 1984.

Taiyo built a large plant in Tochigi Prefecture in 1985 to develop new food products and pharmaceuticals. That same year one of its first projects was completed: an advanced canning process for fish-meat sausages. Within two years, Taiyo had also developed a drug to combat arteriosclerosis.

As pressures from environmentalists and new legal restrictions place limits on large-scale fishing operations in waters where Taiyo's fleets have been active, onshore and coastal businesses have been given greater emphasis in the company's plans. Taiyo will have to meet the challenges of the rapidly changing fishing industry at the same time that it pursues new opportunities in the food industry if its progress toward a future as a good conglomerate is to be steady, but given Taiyo's steady attention to diversification in the past, its prospects look strong.

Principal Subsidiaries: Taiyo Fishery Co., Ltd., Seattle, Washington, (U.S.A.); Taiyo Fishery Co., Ltd., New Jersey (U.S.A.); Taiyo Fishery Co., Ltd. (U.K.); Taiyo Fishery Co., Ltd.. (New Zealand); Taiyo Fishery Co., Ltd. (China); Taiyo Fishery Co., Ltd. (Singapore); Western Alaska Fisheries, Inc. (U.S.A.); Taiyo (U.S.A.) Inc.; Alyeska Seafoods Co., Ltd. (U.S.A.); Trans Ocean Products, Inc., (U.S.A); Sociedad Pesquena Taiyo Chile Ltda. (Chile); Reefer Express Lines Pty. Ltd. (Bermuda); Taiyo (U.K.) Ltd.; Iberia Taiyo S.A. (Spain); Solomon Taiyo Ltd. (Solomon); Amaltal Taiyo Fishery Co., Ltd. (New Zealand); P.T. Nusantara Fishery (Indonesia); China Zhouyang Fishery Co. Ltd. (China); Taiyo Gyogyo Co. (Hong Kong) Ltd., (Hong Kong); Bengal Fisheries Ltd. (Bangladesh); Societe Malgache de Pecherie (Madagascar) Malagasy; Societe des Pecheries du Boina (Madagascar); Efripel (Mozambique); Senepesca (Senegal); New Eastern Ltd. (Liberia).

TATE & LYLE PLC

Sugar Quay
Lower Thames Street
London EC3R 6DQ
United Kingdom
(01) 626–6525

Public Company
Incorporated: 1921
Employees: 18,500
Sales: £3.4 billion (US$6.15 billion)
Stock Index: London

Formed in 1921 by the merger of two family-run sugar refiners founded in the mid-19th century, Tate & Lyle PLC is the largest refiner of raw cane sugar in Europe, and operates in nearly 30 countries worldwide. In addition to cane sugar refining, T&L processes beet sugar, produces starches and cereal sweeteners, and is engaged in a broad spectrum of activities both related and unrelated to the sugar industry. Over the more than one hundred years since its beginnings, Tate & Lyle has successfully adapted to changing conditions, from the threat of government nationalization to the introduction of non-sugar sweetening products. A dramatic company retrenchment in the late 1970s rid the company of unprofitable ventures; today, T&L concentrates on investment in its areas of expertise.

Henry Tate was born in Liverpool in 1819, the seventh son of a Unitarian clergyman. At age 13, he was apprenticed to his older brother Caleb, a grocer, and at 20 he set out on his own. By age 36, he owned a chain of six grocery shops and began to look for other profitable ventures. In 1859, Tate became the partner of Liverpool sugar refiner John Wright and began to learn about sugar.

Use of sugar at the time was burgeoning in Great Britain, where decreasing prices led to a steady increase in consumption. New uses were being developed for sugars, including jams, condensed milk, and desserts, that made it a staple on British tables.

In 1869, Tate, a man who liked to be his own boss, dissolved his partnership with Wright and, with sons Alfred and Edwin, formed Henry Tate & Sons. He began building his new refinery in Liverpool in 1870. In 1878, the business had grown so much that Tate opened a second refinery on the Thames, which specialized in making sugar cubes using a process developed on the continent. His 250 employees at that refinery worked 60-hour weeks in 12-hour shifts.

If Henry Tate was successful in sugar, that wasn't true of all sugar producers, most of them family firms like his own. At the end of the 18th century, about 120 sugar refiners in Great Britain had supplied the growing need for sugar. By 1882, that number had been reduced to 26, and there were only 16 by 1900. But the changing business climate for sugar producers didn't deter Abram Lyle III.

Lyle, born in 1820, had gone from his father's cooperage into shipping, like Tate setting up a business with his sons. The story goes that he got into the sugar business when he accepted a cargo of sugar in lieu of payment and had to find something to do with it. In 1881, Lyle bought Odam's and Plaistow Wharves on the Thames and began to build his own sugar refinery.

Lyle got off to a rocky start. An especially large continental sugar beet crop in 1882 severely depressed the price of sugar. At the same time, the cost of construction for his refinery soared well over the estimates. Lyle was forced to take severe personal measures, including taking his children out of school, to get his fledgling business off the ground.

Lyle's policy at his Plaistow Wharf refinery was to produce a few types of sugar as cheaply as possible. He specialized in Golden Syrup, a low-price sugar product designed to resemble honey (packaging that highlighted a bee motif enhanced the identification). It was said that the poor of the industrialized cities of England lived on bread and cheap sugar products like Golden Syrup and treacle.

Although both their refineries were on the Thames, Henry Tate and Abram Lyle never met. But the two firms seem to have had a tacit understanding: Lyle never produced sugar cubes and Tate never produced syrup. When Tate died in 1890, he left his sons firmly in charge of his business, as Lyle did when he died a year later.

In 1903, Sir William Henry Tate, the founder's oldest son, made a significant change in his father's company by taking it public, perhaps because one of his brother's widows wanted to withdraw her share of the investment. Only 17 shareholders, the majority of them family members, originally invested in the company.

By 1914, both concerns were successful family-run businesses. With the outbreak of World War I, however, they faced a very difficult situation. Between 60% and 90% of the sugar refined at the two Tate factories and at Lyle's Plaistow Wharf had been raw beet sugar, primarily from Germany and Austria. That supply was quickly cut off, and U-boats threatened cane supplies from regular suppliers in the West Indies, Peru, and Mauritius. In 1914, the government took control of sugar refining, confiscating the Lyles' supplies of raw sugar and portioning out supplies of all incoming sugar to the country's sugar producers. Government wartime policy allowed companies the same profit as they had averaged on granulated sugar for the three preceding years. Since granulated sugar was not the major product of either company, this formula was a blow.

Both companies faced other hardships during the war years, including an inability to replace crucial supplies such as the charcoal used as a filter during sugar manufacture, and overworked staffs of women who replaced the soldiers. But both the Tates and Lyles survived.

In 1918, Earnest Tate, the son of Henry Tate's oldest son

William, approached second-generation brothers Charles and Robert Lyle about combining the two firms. The products of the two companies were complementary, and there would be advantages in being able to purchase in larger lots and exchanging technical expertise.

Tate was probably motivated by two factors: although his company had a greater refining capacity, it also made a lower profit per ton of sugar processed and a lower total profit. Also, the Tates saw a coming dearth of family leadership. Although the two founders were virtually the same age, the second- and third-generation Tates were much older than the Lyles and only one grandson, Vernon, was coming into the firm. The Lyles, on the other hand, had two active second-generation brothers and four family members in the firm from the third generation.

Negotiations began in the autumn of 1918 and dragged on until the spring of 1921, although the actual stumbling blocks in the negotiations were minor. Perhaps the most important deterrent was that the Tates and Lyles had different ideas about management. While the Tates hired people to handle purchasing, sales, and management, Lyles handled those positions themselves. Philip and Oliver Lyle, grandsons of Abram III, were said to dislike the Tates on principle.

But the advantages of merger finally outweighed the objections, and the two companies became Tate & Lyle in 1921, with Charles Lyle as the first chairman, to be succeeded by Ernest Tate. The actual mechanics of merger were complicated, especially since Tate's was a public company and Lyle's was privately owned. But the merger was designed to form a 50/50 partnership.

Despite agreements between managements and an exhange of personnel between plants, however, fraternization between Tates and Lyles was slow. As long as 15 years after the merger, old Tate employees were reluctant to mingle with the Lyle group and vice versa.

The first challenge the newly amalgamated company faced was to respond to the postwar economy. The end of World War I meant a growing worldwide demand for refined sugar—in West Africa, in fact, sugar cubes were used as currency after the war. T&L invested in sugar-cane producing land in Africa (an experiment that was later transferred to local government control after political upheavals), expanded capacity with new refining techniques, and became a leader in the distribution of brand-name goods instead of bulk commodities.

T&L also became involved in the effort to develop a homegrown sugar industry so Britain wouldn't have to face the supply crisis precipitated by World War I. The company invested heavily in the Bury Group, which was set up to develop a beet sugar industry in Britain.

But the government also had its eye on beet sugar production. In 1933, national quotas for beet sugar products were established. By 1935, the government was prepared to go even further. Existing beet sugar companies were combined into the British Sugar Corporation under the supervision of a Sugar Commission. The Bury Group received £1.4 million in British Sugar Corporation shares in exchange for its assets; this money was distributed to its shareholders, including Tate & Lyle.

The company was now effectively excluded from the beet sugar industry at home. But with the money from the transaction, T&L looked for new sources of sugar cane to offset the loss. In 1937, T&L formed the West Indies Sugar Company to buy property in Jamaica and Trinidad. The company also built a new central processing center in Frome, Jamaica.

By this time, however, a new crisis was at hand with the opening of hostilities leading to World War II. Sugar rationing began in mid-February 1940 and limited each citizen to 3/4 pounds of sugar a week, later 1/2 pound. That meant a huge reduction in Tate & Lyle production. The directors, still primarily immediate family members, decided to keep both the London and Liverpool refineries open despite the drop in production. Plaistow made Golden Syrup, which was in great demand because of its low price. The Thames facility continued to make sugar cubes, although wartime shortages meant that the quality was lower. Both London factories were hit hard by bombs and required substantial repairs. By 1942 over half of the employees in both refineries were women.

The end of the war again meant increased demand and an abundant work force, but it wasn't long before government intervention in the sugar industry became a direct threat to the company. In 1949, with Socialists in power, it looked as if the government was ready to expand from its base in beet sugar and directly nationalize Tate & Lyle. To avoid becoming a subsidiary of British Sugar, the company enlisted the support of other sugar producers and took its case directly to the people with its "Mr. Cube" campaign. The little square cartoon character told homemakers, "State control will make a hole in your pocket and my packet," and "If they juggle with SUGAR they'll juggle with your SHOPPING BASKET!" The pressure held off the threat to the company's independence, which was further relieved when the Socialists were defeated in 1951.

Tate & Lyle may have been independent, but in the postwar world the company couldn't function freely. The U.S. Sugar Act of 1948 set the price of sugar there to protect its own sugar industry. The act also admitted Cuban sugar under a preferential tariff and regulated other imports under a quota system, thus severely limiting T&L's expansion in the United States.

Other industry regulations followed. In 1951, the Commonwealth Sugar Agreement, an agreement suggested by the British West Indies Sugar Association (which included Tate & Lyle interests in Jamaica and Trinidad) specified quotas and prices for imported sugar in Great Britain. The agreement was monitored by the Sugar Board to provide fixed quantities of sugar at reasonable prices, and it did provide a stability in the industry that Tate & Lyle welcomed.

The 1950s saw T&L begin to branch out into related ventures. In 1951, the company established Tate & Lyle Technical Services to emphasize research and development. That company in turn spawned Tate & Lyle Enterprises, an agricultural planning service to help develop agricultural ventures, especially in the developing world.

The company continued to acquire interests in sugar, buying Rhodesian (later Zimbabwe) Sugar Refineries in 1953. Another major subsidiary, Canada & Dominion Sugar Company (later Redpath Industries), was acquired in 1959, giving T&L a new foothold in the beet sugar industry and a better opportunity to serve the large U.S. market (beet sugar imports were not regulated under the same quotas as cane imports). When the United States slashed Fidel Castro's Cuban sugar quotas in the early 1960s for political reasons, T&L took advantage of additional quotas for Caribbean cane sugar by buying Belize Sugar Industries. And in 1964, the company diversified into a related area when it bought United Molasses. In 1967, as a member of a European consortium, T&L expanded its interests in beet sugar outside of Britain by investing in the Say beet sugar factories in France.

Redpath Industries and United Molasses brought with them business areas outside of T&L's traditional concerns. Subsidiaries of Redpath manufacture automotive parts and vinyl siding for homes, and United Molasses includes shipbuilding capacity.

Tate & Lyle's expansion abroad and diversification proved to be the right course when Britain joined the European Economic Community in 1973. One provision of membership that directly affected the company was the EEC's sugar quotas. Traditional suppliers of cane sugar would continue to supply the EEC with specific annual quotas of raw cane sugar, both to assure British producers of an adequate supply and to protect the economies of developing countries dependent on sugar. The EEC Sugar Protocols guaranteed annual quotas of raw sugar from the African, Caribbean, and Pacific producers. These agreements, embodied in 1975 in the Lomé Convention, completely insulated the EEC from the world price of sugar and tightly controlled sugar trading.

Another provision of membership that affected T&L was the EEC's subsidization of beet sugar production. Locked out of the beet sugar market at home by government-controlled British Sugar, T&L was never satisfied with the EEC's subsidization, as it provided substantial incentives for the beet sugar industry to overproduce and decreased the market for T&L's cane products.

Nonetheless, EEC membership had little impact on the company at first. An acute world shortage of sugar in 1975 meant sugar reached all-time high prices. In 1976, T&L was able to expand both at home and abroad, purchasing the last other independent British sugar refiner, Manbré and Garton (which specialized in starches and glucose), Amylum of Belgium, and Refined Sugars in the United States (which finally gave it a foothold in the U.S. market).

But when sugar prices fell dramatically in 1978 at the same time that worldwide sugar production rose 14%, T&L's earnings plummeted 62% in one year.

That same year Lord Jellicoe became the first non-Tate or Lyle to fill the chairmanship of the company, and T&L began a policy of retrenchment due to "a trading climate which is unlikely to become easier in the near future," according to Jellicoe. Because of the "crisis of overcapacity" since membership in the EEC, the company closed its Liverpool refinery in 1980 to help reestablish a better balance between supply and demand. Liverpool had been in operation for more than 100 years, and some workers there were the third generation of their families to work for the company. T&L also introduced cost cutting measures at the Thames refinerey and terminated the production of starches and glucose. Finally, the company put a new organizational structure in place, marked by a smaller number of chief executives who had clear lines of responsibility and were held personally responsible for the performance of their divisions.

With unprofitable areas of the business gone and a reinvigorated management team in place, Tate & Lyle has moved since 1978 to regain a position of leadership. In the early 1980s, T&L took another step, recognizing that sugar was not the only sweetener consumers wanted. High fructose corn syrup had become an extremely important product early in the 1970s. Corn syrup not only used the bumper corn corps of the United States, but also was easier to use in soft drinks and many types of packaged goods. In 1981 T&L's Redpath Industries entered a joint venture with John Labatt to produce high fructose corn syrup for the soft-drink industry. Redpath withdrew from the venture, called Zymaize, two years later, but T & L was convinced that they would have to compete in the industry to stay on top of sweeteners.In 1985, T&L re-entered the beet sugar processing business by acquiring several U.S. beet factories; seven midwestern factories now operate as The Western Sugar Company.

As the decade went on, T&L bought controlling interests in other foreign sugar producers, Alcantara and Sores refineries in Portugal, and developed new sugar technology with a micro-crystalline process at the Plaistow plant to provide new types of sugar for packaged foods and industry. It also expanded some of its profitable non-sugar interests with the acquisition of Vigortone, a U.S. producer of animal feed, in 1984 and of Heartland Building Products, a producer of vinyl siding, in 1987. The Heartland acquisition put T&L among the top five vinyl siding manufacturers in North America.

At the same time, T&L began another strong public relations effort to counteract a trend toward decreased consumption of sugar in developed countries because it has been implicated as a cause of dental cavities, obesity, diabetes, and hyperactivity.

Three major developments in the late 1980s promise to keep the reinvigorated firm at the forefront of the sweetener industry. In June 1988, T&L purchased Staley Continental, a major corn wet milling business in the United States. The $1.48 billion hostile takeover gave the company 25% of the U.S. high fructose corn syrup market. T&L's aggressive new chairman, Neil Shaw (who took over in 1986 after serving as group managing director), immediately began restructuring the company to fit with Tate & Lyle by selling Staley's foodservice division.

In October 1988, after resolving antitrust problems by selling the refining interests of Refined Sugars, T&L acquired another major U.S. sweetener business, Amstar Sugar, which produces the Domino brand, for $305 million.

Finally, T&L announced its development of sucralose, a calorie-free sweetener that could compete with aspartame (marketed as Nutrasweet). It is developing this discovery in a joint venture with the American company Johnson & Johnson to ensure approval for its use in the United

States. The approval process, however, has proven slower than anticipated, so T&L's position in this new area of the sweetener industry lags far behind the industry leader.

Tate & Lyle's policies under nonfamily leadership since 1978 have given the company a strong market position in cane, beet, and corn-based sweeteners and have positioned it to gain a share of the artificial sweetener market. These policies should keep Tate and Lyle in the forefront of the market for some time to come.

Principal Subsidiaries: Athel Reinsurance Co. Ltd.; Richards (Shipbuilders) Ltd.; Tate & Lyle Holdings Ltd.; Tate & Lyle Industries Ltd.; The Molasses Trading Company Limited; Tate & Lyle International Finance Limited; Tate & Lyle Investments Limited; Tunne Refineries Limited (66.67%); British Charcoals & Macdonalds; Four-F Nutrition; Hugh Baird & Sons; Kentships; Micronized Food Products; Milltech; Rumenco; Speciality Sweeteners; Tate & Lyle International; Tate & Lyle Sugars; Unitank Storage Company; United Molasses Company; Caribbean Antilles Molasses Co. Ltd. (Barbados); Amylum NV (Belgium) (66.67%); Tameco NV (Belgium); Tate & Lyle Management & Finance Ltd. (Bermuda); Tate & Lyle Commodities Ltd. (Bermuda); Tate & Lyle Reinsurance Ltd. (Bermuda); Tate & Lyle do Brasil Servicos e Participacoes Limitada (Brazil); Canada West Indies Molasses Co. Ltd. (Canada); Redpath Industries Ltd. (Canada); Nordisk Melasse A/S (Denmark); Schouten France Sarl (France); Societe Europeene des Melasses SA (France)(50%); Biamyl SA (Greece)(97.5%); Caribbean Molasses Co. Ltd. (Guyana); Melassa Italiana (Melitalia) SpA (Italy); East African Storage Co. Ltd. (Kenya); The Mauritius Molasses Co. Ltd. (Mauritius) (66.67%); Nederlandsche Melasse Handel Maatschappij BV (Netherlands); Tate & Lyle Holland BV (Netherlands); Technostaal Schouten BV (Netherlands); Ten Havc BV (Netherlands); Zetmeelbedrijven de Bijenkorf BV (Netherlands); Tate & Lyle Norge A/S (Norway); Alcantara Sociedada de Empreendimentos Acucareiros, SA (Portugal); Sociedade de Refinadores de Santa Iria, SA (Portgual); Tate & Lyle (Portugal) Importacao e Exportacao Ltda. (Portugal); Campo Ebro Industrial SA (Spain) (91%); United Molasses (Espana) SA (Spain); Caribbean Bulk Storage and Trading Co. Ltd. (Trinidad); Automotive Industries Inc. (USA); Tate & Lyle Inc. (USA); Pacific Molasses Co. (USA); The Western Sugar Co. (USA); AE Staley manufacturing Co. (USA) (92.7%); Amstar Sugar Corp. (USA); Staley Holding Inc. (USA) (92.7%); Technostal Schouten Inc. (USA); Vigortone Ag Products Inc. (USA); Unitank Inc. (USA); Hansa Melasse Handels GmbH (West Germany); Zimbabwe Sugar Refineries Ltd. (Zimbabwe) (50.13%).

Further Reading: Hugill, Antony. *Sugar and All That . . .*, London, Gentry Books, 1978; Mintz, Sidney W. *Sweetness and Power*, New York, Viking Penguin, 1985.

TYSON FOODS, INCORPORATED

2210 West Oaklawn Drive
Springdale, Arkansas 72764
U.S.A.
(501) 756–4000

Public Company
Incorporated: 1947 as Tyson Feed & Hatchery, Incorporated
Employees: 26,000
Sales: $1.94 billion
Stock Index: NASDAQ

During the Depression, John Tyson, an Arkansas farmer, began selling chickens while his son Don was still a toddler. Don Tyson grew up along with the company, and eventually transformed it into a giant in the poultry industry.

In 1935, John Tyson bought 50 "springer" chickens and hauled them to Chicago to sell at a profit. Two years later, he named his business Tyson Feed & Hatchery. Over the next thirteen years the company prospered by buying and selling chickens, especially with the postwar boom that brought, among other things, improved kitchen appliances and the first supermarkets.

Gradually, however, Tyson became involved in raising chickens, which allowed him better control over the quality of what he sold. In 1947, the company was incorporated.,

Five years later, Don Tyson graduated from college and joined the company as head of operations. Father and son were said to have made a dynamic team, the older Tyson more cautious and the younger one pushing forward. For example, Don convinced his father to raise rock cornish game hens, a market that Tyson would one day dominate.

For the next six years, Tyson focused on expanding production facilities, and in 1958, the company opened a processing plant in Springdale, Arkansas, the site of company headquarters. Tyson also introduced its first ice-pack processing line, which brought the company into a more competitive industry bracket. By achieving more complete vertical integration, its dependence on other suppliers lessened.

During the early 1960s, many amateur chicken producers were lured into the market by the drop in feed-grain prices and the easy availability of credit. As a result, broiler production rose about 13% between 1965 and 1967. The glut that followed caused big price cuts and accounted for about $50 million in losses in the industry. Several small companies were forced out of business, but the demand for low-priced chicken soared. People were eating four times as much chicken as they did in 1950.

In 1963, Tyson went public and changed its name to Tyson's Foods, Incorporated. It also made its first acquisition, of the Garrett Poultry Company, based in Rogers, Arkansas.

In 1966, John Tyson and his wife died in an automobile accident, and Don Tyson took over the business as president. The growth of the poultry industry in the 1960s was largely due to technological improvements. Broiler production had become one of the most industrialized, automated parts of American agriculture. Through the development of better feeds and better disease control methods, chickens were maturing more quickly. All of this was good for consumers, but for processors, it meant lower earnings. In 1967, despite a 37% gain in sales, Tyson lost more than a dollar per share in earnings. Nonetheless, the company took advantage of a situation in which several smaller companies were floundering, and with its acquisition of Franz Foods, Inc. continued its pattern of buying out smaller poultry concerns. It also began to give its corporate name more visibility, printing "Tyson Country Fresh Chicken" on its wrappers instead of the name of the supermarket the chickens were sold to.

In 1968, Tyson went to court with two other processors when an Agriculture Department officer alleged that the processors had discriminated against Arkansas chicken farmers who were members of an association of poultry farmers. At that time, it was customary for processors to hire farmers to raise their chickens; Tyson and the others had been accused of "boycotting and blacklisting" association members in 1962. In 1969, a federal appeals court ruled that the Agriculture Department had "erred" in treating the chicken processors like meat packers and therefore did not have the authority under existing laws to take any action against them.

Also in 1969, Tyson acquired Prospect Farms, Inc., the company that became its pre-cooked chicken division. That year Tyson produced more than 2% of the nation's chickens, 70% for retail sale and 30% for institutions. The company had grown from 15 to 3,000 employees and operated five chicken-processing plants and four protein-processing plants in northwest Arkansas and southwest Missouri.

During the 1970s, Tyson continued to grow and diversify. In 1970, a new egg facility was built, and in 1971, a computerized feed mill and a plant in Nashville, Arkansas were completed. Also in 1971 the company's name was changed from Tyson's Foods to Tyson Foods. In 1972, Tyson acquired the Ocoma Foods Division of Consolidated Foods Corporation, including three new plants, as well as Krispy Kitchens, Inc. and the poultry division of Wilson Foods. That year Tyson began selling the Ozark Fry, the first breaded chicken breast pattie, and also bought a hog operation in Creswell, North Carolina from First Colony Farms.

1972 was a shakeout year in the poultry business, and several large processors sold out to those with better prospects of survival, easing competition. Because of the rising prices of beef and pork, chicken consumption was increasing at a rapid rate, and new products and technological developments seemed to promise improved profits for the industry. Tyson was already a leader in introducing new products like its chicken pattie, chicken hotdogs, and chicken bologna—by 1979, it had 24 specialty products. Tyson also operated three plants that used the new deep chill (rather than ice-pack) process, in which the moisture of the bird was frozen at 28°—one degree warmer than the temperature at which chicken meat freezes, leaving the meat still tender and doubling shelf life to about 25 days. In 1973, Tyson bought Cassady Broiler Company, another small poultry concern.

In the early 1970s Tyson closed its money-losing plant in Shelbyville, Tennessee, but reopened it in 1974 to produce more popular processed and pre-cooked chicken products. Tyson also acquired Vantress Pedigree, Inc. in 1974.

A civil antitrust lawsuit brought against Tyson and other broiler processors in 1974 for conspiring to fix, maintain, and stabilize broiler prices was settled in 1977. Tyson agreed to pay a $975,663 fine to about 30 chicken purchasers.

In 1978, Tyson acquired the rest of Wilson Foods Corporation. A year later the company sold its two North Carolina chicken-processing plants.

In 1980, Tyson introduced its Chick 'n Quick line of products, which included a variety of chicken portions that were easy to prepare. By then Tyson was the largest grower of rock cornish game hens and one of the nation's largest hog producers. As it perfected its pre-cooked chicken pattie for restaurants, its institutional sales also grew.

In 1983, Tyson implemented its new advertising slogan, "Doing our best . . . just for you" with television commercials on all three major networks. The company also acquired Mexican Original Products, Inc., a manufacturer of tortillas, taco shells, tostados, and tortilla chips.

By the early 1980s, consumers' nutritional concerns and the continually high prices of beef and pork had caused the nation's poultry consumption to increase 30% since 1970. This increase was also partly due to innovative, easy-to-prepare products from companies like Tyson and the industry's ability to improve breeding and feed techniques. Some of Tyson's experiments had produced six-pound chickens in just six weeks. In 1984, Cobb, Inc. and Tyson began a joint venture called Arkansas Breeders, to breed and develop the Cobb 500, a female with fast growth, low fat, and high meat content.

In September of 1984, Tyson acquired 90% of another poultry firm, Valmac Industries. By then, Tyson had expanded its operations into six states—Georgia, North Carolina, Missouri, Tennessee, Louisiana, and Arkansas—and many of its products were being distributed internationally.

In 1986, *The Wall Street Transcript* named Don Tyson the gold award winner in the meat and poultry industry. The company acquired Lane Processing Inc. a closely held poultry processing firm that had been bankrupt since 1984.

In October, 1988, Tyson made a takeover bid for Holly Farms Corporation, the national leader in brand-name chicken sales based in Memphis, Tennessee. Holly Farms had begun more than a century before as a cotton compressor. Over the years it had evolved into a chicken and food service firm with vast holdings and a 19% share of the brand-name chicken market. It had been the first processor to use its own name rather than the retail seller's on its packaging, which gave the company a long-standing credibility with consumers and made it a very attractive purchase. Holly Farms rejected the bid, nodding to Tennessee takeover laws, and agreed to merge with ConAgra, Inc., one of the nation's largest food companies and a leading poultry producer based in Omaha, Nebraska. Holly Farms also agreed to sell its poultry assets to ConAgra should the merger not come to fruition. In mid-November, Tyson sued Holly Farms and ConAgra to stop the merger. A few days later, a federal judge ruled that Tennessee's anti-takeover laws were unconstitutional and could not be used to halt Tyson's bid, opening an eight-month fight between Tyson and ConAgra for control of Holly Farms.

Tyson's rapid growth in the fast-food chicken business had put a strain on its production facilities, and Tyson needed Holly Farms's chicken supply. More than half of Tyson's business now was with institutions and restaurants, and Tyson's name was not as popular as Holly Farms's in the grocery stores. Finally in June, 1989, Don Tyson agreed to pay $1.3 billion for Holly Farms, and the company was fully merged into Tyson later that year.

Between 1984 and 1989 Tyson's profits more than quadrupled while its revenues nearly tripled. With the acquisition of Holly Farms, Tyson is the new king of the chicken industry—an industry that has seen explosive growth, but can look forward to more if projections that chicken will pass beef as the number-one meat in the early 1990s are true. In an interview with *Forbes* in 1988, Tyson explained that executives at Tyson were required to wear khakis: "If we all wore suits we'd sit here in the office, and we don't make money in here. We make it out in the field." As long as this kind of hard-working lack of pretension characterizes the way Don Tyson does business, and as long as chicken prices stay high enough to keep Tyson's debt load from its Holly Farms acquisition manageable, Tyson's future looks promising.

Principal Subsidiaries: Tyson Carolina, Inc.; Tyson Express, Inc.; Coastals Rentals and Rigging Corp.; Tyson Export Sales, Inc.; Dixie Home Farms, Inc.; Tyson's Pride of Oklahoma, Inc.; Poultry Growers, Inc.

UNIGATE PLC

Unigate House
Western Avenue
London W3 0SH
United Kingdom
(01) 992–3400

Public Company
Incorporated: 1959 as Unigate Limited
Employees: 34,922
Sales: £2.2 billion (US$3.98 billion)
Stock Index: London

The evolution of Unigate PLC has certainly been an interesting story. The company, in its various forms, went from selling liquor in the mid-19th century to selling milk and baby food in the early 20th century, and is now a conglomerate that markets goods and services ranging from turkeys to transportation to Mexican food. But through the decades, Unigate has had two constants: growth, and a dairy business that has remained at the core of its operations for more than a century.

The history of Unigate goes back to 1882, when Charles Gates died and left his Guildford, Surrey grocer's shop to two of his sons, Charles Arthur and Leonard. The Gates' store primarily sold liquor; it was the local agent for Gilbey's wines and spirits and also sold beer. The Gates brothers added tea and coffee to their father's shelves. Then in 1885, according to a story that has become a part of company legend, they were seized by a violent fit of pro-temperance sentiment, vowed never to make money off the liquor trade again, and poured their entire stock of alcoholic beverages into the gutters of High Street, Guildford.

This left them without a source of livelihood, but it occurred to them that the cellars underneath the shop, as well as the yards and stables in back, could be converted into a dairy. They bought a milk separator and started West Surrey Dairy. They purchased milk from local farmers, sold the skim back to them for feeding pigs, and sold the cream to the prosperous citizens of Guildford. In 1888 the company changed its name to West Surrey Central Dairy Company Limited. Three more Gates brothers—Walter, William, and Alfred—and three of their sons joined the family business about this time.

It didn't take long for the business to become successful enough to justify expansion. West Surrey Central Dairy bought creameries in Somerset, Dorset, and even Ireland. Its brown jugs of cream soon became famous throughout England, although the level of artistry on the label left something to be desired. According to one historian of the British dairy industry, they showed "a cow looking uncomfortably through a somewhat untypical four-barred gate, rather as if its neck had got stuck between the bars."

West Surrey Central Dairy entered the baby-food business in 1904 when Dr. Killick Millard, medical officer of health for Leicester, asked it to supply powdered milk to help feed children of poor families. Four years later, its "Cow & Gate Pure English Dried Milk" was first marketed on a large scale. The dried milk became widely popular despite the prevailing belief that breast-feeding was essential to a baby's health. In 1924 the company developed a special export version of its powdered milk, for feeding babies in tropical climates, which became very popular. In fact, an Indian nobleman once placed a rush order for two cases. It turned out, however, that he wanted to feed the milk to his racehorses.

In 1929, the company renamed itself after its popular Cow & Gate product line, becoming Cow & Gate Limited. During the 1930s it worked with scientists to develop specialized formulas to cater to infants with special needs. It came out with Frailac, a milk food for premature infants; Allergiac for babies sensitive to certain constituents of cow's milk; and a cereal food designed to start babies on mixed feeding at an earlier age.

On the corporate side, the company had gone public in 1918 under the chairmanship of Bramwell Gates, the son of Walter Gates. In the 1920s and 1930s, Cow & Gate expanded by acquiring dairies and creameries. Economic conditions were by no means easy in post–World War I Britain, and many of these acquisitions may have been salvages of struggling businesses. Cow & Gate began by purchasing Wallens Dairy Company of Kilburn in 1924 and added companies in Wales, Yorkshire, Lancashire, Cornwall, Devon, and Somerset over the next 15 years. In 1925 the company decided that its operations were large enough to justify setting up its own transportation subsidiary, and over the next seven decades that part of the company's operations (now known as the Wincanton Group) would become one of the nation's largest transport concerns.

Political uncertainty in Europe in the early 1930s convinced the Gates family to seek an overseas source of powdered milk as a way of safeguarding its export business. In 1933 Cow & Gate purchased a controlling interest in General Milk Products of Canada Limited. And indeed, when World War II broke out in 1939, the British government banned all exports of food products, but Cow & Gate was able to keep its overseas markets supplied for the duration through its Canadian facilities.

Bramwell Gates retired in 1958 at the age of 83; he was replaced as chairman by Ernest Taylor. One of Taylor's first acts in office was to begin negotiating a merger with United Dairies, the nation's largest producer of dairy products. United was formed in 1917 when Wiltshire United Dairies, Metropolitan and Great Western Dairies, and Dairy Supply Company merged in an attempt to cope with distribution problems caused in the London market by the loss of men, vehicles, and horses to the war effort. In the late 1920s, United Dairies helped pioneer the sale of pasteurized milk in Britain. During the 1930s and into World War II it expanded into Scotland through the acquisition of dairies, and after the war it spread its presence to Wales, Liverpool, Cheshire, Birmingham, and Sherbourne.

The merger between Cow & Gate and United Dairies was consummated in 1959. The new company was reincorporated as Unigate Limited. Integration was not easy, however, and internal politics and rivalry between factions adhering to old-company loyalties continued to plague Unigate for years. In 1963 Unigate acquired Midland Counties Dairies and began buying up small grocery stores and restaurants soon thereafter, but otherwise the company moved slowly in the early 1960s as it tried to digest the merger.

As milk consumption leveled off in the 1960s and began to decline as the decade ended, Unigate responded by increasing its non-dairy businesses and its non-milk product lines. In 1970 it announced plans to expand its retail activities, which included Kibby's supermarkets, Quids-In clothing shops, Uni-Wash laundrettes, and even some Kentucky Fried Chicken franchises. In 1973 it acquired Scot Bowyers, a meat-processing company. In 1975 it purchased Frigo, an American maker of Italian cheeses, and it acquired another American specialty cheesemaker, Gardenia, in 1978.

Even still, Unigate's financial performance was sluggish through the early and mid-1970s and it continued to be bothered by political infighting, a sign that the merger was still not fully digested. So when John Clement became chairman in 1977, he immediately set about knocking heads in the name of company unity. Over the next five years, Unigate lost a number of senior executives and Clement, a career dairyman, gained a reputation for autocratic rule. But he also put the company on solid financial footing and accelerated the process of diversifying its business.

One of Clement's first major acts as chairman was important in this regard. In 1979, Unigate parted with three-quarters of its manufacturing capacity when it sold 16 of its creameries to the Milk Marketing Board for £87 million. The sale lessened its presence in its traditional mainstay, but raised cash for acquisitions and paying off debt. In 1981 Unigate acquired Giltspur, a moving company; Turner's Turkeys; and Casa Bonita, an American restaurant chain specializing in Mexican food. In 1984 it added another poultry processor, J. P. Wood. In 1985 it acquired Arlington Motor Holdings, followed by Colchester Car Auctions the next year, and added them both to the Wincanton Group. Also in 1986, it added the American restaurant chain Prufrock, which specializes in southern-style food.

In the mid- and late 1980s, however, some of these diversification moves were junked after they proved less than successful. In 1984 Clipper Seafoods, a struggling fish-products business, was sold off. Scot Bowyers was sold to Northern Foods in 1985. And in 1987, Unigate divested several small engineering businesses that had been acquired with Giltspur. To complicate matters further, Unigate also began reinvesting in its milk business in 1987, acquiring the Middlesex dairy H. A. Job for £26 million. As of that year, it was still the United Kingdom's leading milk supplier, despite relying on milk for less than one-third of its business.

In the final analysis, Unigate is both of the things it has appeared to be in the 1980s—both the largest British dairy company and a dairy company that has drastically cut its reliance on its traditional business. The bottom line is that its financial performance improved dramatically during the decade, even as the milk market showed no sign of improving. Unigate's pre-tax profits more than doubled between 1981 and 1986, and its debt load steadily declined. It entered the 1990s with a streamlined management structure and in a state of financial health. The unhappy cow with its neck stuck in a gate may belong to the past as a corporate icon, but the legacy of its creators survives.

Principal Subsidiaries: Arlington Motor Holding Plc; Fermanagh Creameries Ltd.; Hassy Ltd.; Wincanton Vehicle Rentals Ltd.; Turners' Turkeys Ltd.; Unigate (UK) Ltd.; Ashton Foods Ltd.; H. A. Job Ltd.; Panda Van Hire (Exeter) Ltd.; Unigate Poultry Ltd.

Unilever

UNILEVER PLC
UNILEVER N.V.

Post Office Box 68
Unilever House
Blackfriars
London EC4P 4BQ
United Kingdom
(01) 822–5252

Post Office Box 760
3000 DK Rotterdam
The Netherlands
(10) 464–5911

Public Company
Incorporated: 1929 as Unilever Ltd. and Unilever NV
Employees: 291,000
Sales: £17.12/Dfl61.96 (US$31 billion)
Stock Index: London Amsterdam New York Paris Frankfurt Brussels Zurich Luxembourg Vienna

If the adage "two heads are better than one" applies to business, then certainly Unilever is a prime example. The food and consumer products giant actually has two parent companies: Unilever PLC, based in the United Kingdom and Unilever N.V., based in the Netherlands. The two companies, which operate virtually as a single corporation, are run by identical boards of directors, in which the chairman of each automatically becomes vice-chairman of the other. Foods, drinks, and personal products like soap and detergent constitute the majority of Unilever's business. Unilever brands include Imperial and Promise margarines, Lipton tea, Ragu foods, detergent products such as Wisk, Sunlight, and Dove; and personal products like Vaseline, Pond's, and Elizabeth Taylor's passion perfume. Unilever also has specialty chemicals and agribusiness operations.

William Hesketh Lever, later Lord Leverhulme, was born in Bolton, England in 1851. The founder of Lever Brothers, Lever's personality combined "the rationality of the business man with the restless ambitions of the explorer," according to Unilever historian Charles Wilson.

During the depression of the 1880s, Lever, then a salesman for his father's wholesale grocery business, recognized the advantages of not only selling, but also manufacturing, soap, a non-cyclical necessity item. His father, James Lever, was initially opposed to the idea, believing that they should remain grocers, not manufacturers. He softened, however, in the face of his son's determination. In 1885, William established a soap factory in Warrington as a branch of the family grocery business. Within a short time Lever was selling his soap across the United Kingdom, as well as in Continental Europe, North America, Australia, and South Africa. He also began a tradition that to some degree still exists at Unilever—that of producing all its raw components. The vertically integrated company grew to include milling operations used to crush seeds into vegetable oil for margarine as well as packaging and transporting businesses for all its products, which then included Lux, Lifebuoy, Rinso, and Sunlight soaps.

In 1914, as the German navy began to threaten food imports, particularly Danish butter and Dutch margarine, the British government asked if Lever would produce margarine. He eagerly accepted the opportunity, believing that the margarine business would be compatible with the soap business because the products both required oils and fats as raw materials. Lever Brothers' successful diversification, however, now put the company in competition with Jurgens and Van den Berghs, two leading margarine companies.

Fierce competitors in the latter half of the 19th century, Van den Berghs and Jurgens had decided in 1908 to pool their interests in an effort to make the best of the poor economic situation that existed in most of the world. Competition in the margarine industry had intensified, fueled by an increasing number of smaller firms, which were exporting their products and lowering their prices to get a piece of the market. Van den Berghs eliminated the potential for problems such as double taxation, which arose from its interests both in Holland and the United Kingdom, by creating and incorporating two parents companies for itself: one in Holland and one in England. In 1920, Jurgens and Van de Berghs decided there was strength in numbers and joined with another margarine manufacturer, Schicht, in Bohemia. In 1927 the three companies, borrowing the ideal of a dual structure from Van de Berghs, formed Margarine Union Limited, a group of Dutch firms with interests in England, and Margarine Unie N.V., located in Holland.

Through the middle and late 1920s, the oil and fat trades continued to grow. Although the activities of Margarine Unie and Margarine Union were focused on edible fats (margarine), the companies had held soap interests throughout Europe for years. Similarly, although Lever Brothers had produced margarine since World War I, its focus was soap. After two years of discussion, the companies decided that an "alliance wasted less of everybody's substance than hostility," and merged on September 2, 1929.

As it does today, the newly formed Unilever consisted of two holding companies: Unilever Limited, previously Margarine Union; and Unilever N.V., formerly Margarine Unie. The new organization included an equalization agreement, to assure equal profits for shareholders of both companies, as well as identically structured boards.

Unilever's parent companies were actually holding companies supervising the operations of hundreds of manufacturing and trading firms worldwide. The end result of the merger was a company which bought and processed more than a third of the world's commercial oils and fats and traded more products in more places than any other company in the world. Its manufacturing activities—which included detergents and toilet preparations, margarine and edible fats, food products, and oil milling and auxiliary businesses—were joined by a need for similar raw and refined materials, such as coconut, palm, cottonseed, and soybean oil, as well as whale oil and animal fats.

The Great Depression, which struck just after the new company was formed, affected every aspect of Unilever's multi-faceted operation: its raw material companies faced price decreases of 30% to 40% in the first year alone; cattle cake, sold as a product of its oil mills, suffered with the decline of the agricultural industry; margarine and other edible fats suffered from damaging competition as the price of butter collapsed; and its retail grocery and fish shops suffered along with their customers.

As prices and profits threatened to collapse around the world, Unilever had to act quickly to build up an efficient system of control. The special committee was established in September, 1930 to do that. The special committee operates like a board of directors over the two boards the company has. It was designed to balance Dutch and British interests and act as an inner cabinet for the organization. It also oversees two committees established to deal with Unilever's world affairs: a continental committee to deal with businesses on the European Continent, and an overseas committee to supervise business elsewhere.

A new generation of management led Unilever through the 1930s: Francis D'Arcy Cooper, who had been chairman of Lever Brothers since William Lever's death in 1925; Georg Schicht, the former chairman of Schicht Company; and Paul Rijkens, who succeeded Anton Jurgens as chairman of Jurgens in 1933. It was Cooper who seemed to lead the efforts to turn the various companies that comprised Unilever into one Anglo-Dutch team. It was also Cooper who convinced the board of the necessity for a reorganization in 1937, when the relationship between the profit-earning capacities of the Dutch and British companies found itself reversed. Originally, about two-thirds of Unilever's profits were earned by the Dutch group and one-third was earned by the British group. By 1937, however, due to increasing trade conflicts in Europe, particularly in Germany, the situation had reversed. By selling the Lever company's assets outside the British Empire, including Lever Brothers Company in the United States, to the Dutch arm of Unilever, the assets of the two groups were redistributed so that they would be nearly equal in volume and profits, which had always been the objective of the two parent companies.

Before 1945, the oils and fats industries had progressed fairly smoothly. The only major industry discoveries were the discovery of the hydrogenation process just before World War I, which enabled manufacturers to turn oils into hard fats, and the possibility of adding vitamins to margarine in the 1920s, which created an opportunity for new health-related product claims. But it was not until the end of World War II that the industry in general, including Unilever, began to recognize the important relationship between marketing and research.

While Unilever's growth until the mid-1940s was a result of expanded product lines and plant capacities, its greatest achievements between 1945 and 1965 were its adaptation to new markets and new technology. The decade following World War II was a period of recovery, culminating by the early 1950s in rapid economic growth in much of the Western world. Until 1955, demand continued to rise and competition was not a major issue. Afterwards, however, profit margins dropped, competition in Europe and North America sharpened, and success was less assured. Unilever's strategy was to put its eggs into several baskets by acquiring companies in new areas, particularly food and chemical manufacturers.

Before the formation of Unilever, Lever Brothers had coped with overseas expansion by purchasing two factories in the United States, one in Boston and one in Philadelphia. Following World War II, however, Unilever found it lacked the scientific resources needed to compete with American companies in research and development. Previously, key concerns for the soap industry revolved around color, scent, lather, and how well the products adapted to changing fabrics. Following the war, development efforts in the United States succeeded in creating a non-soap synthetic detergent powder, to the dismay of Unilever and its United States subsidiary, Lever Brothers Company. Detergents have superior cleaning powers, and they do not form insoluble deposits in plumbing systems in hard water. The disappointment, however, spurred the company to value research as highly as marketing and sales. Lever Brothers had three detergent plants in production by 1950, but it remained behind in the industry for some time.

Because the primary ingredients of the new detergents were petro-chemicals, the company now found itself involved in chemical technology. In the synthetic detergent market, each geographic area required a different kind of product, depending on the way consumers washed their clothes and the type of water available to them. The new detergents gave rise to new problems, however; the foam detergents left in sewage systems and rivers had become a major issue by the late 1950s. By 1965, Unilever had introduced biodegradable products in the United States, the United Kingdom, and West Germany.

Throughout the postwar era, Unilever continued to invest in research and research facilities. One of its major establishments—its Port Sunlight facility in Cheshire, which William Lever had founded in the 1920s—researched detergents, chemicals, and timber. In Bedfordshire, the Colworth House facility continued research efforts in food preservation, animal nutrition, and health problems associated with toothpaste, shampoo, and other personal products. By 1965, the company had 11 major research establishments around the world, including laboratories in Continental Europe, the United Kingdom, the United States, and India.

One example of how Unilever effectively answered market demands was its continuing research in margarine. When first developed, margarine was simple a substitute for the butter that was in short supply during wartime. But when butter became plentiful again the product needed to offer other advantages to the consumer. Research focused on methods to improve the quality of margarine, such as making it easier to spread, more flavorful, and more nutritional. This was the primary emphasis at Unilever's Vlaardingen laboratory. By improving techniques used to refine soybean oil, the company succeeded in improving the raw materials available for margarine production, while at the same time it achieved vast savings, since soybean oil itself was inexpensive.

The advent of the European Economic Community, or Common Market, also created new opportunities for the company. Unilever held several conferences throughout the 1960s to discuss strategies for dealing with marketing, factory location, tariffs, cartels, and transport issues created by the Common Market. Of particular importance was the need to determine the best places for production under changing economic conditions. Since the late 19th century, when the companies that comprised Unilever had set up factories in other European countries to avoid tariff restrictions, Unilever's products had been manufactured wherever it was most economical. Under the Common Market, many of the tariff restrictions that had spawned the multi-national facilities were eliminated, giving the company an opportunity to consolidate operations and concentrate production in lower-cost countries.

In the 1980s, Unilever undertook a massive restructuring. The company sold most of its service and ancillary businesses, like transport, packaging, advertising, and other services that were readily available on the market and went on a buying spree, snapping up some 80 companies between 1984 and 1988. The restructuring was designed to concentrate the company in "those businesses that we properly understand, in which we have critical mass, and where we believe we have a strong, competitive future," Unilever PLC Chairman M.R. Angus told *Management Today* in 1988. Specifically, Unilever's core businesses are detergents, foods, toiletries, specialty chemicals, and agribusinesses.

In addition to increasing profitability in core areas, restructuring also helped Unilever execute its biggest acquisition to date, when it acquired Chesebrough-Pond's in the United States in 1986. A company with sales of about $3 billion, Chesebrough is the maker of such brands as Vaseline Intensive Care, Pond's Cold Cream, and Ragú spaghetti sauce. The acquisition allowed Unilever to fill out its international personal products business, particularly in the United States, where Unilever sees a higher profit potential.

During the 1980s, Unilever's detergent products posted a 50% growth in operating profit, while food products grew at a faster-than-normal rate. In the United States, plans to take on long-time rival Procter & Gamble were successful in 1984, when Unilever's Wisk moved P&G's Cheer out of the number-two spot in the laundry detergent market. In Europe, Unilever completed its first hostile takeover attempt in 15 years when it acquired the British company Brooke Bond, the leading European tea company, for £376 million, which complimented its Lipton brand, the leader in the United States. Two years later, the company launched Wisk in the United Kingdom, as well as Breeze, its first soap powder launch in the United Kingdom since the debut of Surf more than 30 years before.

In 1989, Unilever became a major player in the world's perfume and cosmetic industry through three more acquisitions. It acquired Shering-Plough's perfume business in Europe; the Calvin Klein business from Minnetonka, Inc.; and, by far the largest purchase of the three, Faberge Inc., the American producer of Chloe, Lagerfeld, and Fendi perfumes, for $1.55 billion. The upper-end cosmetics market is a high margin business, and Unilever plans to step up marketing of its new products to raise sales.

As it entered the 1990s, Unilever had virtually completed reorganizing its European business in order to better compete after the integration of the European Economic Community in 1992. While its existing businesses are primarily in highly competitive, mature markets, recent acquisitions, like its cosmetics, have positioned the company for continued growth.

Principal Subsidiaries: Unifrost GmbH; Österreichische Unilever GmbH; Nordsee GmbH; Hartog; Iglo-Ola; Lever; Union; Uni-Dan A/S; Paasivaara Oy; Suomen Unilever Oy; Astra-Calvé SA; CNF SA; Française de Soins et Parfums SA; 4P Emballages France SA; Lever SA; Niger France SA; Compagnie des Glaces et Surgelés Alimentaires SA; Française d'Alimentation et de Boissons SA; Unilever Export France SA; Unilever France SA; Deutsche Unilever GmbH; Elida-Gibbs GmbH; 4P Folie Forchheim GmbH; 4P Nicolaus Kempten GmbH; 4P Verpackungen Ronsberg GmbH; 4P Rube Göttingen GmbH; Langnese-Iglo GmbH; Lever GmbH; Meistermarken-Werke GmbH, Spezialfabrik für Back-und Grossküchenbedarf; Nordsee Deutsche Hochseefischerei GmbH; Schafft Fleischwerke GmbH; Unichema Chemie GmbH; Union Deutsche Lebensmittelwerke GmbH; Lever Hellas AEBE; Elais Oleaginous Products AE; Lever Brothers (Ireland) Ltd.; W&C McDonnell Ltd.; Paul and Vincent Ltd.; HB Ice Cream Ltd.; 3C Industriale SpA; Lever Sodel SpA; Sagit SpA; Unil-It SpA; Calvé Nederland BV; Crosfield Chemie BV; Elida Gibbs BV; Zeepfabriek de Fenix BV; Inglo-Ola BV; Lever Industrial BV; Lever BV; Loders Croklaan BV; Lucas Aardenburg BV; Naarden International; National Starch & Chemical BV; Nederlandse Unilever Bedrijven BV; Quest International Nederland BV; Exportslachterij Udema BV; Unichema Chemie BV; Unilver Export BV; UniMills BV; UVG Nederland BV; Van de Bergh en Jurgens BV; Vinamul BV; Iglo Indústrias de Gelados, Lda.; Indústrias Lever Portuguesa, Lda.; Agra SA; Frigo SA; Lever España SA; Industrias Revilla SA; Pond's Española SA; Unilever España SA; Glace-Bolaget AB; Margarinbolaget AB; Lever AB; Leverindus AB; Novia Livsmedelsindustrier AB; Elida Robert Group AB; Svenska Unilever Förvaltnings AB; Astra Fett-und Oelwerke AG; Chesebrough-Pond's (Genève) SA; Elida Cosmetic AG; Lever AG; Meina Holdings AG; Sais; A. Sutter AG; Unilever (Schweiz) AG; Unilever-Is Ticaret ve

Sanayi Türk Limited Sirketi; Batchelors Foods Ltd.; Birds Eye Wall's Ltd.; BOCM Silcock Ltd.; Brook Bond Foods Ltd.; Chesebrough-Pond's Ltd.; Jospeh Crosfield & Sons Ltd.; Elida Gibbs Ltd.; Erith Oil Works Ltd.; Lever Brothers Ltd.; Lever Industrial Ltd.; H. Leverton Ltd.; Lipton Export Ltd.; Lipton Tea Company Ltd.; Loders Croklaan Ltd.; Marine Harvest Ltd.; Mattessons Wall's Ltd.; Oxoid Ltd.; Plant Breeding International Cambridge Ltd.; Quest International (Fragances, Flavours, Food Ingredients) UK Ltd.; UAC Ltd.; UAC International Ltd.; UML Ltd.; Unichema Chemicals Ltd.; Unilever Export Ltd.; Unilever UK Central Resources Ltd.; United Agricultural Merchants Ltd.; Van de Berghs and Jurgens Ltd.; Vinamul Ltd.; John West Foods Ltd.; Chesebrough-Pond's (Canada) Inc.; Lever Brothers Limited; Thomas J. Lipton Inc.; A&W Food Services of Canada Ltd.; Unilever Canada Limited; Chesebrough-Pond's Inc.; Lawry's Foods Inc.; Lever Brothers Company; Thomas J. Lipton, Inc.; National Starch and Chemical Corporation; Prince Matchabelli, Inc.; Ragú Foods, Inc.; Sequoia-Turner Corporation; Unilever Capital Corporation; Unilever United States, Inc.; Lever y Asociados sacif; Unilever Australia Ltd.; Lever Brothers Bangladesh Ltd.; Indústrias Gessy Lever Ltda.; RW King SA; Lever Chile SA; Compañia Colombiana de Grasas Cogra-Lever SA; Plantaciones Unipalma de Los Llanos SA; Blohorn SA; CFCI SA; Uniwax SA; Hatton et Cookson SA; UAC of Ghana Ltd.; Lever Brothers (China) Ltd.; Hindustan Lever Ltd.; PT Unilever Indonesia; Nippon Lever BV; Brooke Bond Kenya Ltd.; East Africa Industries Ltd.; Gailey & Roberts Ltd.; Lever Brothers (Malawi) Ltd.; Lever Brothers (Malaysia) Sdn. Bhd.; Pamol Plantations Sdn. Bhd.; Anderson Clayton & Co. SA; Pond's de Mexico SA de CV; Unilever Becumij NV; Unilever New Zealand Ltd.; Niger-Afrique SA; Pamol (Nigeria) Ltd.; Lever Brothers Pakistan Ltd.; Philippine Refining Company, Inc.; UAC of Sierra Leone Ltd.; Lever Brothers Singapore Sdn. Bhd.; Lever Solomons Ltd.; Unilever South Africa (Pty.) Ltd.; Lever Brothers (Ceylon) Ltd.; Formosa United Industrial Corporation Ltd.; UAC of Tanzania Ltd.; Brasseries du Logone SA; Lever Brothers (Thailand) Ltd.; Lever Brothers West Indies Ltd.; Gailey & Roberts (Uganda) Ltd.; Sudy Lever SA; Lever-Pond's SA; Plantations Lever au Zaîre sarl; Compagnie des Margarines, Savons et Cosmétiques au Zaîre sarl; Sedec sarl; Lever Brothers (Private) Ltd.

Further Reading: Wilson, Charles. *The History of Unilever*, London, Cassell & Company, 1970.

UNITED BISCUITS (HOLDINGS) PLC

Grant House
Post Office Box 40
Syon Lane
Isleworth, Middlesex TW7 5NN
United Kingdom
(01) 560–3131

Public Company
Incorporated: 1948 as United Biscuits Limited
Employees: 41,000
Sales: £2.38 billion (US$4.3 billion)
Stock Index: London

A leading British food company, United Biscuits is primarily a manufacturer of biscuits, crackers, and other snack foods. As its name implies, the company was founded when two biscuit makers joined forces, in the wake of World War II. The two original companies, McVitie & Price and Marfarlane Lang & Company, were eventually joined by many other bakers, among them such well-known names as Carr's and Crawford's. One of UB's most significant additions was Keebler Company, the second-largest producer of cookies and crackers in the United States.

Robert McVitie, the son of a prosperous farmer who started a provision store in Edinburgh in the 1830s, was first apprenticed to a baker. He later joined his father in the shop, carrying on the business when his father decided to leave it. By the 1840s, Robert had left the shop on Rose Street (just a few yards away from the Crawford family's business, which became a part of United Biscuits in 1962) and moved to larger quarters. Robert prospered, opened more shops, and, in 1844, married Catherine Gairns, who brought additional wealth to the family.

Robert and Catherine had four children; sons William and Robert Jr. were apprenticed in the bakery trade, and were sent to the Continent to study French, German, and baking. William became a journalist, but Robert returned to introduce Vienna bread into Scotland and inherited the family business in 1884—the year that McVitie Scotch cakes (shortbread, oatcakes, and biscuits) won the gold medal at an international exhibition in Calcutta. Robert decided to concentrate McVitie's resources on biscuits. which at that time would keep better than bread or cakes—an important point in the expansion of sales territory.

Preparing to leave for the United States in 1887 to study American methods, Robert was behind the counter in the Edinburgh shop when Alexander Grant, 22, came in to seek employment. Told that no job was available, Grant replied, "it's a pity, for I'm a fell fine baker." As he lifted a scone and scrutinized it on his way out he added, "Well, onyway, ye canna make scones in Edinburgh"—and Robert, amused, hired him on the spot. Grant did prove to be a fell fine baker, was promoted, and saved enough money to buy a small bakery of his own. But, undercapitalized, the business failed, and Grant returned to McVitie's employ. He devoted himself to further study and hard work and took on increasing levels of responsibility.

Charles Price, a traveling salesman for Cadbury, joined McVitie in 1888 on the understanding, contingent on his sales volume, that he would become a partner. The company was soon McVitie & Price. Thirteen years after he joined, he departed to become a member of parliament, having transformed the company into a national entity.

Londoners' tastes required something smaller, thinner, and lighter than the traditional Scottish fare, according to George Andrews Brown, another outstanding salesman, who was the first to develop the London market. While the company worked to refine its "Rich Tea" biscuit to suit London tastes, Brown invented a sandwich biscuit with cream filling. Alexander Grant meanwhile developed what he called a digestive biscuit, using a formula he kept secret until the 1930s, when he passed it on to his daughter. Because he was the only one who knew how to supervise the biscuit's mixing at the Edinburgh and London factories, he kept a strenuous schedule, traveling by train between the two.

Queen Victoria's daughter, Princess Mary of Teck, pronounced McVitie and Price's cake the best of those made for her wedding in 1893. Later, as Queen Mary, she named the firm the royal family's official supplier of wedding and christening cakes, a tradition that has continued through all its succeeding generations.

Robert McVitie died in 1910 at age 56, his one-man business now a prominent national enterprise. He had guided it through the mechanization necessary to increase volume—the result, in part, of a fire that destroyed the Edinburgh factory in 1894. The business employed thousands of people, and its products had inspired many tributes. Because McVitie had no heirs, he planned to make the firm a limited liability company and nominated Alexander Grant as managing director. The board of directors agreed.

World War I created pressure to supply "iron ration" plain biscuits as government-issued fare. This overtaxed existing factories, so an additional facility was opened in Manchester. Grant, whom the directors had named chairman, wanted to develop the company at a faster pace, so he borrowed the money to buy control of the business in 1916. Grant's son, Robert McVitie Grant, had worked his way up from an entry-level position to managing director, demonstrating his resourcefulness along the way by inventing a product to compete with Scandinavian hardtack: MacVita, still a popular item today.

The hard work Grant demanded from himself and his son was expected of the entire staff. Hector Laing, engaged to Grant's daughter Margaret, began work at McVitie's by stoking ovens when he returned from World War I. Even on the morning of his wedding, in 1922, he had to put in a stint at work.

Grant paid close attention to his sales staff and kept them motivated through special recognition of achievement and through generous commissions. He himself was rewarded in 1924 with a baronetcy. That same year, McVitie & Price received this tribute from the Oxford expedition to the Arctic Circle: "Every brand which you supplied had its devotees and you can be certain that not one crumb was left uneaten. If any Expedition in the future revisits North Eastland it will find many of your tins on these icegirt shores—all empty, mute tokens of our appreciation of your biscuits."

At Sir Alexander's death in 1937, Sir Robert was already in command of a vast business. But World War II brought many changes. The company soon found that, with restrictions on supplies and transportation, cooperation with its competitor, Macfarlane Lang, made good sense. The 370 varieties of biscuits produced in 1939 were reduced to ten by 1945. Robert Grant had begun negotiations for a merger with MacFarlane Lang when, in 1947, he died at the age of 52. He had previously named Peter MacDonald, legal adviser to the company for many years, his successor.

Taxation and death duties, together with the need for a reduction in overhead expenses and the promise of economies of scale, made the merger with Macfarlane Lang a natural union.

Macfarlane Lang began with a bakehouse and small shop opened by James Lang in Glasgow in 1817. At Lang's death in 1841, his nephew, John Macfarlane, took over the business, renaming it Macfarlane and using its assets to open a new bakery on another street in Glasgow. When his sons James and John Jr. joined him in 1878, he had greatly expanded the business and decided to rename it John Macfarlane and Sons. In 1884 his youngest son, George, joined the business. The following year Macfarlane built a new, mechanized bread factory called the Victoria Bread Works. But one of Macfarlane's chief assets was Lang's fine reputation. The name Lang had clung over the years to the bakery's products. Eventually that asset was recognized; in 1885 "Lang" was officially restored and the company became known as Macfarlane Lang.

The bakery continued to grow. A depot in London was built in 1894, and soon the demand for Macfarlane Lang products warranted the construction of a new factory on the Thames River—the Imperial Biscuit Works.

John Macfarlane died in 1908, on the day before the date he had set for his retirement. Despite intense competition from other biscuit companies for the bakery business, his sons capably carried on their father's expansion programs through the succeeding decades. Despite the supply shortages and transportation problems during World War I, the business continued to expand; between 1914 and 1916 the capacity of the London works more than doubled. New and larger factories were built in Osterley, Glasgow, and Tallcross, and extensions were built onto these to meet the burgeoning demand for breads and biscuits. Directorship of Macfarlane Lang remained in the family even after the retirements of each of John's sons, until 1973, when John E. Macfarlane, the grandson of the founder, died in his ninetieth year.

The combined trading profits of Macfarlane and McVitie came to £443,000 in 1947, of which Macfarlane had contributed £164,000. When the merger was finalized and United Biscuits incorporated in 1948, Peter MacDonald was named chairman of the new company. MacDonald concentrated on taking advantage of economies of scale, sticking to a shorter list of biscuit varieties. During his 20 years of leadership, UB achieved market dominance in many products, including digestive biscuits, rich tea biscuits, Homewheat, and Jaffa Cakes.

Despite their merger, however, the two companies continued to operate quite independently until the late 1960s. Independence stretched so far, in fact, that the three McVitie factories were not even using identical recipes for the same products. Nonetheless, United Biscuits soon began to grow. In 1962 William Crawford and Sons, best known for its shortbread, joined United Biscuits.

The oldest of the UB bakeries, Crawford's was founded as a family bakery in Leith in 1813. The bakery eventually expanded into restaurants, meat processing, and jam-making under the leadership of successive generations of Crawfords.

In 1964, William McDonald & Sons, best known for its chocolate-covered biscuits, was the next company to join UB. Formed in 1946 by a former salesman with two favorite recipes, Macdonald & Sons went public in 1954 and was acquired by UB in 1964.

Together these four bakeries are the foundation of today's UB Brands division. Two acquisitions, in 1967 and 1968 respectively, form the basis of today's KP division: Meredith and Drew, a biscuit and crisp manufacturer since 1830, and Kenyon Sons and Craven Ltd., Europe's largest nut processor, dating back to 1891.

After founding his bakery in 1830, William Meredith quarreled with William Drew, his principal assistant, in 1852 and Drew left to set up a rival business. The sons of these two men reunited the two companies in 1890, deciding by coin toss the order of their names. In 1905 Meredith and Drew merged with Wright and Son, a small company known for a cheddar sandwich biscuit—"a meal for a penny." One of the strengths Meredith and Drew brought to United Biscuits was its experience in concentrating on a single product in each plant; adopting this plan helped UB attain dominance in the biscuit market.

Kenyon Sons and Craven dates back to two British factories that began making sugar confectionery, jams, and pickles in 1853. In 1891 the partners and their families formed a limited liability company. For several decades, the company's facilities and products—as well as profits—increased. But the Depression and then World War II sent the company into a steady decline. In September, 1943 the directors resigned, and Simon Heller, of the Hercules Nut Company, became director.

Heller's hard work, ingenuity, and imagination turned the company around. For example, during the war, when there was a glut of vegetables at the local market, the company would fill a van with the low-cost items and rush to the plant to make chutney. In 1953 Heller introduced a twopenny packet of KP Nuts. It became a best seller and stimulated demand for more nut and mixed nut-and-fruit products. So it was with a strong snack food background that Kenyon Sons and Craven came to United Biscuits in 1968.

When United Biscuits formed its Continental businesses division in 1986, it united Westimex (Belguim), Sepa (France), and Productos Ortiz (Spain) under a single management team. Westimex, a crisp manufacturer, had joined United Biscuits in 1970 and had been expanding its line to include lower-fat products; it has been steadily increasing its market share in France and the Netherlands as well as Belgium. Sales of branded crisps and private-label nuts sparked major growth in volume and profits at Sepa. Productos Ortiz, acquired in 1973, profited from increased sales of toasted bread, chocolate granola, and cookies.

The British Carr's of Carlisle, acquired in 1972, was founded in 1831 when Jonathan Dodgson Carr, 25, walked to the town of Carlisle from nearby Kendall to seek his fortune. The bakery he started was so successful that within three years he was able to add a flour mill to the business. In 1841, he became the first biscuit maker to receive a royal warrant from Queen Victoria. At first his biscuits were handmade, but during that decade he designed and installed the first biscuit-cutting machine, based on the hand-operated printing press he had observed at his tin supplier's factory. Described as a giant of a man, Carr was renowned for his work in campaigning for the repeal of the corn tax and for affordable housing. The business expanded until the 1930s, went into a decline, and had recovered to some extent at the time of the United Biscuits purchase.

Kemp's Biscuits Limited was another 1972 acquisition. The business began in 1835 as Watmough and Son Limited, making ship's biscuits—hardtack. During World War I, Watmough made Army biscuits—which were reported on occasion to have been used as money to purchase tram tickets. The market for ship's biscuits was nearly decimated when the Board of Trade passed regulations requiring shipowners to make fresh bread at least three days a week. Ernest Kirman, the founder's grandson, joined the business in 1892. In 1926, the company introduced sweet biscuits for human consumption, and it was producing 300 tons a week at the outbreak of World War II. In 1948, wearied by wartime labor shortages and production schedules for civilian gas masks, Kirman sold Watmough to Scribbans-Kemp Limited, which became Kemps Biscuits.

Reaching across the Atlantic, United Biscuits acquired the Keebler Company in 1974. In many ways, Keebler's development paralleled that of the family-owned bakeries that had come together as United Biscuits.

Godfrey Keebler opened a small Philadelphia bake shop in 1853 and earned a fine reputation for his cookies and crackers. A network of similar bakeries was formed in the United States, coincidentally under the name United Biscuit Company, in 1927 to provide the purchasing economies and transportation that central management made possible. By 1944 United Biscuit had 16 bakeries, from Philadelphia to Salt Lake City, Utah. For the next 22 years, United Biscuit expanded its reach into all but three states, selling products under many brand names. Finally, in 1966 the company adopted Keebler as the single, official corporate and brand name for all these bakeries' products. Keebler is now a unit of UB Foods U.S., a holding company formed in 1986 that operates companies under the Keebler name. With annual sales in excess of $1 billion, Keebler is the second-largest cookie and cracker producer in the United States. The company also produces ice cream cones and salty snacks, and in 1986 opened a product-and-process development center at its headquarters in Elmhurst, Illinois, to develop and test new products.

United Biscuits has continued acquiring bakeries and other types of food companies throughout the 1970s and 1980s, like Shaffer Clarke, in 1978; Terry's of York in 1982; and Callard and Bowser in 1988, all in the United States.

UB's variety of operations and desire to keep brand names and individual company identities intact has necessitated repeated reorganizations. Today the company is divided into five divisions.

Chairman Hector Laing, the son of Hector Laing and Margaret Grant, is mindful of the impact of computerization and other technological advances on the business—and particularly on personnel. Reinvestment in expansion and new equipment is set at a minimum of 5% of profits. That may leave little for raising wages if there are lean years. To offset that possibility, UB workers receive a rare degree of job security: three years' service guarantees the job for the next five years, ten years' service guarantees a job for life. Workforce reductions resulting from technological improvements will be accomplished through normal attrition and incentives for early retirement.

The company established a firm foothold in Europe long before there was talk of a Common Market, and it is well rooted in the Western hemisphere, so it is to Asia that United Biscuits looks for future expansion.

Principal Subsidiaries: United Biscuits (UK) Limited; Keebler Company (U.S.A.); Specialty Brands, Inc. (U.S.A.); NV Westimex Belgium S. A. (Belgium); Productos Ortiz (Spain); U.B. Investments PLC; UB Finance B. V.; Shaffer Clarke & Co., Inc. (U.S.A.)

Further Reading: Adam, James S. *A Fell Fine Baker: The Story of United Biscuits, A Jubilee Account of the Men and the Companies Who Pioneered One of Britain's Most Celebrated Industries*, London, Hutchinson Benham, 1974.

UNITED BRANDS COMPANY

One East Fourth Street
Cincinnati, Ohio 45202
U.S.A.
(513) 579–2115

Public Company
Incorporated: 1899 as United Fruit Company
Employees: 40,000
Sales: $3.5 billion
Stock Index: New York Boston Pacific Midwest Philadelphia

In 1870, Captain Lorenzo Dow Baker joined a growing number of people intrigued by the risky banana business when he bought 160 bunches of bananas for a shilling a bunch in Jamaica and sold them 11 days later in Jersey City for $2 a bunch. He soon became a founding member of the Boston Fruit Company, the predecessor of United Fruit. From its founding in 1899 through the middle of the 20th century, United Fruit continued to grow rapidly, despite the environmental and political setbacks inherent in the banana business. The company not only continued to buy smaller banana producers, but branched out to acquire diverse holdings including control of three sugar companies. Today United Brands' Chiquita brand bananas are the leader in the banana market. United Brands also produces meats under the John Morrell brand, as well as other food products.

United Fruit Company was formed when the Boston Fruit Company, an importer of bananas from the Caribbean islands, merged with Minor Keith, a railroad pioneer who imported bananas from Central America and Colombia. The strategy behind the merger was to create a broad base of operations in an effort to continue trade when droughts, floods, or political upheavals were disrupting one or another of the harvesting lands. Strategies for dealing with unstable conditions in Central America would be the test of the leaders of United Brands for years to come.

From the turn of the century until well into the 1930s, the governments of Honduras, Guatemala, Panama, and other Central American countries were eager to develop. They were unable to finance the construction of railroads and ports themselves, but land in these countries was cheap and readily available to ambitious North American companies who were willing to do the building themselves. United Fruit eventually owned more than 200,000 acres in Central America, of which only 60,000 were fruit producing.

In May, 1924 the company made a typical deal: Chiquita's Guatemalan branch made a 25-year agreement with the Guatemalan government to extend plantations, railroads, and telephone lines and to build a port. Agreements like this resulted in unchecked growth until 1953, when problems concerning domestic growers and land rights prompted the Guatemalan government to seize a great deal of Pacific and Atlantic coastal property from United Fruit. The following spring the U.S. State Department served claim against this expropriation, but it was not until December that Guatemala agreed to return the land to United Fruit for six months, after which the company would give 100,000 west coast acres back to the government and pay a 30% income tax on the remaining west coast lands. Throughout 1954 similar agreements were reached with Panama, Costa Rica, and Honduras. Relations with the Guatemalan government continued to be rough until December 1972, when United Brands sold its Guatemalan banana operations to Del Monte for more than $20 million.

Although World War II had no remarkable effect on United, the company's role in maintaining open relations with Central America was important because of the sugar, rubber plants, and other raw materials that these countries supplied.

United Fruit spent the years between the late 1950s and 1969 acquiring a diverse collection of companies, among them the A & W Root Beer Company and Foster Grant. In 1958, United acquired rights to explore for petroleum and natural gas in Panama, Ecuador, and Colombia. This relatively unfocused stream of acquisitions ended when United Fruit merged with AMK Corporation in June, 1970.

In 1966 AMK, originally a producer of milk-bottle caps, had acquired a third of the common shares of John Morrell and Company, a meat packer, and in December of the following year acquired the rest. Eli Black, the president and chairman of AMK, gained a reputation for financial wizardry with this acquisition—Morrell, the fourth-largest meat packer in the country, was twenty times larger than AMK.

In 1969 AMK acquired a majority share of the United Fruit Company. By February, 1970 John Fox, the chairman of United Fruit, and Eli Black had agreed on a merger. After some negotiation with the Federal Trade Commission, which was concerned by the antitrust implications of the merger, the new United Brands was incorporated on June 30, 1970.

Unfortunately, Black's triumph was short-lived. In the following few years United Brands experienced the worst losses in its history. In April, 1974 Central American governments began levying a large export tax on their bananas. Then in September, 1974 hurricane Fifi hit Central America, wiping out 70% of the company's Honduran plantations and causing losses of more than $20 million. Eli Black sent relief teams to the victims of the hurricane, but he could do nothing to help the company. Losses continued to mount: because of high cattle feed costs, the John Morrell division contributed another $6 million in losses to United Brands' $70 million operating loss in 1974, compared to a $16 million profit the previous year.

Black's final attempt to alleviate the company's troubles was to sell United's interest in Foster Grant for almost $70 million at the very end of the year. The sale was considered a tremendous success, but apparently it was not enough for Black, who committed suicide on February 3, 1975.

Eli Black's death sparked countless investigations into the problems of a businessman who, according to a friend quoted in *The Wall Street Journal* ten days later, "felt deeply his responsibilities to his shareholders, but . . . also believed that business was a human operation." The routine business investigation of Black's death, however, soon revealed more than a personal explanation for his tragic decision. It turned up a bribery scandal that was to plague United Brands for more than three years.

In April, 1975 the Securities and Exchange Commission (SEC) charged United Brands with having paid a bribe of $1.25 million and having agreed to pay another $1.25 million to a Honduran official in exchange for a reduction in export taxes. The SEC also accused United of bribing European officials for $750,000. Trade in United Brands stock was halted for almost a week; among other suits, a shareholder filed a derivative action (for the benefit of the corporation) and class action (for the benefit of the shareholders) suit; the president of Honduras was removed by the Honduran military on suspicion of participating in the bribe; the Costa Rican president threatened to cancel all contracts with United Brands if all Costa Rican officials involved in any bribes were not revealed; and finally, a federal grand jury brought criminal charges against United Brands.

Interestingly, in the midst of litigation over these charges, major investors were faithful to United Brands. One of the largest of these investors was Carl Lindner, owner of the American Financial Corporation in Cincinnati. Elected a director of United Brands in 1976, Lindner attributed his continued investment to the company's turnaround potential. Eight years later, Lindner himself would be the pivotal figure in returning United Brands to profitability.

In January, 1976, a federal judge signed a consent order barring United Brands from further violations and granting the SEC permanent access to the company's records. United Brands agreed to the order without admitting or denying the allegations. Litigation continued until 1978, when the company pleaded guilty to conspiring to pay $2.5 million to the former Honduran minister of economy, Abraham Bennaton Ramos. The company was fined $15,000, the maximum sentence, and the case was officially closed.

In May, 1975 Wallace Booth succeeded the string of chairmen who had headed the company in the wake of Eli Black's death. Booth is credited with leveling the rocky operation by methodically tightening management control, streamlining banana delivery systems, and updating meat-packing technology at John Morrell.

In the wake of the bribery scandal, United Brands agreed in April, 1976 to sell 190 miles of railroad track to the Honduran government for 50¢ and then lease it back for $250,000 a year. It also agreed to operate and maintain the railroad line. Booth furthered such placating efforts, including a similar land deal in Panama, earning himself the nickname "the Good Gringo."

Booth resigned in 1977. Until 1984 a series of chairmen and presidents managed to keep United Brands afloat, but profits slipped and net losses increased steadily. John Morrell came close to closing a plant in the early 1980s, and in 1983 tropical storms in Panama and Costa Rica inflicted further damage.

In 1982, Carl Lindner's American Financial Corporation began substantially increasing its stake in United Brands. A savvy investor and an expert manager, Lindner took over as chairman of United Brands in August, 1984. Lindner shifted the company away from large, diversified operations toward a narrower focus on stable profits throughout the company. He and the four new directors he elected doubled United's cash flow between 1985 and 1988. Lindner streamlined the company's operations by selling some of its extraneous operations, like soft drinks, animal feeds, and international telecommunications, and lowered its overhead by moving the company's headquarters from New York to Cincinnati.

Although Lindner's push to broaden the Chiquita product line with frozen fruit pops lost some $10 million in 1987, the company has been successful in using the Chiquita name to sell other fresh fruit, like grapefruit and pineapples. Chiquita has also recaptured first place in the banana market from Dole, which had taken the lead from Chiquita in the early 1970s.

John Morrell has not fared as well in recent years. Strikes in 1986 and 1987 at two of the largest meatpacking plants were settled in March, 1988 when the company was awarded $24.6 million in damages, as the strikes were ruled illegal. But another suit was filed on behalf of Morrell employees in October, 1988 for $35 million, claiming that workers were not paid for work involving safety equipment that they were required to perform on their own time. A week later the Labor Department's Occupational Safety and Health Administration proposed a $4.3 million fine against Morrell for "willfully ignoring" serious injuries caused by repetitive motions used in the meatpacking business.

The complications inherent in the production, processing, and distribution of perishable fruit grown in politically unstable countries have challenged United Brands since the company's beginnings nearly 100 years ago. After recovering from a severe decline in the mid-1970s, United Brands today is a very successful company. With Carl Lindner in charge, United Brands seems to be on a higher level of financial and managerial operation than it has ever been before. From the time of the company's fragmented origins, the banana business has combined an obvious risk of instability with the potential for great profit. Lindner, who quieted rumors that he planned to take the company private when in 1988 he reduced his stake in the company from 87% to 84%, seems to have achieved an admirably stable balance, promising United Brands a prominent role in the industry for the foreseeable future.

Principal Subsidiaries: Chiquita Brands, Inc.; Compania Mundimar; John Morrell & Company; Polymer United, Inc.

Further Reading: May, S. and Plaza, G. *The United Fruit Company in Latin America*, New York, National Planning Association, 1958.

FOOD SERVICES & RETAILERS

ALBERTSON'S, INC.
AMERICAN STORES COMPANY
ARA SERVICES
ARGYLL GROUP PLC
ASDA GROUP PLC
BURGER KING CORPORATION
CARGILL, INC.
THE CIRCLE K CORPORATION
EDEKA ZENTRALE A.G.
FLEMING COMPANIES, INC.
FOOD LION, INC.
THE GATEWAY CORPORATION LTD.
GEORGE WESTON LIMITED
GIANT FOOD INC.
THE GREAT ATLANTIC & PACIFIC TEA COMPANY, INC.
ICA AB
KONINKLIJKE AHOLD N. V.
THE KROGER COMPANY
MCDONALD'S CORPORATION
THE OSHAWA GROUP LIMITED
PROVIGO INC.
SAFEWAY STORES INCORPORATED
J SAINSBURY PLC
THE SOUTHLAND CORPORATION
STEINBERG INCORPORATED
THE STOP & SHOP COMPANIES, INC.
SUPER VALU STORES, INC.
SUPERMARKETS GENERAL HOLDINGS CORPORATION
SYSCO CORPORATION
TESCO PLC
TW SERVICES, INC.
WETTERAU INCORPORATED
WINN-DIXIE STORES, INC.

ALBERTSON'S, INC.

250 Parkcenter Boulevard
Boise, Idaho 83726
U.S.A.
(208) 385-6200

Public Company
Incorporated: 1945
Employees: 53,000
Sales: $6.77 billion
Stock Index: New York Boston Pacific Midwest

In 1939, Joe Albertson left his position as a district manager for Safeway Stores and, with partners L. S. Skaggs, whose family helped build Safeway, and Tom Cuthbert, Skaggs' accountant, opened his first one-stop shopping market on a Boise, Idaho corner. Albertson thought big from the start—his first newspaper ad promised customers "Idaho's largest and finest food store." And indeed, the store was huge by contemporary standards; at 10,000 square feet it was approximately eight times as large as the average grocery store of that era. The store included specialties such as an in-store bakery, one of the country's first magazine racks, and homemade "Big Joe" ice cream cones. Customers liked what they saw, and the store pulled in healthy first-year profits of $9,000.

Today, Albertson's is the sixth-largest grocery chain in the United States, operating over 500 stores in 17 western and southern states. Yet Albertson's has not forgotten the lessons of its small town beginnings during its expansion. "Albertson's is, in effect, a big store with a specialty store approach," claims its corporate philosophy, adopted in 1973. "We must be 'big' in terms of low prices, convenience and wide selection of brands. We must be a 'specialty' store in terms of quality, personal service and specialized selection."

Albertson's fosters this small-town style both through management and consumer services. The corporation implements a strong employee incentive program which returns 15% of each store's profits directly to its store director and department heads, and store management teams are kept informed of the accounting figures that make or break their unit's profitability.

Among their specialty consumer services, Albertson's stores provide personal service at in-store "scratch" bakeries, delicatessens, and meat departments. Larger stores carry ethnic foods geared toward the neighborhoods in which they are located, and according to *Forbes* Albertson's is cleaned "with a Disney-like fanaticism."

While Albertson's may owe its style to small-town roots, its history turns on the expansion of the one-stop shopping concept, which naturally led to the growth of larger stores carrying more diverse products and eventually to the jumbo food-and-drug stores that were the key to Albertson's tremendous success.

Albertson's grew slowly at first. Sales remained constant during the war years, and in 1945, Joe Albertson dissolved the partnership and Albertson's was incorporated. By 1947, the chain had six stores operating in Idaho, and had established a complete poultry-processing operation. In 1949, the Dutch Girl ice cream plant opened in Boise, and Albertson's adopted the Dutch Girl as its early trademark.

Albertson's expanded during the 1950s into Washington, Utah, Oregon, and Montana. In 1957 the company built its first frozen foods distribution house, which served its southern Idaho and eastern Oregon stores. Albertson's also operated a few department stores during the 1950s but these were phased out rapidly as the company decided to focus on the sale of food and drugstore items. In 1959, Albertson's introduced its private label, Janet Lee, named after the executive vice president's daughter. The company also went public in 1959, and with that capital began to expand its markets aggressively.

Albertson's moved into its sixth state, Wyoming, in 1961, and opened its 100th store in 1962. In 1964, the company broke into the California market by acquiring Greater All American Markets, based in Los Angeles. The same year, Albertson turned the position of chief executive over to J. L. Berlin, although he continued to chair the executive board.

Under Berlin's leadership, the company strengthened its Californian position by merging with Semrau and Sons, an Oakland-based grocery store chain, in 1965. This added eight markets in northern California, which Albertson's continued to operate under the name of Pay Less. In 1967, the company purchased eight Colorado supermarkets from Furr's Inc., a Lubbox, Texas concern. Between these purchases and construction of new units, Albertson's operated more than 200 stores by the end of the decade and annual sales were well over $400 million.

In the late 1960s, Albertson's set several company policies that would secure its snowballing success. One of these was the company's ongoing renovation program. In 1980, vice chairman Bolinder pointed out that "almost every failure of previously profitable supermarket companies can be attributed to stores becoming outdated." Albertson's has avoided this pitfall by constantly upgrading its facilities, remodeling and enlarging older stores, and closing those that have become obsolete.

Anticipating the ever-increasing competition for profitable operating sites, Albertson's also took care during the 1960s to build a sophisticated property-development task force of lawyers, economic analysts, negotiators, engineers, architects, and construction supervisors that has allowed the company to stay on top of industry trends. In addition, it expanded its employee training and incentive programs to encourage employees to make a lifetime career with the company.

During its first three decades Albertson's primarily sold groceries, although it did introduce drugstore departments into units where possible. In 1970, however, the company pioneered a unique and exceptionally profitable concept in supermarket design. J. L. Scott, who had become CEO in 1966, announced in 1969 that Albertson's would enter into partnership with Skaggs Drugs Centers, based in Salt Lake City, Utah and headed by Albertson's former partner, to jointly finance and manage six jumbo combination food and drug stores in Texas. While the average contemporary supermarket was 30,000 square feet or smaller, the combination stores covered as many as 55,000 square feet. And while conventional stores carried strictly grocery items, which have a slim profit margin of 1% to 2%, the Skaggs-Albertson's combination stores stocked not only groceries but also nonfood items such as cosmetics, perfumes, pharmacy products, camera supplies, and electrical equipment. Banking on the higher profit margin of nonfood items as well as on an aggressive five-year plan, Scott also predicted in 1969 that Albertson's sales would double within five years. His optimism was not unfounded. By 1974, sales reached $852.3 million, with net earnings of $8.9 million.

The first Skaggs-Albertson's combination stores were opened in Texas in 1970, the year after the New York Stock Exchange began to trade Albertson's shares. In the early 1970s, Albertson's and Skaggs considered merging, but ultimately decided against the move. Albertson's continued its beneficial partnership with Skaggs until 1977, opening combination drug and grocery stores throughout Texas, Florida, and Louisiana.

Along with rapid growth, Albertson's faced some minor setbacks during the early 1970s. In 1972 Albertson's had acquired Mountain States Wholesale of Idaho, a subsidiary of DiGiorgio Corporation. In 1974, the Justice Department filed a civil antitrust suit against Albertson's, asserting that at the time of the purchase, Albertson's was the largest retail grocer in the southern Idaho and eastern Oregon market, while Mountain States carried 43% of the wholesale grocery market, and that Albertson's purchase created an illegal monopoly.

Robert D. Bolinder, CEO from 1974 through 1976, claimed that the suit was without basis and that Albertson's had in fact preserved competition in the area by acquiring Mountain States. Although Bolinder still claimed that the Justice Department had misunderstood Albertson's reasons for buying the wholesaler, noting that the subsidiary was not financially integral to the company but accounted for only 3.4% of its total sales in 1973, the settlement, in 1977, required Albertson's to divest Mountain States and barred the company from acquiring any retail or wholesale grocery businesses in southern Idaho or eastern Oregon for five years.

Also in 1974, in the Portland, Seattle, and Denver areas, the Federal Trade Commission found fault with Albertson's advertising practices. The company complied with an FTC order requiring that advertised sale items be available to customers and that rainchecks be issued when sale items were out of stock, although Bolinder maintained that Albertson's had not violated any laws and emphasized that compliance would not require any change in the company's previously established advertising policies.

In 1976, after chairing the board for 37 years, Joe Albertson became chairman of the executive committee. Warren McCain, who began his career with Albertson's as a merchandising supervisor in 1951, became chairman of the board and CEO. In the same year, Albertson's began to build superstores, which would carry an even higher ratio of nonfood items. A slightly smaller version of the combination store, the superstores range in size from 35,000 to 48,000 square feet and feature more fresh foods and perishables. It was during 1976 that the corporation slowly began to phase out its conventional markets. Although a few profitable ones are still in existence today, most were closed or converted into larger stores during the late 1970s and early 1980s. Albertson's also installed its first electric price scanner in 1976. By the late 1980s, 85% of Albertson's stores used scanners.

Relying principally on outside distributors, Albertson's successfully penetrated markets located throughout a broad geographic area, but the rapid expansion of its markets during the 1970s called for expansion of company-owned distribution facilities. Two of the company's four full-line distribution facilities were built during this period. The first of these went up in 1973 in Brea, California, and the other was completed in 1976 in Salt Lake City. All Albertson's distribution facilities are built, and operate, as profit centers, contributing a return on investment that equals or exceeds that of the company's retail stores.

In 1977, Albertson's and Skaggs dissolved their partnership amicably, splitting their assets equally. For Albertson's, the breakup resulted in the formation of Southco, the company's southern division. Southco assumed operation of 30 of the 58 combination stores formerly run by the partnership. Albertson's continued opening combination stores, concentrating them principally in southern states, but also opening a few in South Dakota and Nebraska. In 1978, Albertson's strengthened its stronghold in southern California by acquiring 46 supermarkets located in the Los Angeles area from Fisher Foods, Inc.

In 1979, Albertson's took the "bigger is better" concept to the drawing boards again and introduced its first warehouse stores. As inflation drove prices up, Albertson's needed to cut overhead to preserve its profit margin. To this end, it converted, between 1979 and 1981, seven stores into full-line, mass-merchandise warehouse stores run under the name Grocery Warehouse. These no-frills stores carried nonfood items but emphasized groceries, with substantial savings on meat and liquor. While these stores continue to be successful, they did not eclipse the profitability of the more broadly appealing superstores.

The introduction of the combination store and the continuing readaptation of older stores—87% of the company's stores were newly built or completely remodeled during the 1970s—allowed Albertson's to prosper despite the economically hostile environment of the late 1970s and early 1980s. In 1983, just after the country's most severe recession since the Depression, Albertson's boasted 13 years of record sales. The combination stores, both jumbo and smaller, were largely responsible for this success. In 1983, these units accounted for only one-third of the chain's 423 stores but were the source of 65% of its profits.

Since Albertson's had grown by expanding over a wide geographic area rather than increasing its dominance in a smaller area, it did not hold superior market share in many of the areas where it operated. But it was this diversification, in part, that had allowed Albertson's to weather the economic storms of the 1970s and 1980s so successfully. As it happened, the areas of Albertson's concentration were the areas of relative economic prosperity. In fact, in 1981 Albertson's was operating in 17 of the fastest growing standard metropolitan areas, as identified by the U.S. Department of Commerce. Stores in relatively stable areas helped balance losses in more depressed markets.

Although Albertson's did break into the Nebraska and North and South Dakota markets in 1981, during the 1980s it concentrated principally on increasing its presence in established markets. For example, in an effort to expand its market in Texas, Albertson's modified its advertising strategy. In 1984, Albertson's reentered the Dallas–Fort Worth area, a very competitive market that no new firm had entered since Skaggs opened its first store there in 1972. The standard advertising strategy was to offer gimmicks like double-value coupons and promotional games to attract customers. Albertson's had used such techniques, but chose to approach the Dallas–Fort Worth market with an "every day low-cost" image instead. Store circulars explained "we won't be advertising weekly specials . . . we'll pass the savings on advertising costs on to you. Tell your friends and neighbors to help us keep prices down." The campaign sparked fierce competition, but the Albertson's units continued to prosper. Although the company traditionally held an upscale profile, it began to extend the new image to other suitable markets, and today about half of its stores operate on this basis.

As Albertson's continues to build larger concentrations of stores, its behind-the-scenes operations continue to grow. In 1982, retail management was reorganized into four regions: California, northwest, intermountain, and Southco. This subdivision allows each regional director and his management team to more effectively focus marketing and retail sales strategies, and more closely guide employee and real estate development. Albertson's built another distribution center in the Denver area in 1984, and completed its first fully mechanized distribution center in Portland, Oregon in 1988. In addition, the Salt Lake City facility was substantially expanded in late 1988, and the Brea, California center was expanded and mechanized in 1989.

Albertson's is situated in some of the fastest growing markets in the country—California, Arizona, Texas, and Florida—and it plans to open 200 new units, primarily superstores, by 1993. Remodeling, which will include the introduction of in-store computers and installment of scanners, is planned for another 175 existing units. Distribution facilities are also headed for major expansion, as Albertson's seeks to supply all its markets except North Dakota and Florida by 1993.

The key to Albertson's success has been a steady sensitivity to the changing desires of consumers. It continues to groom its top executives the old-fashioned way, promoting from within the corporation. Most of the current top officers began in typical entry-level positions and have seen their careers grow with the company. Years of familiarity with Albertson's strengths and style allow top executives to adapt the company to changing consumer desires effectively. And while this modern business sensibility has cultivated Albertson's billion-dollar success, the solid, small-town philosophy of founder Joe Albertson—giving customers quality merchandise at a reasonable price—is at its root.

Further Reading: Hughes, Terri (ed). "Yesterday and Tomorrow 1939–1989," *Albertson's Today*, July 1989.

AMERICAN STORES COMPANY

5201 Amelia Earhart Drive
Salt Lake City, Utah 84116
U.S.A.
(801) 539-0447

Public Company
Incorporated: 1965
Employees: 130,000
Sales: $18.5 billion
Stock Index: New York Philadelphia Midwest Pacific

If nothing else, the American Stores Company is a testimony to the drive and ambition of one family. Leonard S. Skaggs Jr., who built his father's modest drug-store chain into the largest drug-and-grocery retailer in the United States, comes from a clan of retail entrepreneurs. His grandfather, father, and uncles each staked out an enduring claim in the supermarket and drugstore fields, but Leonard S. Jr. has been even more successful than any of them. Through a frenzy of mergers and acquisitions in the 1970s and 1980s, he brought two Skaggs-founded enterprises into the American Stores fold, and in the process of building his coast-to-coast retail empire he has encountered several people and organizations whose lives were in some way influenced by his family's legacy.

The history of American Stores is inextricably linked to that of the Skaggs family. Samuel Skaggs, the patriarch, opened a drug store in Utah in 1915. In 1926 his six sons, including Leonard S. Sr., helped build Safeway Stores, which still survives as one of the nation's largest supermarket chains. In 1932 L. J. Skaggs split with his brothers and opened his first Pay Less drugstore in Tacoma, Washington. In 1939 Leonard S. Sr. founded the Skaggs Drug Center chain and bought the California operations of Pay Less. And at about the same time, L. L. Skaggs founded the Osco Drug chain.

The combined operations of Skaggs Drug Centers and Skaggs Pay Less was known as Skaggs Companies, and it remained a modest enterprise through the 1940s. In 1950, Leonard S. Sr. died and his 26-year-old son Leonard S. Jr. inherited the business. At the time, Skaggs Companies had posted sales of $9.6 million, .05% of what American Stores would report four decades later.

Leonard S. Skaggs Jr., more familiarly known as Sam, had ambitious plans for the family business. But those plans waited during the 1950s and early 1960s. Skaggs Companies made little news during this time, except in 1956 and 1957 when General Electric sued a group of western retailers over their practice of selling GE products at less than the recommended price. Skaggs filed a counter suit, and as a result of the controversy, courts in Utah and other western states overturned so-called "fair trade" laws that prohibited the discounting of merchandise.

In 1965 Skaggs Companies bought 30 Super-S general merchandise stores from Safeway. By 1969, it had expanded its retail drug operations to 80 stores in 13 western states and in that year earned $4.7 million on sales of $172.2 million. At that point, Sam Skaggs contemplated a merger that would enlarge his company even further. Skaggs Drug Centers negotiated with People's Drug Store, a retailer that would have expanded Skaggs' geographical base with 245 stores in eight eastern states, but talks broke down when the companies could not reach mutually acceptable financial terms. In 1970, however, Skaggs did merge with Katz Drug, a move noteworthy not only because it allowed Skaggs to expand into the Midwest, but also because Katz owned the non-California operations of L. J. Skaggs' old Pay Less chain.

Also in 1970, Skaggs entered into a joint venture with Albertson's, one of the largest supermarket chains in the western United States, that resulted in the first successful combined drug and food superstores. Traditionally, it had been difficult for drugstores and supermarkets to cross over into each other's territory because their goods are marketed differently. Skaggs had experimented with "combo" stores by opening one in Las Vegas, Nevada in 1969, but needed more managerial expertise in grocery retailing to make them succeed on a large scale. A connection between Albertson's Chairman Joe Albertson and the Skaggs family was not unprecedented; Albertson had worked for Safeway when the Skaggs brothers were running the chain.

The joint venture proved to be a considerable success. Over the next seven years, Skaggs-Albertson's Properties opened 58 combo stores in Oklahoma and the Southeast, and in 1976, the last full year of the partnership, it generated $624 million in sales. But in 1977, both Skaggs and Albertson's realized that the venture had grown so large as to become nearly unmanageable. A merger between the two partners would have been an elegant solution, but both feared that it would result in antitrust litigation. Neither had enough money to acquire the other outright, and neither wanted to take on the capital-gains tax obligations of selling out. Irreconcilable differences in management philosophies were also rumored to have played a part in the split. So Skaggs-Albertson's Properties was dissolved, with each partner receiving half of its assets.

Overall, Skaggs Companies prospered during the 1970s. In 1978 it posted earnings of $25 million on sales of $1.1 billion and operated 202 drugstores, most of them in the West and Southwest. And amid widespread concern over the state of the American economy, Sam Skaggs remained confident in the future of his company. "We're more or less recession-proof," he told *Business Week* in 1977. "People are going to brush their teeth and cure their headaches all the time."

Even so, the expansion of Skaggs' combo store operations slowed without the help of Albertson's muscle. In 1978 the company worked out an agreement to merge with Jewel Companies, a major Chicago-based food retailer. Sam Skaggs had tried to merge with Jewel 12 years earlier, and this time around he believed that integrating its decentralized management structure into his own essentially one-man operation would facilitate further expansion. Jewel Chairman Donald Perkins, for his part, saw combo stores as the wave of the future, as supermarkets began to stock more non-grocery items, and sought Skaggs' expertise. The merger seemed mutually advantageous, but was torpedoed at the last moment when some of Skaggs' directors, concerned that they would lose their autonomy under the deal, failed to approve it.

Momentarily set back but undaunted, Sam Skaggs soon resumed his quest for a merger that would further his goal of building a food-and-drug retail juggernaut. He found one in 1979, when American Stores Company agreed to merge with Skaggs Companies. American Stores was by far the larger organization, with 758 supermarkets, 139 drugstores, 53 restaurants, and nine general-merchandise stores in nine states, but Skaggs was the one that survived the merger. The resulting entity bore the American Stores name, but was controlled by Skaggs management.

Thanks to the merger, American Stores posted $83 million in earnings on sales of nearly $8 billion in 1983. But its presence was still weak in the Midwest, New England, and Florida. To help overcome these remaining geographical shortcomings, Sam Skaggs made yet another attempt to merge with Jewel in 1984. But Weston Christopherson, who had succeeded Donald Perkins as chairman of Jewel, was opposed to a merger and Skaggs was forced to engineer a hostile takeover. On June 1, 1984, American Stores tendered an offer worth $1.1 billion for 67% of Jewel's outstanding shares at $70 per share.

For two weeks, Jewel management refused all comment on the offer, maintaining its silence even at a stormy shareholder's meeting before which Jewel shareholder groups controlling 20% of the company's stock had come out in favor of negotiating with American Stores. Finally, on June 14, Sam Skaggs and Jewel President Richard Kline reached an agreement after an all-night bargaining session. American Stores raised its bid for Jewel's prefered stock, increasing the total bid to $1.15 billion in cash and securities. In return, Jewel dropped plans for a defensive acquisition of Household International and accepted American Stores' offer. To help raise cash for the deal, American Stores sold its Rea & Derick drug chain in December, 1984 to People's Drug, which was now a subsidiary of Imasco Limited.

The acquisition of Jewel also returned L. L. Skaggs' Osco Drug chain to the Skaggs family ownership. And Sav-on Drug, another Jewel subsidiary, had been founded by C. J. Call, who had once been a business partner of another of Sam Skaggs' uncles, O.P. Skaggs.

Jewel added 193 supermarkets, 358 drugstores, 140 combo stores, 301 convenience stores, and 132 discount stores to the American Stores empire. But in 1985, American Stores found itself in legal trouble through its new subsidiary. A salmonella food-poisoning outbreak affecting some 20,000 people in the Midwest was traced to a Melrose, Illinois dairy that had supplied tainted milk to Jewel stores. Two years later, Jewel was found not liable for punitive damages in Cook County Circuit Court, but agreed to pay compensatory damages estimated at $35 to $40 million.

After two decades of intense merger-and-acquisition activity, American Stores was the largest drug retailer in the United States, but only the third-largest grocery retailer. Furthermore, its 210-store Alpha Beta chain in California was struggling, plagued by high prices and a reputation for poor service. On March 22, 1988, American Stores made an unsolicited tender offer for Lucky Stores, an Alpha Beta competitor noted for high efficiency and low prices.

Lucky refused American Stores' first offer, worth $1.7 billion, or $45 per share of Lucky stock. By the end of the month, American Stores proposed to up its bid to $50 per share if Lucky would agree to a friendly takeover. Again Lucky rejected the offer as inadequate and was said to be contemplating defensive strategies. In May, Lucky agreed to a $2.4 billion, $61-per-share buyout by a company set up by Lucky management and the investment-banking firm Gibbons Green van Amerongen. On the one hand, this move seemed very much like a bid by Lucky managers to retain control of their company. But on the other, it could also have been a ploy to milk American Stores for a higher bid, since later that month Lucky allowed American Stores to examine confidential financial information that it had been witholding for several weeks and gave its suitor one week to respond with a better offer. On May 17 American Stores upped its bid to $2.5 billion, or $65 per share.

Five days later, Lucky accepted. American Stores was about to become the largest supermarket chain in the nation, leapfrogging over Kroger Company and Safeway Stores. Interest payments alone on its acquisition debt cut the company's earnings in 1988 by 36% from the previous year, but analysts called the deal worthwhile.

But California Attorney General John Van de Kamp took to the warpath against the acquisition. In August, Van de Kamp asked the Federal Trade Commission to void it, claiming that a Lucky-Alpha Beta juggernaut would cost California consumers $400 million by reducing competition. The FTC refused. He then took his case to court, and on September 29, a federal judge in Los Angeles issued a preliminary injunction against the merger. American Stores appealed, and in April, 1989, an appeals court judge in San Francisco overturned the injunction. Van de Kamp has appealed this reversal to the Supreme Court, but American Stores continued to plan its assimilation of Lucky.

In 1988, Sam Skaggs reached the mandatory retirement age of 65, and in December of that year the company named vice chairman Jonathan L. Scott to succeed him as CEO. It marked the end of an era for American Stores in more ways than one; not only would it be without a member of the Skaggs clan to handle day-to-day operations for the first time, but it would experience a profound change in management style as well. "Mr. Skaggs is a builder," Scott told *The Wall Street Journal*. "He's always been aggressive in acquisitions. My forte is more in how we operate those companies and how we grow them." So American Stores finished out the 1980s in a mood to consolidate.

In the space of 20 years, Sam Skaggs single-handedly built his family business into a retailing giant larger than any of his competitors in both the drug and grocery fields through a vigorous program of expansion and acquisition. The time seems right for American Stores to digest and consolidate, but it may miss his aggressive, hard-driving leadership. The Skaggs family has produced more than its share of successful men, but none of them has been more adept at empire building than Leonard S. Skaggs Jr.

Principal Subsidiaries: Acme Markets, Inc.; Alpha Beta Co.; Lucky Stores, Inc.; Jewel Food Stores; Osco Drug, Inc.; Star Market Co.; Skaggs Alpha Beta Co.; American Superstores, Inc.; Alpha Beta Stores, Inc.; Skaggs Telecommunications Service, Inc.

ARA SERVICES

The ARA Tower
1101 Market Street
Philadelphia, Pennsylvania 19107
U.S.A.
(215) 238–3000

Private Company
Incorporated: 1959 as Davidson Automatic Merchandising Company, Inc.
Employees: 120,000
Sales: $3.92 billion

ARA's is a short but eventful history. The company has grown out of the merger of two small vending companies in 1959 to become a huge service management company that today provides or manages services in four diverse areas: food and refreshment services; magazine and book distribution services; uniform rental, maintenance, and airport services; and health and education services. Its growth has come mainly through acquisition; ARA has bought more than 300 companies since 1959. All this activity has not come without strife, however. Over the years the company has been accused of price fixing, monopolization of markets, and infiltration by organized crime.

ARA was incorporated in 1959 when William Fishman merged his Chicago vending machine business with Davre Davidson's Los Angeles operation. The new company, Davidson Automatic Merchandising Company, Inc., rang up $25 million in sales during its first year. By the end of the year, its name had been changed to Automatic Retailers of America, Inc. The first of its many acquisitions came in 1961, with the purchase of Slater Company Foods, the largest company in the industrial and college food-services business.

The Federal Trade Commission (FTC) and ARA first clashed in 1964, when the FTC complained of attempts by ARA to monopolize the vending business. In a consent order, ARA agreed to divest vending companies worth $7.7 million in revenues.

More diversification and acquisitions followed. Almost every year, at least one acquisition was made. The company's strategy was to build national businesses where only local ones existed before. In 1966 ARA formed a division to run parks and resorts. Two years later it acquired a Washington, D.C. company, District News Company, giving it a dominant position in periodicals distribution. Other publication distribution companies were acquired in each of the next three years. In 1969 the company abbreviated its name to ARA Services.

In 1972 the purchase of a California firm, Educational & Recreational Services, Inc., gave ARA entry into the school busing industry. This was just one of nine purchases in fiscal 1972, and in fiscal 1973 ten more companies were acquired.

ARA's next brush with the law came in 1973, when the FTC challenged ARA's purchase of 98 vending-machine companies and 39 local publication distributors. Both complaints charged that ARA's acquisitions created monopolies or illegally reduced competition. Consent orders forced ARA to divest itself of other vending and periodicals companies and to accept a ban on entering certain markets without FTC approval. Also in 1973, the company paid $80,000 in fines after pleading no contest to federal charges of cigarette price-fixing in Cincinnati, Ohio and conspiracy to fix prices of vended drinks in Atlanta, Georgia.

In 1974 and 1975 six more companies became part of ARA. Acquisitions in 1977 included the U.S. rental-service business of Work Wear Corporation, a uniform-rental company. In 1977, ARA conducted an internal investigation and found that certain employees had received $504,000 in illegal rebates from suppliers and shipping businesses. The same inquiry also concluded that employees had paid out $393,000 to politicians and business contacts.

In May 1978, ARA was sued by a former employee, Peter L. O'Neill, who was director of the company's security division from 1974 to 1977 and, prior to that, an FBI agent. O'Neill claimed that he was dismissed because he knew too much about illegal activities carried out by ARA officials and that ARA had tried to cover up illegal payoffs and dealings with underworld figures. The company settled the suit out of court for $250,000, denying any connections with organized crime. It also divested itself of the subsidiary named in the suit.

In March, 1979, ARA agreed to pay a $300,000 fine and sell some assets in settlement of a suit brought by the government in 1977. The suit had charged that the company had violated the 1973 FTC order prohibiting it from acquiring any periodicals wholesalers without prior approval from the commission.

Other purchases over the next few years included a nursing home chain, and, in 1980, a trucking company, Smith's Transfer Corporation. The recession of the early 1980s did not stop ARA. A chain of day-care centers, National Child Care Centers, Inc., was a major purchase in 1981, and in 1982, Means Services, Inc., a uniform and laundry service, was bought for $45.5 million in cash. This acquisition made ARA the world's largest uniform renter. The 1983 purchase of Solon Automated Services, an operator of 200,000 washers and dryers, bolstered this business segment. One analyst attributed ARA's success during the recession to "its ability to manage businesses in which large numbers of employees, often earning below average wages, handle large amounts of cash and operate away from any central control."

The next year, 1984, was a key one in ARA's history. In April, the chairmanship passed from William Fishman, one of the company's founders, to Joseph Neubauer. Neubauer had come to ARA in 1979 from PepsiCo, and was appointed president and CEO before beginning his tenure as chairman. Neubauer began an overhaul of corporate strategy, seeking a higher profile for the company and focusing less on acquisition and more on marketing and internal controls. As part of this quest for a higher profile, for example, employees began to wear ARA uniforms. Advertisements for the company appeared in business and news magazines. To help raise employee morale, and thereby improve performance, an incentive program that rewarded employees for bringing clients of one division into another was initiated. These merit bonuses for managers could amount to as much as 45% of salaries. The company won several contracts, including one for six years with Baltimore's Memorial Stadium and one for 15 years with the New Orleans convention center. In 1984, ARA served the Olympics for the tenth time. During the two weeks of the games, the company served 50,000 meals and provided 20,000 box lunches daily. ARA also had 13,000 drivers shuttling athletes and spectators between sites.

In July, 1984, William M. Siegel, a former director and top manager of ARA, offered to buy the company. Neubauer turned him down. But over the following months Siegel pursued the matter; finally, in December, 1984, an $882.5 million management buyout was announced. Management formed ARA Holding Company to acquire the organization, and ARA Services became a private company, owned by 70 senior executives.

The ARA deal however, was not a typical leveraged buyout. Management did not sell parts of the company to pay back its debt. In fact, it immediately continued its acquisition campaign.

Although, during the previous August, the transportation unit had been sold, in the years immediately following the buyout the company continued to grow. In 1986 the food-services units bought Cory Food Services, Inc., Cory Canada, Inc., and Szabo, while during the same year the uniform-rental business grew with the purchase of Servisco, a company that leased and serviced work garments.

Saga Corporation, another giant food services company, became available for acquisition in 1986. ARA lined up financing to bid for the company, but was outbid by Marriott Corporation. Although the deal did not go through, it was seen as a good sign that ARA could even make a bid just two years after a major transition.

In 1987, major changes included the acquisition of Children's World, the child-care affiliate of Grand Metropolitan; the sale of Smith's Transfer; and the formation of GMARA, a joint venture with General Motors, to serve as industrial cleaners in GM plants.

There were internal changes also: ARA increased its 70-member management group fourfold, increasing management's share of stock from 26% to 34%. In March, 1988 a stock repurchase boosted management's stake to 56%.

ARA's history has been turbulent, but as a service company, it is in the fastest-growing segment of the economy. Since its management buyout in 1984, the company has continued to do well. Operating profits reached a record high of $211 million in 1988 as the company has concentrated on expansion through internal growth, and acquisitions have been made only in what ARA considers its core businesses. Emphasizing client retention as the base of success, ARA's future seems certain to hold continued growth.

Principal Subsidiaries: Aero Enterprises, Inc.; ARA/Cory Refreshment Services, Inc.; ARA Environmental Services, Inc.; ARA Health/Care, Inc.; ARA Health Facilities of Florida, Inc.; ARA Healthcare Management, Inc.; ARA Healthcare Nutrition Services, Inc.; ARA Healthcare Textile Services, Inc.; ARA Leisure Services, Inc.; ARA Transportation Services of Dayton, Inc.; ARA Virginia Sky-Line Co., Inc.; Aramont Properties, Inc.-Delaware; Aramont Risk Management Services, Inc.; ARASERVE, Inc.; ARASERVE of Puerto Rico, Inc.; Aratex Services, Inc.

ARGYLL
GROUP PLC

ARGYLL GROUP PLC

Argyll House
6 Millington Road
Hayes, Middlesex UB3 4AY
01–848 8744

Public Company
Incorporated: 1977 as James Gulliver Associates
Employees: 63,000
Sales: £3.7 billion (US$6.69 billion) (1989)
Stock Index: London

Considering its current annual sales of £3.7 billion, the Argyll Group's history is remarkably short. In 1987, just short of celebrating its tenth birthday, Argyll became the fourth-largest grocer in Britain when it purchased the 133 U.K. Safeway stores from their American parent, Safeway Stores Inc. The Safeway purchase gave Argyll a place in the upper echelon of British retailing and encouraged the company to begin the conversion of its largest Presto stores to the widely recognized and well-respected Safeway name. When its ambitious "Safeway 1990s" program is completed in March of 1991, Argyll will have built its stable of Safeway markets to around 320, comprising some 6.2 million square feet of sales area and contributing all but 20% of Group sales. In addition, Argyll will have some 300 Lo-Cost stores, discount stores that offer a limited range of groceries, and nearly 200 other stores (chiefly Prestos) in Scotland and northeastern England.

James Gulliver is the man most responsible for Argyll's spectacular career. He was born in Cambeltown, Argyllshire (hence the Group's name), in 1930, and graduated from Glasgow University with a degree in engineering. He spent several years with the management consulting firm of Urwick Orr. In the mid-1960s, he joined the supermarket chain Fine Fare, then a division of Associated British Foods. He quickly became chief executive, and in a matter of seven years had more than tripled sales from £60 million to £200 million. One newspaper honored Gulliver as its "Young Businessman of the Year" for 1972, but he resigned shortly thereafter, along with Alistair Grant, then managing director at Fine Fare.

Gulliver promptly bought a significant minorty share Oriel Foods, a wholesaling firm doing about £10 million annually. Together with Grant and David Webster, an investment banker, Gulliver acquired management control of Oriel. Within a year, Oriel was bought out by RCA Inc., which was then trying to build a European food division. The three men stayed on, multiplying Oriel sales tenfold by 1977. That year Gulliver, Grant, and Webster left Oriel and formed James Gulliver Associates. After a first investment in a home improvements company, they began building their own grocery conglomerate, starting with the purchase of two food companies, Morgan Edwards and Louis C. Edwards, a Manchester meat business.

By 1980 the new organization had adopted the name Argyll Foods and made significant inroads into the U.K. grocery trade. Over the next few years Argyll made several major acquisitions. Chief among these purchases were the 1981 acquisition of Oriel Foods for £19 million from RCA, which had apparently tired of the grocery business; and the June, 1982 purchase of Allied Suppliers from James Goldsmith, for £101 million. Between them, these acquisitions gave Argyll a nationwide range of operations, but one concentrated in northern England and Scotland. Presto, the most important of the new holdings, was a chain of 136 large grocery stores. Argyll also now owned Templeton, a line of 84 medium-sized supermarkets in Scotland; Liptons, with some 500 supermarkets in England and Wales; Lo-Cost, which, as its name suggests, occupied the lower end of the price spectrum; and Cordon Bleu, a 125-unit chain selling frozen foods. Along with some limited food wholesaling activity, Argyll also owned a biscuit, tea, and coffee manufacturer and an oil-refining business; both had been divested by 1987.

In 1983 Argyll Foods was merged with Amalgamated Distilled Products (ADP), a liquor company Gulliver and his associates had controlled since 1979. ADP produced Scotch whisky and dark rum, and ran a 300-unit discount liquor chain called Liquorsave. It also owned Barton Brands, a U.S. liquor producer and distributor, which it had acquired in 1982.

In 1985 Argyll began a major reorganization of its food division, realizing that if it was to become a major force in British groceries it would have to simplify and streamline its collected holdings, many of which were old, small, and out of touch with recent trends in marketing. The company therefore began converting all of its stores to either Presto or Lo-Cost, according to the demographics of each store. At the same time, the directors put a great deal of energy into lowering costs by taking advantage of the Group's greatly enhanced purchasing power and improving its distribution network. This reorganization, which was completed in 1986, put Argyll in a strong position to integrate its 1987 Safeway acquisition smoothly and efficiently.

One reason for Argyll's interest in Safeway was the debacle of its 1986 bid for the Distillers Company, Britain's largest producer and distributor of Scotch and other liquor products. Gulliver hoped to use Argyll's relatively minor liquor business as a springboard from which to enter the liquor market in a much more dramatic fashion.

In a carefully planned attack, Argyll made its bid for what Gulliver described as a once-great Scottish concern lately become moribund, offering to its shareholders a higher-than-market price for their stock and the prospect of fresh managerial expertise. Financial analysts heavily favored the proposed merger, which Gulliver and Alistair

Grant hoped to consummate for reasons of Scots pride as well as profitability, but Distillers eventually rejected Argyll and accepted a possibly illegal bid from Guinness, the well-known British brewing conglomerate. The complex legal issues involved have not been fully sorted out, but it was clear that the failure of Gulliver's year-long struggle was a great disappointment to him. Though he remained at Argyll long enough to consummate the Safeway deal, he stepped down as chairman in September, 1988.

Gulliver's successor, and the chief architect of the Safeway deal, was Alistair Grant. For many years Gulliver's closest adviser, Grant is an experienced food retailer who commands great respect in London financial circles, as evidenced by the ease with which he placed the £621 million worth of new stock needed to pay for the Safeway stores. (The total price of £681 million was made up with a £60 million interest-free loan from seller to buyer.)

It has been Grant's job to oversee the integration of Safeway and Argyll. The two companies were well matched: while Argyll's strength lay in the north, Safeway was predominantly a southern chain, though it had a significant business in Scotland. In addition, Safeway, despite its size and high per-unit profits, was widely believed to have a weak purchasing policy, an aspect of the business which Argyll had honed to a fine art. In general, the merger brought together the old and the new: Argyll's older and smaller stores, closer to the English tradition of the independent shopkeeper, with Safeway's more efficient and more fashionable stores. Argyll essentially has set out to capitalize on Safeway's appeal by adopting not only its name but its merchandising concepts as well.

To that end, Argyll converted some 57 of its Presto stores to the Safeway logo in fiscal 1988 (and seven the year before), in addition to opening 19 entirely new Safeways. To supply its vast network of outlets in an efficient manner, Argyll continued to upgrade and consolidate its warehouse distribution centers, most recently adding a 510,000-square-foot facility in Bellshill, Scotland. In accordance with Argyll's policy of operating only in those markets in which it can be a major player, the Group sold off all of its liquor holdings, except its retail operation, Liquor-Save, after failing to capture Distillers. Argyll is now the third-largest grocer in the United Kingdom. The market analysts who once were suspicious of Argyll's unlimited ambition are now the company's most enthusiastic backers, predicting continued success under the Safeway logo and the likelihood of further acquisitions in the coming decade.

Principal Subsidiaries: Safeway PLC; Safeway Properties Ltd.

ASDA GROUP PLC

Asda House, Southbank
Great Wilson Street
Leeds LS11 5AD
United Kingdom
(532) 435435

Public Company
Incorporated: 1949 as Associated Dairies and Farm Stores Limited
Employees: 47,000
Sales: £2.7 billion (US$4.88 billion)
Stock Index: London

In the race currently underway to fill Great Britain with large, brightly decorated supermarkets, Asda Group has the unique distinction of being both an innovator and a latecomer to the field. Asda introduced the concept of the "superstore" as early as 1965 and has never operated anything but these behemoths of the food-retailing world (a superstore is defined as one with 25,000 square feet or more of selling area). But it was not until the mid-1980s that Asda began upgrading its warehouse stores to meet the standards of design appeal and fresh-food selection set by its major competitors. At present, some 85% of the Group's approximately 130 superstores are new or have been recently refurbished, sporting the lively green color and dramatic lighting Asda chose to help shake off its old image. This massive program, begun in 1985 under the direction of the present chairman, John Hardman, has proven highly successful, and in the opinion of many observers saved Asda from falling irretrievably behind in the competitive grocery business.

Under Hardman's guidance, the Group has sold off all of its ancillary interests except one, the 90-unit chain of Allied Stores, retailers of carpeting, draperies, and other household items. Indeed, so great has been Asda's desire to concentrate its energies on the retailing of food that it no longer owns the parent company from which it sprang—a large group of dairies scattered across the North and Midlands known most recently as Associated Fresh Foods. When AFF was sold, in 1987, Asda completed a 60-year metamorphosis from dairy cooperative to supermarket giant.

The origins of the Asda Group are to be found in the efforts of English dairy farmers to protect themselves from falling milk prices after World War I. When wartime price controls were lifted and England began once again to import large quantities of European dairy products, local milk prices fell sharply and showed every sign of continuing to do so. Various legislative remedies were devised, but in the meantime a Yorkshire dairy farmer named J. W. Hindell led a number of his fellows in the creation of Hindell's Dairy Farmers Limited, a 1920 partnership whose purpose was to acquire or build both wholesale and retail outlets for their milk, in that way securing for themselves a steady market and a floor price.

During the next 25 years, Hindell's assembled a wide variety of dairy businesses, founding or purchasing a total of nine operating companies involved in everything from the raising of dairy cattle to the processing and distribution of milk and milk products, as well as the promotion of numerous cafes, retail milk shops, and bakeries.

By the time of World War II, Hindell's, headquartered in Leeds, had extended its interests across the Midlands and diversified as far as meatpacking and even the quarrying of lime. The partnership became a public company in March, 1949, as Associated Dairies and Farm Stores Limited, which included some 26 farms, three dairies, two bakeries, 42 retail shops, and pork-butchering facilities. With 1,200 employees, Associated was already an important part of the relatively quiet economy of northern England.

The next 20 years saw a veritable blizzard of further acquisitions by Associated. Dairies and creameries too numerous to mention became part of the rapidly growing northern conglomerate, but beyond expanding profits, little changed at the company until 1965, when Associated created a subsidiary called Asda Stores Limited. In that year, the parent company, by then known as Associated Dairies Limited, with sales of £13.5 million, was highly profitable and probably did not much concern itself with the tiny food-stores division, which at best could be expected to fill one more niche in the company's overall business plan.

As it turned out, however, the stores were an immediate and immense success. Associated had come up with a merchandising concept entirely new to England, and well tailored to the working-class cities in which it chiefly operated: the company opened extremely large, rather spartan stores in abandoned warehouses or mills, offering to the public a limited selection of goods at the lowest possible prices. These "edge-of-town" stores depended for their success on the rapid proliferation of the automobile in Great Britain and the accompanying decline in local consumer loyalties. As in America, the British public soon decided that it cared less about neighborhood vendors than low prices, and the automobile allowed them to act on their preference. Associated's warehouse stores were an enormous success, and the company quickly set about the program of expansion that would make it one of the leading retailers in the country.

The company thus found itself milking two kinds of cows, dairy and cash, and the latter naturally proved the more attractive as time went on. Associated continued to add to its dairy holdings, but it was apparent by the early 1970s that the Asda Stores division would soon dwarf its parent. At that time, the stores were still operated in a rudimentary fashion, with little centralized administration, primitive marketing, and no attempt at attractive floor displays. But Asda had pioneered not one but two new ideas in British food retailing, the edge-of-town location and the superstore size, and for a long time had the market to itself.

The company opened stores in Scotland and Wales, and began casting about for opportunities to invest its growing cash reserves. In 1972, Asda entered the travel agency business, in 1977 it had a go at furniture with its purchase of the Wade's stores, and at various times in the decade it tried its hand at a number of other diversions, none of them successful and all of them eventually disposed of. But longtime–Chairman Noel Stockdale could hardly be concerned about these minor setbacks; quite reasonably, he did not try to fix what was not broken, but continued building more superstores across the northern half of the country. By 1978, Asda had 60 of these, and two years later they passed the £1 billion sales mark.

As is usually the case, however, the rest of the marketplace had not stood still in the meantime. With Asda's runaway success as a model, the established grocery chains began building similar superstores at out-of-town locations, while London-area stores discovered that low prices were not enough to please more sophisticated shoppers. These shoppers wanted pleasant surroundings as well as low prices, and they soon got both in the more luxurious superstores opened by Adsa's rivals. As a result, by the early 1980s the Asda format of high volume, low price, and no frills had come to seem dated and unappealing. Customer loyalty, never strong in the economy-store sector, shifted away from Asda toward the chains more in tune with the new wave of unabashed materialism in Thatcher's England, leaving the Yorkshire firm in danger of an early death. In a period when everyone had a superstore, Asda's were decidely less "super" than the rest.

Such, at any rate, was the diagnosis of John Hardman when he became managing director of stores in June, 1984. Though the company was in the midst of a profitable, £1.76 billion sales year, Hardman understood that the market had moved ahead of Asda and would soon leave Asda floundering in its wake. Hardman therefore proposed a radical repositioning of the Asda chain, to include the following improvements. First, a completely new look for all of the stores, replacing their stacked-carton, industrial brown decor with a new, appetizing green palette, dramatic lighting, dropped ceilings, and imaginative display racks. Second, the chain would introduce its own "Asda Brand" line of foods, since private-label merchandising generally yields substantially higher gross margins. Third, the stores were to adopt an EPOS system—electronic point of sale registers—to provide more efficient records and inventory control. Fourth, the company would build a centralized network of distribution warehouses, eliminating the scores of trucks that arrived each day at store loading docks. Fifth and last, Asda would push toward the more affluent population in southern England and the London area, where relatively few superstores had as yet been built.

Around the same time Hardman was revamping its stores, Asda made its largest acquisition to date. In 1985 the company purchased the leading retailer of furniture in the United Kingdom, a company known as MFI, which had sales of about £300 million a year. Company spokesmen at the time pointed to the two concerns' similar positions in the marketplace, since MFI also operated large, edge-of-town stores that sold low-price goods; but financial analysts from the beginning doubted the wisdom of the merger, and in this case they were correct. After only two years of an up-and-down marriage, Asda sold its partner in the largest management buyout in British history, receiving £453 million in cash plus 25% of the newly formed "Maxirace."

As a matter of fact, Asda decided at that time to sell everything: under Hardman, now chairman, the company realized that its future lay in superstores and nothing but superstores, and therefore sold off not only MFI but also Associated Fresh Foods, the modest dairy company which at one time had been Hindell's Dairy Farmers Limited—that is, Asda's own parent. Asda would henceforth focus solely on its newly revamped and expanded line of food stores, with the single exception of Allied, a chain of carpet and drapery stores that the Group was unable to sell and has retained.

The superstore facelift and expansion program has succeeded in every respect. Asda Stores are now known for their innovative design, large selection of fresh foods, and equally extensive nonfood offerings, the latter accounting for some 25% of total store sales. The system of nine central warehouses is nearly complete, as is the installation of EPOS and a more advanced data processing network. Profits in the new and redecorated stores are significantly higher than in the older ones, due in part to the ever-increasing number of Asda brand items on the shelves and the more efficient distribution system. The company continues its southern assault, opening an average of 12 to 15 new superstores each year, many of them in the crowded urban areas of the South. And, in the most dramatic proof yet of its commitment to the grocery business, Asda recently acquired 62 of rival Gateway's superstores for £705 million. This mammoth purchase, in a single stroke, increased Asda's selling area by 50%, from 5 million to 7.5 million square feet, and further solidified its position as the largest operator of superstores in the U.K. (The new stores are on average even larger than Asda's.) Asda is the only superstore chain in the country without a tail of smaller, older, and less profitable stores to support, and as the company assimilates its latest acquisition, it will no doubt continue its current surge in bottom line results. Chairman Hardman has said that by 1995 England will be saturated with superstores and that his company will by then have once more diversified. In the meantime, Asda seems to have corrected its mid-life crisis without suffering serious damage, adroitly managing the makeover needed to restore it to the role of superstore leader.

Principal Subsidiaries: Asda Stores Ltd.; Allied Carpet Stores Ltd.; Gazeley Properties Ltd.; McLagan Investments Ltd.

BURGER KING CORPORATION

7360 N. Kendall Drive
Miami, Florida 33156
U.S.A.
(305) 596–7011

Wholly-owned subsidiary of Grand Metropolitan, PLC
Incorporated: 1954
Employees: 250,000
Sales: $2.8 billion

Miami entrepreneurs James McLamore and David Edgerton founded Burger King Corporation in 1954. Five years later, they were ready to expand their five Florida Burger Kings into a nationwide chain. By the time they sold their company to Pillsbury in 1967, Burger King had become the third largest fast-food chain in the country and was on its way to second place, after industry leader McDonald's.

The story of Burger King's growth is the story of how franchising and advertising developed the fast-food industry. McLamore and Edgerton began in 1954 with a simple concept: to attract the burgeoning numbers of postwar baby boom families with reasonably-priced, broiled burgers served quickly. The idea was not unique; drive-ins offering cheap fast food were springing up all across America in the early 1950s. 1954, in fact, was the same year Ray Kroc made his deal with the McDonald brothers, whose original southern California drive-in started the McDonald's empire.

McLamore and Edgerton tried to give their Burger King restaurants a special edge. Burger King became the first chain to offer dining rooms (albeit uncomfortable plastic ones). In 1957 they expanded their menu with the Whopper, a burger with sauce, cheese, lettuce, pickles, and tomato, for big appetites. But prices were kept low: a hamburger cost 18 cents and the Whopper 37 cents. (McDonald's burgers at the same time, however, cost only 15 cents.) In 1958 they took advantage of an increasingly popular medium, television: the first Burger King television ad appeared on Miami's VHF station that year.

By 1959 McLamore and Edgerton were ready to expand beyond Florida, and franchising seemed to be the best way to take their concept to a broader market. Franchising was booming in the late 1950s because it allowed companies to expand with minimal investment. Like many other franchisers, McLamore and Edgerton attracted their investors by selling exclusive rights to large territories throughout the country. The buyers of these territorial rights, many of them large businesses themselves, could do what they wanted to in their territory: buy land, build as many stores as they liked, sell part of the territory to other investors, or diversify. McLamore and Edgerton took their initial payments (which varied with the territory) and their cut (as little as one percent of sales) and left their franchisees pretty much on their own.

The system worked well, allowing Burger King to expand rapidly. By 1967, when the partners decided to sell the company they had founded, the chain included 274 stores and was worth $18 million to its buyer, prepared-foods giant Pillsbury.

The system also worked well for the franchisees. Under the early Burger King system, some of the company's large investors expanded at a rate that rivaled that of the parent company.

Where this loosely knit franchising system failed, however, was in providing a consistent company image. Because McLamore and Edgerton didn't check on their franchises and used only a small field staff for franchise support, the chain was noted for inconsistency in both food and service from franchise to franchise, a major flaw in a chain that aimed to attract customers by assuring them of what to expect in every Burger King they visited.

It was up to the new owner, Pillsbury, to crack down on franchise owners. But some large franchisees thought they could run Burger King themselves better then a packaged-goods company could. Wealthy Louisianans Billy and Jimmy Trotter bought their first Burger King outlet in 1963. By 1969, they controlled almost two dozen Burger King restaurants and went public under the name Self Service Restaurants Inc. In 1970, when the franchisees in control of the lucrative Chicago market decided to sell out, Billy Trotter flew to Chicago in a snowstorm to buy the territory for $8 million. By the time Pillsbury executives got to town the next day, they found they had been bested by their own franchisee.

The Trotters didn't stop there. By 1971 they owned 351 stores with sales of $32 million. They bought out two steak house chains (taking the name of one of them, Chart House), established their own training and inspection programs, and decided on their own food suppliers. By 1972 they were ready to take over altogether; the Trotters made Pillsbury a $100 million offer for Burger King. When that initiative failed, they suggested that both Pillsbury and Chart House spin off their Burger King holdings into a separate company. When that also failed, they continued to acquire Burger King piecemeal, buying nine stores in Boston and 13 in Houston.

But Pillsbury wasn't about to allow Chart House to gain other valuable territories. They sued the Boston franchisees who had sold to Chart House, citing Pillsbury's contractual right of first refusal to any sale. Eventually Chart House compromised, agreeing to give up its Boston holdings in exchange for the right to keep its Houston properties.

Pillsbury's suit was proof of a new management attitude that involved more central control over powerful franchisees. But it wasn't until Pillsbury brought in a hard-hitting executive from McDonald's that Burger King began to exert real control over its franchisees. Donald Smith was third in line for the top spot at McDonald's when Pillsbury lured him away in 1977 with a promises of full autonomy in the top position at Burger King. Smith used it to "McDonaldize" the company, a process that was especially felt among the franchise holders.

While Burger King had grown by selling wide territorial rights, McDonald's had taken a different approach from the very beginning, leasing stores to franchisees and demanding a high degree of uniformity in return. When Smith came on board at Burger King in 1977, the company owned only 34% of the land and buildings in which its products were sold. Land ownership is advantageous because land is an appreciating asset and a source of tax deductions, but more important because it gives the parent company a landlord's power over recalcitrant franchisees.

Smith began by introducing a more demanding franchise contract. Awarded only to individuals, not partnerships or companies, it stipulated that franchisees may not own other restaurants and must live within an hour's drive of their franchise, effectively stopping franchisees from getting too big. He also created ten regional offices to manage franchises.

Smith's new franchise regulations were soon put to the test. Barry W. Florescue, chairman of Horn & Hardart, the creator of New York City's famous Automat restaurants, had recognized that nostalgia alone couldn't keep the original fast-food outlets alive and had decided to turn them into Burger Kings. Smith limited Florescue to building four new stores a year in New York and insisted that he could not expand elsewhere. When Florescue bought eight units in California anyway, Smith sued successfully. Florescue then signed with Arby's, and Smith again effectively asserted Burger King's control in court, based on the franchise contract. His strong response to the upstart franchisee kept Horn & Hardart from becoming too strong a force within Burger King.

Increasing control over franchisees was not the only change Pillsbury instituted at Burger King during the 1970s. Like many other chains, Burger King began to expand abroad early in the decade. Fast food and franchising were unfamiliar outside the United States, making international expansion a challenge. Burger King's international operations never became as profitable as anticipated, but within a decade the company was represented in 30 foreign countries.

At home the company focused on attracting new customers. In 1974 management required franchisees to use the "hospitality system," or multiple lines, to speed up service. In 1975 Burger King reintroduced drive-through windows. While original stands had offered this convenience, it had gradually been eliminated as Burger King restaurants added dining rooms. Drive-throughs proved to be a profitable element, accounting for 60% of fast food sales throughout the industry by 1987.

Smith also revamped the corporate structure, replacing eight of ten managers with McDonald's people. To attack Burger King's inconsistency problem, Smith mandated a yearly two-day check of each franchise and frequent unscheduled visits. He also decided that the company should own its outlets whenever possible, and by 1979 had brought the company's share of outlet ownership from 34% to 42%.

Smith also turned his hand to the food served in his restaurants. He introduced the french fry technique that produced the more popular McDonald's-type fry. In 1978, primarily in response to the appeal that newcomer Wendy's had for adults, he introduced specialty sandwiches—fish, chicken, ham and cheese, and steak—to increase Burger King's dinner trade. Offering the broadest menu in fast food did the trick, boosting traffic 15%. A more radical expansion for the Burger King menu came next. After McDonald's proved that breakfast could be a profitable fast-food addition (offering a morning meal spread fixed costs over longer hours of operation) Smith began planning a breakfast menu in 1979. But Burger King had a problem with breakfast: its flame broilers could not be adapted as easily to breakfast entrees as McDonald's grills could. Smith urged development of entrees that could be prepared on existing equipment instead of requiring special grills. He began testing breakfast foods in 1978, but it wasn't until the Croissan'wich in 1983 and French Toast sticks in 1985 that Burger King had winning entries in the increasingly competitive breakfast market.

Smith left Burger King in June 1980 to try to introduce the same kind of fast-food management techniques at Pizza Hut. (Ironically, when he left Pizza Hut in 1983 he moved into the chief executive position at the franchisee that had given Burger King so much trouble, Chart House.) By following in Smith's general direction, Burger King reached its number-two position within two years of his departure, but frequent changes at the top since then have meant inconsistent management for the company. Louis P. Neeb succeeded Smith, to be followed less than two years later by Jerry Ruenheck. Ruenheck resigned to become a Burger King franchise owner in Florida less than two years after that, and his successor, Jay Darling, resigned a little over a year later to take on a Burger King franchise himself. Charles Olcott, a conservative former chief financial officer, took over in 1987.

Burger King didn't stand still under its succession of heads, though. The company continued to expand abroad, opening a training center in London to serve its European franchisees and employees in 1985. Besides developing successful breakfast entries, Burger King added salad bars and a "light" menu to meet the demand for foods with a healthier, less fatty image. In 1985 the firm began a $100 million program to remodel most of its restaurants to include more natural materials, such as wood and plants, and less plastic. Burger King also completely computerized its cooking and cash register operations so even the most unskilled teenager could do the job. Average sales per restaurant reached the $1 million mark in 1985.

Even some of Burger King's post-Smith successes caused problems, though. The company introduced another successful new entree, Chicken Tenders, in 1986, only to find it that it couldn't obtain enough chicken to meet demand. Burger King was forced to pull its $30 million introductory ad campaign.

Burger King was still bedeviled by the old complaint

that its service and food were inconsistent. The company played out its identity crisis in public, changing ad styles with almost the same frequency that it changed managers. After Smith's departure in 1980, Burger King's old "Have it your way" campaign ("Hold the pickles, hold the lettuce. Special orders don't upset us") was no longer appropriate. That ad campaign emphasized as a selling point what many saw as a drawback at Burger King: longer waiting times. But under Smith's emphasis on speed and efficiency, special orders did upset store owners. So the company turned to the harder sell "Aren't you hungry for Burger King now?" campaign. The hard sell approach moved the chain into second place, and Burger King took an even more aggressive advertising line. In 1982 Burger King directly attacked its competitors, alleging that Burger King's grilled burgers were better than McDonald's and Wendy's fried burgers. Both competitors sued over the ads, and Wendy's challenged Burger King to a taste test (a challenge that was pointedly ignored). In return for dropping the suits, Burger King agreed to phase out the offending ads gradually, but Burger King came out the winner in its $25 million "Battle of the Burgers": the average volume of its 3,500 stores rose from $750,000 to $840,000 in 1982, sales were up 19%, and pretax profits rose 9%.

Burger King's subsequent ad campaigns were not as successful. In 1985 the company added just over half an ounce of meat to its Whopper, making the 4.2 ounce sandwich slightly larger than the quarter-pound burgers of its competitors. The meatier Whopper and the $30 million ad campaign using celebrities to promote it failed to bring in new business. All three of the major campaigns that followed ("Herb the Nerd," "This is a Burger King town," and "Fast food for fast times") were costly flops. "We do it like you'd do it" followed in 1988, and then in 1989 came "Sometimes you've gotta break the rules," a controversial and ambiguous campaign that was poorly received by franchises and customers alike.

Burger King's lack of an identifiable image has contrasted dramatically with McDonald's strong ad showing. The number-one fast food restaurant spends three times as much on advertising as Burger King does. In a mature market in which there are few new converts to fast food and there is a continual battle for the food dollars of those who already buy it, advertising failures are costly.

In 1988, the company faced another kind of threat. Parent Pillsbury, the target of a hostile takeover attempt by the British Grand Metropolitan PLC, devised a counterplan that included spinning off the troubled Burger King chain to shareholders, but at the cost of new debt that would lower the price of both Pillsbury and the new Burger King shares. Such a plan would have made it highly unlikely that Burger King could ever have overcome its ongoing problems of quality and consistent marketing.

Pillsbury's plan didn't work, and Grand Met bought Pillsbury in January 1989 for $66 a share, or approximately $5.7 billion. Pillsbury became part of Grand Met's worldwide system of food and retailing businesses with well-known brand names. In Burger King, Grand Met got a company with some problems but whose 5,500 restaurants in all 50 states and 30 foreign countries give it a strong presence.

With a new owner committed to developing Burger King, the company may have its best chance yet of conquering the problems that have plagued it from the start. In the tough, slow-growth fast food market, Burger King has to succeed if it hopes to keep its place.

Further Reading: Emerson, Robert L. *Fast Food: The Endless Shakeout*, New York, Lebhar-Friedman Books, 1979; Luxenberg, Stan. *Roadside Empires: How the Chains Franchised America*, New York, Viking, 1985.

CARGILL, INC.

15407 McGinty Road West
Minnetonka, Minnesota 55343
U.S.A.
(612) 475-7575

Private Company
Incorporated: 1930
Employees: 53,700
Sales: US$32.28 billion (1986)

Cargill modestly describes itself as a buyer, transporter, and seller of bulk commodities. While accurate, this summary minimizes the variety and importance of the company's operations. Cargill, probably the largest private corporation in the United States, is one of the largest grain and commodities marketers in the world. Substantial interests in corn and oilseed processing, molasses, meat processing, transportation, and steel round out the picture. All Cargill operations require the same basic skills: careful handling, transportation, and marketing. In an interview with *The New York Times*, Chairman Whitney MacMillan compared Cargill to Proctor and Gamble: "we stick to our knitting . . . How many soaps does P. & G. make? In a sense they're all the same. Can you tell me the difference between trading soybeans, cotton and rubber? They're all soaps to us." The diversity of Cargill operations provides an essential protection for the company since many of its operations are subject to serious price fluctuations.

Cargill's corporate philosophy was shaped by its participation in the grain trade. This philosophy emphasizes secrecy and an intricate worldwide intelligence network. Robert Bergland, former secretary of agriculture, told the *Minneapolis Star and Tribune* that "they probably have the best crop-marketing intelligence available anywhere, and that includes the CIA." While secrecy provides an enormous operational advantage to Cargill, it creates problems as well. One frustrated journalist summarized Cargill as a "secretive, inbred and suspicious" company. Cargill's low profile has created no reservoir of favorable public opinion in difficult times. An exasperated Cargill MacMillan complained just after he had become president of Cargill in 1957 that the company rarely received public attention except when it was involved in a court case. As late as 1977, a company survey revealed that while 94% of farmers had heard of Cargill, only 49% knew what the company did.

William Wallace Cargill began his grain-business career in 1865 in Conover, Iowa. The business grew as it followed the expansion of the railroad into northern Iowa in the period after the Civil War. In 1875, William Cargill moved the headquarters of his company to La Crosse, Wisconsin. He formed several different partnerships with his brothers, Samuel and James. With Samuel he formed W. W. Cargill and Brother in 1867, which became the W. W. Cargill Company in 1892. James Cargill and John D. McMillan operated in the Red River Valley in North Dakota and Minnesota. In 1882, they sold their Red River Valley grain elevators to William Cargill in order to raise more capital. Then in 1888, James, William, and Sam Cargill formed Cargill Brothers. In 1890, this firm became the Cargill Elevator Company, headquartered in Minneapolis, Minnesota.

In 1895, William W. Cargill's daughter married John Hugh MacMillan, and later his son William S. Cargill also married a MacMillan. This union would reshape the company. When the elder Cargill died in 1909 the company suffered its greatest crisis. John Hugh MacMillan forced William S. Cargill out and took control of the company. The ensuing feud simmered for decades, but control of the company now rests firmly in the hands of the MacMillan family, though some Cargills still hold stock.

John MacMillan ran the company until 1936. MacMillan led the company through a difficult period after the struggle for power; not until 1916 was its financial situation completely secure. MacMillan was a cautious manager who established the rule that the company would not speculate in commodities, a careful policy that helped establish the company's reputation in banking circles—an important consideration since the large deals which became Cargill's mainstay required huge lines of credit.

After World War I, MacMillan took two steps that helped lay the foundation for the future growth of the company. Since its beginnings in 1865, Cargill had been based entirely in the Midwest, selling to eastern brokers. When Albany, New York brokers began to open offices in the Midwest, bypassing Cargill as a middleman, Cargill opened an office in New York in 1922. In 1929, Cargill opened a permanent office in Argentina in order to secure immediate information on Latin American wheat prices. And in 1930 the Cargill Elevator Company became Cargill, Inc.

John MacMillan Jr. became president of Cargill in 1936. He followed most of his father's cautious policies, but he brought an imaginative and visionary quality to the company. During the Depression, Cargill invested heavily in the storage and transportation of grain, secure in the knowledge that a recovering economy would find Cargill prepared to reap maximum benefit. He also left his mark on grain transportation. Disliking the standard barge design, he and some associates designed a new type of articulated barge and submitted the design to shipyards. When no company would build the barges, Cargill established its own unit to construct them. Soon Cargill built barges at half the typical cost and with twice the capacity of standard barges.

But John Jr.'s aggressiveness also created problems for the company. Most serious was the September Corn Case of 1937. The year 1936 had been a bad one for corn, and the 1937 crop would not be available until October. The Chicago Board of Trade and the United States Commodity Exchange Authority accused Cargill of trying to corner the corn market. When Cargill refused a Board of Trade order to sell some of its corn, the Board suspended Cargill Grain Company, the subsidiary which conducted trading, from membership. Typically, when the Board eventually lifted its suspension, Cargill refused to rejoin. For decades, Cargill carried on its trading through independent traders and proclaimed its satisfaction with the greater security this method afforded. It did rejoin in 1962, however.

World War II created serious problems for Cargill. By 1940, 60% of Cargill's business involved foreign markets. While Cargill did build ships for the navy, this enterprise could not replace its lost international business, so the company began a major diversification and entered the vegetable-oil and animal-feed fields for the first time. The two activities are closely related: pressing oil leaves high-protein meal, which is then used in animal feed. Cargill's first priority was to have some product to sell back to farmers after buying their grain, and animal feed was the logical choice. In 1945, Cargill purchased Nutrena, an animal-feed producer, a transaction which doubled its capacity in poultry and animal feeds. Oil processing soon outstripped the value of animal feeds, however. Corn and soybean processing were two of the most rapidly expanding agricultural areas in the 20 years after World War II. By 1949, Cargill had made a major entry into soybean processing and its researchers were already exploring the value of safflower and sunflower oil.

John MacMillan Jr. and his brother Cargill were determined to expand the company after the war, but they never forgot the lessons of 1909. The company expanded steadily, but in a cautious manner that minimized risk. Cargill took the lead among the major grain companies in efforts to combine a network of inland grain elevators with the ability to export large quantities of grain. Two developments in the 1950s helped to establish Cargill in world trade. In 1955 Cargill opened a Swiss subsidiary, Tradax, to sell grain in Europe. Eventually, Tradax grew into one of the largest grain companies in the world. And in 1960, Cargill opened a 13-million-bushel grain elevator at Baie Comeau, Quebec. This facility allowed Cargill to store grain for shipment during the months that winter weather closed the Great Lakes to traffic. The grain elevator also cut the cost of midwestern grain bound for Europe by 15¢ a bushel. In order to maximize profit, the barges that took grain to Baie Comeau backhauled iron ore. Also in the 1950s, barges that carried grain to New Orleans began to backhaul salt. Both practices would lead to profitable new enterprises for Cargill. Before the end of the decade, Cargill's sales topped the $1 billion mark.

Cargill became involved in grain sales to communist countries at an early date. In the early 1960s, Cargill began to sell grain to Hungary and the Soviet Union, while its Canadian subsidiary also played a significant role in trade with the Soviets. After a lapse of several years in the late 1960s, Soviet leader Leonid Brezhnev's desire to improve the Soviet standard of living led to a renewed interest in grain deals. The United States, anxious to improve relations with the Soviet Union, eased trade restrictions. These developments set the stage for the famous grain purchase of 1972. The U.S.S.R. purchased 20 million tons of wheat—roughly one-fourth of the American harvest, of which Cargill sold one million tons.

While Cargill actually lost money on the sale, the ensuing change in the market was more important. The massive sale of wheat, combined with a worldwide drought, drove up agricultural prices and increased Cargill's profits in all areas of operations. Sales increased from $2.2 billion in 1971 to $28.5 billion in 1981. Together with Cargill's success in high-fructose corn syrup and animal feed, this boom financed a significant expansion: during that decade Cargill's purchases included 137 grain elevators; coal, steel, and flour companies; and Ralston Purina's turkey processing and marketing division.

The 1980s brought economic problems that slowed Cargill's growth. The 1980 embargo on grain sales to the Soviet Union left Cargill long on grain. The Carter administration provided support for the companies which the embargo damaged, but the rise in the value of the dollar and the Third World debt crisis added to the problems of American agriculture. Cargill continued to search for opportunities in the depressed business cycle. Typical of its approach was the purchase of Ralston Purina's soybean-crushing plants in 1985. Overcapacity in the soybean industry did not faze Cargill. Whitney MacMillan pointed out that when a business is not doing well there is more room for improvement. Cargill remained confident that investment during hard times would reap major rewards during the next rise in the business cycle.

Several factors indicate that Cargill will continue to grow. Early in the 1930s, Cargill began one of the first management-trainee programs in the country. Cargill does not rely on business-school graduates but takes trainees from a wide range of backgrounds and introduces them to the company's system. Cargill places young executives in responsible positions quickly and grooms those who succeed. This system proved its worth in 1960 when John MacMillan Jr. died. For 16 years nonfamily employees ran the company under the leadership of Erwin Kelm. When Kelm retired in 1976, Whitney MacMillan became chairman. Most upper-level administrators at the company are graduates of Cargill's training program, and these officers, like family members, take the long view in planning for the welfare of the company. The family has shown a determination to plow back virtually all profits into the company, a dedication that indicates that the company will maintain a strong capital base. It is fair to guess that caution and the search for long-term growth opportunities will continue to characterize Cargill.

Principal Subsidiaries: Cargill Investor Services, Inc; Hohenberg Brothers Company; Tradax America Inc; Cargill Agricola S.A. (Brazil); Dutch General Cocoa-Gerkens Group; North Star Steel Company; North Star Steel Texas Inc; Cargill Marine and Terminal, Inc.; Excel Corporation.

Further Reading: The History of Cargill, Incorporated, 1865–1945, Cargill, Minneapolis, 1945; Work, John. *Cargill Beginnings*, Cargill, Minnetonka, Minnesota, 1965; Morgan, Dan. *Merchants of Grain*, Weidenfeld and Nicholson, London, 1979; Schmitz, Andrew et al. *Grain Export Cartels*, Ballinger Publishing Company, Cambridge, Massachusetts, 1981.

THE CIRCLE K CORPORATION

Post Office Box 52084
1601 North 7th Street
Phoenix, Arizona 85072–2084
U.S.A.
(602) 253–9600

Public Company
Incorporated: 1951 as Circle K Food Stores, Inc.
Employees: 26,000
Sales: $2.7 billion
Stock Index: New York

The Circle K Corporation, the second-largest convenience store operator in the world, runs more than 4,500 stores in 26 states and some 1,100 stores, through joint ventures or licensing agreements, in Canada, the United Kingdom, Finland, Australia, the Caribbean, and much of Asia. Circle K stores sell groceries, fast food, and other convenience items and offer many services such as money orders and movie rentals. About three-quarters of its stores also sell gasoline, making Circle K one of the top independent gasoline retailers in the United States. In addition to its stores, Circle K owns a bottling plant and is one of the largest ice manufacturers in the country.

In 1951, Fred Hervey, a self-made business man, bought three Kay's Food Stores in El Paso, Texas, and began operating them under the name of Kay's Drive-In Food Service. Hervey, who was born in 1909, began his business career in childhood by selling magazine subscriptions and by setting a soda pop stand outside his father's outdoor theater. During the 1930s, Hervey and his brother started a profitable root beer stand. Hervey then went on to other business enterprises and even served two terms as mayor of El Paso before he founded Circle K.

By 1957 Hervey had a ten-store chain in the El Paso area, and he decided to expand his operation to Arizona. The company adopted a new logo and corporate trademark: an encircled K to create a western image. By 1959 the Circle K Food Store chain had 15 units in Arizona in addition to the ten in Texas. In those days, convenience stores were still a new idea—there were only 500 such stores in the country (in 1988, there were 80,000). In 1965 Circle K developed its contract store concept, individual owner-operated stores to serve remote areas. Contract stores still exist, but only 106 stores today are contract, rather than company-owned.

In the early 1960s, the company doubled in size and moved its corporate headquarters to Phoenix, Arizona. In 1963 Circle K went public, issuing 96,000 shares of common stock. Since that original stock offering, Circle K's stock has split eight times.

In 1964 Circle K celebrated the opening of its 100th store. That same year, the board of directors began to think about expanding into non-food activities, and so changed the name of the corporation, eliminating the words "Food Stores." The Circle K Corporation soon began selling gasoline as well as food products—the first convenience store to do so. In 1964 the company also test-marketed manufactured ice under the brand name Crystal Clear Circle K.

By the late 1960s, the company was able to devote more of its resources to technology: in 1967, business operations were computerized, and in 1968, a chemist was hired to develop food products, which eventually led to the Hi Spark'l line and Circle K Frezes. These products, along with others in the Polar Beverage division, such as Del Sol fruit punches and Just Orange juice, developed in the 1970s, continued to be sold until the mid-1980s. Today, however, the trend in convenience stores is to enter into joint ventures with brand name companies to sell fast food such as ice cream, juices, or doughnuts. For example, a Dunkin' Donuts brand program has been successful in many Circle K stores in recent years.

In 1971, with the establishment of the foodservice division, the company began to sell sandwiches, an enterprise which continues to be successful. In 1972, the company was operating in eight western states: Arizona, California, Colorado, Idaho, Montana, Oregon, New Mexico, and Texas. By the mid-1970s Circle K had acquired 26 Quick-Shop stores, thus expanding its base of operation into Oklahoma and Kansas.

Under the leadership of President John Gillet, Circle K began to expand overseas in the early 1970s. In 1972, businessmen from Japan came to the United States to study the convenience store concept; their visit to Circle K in Phoenix led to Circle K's first foreign licensing agreement, in 1979, with the Uny Company of Japan to establish Circle K stores there. Further overseas expansion in Asia, Europe, and Australia occurred in the 1980s. By 1989, Circle K convenience stores existed in 13 foreign countries.

The early 1980s were a period of aggressive growth. Karl Eller, CEO and chairman of the board, with the help of his long-time associate, Carl H. Linder, a director who owns 31% of Circle K, is given credit for Circle K's ambitious posture during this time. Eller, who previously founded Combined Communications Corporation and served as president of Columbia Pictures, has a reputation as an acute dealmaker and business opportunist. (An anecdote reported by *Business Week* claims Eller was once able to strike a good deal buying several television stations by reading about their owner's death in the obituaries.) And, indeed, under Eller's leadership sales soared and the number of Circle K stores nearly tripled, mostly through acquisitions from other chains. During the early 1980s, due to changing consumer needs and the growth of the industry, competition in the convenience food industry was fierce, and Eller's strategy was to buy up units from rivals hurt by this vigorous competition. In 1983 Circle K nearly doubled its size with its acquisition of 960 UtoteM units. Other acquisitions included 435 Little General stores and 21 Day-N-Nite stores in 1984, 449 Shop & Go stores in 1985, and 473 7-Eleven stores and 538 stores from Charter Oil in 1988. Circle K has expanded from its base in the Southwest aggressively into the South and Northwest and to a lesser extent into the East and Midwest, as well as internationally.

In addition to expansion, the early 1980s also brought a number of innovations to Circle K stores. In 1983, stores in the Phoenix area installed automatic teller machines, while commissary operations developed the Deli-Fresh sandwich concept to serve company stores as well as some supermarket and military accounts. A third innovation that year was a redesigning project to establish a unique corporate identity for Circle K. Stores were remodeled in orange, red, and purple, a distinctive color scheme that identifies Circle K today.

In fiscal 1984, Circle K passed the $1 billion sales mark, and the next year it constructed a new corporate headquarters in Phoenix—an elegant four-story building housing a Circle K store in its front section. But the fast growth and creative innovation of the 1980s were not without difficulty and controversy. Circle K's 1980 acquisition of 13.2% of Nucorp Energy, Inc., a petroleum corporation, brought with it a lawsuit by a group of shareholders and officers of companies acquired by Nucorp in 1981. The lawsuit, filed in 1983, questioned the integrity of Nucorp's accounting practices, and threatened the financial stability and ratings of Circle K for five years. It was settled in 1988, when a jury ruled in Circle K's favor.

In 1988, however, there were other problems. Early in that year, Circle K triggered a gasoline price war in Alabama by cutting prices as much as seven cents a gallon. The state's attorney and a group of retailers claimed that Circle K's action violated the state's Motor Fuel Marketing Act and threatened to file a suit. The impetus for legal action was stifled when Circle K raised its gas prices once again. A spokesperson for Circle K told *National Petroleum News*, "As a convenience store chain, we give our customers the best possible convenience and value in pricing, but we don't sell below cost."

Circle K generated further controversy in 1988 when it instituted a new health insurance plan for its employees which sought to exclude "lifestyle-related" health care problems such as drug or alcohol abuse. This policy would also have excluded AIDS victims, except ones who contracted the disease through blood transfusions. It would not have excluded drug and alcohol rehabilitation, however. The plan created a furor among civil libertarians and gay-rights groups, who feared that other self-insured companies would rush to institute similar policies. Brent Nance, insurance case manager for AIDS Project Los Angeles, told *Business Insurance*, "It's almost as if Circle K says there are innocent victims and guilty victims, and they will cover only innocent victims." Criticism also came from less expected quarters such as the insurance industry and the convenience store industry. Circle K eventually withdrew the lifestyle exclusions from its policy.

Circle K's fast growth brought with it a number of personnel problems that the company has had to address in recent years. Numerous acquisitions meant that uniformity of procedures and training simply did not exist. It also led to rapid turnover and a lack of company loyalty on the part of employees who often felt an allegiance to their original employer. Circle K instituted a number of communication and training improvements. Newsletters and a toll free telephone number were designed to allay fears among employees whose stores are in the process of being acquired by Circle K. The No. 1 Club rewards sales effort with cash and recognition; the Management Development Candidate program and the Professional Retail Operator program provide comprehensive training for managers.

The convenience store industry is considered to be in the maturing stage of its life cycle: growth, overall, has slowed, and competition is keen. In order to thrive, convenience stores must keep abreast of new trends and accommodate new customer bases. The traditional customer has been a 35-year-old, male, blue-collar worker. While these customers are still important to the industry, working women and white-collar men are making up a larger percentage of customers.

Karl Eller does not intend to let up on the aggressive growth pattern he has set for the company. New conveniences are the order of the day: Circle K offers lottery tickets, movie rentals, money orders, and Federal Express drop-off boxes. To counter its fiercest competitors—gasoline marketers who have begun to sell food and beverages on prime corner locations—Circle K will soon increase the percentage of stores with pumps from about 75% to 90% of its locations. In a 1988 interview with *National Petroleum News*, Eller was confident of Circle K's ability to check the threat of this new breed of gasoline vendors: "Right now we can go head-to-head with any major oil company on the same corner because I think we can be more responsive to the customer. Also we don't lose sight of the fact that gasoline isn't the top priority in our stores. Customer convenience is." Circle K's service orientation has been its strength since its beginning and over several decades of growth, and promises the company a strong future.

Principal Subsidiaries: Circle K Convenience Stores, Inc.; Circle K General, Inc.; Shop & Go, Inc.; UtoteM, Inc.; Bauman Co.; Idaho Outdoor Advertising, Inc.

EDEKA ZENTRALE A.G.

New York Ring 6
Postfach 60 06 80
2000 Hamburg 60
Federal Republic of Germany
(40) 63–770

Cooperative Company
Incorporated: 1908
Employees: 800
Sales: DM11.98 billion

As a cooperative company, Edeka is made up of a network of small retailers who purchase food and general goods as a group. Small shops that are part of the co-op can be found all across the Federal Republic of Germany, in rural as well as urban regions. Edeka, or EdK as it is also known, is the German acronym for "Central Purchasing Co-op of the Association of German Retail Co-ops."

Edeka's direct predecessor was established in October, 1907 with only 800 marks in capital, at a time when co-ops were a new idea. Fritz Borrmann and Karl Biller were its first managers. This company, the Association of German Retail Co-ops, was soon joined by other co-ops all over the country. At a meeting in May, 1908, a statute was presented to 80 representatives of 23 organizations, and Edeka itself was formally born.

From its first year, Edeka was financially successful, and by 1910 it was able to found an advertising division. EdK did not at first have its own brands, but in 1911 it purchased several famous brands. But the young company soon felt the strength of its competitors, the industry's big retailers. The large retailers pressured suppliers not to sell Edeka goods at a discount, arguing that EdK was too small to receive the discounts big retailers were given. As a result, 44 supply companies boycotted EdK.

In its first years, EdK was very careful abut giving loans and credits to its members, making all money transfers in cash rather than using credit. But it was soon clear that the co-op needed a bank. After long and intense discussion, the Genossenschaftsbank Edeka (Edeka Co-op Bank) was founded to provide loans to Edeka's small retailers.

During the months before World War I, the German economy was in a state of chaos. The government partially restricted free trade, and city and county administrations were ordered to confiscate goods if necessary. People rushed into shops and bought as much food as they could. As a co-op, Edeka's local, decentralized structure meant that it handled the crisis in a steady and reliable fashion. For this, the organization earned a strong reputation among consumers, and within the next several years, many Edeka shops were founded. Local administrations sought Edeka's cooperation, and some city governments even tried—unsuccessfully—to unify all small retailers into a single co-op.

Finally, in 1918 EdK gained legal recognition as a co-op, and as a trader that bought large quantities of goods and was therefore entitled to discounts. With this legal status, there was no question any more about its official place in the German economy.

After World War I, while free trade was still restricted, EdK's members increased from 194 in 1918 to 578 by 1923. As terrible inflation wrought economic havoc, Edeka had to come up with ways to lessen its impact. One way was to issue 20-mark "saving coupons," to strengthen the company's financial base. Edeka suggested that each co-op member purchase at least one coupon each week, and promised to pay 6% interest. Edeka also made a call for solidarity in 1923, when it needed a new office and a warehouse and asked each retailer to contribute 20 marks. Edeka, like many other companies, also began to issue its own money in another effort to combat inflation. EdK retailers were obliged to accept EdK money, which they could use to buy supplies from the central organization. This measure helped insure that people would be able to shop at Edeka.

In 1924, EdK introduced several new policies for members. Each member store was required to use the name "Edeka" and to post an Edeka sign prominently. Shops were also required to sell Edeka brands. In its continuing effort to cope with inflation, in 1925 Edeka restricted its loans to not more than 5,000 reichsmarks per shop, and limited the liability of each shop to 7,500 reichsmarks. A year later, in 1926, new regulations required that all financial transactions be conducted in cash. This was an advantage for Edeka, since immediate payment, in cash, reduced its financial risk. By this time, EdK supplied a wide range of good besides food, like soap, floor wax, candles, and other products.

In a concerted effort to help small retailers, who often lacked experience as well as financial resources, EdK sent trained managers to member stores in trouble. During the Great Depression, customers trusted Edeka because of their experience during and after World War I, when Edeka's special role as a co-op ensured a stable and reliable market.

After Adolf Hitler came to power in 1933, the whole economy was restructured and the government tried to organize institutions to regulate all sections of the economy. This effort was not entirely successful with EdK because of its decentralized organization.

After March, 1934 it became illegal to import goods from foreign companies which were not part of a German company. To cope with this regulation, EdK was eventually forced to establish branches in Italy, Greece, and Turkey. Edeka also formed a subsidiary, Edeka Import and Export, a co-op with limited financial liability.

During the first years of Nazi rule, the large retailers

once again tried to persuade the government to prevent Edeka from enjoying the discount and other advantages of bigger companies. Between 1936 and 1939 Edeka was confronted with intense regulations and controlled prices. At this time Edeka added cigarettes to its goods, which then included some 400 items. Despite huge losses, EdK proved to be a stable company, even when in 1943 its Berlin headquarters office was bombed and burned down. At a time when thousands of companies failed, Edeka was able to stay in business, and its food stamps remained valid until February, 1945, when Germany's food industry collapsed.

After the war, the partition of Germany cut off almost all communication between the eastern and western zones. The situation in Berlin was especially confusing, leading Edeka to establish a second headquarters in Hamburg.

A new generation of managers met in Bad Godesberg in 1945 to reestablish an active Edeka. Their first effort failed, but a second meeting in March, 1946 in Goettingen made it clear that Edeka would continue to work. The company's first annual report, for 1945, was written by both headquarters, in Berlin and Hamburg.

Of the 524 co-ops that existed before World War II, 201 in West Germany and 125 in East Germany survived the war. In 1952, however, the East German state brought an end to all Edeka co-ops in East Germany when it forbade governmental companies to deliver to the private sector. But the situation in the West improved: in 1950 the central office counted 225 co-ops with a total turnover of DM15 million. Each co-op encompassed an average of 124 small retailers.

The 1950s, the years of the economic miracle, were a time of tremendous growth for all sectors of the economy. During this time more than 20% of all small retailers were part of Edeka, and the co-op expanded vigorously, constructing warehouses in Braunschweig for tins and vegetables, in Cuxhaven for fish, and in Kempten for cheese.

Edeka also continued to introduce new ideas and systems to customers and small retailers: Edeka stores were among the first to introduce self service, since new packing machines enabled EdK to sell packaged goods. By 1958, 7,000 of 40,500 stores offered self service. Frozen food and fruits were introduced in 1955, and special diet and health foods were introduced in 1957.

EdK did not stop its modernization. Shops continued to change to self service. In 1962 delegations of the co-op traveled to the United States to compare the Edeka system to similar American companies. Meanwhile Europe took its first steps toward the Common Market. Edeka joined the Union of Food Co-ops (UGAL) in Brussels. Since the foundation of UGAL in 1963 EdK has been part of the lobby for co-op interests in the European market.

In its ongoing effort to sell a greater variety of goods, EdK started to sell meat in 1963. The wider range of EdK's goods enabled the co-op to survive in smaller villages and towns, since it meant that neighborhoods could buy all their necessary food, such as bakery products, fruits, frozen food, and dairy products, from an Edeka store. In 1968 Edeka for the first time began to sell general household goods such as can openers and pens.

But competition was fierce, especially in the early 1960s, and many smaller retailers failed. In order to survive, EdK had to improve its weak points. Restructuring the stocking system through the use of rolling shelf containers helped retailers stock a wider variety of goods in the same space, helping mitigate rising rents. By 1965 regional computer centers were established to simplify communication among small retailers and Edeka's head office. Another important initiative to compete with other companies was education. EdK established a training center and started an international educational program in cooperation with Swiss and Austrian retailers in 1965.

Two years later two new subsidiaries were founded to help with the real estate problems of small retailers, especially retailers located in downtown areas. All these organizational and educational steps, however, could not prevent the failure of 2,500 small retailers between 1968 and 1970.

Edeka decided to tighten its organizational structure; five regional offices were created, in Hamburg, Cologne, Frankfurt, Stuttgart, and Munich. Since 1970 each regional office has been financed equally by the Edeka bank and the co-ops. Despite of this change, however, Edeka was heavily criticized by the department of monopolies, which saw the size of the organization as proof of its monopolistic hold on the retail industry. Edeka claimed that it simply represented small retailers and did not, as state officials assumed, dominate them.

In the economic turmoil that followed the oil shock in 1973, small retailers had a particularly hard time in Germany. Public opinion turned away from Edeka and from co-ops in general, which were seen as old-fashioned. Edeka began to concentrate more on public relations, and recruited employees through workshops and cooperation with local schools. By 1975, 6,000 trainees worked in shops all over Germany. Three of every four EdK shops were remodeled between 1965 and 1975. In 1978, Edeka entered an agreement with the department store Horten in which Edeka rented space in 58 department stores and set up food shops. The agreement came at a time when almost no Edeka stores had survived in the rapidly changing downtown areas. The EdK-Horten arrangement helped many retailers to survive, as renting one section of a department store was much cheaper than the rent for a separate street level shop.

At the beginning of the 1980s, EdK was the biggest independent group of small retailers in Europe, with 18,200 small retailers who owned 20,300 shops. By the end of 1988, Edeka had 11,000 members who operated a total of 13,150 stores and had total sales of more than DM20 billion. Some of this drop can be accounted for by the trend toward fewer, larger stores in the retail industry.

Today each member is a member of a regional co-op; these regional co-ops together run 22 wholesale businesses for the individual stores and each is a member of Edeka Zentrale, the holding company. The regional co-ops are also members of Edekabank, which today handles both credit and insurance for Edeka members. And, in addition to supplying individual retailers and operating their own meat-processing facilities, Edeka wholesale businesses also supply hotels and large restaurants. After surviving more than 80 years of tumultuous change, Edeka remains a powerful force in the German retail industry.

Principal Subsidiaries: EDEKA Fruchtkontor GmbH; EDEKA Zentralhandelsgesellschaft mbH (50%); EDEKA Zentralverwaltung GmbH; GVG Gerbrauchsgueter-Vertriebs-GmbH; Immobilien–Anlagegesellschaft Fonds, Nr. 4 Dr. Baumann—Dr. Sonnemann KG (96.7%); Veritas Vertriebs-GmbH; EDEKA International S.A. Luxembourg (99.5%); EDEKA Frucht Kontor S.a.r.l., Bozen (90%); EDEKA Produktions-und Handelsgesellschaft mbH (98.6%); EDEKA ZENTRALE AG & Co. Beteilingungs KG; EDEKA Datenverarbeitungs-GmbH; EDEKA Betriebsberatungs-und Kapita-beteiligungs GmbH; EDEKA Treuhand Verwaltungs-und Betriebs GmbH; EDEKA Treuhand GmbH & Co. Grundvermoegen Alaskaweg KG.

Further Reading: Edeka: 75 Jahre immer in Aktion, Hamburg, Edeka, 1982.

Fleming Companies, Inc.

FLEMING COMPANIES, INC.

6301 Waterford Boulevard
Post Office Box 2664
Oklahoma City, Oklahoma 73126–0647
U.S.A.
(405) 840–7200

Public Company
Incorporated: 1915 as the Lux Mercantile Company
Employees: 24,600
Sales: $10.5 billion
Stock Index: New York

Fleming Companies is the largest food wholesaler in the United States. The company stocks the shelves of more than 5,000 supermarkets and other retail food stores nationwide, including such familiar names as I.G.A., Piggly-Wiggly, Thriftway, Sentry, Food-4-Less, Shop 'n Bag, and United Supers. Fleming has shown exceptional innovation in meeting the changing needs of the independent grocer over the years. The company's taste for the most up-to-date technology and its knack for making healthy acquisitions has catapulted it to the forefront of the wholesale foods industry. Today the company not only supplies its customers with food products but also assists with new store planning and financing, marketing, accounting, and operations management.

In 1915, O. A. Fleming, E. C. Wilson, and Samuel Lux founded the Lux Mercantile Company in Topeka, Kansas to sell produce to local merchants. The company's name was changed to Fleming-Wilson three years later. In 1921, Ned Fleming, the son of the company's co-founder, joined the firm. He was promoted to general manager a year later, and held that position until he was elected president in 1945.

Throughout the 1920s, the Fleming-Wilson Company operated locally in Kansas. In 1927, it joined the Independent Grocers Alliance (I.G.A.), a voluntary grocery store chain and one of the largest independent chains today. In such voluntary chains, affiliated stores agree to buy most or all of their merchandise from one distributor and receive collective buying power in exchange, enabling them to compete with larger corporate supermarket chains. Voluntary chains have historically made up the largest share of the wholesaler's business, and they contributed significantly to Fleming-Wilson's growth.

The Depression took a particularly heavy toll on the lower Midwest and the Southwest. Though many industries in the region were virtually paralyzed, Fleming-Wilson managed to survive. In 1935, it acquired the Hutchinson Wholesale Grocery Company, another Kansas-based distributor, the start of a period of growth that has continued virtually unbroken to the present day.

In February, 1941 the company changed its name to Fleming Company, Inc. That same year it branched out of Kansas when it acquired the Carol-Braugh-Robinson Company of Oklahoma City. By the end of World War II the fate of the independent grocer was uncertain, Ned Fleming was faced with new challenges. Americans were moving out of the cities and into the suburbs. As shoppers drove their new automobiles to the new supermarkets, independent "mom and pop" corner stores fell by the wayside and supermarket chains grew at a frantic pace. It was the voluntary chain concept that rescued the independent grocer. Voluntary chains expanded tremendously after the war, and as a result so, too, did Fleming. The company reported steadily increasing earnings throughout the late 1940s and the 1950s.

In 1956, Fleming Company bought Ray's Printing of Topeka, renamed General Printing and Paper. Fleming itself was General Printing and Paper's biggest customer, consistently accounting for more than half the company's sales.

The 1960s were a decade of exceptional growth, as Fleming expanded nationwide through the acquisition of other regional wholesalers. Throughout the early 1960s, the company acquired several companies and facilities in the Midwest and Southwest, including the Schumacher Company of Houston, Texas in 1960.

In 1964, Ned Fleming became chairman of the board of directors and Richard D. Harrison became the company's president. Under this new leadership, Fleming began an even more ambitious campaign of expansion and acquisition. In 1965, Fleming purchased Thriftway Foods, which operated in the East. Thriftway, which is headquartered in King of Prussia, Pennsylvania, is one of Fleming's most active units today. Three years later, Fleming tapped West Coast markets when it bought Kockos Brothers, Inc in California. But at the end of the decade profits slowed for the first time in many years.

Fleming began to diversify again in the 1970s. The company bought a semi-trailer manufacturing unit in 1970, and in 1972 it created the Fleming Foods Company, which ran the food distributing operations as a semi-autonomous unit. Later that year Fleming bought the Quality Oil Company, of Topeka, Kansas. Quality Oil operated about 50 retail gas stations in the Midwest and proved to be a wise investment. A year after the acquisition, the subsidiary was contributing more than 10% of Fleming's pretax profits. Fleming also branched into health foods distribution when it bought Kahan and Lessin in 1972. At that time, K&L delivered to about 1,200 health food stores and 1,000 supermarkets. Fleming's venture into health foods proved to be less profitable than petroleum: K&L lost money in 1973 and showed only a slight profit in 1974.

In 1974, Fleming bought Benson Wholesale Company and the Dixieland Food Stores retail chain, both headquartered in Geneva, Alabama. In 1975, the company pushed into the New Jersey and New York markets by purchasing Royal Food Distributors. Finally, in 1979 Fleming acquired Blue Ridge Grocery Company of Waynesboro, Virginia, capping off a decade of acquisition and growth.

In 1981, Fleming Companies reincorporated in Oklahoma and its corporate headquarters moved to Oklahoma City. In March, 1981 Richard D. Harrison was elected chairman of the Fleming Companies board of directors, and E. Dean Werries, who had previously headed the Fleming Foods division, replaced him as president, while Harrison remained CEO.

This new leadership steered Fleming in a slightly different direction. Harrison and Werries stressed wholesale food distribution over diversification. Throughout the 1980s, Fleming made more and larger acquisitions of food wholesalers as part of its growth strategy. In 1981, it bought McLain Grocery in Ohio. In 1982, it bought the Waples-Platter Company for $91 million, which included the White Swan Foodservice division in Texas. A month later, in January, 1983, it purchased the bankrupt American-Strevell Inc. for $14 million. Fleming also purchased Giant Wholesale of Johnson City, Tennessee, that year. In 1984, Fleming acquired United Grocers, a cooperative wholesaler in California. It further strengthened its hold on the northern California region by purchasing a huge distribution center in Milpitas, California, from the Alpha-Beta Company a year later. In 1985, Associated Grocers of Arizona, Inc. was purchased for $47 million. In 1986, it purchased the Frankford-Quaker Grocery Company in Philadelphia, and the Hawaiian distribution warehouse of Foodland Super Markets. In 1987, Fleming acquired the Godfrey Company of Wisconsin, and in July, 1988 Fleming became the largest wholesaler in the country when it acquired the nation's fourth-largest wholesaler, Malone & Hyde Inc.

Fleming's incredible spree of acquisitions was not completely free of complications. In particular, the acquisition of Associated Grocers of Arizona posed some new problems for Fleming. Because the wholesaler had previously operated as a cooperative, owned by those supermarkets it serviced, Fleming had difficulty implementing its own corporate style of management. Associated Grocers customers were not at first supportive of the changes which were necessary to transform the company into a profitable unit for Fleming. Despite such minor setbacks, Fleming continues to look for possible mergers to strengthen the company. Cooperative distributors who lack the capital to reinvest in new facilities and find it increasingly difficult to compete with the streamlined, efficient corporate wholesaler are likely candidates.

At the same time Fleming concentrated on acquiring food wholesalers, it divested some of its other units. In 1982, it sold Quality Oil, and in 1983 it sold General Printing and Paper. In 1984, it sold its health foods specialty distributor, Kahan and Lessin. K&L's performance had been inconsistent ever since its acquisition in 1972. In addition, the Justice Department charged the subsidiary, along with three other health food distributors, with fixing prices in 1982. The company was fined $75,000; Fleming reported a $862,000 expense as a result of the litigation.

Wholesale food distributors traditionally operate on profit margins of less than one percent. Increased productivity of even fractions of a penny on each dollar of volume can make a noticeable difference in earnings. For this reason, Fleming has been quick to implement technological developments to increase productivity. In its newest warehouses, a computer breaks down orders by product, allowing a worker to fill several orders at once. The worker puts the total number of cases of one product ordered on a conveyor belt. A laser scanner sends each unit to the proper shipping bay to be loaded for delivery. This new system increased productivity an average of 11% in those warehouses where it was employed. In those warehouses in which it was impossible to mechanize without significantly disrupting operations, Fleming established standards of productivity as an alternative way to increase its profit margins. The procedure improvement program (PIP) measured each worker's productivity by computer. Before doing a specific task, a worker inserted a card into a computer, which calculated the standard amount of time for the task and evaluated his performance. If a worker consistently fell below standard, he faced dismissal. Such work standards programs were, naturally, not always popular. In early 1986, workers went on strike at Fleming's warehouse in Oaks, Pennsylvania in opposition to the work standards program and an increase in the standard number of cases moved per hour, from 125 to 150. The strike was settled when the Teamsters agreed to the new standard and the company lengthened the five-step disciplinary review procedure to six steps.

The wholesale food industry is not expected to grow much domestically in the future. The aggressive expansion of corporate supermarket chains puts pressure on wholesalers distributing to independent retail stores. Although Fleming's most recent acquisitions give it a very solid share of the market, the company will have to stay innovative to stay on top. International markets are one potential area of growth for wholesale distributors. In the meantime, Fleming expects to continue to expand by acquiring healthy competitors and to improve profit margins by increasing productivity.

Principal Subsidiaries: Crestwood Bakery; Dixieland Food Stores, Inc.; Fleming Co. of Alabama, Inc.; Fleming Finance Co., Inc.; Godfrey Company, Inc.; Malone and Hyde, Inc.; Royal Food Distributors, Inc.; Fleming Foods of Ohio, Inc.; Fleming Foods of Pennsylvania, Inc.; Fleming Foods of Tennessee, Inc.; Fleming Foods of Texas, Inc.; Fleming Foods of Virginia, Inc.; Fleming Foods West; Fleming Guardian Group, Inc.; Fleming Insurance, Ltd.; Fleming Transportation, Inc.; Hub City Foods, Inc.; Selected Products, Inc.; Sentry Markets, Inc; Thrift-Rack, Inc.

FOOD LION, INC.

Harrison Road
Post Office Box 1330
Salisbury, North Carolina 28145-1330
U.S.A.
(704) 633-8250

Public Company
Incorporated: 1957 as Food Town Inc.
Employees: 35,531
Sales: $3.82 billion
Stock Index: New York

Food Lion, Inc. is the fastest growing supermarket chain in the United States: its annual expansion rate has averaged 20% for the past 20 years. The company operates more than 560 stores in the Southeast and has recently been adding nearly 100 each year. Food Lion's success has centered around its low-price, high-volume strategy. The chain sells many items at cost or even below to lure customers through its doors. By cutting its own overhead dramatically, Food Lion has been able to offer "everyday low prices" to consumers and still manage to reap some of the highest profits in the supermarket industry.

In December, 1957 Ralph W. Ketner, Brown Ketner, and Wilson Smith opened a Food Town supermarket in Salisbury, North Carolina. The three men had worked together in the grocery business for some time at a small chain that was owned by the Ketners' father but had recently been sold to Winn-Dixie. Dissatisfied with their new employer, the Ketners and Smith set out to open their own chain of supermarkets. By calling on everyone they knew in Salisbury for a small investment, the trio slowly raised enough capital to begin operations. Although growth was sluggish for the first ten years or so, those early investors made out very well in the long run. After numerous stock splits, an initial investment of 100 shares, originally valued at $1,000, was worth more than $16 million by the end of 1987.

During Food Town's first decade, the company tried every kind of gimmick available to entice customers into its stores. Contests, free pancake breakfasts, trading stamps, beauty pageants, and a slew of other tricks captured shoppers' attention, but not their sustained business. By 1967, after a full decade of operations, Food Town had only seven stores, and earned less than $6 million that year.

In 1967 Ralph Ketner formulated the strategy that would launch Food Town's dramatic rise in the retail food industry. Ketner, the story goes, locked himself up in a Charlotte, North Carolina motel room with six months worth of invoices and an adding machine. When he emerged three days later, he had determined that prices could be slashed on 3,000 items, and, if sales volume increased by 50%, the company would still show a profit. Gambling that the reduced-price strategy would adequately expand its repeat-customer base, Food Town implemented his plan. Ketner later remarked, "One thing about taking a gamble: when you're already broke you can't do much damage." Soon the company adopted an unusual new slogan: "LFPINC," which stood for "Lowest Food Prices In North Carolina," and shifted its advertising emphasis from print to television. Ketner's gamble was a winner: increased volume soon more than made up for the price reductions.

The 1970s were a period of tremendous growth for the company. By 1971, sales were nearly $37 million. Although it occasionally snapped up a particularly appetizing acquisition, Food Town preferred to build its chain from within. The company tended to construct more smaller stores rather than fewer larger ones in order to provide greater convenience. In 1974 the second-largest Belgian supermarket chain, Delhaize Freres & Cie, "Le Lion," purchased a majority of Food Town's shares. Delhaize "Le Lion" signed an agreement to vote with Chairman Ralph Ketner for ten years on all policy issues. The company's growth accelerated dramatically in the late 1970s and the 1980s. Food Town opened stores in Virginia in 1978 and in Georgia in 1981. In 1977 the chain operated 55 stores; by 1987, it ran 475.

In 1982, Food Town was sued by the owner of several supermarkets in Virginia which operated under the name Foodtown. The court restricted the use of Food Town's name in certain markets due to the similarity. As a result of this action and in anticipation of similar problems with another group of stores in Tennessee, the chain decided to change its name. The new name, Food Lion, was selected partly because the Belgian chain Delhaize had a lion logo, but also because the chain could save money in changing the signs on its stores: only two new letters, an "L" and an "I," needed to be purchased since the "O" and the "N" could be shifted over. This type of frugality was characteristic of the chain. In 1983, Food Lion carried its new banner into Tennessee as sales surpassed the $1 billion mark.

In the summer of 1984, the National Association for the Advancement of Colored People (NAACP) organized a boycott of Food Lion stores because the chain refused to sign a "fair share" agreement to raise the number of blacks in management, increase minority employment, and pledge to do business with minority-owned vendors and construction firms. The NAACP moved its annual board meeting from New York to Charlotte, North Carolina to attract attention to its protest. The boycott ended in September when Food Lion signed an agreement with the NAACP to increase minority opportunities with the company.

Food Lion branched into Maryland in 1984. Early in

1985, the company acquired Giant Food Markets Inc. of Kingport, Tennessee. It soon sold the 22 Jiffy Convenience Stores that came with the Giant deal, sticking to what it did best—the conventional supermarket trade.

In January, 1986, Tom Smith became CEO of Food Lion, replacing Ralph Ketner, who remained chairman. Smith, who had once worked as a bagger for a Food Town store, returned to the company in 1971 as a buyer, and became president and chief operating officer in 1980. Smith steered Food Lion on the same course as Ketner had, stressing low prices and efficient service. The company topped the $2 billion sales mark at the end of Smith's first year as CEO.

By the late 1980s, Food Lion had become the dominant force in the regions in which it did business. Stunning earnings and market share encouraged the chain's further expansion. In 1987 Food Lion prepared to extend its territory into Florida. Food Lion saw Florida's increasing population and the relatively high prices of chains already in the area, like Winn-Dixie and Publix, as an excellent opportunity for expansion. The chain planned to double its number of outlets by first tapping Florida's shoppers, then possibly moving westward through Alabama, Mississippi, and Louisiana. After nine months of market-softening advertising proclaiming "when we save, you save," three Food Lion stores opened in Jacksonville, Florida. The response was phenomenal; security guards had to be hired to help people line up at cash registers. By the end of the year, Food Lion had plans for 20 more stores and a one-million-square-foot distribution center to be built in nearby Green Cove Springs. That facility positioned Food Lion for eventual entry into other Florida markets like Tallahassee, Tampa, and Melbourne.

Since Ralph Ketner formulated Food Lion's everyday low-price strategy in 1967, the company has stressed doing "1,000 things 1% better," an attitude that has been responsible for Food Lion's operating expenses of only 13% of sales, compared to a 21% average in the industry. Food Lion has cut costs in a variety of inventive ways: recycling banana boxes to ship cosmetics and health products and using exhaust from freezer motors to help heat the store in the winter, for example. Food Lion also uses aggressive inventory strategies, ordering enormous quantities of products in order to save through volume buying.

By the end of the 1980s, Food Lion was the fastest growing and one of the most profitable supermarket chains in the country. In an industry that is often considered stagnant, Food Lion has found new ways to improve its market penetration and share and held to the philosophy of making "five fast pennies rather than one slow nickel." It is an attitude has paid off handsomely over the years, and promises to do so in the future.

Principal Subsidiary: Save-Rite, Inc.

THE GATEWAY CORPORATION LTD.

Stockley House
130 Wilton Road
London SW1V 1LU
United Kingdom
(01) 233-5353

Private Company
Incorporated: 1974 as Linfood Holdings Ltd.
Employees: 50,000
Sales: £3.7 billion (US$6.69 billion)

It is an indication of the frantic activity in British retailing during the 1980s that the Gateway Corporation has had three names during that period: Linfood Holdings, Dee Corporation, and Gateway itself. Now Gateway has been acquired by Isosceles PLC, a company formed specifically for the purpose of making the acquisition. This nominal uncertainty reflects the extraordinary speed with which Alec Monk, managing director from 1981 until 1989, built a company which at its zenith was England's third-largest retailer of groceries and employed some 85,000 people. But the company soon fell victim to the dangers of rapid expansion and suffered a hostile takeover by a group of investors. Even in the dizzy world of corporate mergers Monk's rise and fall was exceptionally abrupt.

Alec Monk was born in Wales in 1942, the son of a baker. After earning a degree at Oxford, he worked for Esso and then spent a number of years at Rio Tinto-Zinc (RTZ), a mining company, where he became a member of the board of directors at age 31. Apparently frustrated at RTZ, in 1977 Monk moved to New York and took a position with AEA Investors, a prestigious investment firm. After four years with AEA as a specialist in buying and selling of mid-size corporations, Monk was offered a post as managing director at Linfood Holdings Ltd., a British food wholesaler doing about £1 billion a year in sales. Monk admitted that before the offer he had never heard of Linfood, but he took the job and immediately began to shake things up.

Linfood was the result of a 1974 merger between Associated Food Holdings Ltd. and Thomas Linnell & Company Ltd. When Monk arrived in 1981, he decisively reoriented corporate growth in the direction of retailing, eventually restricting wholesale activity to the cash-and-carry supply of independent grocers and caterers. Linfood had acquired a number of Carrefour retail superstores in 1978, and with these as a base Monk began to build his grocery empire. From the start, his reign was marked by continual corporate skirmishing, as Linfood bought one rival chain after another or was itself the object of takeover attempts. Just weeks after Monk had joined his new company, Linfood escaped the clutches of the aggressive James Gulliver when Gulliver's £87 million hostile bid failed to gain approval from the Monopolies and Mergers Commission.

Having survived this early battle, Monk began his own campaign of acquisitions. In 1983 Monk merged Dee supermarkets, which had been acquired by Associated Food Holdings in 1970, with Gateway Foodmarkets, which had been acquired by Linfood in 1977. Monk used Dee as the new name for his corporation. In June, 1983 Dee snapped up the 98 Key Markets, topping Safeway's bid with a £45 million offer, and in 1984 followed up with the purchase of 41 Lennon's stores for £25 million. At the end of that year, Monk and Dee made a quantum leap with the acquisition, for £180 million, of BAT's 380 International stores. For the financial period ending in April, 1985, Dee had amassed sales of £2.43 billion and profits of £64 million, making Monk one of the London financial world's most celebrated stars.

The Dee collection of stores included many small, older markets located primarily on the "high street"—that is, near the center of urban concentrations—as well as a growing number of supermarkets and a sprinkling of superstores (stores larger than 25,000 square feet and including nonfood items). By unifying many regional corporations into one organization, Monk was able to eliminate management positions, benefit from economies of scale in advertising and food distribution, and cut better deals with his wholesale suppliers. With each new acquisition, Dee gained not only additional clout in the marketplace but also the particular expertise of each chain, as one group might have specialized in fresh produce, while another had made a name for its meat departments.

As Dee grew in size, its profits grew proportionately, and it appeared to those in the investment business that Monk might expand his retailing success indefinitely. When, in 1985, no further targets were available in the British food retailing sector, Monk decided to establish a U.S. base with the purchase of Herman's, the largest retailer of sporting goods in America. With 130 stores and a reputation for skilled management, Herman's seemed a good bet; but in retrospect the acquisition proved to be the beginning of the end for Monk and the Dee Corporation.

Like other tacticians before him, Monk had spread his forces too thin, and he compounded the error a few months later when he bought a very large and complex chain of 419 Fine Fare supermarkets. At the time—early 1986—both moves were generally praised, but a series of apparently unimportant events soon combined to thwart Monk's plans. First of all, both the Herman's deal and the

£686 million Fine Fare purchase were financed by means of "vendor placings," in which new shares in a company are sold without first being offered to existing shareholders on a pro-rated basis. This technique, common in America, was new to Britain, and it inevitably angered the institutional investors who held large blocks of Dee stock. Their displeasure became an important, although subtle, drag on the price of Dee shares at a time when Monk was most in need of investor faith in his ambitious plans. The institutional managers felt abused by Monk, and their resentment seemed to color their assessment of his company's prospects.

Those prospects, however, no longer looked quite as outstanding from any angle. Monk's efforts to make Herman's into a nationwide sporting goods chain were a disaster from the beginning. As the chain expanded into new parts of the country it could not keep its shelves stocked efficiently, and when it did have merchandise, it was often poorly suited to varying local tastes. Whiles sales went up, profits did not, and Monk soon found that he had transformed a well run regional chain into a national mess.

Much more significant were the problems at Fine Fare, the chain which had boosted Dee into third place among British food retailers by sales (and largest in terms of square footage), but which proved to be much more difficult to integrate and streamline than Monk's earlier purchases. As it turned out, Fine Fare's stores were not in the excellent condition Monk had expected them to be, but suffered from deteriorated physical settings and widespread pilferage. In addition, Fine Fare's wide range of store formats, from vast suburban "hypermarkets" to hole-in-the-wall city locations, only added to Dee's already complex distribution and administrative problems. Converting all of these stores to Gateway's logo, accounting system, and corporate standards proved to be more difficult than Monk had envisioned, or at least more costly than investors were willing to pay for.

For the year ending in April, 1987, Dee's first after the big mergers, the company was expected to earn around £230 million on sales of £4.8 billion; when the figure came in at £192 million many already-disenchanted analysts said that Monk had gone too far too fast. As a result, Dee's stock price faltered, drifting sideways while the market as a whole was booming along at a 45% faster clip. For the year and a half following the Herman's purchase, Dee's stock was dead last on the *Financial Times*' list of the 100 leading companies in Great Britain. Monk defended the prudence of his moves, noting that he had predicted all along that it would take three years for Dee to assimilate its new acquisitions fully, which by 1987 also included the country's fourth-largest drug chain, Medicare, and two more American sporting-goods outfits. He asked for patience and a little faith, two commodities always hard to buy on the world's stock exchanges. Monk might have come through the crisis if Dee's first half result for 1987–1988 had been outstanding. They proved to be the worst blow yet: the £64 million total announced in the fall of 1987 was 18% below the previous year's midterm figure, and rumors of a takeover immediately began to circulate through the City. When the October 19, 1987 crash ruined the Christmas selling season for Herman's, it was only an appropriate conclusion to Dee's dismal year.

Even the stock crash could not prevent the beginning of a prolonged and bitter bidding war for what was now characterized as an overly diversified, poorly managed conglomerate. In December of 1987, a British confectionery company called Barker & Dobson (B&D) offered Dee shareholders the equivalent of about £2 billion for their stock, charging Monk with incompetence and promising to sell off unprofitable parts of the Dee network. Monk fought back vigorously, however, spending millions of pounds in defense of his company and its future prospects. Second half profits for the fiscal year ending April, 1988 were substantially better, cutting the total annual decline to only 3%, and the chairman could point to the company's remarkable growth and the profits to be realized when all of its stores had organized themselves under the Gateway banner. When the votes were counted in the spring of 1988, Monk had won the battle easily and Dee appeared safe for the time being.

The grace period was short. Although Monk took steps to correct some of the problems Barker & Dobson had harped on, selling, for example, Dee's Spanish distributing business and the original Linfood wholesaling subsidiary, it was only a year later that the second wave of predators made its attack. Dee had changed its name in the summer of 1988 to Gateway Corporation, emphasizing its commitment to the retailing end of its business, but to David Smith it was still the same bloated, underpriced temptation. Smith had been a financial advisor to B&D during its unsuccessful bid, and, backed by a variety of large investors, including the British investment bank S.G. Warburg, he launched his own strike, under the name Isosceles PLC, in April, 1989. After intense competition from a number of other bidders, including a company called Newgateway PLC, put together by the Great Atlantic & Pacific Tea Company and dealmaker Wasserstein Perella & Company, two U.S. companies—Isosceles emerged the winner in July of that year, buying up a bare majority of the stock to force out Monk and his board of directors.

Smith wasted no time implementing the policy B&D had urged two years before, selling off 61 of Gateway's largest superstores to the Asda Group and repositioning the company as an operator of mostly mid-size, high street retail outlets. Gateway will no longer try to compete with the big out-of-town and edge-of-town grocers, but will fill the somewhat smaller niche left in-town by the emergence of the suburban superstore. It will almost certainly sell Herman's and its other nonfood holdings, concentrating wholly on developing its rather delicate market position in groceries.

The Gateway takeover, however, was not altogether successful. In December, 1989 Isosceles launched an offering to help unload some of its US$2.1 billion in debt, but was unable to find buyers, and its 16 underwriters were left holding US$848 million more in paper than they had expected. Isosceles itself must now settle down to cope with the difficulties of consolidating Gateway's operations.

Principal Subsidiaries: Carrefour Ltd.; F.A. Wellworth and Company Ltd. (Northern Ireland); Gateway Foodmarkets Ltd.; International Stores Ltd.; International Stores Properties Ltd.; Lennons Group Ltd.; Herman's Sporting Goods, Inc. (U.S.A.); Gateway Properties Ltd.; Fine Fare Ltd.; Wellworth Properties Ltd. (Northern Ireland); Fine Fare Properties Ltd.; Elder Gate Property Co. (C.B.) Ltd.

Weston

GEORGE WESTON LIMITED

22 St. Clair Avenue East, Suite 1901
Toronto, Ontario M4T 2S7
Canada
(416) 922–2500

Public Company
Incorporated: 1928
Employees: 67,300
Sales: C$10.8 billion (US$9.05 billion)
Stock Index: Toronto Montreal Vancouver

George Weston Limited, a diversified food processor and distributor, carries the name of the baker's apprentice who started this family-run business in 1882 with two bread routes. It has since grown, mainly by acquisition, to become one of the largest companies in Canada.

George Weston's early success selling bread led to a rapid increase in the number of routes he managed, and soon encouraged him to establish a bread and cake bakery in Toronto, in 1897. At George Weston's death in 1924 his son Garfield Weston took over a growing business. In 1928 he incorporated George Weston Ltd.

Under Garfield's leadership, the firm built its bread and biscuit businesses in Canada and the United States. Weathering the Depression without major problems, the company was able to take advantage of its position as a low-cost producer to overtake other competitors in the baking industry. Its 1938 acquisitions of the Inter-City Western Bakeries, Ltd. and the Associated Biscuit Company, for example, provided Weston with the facilities and resources to produce 370 varieties of candy and 100 types of biscuits, in addition to its breads and cakes.

Despite World War II, expansion continued smoothly throughout the 1940s. In 1944 the company bought the Southern Biscuit Company, and the acquisition of Western Grocers marked the firm's initial entry into food distribution. This growth was strengthened by purchases of the Edmonton City Bakery in 1945 and Dietrich's Bakeries in 1946. After the war, the company acquired William Neilson, a major Canadian producer of chocolate, cocoa, milk, and dairy specialty products. In the 1980s Neilson acquired licenses to produce Haagen-Dazs ice cream and Danone yogurt in Canada. This subsidiary's 1987 acquisition of the confectionery operations of Cadbury Schweppes Canada Inc. gave Weston a commanding one-third share of the Canadian chocolate bar market and made it Canada's largest chocolate manufacturer.

During the 1940s and early 1950s, Weston began buying shares of Loblaw Groceterias, a food distributor, as part of a strategy designed to reach consumers directly with its products. By 1953, the firm had acquired a majority interest in Loblaw, a position that made possible Loblaw's subsequent acquisitions of other food distributors across Canada and the midwestern United States, including National Grocers of Ontario in 1955; National Tea, a U.S.–based retailer, in 1956; Kelly, Douglas and Company, a British Columbia wholesaler, in 1958; the Maritime-based Atlantic Wholesalers in 1960; and the Zehrmart supermarket chain in 1963.

During the 1960s the company pursued further diversification in an attempt to improve its value to shareholders by expanding into the natural resources area. Weston bought Eddy Paper Company in 1962, and five years later, British Columbia Packers, a salmon processor, and Connors Brothers, the largest herring and sardine processor in Canada.

Growth was temporarily curtailed in the 1970s as management focused on reorganizing the company's activities and operations to achieve greater control and efficiency. W. Galen Weston, one of Garfield's sons, had become president in 1970, and the firm began to refocus on food as its primary area of emphasis. By the next decade, Weston had successfully consolidated its many businesses into three major groups which manage daily operations autonomously within the framework of defined corporate goals and objectives.

Weston Foods Ltd., the food processing group, was formed in 1986. Its operations include baking and milling, biscuits, chocolate, dairy, and specialty products, providing food and ingredients both to intermediate processors and directly to consumers all over North America. This group employs more than 12,000 workers and accounts for 11% of the company's total sales.

The food processing group includes Weston Bakeries, Canada's largest baker of fresh bread, buns, and cake products (distributed under a variety of brands and private labels), Neilson/Cadbury, and the Stroehmann Bakeries. Stroehmann was acquired in 1980 and today is one of the largest wholesale baked goods producers in the northeastern United States. Another member of the food processing group is the Interbake Foods specialty biscuit division, which consists of the cookie and cracker businesses acquired between 1928 and 1960, including the Southern Biscuit Company, the focus of operations in the United States. This group also includes the Soo Line Mills and McCarthy Milling, which manufacture and distribute various types of flour inside Canada and abroad, and Bowes Company, a food specialties supplier.

Weston Resources, divided into two areas, accounts for 11% of Weston's total sales. Operations of the Forest Products division are handled primarily by the Ontario-based E.B. Eddy Forest Products, established in the mid-1800s. Today this company mills and processes pulp, lumber, and paper products for North American distribution. The Fisheries division, comprised of British

Columbia Packers and Connors Brothers, markets canned, fresh, frozen, and processed fish and herring products throughout the world.

Loblaw Companies, Weston's food distribution group, is the largest wholesale and retail food distributor in Canada, and has a sizeable retail business in the United States as well. Staffed by more than 46,000 employees and representing 78% of total company sales, the group's aim is to customize its stores to meet the needs of specific markets and to develop a large number of products under the private labels of "no name" and "President's Choice."

In 1986 Weston's National Tea subsidiary acquired 26 stores in St. Louis owned by the Kroger Company. Ten years earlier, however, National Tea had encountered serious financial problems in its food distribution area, forcing it to sell 75% of its supermarkets. This set the stage for a period of consolidation which lasted into the 1980s.

The firm also faced major labor problems in the early 1980s involving the unionized employees of its Super Valu stores in Manitoba. These difficulties resulted from Weston's aggressive penetration of the Winnipeg retail food market. In order to convert its existing Loblaw stores in the area to larger-scale supermarkets and hire away experienced employees from other retailers, Weston offered to recognize the Manitoba Food and Commercial Workers Union and to match its current contract with Safeway Foods in return for a six-year, no-strike, no lock-out agreement which effectively eliminated the union's contract negotiation rights. Shortly after consummating this arrangement, Super Valu was accused by its employees of violating a number of contract provisions related to seniority, scheduling, and full-time employment, but a compromise was eventually worked out.

Today, George Weston is a dominant force in its three business segments. Guided by a corporate philosophy that positions the company as a low-cost supplier of superior products, the firm continues to be managed by Galen Weston, who assumed the additional position of chairman in the mid-1970s. Galen Weston has earned a reputation as a turnaround specialist and expert retailer. He maintains a very private lifestyle, particularly after a foiled kidnap attempt by the Irish Republican Army in 1983.

In recent years the company has slowed its growth in favor of improving the profitability of its current activities. Loblaw Companies is once again focusing on consolidation and on maximizing the returns on its recent investments in capital improvements and new stores. Strict control of capital, material, and labor costs will be required for Weston Resources to improve productivity and overcome the business risks involved in matching unpredictable supplies with the peaks and valleys of customer demand. The group's formation of a salmon farming operation and its entry into additional foreign markets should provide major opportunities.

George Weston faces many challenges in the years ahead, as political, social, and regulatory changes occur both domestically and abroad. Although each of its groups of businesses operates independently, they share the need to balance new growth with selective upgrading or divestiture in response to changing conditions.

With a renewed emphasis on product superiority and low-cost production, Weston is positioned to remain a leader in its industry.

Principal Subsidiaries: Weston Bakeries Ltd.; Stroehmann Bakeries, Inc.; Soo Line Mills Ltd.; McCarthy Milling Ltd.; Interbake Foods Inc. (U.S.); William Neilson Ltd.; Cadbury Canada Marketing Inc.; Bowes Co. Ltd.; Atlantic Wholesalers Ltd.; IPCF Properties Inc.; Loblaws Supermarkets Ltd.; National Grocers Co. Ltd.; Zehrmart Ltd.; Kelly, Douglas & Co. Ltd.; Westfair Foods Ltd.; National Tea Co. (U.S.); E.B. Eddy Forest Products Ltd.; E.B. Eddy Paper, Inc.; British Columbia Packers Ltd.; Nelbro Packing Company Ltd.; Connors Bros., Ltd.; Connors Seafoods Ltd.; Connors Bros., Inc.; Port Clyde Canning Co.

GIANT FOOD INC.

6300 Sheriff Road
Landover, Maryland 20785
U.S.A.
(301) 341–4100

Public Company
Incorporated: 1935 as Giant Food Shopping Center Inc.
Employees: 26,000
Sales: $2.9 billion
Stock Index: American Pacific Philadelphia

From its Depression-era beginnings as Giant Food Shopping Center Inc., Giant Food has become a large, vertically integrated regional supermarket and pharmacy chain. Directly and through its 14 subsidiaries, Giant operates 148 retail food and drug stores in the Washington, D.C. and Baltimore, Maryland metropolitan areas. Its stores are large (average size is 55,000 square feet), and focus on providing its customers with quality, value, and service. Giant dominates its market area with 47% of the Washington market and 25% of the Baltimore market. Over the years it has been innovative in its approach to selling in the food industry and willing to take risks in developing a high-quality supermarket chain in a diverse urban market. To achieve its position as one of the largest food retailers in the United States, Giant has been aggressive in its marketing strategies and successful at spotting coming trends and implementing changes that keep it ahead of its competition.

Starting a new business during the Depression was a risk for Giant's founder, Nehemiah Myer (N. M.) Cohen, but he had been watching the progress of the "supermarkets" that had begun to open in the early 1930s and felt that they were the business of the future. Cohen, a rabbi, had immigrated from Palestine after World War I and settled in Carnegie, Pennsylvania, where he soon opened a kosher meat market. He later moved to Lancaster, Pennsylvania and eventually opened three butcher shops there. To open his first supermarket Cohen sought the help of food distributor Samuel Lehrman, who provided the financial backing. Lehrman's son Jacob was also a partner in the venture. They chose Washington, D.C. as their location, figuring that government employment would keep the economy there stable. Giant Food Shopping Center opened its doors in early 1936 as Washington's first mass-merchandised supermarket. Amid the unemployment and breadlines that followed the 1929 stock market crash, Giant Food made its impact on the community by introducing both self-service and one-stop shopping to the consumer. Coupled with its lower prices, these features kept the store busy and crowded from its opening days.

By 1939 Giant had expanded to three stores. Giant's fourth store had a brick-and-glass facade that spelled out its name and was lighted at night, an innovation at the time. Just as the United States entered World War II, Giant opened its sixth store, in Arlington, Virginia, the first outside of the District of Columbia.

The war had a detrimental effect on the supermarket industry as personnel shortages, product shortages, and rationing became prevalent. Giant, like many other businesses, began employing women to counter the manpower shortage, and female checkers soon became a permanent part of the American grocery store.

Giant stopped expanding during the war, but in 1945 it opened two new stores in Washington and one in Virginia. In the late 1940s, Giant began to move toward vertical integration, leasing a slaughterhouse to ship meat to all its stores. In 1948 Giant bought the Sheridan Bakery, which had been supplying baked goods to the chain. Renamed for Jacob Lehrman's daughter, Heidi Bakery has continuously provided bread and baked goods for all Giant stores both from the original bakery location in Silver Spring, Maryland and from the in-store bakeries developed in later years. (In 1965 the bakery baked a 700-pound cake for President Lyndon Johnson's Inaugural Ball.) In 1952 Giant opened the Giant Retail Bakery in downtown Washington to sell only bakery goods, but this venture was not successful and was closed within a few years. By 1949 Giant had 19 stores, including three in Maryland and three in Virginia.

Between 1950 and 1952, Giant added five new stores, joining in the general expansion of the American economy. At this time, the shopping center concept was taking hold in America and Giant put a new store in the Congressional Plaza Shopping Center in Rockville, Maryland. In 1955 Giant Construction Company was incorporated to build Giant stores. Giant Food Properties, an independent company which eventually came under the control of Giant and is now known as GFS Realty Inc., was established to handle the sale and lease of real estate for the company.

In 1955 the chain opened its first store in Baltimore and in 1956, its first in the Richmond, Virginia market. By this time 48% of all its stores were located in shopping centers. In 1958, riding a new merchandising trend of combination supermarket/department/discount stores, Giant opened its first Super Giant store and within a year had opened eight more. Also in 1958 the company opened its new headquarters and distribution center on a 40-acre site in Landover, Maryland. At the same time, an addition to the Heidi Bakery doubled its production capacity.

In 1957, Giant Food Shopping Center Inc. became Giant Food Inc., and fiscal 1958 saw sales of more than $100 million dollars. In 1959 the company, with 53 stores (including nine Super Giants) went public.

During this time Giant computerized its inventory data, customer information, and payroll and bookkeeping operations. Customer service features added in the 1950s included self-opening doors, mechanized checkouts, and open display cases to make meats and frozen food directly accessible to the customer.

In the 1950s, Giant initiated a scholarship program to encourage students to pursue food management careers. Two of the first five recipients are now senior vice presidents at Giant. This scholarship program is only one of the ways in which Giant has contributed to the community over the years. In the aftermath of the racial unrest of the 1960s, Giant took a leading role in providing food for those made homeless by riots. Giant's then-president Joseph B. Danzansky also directed a food drive, in which local and national businesses supplied food for demonstrators camped in "Resurrection City" in Washington during a two-week protest to call attention to the poor in America.

In 1961 Giant's stock began trading on the American Stock Exchange as well as the Washington branch of the Philadelphia-Baltimore Stock Exchange. In its stores, Giant began developing its private-label products and offering plastic housewares and specialty food items in response to customer demands. Giant built its first combination food store and pharmacy in 1962.

Although the company has been criticized for bypassing predominantly black neighborhoods, by the mid-1960s Giant did begin to open stores in the inner city. In the rioting that followed the assassination of Martin Luther King Jr. in 1968, store managers and black employees faced down angry mobs at Giant stores, and the chain escaped much of the looting and damage of the period.

Giant's management implemented three policies during this time which were designed to decrease employee turnover. It began recognizing talented young workers (age 25 and under) and giving them increased management responsibility—the company dedicated itself to promoting from within—and an employee tuition-assistance program was started.

In 1964, founder N. M. Cohen stepped down as president and became chairman of the board, a newly created position. Joseph Danzansky, longtime legal counsel, became president. This election touched off a legal battle for control of Giant between the Cohen family and Jacob Lehrman. The Cohens gained operating control of the company, but Lehrman remained on the board of directors. In 1977, N. M. Cohen was made honorary chairman of the board, Danzansky became chairman, and N. M.'s son Israel became president and CEO. Izzy, as he is known, had been in the business since he was a delivery boy in his father's butcher shops before the days of Giant Food. He continued his father's informal and friendly, but strict, management style.

The 1970s were the "decade of the consumer"; Giant responded to this movement by hiring its own consumer advocate, Esther Peterson, formerly a consumer adviser to the Kennedy and Johnson administrations. The company began a program of providing information to consumers about the food they were buying, and also worked with the Food and Drug Administration to develop and test nutrition labeling. Educational and informational brochures were distributed for free, and unit pricing and open dating were implemented. In 1972 Giant opened its Quality Assurance Laboratory to monitor the quality and safety of the food it sold, and in 1974 the company implemented a toy-safety program by pledging to sell only those toys certified safe by the manufacturer.

In another move toward vertical integration, Giant built a warehouse and grocery-distribution center in Jessup, Maryland. The Jessup center opened in 1973 and was a model of automated operations. Danzansky described it in 1974 to *Nation's Business* as "a Buck Rogers kind of thing. Push a button and the stuff almost jumps on the truck."

In the early 1970s Giant sold its four freestanding Super Giant stores to Woolco and rededicated itself to food retailing. In the inflationary period of the middle 1970s, Giant began discounting its prices, gambling that increased volume would counterbalance lower prices. In fiscal 1979 the company had its first billion-dollar year.

In 1975, Giant began using computer-assisted checkout and in 1979 it installed price-scanning equipment in all of its stores. While Giant was making supermarket history by implementing scanners, consumer activists and legislators in Washington accused the company of using the scanning system to trick unwary customers into paying higher prices since prices were posted only on shelves, not each item. Giant weathered the storm of protests and proved with its data that the system reduced operating costs.

Giant Food in the 1980s continued both expansion and vertical integration to hold and build its place in its market. In 1982 it opened Someplace Special in McLean, Virginia, a gourmet food store that sells specialty items and offers services such as menu planning, flower arranging, delivery service, and catering for its affluent customers. While not its most profitable store, Giant has used Someplace Special to test consumer demand for gourmet food and other specialty items. The chain also experimented with warehouse-type stores, opening three under the name Save Right; these now operate under the Giant name. In 1982, Giant closed its Richmond, Virginia stores after 25 years of operating in that city. By mid-1980s about half of Giant's stores were food and pharmacy combinations. In the 1970s Giant had created Pants Corral stores in its Super Giants as part of a deal to sell Levi's jeans. The Pants Corral division, which also included 30 free-standing stores, was sold in 1985.

Expansion at Giant in the 1980s included increasing store size; in 1983 it opened a 60,000-square-foot store in a former Super Giant. This flagship store stocked some 40,000 items and combined such features as gourmet food, cosmetics, in-store bakery, salad bar, and bulk food items. Vertical integration continued with the opening of an ice cream plant and a soda-bottling plant in 1985. Giant has also focused on remodeling and redesigning existing stores in the late 1980s.

Consumer-oriented programs have continued to be a part of Giant's service. Giant initiated a point-of-purchase "special diet alert" shelf label to increase customer awareness of low-fat, low-calorie, and low-sodium foods. Sales of these items were monitored for two years and data supplied to the United States Food and Drug Administration for use in measuring the effectiveness of such shelf-labeling programs. Giant also participated in an "Eat for Health" campaign with the National Cancer Institute. Bulk food bins, which allow customers to buy the amount they want, and increased availability of specialty food items are offered in response to consumer input, and Giant operates a corporate customer service center to handle questions, concerns, and compliments from both customers and employees.

Giant is located in a market area that is highly transient. The company feels that it must give customers exceptional service to draw them to Giant instead of the familiar national chains. Giant's approach to its "associates," as employees are called, is an important part of achieving this high level of service. Good salaries, employee benefit programs, and intensive training have always been a part of the company's employment philosophy. Associates, many of whom are the second and third generation of their family to work with the company, are motivated through career-development programs, awards, and a company news magazine, started in the 1950s and produced on video in the 1980s.

Giant attributes its success to the principles on which it was founded, the personal philosophy of founder, N.M. Cohen. Cohen not only closely monitored his business to spot trends, but was the force behind the company's continuous emphasis on quality, value and service. Active in the company until he was 90, the elder Cohen died in 1984 at age 93.

Of the future, President Izzy Cohen said, "we've found our best mousetrap—the food/pharmacy combination, married to the gourmet features. We think that's the store of the 90s."

Principal Subsidiaries: Giant of D.C., Inc.; Giant of Maryland, Inc.; Giant of Virginia, Inc.; Giant of Salisbury, Inc.; Warex-Jessup, Inc.; Giant Construction Co., Inc.; GFS Realty, Inc.; Landover Wholesale Tobacco Corp.; Bursil, Inc.; LECO, Inc.

THE GREAT ATLANTIC & PACIFIC TEA COMPANY, INC.

2 Paragon Drive
Montvale, New Jersey 07645
U.S.A.
(201) 573-9700

Public Company
Incorporated: 1902
Employees: 92,000
Sales: $10.07 billion
Stock Index: New York

After a downward spiral that began more than 50 years ago, the Great Atlantic & Pacific Tea Company, better known as A&P, has so forcefully reestablished its foothold in the retail food market that industry analysts have described A&P's current fourth place among competitors as "one of the great success stores in U.S. food retailing." Once the undisputed leader in American supermarkets, A&P experienced management and legal difficulties beginning in the mid-1930s that nearly drove the company into bankruptcy. The company's turnaround began in 1979, when controlling interest of A&P was bought by the West German Tengelmann Group, which brought in James Wood, a noted turnaround manager, as the new CEO. During Wood's tenure, A&P has undergone a radical restructuring that has enabled the company to compete in a market in which both the competition and the consumer have changed drastically since A&P was founded in 1859.

In 1859, George Huntington Hartford and George Francis Gilman became partners. Using Gilman's connections as an established grocer and son of a wealthy ship owner, Hartford purchased coffee and tea from clipper ships on the waterfront docks of New York City. By eliminating middlemen, Hartford and Gilman were able to sell their wares at "cargo prices." The enterprise was so successful that in 1869 Hartford and Gilman opened a series of stores under the name Great American Tea Company. The first of these soon became a landmark on Vesey Street in New York City.

The company's appeal to the 19th-century consumer was enhanced by the lavish storefronts and Chinese-inspired interiors which Gilman designed: inside the Chinese paneled walls, cockatoos greeted customers, who brought their purchases to a pagoda-shaped cash desk. Outside, the red-and-gold storefronts were illuminated by dozens of gas lights that formed a giant "T," and on Saturdays customers were treated to the music of a live brass band.

Despite the company's extravagant trappings, its success was largely due to its innovative strategy of offering savings and incentives to the consumer. A&P's "club plan," which encouraged the formation of clubs to make bulk mail-order sales for an additional one-third discount, was so successful that by 1886 hundreds of such clubs had been formed. Pioneering the concept of private labels and house brands, the Great American Tea Company introduced its own inexpensive tea and coffee blends, continuing to direct its efforts at the price-conscious consumer. Today, A&P's "Eight O'Clock" blend remains a hallmark house brand.

In 1869 the company became the Great Atlantic and Pacific Tea Company, to commemorate the joining of the first transcontinental railroad and to separate its retail stores from its mail-order operations. A&P's gradual national expansion began shortly thereafter. The company established a foothold in the Midwest in the aftermath of the Chicago Fire of 1871, when A&P sent staff and food to help the devastated city, and stayed to open stores in the Midwest.

Careful thought and planning were given to A&P's expansion. New store openings were complemented by promotions and premiums. In the Midwest and the South, new stores gave away items such as crockery and lithographs in order to attract customers, and in other areas, garish "Teams of Eight" became legendary symbols of A&P. The brainchild of the flamboyant John Hartford, parades of teams of eight horses decorated with spangled harnesses and gold-plated bells drew red and gold vehicles through the towns; the person who best guessed the weight of the team was awarded $500 in gold.

In 1878, after Gilman's retirement, Hartford gained full control of the business. His two sons, George and John, were each apprenticed at the age of 16. Years later, a writer in the *Saturday Evening Post* observed that "in discussing the two brothers, tea company employees seldom get beyond the differences between the two." The older brother, who became known as Mr. George, earned a reputation as the "inside man" due to his concern for the books, and was considered to be the "conservative, bearish influence in the business." The younger, flamboyant Mr. John was described as an "old-school actor-manager." He was well-suited for his responsibility for promotions and premiums and generally ensured a "personal touch" in each of A&P's stores, which, by the turn of the century numbered 200 and generated more than $850 million in annual sales. Mr. John was also responsible for A&P peddlers, who by 1910 were carrying A&P products along 5,000 separate routes into rural areas in easily-recognized red-and-black A&P wagons.

Responding to a dramatic rise in the cost of living in the first decade of the 20th century, when food prices increased by 35%, Mr. John devised the first cash-and-carry A&P Economy Store. Initially dismissed by both George Jr. and George Sr., economy stores obviated the problem of capital depletion posed by premiums, credit, and delivery. The cash-and-carry stores followed a simple formula—$3,000 was allotted for equipment, groceries, and working capital. Only one man was needed to run an economy store, and he was expected to adhere strictly to Mr. John's "Manual For Managers of Economy Stores," which outlined, in meticulous detail, how to run the stores. Among other things, Mr. John insisted that all the stores have the same goods at the same location; A&P legend has it that Mr. John could find the beans in any of his stores—blindfolded.

When George Hartford Sr. died in 1917, George Jr. became chairman of A&P, while John became president. By 1925, A&P had 14,000 economy stores, with sales of $440 million, marking one of the greatest retail expansions ever. At this point, the company's national expansion was so far-reaching that A&P had to be divided into five geographical divisions to decentralize management.

During the 1920s, A&P continued to diversify, opening bakeries and pastry and candy shops. It also expanded its manufacturing facilities to produce its own Anne Page brand products, and set up a corporation to buy coffee directly from Colombia and Brazil. "Combination stores" added hitherto unheard-of meat counters to the grocery chain and, when lines at these counters became a problem, A&P devised a system to make prepackaged meats available to customers, who had never before been offered such a convenience. At the same time, A&P introduced food-testing laboratories to maintain quality standards in its manufactured products. When, in 1929, the stock market crashed, causing other retail companies to fold, merge, or sell out in the subsequent Depression, A&P was so firmly established and soundly managed that it was virtually unaffected. Responding to consumers' needs, A&P began publishing literature with money-saving tips and recipes. The public's reception of these publications prompted the company to begin publishing *Woman's Day* magazine in 1937, at two cents per issue.

The 1930s marked the advent of supermarkets in the United States. The Hartfords found the supermarket idea distasteful and were slow to respond to the trend. But as A&P began to lose market share, they were swayed. In 1938, supermarkets made up 5% of A&P's stores—and 23% of its business. By 1939, the total number of A&P stores had dropped to 9,100, of which 1,100 were supermarkets, and A&P's sales had regained the level they were at in 1930. But by this point, the company's size, though smaller than the 15,000 stores it had at its height in 1934, was a distinct liability. In 1936, the Robinson-Patman Act was passed, marking the beginning of the antitrust woes which shook A&P's hegemony. Anti-chain-store legislation, passed at the instigation of small independent grocers who claimed chains practiced unfair competition, imposed severe taxes and regulations on A&P and other chains, limiting pricing and other competitive advantages afforded to them by virtue of their size and purchasing power. Restrictions were based simply on store numbers, hitting A&P particularly hard. The company sought to redeem its damaged public image by publicizing its sense of corporate responsibility to consumers, producers, and employees. The loss of a suit in 1949, however, imposed limitations on A&P's purchasing practices that were more severe than any others in the industry. With this final blow, the company's position as an esteemed industry leader disintegrated.

In 1950 Ralph Burger, who had started at A&P in 1911 as an $11-a-week clerk, became president of the company. Much of A&P's early success had been due to Mr. George and Mr. John's scrupulous attention to the business, or, in Mr. John's term, to "the art of basketwatching." As the *Saturday Evening Post* article on the Hartfords had concluded in 1931, "who will watch the baskets after the Hartfords are gone? Neither has any children and although the ten grandchildren get their due shares of income from the family trust, the direct line of shrewd vigilance will be broken." Burger remained loyal to the Hartford brothers even after their deaths, John in 1951 and George in 1957. As president not only of A&P, but also of the Hartford Foundation, the charity to which the Hartfords had willed their A&P shares, Burger retained full control of A&P, running it, if not imaginatively, then at least reasonably successfully, until his death in 1969. At that point, despite its dusty image, A&P was still the grocery-industry leader, with sales of well over $5 billion a year—more than twice its closest competitor.

With the end of Burger's tenure, and the Hartford heirs' disinclination to enter business, A&P had no clear line of management succession. The "direct line of shrewd vigilance" was indeed broken, and management continued to change throughout the 1970s. The company's direction foundered so much that A&P, once an innovative industry leader, was no longer able even to follow the lead of its competitors. Failing to capitalize on suburban development and to accommodate changing consumer tastes, A&P's sales dropped and its reputation suffered serious injury. A&P's once "resplendent emporiums" were now perceived as antiquated, inefficient, and run-down.

In 1973, as A&P reported $51 million in losses and Safeway took its place as the largest food retailer in the country, Jonathan L. Scott was hired from Albertson's, marking the first time in history that A&P had looked outside its ranks for management. Scott's attempt to revive A&P by closing stores and cutting labor costs only resulted in more dissatisfied customers, and more losses. Finally, in 1979, the Tengelmann Group, a major West German retailer, bought 52.5% of A&P's stock.

The Tengelmann Group soon appointed James Wood, the former CEO of Grand Union, as chairman and CEO of A&P. Wood's reputation as a turnaround manager underwent a trial by fire, but his radical restructuring of the company—the chain was eventually reduced to 1,000 stores—was eventually lauded by analysts as "an outstanding success." By 1982, 600 stores had been closed, virtually all manufacturing facilities had been eliminated, management had won labor concessions in key markets, and the company had returned to profitability. With a formidable cash flow, Wood initiated an aggressive capital-spending program to rejuvenate the store base, develop new store formats, and make prudent acquisitions.

While some markets were abandoned, others were the focus of store recycling and expansion. High-growth areas (such as Phoenix, Arizona and southern California) were avoided in favor of markets in which A&P's presence was firmly established amidst a stable and slow-growing population (such as Philadelphia, New York, and Detroit). Concentrating efforts in the most promising areas of its six major operating regions—the Northeast, the New York metropolitan area, the mid-Atlantic states, the South, the Midwest, and Ontario—the company had the flexibility to tailor store formats, product mixes, service, and pricing to local customer bases.

Initially, tens of millions of dollars were spent to remodel and expand 85% of A&P's extant stores to give them a more up-to-date presentation, rid the company of its tarnished reputation, and add service departments to accommodate consumers' changed tastes. Improved sales allowed the company to begin to undertake new-store construction by 1985: the "new" A&P strives for an upscale, service-orientated image and caters to one-stop shoppers. Two new store formats address different market niches: Futurestores stress A&P's broad variety of quality products, and Sav-A-Centers take a strong promotional approach by offering warehouse prices.

Wood has also focused on growth through the purchase of regional chains, permitting A&P to establish itself as the top food retailer in certain regional markets without the risk and expense of building new facilities and establishing a market niche. With this strategy, A&P has firmly established itself as the fourth-largest U.S. grocery chain. Its 1986 Waldbaum and Shopwell/Food Emporium acquisitions combined to make A&P the market leader in the New York metropolitan area, where the company has its strongest presence, and its 1989 acquisition of Borman's, a Detroit-area chain, resulted in a majority share of the Detroit market. When market share is low and targeted chains resist acquisition, A&P retreats, as is evidenced by the company's diminishing presence in the South since its failure to acquire Delchamps, a chain based in Alabama.

Since its restructuring, operating income per store has more than doubled. Emphasizing high profit margin departments—full service delis, cheese shops, fresh seafood, and floral departments, for example—the company has departed radically from low-price generic product offerings. In 1988, Master Choice, a private-brand label of specialty chocolates, pastas, sauces, and herbal teas was introduced in order to compete with what industry experts consider the real competition: restaurants and fast-food chains.

In 1989 A&P made a bid for Gateway Corporation, the third-largest grocery chain in Britain. Gateway would have offered A&P a whole new arena for growth, one that is of considerable interest to Erivan Haub, Tengelmann's owner, who must shore up his European retailing empire in preparation for the unification of the common market in 1992. Although the Gateway bid ultimately failed, it is clear that, under Wood, who in 1989 renewed his contact through 1995, A&P is back in the first rank of food retailers.

Principal Subsidiaries: ANP Properties Corp.; ANP Sales Corp.; APW Supermarkets Corp. (Waldbaum, Inc.); Great Atlantic & Pacific Tea Co., Ltd. (Canada); Great Atlantic & Pacific Tea Co. of Canada, Ltd.; D/B/A A&P and New Dominion (A&P Drug Mart Ltd.; A&P Properties Ltd.; Jane Parker Bakery Ltd.); Compass Foods Inc.; Family Center, Inc.; Futuresome Food Markets, Inc.; Great Atlantic & Pacific Tea Co., Inc. (N.J.); Great Atlantic & Pacific Tea Co. of Vermont, Inc.; Kohl's Food Stores, Inc.; KwickSave, Inc.; Lo-Lo Discount Stores, Ind.; Richmond, Inc. D/B/A Pantry Pride & Sun, Inc.; St. Pancras Co. Limited; SAV-A-Centre, Inc.; Shopwell, Inc.; South Dakota Great Atlantic & Pacific Tea C., Inc.; Southern Development, Inc. of Delaware; Super Fresh Food Markets, Inc.; Super Fresh Food Markets of Maryland, Inc.; Super Fresh Food Markets of Virginia, Inc.' Super Plus Food Warehouse, Inc.; Supermarket Distributor Service Corp.; Supermarket Distributor Service Corp.—Florence, Inc.; Supermarket Distributor Services, Inc.; Supermarket Systems, Inc.; Supersaver, Inc.; Transco Service—Milwaukee, Inc.; 2008 Broadway, Inc.

Further Reading: Hoyt, Edwin P. *That Wonderful A&P!*, New York, Hawthorne Books, 1969; "Update: The Great Atlantic & Pacific Tea Co. 125th Anniversary Celebration," Great Atlantic & Pacific Tea Co., Summer 1984; Walsh, William I. *The Rise and Decline of The Great Atlantic and Pacific Tea Company*, Secaucus, New Jersey, L. Stuart, 1986.

ICA AB

Odengatan 69
Box 6187
S-102 33 Stockholm
Sweden
(46) 8 728 40 00

Public Company
Incorporated: 1917 as A.B. Hakon Swenson
Employees: 40,310
Sales: SKr 129 billion (US$21.09 billion)
Stock Index: Stockholm

The ICA logo dominates the Swedish grocery-retail industry. It is estimated that ICA outlets are patronized by about two-thirds of the nation's shoppers. In many rural or outlying areas the ICA store is the only outlet—functioning as a general store as well as order-taker for goods not ordinarily stocked. The ICA name is also found on urban and suburban supermarkets and hypermarkets and convenience stores. Underlying their services is a gigantic and complex support system.

In 1917, 34-year-old Hakon Swenson, a minister's son, pioneered what many colleagues called an impossible idea: a cooperative association of independent merchants competing for the same business. He had a strong entrepreneurial spirit and nearly twenty years of business experience behind him. He had worked for a wholesaler for seven years, progressing from messenger to purchasing agent, salesman, and manager. He then left to start his own business, a cigar factory. A change in the tobacco market caused him to close it ten years later, in 1915, but from this experience Swenson recognized that there were economies of scale, efficiencies in deliveries and distribution, and other benefits to be realized from pooling resources with similar firms—benefits that could not easily be obtained by the operator of a small business alone.

Swenson next went to work for a retailer, Manne Tossbergs Eftr., where his experience and talent for business brought him success. Within two years he had enough capital to buy a small but well-established retail business of his own. He opened A.B. Hakon Swenson December 1, 1917. A month later he opened a second store in another town, and on April 1, 1918, he opened one in a third town nearby.

As his ideas proved more and more successful, his contemporaries began to seek his advice on launching their own businesses. Some had worked with him previously and had become enthusiastic about his approach to solving the problems of the small, local entrepreneur. Svenson helped each one get a start in a business of his own, and gradually his idea for a cooperative association of friendly competitors took shape. A group of retailers met to compare notes on problems and opportunities, work out solutions, and improve their service to their respective communities, which were clustered in central Sweden.

By 1923 this group had contributed enough to a mutual fund to build and operate a shared distribution center at Västerås, site of the cooperative association's headquarters. Sharing the cost of shipments to the center made a substantial difference in the cost of doing business in that area, and the group continued to prosper. Swenson studied modern warehousing operations in other parts of Europe and the United States, and continued to provide the kind of leadership to the association that enabled each member's business to progress, which in turn attracted new members.

In the early 1930s, as the effects of the Depression began to erode other types of business, the cooperative association's members still found themselves on firm financial footing since the economies accomplished by working together made it possible to keep prices down.

The number of members grew, spreading out over a wide geographical area, and new distribution centers were built. In 1938, A.B. ICA was formed.

In the early 1940s, there was some pressure from the government to react to wartime shortages by having ICA build its own mill and a margarine factory, but Swenson vetoed the idea. He preferred to concentrate the organization's efforts on expanding the business it had built rather than starting a manufacturing division.

At that point, ICA existed on two levels: the retail stores, independently owned and operated; and the cooperative association, owned jointly by the stores. (ICA retailers agree to purchase 80% of their stock from the cooperative association's wares.) Many of the stores, especially in remote areas, were operated by a husband and wife, and, in some cases, the entire family. As time passed, new generations of the same families took over the operation of the stores.

As the business grew, however, ICA's structure became more complex. Some of the independent stores formed joint ventures with the association, and four main regional centers were established. ICA Hakon A.B., the original distribution center, is based in Västerås and serves central and northern Sweden; ICA Eol A.B., based in Göteborg, serves the South; ICA Essve A.B., based in Stockholm, serves the Southeast; and ICA A.B., which began the organization's flourishing import business following World War II, is based in Stockholm and performs administrative functions. Each one of the distribution centers eventually became a separate company within the organization, creating new distribution centers within its area of operation as business grew.

In 1948, ICA Frukt och Grönsaker A.B. was established in southern Sweden to buy and distribute fruit and vegetables for domestic and international markets. In 1949 ICA acquired Hjalmar Blomqvist A.B. to supply member stores and boutiques with glassware and china; it is Sweden's major supplier of dinnerware. In 1950, ICA bought Svea Choklad A.B., a producer of sweets. That same year, to keep employees and independent retailers informed and in communication with each other, ICA added a publishing arm to print and distribute an in-house newsletter. From that beginning grew one of Sweden's largest publishing operations, ICA-förlaget A.B., which today produces weekly newspapers, trade and consumer periodicals, and books; it also operates a book club.

During the 1950s, consumers' buying habits in urban and suburban areas began to change radically. These changes led to the substitution of self-service facilities for traditional service counters in many of the stores, and sent suppliers scrambling to international markets to meet the new demand for a variety of food choices.

New stores built during the 1950s and the 1960s were usually supermarkets or hypermarkets. These larger stores began to carry a greater number of nonfood household items as well as a wider range of foodstuffs. New stores were typically owned by the association at first, allowing the proprietor to buy it gradually, so that the store could get off to a profitable start without consuming an inordinate amount of the owner's capital.

Hakon Swenson died in 1960, having overseen the creation of a network of retail and wholesale companies that became the largest in the nation. Succeeding administrators of ICA have continued in general to follow his policies and principles.

In 1967 ICA Rosteri A.B. began producing and marketing coffee and importing some from Latin America and Africa. In 1969, ICA Banan A.B. began importing bananas from Central America and ripening them in plants in central and southern Sweden.

ICA purchased Ringköpkedjan, a competing retail food chain, in 1982, and the following year the association purchased and installed a computerized order-preparation system. That year ICA also purchased Lindex, a chain of fashion stores selling women's clothing, and Intervideo TV Productions-A.B. And in 1988, ICA bought Ellos A.B., a major mail order company.

Since its early days, ICA has pooled advertising strategies and resources to reach wider markets and minimize costs. As a part of this advertising effort, Intervideo TV Productions produces educational and advertising programs to be shown in ICA stores.

With an aggressive advertising program, dynamic growth policies, and continuing sensitivity to changes in market needs, ICA should continue to operate the dominant retail and wholesale food-supply network in Sweden.

Principal Subsidiaries: ICA Partihandel AB; ICA Detaljhandel AB; ICA Företagen AB; ICA-handlarnas AB.

KONINKLIJKE AHOLD N.V.

Ankersmidplein 2
1506 CK Zaandam
The Netherlands
(75) 59-9111

Public Company
Incorporated: 1948 as Albert Heijn NV
Employees: 80,284
Sales: Dfl 15.3 billion (US$7.64 billion)
Stock Index: Amsterdam Munich

Koninklijke Ahold N.V. operates more than 650 supermarket or specialty stores in the Netherlands, making it Holland's largest food retailer. Its Albert Heijn, Alberto, and Etos units are familiar names throughout the country. The company also operates several retail chains overseas, where growth potential is much greater. Its Bi-Lo, First National, and Giant supermarket chains in the United States, for instance, account for almost half of Ahold's total profits. Through carefully selected acquisitions, Ahold has managed to record substantial revenue increases in an industry which is generally considered stagnant. Ahold subsidiaries also process food products under a variety of labels, and are active in the restaurant and recreation trades.

In 1887, Albert Heijn and his wife opened a small grocery store in Oostzan, the Netherlands. Holland was in the midst of an economic boom sustained by its colonial network. Heijn's grocery store prospered and soon became a chain, under the name Albert Heijn. By the end of World War I, Heijn was running a bakery and a confectionery to help supply his chain of 50 grocery stores.

Steady growth continued throughout the 1920s, as the company added new stores each year. In 1923 Heijn branched into the restaurant trade, providing his company with a new source of income. By the end of the decade, Albert Heijn was in a very solid position. As a result, the company was able not only to weather the worldwide Depression of the 1930s, but even to grow.

In 1941, the Nazi occupation of the Netherlands brought economic turmoil to the country. Dutch wealth was drained to fuel Germany's war machine. But, as during the Depression, the nature of the food business insulated Albert Heijn from the ruin faced by companies in other industries throughout Holland. By the end of World War II the chain had nearly 250 stores in operation.

In 1948, the company went public in preparation for the challenges of the postwar era. Self-service shopping was clearly the trend. In 1952 the company opened its first self-service store, followed three years later by its first supermarket. Albert Heijn emerged from the 1950s as a leader in its industry, and expansion continued in the 1960s through diversification and the addition of new stores. In 1966 Albert Heijn acquired the Meester meat-packing plant, which produced a wide variety of processed meat products, delicatessen items, and sausages, among other things. In 1969 the company opened the first of its Alberto liquor stores.

As the company began the 1970s it had a firm grip on about 20% of the Dutch market. In 1971 Albert Heijn opened the first Miro hypermarket. In 1972 the company acquired the Simon de Wit chain, bringing 137 new supermarkets under the Albert Heijn banner. In 1973, the company changed its name to Ahold N.V. It also entered the health and beauty care market that year with the purchase of the Etos chain.

A number of adverse conditions combined to slow growth just as Ahold digested its new acquisitions: the energy crisis of 1973 softened consumer demand somewhat, labor costs rose considerably, and the government removed artificial price supports. Ahold's management, accustomed to the often cyclical nature of the food retailing industry, rode out the storm. The company stepped up discount store activities and its roadside restaurant operations. By 1975 Ahold was enjoying rapid growth once again, and was poised to make a major thrust overseas.

After carefully researching European markets, Ahold decided to establish a chain of supermarkets in Spain. Spain had a relatively undeveloped industry and Ahold believed its expertise would go the farthest there. In 1976 the company opened the first "Cadadia" store near Madrid. Ahold planned to develop a major chain in the country, but the Spanish subsidiary got off to a sluggish start, hindered in part by a slow-moving Spanish bureaucracy and a depressed economy.

In 1977 Ahold made a major purchase in the United States when it acquired the Bi-Lo chain for $60 million. Bi-Lo operated 98 stores throughout North and South Carolina and Georgia. The Bi-Lo chain got off to a strong start within the Ahold group, returning a 3% profit margin, compared with 1.7% for Ahold's Dutch operations. Ahold retained Bi-Lo's management in the belief that local autonomy would best serve the company's interests. In 1981, however, the president of Bi-Lo resigned when the chain followed its competitors and began selling beer and wine.

Ahold continued its program of diversification when it purchased ten restaurants from the struggling Jacques Borel group of Belgium in 1978. The acquisition strengthened Ahold's network of AC restaurants, located on roadsides throughout Europe. Ahold's Ostara holiday parks in West Germany and Holland provided strong earnings outside of the retail food sector for the company in the late 1970s.

In 1978 the company set up a foundation to hold Dfl 100,000 in preferred stock as protection against hostile bids, after watching a number of hostile takeover attempts, including a particularly bitter battle between Heineken and Lucas Bols. To the company's relief, no hostile bids for Ahold actually materialized.

In 1981, Ahold made its second major U.S. purchase: the Giant Food Stores chain, of Carlisle, Pennsylvania, for $35 million. Giant had 29 stores, mostly in Pennsylvania, and Ahold planned to add four or so new stores each year. As with the Bi-Lo purchase, the company's management remained autonomous.

In 1981 Ahold bought 50% of the Spanish sherry producer Luis Paez. By the end of the decade Ahold was producing one-third of all sherry sold in the Netherlands. In addition, the company's Alberto liquor store unit had grown to 89 stores in its first 20 years, and continued to improve its share even in a shrinking market.

Ahold recorded vigorous profits in the early 1980s largely on the strength of its American operations. Growth slowed a bit around 1984, as vicious competition in the Netherlands shaved already thin margins and the Spanish chain Cadadia reported a loss.

In 1985 the company sold the 38 Cadadia stores to the British Dee Corporation (now Gateway), having decided not to undertake a major expansion in Spain. It kept its winery holdings, however. The company also acquired the Van Kok-Ede company, a major wholesale foods supplier in Holland, in 1985.

In 1988, Ahold purchased 80% of the American First National Supermarkets chain, an acquisition which doubled the size of its U.S. operations. First National runs the Finast, Pick-n-Pay, and Edwards Food Warehouse chains. The deal gave Ahold a footing in New England, Ohio, and New York. Ahold slowed the expansion of its Giant and Bi-Lo chains in order to concentrate its resources on the First National stores.

Meanwhile Ahold increased its holding in the Dutch supplier Schuitema to 55%. Schuitema, Holland's largest supplier of independent supermarkets in the country, gave Ahold an even stronger grip on the industry in Holland.

Ahold has always been committed to using the latest technology in its stores. In the late 1980s the company piloted a program which allowed customers to self-scan the items they wish to purchase. At the Albert Heijn store in Tilberg, the Netherlands, customers were offered the choice of self-scanning or traditional shopping. Self-scanning shoppers selected a cart equipped to scan each item before they put it in the cart; the scanner also kept a running total on an electronic readout. When customers were finished shopping, they proceeded to a special line, where the cashier entered the data from the cart's scanner into the register. Customers liked the shorter lines at the checkout and the idea of a running total displayed at all times, and Ahold expects the technology to be commonplace in the near future.

In 1989, Pierre J. Everaert, formerly head of the company's overseas operations, replaced Albert Heijn, grandson of the company's founder, as president of Ahold. Heijn had reached the company's mandatory retirement age of 62, and so the company passed out of the direct control of the Heijn family for the first time in three generations.

Ahold is well positioned for the integration of European markets in 1992. The company enjoys substantial market share in the Netherlands and is well diversified throughout the United States. The company's wide variety of operations within the food industry, including food processing, distribution, and restaurant and recreation operations as well as retailing, gives it a very wide base to build on. As Ahold continues to look for possible acquisitions around the world, it can be expected to remain on top of the market at home.

Principal Subsidiaries: Albert Heijn; Albert Heijn Franchising; James Telesuper; Alberto; Etos; Albro Bakkerijen Zwanenburg; Marvelo; Meester Wijhe; AC Restaurants; AC Restaurants (Belgium/Germany); Grootverbruik Ahold; Ahold Recreational Activities; Ahead Advertising; Pensioenfonds Ahold; Ahold Financieringsmaatschappij, Curacao (Netherlands Antilles); Ahold USA Inc.; BI-LO Inc.; Giant Food Stores Inc.; FNS Holding Company Inc.; First National Supermarkets, Inc.

THE KROGER COMPANY

1014 Vine Street
Cincinnati, Ohio 45201
U.S.A.
(513) 762–4000

Public Company
Incorporated: 1902 as Kroger Grocery and Baking Company
Employees: 170,000
Sales: $19.1 billion
Stock Index: New York

The Kroger Company traces its roots back to 1883, when Bernard H. Kroger began the Great Western Tea Company, one of the first chain store operations in America. As his business grew from small neighborhood groceries into the supermarkets and superstores of today, The Kroger Company played a significant part in the evolution of the country's trade practices, owing many of its forward-pushing policies to its founder. The Kroger Company now operates more than 2,000 supermarkets and convenience stores in the United States.

Kroger left school to go to work at age 13 when his father lost the family dry goods store in the panic of 1873. At 16, he sold coffee and tea door-to-door. At 20, he managed a Cincinnati grocery store, and at 24, he became the sole owner of the Great Western Tea Company, which by the summer of 1885 had four stores. Kroger's shrewd buying during the panic of 1893 raised the number to 17, and by 1902, with forty stores and a factory in Cincinnati, Kroger incorporated and changed the company's name to The Kroger Grocery and Baking Company.

Kroger Company historians characterize B. H. Kroger as somewhat of a "crank," fanatically insistent upon quality and service. Profanity was called his second language; he often advised his managers to "run the price down as far as you can go so the other fellow won't slice your throat."

Part of Kroger's success came from the elimination of middlemen between the store and the customer. In 1901, Kroger's company became the first to bake its own bread for its stores, and in 1904, Kroger bought Nagel Meat Markets and Packing House and made Kroger grocery stores the first to include meat departments.

This important innovation, however, was not easy. It was common practice at that time for butchers to short-weigh and take sample cuts home with them, practices that did not coincide with B. H. Kroger's strict accounting policies. When Kroger installed cash registers in the meat departments, every one of them inexplicably broke. When Kroger hired female cashiers, the butchers opened all the windows to "freeze out" the women and then let loose with such obscene language that the women quit in a matter of days. When Kroger hired young men instead as cashiers, the butchers threatened them with physical force. But Kroger was stubborn, and in the long run his money-saving, efficient procedures won out.

From the beginning, Kroger was interested in both manufacturing and retail. His mother's homemade sauerkraut and pickles sold well to the German immigrants in Cincinnati. And in the back of his store, Kroger himself experimented to invent a "French brand" of coffee, which is still sold in Kroger stores.

The Kroger Grocery and Baking Company soon began to expand outside of Cincinnati; by 1920, the chain had stores in Hamilton, Dayton, and Columbus, Ohio. In 1912, Kroger made his first long-distance expansion, buying 25 stores in St. Louis, Missouri. At a time when most chains only hired trucks as needed, Kroger bought a fleet of them, enabling him to move the company into Detroit; Indianapolis, Indiana; and Springfield and Toledo, Ohio.

When America entered World War I in 1917, B. H. Kroger served on the president's national war food board and on the governor of Ohio's food board. His dynamic plain speech raised substantial amounts of money for the Red Cross and Liberty Bonds.

After the war, The Kroger Grocery and Baking Company continued to expand, following Kroger's preference for buying smaller, financially unsteady chains in areas adjacent to established Kroger territories. In 1928, one year before the stock market crashed, Kroger sold his shares in the company for more than $28 million. One of his executives, William Albers, became president. In 1929, Kroger had 5,575 stores, the most there have ever been in the chain.

Since the turn of the century, chain stores had been accused of driving small merchants out of business by using unfair business practices and radically changing the commerce of communities. In the 1920s, an anti–chain store movement began to gain momentum. Politicans, radio announcers, and newspapers talked about "the chain store menace." People feared the rapid growth of chains and their consequent power over their industries. Because the grocery industry was so much a part of most people's lives, food chains like The Kroger Grocery and Baking Company bore the brunt of public complaints.

Chain store company executives soon realized they would have to organize in order to prevent anti-chain legislation. In 1927, the National Chain Stores Association was founded and William Albers was elected president.

When Albers resigned as president of Kroger in 1930, he also resigned as president of the organization. Albert H. Morrill, an attorney who had served as Kroger's general counsel, was elected president of both in his stead. Morrill faced not only the economic challenges of the Depression, but also the political challenges of the growing public distrust of chain stores.

With the limited transportation and communication systems of the time, the company had to decentralize in order to grow. Morrill established 23 branches with a manager for each branch, and hired a real estate manager to close unprofitable stores. He also implemented policies that guarded against anti-chain accusations, while encouraging customers to shop at Kroger stores.

Instead of going through the usual channels for buying produce, The Kroger Grocery and Baking Company began to send its buyers to produce farms so they could inspect crops to ensure the quality of the food their stores sold. This counteracted the frequent complaint that chain stores sold low-quality foods. This policy eventually resulted in the formation of Wesco Food Company, the Kroger Company's own produce procurement organization.

Morrill also began the Kroger Food Foundation in 1930, making it the first grocery company to test food scientifically in order to monitor the quality of products. The foundation also established the Homemakers Reference Committee, a group of 750 homemakers who tested food samples in their own homes.

In 1930, one of the company's southern managers, Michael Cullen, proposed a revolutionary plan to his superiors: a bigger self-service grocery store that would make a profit by selling large quantities of food at low prices that competitors couldn't beat. But at this stage, Kroger executives were wary of the idea, and Cullen went on alone to begin the first supermarket, King Cullen, in Jamaica, New Jersey.

Throughout the Depression, Kroger maintained its business; by 1935, Kroger had 50 supermarkets of its own. During the 1930s, frozen foods and shopping carts were introduced, and the Kroger Food Foundation invented a way of processing beef without chemicals so that it remained tender, calling the process "Tenderay" beef.

Morrill and Colonel Sherrill, vice president of Kroger, became involved with the organization of the American Retail Association in 1935. A report of the organization's publicity release on the front page of *The New York Times* prompted controversy, because the headline stated that the organization would work as a "unified voice" in economic matters, which suggested a kind of "super lobby" to some people. This led to a congressional investigation and in 1938, a bill was introduced imposing a punitive tax against chain stores that would almost certainly force them out of business. Only after much controversy and public debate was the punitive tax bill defeated that year.

In 1942, Morrill died. Charles Robertson, formerly vice president and treasurer, became president. The company's plans for growth were shelved during World War II, with about 40% of its employees serving in the armed forces. The Army Quartermaster Corps commissioned the Kroger Food Foundation to create rations that would boost the morale of soldiers, and the company produced individual cans of date pudding, plum pudding, and fruit cake. Other rations that came from Kroger included cheese bars, preserves, and "C-ration crackers."

After the war, in 1946, Joseph Hall, who had been hired in 1931 to close unprofitable stores, became president. He changed the company name from The Kroger Grocery and Baking Company to The Kroger Company, in keeping with indications that the company was moving into a new period of growth. In 1947, Kroger opened its first egg-processing plant in Wabash, Indiana in order to further ensure egg quality. Hall also saw that 45 private-label brands were merged into one Kroger brand, and introduced the blue-and-white logo with the name change.

Hall's new policy of consumer research was an important change for the company. Decisions about products and methods of selling were to come from the "votes" shoppers left at the cash register. During his years as president, the company moved into Texas, Minnesota, and California. Annual sales grew as small neighborhood stores were replaced with larger supermarkets. In 1952, Kroger sales topped $1 billion.

This was a time of rapid growth for supermarkets. Between 1948 and 1963, the number of supermarkets in the country nearly tripled. Kroger was already testing the specialty shops that would later be integral to its "superstores." As competition in the industry grew more fierce, Kroger joined with six other firms to found the Top Value Stamp Company, which tried to bring customers into the stores with stamp collecting promotions.

In 1960 the company began its expansion into the drugstore business, with an eye on the potential for drugstores built next to grocery stores. The company bought a small drugstore chain and made its owner, James Herring, the head of the drugstore division. The first SupeRx drugstore opened in 1961 next to a Kroger food store in Milford, Ohio.

Discount stores—strategically located stores that aggressively merchandised goods on a low margin basis with minimum service—were the retailing trend of the 1960s. By 1962, Kroger had also gone into discounting.

In 1963 Kroger's sales reached $2 billion. In 1964, Jacob Davis, a former congressman and judge and a vice president of Kroger, replaced Hall as president and CEO. Davis concentrated on the manufacturing branch of Kroger. With the construction of the interstate highway system in the 1950s and 1960s, central manufacturing facilities could now serve larger territories, allowing Kroger to combine small facilities into larger regional ones.

Davis's experience in both retail and law became important to the company as the government began to clamp down on the food industry. During hearings for the 1967 Meat Inspection Act, several chains were exposed for selling adulterated processed meats. The United States Department of Agriculture revealed that Kroger was selling franks and bolognas with two to four times the legal amount of water or extender and pork sausage treated with artificial colors to make it look fresh.

With the rapid growth of food chain stores, the government also began to concentrate on enforcing antitrust laws. Kroger was one of the companies the Federal Trade Commission challenged on its mergers. In 1971, the FTC proposed a consent order that required the company to divest itself of three discount food departments, charging that Kroger stores would "substantially lessen" competition in food retailing in the Dayton, Ohio area.

Kroger settled without admitting any violation of antitrust laws, and sold the three food departments. The order also prohibited Kroger from buying any food store or department in nonfood stores in which the number of stores or sales accrued would indicate a lessening of competition in that city or county.

James Herring became president of The Kroger Company in 1970 and began to take Kroger into the superstore age, closing hundreds of small supermarkets and building much larger ones with more specialty departments.

The 1970s were a turbulent time for the grocery industry in general, but both turbulent and productive for Kroger. The company perfected its "scientific methods" of consumer research, using the results in planning and advertising. In the early 1970s, at the request of consumer groups, Kroger led the industry in marking its perishable products with a "sell by" date. Kroger began to bake only with enriched flour to add nutrition to its bread products. Two years later, nutritional labels were put on Kroger private-brand products. And food and nonfood products were stocked in twice the variety they had been in the previous two decades.

To increase the accuracy and speed of checkout systems, Kroger, in partnership with RCA, became the first grocery company to test electronic scanners under actual working conditions, in 1972. An invention borrowed from the railroad industry, the scanner was originally used as the electric eye that read symbols on the side of railcars. Kroger and other grocery chains decided to try to use it to read prices on products.

While the government controlled prices between 1971 and 1974, grocery stores suffered depressed profits, but by 1974, the net profits of the top food chains were up 57%. As food chains grew into ever larger and more powerful businesses and gained increasing control over the agricultural economy through their enormous wholesalers, there was another round of Federal Trade Commission hearings that revealed the illegal business practices of several chains. In 1974, Kroger settled out of court on an antitrust claim against Kroger and two other chains for fixing beef prices. In 1974 the Federal Trade Commission also sued Kroger for violations of its 1973 trade rule that all stores must stock a sufficient supply of specials to meet anticipated demand and must give rainchecks if the supplies ran out. In 1977 Kroger consented to the FTC order.

But the biggest battle Kroger faced in its tangles with the Federal Trade Commission concerned the company's use of "Price Patrol," an advertising promotion used in certain markets at different times between 1972 and 1978, in which Kroger advertisements compared Kroger prices with the prices of its competitors on 150 products a week. The figures were based upon surveys conducted among housewives. The Federal Trade Commission ruled that slogans like "Documented Proof: Kroger leads in lower prices" were unfair and deceptive because the items surveyed excluded meat, produce, and house brands. A controversy ensued when the Council on Wage and Price Stability expressed concern that tougher standards for Kroger might prevent the dissemination of food price information in the future, but the Federal Trade Commission decided that surveys must be conducted fairly and reliably and that their limitations should be made clear. Kroger appealed; the "Price Patrol" issue was not decided until 1983, when Kroger settled out of court with the Federal Trade Commission.

In 1978, Lyle Everingham, who began his career as a Kroger clerk, became CEO. The company sold Top Value Enterprises and opened Tara Foods, a peanut butter processing plant, in Albany, Georgia. As Kroger moved more towards the "superstore" concept of one-stop shopping, it began to test even more in-store specialty departments such as beauty salons, financial services, cheese shops, and cosmetic counters.

In 1981, Kroger began marketing its Cost Cutter brand products. In 1983, Kroger merged with the Dillon Companies and began operating stores coast to coast. A year later, Kroger formed a grocery wholesaler for Michigan called FoodLand Distributors with Wetterau.

In 1988, Kroger received several takeover bids, mainly from the Dart Group Corporation and from Kohlberg Kravis Roberts, whose highest bid topped $5 billion. Kroger rejected the bids and restructured, expecting that recapitalization would enhance its competitiveness. The reorganization expanded employee ownership to more than 30% of the company's shares. Kroger also awarded its shareholders with a dividend of cash and debentures worth $48.69 per share. Kroger financed the restructuring by selling $333 million worth of unprofitable assets and by assuming $3.6 billion in loan debt.

Throughout its history, the company has followed the policies of continual renewal and expansion that B. H. Kroger established at its outset, making the company an industry leader in innovation. To maintain its trend-setting position, Kroger will have to try to anticipate the problems facing agricultural production in America, and respond to the growing consumer habit of eating away from home.

Principal Subsidiaries: M&M Super Markets, Inc.; Dillon Companies, Inc.

Further Reading: Lebhar, Godfrey M. *Chain Stores in America*, New York, Chain Store Publishing Corporation, 1963; Cross, Jennifer. *The Supermarket Trap: The Consumer and the Food Industry*, Bloomington, Indiana, Indiana University Press, 1976; *The Kroger Story: A Century of Innovation*, Cincinnati, Ohio, The Kroger Company, 1983.

MCDONALD'S CORPORATION

McDonald's Plaza
Oak Brook, Illinois 60521
U.S.A.
(708) 575–3000

Public Company
Incorporated: 1955
Employees: 169,000
Sales: $5.57 billion
Stock Index: New York Midwest Pacific Toronto Frankfurt Munich Paris Tokyo

Since its incorporation in 1955, McDonald's has not only become the world's largest quick-service restaurant organization, but has literally changed Americans' eating habits. On any given day, nearly 7% of the American population will eat a meal at a McDonald's restaurant; in a year, 96% of Americans will visit a McDonald's. The company stands head and shoulders above its competition, commanding by far the leading share of the fast-food market. The company's growth is best described as phenomenal; McDonald's has recorded increasing sales and earnings every quarter since it went public in 1965.

In 1954, Ray Kroc, a Multimixer milkshake machine salesman, heard about Richard and Maurice (Dick and Mac) McDonald, two brothers who were using eight of his high-tech Multimixers in their San Bernardino, California restaurant. His curiosity was aroused, so he went to San Bernardino to take a look at the McDonalds' restaurant.

The McDonalds had been in the restaurant business since the 1930s. In 1948, they closed down a successful carhop drive-in to establish the streamlined operation Ray Kroc saw in 1954. The menu was stripped to the bare essentials: hamburgers, cheeseburgers, french fries, shakes, soft drinks, and apple pie. The carhops were eliminated to make McDonald's self-serve. There were no tables to sit at, no juke-box, no telephone. As a result, McDonald's attracted families rather than teenagers. Perhaps the most impressive aspect of the restaurant was the efficiency with which the McDonalds' workers did their jobs. Mac and Dick McDonald had taken great care in setting up their kitchen. Each worker's steps had been carefully choreographed, like an assembly line, to insure maximum efficiency. The savings in preparation time, and the resulting increase in volume, allowed the McDonalds to lower the price of a hamburger from 30 cents to 15 cents.

Kroc believed that the McDonalds' formula was a ticket to success, and suggested that they franchise their restaurants throughout the country. When they hesitated to take on this additional burden, Kroc volunteered to do it for them. He returned to his home outside of Chicago with rights to set up McDonald's restaurants throughout the country, except in a handful of territories in California and Arizona already licensed by the McDonald brothers.

Ray Kroc's first McDonald's restaurant opened in Des Plaines, Illinois, near Chicago, on April 15, 1955. As with any new venture, Kroc encountered a number of hurdles. The first was adapting the McDonald's building design to a northern climate. A basement had to be installed to house a furnace. Adequate ventilation was difficult: exhaust fans sucked out warm air in the winter, and cool air in the summer.

Most frustrating of all, however, was Kroc's initial failure to reproduce the McDonalds' french fries. The McDonald brothers produced delicious french fries, but when Kroc and his crew duplicated their method—leaving just a little peel for flavor, cutting the potatoes into shoestrings, and rinsing the strips in cold water—the fries turned into mush. After repeated telephone conversations with the McDonald brothers and several consultations with the Potato and Onion Association, Kroc pinpointed the cause of the soggy spuds. The McDonald brothers stored their potatoes outside in wire bins, and the warm California breeze dried them out and cured them, slowly turning the sugars into starch. In order to reproduce the superior taste of these potatoes, Kroc devised a system using an electric fan to dry the potatoes in a similar way. He also experimented with a blanching process. Within three months he had a french fry which was, in his opinion, slightly superior in taste to the McDonald brothers'.

Once the Des Plaines restaurant was rolling, Kroc began to seek franchisees for his McDonald's chain. The first snag came quickly. In 1956 he discovered that the McDonald brothers had licensed the franchise rights for Cook County, Illinois (home of Chicago and many of its suburbs) to the Frejlack Ice Cream Company. Kroc was incensed that the McDonalds hadn't informed him of this arrangement. He purchased the rights back for $25,000—five times what the Frejacks had originally paid—and marched forward.

Kroc decided early on that it was best to set up the restaurants first, and then franchise them out, so that he could control the uniformity of the stores. McDonald's continues to own most of the real estate for its restaurants. Early McDonald's restaurants were situated in the suburbs. Corner lots were usually in greater demand because gas stations and shops competed for them, but Kroc preferred lots in the middle of blocks to accommodate his U-shaped parking lots. Since these lots were cheaper, Kroc could give franchisees a price break.

McDonald's grew slowly for its first three years; by 1958 there were 34 restaurants. In 1959, however, Kroc opened 67 new restaurants, bringing the total to more than 100.

Kroc had decided at the outset that McDonald's would not be a supplier to its franchisees—his background as a salesman warned him that such an arrangement could lead to lower quality for the sake of higher profits. He also determined that the company should at no time own more than 30% of all McDonald's restaurants. But he knew that his success depended upon his franchisees' success, and he was determined to help them any way he could.

In 1960, McDonald's advertising campaign, "Look for the golden arches," gave sales a big boost. Kroc took the view that advertising was an investment that would in the end come back many times over, and advertising has always played a key role in the development of the McDonald's Corporation—indeed, McDonald's ads have been some of the most identifiable over the years. In 1962, McDonald's replaced its "Speedee" the hamburger man symbol with its now world-famous golden arches. A year later, the company sold its billionth hamburger.

In the early 1960s, McDonald's really began to take off. The growth in automobile use that came with the suburbanization of America contributed heavily to McDonald's success. In 1961, Kroc bought out the McDonald brothers for $2.7 million and dreamed of making McDonald's the number-one fast-food chain in the country.

In 1965, McDonald's Corporation went public. Common shares were offered at $22.50 per share; by the end of the first day's trading the price had shot up to $30. A block of 100 shares purchased for $2,250 in 1965 was worth, after nine stock splits, more than $400,000 in 1989. McDonald's Corporation is now one of the 30 companies that make up the Dow Jones Industrial Index.

McDonald's success in the 1960s was largely due to the company's successful marketing and flexible response to customer demand. In 1965, the Filet-o-Fish sandwich, billed as "the fish that catches people," was introduced in McDonald's restaurants. The new item had originally met with disapproval from Kroc, but after its successful test marketing, he eventually agreed to add it. An item that Kroc had backed a year previously had flopped. It was a burger with a slice of pineapple and a slice of cheese known as a "hulaburger." The market was not quite ready for Kroc's taste, however; the hulaburger's tenure on the McDonald's menuboard was short. In 1968 the now-legendary Big Mac made its debut. Its "two all-beef patties special sauce lettuce cheese pickles onions on a sesame seed bun" slogan was a hit. In 1969, McDonald's sold its five-billionth hamburger. A year later, as it launched the "You Deserve a Break Today" advertising campaign, McDonald's restaurants had reached all 50 states.

In 1968 the company opened its one-thousandth restaurant and Fred Turner became president and chief administrative officer of McDonald's. Kroc became chairman, and remained CEO until 1973. Turner had originally intended to open a McDonald's franchise, but when he had problems with his backers over a location he went to work for Ray Kroc in 1956. As operations vice president, Turner helped new franchisees get their stores set up and running. He was constantly looking for new ways to perfect the McDonald's system, experimenting, for example, to determine the maximum number of hamburger patties one could stack in a box without squashing them and pointing out that seconds could be saved if McDonald's used buns that were pre-sliced all the way through and weren't stuck together in the package. Such attention to detail was one reason for the company's extraordinary success.

McDonald's spectacular growth continued in the 1970s. Americans were more on-the-go than ever, and fast service was a priority. In 1972, the company passed $1 billion in annual sales; by 1976, McDonald's had served 20 billion hamburgers, and systemwide sales exceeded $3 billion.

McDonald's pioneered breakfast fast food with the introduction of the Egg McMuffin in 1973 when market research indicated that a quick breakfast would be gobbled up by consumers. In 1977, the company added a full breakfast line to the menu. By 1987 one-fourth of all breakfasts eaten out in the United States came from McDonald's restaurant.

Chairman Ray Kroc was a firm believer in "putting something back into the community where you do business." In 1974, McDonald's acted on that philosophy in an original way by opening the first Ronald McDonald House, in Philadelphia, to provide a "home away from home" for the families of children in nearby hospitals. Twelve years after this first house opened, 100 similar Ronald McDonald Houses were in operation across the United States.

In 1975, McDonald's opened its first drive-thru window in Oklahoma City. This service gave Americans a fast, convenient way to get a quick meal. The company's goal was to provide service within 50 seconds, quicker where possible. Drive-thru sales eventually accounted for more than half of McDonald's systemwide sales.

In the later 1970s competition from other hamburger chains like Burger King and Wendy's began to heat up. Experts believed that the fast-food industry had gotten as big as it ever would, so the companies began to battle fiercely for market share. A period of aggressive advertising campaigns and price slashing in the early 1980s became known as the "burger wars." Burger King suggested that customers "have it their way"; Wendy's offered itself as the "fresh alternative" and asked "Where's the beef?" But McDonald's sales and market share continued to grow. Consumers seemed to like the taste and consistency of McDonald's best.

During the 1980s McDonald's further diversified its menu to suit changing consumer tastes. Chicken McNuggets were introduced in 1983; by the end of the year McDonald's was the second-largest retailer of chicken in the world. In 1987, ready-to-eat salads were introduced to lure more health-conscious consumers. The 1980s were the fastest-paced decade yet. Efficiency, combined with an expanded menu, continued to draw customers. McDonald's, already entrenched in the suburbs, began to focus on urban centers and introduced new architectural styles. Though McDonald's restaurants no longer looked identical, the company made sure food quality and service remained constant.

Despite experts' claims that the fast-food industry was saturated, McDonald's continued to expand. The first generation raised on restaurant food had grown up. Eating out had become a habit rather than a break in the routine, and McDonald's relentless marketing continued to improve sales. Innovative promotions, like "When the U.S. wins, you win" giveaways during the Olympic games in 1988, were a huge success.

In 1982, Michael R. Quinlan became president of McDonald's Corporation and Fred Turner became chairman. Quinlan, who took over as CEO in 1986, had started at McDonald's in the mailroom in 1963, and gradually worked his way up.

The first McDonald's CEO to hold an MBA, Quinlan was regarded by his colleagues as a shrewd competitor. In his first year as CEO the company opened 600 new restaurants.

McDonald's growth in the United States was mirrored by its stunning growth abroad. By the late 1980s, 26% of systemwide sales came from restaurants outside the United States. McDonald's opened its first foreign restaurant in British Columbia, Canada in 1967; since then the company established itself in more than 50 foreign countries and now operates more than 2,500 restaurants outside the U.S. Its strongest foreign markets are Japan, Canada, West Germany, Great Britain, and Australia.

In the mid-1980s, McDonald's, like other traditional employers of teenagers, was faced with a shortage of labor in the United States. The company met this challenge by being the first to entice retirees back into the work-force. McDonald's has always placed great emphasis on effective training. It opened its Hamburger University in 1961 to train franchisees and corporate decision makers. By 1987, more than 30,000 people had received "Bachelor of Hamburgerology" degrees from the 80-acre Oak Brook, Illinois facility. The corporation opened a Hamburger University in Tokyo in 1971, in Munich in 1975, and in London in 1982.

Quinlan continues to experiment with new technology and to research new markets to keep McDonald's in front of its competition. Clamshell fryers, which cooked both sides of a hamburger simultaneously, were tested. New locations such as hospitals and military bases are being tapped as possible sites for new restaurants. In response to the increase in microwave oven usage, McDonald's, whose name is the single most advertised brand name in the world, has beefed up advertising and promotional expenditures, stressing that its taste is superior to quick packaged foods.

It took McDonald's 33 years to open its first 10,000 restaurants. The company plans to open the next 10,000 by 2005, mainly by taking advantage of strong opportunities overseas. McDonald's ability to adapt to the changing tastes and habits of its customers has made it the virtually unassailable leader in the fast-food industry. New challenges will arise, but if McDonald's relatively brief past in any indication of its future, the company has plenty to look forward to.

Principal Subsidiaries: McDonald's Australian Properties Corp.; McDonald's Deutschland, Inc,; McDonald's Restaurant Operations, Inc.; McDonald's Property Co. Ltd.; McDonald's Restaurants of Canada, Ltd.; McDonald's Systems of Australia, Ltd,; McDonald's Properties (Australia) Pty., Ltd.; McDonald's Immobilien GmbH (West Germany); McDonald's Hamburgers Ltd. (U.K.); McDonald's Finance Co., N.V. (Netherlands Antilles).

Further Reading: Kroc, Ray. *Grinding It Out*, Chicago, H. Reguery, 1977; Love, John F. *McDonald's: Behind the Golden Arches*, New York, Bantam Books, 1986.

THE OSHAWA GROUP LIMITED

302 The East Mall
Etobicoke
Ontario M9B 6B8
Canada
(416) 236-1971

Public Company
Incorporated: 1957 as Oshawa Wholesale Ltd.
Employees: 19,000
Sales: C$4.27 billion (US$3.58 billion)
Stock Index: Toronto Montreal

The Oshawa Group is one of Canada's largest suppliers of food, operating in both the wholesale and retail sectors. The company runs 102 supermarkets under a variety of banners, including Food City, IGA, and Dutch Boy. It is also the largest wholesale supplier to independently owned IGA stores in Canada. Oshawa is active in the general merchandise and pharmaceutical market as well, running 39 Towers department stores in Ontario, nine Bonimart stores in Quebec, and 156 drugstores under the Pharma Plus, Drug City, and Metro Drugs chains. The company also operates 25 pharmacy units throughout its department stores and supermarkets.

The Oshawa Group has experienced steady growth since it was established in 1957. It registered record sales and earnings for the 12 consecutive years preceding 1989—a remarkable feat considering the generally cyclical nature of its primary industry—and the company is well positioned to continue its progress.

The company was originally incorporated in Ontario on June 18, 1957 as Oshawa Wholesale Ltd., and operated as a distributor to grocery stores during its first few years. But as the company grew in the early 1960s, it quickly began to diversify. In 1963 Oshawa purchased a controlling interest in the Dominion Mushroom Company, a large mushroom growing and packing concern. Earnings surpassed $1 million in 1963, and Oshawa soon invested heavily in supermarkets. In September, 1964 the company acquired full control of the Independent Grocers Alliance (IGA) Distribution Company. Two months later it purchased the eight units of Bassins Food Chain located in Toronto and Ajax, Ontario, and transformed them into IGA stores. Throughout the rest of the decade the company built a formidable chain of supermarkets through acquisition.

Oshawa diversified into general merchandise retailing in January, 1966 when it purchased a 75% interest and took over management of the six-store Rite-Way Department Store chain, which operated throughout Ontario. A year later the company acquired the rest of Rite-Way's shares and purchased Allied Towers Merchants Ltd., another department store chain, combining the operations of the two under one management group.

Oshawa continued its diversification into other businesses and new geographical areas in the late 1960s. In July, 1968 the company purchased Kent Drugs Ltd. The acquisition added about $7 million to Oshawa's annual sales, and Oshawa President Ray D. Wolfe announced the company's plans to put Kent Drug store units in new Towers Department stores. Also in 1968 Oshawa purchased Rockower of Canada Ltd., a firm which operated the men's and boys' departments in 26 of Oshawa's Towers stores. Oshawa's food distribution unit was greatly expanded late in the year by the purchase of Shop & Save Ltd., an IGA supplier in Quebec. The company branched into Canada's maritime provinces when it acquired Bolands Ltd., which as supplier to 45 IGA stores in that region had accounted for about $27 million in sales the previous year. By the end of its shopping spree Oshawa was the supplier to 325 IGA stores in five provinces and had become well diversified in the general merchandise and drug store markets.

In the 1970s Oshawa became more involved in real estate dealings. In mid-1970 the company purchased an interest in Baxter Estates, a real estate partnership which owned an apartment building in Winnipeg and a shopping center in Calgary. (The company sold its interest in Baxter three years later for a nearly 100% profit).

In November, 1971, three months after it changed its name to The Oshawa Group Ltd. to reflect its diversity, the company purchased the rest of Marchland Holdings Ltd., a real estate developer it already half-owned. At the time of the acquisition Marchland owned four Towers-Food City shopping centers and a commercial complex in Sudbury, Ontario that included a shopping mall, hotel, office center, theater, and parking garage. Oshawa also purchased the remaining third of the modular home developer Systems Construction Ltd. of Ontario.

In early 1972 Oshawa moved into western Canada by acquiring Codville Distributers Ltd. Oshawa's bid was accepted over the competing bid of Westfair Foods Ltd., a subsidiary of George Weston Ltd., because Oshawa's offer was more attractive to Codville's minority stockholders.

In October, 1973, Harvey S. Wolfe succeeded his brother Raphael Wolfe as president of Oshawa; Raphael became chairman and CEO. In 1976 Oshawa bought out its partners in the Decairie Square shopping mall in Montreal. In December, 1977, Norman S. Lipson, former president of Oshawa's Tower Department Stores unit, pleaded guilty to four counts of fraud which involved kickbacks of $411,000. Lipson had resigned from his position in late 1976. He was sentenced to two years' imprisonment and fined $30,000.

In the late 1970s the Wolfes began to slim Oshawa's operations a bit. The company shed its 50% interest in the Consumers Distributing Company, Ltd. in 1978. Consumers Distributing sold brand-name general merchandise at reduced prices in large, no-frills showrooms; Oshawa had entered into a joint venture with the limited-service retailer, providing capital for the chain's expansion eight years before. Oshawa also sold its 90% interest in Coinamatic Laundry Equipment in late 1978.

The early 1980s saw Oshawa emphasize its core businesses—food wholesaling and retailing. In 1983 group sales surpassed $2 billion. In 1985 the company strengthened its presence in the Atlantic provinces when it acquired nine supermarkets and a distribution center in Nova Scotia from Dominion Stores Ltd. and bought 22 Canada Safeway supermarkets in the Toronto-Hamilton area. In 1986, as group sales passed the $3 billion mark, Oshawa divested its Dominion Mushroom farm due to both erratic earnings and the unit's need for a major capital reinvestment, and sold its Decairie real estate in Montreal and its Sudbury shopping center.

In the late 1980s Oshawa took bold steps to improve its food retailing business. Oshawa's corporate-owned Food City stores took on a new "streetscape" look. The store layout was intended to resemble an old-fashioned sidewalk merchant atmosphere, and at the same time appeal to young urban professionals as well as retirees. Oshawa targeted upscale consumers wherever possible with specialized services and fancy merchandising. For example, in 1987 the company's Thornhill, Ontario Food City superstore added a kosher deli, bakery, and meat department to appeal to the community's large Jewish population. By specializing wherever possible, Oshawa commanded beefier margins on premium products and services.

In 1988 Oshawa tripled its drug store chain by acquiring the 109 retail units of Boots Drug Stores for C$45 million. The stores were renamed Pharma-Plus Drugmarts and joined the 34 Kent Drugs and 12 Metro Drugs units in operation. The addition helped Oshawa sales to top $4 billion in 1989.

The Oshawa Group's aggressive management has produced excellent results for a number of years, and the company intends to concentrate on what it calls the mainstream of the market, rather than change store formats to superstores or specialty stores. Although the trend in Europe and the United States has been toward increased size and cross-merchandising between food and nonfood retail stores, Oshawa does not anticipate similar trends in Canada. Instead the company plans to focus on retail presentation in its department stores and drug stores and broader product lines in its existing supermarkets.

Principal Subsidiaries: Bolands Ltd.; Codville Distributors; Dutch Boy Food Markets; Elliot Marr and Company Ltd.; Fieldfresh Farms Inc.; Hudon et Deaudelin Ltee; Oshawa Foods; The Ontario Produce Company; The White and Company; Hickeson-Langs Supply Company; Langs Cold Storage; Model Uniform Rental Services Ltd.; Kent Drugs Ltd.; Pharma Plus Drugmarts Ltd.; Towers Department Stores Inc.

PROVIGO

PROVIGO INC.

800 René-Lévesque Boulevard West
Montreal, Quebec H3B 1Y2
Canada
(514) 878–8300

Public Company
Incorporated: 1961 as Couvrette & Provost Limited
Employees: 22,000
Sales: C$6.42 billion (US$5.38 billion)
Stock Index: Montreal Toronto

Provigo was founded in Montreal when Bernard and Jacques Couvrette and Roland, Ernest, and René Provost decided to link their family businesses. The new wholesale grocer was incorporated in 1961 as Couvrette & Provost Ltd., dealing mainly in dry goods, tobacco, candy, and toiletries.

Couvrette & Provost's first president, Bernard Couvrette, established a precedent for aggressive acquisition, and over the next eight years the company integrated ten food wholesalers in an effort to diversify its food lines with dairy products, meats, vegetables, and health and beauty aids.

As a wholesaler and distributor, the company depended on independent grocers for its business. At the beginning of the 1960s, a supermarket chain boom consumed much of the smaller grocers' market share, but by 1964, in Quebec at least, these independents had won back most of what had been lost and held 70% of the market. Couvrette & Provost was supplying about 800 grocery stores, 300 of them affiliated with the company under various names. The small grocers' success was largely due to their growth in rural Quebec areas, but in some provinces the chains still dominated.

Couvrette & Provost was also diversifying into new areas of the food-service industry. Its subsidiary, Provost & Provost, served restaurants, hotels, schools, and other institutions, and another subsidiary, Les Epiceries Presto Limitée, operated eight cash-and-carry stores. Couvrette & Provost also organized Primes Régal Incorporated, a trading stamp system for retailers to offer their customers. The stamps were redeemable for prizes the shopper could choose from an illustrated catalogue, and the promotion was successful in bringing some of the supermarket glitz to smaller groceries.

In 1965, the company acquired Magasins Régal Stores, a cooperative of several Quebec food retailers that worked through pooled purchases to allow the group to run its own warehouse to keep prices lower. Also that year, Conrad Lajoie Limitée, a small distributor, was acquired as a subsidiary. The company also underwent a five-for-one stock split in 1965, feeling that its C$30 to C$35 unit price was too high for ordinary investors and that the company would benefit from more shareholders and shares outstanding to increase its leverage on the stock market.

During the mid-1960s, profits continued to increase by as much as 29% a year, and in 1967, Couvrette & Provost made a change in capital structure. Previously, the company had used the two-class structure of A and B shares that was common for newly incorporated Quebec companies. Only the B shares, which were held by the Couvrette and Provost families, had voting rights. Under the new plan, both classes of shares were converted into no-par-value common shares.

In August, 1967 Bernard Couvrette became chairman of the board and René Provost was named president. During the next two years, the company became a leader in the Quebec market. It acquired P. D'Aoust Limited, a family-owned wholesale grocery business, and then merged with Lamontagne Limited and Denault Limited through an exchange of shares. This was the first merger of its kind in the province, and it expanded the company into new territories—Saguenay, Quebec City, Sherbrooke, and the Eastern Townships. One of the main results of the merger was an overall reduction of operating costs through the integration of management, distribution, advertising, and purchasing, which helped sales to increase at a rapid rate over the next 20 years. *The Financial Post* called the firm's progress in nine years "most impressive," saying, "management appears to be very aggressive and forward looking and has shown sound judgment in the recent mergers."

In 1969, Antoine Turmel became CEO, while René Provost remained president and general manager. In September of the next year, Couvrette & Provost changed its name to Provigo Inc.

As rural citizens of Quebec began to move to the cities in larger numbers in the early 1970s, their lifestyle changes included patronizing independent grocers less and chain supermarkets more. The chains used modern merchandising techniques and muscular ad campaigns to attract more consumers to their strategically placed sites in shopping centers and suburbs. Because of the volume of their sales and the strength of their purchasing power, the supermarkets could afford to offer lower prices, and soon had launched price wars.

In food distribution, often called the "penny business," profit margins are tiny and must be compensated for with a large sales volume. To counteract the supermarket price war, wholesalers began to band together and distributors forged closer links with their independent grocers by affiliating retailers and franchising convenience stores. In 1970, Provigo merged ProviFruit Inc., and over the next five years, Provigo concentrated on developing its retail sector by establishing a network of 50 supermarkets and 800 affiliated or franchised stores. The company had opened its first warehouse market in 1969; by 1972, it had a dozen warehouse operations. Because of this wise planning during the price wars, Provigo was the only publicly owned food distributor in Canada whose earnings did not decline at all but, in fact, increased.

In 1974, Provigo implemented a new approach to retailing and developed a chain of franchised convenience stores under the name Provi-Soir. In 1975, Provigo purchased Jato, a company operating nine supermarkets. In November, 1976 the company moved into the meat sector and created its own subsidiary, Provi-Viande.

Provigo made an audacious move in 1977 when it acquired M. Loeb Limited, a company with larger sales and territories than its own, more than doubling Provigo's size. The company's sales rose from C$500 million to C$2 billion in the next two years. The acquisition was not only shrewd but well timed, since price competition in food retailing lessened during 1977 and sales growth was outrunning inflation. Along with M. Loeb, Provigo acquired Loeb's subsidiaries in Washington, D.C. and northern California, thus gaining a foothold in America. Provigo also acquired National Drug Limited, a pharmaceutical distributor.

Provigo's dominance in the food industry so far was mainly due to its wholesale activities, which still earned about 75% of the company's sales. In Quebec, the market for independent grocers was growing again as more women were working, families were smaller, and fewer people were shopping in large supermarkets.

Provigo decided to expand its retail operations, extending its Jovi, Provibec, and Provigo stores into all areas of Quebec City. In November, 1980, it bought all the shares of Abbatoir St.-Valerien Inc., which operated a large slaughterhouse. And in January, 1981, the company acquired Sports Experts Inc. In February, Provigo bought 87 of Dominion Stores' Quebec operations and distributing facilities. Pierre Lessard, who had become president and general manager in 1976, told *The Wall Street Journal* that "getting a larger presence in Montreal was the key to the transaction."

From the beginning, the Dominion stores had trouble. The managers responsible for integrating the new stores did not always agree with the managers of other Provigo supermarkets, and because of their differences, the stores had to be transformed one by one, taking six months longer than expected. As operational losses grew, the acquisition put several other projects on the shelf and cost the company a great deal of money and work. By 1984, Richard Constantineau, who had managed the Dominion stores, had resigned. Several of the Dominion stores were sold to affiliates and about 30 were closed. Others continued to do business until 1986, when the last were closed.

Provigo was involved in another price war in 1983, this time as a retailer. It began when Provigo's competitor, Steinberg Inc., started giving its customers coupons worth 5% of their total purchase, redeemable at the next purchase, a plan that won over shoppers immediately. Two days later, Provigo retaliated by offering a 6% discount on most products, which could be applied immediately to the purchase, as well as accepting discount coupons issued by Steinberg. When asked what it would take to end the price war, Turmel told *The Globe and Mail*, "I think it will be over when our competitor sees our results. They'll see we can withstand it better than they can . . . . We don't like it, but we can stand it." Provigo's colorful advertisements drew more customers during the war, and attracted wide press coverage.

In October, the company suffered another crisis when 45 of its Montreal-based Provigo stores were shut down by a strike, following a one-week strike at Steinberg. About 2,200 workers asked for increased job security and wages. After four weeks, Provigo offered a contract that matched Steinberg's contract with its workers, and the Provigo labor force accepted.

In 1984, Provigo extended its reach in the fast-food area by becoming a majority owner of Restaurants Les Pres Limitée, which operated four restaurants and was set to open eight more. Provigo also planned to focus on the convenience-store industry, which was blossoming in Quebec. And the company began installing automatic banking machines in its major stores. In July, company stores also announced price cuts on many items with a campaign called Permaprix. Between 1980 and 1985, Provigo more than doubled its profits.

In April, 1985, Antoine Turmel retired, and the president of the Montreal stock exchange, Pierre Lortie, resigned that post to take control of Provigo as CEO. Later in the year, Pierre Lessard, who many had believed would take Turmel's place, stepped down from his position as president.

That year was also full of new ventures. Capitalizing on the many young couples who were buying and repairing old houses, Provigo went into the home-renovation business in February, becoming partners with a building supply firm, Val Royal LaSalle, to open a large home-renovation center in Montreal. That month the company also joined with Collegiate-Arlington Sports Inc. in Toronto, merging its Sports Experts division to form a new national business called Sports Experts Inc. In August, Provigo purchased a majority stake in Consumers Distributing Company, a catalogue showroom firm in Ontario. And the company decided to broaden its presence in eastern Quebec by purchasing Alphonse Allard Inc. and Approvisionnement Atlantique, both food wholesalers.

In an effort to increase profits as well as geographical growth, Provigo divided its businesses into five groups: food distribution (still comprising about two-thirds of its business), pharmaceuticals, convenience stores, nonfood distribution, and Provigo U.S.A. Lortie believed this restructuring would enhance Provigo's national presence and help block competition from other firms. Provigo's American subsidiaries had merged under the new restructuring, and sales increased to account for about 14% of the annual total.

In 1986, Provigo acquired Pharmacom Systems Limited, a supplier of computer systems to pharmacies. The Sports Experts subsidiary opened five stores, the National Drug subsidiary opened a new distribution center, and several new food-distribution centers and cash-and-carry warehouses were also opened. Provigo undertook a joint venture with McKesson Corporation in San Francisco to distribute health supplies and equipment in Canada. In the supermarket division, the company expanded its fresh-foods and specialty departments.

By 1987, the pharmaceuticals operation was Provigo's fastest-growing business, and in February, the company consolidated its C$1 billion operation into one company called Medis Health and Pharmaceuticals Services Inc. The move was viewed by many as a guard against Steinberg, Provigo's fiercest competitor; analysts had predicted that Steinberg would enter the drug-distribution market soon. Provigo also planned to spend C$18 million building drug-distribution warehouses in Montreal and Toronto. In November, the company bought the remaining shares of Consumers Distributing Company.

In 1988, Unigesco Inc., a holding company, and Empire Company, a supermarket concern, raised their joint stake in Provigo stock from about 41% to 51%, and the president of Unigesco, Bertin Nadeau, who had been a director at Provigo since 1985, gained control of the company as the head of this 51% consortium.

Steinberg had been seeking bids for its supermarkets due to a quarrel in the Steinberg family, and in April, 1988 Provigo and Metro-Richelieu Inc., another food wholesaler, made a joint bid for its Quebec stores, planning to convert them into their own. Provigo and Metro-Richelieu were very competitive, and the joint bid insured that a bidding war would not occur between them. In the end however, with a new labor agreement, Steinberg opted not to sell its supermarkets after all.

In June, 1988, Provigo began to act on its plans for expansion in the United States, purchasing the Petrini's upscale supermarket chain in San Francisco, ten Alpha Beta stores, and five Lucky Supermarkets throughout northern California. The company is also positioning to establish itself in Europe and Japan by organizing Provigo International to increase exports.

Provigo's foundation is in wholesaling. Instead of focusing on vertical expansion into food manufacturing like many similar companies, it chose to test its retail and distribution skills in businesses other than groceries. In a country as large and diverse as Canada, Provigo faces the task of predicting the social, economic, and regional trends that influence shoppers' desires. Provigo's future, therefore, will depend largely on its local retailers' sensitivity to the people who walk through their stores.

Principal Subsidiaries: Loeb Inc.; Horne & Pitfield Foods Ltd.; Provigo Distribution Inc.; Sports Experts Inc.; Provigo Corp.; Dellixo Inc.; Medis Health and Pharmaceutical Services Inc.; C Corp. Inc.; Consumers Distributing Co., Ltd.

Further Reading: Provost, René and Chartrand, Maurice. *Provigo: The Story Behind 20 Years of Entrepreneurial Success*, Prentice Hall, 1989.

SAFEWAY STORES INCORPORATED

4th and Jackson Streets
Oakland, California 94660
U.S.A.
(415) 891–3000

Private Company
Incorporated: 1926
Employees: 130,922
Sales: $13.76 billion

With 1,118 stores in the United States and Canada, Safeway Stores is one of the largest food chains in the world. Safeway's ten major distribution centers deliver thousands of food and nonfood items, both national and private-label brands, to its retail outlets around North America. Acquired by Kohlberg, Kravis & Roberts Company and taken private in 1986, Safeway was radically downsized in the following two years. Yet Safeway's streamlining efforts have been so successful at reducing the debt incurred during the leveraged buyout that the company may soon go public again.

In the early days of this century S. M. Skaggs saw that the grain farmers in his community of American Falls, Idaho were poorly served by their local grocery stores. Without money except at harvest-time, their buying power was considerably reduced by the heavy credit charges that store owners levied. Also, the variety and quality of goods was poor, causing much customer dissatisfaction. As a minister, Skaggs was interested in solving these problems. He talked a local bank president, D. W. Davis (later the governor of Idaho), into a loan, and then set himself up in an 18-by-32-foot store and opened for business.

Despite his zeal, Skaggs could not make his store particularly profitable, so in 1915 he sold it to his son, M. B. Skaggs, who at age 27 had already been involved in business for years. The younger Skaggs added energy and sound business sense to his father's sense of mission, and by 1926 he was running a chain of 428 grocery stores throughout California and the Pacific Northwest. People flocked to Skaggs's stores, not only for the cash-and-carry plan which his father helped to create, but because Skaggs used every inch of store space to stock a large variety of goods and worked hard to get quality meat and other perishables.

In 1926 Charles Merrill, one of the founders of Merrill Lynch, was looking to expand his investment firm's involvement in the retail chain store business. Seeing a huge potential for growth in the West, he purchased Safeway Stores, a chain of some 240 stores founded by Sam Seelig in 1914 that covered most of the Pacific coast. Merrill had the capital and the stores to do business; all he needed was experienced management. Merrill asked the president of Safeway, James Weldon, who the best man to run the new venture was. Weldon named M. B. Skaggs as his only choice, and soon Skaggs had been persuaded to add his chain of 428 stores to Safeway's 240. The newly expanded venture kept the Safeway name and Skaggs was made president of Safeway's operating subsidiaries in California and Nevada in addition to retaining control over his own stores.

Merrill had insisted his deal with Skaggs be profitable, so Skaggs expanded the business at a tremendous pace during its early years. By 1928 Safeway had expanded to 2,020 stores and its stock was listed on the New York Stock Exchange. All of this pleased Merrill so much that he made Skaggs president of the entire company. The following year Safeway even ventured into international expansion, establishing Canada Safeway Ltd. in Winnipeg. Noting the different distribution system used in Canada, Safeway acquired a Canadian wholesaling business to eliminate the usual high price markup there.

The Depression years decreased consumers' food budgets dramatically, creating difficulty in the low-profit-margin grocery industry, but Safeway was able to survive, thanks once again to Charles Merrill. In 1928 Merrill had sent Lingan Warren to run a string of about 1,400 grocery stores in the Pacific Northwest known as the MacMarr Stores. Warren had earned Merrill's confidence through his insight into the mechanics of store management. In 1931, with both the MacMarr and Safeway chains hurt by sliding profits, a deal was brokered to unite the two chains, and Lingan Warren became a part of Safeway. Assuming the presidency of the company in 1934 and holding it until 1955 (Skaggs became chairman of the board), Warren exerted a huge influence on Safeway throughout his tenure with the firm. He helped to innovate policies that educated consumers about what they were getting, such as supplying scales to price fruits and vegetables by the pound rather than the piece. Warren pushed the idea of allowing customers to serve themselves whenever possible, cutting overhead costs, and he also involved the company in special merchandising campaigns that served more individual grocery needs. Together Skaggs's energy as chairman of the board and Warren's nuts-and-bolts insight gave Safeway the strength to weather the Depression.

World War II brought much-needed relief to the grocery business, as the general economic turnaround created by huge government spending put money back into consumers' hands. After the war, Safeway shared in the economic explosion that America, and particularly the West, experienced. Soldiers returning from the Pacific theater liked what they saw of the West Coast, and by 1947 they made up a third of Safeway's work force and helped the firm reach $1 billion in sales. In 1949 Safeway launched a massive building campaign to replace more than 1,000 old stores with newer, larger models. The $200 million project brought many conveniences such as dairy sections, self-help meat stands, and frozen food cases into the Safeway mainstream.

Despite the Korean War, when wage and price controls as well as material rationing were still in effect, Safeway prospered enough to improve and expand its warehousing and distribution operations. The famous "S" insignia, adopted in 1952, could be seen on vast new warehouses in most western states. This extensive warehousing system quickly gave it a reputation for stocking high-quality meats, which meant that many consumers felt that Safeway was the only major grocery chain that could offer them the chance to fill all their food needs under one roof.

In 1954 Safeway joined the list of firms that offered their employees major medical coverage, a move that helped cement good labor relations. In 1955 an era ended at Safeway when Lingan Warren retired from his posts as president, general manager, and director of the company. The slight, bespectacled, reedy-voiced superclerk had been one of the driving forces in the firm for almost a quarter century. Warren was succeeded as president by Milton Selby, a longtime member of Safeway management. Robert Magowan, Charles Merrill's son-in-law, was named company director and chairman of the board, leaving his post as securities and marketing services director at Merrill Lynch.

Magowan took over Safeway completely when he was named president of the firm in 1957. That same year the company reached $2 billion in sales, a doubling of total volume in only ten years. Safeway was the only firm west of the Mississippi selling at that volume. Under Magowan, Safeway would expand at an even faster rate than ever before, becoming the first retail food chain to sell more than $10 billion worth of merchandise. Magowan's aggressive marketing strategy and hunger for expansion attracted national attention and greatly enhanced the public profile of the company. By 1959, under Magowan's leadership, Safeway had moved into Alaska and Iowa.

At the beginning of the 1960s, Safeway's construction program had ensured that almost half of the firm's retail outlets were less than five years old and close to two-thirds were less than a decade old. In 1960 the company opened operations in Louisiana. Safeway's first overseas expansion campaign came in 1962, when the company bought a string of 11 stores in England. The following year Safeway crossed the Pacific to open stores in Australia and Hawaii, and strengthened its presence in Alaska. In 1964 Safeway moved into West Germany and opened the first "international" supermarket in Washington, D.C. Stocking food products from all of the world's major cuisines, this store was built to be a kind of United Nations of food, offering Washington's shoppers everything they needed to prepare native dishes from around the world.

In 1965 the Amalgamated Meat Cutters and Butchers Workmen's Local 576 picketed Safeway's Kansas City Stores. Most stores in the area were able to operate, but some were shut down and business was hurt at almost all local stores. This was one of several labor disputes that occurred in the 1960s and 1970s.

When the company reached its 40th anniversary in 1966 it proudly announced that it had reached $3 billion dollars a year in sales—and had paid a dividend through the Depression, World War II and ten years of material shortages and price controls. During the same year, Quentin Reynolds succeeded Robert Magowan as president of the company.

In 1969 Robert Magowan resigned as CEO of the firm, phasing out his active involvement in the company. This created some uncertainty since his tenure as Safeway's lead manager had been spectacularly successful.

In 1970 Quentin Reynolds became Safeway's CEO and William Mitchell succeeded Reynolds as president; Robert Magowan kept only his post as chairman of the executive committee. Mitchell would lead the firm to yet more expansion—in 1972 Safeway surpassed the Great Atlantic & Pacific Tea Company (A&P) as the world's largest food retailing chain. In 1971 Safeway was among the first to adopt the now-common practice of labeling ground beef by fat content rather than by weight alone, continuing the firm's tradition of supplying consumers with all the facts they needed to make a purchasing decision.

In the mid-1970s several legal issues surrounding the company came to a head. In 1973 a suit filed against Safeway by the United Farm Workers (UFW), led by Cesar Chavez, was denied class action status, a major victory for Safeway. The UFW, along with other groups, had wanted Safeway to pressure lettuce and grape growers to accept the UFW as the employees' collective bargaining agent. Safeway claimed that when it refused, the UFW undertook a campaign of harassment and sabotage, and countersued the UFW for $150 million.

Then in 1974 Safeway was named with most of its competitors in a $1.5 billion suit brought by a group of cattlemen for allegedly fixing prices in the purchase of dressed beef. Although Safeway only paid the cattlemen $150,000, in making the payment the firm agreed "to continue to comply with the antitrust laws."

Dale L. Lynch was named president of Safeway in 1977, taking William Mitchell's place. Lynch thought that Safeway needed to offer a greater variety of goods and services to maintain its position as the leading food retailer. Eventually Lynch's idea led to the execution of the one-stop-shopping concept.

Robert Magowan officially ended his active role in Safeway in 1979, serving only as honorary director of the firm after this time. He had resigned his post as a company director and chairman of the executive committee in the previous year. That year Safeway was involved in another legal case. A young shelf-stocker challenged his dismissal by the firm for violating a "no beard" policy and took his case all the way to the Supreme Court. The Court upheld Safeway's position, setting an important precedent regarding a company's right to regulate workers' appearances.

In 1980 Peter Magowan, Robert Magowan's son, succeeded William Mitchell as chairman and CEO of the firm. Peter Magowan's corporate strategy stressed state-of-the-art technology in retailing and merchandising, aggressive marketing campaigns, and incentive programs for employees.

Magowan, as part of his expansion plans, reached agreements to buy a chain of stores in Australia. This heightened internationalism helped to compensate for price wars with A&P and Giant Food Inc. Even though Safeway was selling about $16 billion worth of goods each year, any dip in consumer interest hurt profits because the profit margin in the retail food business is only about 1%.

In 1982 Safeway increased its appeal to customers by beginning to sell many health-oriented products, implementing Dale Lynch's concept of one-stop shopping. The firm also formed a joint venture with the Knapp Communications Corporation to create a string of gourmet food stores called Bon Appetit. Two such stores in the San Francisco Bay area offer delicacies like truffles and rare cheeses in a supermarket setting.

James A. Rowland replaced Dale Lynch as president and CEO in 1983. Rowland was known for his sensitive management style; his appointment heralded a new era of improved employee relations. One innovation Rowland introduced was the PAYSOP program, which linked employees' success to Safeway's by granting most workers stock in the company as part of their payment. At this time Safeway also began offering bulk food items and installed salad bars to keep pace with its customers' desires.

In 1985 Safeway merged its Australian operations with Woolworth's Ltd. amid increasing speculation that the chain would be the victim of a takeover bid. The merger between Safeway and Woolworth's gave Safeway a large pretax cash bonanza, leading to speculation that the firm might be trying to liquidate some of its assets to slim down and create a cash pool to buy its own stock and thwart any unfriendly bids.

In June, 1986 all speculation ended when the Dart Group Corporation, led by the Haft family, announced that it had acquired about 6% of Safeway's stock and would try to gain a controlling interest. Since the Hafts were known raiders and had no food retail experience, Safeway never believed that the takeover would be anything but unfriendly. Dart ultimately offered $64 a share for Safeway. Safeway management rebuffed the takeover bid with talk of breaking up the company. The matter was finally resolved in August, 1986, when Safeway was acquired and taken private by Kohlberg, Kravis, Roberts & Company (KKR) for $69 a share or $4.3 billion. The Hafts ended their hostile takeover bid for an option to buy 20% of the holding company that was founded to buy Safeway.

Saddled with enormous debt after the buyout, Safeway was forced to streamline its operations and sell a large number of its stores to reduce the crushing interest burden it had assumed. In 1987 Safeway sold its Liquor Barn retail outlets to Majestic Wine Warehouses Ltd., its 59 grocery stores in Texas and New Mexico, its entire Oklahoma division, and announced plans to sell 172 stores in southern California to the Vons Companies. The biggest sale of all was that of Safeway's British operations to the Argyll Group PLC.

The streamlining of Safeway ended in 1988 when the firm sold its 99 Houston-area stores to an investment group led by local Safeway management. The sale and trimming of unprofitable operations reduced Safeway's debt and increased its profitability so much that KKR announced in 1988 that Safeway might go public again within a year or two. Chairman and CEO Magowan claimed that the leveraged buyout of Safeway forced it to become more competitive than it had been, so much so that in 1988 the firm made a greater operating profit on $14 billion in sales than it did on $20 billion in sales in 1985. By selling a total of around 1,100 stores for about $2.4 billion, Safeway was able to slash its debts while losing assets that only created $50 million in profits a year after taxes.

The leveraged buyout of Safeway became a lightning rod for discussion about the merits of corporate takeovers in general. The firm itself feels that the experience has led to a smaller but more efficient company. Safeway has shown unusual flexibility for a giant in its field. Its success in weathering a takeover would seem to promise no shortage of buyers when the company does go public again, demonstrating as it does that Safeway should be able to maintain its remarkable success in the future.

Principal Subsidiaries: Safeway Holdings, Inc.; Glencourt, Inc.; Casa Ley, S.A. Mexico (49%); Controladora de Empresas del Noroeste, S.A. de c.v. (49%)(Mexico); Brentway, Inc.; Salvage, Inc.; Safeway International Disc. Inc.; Oakland Property Brokerage, Inc.; H.J.M. Properties; Hobbiton Holdings, Inc.; Safeway Foreign Sales (Virgin Islands); Safeway Netherlands (Antilles) Finance Corp. N.V. (Netherlands).

J SAINSBURY PLC

Stamford House
Stamford Street
London SE1 9LL
United Kingdom
(1) 921–6000

Public Company
Incorporated: 1922 as J. Sainsbury Ltd.
Employees: 82,000
Sales: £5 billion (US$9.04 billion)
Stock Index: London

Supermarkets, hypermarkets, and other grocery outlets clustered tightly in the south of England form the nucleus of Britain's largest food and wine retailer: J Sainsbury plc, or Sainsbury's, as it is widely known. The company's expansion over a period of 120 years has been cautious but inexorable, accelerating in the past two decades, and recently venturing overseas. Unlike other major food companies that have diversified into other business areas to counter the slow growth expected in the food market, Sainsbury's is simply building the retailing business in which it excels.

Sainsbury's is not only Britain's largest retailer of food and wine but also its most respected, according to nationwide surveys of city analysts and company directors. The company has earned top or near-top ratings for product and service quality, successful development, profitable pricing, overall financial performance, advertising and marketing, superior management, and recruitment, training, and retention of high-caliber employees. More than a third of Sainsbury's employees own shares in the company.

Sainsbury's was off to a romantic but practical start in 1869 when two young employees of neighboring London shops met, married, and started a small dairy store in their three-story Drury Lane home. Mary Ann Staples, 19, had grown up in her father's dairy business. John James Sainsbury, 25, had worked for a hardware merchant and grocer. Their shop was a success from the start, as both John and Mary Ann had the business knowledge and capacity for hard work that it took to win the loyalty of the local trade. Their passion for order, cleanliness, and high-quality merchandise made the shop an inviting place, in contrast to the prevalent clutter of many tiny family-owned shops and the insanitary conditions of the street vendors' stalls and carts.

Seven years later the Sainsburys opened a second shop in a newly developed section of town and moved into the upper portion of the building. Within a few years, they had opened several similar branches, planning to have a shop for each of their sons to manage when he grew up. By the time their six sons were adults, the branches far outnumbered them. Yet caution has always been characteristic of Sainsbury expansion; they regularly passed up opportunities to buy groups or chains of stores, preferring to develop each new store independently.

The passion for high quality led them to a turning point in 1882, when they opened a branch in Croydon. They used advanced design and materials that had an elegance not attempted in the other shops and made the store easy to keep clean. The walls, floor, and counter fronts were tiled, the countertops were marble slabs. Customers were seated on bentwood chairs. The store's cleanliness—still a rarity in food shops of that time—and elaborate decor helped attract more prosperous customers; it was an instant success. Several similar shops were added during that decade, while Sainsbury's also developed a less elaborate design for suburban branches opened during those years. In these, business could be done through open windows, as in the common market areas, but the design also attracted customers to come into the store to see a greater variety of food.

In 1891, Sainsbury's moved its headquarters to Blackfriars, where it remains. The location provided easy access to wholesale markets and transportation. To obtain the best quality in food, Sainsbury's has always kept in close touch with suppliers, and it controlled and distributed stock from a central depot until the 1960s.

By the turn of the century sons John Benjamin, George, and Arthur were working in the family business; they and other company employees were trained with equal care and attention to detail. Alfred and Paul went through the same training when they joined the company in 1906 and 1921 respectively. Frank, the third son, took up poultry and pork farming in 1902 and became a major supplier.

By the turn of the century, in terms of numbers, rivals seemed to be outdistancing Sainsbury's. Lipton's, the largest, had 500 stores. It took Sainsbury's another 14 years to open its 115th branch. But Sainsbury's continued to place the highest priority on quality, taking the time to weigh each decision, whether it meant researching suppliers for a new product, assessing the reliability of a new supplier, or measuring the business potential of a new site.

The outbreak of World War I slowed expansion plans even further. Rationing and shortages of food, particularly fresh produce, led to the creation of grocery departments selling jams, spices, potted meat, and flour—all bearing Sainsbury's own label. Women began attending the training classes at the Blackfriars headquarters, to replace the male employees who had left for military service. Some worked in the packing plant on Sainsbury-label foods; others served as salespeople in the stores.

Eldest son John Benjamin took much of the initiative in

the postwar years, adding new grocery lines while retaining his father's insistence on high quality. By 1922 there were 136 branches, many of them along the new suburban rail lines, and the firm was incorporated. Mary Ann died in 1927 and her husband in 1928, leaving John Benjamin in charge. By this time, so much public attention accompanied branch openings that when Sainsbury's opened a branch in Cambridge, it published an apology in the local newspaper for the impact of a huge opening day crowd. Altogether, 57 new branches were opened between 1919 and 1929, and the gilded glass Sainsbury sign had become a universal symbol of a spacious, orderly interior displaying foods of the finest quality.

There was an apparent break with tradition in 1936 when Sainsbury's bought the Thoroughgood stores, a chain of nine shops in Britain's Midlands. But the purchase was made with the same care and emphasis on quality that had distinguished all other Sainsbury branches. Stamford House, which had been built in 1912 as an extension of the headquarters at Blackfriars, was extended to provide more space for the centralized supply procurement and distribution that maintained quality control for all branches, which by this time numbered 244. Specially designed lightweight vans had replaced horse-drawn vehicles, further speeding deliveries.

World War II not only slowed Sainsbury's growth, through shortages of food and labor, but also brought the stores into the line of fire. Some branches were totally destroyed; others were extensively damaged. Vehicles carrying mobile shops carried on trade as far as possible in the areas affected by the Blitz. But the evacuation of bomb-damaged areas made it impossible to carry on the centralized procurement and distribution operation that had provided efficiency, economy, and standardization of products and services. Along with other wartime restrictions, this caused sales to dwindle to half the prewar level.

John Benjamin's sons Alan and Robert, who had shared the general manager's post since their father's retirement in 1938, became deeply aware of the crucial role of communications during the trying days of this wartime decentralization. The *JS Journal*, begun in 1946 (and its sister publication, the *Employee Report*, begun in the late 1970s) exemplifies the thorough job of reporting that to this day keeps staff members abreast of company developments and business conditions. Both publications have won national awards for excellence.

Long before the last of the wartime restrictions were lifted in 1954, the brothers had begun an aggressive recovery program. Basic operations were recentralized to regain the economies of scale that kept prices down while retaining a substantial profit margin. Alan studied America's burgeoning supermarkets and opened the first self-service Sainsbury's in June, 1950 in Croydon, where his grandfather had opened his "turning point" store nearly 70 years earlier.

Expansion in the 1950s often meant converting existing stores to supermarkets in addition to adding new outlets. In 1955, the 7,500-square-foot Sainsbury's at Lewisham was considered the largest supermarket in Europe. By 1969, Sainsbury supermarkets had an average of 10,000 square feet of space. Today's supermarkets and hypermarkets have tripled that amount.

John Benjamin and Arthur were the only two of the founders' sons whose own sons joined the family business. Arthur's son James, who had joined the company in 1926, was named Commander of the Order of the British Empire for his accomplishments. He created new factory facilities at Sainsbury's headquarters in 1936 and also set up the Haverhill line of meat products.

John Benjamin's sons Alan and Robert, and Alan's son John, were also honored for their work. Alan was made Baron Sainsbury of Drury Lane in 1962, and his son John was made Baron Sainsbury of Preston Candover in 1989. Robert was knighted in 1967. Today Alan and Robert share the presidency of Sainsbury's, John is chairman, and Robert's son David is deputy chairman.

With typical caution, Sainsbury's did not actually use the word supermarket in its own communications until the late 1960s, even though it owned almost a hundred. Nonetheless, the company was at the forefront of new technology. In 1961, for example, Sainsbury's became the first food retailer to computerize its distribution system. In the late 1980s, electronic cash registers at the checkout counter were replaced by scanning. Multibuy, a special feature of the scanning system, automatically applies a discount to multiple purchases of certain designated items. Spaceman, a microcomputer planning system, uses on-screen graphics to plot the allocation of merchandise to specific shelf space in the stores. EFTPOS, an electronic funds transfer system, allows customers to use debit cards to make purchases.

Sainsbury's centenary, 1969, sparked a series of rapid changes. Alan's son, John, became chairman of a new management tier, which now reported directly to the board of directors. Departmental directors were given greater responsibility for operating functions to strengthen the centralized control that had always been company policy. With ordering, warehousing, and distribution computerized, strict controls on the speeded-up activity were vital. Sainsbury's became a public company in 1973, two years after making a name change: the period after the initial J was dropped.

In the 1970s Sainsbury's began to make significant additions to its nonfood merchandise for the first time. The company's first petrol station, a convenience for shoppers, was opened in 1974 at a Cambridge store. To gain the economies of direct supplier-to-store deliveries, Sainsbury's formed a joint venture with British Home Stores in 1975, launching a chain of hypermarkets called Savacentre. Sainsbury's retained control of all food-related operations, leaving nonfood lines to its partner until 1988, when Savacentre became a wholly owned subsidiary of Sainsbury's.

Homebase, another chain, was in the planning stage by 1979. In 1981, the first Homebase home and garden center was opened. Sainsbury's owns 75% of Homebase; the other 25% is owned by GB-Inno-BM, the largest Belgian retailer, known for its worldwide leadership in merchandising products for do-it-yourselfers.

In 1983, Sainsbury's began to acquire an interest in Shaw's Supermarkets, a New England supermarket chain.

Shaw's was founded in 1860, and has a similar history of high-quality food at the lowest prices obtainable through efficiency of management and distribution. And like Sainsbury's, Shaw's has also been at the forefront of computer technology. By 1987, Sainsbury's had completed purchase of 100% of the 60 stores in Massachusetts, Maine, and New Hampshire, and had plans to open additional stores in that area.

Personnel policies at Sainsbury's have adhered closely to the principles established at its founding: thorough training, open communication, and continuing training on the job. The company recruits actively at schools and universities, preferring to "grow its own talent," but holding employees to high standards of performance. With other leading companies and the City University Business School, Sainsbury's conducts a practical management course, the Management MBA. Sainsbury's employees participate in profit sharing and share option schemes.

The company's community involvement has been active, taking many forms. John Sainsbury addressed the London Conference on saving the ozone layer early in 1989. The only retailer invited to take part in the conference and the associated exhibition, he presented details of the technological changes made in Sainsbury's aerosol products and plant operations to eliminate chlorofluorocarbons from their operations. (Sainsbury's high-quality private-label products are a booming business.) Incubation of small start-up businesses, arts sponsorships, and grand-scale charity drives are other ongoing projects.

John James Sainsbury's principles and passions are alive and well, and continuing to foster cautious growth under the leadership of the family business's fourth generation. The company and family continue to control the majority of shares, and management seems intent on continuing the practices that have brought it success.

Principal Subsidiaries: Homebase Ltd. (75%); J Sainsbury Properties Ltd.; J Sainsbury Farms Ltd.; The Cheyne Investments Ltd.; The Cheyne Investments, Inc. (USA); The Sainsbury Charitable Fund Ltd.; J Sainsbury (Finance) B.V. (Netherlands); Savacentre Ltd.; Shaw's Supermarkets, Inc. *Associates*; Haverhill Meat Products Ltd. (50%); Breckland Farms Ltd. (50%); Kings Reach Investments Ltd. (28.76%).

THE SOUTHLAND CORPORATION

Post Office Box 719
2828 Haskell Avenue
Dallas, Texas 75221
U.S.A.
(214) 828-7011

Private Company
Incorporated: 1961
Employees: 50,724
Sales: $12.7 billion

In 1927 John Jefferson approached Joseph C. Thompson, one of five founding directors of the Dallas Southland Ice Company, with a new idea. He wanted to sell milk, eggs, and bread through his retail ice dock. "You furnish the items," he suggested, "and I'll pay the power bills." Thompson agreed, and together they established the first known convenience store.

The newly formed Southland Ice Company was comprised of four separate ice companies and operated eight ice plants and 21 retail ice stations. Today, the Southland Corporation is the nation's largest operator and franchisor of convenience stores, with five distribution centers, six food-processing centers, and a 50% interest in the refining and distribution of Citgo Petroleum.

After a visit to Alaska in 1928, one Southland manager traveled home to Texas and planted a souvenir totem pole in front of his store. The pole attracted so much attention that the employee suggested placing one at every Southland-owned retail ice dock and naming the stores "Tote'm Stores," since the consumers toted away their purchases.

Southland decided to go with the new name; it unified the company's diversified stores and provided a distinct identity, a key ingredient in the successful operation of numerous retail outlets. Joseph Thompson, secretary-treasurer of Southland Ice, unified the stores further by training staff with daily sales talks. He also chose a company uniform for ice station service men. Thompson recognized early on that consumers should receive the same quality and service at every store. During this time Southland also began to experiment with constructing and leasing gasoline stations at ten of its Dallas-area stores.

The Depression plunged Southland into bankruptcy in 1931. During a period of receivership and reorganization, Joseph Thompson was named president, a move which ensured continuity during the rocky period. The management team chosen during this time was especially strong, and led Southland for a number of years. W. W. Overton Jr., a Dallas banker, helped disentangle the young company's finances by organizing the purchase of all Southland bonds for seven cents on the dollar, which eventually put ownership of the company under the control of the board of directors.

Despite the financial confusion, profits from the Tote'm Stores continued to climb, and with the repeal of Prohibition in 1933, ice and beer sales surged.

Once it was on more stable footing, Southland began vertical integration with construction of Oak Farms Dairies in 1936, using public relations to market its new dairy products by offering a free movie for six of its milk-bottle caps. A crowd of 1,600 attended the Dallas theater sponsoring the event. By 1939 Southland operated 60 Tote'm Stores in the Dallas–Fort Worth area, triple the number operating when the company was founded 12 years earlier.

With the onset of World War II, demands for ice peaked; Southland became the chief supplier of ice for the construction and operation of Camp Hood, the United States Army's largest training camp. The dramatic increase in business prompted reorganization of the company. Southland bought City Ice Delivery, Ltd.; the acquisition included two modern ice plants, 20 retail stations, and property on Haskell Avenue, where the new company headquarters was sited. Southland became the largest ice operator in Dallas.

By 1945 Southland owned stores scattered over north-central Texas, operating from seven in the morning to 11 at night, seven days a week. The firm Tracey-Locke, commissioned to create a new name, chose "7-Eleven" to emphasize the firm's commitment to long operating hours to serve customers better. At this time Southland remodeled all 7-Eleven stores, doubling the amount of floor space at each retail outlet.

After the war, America's pent-up consumer appetite surged. Refrigerators, however, were not yet readily available to the public. To meet demands for block ice, Southland bought Texas Public Utilities, which owned 20 ice plants, in 1947, making Southland the largest ice operator in Texas. In 1948, Joseph Thompson's oldest son, John P. Thompson, was named to the board of directors.

At a management meeting in Washington, D.C. in 1956, a blizzard blanketed the city. John Thompson noticed that in densely populated areas, people could walk to the stores even when the weather made driving impossible, and that 7-Eleven's long operating hours and unusual stock could provide exactly what customers might need, from canned soup to tissues to aspirin. Southland began to focus on the traffic patterns around potential store sites, choosing high-volume corners whenever possible.

At the end of the 1950s, John Thompson, now vice president, began to introduce 7-Eleven stores outside of Texas, in Virginia, Maryland, and eastern Pennsylvania. In reaction to mass-migration to the suburbs, Southland opened more suburban stores. Southland also refined its marketing by studying customer traffic in its stores and eliminating products that moved slowly.

In 1961 Joseph Thompson named his son John as the second president of Southland. His son Jere W. Thompson also was elected vice president of sales. Upon the elder Thompson's death that year, the *Dallas Morning News* credited Thompson with transforming "the ordinary corner ice house from an ice dispensary to a multi-million-dollar drive-in grocery enterprise." John Thompson's first goal as president was to propel Southland from $100 million in annual sales to $1 billion within ten years.

Southland, incorporated in 1961, moved quickly to national prominence. The unprecedented expansion began with dairy acquisitions, notably Midwest Dairy Products in 1962, with production plants and branches in Illinois, Arkansas, Louisiana, and Alabama. Purchasing continued through the 1960s and 1970s, as Southland bought existing convenience market chains in Arizona, New Jersey, Colorado, Illinois, Georgia, and Tennessee. In addition, Southland experimented with its first 24-hour store, in Las Vegas, and expanded to the East Coast and into Canada in 1969.

With the acquisition of 100 SpeeDee Marts in California in 1963, Southland was introduced to the concept of franchising, a system already in operation at the very successful SpeeDee Mart stores. The company developed two-week training sessions for prospective franchisees, which allowed greater decentralization of stores. By 1965, Southland had climbed to 49th in *Fortune*'s top 50 merchandising firms.

In January, 1965, 1,519 7-Eleven stores were operating; by December, 1969 the number had exploded to 3,537. Through a new computer inventory system, 7-Eleven was able to pinpoint its strengths and discover that single purchase items were its best sellers. But with such growth, problems began to surface: due partly to the operation of 24-hour stores, high employee turnover and insufficient security systems drew management attention. The company committed itself to the 24-hour store nonetheless, and the number of 24-hour 7-Eleven stores rose from 817 in 1972 to 3,703 by the end of 1975.

Southland reached $1 billion in sales by 1971, and became a member of the New York Stock Exchange the following year. The first regional distribution center was opened in Florida in 1971; by 1977 several such centers were fully functioning and serving more than 3,000 7-Eleven stores. Jere Thompson, named president of Southland in 1973, continued Southland's American retail store expansion.

Southland began to use microwaves for fast-food sales and introduced self-service gasoline through its newly acquired Pak-a-Sak stores. In 1974, the five-thousandth 7-Eleven store opened in Dallas at the site of John Jefferson's original ice dock.

Penetration of the European market occurred with Southland's purchase of a 50% interest in Cavenham Ltd., a manufacturing corporation controlling 840 retail outlets in Great Britain. By early 1974, Southland's international operations included 50% interest in 1,096 United Kingdom outlets, 75 7-Eleven stores in Canada, and four Super-7 Stores in Mexico.

Negotiations for the introduction of 7-Eleven to Japan were completed in December, 1973, when Southland granted Ito-Yokado, one of Japan's largest retailers, an area license. Like the franchise concept in the U.S., area licensing worked well in Japan because of its emphasis on the individual businessperson operating a store but able to take advantage of 7-Eleven's name and established systems of management and accounting. By late 1978, 188 7-Eleven stores were open for business in Japan.

Also in 1978, Southland bought Chief Auto Parts, a California chain of 119 retail automobile-part stores. By 1986 Chief Auto Parts was the largest convenience retailer of automobile parts in the nation, operating 465 stores. Another Southland acquisition was Tidel Systems, a manufacturer of cash-dispensing systems and underground gasoline-tank-monitoring systems.

But Southland's most significant acquisition by far was the Citgo Petroleum Corporation, purchased in August, 1983. Southland hoped that the $780 million acquisition would provide a smooth supply of gasoline for its convenience stores. But because of a decrease in demand and a glut in capacity throughout the oil-refining industry, the Citgo purchase resulted in a pretax loss of $50 million for Southland. Profits in 1985 exceeded the previous year's loss by $20 million, but nevertheless, Southland cut Citgo's petroleum production in half, expecting Citgo's Lake Charles, Louisiana refinery to be unprofitable. In September, 1986 Southland decided to sell a 50% interest in Citgo to a subsidiary of Petroleos de Venezuela, S.A.

In mid-1987 the Thompson brothers, spurred in part by the threat of a hostile takeover bid by Canadian raider Samuel Belzburg, initiated a leveraged buyout. The buyout, which involved the formation of a temporary holding company called JT Acquisitions, was completed on July 6, 1987.

By the end of 1988 Southland had completed a series of divestitures in order to streamline operations. Southland sold Chief Auto Parts, the snack foods division, the dairies group, Reddy Ice, Chemical/Food Labs, Tidel Systems, 1,000 convenience stores, and related real estate properties. Proceeds from the divestitures, as well as the transfer of royalties from licensees in Japan, went to repay a portion of the $4 billion debt Southland had incurred through the leveraged buyout.

The Southland Corporation, led by the sons of Joseph C. Thompson, entered the 1990s going back to the basics: minding the neighborhood store. As one of the leading retailers in the United States, Southland—still the nation's largest operator and franchisor of convenience stores—commands a reputation its first president would be proud of.

Principal Subsidiary: Citgo Petroleum (50%).

Further Reading: Liles, Allen. *Oh Thank Heaven! The Story of the Southland Corporation*, Dallas, Texas, The Southland Corporation, December 1977.

STEINBERG INCORPORATED

2 Place Alexis Nihon
3500 de Maisonneuve West
Montreal, Quebec H3Z 1Y3
Canada
(514) 931–9131

Public Company
Incorporated: 1930 as Steinberg's Service Stores Limited
Employees: 26,000
Sales: C$4.58 billion (US$3.84 billion)
Stock Index: Montreal Toronto

In 1917, Ida Steinberg opened a small grocery store in Montreal, determined to "give customers a little more than they expect." From this modest beginning the Steinberg family created the empire of food stores, department stores, restaurants, and real estate that Steinberg, Inc. is today.

Ida's son Sam rented an adjacent store in 1919, and seven years later, the second independent store opened in Montreal. By 1930 Sam was operating four stores. He decided to incorporate the company under the name Steinberg's Service Stores Limited that year, and became president.

Like many grocers of that time, the stores were full-service grocery stores that offered delivery services. But in 1933, Steinberg opened a tenth store that was its first self-service one. Self service was a new idea at the time, but as this was during the Great Depression it quickly became a very popular one: at this "cash-and-carry" operation, prices were as much as 20% lower. Steinberg continued to be a trendsetter in the industry when, in 1937, it opened its first two supermarkets, the first in Canada equipped with separate coolers for meat, dairy products, and produce. At these stores Steinberg was also a pioneer in the use of cellophane packaging, as well as in providing parking lots for each store. Six years later, Steinberg installed its first self-service meat counters, where customers could select their own cuts of meat without the help of a butcher.

In 1953, Steinberg entered the real estate market when it established a subsidiary called Ivanhoe, Inc., a real estate–development company. Meanwhile, Steinberg's core grocery division began to experiment with the sale of small nonfood items such as toiletries, cosmetics, housewares, and hardware.

Steinberg became a public company in 1958, and the next year it doubled its outlets when it acquired the 38 Grand Union food stores in Ontario; Ottawa Fruit Supply Ltd.; and Allied Food Markets. In 1961 Steinberg established a general merchandising division called Miracle Mart to enter the general retail industry. In 1962, Steinberg's Shopping Centres was formed to build and acquire shopping centers in Ontario and Quebec, and that year Steinberg opened its first restaurants.

Two years later, the company tallied record sales and net profits due to the steady progress of its food stores and the fortunate beginnings of its eight Miracle Mart department stores. Steinberg expanded from the selling of food to its actual production in 1963, and the company's food stores now had their own private brands of dairy products, fruits and juices, baked goods, and nonfood items.

The company continued its vertical expansion with a 1966 investment of C$8 million in a new Montreal bakery and better manufacturing facilities, and food-production operations were incorporated as Steinberg Foods Limited. The bakery was the largest of its type in Canada, with completely automated assembly and shipping areas, high-speed bread wrappers, an electronic cake line, an automatic pie line, and equipment that produced 2,460 dozen doughnuts an hour.

About this time, chain operations of small milk and grocery stores in urban areas began to spring up, offering new competition for supermarkets. One important advantage convenience stores had was that they were permitted later closing hours in the evening by law. Meanwhile, because of rising prices, the supermarket industry in general came under severe consumer attack. While profits at most supermarket companies suffered, however, Steinberg's finances remained stable, and in the years between 1958 and 1967, it was able to maintain a higher-than-average growth rate.

In 1966, the company bought a substantial interest in Cartier Refined Sugars Limited, a sugar refinery which it later acquired, and that year Steinberg also opened a new chain of drive-in restaurants under the name Pik-Nik.

When industries in Quebec and France began to strengthen their ties, Sam Steinberg joined a group of French businessmen in building a chain of supermarkets in Parisian suburbs; Steinberg retained a 49% interest in the company. The first of these Supermarchés Montréal stores was the largest in the Steinberg chain.

In 1967, Steinberg's 50th anniversary, the company was operating 171 food stores and 15 Miracle Mart department stores. That year it acquired a 30% interest in Phenix Mills Ltd., one of the largest flour mills in Canada.

Investors watched the company closely as, in the midst of its expansion, major changes occurred in the Steinberg family. Leo Goldfarb, an executive vice president and a son-in-law of Sam Steinberg's, left the company to begin his own business in real estate. This left only one other executive vice president, another son-in-law, Melvyn Dobrin.

The company had discontinued its trading stamps in 1967, and two years later had stopped weekend specials, in an attempt to lower prices—its advertisements now claimed the lowest prices in eastern Canada. Arnold

Steinberg, a vice president and Sam Steinberg's nephew, told *The Financial Post* in 1969 that "the customer who shops at Steinberg's week in, week out, can always buy her order cheaper with no strings attached." To combat consumer skepticism, Steinberg began a clever advertising campaign. Randomly picking shoppers who had finished buying their food for the week, it asked them to duplicate their purchases at the company's expense at a competitor's store. The shopper's story and photograph were then used in Steinberg ads. Steinberg hoped for a big jump in sales in the midst of heavy competition, although at first it took a profit loss after cutting prices as much as 15% on some items.

In 1969, Melvyn Dobrin became president. His first challenge was to bring profits up, while preserving the new "miracle" prices. By 1970, profit margins had recovered a bit and sales continued to show a sharp increase over the next four years—Steinberg's share of the Ontario market doubled. The company's recently organized subsidiary, Intercity Food Services, Inc., was also doing well, operating restaurants, snack bars, and doughnut kiosks in Steinberg's and others' shopping centers. But the firm was struggling with its 28 Miracle Mart department stores, which were not as successful.

In 1972, the company made arrangements with Premisteres S.A. to sell its 49% interest in Supermarchés Montréal. The profits of the French concern had not kept pace with sales increases, and Steinberg found it difficult to provide adequate operating controls.

In 1973, the Miracle Food Mart division made a revolutionary move to abolish its general-image advertising and to mount a "give-'em-the-facts" consumer-oriented campaign. The program included a formal Consumer Bill of Rights, nutrition booklets, a key to the codes used to mark perishables, and clearly labeled price tags. Fierce competition continued in the supermarket industry. Although other stores began to revert to using coupon and game promotions, Steinberg concentrated on maintaining its low prices. In general, stores began to get bigger, including bakeries and delicatessens to encourage one-stop shopping, and where the law permitted it, they began to keep late-night hours.

Steinberg showed almost a 30% decline in 1975 earnings as a result of losses suffered by Cartier Sugar Limited, which had been unprotected against wide price fluctuations in the world sugar market.

In 1978 Sam Steinberg died, and Jack Levine became president. Steinberg left his voting shares to his family. Melvyn Dobrin stayed on as CEO. The company adopted its present name, Steinberg Inc., and opened a chain of small, limited-assortment grocery stores in Ontario in 1979 under the "Valdi" name. A year later it purchased three Hypermarches stores in Toronto.

The company began to withdraw from food production and distribution in 1981, closing its Cartier Sugar Plant and its specialty bakery and delicatessen operations. It also sold its nonfood retail companies, Cardinal Distributors Limited, and its 50% interest in Pharmaprix Ltd. In 1983, it also sold its flour mill, Phenix Flour Ltd. Steinberg began to focus less on Quebec as it diversified geographically with the 1981 purchase of Smitty's Super Valu, Inc., a food-store chain in Phoenix, Arizona, and a 1,000-acre parcel of land in Austin, Texas. The company also took steps toward franchising, opening its first La Maisonnée convenience store.

After Jack Levine's retirement in 1982, Peter McGoldrick, a U.S. citizen, took over as president and CEO. He had previously been connected to major supermarket companies in Chicago and Philadelphia. The 18 months he led Steinberg were tumultuous ones.

As the industry leader in Quebec, with mostly unionized employees, Steinberg had been a union target for several years. In October, 1982, the company managed to avert a 5,000-worker strike in its Miracle Food Mart division by reaching a tentative two-year contract with the United Food and Commercial Workers Union. That year, market conditions caused the company to lay off about 800 workers in its Quebec division supermarket, food-manufacturing, and warehousing units. The company sought to renegotiate its labor contract, calling for a two-year wage freeze; the union sought an increase of 11% over two years. In early November, Steinberg was forced to close its Montreal-area supermarkets when the union struck. As a result, almost half of the 835 workers at the warehouse were laid off, and the company lost an estimated C$40 million in sales during the two weeks of the strike. By the end of the month, the company's Montreal-area Miracle Mart employees had also gone on strike. The company warned that unless workers accepted its offer within a week, Christmas sales would plummet and it would be necessary to close stores for about five months. After five days, the union accepted Steinberg's new two-year contract, which included raised wages.

Before the strikes, Steinberg was already losing its number-one spot in the Montreal food market, partly due to labor-connected losses and partly due to a strong competition from cooperative-type supermarkets, which, because they were independently owned, were allowed to sell beer and wine, unlike Steinberg stores. (The Quebec Liquor Permit Board prohibited chains like Steinberg from selling beer or wine to compensate small grocers for the chains' power in food pricing.) It wasn't until 1984 that the board allowed Steinberg stores located in shopping centers to sell beer and wine.

In March of that year, McGoldrick resigned in order to return to the United States. In April, Irving Ludmer became president and CEO. Ludmer had worked for the company between 1957 and 1971, when he left to begin his own real estate firm. He had just rejoined the company in May, 1983.

Ludmer faced the task of turning around profits in a flat market. He reasoned that stores should be adapted to consumer needs, which varied according to environment. Almost immediately, Ludmer brought about major management changes, hiring a team of consultants to offer suggestions. By 1985, store managers were put on an incentive program based on their stores' performances and were given more authority to make changes.

Ludmer made other changes too. In Laval, Quebec, the company opened it first giant supermarket, Marche du Jour, hoping to remedy its ailing sales in Quebec.

The store included a traditional supermarket, a discount warehouse store, and various boutiques. The company also began to update its larger supermarkets, widen the appeal of its convenience stores, and develop its warehouse outlets in Quebec. Steinberg had to make the decision either to pull out of Ontario or to try to gain share rapidly in its slow-growing market; in 1985, Ludmer began to concentrate on Ontario. The company opened several large combination food-and-drug stores and revamped its conventional supermarkets, emphasizing specialty departments. Steinberg also opened a chain of neighborhood perishable-food stores under the name "Les 5 Saisons," and its Multi Restaurants subsidiary opened several new fast-food places. Steinberg and the Price Company of San Diego, California also formed a joint venture to open a maximum of 20 wholesale outlets in Canada by 1990. The Valdi limited-assortment stores in the western provinces were scheduled to be closed in the next two years, and several of the lagging Miracle Mart department stores were to be regional mass-merchandise stores called simply M. In the meantime, Steinberg also set up a real estate subsidiary in the United States.

In 1987, Steinberg began a new strategy to change from a mostly retail organization into a wholesale-retail organization that made use of the synergies between the two. The company acquired Aligro, a large food wholesaler in Quebec, which continued to operate under its original name and management. The company had already acquired in 1986 a 60% interest in Legault and Masse, a Montreal-based wholesaler, to support its La Maisonnée stores.

In October that year the company closed several unconverted Miracle Mart department stores and the Jadis warehouse stores. In the reorganization, Steinberg created a new wholesale division called Steinberg Distribution, a centralized wholesaler, and the company continued to franchise, offering individual grocers the option to join the Steinberg chain.

The company spent C$30 million in improvements for its Miracle Food Marts, creating several large 24-hour food-and-drug stores called Miracle Ultra-Marts. The stores offered fresh fish and deli departments, party-planning services, kitchen centers selling microwave ovens, and hardware and electronic centers.

In August, 1987 an informal takeover bid was made for the company, but it was rejected by most of the Steinberg family members, who now held 90% of the voting shares. This prompted a feud among Steinberg's three daughters and their husbands over whether or not the company should be sold. Mitzi Steinberg Dobrin, the wife of former president Melvyn Dobrin, filed suit against her two sisters, Marilyn Cobrin and Evelyn Alexander, for control of the family's stake in Steinberg.

Early in 1988, several offers were made for the company. In February, the company changed it strategy and began to negotiate for the sale of just its wholesale division and supermarkets, which had suffered chronic losses in recent years. The sale would leave Steinberg with its real estate holdings, its Smitty's supermarket chain in Arizona, and a 50% stake in Lantic Industries, Inc., a large Canadian sugar refinery. In February, a union representing 8,000 of the company's employees offered Steinberg a five-year no-strike contract if it agreed not to sell its supermarkets.

In March, Mitzi Dobrin dropped the lawsuit against her sisters, but that did not halt Steinberg's plans to sell its core supermarkets. In May, the company announced ten supermarket closings. Steinberg had offered its employees a package of wage concessions, but they rejected it.

Soon after, Steinberg's 8,000 unionized employees came to an agreement with the company for less-severe wage concessions and five years without strikes. Because the company had achieved long-term labor peace with its major unions, it agreed not to sell its core of supermarkets in the Montreal area for the next three years.

In November, the Steinberg sisters also came to an agreement. Mitzi Dobrin resigned as a director and Marilyn and Evelyn joined the board. The following year, one sister would step down and allow Mitzi a place on the board, beginning a cycle of rotating membership that insured that two of the sisters would always be on the board.

The company put Smitty's Super Valu, Inc. up for sale and planned to reinvest the proceeds within the company. That same year, the company sold its chain of franchised La Maisonnée convenience stores. In March, 1989, Oxdon Investments made an offer to acquire Steinberg for C$1.1 billion, but the board rejected the bid, sayings its financial viability was questionable. The acquisition would have left Steinberg restructured as a real estate firm. The board decided that it was in Steinberg's best interests to continue its store operations, despite its previous year, which Ludmer called the most difficult in the company's history.

Soon after, Oxdon came back with another offer; meanwhile, a second purchase offer was made by the Corporation d'acquisition Socanav-Caisse Inc., representing Socanav Inc. and the Caisse de dépôt et placement du Quebec. The Steinberg sisters had entered into an agreement with Socanav-Caisse whereby they would not sell to anyone else. Socanav, Canada's leading marine carrier of bulk liquids, is owned by Montreal entrepreneur Michel Gaucher.

After a battle to win the shareholders' favor, Oxdon withdrew its bid and, on August 22, 1989, Steinberg Inc. was sold to Socanav-Caisse Inc. for C$1.8 billion.

In their agreement to purchase Steinberg, Socanav and the Caisse de dépot had decided that the real estate subsidiary, Ivanhoe Inc., would be sold immediately to the Caisse de dépôt, leaving Socanav with the retailing and wholesaling end of the business. Soon after, the new president and CEO of Steinberg Inc., Michel Gaucher, announced his intention to sell Smitty's Super Valu, Inc., the company's 50% equity in Lantic Sugar Limited, and its restaurant group, in addition to stepping up the store franchising progam. In January, 1990 Lantic was sold to B.C. Sugar.

Since Ida Steinberg opened the first Steinberg store, the company has continued to anticipate the customer's expectations, diversifying in order to meet them. Steinberg's future now rests on its new multi-format wholesale and retail ventures, as well as on its new owner's ability to maintain peace with its employees.

Principal Subsidiaries: Aligro Inc.; Franchise 5–16–11 (1987) Inc.; Valdi Foods (1987) Inc.; Invanhoe Inc.; M Stores Inc.; Oak Pharmacies Ltd.; Smitty's Super Valu, Inc.; Steinberg B.V.

THE STOP & SHOP COMPANIES, INC.

Post Office Box 369
Boston, Massachusetts 02101
U.S.A.
(617) 770–8000

Private Company
Incorporated: 1925 as Economy Grocery Stores Corporation
Employees: 44,000
Sales: $4.34 billion

Like all supermarketing giants, Stop & Shop Companies, Inc. has played a major role in the dramatic transformation of American food retailing in this century. Unlike most of its competitors, however, at Stop & Shop the family that oversees the nation's ninth-largest chain of supermarkets also struggled with the company's first growing pains after World War I, some 70 years ago. Sidney R. Rabb joined his uncle Julius in the grocery business outside Boston in 1918. When he died in 1985 his lifelong position as Stop & Shop's chairman of the board was filled by his son-in-law, Avram Goldberg, while his daughter, Carol Goldberg, became president and chief operating officer.

When Sidney Rabb went into his uncle's business, it was a small chain of stores known as the Economy Grocery Stores Company specializing in the sale of grocery products. Such specialization was hardly new—the Great American Tea Company (later A & P) had begun to modify the traditional general store as early as 1859, and even the practice of chain store ownership dated back into the 19th century. The chains did not begin until after 1912, however, when A & P introduced the "economy store," using efficient management and smaller store size to offer lower prices on a cash-only basis—no credit, and no home delivery. The idea rapidly caught on across the country, and it was this merchandising trend which Julius Robbins, his brother Joseph, and his nephew Sidney Rabb followed after the war. Following a period of instability, their chain, Economy, righted itself, and, buoyed by the surging economy of the 1920s, began a program of rapid growth through acquisition in Massachusetts.

As chain store operators gained in strength they were soon able to convince manufacturers to sell to them directly instead of through the usual wholesalers, thus vastly reducing their costs and increasing the competitive advantage they already enjoyed over the traditional independent owner. Consumers preferred the lower prices of the chains—by the mid-1920s, Economy had expanded to 262 stores. In 1925 Sidney Rabb was named chairman, a post he would hold for the next 60 years; Economy issued its first shares of public stock; and Norman S. Rabb joined his brother Sidney in the business. Ten years later, Irving Rabb, youngest of the brothers, also joined. Now operating with considerable momentum, the brothers bought a chain of meat retailers and gave them space in each of their grocery stores.

Although the Great Depression brought many industries to a stand-still, the resulting need for tight household budgeting was in many respects a boon to the economy chain stores. The Rabbs continued to expand with the purchase in 1932 of 106 Grey United Stores located throughout northern New England. The supermarket, a concept that had originated in southern California, based its customer appeal on rock-bottom prices, increased product selection, self service (the customer roamed about the store while the clerk remained at a cash register), and intensive advertising. To the store owner, the new format promised streamlined operation and excellent overall profit. In 1935 the Rabbs opened New England's first supermarket in Cambridge, Massachusetts, in a converted automobile assembly plant. First-year sales were nearly $2 million, equivalent to the revenue of 45 conventional stores.

The Rabbs built more of the new stores as fast as they could, calling them "Stop & Shop Supermarkets." The program continued to do well until the onset of World War II in 1941, when the food industry was swept up in the war effort and had little money or manpower with which to expand. On the other hand, the labor shortage during the war years proved to be another unexpected advantage for the supermarket business, as housewives grew accustomed to serving themselves in all departments of the store, including the meat section; such total self-service meant lower labor costs and increased number of purchases per customer. When the war ended, Economy was well-positioned to proceed with the conversion of its entire chain to the supermarket format, effectively reducing its number of stores while increasing total sales and profits. By 1947 annual sales topped $47 million and the company had changed its name to Stop & Shop, Inc., signaling its total commitment to the supermarket concept.

The postwar boom years saw another period of tremendous growth for Stop & Shop. In order to distribute products more efficiently the company built, between 1948 and 1960, a central bakery, a perishable goods distribution warehouse, and a grocery distribution center in strategic Massachusetts locations. Stop & Shop also quickly established itself in Rhode Island and Connecticut, and by the end of the 1950s was nearing $200 million in sales. The company made an important decision in 1961 to diversify outside the food business with its purchase of Bradlees, a small chain of discount department stores operating largely in shopping centers which already featured a Stop & Shop supermarket. The Rabbs saw in Bradlees a company based on the same high-volume, low-margin marketing used in the food industry. Their expertise soon turned a few moribund stores into a thriving chain. Adding new outlets each year, Bradlees increased its sales from $5 to $107 million between 1962 and 1968.

Over the years Stop & Shop has tried to develop and maintain excellent relations with the communities in which it does business. The company was one of the first to unionize in the 1930s; it created the Stop & Shop Foundation in 1951 to support various civic and cultural projects; and in 1967 it initiated its Consumer Board Program in response to growing public concern about health and environmental issues. In a further move to accommodate changing customer demands, in 1971 the company gave far greater autonomy to each of its store managers, freeing them to respond more directly to the needs of local customers. On the other hand, the company has twice been sued in recent years for allegedly conspiring to fix the prices of certain grocery, meat, and dairy products. Both suits were settled.

Since the late 1960s both Stop & Shop and the Bradlees chain have continued their robust growth. Building on an ever more sophisticated network of warehouse distribution centers, the two chains have expanded geographically, in the total number of stores, and in sales dollars. In addition, in 1968 and 1969 respectively, the company established the Medi Mart Drug Store Company and acquired the Charles B. Perkins Company, a 21-unit New England retailer of tobacco and sundries. A year later all four retailing chains were brought together as divisions of a newly renamed Stop & Shop Companies, Inc., which at that point included 150 supermarkets, 52 Bradlees Department Stores, 10 Medi Marts, and 25 Perkins Tobacco Shops, together totaling about $750 million in sales. Four years later the company celebrated its first $1 billion year; it had doubled that figure by 1980.

Other acquisitions were not as successful. In 1978 Stop & Shop bought Off the Rax, a discount women's clothing store chain, but sold it after six less-than-spectacular years. Similarly, a venture into a more upscale segment of the department store world ended in 1987 with the sale of Almys, a 19-store chain the company had purchased just two years before. And despite a history of steady growth and good profits, Medi Mart and Perkins were also put on the block in the mid-1980s as Stop & Shop decided to concentrate its resources on its two biggest and most lucrative divisions, supermarkets and Bradlees. Bradlees reached a high of 169 units in 1987, combining with the 113 supermarkets to amass $4.34 billion in sales.

In 1985 "Mr. Sidney," Sidney R. Rabb, died and was succeeded as chairman by his son-in-law Avram J. Goldberg. Mr. Goldberg and his wife Carol, now the president of the company, have moved decisively to keep pace with the current trend toward the "superstore," a greatly enlarged and further diversified model of the traditional supermarket. These immense stores average 55,000 to 60,000 square feet in size and are planned around the "street of shops" concept, in which each class of product receives its own well-defined and suitably decorated segment of the store and is offered to the consumer in an ever-larger variety of brands and packaging. Stop & Shop completed its first superstore in 1982 and hopes to finish converting its entire chain by the early 1990s. Thus, after a long and circuitous development, supermarket shopping in the next decade will curiously resemble that of 100 years ago, when families made their progress through a series of neighborhood stores each specializing in a different product line. The "street of shops" has simply moved indoors.

Stop & Shop recently took another step forward into the past when, for the first time since 1924, it once again became a privately owned corporation. Responding to a hostile 1988 takeover bid by the Dart Group Corporation, Stop & Shop's board of directors enlisted the aid of Kohlberg Kravis Roberts in forming a privately held acquisition company to buy all outstanding shares for approximately $1.23 billion. The acquisition company merged with Stop & Shop, whose top management was largely unaffected. To pay down some of its debt, Stop & Shop sold 33 southern Bradless stores and plans to sell more. As it moves into the 1990s, Stop & Shop continues to focus its energy on Sidney Rabb's original business, the retailing of food.

Further Reading: Zimmerman, M.A. *The Super Market: A Revolution in Distribution*, New York, McGraw-Hill, 1955; Peak, Hugh S. and Ellen F. *Supermarket Merchandising and Management*, Englewood Cliffs, N.J., Prentice-Hall, 1977.

SUPER VALU STORES, INC.

11840 Valley View Road
Eden Prairie, Minnesota 55344
U.S.A.
(612) 828–4000

Public Company
Incorporated: 1926 as Winston & Newell Company
Employees: 40,000
Sales: $10.3 billion
Stock Index: New York

Super Valu Stores, Inc. was born of a merger, and a pattern of mergers, acquisitions, and divestitures has marked its rise to eminence in the food wholesale and distribution industry. Minnesota-based Super Valu is the second-largest wholesaler and distributor in the United States, with retail support and distribution centers nationwide. The company operates and franchises retail stores and provides highly developed retail support for the independent grocery store operators who belong to its network of subsidiaries, franchises, and customers. Super Valu also owns, operates, and services a nonfood chain.

Super Valu's origins lie in the merger of the Minneapolis wholesale grocery firms B.S. Bull & Company and Newell and Harrison in the late 19th century. A series of subsequent mergers during the early 20th century culminated in the joining of the Winston, Harper, Fisher Company with the George R. Newell Company to form the Winston & Newell Company. Winston & Newell was incorporated in 1926 in response to the threat that independent retailers faced from the emerging grocery store chains that began developing in the 1920s. Winston & Newell hoped to improve services to these independent retailers so they could withstand the competitive impact of the chain stores; this remains Super Valu's objective today. At the time of its creation, Winston & Newell was serving some 5,000 small grocery stores and had sales of $6 million.

With Minnesotan Thomas G. Harrison at its helm, Winston & Newell became one of the first wholesale distributors in the nation to join the Independent Grocers Alliance (IGA). Harrison, the son of Perry Harrison, a principal in one of the predecessor firms, had joined Winston, Harper, Fisher Company in 1919 as an assistant sales manager. He successively became assistant treasurer and executive vice president, directing the operations of Winston & Newell and later Super Valu in a variety of executive positions from 1926 until his retirement as CEO in 1958.

Harrison, in guiding the company through the Depression, was primarily responsible for introducing many practices which changed the way in which grocery stores conducted business. Cash-and-carry and self-service shopping, almost unheard of at the time, were two of his innovations at Winston & Newell. He broke with tradition again when he stopped using a pricing structure with an arbitrary markup and began charging instead the manufacturer's price plus a percentage fee that declined with volume. This practice gave the company impressive cumulative profits. During the 20-year period from 1942 to 1962, *Fortune* reported that the company's sales volume increased from about $10 million to more than $300 million.

It was during World War II that Winston & Newell began the march to becoming Super Valu Stores and attaining its position as the world's largest food wholesaler and distributor, a position it held until the late 1980s. Although no acquisitions were made during the 1940s, in 1942 the company ended its affiliation with IGA and formed its own association, known in the industry as a "voluntary." Winston & Newell offered independent retailers services such as food processing and packaging, preparation of advertising for individual store use in local newspaper advertising, and store planning assistance, in addition to supplying most of the merchandise sold. This voluntary association introduced the Super Valu name and operated independently from the wholesale business. Super Valu and another voluntary association called U-Save (which was also formed under the auspices of Winston & Newell) were familiar to grocers in Iowa, Minnesota, and North Dakota. By 1942 the company had wholesale sales of $10 million and some 400 stores belonged to its wholesale-retail team.

In 1954 Winston & Newell Company changed its name to Super Valu Stores, Inc. in order to clarify the connection between itself and the voluntary association. In the 1950s Super Valu began to grow by acquiring other voluntary associations. In 1955 it purchased Joannes Brothers of Green Bay, Wisconsin, a firm which had begun serving stores in northern Michigan and northeastern Wisconsin in the 1870s. In 1961 Super Valu moved into the Ohio Valley with the purchase of the Eavey Company, one of the nation's oldest food wholesale distributors.

Acquisition followed acquisition during the 1960s as Super Valu expanded throughout the Midwest. In 1963 the company acquired the J.M. Jones Company of Champaign-Urbana, Illinois and the Food Marketing Corporation of Fort Wayne, Indiana. Each of these companies could trace its beginnings to the early days of the grocery business. Jones began as a general store and developed into a large wholesale business; Food Marketing dated back to the early 1800s, as Bursley & Company and the Bluffton Grocery Company. The Food Marketing acquisition also brought Super Valu into the institutional market.

After acquisition, these two companies were operated as autonomous divisions in a company that has historically given its divisions and stores as much free rein as possible.

Russell W. Byerly became president of Super Valu in 1958. Byerly, a North Dakota native who joined Winston & Newell in 1932 as a bookkeeper, served as president until 1964 and later was chairman of the board and chief executive officer.

In 1964 Super Valu expanded its area of operation outside the Midwest by acquiring Chastain-Roberts Company, which had begun in 1933 as a wholesale flour and feed company, and the McDonald Glass Grocery Company, Inc. of Anniston, Alabama.

In 1965 Super Valu acquired the Lewis Grocer Company of Indianola, Mississippi. The Lewis Grocer Company was founded by Morris Lewis Sr. and eventually became a multi-million dollar wholesale grocer, branching out later into the retail grocery business.

The 1960s were a growth period for Super Valu in ways other than acquisition. The company expanded its retail support services to include accounting, efficiency studies, budget counseling, and store format and design advice. In 1962 Super Valu established Planmark, a department which offers engineering, architectural, and design services to independent retailers, subsidiaries, and corporate stores. Planmark became a division in 1975; with Studio 70, its commercial design arm, Planmark uses computer-assisted design to analyze and develop plans for construction, expansion, or remodeling. This innovation, implemented in the recessionary years of the late 1970s, allows Super Valu retailers to take a project from planning to opening faster than their competition. Super Valu also began providing financial assistance for retailers building new stores, bankrolling some 500 stores in a three-year period in the 1960s. Super Valu also signed leases on its retailers' behalf, allowing them to locate in prime space in shopping centers and other locations.

In 1968 Preferred Products, Inc. (PPI) was incorporated as a subsidiary of Super Valu. A food packaging and processing division, it was started in the 1920s as a department of Winston & Newell. At the time of PPI's incorporation, Super Valu began to develop its private label program; today PPI "processes a limited line of food products under a variety of private labels," according to the company.

Super Valu also formed an insurance agency, Risk Planners, in 1969. This wholly owned subsidiary began by providing insurance on retail property for the company and its retail affiliates. Tailored specifically to the needs of retailers, its products have expanded to include all types of insurance for Super Valu and its stores and franchisees, as well as independent retailers' employees and families.

Diversification was the moving force at Super Valu in the 1970s. Beginning with the 1971 acquisition of ShopKo, a general merchandise discount chain, Super Valu began what has proved to be a highly profitable program of nonfood marketing operations. ShopKo, founded by James Ruben in Chicago in 1961, opened its first store in Green Bay, Wisconsin in 1962. In 1971 Super Valu acquired Daytex, Inc., a textile goods company, but the venture proved unsuccessful and its assets were liquidated in 1976.

When Jack J. Crocker became chairman and CEO of Super Valu in 1972, he initiated another diversification venture, County Seat. A success story in its own right, County Seat opened its first store in 1973 selling casual apparel, including the complete Levi's jeans line. By 1977 there were 183 County Seat stores, and the chain's earnings were $8 million in that fiscal year. When it was sold for $71 million to Carson Pirie Scott and Company of Chicago in 1984, there were 269 stores in 33 states.

Crocker, a CPA who came to Super Valu from the presidency of the Oregon-based grocery and pharmacy chain Fred Meyer, Inc., also directed the company's continuing acquisition and expansion program. Very much a part of the trend toward consolidation in the food wholesale industry, Super Valu continued to purchase smaller food wholesalers, acquiring Pennsylvania-based Charley Brothers in 1977. Charley Brothers, which began as a retail grocery store and moved into wholesaling in 1918, served Shop 'n Save stores and other independent retailers in Pennsylvania.

The advent of universal price codes and scanning equipment in the grocery business led to the introduction, in the mid-1970s, of Testmark, an independent research center providing store measurement data. This data had been available from Super Valu stores since 1965 and, during the period before Testmark was established, had been handled by Super Valu merchandising research, an internal department for clients who preferred not to use commercial research companies. In direct competition with these commercial research companies, Testmark, with Super Valu's backing, offered its customers the advantage of cooperation within the Super Valu network and with major chains and independents nationwide. Testmark's autonomy is enhanced by its Hopkins, Minnesota location, separate from Super Valu's corporate headquarters.

Crocker's tenure at Super Valu was characterized by his success in running what was one of the better-capitalized and stronger wholesalers in the country and by the casual no-frills operation he ran. Company headquarters were in a warehouse, not a plush office. Crocker personally founded a professional soccer team, the Minnesota Kicks, in 1976. They, too, were a Crocker success story, becoming popular in their home territory.

Crocker's successes were apparent on the bottom line, as well. By fiscal 1978 earnings per share had increased approximately 50% since Crocker's first year with Super Valu, but, Crocker explained to *Financial World* in 1977, "I don't think about profits very much. If you're doing things right, profits always follow." By the end of the 1970s Super Valu's sales were $2.9 billion.

Super Valu ushered in the 1980s with the acquisition of Cub Foods, a discount grocery store operation. Warehouse stores, with bare bones facilities and prices, were a phenomenon of the 1970s. Cub Foods was founded by the Hooley family, grocers since 1876 in Stillwater, Minnesota. The Hooleys opened their first warehouse store with the Cub name in a Minneapolis suburb in 1968. When Super Valu purchased the chain in 1980, there were five Cub stores and a Hooley supermarket in Stillwater. Culver M. Davis was appointed president and chief executive officer of Cub Foods in 1985. Davis had joined the Hooley organization in 1960 and was a founder, with the Hooley family, of the discount stores.

Super Valu originally acquired the Cub chain to boost its wholesale sales, but, *Business Week* reported in 1984, soon realized it had a "tiger by the tail," and that Cub had "taken on a (retailing) life of its own." The company improved the atmosphere of Cub Foods stores by using attractive decor, keeping the stores clean, and increasing product offerings, including perishables, which the early warehouse stores did not offer. As a result, Cub Foods evolved into a combination of the conventional grocery store and the warehouse store, known in the industry by the late 1980s as a "super warehouse."

Although Cub Foods competes directly with a number of Super Valu's customers' stores and its own corporate stores, the company saw a benefit in the opportunity Cub offered its retailers to learn about warehouse-store operations from the inside. Several of its retailers did not totally agree, citing a 10% to 15% reduction in business when a Cub Foods store opened in their market area. To address this complaint, Super Valu started franchising its Cub stores and also developed County Market, a downsized version of Cub with the same low prices, but aimed at smaller communities and at independent retailers who could not meet the financial commitment that buying a Cub franchise required. By 1989, Cub Foods's 74 stores (of which Super Valu owned 34) were in nine states and had sales of approximately $3 billion.

By 1986 Super Valu had introduced another variation on the Cub theme. Developed for retailers who needed to improve their stores' look and style to meet competition, the Newmarket format combined warehouse pricing with an upscale product line and services such as video rental, check cashing counters, and baggers. The first Newmarket store opened in the St. Paul–Minneapolis area, and has been so successful that the company is offering it in other locations.

In June, 1981 Jack Crocker, at age 57, stepped down from his position as CEO. Crocker, who headed Super Valu for nine years, brought the company to just over $4 billion in sales. He is reported to have handpicked Michael W. Wright, who had joined Super Valu as an executive vice president in 1977 and become president in 1978, to be the next CEO. Wright had first come to Crocker's attention when he handled some legal matters for the company in Minneapolis. Wright, a former captain of the University of Minnesota football team, had put himself through law school by playing professional football with the Canadian Football League.

Super Valu took its expansion west in 1982 when it acquired Western Grocers, Inc. Western had distribution centers in Denver, Colorado and Albuquerque, New Mexico; in 1984 these two centers became separate divisions. Super Valu also moved into Nebraska in 1982 by acquiring the Hinky Dinky distribution center near Omaha from American Community Grocers, a subsidiary of the Texas-based grocers Cullum Companies. In 1984 Super Valu sold the center back to Cullum.

With intentions of gaining a strong market presence in Florida, in 1983 and 1984, respectively, Super Valu purchased Pantry Pride's Miami and Jacksonville distribution centers. In what Super Valu considered a breach of their agreement, Pantry Pride began selling off its stores. With this and the fact that the Florida market had historically been dominated by the chains, Super Valu, claiming that the Florida market would take a large amount of capital to develop, sold the Miami center to Malone & Hyde in 1985, and the Jacksonville center to Winn-Dixie in 1986.

In 1985, Super Valu created its Atlanta division when it acquired the warehouse and distribution facilities of Food Giant. Through this division the company supplies Food Giant, Big Apple, Cub Foods, and independent stores. Food Giant, according to a 1988 *Financial World* report, "refused to implement Super Valu's turnaround plan for store upgrading," and the retail stores that Super Valu owned through the original transaction and a later acquisition of stock lost money for the company. By 1988 the company had divested itself of these stores, but operated or franchised seven Cub stores in the Atlanta area.

Also in 1985, Super Valu acquired West Coast Grocery Company (Wesco) of Tacoma, Washington. Wesco, founded by the Charles H. Hyde family in 1891, was Super Valu's largest acquisition to that time. Wesco has distribution centers in two Washington cities and Salem, Oregon and a freezer facility in another Washington city. Super Valu's West Coast operations were hurt when the Albertson's chain opened a distribution center to supply its own stores in Washington.

In 1986 and 1987 Super Valu acquired two more distribution centers in Albuquerque and Denver, respectively. These centers were owned by Associated Grocers of Colorado which, at the time of the Denver purchase, was in Chaper 11 bankruptcy proceedings. In December, 1988, Super Valu acquired the Minneapolis; Fargo, North Dakota; and Green Bay, Wisconsin distribution centers of Red Owl Stores, Inc. The former Denver and Albuquerque divisions of Western Grocers were moved into these new facilities.

By the mid-1980s Super Valu had developed a substantial presence in the military-commissary marketplace. The company had been supplying both product and retail support to military commissaries in the United States and abroad and, in 1986, demonstrated its commitment to international operations by appointing a military and export product director. Super Valu International had its beginnings with the caribbean and Far East markets and now supplies fresh goods and private label canned goods, general merchandise, and health and beauty aids to most countries of the world.

During the 1980s ShopKo continued to expand and to turn in substantial profits for the company. At the end of fiscal 1989 ShopKo operated 87 stores in 11 states from the Midwest to the Pacific Northwest and had sales of $1.28 billion. Now Super Valu's only nonfood retail operation, ShopKo has its headquarters and distribution center in Green Bay, Wisconsin, and distribution centers in Omaha, Nebraska and Boise, Idaho.

It was perhaps the successes of ShopKo and of Cub Foods that led Super Valu to its biggest venture in retailing in the 1980s—the "hypermarket," a retailing concept that originated in Europe after World War II. The first hypermarkets introduced in America in the early 1970s were not successful, but in the mid-1980s Hyper Shoppes, Inc., a predominantly French consortium, reintroduced the hypermarket in the United States. Super Valu was a 10% investor in the venture, which opened Bigg's, a 200,000-square-foot food and general merchandise store in the Cincinnati, Ohio area.

With the experience of this venture under its belt, Super Valu created its own version of the hypermarket, Twin Valu. A combination of a Cub Foods and a ShopKo, this 180,000-square-foot store opened in early 1989 in Cleveland. The hypermarket concept as executed by Super Valu emphasizes low prices, good selection, and brand-name merchandise.

In 1988 Super Valu lost its position as the world's largest wholesaler when Oklahoma City–based Fleming Companies bought Malone & Hyde, a purchase Super Valu declined to make. At the end of the 1980s, Super Valu's empire served some 3,000 independent retailers in 33 states. The company still owns and operates 70 conventional grocery stores and some Cub Foods stores and serves its corporate stores and customers from 18 retail support and distribution centers.

One of the problems that Super Valu will face in the 1990s is the loss of business through acquisition of its independent retail customers by chains. Not content to stand still, however, Super Valu began construction of a 300,000-square-foot grocery warehouse in Kenosha, Wisconsin in 1989, with plans for additional facilities to be built on the site in 1990 and 1991. Other plans for the company in the early 1990s include an additional Twin Valu store in Cleveland and expansion of the hypermarket concept to other cities. The main focus at Super Valu has always been helping its retailers stay competitive, and this remains the company's standard for the 1990s and beyond.

Principal Subsidiaries: Cub Foods; Food Giant, Inc.; J. M. Jones Co.; Lewis Grocer Co.; Planmark, Inc.; Preferred Products, Inc.; Risk Planners, Inc.; ShopKo Stores, Inc.; Charley Brothers; Food Marketing Corporation; Ryans; West Coast Grocery Co.; Studio 70.

SUPERMARKETS GENERAL HOLDINGS CORPORATION

200 Milik Street
Carteret, New Jersey 07008
U.S.A.
(201) 499–3000

Private Company
Incorporated: 1966
Employees: 52,000
Sales: $5.96 billion

Supermarkets General Corporation (SGC) operates the Pathmark supermarket chain, one of the top ten grocery stores in the United States. The company met with great success as one of the first grocery chains on the East Coast to open large discount stores offering a wide variety of groceries as well as non-food items.

After World War II, the Mom-and-Pop grocery stores that dotted neighborhoods throughout the United States were in danger of being run out of business by the proliferation of large grocery chains. Among the independent grocers were three men in New Jersey who were working in family-owned businesses.

Alex Aidekman's father had emigrated to the United States from Russia in the early 1900s and started a dairy farm. His sons, Alex, Ben and Sam, opened a roadside stand where they sold produce and dairy products. The stand soon made enough of a profit that Sam opened two of his own stores and Alex and Ben became partners in another one.

Herb Brody also came into the grocery business at a young age. After learning the ropes as an employee in several stores, Brody and a friend decided to open their own store in East Orange, New Jersey. Typical of grocery stores at the time, Brody's store carried groceries, produce, and dairy products (meat was usually only available at the local butcher shop). Brody later opened his own store in Scotch Plains.

Milt Perlmutter's father owned a series of small neighborhood stores. The Perlmutters were successful entrepreneurs, and Milt was able to attend the Wharton School of Finance. Upon graduation, he enlisted in the army. After World War II, Perlmutter spent a year working for the Colgate Palmolive Company and then rejoined the family business.

About the same time, a grocery distributor named Bob Casson mentioned to Sam Aidekman that some of his other grocer-customers were also concerned about their ability to compete with the large grocery chains. A group of eight men, including Alex Aidekman, Herb Brody, and Milt Perlmutter, eventually met and decided to form a merchandising cooperative to pool their resources and create more buying power for their individual stores. The Wakefern Cooperative was established in 1947.

With this cooperative these neighborhood grocery stores were able to stock many of the same items as the chains at competitive prices. Their next challenge was to find a way to advertise. Newspaper advertising was too expensive for an independent grocer. In 1951, some members of Wakefern proposed that they also pool resources to buy advertising space. In order to form an advertising cooperative, they decided that the stores would have to share a common name, an idea that did not appeal to all members of the group, who were unwilling to let the group decide what to stock or tell them how to run their businesses.

A small group of ambitious owners decided to take the risk, however, and began to operate their stores under the name of Shop-Rite. Herb Brody was elected president of Shop-Rite, and Alex Aidekman served as president of Wakefern. At weekly meetings, owners decided which items would be sale-priced for a given period and placed ads in area newspapers. The ads themselves were created by an ambitious advertising representative named Zal Venet. Primitive by today's slick advertising standards, these ads were nonetheless striking at the time, with cartoon-like drawings of elephants charging and firecrackers exploding. Venet also created Shop-Rite's "Why Pay More?" slogan.

The requirements for buying into the Shop-Rite franchise were relatively simple. A store had to be a member of the Wakefern cooperative, have the necessary financial resources, display the Shop-Rite emblem, be located outside the market area of another Shop-Rite store, and sell the advertised items at the indicated prices.

With both a wholesale and a retail cooperative in operation, the Shop-Rite stores began to expand quickly. Through Wakefern's wholesale operation, the Shop-Rite stores were able to stock new frozen items, such as ice cream. Store owners installed refrigerated cases, and the cooperative developed new packaging to promote the products as Shop-Rite's house brand. In addition, the stores began to stock meat.

The first major test of the new venture came in 1956, when the supermarket chains began to offer trading stamps that could be exchanged for gifts ranging from dishes to badminton sets to lawnmowers. Although some members of Wakefern wanted to join the stamp program, the general consensus was that the stamps would eventually cause food prices to rise. As a line of defense against the stamps, fifty to a hundred items were advertised at outrageously low prices each week. Business at the Shop-Rite stores slumped for several weeks and store owners in favor of offering stamps continued to push for the program. But none of the stores left the cooperative, and within a few months customers began to return.

By holding firm during this time, the cooperative added

to its strength and was able to step up expansion. Within the stores, customer service was given high priority, and non-food items were added to the inventory. Mailer programs also allowed each store to have its own specials.

Soon members began to search for larger quarters. The goal was to build large supermarkets, but this was prohibitively expensive. Again, members pooled resources for greater strength. Small groups within Shop-Rite banded together and began to lease the buildings of failed supermarkets in the New Jersey area. One of these small groups, formed in 1956 by Aidekman, Brody, and Perlmutter, was the Supermarkets Operating Company (SOC). During the next ten years, SOC expanded into the northern New Jersey and middle Atlantic markets by acquiring failed stores, remodeling them, and adding the Shop-Rite name. SOC also branched into nonfood retail items and in 1963 acquired Crown Drugs.

The Shop-Rite cooperative continued to be in the forefront of grocery store innovations. In the early 1960s, Shop-Rite stores were the first to offer late night and Sunday hours, drugstores within the stores, fresh fish counters, liquor departments, and bag stuffer coupons. Aggressive merchandising techniques such as watermelon contests, carnival games, pony rides, and 10¢ coupons toward purchases in any Shop-Rite stores, together with Shop-Rite's low prices, brought large crowds and lent an air of excitement to the stores.

In 1966, Supermarkets Operating Company and General Supermarkets, another small group within the Wakefern and Shop-Rite cooperatives whose owners included other original members of Wakefern, merged to become Supermarkets General Corporation (SGC). The resulting corporation held 71 supermarkets, ten drug stores, six gas stations, a wholesale bakery, and a discount department store. By 1968, SGC had acquired Genung's, a department store chain with 22 locations; Rickel Home Centers; Hochschild, Kohn Department Stores; and Value House, a catalog and showroom operation in Maine.

The final step to independence came in 1968, when Supermarkets General broke away from Wakefern and Shop-Rite and renamed its grocery stores Pathmark, a name that is also used today on its house brands and nonfood merchandise. Milton Perlmutter was elected president of Pathmark; Herb Brody and Alex Aidekman were elected vice chairman and chairman, respectively, of the parent company, SGC. The company began to build warehouses near its stores and built a $70 million distribution center.

Such rapid growth and diversification was costly. During its first year, Pathmark's earnings remained at the same level as the previous year. Ultimately, the company had to sell some of its divisions and seek financial backing in the private sector. Value House was sold in 1978, and the assets of the Howland-Steinback (originally Genung's)—Hochschild division were eventually sold in 1986.

Although Pathmark was now a large chain, the organization encouraged individual stores to tune into the tastes and preferences of their neighborhoods. The company began holding weekly in-house seminars to keep clerks abreast of specials and changes in the food industry. It was not unusual to see corporate officers wandering around the aisles, collecting ideas from employees and customers.

Pathmark began using open dating in the early 1970s and was one of the first food chains to adopt unit pricing. Pathmark maintained its position at the forefront of the industry as it continued to discount more deeply than other large retailers and began to concentrate on building giant outlets in suburban shopping centers. Also, in 1971, SGC spearheaded the movement to challenge statutes in New York, New Jersey, and Connecticut that prohibited the advertisement of prescription drug prices.

When the 1973 oil crisis and recession caused food prices to skyrocket, Pathmark met the problem head-on by airing television commercials for a "food facts hot line." Callers could get information on which items were in short supply and which prices were likely to rise in the future. Initiated in 1973, the hot line generated a great deal of positive media attention for Pathmark. Pathmark also announced a price freeze that February on 600 non-commodity private label items for 60 days.

By 1975, SGC's phenomenal growth had begun to slow as competitors adopted the deep discount methods Pathmark originated. After almost 20 years, the high-volume, low-margin merchandising techniques that had made Aidekman, Brody, and Perlmutter giants in the food industry were no longer unique. In addition, analysts pointed out that SGC's general merchandise store acquisitions were not as structurally sound as the Pathmark organization.

SGC did continue to grow, however, and in 1977, Pathmark opened the first of its "super centers"—enormous discount grocery stores that also offered a large line of health and beauty aids, small appliances, and video-tape rentals. Largely through the expansion and renovation of existing units, Pathmark was operating a remarkable 117 super centers, accounting for 88% of the company's sales, by the end of 1977.

Beginning in the late 1970s, top management positions began to change. When Milton Perlmutter died in 1978, Louis Lowenstein, an attorney specializing in acquisitions and a member of the board of directors and the executive committee of SGC since 1966, became president of the corporation, but he resigned after only 17 months. According to rumors within SGC and industry speculation, Brody and Aidekman had not been comfortable with Lowenstein's fast-paced style. Brody in particular had not favored Pathmark's recent acquisitions. In any event, Brody was elected to replace Lowenstein.

Despite these administrative upheavals, Pathmark continued to operate with its same enormous volume. Stores were computerized and the distribution system became increasingly sophisticated. The company also continued its policy of community involvement. In 1977, SGC entered into an agreement with the Bedford-Stuyvesant Restoration Corporation to build a supermarket in Brooklyn's inner city. Modeled on a similar project in Chicago, financing was provided by the Restoration Corporation and employee training, management, supervision, and stock was supplied by Supermarkets General.

In 1982, Pathmark was the tenth-largest supermarket in the United States and Leonard Lieberman was elected president of Supermarkets General Corporation. Lieberman, an attorney who had been with the organization since Shop-Rite was created, had been the chairman of Pathmark. Many, in fact, had been surprised when Lowenstein had been chosen over Lieberman as president in 1978. Under him, SGC remained committed to the consumer and the community in a vastly different world than the one Aidekman, Brody, and Perlmutter had known.

As, Lieberman explained to *Business Week*, in 1987, "There aren't as many good sites today, and there is a proliferation of local regulations. In the old days, all you needed was a zoning variance. Now you have to consider the sociological infrastructure and have an environmental impact study. It is a fact of life. For some New York City stores, you need a five-year gestation period just to get through the regulations."

But Pathmark also grew by acquisition. It bought Purity Supreme, Inc. in 1984, and Angelo's Supermarkets, Inc. in 1986. SGC had agreed to acquire the grocery chains owned by Pantry Pride in 1982, but when Pantry Pride stockholders filed a complaint the agreement was canceled.

A strike by butchers and delicatessen workers in 1984 temporarily slowed Pathmark's sales, but it was settled within a month. Although details of the pact were not released to the press, union leaders reported that SGC compensated for a cut in Sunday pay by increasing benefits. More serious problems developed later that year when a federal grand jury indicted SGC and three other supermarket chains on charges of conspiring to limit the amounts paid on coupons for grocery and meat products. By agreeing to halt the awarding of double values on cents-off coupons, the grand jury said, the four firms had violated the Sherman Antitrust Act. Eventually, all four grocery chains pleaded no contest and were ordered to pay a combined fine of $830,000.

That the organization has now become the kind of giant conglomerate it once challenged is evident in the controversy that surrounded the opening of Pathmark's Pike Slip store in Manhattan. Although local groups had been pushing for a modern supermarket in the neighborhood, independent store owners in the area campaigned against the store. SGC's traditional community-oriented approach worked to its advantage. According to a company spokesperson, the company typically works with local consumer groups who are expressing the need for a major supermarket and merchants who are afraid that their businesses are in jeopardy. "We explain to the consumers how important it is that their voices be heard. Community boards, particularly in New York, are almost always made up of local merchants who do not want a large supermarket like Pathmark to move into the neighborhood. When the customers become involved, it helps to ease the tension and makes it easier for us to open a store in the area." SGC officials also make presentations to the local merchants' groups to demonstrate how a large establishment acts as an anchor and actually draws traffic to the area.

Another factor that could affect Pathmark's future growth is the lack of entry-level workers, a problem that it shares with others in the food industry. The solutions some companies have found so far include paying higher wages to beginning part-timers, hiring workers older and younger than federal guidelines allow, and keeping stores undermanned. It is a problem with no easy solution, and labor cost and availability will certainly be a consideration in further plans for growth.

In 1987 the SGC successfully fought off a takeover bid by Dart Group Corporation, which offered $1.6 billion after buying 5% of SGC's stock. The hostile bid was averted by a management-led leveraged buyout, and SGC is now a privately owned company. During this period, Leiberman and Aidekman retired. Kenneth Peskin, who had headed the Pathmark division after Leiberman and has an MBA rather than a family history of corner grocery stores, became CEO of SGC. How these changes will affect Pathmark's corporate policies remains to be seen.

Principal Subsidiaries: Pathmark Supermarkets; Purity Supreme Supermarkets; Heartland Warehouse Stores; Angelo's Supermarkets; Rickel Home Centers.

SYSCO CORPORATION

1390 Enclave Parkway
Houston, Texas 77077–2027
U.S.A.
(713) 584–1390

Public Company
Incorporated: 1970
Employees: 18,700
Sales: $6.9 billion (1989)
Stock Index: New York

The Sysco Corporation (an acronym for Systems and Services Company) is the largest marketer and distributor of food-service products in the United States. With 89 distribution facilities serving nearly 150 of the largest cities in the continental United States, SYSCO provides products and services to approximately 225,000 institutions. The company provides food—fresh produce, meat, and canned and dried food—to restaurants of all sizes and styles, hotels and motels, universities, convenience stores, airlines, and other organizations. It also supplies frozen foods to supermarkets, and supplies all of these institutions with nonfood products such as paper goods, janitorial supplies, cutlery, and chinaware.

The Sysco Corporation has been growing steadily since its founding in 1969. John Baugh, a Houston-based distributor, formed SYSCO by pooling nine small food distributors. Baugh's goal was to provide a national food service able to distribute any food despite its regional availability. Since that time, SYSCO has grown to become the leader in food distribution, with annual sales well above $6 billion. SYSCO's phenomenal growth has coincided with the boom in America's interest in eating out. But the company's success can be credited to more than luck. In the 20 years after it was founded, SYSCO made more than 43 major acquisitions and saw an annual increase in sales and earnings of 20% nearly every year.

SYSCO went public in 1970 and that year made its first acquisition, of Arrow Food Distributor. In its early years the company grew by acquiring a number of small distribution companies, carefully chosen for their geographic regions. These acquisitions helped to realize Baugh's early goal of providing uniform service to customers across the country. Throughout the 1970s the Sysco Corporation built many new warehouses to deal with this rapid expansion, later incorporating freezers into its warehouses and adding refrigerated trucks to transport produce and frozen foods.

During the 1970s SYSCO grew steadily except for a brief earnings drop in 1976 caused by a canned food glut and excessive startup costs due to increasing capacity. One reason for such rapid recovery and regular growth was SYSCO's continuing diversification into new products like fish, meat, and frozen entrees. In 1976 SYSCO acquired Mid-Central Fish and Frozen Foods Inc. and began providing frozen foods to supermarkets around the nation. In 1979 SYSCO's sales passed the $1 billion mark for the first time; by 1981 the company was rated as the largest U.S. food-service company. That year SYSCO set up Compton Foods in Kansas City to purchase meat, and began to supply supermarkets and other institutions with meat and frozen entrees.

In 1984 the Sysco Corporation continued its policy of acquiring its competitors when it purchased three operations of PYA Monarch, then a division of Sara Lee. SYSCO's largest acquisition to date occurred in 1988, when the company bought CFS Continental, at that time the third-largest food distributor in the country, which added 4,500 employees and brought the market it served to 148 out of the top 150 markets. Although much of the United States and especially Texas experienced hard financial times during the 1980s, as a national company in a relatively recession-proof industry, the Sysco Corporation was not adversely affected.

Through diversification and with each acquisition, SYSCO has continued to increase its market throughout the 1980s, even providing food for fast-food chains. There is plenty of room for growth, however, since the top 50 food distributors account for less than 20% of the available market. The Sysco Corporation is likely to maintain its growth in the food-distribution market as it continues to anticipate and supply consumer needs.

Principal Subsidiaries: Allied-Sysco Food Services, Inc.; Arrow-Sysco Food Services, Inc.; Baraboo-Sysco Food Services, Inc.; Bell/Sysco Food Services, Inc.; Cochran/Sysco Food Services.; Deaktor/Sysco Food Services Co.; DiPaolo/Sysco Food Services, Inc.; Food Service Specialists, Inc; Glencoe-Sysco Food Services Co.; Global Sysco; Grants-Sysco Food Services, Inc.; HFP-Sysco Food Services, Inc.; Hallsmith-Sysco Food Services; Hardin's-Sysco Food Services, Inc.; Sysco/Konings Wholesale; Koon-Sysco Food Services, Inc.; Lankford-Sysco Food Services, Inc.; Maine/Sysco, Inc.; Major-Sysco Food Services, Inc.; Mid-Central/Sysco Food Services, Inc.; Miesel/Sysco Food Service Co.; New York Tea-Sysco Food Service Co.; Nobel/Sysco Food Services Co.; Robert Orr–Sysco Food Services Co.; Olewine's/Sysco Food Services Co.; Pegler-Sysco Food Services Co.; Select-Sysco Foods, Inc.; Sugar Food Corp.; The SYGMA Network, Inc.; Sysco/Avard Continental Food Services, Inc.; Sysco/Continental Food Services of Indianapolis, Inc.; Sysco/Continental Food Services of Los Angeles, Inc.; Sysco/Continental Food Services of Minnesota, Inc.; Sysco/Continental Food Services of Pittsburgh,

Inc.; Sysco/Continental Food Services of Portland, Inc.; Sysco/Continental Food Services of Seattle, Inc.; Sysco/Continental Institutional Food Services, Inc.; Sysco/Continental Keil Food Services, Inc.; Sysco/Continental Mulberry Food Services, Inc.; Sysco/Continental Smelkinson Food Services, Inc.; Sysco Food Services of Austin; Sysco Food Services of Atlanta, Inc.; Sysco Food Services of Beaumont, Inc.; Sysco Food Services of Central Florida, Inc.; Sysco Food Services of Chicago Inc.; Sysco Food Services, Inc.; Sysco Food Services of Iowa, Inc.; Sysco Food Services–San Antonio; Sysco Food Services of South Florida, Inc.; Sysco Food Systems, Inc.; Sysco/Frost-Pack Food Services, Inc.; Sysco Frosted Foods, Inc.; Sysco/General Food Services, Inc.; Sysco Intermountain Food Services; Sysco/Louisville Food Services Co.; Sysco Military Distribution Division; Sysco/Rome Food Service, Inc.; Theimer-Sysco Food Services; Thomas/Sysco Food Services; Vogel/Sysco Food Service, Inc.

TESCO PLC

Tesco House
Delamare Road
Cheshunt, Hertfordshire EN8 9SL
United Kingdom
(0992) 3222

Public Company
Incorporated: 1932 as Tesco Stores Limited
Employees: 75,658
Sales: £5 billion (US$9.04 billion)
Stock Index: London

When John Edward Cohen opened his small grocery stall in the East End of London in 1919, he could hardly have known that he had set the wheels in motion for the development of one of the leading food retailers in the United Kingdom. Today, Tesco PLC consists of 371 stores in England, Scotland, and Wales, including more than 150 superstores—stores that sell food items in addition to a variety of other products, including fuel, clothing, housewares, and liquor.

In Jack Cohen's day, a retailer's product line was comprised of whatever could be housed in a tiny stall. Cohen invested his £30 stipend from his service in the Royal Flying Corps in stock for his stall and began his career as a market trader. He soon became a successful trader in other London markets outside of the East End and also branched out into wholesaling for other market traders. In 1931, Cohen officially founded Tesco Stores Limited. The name was originally that of a brand of tea Cohen sold, created from the initials of T. E. Stockwell, a merchant from whom he bought tea, and the first two letters of his last name.

Over the next eight years, the company grew rapidly, as Cohen opened more than 100 small stores, mainly in the London area. In 1935 Cohen was invited to the United States by several major American suppliers and became an eager student of the American food-retailing system. His vision of taking the American self-service supermarket concept back to the United Kingdom was thwarted temporarily by World War II. But Cohen's dream became a reality in 1947 when Tesco opened its first self-service store, in St. Albans, Hertfordshire, the same year that shares in Tesco Stores (Holdings) Limited were first offered for sale to the public. Although the St. Albans store closed in 1948 after failing to capture the interest of British shoppers, it reopened one year later to a much warmer reception.

Over the next two decades, Tesco expanded quickly across the United Kingdom. This growth was accomplished almost exclusively by the acquisition of smaller grocery chains, including Burnards in 1955, Williamsons Ltd. in 1957, Harrow Stores Ltd. in 1959, Charles Phillips & Company Ltd. in 1964, and the Adsega chain in 1965. In 1956, the company opened its first supermarket, in Maldon, Essex, to carry fresh foods in addition to its traditional dry goods.

In 1960, Tesco established a special department in its larger stores called Home 'n' Wear to carry higher-margin, nonfood merchandise, including apparel and household items. Eight years later, Tesco opened its first 40,000-square-foot "superstore" at Crawley, Sussex. The term superstore referred not only to the store's size but also to its vast selection of inexpensive food and nonfood items.

By 1976 Tesco operated nearly 900 supermarkets and superstores on the "pile it high, sell it cheap" formula that Cohen had imported from America. The firm's management found that the effectiveness of this strategy had deteriorated over time, however, leaving the company with uncomfortably slim margins and a serious image problem among consumers. While Tesco had been preoccupied with opening as many stores as possible and loading them with merchandise, the company had missed important signs that its market was changing, and had come to value merchandise quality over quantity.

The task of turning the company around fell on the shoulders of Ian MacLaurin, who had risen through the Tesco ranks to become managing director in 1973. In the first phase of his rescue plan Tesco discontinued the use of Green Shield trading stamps, an action that major stores in the United States had also taken recently. This was followed in 1977 by a controversial tactic dubbed Operation Checkout, in which Tesco cut prices across the board in an attempt to increase sales and market share during a period when consumers were spending less money on food purchases. Although the company accomplished these original objectives, Operation Checkout did little to improve Tesco's sagging image among consumers. Most of Tesco's stores were cramped, difficult to operate, and even harder to staff. Customer service was poor and merchandise selection in many outlets was limited. Tesco also touched off a price war with J Sainsbury, one of its major rivals, which ended up driving a number of smaller retailers and independent grocers out of business or into the arms of larger companies when they found themselves unable to compete with the prices offered by the two warring retailers.

Next, in order to reposition itself, Tesco embarked upon a massive modernization program. It closed 500 unprofitable stores, and extensively upgraded and enlarged others. Tesco pursued the superstore concept much more aggressively than it had in the past in order to compete more successfully with other major retailers and be more responsive to consumers who preferred to shop where parking was convenient and the selection of goods was broad. The company made a significant investment not only in improving the physical appearance of its stores but also in providing the higher-quality merchandise consumers wanted. Superstores were also seen as a way to generate a higher volume of business at increased margins while reducing overhead.

The superstores averaged 25,000 square feet to begin with, but eventually grew as large as 65,000 square feet. Each superstore functioned as a self-service department store coupled with a supermarket. The company places a heavy emphasis on having a varied selection of fresh, high-quality foods available, as well as a wide range of general merchandise such as household items and clothing designed to appeal to more sophisticated tastes.

To support these stores and its new high-quality, service-oriented image, Tesco introduced its own private-label product lines, developed through an extensive research-and-development program. Tesco also restructured and computerized its distribution system, opening its own centralized warehouses for storing inventory which could then be supplied to its stores as needed, instead of having to rely on manufacturers' delivery schedules.

In 1979, in an attempt to increase its overall sales volume through larger stores, Tesco acquired 17 outlets affiliated with Cartiers Superfoods. This acquisition and another involving Ireland's Three Guys store chain, together with lower sales in nonfood merchandise than the company had expected, drained Tesco's profits the following year.

By late 1981, food sales also appeared to be settling into another slump, placing additional pressure on Tesco's bottom line. In an effort to rekindle activity, MacLaurin initiated Checkout '82, cutting prices between 3% and 26% on approximately 1,500 food items. Like the strategy employed in 1977—but operating in an environment of smaller net profit margins—Checkout '82 touched off renewed price wars between Tesco and J Sainsbury, in which each chain devoted all of its energies to outdoing the other to win customer loyalty.

In the midst of this ongoing battle, Tesco also established its Victor Value chain of discount stores. Growing over the next four years to a total of 45 outlets, the stores were sold to the Bejam Group PLC in 1986, the same year in which the Three Guys chain, renamed Tesco Stores Ireland Ltd., was sold to H. Williams and Company, Ltd., a Dublin-based supermarket chain. This divestiture resulted primarily from the company's inability to operate effectively in Ireland from its home base in England.

In 1983, the company changed its name to Tesco PLC. The following year, it joined forces with Marks & Spencer, the upscale British variety store, to develop shopping centers in areas outside the country's major cities. Their first venture, which became a model for subsequent centers, was established at Brookfield Centre, near Cheshunt, and placed a 65,000-square-foot Tesco superstore next to a 69,000-square-foot Marks & Spencer department store. Supported by 42 computerized checkout counters and 900 employees, the Tesco store offered a variety of food and nonfood departments, in addition to services ranging from a bank to a gas station to baby-care facilities to a consumer advisory kitchen staffed by home economists. The Marks & Spencer store featured mostly nonfood merchandise, although it devoted a small amount of space to the popular specialty food items it markets under its own St. Michael label.

In 1985 Ian MacLaurin became chairman of Tesco, the same year that Tesco opened its 100th superstore in the United Kingdom. The construction of this outlet, located in Brent Park, Neasden, was a source of controversy between the company and the local governing council from the date Tesco first acquired the 43-acre site in 1978. The council made a number of objections to the proposed development, maintaining that the store did not fit the planning needs of the area and did not make adequate allowances for future warehousing requirements. The council's greatest concern was the threat the Tesco store would pose to existing shopping centers and local merchants. Once Tesco's store finally opened for business it became London's largest food store.

Also in 1985,Tesco launched a major capital spending program for aggressive store and warehouse expansion and for more efficient technology in existing stores, both at the checkout counters and behind the scenes. Tesco's investment in the development of a sophisticated distribution system, together with other facility improvements, enabled the company to incorporate its 1987 acquisition of the 40-store Hillards PLC chain easily. This expansion also gave Tesco increased visibility in Yorkshire.

Led by Sir Ian MacLaurin, who was knighted in 1989, Tesco, already one of the United Kingdom's top three food retailers, continues to compete aggressively for the right to claim the industry's leadership position. With ambitious plans for growth through the opening of additional stores throughout England, Wales, and Scotland, the company will require substantial capital investment—in property as well as in technology—to ensure efficient operations from the loading dock to the sales floor.

The company is currently engaged in a £1 billion development program, which will yield 60 new stores in the United Kingdom by 1993. At the end of 1989, 100 of Tesco's stores had been equipped with electronic scanning checkout devices. The company also introduced a composite warehouse distribution system to serve its stores, resulting in increased efficiency and improved service.

Although Tesco sees expansion to Europe and other countries overseas, including the United States, as prime opportunities for future growth, it intends to maintain a sharp focus on its home territory as it strives to become the United Kingdom's premier food retailer.

Principal Subsidiaries: Tesco Stores Limited; Tesco Holdings Limited; Tesco Insurance Limited.

Further Reading: Corina, Maurice. *Pile It High, Sell It Cheap*, London, Weidenfeld & Nicolson, 1971.

TW SERVICES, INC.

Post Office Box 904
Paramus, New Jersey 07653–0904
U.S.A.
(201) 712–0500

Public Company
Incorporated: 1980
Employees: 120,000
Sales: $3.57 billion
Stock Index: New York Midwest Pacific

TW Services has had a short but turbulent history. Although it was incorporated in 1980, for several years it conducted no significant business operations and all of its common stock was owned by Trans World Corporation. It only came into its own on December 30, 1986, when all of the voting shares of TWS were distributed to Trans World stockholders.

Trans World Corporation, formed in 1978, was a holding company that owned TWA, Hilton International, Spartan Food Systems, Inc., Canteen Corporation, and Century 21 Real Estate. Although its major holding was the airline, Trans World's many other subsidiaries made it the most diversified of all the airline companies.

In 1980, Trans World's efforts to rescue its ailing airline caused the chairmen of its other subsidiaries much frustration as they had to hold back their expansion plans in order to leave funds available for TWA. For example, the chairman of Spartan, Charles J. Bradshaw, had to scale down plans to build 250 new Quincy Family Steak House units over five years to 50 over two years.

In April, 1983, Odyssey Partners, a private Wall Street group, tried to press Trans World to separate its various units, but the company didn't make the move at the time. Instead, to fend off raiders, Trans World's management decided in December of that year to spin off the airline from the rest of the company; the move was completed in February, 1984.

Once the airline was gone, the remaining subsidiaries were all profitable. Chairman and CEO L. Edwin Smart planned to make the company more service-oriented. The recession of the early 1980s had affected some of Trans World's units more than others. Canteen Corporation, an operator of vending machines and factory cafeterias, saw revenues dip as industrial workers were laid off. As a result, Canteen shifted its focus, becoming an institutional supplier. It also looked for more business at service-oriented firms, especially in the health-care and recreational fields.

Century 21, Trans World's real estate subsidiary, suffered from the slow housing market, but by 1983 it had an 11% market share of retail home sales. Expansion plans for the subsidiary included moves into related service areas. A franchise agreement with C. Itoh to open a network of offices in Japan was also signed.

The Spartan division did well throughout the period. Its Hardee's operation, which generated more than half of Spartan's sales, prospered, and its Quincy Family Steak House chain continued to expand successfully in the South.

In 1983, Hilton International was the only subsidiary still having problems. Although still making a profit, it continued to be affected by recession that lingered in other parts of the world, even though it had lifted domestically.

Trans World continued its expansion into the food service business in 1985 with the purchase of Interstate United, a Chicago-based company. Interstate's business concentrated on schools, sports arenas, and hospitals. Also in 1985, Smart agreed to sell Century 21 to Metropolitan Life Insurance Company as part of his strategy to concentrate on Trans World's "core" food and lodging businesses.

The next year Smart decided that he wanted to acquire a nursing home corporation, American Medical Services. Charlie Bradshaw, president and CEO of Trans World, disagreed with the purchase—not his first entanglement with Smart, but his last. Bradshaw had come to Trans World by way of Spartan Food Systems, and Smart had hoped to make Bradshaw his successor. Bradshaw and his partner had built up Spartan from one Hardee's franchise in 1961 to 250 Hardee's and Quincy Family Steakhouses when Trans World bought it in 1979. Bradshaw then continued to run Spartan from its headquarters in South Carolina. But in 1984, bored and tired of corporate bureaucracy, he told Smart that he wanted out. Smart convinced him to move to New York as president of Trans World, not anticipating the clash of styles that subsequently erupted. Bradshaw kept trying to buy one restaurant chain after another; Smart and Frank L. Salizzoni, vice chairman, kept finding reasons to reject each potential acquisition. When Salizzoni and Smart came up with the American Medical Services deal, Bradshaw disagreed with the argument that hotel management expertise would apply to nursing home management and felt that the purchase would pull Trans World away from its principal businesses. At the board meeting where the issue was discussed, Bradshaw was the only one to vote against the nursing home deal. Before the day was over, he had resigned from his position at Trans World and was back home in South Carolina.

The last quarter of 1986 brought upheaval to Trans World. In October, Ronald O. Perelman, owner of MacAndrews and Forbes Holdings, Inc. and the chairman of the Revlon Group, Inc., made a bid for the company. In response, and to repel Perelman, the company announced a liquidation plan in November that called for the sale of Hilton International and the possible sale or recapitalization of its other subsidiaries. The pieces of the company that were left would be known as TW Services. On December 30, 1986, Canteen, Spartan, and all other directly owned subsidiaries except Hilton International were merged into TW Services. Hilton International was soon sold to UAL, Inc., the parent company of United Airlines. With the merger, Canteen and Spartan became divisions of the TW Services, and American Medical Services became a subsidiary.

Smart retired as chief executive in April, 1987. Frank Salizzoni took the job and immediately set to work. Just as he warmed his seat, an investment banker from Merrill Lynch & Co. called to ask him if TW Services would be interested in buying DHI, the parent of Denny's and several other restaurant chains. Salizzoni was, and the deal was completed in September, only two and a half months later, making TW Services the owner of 1,200 Denny's restaurants, 70 El Pollo Loco chicken restaurants, and a 42% interest in the Winchell's Donut Shops chain. Management believed that this acquisition would complement TW's strong holdings in institutional services and its fast-food restaurants and steak houses.

By the end of 1988, not even two years after the company had assumed its present form, rumors about another takeover attempt, this time by Coniston Partners, started to surface. After months of haggling and the adoption of the "poison pill" measure, TW finally agreed to a buyout by Coniston in June, 1989. Under the agreement, Coniston bought 30 million TW shares, bringing its ownership to about 80% of TW.

TW Services, in all its incarnations, has gone from a company based in the travel industry to one primarily involved with supplying food, both on an institutional level to schools, sports facilities, and cafeterias, and on the retail level at both fast-food restaurants and mid-priced sit-down steak houses and coffee houses.

Despite the company's protean tendencies, TW's core businesses today are well-established ones. Though the company's future under is new owner is still uncertain, TW looks settled for now in the food industry.

Principal Subsidiaries: American Medical Services, Inc.; DHI Corp.

WETTERAU INCORPORATED

8920 Pershall Road
Hazelwood, Missouri 63042
U.S.A.
(314) 524–5000

Public Company
Incorporated: 1961 as Wetterau Foods Incorporated
Employees: 14,000
Sales: $4.9 billion
Stock Index: NASDAQ

In 1867 young George H. Wetterau left Germany to seek opportunity in the bustle of post–Civil War America. George joined his brother in St. Louis, where many other Germans had also settled. While studying business at night school, he joined J.F. Lauman and Company, a local wholesale grocery firm, in 1868. J. F. Lauman retired a year later, leaving the young Wetterau to assume the leadership of the firm. George Wetterau persuaded Frederick Goebel to invest in the company, which became the Goebel & Wetterau Grocery Company.

During its early years the new venture thrived as a distributor of groceries in the booming St. Louis economy. St. Louis thrived during and after Reconstruction as the new transcontinental railway was completed and the city became the "gateway to the West" for the huge influx of pioneers drawn westward by the Homestead Act and the lure of a new life.

In 1899, the Goebel & Wetterau Grocery Company changed from a partnership to a corporation called the G. H. Wetterau & Sons Grocery Company, since two of Wetterau's sons, George Jr. and Otto, had joined the business. At the same time, the company moved into a new building described in a newspaper account of the time as "one of the most modern wholesale grocery stores in the western country." George Wetterau, starting another tradition that would be one of the hallmarks of his firm, was also quick to get involved with the new technology of the 1890s; Wetterau was among the first firms in St. Louis to be part of the telephone system.

In the first decade of the 20th century, G. H. Wetterau & Sons continued to share in the growth of a booming American economy. As immigrants poured into the cities there were more and more mouths to feed, and George Wetterau made sure that his company filled his clients' every need. Wetterau also grew as a family business when George's third son, Theodore, joined the firm in 1909. All three sons learned the business the hard way—from the ground up. This old school management training method assured that the future leadership of Wetterau appreciated the complexities of each stage of wholesaling operations.

During World War I Wetterau thrived, despite having no share of the lucrative government contracts for supplying canned food. But the increased military spending necessitated by the war served as an economic spur, and Wetterau prospered.

The booming 1920s meant even more expansion for Wetterau. When Otto Wetterau was named head of the firm in 1923, he set Wetterau firmly on a course of innovation and expansion. During the 1920s Wetterau was a pioneer in pallet-loading techniques and in the use of fork trucks. Wetterau was also quick to see the value of the wholesale warehousing of produce, which made daily trips to the produce market unnecessary. It was during this decade that Wetterau also expanded its operations into other parts of Missouri—to Desloge in 1925 and Mexico in 1928.

During the Depression, despite widespread unemployment and wage cuts for those still working, Wetterau continued to prosper. The company's affiliation with the Independent Grocer's Alliance (IGA), arranged at the urging of Theodore Wetterau, helped to keep the firm, along with 50 St. Louis retailers it urged to join, free from the threat of absorption by the retail chains beginning to spring up across the country. In 1936 the company relocated again to keep up with its growth, and was renamed Wetterau Grocery Company. The company made its first acquisition in 1938, buying the Niese & Coast Products Company, a St. Louis food wholesaler.

World War II brought an abrupt halt to Wetterau's plans for geographic expansion. Wetterau contented itself with enlarging and improving its warehouses and consolidating its Mexico, Missouri operation with the Nowell Wholesale Grocery Company.

During the postwar years Wetterau resumed the growth that the war had thwarted. In 1954 Theodore Wetterau, George Wetterau's youngest son, became president of the company. Five years later, in 1959, Wetterau finally outgrew its St. Louis facilities and moved to the complex in suburban Hazelwood where its main branch is still located.

Wetterau's modern history began in 1961, when the company went public with the sale of 100,000 shares of stock and changed its name to Wetterau Foods Incorporated. In 1963 total sales passed $100 million, Oliver S. Wetterau, grandson of the founder, became president, and John R. Figg Inc., now Wetterau's Bloomington Division, was acquired.

Under the leadership of "Ollie" Wetterau, the company looked for a plan that would help its retail customers to start up new outlets. Ted Wetterau, another of the founder's grandsons, developed the Package Store concept. Using this plan a local store owner could bypass designers and architects and set up a completely prefabricated store within ten weeks. The Package Store concept was the key to Wetterau's plan to expand the support services if offered retailers to meet virtually all their needs.

Wetterau later granted the right to use the Package Store program to all IGA wholesalers.

In 1968 Wetterau advanced its communications capabilities by tying all its information systems into a central computer. A year later, Wetterau acquired the Thomas & Howard Company, now its Charleston division, and the Holbrook Grocery Company of New England, becoming the supplier to an additional 367 retail outlets.

In 1970 Ted Wetterau became president. He continued to make innovation, as well as growth, the watchword of the 1970s for Wetterau.

In 1973 the firm's name was changed to Wetterau Incorporated to describe more accurately a newly restructured company based on two major operating groups: Wetterau Food Services, its food wholesaling business, and Wetterau Industries, its retailer support services business.

Several more innovations during the 1970s helped to establish Wetterau as an industry leader. Wetterau's shelf space allocation and inventory control system, nicknamed HOPE, was unveiled in 1971. This revolutionary system used sales figures to determine how much of each product to display on store shelves. During this decade Wetterau also began to use computers to schedule its truck routes and developed a semi-automatic mechanization system for operating its large warehouses more efficiently.

Wetterau's talent for innovation was always tailored to the needs of retail customers, and Wetterau grew as its ability to please its customers increased. In 1972, pushing southeast, Wetterau established a nonfood concern in South Carolina to supply local Red & White retailers. The following year Wetterau bought out the J. Zinmeister Company of Kentucky, which supplied 80 IGA supermarkets in Kentucky, Tennessee, and Indiana. Other acquisitions made in 1976 and 1979 continued to expand the number of retail stores which Wetterau served. This whole period of diversification and acquisition culminated in a sales volume of over $4 billion for the first time in 1979.

Wetterau began the 1980s with still more acquisitions—the Milliken, Tomlinson Company, which added a 145,000-square-foot distribution center to the firm, in 1980, and the Fox Grocery Company, supplier to 300 retailers in six states, in 1981. But in 1981 Wetterau was the object of a hostile takeover attempt by Empire Inc., a propane fuel distributorship. For two months Wetterau battled to maintain the autonomy that it so valued. After wasting much time and energy in keeping Empire at bay, Wetterau committed itself to an aggressive expansion policy to guarantee that it would never again be threatened with the loss of its identity.

The takeover bid, combined with the startup costs of a new marketing program and a change in accounting procedures, caused a steep earnings drop in fiscal 1982, though the drop was only Wetterau's second in 50 years. By 1983 Wetterau's earnings had recovered, and the company continued to acquire.

Wetterau had entered the retail market in 1982 when it purchased Shop 'n Save, a string of 13 supermarkets in Missouri. A year later the company bought Laneco, Inc. of Pennsylvania, the operator of 31 stores. And in 1984 Wetterau bought Milgram Food Stores, Inc., whose 36 retail stores Wetterau sold, keeping Milgram's warehouse and dairy businesses. That same year Wetterau formed Foodland Distributors in a joint venture with the Kroger Company, the first time that a major retailer and wholesaler had combined forces to form their own distribution company.

1985 was Wetterau's biggest year yet: its four purchases that year solidified its position as a major force in food wholesaling. In June, Wetterau bought the Creasy Company Inc., a $280 million supplier in eight states and the District of Columbia; in August it bought Cressey Dockham & Company, a $250 million New England wholesaler supplying 300 retailers; in October it bought a $250 wholesaler to some 325 retailers in three southern states; and in December it bought Amerimark Inc., a food service and convenience store company. With all of these firms now under the Wetterau flag, the company was organized into three business groups. The first was food distribution, the wholesaling group that formed the core of Wetterau. The second group was retail outlets, businesses that allowed Wetterau itself to profit from the mark-ups of the goods it distributed. The last group was Wetterau's support service group, which offered retailers a range of services that included financing, construction, advertising, bakery goods, and communication services.

In 1987 Wetterau moved all the way to the West Coast when it acquired USCP-WESCO Inc., a company that supplied store owners in 13 western states as well as Mexico and Asia, making Wetterau an international company. And in 1988 Wetterau again made dramatically large acquisitions when it absorbed both the Moran Group Inc., the parent company of Save-A-Lot, and Roger Williams Foods. Together these businesses conducted nearly $650 million worth of business annually.

In 1988 Wetterau restructured its senior management to allow for greater future growth and appointed a new CEO and president, George H. Thomazin. A year later Wetterau was named to Standard & Poor's 500 Index, a fitting acknowledgement of the company's successful growth and strong position for the future.

Principal Subsidiaries: Wetterau Finance Co.; Glenn-Wohlberg & Co.; Transcontinental Leasing Co.; Wetterau Insurance Co., Ltd.; Laneco, Inc.; Shop 'n Save Warehouse Stores; Wetterau Builders, Inc.; Food Lane Supermarkets; Milgram Supermarkets; Bright Dept. Stores; Lane Dept. Stores; Carriage Drugs; Just Be Natural.

Further Reading: Humiston, Ron. *120 Years of Progress*, Wetterau Inc., Hazelwood, Missouri, 1989.

WINN-DIXIE STORES, INC.

5050 Edgewood Court
Post Office Box B
Jacksonville, Florida 32203
U.S.A.
(904) 783–5000

Public Company
Incorporated: 1929 as Rockmoor Grocery
Employees: 84,000
Sales: $9.0 billion
Stock Index: New York

Winn-Dixie is America's fourth-largest supermarket chain. It operates some 1,230 stores in 13 states throughout the sunbelt, a third of them in Florida, making W-D by far the largest Florida based corporation.

W-D's founder, William M. Davis, was the owner of an old-fashioned charge and deliver general store in Idaho before World War I. The advent of self-serve, cash and carry chain stores after the war drove many old-fashioned independent grocers out of business. Davis, however, saw the potential of this new kind of grocery store. He moved his family to Miami, Florida and, borrowing $10,000, entered the self-serve grocery business. He bought his first store, the Rockmoor Grocery, in the Miami suburb of Lemon City in 1925. Davis, his wife, and their four sons ran the store; the Davis family has provided the leadership for W-D ever since.

In the early years Davis found it difficult to expand. Three times he attempted to open a second store and three times the store failed. Chain stores had demonstrated their ability to deliver a wider variety of high quality goods at lower prices than had ever before been possible, but many a tradition-bound consumer preferred the old way of doing business. Independent grocers had local support and political connections, but life could be made rather difficult for a chain-store or supermarket operator. After consumers' initial resistance was overcome, however, it was impossible to deny that supermarkets were the wave of the future. By 1934, the year W.M. Davis died, the Rockmoor Grocery had spawned 34 Table Supply Stores, as they were called, in South Florida.

Davis's four sons took control of the company at their father's death and set out on a course of further expansion. In 1939 they acquired control of the 78 stores of the Winn & Lovett Grocery Company of Florida and Georgia, and in 1944 the company established its headquarters in Jacksonville, Florida and officially adopted the Winn & Lovett name.

The war years brought a lull in the supermarket industry. Food rationing, labor shortages, and price increases forced supermarkets to tighten their belts with the rest of the nation. Winn & Lovett, along with most of the supermarket industry, cooperated with the government by maintaining a lid on prices during and immediately following the war. During this time nonfood products filled what would otherwise have been empty shelves, and began to assume a more prominent place in supermarkets. The higher profit margins on nonfood products allowed supermarkets to maintain food prices at relatively low levels without jeopardizing overall profitability.

Once the economy had returned to normal, Winn & Lovett picked up where it had left off before the war, adding, in 1955, several more grocery chains in Florida and the deep South to its company rolls. Later in the same year, Winn & Lovett merged with Dixie Home Stores of Greenville, South Carolina, and changed its name to Winn-Dixie Stores Inc. With this merger, W-D broke into the top ten supermarket chains and from the mid-1950s through to the mid-1960s was the most profitable company in the industry. Profits in the supermarket industry are more dependent on high volume than high profit margins, but W-D's profit margins in this period were exceptionally high. This was due to both an increase in sales (fourfold between 1954 and 1964) and lower labor costs in the non-union South. W-D's workforce remains entirely non-union today.

W-D continued to expand and prosper in the 1960s, acquiring the Ketner and Milner Stores in the Carolinas and the Hill Stores in Louisiana and Alabama. W-D not only acquired more retail outlets but also branched out into processing, manufacturing, and distribution. At present W-D operates 29 of these support facilities, producing a wide variety of store brand products. With profits increasing each year and with 23 consecutive years of cash dividend increases, Chairman J.E. Davis (one of W.M. Davis's sons) could confidently predict in the *Wall Street Journal* in 1966 that W-D would shatter all previous sales and profit records in fiscal 1967.

The year 1966 also brought some bad news, however. The Federal Trade Commission had been investigating the increasing concentration in the supermarket industry and had concluded that mergers and acquisitions in the industry had unfairly limited competition, in violation of the Clayton Anti-Trust Act. W-D, as the most profitable and one of the fastest growing chains, was an obvious target. The investigation showed that, in fact, a third of W-D's increase in sales over the previous ten years had been generated by stores acquired during that period. As a result, the FTC ruled that for ten years W-D was forbidden to acquire any retail grocery stores in the United States without FTC approval. The ruling was not as much a punishment of W-D as it was a settlement between the firm and the FTC. "The principal practical effect," W-D President Bert L. Thomas told *The Wall Street Journal* at the time, "is to clear all Winn-Dixie's past mergers and acquisitions from future challenge." All that was required of W-D was obedience to the ruling. W-D used the ten year period for "internal" expansion, adding stores by leasing new stores and improving existing retail and support facilities. W-D did acquire 11 stores in the Bahamas which were not covered by the FTC order. When the ban was lifted in 1976, W-D acquired the 135 stores and the support facilities of Kimbell Inc. in Texas, Oklahoma, and New Mexico.

In 1983 J.E. Davis stepped down as chairman of Winn-Dixie, and a member of the third generation of the Davis family, Robert D. Davis, assumed control. Robert's five years at the helm were marked by a virtually flat rate of growth in gross profits, although net earnings did not suffer because of lower tax rates. W-D has faced increasing competition in the 1980s, not only from its traditional competitors—the other large chains—but also from convenience stores, which have made a large dent in the market. In 1988, Robert stepped down as chairman (he remains vice chairman) and his cousin, A. Dano Davis, was elected to succeed him.

Dano Davis's new management team implemented measures to cut operating costs and raise gross profit margins. Management costs were also pared, and 60 management positions were eliminated. W-D is selling off its smaller, less efficient stores and is also unloading some of its less productive baking facilities. The prevailing trend is toward larger, more modern stores offering more merchandise.

Despite these very positive moves, W-D does face some problems. It has been notified by the EPA that it is a PRP (potentially responsible party) for the cleanup of two dumping grounds designated as "superfund sites" in Florida; the company estimates cleanup costs at about $200,000. W-D is also spearheading a battle between grocery retailers and large producers of packaged goods over who will determine the shape of the market for retail food. W-D announced in 1988 that it would no longer accept promotion allowances for products on a market by market basis, but only chain wide. W-D has demanded a consistent national pricing policy from major suppliers such as Campbell Soup, General Mills, Quaker, Proctor & Gamble, and others. So far the companies have refused to meet W-D's demands and W-D has retaliated by dropping certain of their products from its inventory. According to *Fortune*, W-D's crusade is a response to the declining profitability of the past five years. W-D is negotiating with each of the producers separately and hopes to solve the impasse and preserve its market position.

The overall picture at Winn-Dixie remains positive. Cash reserves and working capital remain strong and steady. For the 45th consecutive year W-D reported an increase in cash dividends. The firm has shifted from a productivity-driven strategy to a customer-driven strategy in order to maintain the loyalty of present customers and attract new ones in this time of increased competition. Winn-Dixie's stated goal for the future is to become *the* low-cost operator of full-service supermarkets with a full range of specialty departments.

Principal Subsidiaries: Astor Products, Inc.; Crackin' Good Bakers, Inc.; Deep South Products, Inc.; Dixie Darling Bakers, Inc.; Dixie Packers, Inc.; Economy Wholesale Distributors, Inc.; Fairway Food Stores Co., Inc.; Monterrey Canning Co.; Save Rite Foods, Inc.; Sunbelt Products, Inc.; Superbrand Dairy Products, Inc.; Superior Food Co.; Table Supply Food Stores Co., Inc.; W-D (Bahamas) Ltd.; W-D Atlanta, Inc.; W-D Charlotte, Inc.; W-D Greenville, Inc.; W-D Louisiana, Inc.; W-D Louisville, Inc.; W-D Montgomery, Inc.; W-D Raleigh, Inc.; W-D Texas, Inc.

Further Reading: Zimmerman, M. *The Supermarket: A Revolution in Distribution*, New York, McGraw-Hill, 1955; Herbert R. Northrup et al. *Restrictive Labor Practices in the SuperMarket Industry*, Philadelphia, University of Pennsylvania Press, 1967.

INDEX TO COMPANIES AND PERSONS

Listings are arranged in alphabetical order under the full company name, so that Eli Lilly & Company will be found under the letter E; definite articles (The) and forms of incorporation that precede the name (A.B. and N.V.) are ignored for alphabetical purposes. Company names appearing in **bold** have separate entries on the page numbers appearing in **bold**.